Central Asia

Bradley Mayhew
Richard Plunkett
Simon Richmond

D0041504

LONELY PLANET PUBLICATIONS
Melbourne • Oakland • London • Paris

RUSSIA

Ulyanovsk

Penza

Togliatti

Samara

Ufa

M5

M5

Chelyabinsk

Kurgan

Kostanay

Rudny

Petropavlovsk

Kökshetau

M36

Saratov

Volga River

Orenburg

Oral

Volga River

Orsk

Aktöbe

ASTANA

Arkalyk

Lake Tenghiz

KAZAKSTAN

Volgograd

Ural River

Astrakhan

Atyrau

M32

Zhezkaghan

North Aral Sea

Aralsk

Sha River

M6

Aktau

Ustyurt Plateau

South Aral Sea

Moynaq

Kyzylorda

Muyunkum Desert

Turkistan

Shymkent

CASPIAN SEA

Nukus

Konye-Urgench

Dashoguz

Urgench

Khiva

Kyzylkum Desert

UZBEKISTAN

Uchquduq

Zeravshan

Syr-Darya

TASHKENT

Angren

M39

Almalyk

Kokand

BAKU

Sarykamish Lake

Aidarkul Lake

Guliston

Khojand

AZERBAIJAN

Turkmenbashi

Karakum Desert

Balkanabat

TURKMENISTAN

Navoi

Bukhara

Jizzakh

Samarkand

DUSHANBE

Kulyab

Kurgan-Tyube

TEHRĀN

M37

ASHGABAT

Turkmenabat

Qarshi

M37

M39

Mary

Amu-Darya

Termiz

HINDUKUSH

Mashhad

Mazar-i-Sharif

KABUL

Herat

IRAN

Kabul River

AFGHANISTAN

Eşfahān

Ferah River

Kandahar

Quetta

The Gulf

Zāhedān

Helmand River

TURKISTAN
Kazakstan's greatest architectural monument

KONYE-URGENCH
Tantalising remains of the city ravaged by Jenghiz Khan

KHIVA
Mosques, medressas and minarets in this Silk Road city frozen in time

BUKHARA
Central Asia's densest collection of Islamic monuments, with some fascinating backstreets

SAMARKAND
Tamerlane's vision, with the spectacular Registan square and Shahr-i-Zindah street of tombs

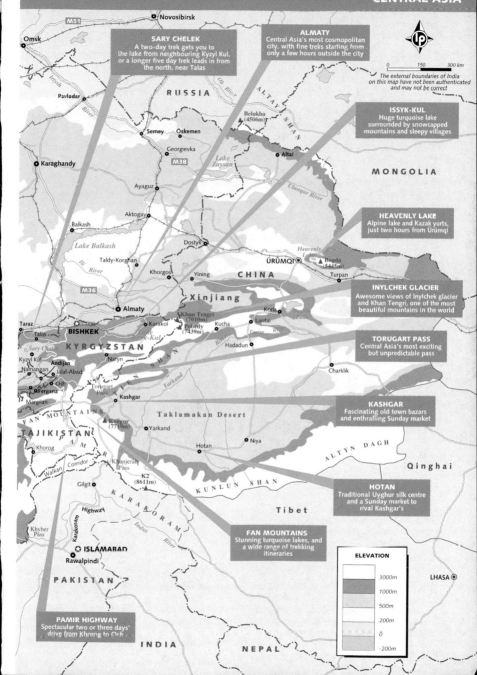

CENTRAL ASIA

SARY CHELEK
A two-day trek gets you to the lake from neighbouring Kyzyl Kul, or a longer five day trek leads in from the north, near Talas

ALMATY
Central Asia's most cosmopolitan city, with fine treks starting from only a few hours outside the city

0   150   300 km

The external boundaries of India on this map have not been authenticated and may not be correct

ISSYK-KUL
Huge turquoise lake surrounded by snowcapped mountains and sleepy villages

HEAVENLY LAKE
Alpine lake and Kazak yurts, just two hours from Ürümqi

INYLCHEK GLACIER
Awesome views of Inylchek glacier and Khan Tengri, one of the most beautiful mountains in the world

TORUGART PASS
Central Asia's most exciting but unpredictable pass

KASHGAR
Fascinating old town bazars and enthralling Sunday market

HOTAN
Traditional Uyghur silk centre and a Sunday market to rival Kashgar's

FAN MOUNTAINS
Stunning turquoise lakes, and a wide range of trekking itineraries

PAMIR HIGHWAY
Spectacular two or three days' drive from Khorog to Osh

ELEVATION

3000m
1000m
500m
200m
0
-200m

LHASA

Novosibirsk

M51

Omsk

RUSSIA

Pavlodar

Irtysh River

Ob River

ALTAY SHAN

Belukha (4506m)

Semey   Öskemen

Georgievka

M38

Lake Zaysan

Altai

Karaghandy

MONGOLIA

Ayaguz

Ulungur River

Aktogay

Balkash

Lake Balkash

Dostyk

Heavenly Lake

Taldy-Korghan

Ili River

Khorgos   Yining

CHINA

ÜRÜMQI   Bogda (5445m)

Turpan

M36

Xinjiang

Almaty

Khan Tengri (7010m)

Korla

Taraz   Talas

Karakol   Pobedy (7439m)   Kucha   Luntai

BISHKEK   Issyk-Kul   Tarim River

KYRGYZSTAN

Sary Chelek   Hadadun

Kyzyl Kul   Naryn

Namangan   Andijan   Jalal-Abad

Osh   Charklik

Fergana

Margilan

Torugart Pass   Kashgar

FAN MOUNTAINS

Kungur (7719m)   Taklamakan Desert

TAJIKISTAN   Yarkand

Khorog   PAMIR   Hotan   Niya

Walkan   Corridor   Khunjerab Pass   ALTYN DAGH

Gilgit   K2 (8611m)   KUNLUN SHAN   Qinghai

KARAKORAM

Highway   Indus River   Tibet

Khyber Pass   Karakoram

ISLAMABAD

Rawalpindi

PAKISTAN

INDIA   NEPAL

Central Asia
2nd edition – April 2000
First published – June 1996

Published by
Lonely Planet Publications Pty Ltd A.C.N. 005 607 983
192 Burwood Rd, Hawthorn, Victoria 3122, Australia

Lonely Planet Offices
Australia PO Box 617, Hawthorn, Victoria 3122
USA 150 Linden St, Oakland, CA 94607
UK 10a Spring Place, London NW5 3BH
France 1 rue du Dahomey, 75011 Paris

Photographs
All of the images in this guide are available for licensing from
Lonely Planet Images.
email: lpi@lonelyplanet.com.au

Front cover photograph
The colours of Central Asia – detail of painted ceiling from a mosque
in Bukhara. (Bradley Mayhew)

ISBN 0 86442 673 9

Contents – Text

2 Contents – Text

MAP LEGEND   back page

METRIC CONVERSION   inside back cover

Contents – Maps

The Authors

Bradley Mayhew

Bradley started travelling in South-West China, Tibet and northern Pakistan while studying Chinese at Oxford University. Upon graduation he fled to Central America for six months to forget his Chinese and then worked in Beijing in a futile attempt to get it back. Since then he has spent two months in the Silk Road cities of Bukhara and Khiva, two months trekking in Kyrgyzstan and has enjoyed extended trips to Iran, eastern Turkey and Ladakh. He has also worked on Lonely Planet's *India*, *Indian Himalaya*, *Pakistan*, *Karakoram Highway*, *South-West China* and *Tibet* guides.

Bradley is also the co-author and photographer of the *Odyssey Guide to Uzbekistan*, and has lectured on Central Asia at the Royal Geographical Society. He splits his time between Sevenoaks in south-east England and Las Vegas, Nevada.

Richard Plunkett

Richard grew up on a farm/vineyard in central Victoria, and got the travel bug during a solo journey around India aged 18. He started work as a cadet journalist on the Melbourne *Age* after dropping out of university, left for an extended trip through the Middle East, went broke, came home, and got a job as an editor at Lonely Planet. Besides covering Uzbekistan and Turkmenistan for this book, he's worked on the *India*, *Indian Himalaya* and *Delhi* guides; next up is *Bangladesh*.

Simon Richmond

Simon's first experience of Central Asia was in 1994 when he backpacked from Europe to Hong Kong, making the notorious crossing into China by train from Almaty. Co-author of guidebooks on Japan, South-East Asia and South America for other publishers, this is Simon's first update for Lonely Planet, although he has also contributed to the new Lonely Planet *Out to Eat* series of restaurant guides for Sydney and London. His features have been published in major newspapers and magazines in the UK, Australia and Japan and he has been a presenter on BBC radio. Simon currently lives in Sydney.

John King

John King grew up in the USA but now resides in the UK. He has spent over four months in Central Asia and 13 months in China at various times. Among the other Lonely Planet guides he has worked on are *Karakoram Highway*; *Russia, Ukraine & Belarus*; *Pakistan*; *Prague*; and *Czech & Slovak Republics*. In the first edition, John was coordinating author and concentrated his research on Kyrgyzstan, eastern Uzbekistan and Xinjiang.

John Noble

John Noble comes from the valley of the River Ribble in northern England. In 1989 he found himself taking on Lonely Planet's *USSR* guide with John King. He has also worked on the *Baltic States* and *Russia, Ukraine & Belarus* guides. John's main turf for the first edition was Kazakstan, western Uzbekistan and northern Turkmenistan. He also wrote about the Aral Sea and the Semey polygon.

Andrew Humphreys

Born in England, Andrew has spent most of the last 10 years on the road. While living in Estonia, he updated the Baltic chapters of Lonely Planet's *Scandinavian & Baltic Europe on a shoestring*, which earned him the dubious privilege of being despatched to Siberia for *Russia, Ukraine & Belarus*. For the first edition of this book, Andrew concentrated his efforts on southern Turkmenistan, south-east Uzbekistan and war-weary Tajikistan. He also prepared the Arts section.

FROM THE AUTHORS

From Bradley

Thanks first of all to John King for putting together a solid first edition of Central Asia and for sending us huge steaming piles of notes for use on the second edition. At Lonely Planet, thanks to fellow author Alex English for fine Xinjiang information, Thalia Kalkipsakis who regularly gets stuck editing my books and Maree Styles, for allowing us to dabble in the design decisions. This trip began with the help of the Roza Otunbayeva, Kyrgyz Ambassador to the UK, and Ainor Toktorbaeva, the Consul.

In Kashgar, thanks to Akbar, Abdul and especially Elvis (Ablimit Ghopor) for information and insight. Thank you to all the shopkeepers, hotel owners and friends in Hunza, who helped us out, and to Abdullah Baig and Mohammed (Medina) in Gilgit; apologies for not being able to squeeze the KKH into this second edition. Thanks to Anwar Sajid in Rawalpindi for continued help over the years, and to Osman Sakiin for filling out some holes in the Tajikistan chapter. Thanks to Martin Moos for his contributions.

Thanks to Jeff Whitbeck, Chris Pemberton, Kevin Tillman and all the Peace Corps workers in Krygyzstan for their time. Theodor Herzen provided splendid artwork for this book, as well as patience as we made our selections. Special thanks to Valentin in Karakol for his support of Lonely Planet and his eager help; likewise to Baba Lena, the best cook in Kyrgyzstan. Also in Karakol, thanks to Sergey Pyshchenko. Thanks to Max Haberstroh for posting us valuable information from Kyrgyzstan. Thank you to the superb English Faculty in Osh, especially head of the English chair, Kamil, for his guidance. Philip Micklin, Professor of Geography at the Western Michigan University USA helped with info on the Aral Sea for the first edition.

Howdy to Timur, in Osh, may we meet again. Much gratitude to Lynn Tracy of the US embassy in Bishkek, and to Walter Schlaeppi of Shepherd's Life for their professional assistance. Humble thanks to Kadirov Abdi Mital in Suusamyr, who saved us from a night in the cold. Celestial Mountains' Ian Claytor provided much appreciated information on crossing the Torugart. Hats off to our determined driver, Nicolai, of Kyrgyz concept, who literally pushed our van through the snow halfway to Torugart and back. Our deepest appreciation to Alex Timofeev of ITMC who worked around the clock to make sure we made it over the pass. Cheers to Thea and Mennu – may all your other trips be easier, warmer and better-fed than the Torugart! Warm thanks to Tursan, Miriam and Beyshanbek in At-Bashy for fine hospitality and then unexpectedly taking care of us, our friends and our exhausted driver. And *chong rakhmat* to two lonely shepherds and their powerful horses at Song-Köl for epitomising the essence of Kyrgyz hospitality (and getting our Zhiguli out of the mud).

Finally, thanks and love to Kelli, who valiantly managed to keep down bowls of yoghurt and mutton fat (yet again) and helped out with every stage of this book, without getting much credit. Thank you for your hard work, love, care and patience, as always.

From Richard

In Uzbekistan my thanks go to Airat and Goumira Yuldashev, Gairat Sharahmatov, Anwar & the Brothers, Xavier & Aude, Bett Gottschling, Richard Jones, Andy, Vera, Romi, Raisa Gareyeva, Yuliya Shishova, Farkhad Bakhramov and Mrs Akhmedov.

In Turkmenistan huge thanks go to the Peace Corps volunteers at the summer camp, and to Hunter de Butts, Billy McCallum, Paul Dryden, Vernon King, Alex Brown, Djora, Tatyana Mitelman, Aman Meredov, Golubeva Yevgeniya, Leonardo and Natalya.

Thanks to Rebecca Mullins for the preliminary arrangements and to Leonie Plunkett for the emergency loan, to Andrew Humphreys, John Noble and John King for the first edition, to Brad Mayhew for all his help, and to Thalia, Maree, Adriana, Sharan and Geoff at LP. Thanks also to all the people who gave their time to write such detailed letters, and to all the hospitable, honest and helpful people I met on the way.

Most of all, thanks to Hannah Lawrence.

From Simon

There were many people who made my journey around Kazakstan so much more enjoyable, interesting and productive than it might have been; I apologise if your name is not mentioned here, but my sincere thanks goes to you also. Paul and Jane Edwards of the British embassy provided a warm and much appreciated welcome. Thanks also to Liliana Biglou and Louise Cowcher of the British Council for extending their hospitality and assistance. Simon Forrester and his UN colleagues around the country were an invaluable source of help; in particular, thanks to Bruno de Cordier, Helen Allen, Matilda Bolger, Yves van Loo, Svetlana Kamal-ad-Din and Sergei Ramonov.

Seamus Bennett, Daniella Morini and Molly Graves at KIMEP freely provided their insiders' knowledge of the city and allowed me to keep in touch with the world via email. Oleg Samukhin was an ideal hiking guide. Thanks also to Jennifer Gable, Amy Forster, Micheal Rothburt, Scott Browder, Stan Veitsman and Katya Brightwell all for shedding light on various aspects of Almaty life.

In Astana, I owe much to the unstinting assistance of Anne Marie Bereschak and her colleagues. Thanks also to Peace Corps volunteer David Beutel and his Kazak 'father' Talgat. In Kostanay, Marina Burdyga came to my rescue. In Petropavlovsk, I enjoyed the company and expertise of David Mikosz and Lance Shumway. Thanks to Peace Corp volunteer Andrew in Pavlodar and to Anne in Semey for impromptu guiding duties. In Öskemen, many thanks to Daulet at the library and Andrei Tselichev for pulling out all the stops to get me to the end of the road. Thanks to Shamiel Raifikov, Viktoria Vorobiyova and Artur for their help around Shymkent and to Nelly Davietyarova for arranging that section of my travels. In Burabay, I will long treasure the afternoon spent in the company of Gulira Nursharipova and her class of 11-year-olds. Finally, Alex Newton and Betsy Wagenhauser, fellow LP scribes and Almaty residents, were the most generous and supportive hosts. Thanks for treating me as well as you would your own Simon.

This Book

The first edition of this book was researched and written by John King, John Noble and Andrew Humphreys. In this second edition, Bradley Mayhew coordinated the project and updated Kyrgyzstan, Tajikistan, Afghanistan, Xinjiang and the introductory chapters; Richard Plunkett updated Uzbekistan and Turkmenistan; and Simon Richmond updated Kazakstan.

This edition features expanded Xinjiang coverage, an informative Afghanistan chapter, additional trekking information, plus expanded sections on architecture, the Silk Road and peoples of Central Asia.

FROM THE PUBLISHER

This edition was produced at Lonely Planet's Melbourne office. Thalia Kalkipsakis headed the editorial team with assistance from Adam Ford, John Hinman and Michelle Coxall. Maree Styles coordinated the mapping, design and layout, with assistance from Shahara Ahmed and Mark Germanchis. Quentin Frayne and Vicki Webb compiled and edited the Language chapter and the cover was designed by Maria Vallianos. Tim Uden provided Quark support; he also compiled the index with Darren Elder and Carolyn Papworth.

Thanks to Sharan Kaur and Adriana Mammarella for their time and support throughout the project.

Special Thanks

Special thanks to Bruno de Cordier, who updated most of the Pamir Highway and Alay Valley sections and helped with the Kyrgyzstan, Tajikistan and Kazakstan chapters, especially Bishkek and around. For the last three years Bruno has been travelling and working in Central Asia for various international agencies. He currently resides in Bishkek.

Bruno would like to thank the following for their great help with his update: Steven Descamps and Torstem Swobeda for being solid and enthusiastic travel partners, Sasha Zelichenko and Irina Blhovskaya (UNODCCP in Osh) for advice and logistic help, Jean-Christian Dumas (MSF Khorog) and the MSF gang in Osh for their hospitality, Mirzohayat Khudonazar (WFP Khorog), Abubakir Ubaderdiev (MSDSP Murgab) and Edik Smirnov (CIS Border Guards in Kara Kul), Slava Musienko, Togai (Kashka-Suu), and the Atyrov (Sary Tash) and Ashymov (Ottyk) families for their hospitality. Last, but not least, thanks to Bugu.

THANKS
Many thanks to the travellers who used the last edition and wrote to us with helpful hints, advice and interesting anecdotes. Your names appear in the back of this book.

Foreword

ABOUT LONELY PLANET GUIDEBOOKS

The story begins with a classic travel adventure: Tony and Maureen Wheeler's 1972 journey across Europe and Asia to Australia. Useful information about the overland trail did not exist at that time, so Tony and Maureen published the first Lonely Planet guidebook to meet a growing need.

From a kitchen table, then from a tiny office in Melbourne (Australia), Lonely Planet has become the largest independent travel publisher in the world, an international company with offices in Melbourne, Oakland (USA), London (UK) and Paris (France).

Today Lonely Planet guidebooks cover the globe. There is an ever-growing list of books and there's information in a variety of forms and media. Some things haven't changed. The main aim is still to help make it possible for adventurous travellers to get out there – to explore and better understand the world.

At Lonely Planet we believe travellers can make a positive contribution to the countries they visit – if they respect their host communities and spend their money wisely. Since 1986 a percentage of the income from each book has been donated to aid projects and human rights campaigns.

Updates Lonely Planet thoroughly updates each guidebook as often as possible. This usually means there are around two years between editions, although for more unusual or more stable destinations the gap can be longer. Check the imprint page (following the colour map at the beginning of the book) for publication dates.

Between editions up-to-date information is available in two free newsletters – the paper *Planet Talk* and email *Comet* (to subscribe, contact any Lonely Planet office) – and on our Web site at www.lonelyplanet.com. The *Upgrades* section of the Web site covers a number of important and volatile destinations and is regularly updated by Lonely Planet authors. *Scoop* covers news and current affairs relevant to travellers. And, lastly, the *Thorn Tree* bulletin board and *Postcards* section of the site carry unverified, but fascinating, reports from travellers.

Correspondence The process of creating new editions begins with the letters, postcards and emails received from travellers. This correspondence often includes suggestions, criticisms and comments about the current editions. Interesting excerpts are immediately passed on via newsletters and the Web site, and everything goes to our authors to be verified when they're researching on the road. We're keen to get more feedback from organisations or individuals who represent communities visited by travellers.

> Lonely Planet gathers information for everyone who's curious about the planet – and especially for those who explore it first-hand. Through guidebooks, phrasebooks, activity guides, maps, literature, newsletters, image library, TV series and Web site we act as an information exchange for a worldwide community of travellers.

Research Authors aim to gather sufficient practical information to enable travellers to make informed choices and to make the mechanics of a journey run smoothly. They also research historical and cultural background to help enrich the travel experience and allow travellers to understand and respond appropriately to cultural and environmental issues.

Authors don't stay in every hotel because that would mean spending a couple of months in each medium-sized city and, no, they don't eat at every restaurant because that would mean stretching belts beyond capacity. They do visit hotels and restaurants to check standards and prices, but feedback based on readers' direct experiences can be very helpful.

Many of our authors work undercover, others aren't so secretive. None of them accept freebies in exchange for positive write-ups. And none of our guidebooks contain any advertising.

Production Authors submit their raw manuscripts and maps to offices in Australia, USA, UK or France. Editors and cartographers – all experienced travellers themselves – then begin the process of assembling the pieces. When the book finally hits the shops, some things are already out of date, we start getting feedback from readers and the process begins again ...

WARNING & REQUEST

Things change – prices go up, schedules change, good places go bad and bad places go bankrupt – nothing stays the same. So, if you find things better or worse, recently opened or long since closed, please tell us and help make the next edition even more accurate and useful. We genuinely value all the feedback we receive. Julie Young coordinates a well travelled team that reads and acknowledges every letter, postcard and email and ensures that every morsel of information finds its way to the appropriate authors, editors and cartographers for verification.

Everyone who writes to us will find their name in the next edition of the appropriate guidebook. They will also receive the latest issue of *Planet Talk*, our quarterly printed newsletter, or *Comet*, our monthly email newsletter. Subscriptions to both newsletters are free. The very best contributions will be rewarded with a free guidebook.

Excerpts from your correspondence may appear in new editions of Lonely Planet guidebooks, the Lonely Planet Web site, *Planet Talk* or *Comet*, so please let us know if you *don't* want your letter published or your name acknowledged.

Send all correspondence to the Lonely Planet office closest to you:

Australia: PO Box 617, Hawthorn, Victoria 3122
USA: 150 Linden St, Oakland, CA 94607
UK: 10A Spring Place, London NW5 3BH
France: 1 rue du Dahomey, 75011 Paris

Or email us at: talk2us@lonelyplanet.com.au

For news, views and updates see our Web site: www.lonelyplanet.com

HOW TO USE A LONELY PLANET GUIDEBOOK

The best way to use a Lonely Planet guidebook is any way you choose. At Lonely Planet we believe the most memorable travel experiences are often those that are unexpected, and the finest discoveries are those you make yourself. Guidebooks are not intended to be used as if they provide a detailed set of infallible instructions!

Contents All Lonely Planet guidebooks follow roughly the same format. The Facts about the Destination chapters or sections give background information ranging from history to weather. Facts for the Visitor gives practical information on issues like visas and health. Getting There & Away gives a brief starting point for researching travel to and from the destination. Getting Around gives an overview of the transport options when you arrive.

The peculiar demands of each destination determine how subsequent chapters are broken up, but some things remain constant. We always start with background, then proceed to sights, places to stay, places to eat, entertainment, getting there and away, and getting around information – in that order.

Heading Hierarchy Lonely Planet headings are used in a strict hierarchical structure that can be visualised as a set of Russian dolls. Each heading (and its following text) is encompassed by any preceding heading that is higher on the hierarchical ladder.

Entry Points We do not assume guidebooks will be read from beginning to end, but that people will dip into them. The traditional entry points are the list of contents and the index. In addition, however, some books have a complete list of maps and an index map illustrating map coverage.

There may also be a colour map that shows highlights. These highlights are dealt with in greater detail in the Facts for the Visitor chapter, along with planning questions and suggested itineraries. Each chapter covering a geographical region usually begins with a locator map and another list of highlights. Once you find something of interest in a list of highlights, turn to the index.

Maps Maps play a crucial role in Lonely Planet guidebooks and include a huge amount of information. A legend is printed on the back page. We seek to have complete consistency between maps and text, and to have every important place in the text captured on a map. Map key numbers usually start in the top left corner.

Although inclusion in a guidebook usually implies a recommendation we cannot list every good place. Exclusion does not necessarily imply criticism. In fact there are a number of reasons why we might exclude a place – sometimes it is simply inappropriate to encourage an influx of travellers.

Introduction

The region known loosely as Central Asia or 'Turkestan' is a vast arena of desert, steppe and knotted mountain ranges stretching from the Caspian Sea in the west to Mongolia in the east, from Siberia in the north to the Hindu Kush in the south. It forms a bridge and barrier where Europe and Asia meet on the Eurasian steppes. It spans five former Soviet republics, parts of western China and Afghanistan. Until recently it was inaccessible and unfamiliar to the outside world, thanks in part to its isolation within the former Soviet Union and communist China. Even now, most westerners think of it as a desert wasteland of illiterate nomads. Nothing could be further from the truth.

For more than 2000 years Central Asia has been the locus of ancient east-west trade routes collectively called the Silk Road, and at various points in history a cradle of scholarship, culture and power. It was the board on which the 19th and 20th centuries' greatest geopolitical chess match, the 'Great Game' between imperial Britain and imperial Russia, was played.

It's as geographically diverse as it is historically rich. Along with ferocious deserts it takes in fertile valleys of shoulder-high pasture, and some of the highest mountain peaks on the planet. The nomadic population, now live in thousands of small towns and a score of Russianised oasis-cities (whose people

---

Surreal Central Asia

There's something about the ex-Soviet republics that is just, well, *weird*. From the deserted *why would anyone live here* cities of western Kazakstan to the Vegas-style strip of neon hotels in the middle of sullen Ashgabat and from the world's grandest orphanage in Turkmenistan to the fishing trawlers beached in the desert sands of the Aral Sea – the region is punctuated by monuments of wonderful strangeness.

Scouring the news agencies can produce some fine surreal stories, from huge meteors landing in the Karakum desert to yeti hunters scouring the Kyrgyz mountains. From the Hannibal Lector school of journalism comes the three psychiatric nurses in Almaty charged with drugging, killing and eating seven prostitutes, or the female doctor (also in Almaty) who mummified her mother and three sisters and kept them in the family cupboard when she couldn't afford to bury them. Or how about the crack squad of 10,000 chickens trained up by the People's Liberation Army to deal with a plague of locusts in northern Xinjiang?

Travel in the region reveals daily Twilight Zone encounters. The prize for 'Weirdest Accommodation in Central Asia' surely goes to the travellers' dormitory in Ashgabat's psychiatric institute. The 'Most Surreal Place to Eat' award goes to the Hound Dog Hole in the US embassy (guests only), where food is prepared in Elvis Presley's kitchen (he bought it while serving in the military). I particularly admired the sheep who boarded the local bus in Tajikistan alone and then got off two stops later, *without paying*. Or the old man on a bus in Tajikistan who handed me a light bulb and absolutely refused to take it back until he got off the bus eight hours later. For those who like to live on the edge I wholeheartedly recommend the one-legged taxi driver who drove me to Ala-Archa in Kyrgyzstan (where *was* that brake?). But don't wear your seatbelt in Uzbekistan – I almost made this fatal mistake until the driver told me 'people will think we're rebels from Tajikistan!'.

Of course they will.

Bradley Mayhew

---

are, if not worldly, at least intensely interested in the outside world).

Though the people of Central Asia have had fairly distinct cultural identities for centuries, the separate countries that this book is mostly about – Uzbekistan, Kyrgyzstan, Tajikistan, Turkmenistan and vast Kazakstan – were more or less invented in the 1920s as republics of the USSR, and only became sovereign states upon the collapse of that union. Despite serious post-partum blues, Central Asia is again at a geopolitical pivot-point – a repository of immense natural wealth and a reservoir of potential converts to Islam, Pan-Turkism or the free market. This former blank on the map is being 'discovered' again by scholars, aid workers and travellers.

There is of course much that's *not* romantic about the region. In the name of Soviet ideals, its people have for two generations been severed from their past and taught to pity their ancestors' ways with condescending museums of history and applied arts, empty architectural monuments and slick music-and-dance troupes. Now they are struggling to cope with the sudden death of those Soviet ideals, the loss of cultural reference points and the failure of the economic and political life-support system that gave them all a minimal share of the pie.

In this vacuum poverty, unemployment and crime are on the rise, and one state (Tajikistan) has been shattered by civil war. The natural desolation of desert and steppe now seems overlaid with human desolation: impoverished towns and broken-down housing blocks, corrupt and suffocating bureaucracy, ethnic unease and ecological disaster zones like the dying Aral Sea and the Semey nuclear 'polygon'. Everyone is waiting for the answer – a strong leader, a revived union, a heroic past, Islam or the free market – to put things right again, and to help with the recovery of their stolen cultural identities.

Not surprisingly, travel here can be a struggle, especially for independent travellers. Getting visas can be like pulling teeth. Hotels tend to be shoddy and overpriced, food cheap but unvarying, transport unpredictable. Outside the cities little English is spoken. Greedy officials abound with their obscure, mutable and sometimes fictional 'regulations'. The widespread use of alcohol can turn the friendliest daytime scene ugly after dark.

In spite of the difficulties, the region's story-book history, its present ferment, and the sense of mutual rediscovery between Central Asians and the rest of the world, make it a gripping place to visit. Restaurants are popping up everywhere, advantageous exchange rates make the region cheaper than ever, shops are well stocked, transport along the Silk Road is cheap and everywhere you turn is a helping hand.

The ancient pace and Silk Road flavour are still there if you look, especially outside the cities. Open markets in storied caravan stops seem lifted from the days of Timur, the 14th century despot-turned-cultural-icon whose capital, Samarkand, has become a symbol of Central Asia's past and future potential. The region's backdrop, especially the snowcapped mountains, offers some fantastic trekking and mountaineering.

Uzbekistan, with the longest settled past, has the most interesting historical and architectural heritage, but is the most like the old USSR and the most difficult for independent travellers. Kyrgyzstan and Kazakstan are the most welcoming, though their attractions are mainly human or geophysical. Turkmenistan is the least familiar and least connected to the outside world. Tajikistan remains the most tantalising because it is presently the least accessible.

It's easy to burn out on the standard hotels-and-monuments route. Combat this by making friends. You'll understand and remember Central Asia best through individual contacts and insights (and you may also discover how pliant rules and prices can be). This is partly a matter of luck but partly a matter of attitude. Central Asians are softies for a handshake and a *salam aleykum* (the traditional Islamic greeting, 'Peace be with you'), and Russians for a smile and a few words of pidgin Russian. Most of them are keen to learn about you, to tell their stories and to help you discover Central Asia.

Facts about Central Asia

HISTORY

Central Asia is perhaps the best place on earth to explore the reality of the phrase 'the sweep of history'. Populations, conquerors, cultures and ideas have swept colourfully across the region's steppes, deserts and mountains for thousands of years. The notion of the Silk Road stresses Central Asia's important linking role as the territory through which the great civilisations of the east and the west made contact and carried on cultural exchange. But Central Asia was, and is, more than just a middle ground, and its cultural history is far more than the sum of the influences brought from the east and the west.

Scholar and writer, Stuart Legg, dubbed Central Asia, together with Mongolia and Siberia, the 'Heartland' and wrote a book with the same title. Here in the heart of the largest landmass on earth, vast steppes provided the one natural resource, grass, required to build one of this planet's most formidable and successful forms of statehood, the nomadic empire. The grass fed horses by the millions, and mounted archers (a Heartland invention) remained the unstoppable acme of open-ground warfare for over 2500 years. The Heartland was a hotbed of social energies and explosions of conquest which reached the farthest corners of Eurasia.

How the settled civilisations on the periphery of Eurasia interacted with successive waves of mounted nomadic hordes is the main theme of the story of Central Asia's.

Prehistory & Early History

In the Middle Palaeolithic period, from 100,000 to 35,000 years ago, people in Central Asia were isolated from Europe and elsewhere by ice sheets, seas and swamps. The *Homo sapiens neanderthalensis* remains found at Aman-kutan cave near Samarkand date roughly from 100,000 to 40,000 years ago, and are the earliest known human remains in Central Asia.

Cultural continuity begins in the late 3rd millennium BCE (before common era) with the Indo-Iranians, speakers of an unrecorded Indo-European dialect related distantly to English. The Indo-Iranians are believed to have passed through Central Asia on their way from their Indo-European homeland in southern Russia. From Central Asia, groups headed south-east for India and south-west for Iran. These peoples herded cattle, went to battle in chariots, and probably buried their dead nobles in mound-tombs *(kurgans)*. The Tajiks are linguistic descendants of these ancient migrants.

Central Asia's recorded history begins in the 6th century BCE, when the large Achaemenid empire of Iran held three client kingdoms beyond the Amu-Darya river: Sogdiana, Khorezm and Saka. These territories changed hands and fluctuated in relative importance countless times over the next 2500 years, but their outlines remained principally the same and helped shape the destiny of Asia.

Sogdiana was the land between the Amu-Darya and Syr-Darya, called Transoxiana by the Romans and Mawarannhr by the Arabs. Here Bukhara and Samarkand later flourished. Khorezm lay on the lower reaches of the Amu-Darya south of the Aral Sea, where one day the khans of Khorezm would lord it from the walled city of Khiva until well into the 20th century. Saka (called Semireche by the Russians), extending indefinitely over the steppes beyond the Syr-Darya and including the Tian Shan range, was the home of nomadic warriors until the Heartland way of life ended in the late 19th century.

Alexander the Great

In 330 BCE this former pupil of Aristotle, from Macedonia, led his army to a key victory over the last Achaemenid emperor, Darius III, in Mesopotamia. With the defeat of the Persian nemesis, Alexander (356-323 BCE) developed a taste for conquest. By 329 he had reached modern Kabul. Crossing the Hindu Kush, he pressed northward across the Oxus (Amu-Darya) and proceeded via

Marakanda (Samarkand) towards the Jaxartes (Syr-Darya), which he crossed in order to crush Scythian defenders. Perhaps in celebration he founded the city of Alexandria Eschate (Farthest Alexandria) near the site of modern Khojand.

Alexander met the most stubborn resistance of his career in the Sogdians, who in concert with the Massagetes, a Saka clan, revolted and held the mountainous parts of their homeland until 328. After an 18-month guerrilla war, the rebels' fall was a poignant one: attacked and defeated at their last redoubt, the 'Rock of Sogdiana' (whose location today in the Hissar mountains is a mystery), their leader yielded his daughter, the beautiful Bactrian princess Roxana into captivity, and marriage to Alexander.

The Macedonian generalissimo's sojourn in Central Asia was marked by a growing megalomania. It was at Marakanda that Alexander murdered his right-hand general, Cleitus. He tried to adopt the dress and autocratic court ritual of an Oriental despot. However his Greek and Macedonian followers refused to prostrate themselves before him.

When he died in Babylon in 323, Alexander had no named heir. But his legacy included nothing less than the west's perennial romance with exploration and expansion.

East Meets West

The aftermath of Alexander's short-lived Macedonian empire in Central Asia saw an increase in east-west cultural exchange and a chain reaction of nomadic migrations. The Hellenistic successor states of the Seleucid empire disseminated the aesthetic values of the classical world deep into Asia, while trade brought such goods as the walnut to Europe. Meanwhile, the grassy plains of the Heartland had been the scene of fomentation among the nomad clans.

Along the border of Mongolia and China, the expansion of the warlike Xiongnu (Hsiung-nu) confederacy (probably the forebears of the Ephalites, or Huns) uprooted the Yüeh-chih of western China (the Yüeh-chih ruler was slain and his skull made into a drinking cup). The Yüeh-chih were sent packing westward along the Ili river into

Saka, whose displaced inhabitants in turn bore down upon the Sogdians to the south.

The Xiongnu were also irritating more important powers than the Yüeh-chih. Though protected behind its expanding Great Wall since about 250 BCE, China eagerly sought tranquillity on its barbarian frontier. In 138 BCE the Chinese emperor sent a brave volunteer emissary, Zang Qian, on a secret mission to persuade the Yüeh-chih king to form an alliance against the Xiongnu.

When he finally got there, 13 years later, Zang found that the Yüeh-chih had settled down in Bactria to a peaceable life of trade and agriculture, and no longer had an axe to grind with the Xiongnu. But Zang Qian's mission was still a great success of Chinese diplomacy and exploration and the stage had been set for major east-west contact and the birth of the Silk Road (see the 'Silk Road' section in the Kyrgyzstan chapter).

The Kushans

The peaceable, put-upon Yüeh-chih finally came into their own in the 1st century BCE when their descendants, the Kushan dynasty, converted to Buddhism. The Kushan empire controlled northern India, Afghanistan and Sogdiana from its core in the Gandhara region of north-west Pakistan. At its height in the first three centuries after Christ, it was one of the four great powers of the world, along with Rome, China and Parthia.

Vigorous trade on the Silk Road helped spread Kushan culture. The rich Kushan coinage is concrete testimony to this classic Silk Road power's lively religious ferment: the coins bear images of Greek, Roman, Buddhist, Iranian and Hindu deities. The art of the empire fused Iranian imperial imagery, Buddhist iconography and Roman realism. It was carried out from Gandhara over the mountainous maze of deepest Asia to the farthest corners of Transoxiana, Tibet and the Tarim basin. Indian, Tibetan and Chinese art were permanently affected.

Sassanids, Huns & Sogdians

For a thousand years after the birth of Christ, Central Asia was the scene of pendulum-like shifts of power between the

Great Chinese Explorers

Zang Qian (Chang Ch'ien)

Zang Qian's 13-year voyage to Central Asia in 138 BCE (and his return in 119) is the first great traveller's saga of Central Asia. Taken prisoner by the Xiongnu soon after departure, he spent 10 years in captivity, then escaped and wandered west over the Pamir Alay to the Fergana valley. There the fertile land yielded the pleasures of the vine, knowledge of which Zang Qian brought back to China. Other discoveries were in store – the Heavenly Horses, untiring tiger-striped steeds which sweated blood and captured the imagination of Chinese militarists and poets for centuries to come; booming trade in Hellenistic Bactria, which featured standardised coinage in the likeness of the king; and reports of two rich, distant lands: one called India; the other Daqin, otherwise known as Rome.

Xuan Zang

Travelling through Chinese Turkestan with insufficient documents along a string of tenuously Han-controlled frontier outposts, a lone traveller is repeatedly asked by officials to return to the safety of China proper. At the jumping-off place, a sympathetic local governor burns his orders to seize the man and tells him to make a run for it. At a loose end, the traveller meets a self-styled local guide with a plan to get him across the border. With no other option, he follows the guide, who then leaves him stranded in the middle of a dreadful stretch of desert.

Sound like a recent backpacker's nightmare? Guess again. This scenario took place in 630 CE, when a tall, handsome, 28-year-old Buddhist monk named Xuan Zang (Hsüan-tsang) (602 to 664) set out from China for the holy places of India, the homeland of his faith. In his day, the available Chinese copies of Buddhist sacred texts were corrupt and inaccurate. In visiting India, his most pious wish was to procure good copies of the *sutras* to take back to China.

In the 16 years of his pilgrimage, Xuan Zang bracketed his grand tour of Indian sacred sites with extensive travels through Central Asia. Turfan, Kucha, the Bedel pass, Lake Issyk-Kul, the Chuy valley (near present-day Bishkek), Tashkent, Samarkand, Balkh, Kashgar and Khotan were all blessed by the footsteps of the pilgrim, whom Buddhists (and readers of the Chinese classic *Monkey*) know as Tripitaka.

Fa Xian (Fa Hsien)

Fa Xian was an earlier Buddhist pilgrim whose mission was to fetch Buddhist sutras and relics from India and who left a fascinating account of a Central Asia dominated by monasteries, monks and pagodas. Fa Xian set off in 399 CE, following the southern Silk Road, over the Hindu Kush into India and on to Sri Lanka. He eventually returned to China by boat after a 15-year trip loaded with texts to boost the growth of Buddhism in China.

nomadic hordes of the Heartland and the sedentary civilisations of Eurasia's periphery. Both sought to profit from Central Asia's long-distance trade routes. With the push and pull of a piston gathering steam, the continent's two major lifestyles played an extended overture to the Mongol conquest. Meanwhile the Turks, namesake of today's Turkestan, appeared on the scene at this time.

The Silk Road's first flower faded by about 200 CE (common era), as the Chinese, Roman, Parthian and Kushan empires went into decline. Sogdiana came under the control of the Sassanid empire of Iran. As the climate along the middle section of the Silk Road became drier, the Heartland nomads increasingly sought wealth by plundering, taxing and conquering their settled neighbours. The Sassanids lost their Inner Asian possessions

Unearthing the Amazons

As early as the 5th century BCE the Greek historian Herodotus knew of an army of women warriors, known as the Amazons, who were so dedicated to warfare that they allegedly cut off their own right breast in order to improve their shot with bows and arrows.

Recent excavations of burial mounds, or *kurgans* on the Kazak border with Russia are unearthing some intriguing links to these perhaps not so mythical warrior women.

Archaeologists have discovered skeletons of women, bow-legged from a life in the saddle, buried with swords, daggers and bronze-tipped arrows. Some appear to be priestesses buried with cultic implements, bronze mirrors and elaborate headdresses.

The finds indicate that women of these early steppe civilisations were trained from the outset to be warriors, fighting alongside men, perhaps even forming an elite social group. The status of these steppe women seems far higher than that of sedentary civilisations of the same time, challenging the stereotypical macho image of the Central Asian nomad.

in the 4th century to the Huns, who ruled a vast area of Central Asia at the same time that Attila was scourging Europe.

The Huns were followed south across the Syr-Darya by the western Turks (the western branch of the empire of the so-called Kök Turks or Blue Turks), who in 559 made an alliance with the Sassanids and ousted the Huns. The western Turks, who had arrived in the area from their ancestral homeland in southern Siberia, nominally controlled the reconquered region.

The mixing of the western Turks' nomadic ruling class with the sedentary Sogdian elite over the next few centuries produced a remarkable ethnic mix in cities like Penjikent, Afrosiab and Varakhsha. The populations thus invigorated by tolerant interchange would need every ounce of courage they could muster to weather the coming centuries of turmoil.

The Arrival of Islam

When the western Turks faded in the late 7th century, an altogether new and formidable kind of power was waiting to fill the void – the religious army. The new faith was Islam. Bursting out of Arabia just a few years after the Prophet Mohammed's death, the Muslim armies rolled through Persia in 642 to set up a military base at Merv but met stiff resistance from the Turks of Transoxiana. The power struggle in between the Amu-Darya and Syr-Darya rivers ebbed

and flowed, while Arab armies spread to take Bukhara in 709, Samarkand in 712 and Kashgar by 714.

China, meanwhile, had revived under the Tang dynasty. The Tang presence in 8th century Central Asia was a classic image of great-power expansionism, with colonial governors and over-extended expeditionary forces policing the dynasty's interests outside its borders, deep into Sogdiana, Kashmir and even Bactria. Provided the Chinese and the Arabs avoided confrontation, the resulting security on the trade routes meant more wealth and prosperity for all.

But one Chinese viceroy wanted more than his share, and murdered the khan of the Tashkent Turks to get it. It was perhaps the most costly incident of skulduggery in Chinese history. The enraged Turks were joined by the opportunistic Arabs and Tibetans; in 751 they squeezed the Chinese forces into the Talas valley (in present-day Kazakstan and Kyrgyzstan) and sent them flying back across the Tian Shan. Many soldiers and colonists were taken prisoner. From the south the Tibetan empire moved quickly to exert its control over vast areas of the Tarim basin.

From the north, the Uyghur Turks swept down to make their debut, as saviours of the Tang throne. As a direct result of their political alliance with Tang China, the Uyghurs began to live the settled and literate life which later bore the first flowering of Turkic culture.

Lost Battle, Lost Secrets

The Chinese lost big to the Arabs at the Battle of Talas in 751. The defeat marked the end of Chinese expansion west and secured the future of Islam as the region's foremost religion. But to add insult to injury, some of the Chinese rounded up after the battle were no ordinary prisoners: they were expert at the crafts of paper and silk making. Soon China's best-kept secrets were giving Arab silk makers in Persia a commercial advantage all over Europe. It was the first mortal blow to the Silk Road. The spread of paper-making to Europe sparked a technological revolution, the impact of this on the development of civilisation cannot be underestimated.

After Talas, the Arab's Central Asian territories receded in the wake of local rebellions. By the 9th century, Transoxiana had given rise to the peaceable and affluent Samanid dynasty. It generously encouraged the development of Persian culture while remaining strictly allied with the Sunni caliph of Baghdad. It was under the Samanids that Bukhara grew into a world centre of Muslim culture and garnered the epithet 'Pillar of Islam'. Some of the Islamic world's best scholars were nurtured in its 113 *medressas* (Islamic seminaries), including the physician Abu Ali ibn-Sina (Avicenna), the mathematician and encyclopaedist al-Beruni, and many poets and writers.

Karakhanids to Karakitay

By the early 10th century, internal strife at court had weakened the Samanid dynasty and opened the door for two Turkic usurpers to divide up the empire: the Ghaznavids in Khorasan, south of the Amu-Darya; and the Karakhanids in Transoxiana and the steppe region beyond the Syr-Darya. The Karakhanids are credited with finally converting the populace of Central Asia to Islam. They held sway from three mighty capitals: Balasagun (now Burana in Kyrgyzstan) in the centre of their domain, Talas (now Taraz in Kazakstan) in the west, and Kashgar in the east. Bukhara continued to shine, and Karakhanid Kashgar was the home of rich culture and science.

The Karakhanids and Ghaznavids coveted each other's lands. In the mid-11th century, while they were busy invading each other, they were caught off guard by a third Turkic horde, the Seljuqs, who annihilated both after pledging false allegiance to the Ghaznavids. In the Seljuqs' heyday their sultan had himself invested as emperor by the caliph of Baghdad. The empire was vast. On the east it bordered the lands of the Buddhist Karakitay, who had swept into Balasagun and Kashgar from China; to the west it extended all the way to the Mediterranean and Red seas.

An incurable symptom of Heartland dynasties through the ages was their near inability to survive the inevitable disputes of succession. The Seljuqs lasted a century before their weakened line succumbed to the Karakitay (who would in time lend their name to Cathay and Kitai, the Russian word for China) and to the Seljuqs' own rearguard vassals, the Khorezmshahs. From their capital at Gurganj (present-day Konye-Urgench), the Khorezmshahs burst full-force into the tottering Karakitay. They emerged as rulers of all Transoxiana and much of the Muslim world as well.

And so Central Asia might have continued in a perennial state of forgettable wars. As it is, the Khorezmshahs are still remembered primarily as the unlucky stooge left holding the red cape when the angry bull was released.

Mongol Terror, Mongol Peace

Jenghiz Khan felt he had all the justification in the world to ransack Central Asia. In 1218 a Khorezmian governor in Otyrar (now in Kazakstan) received a delegation from Jenghiz to inaugurate trade relations. Scared by distant reports of the new Mongol menace, the governor assassinated them in cold blood. Up until that moment Jenghiz, the intelligent khan of the Mongols who had been lately victorious over Chungtu (Beijing), had been carefully weighing the alternative strategies for expanding his power: commerce versus conquest. Then came the crude Otyrar blunder, and the rest is history.

In early 1219 Jenghiz placed himself at the head of an estimated 200,000 men and began to ride west from his Altay mountain stronghold. By the next year his armies had sacked Khojand and Otyrar (the murderous governor was dispatched with savage cruelty in Jenghiz's presence), and Bukhara soon followed.

It was in that brilliant city, as soldiers raped and looted and horses trampled Islamic holy books in the streets, that the unschooled Jenghiz ascended to the pulpit in the chief mosque and preached to the congregation. His message: 'I am God's punishment for your sins'. Such shocking psychological warfare is perhaps unrivalled in history. This was no heavy metal rock video, but the real thing.

Bukhara was burned to the ground, and the Mongol hosts swept on to conquer and plunder Samarkand, Merv, Termiz, Kabul, Balkh and, eventually under Jenghiz's generals and heirs, most of Eurasia.

Methods were bloody, brutal, meticulously destructive and, according to historians, each conceived with a definite goal in mind. For instance, in massacring populations (a common practice only when cities resisted), Mongol officers were instructed to spare artisans, architects, clerks and other professionals; these were appointed to run the empire. And the Mongol armies were

Jenghiz Khan & the Mongol Horde

The reign of Jenghiz Khan (1167 to 1227) is all the more remarkable for the fact that he started with nothing. The story (as preserved in the Mongolian *Secret History*) goes that the boy Temujin was born with noble blood in a clan down on its luck. His fatherless childhood was an unending series of hardships as he hid and fled from rival clan leaders bent on extinguishing his line. This experience bred a certain hardness of heart in Temujin: he killed his half-brother in cold blood when still in his teens.

With a combination of skill, luck and chutzpah perhaps unmatched by anyone before or since, Temujin managed to gather together a group of loyal clans around his stamping-ground, the Orkhon river region. By the age of 39 he was elected supreme khan, having taken the name Jenghiz (Mongolian for 'ocean') and it seems the ruler had no intention of stopping until his Heartland energy had inundated the world, like the oceans towards which his ambitions were expanding.

His war/state machine was a confederation of both Mongol and Turkic clans, and hence the group he controlled is correctly called Mongol Tatars (the western term *Tartar* comes from *Tatar* via association with *Tartaros*, the Greek name for hell, from whence the barbarians were said to have sprung). Once things got rolling, ethnic Mongols actually made up a very small percentage of the fighting force outside Mongolia, mainly occupying command positions.

When Jenghiz Khan's realm disintegrated a generation after his death, it was the beginning of the end for the Heartland, and the steppe was gradually eclipsed as a factor in world history. This was partly because the Mongol conquerors implanted the techniques necessary for victory among the peoples they conquered. The settled states of the Eurasian periphery, adopting and then adapting horse warfare, began to raise armies that could challenge the steppe invaders. Over the centuries, these states combined technological and military superiority in a new way. Eventually their expanding empires devoured the steppe. Grass, after centuries of enjoying special geopolitical status, became just a plant again.

Social historians point to Mongol roots in medieval chivalry. The horseback military culture of the Mongol elite was adapted and changed by their vassal rulers in Europe, acquiring the air of refined gallantry and romance associated with knights of old.

The Travelling Polos

In the 1250s Venice was predominant in the Mediterranean and looking for new commercial routes. The Venetian brothers Nicolo and Maffeo Polo set out to do some itinerant trading. Sailing from Constantinople with a cargo of precious stones, they made their way to the Crimea. Choice business deals followed and took them gradually up the Volga (they stayed a year at the Mongol khan's encampment), eastward across the steppes, south to Bukhara (for a three year stay), then across Central Asia to Karakoram (now in Mongolia), the seat of Kublai Khan, grandson of Jenghiz.

Kublai welcomed the Europeans warmly and questioned them at length about life and statecraft in Europe. Such was the style of hospitality on the steppe that the khan couldn't bear to let them go (modern travellers know similar treatment!). The Polos remained at Kublai's court for some four years.

In the end Kublai made them ambassadors to the Pope in Rome. Always searching for worthy doctrines from settled civilisations, Kublai requested that the Pope send him 100 of his most learned priests. They were to argue the merits of their faith over others, and if they succeeded, Kublai and his whole empire would convert to Christianity. It took the Polos three difficult years to get home; when they arrived, no one believed their stories.

Marco Polo, the teller of the world's most famous travel tale, was not born when his father Nicolo and uncle Maffeo set out on their journey. When they returned he was a motherless teenager. After a couple of years the elder Polos set off once more for Kublai's court, this time with Marco along.

The Pope had supplied only two monks, and they stayed behind in Armenia when the going got tough. It is tempting to conjecture how the fate of Eurasia might have been different if the requested 100 doctors of religion had shown up at Karakoram and converted the entire Mongol empire. But it is more probable that they would have been politely detained and made into imperial bureaucrats. The Mongols liked to use the services of foreigners whenever possible.

The Polos made their way from Hormuz on the Persian coast, to Balkh, and on through the Hindu Kush and Pamir (stopping by Lake Kara-Kul, now in Tajikistan, on the way), then on past Kashgar, Yarkand and the southern route around the Taklamakan desert, reaching China via Unhung and the Gansu Corridor. They found the khan dividing his time between Khanbaligh (now Beijing) and his nearby summer capital of Chung-tu (Xanadu of the Coleridge poem).

Marco was exceptionally intelligent and observant, and Kublai took a great liking to him. He was soon made a trusted adviser and representative of the ageing khan. The three Polos spent about 16 years in China; Marco travelled far afield and brought the khan news of his far-flung and exotic empire, little of which he had seen.

The Polos were only allowed to go home when they agreed to escort a Mongol princess on her way to be married in Persia. To avoid long hardship the party took the sea route from the east coast of China around India and up the Persian Gulf. Back in Venice, *still* no one believed the Polos' tales.

Many years later during a war with Genoa, Marco Polo was captured in a naval battle. While in prison he dictated the story of his travels. The resulting book has become the most-read travel account ever written. Hounded all his life by accusations that the exotic world he described was fictitious, Marco Polo was even asked to recant on his deathbed. His answer: 'I have not told the half of what I saw'.

employed with an understanding of grand strategy which not a single opposing general could even remotely match. The condescending western attitude that the uncivilised, almost subhuman Tatars conquered the civilised world by force of overwhelming numbers may have contributed to the persistent schism between east and west.

It is difficult to deny that Central Asian settled civilisation took a serious blow, from which it only began to recover 600 years later under Russian colonisation. The Mongols' ravages were largely to blame, while other circumstances also caused damage. Jenghiz's descendants controlling Persia favoured Shia Islam over Sunni Islam, a development which over the centuries isolated Central Asia from the currents of the rest of the Sunni Muslim world.

But there was stability, law and order under the *Pax Mongolica*. Like their numerous nomadic predecessors, it was a cherished wish of the Mongols to sit astride flourishing trade routes. Jenghiz Khan perceived that his large empire would not survive him without swift, reliable communications. To achieve these ends he laid down a thorough network of guard and post stations, employed express mail riders who could cover over 300km a day, and gave tax breaks to traders. In 20th century terms, the streets were safe and the trains ran on time. The resulting modest flurry of trade on the Silk Road was the background to many famous medieval travellers' journeys, including the greatest of them all, Marco Polo's.

On Jenghiz Khan's death in 1227, his empire was divided among his sons. By tradition the most distant lands, stretching as far as Ukraine and Moscow and including western and most of northern Kazakstan, would have gone to the eldest son, Jochi, had Jochi not died before his father. They went instead to Jochi's sons, Batu and Orda, and came to be known collectively as the Golden Horde. The second son, Chaghatai, got the next most distant portion, including most of Kazakstan, Uzbekistan and western Xinjiang; this came to be known as the Chaghatai khanate. The share of the third son, Ogedei, seems to have eventually been divided between the Chaghatai khanate and the Mongol heartland inherited by the youngest son, Tolui. Tolui's portion formed the basis for his son Kublai Khan's Yüan dynasty in China.

Unlike the Golden Horde in Europe and the Yüan dynasty, the Chaghatai khans tried to preserve their nomadic lifestyle, complete with the khan's roving tent encampment as 'capital city'. But as the rulers spent more and more time in contact with the Muslim collaborators who administered their realm, the Chaghatai line inevitably began to settle down. They even made motions towards conversion to Islam. It was in a fight over this issue, in the mid-14th century, that the khanate split in two, with the Muslim Chaghatais holding Transoxiana and the conservative branch retaining the Tian Shan, Kashgaria (the region around Kashgar at the west end of the Taklamakan desert) and the vast steppes north and east of the Syr-Darya, an area collectively known as Moghulistan.

Timur & the Timurids

One clear sign of the perennial viability and vitality of the steppe-based, nomadic-military form of government was that it appeared like crab grass at any crack in the status quo. The fracturing of the Mongol empire immediately led to resurgence of the Turkic peoples. From one minor clan near Samarkand arose a tyrant's tyrant, Timur ('the Lame', or Tamerlane). After assembling an army and wresting Transoxiana from Chaghatai rule, Timur went on a spectacular nine-year rampage which ended in 1395 with modern-day Iran, Iraq, Syria, eastern Turkey and the Caucasus at his feet. He also despoiled northern India (the founder of India's Moghul dynasty, Babur, was his grandson).

All over his realm, Timur plundered riches and captured artisans and poured them into his capital at Samarkand. The city grew, in stark contrast to his conquered lands, into a lavish showcase of treasure and pomp. The postcard skyline of today's Samarkand dates to Timur's reign, as do many fine works of painting and literature. Foreign guests of Timur's, including the Spanish envoy Ruy

MICK WELDON

'Timur the Lame' (Tamerlane), the tyrants' tyrant and patron of the arts.

Gonzales de Clavijo, took home stories of enchantment and barbarity which fed the west's dream of remote Samarkand.

Timur claimed indirect kinship with Jenghiz Khan, and his exploits certainly show that he was a pretender to Jenghiz's destiny. But it seems he had none of his forerunner's good sense and gift for statecraft. History can be strange: both conquerors savagely slaughtered hundreds of thousands of innocent people, yet one is remembered as a great ruler and the other not. The argument goes that Timur's bloodbaths were insufficiently linked to specific political or military aims. On the other hand, Timur is considered the more cultured and religious of the two men. At any rate, Timur died an old man at Otyrar in 1405, having just set out in full force to conquer China.

Important effects of Timur's reign can still be traced. For instance, when he pounded the army of the Golden Horde in southern Russia, Timur created a disequilibrium in the bloated Mongol empire which led to the seizure of power by its vassals, the petty

and fragmented Russian princes. This was the pre-dawn of the Russian state. Like the mammals after the dinosaurs, Russia had small beginnings.

For a scant century after Timur's death his descendants ruled on separately in small kingdoms and duchies. From 1409 until 1449, Samarkand was governed by the conqueror's mild, scholarly grandson, Ulughbek. Gifted in mathematics and astronomy, he built a large celestial observatory and attracted scientists who gave the city lustre as a centre of learning for years to come (Ulughbek was the victim of a cultural and religious backlash, and beheaded as part of a plot that involved his own son Abdul Latif).

The Timurids were generous patrons of art and literature. In addition to Persian, a Turkic court language came into use, called Chaghatai, which survived for centuries as a Central Asian lingua franca.

Uzbeks & Kazaks

Modern Uzbekistan and Kazakstan, the two principal powers of post-Soviet Central Asia, eye each other warily across the rift dividing their two traditional lifestyles: sedentary agriculture (Uzbeks) and nomadic pastoralism (Kazaks). Yet these two nations are closely akin, and parted ways with a family killing.

The family in question was the dynasty of the Uzbek khans. These rulers, one strand of the modern Uzbek people, had a pedigree reaching back to a grandson of Jenghiz Khan and an original territory in southern Siberia. In the 14th century they converted to Islam, gathered strength, and started moving south. Under Abylqayyr (or Abu al-Khayr) Khan they reached the north bank of the Syr-Darya, across which lay the declining Timurid rulers in Transoxiana. But Abylqayyr had enemies within his own family. The two factions met in battle in 1468, and Abylqayyr was killed and his army defeated.

After this setback, Abylqayyr's grandson Mohammed Shaybani brought the Uzbek khans to power once more. He invaded Transoxiana and established Uzbek control over the territory between the Syr-Darya and Amu-Darya, the same land which Alexander and Ptolemy had known as Transoxiana, and which is now Uzbekistan. Abylqayyr's rebellious kinsmen became the forefathers of the Kazak khans.

The Uzbeks gradually adopted the sedentary agricultural life best suited to the fertile river valleys they occupied. Settled life involved cities, which entailed administration, literacy, learning and, wrapped up with all of these, Islam. The Shaybanid dynasty, which ruled until the end of the 16th century, attempted to out-do the Timurids in religious devotion and to carry on their commitment to artistic patronage. But the Silk Road had disappeared, usurped by spice ships, and Central Asia's economy had entered full decline. As prosperity fell, so did the region's importance as a centre of the Islamic world. The Astrakhanid khans and Iranian Safavids held sway over the benighted remains of Transoxiana until the mid-18th century.

The Kazaks, meanwhile, stayed home on the range, north of the Syr-Darya, and flourished as nomadic herders. Their experience of urban civilisation and organised Islam remained slight compared with their Uzbek cousins. By the 16th century the Kazaks had solidly filled a power vacuum on the old Saka steppes between the Ural and Irtysh rivers and established what was to be the world's last nomadic empire. In their heyday in the late 15th and 16th centuries the Kazaks controlled a vast region of grassland with as many horse soldiers as Jenghiz Khan and the Seljuqs had commanded.

Inevitably the political 'cell division' of the nomads produced three distinct Kazak groups or hordes, each centred in a separate area on the steppe (the word *horde*, which conjures up images of immense swarms of people, comes through French from the Turkic word *orda*, meaning the yurt or pavilion where a khan held his court). The Great Horde roamed the steppes of the Jetisuu region (Russian: Semireche) north of the Tian Shan; the Middle Horde occupied the grasslands extending east from the Aral Sea; and the Little Horde nomadised west of there as far as the Ural river.

In good times, such as the reigns of Qasym Khan and his son Haq Nazar in the 16th century, the Kazak hordes were a unified nation acting under the firm control of a single khan. Unity brought military might and expansion; the Kazaks menaced the dying Chaghatai khanate of the Tian Shan and Kashgaria, invaded Transoxiana, and even entered Samarkand as conquerors. But during the years when the power of the principal khans waned and the individual hordes split apart, the Kazaks suffered badly at the hands of another steppe power whose star was briefly on the rise.

The Zhungarian Empire

The Oyrats were a western Mongol clan who had been converted to Tibetan Buddhism. Their day in the sun came when they subjugated eastern Kazakstan, the Tian Shan, Kashgaria and western Mongolia to form the Zhungarian (or Dzungarian) empire (1635-1758). During this time the Oyrats exploited the weaknesses of their neighbours well, and sent alarms sounding through the courts of Manchu (Qing) China and Russia. Russia's frontier settlers were forced to pay heavy tribute, China lost large amounts of territory, east Turkestan and Tibet were invaded, and the Kazak hordes, with their boundless pasturage beyond the mountain gap known as the Zhungarian Gate, were cruelly and repeatedly pummelled.

All this continued until the death of the Zhungarian emperor Galdan Tseren, when – surprise, surprise – a struggle for the succession caught the inheritors off guard. Alert for an opportunity to make an economical strike, in 1758 the exasperated Manchu Chinese emperor took a large force and fell upon the Oyrat armies. The Zhungarian state was liquidated and Oyrat men, women and children were massacred to a fraction of their former population.

Memory of the Oyrat legacy has been preserved in epic poetry by the Kazaks and by their mountain-dwelling relatives the Kyrgyz, who both suffered under the Oyrats' ruthless predations. The Kyrgyz epic poems of the *Manas* cycle have preserved the general national anxiety (though few actual historical details) from a time when the Oyrat Mongols (as Kalmaks) seemed poised to crush all resisters. Descendants of the Oyrats continue to live in China and in the Altay Republic in Russia.

Central Asia after the fall of the Zhungarian empire was an anarchic place, lulled by the uneasy peace of exhaustion. The Manchu court was weak and could expend little effort on policing the huge territory which it had garnered. The Chaghatai khans of the Tian Shan and Kashgaria were powerless figure heads. Their mountain provinces were claimed by hard-bitten Kyrgyz, and their cities were governed by an Uyghur dynasty of priest-kings (Khojas). On the steppes, the Kazak khans were reeling from the Zhungarian years. Gradually over the mid-18th century, the Kazaks accepted Russian protection – first the Little Horde, then the Middle Horde, then part of the Great Horde. But the protection did little to improve the Kazaks' fate at the hands of the Oyrats.

The Russians had by this time established a line of fortified outposts on the northern fringe of the Kazak Steppe. However, it appears that there was no clear conception in St Petersburg of exactly where the Russian Empire's frontier lay. Slow on the uptake, Russia at this stage had little interest in the immense territory it now abutted.

The Khanates of Kokand, Khiva & Bukhara

In the fertile land now called Uzbekistan, the military regime of an Iranian interloper named Nadir Shah collapsed in 1747, leaving a political void which was rapidly occupied by a trio of Uzbek khanates.

The three dynasties were the Kungrats, enthroned at Khiva (in the territory of old Khorezm), the Manghits at Bukhara and the Mins at Kokand. They were all rivals of one another. The khans of Khiva and Kokand and the emirs of Bukhara seemed able to will the outside world out of existence as they stroked and clawed each other like a box of kittens. Boundaries were impossible to fix as the rivals shuffled their provinces in endless wars.

Unruly nomadic tribes produced constant pressure on their periphery. Bukhara and Khiva vainly claimed nominal control over the nomadic Turkmen, who prowled the Karakum desert and provided the khanates with slaves from Persia. Kokand expanded into the Tian Shan mountains and the Syr-Darya basin in the early 19th century, but there it encountered cagey Kyrgyz and Kazak tribes who proved to be more than a handful. Farther afield, various provinces of all three khanates were disputed with Persia, Afghanistan or Chinese Kashgar.

The khans ruled absolutely as feudal despots. Some of them were capable rulers; some, such as the last emir of Bukhara, were depraved and despised tyrants. The social sphere was dominated by the mosque. In the centuries since Transoxiana had waned as the centre of Islam, the mullahs had slipped into hypocrisy and greed. The level of education and literacy was low, and the *ulama* or intellectual class seems to have encouraged superstition and ignorance in the people.

It was no dark age, however. Trade was vigorous. This was especially true in Bukhara, where exports of cotton, cloth, silk, karakul wool and other goods gave it a whopping trade surplus with Russia. Commerce brought in new ideas, with resulting attempts to develop irrigation and even to reform civil administrations. European travellers in the 19th century mentioned the splendour of the Islamic architecture in these exotic capitals.

In none of the three khanates was there any sense among the local people that they belonged to a distinct *nation* – whether of Bukhara, Khiva or Kokand. In all three, *sarts* (town dwellers) occupied the towns and farms, while tribes who practiced nomadism and seminomadism roamed the uncultivated countryside. Sarts included both Turkic-speaking Uzbeks and Persian-speaking Tajiks. These two groups had almost identical lifestyles and customs, apart from language.

In many respects, the three khanates closely resembled the feudal city-states of late medieval Europe. But it is anybody's guess how they and the Kazak and Kyrgyz nomads might have developed had they been left alone.

The Coming of the Russians

Russia has two faces, an Asiatic face which looks always towards Europe, and a European face which looks always towards Asia.

Benjamin Disraeli

By the turn of the 19th century Russia's vista to the south was of anachronistic, unstable neighbours. Flush with the new currents of imperialism sweeping Europe, the empire found itself embarking willy-nilly upon a century of rapid expansion into its own 'heart of darkness'.

The reasons were complex. The main ingredients were the search for a secure, and preferably natural, southern border, nagging fears of British expansion from India, and the boldness of the tsar's officers. And probably, glimmering in the back of every patriotic Russian's mind, there was a vague notion of the 'manifest destiny' of the frontier.

The first people to feel the impact were the Kazaks. Their agreements in the mid-18th century to accept Russian 'protection' had apparently been understood by St Petersburg as agreements to annexation. A few decades later Russia began at last to turn its attention to controlling and using its 'new possessions'. Tatars and Cossacks were sent to settle and farm the land. Angered, the Kazaks revolted. As a consequence, the khans of the three hordes were one by one stripped of their autonomy, and their lands were made into bona fide Russian colonies. In 1848, as the USA was gaining land stretching from Texas to California, Russia abolished the Great Horde. Theirs was the last line of rulers in the world directly descended, by both blood and throne, from Jenghiz Khan.

The Kyrgyz were close relatives of the Kazaks, but with no khans and no state. At the turn of the 19th century they were already cornered in the Tian Shan mountains when the long arm of Kokand began to encircle them. As Russia approached from the north, each of the splintered Kyrgyz chiefs acted in his own interests to buy security for his clan. Kokand took taxes and military conscripts, and promised agreeable Kyrgyz leaders a piece of the pie. Russia exacted assurances of support in the coming confrontation with Kokand, and offered protection. Mostly the Kyrgyz waffled, perhaps wisely. In lieu of unity they opted to continue their age-old feuds and mutual cattle raids.

By the 1860s Russia had received a disappointing rebuke in the Crimean War. Checked in the west, the empire began to focus on eastward expansion. Job one was to stabilise the frontier areas occupied by the nomads, to woo the Kyrgyz and Kazaks into submission. This happened piecemeal, almost clan by clan.

Kokand, the nomads' other major suitor, was thus the first of the three Uzbek khanates to be swamped. In 1864 the Kokand city of Turkistan was taken by the Orenburg Corps from the north. That same year, Aulie-Ata (now Taraz) fell to a Russian force from Verny (Almaty) in the east. The Kokand fortress of Pishpek (Bishkek) had been wiped out two years before by a combined Kyrgyz and Russian siege. Chimkent (Shymkent) fell in 1864, followed by Tashkent.

The assault on Tashkent in May and June 1865 was as dramatic a moment as any in the conquest. General Mikhail Grigorevich Chernyayev, against explicit orders from St Petersburg, marched a tiny regiment to the outskirts of the medieval walled city and cut off the water supply. But while waiting for thirst to set in, his men were raided by the Kokand army, four times greater in number. The counter-attackers were beaten off, and at dawn on June 14 Chernyayev lead his men through the gates of Tashkent. The Russians were outnumbered by more than 20 to one; their chaplain led one charge armed only with a cross. Yet the city surrendered after two days of bloody street fighting.

The capture of Tashkent from Kokand closed the gap between two fortified lines on Russia's southern frontier.

For his shrewd disobedience, Chernyayev earned a diamond-encrusted sword from the tsar, and his dismissal. From his vanquished foes he received the nom de guerre 'Lion of Tashkent'.

Bukhara was understandably worried by the news. At about the time General Konstantin Petrovich Kaufman was inaugurated

Renaissance Boy of the Steppes

Shoqan Ualikhanov (1835-65) was one of the most remarkable personalities of Russian Central Asia. A grandson of the last khan of the Kazak Middle Horde, Shoqan (the Russian spelling of his name is Chokan Valikhanov) was educated in the prestigious Orenburg Cadet Corps and rose to become an army captain. He served as an intelligence agent among the Kazaks and Kyrgyz, befriended the exiled Dostoevsky and the explorer Nikolai Przhevalsky, and drew and painted with great skill.

He earned his place in history as a member of military-political-scientific expeditions through Semireche and Kashgaria. His notebooks from these journeys are crammed with observations on geography, botany, zoology, ethnography, history, folklore, archaeology, linguistics, literature and politics. Shoqan was also the first person to take down a fragment of the *Manas* epic from the mouth of a Kyrgyz oral bard.

His main claim to fame, though, was his daring infiltration of Kashgar in 1858 and 1859. Arriving by caravan disguised as the son of a Kokand merchant, the 23-year-old officer began his observations with a laconic note in his diary:

> In Kashgar, and in the Six Cities in general, there is a custom that all foreigners upon arrival must enter into marriage ... The wedding is conducted in due form, and all that is required of the groom is that he consummate the union with the bride. So as not to depart from common procedure, and at the insistence of our new friends, we too were obliged to submit to this custom ...

Shoqan stayed under cover for five months, befriending Kashgarians of all sorts and gathering political intelligence. The job was not without risk, however. Only a year before, the second European to enter Kashgar since Marco Polo had been unmasked and beheaded. Shoqan escaped that fate.

Leaving Kashgar, Shoqan made his way to St Petersburg. There he lived for a year and a half, writing, reporting to the government on his adventures, and meeting the literati. His liberal sentiments began to run him up against authority during the Russian conquest era of the 1860s. Those were his fellow Muslims, and his fellow Turks, being carved up by the Russian army he was serving. He is said to have had an argument with General Chernyayev himself, in which he condemned unnecessary violence by Russian storm troopers.

His early death in April 1865 is shrouded in mystery. Some say his final illness was tuberculosis; others claim it was syphilis contracted at Kashgar. He died in a simple Kazak *aul* (nomadic encampment). His last letters to his commander, the governor general of Semireche, continued to contain valuable briefings on the political situation in the hinterlands.

Yet in spite of his intelligence work and his illness, the young Kazak kept his priorities straight to the bitter end. One of the last letters the governor general received ended: 'PS Your Excellency would render a great favour if he would send me a few boxes of Havana cigars ...'

Shoqan Ualikhanov's reputation suffered relatively little distortion as the Soviets turned him into a national hero for the Kazaks – explorer, scholar, democrat. He is now universally revered in his homeland.

as military governor general of the Russians' new Turkestan province, the Bukhara mullahs issued a fatwah declaring holy war on Russia. In April 1868 the emir and his army clashed with Kaufman and a small body of Russian troops near Samarkand. It was an overwhelming defeat for Bukhara: everyone fought, including the emir. The very next day Kaufman was presented with the keys to the city of Samarkand.

By late June 1868, after quashing a popular uprising in Samarkand, Kaufman at last brought the Bukharan government to the table for a meal of humble pie. The peace treaty ceded three provinces to the empire, while the rest of the Bukhara emirate was made a protectorate. The emir also had to pay a hefty war indemnity and allow free access to local markets for Russian businesses.

Khiva, remote and ringed by deserts, held out a little longer. Four forces converging from Tashkent, Orenburg, Mangghyshlak and the Caspian port of Krasnovodsk finally pinched the khanate in 1873. In its place remained a protectorate with status similar to Bukhara's. In the meantime Kokand had been losing provinces right and left to the mushrooming Russian Turkestan. The rump Kokand khanate, stripped of all its territories, was finally abolished and annexed in 1877.

The last and fiercest people to hold out against the tsarist juggernaut were the Tekke, the largest Turkmen tribe. Of all nomad groups, the Tekke had managed to remain the most independent of the khanates, in this case Khiva. Some Turkmen tribes had asked to be made subjects of Russia as early as 1865, for convenient help in their struggle against the Khivan yoke. But none were in a mood to have their tethers permanently shortened as Russia expanded into their territory. To add rancour to the pot, the Russians were anguished by the Tekkes' dealings in slaves, particularly Christian ones.

Much blood was spilled in the subjugation of the Tekke. The Russians were trounced in 1879 at Teke-Turkmen, but returned with a huge force under General Mikhail Dmitrievich Skobelev in 1881. The siege and capture of Geok-Tepe, the Tekkes' last stronghold, resulted in staggering casualties among the defenders.

With resistance ended, the Russians proceeded along the hazily defined Persian frontier area, occupying Merv in 1884 and the Pandjeh oasis on the Afghan border in 1885. It was the southernmost point they reached.

During this conquest, the government in St Petersburg had agonised over every advance. In the field, however, their hawkish generals took key cities without asking for permission. It all seems to have gone according to the precepts of General Skobelev, who is quoted as having said:

> I hold it as a principle that in Asia the duration of peace is in direct proportion to the slaughter you inflict upon the enemy. The harder you hit them the longer they will be quiet afterwards.

When it was over, Russia found it had bought a huge new territory, half the size of the USA, geographically and ethnically diverse, and economically rich – fairly cheaply in terms of money and lives, and in just 20 years. But while the dysfunctional grabbing-binge was going on upstairs in Central Asia, down in India the other great empire of the 19th century had found it difficult to get any rest. And some disturbing noises from India had caused due alarm in Russia.

The Great Game

What do two expanding empires do when their fuzzy frontiers draw near each other? They scramble for control of what's between them.

The British called it the Great Game; in Russia it was the Tournament of Shadows. Its backdrop was the first cold war between east and west. All the ingredients were there: spies and counter-spies, demilitarised zones, puppet states and doom-saying governments whipping up smokescreens for their own shady business. All that was lacking was the atom bomb and a Russian leader banging his shoe on the table. Diplomatic jargon acquired the phrase 'sphere of influence' during this era.

The story of the Great Game would be dull as dishwater except that its centre arena was the Roof of the World (a common term for the Pamir range). The history of Central Asia from the beginning of the 19th century onward must be seen in the context of the Great Game, for this was the main reason for Russian interest in the region.

Kashgaria Stage: Yakub Beg The Great Game era is perhaps unique in history for the way it made the British empire abase itself to local tyrants in exchange for elusive 'favours'. Yakub Beg is a case in point.

In the mid-19th century Uyghurs and Dungans (Chinese Muslims) rose up and wrested the Ili river region and Zhungaria (now in north-west Xinjiang) from the feeble rule of the Chinese Manchu dynasty. In 1863 Kokand sent its own pretender out to vie for Kashgar. The mission's military officer was one Yakub Beg, a Tajik of low birth and high aspirations. He dumped the would-be puppet ruler he was accompanying and manoeuvred himself into power. By 1867 he had emerged as supreme potentate of Kashgaria, the Ili river region and Zhungaria, a region known as Alty Shaar or 'the Six Cities'.

Soon Yakub Beg found himself officially recognised by Great Britain and Turkey. The Russians went for economic ties, and swiftly sent trading caravans to Kashgar. Spies and shadowy traders from Britain lined up to whisper sweet nothings in Yakub Beg's ear. Through it all, he played the Russians and British off against each other.

But Yakub Beg's diplomatic overtures to Russia were spurned; St Petersburg still had friendly relations with the Manchu regime he had usurped. In 1871 Russia decided to stabilise its frontier. Troops crossed the 'Chinese' border and captured the rebellious Ili region, including its centre, Kulja (Yining).

Yakub Beg died mysteriously in 1877, and his regime toppled in the succession struggle. The moment the outcome was inevitable, Britain changed course and lavishly financed the Chinese recapture of Kashgaria. The crackdown was savage.

The fortunes of the locals reached a low ebb when Russia evacuated its troops from the Ili region. Fearing Chinese reprisals, tens of thousands of Uyghurs, Dungans and Kazaks fled in 1882 as the Russians pulled out (these refugees are the ancestors of the Dungan and Uyghur communities of modern Kazakhstan and Kyrgyzstan). The Chinese organised their recaptured territories into Xinjiang province, the 'New Dominions'.

Ground gained by Russia: zero. Ground gained by Britain: zero.

Pamir Stage The Russian occupation of Merv in 1884 immediately raised blood pressures in Britain and India. Merv was a crossroads leading to Herat, an easy gateway to Afghanistan which in turn offered entry into British India. The British government finally lost its cool when the Russians went south to control Pandjeh. But the storm had been brewing long before 1884.

In 1839 Britain installed a hand-picked ruler of Afghanistan, which resulted in an uprising, a death march from Kabul by the British garrison, and a vengeful 'First Afghan War'. By the end of it, Britain's puppet-ruler was murdered and his predecessor was back on the throne. This failure to either control or befriend the headstrong Afghans was repeated in an equally ill-fated 1878 invasion (the Russians likewise failed from 1979 to 1988).

By 1848 the British had defeated the Sikhs and taken Punjab and the Peshawar valley. With a grip now on the 'Northern Areas' Britain began a kind of cat-and-mouse game with Russia across the vaguely mapped Pamir and Hindu Kush. Agents posing as scholars, explorers, merchants – even Muslim preachers and Buddhist pilgrims – crisscrossed the mountains, mapping them, spying on each other, courting local rulers, staking claims like dogs in a vacant lot.

In 1882 Russia established a consulate in Kashgar. A British agency at Gilgit (now in Pakistan), which had opened briefly in 1877, was urgently reopened when the Mir of Hunza entertained a party of Russians in 1888. Britain set up its own Kashgar office in 1890.

Also in 1890, Francis Younghusband (later to head a British incursion into Tibet) was sent to do some politicking with Chinese officials in Kashgar. On his way back through the Pamir he found the range full of Russian troops, and was told to get out or face arrest.

This electrified the British. They raised hell with the Russian government and invaded Hunza the following year; at the same time Russian troops skirmished in north-east Afghanistan. After a burst of diplomatic manoeuvring, Anglo-Russian boundary agreements in 1895 and 1907 gave Russia most of the Pamir and established the Wakhan Corridor, the awkward tongue of Afghan territory that stretches across to meet Xinjiang.

The Pamir settlement merely shifted the focus of the Great Game back towards Kashgar, where the two powers went on conniving. Their consulates in Kashgar became 'listening posts' which buzzed with intelligence and rumours. Local ears were employed, and travellers passing through the consulates' doors were apt to be debriefed exhaustively about what they had seen.

The Great Game was over. The Great Lesson for the people of the region was: 'No great power has our interests at heart'. The lesson has powerful implications today.

Colonisation of Turkestan & Semireche

In 1861, the outbreak of the US Civil War ended Russia's imports of American cotton. To keep the growing textile industry in high gear, the natural place to turn to for cotton was Central Asia. Other sectors of Russian industry were equally interested in the new colonies as sources of cheap raw materials and labour, and as huge markets. Russia's government and captains of industry wisely saw that their own goods could not compete in Europe against products from the more industrialised west. But in Central Asia they had a captive, virgin market. Gradually, Russian Turkestan was put in line with the economic needs of the empire.

The Trans-Caspian Railway was begun at Krasnovodsk in 1880 and reached Samarkand in 1888. The Orenburg-Tashkent line was completed in 1905.

In the late 19th century, Europeans began to flood the tsar's new lands, a million in Kazakstan alone. The immigrants were mostly freed Russian and Ukrainian serfs who wanted land of their own. Central Asia also offered a chance for enterprising Russians to climb socially. The first mayor of Pishpek (Bishkek) left Russia as a gunsmith, married well in the provinces, received civil appointments, and ended his life owning a mansion and a sprawling garden estate.

The middle class brought with them straight streets, gas lights, telephones, cinemas, amateur theatre, charity drives, parks and hotels. All these were contained in enclaves set apart from the original towns (the central district of Karakol, on Lake Issyk-Kul in Kyrgyzstan, is probably the best-preserved relic of this colonial environment).

Through their lace curtains the Russians looked out on the Central Asian masses with a fairly indulgent attitude. The Muslim fabric of life was left alone, as were the mullahs, as long as they were submissive. Some Russian politicos even maintained that Islam would surely wither and die in the face of enlightened western society.

Development, both social and economic, was initially a low priority. When it came, it took the form of small industrial enterprises, irrigation systems and a modest program of primary education.

In culture it was the Kazaks, as usual, who were the first to be influenced by Russia. A small, Europeanised, educated class began for the first time to think of the Kazak people as a nation. In part, their ideas came from a new sense of their own illustrious past, which they read about in the works of Russian ethnographers and historians. Their own brilliant but short-lived scholar, Shoqan Ualikhanov, was a key figure in Kazak consciousness-raising. Kazak politics of the day were also shaped by contact with the Tatars, a Turkic people of Russia with a strong early sense of nationality.

The Uzbeks were also affected by the 19th century cultural renaissance of the Tatars. The Jadidists, adherents of educational reform, made small gains in modernising Uzbek schools. The Pan-Turkic movement found fertile ground among educated Uzbeks at the beginning of the 20th century, and took root.

The 1916 Uprising

Resentment against the Russians ran deep and occasionally boiled over. Andijan in Uzbekistan was the scene of a holy war from 1897 to 1898 which rocked the Russians out of complacency. After the insurrection was put down, steps were taken to

Russify urban Muslims, the ones most under the influence of the mullahs and most likely to organise against the regime.

The outbreak of WWI in 1914 had disastrous consequences in Central Asia. In Semireche, massive herds of Kazak and Kyrgyz cattle were requisitioned for the war effort, while Syr-Darya, Fergana and Samarkand provinces had to provide cotton and food. Then, in 1916, as Russia's hopes in the war plummeted, the tsar demanded men. Local people in the colonies were to be conscripted as noncombatants in labour battalions. To add insult to injury, the action was not called 'mobilisation' but 'requisition', a term usually used for cattle and materiel.

Exasperated Central Asians just said no. Starting in Tashkent, an uprising swept eastwards over the summer of 1916. It gained in violence, and attracted harsher reprisal, the farther east it went. Kazak and Kyrgyz nomads were indeed a force to be reckoned with. Colonisation of their ancestral grasslands had squeezed them into smaller and smaller areas. In some cases the nomads were forced by the tsarist administration to rent back their own land. Taxed into destitution, they had nothing to lose in fighting.

Accounts of what happened vary. It appears that the Kazaks and Kyrgyz began their uprising under strict discipline, but things quickly got out of hand. Purposeful attacks on Russian militias and official facilities gave way to massive rioting, raiding and looting. Colonists were massacred, their villages burned, and women and children carried off.

The resulting bloody crackdown is a milestone tragedy in Kyrgyz and Kazak history. Russian troops and vigilantes gave up all pretence of a 'civilising influence' as whole Kyrgyz and Kazak villages were brutally slaughtered or set to flight. Manhunts for suspected perpetrators continued all winter, long after an estimated 50,000 Kyrgyz and Kazak families had fled towards China. The refugees who didn't starve or freeze on the way were shown little mercy in China.

But not all unrest among Muslims was directed against Russia. The Young Bukharans and Young Khivans movements agitated for social self-reform, modelling themselves on the Young Turks movement which had begun transforming Turkey in 1908. Though small in number, these groups attracted serious opposition and even repression from the ruling Muslim elite, a measure of their importance.

Revolution & Civil War

For a short time after the Russian Revolution of 1917, which toppled the tsar, there was a real feeling of hope in some Central Asian minds. The society which the west, out of ignorance and mystification, had labelled backward and inflexible had actually been making preparations for impressive progress. The Bolsheviks made sure, however, that we will never know how Central Asia might have remade itself.

The Kokand Government In 1917 an independent state was launched in Kokand by young nationalists under the watchful eye of a cabal of Russian cotton barons. This new government intended to put into practice the philosophy of the Jadid movement: to build a strong, autonomous Pan-Turkic polity in Central Asia by modernising the religious establishment, westernising, and educating the people.

Kokand, its khanate long gone, was politically far ahead of Bukhara and Khiva, where the ruling elite still wallowed in feudal intrigues. The Bolsheviks seized power in Russia in November 1917, and within five months of its inception the Kokand government was smashed by the Red Army's newly formed Trans-Caspian front. Over 5000 Kokanders were massacred after the city was captured. Central Asians' illusions about peacefully coexisting with Bolshevik Russia were shattered as well.

Bolshevik Conquest Like most Central Asians, Emir Alim Khan of Bukhara hated the Bolsheviks. In response to their first ultimatum to submit, he slaughtered the Red emissaries who brought it and declared a holy war. A truce from spring 1918 to spring 1919 gave the Bolsheviks and the emir time to build up their offensive strategies. The

Enver Pasha & the Basmachi

As the Bolsheviks were celebrating their victory in Central Asia, a dashing, courageous Ottoman Turkish soldier named Enver Pasha was making his way towards Central Asia. A Young Turk, Enver had served as the Ottoman empire's minister of war during WWI but was forced to flee his homeland after the empire's defeat in 1918. He wound up in Moscow, where he bent Lenin's ear and convinced the Soviet leader that he was just the person to bring him Central Asia and British India on a platter. In exchange, Lenin was to help him win control of what was left of the Turkish empire.

Enver left Moscow for Bukhara in November 1921, ostensibly to make ready an army for his benefactor. In reality he had already decided to jilt Lenin and look after his own dream: to conquer and rule a Pan-Turkic state with Central Asia as its core.

In Bukhara he made secret contact with leaders of the *basmachi* – local bands of Turkic and Tajik freedom fighters (the Russians had given them the name, with its overtones of banditry and murder, and it has unfortunately stuck). The basmachi guerrillas (today they would be called mujaheddin), with their grass-roots base and intimate knowledge of the mountain geography, had already proven to be worthy foes of the infant Red Army. But to make great and lasting gains they needed a leader to unify them. It was love at first sight between Enver and the basmachi. He gave his Bolshevik hosts the slip and rode east from Bukhara. In the countryside, exulting like a bridegroom, he gathered up to 20,000 recruits.

Enver Pasha could never be accused of underestimating himself. As support and material aid began to pour in from the exiled Emir of Bukhara and his host the Emir of Afghanistan, Enver styled himself 'Commander in Chief of All the Armies of Islam', a relative of the caliph by marriage, and Representative of the Prophet. The people flocked to his campaign as to a holy war.

Initial successes were stunning. Enver's small army took Dushanbe in February 1922. By the spring they had captured much of the former emirate of Bukhara. The egotistical Enver refused to negotiate with the Bolsheviks until they evacuated Central Asia.

Enraged, the Bolsheviks sent 100,000 additional troops in to crush him. Moscow also played an important political card: it permitted the Islamic courts to reconvene, gave residents of the Fregon valley a massive tax cut, and returned confiscated land. Support for the basmachi faltered.

Enver also discovered the downside of his fanatical host of irregulars: they simply dissolved back into the countryside as things started to go against their leader. With his rural support drying up, and with the Emir of Afghanistan turning a cold shoulder, he still refused to surrender. He and a small band of his closest officers set out for the Pamir east of Dushanbe, never to emerge again.

On 4 August 1922, less than nine months after his portentous arrival at Bukhara, Enver Pasha met his end like a hero. Accounts of the final moments differ. The most popular holds that he galloped headlong with sabre drawn at the head of a suicidal charge against the machine-gun fire of a Bolshevik ambush. In any case the few survivors of the raid scattered, and immediately began feeding the legend of their fallen leader. Had he succeeded in his grandiose vision, Enver Pasha would have been the first Turkic conqueror of all Turkestan since Timur. The fact that he made the attempt is ample fuel for myth.

The basmachi fought on, scattered and dwindling, until the early 1930s. They are now the subject of intensive research by post-Soviet historians, the first generation able to commemorate the basmachi without fear of repression.

emir conspired with White (ie anti-Bolshevik) Russians and British political agents, while the Reds concentrated on strengthening Party cells within the city.

The end came swiftly after the arrival in Tashkent of the Red Army commander Mikhail Frunze. Khiva went out with barely a whimper, quietly transforming into the Khorezm People's Republic in February 1920. In September Frunze's fresh, disciplined army captured Bukhara after a four day fight. The emir fled to Afghanistan, taking with him his company of dancing boys but abandoning his harem. These women were 'liberated' by Bolshevik soldiers.

Tashkent and much of Semireche, had fallen to the Bolsheviks soon after the October revolution. Then in December 1918 a counter-revolution broke out, apparently organised from within Tashkent jail by a shadowy White Russian agent named Paul Nazaroff. Several districts and cities fell back into the hands of the Whites. The bells of the cathedral church in Tashkent were rung in joy, but for the last time. The Bolsheviks defeated the insurrection, snatched back power, and kept it. Nazaroff, freed from jail, was forced to hide and flee across the Tian Shan to Xinjiang, always one step ahead of the dreaded secret police.

The Soviet Era

The Communist Party is the mind, honour and conscience of our era.

Vladimir Ilych Lenin

From the start the Bolsheviks ensured themselves the universal hatred of the people. Worse even than the tsar's bleed-the-colonies-for-the-war policies, the revolutionaries levied grievous requisitions of food, livestock, cotton and land. Turks were even subjected to forced farm labour. Trade and agricultural output in the once-thriving colonies plummeted. The ensuing famines claimed nearly a million lives; some say many more.

Forced Collectivisation Forced collectivisation was the 'definite stage of development' implicit in time-warping the entire population of Central Asia from feudalism to Communism. This occurred during the USSR's grand First Five Year Plan (1928-32). The intent of collectivisation was first to eliminate private property and second, in the case of the nomadic Kazaks and Kyrgyz, to put an end to their wandering lifestyle.

The effect was disastrous. When the orders came down, most people simply slaughtered their herds and ate what they could rather than give them up. This led to famine in subsequent years, and widespread disease. Resisters were executed and imprisoned. Millions of people died. Evidence exists that during this period Stalin had a personal hand in tinkering with meagre food supplies in order to induce famines. His aims seem to have been to subjugate the people's will and to depopulate Kazakstan, which was good real estate for Russian expansion.

The basmachi (see the boxed text 'Enver Pasha & the Basmachi'), in twilight for some time, renewed their guerrilla activities briefly as collectivisation took its toll. It was their final struggle.

Political Repression Undeveloped Central Asia had no shortage of bright, sincere people willing to work for national liberation and democracy. After the tsar fell they jostled for power in their various parties, movements and factions. Even after they were swallowed into the Soviet state, some members of these groups had high profiles in regional affairs. Such a group was Alash Orda, which was formed by Kazaks and Kyrgyz in 1917. Alash Orda even held the reins of a short-lived autonomous government.

By the late 1920s, the former nationalists and democrats, indeed the entire intelligentsia, were causing Stalin serious problems. From their posts in the Communist administration they had front-row seats at the Great Leader's horror show, including collectivisation. Many of them began to reason, and to doubt. Stalin, reading these signs all over the USSR, foresaw that brains could be just as dangerous as guns. Throughout the 1930s he proceeded to have all possible dissenters eliminated. Alash Orda members were among the first to die, in 1927 and 1928.

Thus began the systematic murder, the Purges, of untold tens of thousands of Central Asians. Arrests were usually made late at night. Confined prisoners were rarely tried; if any charges at all were brought, they ran along the lines of 'having bourgeois-nationalist or Pan-Turkic attitudes'. Mass executions and burials were common. Sometimes entire sitting governments were disposed of in this way.

Construction of Nationalities The solution to the 'nationality question' in Central Asia remains the most graphically visible effect of Soviet rule: it drew the lines on the map. Before the revolution the peoples of Central Asia had no concept of a firm national border. They had plotted their identities by a tangle of criteria: religion, tribe, location, way of life, even social status. The Soviets, however, believed that such a populace was fertile soil for Pan-Islamism and Pan-Turkism. These philosophies were threats to the regime.

So, starting about 1924, nations were invented: Kazak, Kyrgyz, Tajik, Turkmen, Uzbek. Each was given its own distinct ethnic profile, language, history and territory. Where an existing language or history did not exist or was not suitably distinct from others, these were supplied and disseminated. Islam was cut away from each national heritage, relegated to the status of an outmoded and oppressive cult, and severely suppressed throughout the Soviet period.

Ultimately, each nation became the namesake for a Soviet Socialist Republic (SSR). Uzbek and Turkmen SSRs were proclaimed in 1924, the Tajik SSR in 1929, and the Kazak and Kyrgyz SSRs in 1936.

Some say that Stalin personally directed the drawing of the boundary lines. If he did not, he should have rewarded the mapmaker handsomely. Each of the republics (referred to as 'Central Asia & Kazakstan' in the strict usage of the Soviets, because Kazakstan's boundary extends into the traditionally defined territory of Europe) was shaped to contain numerous pockets of the different nationalities, each with long-standing claims to the land. Everyone had to admit that only a strong central government could keep order on such a map. The present face of Central Asia is a product of this 'divide and rule' technique.

WWII 'The Great Patriotic War Against Fascist Germany' galvanised the whole USSR. It is widely acknowledged that the USSR could not have driven back Hitler's invasion without the unified mentality and productive strength which Stalin's totalitarian regime had begun to build.

In the course of the war Central Asia was drawn further into the fold. Economically the region lost ground from 1941 to 1945 but soon gained it back and surged forward. A sizable boost came in the form of industrial enterprises arriving ready-to-assemble in train cars: evacuated from the war-threatened parts of the USSR, they were relocated to the remote safety of Central Asia. They remained there after the war and kept on producing.

Other wartime evacuees – people – have made a lasting imprint on the face of Central Asia. These are the Koreans, Volga Germans, Chechens and others whom Stalin suspected might aid the enemy. They were deported from the borderlands and shuffled en masse. They now form sizable minority communities in all the former Soviet Central Asian republics.

For many wartime draftees, WWII presented an opportunity to escape the oppressive Stalinist state. One Central Asian scholar claims that over half of the 1.5 million Central Asians mobilised in the war deserted. Large numbers of them, as well as POWs, actually turned their coats and fought for the Germans against the Soviets.

Agriculture The tsarist pattern for the Central Asian economy had been overwhelmingly agricultural; so it was with the Soviets. Cotton was chosen for intensive production. Almost all the land that could be, and much which shouldn't have been, was planted with cotton. The labour-intensive 'cotton bowl' covered Uzbekistan as well as sizable chunks of the other republics.

Into the cotton bowl poured the diverted waters of the Syr-Darya and Amu-Darya, while downstream the Aral Sea was left to dry up. Over the cotton-scape was spread a whole list of noxious agricultural chemicals, which have wound up polluting waters, blowing around in dust storms, and causing serious health problems for residents of the area. For further detail, see the Ecology & Environment section later in this chapter.

Another noxious effect of cotton monoculture was the 'cotton affair' of the Brezhnev years. A huge ring of corrupt officials habitually over-reported cotton production, swindling Moscow out of billions of roubles. When the lid finally blew off, 2600 participants were arrested and over 50,000 were kicked out of office. Brezhnev's own son-in-law was one of the fallen. For more on this, see the boxed text 'The Great Cotton Flim-Flam' in the introduction to the Uzbekistan chapter.

In 1954 the Soviet leader Nikita Khrushchev launched the Virgin Lands campaign. The purpose was to jolt agricultural production, especially of wheat, to new levels. The method was to put Kazakstan's enormous steppes under the plough and resettle huge numbers of Russians to work the farms. Massive, futuristic irrigation schemes were drawn up to water the formerly arid grassland, from as far away as the Ob river in Siberia. The initial gains in productivity soon dwindled as the fragile exposed soil of the steppe literally blew away in the wind. The Russians, however, remained.

Benefits of the Soviet Era In spite of their heavy-handedness the Soviets made profound improvements in Central Asia. Overall standards of living were raised considerably with the help of health care and a vast new infrastructure. Central Asia was provided with plants, mines, farms, ranches and services employing millions of people (never mind that no single republic was given the means for a free-standing economy, and that most operations were coordinated through Moscow).

Education reached all social levels. Pure and applied sciences were nurtured. Literacy was made almost universal, and the languages of all nationalities were given standard literary forms. The Kyrgyz language was even given an alphabet for the first time.

Artistic expression was encouraged within the confines of Communist ideology. The Central Asian republics now boast active communities of professional artists who were trained, sometimes lavishly, by the Soviet state. And through the arts, the republics were allowed to develop their distinctive national traditions and identities (again, within bounds).

To the extent that the Central Asian republics were prepared at all when independence came, they were prepared by the Soviet era.

'Ethnic' Violence
Mikhail Gorbachev's debut at the helm of the USSR in 1985 led to the linked policies of *glasnost* (openness) and *perestroika* (restructuring). In Central Asia, as throughout the USSR, these devolved into explosion and disintegration.

Almaty, 1986
> Kazaks riot in response to the replacement of the Kazak Communist Party chief, Dinmukhamed Konaev, with a Russian.

Andijan, 1989
> Jews are chased and burned out of the area in what observers call a pogrom.

Tashkent & Fergana valley, 1989
> Meskhetian Turks, a tiny minority, are attacked by Uzbeks; 150 deaths are reported; 15,000 Meskhetians are made refugees.

Osh region, 1990
> Kyrgyz and Uzbeks clash in a month of carnage and destruction. Estimates of deaths start at 200; thousands of homes are destroyed. During the bloodiest days in Özgön, police and security forces are strangely absent.

Moscow was quick to suggest that these episodes of violence were outbreaks of nationalism, ethnic tensions, or even a resurgence of Islamic fundamentalism. But some facts were ignored. There was often no police or army intervention during the worst atrocities (yet at times helicopters were seen hovering overhead). Rioters sometimes arrived at the scene in bus or truck convoys.

Agitators frequently had modern communications equipment.

It is now widely accepted that some people in the foundering hard-line part of the Communist regime were doing what they could to harness social discontent for their own ends. Made desperate by their crumbling rule, the conservative camp sought to reassert Moscow's relevance as peacekeeper in a classic divide-and-rule play. Social discontent there surely was: living standards were poor, competition was strong for scarce housing and water, and unemployment was high. Interestingly, 'ethnic' rioting virtually ceased after the collapse of the USSR.

Post-Soviet Central Asia

One Russian humorist has summed up his county's century in two sentences. After titanic effort, blood, sweat and tears, the Soviet people brought forth a new system. Unfortunately, it was the wrong one.

By the spring of 1991 the parliaments of all five republics had declared their sovereignty. However, when the failure of the August coup against Gorbachev heralded the end of the USSR, none of the republics was prepared for the reality of independence.

On December 8 the presidents of Russia, Ukraine and Belarus met near Brest in Belarus to form the Commonwealth of Independent States (CIS). Feeling left out, the Central Asian presidents convened and demanded admission. On December 21, the heads of 11 of the former Soviet states (all except the three Baltic states and Georgia) met in Almaty and refounded the CIS. Gorbachev resigned three days later.

Independence has put the Central Asian republics' similarities and differences under a strong light. All are grappling with huge population shifts as minorities, especially Slavs and Germans, emigrate. All are weathering pressing economic crises while nursing economic disputes with each other. All are experiencing rising nationalism, and are attempting to modernise and westernise while maintaining and redefining their national character. All are reinventing the past, rehabilitating fallen local leaders, reintroducing historical heroes and reinforcing their national languages. All are feeling pressure from an unhappy Russia seeking to reassert its interests. All are opening themselves more or less to new spheres of influence from Turkey, Iran, China and the industrialised west. And in all of the republics the initial rush of post-independence joy has been replaced by a yearning for stability and the search for new ideals. There are still a lot of ordinary people who complain that things were fine until 'that idiot Gorbachev ruined everything with perestroika'.

But there are differences. Kyrgyzstan is the odd one out politically: its president, Askar Akaev, is the only one to have professed aspirations to swift democratisation and free market reform, while his neighbours are unabashedly authoritarian. Turkmenistan is the only republic which seems to have bright economic possibilities – sitting pretty on enormous reserves of oil and gas. Tajikistan is the only one which has experienced civil war, while the others are all in dread that they will be next to succumb to political meltdown and recolonisation by Russia.

The region is undergoing a serious strategic realignment as it turns away from Russia towards traditional and cultural allies. Russia and China are both particularly worried about the expansion of NATO into Central Asia. In September 1997, 500 crack US paratroopers parachuted into the Fergana valley in joint military exercises, only 200km from China's sensitive Xinjiang border. Recent border agreements have settled disputes which led to Sino-Soviet clashes in 1969 but the issue remains a touchy one to China.

Meanwhile Russian plans to establish a military base in Tajikistan angered Afghanistan and Uzbekistan, which already has quite tense relations with its neighbouring republic. Russia already has 30,000 troops in Tajikistan, most defending CIS borders against drug smugglers and Islamic infiltrators. Islam is the strength which most Central Asian leaders fear the most. Islamists were rounded up in the wake of a bombing attempt on the life of Uzbek president, Islam Karimov, on 16 February 1999.

As Central Asia gets into its post-independence stride and as new economic and cultural ties strengthen, oil routes open and Silk Roads are redrawn, this hitherto unknown region will undoubtedly become increasingly important to the security, economy and politics of Russia, Asia and even the world.

GEOGRAPHY

The Central Asia of this book includes Kazakstan, which in Soviet parlance (still lingering even in the west) was considered a thing apart. It is true that Kazakstan's enormous territory actually extends westward across the Ural river, the traditional boundary between Europe and Asia, and that parts of the north have been settled by Russians for centuries. But Kazakstan still shares many geographic, cultural, ethnic and economic similarities and ties with Central Asia 'proper'.

Even the term 'Central Asia' does not unify the republics: some residents of huge Kazakstan live about as far away from Vienna as they do from their own capital, and Kazaks are a minority in the country.

Kazakstan, Kyrgyzstan, Tajikistan, Turkmenistan and Uzbekistan together occupy 5.8 million sq km; including Xinjiang, Central Asia's area is 7.5 million sq km, the size of the Australian continent.

A quick spin around the territory covered in this book would start on the eastern shores of the Caspian Sea; then dip southeast along the low crest of the Kopet Dag mountains between Turkmenistan and Iran; follow the Amu-Darya river swing down into the deserts of Afghanistan, northeast over the Hindu Kush to the Amu-Darya and then its headstream, the Pyanj, up into the high Pamir; glide eastward along the Kunlun range as it skirts the southern rim of the Tarim basin; round the eastern nose of the Tian Shan range; traverse the Zhungarian basin; skip north-westward over the Altay mountains to float down the Irtysh river; and then turn west to plod along Kazakstan's flat, farmed, wooded border with Russia, ending in the basin of the Ural river and the Caspian Sea.

The sort of blank which is drawn in the minds of many people by the words 'Central Asia' is not entirely unfounded. The over-whelming majority of the territory is flat steppe (arid grassland) and desert. These areas include the Kazak Steppe, the Betpak Dala (Misfortune) Steppe, the Kyzylkum (Red Sands) desert, the Karakum (Black Sands) desert and the Taklamakan (Go-In-and-You-Won't-Come-Out) desert. The Kyzylkum and Karakum combined make the fourth largest desert in the world. Xinjiang's landscape includes two large basins, the Zhungarian (Jungarian) and the Tarim – the latter is the largest inland basin in the world.

Central Asia's mountains are part of the huge chain which swings in a great arc from the Mongolian Altay to the Tibetan Himalaya. Central Asia's high ground is dominated by the Pamir, a range of rounded, 5000 to 7000m mountains, which stretch 800km across Tajikistan. With very broad, flat valleys nearly as high as the lower peaks, the Pamir might be better described as a plateau. The valleys are treeless, grassy (*pamir* roughly means 'pasture' in local dialects) and often swampy with meandering rivers. They remain among the least explored mountain ranges left on earth. Over the ages the Pamir have been called the Bam-i-Dunya (Roof of the World), 'the Mid Point between Heaven and Earth' and the 'Foot of the Gods'. The Chinese called them the Congling Shan, or Onion Mountains. The roof of the Pamir, Tajikistan's 7495m Kommunizma, is the highest point in Central Asia and was the highest in the USSR.

The Tian Shan, extending over 1500km from south-west Kyrgyzstan to beyond Hami in eastern Xinjiang, forms the backbone of eastern Central Asia. The jagged, ice-clad 4000 to 7000m crests are grooved by canyons, which shelter dense evergreen forests and lush summer pastures or *jailoo*. The summit of the range is 7439m Pobedy on the Kyrgyzstan-China border. Tian Shan is Chinese for Celestial Mountains; the local translation is Tengri Tau. The range was a favourite among Russian explorers such as Fedchenko, Kostenko, Semenov and Prezhevalski.

These two mountain ranges hold some of the largest glaciers and fresh water supplies on earth (around 17,000 sq km) and are one of the region's most significant natural resources. The 72km-long Fedchenko glacier, which is the longest in the USSR, contains more water than the Aral Sea.

The Caspian Sea is called either the world's biggest lake or the world's biggest inland sea. The Caspian Depression in which it lies dips to 132m below sea level. Lake Balkash, a vast, marsh-bordered arc of half-saline water on the Kazak Steppe, is hardly deeper than a puddle, while mountain-ringed Lake Issyk-Kul in Kyrgyzstan is the fourth deepest lake in the world. Other glacially fed lakes dot the mountains, including Song-Köl in Kyrgyzstan and Kara-Kul, first described by Marco Polo, in Tajikistan (another Kara-Kul lies nearby in the Muztagh Ata/Kongur area of Xinjiang). Down in the Tarim basin, the salt lake Lop Nor and the surrounding Lop desert are the site of China's former nuclear weapons testing ground.

What little water flows out of Central Asia goes all the way to the Arctic Ocean, via the Irtysh river. Most of Central Asia's rainfall drains internally. The Ili river waters Lake Balkash; the Ural makes a short dash across part of Kazakstan to the Caspian Sea. Numerous rivers rise as cold streams in the mountains only to lose themselves on the arid steppes and sands below. The region's two mightiest rivers, the Syr-Darya (Jaxartes) and Amu-Darya (Oxus), used to replenish the Aral Sea. Now most of their waters have been diverted onto vast areas of cotton fields, and the Aral Sea is virtually disappearing. High in the mountains, these rivers make the big wheels turn in hydroelectric plants, such as the impressive Toktogul dam on Kyrgyzstan's Naryn river (the Syr-Darya's headstream). There is evidence that Amu-Darya once flowed into the Caspian, along the now dry Uzboy channel.

GEOLOGY

The compact, balled-up mass of mountains presided over by Pik Kommunizma is often called the Pamir Knot. It's the hub from which other major ranges extend like radiating ropes: the Himalaya and Karakoram to the south-east, the Hindu Kush to the south-west, the Kunlun to the east and the Tian Shan to the north-east. These young mountains all arose (or more correctly, are arising still) from the shock waves created by the Indian subcontinent smashing into the Asian crustal plate over a hundred million years ago. Amazing as it seems, marine fossils from the original Tethys Ocean have been found in the deserts of Xinjiang as a testament to the continental collision. The Tian Shan are currently rising at the rate of around 10mm per year.

Central Asia is therefore unsurprisingly a major earthquake zone. Ashgabat was destroyed by earthquake in 1948 and Tashkent was levelled in 1966. More recently, five quakes of over six on the Richter scale rocked Artush, in the Kashgar region, between March 1996 and 1998. Devastating earthquakes also hit the Tajikistan-Afghanistan border in 1997 and 1998.

CLIMATE

Central Asia has an extreme continental climate. Temperatures are wildly variable, with a record 26.4°C (80°F) change in temperatures recorded in the desert in a single day, dramatic differences between the deserts and mountains, and seasonal transitions full of false starts. Rain is minimal except at higher altitudes; what there is falls mainly in March/April and October/November and turns everything to mud.

The finest times in the lowlands are May to early June (also good for wildflowers) and September to early October (also good for fruit in the markets). Midsummer is for mad dogs, with daytime averages of 30°C to 35°C in foothill cities like Dushanbe, Bishkek and Almaty, and 40°C or more in Tashkent, Samarkand, Bukhara and Ashgabat. The hottest city in Central Asia is Termiz in southern Uzbekistan, with summer days over 50°C.

By November, it turns fairly cold everywhere, in fits and starts. January to February days are typically -5°C to 10°C, sometimes much colder. Winter snow stays on the ground in the north and east, and snow and cold are severe in the mountainous interiors of Kyrgyzstan and Tajikistan.

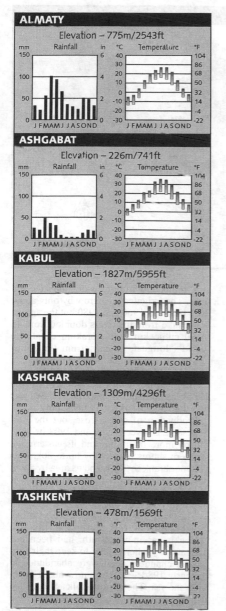

ALMATY
Elevation – 775m/2543ft

ASHGABAT
Elevation – 226m/741ft

KABUL
Elevation – 1827m/5955ft

KASHGAR
Elevation – 1309m/4296ft

TASHKENT
Elevation – 478m/1569ft

ECOLOGY & ENVIRONMENT

Central Asia is home to a unique range of ecosystems and an extraordinary variety of flora and fauna. But as with many places in the former USSR, its amazing landscapes also served as testing grounds for some of the worst cases of Soviet megalomania. Land and water mismanagement and destruction of natural habitat were part of a conscious effort to tame nature, or 'harness it like a white mare' as the propaganda had it. The results are almost beyond belief and on a staggering scale.

Even casual students of the region are familiar with some of the most infamous catastrophes of Soviet environmental meddling: the gradual disappearance of the Aral Sea, the excessive levels of radiation around the Semey (Semipalatinsk) Nuclear Testing site, and the consequences of Khrushchev's Virgin Lands scheme (which, according to Soviet theoreticians, should have allowed the USSR to overtake the USA in grain production). For information on these last two issues see Ecology & Environment in the Kazakstan chapter.

In the economic malaise of the post-Soviet years the environment has taken a back seat to survival. Whether it is poaching, hunting tours or pollution from gold mining operations, with the promise of hard-currency earnings in an otherwise bleak economic landscape, nature is always the victim.

The Aral Sea

One of the most amazing things about the Aral Sea disaster is that it was no accident. The Soviet planners who fatally tapped the rivers that fed the Aral Sea, to irrigate new cotton fields, *expected* the sea to dry up. They also wanted to bring water to Central Asia by a huge canal from Siberia, not to replenish the Aral Sea but to expand cotton production still further. They either didn't understand that drying up the world's fourth largest lake would wreck a whole region's climate and ecology, and cause untold suffering to its people, or didn't care.

The Aral Sea, or rather seas, since it split into two in 1987, straddles the border between western Uzbekistan and southern

THE SHRINKING ARAL SEA

Based on information supplied by Philip Micklin

Kazakstan. It's fed, in the years they actually reach it, by the Syr-Darya and Amu-Darya rivers, flowing down from the Tian Shan and Pamir. Back in the 1950s these rivers brought an average 55 cubic km of water a year to the Aral Sea, which stretched 400km from end to end and 280km from side to side, covering 66,900 sq km. The sea had by all accounts lovely clear water, pristine beaches, plenty of fish to support a big fishing industry in the ports of Moynaq and Aralsk, and even passenger ferries crossing it from north to south. The extensive deltas of the Syr-Darya and Amu-Darya were ecologically unique networks of rivers, lakes, reedbeds, marshes and forests supporting very diverse flora and fauna.

Then the USSR's central planners decided to boost cotton production in Uzbekistan, Turkmenistan and Kazakstan, to feed a leap forward in the Soviet textile industry. Although by 1960 the Amu-Darya and Syr-Darya already supported an estimated 50,000 sq km of irrigation, mainly for cotton, the Aral Sea had survived that sort of 'take' without shrinking. But the new cotton fields, many of them on poorer desert soils and fed by long, unlined canals open to the sun, drank much more water than the old ones. The irrigated area grew by only about 20% between 1960 and 1980 but the annual water take from the rivers doubled from 45 to 90 cubic km. The Karakum canal, the world's longest, reaches from the Amu-Darya far across southern Turkmenistan, and takes 14 cubic km a year, nearly a quarter of the Aral Sea's old supply. By the 1980s the annual flow into the Aral Sea was less than a tenth of the 1950s supply.

Production of cotton rose, but the Aral Sea, sank. Between 1966 and 1993 its level fell by more than 16m and its eastern and southern shores receded by up to 80km. Its volume shrank by 75%, and its area by about half. In 1987 the Aral divided into a smaller northern sea and a larger southern one, each fed, sometimes, by one of the rivers.

The two main fishing ports, Aralsk (Kazakstan) in the north and Moynaq (Uzbekistan) in the south, had been left high and dry when efforts to keep their navigation channels open were abandoned in the early 1980s. Both are now about 40km from the sea. The rusting hulks of beached fishing boats are scattered along what were once their shores.

In any case there are hardly any fish left in the Aral Sea: the last of its 20-odd indigenous species disappeared in about 1985, wiped out by the loss of spawning and feeding grounds, rising salt levels and, very likely, residues of pesticides, fertilisers and defoliants used on the cotton fields which found their way into the sea. Only introduced species like the Black Sea flounder remain – though a few indigenous ones survive in the deltas and around the mouth of the Syr-Darya. Of the 60,000 people who used to live off the Aral fishing industry, many are now gone: Moynaq and Aralsk (which used to harvest 20,000 tons of fish a year) are ghost towns.

In 1992 the little channel still connecting the northern and southern seas was blocked by a 16km-long dike to prevent further water loss from the northern sea (see the boxed text 'Hope for the Little Aral Sea' in the Kazakstan chapter). The northern sea has since risen almost 3m and it is forecast that the northern sea will reach a state of equilibrium, with an area of 3500 sq km, by about 2025. But if recent rates of depletion continue, the southern sea is expected to split again by 2005 into western and eastern parts. The eastern part will receive the Amu-Darya and is expected eventually to stabilise at about 7000 sq km, but the western part will go on shrinking.

The Aral Sea's shrinkage has devastated the land around it, and a visit to anywhere near the sea is a ride into a nightmare of blighted towns, blighted land and blighted people. Locals talk of a new Akkum (White desert) forming an unholy trinity with the Kyzylkum (Red desert) and Karakum (Black desert).

The climate around the lake has changed: the air is drier, winters are a few degrees colder and a month longer and summers are hotter. The average number of rainless days has risen from 30 to 35 in the 1950s to 120-150 at the time of research. Salt, sand and dust from the exposed bed is blown hundreds of kilometres in big salt-dust sandstorms, which also pick up residues of the chemicals from cultivated land. Aralsk suffered an average 65 days of dust storms a year from 1966 to 1985. The damage caused by these storms to human health and agriculture is huge.

Further grave problems have resulted directly from methods of irrigation and cotton cultivation. Soils have been salinised not only by salt-dust sandstorms but also by evaporation of the river water brought to irrigate them. In 1994 *Newsweek* reported that the Central Asian cotton harvest was actually shrinking because the soil was now so salinised.

In addition to salt, residues of the huge doses of defoliants, pesticides and fertilisers used on the cotton fields have inevitably found their way into irrigation drainage channels and from there into the Syr-Darya and Amu-Darya, all of which provide drinking water. DDT pesticide was widely used till about 1982 and is still present in high concentrations in soils. Defoliants are used to make cotton harvesting easier but one variety, Butifos, used till about 1990, was so toxic that according to some reports it killed thousands of people. Much food grown in the Aral basin contains residues of these chemicals and is lacking in vitamins.

In human terms, the worst affected areas are those to the Aral sea's south (as far as northern Turkmenistan) and east (the areas north and west of the Aral Sea are very sparsely populated). The catalogue of health problems is awful: salt and dust are blamed for respiratory illnesses and cancers of the throat and oesophagus; poor drinking water has been implicated in high rates of typhoid, paratyphoid, hepatitis and dysentery; the area has the highest mortality and infant mortality rates in the former USSR, and in parts of Karakalpakstan (far west Uzbekistan) more than one baby in 10 dies (compared to one in 100 or more in Britain or the USA). Karakalpakstan also has high rates of birth deformities and in Nukus, the Karakalpak capital, virtually all pregnant women are anaemic, which leads to many premature births. In Aralsk, tuberculosis is common.

Of the 173 animal species that used to live around the Aral Sea, only 38 survive. Especially devastating has been the degradation of the big Amu-Darya and Syr-Darya deltas, with their very diverse flora and fauna. The deltas have supported irrigated agriculture for many centuries, along with hunting, fishing, and harvesting of reeds for building and papermaking. The dense *toghay* forests, unique to the valleys of these desert rivers, have shrunk to a fifth of their old size, causing a catastrophic drop in the once abundant waterbird population.

The local name for the Aral is the Aral Tenghiz, or Sea of Islands. Barsakelmes (The Place of No Return) Island, a nature reserve protecting the saiga antelope and the rare Asiatic wild ass, has reportedly become an unviable habitat because it is now so arid.

Nor can matters have been helped by the use of Vozrozhdenia island as a Soviet biological warfare testing site: locals have blamed Vozrozhdenia for mass deaths of saiga antelope on the Ustyurt plateau southwest of the Aral in the 1980s, and suspicions remain over human illnesses in and near Moynaq. Ironically, the island's name in pious Russian means 'rebirth'.

Long-Term Solutions Dozens of inquiries, projects and research teams have poked and prodded the Aral problem; locals joke that if every scientist who visited the Aral region had brought a bucket of water the problem would be over by now. The initial outcry over the disaster seems to have largely evaporated, along with the sea, and the focus has shifted from rehabilitating the sea, to stabilising the sea and now stabilising the environment around the sea.

To restore the Aral would require that irrigation from the Amu-Darya and Syr-Darya cease for three years, or at least a slashing of the irrigated area from over 70,000 to 40,000 sq km, combined with a big improvement in irrigation techniques reducing water use per sq km by a third. In other words, a complete restructuring of the economies of Uzbekistan (which has over half the Aral basin's irrigated land) and Turkmenistan (also heavily dependent on cotton). No one is seriously considering this.

The Aral crisis became apparent to Soviet scientists in the 1970s, and finally in 1988 a gradual increase in water flow to the sea was ordered, to be achieved by more efficient irrigation and an end to the expansion of irrigation. Before the collapse of the USSR some steps were taken to improve human conditions in the Aral area with the building of new water mains, hospitals and desalination plants. But the crack-up of the old empire led to a breakdown of planning and, worse, fears of conflict over rights to the waters of the Syr-Darya and Amu-Darya between the Central Asian republics – two of which, Kyrgyzstan and Tajikistan, hold the rivers' upper reaches while the other three, downriver, are economically dependent on the rivers.

Early promises of cooperation and money from the Central Asian leaders bore little fruit and in 1995 the president of Uzbekistan, Islam Karimov, was still regurgitating the old idea of diverting water from Siberian rivers. The now annual Aral Sea convention of Central Asian leaders has achieved little, except to highlight conflicting claims to sections of the Amu-Darya. International schemes organised by the World Bank, USAID and the European Union seem to offer more hope. The three-year first phase of the World Bank scheme, with a projected budget of US$250 million, aims to clean up water supplies, improve sanitation and public health, restore some economic viability and biodiversity to the Amu-Darya delta, and stabilise the Aral's northern sea.

Longer-term efforts may focus on building more dikes around parts of the sea that can be maintained, rehabilitating the blighted region around the sea and stabilising its fragile environment, improving water management and building up local institutions to manage these projects. Whether the will exists among Central Asia's politicians to introduce less water-intensive irrigation methods, or even less thirsty crops than cotton, remains to be seen.

Caspian Sea

Ironically, as the Aral sinks the Caspian is rising, flooding out many coastal communities in Turkmenistan, Kazakstan, Russia, Azerbaijan and Iran. The 'sea' has risen 2.25m since 1978, mostly due to higher levels of river inflow and rainfall. The rise is thought to be largely natural, part of a cycle of ebb and flow over hundreds of years. The Caspian actually fell in the 1980's and a dam was built over the Kara-Bogaz-Gol inlet in Turkmenistan to halt the fall but these dam gates are now left permanently open. Potential pollution from flooded oil wells and even nuclear waste dumps near the shoreline may prove to be what has already been called a 'slow motion environmental disaster'.

There's not much anyone can do about this, though some have suggested pumping water from the Caspian to the Aral. As with the Aral, this is a regional problem.

Overgrazing

Overgrazing and soil degradation is a major problem affecting all the Central Asian republics. The steady rise in livestock grazing has unhinged delicate ecosystems and accelerated desertification and soil erosion. From 1941 to 1991 the population of sheep and goats more than doubled to 5.5 million in Turkmenistan and quadrupled to 10 million in Kyrgyzstan, while a third of Kyrgyzstan's available grasslands has disappeared.

In Kazakstan much of the semi-arid steppe, traditionally used as pasture over the centuries, was put to the plough under the Virgin Lands campaign. Wind erosion in the steppes of north Kazakstan has accelerated soil depletion.

Soil degradation is also activated by failure to rotate crops and by excessive use of chemicals, and aggravated by irrigation water mismanagement. In Kazakstan, 40% of rangeland is considered to be overused, and will need 10 to 50 years to be restored to its original fertility. In Kyrgyzstan an estimated 70% of pastureland suffers erosion above acceptable levels. In Tajikistan the productivity of summer pastures in the mountains has dropped by 50% over the last 25 years and large areas of the Pamirs are threatened by desertification.

Central Asia suffered from a plague of locusts of almost biblical proportions in 1999, affecting 8.5 million hectares in Kazakstan and 330,000 hectares in Uzbekistan.

Pollution

Cotton is to blame for many of Central Asia's ills. Its present cultivation demands high levels of pesticides and fertilisers, which are now found throughout the food chain – in the water, in human and animal milk, in vegetables and fruit, and in the soil itself.

In Kyrgyzstan, soils are seriously contaminated with DDT, especially in the Osh region where 94% of soils contain DDT. See The Aral Sea in this section to read about the appalling situation in Karakalpakstan.

Kazakstan, the third largest industrial power in the CIS, suffers particularly from industrial pollution, the worst culprits being power stations running on low-grade coal and metallurgical factories. Lake Balkash has been polluted by copper smelters established on its shores in the 1930s; bird and other lake life is now practically extinct.

Uzbekistan, also heavily industrialised during the Soviet period, has a concentration of polluting industries in the Fergana valley (Fergana ranked as one of the 30 most polluted Soviet towns in 1989) and in Tashkent. Problem areas in Turkmenistan include oil pollution along the shore of the Caspian Sea.

Following the same pattern as industrial development, mining techniques are inefficient, outdated and environmentally hazardous. In 1998 almost two tonnes of sodium cyanide destined for the Kumtor gold mine in Kyrgyzstan was spilled into the Barskoön river and thence Issyk-Kul.

Uranium for the Soviet nuclear military machine was mined in both Tajikistan and Kyrgyzstan (the Kyrgyz SSR's uranium sector earned the sobriquet 'Atomic Fortress of the Tian Shan'), and as many as 50 abandoned mine sites in Kyrgyzstan alone may now leak unstablised radioactive tailings or contaminated groundwater into their surroundings; some are along major waterways which drain eventually to the Aral Sea.

FLORA & FAUNA

Central Asia covers only 17% of the former USSR's territory, but contains over 50% of its variety in flora and fauna. Though environmental pressures are as bad in Central Asia as anywhere, there's a reasonably good chance you will see some memorable beasts and plants.

The mountains of Kyrgyzstan, Kazakstan, Tajikistan, Xinjiang and (to a lesser extent) Uzbekistan are the setting for high, grassy meadows known as jailoos. In summertime the wildflowers (including wild irises and edelweiss) are a riot of colour. Trout lurk in the rushing streams. Marmots and pikas provide food for eagles and lammergeiers; the elusive snow leopard preys on the ibex, with which it shares a preference for crags and rocky slopes, alongside the Svertsov ram, named after the Russian father of Central Asian zoology. Forests of Tian Shan spruce, ash, larch and juniper provide cover for lynxes, wolves, wild boars and brown bears.

Higher up on the tundra-like grasslands, Marco Polo sheep roam in herds, and flamingos can be seen around lowland lakes as well as swamps. The Kyrgyz of the Pamir valleys, between 3000 and 4000m high, keep herds of domestic yaks. High-altitude herders and mountain climbers share stories of yeti sightings. The high Pamir is completely treeless.

Lower down in the mountains of southern Kyrgyzstan, Uzbekistan, Tajikistan and Turkmenistan are ancient forests of wild walnut, pistachio, juniper, apricot, and apple. The steppes (what's left of them after massive cultivation projects) are covered with grasses and low shrubs such as saxaul. Where they rise to meet foothills, the steppes bear vast fields of wild poppies (including some opium poppies) and tulips. Chiy, a common grass with whitish, cane-like reeds, is used by nomads to make decorative screens for their yurts. The nomads sometimes keep Bactrian or two-humped camels in addition to horses and sheep.

Roe deer, wolves, foxes and badgers have their homes on the steppe, as do the saiga, a species of antelope. The ring-necked pheasant, widely introduced in North America and elsewhere, is native to the Central Asian steppe, as are partridges, black grouse, bustards, and the falcons and hawks that prey on them. The ubiquitous tortoise and hedgehog are often the first wild acquaintances made by children.

Rivers and lakeshores in the flatlands are a different world, with dense thickets of elm, poplar, reeds and shrubs. Wild boar, jackal and deer make their homes in these jungle belts – the Amu-Darya is the habitat of a variety of pink deer. Geese, ducks and numerous species of wading birds migrate through the marshes. A carp-like fish called the sazan is the most popular catch.

In the Karakum, Kyzylkum and Taklamakan, as in all deserts, there is more than meets the eye. The goitred gazelle (also called jeran) haunts the deserts of western Uzbekistan and Turkmenistan. Gophers, sand rats and jerboas (small jumping rodents with long hind legs) are abundant wherever it's possible to make a hole in the ground. They provide food for foxes, lizards and various kinds of snakes. Turkmenistan is noted for its big poisonous snakes, including vipers and cobras.

Turkmenistan's wildlife has a Middle Eastern streak, understandable when you consider that parts of the country are as close to Baghdad as they are to Tashkent. Leopards and porcupines inhabit the parched hills. The varan (sand crocodile) is actually a type of large lizard of the region.

The Altay has large forests of Siberian pine, birch, larch and fir. Hanas Lake in Xinjiang is a rare example of taiga forest.

Poaching

In many former Central Asian republics, poaching has always been a problem, despite official attempts at control. Now it's on the rise, both as a food source and for trophies to sell for hard currency, and goes almost totally unchallenged.

Several private and government travel agencies run hard currency hunting expeditions, luring wealthy foreigners to slaughter bustards, wolves, mountain ibex and bears. Falconers from the Middle East have found Central Asia to be an exciting new source of hunting birds. Encouraged by stories of fanatic western hunter-tourists knocking off Marco Polo sheep and snow leopards, local people have joined the trade. The economic pressures felt by locals cannot be overemphasised. Some countries, like the

Heavenly Horses

Central Asia has been famed for its horses for millennia. The earliest Silk Road excursions into Central Asia were made to bring back the famous blood-sweating (due to parasites or a skin infection) horses of Fergana (based on the ancient kingdom of Davan, near modern day Osh), to help Han China fight incursive nomadic tribes. Kucha and Ili in Chinese Turkestan were also famed for their Heavenly Horses, thought to be the offspring of dragons and divine steeds. Much of the highly-coveted silk which made its way into Central Asia and beyond came from the trade of horses.

Today's most famous horses are the Akhal Teke of Turkmenistan, the forefather of the modern Arabian steed. The Roman historian Appian wrote that the horses of Parthian Nisa excelled in all beauty, 'for their golden manes whirl with glory in the air'. Today there are around 2000 thoroughbred Akhal Teke in the world, of which 1200 are in Turkmenistan. Turkmenistan's state emblem and banknotes feature a descendant and there's even a national holiday named after them. Akhal Teke are regularly handed out as diplomatic gifts (Francois Mitterrand, John Major and Boris Yeltsin each have one), much as they were two thousand years ago.

The region's other famous breed is the diminutive Prezhevalski, or Wild Asiatic horse, the last remaining species of wild horse. These horses are now almost exclusively in zoos, though a few wild examples have been spotted in Xinjiang's remote Altyn Dagh mountains and reintroduced to parts of Mongolia.

Other regional breeds include the Lokai of Tajikistan and Karabair of Uzbekistan. These stocky horses are used in sports such as *buzkashi* (a traditional polo-like game played with a headless goat carcass) and are descendants of horses which played such a fundamental role in the Mongol conquest of Eurasia.

US, have banned the import of Marco Polo sheep horns, as they are from an endangered species.

Tens of thousands of saiga antelope are killed every year by gangs of poachers, intent on selling their horns to Chinese medicine makers. Musk deer, currently found in Kyrgyzstan, Uzbekistan and Russia are killed for their musk glands. Around 160 deer are killed for every 1kg of musk, making the musk worth three to four times its weight in gold. Tens of thousands of the deer have been killed in the last 20 years and numbers in Russia have fallen by 50%.

Endangered Species

In 1985 the Kyrgyz 'Red Book' – the regional edition of *Krasnaya Kniga SSSR* (The USSR Red Book), bible of endangered species – stated that 15% of mammals and 10% of birds in Kyrgyzstan were threatened with extinction. Since then the situation has further deteriorated.

Kyrgyzstan, annual refuge for thousands of migrating birds, enjoys a unique position among researchers. The mountain goose, among other rare species, nests on the shores of its mountain lakes, but the population has shrunk over the years to less than 15 pairs worldwide.

Kyrgyzstan was once believed to have had the world's second largest snow leopard population, though numbers are declining rapidly. The population of snow leopards in the former USSR (Central Asia and the Russian Altay) is estimated at about 1000, out of a global population of around 7000. Only 5% of the snow leopard's habitat is currently protected. The last Turan (or Caspian) tiger was killed in the Amu Darya delta in 1972.

Wild Bactrian camels, once the quintessential Silk Road sight are now only found in very remote areas of Xinjiang. Perhaps 1000 remain. The animals are superbly adapted to cope with the Central Asian deserts; they have double sets of eyelids and eyelashes, can completely close their nostrils and can survive for a week without water and for a month without food.

National Parks

Many of the region's approximately two-dozen nature reserves (*zapovedniki* and protected areas *zakazniki*) and nine or so national parks (*gosudarstvenny prirodny park*), founded for a mixture of preservation and recreation) are accessible for tourists.

The existing system, one of the rare positive legacies of the USSR, is nevertheless antiquated and inadequate. Unfortunately all suffer from a lack of government funding and are under increasing pressure from grazing, poaching, firewood gathering and even opium poppy plantations. Staff are few and management tends to be incompetent or toothless.

In Kyrgyzstan, for example, just 2% of the country's area is dedicated to land conservation, of which most is only semiprotected and commercially managed, often as hunting reserves. In Kazakstan, only 2.5% of the land area is protected, and although an additional three national parks and 14 nature reserves have been proposed, this would only add an extra 1%, well below the minimum 10% recommended by the World Conservation Union. In Tajikistan, civil strife has halted all environmental initiatives; nature reserves have been theatres of battle, with disastrous consequences for their fauna and flora.

UNESCO-sponsored biosphere reserves include Sary-Chelek, Ugam-Chatkal, Repetek, and soon, Issyk-Kul.

The most easily visited and scenically beautiful national parks are both in Kyrgyzstan; at Ala-Archa, outside Bishkek, and Karakol in the south east corner of Issyk-Kul.

In southern Kazakstan the Aksu-Zhabaghly Nature Reserve, with its beautiful tulips, is easily visited with the help of a travel agency. Outside Almaty, the Almatinsky Nature Reserve has big horned sheep, gazelle, and hiking trails.

Uzbekistan has fewer user-friendly reserves. The Ugam-Chatkal National Park has juniper forests, birch groves and wildlife such as wild boars, bears, and snow leopards. The Badai-Tugai Nature Reserve in Karakalpakstan protects a strip of *tugai* riverine forest on the eastern bank of the Amu-Darya. Once off-limits, it today welcomes foreign tourists as the entry fee pays for food for a Bukhara deer breeding centre.

The Repetek Desert Reserve, between Mary and Turkmenabat, is Turkmenistan's most famous reserve and features a desert research centre studying species such as *zemzen* lizards, cobras and scorpions.

In Xinjiang the most accessible reserves are the much-visited Tianchi (Heavenly Lake) Nature Reserve and more remote Hanas Nature Reserve.

GOVERNMENT & POLITICS

Former Soviet Central Asia now consists of five independent republics with their own ambitions and opportunities, but also with a common legacy. The Central Asian republics as such never enjoyed any pre-Soviet political independence and democratic rule. Thus democracy, as the west knows it, is a recent and even alien notion, and it shows.

Authoritarian Habits

In recent years, most Central Asian leaders have expressed at least some admiration for South-East Asian models of development which link authoritarian rule and economic development. And all the Central Asian governments are authoritarian to some degree, running the gamut from pure *ancien regime* style autocracy (Turkmenistan), to a tightly controlled mixture of neo-communism and spurious nationalism (Uzbekistan and Tajikistan), to a more enlightened 'channelled transition' to democracy and a market economy (Kazakstan). Even liberal-minded Kyrgyzstan shows occasional signs of tightening up. Human rights abuses are common.

In most of the republics the old Communist Party apparatus remains more or less in place under new names: People's Democratic Party (Uzbekistan), Democratic Party (Turkmenistan), Party of People's Unity (Kazakstan), and another People's Democratic Party (Tajikistan). The Central Asian presidents have been either elected by the obligatory 99.9% vote (Uzbekistan and Turkmenistan), furnished with strong executive power (Kazakstan and Kyrgyzstan), or installed in an armed coup (Tajikistan).

Political opposition is completely marginalised (Turkmenistan), brought to heel or banned (Uzbekistan), or tolerated but closely watched (Kazakstan and Kyrgyzstan).

The added importance of family networks and clan ties to Central Asian politics was highlighted when the daughter of Kazak president Nazarbaev married the son of Kyrgyz president Akaev in 1998.

That old habits die slowly is not surprising after three generations of Soviet rule, and three of tsarist paternalism before that. The absence of clear historical identities and precedents of independence (such as in the Baltic and Transcaucasian states) means there was no strong nationalist or intellectual movement that was capable of articulating alternatives to centralised rule.

Militant Islam has begun to fill this void since the Soviet invasion of Afghanistan in 1979, with open or clandestine backing from the Arab Gulf States, Egypt, Iran and Afghanistan. Central Asians gained their independence essentially as a *fait accompli* rather than as the culmination of a long struggle.

Consequently the old Soviet nomenklatura were essentially the only group with the experience and the means to rule after 1991, and there is scant sign that this will change soon. Despite lip service to the concepts of 'democracy' and 'market economy' – largely to please the USA and the European Union – most Central Asian governments are wary of quick political and economic liberalisation. With the Tajik and Afghan civil wars and Russian economic chaos in mind, they argue that rapid change will only open the door to Islamic fundamentalism and ethnic strife, and that a strong hand is the only answer.

At the same time they are ready to play both the Islamic and nationalist cards to legitimise themselves in the eyes of their own disoriented subjects. One can only wait and see where this double standard will lead.

Uzbek and Kyrgyz elections are due to take place in 2000 and Kazak elections are due in 2006.

Commonwealth of Independent States (CIS)

With all this in mind, it is no surprise that the Central Asian states were among the most fervent supporters of the Commonwealth of Independent States, or CIS (Russian: Sodruzhestvo Nezavisimykh Gosudarstv, or SNG), to which all five belong. Seen as a plain tool of Russian neocolonialism by some and as a guarantor of regional security by others, the CIS was founded in late 1991 with its administrative centre in the Belarussian capital of Minsk. With the belated entry of Georgia in 1993, the CIS now includes all the former Soviet republics except the Baltic states.

The CIS is *not* a successor state to the USSR, and in fact is not a state at all but a community of independent states which has taken over some of the international functions of the old USSR. Its original aims were the creation of a common economic zone and a common currency (quite unlikely these days), the setting up of a joint peacekeeping force, and the retention of unitary control over strategic armed forces and nuclear arms in what Russia likes to call its 'near abroad'. The CIS is the formal manifestation of what is, in any case, a huge Russian finger in the Central Asian pie, thanks to the legacy of Soviet interdependence and the rule of Russified Soviet elites in the republican capitals.

The defence aspect is especially important to the Central Asian republics, having inherited vulnerable borders (including Turkmenistan, Tajikistan and Kyrgyzstan), a nuclear arsenal (Kazakstan) and an ongoing civil war next door in Afghanistan. Furthermore, the individual republican armies either still depend heavily on Russian personnel and supplies (Kazakstan and Uzbekistan), are simply Russian expeditionary forces (Tajikistan) or have been abolished and replaced by collective assistance in case of emergency (Kyrgyzstan and Turkmenistan).

Administrative Structures

All the Central Asian republics have maintained the general administrative structures that were in place under the Soviets. The major administrative divisions are national; provincial or regional, corresponding to the Russian oblasts (Turkmen: *velayat*, Kazak: *oblys*, Kyrgyz: *duban*, Uzbek: *viloyat*); extra-municipal, corresponding to the Russian *rayon* (Uzbek: *tuman*, Kazak: *audan*); and municipal, corresponding to the Russian *gorod* or city (Uzbek: *shakhar*, Kazak: *kala*).

The individual traveller is likely to encounter various reincarnations of all-too-familiar Soviet police authorities, in particular the Interior Ministry's branch for keeping track of foreigners, the Office of Visas & Registration, or OVIR (Russian *Otdel Vis i Registratsii*); the state police or *militisia*; and the traffic police or GAI (DAN in Uzbekistan, MAI in Kyrgyzstan).

ECONOMY

The Central Asian economies remain heavily dependent on that of Russia, itself in a state of profound shock. All partook of the same over-specialisation, over-dependencies and inefficiencies of the centralised Soviet system, and all are paying the morning-after price now that the system has collapsed. But by and large, all are slowly picking themselves up and reinventing their economies.

The Legacy of Russian & Soviet Colonialism

The Russian annexation of Central Asia in the 19th century was not just a geo-strategic move in the Great Game, but an economic move. The Kazak Steppe and Central Asia promised not only indirect access to warm seas and to the rich Persian and Indian markets, but a demographic safety valve and, with their warm climate and traditional irrigated agriculture, an ideal supplier of cotton.

In the 1850s the booming Russian textile industry got much of its raw cotton from the USA, but experienced shortages and steep price rises when the US Civil War broke out. Because imports from British India and Egypt were politically taboo, the alternative was domestic plantations. So, while the grasslands of Kazakstan became a peasant settlement colony, the rest of Central Asia was harnessed to cotton. This criminal waste of its most fertile lands displaced food production, marginalised traditional practices, introduced heavy herbicide use, and created the spectre of crop disease that could in a stroke obliterate vast areas economically. Subsequently Central Asia was physically grafted onto the Russian economy with the completion of the Trans-Caspian (1899) and Tashkent-Orenburg (1906) railways.

Despite rhetoric about the 'liberation of the peoples of the east', Soviet economic policy in the 1930s only made matters worse. The closing of borders and Stalin's genocidal collectivisation programs struck the final blow to nomadic animal breeding.

In an attempt to make the USSR economically self-sufficient, each republic (and Soviet satellite country) was 'encouraged' to specialise in a limited range of crops, raw materials and/or industrial products. Uzbekistan alone soon supplied no less than 64% of Soviet cotton, making the USSR the world's second largest cotton producer after the USA. Tajikistan built the world's fourth-largest aluminium plant but all the aluminium had to brought in from outside.

Most raw materials were shipped to other parts of the USSR for processing – for example 90% of Central Asian cotton went to Russian and Ukrainian mills. Conversely, Central Asia depended for the bulk of its food, machinery, fuels and consumer goods on Russia and Ukraine, mostly at below-market internal rates. Three-quarters of Central Asia's skilled labourers and factory and farming managers were settlers from Russia and the Ukraine.

While Russian and Soviet development brought some modernisation and progress, on the whole Central Asia received less than its share of the heralded social advantages of the Soviet system. In the last years of the USSR, official reports revealed that while Central Asia proper (without Kazakstan) was home to some 16% of the USSR's population, it held about 64% of its poor. Rates of child mortality and life expectancy were worse than in other Soviet republics.

Post-Independence

The newly independent Central Asian republics have been harshly affected by the price liberalisation in Russia from 1992, and plagued by the same shortages, collapse of infrastructure and plunging production that hit Russia after the end of the USSR. The region was further hurt badly in 1998 by the Russian economic crisis and a slump in raw material prices especially oil, gas, gold and copper. All are suffering from the exodus of Russian and Ukrainian engineers, technicians and skilled workers.

The deepest economic trauma is in the countryside, but even many urbanites are just scraping by. Factory workers and professionals in Bishkek (for example) earn perhaps US$35 to US$50 a month, and factory managers up to US$80. Many Tashkenters make do with less than US$5 a week for food and clear as little as US$25 to US$35 a month. Most heart-rending are the pensioners, especially the Slavic ones whose children have fled Central Asia and whose pensions are currently worthless. Watery-eyed babushkas (old women) sit quietly along the pavements, trying not to look like beggars. Kazakstan alone owes over US$800 million in back wages and pensions.

Central Asia has a young, fairly skilled and entrepreneurial population capable of starting small manufacturing enterprises to fill out the present lack of industrial diversity, but bureaucratic obstacles abound.

So far the main form of capitalism in Central Asia is the 'kiosk economy': small-time dealers buying goods (mostly cigarettes, sweets, alcohol, cheap Chinese, Iranian and Russian clothes and furnishings) and reselling them at a higher price. Longer-term projects are frustrated by banks willing to make only the shortest of short-term loans.

There are signs of economic cooperation. Tajikistan, Kazakstan, Kyrgyzstan, Belarus and Russia are all members of the CIS Customs Union. A Central Asian Economic Community was set up in 1997 and now includes Uzbekistan, Kazakstan, Tajikistan and Kyrgyzstan. Kyrgyzstan was the first of the Central Asian republics to join the World Trade Organisation (WTO) in 1998.

Rebirth of the Silk Road?

Sitting strategically between east Asia, the Indian subcontinent and the Arabian peninsula, Central Asia has a potential role as an economic transit zone and transport corridor, rather like the Silk Road days of old.

Central Uzbekistan, with its historically resonant cities like Bukhara, Samarkand and the Fergana valley, stands to benefit particularly; Tashkent after all is closer to Kashgar and Tehran than to Moscow or Kiev. The re-establishment of rail links to Xinjiang and Turkmenistan, the growth of border trade over the Torugart and Khunjerab passes and the increase in oil piped along the silk routes all offer the republics a means to unlock their natural reserves and shake off ties with Moscow. China is becoming an increasingly important trade partner with the region.

In 1969 Turkey, Iran and Pakistan founded the Economic Cooperation Organisation (ECO) in the hope of integrating their transport systems. After a slow start it was opened in 1992 to Azerbaijan, Afghanistan and the five Central Asian republics. One of the enlarged ECO's first acts was a decision to complete a railway link between the Iranian city of Mashad and the Turkmen capital, Ashgabat, thus offering access to Persian Gulf ports for Turkmen gas.

Resources The region is a mother lode of energy and raw materials, notably oil and gas but also a range of minerals including coal, copper, silver, gold, iron ore, chromium, bauxite and uranium, while mountainous Kyrgyzstan and Tajikistan offer hydroelectric power. Uzbekistan is the world's fifth largest producer of gold, while Kyrgyzstan holds the world's fifth largest gold mine. The biggest problem landlocked countries like Turkmenistan face is how to get their gas and oil to countries which can actually afford to pay for it, unlike their skint ex-Soviet neighbours. For details in the superpower scramble for oil and gas in the region see the boxed text 'Pipe Dreams'.

Agriculture Despite its overspecialisation in cotton, Central Asia is a major producer

Pipe Dreams

Central Asia and the Caspian region represent the most concentrated mass of untapped wealth in the world; a wealth measured in *trillions* of dollars. The Caspian Sea hides an ocean of oil, around 200 billion barrels, and foreign companies are falling over themselves to invest the US$50 billion needed just to extract it. The best-endowed republic is Kazakstan, whose oil reserves rank third after those of the Persian Gulf and Siberia. Turkmenistan is sitting on the world's fourth largest reserves (three trillion cubic metres) of gas. Kazakstan and Uzbekistan also have major natural gas reserves.

These riches are becoming the stake in a new economic Great Game, as western energy and mining firms scramble to strike high-stake deals. And in a region of interlocking interests this scramble is taking on a geopolitical significance. Chevron's multibillion dollar agreement with Kazakstan for its Caspian oil fields was just the first of many gigantic multinational deals.

Until recently the only regional pipeline was through Russia, which imposed restrictive quotas on the amount of Kazak oil allowed to flow through it and demanded high fees. The Central Asian republics are anxious to lessen reliance on Russia and re-tie regional trade links. Countries as varied as the US, Britain, Russia, Turkey, Japan, Iran, China and Pakistan are all jostling to promote their own particular pipelines through the Eurasian energy corridor and grab a slice of the billion dollar action. Iran has been pushing itself as the shortest, cheapest and most obvious choice, making use of existing pipelines from Turkmenistan to the Persian Gulf, but politically-motivated US trade sanctions have straight-jacketed investment.

In May 1999 Turkmenistan finally signed a deal to build a 2000km pipeline under the Caspian to Azerbaijan, Georgia to Turkey, bypassing Russia and Iran (much to the US's pleasure and Iran's fury). Kazakstan is also keen to construct a pipeline under the Caspian, if it can get Russia's approval. Both of these plans depend on the redrawing of national borders, to split the Caspian between Turkmenistan, Kazakstan, Russia, Azerbaijan and Iran (previously divided between Iran and the USSR). The northern half of the sea was recently split down the middle between Kazakstan and Russia.

The US company UNICOL has an even grander plan – to build a 1300km pipeline from the Dauletabad gas fields of Turkmenistan, across Afghanistan to Pakistan and thence down to the Arabian Sea, with a second 700km oil line leading from Turkmenabat (Charjou) across Afghanistan to the Arabian sea that is capable of delivering one billion barrels a day. The big snag in this particular pipe dream is that it requires political stability in Afghanistan, probably the region's biggest 'if', as well as international recognition of the Taliban regime. UNICOL is confident and has already invited the Taliban to Texas and begun training Afghans in Nebraska.

Even China has joined the scramble for influence. It recently spent US$9 billion securing the rights to Kazakstan's second largest oilfield, in what has been called 'the contract of the century', and is currently building a 3000km-long pipeline to Ürümqi. There are epic plans to construct a further 8000km-long pipeline along the former Silk Road to Japan, making China the energy corridor of the east. For the Kazaks, China is exactly the kind of important partner it is looking for to counterbalance Russia's stranglehold on the economy. The Chinese themselves are eager to find extra reserves to fuel its juggernaught economy, after initial exploration for oil in Xinjiang's Tarim basin proved disappointing.

Governments are well aware of the dangers of laying major oil pipelines through volatile Kurdish, Chechen, Afghan, and Caucasian territories, but the rewards are simply too fantastic to walk away from. The competition can only intensify and it is a game which will have resonance deep into the 21st century.

of agricultural goods. Agriculture accounts for one quarter to one third of the gross national product of all republics, and employs one third to one half of their workforces. The dominant areas are the grain producing Virgin Lands of northern Kazakstan (see Ecology & Environment in the Kazakstan chapter) and the cotton belt centred around the Fergana valley. Other important sectors are cereals, fruit and vegetables, and animal husbandry (mostly sheep, cattle and horses).

Reform and diversification is proving more difficult in agriculture than in most other fields. Dependence on 'white gold' (cotton), for example, will not be easily kicked. In 1993, 80% of Uzbekistan's export revenues came from cotton, and plantations and associated industry still employ more than a quarter of its workforce. Land reform in favour of small and medium sized farms is a way out, but raises other problems, including the resistance to change of apparatchik landowners, and more importantly the threat of land-related ethnic strife. In 1998 Kyrgyzstan became the first, and so far only, Central Asian government to pass a referendum allowing the private ownership of land.

POPULATION & PEOPLE

The total population of the former Soviet Central Asia is about 60 million, with a 2.4% annual growth rate. With China's Xinjiang Autonomous Region and Afghanistan, the region's total is some 100 million. Few areas of its size are home to such tangled demographics and daunting transitions.

It's a social rollercoaster in Central Asia: the overall birth rate is down, deaths from all causes are up, economies are plummeting, crime is skyrocketing, life expectancies have dropped and migration (most especially emigration) is on the rise. Many elder Central Asians lost their social and cultural bearings with the fall of the Soviet Union. Health levels are plummeting, drug addiction is up and alcoholism has acquired the proportions of a national tragedy.

But in a few years these setbacks to population growth will probably look like small blips on a steep upward curve. Central Asia has shown high birth rates and population

growth ever since the Russians started taking censuses.

Each republic has inherited an ethnic grab-bag from the Soviet system. Thus you'll find Uzbek towns in Kyrgyzstan, legions of Tajiks in the cities of Uzbekistan, Kazaks grazing their cattle in Kyrgyzstan, Turkmen in Uzbekistan – and Russians and Ukrainians everywhere. In Xinjiang, Uyghurs are joined by hordes of Chinese and some Kazaks and Kyrgyz.

Tajikistan exemplifies how a Central Asian republic can be demographically complex. Its 4.4 million Tajiks constitute only 65% of the country's population, and fewer than half of the world's Tajiks (more Tajiks inhabit Afghanistan than Tajikistan, and large groups also live in Uzbekistan, Kazakstan and Xinjiang). Some 25% of Tajikistan's population are Uzbeks, with whom there is considerable ethnic rivalry. And on an urgent note, Tajikistan's annual birth rate is an astonishing 5% (in Bangladesh it's 2.2%, in the USA 0.9%), perhaps due to early marriage and the remoteness of the region.

Ethnic Conflicts

Given the complicated mix of nationalities across national boundaries, Central Asia's ethnic situation is surprisingly tranquil, but it was not always so. From the late 1980s until independence in 1991, there were numerous flare-ups: Kazaks against Russians, Uzbeks against Jews and Meskhetian Turks, Kyrgyz and Uzbeks against each other. Moscow described the violence as 'ethnic', ignoring more complicated causes such as land and water rights and housing space.

The most noticeable divide (and a largely amicable one) is between the traditionally sedentary peoples, the Uzbeks, Tajiks and Uyghurs, and their formerly nomadic neighbours, the Kazaks, Kyrgyz and Turkmen.

One serious old wound remains which binds Central Asians together – all share bitter memories of subjugation by two Russian empires, reaching its depths during the Stalin years, and extending right up to 1991. The Uyghurs of Xinjiang hold similar grievances against China (see the boxed text 'The Beginning or the End?' in the Xinjiang chapter).

Migration

Most emigration from Central Asia consists of minority groups (Russians, Ukrainians, Germans, Koreans) going to their 'homelands', though the individuals may have spent their entire lives in Central Asia. At the height of the migration, in 1994, over 280,000 Russians left Kazakstan. Almost the entire Jewish population, even the venerable Bukharan Jewish community with roots to the 9th century, has left for Israel. Dungans (Chinese Muslims) and Uyghurs, however, are understandably not flocking to Xinjiang. Those minority groups that do stay are beginning to speak up for recognition and rights.

Immigration is relatively low and is mostly intra-regional and intra-CIS – for example, Uzbeks from Kyrgyzstan moving to Uzbekistan. Tens of thousands of Tajik war refugees are marking time in neighbouring republics, especially Kyrgyzstan. Of Turkic groups living in the so-called 'far abroad' (outside the CIS), few members have immigrated to their Central Asian motherlands.

EDUCATION

Before the revolution of 1917, education in Central Asia was largely through the limited, men-only network of Islamic schools and medressas.

As part of the early Bolshevik drive to educate and bring minority nations into the socialist fold, largely state-financed national education, obligatory to the end of secondary school, was provided across the board. Today mobile primary schools are taken out on the grasslands in Xinjiang, when children cannot make it into the village classrooms.

The old Arabic alphabet was replaced with a simpler Roman one, and later with a modified Cyrillic script. As a result, male and female literacy shot up during the Soviet years. In Central Asia in 1926, the literacy rate ranged from 2.2% among Tajiks to 7.1% for Kazaks. By 1970 all ethnic groups in the USSR had achieved literacy rates in excess of 97%, largely in their own languages. This contrasts greatly with Afghanistan, where literacy rates are as low as 47% for men, and 15% for women.

Presently in Central Asia, general education is compulsory from ages six to 14. Some 58% over age 25 has full secondary or some post-secondary education, with about 10% of the population receiving higher education.

But statistics don't tell it all. Many badly paid and disillusioned teachers are moving on to more lucrative 'businesses'. The end of the old Soviet subsidies means the quality and supporting infrastructure of public schools is deteriorating.

While the Soviet system produced excellent technicians and engineers, the human sciences (eg economics, history, public administration, international relations) were so heavily ideologised that the old textbooks are now worthless. Meanwhile, the newly independent republics cannot get their own textbooks into print for lack of funds and even of paper.

The rapid shift from Arabic to Roman and then to Cyrillic as the official script (and recent decisions by several republics to return to Roman) has led to a kind of 'virtual illiteracy', with older people using alphabets incomprehensible to their children and grandchildren.

Free Islamic schools (often financed by Middle Eastern foundations) are multiplying in rural, conservative areas like the Fergana valley and southern Tajikistan. Islamic education clearly offers Central Asians a return to old values but is seen by some as simply a conduit for imported fundamentalist ideas.

In Uzbekistan, a university planned in Margilan and several Saudi-financed medressas of the Wahhabi branch of Sunni Islam were prevented from opening by 1993 legislation banning private schools, a result of the government's unease about fundamentalism.

Under the Soviet system, women had 'economic equality' – meaning that they had the chance to study and work alongside men while retaining all the responsibilities of homemakers. Female literacy approached male levels and women readily assumed positions of responsibility in middle-level administration positions as well as academia.

[Continued on page 61]

PEOPLES OF THE SILK ROAD

Centuries of migrations and invasions have ensured Central Asia's ethnic diversity. A trip from Ashgabat to Kashgar reveals an array of faces, ranging from Turkish, Slavic, Chinese and Middle Eastern to downright Mediterranean – surmounted, incidentally, by a vast array of hats.

Before the Russian Revolution of 1917, Central Asians usually identified themselves 'ethnically' as either nomad or sart (settled), as Turk or Persian, as simply Muslim, or by their clan. Later, separate nationalities were 'identified' by Soviet scholars as ordered by Stalin. Central Asia's linguistic continuum was artificially teased apart into five standardised languages (Tajik, an Indo-European language, was the easiest to distinguish), with a host of in-between dialects lost in the process. Similarly, the ethnic blur was vivisected and its five most distinguishable parts bottled in separate republics. Distinct, carefully crafted 'traditions' were formulated and parcelled out to each of these nationalities, mostly to prevent any pan-Islamic or pan-Turkic tendencies.

While it is easy to see the problems this has created, some Kazaks and Kyrgyz at least will admit that they owe their survival as a nation to the Soviet process of nation-building. The following sections are a summary of who's who.

Kazaks

Kazakstan: 8 million	**Turkmenistan:** 90,000
Xinjiang: 1.1 million	**Western Mongolia:** 70,000
Uzbekistan: 900,000	**Kyrgyzstan:** 50,000
Russia: 740,000	**Afghanistan:** 30,000

The Kazaks were nomadic horseback pastoralists until the 1920s; indeed the name kazak is said to mean 'free warrior' or 'steppe roamer'. Kazaks trace their roots to the 15th century, when rebellious kinsmen of an Uzbek khan broke away and settled in present-day Kazakstan. They divide themselves into three main divisions, or zhuz, corresponding to the historical Great (southern Kazakstan), Middle (the north and east) and Little (the west) Hordes (see Uzbeks & Kazaks under History in the Facts about Central Asia chapter). Family and ancestry remain crucial to Kazaks. 'What zhuz do you belong to?' is a common opening question.

Kazaks are the most Russified of Central Asians, due to their long historical contact with Russia, though some maintain a seminomadic existence, moving out with herds, flocks and yurts from their collective farms to summer pastures every year.

Most Kazaks have Mongolian facial features similar to the Kyrgyz. Most wear western or Russian clothes, but you may see women – particularly on special occasions – in long dresses with stand-up collars or brightly decorated velvet waistcoats and heavy jewellery. Sometimes they also wear fur-trimmed headdresses topped with crane plumes. Some men still wear baggy shirts and trousers and sleeveless jackets and wool or cotton robes. This outfit may be topped with either a skullcap or a high, tasselled felt hat resembling nothing so much as an elf-hat.

SIMON RICHMOND

Kazak 'literature' is based around heroic epics, many of which concern themselves and the 16th century clashes between the Kazaks and Kalmyks, and the heroic *batyrs* (warriors), of that age. Apart from various equestrian sports (see the Spectator Sports section in the Regional Facts for the Visitor chapter), a favourite Kazak pastime is *itys*, which involves two people boasting about their own town, region or clan and ridiculing the other's in verses full of puns and allusions to Kazak culture. The person who fails to find a witty comeback loses.

Kazaks adhere rather loosely to Islam. Reasons for this include the Kazaks' location on the fringe of the Muslim world and their traditionally nomadic lifestyle, which is unsuited to central religious authority. Their earliest contacts with the religion, from the 16th century, came courtesy of wandering Sufi dervishes or ascetics. Many were not converted till the 19th century, and shamanism apparently coexisted with Islam even after conversion.

Kazak women appear the most confident and least restricted by tradition in Central Asia. All this is despite the lingering custom of wife-stealing, whereby a man may simply kidnap a woman he wants to marry (often with some collusion it must be said), leaving the parents with no option but to negotiate the bride-price.

The eight or so million Kazaks have only recently become a majority in 'their' country, Kazakstan. A further 1.1 million Kazaks live in northern Xinjiang, mostly in the Ili, Mori and Burqin autonomous regions. Over 200,000 Kazaks fled to China in 1916 after an uprising over forced labour conscription during WWI, and more fled in the wake of the Bolshevik uprising and forced collectivisation in the 1920s.

Top: Kazak man in uniform. While national pride is being encouraged, family and ancestry remain crucial to Kazaks.

Kyrgyz

Kyrgyzstan: 3 million **Xinjiang:** 143,000
Uzbekistan: 180,000 **Afghanistan:** 3,000

Some Kyrgyz are fond of suggesting that long ago some of their ancestors from Siberia crossed the Bering land bridge to become the forebears of native Americans (there are indeed some resemblances). Many Kyrgyz derive their name from *kyrk kyz*, which means '40 girls' and goes along with legends of 40 original clan mothers. Today, ties to such clans as the Bugu (the largest clan), Salto (around Bishkek), Adigine (around Osh) and Sary Bagysh (President Akaev's clan) remain relevant. Clans are divided into two federations, the Otuz Uul (30 Sons) and the Ich Kilik of southern Kyrgyzstan.

The name 'Kyrgyz' is one of the oldest recorded ethnic names in Asia, going back to the 2nd century BCE in Chinese sources. At that time the ancestors of the modern Kyrgyz are said to have lived in the upper Yenisey basin in Siberia. They migrated to the mountains of what is now Kyrgyzstan from the 10th to 15th centuries, some fleeing wars and some in the ranks of Mongol armies. Kazaks and Kyrgyz share many customs and have similar languages, and in a sense they are simply the steppe (Kazak) and mountain (Kyrgyz) variants of the same people.

For special events Kyrgyz women's dress is similar to Kazak women's. Older women may wear a large white wimple-like turban (known as a *elechek*) with the number of windings indicating her status. Kyrgyz men wear a white, embroidered, usually tasselled, felt cap called an *ak kalpak*. In winter, older men wear a long sheepskin coat and a round fur-trimmed hat called a *tebbetey*.

Traditions such as the Manas epic (see the Arts entry of the Facts about Kyrgyzstan section of the Kyrgyzstan chapter), horseback sports and eagle hunting remain important cultural denominators.

Northern Kyrgyz are more Russified and less observant of Muslim doctrine than their cousins in the south (in Jalal-Abad and Osh provinces). Like the Kazaks, they adopted Islam relatively late and limited it to what could fit in their saddlebags.

Tajiks

Tajikistan: 4.4 million **Kazakstan:** 100,000
Afghanistan: 3.5 million **Xinjiang:** 33,000
Uzbekistan: 630,000

With their Mediterranean features and the occasional green-eyed redhead, Tajiks like to recall that their land was once visited by Alexander the Great and his troops, who are known to have taken local brides. Whether that blood is still visible or not, the Tajiks are in fact descended from an ancient Indo-European people, the Aryans, making them relatives of present-day Iranians. Before this century, *taj* was merely a term denoting a Persian speaker (all other Central Asian peoples speak Turkic languages).

Tajiks have been in Tajikistan for thousands of years, making them the oldest of all Central Asian groups. They often consider themselves to be the most civilised as well, pointing out that many great 'Persian' literary figures in fact hailed from parts closer to Tajikistan. Some Tajik nationalists have even demanded that Uzbekistan 'give back' Samarkand and Bukhara, as these cities were long-time centres of Persian culture. Tajiks trace their history back to the Samanids, Sogdians and Bactrians.

There are in fact many Tajik subdivisions and clans, such as the Kulyabis and Khojandis. The main sub-group is Pamiri Tajiks (or Badakhshanis), but even these are again subdivided into clans such as the Shugnis, Rushanis, Wakhis and Ishkashims.

MICK WELDON

Traditional Tajik dress for men includes a heavy quilted coat *(tapan)*, tied with a sash that also secures a sheathed dagger, and a black embroidered cap *(tupi)*. Tajik women could almost be identified in the dark, with their long, psychedelically coloured dresses *(kurta)* with matching head scarves *(rumol)*, and underneath the dress striped trousers *(izor)* and bright slippers. In Xinjiang, Tajik women wear embroidered pillbox hats, sometimes with silver chains hanging down the front.

Most Tajiks are Sunni Muslims, but Pamiri Tajiks of the Gorno-Badakhshan region belong to the Ismaili sect of Shia Islam, and therefore have no mosques.

Most of China's 33,000 Tajiks live in the Tashkurgan Tajik Autonomous County. Most evident in this region are Sarikol and Wakhi Tajiks. Wakhi Tajiks also live in northern Pakistan.

The 3.5 million Tajiks in Afghanistan speak Dari and resemble Pashto society. They follow a code of conduct called Abdurzadagai, similar to the Pashto Pakhtunwali. Most Afghani Tajiks share closer ties to the valley they live in than their ethnic group. The most famous Tajik Afghan is the alliance leader Ahmed Shah Masood.

There are also large, historical communities of Tajiks in Uzbekistan. Tajiks have the highest population growth in Central Asia.

Like all countries in Central Asia, Kyrgyzstan is a mix of nationalities and the Kyrgyz themselves are a mix of clans. The Kyrgyz men are most easily recognised by their *ak kalpak* (felt hats).

MARTIN MOOS

MARTIN MOOS

BRADLEY MAYHEW

Top Right & Top Left: Turkmen males traditionally wear huge, sheepskin *telpek* hats – worn on top of a scullcap year-round, rain or shine.

Bottom: Tajiks are the oldest of all Central Asian groups, being related to present-day Iranians. Traditional dress for men includes a *turpan* (a quilted coat) tied with a sash.

SIMON RICHMOND

MARTIN MOOS

MARTIN MOOS

BRADLEY MAYHEW

Top: Kazaks picnicking amid alpine meadows, Aksu-Zhabaghly Nature Reserve.
Bottom Left: Uzbek man wearing a traditional *doppe* – a four-sided black scullcap embroidered in white.
Middle Right: Fashionable Uzbek women outside Guri Amir mausoleum, Samarkand.
Bottom Right: An *aksakal* (elder), Samarkand. Aksakal tranlsates literally as 'white beard'.

Male and female, young and old – the Uzbek people emerged from Soviet rule with a strong concept of their cultural heritage. Uzbek women are proud of dresses made from sparkly *ikat* cloth **(bottom left)**.

Turkmen

Turkmenistan: 3.6 million
Iran: 1 million
Afghanistan: 650,000

Legend has it that all Turkmen are descended from the fabled Oghuz Khan or from the warriors who rallied into clans around his 24 grandsons. Most historians believe that they were displaced nomadic horse-breeding clans who drifted into the oases around the Karakum desert (and into Persia, Syria and Anatolia) from the foothills of the Altay mountains in the wake of the Seljuq Turks.

The hardships of desert-based nomadism forged them into a distinct group long before Soviet nation-building, though centuries-old clan loyalties still exist and play a major role in politics. The largest of the 100 or so Turkmen clans are the Yomud (Caspian shore and northern Iran), Tekke (Merv, Ashgabat and central Turkmenistan), Ersari (Turkmenistan-Afghanistan border), Sarik (south, around Kushka) and Salor (eastern Turkmenistan and northern Afghanistan), each distinguished by their dialect, style of clothing and jewellery, and the patterns woven into their famous Turkmen *gillams* (carpets). The Tekke and Yomud dominate the ruling circles. Even the most urbane Turkmen retains allegiance to his clan, while in the more remote regions clan loyalty dominates to such an extent that Ersari marry only Ersari, Yomud only Yomud and so on.

Interestingly, there was a Turkmen literary language as early as the mid-18th century. The Turkmen were the last of the Central Asian people to fall to Russian expansion (rebels were still fighting in 1936) and they remain among the least Russified.

Turkmen tend to be tall, and their faces show a mixture of Mongolian and Caucasian features. Turkmen males are easily recognisable in their huge sheepskin hats *(telpek)*, either white (for special occasions) or black with thick ringlets like dreadlocks, worn year round on top of a skullcap, even on the hottest days. As one Turkmen explained it, they'd rather suffer the heat of their own heads than that of the sun. Traditional dress consists of baggy trousers tucked into knee-length boots, and white shirts under the knee-length *khalat*, a cherry red cotton jacket. Older men wear a long belted coat.

Turkmen women wear heavy, ankle-length velvet or silk dresses, the favourite colours being wine reds and maroons, with colourful trousers underneath. A woman's hair is always tied back and concealed under a colourful scarf. Older women often wear a khalat but, curiously, it is always thrown over their heads.

The Turkmen shared the nomad's liking for Sufism, and that sect is now strongly represented in Turkmenistan. The Turkmen language is closest to Azeri.

Turkmenistan's population is now 82% Turkmen, giving it the highest proportion of the titular nationality of any Central Asian republic.

Uzbeks

Uzbekistan: 18 million **Kyrgyzstan:** 690,000
Tajikistan: 1.6 million **Turkmenistan:** 396,000
Afghanistan: 1.3 million **Xinjiang:** 14,700

The Uzbek khans, Islamised descendants of Jenghiz Khan, left their home in southern Siberia in search of conquest, establishing themselves in what is now Uzbekistan by the 15th century, clashing and then mixing with the Timurids. The Uzbek Shaybanid dynasty oversaw the transition from nomad to settler, though the original Mongol clan identities (such as the Kipchak, Mangit and Karluks) remain.

Uzbeks resisted Russification and have emerged from Soviet rule with a strong sense of identification with their rich heritage. Uzbek neighbourhoods *(mahalla)* and villages *(kishlak)* are coherent and solid, both physically and socially. Houses are built behind high walls, sometimes with handsome gates.

Uzbeks are the largest Turkic group outside of Turkey and were the third largest ethnic group of the Soviet Union. With their high profile and numbers in all the former USSR republics, Uzbeks are often cast as the regional bogeyman, seeking political hegemony over Central Asia.

Uzbek men traditionally wear long quilted coats tied by a bright-coloured sash. Nearly all wear the *doppilar* or *dopy*, a black, four-sided skullcap embroidered in white. In winter, older men wear a furry telpek. Uzbek women are fond of dresses in sparkly, brightly coloured ikat cloth, often as a knee-length gown with trousers of the same material underneath. One or two braids indicates a married woman; more means that she is single. Eyebrows that grow together over the bridge of the nose are considered attractive and are often supplemented with pencil for the right effect. Both sexes flash lots of gold teeth.

Uzbeks in general seem to be the most Islamised of ex-Soviet Central Asia; the most devout and conservative of these are to be found in the Fergana valley.

There are around 1.3 million Uzbeks in northern Afghanistan, north of the Hindu Kush, who mostly grow cotton or trade in karakul fleeces. Ties to the local landlord *(arbab)* are still strong in this region.

Uyghurs

Xinjiang: 7.2 million (1990)
Kyrgyzstan: 50,000

The Uyghurs have a proud heritage stretching over 1000 years to the Uyghur khanate of southern Siberia, which ruled from Lake Baikal to the Karakoram. Uyghurs were the first Turkic people to settle, populating Xinjiang during the days of Silk Road trade, perhaps around the 5th century CE. Later branches include the Buddhist 'Yellow Uyghurs' of Gansu, the Buddhist Karakhoja Uyghurs of Gaochang (modern day

Turpan) and the great Muslim Qarakhan dynasty that held sway from Balasagun (now Burana in Kyrgyzstan), Talas (now Taraz in Kazakstan) and Kashgar.

Uyghur legends put their genesis down to one Wugusi, who lived on raw meat and wine as a baby, talked immediately after birth and who started to walk at the age of 40 days. Wugusi's grandsons formed the 24 clans of the Uyghurs. Wolves are an important aspect of Uyghur mythology.

Their first writing system, long since discarded, became the basis of Mongolian script. Uyghurs of Xinjiang now write with Arabic letters. Their language is similar to Uzbek. Uyghur medicine is famous throughout Central Asia; some sources even claim that the Uyghurs invented acupuncture.

In Xinjiang, Uyghurs are immediately distinguishable from the Han, or ethnic Chinese. They are larger and have generally darker complexions and more Mediterranean features. The four-sided skullcap of the men is also a giveaway, though older Uyghur men may wear a tall black cotton hat with a narrow fringe of fur at the bottom. Uyghur men seem to wear a long black coat and leather boots whatever the weather. Uyghur women often wear long and elaborate braids and a colourful skullcap. Married Uyghur women in Kashgar often wear a brown *paranja* veil.

Uyghurs make up only around half of Xinjiang's population. The reason is 'sinicisation' – China has sought to dilute Uyghur nationalism by flooding the region with Han immigrants.

It is estimated that there are a further half-million Uyghurs in the former Soviet Central Asian republics (having moved there after heavy Chinese persecution in the late 19th century), plus a total of about 75,000 in Pakistan, Afghanistan, Turkey and the west.

Slavs

Russians and Ukrainians have settled in Central Asia in several waves, the first in the 19th century with colonisation and the latest in the 1950s during the Virgin Lands campaign (see the Revolution & Civil War entry in the History section of the Facts about Central Asia chapter). Numerous villages in remoter parts of Central Asia with names like Orlovka or Alexandrovka were founded by the early settlers and are still inhabited by their descendants.

Many Slavs, feeling deeply aggrieved as political and administrative power devolves to 'local' people, have emigrated to Russia and Ukraine. Some have returned, either disillusioned with life in the Motherland or reaffirmed in the knowledge that Central Asia is their home, like it or not.

It is a surprise to come across the occasional Slav living in Xinjiang (and thus 'Chinese'), descendants of White Russians who fled after the 1917 Bolshevik Revolution.

Other Nationalities

Dungans are Muslim Chinese who first moved across the border in 1882, especially to Kazakstan and Kyrgyzstan, to escape persecution after failed Muslim rebellions. Few still speak Chinese, though their cuisine remains distinctive.

Koreans arrived in Central Asia as deportees in WWII. They have preserved little of their traditional culture. They typically farm vegetables and dominate the grocers' stalls of some bazars.

Germans were deported in WWII from their age-old home in the Volga region, or came as settlers (some of them Mennonites) in the late 19th century. Most are now departing en masse to Germany at a rate of some 150,000 a year. Likewise, **Jews**, once such an important part of Bukharan commerce, are making for Israel (and Queens, New York).

Tatars, a Turkic people from Russia (descended from the Mongol Golden Horde), began settling in Central Asia with the tsar's encouragement in the mid-19th century. Most look more like Russians than like other Turkic peoples. **Meskhetian Turks** have groups in the Fergana (the largest concentration), Chuy and Ili valleys. There are around 120,000 **Mongolians** living in Xinjiang.

Karakalpaks occupy their own republic in north-west Uzbekistan and have cultural and linguistic ties with Kazaks, Uzbeks and Kyrgyz (see the boxed text 'Karakalpakstan' in the Nukus section of the Uzbekistan chapter). **Kurds** are another WWII-era addition to the melting pot, with many living in Kazakstan. Estimates of their numbers in Central Asia range from 150,000 to over a million.

Cossacks, fearsome cavaliers with legendary prowess in war, were instrumental in the Russian empire's subjugation of Central Asia. By origin they are part social class, part profession and part ethnic group. Back in the 16th century, the Cossacks were Russian serfs who had escaped from their estates and settled on the wild frontier.

In the 19th century, their rugged lifestyle and fighting mettle made them a perfect choice for relocation onto the newly acquired Kazak steppe. Today the Cossacks are leading demands that parts of Kazakstan be returned to Russia.

Pashtos are the largest ethnic group in Afghanistan, totalling over seven million. Many Pashtos, or Pakhtuns, live over the border in Pakistan's Tribal Areas and North-West Frontier Province. Pashtos are divided along clan lines, the largest of which are the southern Durranis and eastern Ghilzai. Over the centuries they have been characterised as loyal, honest, brave and wily, perpetually waiting in ambush somewhere, with a love of freedom and guns.

Hazaras, or Hazarajat, are the second largest ethnic group in Afghanistan, totalling over 1.5 million. Descendants of Mongol troops, they have very Mongolian faces and follow Shia Islam. They speak a dialect of Dari. They have traditionally suffered much discrimination within Afghanistan as they are non-Sunni and non-Pashto.

[Continued from page 52]

But the combination of rising unemployment in post-Soviet economies, and the resurgence of traditional values, which favour early, arranged marriages and large families, has eroded these gains in rural areas. And while some Islamic schools are co-educational, there are still no women found in medressas.

Despite this somewhat gloomy picture, education reforms have included increased emphasis on Central Asian history and literature, the renewed study of Arabic script, and the adoption in 1992 of the US university degree system. Turkey is playing an important role in education, and Turkish lycees are the best schools in many Central Asian towns.

SCIENCE & PHILOSOPHY

Central Asia has produced some of history's most important thinkers. Abu Ali Ibn-Sina (Latinised as Avicenna, 980 to 1037), from Bukhara, was the greatest medic of his age, whose *Canon of Medicine* was the standard textbook for western doctors until the 17th century.

Al-Khorezmi (Latin: Algorismi) was a mathematician who gave his name to algorithm, the mathematical process behind addition and multiplication. The title of another of his mathematical works, Al-Jebr, became algebra.

Al-Beruni, from Khorezm, was the world's foremost astronomer in the 11th century when he worked in Gurganj (modern day Konye-Urgench). He knew that the earth rotated and that it circled round the sun, estimating the distance to the moon to within 20km. He also produced the world's finest encyclopedia.

ARTS
Fine Art

Rendered in a style that foreshadows that of Persian miniature painting, some splendid friezes were unearthed in the excavations of the Afrasiab palace (6th to 7th century) on the outskirts of Samarkand, depicting a colourful caravan led by elephants. Similar wall frescoes were discovered at Penjikent showing men and women tossed in a sea filled with monsters and fish.

During their campaigns of terror both Jenghiz Khan and Timur collected artisans, dispersing them anywhere from Beijing to Baghdad, resulting in a splendid fusion of styles in textiles, paintings, architecture, and toreutic (embossed metal) arts.

This promise of a great artistic heritage for Central Asia failed to develop any further when the Sogdians of Afrasiab and Penjikent fled into the mountains, and into historical obscurity, in the face of the Arab invasion. As a result, representational art in Central Asia was put on hold for the better part of 1300 years.

Islam prohibited the depiction of the living, so traditional arts developed in the form of calligraphy, combining Islamic script with arabesques, and the carving of doors and screens. Textiles and metals took on floral or repetitive, geometric motifs. Examples of this kind of work can be found in museums in Central Asia's capital cities, particularly in Tashkent's Museum of Applied Arts.

Painting and two-dimensional art were only revived under the Soviets who introduced European ideas and set up schools to train local artists in the new fashion. Under Soviet tutelage the pictorial art of Central Asia became a curious hybrid of socialist realism and mock traditionalism – Kyrgyz horsemen riding proudly beside a shiny red tractor, smiling Uzbeks at a *chaykhana* (teahouse) with futuristic chimneys thrusting skywards in the background.

Folk Art

Central Asian folk art developed in tune with a nomadic or seminomadic way of life focusing on transport (horses) and home (*yurts*). Designs followed the natural beauty of the earth: snow resting on a leaf, the elegance of an ibex horn, the flowers of the steppe. Status and wealth were apparent by the intricacy of a carved door or a richly adorned horse. Art was not merely created for pleasure; each item had a useful function in everyday life. From brightly colored carpets used for sleeping, to woven reed mats used to block the wind, to leather bottles used for carrying *kumys* (fermented mare's milk), many of the souvenirs dispersed throughout Kyrgyzstan and Kazakstan in particular are remnants of a nomadic past.

With such emphasis on equestrian culture it is not surprising that horses donned decorative blankets, inlaid wooden saddles, and head and neck adornments. Men hung their wealth on their belts with daggers and sabres in silver sheaths, and embossed leather purses and vessels for drink. Even today the bazars in Tajikistan, the Fergana valley and Kashgar, are heavy with carved daggers and knives *(pichok)*.

During this time when wealth had to be portable and useful, nomadic women wore stupendous jewellery, mostly of silver incorporating semiprecious stones like lapis lazuli and carnelian (believed to have magical properties); there was sometimes enough jewellery on marriageable women to make walking difficult.

To remain portable, furnishings consisted of bright quilts and carpets and woven bags *aiyk kap* to hang on yurt walls for storing plates and clothing. Embossed leather bottles *(sabaa, chanach* and *kökör)* were used for preparing, transporting and serving kumys. Decorative woven mats made of *chiy* (or *chij*) served as room partitions and entryways.

Kyrgyz specialise in felt rugs with appliqued coloured panels *(shyrdak)* or pressed wool designs *(ala-kiyiz)*. See the Shopping section in the Kyrgyzstan chapter.

Kazaks also specialise in multicoloured felt mats *(koshma)*, brightly coloured rugs, wall coverings and bedspreads, traditionally used to furnish the inside of yurts. Possibly the most accessible Kazak textile souvenir (with the exception of floor carpets) is a *tus-kiiz* (*tush-kiyiz* in Kyrgyzstan) or 'wall carpet' (*tus* literally means colour and *kiiz* means felt). These colourful wall hangings, made of cotton and silk, were traditionally used for decoration, quite often to cover the bedding. Designs vary, but generally tus-kiiz are made of red or brightly coloured velvet bordered at the top and sides with embroidered silk panels, sometimes dropping into one or more triangles.

Plant and flower motifs are most common, though some feature birds and animals.

It seems the best wall carpets of all originate in north-east Kazakstan, near the 'four corners' region of Kazakstan, Russia, China and Mongolia. The mixed Kazak-Mongolian influences here appear to produce the most intricate and colourful textiles in the whole of Kazakstan.

Most Central Asian peoples have traditional rug or carpet styles and some, like the Turkmen, have gone quite commercial in this century. Most 'Bukhara' rugs – so called because they were mostly sold, not made, in Bukhara – are made by Turkmen. See the colour section on 'Bukhara' Rugs in the Turkmenistan chapter.

Uzbeks make silk and cotton wall hangings and coverlets such as the beautiful *suzani* (*suzan* is Persian for needle). Though enjoyed by nomads and settled families alike, most suzanis were found in established earth-rammed homes. Suzanis are made in a variety of sizes used as table covers, cushions, and *ruijo* (a bridal bed spread) and thus were important for the bride's dowry. Generally using floral or celestial motifs (depictions of people and animals are against Muslim beliefs) an average suzani requires about two years to complete. Nice examples of suzani can be found in Tashkent's Museum of Applied Arts.

The colourful *atlas* tie-dyed silks of Xinjiang, known as *khanatlas* or *ikat* in Uzbekistan, are popular throughout the region. The Uzbeks sport them with a flourish: from the psychedelic dresses and trousers of the women to the traditional male *khalat* (quilted cloak).

Literature

The division into Kazak literature, Tajik literature, Uzbek literature and so on, is a modern one; formerly there was simply literature in Chaghatai Turkic and literature in Persian. With most pre-20th century poets, scholars and writers bilingual in Uzbek and Tajik, literature in Central Asia belonged to a shared universality of culture.

For example, Abu Abdullah Rudaki, a 10th century Samanid court poet considered the father of Persian literature, stars in the national pantheons of Afghanistan, Iran and Tajikistan (he is buried in Penjikent) and is also revered by Uzbeks by dint of being born in the Bukhara emirate. Omar Khayyam, famed composer of *rubiayyat* poetry, although a native of what is now north-east Iran, also has strong if indistinct ties to Tajikistan and to Samarkand where he spent part of his early life at the court of the Seljuq emir.

A strong factor in the universal nature of Central Asian literature was that it was popularised not in written form but orally by itinerant minstrels in the form of songs, poems and stories. Known as *bakshi* or *dastanchi* in Turkmen and Uzbek, *akyn* in Kazak and Kyrgyz, these story-telling bards earned their living travelling from town to town giving skilled and dramatic recitations of crowd-pleasing verse tales and epics to audiences gathered in bazars and chaykhanas. *Manaschi* are a special category of akyn who sang the traditional Kyrgyz *Manas* epos. *Askiyachi* are humorists who play on words.

Certain bards are folk heroes, regarded as founders of their 'national literatures', even memorialised in Soviet-era street names (eg Toktogul, Zhambyl and Abay). Bardic competitions are still held in some rural areas. In Kyrgyzstan the epic *Manas* celebrated its 1000th anniversary in 1995, and following suit, Uzbekistan celebrated the 1000th anniversary of its national epic *Alpamish* in 1999.

It was only with the advent of Bolshevik rule that literacy became widespread. Unfortunately, at the same time, much of the region's classical heritage never saw print because Moscow feared that it might set a flame to latent nationalist sentiments. Instead writers were encouraged to produce novels and plays in line with official Communist Party themes. While a number of Central Asian poets and novelists found acclaim within the Soviet sphere, such as the Tajik Sadruddin Ayni (1878-1954) and the Uzbeks Asqad Mukhtar and Abdullah Kodiri, the only native Central Asian author to garner international recognition has been the Kyrgyz Chinghiz Aitmatov, who has had novels translated into English and other

European languages (see the Books section in Regional Facts for the Visitor). His works have also been adapted for the stage and screen, both in the former USSR and abroad.

Music

While visual arts and literature succumbed to a stifling Soviet-European influence (which they're presently struggling to shrug off), the music of Central Asia remains exotic and untainted, still closely related to the swirling melodies of the Middle East and Persia. The instruments used are similar to those found in the Arab world; the *rabab* (six stringed mandolin), *dutar*, a two stringed guitar, *dombra* (two stringed Kazak guitar) and *doira* (tambourine/drum).

In the past the development of music was closely connected with the art of the bards (see the Literature section), but these days the traditions are continued by small ensembles of musicians and singers, heavily in demand at weddings and other festivals. In Uzbek and Tajik societies there's a particularly popular form of folk music known as *sozanda*, sung primarily by women

A Kyrgyz folk hero, Toktogul recited his poetry orally, as songs.

accompanied only by percussion instruments like tablas, bells and castanets. Performances can last as long as eight hours, although for the novice ear eight minutes is probably more than enough.

Much more accessible is the folk music of Turkmenistan, which mixes influences from Persia, Azerbaijan and Turkey to create a sound driven by a clattering drumbeat and rounded out with swaying accordions and ferocious strumming of the *dutar*, a two-stringed lute.

One of the best introductions to Central Asian music that we've heard is the superb, lilting, *City of Love* CD (Real World CDRW 34), performed by a five-piece Turkmen ensemble called Ashkhabad. If you only try one CD of Central Asian music this should be it.

One Uzbek group that has successfully mixed Central Asian and Middle Eastern folk melodies and poetry with modern pop and dance influences is Yalla; for information on their popular *Beard of the Camel* and *Jinouni* albums, contact Imagina Productions, 2545 Warren Avenue N, Seattle, WA 98109-1836, USA (☎ 1206-284 8381, fax 284 9426, ✉ imagina@msn.com, Web site http: //imagina.base.org).

Other Central Asian musicians released by Imagina include Yulduz Usmanova, an Uzbek pop superstar, Oleg Fesov, an emigre Tajik from Badakhshan, Ziyod Ishankhojaev and Kumush Razzakov, both Uzbek.

Other, less accessible, recordings of Central Asian music include:

Asie Centrale Traditions Classique, Muridjat Yulchieva & Ensemble (World Network)
At the Bazaar of Love, Ilyus Malayev Ensemble (Shanachie Entertainment, 1997)
  Bukharan Jews living in New York play *shash maqam*, the classical music of Bukhara
Bukhara, Musical Crossroads of Asia (Smithsonian Folkways, 1991) Includes songs from a *sozanda* group, and shash maqam, classical instrumental pieces thought to have developed at the court of the Bukhara emirs
Ouzbekistan – L'Art du Dotar (Ocora)
Secret Museum of Mankind, The Central Asia Ethnic Music Classics: 1925-48 (Yazoo, a division of Shanachie Entertainment, 1996)
Uzbekistan, Harmonia Mundi (Radio France, Paris, 1995) Classical lute folksongs

Anyone interested in the music of the region should pick up *The Hundred Thousand Fools of Gold: musical travels in Central Asia* by Theodore Levin. The book, which traces a journey through Uzbekistan, is part-travel, part-ethnomusicology and comes with a CD of on-site recordings.

Cinema

Central Asian films rarely make it to foreign film festivals but the region has a history of producing films, mainly for the Soviet market. Film output dropped drastically after the fall of the Soviet Union but a mini-renaissance is underway. The first Eurasia Film Festival was held in Almaty in 1998.

Kazakstan is the largest film producer in the region. Recently released are *Abay*, a dramatisation of the bard's life, *Shankhai*, a drama about urban life, and *Lost Love of Genghis Khan*, a cheesy period drama.

Kyrgyzstan's Aktan Abdykalykov is a rising star of Central Asian cinema. His film *Besh Kumpyr* (Five Old Ladies) made it to the final of the Grand Prix in Cannes and is well worth a viewing.

Other titles to look out for include *The Snowstorm Station*, a filmed version of the Chinghiz Aitmatov novel, *Yandym*, a 1995 Turkmen film, and *And the Days Passed* from Uzbekistan.

Valentin of Yak Tours in Karakol in Kyrgyzstan has several videos, which travellers can watch for free. Of these, *Yak Born in Snow* is a fascinating Soviet documentary of Kyrgyz yak herders.

SOCIETY & CONDUCT
Traditional Culture

In Islam, a guest – Muslim or not – has a position of honour not very well understood in the west. If someone visits you and you don't have much to offer, as a Christian you'd be urged to share what you had; as a Muslim you're urged to give it all away. Guests are to be treated with absolute selflessness.

For a visitor to a Muslim country, even one as casual about Islam as Kazakstan or Kyrgyzstan, this is a constant source of pleasure, temptation and sometimes embarrassment. You may find yourself eating a lavish meal with the head of the family while all around, other adults and children look on, unlikely to eat any of it themselves.

The majority of Central Asians, especially rural ones, are poor with little to offer *but* their hospitality. Poorer families may put themselves under financial strain to show you a proper evening, possibly slaughtering a sheep if they have one, and a casual guest could drain a host's resources and never know it. And yet to refuse such an invitation (or to offer to bring food or to help with the cost) would almost certainly be a grave insult.

All you can do is enjoy it, honour their customs as best you can, and take yourself courteously out of the picture before you become a burden. If for some reason you do want to decline, couch your refusal in gracious and diplomatic terms, allowing the would-be host to save face.

If you are really lucky you might be invited to a celebration, or *toi*, such as a *kelin toi* wedding celebration, *beshik toi*, nine days after the birth of a child, or *sunnat toi*, circumcision party. Other celebrations are held to mark the birth, name-giving and first haircut of a child.

Hospitality

If you're invited home for a meal this can be your best introduction to local customs and traditions as well as to local cuisine. Don't go expecting a quick bite. Your host is likely to take the occasion very seriously. Uzbeks, for example, say *mehmon otanda ulugh*, 'the guest is greater than the father'.

It's important to arrive with a gift. Something for the table (eg a bunch of fruit from the market) will do. Better yet would be something for your hosts' children or their parents, preferably brought from your home country (eg sweets, postcards, badges, a picture book). Pulling out your own food or offering to pay someone for their kindness is likely to humiliate them (though some travellers hosted by very poor people have given a small cash gift to the eldest child, saying that it's 'for sweets'). Don't be surprised if you aren't thanked: gifts are taken more as evidence of God's grace than of your generosity.

A traditional meal in Central Asia may begin with tea and bread or nuts to 'open the appetite.'

THEODOR HERZEN

You should be offered water for washing, as you may be eating with your hands at some point (shaking the water off your hands is said to be impolite). Remember that more devout Muslims avoid taking food to the mouth with the left hand; in the same vein, accept cups of tea and plates of food only with the right hand. Men (and foreign women guests) may eat separately from women and children of the family.

Wait until you are told where to sit; honoured guests are often seated by Kyrgyz or Kazak hosts opposite the door (so as not to be disturbed by traffic through it, and because that is the warmest seat in a yurt). The meal might begin with a mumbled prayer, followed by tea. The host breaks and distributes bread. After bread, nuts or sweets to 'open the appetite', business or entertainment may begin. The eldest person normally serves and either he or the guest is expected to tuck in before the others do.

The meal itself is something of a free-for-all. Dozens of dishes may be spread over a low table, or on a cloth on the floor (the *dastarkhan*) surrounded by pillows. Food is served, and often eaten, from common plates, with hands or big spoons. It will be heaped on your plate by everyone. Pace yourself – eat too slowly and someone may ask if you're ill or unhappy; too eagerly and your plate will be immediately refilled. Praise the cook early and often; your host will worry if you're too quiet. If you find a dish you like, make a show of refilling your plate.

Traditionally, a host will honour an important guest by sacrificing a sheep for them. During these occasions the guest is given the choicest cuts, such as the eyeball, brain or meat from the right cheek of the animal. If you're offered sheep's eyeballs or anything else you really can't face, refuse firmly and solemnly, saying something like 'this is not the custom of my people'. The parts of the body served are often symbolic; the tongue is served to someone who should be more eloquent and children get the ears, to help them be better listeners.

If alcohol consumption is modest, the meal may end as it began, with tea and a prayer, but don't count on it (see Alcohol & Assault-by-Hospitality in the Dangers & Annoyances section of the Regional Facts for the Visitor chapter).

Dos & Don'ts

Clothing Dress codes vary throughout Central Asia. The main places where you should dress conservatively are in Xinjiang (especially Kashgar) and Uzbekistan's Fergana valley. Western-style clothes are acceptable in the capital cities and in large towns like Samarkand that see a lot of tourist traffic. For more information about clothing conventions in Central Asia, see the Clothing entry of the What to Bring section of the Regional Facts for the Visitor chapter.

Blowing Your Nose in Public Despite the early morning sinus-clearing rituals you may hear in your hotel, most Central Asians are disgusted with the thought of emptying the contents of your nose into a cloth, especially if you then carry it around in your pocket all day. This is especially revolting when done at the table. In Shakhrisabz a western friend blew her nose at length into a restau-

Body Language

A heartfelt handshake between Central Asian men is a gesture of great warmth, elegance and beauty. Many Central Asian men also place their right hand on the heart and bow or incline the head slightly, a highly addictive gesture that you may find yourself echoing quite naturally.

Good friends throughout the region shake hands by gently placing their hands, thumbs up, in between another's. There's no grabbing or western-style firmness, just a light touch. Sometimes a good friend will use his right hand to pat the others'. If you are in a room full of strangers it's polite to go around the room shaking hands with everyone. Don't be offended if someone offers you his wrist if his hands are dirty. Some say the custom originates in the need to prove that you come unarmed as a friend.

Women don't usually shake hands but touch each others' shoulders with right hands and slightly stroke them. Younger women in particular will often kiss an elder woman on the cheek as a sign of respect.

Afghans and Pakistanis are great huggers. Offering a handshake to a Pakistani of the opposite sex may put them in an awkward position; let them make the first move. If you try to shake hands with a Han Chinese on the other hand they may act as if you are mad.

After a meal or prayers, or sometimes when passing a grave site, you may well see both men and women bring their cupped hands together and pass them down their face as if washing. This is the *amin*, a Muslim gesture of thanks, common throughout the region.

rant napkin, until finally a man sitting nearby uttered a shout of disgust and spat at her feet.

Eating with Your Hands Devout Muslims consider the left hand unclean, and handling food with it at the table, especially in a private home and with communal dishes, can be off-putting to them. At a minimum, no one raises food to the lips with the left hand.

Tea Etiquette The first cup or *piala* (bowl) of tea is often poured away (to clean the piala) and then two piala are poured back into the pot to brew the tea. Hosts normally fill a guest's cup only half-full, and fill it frequently to keep it hot; the offer of a full piala of tea is a subtle invitation that it's time to leave.

Bread Bread is considered sacred in Central Asia. Don't put it on the ground, turn it upside down or throw it away (leave it on the table or floor cloth). If someone offers you tea in passing and you don't have time for it, they may offer you bread instead. It is polite to break off a piece and eat it, followed by the *amin* (bring your cupped hands together and pass them down their face as if washing). This is a Muslim gesture of thanks, common throughout the region after a meal or prayers. If you arrive with nan bread at a table, break it up into several pieces for everyone to share.

Other Customs Never point the sole of your shoe or foot at a Muslim, step over any part of someone's body, or walk in front of someone praying to Mecca.

When you enter a private house, take your shoes off at the door unless told not to. You will often find a pair of undersized thongs (flip-flops) waiting for you at the door. (Traditional Central Asian footwear consists of overshoes, which can be taken off without removing the soft leather under boots, or *massi*.) Avoid stepping on any carpet if you have your shoes on. Never put your feet on a table, nor near any food spread on a cloth on the floor. There are other things people do as well (for example Uzbeks enter others' homes with the right foot) but foreigners are forgiven for not knowing everything.

Men & Women In bigger cities of the former Soviet republics there is no apparent taboo on unaccompanied local women talk-

ing to male visitors in public (as there is in Middle Eastern Islamic countries).

But despite the imposition of Soviet economic 'equality', attitudes in the Central Asian republics remain fairly male-dominated. Local men addressed by a woman in a couple direct their reply to the man, you should try to follow suit. Local women tend not to shake hands or lead in conversations. Because most local women don't drink in public, female visitors may not be offered a shot of the vodka or wine doing the rounds. But these are not taboos as such, and as usual, foreigners tend to be forgiven for what locals might consider gaffes.

Some travellers report unmarried couples being refused shared hotel rooms in Osh, and the same may occasionally be true elsewhere in the Fergana valley.

Mosques Working mosques are closed to women and often to non-Muslim men, though men may occasionally be invited in. When visiting a mosque, always take your shoes off at the door, and make sure your feet or socks are clean (dirty socks, like dirty feet, are an insult to the mosque). It is polite to refer to the Prophet Mohammed as such, rather than by his name alone.

White Beards Central Asian society devotes much respect to its elderly, known as *aksakals*, or white beards. Always make an effort to shake hands with an elder, younger men give up their seats, and foreigners should certainly offer their place in a crowded chaykhana. Some Central Asians address elders with a shortened form of the elders' name, adding the suffix 'ke'. Thus Abkhan becomes Abeke, Nursultan becomes Nureke, and so on.

RELIGION

With the exception of rapidly shrinking communities of Jews and Russian Orthodox Christians, small minorities of Roman Catholics, Baptists and Evangelical Lutherans, and a few Buddhists among Koreans of the Fergana valley and Kyrgyzstan, nearly everyone from the Caspian Sea to the Taklamakan desert is Muslim, at least in principle.

The intensity of faith varies from faint to fanatical, although after the 'militant atheism' of the Soviet years, few now appear to understand Islam very deeply. Sectarianism is almost nonexistent in the former Soviet republics because, with the exception of the Ismailis of eastern Tajikistan, nearly everyone is of the Sunni branch of Islam.

Islam

History & Schisms In 612 CE, the Prophet Mohammed, then a wealthy Arab of Mecca in present-day Saudi Arabia, began preaching a new religious philosophy, Islam, based on revelations from Allah (Islam's name for God). Islam incorporated elements of Judaism, Christianity and other faiths (eg heaven and hell, a creation story much like the Garden of Eden, myths like Noah's Ark) but treated their prophets simply as forerunners of the Prophet Mohammed. These revelations were eventually to be compiled into Islam's holiest book, the Quran (or Koran).

In 622, Mohammed and his followers were forced to flee to Medina due to religious persecution (the Islamic calendar counts its years from this flight or *hejira*). There he built a political base and an army, taking Mecca in 630 and eventually overrunning Arabia. By the end of his life Mohammed ruled a rapidly growing religious and secular dynasty. The militancy of the faith meshed nicely with a latent Arab nationalism, and within a century Islam reached from Spain to Central Asia.

Succession disputes after the Prophet's death soon split the community. When the fourth caliph, the Prophet's son-in-law Ali, was assassinated in 661, his followers and descendants became the founders of the Shia (or Shi'ite) sect. Others accepted as caliph the governor of Syria, a brother-in-law of the Prophet, and this line has become the modern-day orthodox Sunni (or Sunnite) sect. In 680 a chance for reconciliation was lost when Ali's surviving son Hussain and most of his male relatives were killed at Karbala in Iraq by Sunni partisans.

Among Shia doctrines is that of the imam or infallible leader, who continues to unfold the true meaning of the Quran and provides guidance in daily affairs. Most Shias recognise an hereditary line of 12 imams ending in the 9th century (though imam is still used, loosely, by modern Shias). These Shias are known as Ithnashari (Twelvers). This book refers to them simply as Shias.

An 8th century split among Shias gave rise to the Ismaili or Maulai sect, who disagreed with the Ithnasharis on which son of the sixth imam should succeed him. For Ismaili Shias the line of imams continues into the present. Ismailis today number up to 15 million in pockets of Asia, India, East Africa and the Middle East, and their present leader, the billionaire Prince Karim Aga Khan, is considered to be imam No 49. Doctrines are more esoteric and practices less regimented than those of Sunnis or Ithnashari Shias.

Today some 85% to 90% of Muslims worldwide are Sunni. About 80% of all Central Asians are Muslim, nearly all of them Sunni (and indeed nearly all of the Hanafi school, one of Sunnism's four main schools of religious law). The main exception is a tightly knit community of Ismailis in the remote mountainous region of Gorno-Badakhshan in eastern Tajikistan (see the Population & People section in the introduction to the Tajikistan chapter). A small but increasingly influential community of another Sunni school, the ascetic, fundamentalist Wahhabi, are found mainly in Uzbekistan's Fergana valley; sources differ on their links to Saudi Arabia, where Wahhabism dominates.

Practice The word 'Islam' translates loosely from Arabic as 'the peace that comes from total surrender to God'. The Quran is considered above criticism: the word of God as spoken to his Prophet. This is supplemented by various traditions such as the *hadith*, the collected acts and sayings of the Prophet.

Devout Muslims express their surrender in the 'Five Pillars of Islam':

1. The creed that 'There is only one god, Allah, and Mohammed is his Prophet'
2. Prayer, five times a day, prostrating towards the holy city of Mecca, in a mosque (for men only) when possible but at least on Fridays, the Muslim holy day
3. Dawn-to-dusk fasting during Ramadan

4. Making the *hajj* (pilgrimage to Mecca) at least once in one's life (many of those who have done so can be identified by their white skullcaps)
5. Almsgiving, in the form of the *zakat*, an obligatory 2.5% tithe (alms-tax)

Devout Sunnis pray at prescribed times: before sunrise, just after high noon, in late afternoon, just after sunset and before retiring. For Shias there are three fixed times, before sunrise and twice in the evening at one's discretion. Prayers are preceded if possible by washing, at least of hands, face and feet. For Ismailis the style of prayer is a personal matter (eg there is no prostration), the mosque is replaced by a community shrine or meditation room, and women are less excluded.

Just before fixed prayers a muezzin calls the Sunni and Shia faithful, traditionally from a minaret, nowadays often through a loudspeaker. The melancholy sounding Arabic azan (call to prayer) translates roughly as, 'God is most great. There is no God but Allah. Mohammed is God's messenger. Come to prayer, come to security. God is most great'.

In its fullest sense Islam is an entire way of life, with guidelines for doing nearly everything. For example, Muslims do not eat pork or drink alcohol.

Islam has no ordained priesthood, but members of the *ulama* or class of religious scholars (often called mullahs) are trained in theology, respected as interpreters of scripture, and are sometimes quite influential in conservative rural areas.

Islam in Central Asia Islam first appeared in Central Asia with Arab invaders in the 7th and 8th centuries. In the following centuries many conversions were accomplished by teachers from Islam's mystic Sufi tradition who wandered across Asia (see Sufism following). Tsarist colonisers largely allowed Central Asians to worship as they pleased. Indeed, proselytising by Christian missionaries was forbidden (the intent being to spare local people too much enlightenment). But the Bolsheviks feared religion in general and Islam in particular because of its potential for coherent resistance, both domestic and international.

Three of the Five Pillars of Islam (the fast of Ramadan, the hajj and the alms-tax) were outlawed in the 1920s. Polygamy, the wearing of the veil *(paranjeh)*, and the Arabic script in which the Quran is written were forbidden. Clerical (Christian, Jewish and Buddhist as well as Muslim) land and property were seized. Medressas and other religious schools were closed down. Islam's judicial power was curbed with the dismantling of traditional sharia courts (based on Quranic law).

From 1932 to 1936 Stalin mounted a concerted antireligious campaign in Central Asia, a 'Movement of the Godless', with mosques closed and destroyed, and mullahs arrested and liquidated as saboteurs or spies. By the early 1940s only 1000 of Central Asia's mosques remained standing, of some 25,000 to 30,000 in 1920. All its 14,500 Islamic schools were shut, and only 2000 of its 47,000 mullahs remained alive. Control of the surviving places of worship and teaching was given to the Union of Atheists, which transformed most of them into museums, dance halls, warehouses or factories.

During WWII things improved marginally as Moscow sought domestic and international Muslim support for the war effort. In 1943 four Muslim Religious Boards or 'spiritual directorates', each with a *mufti* (spiritual leader), were founded as administration units for Soviet Muslims, including one in Tashkent for all of Central Asia (in 1990 one was established for Kazakstan). Some mosques were reopened and a handful of carefully screened religious leaders were allowed to make the hajj in 1947.

But beneath the surface little changed. Any religious activity outside the official mosques was strictly forbidden. By the early 1960s, under Khrushchev's 'back to Lenin' policies, another 1000 mosques were shut. By the beginning of the Gorbachev era, the number of mosques in Central Asia was down to between 150 and 250, and only two medressas were open – Mir-i-Arab in Bukhara and the Islamic Institute in Tashkent.

Following bloody inter-ethnic violence, particularly around the Fergana valley in 1989 and 1990, the Soviet authorities fell

The Lost Religions of Central Asia

Manicheism

Inspired by Babylonian prophet Mani, or Manes, (216 to 277 CE), Manicheism a mix of Zoroastrianism, Buddhism, Gnosticism and Christianity, the basis of which is grounded in the duality of being, the opposing principles of light and darkness and the belief that all light is held in dark captivity until liberated by certain intermediaries: Zoroaster, Buddha, Mani or Jesus.

Mani was flayed alive by Sassanian King Braham I in 277 and subsequent religious persecution forced his disciples to flee to the four corners of the Sassanian empire. Exiled Manicheists began arriving in Central Asia in the 5th century and the religion remained popular until the 13th century. Manicheism was made the official Uyghur religion in 763.

Remnants of a Gnostic orientation can be found in scattered works and quotes found in Turpan; in particular, a handbook of principles for confession of the sins, found in Uyghur text.

Nestorian Christianity

Named for Nestorius, patriarch of Constantinople, Nestorian Christianity pushes the idea of the dual nature (man and divine) of Christ to make a distinction between Christ the man and God, thereby maintaining that Mary should not be called the mother of God, only the mother of Christ. Nestorius was banished to Egypt in 431 at the Council of Ephesus, and died in exile. Believers fled persecution from the Church, which decried them as heretics, and the exiled religion spread into Assyria, Iran, China and even parts of India.

After arriving in China in the 6th century, Nestorianism filtered into Central Asia in the 7th century and was designated as an official religion in the 13th century. In the 8th century there were bishoprics in Herat and Samarkand.

The religion was eventually pushed into remotest Kurdistan by the Mongol and Turkic invasions, where tiny pockets remain to this day.

---

over themselves to allow the construction of new mosques. Since the republics' respective declarations of independence, mosques and medressas have sprouted like mushrooms, often with Saudi or Iranian money.

But Islam never was a potent force in the former nomadic societies of the Turkmen, Kazaks and Kyrgyz, and still isn't (some researchers suggest that Islam's appeal for nomadic rulers was as much its discipline as its moral precepts). The nomad's customary law, known as *adat*, was always more important than Islamic sharia. Even in more conservative Uzbekistan and Tajikistan, all those new mosques are as much political as religious statements. The majority of Central Asians, though interested in Islam as a common denominator, seem quite happy to toast your health with a shot of vodka.

The Central Asian brand of Islam is also riddled with outside influences – just go to any important holy site and notice the kissing, rubbing and circumambulating of venerated objects, women crawling under holy stones to boost their fertility, the shamanic 'wishing trees' tied with bits of coloured rags, the cult of *pirs* (holy men), the Mongol-style poles with horse-hair tassel over the graves of revered figures, the Russian-style gravestones, and sometimes candles and flames harking from Zoroastrian times. The Turkmen place particular stock in amulets and charms. There is also a significant blurring between religious and national characteristics.

And yet the amazing thing is that, after 70 years of concerted Soviet repression, with mainstream Islam in an official hammerlock, so much faith remains intact. Some rural Central Asians in fact take Islam very seriously, enough to create substantial political muscle. The real power in the coalition that seized control of Tajikistan in 1992, and almost won the civil war, was the Islamic Renaissance Party (IRP), with heavy support in the Garm valley. The IRP, though outlawed by the other Central Asian republics, enjoys enormous support in the Fergana valley of Uzbekistan; the epicentre of what fundamentalism exists is here.

Credit for any continuity from pre-Soviet times goes largely to 'underground Islam', in the form of the clandestine Sufi brotherhoods (and brotherhoods they were, being essentially men-only) which preserved some practice and education – and grew in power and influence in Central Asia as a result (see the following section on Sufism for more information).

Islam has faced a similarly rocky road in Communist China. During the Cultural Revolution, in particular, it was dangerous to be seen to be a Muslim, and many mosques were closed and even converted into pigsties. Even in post-Deng China, Islam is under considerable political pressure and is being pushed underground into secretive Sufi brotherhoods known as *mashrab*.

Sufism The original Sufis were simply purists, unhappy with the worldliness of the early caliphates and seeking knowledge of God through direct personal experience, under the guidance of a teacher or master, variously called a *sheikh, pir, ishan, murshid* or *ustad*. There never was a single Sufi movement; there are manifestations within all branches of Islam. For many adherents music, dance or poetry about the search for God were routes to trance, revelation and direct union with God. Secret recitations, known as *zikr*, and an annual forty-day retreat known as the *chilla* remain cornerstones of Sufic practice. This is the mystical side of Islam, parallel to similar traditions in other faiths.

Sufis were singularly successful as missionaries, perhaps because of their tolerance of other creeds. It was largely Sufis, not Arab armies, who planted Islam firmly in Central Asia and the subcontinent. The personal focus of Sufism was most compatible with the nomadic lifestyle of the Kazak and Kyrgyz in particular. While abhorred nowadays in the orthodox Islamic states of Iran and Saudi Arabia, Sufism is in a quiet way dominant in Central Asia. Most shrines you'll see are devoted to one Sufi teacher or another.

When Islam was itself threatened by invaders (eg the Crusaders), Sufis assumed the role of defenders of the faith, and Sufism became a mass movement of regimented *tariqas* or brotherhoods, based around certain holy places, often the tombs of the tariqas' founders. Clandestine, anti-Communist tariqas helped Islam weather the Soviet period, and the KGB and its predecessors never seemed able to infiltrate.

The moderate, non-elitist Naqshbandiya tariqa was the most important in Soviet times, and probably still is. Founded in Bukhara in the 14th century, much of its influence in Central Asia may come from the high profile of Naqshbandi fighters in two centuries of revolts against the Russians in the Caucasus. In 1940 one of the last of these, in Chechnya, was crushed, and in February 1944 the entire Chechen and Ingush populations were deported to Siberia and Kazakstan. When, after Stalin's death, the survivors were permitted to return to their homeland, they left behind several well-organised Sufi groups in Central Asia. A number of well-known basmachi leaders were Naqshbandis.

Another important Sufi sect in Central Asia is the Qadiriya, founded by a teacher from the Caspian region. Others are the Kubra (founded in Khorezm) and Yasauia (founded in Turkistan, in Kazakstan). All these were founded in the 12th century.

Regional Facts for the Visitor

Most of the information in this chapter is generally relevant to the ex-Soviet republics. For specific information, plus details on Xinjiang, see the Facts for the Visitor sections in the individual country chapters.

SUGGESTED ITINERARIES

Central Asia is a vast, largely untravelled region. You could spend months exploring mountain villages or obscure historical sites. There is a danger in proscribing suggested itineraries, as one of the inherent joys of travel is the element of surprise. Nevertheless, time and especially visa constraints limit most peoples' time in the region, so here are a few of the many possible regional itineraries.

Silk Road Cities of Uzbekistan (10 days to two weeks)

Fly into Tashkent and get the feel of the place before taking a domestic flight to Urgench and then a short bus or taxi ride to Khiva. Khiva can be comfortably seen in a day. Take a side trip to Konye-Urgench if you can arrange a Turkmen visa. From Urgench take the long bus ride down to Bukhara, which deserves the most time of all the Silk Road cities. Try to budget a minimum of three days to take in the sights and explore the backstreets. From here take the tarmac road to Samarkand and soak in the glories of the Registan and Shahr-i-Zindah for a day or two.

An alternative to this route is to travel from Konye-Urgench to Ashgabat and then travel to Bukhara via the Sultan Sanjar mausoleum at Merv.

Silk Road by Rail (two to four weeks)

From Moscow (or even St Petersburg) take in the transition to Central Asia on the three or four day train to Tashkent or Almaty. From here you can add on any number of side trips to Samarkand, Bukhara or even Urgench (Khiva), all of which are on the railway line. From Almaty, it's possible to continue on the train to Ürümqi in China and even to Kashgar along the newly completed rail link. From Ürümqi you could continue along the Silk Road by train east to Unhung, Xi'an and even Hong Kong.

Bishkek to Gilgit (two to three weeks)

Fabulous scenery and natural beauty is the focus of this rollercoaster ride over the Torugart pass to Kashgar, and then over the Khunjerab pass to Pakistan's Hunza valley, along the Karakoram Highway. This is surely one of the world's most beautiful road trips.

The Central Asian Loop (one month)

Fly into Tashkent or Bishkek, and then arrange a Kazak visa and transport over the Torugart pass to Kashgar to catch the Sunday market. From Kashgar, catch the train or flight to Ürümqi, make a side trip to Turpan or Heaven Lake and then take the train or bus back to Almaty.

Alternatively, take the overnight bus from Kashgar to Hotan for its Sunday market and then continue to Ürümqi by plane or bus.

Central Asia Overland

Central Asia fits well into an overland route from the Middle East to Asia, which can last as long as you like. Western roads into Central Asia lead from Mashad in Iran to Ashgabat, or from Baku in Azerbaijan by boat to Turkmenbashi in Turkmenistan. From Ashgabat the overland route leads to Merv, Bukhara, Samarkand and Tashkent. From here you can continue to Almaty and then by train or bus to Ürümqi and into China proper.

Alternatively, head into the Fergana valley from Tashkent and swing north along the mountain roads to Bishkek. From here arrange a trip over the Torugart pass to Kashgar. You can then continue down into Pakistan to join the main overland trail into India and Nepal.

Personal Highs & Lows of Central Asia

Favourites

- Sitting in a teahouse with a cold Kashgar beer, a round of kebabs and hot nan bread – magic!
- Cheap taxis in Kyrgyzstan
- Finally crossing the Torugart pass
- White bearded *aksakals* in stripy cloaks and turbans
- Turquoise blue domes and mesmerising Timurid tilework
- Trekking, almost anywhere
- Central Asian handshakes, with a slight bow and a hand on the heart
- Staying in a yurt in Kyrgyzstan or a traditional courtyard house in Uzbekistan
- Central Asian melons and grapes
- White Rabbit sweets in Xinjiang

Pet Peeves

- The taste of congealed mutton fat on the roof of your mouth
- Local bus trips that take seven hours to go 100km, when you don't have a seat, and there's sweaty armpits in your face
- Getting turned back at the Torugart pass
- Aggressive drunks who think you are Russian
- Soviet hotel architecture
- Bride of Frankenstein receptionists with dyed cherry-red hair, all mysteriously called Svetlana
- Vodka terrorism
- Visa hassles and *militsia* checks
- Russian techno music, turned up especially loud when you walk into a cafe
- The smell of Soviet canteens

Bradley Mayhew

The Silk Road

Almost any route through Central Asia follows at least one branch of the Silk Road network, but for those travellers intent on following the Silk Road's presumed paths, the following itinerary provides the approximate route.

From China's Gansu province, branch off south-west to follow the remote southern road, via Hotan and Yarkand. Alternatively take the northern route via Turpan, Kucha and Aksu, to Kashgar. From here, cross the Torugart pass into Kyrgyzstan and visit the atmospheric Tash Rabat caravanserai. From Naryn you can take the popular route to Bishkek via Song-Köl, or more authentically, take a taxi along the little-used road into the Fergana valley via Kazarman.

(A more direct Silk Road link leads from Kashgar to Osh in the Fergana valley over the Irkeshtam pass. This route is currently closed, though it may open soon.)

From the Fergana valley continue to Samarkand, Bukhara and Merv, and from here cross into Iran's Khorasan province to reach the holy Shia city of Mashad.

Highlights of Central Asia

Architecture

Samarkand, Uzbekistan – Featuring the Registan ('the noblest public square in the world'), the Guri Amir, the wonderfully restored tomb of Timur (Tamerlane), and the Shahr-i-Zindah, a street of tombs, which features the most stunning tilework in Central Asia.

Bukhara, Uzbekistan – Winding backstreets and stunning Islamic architecture, featuring the Kalon Minaret, which took Jenghiz Khan's breath away, and dozens of mosques, medressas and caravanserais.

Khiva, Uzbekistan – Central Asia's most homogenous old town, an open-air museum.

Shakhrisabz, Uzbekistan – Timur's home town, with tantalising vestiges of faded grandeur.

Konye-Urgench, Turkmenistan – Scattered remains of the glorious city destroyed by Jenghiz Khan

Turkistan, Kazakstan – The majestic mausoleum of Kozha Akhmed Yasaui was a blueprint for more famous ones in Samarkand.

Natural Scenery

Ala-Archa Park, Kyrgyzstan – Stunning alpine scenery just one hour's ride from Bishkek.

Altyn Arashan Valley, Kyrgyzstan – Great place to relax, hike, take a bath in hot springs and ride horses.

Karakul Lake and Muztagh Ata, Xinjiang – A pit stop on the Karakoram Highway; a beautiful turquoise lake at the foot of two muscular Pamir giants.

Heavenly Lake, Xinjiang – Alpine scenery 2½ hours drive from Ürümqi. Try to stay the night at one of the Kazak yurts.

Inylchek Glacier and Khan Tengri, Kyrgyzstan – Helicopter rides are possible here but expensive; try to tag along with an existing group.

Fan Mountains, Tajikistan – Fine trekking around these turquoise lakes, well away from Tajikistan's civil strife. Most easily accessed from Samarkand.

Bazars

Kashgar Sunday Market, Xinjiang – The largest and most touristed bazar in Central Asia. Go early and bring lots of film.

Hotan Sunday Market, Xinjiang – Just as good as the Kashgar market but little visited. A 10 hour bus ride from Kashgar.

Ashgabat's Sunday Bazar, Turkmenistan – A Cecile B De Mille production of carpets and turbans.

Cultural Experiences

Kochkor Home-Stays, Kyrgyzstan – An excellent opportunity to experience traditional Kyrgyz life. Can be done for less than US$10 a day, so budget a few extra days here.

Arasan Baths, Almaty, Kazakstan – A choice of three styles of bath in this monumental Almaty complex. Pay extra for a heavy duty massage.

Tea at the Labi-Hauz, Bukhara – Green tea and kebabs make this the quintessential Central Asian experience.

Highlights of Central Asia

Russian Orthodox Cathedrals – Best visited on Sundays at service times to get the full-on Russian Orthodox experience. The best ones are Tashkent's Assumption Cathedral or Almaty's Zenikov Cathedral.

Great Journeys

Torugart Pass (Kyrgyzstan/China) – Central Asia's most exciting overland crossing. Scenically impressive but logistically complicated and potentially expensive.

Karakoram Highway (China/Pakistan) – Simply the most breathtaking overland trip in the world, from Kashgar to Islamabad. The Khunjerab pass is officially open from 1 May to 30 November.

Silk Road by Rail – Take in the transition from Russia to Central Asian steppe, desert and mountains at an easy 30 km/h. The down side is that trains can be uncomfortable, unreliable and run down.

Pamir Hwy, Tajikistan – Little-trafficked mountain rollercoaster road from Osh to Khorog, passing through Tajikistan's remote Gorno-Badakhshan region. Permits are needed. Check the security situation before setting off.

Dushanbe-Khorog Flight, Tajikistan – *Through*, not over, the Pamir mountains. Again, check the security situation in Tajikistan before setting off.

Activities

Trekking – A trekker's paradise of alpine valleys and snowy peaks that you will probably have to yourself. The best spots are in Kyrgyzstan and south-east Kazakstan. See trekking in the Activities section for information and a map of trekking highlights.

Horse Riding – Realise the nomadic dream. In Kyrgyzstan take a horse trek to Song-Köl or up the alpine valleys around Karakol.

Mountaineering – Central Asia has many unclimbed peaks, as well as high-altitude 7000m-plus giants such as Pik Lenin and Kommunizma. Ak Suu peak's 2km sheer wall is one of the prime rock climbing locations in the world.

Surreal Central Asia

Aral Shipwrecks – Witness the wreckage of the Aral Sea at Moynaq in Uzbekistan or Aralsk in Western Kazakstan.

Beaches on Issyk-Kul, Kyrgyzstan – Sunbathe on a sandy beach thousands of kilometres from the sea.

Festivals

Navrus – Central Asia's main holiday and the best time to see traditional horse races and sports such as buzkashi. Hissar Fort outside Dushanbe is a good place to catch buzkashi.

Kurban Festival, Kashgar, Xinjiang – Thousands descend on Id Kah Mosque in Kashgar for this Muslim holy day.

Independence Day – Pomp and bravado as the new republics celebrate the break up of the Soviet Union. The celebrations fall on different dates – see the Public Holidays & Special Events section later in this chapter.

PLANNING
When to Go

Weather Although it is difficult to generalise about such a large region, there are some basic factors to consider. At lower elevations spring and autumn are the overall best seasons, in particular April to early June and September through October. In April the desert blooms briefly and the monotonous ochre landscapes of Turkmenistan, Uzbekistan and Kazakstan become a Jackson Pollock canvas of reds, oranges and yellows. Autumn is harvest time, when market tables heave with freshly picked fruit.

Summer is ferociously hot in the lowlands, with sizzling cities and desert temperatures as high as 40°C or more. November is changeable but mostly chilly, with first snows at higher elevations. Mountain passes fill with snow until April or even May. Winters are bitterly cold even in the desert, and food is a problem, with many eateries closed for the season. Many domestic flights are grounded in winter.

July through August is the best time to visit the mountains and to trek (earlier and later than that, herders and other summer residents will have returned to the lowlands). Bishkek and Almaty may have snow in April. Northern Kazakstan is comfortable right through the summer.

If you're heading to or from Pakistan, bear in mind that while the Khunjerab pass is officially open from 1 May to 30 November, it tends to close early around mid-November or even sooner because of snow.

For more details see the When to Go and Climate sections of the individual country chapters.

Other Factors You may want to time your visit with the region's two major celebrations – Navrus (around 21 March) and Independence Day (around October). See the Public Holidays & Special Events section later in this chapter for details.

Border crossings to/from China, especially the Torugart pass, take every opportunity to close, in particular on Chinese holidays and sometimes several days either side of them.

Government Travel Advice

The US State Department's Bureau of Consular Affairs issues travel warnings and periodically updated Consular Information Sheets that include entry requirements, medical facilities, crime information and other topics at http://travel.state.gov/travel_warnings.html. They also publish a brochure called *Tips for Travellers to Russia and the Newly Independent States,* which is available from the Superintendent of Documents, US Government Printing Office, Washington DC 20402 or via the Internet at www.access.gpo.gov/su_docs or travel.state.gov/tips_russia.html.

You can listen to 24 hour recorded government travel information at ☎ 202-647 5225 or you can receive copies of these bulletins by sending a self-addressed, stamped envelope to the Overseas Citizens Services, Room 4800, Department of State, Washington, DC 20520-4818. (Write the name of the requested country or countries on the outside of the envelope.) To receive them by fax, dial 202-647-3000 from a fax machine, using the machine's telephone receiver, and follow the instructions.

If you're on the Internet, you can subscribe to a mailing list for all current State Department travel advisories by sending a message containing the word 'subscribe' to travel-advisories-request@stolaf.edu (St Olaf College, Northfield MN, USA).

Get British Foreign Office travel advisories from the Travel Advice Unit (☎ 020-7238 4503, fax 7238 4545), Foreign & Commonwealth Office, 1 Palace St, London SW1E 5EH, UK. It's Web site is at www.fco.gov.uk/. Regularly updated Foreign Office travel advice is also displayed on BBC2 Ceefax, pp 470ff. It also has a regularly updated travel advice line at ☎ 0374-500900.

Australians can contact the Department of Foreign Affairs advice line in Canberra on ☎ 06-6261 3305 or visit its Web site at www.dfat.gov.au/consular/advice/.

Citizens of Canadians can get Department of Foreign Affairs travel advice by calling ☎ 1-800-267 6788, fax 1-800-575 2500, or by visiting its Web site at www.dfait-maeci.gc.ca.

What Kind of Trip?

A fully independent trip to and around Central Asia is perfectly feasible, though you'll need to devote some time to the visa chase, both at home and in Central Asia. If you don't have much time you might want to consider arranging the odd airport transfer, hotel and flight or train booking, and visa support through a specialist travel agency (see Travel Agencies & Organised Tours in the Getting There & Away chapter for a list of these). Treks of more than a few days are generally best organised through an agency.

Maps

Abroad Get your big-scale maps before you go. Most Commonwealth of Independent States (CIS) maps reduce Central Asia to the size of a postcard, but Hildebrand's 1:3,500,000 *CIS* (1993) is fairly well updated, and of a useful scale, though it does not contain many of the recent city name changes.

Central Asia (Gizimap, 1999) is a good 1:750,000 general elevation map of the Central Asian republics (plus Kashgar), though it excludes northern Kazakstan. It usefully marks many trekking routes.

Central Asia – The Cultural Travel Map along the Silk Road is a similar (but not as good) 1:1.5 million Italian map, which concentrates on Uzbekistan and Tajikistan.

Tourist Map of Eastern Kyrgyzstan, published by JS Company Turkestan, covers Issyk-Kul and the surrounding mountains. It's available from Stanfords and direct from the publishers in Karakol, Kyrgyzstan.

Trekking Maps US-published air navigation charts make fine wall hangings but are expensive at US$10 or more per sheet. The 1:1,000,000 ONC series covers all of Central Asia, while coverage by the 1:500,000 TPC series is patchy. Specific trekking maps available abroad include:

Central Tian Shan (EWP, @ ewp-uk@compuserve .com), 1:150,000; Inylchek glacier and surroundings.

Fann Mountains (EWP, 1994), 1:100,000; Fann mountains in Tajikistan.

Kongur Tagh-Muztagh Ata (Xi'an Cartographic Publishing House), 1:100,000; Chinese-made climbing map. Available from Stanfords (UK) or Kashgar Mountaineering Association (☎ 0998-282 3680, fax 282 2957, 45 Tiyu Lu, Kashgar).

Pamir Trans Alai Mountains (EWP), 1:200,000; Pik Lenin and the Fedchenko glacier.

Pik Lenin (Karto Atelier, 1996), 1:100,000; topographical map of the mountain.

Map Sources Several map suppliers have Web sites where you can view catalogues or even the actual maps. Mail order suppliers include:

Arguments & Facts Media Ltd
  (☎ 01424-442741, fax 442913,
  @ Caspian@afmltd.demon.co.uk)
  PO Box 35, Hastings, East Sussex TN34 2UX, UK – sells a UK£36 paperback *Atlas of Russia and the Post Soviet Republics* (1994), with country and capital city maps, though these now have a few outdated street and place names. Web site www.caspiantimes.com.

Chessler Books
  (☎ 800-654 8502, 303-670 0093, fax 670 9727,
  @ chesslerbk@aol.com)
  PO Box 4359, Evergreen, CO 80437, USA. Web site www.chesslerbooks.com.

Edward Stanford Ltd
  (☎ 020-7836 1321, fax 7836 0189)
  12-14 Long Acre, Covent Garden, London WC2E 9LP, UK.

A Galaxy of Maps
  (☎ 800-388 6588, fax 954-267 9007,
  @ sales@galaxymaps.com)
  Fort Lauderdale, Florida, USA – stocks US Defense maps.

GeoCenter ILH
  (☎ 0711-788 93 40, fax 788 93 54,
  @ geocenterilh@t-online.de)
  Schockenriedstrasse 44, D-70565 Stuttgart, Germany.

Map Link, Inc.
  (☎ 805-692 6777, fax 692 6787,
  @ custserv@maplink.com)
  30 S La Patera Lane, Unit #5, Santa Barbara, CA 93117. Web site www.maplink.com.

Upton Map Shop
  (☎ 01684-593146, fax 594559)
  15 High St, Upton-upon-Severn, Worcs WR8 0HJ, UK.

Maps in Central Asia Reliable locally produced city and regional maps can be found in Kazakstan and Kyrgyzstan, but are hard to find elsewhere. The occasional Soviet-era city map, full of errors, languishes on the back shelf of some bookshops. Especially in Uzbekistan, where Soviet-era street names were jettisoned en masse, any map older than about 1994 will drive you crazy (check the title box or the back of the map for its copyright date). In Ashgabat's top-end hotels you can buy good Turkish-made maps of Ashgabat, Nebit Dagt, Dashoguz, Mary and Turkmenbashi.

Especially for trekking, you should avoid all Soviet-era maps, which were deliberately distorted (except military ones). There are several useful sources of maps inside Central Asia, most of which produce trekking route maps, topographical maps or political republic maps.

The Kyrgyz Cartographic Agency (see the Bishkek Information section of the Kyrgyzstan chapter) sells useful maps of major Central Tian Shan trekking regions for the equivalent of about US$0.25. They also reprint good general topographic maps covering all of Kyrgyzstan plus the Kashgar region. They also sell a good Silk Road of Kyrgyzstan and general republic map. See the Bishkek section of the Kyrgyzstan chapter for a list of available trekking maps.

Asia Travel in Tashkent can supply good 1:100,000 Uzbek topographical maps printed in 1992, which are essential for trekking. These include:

Bisokiy Alay: Treks from Shakhimardon, Khaidakan and the Sokh valley in southern Kyrgyzstan
Fanskie Gori: Tajikistan's Fan mountains
Matcha Palmiro-Alay Tsentralnaya Chast: Treks from Vorukh and Karavsin valley, southern Kyrgyzstan

JHER (also known as GEO) in Almaty sells a wide variety of topographic and trekking maps from 1:25,000 to 1:100,000, as well as more general maps.

What to Bring

Of course, bring as little as you can. You can usually find batteries, laundry soap, toothbrushes, razor blades, toilet paper, tampons and shampoo in big-city department stores and bazars, and aspirin in pharmacies, but it is good to keep a small emergency stash of these items.

Carrying Bags An internal-frame or soft pack is most manageable on buses and trains – though easy for someone to slash. The 'expandable' types are most convenient – a clever arrangement of straps causes these packs to shrink or expand according to how much is inside. Packs that close with two zippers can be secured with a padlock. Otherwise you can make your bag more thief-proof by sewing on tabs so you can padlock it shut. Forget suitcases unless you are on a tour.

A day pack is good for hiking and for carrying extra food, books, etc on long bus rides. You can even dump your main luggage in a (secure) hotel's storage and travel light for a few days with a full day pack. A belt pack is okay for maps, extra film and other miscellanea, but don't use it for valuables such as travellers cheques, plane tickets and passports – it's an easy target for pickpockets.

Clothing With strong social overtones in Islamic countries, in no other way have westerners managed to offend Central Asians more than by the way they dress. To a devout Muslim (and there are quite a few in Central Asia, especially in Uzbekistan's Fergana valley and around Kashgar), clothes that reveal flesh other than face, hands and feet, or the shape of the body, look ridiculous on men, and scandalous on women. Shorts and singlets are especially offensive. For women visitors this is not only an elementary courtesy but may also reduce hostility or harassment; ignore the mini-skirts of the Russian women and cover up.

This doesn't mean you have to wear a choir-robe – just long, loose, nonrevealing shirts, trousers or skirts (which, in any case, are the most comfortable in summer). In bigger cities in ex-Soviet Central Asia you can pretty much wear what you want, except for shorts.

The region swings wildly in climate. If you are going only to Uzbekistan or Turkmenistan, there is no need for a fleece. However, higher elevations in Kyrgyzstan and Kazakstan have snow even in July. Any Central Asian bazar will have a low-quality assortment of flip-flops, T-shirts and thermal underwear in case you end up in a warmer or cooler climate than you anticipated. They are also a good place for women to pick up headscarves if travelling to the Fergana valley, Kashgar or Pakistan, or if you'll be visiting Russian Orthodox churches.

Light walking shoes are adequate for all but long or snowy treks; heavy, waterproof boots are only essential in high mountain areas. Trekking sandals are a relief in warm, dry weather. Keep lightweight flip-flops handy for showers and for replacing your shoes when entering homes.

Wide-brimmed pork pie hats and baseball caps can be bought cheaply in Central Asia, but the latter won't protect your ears from the sun.

Gifts If you intend to stay in (or even just visit) private homes you should never arrive empty-handed. Some portable but well-received gifts are international stickers, postage stamps, badges, pins, key rings, postcards and flower seeds from home. It's nice to have small gifts for the children of families who helped you out – funny stickers, interesting pencils, pass around mints for the dinner table – but don't hand these things out in the street. If nothing else take a family photo and be sure to post it when you arrive home. Photographs of your own family and country are lifesavers during awkward home-stay moments.

Drivers are especially keen on stickers and anything that can hang from the mirror, like air fresheners (which also keep your pack smelling nice). Bring a few cassette tapes to vary the music on bus rides and car journeys, but don't put anything into a Soviet cassette deck that you can't do without.

Western cigarettes are available in Central Asia, so they don't make as good a gift as they did in Soviet days, but they are nice to offer men to establish rapport.

Miscellaneous A Russian phrasebook (and a dictionary if you have room) will definitely come in handy. Basic Turkish will be helpful, since all but Tajiks speak languages closely related to Turkish. Lonely Planet publishes a *Russian phrasebook* and a *Central Asia phrasebook*.

Besides the usual items, essential items for Central Asia include a water bottle (one that won't melt with boiling water), sun hat, light day pack, penknife and flip-flops for showering in. Sunglasses (which filter UV rays), sunscreen and lip salve are especially important if you'll be doing any mountain trekking.

A torch (flashlight) is essential where the electricity is dodgy and for trotting out to the pit toilet in the middle of the night. A mini alarm clock will help you catch those 5 am buses. Earplugs are essential in China to block out the 24 hour noise. A universal sink plug is very handy, as few hotels have plugs. Bottom-end hotels tend not to give you towels either.

Bring mosquito repellent, especially if you'll be travelling in the lowland southern border regions of Tajikistan, where malaria is a risk (see the Health section later in this chapter for more information).

Seasoned travellers will already have a secure passport-and-money pouch. Half a dozen passport-sized photos will save you trouble in case of paperwork, though it's possible to get them en route. Photocopies of the first few pages of your passport and air ticket will ease the headaches if you lose the originals.

A padlock is a virtual necessity and a heavy-duty chain will enable you to padlock your pack to the luggage racks of trains and buses. It's worth bringing several sizes, to fit both a day pack and a hotel door. Some women carry a high-pitched whistle, which may act as a deterrent to would-be assailants.

An oversized cup is useful if you're self-catering. You can even boil an egg in one, using a heating coil *(kipyatelnik)*, which you can buy in department stores and electrical shops for a few US dollars. This way you don't have to depend on hotel floor ladies for hot water. You can get tins of instant coffee in most large towns, but bring along some sachets of hot chocolate for when you need a moment of luxury.

Women should buy tampons before coming to Central Asia, although you can find them in department stores and supermarkets. Likewise, bring condoms from home.

For a suggested medical kit see the Health section later in this chapter. For photography prerequisites see the Film & Photography section later in this chapter.

Other ideas worth considering are:

Calamine lotion or anti-itch preparation (for insect bites), elastic 'pegless' washing-line, tape, 'ziplock' bags and plastic containers (for carrying half-opened boxes of laundry soap etc), a sewing kit, dental floss, vitamins, Lomotil (for diarrhoea), contact lens cleaning solution, special medications, scrubbing brush for laundry, a short-wave radio, a copy of your address book, pens, compass, extra camera battery, emergency toilet paper stash (cheaper hotels don't supply toilet paper), a string shopping bag for the bazars, eating utensils and a small plastic bowl for self-caterers.

Sleeping Bags & Trekking Equipment

If you are only doing light occasional trekking, there are a few places where you can rent equipment (eg at Karakol in Kyrgyzstan). If you go on an organised trek, equipment hire is often thrown in. Otherwise you are better off bringing your own.

A sleeping bag is a nice luxury even if you are not camping, especially if you will be travelling at altitude, in the winter, off the beaten track or staying in the cheapest accommodation. It's especially useful for home-stays or if you get invited to stay in a yurt. A plastic mat or groundsheet will shield you from any bugs.

The easiest stove fuels to obtain in Central Asia are petrol (gasoline) and medicinal spirits. Dried fruits and nuts, instant noodles, rice and tinned foods are available in the big city department stores.

RESPONSIBLE TOURISM

Tourism is still relatively new to Central Asia, so please try to keep your impact as low as possible and create a good precedent for those who follow you. Following are a few tips for responsible travel:

- Be respectful of Islamic traditions and don't wear singlets or short skirts in Kashgar or the Fergana valley.
- Don't hand out sweets or pens to children on the streets, since it encourages begging. Similarly, doling out medicines can encourage people not to seek proper medical advice. A donation to a project, health centre or school is a far more constructive way to help.
- You can do more good by buying your snacks, cigarettes, bubble gum etc from the enterprising grannies trying to make ends meet rather than state-run stores.
- Try to support local services and guides when possible rather than paying a large travel agency in the capital. Support eco-friendly tourist initiatives wherever you see them.
- Don't buy items made from endangered species.
- Don't pay to take a photo of someone and don't photograph someone if they don't want you to. If you agree to send someone a photo, make sure you follow through on it.
- Try to give people a balanced perspective of life in the west. Point out that you are only temporarily rich in Central Asia and that income and costs balance out in Amsterdam just as they do in Almaty. Try also to point out the strong points of the local culture – strong family ties, comparatively low crime etc.

TOURIST OFFICES
Local Tourist Offices

Intourist, the old Soviet travel bureau, gave birth to a litter of Central Asian successors – Yassaui in Kazakstan, Kyrgyzintourist in Kyrgyzstan, Tajik Intourist in Tajikistan, Turkmensiyahat in Turkmenistan, and Uzbektourism in Uzbekistan. Kyrgyzintourist has since folded and Tajikistan Intourist and Yassaui are mostly redundant. On the whole these offices are dedicated to hard-currency group and package tourism; the spectrum of help for individuals ranges from modest to none at all.

Uzbektourism wins the booby prize – at best uninterested in individual travellers, at worst hostile to them, with few points for public interface beyond the service bureaus; exceptions include the good offices in Fergana, Urgench and Nukus.

You are almost always better off with one of the growing number of private agencies, if you can find one, though their prices tend to be high. The details for local offices of both private and state agencies can be found in the Information section for each large town in the relevant country chapters.

The best sources of information at home tend to be foreign travel firms specialising in Central Asia or the CIS (see the Travel Agencies & Organised Tours section in the Getting There & Away chapter for more information on these firms).

For a list of China National Tourism Organisation offices abroad, see the Xinjiang chapter.

VISAS

To enter forbidden Turkistan without papers? I would sooner pay a call on the Devil and his mother-in-law in Hell.

Gustav Krist, Alone in the Forbidden Land, 1939

Visas can be the single biggest headache associated with travel in Central Asia, especially in the former Soviet republics, where regulations are still mutating. Up-to-date information is hard to find and there's a loophole for every rule. Collecting visas for a multi-country trip can take months. Things are, however, getting easier.

Don't consider getting on a plane to Central Asia without a visa for your destination unless you have a letter of support and will be met at the airport by a local travel agency. In fact, you probably won't even be allowed on a plane coming from outside the CIS without a visa for your destination or at least a letter of support (see the following Visas by Invitation entry in this section). Airlines are keen to avoid the costs and fines associated with bringing you back if your papers aren't in order. The one exception is flying to Almaty, which is currently permitted without a Kazak visa if you have a Kyrgyz or Uzbek visa (although you should check this with your airline).

The steps to obtain a visa and the attention it gets after you arrive differ for each republic, but their outlines are similar. The following information is general, with individual country variations detailed in the Facts for the Visitor sections of the relevant country chapters.

Without an Invitation

Some republics have taken the first steps towards scrapping the clumsy, counterproductive invitation system. Kyrgyzstan now issues month-long tourist visas without the need for a letter of support and is even planning to introduce visa-free travel for most western countries. In 1999 Uzbekistan began to issue tourist visas to US citizens without an invitation, though it still makes life difficult for everyone else.

By Invitation

The key to getting a visa for Turkmenistan, Uzbekistan, Kazakstan and Tajikistan is 'visa support' or 'sponsorship', which means an invitation, approved by the ministries of Foreign Affairs &/or Interior, from a private individual, company or state organisation in the country you want to visit. After obtaining ministry approval, your sponsor sends the invitation (also known as a letter of support) to you, and when you apply at a consular office for your visa it's matched with a copy sent directly to them from the Ministry of Foreign Affairs.

The invitation should include your name, address, citizenship, sex, birth date, birthplace and passport details; the purpose, proposed itinerary and entry/exit dates of your visit; and the type of visa you will need and where you will apply for it.

The cheapest way to get a visa invitation is directly, by fax or email, through a Central Asian travel agency. Many agencies in Kyrgyzstan, Kazakstan, Turkmenistan and Uzbekistan will just sell you a letter of visa support for between US$20 and US$40, which you pay when you arrive in the country. Others require you to book at least a night or two's accommodation or an airport transfer. See Travel & Visa Agencies in the Getting There & Away chapter for some trustworthy agencies in Central Asia.

A few western travel agencies can arrange visa invitation but most require you to book a package of hotel and transport services. Regulations do change, see the agencies listed in the Getting There & Away chapter.

The most expensive way to get sponsored is to arrange your trip through one of t' state-run successors to Intourist, the old Soviet travel bureau, and pay in advance for their overpriced accommodation and other services. That bureau becomes your sponsor and, along with a letter of support, you get travel vouchers to present for those services.

Applying for a Visa

Visa applications can be made at some or all of the republics' overseas embassies or consulates, the addresses of which are listed in the individual country chapters. In countries without Central Asian representation, Russian embassies may issue a visa (see the following Russian Visas entry in this section). Kazak embassies will often issue visas for Kyrgyzstan if there is no Kyrgyz representation.

In addition to a letter of support and/or travel vouchers, embassies may want a photocopy of the validity and personal-information pages of your passport, two or three passport-size photos and a completed application form. Some may want more. The Kazak embassy in Moscow wants a photocopy of your Russian visa and Uzbek embassies may ask to see an onward visa.

Visas for Kyrgyzstan, Uzbekistan and Kazakstan do not list the towns to be visited and you are free to travel almost everywhere in these republics. The visa application for Turkmenistan and Tajikistan requires you to list the name of every town you want to visit, and these will normally be printed on your visa. It's a good idea to ask for every place you might conceivably want to see, unless these are sensitive border towns or off limits to foreigners. There's no charge for listing extra destinations.

If there's no convenient embassy and you're planning to fly in from outside the former USSR, you may be able to get a visa when you arrive, as long as this has been arranged with a travel agency in that country and you have a letter of visa support to prove it. Responsible sponsors and agencies send representatives to meet their invitees at and smooth their way through immigration. Even so, consular officials at the airport can be notoriously hard to find, especially if your flight arrives in the mid-

dle of the night, and may not be able to find your records scribbled in their big black book. Try to get a visa in advance if it's at all humanly possible.

Visas are normally stamped or pasted into your passport, though they can be a separate document (as with Russian visas). Errors happen – check the dates and other information carefully before you hit the road, and try to find out what the Russian or other writing says.

Getting Central Asian Visas in Central Asia

Some (not all) visas are simple and cheap to get after you arrive. It's relatively easy, for example, to get an Uzbek visa in Kazakstan, or a Kazak or Uzbek visa in Bishkek (Kyrgyzstan), by getting a letter of support from a travel agency.

This could make your pre-trip visa search much simpler, if you're willing to take some chances and have a week or so in a Central Asian republic to deal with the bureaucracy. Indeed, it might be possible (though we have not tried it) to leave home without any visas at all – eg fly to Bishkek from Istanbul, Ürümqi or Birmingham and get a visa on arrival, then get a Kazak or Uzbek visa in Bishkek and continue your trip there. In general, though, you are better off getting at least one visa (Kyrgyz is the easiest) before you board a plane to Central Asia.

Chinese and Pakistan visas can be arranged in Tashkent. They are a pain to organise in Almaty and Bishkek. Try to get a Chinese visa before you set off. See the Visa section in the Xinjiang chapter for more details.

Note that you cannot get a tourist visa at a land border of any Central Asian republic.

Business Visas

A business visa always requires a letter of support. Some travel and visa agencies like them because they can be obtained quickly, but embassies may give business visa applications closer scrutiny than tourist ones. Travellers who hold business visas but don't look like business people may attract more police attention, especially in Uzbekistan.

Russian Visas

In countries where there is no Central Asian representation, the Russian embassy will issue a visa valid for Central Asia, or transmit applications to the relevant Central Asian foreign ministries. The same conditions apply to get the visa as they do if you were applying at a Central Asian embassy, ie you will need a letter of visa support and the Russian embassy will need to receive authorisation from the relevant republic's Ministry of Foreign Affairs. In fact, Russian embassies are often stricter about these requirements than the actual Central Asian republics. For example, it is unlikely that you will get a Russian visa for Kyrgyzstan without an invitation.

Visas fees will also be different. Some travel agencies charge more for a visa invitation to be processed through a Russian embassy, to compensate for the extra work involved.

A Russian visa is normally a paper document; nothing goes into your passport. It lists cities, but this doesn't matter much in terms of where you can go.

For details on getting a Russian visa for Russia, see Lonely Planet's *Russia, Ukraine & Belarus*.

Russian Transit Visas If you're passing through Russia by air en route to Central Asia, a regular transit visa is usually good for 48 hours. For a nonstop Trans-Siberian Railway journey it's valid for 10 days.

Under certain circumstances, travellers who hold visas for Armenia, Belarus, Kazakstan, Kyrgyzstan, Tajikistan or Uzbekistan are entitled to 72 hour transit permission without a Russian transit visa, but you may have trouble convincing some border officials of this. Play it safe and get a transit visa.

Russian Embassies & Consulates Some (not all) Russian consular addresses overseas include the following; addresses are for embassies unless otherwise stated:

Australia
 (☎ 02-6295 9033, fax 6295 1847)
 78 Canberra Ave, Griffith, Canberra, ACT 2603
 Consulate: Woollahra

Canada
 (Visa Department ☎ 613-236 7220, 236 6215, fax 238 6158, Consular Section)
 285 Charlotte St, Ottawa, Ontario K1N 8J5
 Consulate: Montreal
China
 (☎ 10-532 2051, Visa Section ☎ 532 1267)
 4 Baizhongjie, Beijing 100600
 Consulate: Shanghai
France
 (☎ 1-45 04 05 50, 45 04 71 71, fax 45 04 17 65)
 40-50 Boulevard Lannes, F-75116 Paris
 Consulate: Marseille
Germany
 (☎ 0228-312 08 5/6/7/9, fax 311 56 3)
 Waldstrasse 42, 53177 Bonn
 Consulates: Berlin, Munich
Ireland
 (☎ 01-494 3525, 492 2048, fax 492 3525)
 186 Orwell Rd, Rathgar, Dublin 6
Latvia
 (☎ 2-33 21 51, 22 06 93, fax 21 25 79)
 Paeglesiela 2, LV-1397 Riga
Lithuania
 (☎ 22-35 17 63, fax 35 38 77)
 Juozapaviciaus gatve 11, LT-2000 Vilnius
Moldova
 (☎/fax 2-23 26 00), bulvar Stefan del Mare 151, 277019 Chisinau
Mongolia
 (☎ 1-7 28 51, 2 68 36, 2 75 06)
 Friendship St A 6, Ulan Bator
Netherlands
 (☎ 070-345 13 00/01, 346 88 88, 34 10 75 06, fax 361 7960)
 Andries Bickerweg 2, NL-2517 JP,
 The Hague
New Zealand
 (☎ 04-476 6113), 57 Messines Rd, Karori, Wellington
UK
 (☎ 020-7229 3628/29, fax 7727 8624/8625, 7299 5804)
 13 Kensington Palace Gardens, London W8 4QX
 Consular Section:
 (☎ 020-7229 8027, premium-rate recorded visa information ☎ 0891-171 271, fax 020-7229 3215)
 5 Kensington Palace Gardens, London W8 4Q℠
 Consulate: Edinburgh
USA
 (☎ 202-298 5700, 298 5772, fax 298 5749 2650 Wisconsin Ave, NW, Washington D 20007
 Visa Department:
 (☎ 202-939 8907, fax 939 8909)
 1825 Phelps Place NW, Washington
 Consulates: New York, San Franci

For Russian embassies in Central Asia see Embassies & Consulates under Facts for the Visitor of the relevant country chapter.

Transit Visas & the '72 Hour Rule'

Some CIS countries allow a non-CIS visitor with a valid visa for one CIS country to spend up to 72 hours in another at no further cost. But not all CIS visas are honoured in all other CIS countries, and officials contradict one another on which visas are acceptable and for how long. Current '72-hour' agreements that might get you in the door are noted in the Information entries in the Facts for the Visitor sections of the relevant country chapters. Turkmenistan does not honour the 72 hour rule and is the only republic to require a visa from nationals of other CIS republics. Uzbekistan does not honour the rule if you have only a Tajik visa. The Russian text of the 72 hour agreement is printed in the Language chapter.

The system is fraught with vagaries. There are no visa checks at most CIS borders, so immigration officials never know when you arrived in a republic, or when your 72 hours are up. In general the burden of proof lies upon you, so keep all hotel receipts, bus tickets etc that show when you arrived in a republic. In rare cases you may need to prove that you have a flight out of the republic within three days.

This 'rule' is not the same as a transit visa, which you can usually apply (and pay) for in advance. You normally don't need a letter of support or prebooked accommodation for a transit visa, though you may have to show an onward ticket or visa. Transit visas are normally only valid for three to five days and are normally nonextendable.

Visa Extensions

Extending an ordinary visa after you get here is tedious, but usually straightforward you have a sponsor, who must prepare a ~r of support in the same way as they did he original visa. If your sponsor is a agency, or if you have no sponsor and a agency for help, you'll have to pay d the relevant ministry will charge e too.

Exit Visas

You don't need a separate visa to exit from any republic, which means that if someone asks for one, they're probably trying to shake you down. The only exit permission that is apparently required is associated with some excursions crossing briefly into another republic, eg from Samarkand to Penjikent. An Uzbek agency arranging such a trip might need to get both entry and exit visas for the adjacent republic to ensure that your Uzbek visa is not cancelled by this temporary departure.

Border Controls & Visa Checks

By agreement with the relevant republics, Russian border troops are still in charge of immigration control between CIS and non-CIS countries, except in Kyrgyzstan. This means thorough visa checks if you fly to Central Asia directly from any non-CIS country (with this in mind, major international carriers may not even let you on board without a visa, letter of support or vouchers) or if you cross any land border between a Central Asian republic and Iran, Afghanistan or China. Therefore you may well have problems trying to cross into Kazakstan or Kyrgyzstan from China with only an Uzbek visa if you intend claiming the 72 hour transit rule.

On the other hand, if you cross a land border between two Central Asian republics you may well be waved straight through without a visa check, though there may be a perfunctory passport check. Even the border between Russia and Kazakstan is fairly porous. There aren't always arrival checks on flights between Central Asian republics either, though there are usually exit checks.

This is not to recommend visa-less travel, since it's hard to keep a low enough profile inside a republic. You'll usually be asked for your visa when you register at a tourist hotel or buy an air ticket (and sometimes a train or bus ticket). Some travellers have deflected demands to see a visa by saying they're in transit, but you may have to prove this.

Border crossings between Uzbekistan and surrounding countries have become increasingly strict since the bombings in Tashkent in 1999, particularly between Tajikistan and Uzbekistan. Make sure your paperwork is watertight at these crossings.

Registration
This relic of the Soviet era allows officials to keep tabs on you once you've arrived. In Uzbekistan you're expected to register in every town in which you stay the night. In Kyrgyzstan you only need to register once, within 72 hours of arriving. Registration in Kazakstan is more involved and is normally handled by a travel agency for around US-$15. Registration is often automatic if you check into a tourist hotel, but not if you're staying in a private home or smaller hotel.

The place to register is the Office of Visas & Registration (OVIR, Russian – Otdel Vis i Registratsii). There's one in every town, sometimes in each city district, functioning as the eyes and ears of the Ministry of the Interior's administration for policing foreigners. Though it has a local name in each republic (eg OPVR in Kazakstan, IIB in Uzbekistan, UPVR in Kyrgyzstan), everybody still calls it OVIR. In some remote areas where there is no OVIR office you may have to register at the *passportny stol* office.

Planning Ahead
Travel and visa agencies at home prefer to hear from you six weeks to two months before you leave, although they can get visa support more quickly if you pay extra. Individual sponsors may need months to get their invitations approved before they can even be sent to you.

Once you have visa support, even the most helpful Central Asian embassies in the west normally take a week or two to get you a visa, and getting one through a Russian embassy takes longer. Most embassies will speed the process up for an extra fee. Central Asian embassies within the CIS seem to be quicker, eg a day or less at Kyrgyz embassies in other Central Asian republics, a week or less at Kazak embassies.

Try to allow time for delays and screwups. And in the end, despite carefully laid plans, your visa probably still won't be ready until the last minute.

Getting Current Information
As with all official mumbo-jumbo in Central Asia, the rules change all the time, so the information here may be out of date by the time you read it. Check with Central Asian embassy Web sites (see the Embassies & Consulates entry in the Facts for the Visitor section of the various country chapters), travellers just back from the region, and with one or more CIS-specialist travel or visa agencies.

DOCUMENTS
Passport
Ensure that your passport will be valid for at least six months beyond your expected return. If you need to get a new passport, do so early as there can be waiting lists of several months during the high summer season.

Travel Permits
Uzbek, Kazak and Kyrgyz visas allow access to all places in the republics, save for a few strategic areas that need additional permits. In Kazakstan the Altay region requires a special permit and Baikonur Cosmodrome and the Polygon nuclear testing site at Semey are off limits to travellers. In Uzbekistan, Termiz is currently off limits to individual tourists.

In Kyrgyzstan any place within 50km of the Chinese border (such as the Inylchek glacier, Torugart pass and Alay valley) requires a military permit, as do many popular trekking routes. See the Visas entry of the Facts for the Visitor section of the relevant country chapters for more information.

A few off-the-beaten-track towns and nature reserves near the border in Turkmenistan require special permits, and you'll need the help of a travel agency to get these.

In theory the Gorno-Badakhshan region of Tajikistan needs a permit, but you can probably get away without one as long as you have the towns of Khorog and Murgha written on your visa.

Some remote areas in Xinjiang require Alien Travel Permit (*wàibīn tōngxíng zh*

For information on these permits s formation in each city entry in the r country chapters

Travel Insurance

A travel insurance policy to cover theft, loss and medical problems is an excellent idea for a trip to Central Asia. If you're a frequent traveller it's possible to get year-round insurance at reasonable rates. Agencies like Council Travel, Trailfinders, Flight Centre and Campus Travel sell insurance along with tickets.

There is a wide variety of policies available, so check the small print. Most policies offer lower and higher medical-expense plans; Central Asia generally falls into the lower one. A minimum of US$1 million medical cover and a 'medivac' clause or policy covering the costs of being flown to another country for treatment is essential as few reliable emergency services are available in the CIS.

Some policies specifically exclude 'dangerous activities', which can include scuba diving, skiing, motorcycling, even trekking or horse riding. If these are on your agenda, ask about an amendment to permit some of them (at a higher premium).

Few medical services in Central Asia will accept your foreign insurance documents for payment; you'll have to pay on the spot and claim later. Get receipts for everything and save all the paperwork. Some policies ask you to call back (reverse charges) to a centre in your home country where an immediate assessment of your problem is made.

Some policies offer a cheaper plan, which covers only medical emergencies and not baggage loss. This can be worthwhile if you're not carrying any valuables in your grotty 10-year-old backpack. Most policies require you to pay out the first US$100 or so anyway and only cover valuables up to a set limit. (Thus if you lose a US$1000 camera you might find yourself only covered for US$400 and having to pay the first US$100.) In the case of theft you will almost certainly need a police report to show your insurance company.

Insurance policies can normally be extended on the road by a simple phone call, but make sure you do this *before* it expires or you may have to buy a new policy, at a higher premium.

The UK has reciprocal agreements with all the former Soviet republics except the Baltic states, theoretically allowing UK nationals and their dependents (who are normally resident in Britain) *emergency* treatment – such as it is – on the same terms as local people get; you must show your British passport. If you plan to live or work in Central Asia, other agreements may apply instead; contact the UK Department of Health, International Relations Unit (☎ 020-7210 4850), Room 518, Richmond House, 79 Whitehall, London SW1A 2NS.

Student & Youth Cards

These are of little use in Central Asia, though flashing a laminated card to hotel staff can occasionally get you a useful discount (one traveller waved a diving club card!). They are mainly of use to get cheap international airfares to Central Asia. They are also useful as a decoy if someone wants to keep your passport, for example when you rent a bicycle in China. You can get an ISIC card at Jibek Joly Travels in Almaty for US$8.

Other Documents

Besides your passport and visa, there are a number of other documents you may need to keep track of:

- Customs declaration form filled out when you first enter the CIS – you're unlikely to have to show this when you leave for another CIS country (though you may have to fill in another one when you *enter* another CIS country). You may then have to show it (or them) when you finally leave the CIS, and to any bank where you want to sell back local money. Hang onto them in any case. If they're lost or stolen, a police certificate to this effect may satisfy officials on departure.
- Currency-exchange and hard-currency purchase receipts – you may need to show these when you sell back local money. The total should be more than the amount you want to sell back.
- Vouchers – if you prepaid accommodation, excursions or transport, these are the only proof that you did so.
- Hotel registration chits – in Uzbekistan you may need to show these little bits of paper (showing when you stayed at each hotel) to OVIR officials at the stations in order to buy bus or train tickets.

- HIV certification – long-term visitors to Uzbekistan, Kyrgyzstan, Kazakstan or China require proof of a negative HIV test (see the Health section for details).
- Other health certifications – travellers coming to Kazakstan or Kyrgyzstan directly from other Asian countries or Africa may need to show a cholera vaccination certificate. Anyone required to take medication containing a narcotic drug should have a doctor's certificate.

Lost or Stolen Documents

If you have your passport stolen you must immediately contact your nearest embassy (which might be in a neighbouring republic if you are in Kyrgyzstan, Tajikistan or Turkmenistan – see the Embassies & Consulates entry in the Facts for the Visitor section of the relevant country chapter). The UK embassies in Tashkent and Almaty can issue an emergency passport to Brits, enough to get you home only. The US embassies can normally issue 10-year replacement passports. It will help if you have a photocopy of your passport to verify who you are (see the following Copies entry in this section).

Replacing a visa is another matter. The loss must be reported to the police and to OVIR. If you don't have a record of the visa number you could end up having to track it back to the issuing embassy.

Copies

It's wise to have at least one photocopy of your passport – front and visa pages, a copy of your OVIR registration, your travel insurance policy and your airline tickets on your person and another set of copies with a fellow traveller. Freshen them up as needed at copy shops in department stores in the larger cities. It's also a good idea to leave a photocopy of your passport, travel insurance and airline ticket with someone you can contact at home.

CUSTOMS

Barring the occasional greedy official at a remote posting, few western tourists have major customs problems in Central Asia. When they do, it's usually over the export of 'cultural artefacts' from the former Soviet republics or the import of politically sensitive material into China.

In the former Soviet republics you're most likely to encounter customs formalities when you fly between the republics and when you enter and leave the CIS by air or overland. Some remote overland customs posts between Central Asian countries may want to snoop around your vehicle. Westerners' bags tend to be examined less readily than those of local people, except when it comes to rugs and antiques (see the following Exporting Antiques entry in this section).

Customs Declaration

On arrival in the CIS you fill out a customs declaration, listing all your money and valuables including cameras, electronics and jewellery. Hang onto your declaration and, when you leave, turn it in along with another declaration of what you're taking out. If you lose it your embassy might help with a letter to Central Customs requesting a replacement. Failing this, arrange to have the absolute minimum of hard-currency cash when you leave and cross your fingers.

When you finally leave after a multi-country Central Asia trip, you may well be asked for the declaration you filled out when you entered your first CIS state, even if this is Russia. A traveller who had been living in Tashkent for five years was asked for his original Uzbekistan declaration when he crossed from Kyrgyzstan to China at the Torugart pass. The moral is: save *everything*.

Declaring money on entry to a former Soviet republic is an awkward matter – total honesty reveals how much cash you're carrying to possibly dishonest officials, while fudging can create problems later. In general you are better off declaring everything to the dollar. On arrival in Tashkent and Almaty officials may want you to pull out and display everything you've declared. Count up your money privately before you arrive. Women are rarely asked to show currency.

Travellers leaving Kazakstan for China b
bus through Zharkent and Khorgos have be
allowed to take out up to US$500 with
showing an entry customs declaration. I
have more than that, be sure you ha
entry customs declaration from so
country that shows that you arrived

least the amount you're leaving with. It's illegal to carry Kazak tenge out of the country.

Chinese customs are quick and straightforward compared to that on the other side and most travellers aren't even given customs declarations any more.

What You Cannot Bring In

There are no significant limits anywhere on items for personal use, except on guns and drugs. Cameras, video cameras, radios and personal stereos are OK. You are allowed to bring in 400 cigarettes and 2L of alcohol. Large amounts of anything saleable are suspect, and pornography tends to raise alarms. Uzbek officials are also on the lookout for 'anti-Uzbek propaganda', and Chinese officials are after printed material, film and tapes 'detrimental to China's politics, economy, culture and ethics' – but don't worry too much about your own reading material.

What You Cannot Take Out

The main prohibitions are 'antiques' and local currency. Certain electrical appliances bought in the former USSR are apparently unexportable, though it remains a mystery which appliances. Every country's regulations prohibit the export of endangered animals and plants, though few officials would recognise an endangered species if it bit them.

There is little customs control in Tajikistan, except at the border with Kyrgyzstan, where opium is the worry. Vehicles and baggage are searched frequently and exhaustively on the Murgab-Osh road.

Chinese officials seldom search westerners. If you buy a Uyghur knife at Kashgar market do not carry it onto the plane to Ürümqi in your hand luggage, as it will be confiscated.

Exporting Antiques

From the former Soviet republics, you cannot export antiques or anything of 'historical or cultural value' – including art, furnishings, manuscripts, musical instruments, clothing and jewellery – without an licence and payment of a stiff export

Get a receipt for anything of value that you buy, showing where you got it and how much you paid. If your purchase looks like it has historical value, you should also have a letter saying that it has no such value or that you have permission to take it out anyway. Get this from the vendor, from the Ministry of Culture in the capital, or from a curator at one of the state art museums with enough clout to do it. Without it, your goodies could be seized on departure, possibly even on departure from *another* CIS state. If you wait until you get to the airport you could be out of luck. Some travellers end up abandoning their purchases in order to catch their flights, or handing them over to local friends seeing them off.

In Uzbekistan any book or artwork made before 1945 is considered antique. In Turkmenistan 'cultural artefacts' seems to embrace almost all handicrafts and traditional-style clothing, no matter how mundane, cheap or new. One traveller reported that he had to surrender a pair of socks knitted as a gift by the grandmother in a family he visited, because they were 'traditional'. Airport searches at Ashgabat are thorough and time-consuming. Rules on the export of carpets from Turkmenistan are also stringent (see Customs in the Regional Facts for the Visitor chapter).

You're expected to show Chinese officials any cultural relics, handicrafts, gold and silver ornaments, and jewellery you bought there, as well as your receipts for them.

MONEY

The Kazakstan, Uzbekistan and Kyrgyzstan banking systems have improved greatly in the last few years, with credit card transactions, wire transfers and regulated foreign exchange. In the countryside there are no facilities, so change enough to get you back to a main city.

If you will be travelling a lot in the region it's worth bringing a flexible combination of cash US dollars, US dollar travellers cheques and a credit card to cover every eventuality. Prices in this book are mostly given in US dollars, although you may have to pay in local currency. Prices quoted in the Uzbek-

The Relative Value of Money

The manat, *sum*, tenge and Tajik rubl are still relatively unstable and so prices quoted in this book are quoted in US dollar equivalents. This doesn't mean that you have to pay in dollars – in fact this is technically illegal in Uzbekistan. Rather, it gives a more stable indication of costs. In Kyrgyzstan it seems that the som prices are more stable than dollar equivalents and so rates are quoted in som.

The Central Asian economies are all unstable and you can expect prices to jump (or fall) every year; rates in this book are therefore an indication more of *relative* than absolute values.

istan and Turkmenistan chapters are given in US dollars worked out at the black market rate; see the Black Market section later.

Exchanging Money

Nearly all tourist hotels have branch-bank exchange desks where you can at least swap US dollars cash for local money.

Because officially you cannot use foreign currency for anything, many shops, post offices, airline booking offices, airports and train stations in the former Soviet republics also have their own exchange kiosks – with signs in Russian like:

О МЕН ВАЛЮТЫ

(*obmen valyuty*; currency exchange)

О МЕННЫЙ ПУНКТ

(*obmennyy punkt*; exchange point)

Banks in Turkmenistan and Tajikistan may not even have a currency exchange counter. The best places to try in such cases are tourist hotels. At the time of writing, in most of Tajikistan (except the Khojand area) there was simply a physical scarcity of money.

Swapping between currencies can be a pain, with most former Soviet republics uninterested in the others' money (an exception is Kazakstan and Kyrgyzstan). In border areas you may need to deal with several currencies simultaneously; when trekking in the Khojand region it's necessary to carry a mix-

ture of Russian roubles, Tajik rubls, Uzbek *sum*, US dollars and Kyrgyz som.

Of course you can often change money personally, eg with hotel waiters or receptionists, or with dealers who approach you at markets, stations or your hotel (see the following Black Market entry in this section). In the former Soviet republics everybody, but everybody, wants dollars; even your truest friends and hosts will ask you to change a little with them. It can be hard to refuse, although saying that you need official exchange receipts at the border in order to sell back local currency usually closes the matter.

Try to avoid large notes in local currency (except to pay your hotel bills), since few people can spare much change.

Moneychangers Licensed moneychangers are the easiest way to change money in Kyrgyzstan, Kazakstan and Tajikistan. They are readily found in small kiosks on nearly every block, and most will give a receipt (*spravka*) if you ask them; rates may vary by 1% to 2% at most. Licensed changers are completely legal.

Cash US dollars cash is by far the easiest to exchange, followed by Deutschmarks in the former Soviet republics, or UK pound sterling in western China. US dollars can also be exchanged unofficially when nothing else can, making them good emergency money. You will need cash US dollars when paying for services with a private travel agency, though many now accept credit cards. Though officially you cannot spend foreign currency anywhere in Uzbekistan, private hotels and home-stays normally take US dollars or even Deutschmarks. Most people, however, still seem to expect payment in local money.

Take a mixture of denominations – larger notes (US$100, US$50) are the most readily accepted and get a better rate, but a cach of small ones (US$10, US$5) is handy when you're stuck with a lousy excha rate or need to offer a wee inducement

Make sure notes are in good conditic worn or torn bills – and that they ar post-1994. Bills issued before 1990 are generally not accepted – if they are, the rate is often 30% less the normal US dollar rate. The newest US$20, US$50 and US$100 notes have an embedded thread running approximately beneath the words 'This Note Is Legal Tender ...', visible when held against the light. Moneychangers may check for it. New US$5 and US$10 bills will debut in the year 2000. New-style US$100 bills were added in 1996, US$50 in 1997 and US$20 in 1998.

You may raise eyebrows at your bank back home, asking for large amounts of US dollars cash in small, brand-new notes, but rest assured it is worth the trouble.

Taxi drivers and market-sellers often fob off their own ragged foreign notes on tourists as change, so of course *you* should refuse to accept old notes too.

You may want to take a bag or an expandable moneybelt when you change money; at the time of research US$100 gave you a pile of Uzbek *sum* as thick as an airport paperback.

Travellers Cheques Travellers cheques can now be cashed in all the major Central Asian capitals. American Express is the most widely recognised brand, but others can normally be cashed. Only Visa travellers cheques can be changed in Turkmenistan. US dollar cheques are the best currency to bring. Commissions run at between 1% in Kazakstan to 3% or 5% in Kyrgyzstan; it is possible to get your money in dollars instead of local currency, though the commission rate may be a little different. Travellers cheques can also make good decoy money if pressed for a bribe, as most people don't know what to do with them.

In China, travellers cheques actually get better rates than cash, commissions are low and all major brands and currencies are accepted, so this is the best way to bring money if you will be spending much time in ʼinjiang. Cheques can be cashed at the ▪nk of China and most tourist hotels. Ex-▪nge rates are uniform.

▪t Cards It's an excellent idea to bring ʼit card as an emergency back up,

though you shouldn't rely on it completely to finance your trip as there are still only a limited number of places where it can be used.

Major credit cards can be used for payment at top-end hotels, restaurants, airline offices, major travel agencies and shops throughout the region, at Uzbektourism hotels in tourist centres of Uzbekistan, and at a few posh hotels in Ashgabat. Visa seems the most widely recognised brand, but others (American Express, Diners Club, Eurocard, MasterCard) are accepted in some places.

Cash advances are possible – for commissions of 1% to 5% – in Almaty (and a few other Kazakstan towns), Ashgabat, Bishkek and Tashkent, with a Visa card and Master-Card. By using credit cards in Uzbekistan and Turkmenistan you fail to make use of the black market (see the Black Market section following).

You can get cash advances easily with a Visa card at the Bank of China in Kashgar and Ürümqi. In Almaty it is also possible to use western credit cards in cash machines to get cash tenge. See the individual city entries for details.

International Transfers Direct bank-to-bank wire (telegraphic) transfer is possible through some banks in Almaty, Bishkek, Ashgabat and Tashkent, as noted. Commissions of 1% to 4% are typical, and service takes one to five days. Western Union has branch partners at the Centre Credit Bank in Kazakstan and Rossiyski Kredit Bank in Turkmenistan.

Exchange Receipts Whenever you change money, ask for a receipt *(kvitantsiya* or *spravka* in Russian)* showing your name, the date, the amounts in both currencies, the exchange rate and an official signature. Not everyone will give you one (Kyrgyzstan's licensed private dealers rarely do), but if you need to resell your local currency through the banks you may need enough recent ones to cover what you want to resell. You will not need a receipt to sell local currency into US dollars at moneychangers. Customs officials may want to see exchange receipts at crossings to non-CIS countries.

Try to avoid receipts without the bottom portion that you fill out when reselling. In Uzbekistan receipts like this, which explicitly say they confer no right of re-exchange, might be handed out.

Black Market The existence of licensed moneychangers in every town has done away with the black market in most republics. The main exceptions are Turkmenistan and Uzbekistan, where the black market rates were three times the official rate. In both countries the market rate is the acknowledged rate when dealing with taxi drivers and guides (ie if you agree on paying US$10 in Uzbekistan they expect 4500 *sum*, not 1570 *sum*). Changing on the black market in these two republics can seriously cut your costs for transactions that don't require an exchange receipt (some Uzbekistan hotels ask for receipts to prove you got your *sum* legitimately), but there are risks involved.

Police often prey not on local dealers, but on foreign customers, from whom they can then extort a bribe (one traveller was arrested three times in one morning in Tashkent). If you must, at least confine your transactions to trustworthy local friends or B&B owners.

In Xinjiang (and elsewhere in China), Uyghurs have been changing money for centuries, and you'll be asked to change money at every turn, especially outside Kashgar's Chini Bagh hotel. Rates are only a little higher than the bank so there is little to gain except the convenience or the facility to change neighbouring currencies. Many dealers are skilled sleight-of-hand artists, so if you must use them, be very careful.

- Trade a round sum, for quick mental calculations.
- Fold it up in a pocket, to avoid fumbling in an open purse or wallet.
- Isolate yourself and the dealer from his friends; never let yourself be at the centre of a group.
- Tell them what you have, but don't pull it out; some claim they want to check it for counterfeit, and may substitute smaller notes.
- Insist on their money first, and take your sweet time counting it. Once you're sure it's right, do *not* let the dealer recount it (a common scam – you find some missing, he adds the missing Y20 or whatever and hands it back, palming Y500 off the bottom); hand over your little wad, and split.

- Souvenir shops can be a good place to change money as they are less likely to split and you always know where to go back to if there is a problem.

Changing Local Currency

Exchange kiosks in Kazakstan and Kyrgyzstan will change tenge or som into dollars without a problem – locals do it all the time. At times of financial instability there may be a freeze for a few days.

To sell back currency at any official exchange point you will probably need your customs declaration, plus the originals of enough recent exchange receipts to cover the amount you want to resell. Exchange receipts normally have a resale form at the bottom, which you sign at this time.

At the time of research you had to sell Uzbek *sum* back at a main city office of the National Bank – *not* at the airport or the hotels, or the border. In Xinjiang you can change yuan back into dollars only if you have an exchange receipt covering the total amount. The easiest thing, of course, is to spend it up before you leave, or swap it with travellers going the other way.

Security

Thankfully, credit cards and travellers cheques are becoming more common in the CIS, but you may still end up carrying large wads of cash. All you can do is bury it deeply and in several different places, with only tiny sums in wallets, purses and outside pockets (the exception is at customs, where some travellers have been made to display their entire hoard).

Petty crime is a growing problem in all the former Soviet republics (see also Crime under Dangers & Annoyances in this chapter). Don't leave money in any form lying around your hotel room. Carry it securely zipped in one or more moneybelts or shoulder wallets buried deep in your clothing, with only what you'll immediately need (what you would be willing to hand over to a thief to an official on the take) accessible in exterior pocket, wallet or purse.

When paying for anything substantial a hotel bill or an expensive souvenir out the money beforehand, out of public sight. At exchange kiosks, have your money in hand; don't go fumbling in your money-belt in full view.

Be careful when paying by credit card that you see how many slips are being made from your card, that you destroy all carbon copies, and that as few people as possible get hold of your card number and expiry date. There are tales of thieves targeting people coming out of banks with fat cash advances, so keep your eyes open.

Make sure you note the numbers of your cards and travellers cheques, and the telephone numbers to call if they are lost or stolen – and keep all numbers separate from the cards and cheques.

Costs

By travelling with a friend, staying in mid-range hotels, eating in cheaper restaurants, and taking the odd cheap flight or hiring a car when there is no public transport, you can get around Central Asia for between US$20 to US$30 per person per day (at the time of research). For a minimum of comfort you'll probably have to part with US$20 for a hotel in bigger towns. It's easy to blow your budget with imported beer and Mars bars.

Changing money on the black market will reduce costs considerably in Uzbekistan and Turkmenistan if you can pay for official services such as telephone calls etc in *sum*, as US dollar rates are converted to *sum* at the government rate, one third the black market rate (see the Black Market entry earlier in this section).

With money changed on the black market and staying at government hotels, eating at stalls or buying food in the markets and catching buses or trains, budget travellers can get by on US$8 to US$12 in Uzbekistan and Turkmenistan.

Kyrgyzstan has no black market, but it an be even cheaper as there are fewer fa-'ities and tourist traffic. Kazakstan is gen-'ly more expensive and you'll need a 'mum budget of around US$25 per day 'naty, or US$15 outside of the capital. 'able Tajikistan, outside of Dushanbe 'jand, services are scarce and costs

are highly unpredictable. China can be expensive or cheap, depending how you live.

You can shave down costs by self-catering in shops and bazars, staying in private homes and the occasional bottom-end place, sharing larger hotel rooms with more people, getting around town by local bus instead of taxi, taking trains instead of buses, riding overnight trains or buses to save hotel costs, and spending less time in (expensive) cities. Don't forget to bargain in the bazars. You can save money by being smart on taking selective transport (eg Tashkent to Almaty by bus is about US$8, Almaty to Tashkent about US$11; Almaty to Tashkent by air is about US$69 with Kazakstan Airlines, US$105 with Uzbekistan Airways). Take planes in Kyrgyzstan, where there are no foreigners' fares and local fares are dirt cheap.

Don't forget visa costs, which can add a bundle, and of course long-haul transport to get you to and from Central Asia, which isn't all that cheap wherever you are flying from.

Two-Tier Pricing Foreigners have traditionally paid substantially more than local people for airfares, train fares, hotel rooms, even museums in the former Soviet republics and China. Two-tier pricing continues in Uzbekistan and Tajikistan, but has now been abolished in China, Kazakstan and Kyrgyzstan.

There's little you can do if you are faced with a foreigners' price except speak your best Russian, proffer the local price, don't show your passport unless asked, or have local friends buy your tickets for you (this last option doesn't always work; in Uzbekistan, for example, police often check departing buses and trains).

It's fair, and it's unfair. Before you complain, however, ponder the fact that in Uzbekistan at the time of research, the typical monthly wage for a professional such as a university professor was less than a single tank of black-market petrol or 10kg of meat.

Tipping & Bargaining

Tipping is not common anywhere in Central Asia or western China. A few top-end restaurants in the capital cities automatically add a 5% to 15% service charge to the bill, or expect you to round the total up. In the smaller Muslim areas tipping runs counter to many people's Islamic sense of hospitality, and may therefore even offend them.

Bribery, on the other hand, clearly can work in Central Asia, especially Uzbekistan; it almost certainly won't in China. Try to avoid it where possible – it feeds the already-widespread notion that we all just love throwing our money around, and makes it harder for future travellers. In fact a combination of smiles (even if over gritted teeth) and patient persistence can very often work better.

Shops have fixed prices but in markets (food, art or souvenirs) bargaining is usually expected. For food, initial asking prices tend to be in a sane proportion to the expected outcome. Sellers will be genuinely surprised if you reply to their '5000' with '1000'; they're more likely expecting 3500, 4000 or 4500 in the end. Press your luck further in places like art and craft markets heavily patronised by tourists. In Kyrgyzstan bargaining is usually reserved only for taxi drivers. In the markets you may be able to knock off a couple of som, but for the most part tourists are charged the same reasonable prices as locals. Bargain heavily in Xinjiang, but don't lose sight of how much money you are really quibbling over.

POST & COMMUNICATIONS
Postal Rates
See the Post & Communications entry in the Facts for the Visitor section of the individual country chapters for specific rates.

Sending Mail
The postal systems of the former Soviet republics are definitely not for urgent items – due in part to the scarcity of regional flights. In fact, you'll probably get home before your postcards do. An airmail letter to anywhere outside the CIS, if it arrives at all, may take four to eight weeks or more. China is the most reliable place from where to send packages, followed by Kyrgyzstan and Kazakstan.

Tourist hotels and central post offices are the safest places to post things. Address

mail as you would from any country, in your own language, though it will help to write the destination country in the local language too – in Central Asia put the Cyrillic name *before* the address; in China put the Chinese characters after the address.

Courier Services If you have something that absolutely must get there, use an international courier company. DHL has offices in Khojand and Dushanbe in Tajikistan, Bishkek in Kyrgyzstan, Tashkent in Uzbekistan and Almaty in Kazakstan. Federal Express has offices in Almaty. UPS has an office in Almaty as well. (See individual city entries for further details.) A letter to a western country is about US$40, a 500g package around US$42 to US$60, and it takes about a week.

Express Mail Service (EMS) is a priority mail service offered by post offices that ranks somewhere between normal post and courier post. Prices are considerably cheaper than courier services.

Receiving Mail
Incoming mail service is so flakey in Central Asia that it's rare for anyone on the move to find anything at poste-restante. In general you are better off using a Web-based email system (see Email & Internet Access, later). If you do decide to test the system you can improve the chances of getting mail by following these pointers:

- A private or company address is best. A hotel address might work, though staff tend to be careless with mail.
- Few western embassies are keen to hold mail, though some (eg the US embassy in Tashkent) will do so for a couple of months for their own nationals.
- Mail to former Soviet republics should be addressed in the reverse order from western practice, ie country, postal code, town, street or PO box address, addressee (family name first). Try to write the address a second time in Russian. To avoid confusing your own post office, add country name again at the bottom, in Engli
- The 'street' address for poste-restan Главпочтамт, до востребования (R for 'main post office, for collection' *pochtamt, do vostrebovania*).

- Capitalise and underline the addressee's family name. Check for mail under both your surname and Christian name.
- To check for poste-restante mail, bring your passport to the main post office and ask for *do vostrebovania.*
- For letters within the CIS, the address is best written in Russian. The return address is written below the main address.

China has fairly reliable poste restante services at the main post offices of major towns. The Kashgar post office has even returned unclaimed mail.

Telephone

International Calls You can place international calls (as well as local and intercity ones) from the central telephone and telegraph offices in most towns. You tell a clerk the number and prepay in local currency. After a wait of anything from half a minute to several hours, you're called to a booth (they usually shout out the destination and a booth number, in Russian). Early-morning and late night calls, and those from capital cities, go through faster.

Hotel operators will also place your calls, but it takes longer and costs more (typically 20%, though the business centre at the Hotel Dostuk in Bishkek slaps on 55%).

You can set up your own calls – theoretically from anywhere in Central Asia – by dialling 062. This gets you a local operator who speaks at least minimal English and will book the call and ring you back within about half an hour. If you do this from a private telephone, the operator rings afterward with the call length and charges, which are the same as at a telephone office. Doing this from your hotel generates hotel surcharges.

In Tajikistan it's almost impossible to make international calls from anywhere outside Dushanbe or Khojand.

International calls generally cost around US$2 or US$3 per minute.

llect Calls US citizens can call home *ct from anywhere in Central Asia by di-* AT&T in Moscow (☎ 095-155 50 42; h-speaking operator). You can also AT&T calling card on this number.

There looks to be no other way to make a collect call (Russian: *obratnaya oplata*) from Central Asia. The next-cheapest strategy is a quick call to ask your party to call you back – if possible to one of those satellite-linked services. Most hotel-room telephones in the former Soviet Union are not connected to a switchboard but have direct-dial numbers (on a card in the room, or ask reception).

Calling into the CIS from Outside To call a number in any CIS country, dial the following:

☎ caller's country international access code + country code + city code + number

The republics were given separate country and city codes in 1998/1999. See the country chapters for individual republic codes, and the individual city entries for their telephone codes.

Calls within the CIS Calls between CIS countries are now treated as international calls, so for example to call Uzbekistan from, say, Kyrgyzstan you would need to dial Kyrgyzstan's international access code and then the Uzbek city code.

Local Calls Placing a local or trunk call on Central Asia's decomposing telephone systems is usually harder than placing an international one. There are token-operated telephones on the streets of bigger cities (though many seem to be permanently out of order) and in municipal telephone offices. Tokens *(jeton)* are sold at post and telephone offices and some kiosks for the equivalent of about US$0.05.

Local calls are free from most hotels.

Telegram The cheapest way to stay in touch is by short telegram, sent from the central telephone and telegraph offices in most towns, and from some top-end hotels. They usually arrive within a day, almost always within two. A message in English is no problem if it's clearly printed, though you may have to pay a surcharge.

Fax

Faxes can sometimes be sent from post, telephone and telegraph offices, and some top-end hotels. Note that they're charged at telephone rates for the time it takes to transmit them – about one minute per page in China, but up to *five* minutes or more on Central Asia's dicey telephone lines. Moreover there may be a three minute minimum, and you pay for failed attempts too, so the total cost is unpredictable and often huge.

Email & Internet Access

You may want to open a free Web-based email account such as Lonely Planet's eKno (www.ekno.lonelyplanet.com), HotMail (www.hotmail.com) or Yahoo! Mail (mail .yahoo.com). You can then access your mail from anywhere in the world using any net-connected computer.

There are now several commercial Internet providers in capital cities of Central Asia, where short-term visitors can surf the Web for an hour for around US$3 in Kazakstan and Kyrgyzstan, or US$1 or US$2 in Uzbekistan. It's much cheaper to send and receive email messages, although some companies require you to set up a temporary account. In Uzbekistan and Turkmenistan the best place to go is the American Center or Library, or a private travel agency. See the individual city entries for further details of such locations. Even minor cities and towns will have a library or university that has an Internet connection and will let you use their facilities for a small fee.

.tm – Trademark for Sale!

One of Turkmenistan's more unexpected sources of income has come from the Internet. The country's domain name '.tm' is very much in favour by companies whose '.com' address has already been registered by another company, and with companies wishing to use the tm abbreviation to stand for 'trademark'. The domain name has already been sold to thousands of companies, and Turkmenistan gets a slice of every fee.

INTERNET RESOURCES

The Internet is a rich resource for travellers and there's no better place to start than the Lonely Planet Web site (www.lonelyplanet .com). Here you'll find summaries on travelling to most places on earth, postcards from other travellers and the Thorn Tree bulletin board, where you can ask questions before you go or dispense advice when you get back. You can also find travel news and updates to many of our guidebooks, and the subWWWay section links you to useful travel resources elsewhere on the Web.

Many travel agency Web sites contain general travel information (see the Travel Agencies & Organised Tours section in the Getting There & Away chapter). Central Asian embassies abroad and US embassies in Central Asia have some of the most useful sites (see Embassies & Consulates in the Facts for the Visitor section in the various country chapters). Other Web sites are listed in the Government Travel Advice, Maps, Books, Newspapers & Magazines, Radio, Health, Disabled Travellers and Senior Travellers sections. Some good general Central Asian Web sites are listed below:

BISNIS (Business Information Service for the
   Newly Independent States)
   www.bisnis.doc.gov
   (up-to-date business, statistical and some travel
   information)
Caspian Times
   www.caspiantimes.com
   (essentially a business service for the oil industry but has news, maps and travel information on the Central Asian states)
Harvard Forum for Central Asian Studies
   www.fas.Harvard.edu/~centasia/
   (useful mainly for students of the region, with information on courses, libraries, periodicals and magazines that specialise in Central Asia)
Interfax News Agency
   www.interfax-news.com
   (detailed news-gathering site focusing on tᵉ
   old USSR)
Silk Road Foundation
   www.silk-road.com
   (workshops, travel, lectures, music, arti
   Silk Road cities)
Soros Foundation
   www.soros.org/central_eurasia.html
   (links to general information on all ᵗ

Kazakstan

A couple of Kazak cities have their own Web sites. Karaghandy, *www.karaganda.kz* and Atyrau, *www.atyrauobl.kz* are both useful if you have business in these areas.

General Kazakstan
www.kz/firsteng.html
(people, jewellery, architecture, cooking, chat rooms)
Kazakstan
www.welcome.to/kazakstan
(photo gallery, airlines, chat rooms, Almaty radio)
President of Kazakstan
www.president.kz/
(information on the country's economy, culture, nature reserves, history and geography)

Kyrgyzstan

Kyrgyzstan Business & Tourism Directory
www.geocities.com/thetropics/shores/7432/
(tourist information, general information on Kyrgyzstan and lots of links)
Kyrgyzstan embassy
www.kyrgyzstan.org
(general info, travel advice, visa regulations, events links)

Tajikistan

Asia Plus
www.internews.ru/tj/index.html
(regular round-up of news in Tajikistan)
Personal Web Site
www.angelfire.com/sd/tajikistanupdate/
(good news site with lots of Tajikistan-related links)

Turkmenistan

Latif Tours
www.Turkmenistan-travel.com
(excellent tourist and travel information)
Turkmenistan Information Center
www.turkmenistan.com
(general background information on the country)
Turkmenistan Sibnet Network
www.sibnet.tm/ENG/index.htm
(some info on museums, holidays, news, maps)

~bekistan
er Uzbekistan
vw.cu-online.com/~k_a/uzbekistan/
ercafe locations in Uzbekistan, classified
message boards, news, travel)
of Uzbekistan
zbekistan.org
nd visa info)

Government of Uzbekistan
www.gov.uz/
(tourist information, statistics and virtual tours)
Uzbekistan
www.Uzbekistan.com
(Internet cafes, city guides, news)
UzOnLine
www.angelfire.com/ak/Uzonline/main.html
(arts, education, news, festivals, maps, travel and chatrooms)

Afghanistan

Afghanistan Online
www.afghan-web.com
(news searches, books, cultural information and cookery)
Afghanistan Today
http://frankenstein.worldweb.net/afghan/
(music, history, culture, restaurants, publications, news and aid organisations)

Email Discussion Lists

Internetters can take part in, or just listen in on, informal electronic conversations among a constantly changing group of Central Asia scholars, expatriate workers and travellers on topics as varied as politics, semantics and music. Bulletins also pop up all the time for specialist conferences and other events. There's no charge, of course.

CentralAsia List is aimed at students of Central Asia and includes courses, jobs, seminars, publications and cultural events. To subscribe send an email message to majordomo@fas.harvard.edu and write 'subscribe CentralAsia-L' in the message.

The Central Asia Political Discussion List (Cenasia) isn't your usual 'bulletin board', but a serious discussion forum. To subscribe send an email to listserv@lists.mcgill.ca with a message containing the words 'subscribe cenasia'.

Oxiana is a similar mailing list of Central Asian specialists, but with a travel-related slant. To subscribe send a blank message to ❂ Oxiana-subscribe@onelist.com.

The Silk Road List concerns itself with often quite scholarly aspects of the Silk Road. To subscribe send the message 'subscribe' to ❂ silkroad-l-request@list-server.net.

BOOKS

Most books are published in different editions by different publishers in different countries. As a result, a book might be a hardcover rarity in one country while it's readily available in paperback in another. Fortunately, bookshops and libraries search by title or author, so your local bookshop or library is best placed to advise you on the availability of the following recommendations.

All books listed here are available in paperback unless noted otherwise. For specific books on Xinjiang and Afghanistan see those country chapters.

Lonely Planet

Other Lonely Planet guidebooks with further information on areas covered by this book are *Karakoram Highway* and *China*. Coverage of neighbouring countries extends to *Pakistan*, *Trekking in the Karakoram & the Hindukush*, *Iran*, *Georgia*, *Armenia & Azerbaijan* and *Russia, Ukraine & Belarus*. Lonely Planet also produces an essential *Central Asia* phrasebook.

Other Guidebooks

China: the Silk Routes, by Peter Neville-Hadley, Cadogan (1st ed), 1997. Detailed guide concentrating on China, with some information on travelling from Ürümqi to Almaty, and Kashgar to Bishkek. Much of the information consists of rehashed past travelogues.

The Silk Road, by Judy Bonavia, Odyssey (5th ed), 1998. Excellent guide to the Chinese section of the Silk Road from Xi'an to Kashgar, with fine photos and historical tidbits, though short on practical information.

Silk Route by Rail, by Douglas Streatfield-James (2nd ed), 1997. The first and only dedicated guide to the railway line across China from Beijing, through Xinjiang, to Almaty in Kazakstan, through Uzbekistan and on to Moscow. If you are crazy enough to try it, this book has detailed planning tips, a bit of history, and very basic information and maps for major cities en route.

Trekking in Russia & Central Asia, by Frith Maier. This is an unrivalled guide to the former USSR's wild places by an American who first started exploring them as a student in 1984, and pioneered the US firm REI's adventure travel program there. It has 77 pages of Central Asia route descriptions, plus chapters of useful background and planning info. The biggest problem is that the maps simply bear little resemblance to the text.

Uzbekistan – the Golden Road to Samarkand, by Calum Macleod & Bradley Mayhew (3rd ed), 1998. This Odyssey guide (co-written by one of the authors of this guide) offers detailed historical and practical coverage of Uzbekistan's Silk Road cities and touches on the main historical sites in the neighbouring republics. It also features literary excerpts by the likes of George Curzon, Fitzroy Maclean and Colin Thubron, as well as some fine photography.

Travel

Danziger's Travels, by Nick Danziger. An incredible modern-day overland odyssey through Turkey, Iran, Afghanistan, Pakistan, China and Tibet – without much regard for visas, immigration posts, civil wars and the like. He's entitled to sound a bit self-important and melodramatic about it.

Eastern Approaches, by Sir Fitzroy Maclean. Sir Fitzroy Maclean, a young British diplomat in Moscow, managed by guile or stealth to snoop into many corners of Central Asia and the Caucasus during the bloody years from 1937 to 1939, usually with the NKVD (a KGB forerunner) hot on his heels. This old but reprinted book recounts these forays, as well as Maclean's celebrated adventures in wartime Yugoslavia. A much more interesting Maclean book – in hardback and now unfortunately out of print – is his detailed and reflective *To the Back of Beyond; An Illustrated Companion to Central Asia and Mongolia.*

Extreme Continental: Blowing Hot and Cold Through Central Asia, by Giles Whittell. Undeterred by the theft of his money, a motorbike that needed more attention than a baby and a host who used him as a punching bag, Whittell in 1991 completed a comprehensive tour across Central Asia, researching his own guidebook. This is the personal version of that trip, against which independent travellers can check off their own experiences, good and bad.

Goodnight Mr Lenin, by Tiziano Terzani. This Italian journalist happened to be in the USSR when it collapsed, and decided to stay and take the pulse of Siberia, Central Asia and the Caucasus in those first post-Soviet months. The result is personal and unpolished, full of small factual errors (eg China and Uzbekistan have a common border) and irritating references to girls when he means women, but his interviews and encounters make for a unique and occasionally very perceptive chronicle, sympathetic to the huge problem of creating a new non-Soviet reality.

Journey to Khiva, by Philip Glazebrook, and *A ples in the Snow and A Journey to Samarkc* by Geoffrey Moorhouse. Two travel wri Central Asian voyages on what turned out the eve of independence, weaving histo contemporary observation around its cities and sites. Moorhouse's book was published in the USA as *On the Other Side; A Journey Through Soviet Central Asia.*

The Lost Heart of Asia, by Colin Thubron. Thubron is deservedly praised for his careful research, first-hand explorations, delicate observations and Baroque prose. But his books make poor travelling companions because they can be more compelling than being there. This one is relentlessly downbeat.

Red Odyssey, by Marat Akchurin. In 1990 Akchurin, a Russian-Tatar poet and journalist, toured the Soviet Muslim republics 'witnessing the violence and misery brought about by the dying Communist system'. Definitely not of the 'historical sketches and sightseeing' school of travel writing, this is gritty stuff – concrete and vomit, blood and bribery.

Sacred Horses: The Life of a Turkmen Cowboy, by Jonathon Maslow. Fired by a desire to ride a legendary Akhal-Teke horse across the sands of the Karakum desert, naturalist Maslow made two extended visits to Turkmenistan, recounted here. The abrasive Maslow is not always easy to get along with but he has written a very good account of the modern-day Turkmen's struggle to maintain traditions while simultaneously making a few bucks.

Turkestan Solo, by Ella Maillart. This is the engaging account of a Swiss woman adventurer's low-budget solo travels in Soviet Central Asia in the early 1930s, including a winter camel ride across the Kyzylkum desert, and a show-trial of *basmachi* guerillas in Samarkand's Registan. 'Kini' Maillart was an internationally known sportswoman as well as a traveller and writer. Not long after this trip she joined Peter Fleming in a tempestuous seven month journey across remote western China, out of which came two amazingly different books, her *Forbidden Journey* and Fleming's *News from Tartary.*

History & Politics

The Aral Sea Tragedy, by Grigori Reznichenko. Grimly amusing diary of a 1998 expedition throughout Central Asia to pin down the causes and effects of the death of the Aral Sea. Available at the Karakalpakstan Art Gallery in Nukus, Uzbekistan.

Beyond the Oxus; Archaeology, Art & Architecture of Central Asia, by Edgar Knobloch. An oddly appealing book for a specialist cultural history of Central Asia, perhaps because it's so ʁch in all the background information, reconʣuctions, floor-plans and close-ups that nobody ʤCentral Asia seems to know about any more.

Central Asia; A Travellers' Companion, by Kathleen Hopkirk. Handy and very readable historical background on the region (though not half as entertaining as her husband Peter's books), an excellent companion book for those keen to know more about the places they're seeing.

The Great Game, by Peter Hopkirk. A fast-paced, very readable history of the Great Game – the 19th century cold war between Britain and Russia – as it unfolded across Europe and Asia. It's carried along in Hopkirk's trademark style, in a series of personal stories – all men, all westerners, all resolute and square-jawed, with Victoria Crosses for everybody – real Boys' Own stuff, melodramatic, but essentially true.

Life along the Silk Road, by Susan Whitfield. A scholarly yet intriguing book that brings alive the Silk Road through a variety of characters (including a Sogdian merchant from Penjikent) that resemble the *Canterbury Tales* set in Central Asia. Required reading for Silk Road obsessives.

Mission to Tashkent, by FM Bailey. One of the best reads of any kind about Central Asia. Bailey, a British intelligence officer sent to the region in the wake of the Revolution of 1917, pulled off a sequence of hair's-breadth escapes from the Bolsheviks, too implausible to be fiction, which he recounts in a disarmingly understated way. At one stage, under an assumed identity, he was even employed as a Bolshevik agent with the job of tracking himself down.

Setting the East Ablaze, by Peter Hopkirk. Takes up where *The Great Game* stops – a gripping cloak-and-dagger history of the murderous early years of Soviet power in Central Asia, and Communist efforts to spread revolution to British India and China. Of the many original books upon which Hopkirk's research is based, the best, now reprinted in paperback, are FM Bailey's *Mission to Tashkent* (see the previous review in this section) and Paul Nazaroff's *Hunted Through Central Asia.*

The Silk Road: A History, by Irene Franck & David Brownstone. Three hundred well-illustrated, well-mapped pages of history of the multi-stranded caravan routes that began crossing Central Asia in the 2nd century BCE (before common era).

Storm from the East, by Robert Marshall. A good way to get to grips with just who Jenghiz Khan was, which cities his hordes annihilated and when, and what happened to his empire afterwards, based on a BBC television series. The paperback version is not so lavishly illustrated as the hardback.

Tournament of Shadows, by Karl E Meyer. From the Peter Hopkirk school of history, this new book (published 1999) looks at some lesser known Great Game characters and brings the Game up to date with the present scramble for oil in the Caspian.

Younghusband, by Patrick French. Sir Francis Younghusband is known to Asia scholars (and Peter Hopkirk fans) as the archetypal Great Gamester – crossing China solo, facing down Hunza bandits and Russian spies in the Karakoram, and leading the British invasion of Tibet. He was also a detached and stubborn individual, a dyed-in-the-wool imperialist (some say racist), and at the end of his life a raging mystic. This excellent biography intertwines the lives of its subject and of its author as he tracks the story down.

Islam

Living Islam, by Akbar Ahmed. Highly recommended, a sensitive introduction to Islam by a Pakistani scholar who has dedicated himself to bridging the mutual ignorance and misunderstanding between the Muslim and non-Muslim worlds. It is based in part on a BBC television series.

Ethnography & Arts

The Arts and Crafts of Turkestan, by Jahannes Kalter. A detailed, beautifully illustrated, historical guide to the nomadic dwellings, clothing, jewellery and other 'applied art' of Central Asia. A similar work for anyone with a serious interest in traditional Turkmen ways and lifestyles is George O'Bannon's *The Turkoman Carpet.*

The Kazakhs, by Martha Brill Olcott. The ultimate English-language tome on that people, several hundred pages of great detail that could keep you quiet for many a long evening on the steppe.

The Mummies of Ürümchi, by Elizabeth Wayland Barber. This erudite but enjoyable book faces the politically sensitive question of why 3000-year-old mummies found in the Tarim basin are of Caucasoid origin. Focussing on fragments of weaving and embroidery, Barber painstakingly pieces together the fascinating history of Central Asia's early Indo-European migrations.

Flora & Fauna

Realms of the Russian Bear, by John Sparks. An elegant, beautifully illustrated work focusing on the flora and fauna of the old Soviet empire, including 80-plus pages on the Tian Shan mountains and Central Asia's steppes, deserts and seas.

Fiction

The Kyrgyz writer Chinghiz Aitmatov (born 1928) is among the few Central Asian writers whose stories are even remotely familiar to western readers. One of his earliest and best known books is *Djamila* (1967). Aitmatov lost his father in Stalin's purges and the loss of a father is a recurring theme, eg in the gripping 1978 novella *Piebald Dog Running Along the Shore* (made into a prize-winning Russian film in 1990), the 1970 *The White Steamship* and the 1975 *Early Cranes.* In *The Day Lasts Longer Than a Century* (1980) two boys witness the arrest by the NKVD of their father, who never returns. Aitmatov's *The Place of the Skull* (1986) confronted previously taboo subjects like drugs and religion and was an early attack on bureaucracy and environmental destruction. Many of his books have been translated into German and French and a few, like *Djamila* and *The Day Lasts Longer Than a Century,* are fairly easy to find in English.

Kim, by Rudyard Kipling. The master storyteller's classic epic of the Raj during the Great Game.

Perhaps also worth a look are various novels that use Central Asia as a backdrop, including Brian Aldiss' *Somewhere East of Life,* set in Ashgabat; Amin Malouf's *Samarkand,* a fictionalised account of the life of the Persian poet and mathematician Omar Khayyam; and Alexander M Grace's *Sky Blue,* a political thriller set in Kazakstan.

Bookshops

You won't find very much in English at any of the bookshops in Central Asia. Searchable sites such as Amazon (www.amazon .com), Waterstones (www.waterstones.co .uk) and Barnes & Noble (www.bn.com) can be a useful resource for tracking down books and receiving them via post.

The following bookshops have the best selection for Central Asia.

Adventurous Traveller Bookstore
American online travel bookstore, claims to have the world's largest colle travel books and guides. Web site w .com/atbook.htm.

Chessler Books
(☎ 800-654 8502, 303-670 0093, fax 303-670 9727, @ chesslerbk@aol.com)
PO Box 4359, Evergreen, CO 80437, USA – new and used books and maps; send for a catalogue. Web site www.chesslerbooks.com.
The Complete Traveller
(☎ 212-685 9007)
199 Madison Avenue, New York 10016
Distant Lands
(☎ 626-449 3220, fax 310 3220)
56 So. Raymond Ave, Pasadena, CA 91105.
Web site www.distantlands.com.
Edward Stanford
(☎ 020-7836 1321, fax 836 0189)
12-14 Long Acre, Covent Garden, London WC2E 9LP, UK.
The Travel Bookshop
(☎ 0171-229 5260, fax 243 1552, @ post@thetravelbookshop.co.uk)
13-15 Blenheim Crescent, W11 2EE, London; Web site www.thetravelbookshop.co.uk.
Zwemmer
(☎ 020-7379 6253)
28 Denmark St, London WC2H 8NJ – devoted to the former USSR and Eastern Europe, with a fair range of current Central Asia titles. You can send for their catalogue.

FILMS

Lonely Planet produces a video featuring Uzbekistan and Kyrgyzstan, starring Ian Wright in top form riding with eagle hunters and trying to keep down sheep's eyeballs. Travellers have recommended a recent documentary on Kyrgyzstan called *Where the Sky Meets the Land*.

For a rundown of locally made films, see the Arts section in the Facts about Central Asia chapter.

NEWSPAPERS & MAGAZINES

The Kazakstan press is theoretically free, but stories unfavourable to the powerful are scarce except in *Karavan*, the weekly Russian-language paper, which has broken several scandals. The Almaty Herald can be viewed online at www.herald.asdc.kz/. English-language magazines are occasionally produced locally – the ones to look out for are *...s Central Asia* and *All Over the Globe*. ...Kyrgyzstan some international English-...ge papers and magazines can be found ...restaurants in Bishkek. The *Times of*

Central Asia (Web site www.times.elcat.kg) is an eight page English-language weekly sold in tourist hotels and bookshops in Bishkek, with news and features aimed at business people and Central Asia watchers, and a strong editorial line on rounding up crooks.

Foreign journalists crazy enough to set up in what the *Economist* calls Uzbekistan's 'information-free capital, Tashkent' are constantly harassed and intimidated. The officially 'free' Uzbek press is monitored to ensure conformity and is frequently used to denounce foreign journalists critical of the state. The Tashkent expat newsletter *Odds & Ads* has useful listings of restaurants and cultural events.

The printed media are very unhealthy in both Tajikistan and Turkmenistan. Neither country has outright censorship, but if a paper is not singing the right tune, essential supplies like newsprint and ink suddenly become hard to find. There is nothing published in English in Tajikistan, nor anything in Turkmenistan apart from one glossy cultural magazine, *Tourism & Development*, with some interesting, but slightly garbled, articles in English.

Western news magazines such as the *Economist*, *Newsweek*, *International Herald Tribune*, plus major German and French newspapers, are available in Tashkent and Almaty.

National Geographic has published several interesting articles on Xinjiang, including an excellent March 1996 general article on the province, an April 1996 photo-article on Kyzyl caves in Xinjiang and an early March 1980 look at Xinjiang just after China opened to the West. Articles on ex-Soviet Central Asia include a December 1996 look at the Mongol conquests (with several reports from Central Asia) and an August 1986 piece on the ascent of Pobedy peak in Kyrgyzstan. A January 1984 article examined silk and the Silk Road. A September 1999 photo-essay focussed on the Kazak eagle-hunters of Mongolia's Bayan-Olgiy province.

Foreign scholarly periodicals on Central Asia include the American *Central Asian Monitor* and British *Central Asian Survey*.

RADIO

Bring your short wave radio if you want to keep up with the outside world. Nothing in English (other than Radio Moscow) seems to be actually beamed *towards* Central Asia, so reception is often poor. The strongest reception comes from Radio Australia, followed by Voice of America (VOA) and the BBC World Service.

Look for the BBC World Service around MHz 17.64, 15.565, 12.095, 11.97, 11.76, 9.410, 6.195 or 3.955, and VOA at 17.74, 15.20, 9.760, 1.548, 1.260 or 6.045. VOA can also be found on 1341 KHz medium wave in Almaty.

For current schedule and frequency information, contact:

BBC
  (☎ 020-7240 3456)
  PO Box 76, Bush House, London WC2B 4PH;
  Web site www.bbc.co.uk/worldservice/tuning/.
Radio Australia
  (☎ 03-9626 1825, ✉ raust@ozemail.com.au)
  PO Box 428G, Melbourne, Vic 3001;
  Web site www.abc.net.au/ra/.
Voice of America
  (fax 202-619 0211) VOA,
  Washington, DC 20547; Web site www.voa.gov/.

In Almaty and some other cities in Kazakstan the main pop music channel is Radio Khavar on 102.2 FM. It sometimes has English-language programs.

TV

In the popularity stakes the soaps and glitzy cabaret shows of Moscow One and Ostankino, beamed from Russia, win hands down over the dour national channels. At 7.30 pm Moscow time (9.30 or 10.30 pm in Central Asia) most sets are tuned to *Dika Rosa*, a hugely popular Mexican soap opera dubbed into Russian, featuring the misadventures of the eponymous heroine, a former street urchin married to a rich socialite

Uzbekistan has five channels – one from Russia and two each from Tashkent and Samarkand – but with little of interest other than concerts, and dubbed western films. BBC World Service News, over-dubbed with Uzbek, is on Tashkent-2 late in the evening.

In Kyrgyzstan, channel 1 is Kyrgyz TV, 2 and 3 are from Moscow, 4 from Turkey, and 5 is the private Pyramid channel, broadcasting alternately from Almaty and Tashkent with news, music videos, and dubbed B-grade movies from overseas.

Most places in Kazakstan should be able to pick up at least two TV channels, the main one being Khavar, the prime commercial channel (owned by one of President Nazarbaev's daughters) broadcast out of Almaty, which shows a mixture of news, documentaries, game shows and poorly over-dubbed foreign films. There'll often be a Russian-language channel, especially in the major cities and close to the border in northern Kazakstan.

Turkmen TV is quite bizarre. The logos for TVT1 and TVT2 are both golden profiles of Turkmenbashi, and both channels seem to feature the same mix of traditional musicians singing about Turkmenbashi, and young girls singing awful Europop tunes about Turkmenbashi.

PHOTOGRAPHY & VIDEO
Film & Equipment

Most department stores have Kodak franchise outlets that sell 35mm print film and some Ektachrome (but not Kodachrome) slide film and video cassettes, but prices are high, so it's wise to bring your own (more than you think you'll need – Central Asia is a photographer's dream). It's safest to get film developed at home too, though most of the above franchises can develop print film (Kodak C41 process) for prices in line with their film prices.

Xinjiang department stores have cheap Chinese film (Fujicolor and Konica), though processing is second-rate and dusty. Posting film from anywhere in Central Asia is asking for trouble; take it home or to a reliable place like Hong Kong for posting or processing.

Equipment is a personal matter, but with an SLR camera, a mid-range zoom (eg 35mm to 135mm) covers a wide range of situations; a good second lens might be 28mm for panoramas and indoors. Strong summer sunlight has a tendency to bleach out shots, so anybody serious about photography should pack the relevant filters. Similarly, when shooting in the mountains you get the best results with a UV or skylight filter and a lens shade.

Technical Tips

Heat To avoid magenta-tinted memories of Central Asia, keep film away from heat. If you line a stuff-sack with a patch cut from an aluminised 'survival blanket', film will stay cool inside even on fierce summer days.

Cold & Condensation Camera batteries get sluggish in the cold, which can be a problem on mountain treks. Carry the camera inside your coat and keep some spare batteries warm in your pocket. In very cold weather, avoid ruinous moisture on film and inside the camera by putting them in plastic bags *before* going indoors, and leaving them there until they're warm.

Dust Some back roads are a wallow of fine dust that gets into everything. Keep everything bagged up and carry a squeeze-bulb for blowing dust from inside the camera.

Restrictions

There are no significant customs limits on camera equipment and film for personal use.

There are few major restrictions on what you can photograph in Central Asia any more, though military installations and border zones are still taboo. Surprisingly, so is the Tashkent Metro (beware the red-capped attendants). Some museums and galleries forbid flash photography.

In China you can't photograph military sites, factories, airports, railway stations or bridges, and often there are people nearby who'll collar you and take your film. You're not supposed to take pictures from aeroplanes but there's never been a report of a flight attendant swooping down on anybody. Some older Chinese shy away from cameras but nearly everyone loves having their kids photographed.

Photographing People

...fetime with the KGB has made many ...r people uneasy about having their pic-

ture taken. Many people are also touchy about you photographing embarrassing subjects like drunks, run-down housing or consumer queues. You may find people sensitive about you photographing women, especially in rural areas and even among Ismailis; if a husband or brother is nearby it's risky as well. Women photographers may get away with it if they've established some rapport. The Russian for 'may I take a photograph?' is *fotografirovat mozhno?* ('fa-ta-gruh-**fee**-ra-vut **mozh**-na?').

Airport Security

One dose of airport x-rays won't harm slow or medium-speed films, but the effects are cumulative and too much will fog your pictures. Lead 'film-safe' pouches help, but the best solution is hand inspection. Officials will hate you for asking but most will do it if you persist. Having all your film in one or two clear plastic bags makes it easier.

Video

Properly used, a video camera can give a fascinating record of your holiday. As well as recording the obvious things, remember that, unlike still photography, video 'flows' – so, for example, you can shoot scenes of countryside rolling past the train window to give an overall impression that isn't possible with ordinary photos.

Bringing a video camera into Central Asia is a tricky proposition. There are very few video cartridges available along the way and electricity in most cities is unreliable at best, so recharging a battery pack can be a problem. Furthermore, extreme heat can be disastrous for tapes, severe cold can drain batteries, and sand can make the camera freeze up altogether. Finally, be prepared to dismantle the camera completely in front of customs officials and avoid all x-ray machines.

If you still want to try recording your Central Asia experience then be sure you have a quality camera. Bring enough tapes, at least two four-hour batteries, battery charger, electricity converter and plugs, and a battery eraser (if you recharge batteries before they are empty they may develop a 'memory', limiting the charge capacity). Also bring a good lockable, hard-sided carrying case, and the service manual.

Declare the camera on customs forms and carry it by hand through customs, but don't leave the tape in it as it may be confiscated. Drain and recharge both batteries anytime you find a reliable source of electricity. And of course, label your tapes.

Finally, remember to follow the same rules regarding people's sensitivities as for still photography – having a video camera shoved in their face is probably even more annoying and offensive for locals than a still camera. Always ask permission first.

TIME

The official time in most of Central Asia is Greenwich Mean Time (GMT) plus five hours, but giant Kazakstan straddles GMT plus four, five and six hours. All China officially runs on Beijing time (GMT plus eight hours), though Kashgar also runs unofficially on 'Xinjiang time' (two hours earlier) which means visitors must keep track of both.

To complicate matters, Kazakstan and Kyrgyzstan have Daylight Savings Time (DST), setting their clocks forward by one hour from the last Sunday in March until the last Sunday in September. Tajikistan, Turkmenistan, Uzbekistan and China don't have DST.

Countries outside Central Asia switch to DST on their own schedules, so in early spring and early autumn, expect other one-hour differences to come and go.

Timetables

Amazingly, trains (but not buses or flights) in Kazakstan and Kyrgyzstan were still running on Moscow time at the time of research.

ELECTRICITY

The entire former USSR is the same – nominal 220v at 50 cycles, using European two-pin plugs (round pins, with no earth connection) everywhere. Bring candles and a torch (flashlight) – light bulbs are in short supply. Chinese plugs are the same, but often also have two flat pins (American Style), three-pronged angled pins (Australian-style), and, sometimes, three rectangular pins (British style). Adaptors are available in department stores.

WEIGHTS & MEASURES

Central Asia is metric. When buying produce in markets make sure you know whether the price is per piece *(shtuk)* or by the kilo. It's also worth knowing that while Russian dictionaries define *choot choot* as 'a little bit', when applied to a shot of vodka it would appear to mean 'up to the rim'.

LAUNDRY

Nearly all hotels have a place where the bed linen and towels are washed; there you're sure to find someone who can do washing and ironing fairly cheaply. In better hotels, just ask your floor-lady, who might do it herself. Figure on about US$0.50 per piece. But don't give her anything you're particularly fond of; one female traveller got her pair of leggings back, hacked off at the knees.

Of course you can do it yourself, but be sure to bring a universal sink plug, since almost no hotel bathrooms have them. Laundry soap is easy to find in department stores or markets of larger towns. *Banyas* (bathhouses) can be a great place to wash your self and your clothes.

You'll find occasional dry-cleaning sh in the cities, but you take your chances the quality of the job.

TOILETS

Public toilets are as scarce as h Those that you can find – eg ir

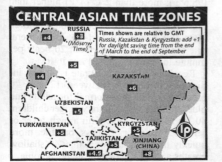

CENTRAL ASIAN TIME ZONES

RUSSIA +4 (Moscow Time)

Times shown are relative to GMT
Russia, Kazakstan & Kyrgyzstan: add +1 for daylight saving time from the end of March to the end of September

+3

+5

+4

KAZAKSTAN +6

UZBEKISTAN +5

TURKMENISTAN +5

KYRGYZSTAN +5

TAJIKISTAN +5

XINJIANG (CHINA) +8

AFGHANISTAN +4.5

bus and train stations – charge the equivalent of US$0.10 or so to use their squatters, either flush or pit. Most are fairly awful. Some have someone out front selling sheets of toilet paper. Capitalism may prevail, however; a few privately run toilets have already appeared, where you pay more and get paper, running water, soap and reasonable hygiene. Carry a small pencil-torch for restaurant toilets, which rarely seem to have functioning lights, and for trips out to the pit toilet in the back. Always have an emergency stash of toilet paper on your person.

Toilet paper appears sporadically for sale in markets and department stores, buy a roll whenever you are running low. Flush systems don't like toilet paper (some people don't even seem to like it in their pit toilets). The waste-basket in the loo is for used paper and tampons (wrapped in toilet paper).

In Russian look for '‎Ж', meaning zhenski for women or 'M', meaning muzhskoy for men. In Xinjiang the symbols are:

men: 男   women: 女

HEALTH

Travel health depends on your pre-departure preparations, your daily health care while travelling and how you handle any medical problem that does develop. While the following potential dangers can seem quite frightening, in reality few travellers experience anything more than an upset stomach in Central Asia.

Summary of Risks

Gut infections, in particular hepatitis A and undulant fever (from bacteria in unpasteurised milk products), are a significant risk, but are easily avoidable with good sense. Hepatitis B is avoidable with care about unprotected sex and the use of needles. There are also effective vaccines for hepatitis A and B, as well as for other diseases considered significant in at least some areas – diphtheria, typhoid and, less importantly, cholera, tuberculosis, polio and tetanus. A low malaria risk exists in the lowland southern border regions of Tajikistan and Afghanistan. Rabies has been reported in the region.

With falling health rates, many diseases formerly eradicated or controlled in the time of the USSR have returned. TB and diphtheria are up 100% in much of the region. In 1994 the World Health Organization noted large increases in TB deaths in Turkmenistan and Kyrgyzstan, and a diphtheria epidemic hit Kyrgyzstan in 1996. Southern Kazakstan experienced a hepatitis A epidemic in 1998. In 1999 cases of anthrax were discovered in Kostanay (Kazakstan), and around Osh (southern Kyrgyzstan), cases of Crimean-Congo haemorrhagic fever (a tick-borne disease) were detected around Taraz (Kazakstan) and there were several outbreaks of bubonic plague in Aktau and Kyzylorda, both also in Kazakstan.

Tick-borne haemorrhagic fever also occurs in Afghanistan, and there have also been occurrences of typhus in parts of Afghanistan. Cutaneous leishmaniasis occurs in Afghanistan and Tajikistan; there has been a recent resurgence of visceral leishmaniasis in Xinjiang and China.

Trekkers must of course beware of hypothermia and altitude sickness, and be cautious in tick habitats (high grass and woodlands) to avoid two tick-borne diseases, haemorrhagic fever and Lyme disease, for which there are no vaccines. Rabies is significant, mainly in connection with guard dogs in remote areas. For more information about any of these diseases, see the relevant entry later in this section.

Everyday Health

Normal body temperature ranges up to 37°C (98.6°F); more than 2°C (4°F) higher than this indicates a high fever. The normal adult pulse rate is 60 to 100 per minute (children 80 to 100, babies 100 to 140). As a general rule the pulse increases about 20 beats per minute for each 1°C (2°F) rise in fever.

Respiration (breathing) rate is also an indicator of illness – between 12 and 20 breaths per minute is normal for adults and older children (up to 30 for younger children, 40 for babies). People with a high fever or serious respiratory illness breathe more quickly than normal. More than 40 shallow breaths a minute may indicate pneumonia.

Health Regulations

Kazakstan and Uzbekistan require visitors staying longer than 90 days to present a medical certificate, less than one month old, proving that they are HIV negative. Turkmenistan has similar legislation pending. Kyrgyzstan theoretically demands a similar test after 30 days, but this regulation is rarely enforced. Visitors staying in China longer than six months must give proof of a negative HIV test when they apply for a visa.

In Kazakstan you can get an AIDS test at the Center for Prevention and Control of AIDS at 7 Talgarskaya in Almaty.

Predeparture Planning

Immunisations It is recommended that you seek medical advice at least six weeks before travel. Some jabs cannot be given simultaneously, some require more than one injection, and some take weeks or months for the onset of full protection. Be aware that there is often a greater risk of disease with children and during pregnancy. Make sure you discuss this with your doctor.

No immunisations are mandatory for travellers to Central Asia, but a yellow fever vaccination certificate is required for entry to Kazakstan and Afghanistan if you are coming from an infected area. You should consider the kind of protection you would want for off-the-beaten-track travel anywhere in Asia. Most western travellers will have been immunised in childhood against measles, polio and 'DPT' (diphtheria, pertussis and tetanus), and you should get any boosters necessary to bring you up to date with these. Children of any age should be immunised against tuberculosis.

Several private travel clinics, such as BA Travel Clinics (for locations call ☎ 01276-685040) or Trailfinders clinic (☎ 020-7938 3999) in London, can provide information and cheap immunisations.

Carry proof of your vaccinations, especially yellow fever. They're best recorded on an official-looking International Health Certificate, available from your physician or government health authority – some border officials are especially fond of these.

Discuss your requirements with your doctor, but vaccinations you should consider for this trip include the following (for more details about the diseases themselves, see the individual disease entries later in this section).

Cholera The current injectable vaccine against cholera is poorly protective and has many side effects, so it is not generally recommended for travellers. However, in some situations it may be necessary to have a certificate as travellers are very occasionally asked by immigration officials to present one, even though all countries and the WHO have dropped cholera immunisation as a health requirement for entry.

Diphtheria & Tetanus Diphtheria immunisation is highly recommended for travel anywhere in the former USSR. Vaccinations for these two diseases are usually combined and are recommended for everyone. After an initial course of three injections (usually given in childhood), boosters are necessary every 10 years.

Hepatitis A Hepatitis A vaccine (eg Avaxim, Havrix 1440 or VAQTA) provides long-term immunity (possibly more than 10 years) after an initial injection and a booster at six to 12 months.

Alternatively, an injection of gamma globulin can provide short-term protection against hepatitis A – two to six months, depending on the dose given. It is not a vaccine, it is a ready-made antibody collected from blood donations. It is reasonably effective and, unlike the vaccine, it is protective immediately, but because it is a blood product, there are current concerns about its long-term safety.

Hepatitis A vaccine is also available in a combined form, Twinrix, with hepatitis B vaccine. Three injections over a six month period are required, the first two providing substantial protection against hepatitis A.

Hepatitis B Travellers who should consider vaccination against hepatitis B include those on a long trip, as well as those visiting countries where there are high levels of hepatitis B infection, where blood transfusions may not be adequately screened, or where sexual contact or needle sharing is a possibility. Vaccination involves three injections, with a booster at 12 months. More rapid courses are available i necessary.

Malaria Medication Malaria is only prevalen parts of Afghanistan and southern Tajikista altitudes below 2000m, from May to Nove

Antimalarial drugs do not prevent yo being infected but kill the malaria during a stage in their development nificantly reduce the risk of becomi or dying. Expert advice on medication should be sought, as there are many factors to consider, including the area to be visited, the risk of exposure to malaria-carrying mosquitoes, the side effects of medication, your medical history and whether you are a child, an adult or pregnant. Travellers to isolated areas in high-risk countries may like to carry a treatment dose of medication for use if symptoms occur.

Meningococcal Meningitis Vaccination is recommended for travellers to Tajikistan and possibly other areas. A single injection gives good protection against the major epidemic forms of the disease for three years. Protection may be less effective in children under two years.

Polio Everyone should keep up to date with this vaccination, which is normally given in childhood. A booster every 10 years maintains immunity.

Rabies Rabies has been detected in Central Asia, but it is not common. Vaccination should be considered by those who will spend a month or longer in rural areas, especially if they are cycling, handling animals, caving or travelling to remote areas, and for children (who may not report a bite). Pretravel rabies vaccination involves having three injections over 21 to 28 days. If someone who has been vaccinated is bitten or scratched by an animal, they will require two booster injections of vaccine; those not vaccinated require more.

Tick-Borne Encephalitis Recommended if you plan some long treks in Central Asia. A treatment of three shots gives full protection.

Tuberculosis TB is on the rise in Central Asia, though the risk to travellers is relatively low, unless you will be living with or closely associated with local people. Vaccination against TB (BCG) is recommended for children and young adults living in Central Asia for three months or more.

Typhoid Vaccination against typhoid may be required if you are travelling for more than a couple of weeks. It is now available either as an injection or as capsules to be taken orally.

A combined hepatitis/typhoid vaccine has recently been developed, although its availability is limited – check with your doctor to find out its status in your country.

Yellow Fever A yellow fever vaccine is now the only vaccine that is a legal requirement for entry into Afghanistan and Kazakstan, usually only enforced when coming from an infected area. Vaccination is recommended for travel in areas where the disease is endemic (parts of Africa and South America). You may have to go to a special yellow fever vaccination centre.

Health Insurance Make sure that you have adequate health insurance. See the Travel Insurance entry in the Visas & Documents section of this chapter for details.

Travel Health Guides If you are planning to be away or travelling in remote areas for a long period of time, you may like to consider taking a more detailed health guide.

CDC's Complete Guide to Healthy Travel, Open Road Publishing, 1997. Lists the US Center for Disease Control & Prevention recommendations for international travel.

Staying Healthy in Asia, Africa & Latin America, by Dirk Schroeder, Moon Publications, 1994. A good all-round guide; it's detailed and well organised.

Travel with Children, by Maureen Wheeler, Lonely Planet Publications, 1995. Includes advice on travel health for younger children.

Travellers' Health, by Dr Richard Dawood, Oxford University Press, 1995. Comprehensive, easy to read, authoritative and highly recommended, although it's rather large to lug around.

Where There Is No Doctor, by David Werner, Macmillan, 1994. A very detailed guide intended for someone, such as a Peace Corps worker, going to work in an underdeveloped country.

Other Travel Advice Medical Advisory Services for Travellers Abroad (MASTA), a private UK group associated with the London School of Hygiene & Tropical Medicine, has a travellers' health line (☎ 0891-224100) where you can order a basic 'health brief' with information on immunisations, malaria, Foreign Office advisories and health news, for the cost of the (premium-rate) call. They also offer more detailed briefs for long or complex trips, plus mail-order health supplies. Also in the UK, the Malaria Reference Laboratory has a 24 hour premium-rate help line at ☎ 0891-600 350.

MASTA in Australia (☎ 02-971 1499, fax 971 0239), associated with the Tropical Health Program of the University of Queensland, offers similar services. Alternatively, call the Australian Government Health Service or a clinic like the Travellers' Medical & Vaccination Centre (☎ 03-9670 3969) at Level 2, 393 Little Bourke St, Melbourne, Victoria.

In the USA the Center for Disease Control & Prevention has a travellers' hotline (☎ 877-394 8747), or call the International Medicine Program at Cornell University Medical Center in New York (☎ 212-746 5454). Another resource is the International Association for Medical Assistance to Travellers (☎ 716-754 4883), 417 Center St, Lewiston, NY 14092.

There are also a number of excellent travel health sites on the Internet. From the Lonely Planet home page there are links at www.lonelyplanet.com/weblinks/wlprep.htm#heal to the World Health Organization (www.who.int) and the US Center for Disease Control & Prevention (www.cdc.gov). Canada's Laboratory Centre for Disease Control has a Web site at www.hc-sc.gc.ca/hpb/lcdc.

Other Preparations Make sure you're healthy before you start travelling. If you are going on a long trip make sure your teeth are OK. There are few good dentists anywhere in Central Asia (as evidenced by nations of gold-clad teeth). If you wear glasses take a spare pair and your prescription.

If you require a particular medication take an adequate supply, as it may not be available locally. Take part of the packaging showing the generic name rather than the brand, which will make getting replacements easier. It's a good idea to have a legible prescription or letter from your doctor to show that you legally use the medication to avoid any problems.

Basic Rules

Food There is an old colonial adage that says: 'If you can cook it, boil it or peel it you can eat it .. otherwise forget it'. Vegetables and fruit should be washed with purified water or peeled where possible. Beware of ice cream that is sold in the street or anywhere it might have been melted and refrozen; if there's any doubt (eg a power cut in the last day or two), steer well clear. Avoid undercooked meat, particularly in the form of mince; have your shashlyk cooked fresh in front of you, and look for a refrigerator. Use your own utensils whenever possible.

Medical Kit Check List

Following is a list of items you should consider including in your medical kit – consult your pharmacist for brands available in your country.

- ☐ **Aspirin or paracetamol (acetaminophen in the USA)** – for pain or fever
- ☐ **Antihistamine** – for allergies, eg, hay fever; to ease the itch from insect bites or stings; and to prevent motion sickness
- ☐ **Cold and flu tablets, throat lozenges and nasal decongestant**
- ☐ **Multivitamins** – consider for long trips, when dietary vitamin intake may be inadequate
- ☐ **Antibiotics** – consider including these if you're travelling well off the beaten track; see your doctor, as they must be prescribed, and carry the prescription with you
- ☐ **Loperamide or diphenoxylate** – 'blockers' for diarrhoea
- ☐ **Prochlorperazine or metaclopramide** – for nausea and vomiting
- ☐ **Rehydration mixture** – to prevent dehydration, which may occur, for example, during bouts of diarrhoea; particularly important when travelling with children
- ☐ **Insect repellent, sunscreen, lip balm and eye drops**
- ☐ **Calamine lotion, sting relief spray or aloe vera** – to ease irritation from sunburn and insect bites or stings
- ☐ **Antifungal cream or powder** – for fungal skin infections and thrush
- ☐ **Antiseptic (such as povidone-iodine)** – for cuts and grazes
- ☐ **Bandages, Band-Aids (plasters) and other wound dressings**
- ☐ **Water purification tablets or iodine**
- ☐ **Scissors, tweezers and a thermometer** – note that mercury thermometers are prohibited by airlines
- ☐ **Syringes and needles** – in case you need injections in a country with medical hygiene problems; ask your doctor for a note explaining why you have them

If a place looks clean and well run and the vendor also looks clean and healthy, then the food is probably safe. In general, places that are packed with travellers or locals will be fine, while empty restaurants are questionable. The food in busy restaurants is cooked and eaten quite quickly with little standing around and has probably not been reheated.

Water The number one rule is *be careful of the water* (including brushing your teeth) and especially ice. If you don't know for certain that the water is safe, assume the worst. You should definitely avoid drinking the tap water in the Karakalpakstan and Khorezm regions of Uzbekistan and most of remoter Kazakstan. Even in the mountains streams may be contaminated with giardia parasites (see the following Diarrhoea entry in this section for more information).

Reputable brands of bottled water or soft drinks are generally fine, although in some places bottles may be refilled with tap water. Only use water from containers with a serrated seal – not tops or corks. Take care with fruit juice, particularly if water may have been added. Milk and nomadic-inspired dairy products should be treated with suspicion as they are unpasteurised, though boiled milk is fine if it is kept hygienically. Tea or coffee should also be OK, since the water should have been boiled.

Water Purification The simplest way of purifying water is to boil it thoroughly. Vigorous boiling should be satisfactory; however, at high altitude water boils at a lower temperature, so germs are less likely to be killed. Boil it for longer in these environments.

Consider purchasing a water filter for a long trip. There are two main kinds of filter. Total filters take out all parasites, bacteria and viruses and make water safe to drink. They are often expensive, but they can be more cost effective than buying bottled water. Simple filters (which can even be a in mesh bag) take out dirt and larger n bodies from the water so that chemical solutions work much more effectively; is dirty, chemical solutions may not work at all. It's very important when buying a filter to read the specifications, so that you know exactly what it removes from the water and what it doesn't. Simple filtering will not remove all dangerous organisms, so if you cannot boil water it should be treated chemically. Chlorine tablets will kill many pathogens, but not some parasites like giardia and amoebic cysts. Iodine is more effective in purifying water and is available in tablet form. Follow the directions carefully and remember that too much iodine can be harmful.

Nutrition You're likely to find enough edible and fairly healthy food at most bazars, but the difficulty of finding decent eateries off the beaten track can lead you to skip meals, lose weight and put your health at risk. Keep your diet balanced – eggs, beans, lentils and nuts are safe protein sources; fruit and vegies that you can peel are normally safe and a vitamin-mineral supplement is not a bad idea. Make sure you drink enough – don't rely on feeling thirsty to indicate when you should drink.

Medical Problems & Treatment

Self-diagnosis and treatment can be risky, so you should always seek medical help. Tashkent, Almaty, Atyrau (in western Kazakstan) and Bishkek all have decent clinics; see the relevant country chapters for details. An embassy, consulate or five star hotel can usually recommend a local doctor or clinic (see the Embassies & Consulates entry in the relevant country chapter for details). Some public hospitals have agreements for the treatment of foreigners. In remote areas (especially in Tajikistan) you may find a western-trained doctor working for one of the relief agencies. In general if you require hospitalisation you should consider evacuation – one reason why a comprehensive insurance policy is essential.

Although drug dosages are given in this section, they are for emergency use only. Correct diagnosis is vital. This section uses the generic names for medications – check with a pharmacist for brands available locally. In Central Asia a pharmacist is known as an *upteka* in Russian, or *dorikhana* in Turkic. Clinics are widely known as *poliklinik*.

Note that antibiotics should ideally be administered only under medical supervision. Take only the recommended dose at the prescribed intervals and use the whole course, even if the illness seems to be cured earlier. Stop immediately if there are any serious reactions and don't use the antibiotic at all if you are unsure that you have the correct one. Some people are allergic to commonly prescribed antibiotics such as penicillin; carry this information (eg on a bracelet) when travelling.

Environmental Hazards

Altitude Sickness This is a particular problem in high-altitude regions of Kazakstan, Kyrgyzstan, Tajikistan and south-east Xinjiang. With motorable roads climbing passes of up to 4700m, it's a problem not just restricted to trekkers.

Lack of oxygen at high altitudes (over 2500m) affects most people to some extent. The effect may be mild or severe and occurs because less oxygen reaches the muscles and the brain at high altitude, requiring the heart and lungs to compensate by working harder.

Symptoms of Acute Mountain Sickness (AMS) usually develop during the first 24 hours at altitude, but may be delayed up to three weeks. Mild symptoms include headache, lethargy, dizziness, difficulty sleeping and loss of appetite. AMS may become more severe without warning and can be fatal. Severe symptoms include breathlessness, a dry, irritative cough (which may progress to the production of pink, frothy sputum), severe headache, lack of coordination and balance, confusion, irrational behaviour, vomiting, drowsiness and unconsciousness. There is no hard-and-fast rule as to what is too high – AMS has been fatal at 3000m, although 3500 to 4500m is the usual range.

Treat mild symptoms by resting at the same altitude until recovery, usually a day or two. Paracetamol or aspirin can be taken for headaches. If symptoms persist or become worse, however, *immediate descent is necessary*; even 500m can help. Drug treatments should never be used to avoid descent or to enable further ascent.

The drugs acetazolamide (Diamox) and dexamethasone are recommended by some doctors for the prevention of AMS, but their use is controversial. They can reduce the symptoms, but they may also mask warning signs; severe and fatal AMS has occurred in people taking these drugs. In general we do not recommend them for travellers.

To prevent acute mountain sickness:

- Ascend slowly – take frequent rest days, spending two to three nights at each rise of 1000m. If you reach a high altitude by trekking, acclimatisation takes place gradually and you are less likely to be affected than if you fly directly to high altitude.
- It is always wise to sleep at a lower altitude than the greatest height reached during the day if possible. Also, once above 3000m, care should be taken not to increase the sleeping altitude by more than 300m per day.
- Drink extra fluids. The mountain air is dry and cold and moisture is lost as you breathe. Evaporation of sweat may occur unnoticed and result in dehydration.
- Eat light, high-carbohydrate meals for more energy.
- Avoid alcohol, as it may increase the risk of dehydration.
- Avoid sedatives.

Heat Exhaustion Dehydration and salt deficiency can cause heat exhaustion. Take time to acclimatise to high temperatures, drink sufficient liquids and do not do anything too physically demanding.

Salt deficiency is characterised by fatigue, lethargy, headaches, giddiness and muscle cramps; salt tablets may help, but adding extra salt to your food is better.

Anhidrotic heat exhaustion is a rare form of heat exhaustion that is caused by an inability to sweat. It tends to affect people who have been in a hot climate for some time rather than newcomers. It can progress heatstroke. Treatment involves removal cooler climate.

Heatstroke This serious, occas fatal, condition can occur if the bod regulating mechanism breaks dov body temperature rises to dangerous levels. Long, continuous periods of exposure to high temperatures and insufficient fluids can leave you vulnerable to heatstroke.

The symptoms are feeling unwell, not sweating very much (or at all) and a high body temperature (39° to 41°C). Where sweating has ceased, the skin becomes flushed and red. Severe, throbbing headaches and lack of coordination will also occur, and the sufferer may be confused or aggressive. Eventually the victim will become delirious or convulse. Hospitalisation is essential, but in the interim get victims out of the sun, remove their clothing, cover them with a wet sheet or towel and then fan continually. Give fluids if they are conscious.

Hypothermia Too much cold can be just as dangerous as too much heat. If you are trekking at high altitudes or simply taking a long bus trip over mountains, particularly at night, be prepared. Along the Pamir Hwy in Tajikistan, Karakoram Highway in Xinjiang, and the road to the Torugart pass in Kyrgyzstan you should always be prepared for cold, wet or windy conditions even if you're just out walking or hitching.

Hypothermia occurs when the body loses heat faster than it can produce it and the core temperature of the body falls. It is surprisingly easy to progress from very cold to dangerously cold due to a combination of wind, wet clothing, fatigue and hunger, even if the air temperature is above freezing. It is best to dress in layers; silk, wool and some of the new artificial fibres are all good insulating materials. A hat is important, as a lot of heat is lost through the head. A strong, waterproof outer layer (and a 'space' blanket for emergencies) is essential. Carry basic supplies, including food containing simple sugars to generate heat quickly, and fluid to drink.

Symptoms of hypothermia are exhaus~n, numb skin (particularly toes and fins), shivering, slurred speech, irrational ʻolent behaviour, lethargy, stumbling, spells, muscle cramps and violent ɔf energy. Irrationality may take the sufferers claiming they are warm g to take off their clothes.

To treat mild hypothermia, first get the person out of the wind and/or rain, remove their clothing if it's wet and replace it with dry, warm clothing. Give them hot liquids – not alcohol – and some high-kilojoule, easily digestible food. Do not rub victims – instead, allow them to slowly warm themselves. This should be enough to treat the early stages of hypothermia. Early recognition and treatment of mild hypothermia is the only way to prevent severe hypothermia, which is a critical condition.

Jet Lag Jet lag is experienced when a person travels by air across more than three time zones (each time zone usually represents a one hour time difference). It occurs because many of the functions of the human body (such as temperature, pulse rate and emptying of the bladder and bowels) are regulated by internal 24-hour cycles. When we travel long distances rapidly, our bodies take time to adjust to the 'new time' of our destination, and we may experience fatigue, disorientation, insomnia, anxiety, impaired concentration and loss of appetite. These effects will usually be gone within three days of arrival, but to minimise the impact of jet lag:

• Rest for a couple of days prior to departure.
• Try to select flight schedules that minimise sleep deprivation; arriving late in the day means you can go to sleep soon after you arrive. For very long flights, try to organise a stopover.
• Avoid excessive eating (which bloats the stomach) and alcohol (which causes dehydration) during the flight. Instead, drink plenty of non-carbonated, nonalcoholic drinks such as fruit juice or water.
• Avoid smoking.
• Make yourself comfortable by wearing loose-fitting clothes and perhaps bringing an eye mask and ear plugs to help you sleep.
• Try to sleep at the appropriate time for the time zone you are travelling to.

Motion Sickness Eating lightly before and during a trip will reduce the chances of motion sickness. If you are prone to motion sickness try to find a place that minimises movement – near the wing on aircraft, close to midships on boats, near the centre on buses. Fresh air usually helps; reading and cigarette smoke don't. Commercial motion-sickness preparations, which can cause drowsiness, have to be taken before the trip commences. Ginger (available in capsule form) and peppermint (including mint-flavoured sweets) are natural preventatives.

Prickly Heat Prickly heat is an itchy rash caused by excessive perspiration trapped under the skin. It usually strikes people who have just arrived in a hot climate. Keeping cool, bathing often, drying the skin and using a mild talcum or prickly heat powder, or resorting to air-conditioning may help.

Sunburn In the deserts and mountains of Central Asia you can get sunburnt surprisingly quickly, even through cloud. Use a sunscreen, a hat and a barrier cream for your nose and lips. Calamine lotion or a commercial after sun preparation are good for mild sunburn. Protect your eyes with good quality sunglasses, particularly if you will be near water, sand or snow.

Infectious Diseases

Diarrhoea Simple things like a change of water, food or climate can all cause a mild bout of diarrhoea, but a few rushed toilet trips with no other symptoms is not indicative of a major problem.

Dehydration is the main danger with any diarrhoea, particularly in children or the elderly, as dehydration can occur quite quickly. Under all circumstances *fluid replacement* (at least equal to the volume being lost) is the most important thing to remember. Weak black tea with a little sugar, soda water, or soft drinks allowed to go flat and diluted 50% with clean water are all good. With severe diarrhoea a rehydrating solution is preferable to replace minerals and salts lost. Commercially available oral rehydration salts (ORS) are very useful; add them to boiled or bottled water. In an emergency you can make up a solution of six teaspoons of sugar and a half teaspoon of salt to a litre of boiled or bottled water. You need to drink at least the same volume of fluid that you are losing in bowel movements and vomiting. Urine is the best guide to the adequacy of

replacement – if you have small amounts of concentrated urine, you need to drink more. Keep drinking small amounts often. Stick to a bland diet while you recover.

Gut-paralysing drugs such as loperamide or diphenoxylate can be used to bring relief from the symptoms, although they do not actually cure the problem. Only use these drugs if you do not have access to toilets, eg if you *must* travel. Note that these drugs are not recommended for children under 12 years.

In certain situations antibiotics may be required – diarrhoea with blood or mucus (dysentery), any diarrhoea with fever, profuse watery diarrhoea, persistent diarrhoea that doesn't improve after 48 hours and severe diarrhoea. These suggest a more serious cause of diarrhoea and in these situations gut-paralysing drugs should be avoided.

In these situations, a stool test may be necessary to diagnose what bug is causing your diarrhoea, so you should seek medical help urgently. Where this is not possible the recommended drugs for bacterial diarrhoea (the most likely cause of severe diarrhoea in travellers) are norfloxacin 400mg twice daily for three days or ciprofloxacin 500mg twice daily for five days. These are not recommended for children or pregnant women. The drug of choice for children would be co-trimoxazole with dosage dependent on weight. A five day course is given. Ampicillin or amoxycillin may be given during pregnancy, but medical care is necessary.

Two other causes of persistent diarrhoea in travellers are giardiasis and amoebic dysentery.

Giardiasis is caused by a common parasite, *Giardia lamblia*. Symptoms include stomach cramps, nausea, a bloated stomach, watery, foul-smelling diarrhoea and frequent gas. Giardiasis can appear several weeks after you have been exposed to the parasite. The symptoms may disappear for a few days and then return, this can go on for several weeks.

Amoebic dysentery, caused by the protozoan *Entamoeba histolytica*, is characterised by a gradual onset of low diarrhoea, often with blood and Cramping abdominal pain and vom less likely than in other types of diarrhoea, and fever may not be present. It will persist until treated and may recur and cause other health problems.

You should seek medical advice if you think you have giardiasis or amoebic dysentery, but where this is not possible, tinidazole or metronidazole are the recommended drugs. Treatment is a 2g single dose of tinidazole or 250mg of metronidazole three times daily for five to 10 days.

Fungal Infections Fungal infections occur more commonly in hot weather and are usually found on the scalp, between the toes (athlete's foot) or fingers, in the groin and on the body (ringworm). You get ringworm (which is a fungal infection, not a worm) from infected animals or other people. Moisture encourages these infections.

To prevent fungal infections wear loose, comfortable clothes, avoid artificial fibres, wash frequently and dry yourself carefully. If you do get an infection, wash the infected area at least daily with a disinfectant or medicated soap and water, and rinse and dry well. Apply an antifungal cream or powder like tolnaftate. Try to expose the infected area to air or sunlight as much as possible and wash all towels and underwear in hot water. You should also change them often and let them dry in the sun.

Hepatitis Hepatitis is a general term for inflammation of the liver. It is a common disease worldwide. There are several different viruses that cause hepatitis, and they differ in the way that they are transmitted. The symptoms are similar in all forms of the illness, and include fever, chills, headache, fatigue, feelings of weakness and aches and pains, followed by loss of appetite, nausea, vomiting, abdominal pain, dark urine, light-coloured faeces, jaundiced (yellow) skin and ellowing of the whites of the eyes. People ᵃo have had hepatitis should avoid alcohol some time after the illness, as the liver s time to recover.

ᵃatitis A is transmitted by contami-ood and drinking water. You should dical advice, but there is not much

you can do apart from resting, drinking lots of fluids, eating lightly and avoiding fatty foods.

Hepatitis E is transmitted in the same way as hepatitis A; it can be particularly serious in pregnant women. Large epidemics can occur in the Central Asia region, generally causing mild hepatitis.

There are almost 300 million chronic carriers of **hepatitis B** in the world. It is spread through contact with infected blood, blood products or body fluids, for example through sexual contact, unsterilised needles and blood transfusions, or contact with blood via small breaks in the skin. Other risk situations include having a shave, tattoo or body piercing with contaminated equipment. The symptoms of hepatitis B may be more severe than type A and the disease can lead to long-term problems such as chronic liver damage, liver cancer or a long-term carrier state. **Hepatitis C and D** are spread in the same way as hepatitis B and can also lead to long-term complications.

There are vaccines against hepatitis A and B, but there are currently no vaccines against the other types of hepatitis. Following the basic rules about food and water (hepatitis A and E) and avoiding risk situations (hepatitis B, C and D) are important preventative measures.

HIV & AIDS Infection with the human immunodeficiency virus (HIV, or SPID in Central Asia) may lead to acquired immune deficiency syndrome (AIDS), which is a fatal disease. Any exposure to blood, blood products or body fluids may put the individual at risk. The disease is often transmitted through sexual contact or dirty needles – vaccinations, acupuncture, tattooing and body piercing can be potentially as dangerous as intravenous drug use. HIV/AIDS can also be spread through infected blood transfusions (Central Asian doctors administer on average 70 injections a day).

All the Central Asian republics have reported cases of AIDS, 80% of which have been contracted by drug users. The town of Temirtau near Karaghandy has 80% of all the HIV infected cases in Kazakstan.

Some republics, such as Uzbekistan and Kazakstan, require visitors who stay longer than three months to present a certificate that states that they are HIV-negative.

Some Central Asian countries cannot afford to screen blood used for transfusions, so if you need an injection, ask to see the syringe unwrapped in front of you, or take a needle and syringe pack with you. Fear of HIV infection should never preclude treatment for serious medical conditions.

Sexually Transmitted Infections HIV/AIDS and hepatitis B can be transmitted through sexual contact – see the relevant entries earlier in this section for more details. Other STIs include gonorrhoea, herpes and syphilis; all are on the rise in Central Asia. Sores, blisters or rashes around the genitals and discharges or pain when urinating are common symptoms. In some STIs, such as wart virus or chlamydia, symptoms may be less marked or not observed at all, especially in women. Chlamydia infection can cause infertility in men and women before any symptoms have been noticed. Syphilis symptoms eventually disappear completely but the infection continues and can cause severe problems in later years. While abstinence from sexual contact is the only 100% effective prevention, using condoms is also effective. Treatment of gonorrhoea and syphilis requires antibiotics. The different sexually transmitted infections each require specific antibiotics.

Typhoid Typhoid fever is a dangerous gut infection caused by contaminated water and food. Medical help must be sought.

In its early stages sufferers may feel they have a bad cold or flu on the way, as early symptoms are a headache, body aches and a fever that rises a little each day until it is around 40°C (104°F) or more. The victim's pulse is often slow relative to the degree of fever present – unlike a normal fever where the pulse increases. There may also be vomiting, abdominal pain, diarrhoea or constipation.

In the second week the high fever and slow pulse continue and a few pink spots may appear on the body; trembling, delirium, weakness, weight loss and dehydration may occur. Complications such as pneumonia, perforated bowel or meningitis may occur.

Rabies Rabies is a significant risk in Central Asia, spread by infected animals – most commonly dogs, but also cats, foxes and other animals, even cattle. Animal herders' guard dogs are a major risk. Rabies not treated before the onset of symptoms (a few days to as much as several years later) is almost always fatal. Avoid it simply by avoiding all animals, domestic or wild.

Any bite or scratch (or even a lick at the site of one) should be cleaned immediately and thoroughly with soap and running water and, if possible, with alcohol solution. If the offending animal cannot be caught alive or the owner cannot be identified (a rabid animal usually acts strangely and dies within a week), seek medical attention at once. A rabies vaccine is available.

Insect-Borne Diseases
Leishmaniasis and typhus are insect-borne diseases, which are prevalent in Central Asia (particularly Afghanistan), but they do not pose a great risk to travellers. For more information on them see the Less Common Diseases entry later in this section.

Malaria
This serious and potentially fatal disease is spread by mosquito bites. If you are travelling in endemic areas (southern Tajikistan and areas of Afghanistan under 2000m) it is extremely important to avoid mosquito bites and to take tablets to prevent this disease. Symptoms range from fever, chills and sweating, headache, diarrhoea and abdominal pains, to a vague feeling of ill-health. Seek medical help immediately if malaria is suspected. Without treatmen malaria can rapidly become more serio and can be fatal.

If medical care is not available, ma tablets can be used for treatment. You to use a malaria tablet that is differe the one you were taking when y tracted malaria. The standard t dose of mefloquine is two 250mg tablets and a further two six hours later. For Fansidar, it's a single dose of three tablets. If you were previously taking mefloquine and cannot obtain Fansidar, then other alternatives are Malarone (atovaquone-proguanil; four tablets once daily for three days), halofantrine (three doses of two 250mg tablets every six hours) or quinine sulphate (600mg every six hours). There is a greater risk of side effects with these dosages than in normal use if used with mefloquine, so medical advice is preferable. Be aware also that halofantrine is no longer recommended by the WHO as emergency stand-by treatment because of side effects, and should only be used if no other drugs are available.

Travellers are advised to prevent mosquito bites at all times. The main messages are:

- Wear light-coloured clothing.
- Wear long trousers and long-sleeved shirts.
- Use mosquito repellents containing the compound DEET on exposed areas (note that prolonged overuse of DEET may be harmful, especially to children, but its use is considered preferable to being bitten by disease-transmitting mosquitoes).
- Avoid perfumes or aftershave.
- Use a mosquito net impregnated with mosquito repellent (permethrin) – it may be worth taking your own.
- Impregnate clothes with permethrin to effectively deter mosquitoes and other insects

Japanese B Encephalitis This viral infection of the brain is transmitted by mosquitoes. Most cases occur in rural areas of China, as the virus exists in pigs and wading birds. Symptoms include fever, headache and alteration in consciousness. Hospitalisation is needed for correct diagnosis and treatment. There is a high mortality rate among those who have symptoms; of those who survive many are intellectually disabled.

s, Bites & Stings

& Scratches Wash well and treat any 'th an antiseptic such as povidone- Where possible avoid bandages and ds, which can keep wounds wet.

Bedbugs & Lice Bedbugs live in various places, but particularly in dirty mattresses and bedding, evidenced by spots of blood on bedclothes or on the wall. Bedbugs leave itchy bites in neat rows. Calamine lotion or a sting relief spray may help.

All lice cause itching and discomfort. They make themselves at home in your hair (head lice), your clothing (body lice) or in your pubic hair (crab lice). You catch lice through direct contact with infected people or by sharing combs, clothing and the like. Powder or shampoo treatment will kill the lice and infected clothing should then be washed in very hot, soapy water and left in the sun to dry.

Bites & Stings Bee and wasp stings are usually painful rather than dangerous. However, if people are allergic to them severe breathing difficulties may occur and require urgent medical care. Calamine lotion or a sting relief spray will give relief and ice packs will reduce the pain and swelling. There are some spiders with dangerous bites but antivenins are usually available. Scorpion stings are notoriously painful and in some parts of Asia, the Middle East and Central America they can actually be fatal. Scorpions often shelter in shoes or clothing.

Ticks You should always check all over your body if you have been walking through a potentially tick-infested area (most of alpine Central Asia), as ticks can cause skin infections and other more serious diseases. If a tick is found attached, press down around the tick's head with tweezers, grab the head and gently pull upwards. Avoid pulling the rear of the body as this may squeeze the tick's gut contents through the attached mouth parts into the skin, increasing the risk of infection and disease. Smearing chemicals on the tick will not make it let go and is not recommended.

Crimean-Congo Haemorrhagic Fever This severe viral illness is characterised by the sudden onset of intense fever, headache, aching limbs, bleeding gums and sometimes a rash of red dots on the skin, a week or two after being bitten by an infected tick. Though not all ticks are infected, it's a risk for trekkers and campers in Central Asia during the summer months.

There is no vaccine, so you need to know what to do about ticks (*kleshch* in Russian). Search for them during and after walking in scrubland, pasture or forests, where the little blighters hitch rides on anything passing by. If you find one on your skin, *don't* just pull it off, as that can leave the head in place and increase the risk of infection. If it has been there for some time, a red blotch may appear around the site.

A strong insect repellent may discourage ticks in the first place, and long trousers tucked into your socks will give them less flesh to burrow into.

Lyme Disease This tick-borne bacterial disease causes a form of arthritis. Infected ticks live on horses or deer, usually in rural areas in April through September. Along with a rash around the bite comes aching joints, and the disease can have serious long-term effects. There is no vaccine. See earlier in this section for what to do about ticks.

Tick-Borne Encephalitis This tick-transmitted viral disease of moderate to low risk occurs mainly from mid-May to mid-June or July. Symptoms – an enlarged red blotch at the bite site, headache, fever, stiffness, extreme weakness and tiredness, cold sweat and confusion – appear a week or two after being bitten, and it can be fatal if it's not treated fairly quickly. A vaccine is available. See earlier in this section for what to do about ticks.

Snakes To minimise your chances of being bitten always wear boots, socks and long trousers when walking through undergrowth where snakes may be present. Don't put your hands into holes and crevices, and be careful when collecting firewood.

Snake bites do not cause instantaneous death and antivenins are usually available. Immediately wrap the bitten limb tightly, as you would for a sprained ankle, and then attach a splint to immobilise it. Keep the victim still and seek medical help, if possible with the dead snake for identification. Don't attempt to catch the snake in the possibility of being bitten again. Tourniquets and sucking out the poison are now comprehensively discredited.

Less Common Diseases

The following diseases pose a small risk to travellers, and so are only mentioned in passing. Seek medical advice if you think you may have any of these diseases.

Cholera Though all countries have dropped cholera immunisation as a requirement, there have been small outbreaks in Kazakstan, Tajikistan and China. Also, travellers often face bureaucratic problems over it (eg on entering China, and also on coming from African or Latin American countries), so it can help to have it on your certificate. Protection is limited and lasts only three to six months.

Cholera is the worst of the watery diarrhoeas and medical help should be sought. Outbreaks of cholera are generally widely reported, so you can avoid such problem areas. *Fluid replacement is the most vital treatment* – the risk of dehydration is severe as you may lose up to 20L a day. If there is a delay in getting to hospital, then begin taking tetracycline. The adult dose is 250mg four times daily. It is not recommended for children under nine years or for pregnant women. Tetracycline may help shorten the illness, but adequate fluid replacement is required to save lives.

Leishmaniasis This is a group of parasitic diseases transmitted by sandflies, which are found in many parts of the Middle East, Africa, India, Central and South America and the Mediterranean. Cutaneous leishmaniasis affects the skin tissue, causing ulceration and disfigurement, and visceral leishmaniasis fects the internal organs. Seek medical vice, as laboratory testing is require diagnosis and correct treatment. Av sandfly bites is the best precaution. F usually painless, itchy and yet anoth to cover up and apply repellent.

Tetanus This disease is caused by a germ that lives in soil and in the faeces of horses and other animals. It enters the body via breaks in the skin. The first symptom may be discomfort when swallowing, or stiffening of the jaw and neck; this is followed by painful convulsions of the jaw and whole body. The disease can be fatal. It can be prevented by vaccination.

Tuberculosis (TB) TB is a bacterial infection usually transmitted from person to person by coughing, but which may be transmitted through consumption of unpasteurised milk. Milk that has been boiled is safe to drink, and the souring of milk to make yoghurt or cheese also kills the bacilli. Travellers are usually not at great risk as close household contact with the infected person is usually required before the disease is passed on. You may need to have a TB test before you travel as this can help diagnose the disease later if you become ill.

Typhus This disease is spread by ticks, mites or lice. It begins with fever, chills, headache and muscle pains followed a few days later by a body rash. There is often a large painful sore at the site of the bite and nearby lymph nodes are swollen and painful. Typhus can be treated under medical supervision. Seek local advice on areas where ticks pose a danger and always check your skin carefully for ticks after walking in a danger area such as a tropical forest. An insect repellent can help, and walkers in tick-infested areas should consider having their boots and trousers impregnated with benzyl benzoate and dibutylphthalate.

Women's Health

Gynaecological Problems Antibiotic use, synthetic underwear, sweating and contraceptive pills can lead to fungal vaginal infections, especially when travelling in hot climates. Thrush, or vaginal candidiasis, is characterised by itching, discharge and a ... Nystatin, miconazole or clotrimazole ..., or vaginal cream are the usual ..., but some people use a more traditional remedy involving vinegar or lemon-

juice douches, or yoghurt. Maintaining good personal hygiene and wearing loose-fitting clothes and cotton underwear may help prevent these infections.

Sexually transmitted infections are a major cause of vaginal problems. Symptoms include a smelly discharge, painful intercourse and sometimes a burning sensation when urinating. Medical attention should be sought and male sexual partners must also be treated. For more details see the Sexually Transmitted Infections entry earlier in this section. Besides abstinence, the best thing is to practise safer sex by making sure that you use condoms.

Pregnancy It is not advisable to travel to some places while pregnant as some vaccinations normally used to prevent serious diseases are not advisable during pregnancy (eg yellow fever). In addition, some diseases are much more serious for pregnant women (eg malaria) and may increase the risk of a stillborn child.

Most miscarriages occur during the first three months of pregnancy. Miscarriage is not uncommon and can occasionally lead to severe bleeding. The last three months should also be spent within reasonable distance of good medical care. A baby born as early as 24 weeks stands a chance of survival, but only in a good modern hospital. Pregnant women should avoid all unnecessary medication, although vaccinations and malarial preventatives should still be taken where needed. Additional care should be taken to prevent illness and particular attention should be paid to diet and nutrition. Alcohol and nicotine, for example, should be avoided.

WOMEN TRAVELLERS

Central Asia can be hard work for the lone woman traveller. Many local men cannot understand why women (in groups of any size, for that matter) would travel without men, and assume they have ulterior sexual motives. Although harassment is not so unrelenting as in some Middle Eastern countries, it tends to be more physical. Macho Uzbekistan tops the list, with Kyrgyzstan by far the least sexist.

You may find that many men will not address you directly, but will instead address any male companions you are travelling with. Don't jump to the conclusion that they are dismissing you because you are a woman – it is regarded as impolite to speak to another man's wife, which is what most men will assume you are (out of politeness, not presumption).

Of course it is easy to say that the best option is for women not to travel alone. However, keen sensibilities and a few staunch rules of thumb can make a solo journey rewarding.

- Register with your embassy when arriving in the CIS (see the Embassies & Consulates entry in the relevant country chapter for details).
- Clothes *do* matter: a modest dress code is essential (even if local Russian women don't seem to have one). See the Dos & Don'ts entry in the Society & Conduct section of the Facts about Central Asia chapter, for more on the important matter of clothing.
- Walk confidently with your head up but avoid eye-contact with men (smile at everybody else).
- Never follow any man – even an official – into a private area. If one insists on seeing your passport, hand over a photocopy as well as a photocopy of your OVIR registration (have quite a few of these); if he pushes you to follow him, walk away into a busy area.
- Ride in taxis that already have other women passengers.
- Sit at the front of the bus, always between two women, if you can.
- When seeking information, always ask a local woman. Most matronly types will automatically take you under their wing if you show enough despair.
- If you feel as though you are being followed or harassed, seek the company of a group of women, or even children; big smiles will get you a welcome.
- Ignore any late night raps at your door; utilise home-stays whenever possible. Never wander around alone at night.
- If you are arranging a trek or car hire, ask the agency to include female travellers.
- Some local men will honestly want to befriend and help you; if you are unsure and have a difficult time shaking them, mention your husband (See the boxed text 'The Invisible Husband').
- Wear a whistle around your neck in case you somehow get into trouble. Blow it on relentlessly if you are absolutely in danger.

The Invisible Husband

Problems can arise in countries in which men are unused to seeing women travelling by themselves – some less admirable characters may try to take advantage of solo female travellers.

Sometimes, the best defence is to play along. In fact, the system can often work in the lone woman's favour. So slip on a fake wedding ring and invent the invisible husband (In Russian: 'moy moosh' means 'my husband'), who can then be used in uncomfortable situations. When being pressured to buy something in a shop, cast your eyes downward and murmur 'moy moosh' (my husband doesn't give me any money). When a strange man tries to befriend you and you can't shake him, give a frantic glance at your watch and shout 'moy moosh' (I am meeting my husband at any moment). When officials, guards or policemen demand a bribe, shrug your shoulders helplessly and cry 'moy moosh' (my husband has left me here and there's nothing I can do!).

Bear in mind, however, that this is not an infallible plan. Some baddies may well have been following you for a while, and may have ascertained that you are indeed alone, and hence the 'moy moosh' ploy may well fall on deaf ears.

But it isn't all bad! The opportunities for genuine cross-cultural woman-to-woman interactions can generally be had during home-stays, and usually outside the cities. Everyone loves to have their children cooed over and doing so will gain you friends as well as unique experiences. You may well see a side of Central Asia hidden to male travellers.

GAY & LESBIAN TRAVELLERS

There is little obvious gay/lesbian community in Central Asia, though there are a couple of gay bars in Almaty. It's not unusual to see young women showing affection towards each other, nor is it uncommon to men holding hands. However, this is a reflection of Asian culture rather than homosexuality.

In Uzbekistan, Turkmenistan and Tajikistan, gay male sex is illegal, but lesbian sex does not seem to be illegal. Kazakstan and Kyrgyzstan have lifted the Soviet-era ban on homosexuality. However, whether you're straight or gay, it's best to avoid public displays of affection.

In Bishkek (Kyrgyzstan) the Oasis organisation (☎ 312-54 19 17), Mira prospektesi 60, is an underground gay and lesbian group (and also an anti-AIDS organisation).

DISABLED TRAVELLERS

Central Asia is a difficult place for wheelchair travellers, as older Soviet buildings and buses are not wheelchair accessible. There is also a severe lack of any services catering to the visually or hearing impaired.

If any specialised travel agency is interested in arranging trips to Central Asia, the best bet is Accessible Journeys (☎ 1-800-TINGLES, 610-521 0339, fax 521 6959, @ sales@disabilitytravel.com) in Pennsylvania, USA. They have a Web site at www.disabilitytravel.com. At the very least, hire your own transport and guide through one of the agencies listed in the Travel Agencies section of the Getting There & Away chapter. If you explain your disability, they may be able to accommodate you.

The following organisations offer general travel advice for the disabled but provide no specific information on Central Asia:

Australia
Independent Travellers
    (☎ 08-232 2555, toll-free ☎ 008-811 355, fax 232 6877)
    167 Gilles St, Adelaide SA 5000 – specialised advice for disabled travellers.
NICAN
    (☎ 02-6285 3713, fax 6285 3714)
    PO Box 407, Curtin, ACT 2605

UK
Travelcare
    (☎ 0120-8295 1797, fax 8467 2467)
    5A High St, Chislehurst, Kent BR7 QAE – specialises in travel insurance for the disabled.

USA
SATH (Society for the Advancement of Travel for the Handicapped)
    (☎ 212-447 0027, fax 725 8253)
    347 Fifth Ave No 610, New York, NY 10016 – good Web site containing tips on how to travel with diabetes, arthritis, visual and hearing impairments, and wheelchairs: www.sath.org.
Twin Peaks Press
    (☎ 202-694 2462, toll free in the USA or Canada ☎ 800-637 2256)
    PO Box 129, Vancouver, WA 98666 – publishes several useful handbooks for disabled travellers, including *Travel for the Disabled* and *Directory of Travel Agencies for the Disabled*.

For general advice, bulletin boards and searchable databases on the Internet try the following links:

- www.access-able.com
- www.newmobility.com
- www.travelhealth.com/disab.htm
- www.dpi.org
- www.eka.com

SENIOR TRAVELLERS

There is no reason that senior travellers can't enjoy Central Asia. Indeed Central Asian culture extends great courtesies (and discounts) to their own senior members. The extremes of temperatures in deserts and mountains may pose a risk, as may altitude if crossing the Torugart or other passes. Consult your doctor before travelling and let any of the agencies listed in the Organised Tours section of the Getting There & Away chapter know of your medical conditions.

Seniors Travel (☎ 02-6285 2644, fax 6285 2430, @ tbriton_justtravel@atlasmail.com) in Australia arranges group tours for clients over the age of fifty. It has a Web site at www.seniorstravel.com.au. If you wish to travel more independently but still require some health care try Travel Aides International (☎ 530-873 2977, @ travel@c-zone.net), 14885 Snowberry Cir, Magalla USA, a travel agency that also provides health care companions. It's Web site is at: members.tripod.com/~Travel_us/index.html. Neither company has much, if any, experience in Central Asia.

TRAVEL WITH CHILDREN

Children can be a great icebreaker and a good avenue for cultural exchange, but travelling in Central Asia is difficult for even the healthy adult. Long bus and taxi rides over winding mountain passes are a sure route to motion sickness. Central Asian food is difficult to stomach no matter what your age, and extreme temperatures – blistering hot in the city; freezing in the mountains – lead to many an uncomfortable moment. Islamic architecture and ruined Karakhanid cities may well leave your children comatose with boredom. A few places of added interest to children include water parks in Almaty and Tashkent, the beaches of Cholpon-Ata and Valentin's mini-zoo in Karakol.

If you are bringing very young children into Central Asia, nappies are available at department stores, but bring your own bottles and medicines. Forget about car seats, high chairs, cribs or anything geared for children, though you'll always find a spare lap and helpful hands when boarding buses. It's possible to make a cot out of the pile of duvets supplied in most home-stays. *Lux* (deluxe) hotel rooms normally come with an extra connecting room, which can be ideal for children. For more advice on travelling with children, pick up *Travel with Children* by Maureen Wheeler, Lonely Planet Publications, 1995.

USEFUL ORGANISATIONS

There are presently thousands of western technical assistance workers all over Central Asia. Of course they all have their own jobs to do, but many are happy to chat with visitors and help them to see beneath the surface of life here.

One of the single biggest representations is the US Peace Corps, involved in both English-language teaching and business development. Peace Corps volunteers in more remote places may be delighted to speak their own language, see faces from home and offer useful tips, though they also seem to be incredibly busy. In smaller towns they tend to have a high profile, and almost everybody knows where to find them (Peace Corps is *Korpus Mira* in Russian).

Many of these volunteers have moved on to kick-start locally staffed 'networking' organisations to put local people in touch with foreign resources. These outfits are often happy to have visitors, especially those with something to offer, eg a little volunteer time, expertise or useful contacts. Some may also know of volunteer or other work opportunities. We have identified these under individual cities, including Tashkent, Samarkand and Bishkek.

Cultural Exchange

The Britain Russia Centre (☎ 020-7235 2116, 14 Grosvenor Place, London SW1X 7HW) and the Britain East-West Centre (☎ 0131-452 8132, 4 Bruntsfield Crescent, Edinburgh EH10 4HD) encourage nonpolitical contacts between Britons and the peoples of the old Soviet empire, with talks, films and other events.

The Society for Co-operation in Russian & Soviet Studies (☎ 020-7274 2282, fax 274 3230, 320 Brixton Rd, London SW9 6AB, UK) organises artistic/cultural exchanges and study tours. All have good libraries, publish small journals, sponsor talks, and offer student memberships.

The Seattle-Tashkent Sister City Association (☎ 206-24 6258, ☻ bruceh@synapps .com) can be contacted at 630 Randolph Place, Seattle, WA 98122, USA.

The Royal Society for Asian Affairs

This small but venerable organisation on London's fashionable Belgrave Square has one of the best specialist libraries anywhere devoted to Central Asia (or rather, westerners' views of the region), including many out-of-print editions. Membership is steep, however, at about UK£55 a year if you live within 60 miles of London, £45 if you live outside. They're at 2 Belgrave Square, London SW1X 8PJ (☎ 020-7235 5122, fa 259 6771, ☻ info@rsaa.org.uk), and hav Web site at www.rsaa.org.uk.

DANGERS & ANNOYANCES

Travel in Central Asia can be a del` those who are ready for it, but a n` for the unprepared. Starting before go, with the visa chase, don't expect anything to go smoothly.

Crime is minimal by western urban standards, but is on the rise everywhere, and visitors are tempting, high-profile targets. In some conservative areas like the Fergana valley you may find a few sour faces shown to non-Muslims, especially women. Local and regional transport can be unpredictable, uncomfortable and occasionally unsafe. And, churlish as it sounds, some Central Asian 'hospitality' can be just too much to bear.

This section, all about the headaches, is not meant to put you off. Rather, it is intended to prepare you for the worst. Patience, tolerance, a thick skin and a good sense of humour are a big help too. Here's hoping you run into none of these problems.

Emergencies

Many kinds of emergencies are covered in other sections of this chapter. See the Health section for medical emergencies; the Money section for lost or stolen travellers cheques, credit cards and money; and the Lost or Stolen Documents entry in the Documents section for lost or stolen passports and visas.

Your embassy in the nearest capital city is your best first stop in any emergency (see the Embassies & Consulates entry in the relevant country chapter for details), but bear in mind that there are some things they cannot do for you. These include getting local laws or regulations waived because you are a foreigner; investigating a crime; providing legal advice or representation in civil or criminal cases; getting you out of jail or getting you better treatment there than local people get; lending money (the UK embassy can do this in exceptional circumstances); or paying your bills.

It's a good idea to register with your embassy upon arrival in Central Asia and to carry the telephone numbers of your embassies in the region. See the Embassies & Consulates section of the relevant country chapter for details.

Emergency telephone numbers throughout the ex-Soviet republics are ☎ 01 for the fire brigade, ☎ 02 for police, and ☎ 03 for ambulance.

Places to Avoid

Civil strife in Tajikistan presents extraordinary dangers for travellers in certain areas such as the Garm valley, the road from Dushanbe to Khorog and anywhere within 25km of the Afghan border. See the Safety in Tajikistan boxed text in the Tajikistan chapter for more information.

At the time of research several incidents of kidnapping, bombing and shoot-outs had made remote western areas of Kyrgyzstan's southern arm, close to the borders of Tajikistan and Uzbekistan, unsafe. Any remote area in this region carries a potential danger; remote valleys are home to the odd rebel and/or opium farmer.

There have been bombings on buses in several locations in Xinjiang by disaffected Uyghurs, though these are not targeted at foreigners and none have so far been affected.

Afghanistan remains firmly off limits to casual travellers.

See the Tajikistan, Kyrgyzstan, Xinjiang and Afghanistan chapters for further details.

Alcohol & Assault-by-Hospitality

Whether it's being poured down your throat by a zealous host, or driving others into states of pathological melancholy, brotherly love, anger or violence, alcohol is one of the biggest problems travellers now face in the former Soviet Union. The Islamic injunction against alcohol has had little obvious impact in Central Asia.

Many foreigners fall victim to what one worn-out expatriate resident calls 'terrorist hospitality'. Initially flattered by the attention and afraid of giving offence by refusing, they end up bullied by would-be hosts into going places they don't want to go, eating things they don't want to eat, and of course washing it down with more vodka than their systems can stand – all administered with toasts to international friendship that boost the moral pressure and magnify their guilt. The host-cum-captor rarely pays any attention to their condition, wishes or alibis. Such overbearing treatment can come not just from the odd garrulous drunk but from the most apparently urbane of dinner hosts.

Your only recourse is to refuse politely but firmly, without wavering or falling for the 'just one little drink' line. 'Weak stomach' won't work, for everyone appears to believe that vodka is excellent for killing every sort of microbe. However, many Central Asians know from personal experience about the dysentery medication metronidazole (brand name Flagyl, or *trikhopol* in Russian) and the results of mixing it with alcohol, so this makes a good excuse. Religious beliefs are a possibility if you're prepared for a theological discussion. Oddly enough, claiming to be an alcoholic sometimes works, though you have to be pretty consistent about it. Men generally experience far more pressure to drink than women.

Alcoholism is epidemic in the former USSR, and after dark the streets of many Central Asian towns fill with drunks – ranging from the obnoxious to the downright dangerous. This is especially true in economically depressed areas, where violence hovers just below the surface and young men may grow abruptly violent, seemingly at random. Take your strolls during the day, and stay inside or travel by taxi after dark.

Crime

With the lifting of the Soviet lid, incidents of mugging, theft and pick-pocketing are on the rise in cities and towns of all the former Soviet republics (though it must be said that these have risen from near-zero levels in Soviet days, and don't even approach the levels of most western cities). The best defence is common sense. Don't be paranoid but be careful. See the Security entry of the Money section in this chapter for sensible ways to handle your money.

Other tips, especially for individual travellers, include:

- Dress down, and keep expensive jewellery, watches and cameras out of sight; carry only as much cash as you would be willing to surrender to a thief (which is the sensible alternative to resistance in every case).
- Be especially alert in crowded situations such as bazaars and bus station ticket scrums, where pockets and purses may be easily picked.

- Avoid parks at night, even if it means going a long way out of your way.
- Do not approach groups of men after dark or even pass close by and, at all costs, stay away from drunks.
- Take officially licensed taxis in preference to private ones; some people also advise against climbing into any taxi with more than the driver in them and sharing with other passengers.
- Travellers who rent a flat are warned to be sure the doors and windows are secure, and *never* to open the door – day or night – to anyone they do not clearly know.
- Western men who speak Russian have on rare occasions been mistaken for Russians by drunken young Central Asians out for an evening of Slav-bashing. If you're physically threatened under these circumstances, you're somewhat less likely to have a punch thrown at you if you make it clear you're a westerner.

If you're the victim of a crime, contact the *militsia* (police), though you may get no help from them at all (see the following Crooked Officials entry in this section). Get a report from them if you hope to claim on insurance for anything that was stolen, and contact your own closest embassy for a report in English. If your passport is stolen, the police should also provide a letter to OVIR, which is essential for replacing your visa. See the Money section in this chapter about loss or theft of credit cards or travellers cheques.

Crooked Officials

The number of corrupt officials on the take has decreased dramatically since the first edition of this book and most travellers make their way through Central Asia without a single run-in with the local militsia. (That said, during the research of this book one of the writers was arrested three times in one morning in Tashkent, another writer was robbed by a drunk policeman, again in Tashkent, and yet another had a gun drawn on him by a policeman in Medeu, Kazakstan.)

The strongest police presence is in Uzbekistan, where there are police checkpoints at most municipal and provincial borders. It's a near certainty you'll meet gendarme or two in every bus and train tion, though most only want to see papers and know where you're going.

The particularly vague 72 hour transit rule is vulnerable to corrupt interpretation (see the Transit entry of the Visa section earlier in this chapter). For this reason always keep hotel and bus receipts as proof of your movements.

If you are approached by the police, there are several rules of thumb to bear in mind:

- Your best bet is to be polite, firm and jovial; cringing tends to make you more of a target, while an uncooperative attitude will only get their backs up. A forthright, friendly manner – starting right out with a *salam aleykum* (peace be with you) and a handshake for whomever is in charge – may help to defuse a potential shakedown, whether you are male or female.
- If someone refers to a 'regulation', ask to see it in writing. If you are dealing with lower-level officers, ask to see their *administrator* (chief).
- Ask to see a policeman's ID and, if possible, get a written copy of the ID number. Do not hand over your passport unless you see this ID. Even better, only hand over a photocopy of your passport; claim that your passport is at your hotel or embassy.
- Try to avoid being taken somewhere out of the public eye, eg into an office or into the shadows; it should be just as easy to talk right where you are. The objective of most detentions of westerners is simply to extort money, and by means of intimidation rather than violence. If your money is buried deeply, and you're prepared to pull out a paperback and wait them out, even if it means missing the next bus or train, most inquisitors will eventually give up.
- Make it harder for police on the take by speaking only in your own language.
- If officers show signs of force or violence, and *provided they are not drunk*, do not be afraid to make a scene – dishonest cops will dislike such exposure.
- Never sign anything, especially if it's in a language you don't understand. You have the right not to sign anything without consular assistance.
- Recent anti-narcotics laws give the police powers to search passengers at bus and train stations. If you are searched, never let the police put their hands in your pockets – take everything out yourself and turn your pockets inside out.

If police officers want to see your money (to check for counterfeit bills) try to take it out only ʼn front of the highest ranking officer. If any is ʼken insist on a written receipt for the sum. If ʼu do have to pay a fine, insist that you do so ʼ bank and get a receipt for the full amount.

Crime on the Rails

Robberies on long-distance trains have increased. Try to get a compartment with friends, be careful about who you invite in, never leave the compartment unattended and keep the door securely locked at night. The UK Foreign Office advises tying the door closed from the inside with wire or strong cord; paranoid as that may sound, travellers have indeed reported attempts by strangers to enter their compartments at night. Stash your bags in the compartment under the lower bunk, not in the overhead spaces.

The Almaty-Ürümqi train trip has long been notorious for its corrupt officials at the Kazak border post at Dostyk, though in recent times the situation appears to have improved. For more information on this, see the Dostyk entry in the South-East Kazakstan section of the Kazakstan chapter.

Trekking Problems

While most commonly used trekking routes are quite safe, there have been problems in the past with bandits in the mountains between Almaty and Lake Issyk-Kul. Reliable trekking guides (including those listed in this book) have thought about this already; some take guards or dogs along for protection, while others do careful advance PR along their routes.

Some trekking routes, especially in southern Kyrgyzstan and Tajikistan, traverse some remote areas, which are prime opium-growing and rebel hide-out territory. Discuss your route with a trekking agency before you wander off into these hills and if possible take a local guide.

Domestic Flights

Not everyone is happy with the thought of flying in an ageing Soviet or Chinese-built aeroplane, and aircraft maintenance is not always up to snuff with the descendants of Aeroflot (the old Soviet mega-airline), or with the many regional splinter airlines now operating throughout China. Uzbekistan Airways aeroplanes, however, are maintained by Lufthansa-trained staff. Refer to the Getting Around chapter for more on travel safety in Central Asia.

LEGAL MATTERS

It's unlikely you will ever be actually arrested, unless there are supportable charges against you. If you are arrested, authorities in the former Soviet states are obliged to inform your embassy (*pasolstvah* in Russian) immediately and allow you to communicate with a consular official without delay. Always keep the contact details of your embassy on your person (see the Embassies & Consulates entry in the relevant country chapter for details). Most embassies will provide a list of recommended lawyers. Several western law companies operate in Central Asia, such as Arthur Anderson and Baker & McKenzie.

Kyrgyzstan remains the most liberal of the ex-Soviet republics when it comes to legal matters. Here, foreigners can own vehicles, houses, stocks and even companies.

Drugs

Marijuana grows openly in many parts of Turkmenistan, Kyrgyzstan and Kazakstan, and is seen as an increasingly profitable cash crop. Moreover, there are several hundred thousand hectares of opium poppies in Kyrgyzstan and Kazakstan and the region is one of the world's major smuggling arteries.

Visitors are subject to the laws of the country they're visiting. All Central Asian republics carry the death sentence for drug-related offences, though Kyrgyzstan and Turkmenistan recently announced a moratorium on the death penalty.

BUSINESS HOURS

All business hours seem mutable in the former Soviet republics. Foreign exchange banks usually open Monday to Friday 9 or 10 am to noon or 1 pm, and those in major cities sometimes open in the afternoon and evening too. Exchange offices keep longer hours, including weekends. Post and telephone offices are typically open Monday to Friday 8 am to 5 pm, with the central offices sometimes open Saturday and Sunday too. Government office hours are usually Monday to Friday 9 or 10 am to 5 or 6 pm, with an hour or two off for lunch.

Museum hours change frequently, as do their days off. Most shut their entrance doors

> ### Nasvai
>
> You may notice some men chewing and copiously spitting, or talking as if their mouth were full of saliva. *Nasvai, nasvar* or *noz* is basically finely crushed tobacco, sometimes cut with spices, ash or lime. As a greenish sludge or as little pellets, it's stuffed under the tongue or inside the cheek, from where the active ingredients leach into the bloodstream, revving up the user's heart rate and self-image. Amateurs who fail to clamp it tightly in place, thus allowing the effluent to leak into the throat, may be consumed with nausea.
>
> Before you try it, bear in mind that nasvai is often cut with opium, and can be quite potent.

30 minutes or an hour before closing time, and have shorter hours on the day *before* their day off. Some just seem to close without reason and a few stay that way for years.

Public places in the former Soviet republics often display their business days visually, as a stack of seven horizontal bars with the top one representing Monday; blue means open, red means closed.

In Xinjiang the official day of rest is Sunday; a few offices may take a half-day off on Saturday too.

PUBLIC HOLIDAYS & SPECIAL EVENTS

Public Holidays

Banks, businesses and government offices are closed on the following dates (listed in chronological order) throughout the region, unless otherwise stated. Though single dates are listed for most, you may find offices close early on the day before as well. Pakistan and Russian holidays are included because the opening days of the Torugart and Khunjerab passes depend on these.

New Year's Day
    1 January – all countries except Afghanistan (31 December to 1 January in Tajikistan and to 2 January in Kazakstan)

Russian Orthodox Christmas
   7 January – Kyrgyzstan and Russia
Remembrance Day
   12 January – Turkmenistan; the anniversary of
   the Battle of Geok-Tepe
Constitution Day
   28 January – Kazakstan
Chinese New Year
   Between late January and early March – China;
   The exact dates for the next five year are: 5
   February (2000), 24 January (2001), 12 February (2002), 1 February (2003), 22 January
   (2004), 9 February (2005)
National Flag Day
   19 February – Turkmenistan
Army Day
   23 February – Tajikistan
International Women's Day
   8 March – all countries except Afghanistan
Navrus
   21 March – all countries; the exact timing of
   Navrus (see the following Navrus entry at the
   end of this section), as with many Muslim festi-
   vals, is determined by the sighting of the moon
Pakistan Day
   23 March – Pakistan
Drop of Water is a Grain of Gold Holiday
   6 April – Turkmenistan
Liberation Day
   18 April – Afghanistan
Revolution Day
   27 April – Afghanistan
Horse Day
   Last Saturday of the month – Uzbekistan
International Labour Day
   1 May – all countries
Youth Day
   4 May – China
Constitution Day
   5 May – Kyrgyzstan
Victory Day
   9 May – all countries except Afghanistan and
   China
Day of Revival & Unity
   18 May – Turkmenistan
Holiday of Poetry of Magtymguli
   19 May – Turkmenistan
Carpet Day
   25 May or last Sunday in May – Turkmenistan
Armed Forces Day
   29 May – Kyrgyzstan
Children's Day
   1 June – China
Capital Day
   10 June – Kazakstan; celebrates the establishment of Astana as Kazakstan's capital
Independence Day
   12 June – Russia

Commemoration Day
   13 June – Kyrgyzstan
Day of Election of First President
   21 June – Turkmenistan
Anniversary of the Founding of the Communist
Party
   1 July – China
Bank Holiday
   1 July – Pakistan
Melon Holiday
   10 July – Turkmenistan
Turkmenbashi Holiday
   14 July – Turkmenistan
Anniversary of the Founding of the People's Liberation Army
   1 August – China
Independence Day
   18 August – Afghanistan, 31 August – Kyrgyzstan
Constitution Day
   30 August – Kazakstan
Independence Day
   1 September – Uzbekistan, 9 September –
   Tajikistan
Defence of Pakistan Day
   6 September – Pakistan
Anniversary of the Death of Mohammed Ali
Jinnah
   11 September – Pakistan
National Day
   1 October – China
Remembrance Day
   6 October – Turkmenistan
Republic Day
   25 October – Kazakstan
Independence Day
   27-28 October – Turkmenistan
Day of Reconciliation and Accord
   7 November – Russia
Iqbal Day
   9 November – Pakistan
Student Youth Day
   17 November – Turkmenistan
Harvest Festival
   30 November, or the last Sunday in November
   – Turkmenistan
Good Neighbourliness
   7 December – Turkmenistan
Constitution Day
   8 December – Uzbekistan
Neutrality Day
   12 December – Turkmenistan
Independence Day
   16 December – Kazakstan
Birthday of Mohammed Ai Jinnah
   25 December – Pakistan
Bank Holiday
   31 December – Pakistan

Navrus

By far the biggest Central Asian holiday is the spring festival of Navrus ('New Days' – *Nauryz* in Kazak, *Novruz* in Turkmen, *Nooruz* in Kyrgyz, *Nauroz* in Urdu, etc), an Islamic adaptation of pre-Islamic vernal equinox or renewal celebrations, celebrated approximately on the spring equinox, though now normally fixed on 21 March.

In Soviet times this was a private affair, even banned for a time. In 1989, in one of several attempts to deflect growing Muslim nationalism, Navrus was adopted by the then Soviet Central Asian republics as an official two day festival, with traditional games, music and drama festivals, street art and colourful fairs, plus much partying and visiting of family and friends.

Special foods are prepared at home, including a wheat dish called *sumalakh* for women and a dish from young beef, *khalem*, for men. To add to this, seven items, all beginning with the Arabic sound 'sh', are laid on the dinner table – wine *(sharob)*, milk *(shir)*, sweets *(shirinliklar)*, sugar *(shakar)*, sherbet *(sharbat)*, a candle *(sham)* and a new bud *(shona)*. Candles are a throwback to pre-Islamic traditions and the new bud symbolises the renewal of life. Families traditionally pay all their debts before the start of the holiday.

Navrus is also celebrated in parts of Afghanistan, Pakistan, Iran, Azerbaijan and India.

Muslim Holy Days

The Islamic calendar is lunar, and shorter than the western solar calendar, beginning 10 to 11 days earlier in each solar year. Modern astronomy notwithstanding, religious officials have formal authority to declare the beginning of each lunar month, based on sightings of the moon's first crescent. Future holy days can be estimated, but are in doubt by a few days until the start of that month, so dates given here are only approximate. They normally run from sunset to the next sunset.

Ramadan and Qurban are observed with little fanfare in most of Central Asia (where travellers will find plenty of food available in any case). The first day of each Eid festival is a public holiday in Uzbekistan.

Eid-ul-Fitr
8 January (2000), 28 December (2001), 17 December (2002), 6 December (2003)
Also called *Hayit* in Uzbekistan, *Orozo Ait* in Kyrgyzstan and *Ruza Eid* in Xinjiang, this involves two or three days of celebrations at the end of Ramadan, with family visits, gifts, banquets and donations to the poor.

Eid-ul-Azba
16 March (2000), 6 March (2001), 23 February (2002), 12 February (2003)
Also called *Qurban, Korban* or *Qurban Hayit* in Central Asia, this is the Feast of Sacrifice. It is celebrated over several days. Those who can afford it buy and slaughter an animal, sharing the meat with relatives and with the poor. This is also the season for hajj (pilgrimage to Mecca). Large celebrations are held at Kashgar's Id Kah Mosque at this time.

Mawlid-an-Nabi
15 June (2000), 4 June (2001), 24 May (2002), 14 May (2003)
The Birthday of the Prophet Mohammed (PBUH, Peace Be Upon Him). A minor celebration in Central Asia, though you might notice mosques a little fuller, especially in Xinjiang.

Ramadan
28 November (2000), 17 November (2001), 6 November (2002), 27 October (2003)
Also known as Ramazan, the month of sunrise-to-sunset fasting (see Religion in the Facts about Central Asia chapter for more information).

Other Events

Every September, Tashkent hosts a festival featuring Asian, African and Latin American films. For three or four days in early August each year, Medeu (outside Almaty) hosts the Voice of Asia rock festival, with bands from all over the CIS and Asia.

One upshot of the post-Soviet urge to establish national identities (and coax in a few more tourist dollars) is a rash of anniversaries, some of them fairly preposterous – eg 1000 years of *Manas*, the Kyrgyz collection of oral epics (though they were not based on any single person or event), 600 years of Ulughbek and so on. The Kyrgy authorities are supposed to be celebrating t 3000th birthday of Osh in the year 20 though this depends on whether or no government can rustle up enough mo fund the celebrations.

ACTIVITIES

Following is an indication of the possibilities for adventure travel in the region. Refer to the individual country chapters for more details on where to go, what to do, and with whom. Overseas agencies with Central Asian adventure-travel programs are listed in the Travel & Visa Agencies section in the Getting There & Away chapter.

Hiking

Hiking (as opposed to trekking) is a major outdoor pursuit for Almaty residents. The Aksu-Zhabaghly nature reserve is another beautiful area of hiking country between the southern Kazakhstan cities of Shymkent and Taraz; it's also a must do for bird-watchers and flower lovers, as is the much more remote Lake Markakol close to the Altay mountains in East Kazakhstan.

You can make nice day hikes from bases in Ala Archa National Park near Bishkek, and Altyn Arashan near Karakol, both in Kyrgyzstan.

Trekking

The various arms of the Tian Shan and Pamir ranges present some grand opportunities for both trekking and climbing. See the map for some of the most popular trekking locations. Other less-visited regions include the Zhungar Alatau range east of Taldy-Korghan in Kazakhstan, and the Altay mountains in far north-east Kazakhstan.

Self-supported trekking is difficult (though not impossible) in Central Asia. A week-long trek is about as much as you can do in one go by yourself. Transport to the trailheads can be patchy, slow and uncomfortable. Some trekking areas are at the junction of several republics, requiring you to carry multiple simultaneous visas and a fistful of different currencies. There are no trekking lodges like the ones you find in Nepal, so you will have to carry all your own food for the ¨rek. It is possible to hire donkeys at many ¨ilheads (eg in the Fan mountains) and ¨e towns, such as Karakol in Kyrgyzstan, reliable and experienced local guides. ¨ou are considering a trek of more than ¨two nights bring your own equipment.

You can rent tents, sleeping bags and stoves from trekking agencies such as JS Turkestan in Karakol for about US$5 per day, but in general good gear is hard to find anywhere in the region. Sleeping bags are especially scarce. A multi-fuel (petrol) stove is most useful, though you will need to clean the burners regularly as old Soviet fuel is of extremely poor quality. Petrol is now fairly easy to find in most towns, as are trekking food supplies such as rice, soups, mashed potato, dried pasta, etc. Most drivers carry jerry cans of petrol in the back of their cars and will sell you one or two litres.

Make sure you are well equipped for these unforgiving environments. In May 1995 an American trekker died of exposure in the mountains above Almaty after being caught, dressed in shorts and T-shirt, in a sudden spring storm.

The best walking season is June through September, but be ready for bad weather at any time. Most high-altitude treks or climbs take place in July or August. Treks in areas around the Fergana valley or Tajikistan's Fan mountains can be scorching hot in July and August.

Banditry is a problem in some areas – eg the Zailiysky and Küngey Alatau between Almaty and Issyk-Kul, and parts of southern Kyrgyzstan (see the Dangers & Annoyances section earlier in this chapter). Trustworthy local knowledge, and preferably a local guide, are essential for trekking in Central Asia. The safest way to go is with a reliable agency, though this will cost somewhere in the region of US$25 to US$40 per person per day. Most agencies can find you a porter for around US$10 per day, or a guide for around US$20.

An essential resource for all serious trekkers and climbers is Frith Maier's *Trekking in Russia & Central Asia*. It provides information on seasons, paperwork, safety, equipment, detailed routes and more; see the Books section earlier in this chapter for further details.

For help finding the page numbers of specific treks covered in this guide, look under 'trekking' in the Boxed Text Index at the very back of this book.

Mountaineering & Rock Climbing

Top of the line for altitude junkies are Khan-Tengri, Pobedy and other peaks of the central Tian Shan in eastern Kyrgyzstan and south-east Kazakstan. Several Almaty and Bishkek tour agents can arrange trips to this region, including helicopter flights to the base camps, during the climbing season from the end of June to early September.

The other prime high-altitude playground is the Pamir in southern Kyrgyzstan and eastern Tajikistan, especially Pik Lenin, accessed from Achik Tash base camp.

One of the prime rock-climbing areas is Ak Suu peak and the neighbouring Karavsin valley in southern Kyrgyzstan. Climbers compare the 2km-high rock walls of this region to the Patagonian peaks of South America.

Other 4000m-plus peaks that you can undertake organised climbs of are Mt Korona in Ala-Archa park in Kyrgyzstan, Mt Sayramsky in the Aksu-Zhabaghly Nature Reserve and Mt Belukha in East Kazakstan's Altay mountains.

Horse & Camel Trips

Some of the agencies that arrange treks can also set up mountain or desert horse treks. For information about horse and camel treks in Turkmenistan, see the Travel Agencies section of the Ashgabat entry in the Turkmenistan chapter.

Tashkent travel agencies arrange camel treks around Ayderkul lake and Nurata in northern Uzbekistan.

Kyrgyzstan is a perfect place for travel on horseback. Shepherd's Life in Kyrgyzstan arranges horse treks to *jailoos* (summer pastures) around central Kyrgyzstan. Horseback is the perfect way to arrive at Song-Köl. Altyn Arashan offers some lovely day trips on horseback. Kegeti Canyon, east of Bishkek is another popular place for horse riding, as are the Köl-Say lakes in south-east Kazakstan.

Eldiyar Tur in Naryn, and Yak Tours in Karakol can arrange longer expeditions on horseback. If you hire horses directly from local herders or farmers you can get a horse for as little as US$5 per day, though agencies will charge two or three times this.

Winter Sports

Central Asia's ski season is approximately November or December to March or April, with local variations. The region's best-known and best-equipped downhill area is Shymbulak (Russian: *Chimbulak*), a day-trip distance from Almaty. Ski rental costs around US$1 per day; a day lift-pass costs US$40. February is the best time to be there.

Second best are the Kyrgyz Alatau valleys (especially Ala-Archa) south of Bishkek, and the Chimgan area above Tashkent. Another possible base for skiing is Karakol on Lake Issyk-Kul. Summer skiing is sometimes possible at Ala-Archa and above Karakol.

Kazakstan's pristine Altay mountains are renowned for cross-country skiing; the best place to do this is Rachmanov's Springs.

A few travel firms in Kazakstan and Kyrgyzstan offer ski-mountaineering trips in the central Tian Shan in July and August, and in the Alatau ranges between Almaty and Lake Issyk-Kul from February through April.

Nearly every sports-related agency in Central Asia offers heli-skiing, in which old Aeroflot helicopters drop you off on remote high peaks and you ski down. Most guarantee 3000 to 4000m vertical per day but require a group of between 12 and 15 people. The Alatau range behind Bishkek is one of the cheapest places to do this. It's possible to heli-ski in the Chimgan range behind Tashkent from January to May.

The Medeu ice rink just outside Kazakstan is one of the largest speed skating rinks in the world and is open to the public from about November to March.

Rafting

A good venue for rafting and kayaking at all skill levels is Tashkent, where you can find flat water on the Syr-Darya and Angren rivers, and more exciting stretches on the Ugam, Chatkal and Pskem. The best season is September through October. There is easy rafting and canoeing on the Ili river between Lake Kapshaghay and Lake Balkash north of Almaty, from mid-April to October. Another rafting location is the river outside Bishkek. Several agen

Kazakstan, Kyrgyzstan and Uzbekistan will arrange multi-day descents of remote rivers for groups.

You can rent boats on Issyk-Kul from Cholpon-Ata, though these are expensive.

Mountain Biking

Several western tour companies offer supported biking trips over the Torugart and a few die-hards actually do the trip themselves. The Kegeti Canyon and pass is another biking location favoured by adventure travel companies. Dostuk Trekking even offers an amazing mountain biking itinerary to Merzbacher lake in the Central Tian Shan. Mountain biking trips arranged through Central Asian trekking agencies cost around US$50 per person per day.

Jeep Trips

The back roads of Kyrgyzstan, and to a lesser extent Tajikistan, offer great scope for adventure travel in a sturdy 4WD. One road leads from Talas over the Kara Bura pass into the Chatkal river valley and then loops around to Sary Chelek. Other tracks lead from Naryn to Barskoön, and Barskoön to Inylchek, through the high Tian Shan. You'd need a tent, a driver and all your supplies to undertake such a trip.

Other Activities

Several companies organise caving trips, especially around Osh in Kyrgyzstan and around Chimgan, north of Tashkent. It's possible to scuba dive in Issyk-Kul, though it is pricey and some of the equipment used looks like a prop from a 1960s Jacques Cousteau documentary.

ACCOMMODATION

Accommodation alternatives are springing up all over Central Asia, so thankfully the smoky Soviet leftovers need only be used as a last resort.

Places once closed to foreigners, such as ▪tels and resorts for Party bigwigs, and tels and *turbaza*s (holiday camps) for ▪roletariat, have opened their doors to ▪igh-elevation camps once reserved for of state sports organisations have

done the same. You can pitch your own tent at these and at most turbazas. You can even sleep in a medressa in Khiva or an astronomical observatory outside Almaty.

Best of all, some sensibly priced guesthouses have appeared, along with a growing number of private homes where spare rooms are being turned into money-spinners. These cast a harsh light on the hideously bad deals at most former Soviet hotels; the difference between what US$15 gets you at Tashkent's Hotel Rossiya and at a private home in Samarkand, for example, is staggering.

Changes are uneven across the region. While Kazakstan, Kyrgyzstan and Uzbekistan still abound in Soviet-era fossils, they also have some of the best alternatives. Turkmenistan has few alternatives to hotels. In Tajikistan, Dushanbe and Khojand are stuck in the Soviet era, while much of the civil-war-ravaged interior has nothing at all.

Thankfully, it's no longer essential to book all your accommodation in advance at exorbitant prices, as it was before independence, although Uzbektourism is trying hard to carry on that old Intourist tradition.

Camping

In the wilds there's normally no problem with you camping, though there is always an inherent security risk with this. If you are obviously on someone's land then you should try to ensure that you have permission. Anywhere near habitation will result in an immediate audience. Popular trekking routes have established camping areas, frequented by Soviet alpinists during the Soviet era and locals will be well accustomed to the sight of a bright tent. You can normally camp in a turbaza or yurt camp for a minimal fee.

Hotels

Though some are better than others, you almost never get what you pay for in Soviet-era tourist hotels. Many were in better shape before 1991, but the subsidies have now run out. Doorknobs may come off in your hand; windows may not open or close. Electricity is usually dicey with dim or missing light bulbs. Toilets that leak but don't flush give bathrooms a permanent aroma and some bathrooms have long-term cockroach colonies. Despite the dry climate, hotel room walls are often mouldy. All beds are single, with pillows the size of suitcases. Guests themselves are essentially viewed as a dispensable inconvenience, ranking somewhere below room cleaners in the hotel pecking order, with nongroup guests often effectively invisible.

If the receptionist says there are no rooms there may be one anyway, though you probably won't get it by demanding it or going to the manager. Instead, take advantage of the Islamic habit of hospitality to strangers, or any residual Slavic instinct for generosity – hang around in the lobby looking desperate; ask kindly looking older ladies (not younger men) behind the counter if they know of anyone with a room to let. Someone may relent, or suggest something better.

Where, you may ask, do ordinary local people stay? Some stay at these very places, at more fitting rates from 50% to 90% below yours. Some stay in municipal hotels that don't want foreign guests – perhaps because they're still unsure what the post-Soviet rules are, perhaps because they can't be bothered dealing with foreigners' high expectations. These days, of course, most local people cannot afford to leave home in the first place.

A limited number of elegant Party or government places, eg Samarkand's mayoral

guesthouses, and the spas of Lake Issyk-Kul in Kyrgyzstan, are now open to all, though even these are not all bargains. Truly international standard hotels – eg Almaty's Rachat Palace, The Hyatt Regency in Bishkek and several Indian-financed hotels in Uzbekistan – are creeping in slowly.

If you're staying at a budget hotel that doesn't have hot water, ask about the local *banya* (public bath), which does. See the Public Baths entry in this chapter for more information.

Most hotels take your passport and visa for anywhere from half an hour to your entire stay, to do the required registration paperwork, and to keep you from leaving without paying. Don't forget them when you leave – no-one is likely to remind you.

Rates given are, unless otherwise noted, for the most basic double room with attached toilet and shower, without breakfast, for individual travellers without advance bookings. Some government hotels charge foreigners double the local rate. Waving a student or other card can get worthwhile discounts here and there; a traveller with a diving-club card got 50% off in one smaller place. Budget hotel room rates range from a few dollars in the countryside to around US$20 in the cities.

We do not mention all of a hotel's top-end options. Even the worst often have a few *lux* (deluxe) or *pol-lux* (semi-deluxe) suites for about twice the price, sometimes with a bathtub, to which they may try to steer you by saying nothing else is available.

Take note that in the former USSR, floors start at '1st' (instead of 'ground') and this convention may still be in use in some areas.

Private Guesthouses

Private places are almost always the best places to stay. The best are to be found in the Uzbek cities of Bukhara, Khiva and Samarkand. Rates tend to be around US$20 per person, and include breakfast. Meals are extra but can normally be provided for around US$5 each.

Home-Stays

These are happily on the rise, though potential hosts still usually face burdensome OV

Late-Night Telephone Calls

Those late-night calls to your room aren't wrong numbers. All hotels with significant numbers of foreigners attract prostitutes. Women guests rarely seem to get unexpected calls and several men have received calls from someone who knew their name, so somebody at the front desk knows what's going on. All you can do is work out how to temporarily disable your telephone.

requirements about registration of guests. For your own room and a breakfast of some description you'll probably pay anywhere from US$1 (in rural Kyrgyzstan) to US$20 per person (Uzbekistan and cities) per night.

Don't expect hotel-style comforts; toilets, for example, are likely to be squatters. Don't expect anything exotic either – you may well end up in a block of flats, in front of a TV all evening. And you may not get as much privacy as you'd like, as hosts are often hungry to learn all about you and your country. Most home-stays in Kyrgyzstan offer a *shyrdak* rug and a snuggly pile of duvets and pillows as bedding and an *umuvalnik* – a portable washbasin that stores water in a top compartment – for washing.

Potential hosts may buttonhole you as you alight at a station or enter a tourist hotel. You may also hear of contacts from sympathetic hotel staff. Many private travel agencies (see the listings under each city entry) can set you up with someone, and these are probably the most reliable and most experienced with foreigners, though prices may be a shade higher. Some agencies in the west specialise in advance-booked home-stays; see the Travel Agencies & Organised Tours section of the Getting There & Away chapter for a list of some.

The Shepherd's Life program in Kochkor and surroundings is a particularly good home-stay program. See the boxed text in the Kochkor section of the Kyrgyzstan chapter.

It seems to be the case that older people, women and Russians tend to be the most honest to deal with. Find out exactly what

you're paying for, where the place is, and what kind of transport is available. Some offer a gas cooker, while others will cook for a small fee. Verify that you'll have a room of your own and breakfast, if you want them.

Friends you meet on the road may invite you home and ask nothing for it, but remember that most ordinary people have very limited resources (see Hospitality in the Culture section of the Facts about Central Asia chapter). And staying with someone who hasn't gone through official channels with OVIR could put them at risk, especially if your own papers aren't in order.

Resident westerners may also offer you a place to sleep – they're a friendly bunch by and large.

Other Possibilities

Turbazas are former Soviet holiday camps that are now open to all, though mostly only in summer. The best ones are mostly in out-of-the-way places (though they are accessible by road), surrounded by grand scenery. Most have bungalows and places to pitch your own tent. Turbazas near towns and cities are sometimes downright awful – run down, grotty and depressing.

Another place to check for rock-bottom accommodation in larger towns is the main sports stadium, which may have an athlete's hostel (often called *Spartak* or *Stadium*) that will accept foreigners.

Some nature reserves (eg Aksu-Zhabaghly Nature Reserve in Kazakstan) have sleeping huts for visitors. Some train stations in Kazakstan still have *komnaty otdykha* (resting rooms) where a bed in a triple, quad or big dormitory with minimal security, costs a few dollars.

Trade-union run sanatoria were once common around Issyk-Kul in Kyrgyzstan, though most are now run down. The ones that remain generally offer a fully-inclusive package of room, board and activities. *Pansiyonats* are similar arrangements on a smaller, more basic scale.

PUBLIC BATHS

Public baths are not just a way to get clean. They also offer the budget traveller the sublime experience of endless hot water. Most sizable towns have at least one. Some are grottier than others. Typically there are men's and women's common rooms, where you can spend a couple of hours soaping and rinsing for less than a dollar. Some have private rooms with tubs; some also have steam rooms. The best of the bunch is probably the Arasan Baths in Almaty.

FOOD

The Central Asian culinary experience is unlikely to be a highlight of your trip. Most visitors encounter Central Asian cuisine only in dismal tourist restaurants or grotty kebab stands. You'd be forgiven for not noticing it, but a large repertoire of dishes is common to most of the region, and every locale has its own specialities as well. The best way to appreciate this, and the region's extraordinary hospitality, is at a meal in a private home. Unfortunately, most restaurants and canteens serve only standard slop, which somehow seems to taste (and smell) indelibly of the old USSR.

Local Food

Central Asian food resembles that of the Middle East or the Mediterranean in its use of rice, savoury seasonings, vegetables and legumes, yoghurt and grilled meats. Many dishes may seem familiar from elsewhere – *laghman* (like Chinese noodles), *plov* (similar to Persian rice pilafs), *nan* or flat-breads (found all over Asia), and pumpkin-filled *samsa* (the 'samosa' of India). Others are more unusual, like Kazak horsemeat sausage and Uyghur goat's-head soup.

The cuisine falls into three overlapping groups. First is the once-nomadic subsistence diet in large areas of Kazakstan, Kyrgyzstan and Turkmenistan – mainly meat (including entrails), milk products and bread. Second is the diet of the Uzbeks and Uyghurs (settled Turks), including pilafs, kebabs, noodles and pasta, stews, elaborate breads and pastries. The third group is Persian, from southern Uzbekistan and Tajikistan to northern Pakistan and on into India, distinguished by subtle seasoning, extensive use of vegetables, and fancy sweets.

Seasoning is usually mild, though sauces and chillies are offered to turn up the heat. Principal spices are black cumin, red and black pepper, barberries, coriander and sesame seeds. Common herbs are fresh coriander *(cilantro)*, dill, parsley, celeriac and basil. Other seasonings include wine vinegar and fermented milk products.

In the heavily Russian-populated cities of northern Kazakstan, and in all the Central Asian capitals, the dominant cuisine is Russian.

Meat

Mutton is the ever-present and preferred meat. Big-bottomed sheep are prized for their meat, fat and wool, and fat from the sheep's tail actually costs more than the meat. The meat-to-fat ratio is generally stacked heavily in favour (and flavour) of the fat, and you will soon find that everything smells of it. You may begin to feel your insides getting plugged up with it (so do locals, who keep themselves unplugged with lots of tea). Sheep's head is a great delicacy, which may be served to honoured guests in some homes.

Beef and horsemeat and, in the countryside, camel and goat are also common. Horsemeat, especially as sausage, is often served at special occasions.

Pork is only found in Russian and Chinese restaurants. Don't ask for pork at Uyghur or Muslim restaurants in China because pork is taboo to Muslims.

Produce

Almost all produce is locally grown, and seasonal. The long growing season means many fruits and vegetables have early, middle and late harvests, though produce is at its most bountiful around September.

In general, May is the best time for apricots, strawberries and cherries, June for peaches, and July for grapes and figs. Autumn brings apples, quinces, persimmons, dates, pomegranates and pears. Melons, watermelons and lemons ripen in late summer, but are available in the markets as late as January.

Fruits are eaten fresh, cooked, dried, made into preserves, jams and drinks kn

The diet of the once-nomadic Kazaks and Kyrgyz consists mainly of meat, dairy products and bread.

as *kompot* or *sokh*. Central Asians are fond of dried fruits and nuts, particularly apricots and apricot stones, which when cracked open have a pith that tastes like pistachios. The white ones are from around Samarkand and the small brown ones from around Bukhara; they're cooked in ash and the shells are cracked by the vendor before they reach the market.

Vegetables include aubergines, peppers, turnips, cucumbers, splendid tomatoes and dozens of pumpkin and squash varieties, plus lesser known items like green radishes and yellow carrots. At any time of year you'll find delicious nuts – walnuts, peanuts, pistachios and almonds – and fine honey from the mountains.

This bounty of fresh fruits and vegetables remains a mystery to most restaurants and even some home cooking, though some kitchens and home-stays will cook the ingredients if you bring them. Vegetarians will find it more rewarding to cook for themselves.

Shashlyk

The ubiquitous *shashlyk* – kebabs of fresh or marinated mutton, beef, liver, minced meat or, in restaurants, chicken – is usually served with nan bread and vinegary onions. The quality varies from inedible to delicious (with the latter occurring mainly in Xinjiang).

Plov

Plov (or *palov* or *palu*) – Central Asian pilaf – consists mainly of rice with fried and boiled meat, onions and carrots, and sometimes raisins, chickpeas or fruit slices, all cooked up in a hemispherical cauldron called a *kazan*. While Uzbek men usually stay out of the kitchen, they pride themselves on preparing good plov; an *oshpaz*, or master chef, can dish up a special plov for thousands on a special occasion like a wedding. Plov is always the piece de resistance when entertaining guests – hence the mistaken impression that Central Asians can prepare only one dish.

Noodles

Long, stout noodles (laghman, or *la miàn* to Xinjiang Chinese) distinguish Central Asian cuisine from any other. Laghman is served everywhere, especially as the base for a spicy soup (usually called laghman too) with fried mutton, peppers, tomatoes and onions. In Xinjiang, *suoman* is roughly the same ingredients on a 'bed' of noodle squares.

A special holiday dish in Kazakstan and Kyrgyzstan is *besbarmak*, which is large flat noodles topped with lamb and/or horsemeat cooked in vegetable broth. The name means 'five fingers' since it was traditionally eaten with the hand. Uzbeks call it *shilpildok*, and Russians *myasa po-kazakhskiy*.

Uyghurs are the undisputed Central Asian masters of the dying art of noodle-making – rolling, stretching, slapping, twirling or folding, and defying the laws of physics with flour, water, salt and oil.

Korean and Dungan noodles are also generally excellent.

Meat & Dough

There are four other variations on the meat and dough theme – steamed, boiled, baked and fried. *Manty* (steamed dumplings) are a favourite from Mongolia to Turkey. *Chuchvara* (Tajik – *tushbera*, Uyghur – *chuchureh*, Russian – *pelmeny*, Chinese – *jia*) are a smaller boiled cousin of manty, served plain or with vinegar, sour cream, butter or whatever, or in soups. Manty and chuchvara are sometimes fried or deep-fried.

A favourite snack is *samsa* (Uyghur: *samsi*, Tajik: *sambusa*), a version of manty usually baked in a tandoor oven – at their best made with flaky puff pastry, distinguishable by a spiral pattern on top. The deep-fried version is an originally Crimean Tatar speciality called *chebureki*.

One of the most common prepared foods in markets and on the street are *piroshki*, greasy Russian fried pies filled with potatoes or meat. A mixture of fat, mutton and onions is the customary filling in all these, but you can also find them filled with potato, pumpkin, chickpeas, curd (*tvorog* in Russian) or, in spring, greens. As with everything made with sheep's fat, they get

gummy if you don't eat them straight from the fire or the pot.

Soups

In addition to laghman, other soups you may come across frequently are *shorpa* (or *shurpa* or *sorpo*), a broth with chickpeas, a few vegetables, herbs and a chunk of mutton on the bone; *manpar*, noodle bits, meat, vegetables and mild seasoning in broth; and Russian borshch (beetroot soup). *Lapsha* is not a 'national dish', just the Russian word for 'noodle', or generically for noodle soup.

Bread

The wide array of cheap breads, leavened and unleavened, is a staple for most of the population. Nan (*non* to Uzbeks and Tajiks), usually baked in tandoor ovens, is served at every meal. Some varieties are prepared with onions, meat or sheep's-tail fat in the dough; others are topped with nigella (the black, onion-tasting seed of a flower from the fennel family) or anise, poppy or sesame seeds. Flat-bread also serves as an impromptu plate for shashlyk kebabs.

You may also find breads made from corn or chickpea flour, and pancakes without yeast are common. *Katlama* is an incredible flaky bread made by repeatedly folding oil or butter into the dough and frying in a skillet or cauldron. Home-made breads are often thicker and darker than normal nan.

Russians call nan *lepyoshka*. Boring, square, white-flour Russian loaves are *khleb* (but to confuse things, some Central Asians use *nan* for this too).

Milk Products

Central Asia is known for the richness and delicacy of its fermented dairy products, which use cow, sheep, goat, camel or horse milk. The milk itself is probably unpasteurised, but its cultured derivatives are safe if kept in hygienic conditions.

Soured milk is used to make yoghurt (*katyk*) with the addition of bacterial culture. Katyk can be strained to make *suzma*, like tart cottage or cream cheese, used as a garnish or added to soups. *Ayran* is a salty yoghurt water mix (the Russian equivalent is call *kefir*; don't confuse this with the Russians' beloved *smetana*, or sour cream). Many doughs and batters incorporate sour milk products, giving them a tangy flavour. Milk-based soups, hot and cold, are common.

The final stage in the 'milk cycle' is *kurtob* or *kurut,* which is dried suzma (often rolled into marble-size balls), a tasty travel snack or soup additive. The pink ones from the Fergana valley have chili pepper added. Scrape away the outer layer if you're uneasy about who's been handling them.

Tvorog is a Russian speciality, made from soured milk, heated to curdle. This is hung in cheesecloth overnight to strain off the whey. The closest Central Asian equivalent is suzma. *Qaymok (*or *kaimak)* is pure sweet cream, skimmed from fresh milk that has sat overnight. This wickedly tasty breakfast item, wonderful with honey, is available in many markets in the early morning, but sells out fast, usually by sunrise.

Fish

You can find caviar and sea-fish dishes in western Kazakstan, by the Caspian Sea. Dried and smoked fish are sold near Issyk Kul. River fish are not recommended, considering the chemical brew they probably swim around in.

Salads

Salads are a refreshing break from heavy main courses. Tomatoes dominate in summer, green radishes in winter. Greens – parsley, fresh coriander, green onions and dill – are served and eaten whole. In state-run restaurants you'll probably be offered a plate of tomatoes or cucumbers, or the ubiquitous Russian *salat stolichny*, a 'Russian Salad' made with carrots, beets, bits of beef, potato and egg in sour cream and mayonnaise.

Desserts

Raisins, nuts, fruit, confections, cookies and a hundred types of halvah are generally served with tea. Cakes and pastries are a European addition to the end of a meal. Almost all Central Asians, of every ethnic group, love ice cream (Russian: *morozhenoe*). You'll find a freezer of the stuff almost anywhere.

Turkish Food

Turkish restaurants are popping up everywhere in Central Asia and most are excellent value. Dishes are almost the same as in Turkey. *Pides* are similar to thin crust pizzas; *lahmacun* is a cheaper, less substantial version. Kebabs are popular, especially Adana kebabs (mincemeat patties) and delicious Iskander kebabs (thinly sliced mutton over bread, with yoghurt and rich tomato sauce). *Patlican* (aubergine) and *dolma* (stuffed peppers) are the most common vegetable dishes. *Çaçik* is a delicious yoghurt, cucumber and mint dip and makes a great snack with *lavash*, a huge bread similar to nan but lighter. Desserts include *baklava* (light pastry covered in syrup) and *sutlaç* (rice pudding).

Where to Eat

You can eat in street-side stalls and cafes, cheap canteens, private restaurants and state-run ones and, best of all, in private homes. In smaller towns, restaurants, if they exist at all, can be pretty dire, and hotels may have the only edible food outside private homes. Many of the cheaper places are only open for lunch and close whenever the food runs out. There has recently been an explosion of private restaurants in the major cities and you can now eat well and cheaply, a great improvement on a few years ago.

Hygiene Most cafes and restaurants have a wash-stand somewhere, and even street stalls may have running water (or you could pack a supply of pre-moistened towelettes, or antibacterial hand gel). Kitchen hygiene is unpredictable except in the best restaurants. Those in the markets tend to use the freshest ingredients. The food is generally hygienic if it's straight off the fire. For street food, it can't hurt to carry your own cup and utensils. The rule for market food is 'peel it or boil it'.

In restaurants, salt is usually provided in common bowls, and looks dirty because it's unrefined.

Pitfalls Beware the *zakuski* (starters), which can kill off (a) your appetite and (b) your budget. One way to save money is to order only from the first-course menu.

A few places run a nasty little scam. You sit down at a table set with zakuski, push them aside and order, but though you didn't ask for them and didn't touch them, you find them all on your bill. In general you must pay for what's on your table; if you don't want it, ask on arrival for *chistyy stol*, Russian for 'clean table'. Some top-end places may also have steep door, music or 'seating' charges. You will normally pay extra for your own booth or curtained off seating area.

The bill may be no more than a scrap of paper showing the total. Ask for an itemisation if you have any doubts. You won't make any friends doing this, but cheating foreigners is not uncommon.

Restaurants A few restaurants in bigger cities offer interesting Central Asian or European dishes and earnest service, though they almost have to be overpriced just to keep up with their own costs. Choice tends to be limited, and they may close altogether outside the summer season. In the capitals you'll also find some international eateries, especially Turkish, Korean and Chinese, with meal prices from US$5 to US$25.

The fare in state-run places is modestly priced and boring, tending towards Russian meat and potatoes. For a list of standard restaurant dishes see the Language chapter.

Russians and Russianised locals don't expect good food from restaurants. What they want at midday is a break. What they want in the evening is a night out – lots of booze and gale-force music or a variety show. Most restaurants play hideous Eurobeat or techno music, specifically designed, it seems, to put you off your food. If you're just looking for a quiet meal, go in the afternoon when there's no music and sometimes a cheaper set menu. Even then the kind staff will most likely turn on the beat especially for the foreigners. Consider checking out an evening variety show just once, however, just to sample the rich mix of debauchery and questionable taste.

Russian is spoken in all but the cheapest rural eateries. *Mozhna pa-yest?*, 'May I eat?', gets the ball rolling. Don't be awed by the *menyu*; they don't have most of it anyhow, just possibly the items with prices typed or pencilled in. Alternatively you could point at what others have. Visits to the kitchen are frowned upon except in very small villages. *Mozhna zakazat?* is 'May I order?'. To pay the bill, say *schyot*.

Don't misread meat prices on menus in fancier restaurants – they are often given as per 100g, not per serving (which is often more like 400g). Bear in mind that many Russian dishes come with nothing, so you'll have to order rice or vegetables separately. Some restaurants offer a set meal, known as a *kompleks*. Finally, always check the bill, and your change.

Hotel Restaurants Every tourist hotel has a restaurant, usually modestly priced and dreary; outside the cities a hotel meal will rarely be more than about US$2. Staff are generally accustomed to undemanding groups and tend to be confused or annoyed by individual diners.

Larger hotels also have alternatives. A *bufet* ('bu-**fyet**') is not a buffet but a little deli with cheap cold meats, boiled eggs, salads, bread and pastries. To take something back to your room, say *soboy* ('sa-**boy**').

One solution to the problem of booked-out hotel restaurants is to pig out with an early or late lunch and go to the bufet or a street stall for an omelette or shashlyk when it's dinnertime. Lunchtime hotel restaurant meals often feature 'national' dishes, and you can fill up on laghman and salad at cold-course prices.

Teahouses The teahouse (*chaykhana* in Turkmen, *chaykana* in Kyrgyz, *choyhona* in Uzbek and Tajik, *shaykhana* in Kazak) is male Central Asia's essential socio-gastronomic institution, especially in Uzbekistan. Usually shaded, often by a pool or stream, it's as much a men's club as an eatery – though women, including foreigners, are tolerated, and local women may be seated at separate places or times. Old and young congregate to eat or to drink pot after pot green tea and talk the day away.

Traditional seating is on a bed-like form (Uzbeks call it a *takhta*, Taji chorpoy), covered with a carpet and topped with a low table. Take your shoes off to sit on the platform, or leave them on and hang your feet over.

Many chaykhana cooks will accept special orders in the morning or the day before. For the equivalent of a few dollars, some places will provide a cauldron, utensils and firewood for those who bring their own ingredients.

Cafes & Canteens A *kafe* can be anything from an ice cream parlour to an elegant place with supper music. Most are mini-restaurants with small menus and no entertainment. They tend to open and close earlier than restaurants and be a bit cheaper.

The canteen (Kazak: *askhana*, Kyrgyz: *ashkana*, Uzbek: *oshhona*, Russian: *stolovaya*) is the ordinary citizen's eatery – dreary but cheap, usually self-service, with a limited choice of cutlet or meatballs, sometimes laghman, soup, boiled vegetables, bread, tea and awful coffee. Some are decent, most are very grotty and there's often that pervading canteen smell. Two good places to sniff out cheap canteens are at universities or government offices.

Home Restaurants Those not lucky enough to get a personal invitation to dinner can still enjoy some fine home-cooked food in certain old-town neighbourhoods of Tashkent and Samarkand (see the respective sections of the Uzbekistan chapter). Private citizens convert their own courtyards into little unofficial restaurants at midday and in the evening, serving a few simple dishes, and sometimes rarities like quail or other wild game.

There are no signs; family members simply solicit customers on the street, and the competition can be intense. Most places are reasonably clean, though you might want to bring your own utensils. Bring your own beer or wine, or buy theirs.

For tips on the protocol of being invited to ~meone's house for dinner (this is different ~n home restaurants), see the Hospitality ~ in the Society & Conduct section of the about Central Asia chapter.

Holy Smoke

In markets, stations and parks all over Central Asia you'll see gypsy women and children asking for a few coins to wave their pans of burning herbs around you or the premises. The herb is called *isriq* in Uzbek, and the smoke is said to be good medicine against colds and flu (and the evil eye?), and a cheap alternative to scarce medicines. Some people also burn it when they move into a new flat.

Self-Catering

Markets Every sizable town has a colourful *bazar* (Russian: *rynok*) or farmers' market with hectares of fresh and dried fruit, vegetables, walnuts, peanuts, honey, cheese, bread, meat and eggs. On weekends the collective farmers come in, so everybody else comes too, for the best deals and freshest goods. Go early in the morning for the liveliest scene and the best selection.

Korean and Dungan vendors sell spicy *kimchi* (vegetable salads), a great antidote for mutton overdose (though some may have MSG). Russians flog pelmeny, *pirozhki* (deep-fried meat or vegetable turnovers) and yoghurt. Watch for snacks like salted apricot seeds (a Samarkand and Bukhara speciality), roasted chickpeas and puffed wheat and rice. Fresh honey on hot-from-the-oven bread makes a splendid breakfast.

Don't be afraid to haggle (with a smile) – everybody else does. As a foreigner you may be quoted twice the normal price or, on the other hand, given a bit extra. Insist on making your own choices or you may end up with second-rate produce. Most produce is sold by the kilo.

State Food Shops & Supermarkets Soviet-style state food shops are slowly being replaced by western supermarkets and kiosks, featuring European or American tinned foods, biscuits, dried soups, tea, coffee and alcohol. The state food stores (*gastronom*) still exist here and there, stocked with a few bits of cheese, lonely bottles of milk or 200 cans of Soviet-made 'Beef in its own Juice' stacked up along the windowsill.

Vegetarians

Central Asia can be hell for vegetarians; indeed the whole concept of vegetarianism is unfathomable to most locals. We met many travellers who had suspended their principles just to survive, though with persistence and a few food tips this needn't be the only option. Those determined to avoid meat will need to visit a lot of farmers' markets (see the Markets entry earlier in this section) and should preferably carry their own stove. Vegetarians will have fewer problems in Kashgar's Chinese restaurants, where there are many vegetable or tofu dishes.

In restaurants, you'll see a lot of tomato and cucumber salads. Zakuski (cold appetisers) may include things like eggs and mushrooms. Laghman or soup may be ordered without meat, but the broth is usually meat-based – you can always just ask for the noodles. In private homes there is always bread, jams, salads, whole greens and herbs on the table, and you should be able to put in a word to your host in advance. Even if you specifically ask for vegetarian dishes you'll often discover the odd piece of meat snuck in somewhere – after a while it all seems a bit of a conspiracy.

Oddly, many Central Asians don't consider sausage, or even fat, as 'meat'. Potatoes (kartoshka; kartofel in Russian) don't seem to be filed under 'vegetable' in the former Soviet mind either, so you must ask for them separately.

For specifically veg fare in Uzbekistan, try asking for katykli sholghom hurda (dish with rice, turnips, carrots, onions and yoghurt); mosh qovoq (mung beans and pumpkin porridge); shir qovoq (milk soup with rice and pumpkin); or mutkhurak (chickpeas).

If you are vegetarian, say so, early and often – when you check into your hotel, when you book a restaurant, when you order. 'I'm a vegetarian' in Russian is ya vegeturianka (females) or ya vegetarianets (males). 'Without meat' is etsiz in Turkmen, atsiz in Kazak and Kyrgyz, goshsiz in Uyghur, gushtsiz in Uzbek, and bez myasa in Russian.

Holiday Food

Ramadan is the Muslim month of fasting, when the devout abstain from eating, drinking and smoking from sunrise to sunset. Since the collapse of the USSR, this has become more popular as a holiday in Central Asia, though relatively few maintain the fast strictly. See the Religion section in the Facts about Central Asia chapter for more about Ramadan.

A big occasion for eating is Navrus (see the Public Holidays & Special Events section earlier in this chapter). Along with plov and other traditional fare, several dishes are served particularly at this time. The traditional Navrus dish, prepared only by women, is sumalak – wheat soaked in water for three days until it sprouts, then ground, mixed with oil, flour and sugar, and cooked on a low heat for 24 hours. Halim is a porridge of boiled meat and wheat grains, seasoned with black pepper and cinnamon. Nishalda – whipped egg whites, sugar and liquorice flavouring – is also popular at Ramadan.

DRINKS
Tea

Chay (choy to Uzbeks and Tajiks, shay to Kazaks) is drunk with some reverence in Central Asia. An array of customs surrounds it, and an entire branch of Central Asian cuisine – samsas, bread, halvah and various fried foods – is aimed at tea-time.

It's the drink of hospitality, offered first to every guest, usually in a little cup with no handles. From a fresh pot, an Uzbek host will pour tea into one cup, twice returning it to the pot before offering it the third time to the guest as a sign of respect (or taking it himself to prove it's not tainted). A cup filled only a little way up is a compliment, allowing your host to refill it often, and keep its contents warm (if your host pours to the brim, it may be a signal that he'd prefer you didn't stay too long). Pass and accept tea with the right hand; it's extra polite to put the left hand over the heart as you do this. If your tea is too hot, don't blow on it, but swirl it gently in the cup without spilling any. If it has grown cold, your host will throw it away before refilling the cup

Straight green *(kok)* tea is the favourite; locals claim it beats the heat and unblocks you after too much greasy plov. Black tea is preferred in Samarkand and Urgench, and by most Russians. Turkmen call green tea *gek* and black tea *gara*; to Russians, green tea is *zelyonnyy chay*, black tea *chyornyy chay*. Western Turkmen brew tea with *chal*, camels' milk, and Pamir Tajiks use goats' milk. Kazak tea is taken with milk, salt and butter – the nomadic equivalent of fast food – hot, tasty and high in calories. Cardamom or star anise from the market will jazz up boring restaurant tea anywhere.

In Xinjiang you can get Chinese jasmine tea *(cha)* everywhere.

Nonalcoholic Drinks

Don't drink the tap water. Cheap bottled mineral water is easy to find, but it's normally gassy and very mineral tasting. Modern joint venture brands are more expensive but taste a lot better, though most are carbonated. Companies like Coca-Cola have factories in all the republics and their products are everywhere.

Old Soviet-style street side machines dispense soda water *(chesti)*, but everybody uses the same glasses so bring your own container if that worries you. Portable kiosks offer the same, often with a dash of cordial, though this is often just tap water with added fizz from a gas bottle under the table. In any case both methods are gradually dying out.

Napitok (Russian for 'beverage') is usually diluted, sweetened fruit juice served from pitchers at cafes and restaurants for next to nothing, but it is definitely not safe. *Sok* and *compot* are similar but more natural forms of fruit juice. *Limonad* is not lemonade but an awful-tasting fizzy drink of dubious origin.

Ayran is a popular liquid-yoghurt drink, sometimes slightly salty; the Russian equivalent is *kefir*. In Xinjiang, little 200ml sealed bottles of sweet yoghurt drink are available everywhere.

Restaurant coffee, usually made in large vats with second-rate ingredients, bears no resemblance to what westerners think of as coffee. Tins of cheap imported instant coffee can be found in shops in Uzbekistan,

Kyrgyzstan and Kazakstan. If you're a serious coffee or black-tea drinker, bring your own, plus a mug and/or thermos; hot water *(tipitok)* is easy to drum up from a bufet or the floor-lady.

Alcoholic Drinks

Vodka & Spirits Despite their Muslim heritage, most Central Asians drink, at least with guests. If you don't enjoy hard booze and heavy drinking, make your excuses early (see the Alcohol and Assault-by-Hospitality entry in the Dangers & Annoyances section of this chapter, earlier).

In a private home or at a restaurant with local friends, a male guest may be expected to offer the first toast. You'll be expected to offer one eventually in any case. Like the Russians who introduced them to vodka, Central Asians take their toasts seriously – small speeches encapsulating their hopes for their guests' well being. Even some of our local friends who don't drink much say it's impolite to refuse the initial 'bottoms up' (Russian – *vashe zdarovye!*), and/or abstain from at least a symbolic sip at each toast. But there's usually heavy pressure to drain your glass every time – so as not to give offence, it is implied – and the pressure only increases as everybody gets loaded.

It is possible to stop at any number of tatty kiosks all over Central Asia and choose from a vast array of industrial-strength spirits with names like Yeltsin or Terminator Vodka, and cheap, drinkable *champanski*. Beware of imitations and counterfeits, usually awful and sometimes lethal. Check the labels, certifications and seals.

You'll also find European beers *(piva)* for around US$1 to US$2 a can, dubious Russian beer, and sometimes cheap, decent Chinese beer. Efes is a popular Turkish beer.

If you order a bottle of restaurant vodka, check the seal; waiters sometimes dilute it and keep a share. Most hotel restaurants have a bufet window somewhere back by the kitchen, where attendants buy the drinks by the bottle or the carafe, that they resell to diners. For takeaway beer, booze, mineral water or soft drinks, put on your I-know-what-I'm-doing face, walk back and buy your own there for noticeably less than they charge you at the table.

Kumys & Other Attractions Kumys (properly *kymys* in Kyrgyz, *qymyz* in Kazak) is fermented mare's milk, a mildly alcoholic drink appreciated by Kazaks and Kyrgyz, even those who no longer spend much time in the saddle (nonalcoholic varieties are also made). It's available only in spring and summer, when mares are foaling, and takes around three days to ferment. The best kumys comes from the herders themselves;

the stuff available in the cities is sometimes diluted with cow's milk or water. Drinking too much of it may give you diarrhoea. Kazaks and Kyrgyz also like a thick, yeasty, slightly fizzy concoction called *bozo*, made from boiled, fermented millet or other grains. Turkmen, Kazak and Karakalpak nomads like *shubat*, fermented camel milk.

ENTERTAINMENT

Theatre, opera and ballet struggle on in Central Asia, and performances and venues are still excellent, especially in Tashkent.

Buzkashi

In a region many of whose people are descended from hot-blooded nomads, no-one would expect cricket to be the national sport. Even so, *buzkashi* (literally 'grabbing the dead goat') is wild beyond belief. As close to warfare as a sport can get, buzkashi is a bit like rugby on horseback in which the 'ball' is the headless carcass of a calf, goat or sheep (whatever is handy).

The day before the kick-off the carcass (or *boz*) has its head, lower legs and entrails removed and is soaked in cold water for 24 hours to toughen it up. The game begins with the carcass in the centre of a circle at one end of a field; at the other end is a bunch of wild, adrenaline-crazed horsemen. At a signal it's every man for himself as they charge for the carcass. The aim is to gain possession of the boz and carry it up the field and around a post, with the winning rider being the one who finally drops the boz back in the circle. All the while there's a frenzied horse-backed tug-of-war going on as each competitor tries to gain possession; smashed noses, wrenched shoulders and shattered thigh bones are all part of the fun.

Not surprisingly, the game is said to date from the days of Jenghiz Khan when, tradition has it, human carcasses were used rather than those of sheep. More importantly, the game traditionally enforced the nomadic values necessary for collective survival – courage, adroitness, wit and strength, while propagating a remarkable skill on horseback. The point of the game used to be the honour, and perhaps notoriety, of the victor, but gifts such as silk *chapans* (cloaks), rifles or cash are common. In 1995 at a Navrus festival game at Tajikistan's Hissar fortress, the prize was a new Lada (an Eastern European car).

Buzkashi takes place mainly outside of the pastoral season, in the cooler months of spring and autumn, at weekends, on feast days or to mark special occasions such as weddings. If you're lucky you'll catch it during Navrus or some local celebration. You can also see it in Pashtun areas of Pakistan's North-West Frontier Province and, in theory, in the towns of Mazar-i-Sharif and Kunduz in the north of Afghanistan, though recent reports suggest that the spoilsport Taliban have banned the sport as un-Islamic.

BRADLEY MAYHEW

National folk dance and song troupes are popular, and some better-known ones are mentioned in the country chapters.

Modern distractions are beginning to creep in to the major cities. Almaty has a popular bowling alley, and Kazakstan has a nationwide chain of tame amusement parks, called Fantasy World.

Outside of the capital cities you'll be hard pressed to come across much in the way of performed entertainment. Cinemas are generally now closed down or showing dated second-rate American films and some foreign pornography, mostly dubbed into Russian. Video parlours showing imported Indian musicals and pirated copies of *Titanic* are much more popular.

Restaurants still serve as a mainstay of nightlife, with diners passing over their shashlyk for another slammer of vodka and a lurch around the floor to a jackhammer Casio-beat. A few western-style disco-cum-nightclubs have appeared, but the western-style cover charges tend to limit the clientele to the nouveaux riche and Mafiosi types.

SPECTATOR SPORTS

In regions with significant nomadic or animal-raising traditions, you may be lucky enough to see traditional horseback games at certain local festivals or on national holidays. The spectacular Central Asian sport, in which two large teams of horsemen play a kind of wild, no-holds-barred polo without sticks and with a beheaded goat carcass instead of a ball, is known in Tajikistan, Afghanistan and Pathan areas of Pakistan as *buzkashi*, in Kazakstan as *kökpar*, in Karakalpakstan as *ylaq oyyny* and in Kyrgyzstan as *ulak-tartysh*; Russians call it *kozlodranie*.

In another traditional horseback game, called *kyz-kumay* in Kyrgyzstan ('kiss-the-girl') and *kyz kuu* in Kazakstan, a man chases a woman on horseback and tries to kiss her, or gets chased and whipped if he fails. This allegedly began as a formalised alternative to abduction, the traditional nomadic way to take a bride.

Other equestrian activities in Kyrgyzstan include *at chabysh*, a horse race over a distance of 20 to 30km, *jumby atmai*, horseback archery, *tiyin enmei*, where contestants pick up coins off the ground while galloping past, and *udarysh*, horseback wrestling. Eagle hunting contests take place during festivals or special celebrations. Don't pass up the chance to view these spectacles. Other popular sports include wrestling *(kuresh)* and soccer. In Uzbekistan you may see circus-style high wire acts during public holidays.

SHOPPING

Potential Central Asian buys include carpets, felt rugs, wall hangings, silk, traditional clothing, ceramic figurines and even nomadic accessories such as horse whips and saddles. Hats are a particularly good buy throughout the region and they make nice presents for the folks back home.

Central Asian bazars are enjoyable even if you're just looking, with everything from Russian champagne to cow's heads, plus hectares of seasonal produce and preserved foods. The best bargains, often at a fraction of the cost in hotel gift shops and cute tourist bazars, are found outside heavily touristed areas entirely, eg in small-town bazars. Another surprising souvenir source right under your nose is the local TsUM (department store).

For any shop licensed to accept credit cards, allow for a hefty service charge when you pay the bill back home. See the Customs section earlier in this chapter about buying antiques or items that look antique. For more details on shopping see the individual country chapters.

Getting There & Away

This chapter deals with travel into or out of the area consisting of the ex-Soviet Central Asian republics and Xinjiang (China). See Getting There & Away under the relevant city section in each country chapter for travel *between* Central Asian countries.

The region's main air links to the 'outside' are through the ex-Soviet republican capitals of Almaty, Bishkek, Tashkent and Ashgabat. A few smaller cities have connections to CIS countries outside of Central Asia, especially Russia. The long-distance rail connections are mostly with Mother Russia – from Moscow to Tashkent and Almaty, and from the Trans-Siberian Railway to Almaty and Tashkent. Others are the relatively new lines between Almaty and Ürümqi (and beyond) in China, and between Ashgabat and Iran.

The other main overland links are two roads from China – one accessible year-round via Ürümqi to Almaty, and a warm weather one via Kashgar, over the Torugart pass into Kyrgyzstan. Kashgar in turn can be reached by road over the Khunjerab pass on Pakistan's amazing Karakoram Highway. A recently opened road link connects Mashad in Iran to Ashgabat.

Finally there is a hybrid journey from Turkey through the Caucasus mountains by bus to Baku (Azerbaijan), across the Caspian Sea to Turkmenbashi (Turkmenistan) and by train to Ashgabat, Bukhara and beyond. See Turkey under Air in this chapter for details.

AIR

Many European and Asian cities now have direct flights to the Central Asian capitals. From North America and Australasia you will have to change planes at least once en route. Of the many routes in, two handy corridors are via Turkey (thanks to the geopolitics of the future) and via Russia (thanks to the geopolitics of the past). Turkish Airlines seems to have more good deals than anyone else (to Almaty, Ashgabat, Bishkek and Tashkent), while Russian and Central Asian carriers have the most connections. Turkey also has the advantage of a full house of Central Asian embassies, airline offices and plenty of travel agencies. Moscow has four airports and connections can be inconvenient.

Tashkent – seven hours from London, 3½ from Moscow, Tel Aviv and Delhi, 4½ from Istanbul, 5½ from Beijing and 6½ from Bangkok – may have the most central airport in Eurasia. More flights go to Tashkent than to any other city in the region. Almaty's airport burned down in 1999; it is to be replaced in 2002 by the region's smartest airport. In the meantime all flights are funnelled through the smaller, but still standing, international terminal.

Almaty is also a useful gateway to Bishkek. No Kazakstan transit visa is necessary if you're going straight to Bishkek (three hours by road). KLM is planning to run its own free Almaty-Bishkek ground shuttle service.

Air Travel Glossary

Cancellation Penalties If you have to cancel or change a discounted ticket, there may be heavy penalties involved; insurance can sometimes be taken out against these penalties. Some airlines impose penalties on regular tickets as well, particularly against 'no show' passengers.

Full Fares Airlines traditionally offer first class (coded F), business class (coded J) and economy class (coded Y) tickets. These days there are so many promotional and discounted fares available that few passengers pay full economy fare.

Lost Tickets If you lose your airline ticket, an airline will usually treat it like a travellers cheque and, after inquiries, issue you with a replacement. Legally, however, an airline is entitled to treat it like cash, so if you lose a ticket, it could be forever.

Open Jaw Tickets These are return tickets that allow you to fly to one place but return from another, and travel between the two 'jaws' by any means of transport at your own expense. These are particularly useful if you are flying in to one end of Central Asia and out of the other.

Overbooking Airlines hate to fly empty seats and will often book more passengers than they have seats and occasionally someone gets bumped. Guess who it's most likely to be? Passengers who check in late.

Reconfirmation If you don't reconfirm your flight at least 72 hours before departure, the airline may delete your name from the passenger list. This is essential for any flight out of Central Asia, where overbooking is common and schedules change unpredictably. Airline booking offices will reconfirm for you free of charge; hotel airline desks may slap on fees.

Round-the-World Tickets RTW tickets give you a limited period (usually a year) in which to circumnavigate the globe. You can go anywhere the carrying airlines go, as long as you don't backtrack. The number of stopovers or total number of separate flights is decided before you set off and they usually cost a bit more than a basic return flight.

Transferred Tickets Airline tickets cannot be transferred from one person to another. Travellers sometimes try to sell the return half of their ticket, but officials can ask you to prove that you are the person named on the ticket. This may not be checked on domestic flights, but on international flights, tickets are usually compared with passports.

Travel Periods Some officially discounted fares, advance purchase fares in particular, vary with the time of year. There is often a low (off-peak) season and a high (peak) season. Sometimes there's an intermediate or shoulder season as well. Usually the fare depends on your outward flight – if you depart in the high season and return in the low season, you pay the high-season fare.

Airlines

Air Kazakstan, Kyrgyzstan and Turkmenistan Airlines, and Uzbekistan Airways (the best of the lot) serve the region. Tajikistan International Airlines is in a state of near collapse. Xinjiang Airlines is devolved from Air China (CAAC) and leases some of its planes from Russian carriers (our Ürümqi-Kashgar run was on a less-than-inspiring plane).

Russia has a host of Aeroflot spin-off airlines and a good, new long-haul airline called Transaero (www.transaero.ru). Transaero offers connections between Tashkent and Almaty to many cities in Europe with a change of plane in Moscow.

Other international carriers with scheduled Central Asia connections include Austrian Air, British Airways (www.british-airways.com) operating as British Mediterranean, Iran Air, KLM (www.klm.nl), Lufthansa (www.lufthansa.com), Turkish Airlines, PIA and Asiana. Azerbaijan Airlines flies to/from Baku, across the Caspian Sea from Turkmenistan.

Airline Safety

Aeroflot, the former Soviet state airline, has been decentralised into around four hundred splinter airlines. The International Airline Passengers' Association (IAPA), a consumer watchdog, says that collectively these 'baby-flots' now have the worst regional safety record in the world, thanks to poor maintenance, ageing aircraft and gross overloading – and little money to remedy the situation. After several highly publicised disasters, the IAPA in January 1994 advised travellers to avoid *Russian* domestic carriers.

But of course the Central Asian carriers are not Russian domestic airlines, and in fact most have at least lifted their *international* services towards international safety standards. The US Federal Aviation Administration (FAA) at the end of 1994 found Uzbekistan Airways (which has a cooperative agreement with Lufthansa for the maintenance of its international Airbus fleet and the training of flight crew) to be in compliance with international standards. Transaero also has notably higher standards than most. In general, however, the Central Asian carriers' domestic flights are not up to the same standards.

In December 1997 a Tajikistan Airlines plane crashed in Sharjah, killing 85 passengers, and a Kazakstan Airlines plane collided with a Saudia jet over Delhi killing 350 people.

Airline Offices

You may need to contact airlines directly for schedules, connections and special fares, and to reconfirm flights, though discounted fares are usually offered by a sales agent. The airlines can give you the contact details of their sales agents. For airline offices in Central Asia see Getting There & Away in the relevant capital city in each country chapter. Contact details change with notorious regularity so double check before heading off to one of the following offices.

Air Kazakstan (9Y) Air Kazakstan has connections between Almaty and Baku, Beijing, Budapest, Delhi, Frankfurt, Istanbul, Kiev, Moscow, Seoul, Sharjah, Tehran and Tel Aviv. It has offices in Vienna, Beijing, Frankfurt, Hannover, Moscow and Istanbul.

Kyrgyzstan Airlines (K2) Kyrgyzstan Airlines flies between Bishkek and Beijing, Birmingham, Delhi, Frankfurt, Hannover, Istanbul, Karachi, Moscow, Sharjah and Ürümqi. Offices outside Central Asia are:

China
  (☎ 10-6522 9799) Beijing International
  Hotel, 9 Jianguomenwai Dajie, Beijing. See
  the Xinjiang chapter for the Ürümqi office.
Germany
  (☎ 069-6907 3962, fax 496 0224) Frankfurt
  (☎ 511-7261 959) Hannover
India
  (☎ 11-687 7715, 336 8713)
  72 Regal Bldg, Connaught Place, Delhi
Russia
  (☎ 95-237 6304)
  Apt 1009, 37/3 Leningradskiy Prospekt, Moscow
Turkey
  (☎ 212-237 2491)
  39/2 Cumhuriyet Caddesi, Taksim, Istanbul
UK
  (☎ 0121-523 5277, fax 507 1800)
  358 Soho Rd, Birmingham

Turkish Airlines (TK) Turkish Airline (www.turkishairlines.com) offices include:

Australia
  (☎ 02-9299 8400, fax 9299 8443,
  ✉ turkair@mt.net.au)
  603/16 Barrack St, Sydney NSW
France
  (☎ 33-1 42 66 47 20) 1 rue Scribe, 75009, Paris
Germany
  (☎ 069-27 300720/721, fax 259123)
  Baseler Str 35-37, 60329 Frankfurt-am-Main
Turkey
  (☎ 212-663 6363, fax 240 2984)
  Cumhuriyet Caddesi No 199/201 Kat: 3,
  Istanbul
  (☎ 312-428 0200, fax 428 1681)
  Ataturk Bulvari No 154, Bakanliklar, Ankara
UK
  (☎ 020-7766 9300/9333, fax 7976 1733,
  ✉ turkishairlines.uk@btinternet.com)
  125 Pall Mall, London SW1Y 5EA
USA
  (☎ 800-874 8875, 212-339 96 50,
  ✉ info@tknyc)
  437 Madison Ave 17-B, New York, NY 10022

Turkmenistan Airways (T5) Also known as Avia Company Turkmenistan, this airline has connections between Ashgabat and Abu Dhabi, Baku, Bangkok, Birmingham, Delhi, Frankfurt, Istanbul, Karachi, Kiev, London, Moscow and Yerevan. Offices outside Central Asia include:

China
(☎ 10-6529 799) Beijing International Hotel, 9 Jianguomenwai Dajie, Beijing
India
(☎ 11-331 2916/1593, fax 371 3869, 332 5521) Delhi
Russia
(☎ 095-290 5483, 291 2481, fax 291 1233) Moscow
Turkey
(☎ 212-241 4601, 233 9309, fax 246 2209) Istanbul
UK
(☎ 020-8577 2212, fax 8893 5400) Hounslow, London

Uzbekistan Airways (HY) Uzbekistan Airways has connections between Tashkent and Amsterdam, Athens, Baku, Bangkok, Beijing, Delhi, Dhaka, Frankfurt, Istanbul, Jeddah, Karachi, Kiev, Kuala Lumpur, Lahore, London, Moscow, New York, Paris, Riyadh, Seoul, Sharjah and Tel Aviv. New routes are planned to Japan and Indonesia. See its Web site www.uzbekistanairways.nl. Offices outside Central Asia include:

China
(☎ 10-6500 6442) 304 CITIC Rear Bldg, 19 Jianguomenwai Dajie, Beijing
France
(☎ 1-42 96 10 10) RPTA, 19 rue St Roch, Paris
Germany
(☎ 69-1337 6168) 7 Kaiser St, Frankfurt-am-Main
India
(☎ 11-335 8687) Prakash Deep Bldg, Tolstoy Marg, New Delhi
Israel
(☎ 3-510 4685) 1 Ben Yehuda St, Tel Aviv
Pakistan
(☎ 21-567 5943) 7 Avari Towers, Karachi
Russia
(☎ 095-155 6851) 709/KOR3 Leningradsky Prospekt, Moscow
(☎ 095-238 2124) 1U, 11/2 Kazachi Berulok, Moscow

South Korea
(☎ 822-722 68 56/57) Suite 934, Royal Bldg, 5 Dangju-Ding, Chongro-Ku
Thailand
(☎ 2-261 5084/5) 191/68, 15th Floor, CTI Tower, 191 Rajadapisolke Rd, Klongtoey, Bangkok
Turkey
(☎ 212-296 4632) N-141 Cumhuriyet Caddesi, El Madag, Istanbul
UK
(☎ 020-7935 1899, fax 935 9554,
✉ 106374.34@compuserve.com)
70 Marylebone Lane, London WIM 5FF
USA
(☎ 212-489 3954/3956) Suite 1401, 630 Fifth Ave, New York, NY 10111

Xinjiang Airlines (XO) Xinjiang Airlines is part of CAAC, China's aviation authority, so you can book its flights at most CAAC/Air China offices inside China. It flies between Ürümqi and Almaty, Islamabad, Moscow and Novosibirsk. There are no international flights to/from Kashgar.

Within China it flies from Ürümqi to Beijing, Changsha, Chengdu, Hong Kong, Lanzhou, Shanghai, Tianjin, Wuhan, Xi'an, Xining and Zhengzhou, as well as throughout Xinjiang.

The office in Russia (☎ 095-209 3344) is at Room 7702, Beijing Hotel, Bolshoya Sadovaia, Moscow. Pakistan's office (☎ 051-273446) is in Sohrab Plaza, Block 32, Jinnah Ave, F-6/4, Blue Area, Islamabad.

Visa Checks

You can buy air tickets without a visa or letter of support (see Visas in the Regional Facts for the Visitor chapter), but in most places outside Central Asia you will have trouble getting on a plane without one – even if embassies and travel agents tell you otherwise. And no wonder: airlines are obliged to fly anyone rejected because of improper papers back home, and in the UK, at least, airlines are fined UK£2000 (either by the Civil Aviation Authority or the Central Asian airports) for every such reject. So check-in staff tend to act like immigration officers. If you have made arrangements to get a visa on arrival, have your letter of support handy at check-in.

Buying Tickets

The plane ticket will probably be the single most expensive item in your budget, and buying it can be an intimidating business. Finding flights to Central Asia isn't always easy, as travel agents are generally unaware of the region (you'll have to help with the spelling of most cities and airlines) and many don't book flights on Russian or Central Asian airlines. Airlines can give you contact details of their consolidators, or sales agents, who often sell the airlines' tickets cheaper than the airlines themselves.

One thing to consider when arranging your itinerary is your visa situation. You may find it easier flying into, say, Bishkek if that's the easiest place to arrange a visa from home. You might consider that it's worth paying a little extra for a reliable airline such as KLM or Turkish Airlines, rather than a relatively inexperienced one, such as Kyrgyzstan Airlines or Air Kazakstan. Also check at what time you arrive in Central Asia; KLM arrives and departs Almaty in the dead of night.

Start early: some of the cheapest tickets have to be bought months in advance. Find out the fare, how many and for how long are the stopovers, the duration of the journey, whether you can get a free stopover, what time the flight arrives and any restrictions on the ticket (ie changing the return date, refunds etc).

Especially in London and some Asian capitals (notably Delhi and Bangkok), you will probably find that the cheapest flights are being advertised by obscure bucket shops taking advantage of last-minute airline discounts and other deals. Many are honest and solvent, but not all. You're safest if an agency is a member of the International Air Transport Association (IATA), or a national association like the American Society of Travel Agents (ASTA) in the USA, the Association of British Travel Agents (ABTA) in the UK or the Australian Federation of Travel Agents (AFTA) in Australia.

Firms such as STA Travel and Trailfinders, which have offices worldwide, Council Travel in the USA or Travel CUTS in Canada are all reliable. Most offer the best deals to students and people aged under 26 but are open to all, and they won't play tricks on you.

If any agency insists on cash in advance, go somewhere else. And once you have the ticket, ring the airline to confirm that you are actually booked on the flight. Paying by credit card generally offers some protection.

Watch for extra charges, eg credit card surcharges. Ask whether all your money will be refunded if the flight is cancelled or changed to a date that is unacceptable to you. Once you have your ticket, photocopy it or write down its number, together with the flight number and other details, and keep the information somewhere separate. If the ticket is lost or stolen, this will help you get a replacement. It's sensible to buy travel insurance as early as possible.

Another source of bargain fares is the Internet. Many airlines and travel agencies offer special online fares to reflect the reduced cost of electronic sales. The system works well if you know exactly how and when you want to go but is no substitute for an on-the-ball travel agent who knows the region.

Fares to the region tend to be 10% to 20% higher in peak travel season (roughly July to September and December in North America and Europe; December to January in Australia and New Zealand). Use the fares quoted in this book as a guide only. They are approximate high-season, discounted economy fares advertised at the time of research. None constitutes a recommendation for any airline.

Departure

A week's advance booking is good enough for nearly any domestic or international flight out of Central Asia, even in summer, and two or three days is still pretty safe. You must show an onward visa to buy a ticket within Central Asia, even to Moscow.

Departure Tax You'll pay this for most departures from Central Asian republics to points outside the CIS, though the rules vary – eg from Tashkent, it is US$10 (often included in the price of the ticket), with no tax for departures to domestic or CIS points; from Bishkek, it's US$10 for international departures, nothing for domestic departures.

At Ashgabat you'll be charged US$25 for international flights, US$15 for CIS flights and (probably) US$5 for domestic flights. There is no departure tax from Almaty.

Always check that the departure tax has not already been worked into the price of your air ticket.

Travellers with Special Needs

Most international airlines (though less so with the Central Asian carriers) can cater for people with special needs – travellers with disabilities, people with young children and children travelling alone. They can also cater for special dietary preferences (vegetarian, low-fat, non-shashlyk), though they need advance warning.

Most international airports will provide escorts from check-in desk to plane where needed, and there should be ramps, lifts, accessible toilets and reachable phones. Aircraft toilets, on the other hand, are likely to present a problem; travellers should discuss this with the airline at an early stage and, if necessary, with their doctor.

Guide dogs for the blind will often have to travel in a specially pressurised baggage compartment with other animals, away from their owner; smaller guide dogs may be admitted to the cabin. All guide dogs will be subject to the same quarantine laws (six months in isolation etc) as any other animal when entering or returning to countries currently free of rabies such as Australia.

Children under two travel for 10% of the standard fare (or free, on some airlines), as long as they don't occupy a seat. They don't get a baggage allowance either. 'Skycots' should be provided by the airline if requested in advance; these will take a child weighing up to about 10kg. Children between two and 12 can usually occupy a seat for half to two-thirds of the full fare and do get a baggage allowance. Pushchairs can often be taken as hand luggage.

The USA & Canada

From North America you generally have the choice of routing your trip via Istanbul (Turkish Airlines) or a major European city (KLM, British Airways, Lufthansa, etc).

From the west coast it's possible to fly via Seoul on Asiana. It's always worth asking whether the airline will give you a free stopover.

From the USA, the best return fares to Central Asia were with Turkish Airlines, via Istanbul, departing twice a week in summer. Return fares from the east/west coast were around US$1575/1810 to Almaty, US$1470/2313 to Ashgabat or US$1470/1710 to Tashkent. Uzbekistan Airways flies from New York JFK to Tashkent via Amsterdam, three times a week, an 18 hour flight for almost the same fare.

The *New York Times, LA Times, San Francisco Examiner, Chicago Tribune,* Toronto *Globe & Mail* and *Vancouver Sun* all have big weekly travel sections with lots of travel agent ads.

Council Travel (www.ciee.org) and STA Travel (www.sta-travel.com) are reliable sources of cheap tickets in the USA. Each has offices across the country. Council's headquarters (☎ 212-822 2600, or toll-free from the USA and Canada ☎ 800-226 8624, fax 822 2699, @ info@ciee.org) is at 205 East 42nd St, New York 10017-5706. STA's main US offices are at 7202 Melrose Ave, Los Angeles 90046 (☎ 213-934 8722) and 10 Downing St, New York 10014 (☎ 212-627 3111, or toll free ☎ 800-777 0112). Or try Gateway Travel (☎ 800-441 1183).

The best bargain-ticket agency in Canada is Travel CUTS (www.travelcuts.com), with around fifty offices located in all major cities. The parent office (☎ 416-979 2406, fax 979 8167) is at 187 College St, Toronto M5T 1P7.

Australia & New Zealand

Most flights to Central Asia go via Seoul (to pick up Asiana flights to Tashkent or Air Kazakstan to Almaty), Kuala Lumpur (Uzbekistan Airways to Tashkent), Bangkok (Uzbekistan Airways to Tashkent) or Karachi (PIA to Almaty or Tashkent or Kyrgyzstan Airlines to Bishkek). Sample fares included: Sydney to Tashkent A$1849 on Malaysia Airlines via Kuala Lumpur, or A$1796 via Karachi on Qantas/BA/PIA; and Sydney to Almaty A$1313 via Seoul on

Korean Airlines. STA Travel, Trailfinders and Flight Centre are major dealers in cheap airfares, each with dozens of offices:

Flight Centre
(☎ 131 600 Australia wide)
(☎ 09-309 0458 New Zealand)
Many offices in Australia and New Zealand. They book tickets on the Internet or by phone. Web site www.flightcentre.com.au.
Gateway Travel
(☎ 02-9745 3333, fax 9745 3237,
✉ agent@russian-gateway.com.au)
48 The Boulevarde, Strathfield NSW 2135 – ex-USSR specialists, they have experience booking flights to Central Asia. Web site www.russian-gateway.com.au.
STA Travel
(☎ 131 1776 Australia wide)
(☎ 02-9212 1255, fax 9281 4183)
855 George St, 6911, Sydney
(☎ 09-309 0458, fax 309 2059)
Ground floor, 10 High St, PO Box 4156 Auckland – Web site at www.statravel.com.au.
Trailfinders
(☎ 02-9247 7666) 8 Spring St, Sydney
(☎ 07-4041 1199) Hides Cnr, Shields St, Cairns
(☎ 07-3229 0887) 91 Elizabeth St, Brisbane

The UK

The best summer fares to Almaty are about UK£265/350 one way/return on KLM via Amsterdam. It's possible to buy an open-jaw return on this airline, say into Almaty and out of Karachi for around UK£480.

To Tashkent the cheapest return fare is around UK£324 with Transaero, a reliable Russian airline. Other fares, with Turkish Airlines or Lufthansa, are UK£500 return.

Uzbekistan Airways' London-Tashkent (-Delhi) run (four per week, UK£500 return) is comfortable, with good service and decent food (but the return is no match, with exhausted Delhi passengers sprawled everywhere and poor food from Tashkent). The routing means that for not much extra you can continue on from Tashkent to Delhi or Bangkok, thus treating Tashkent as a stopover. Uzbekistan Airways also flies from Manchester. For details and prices contact HY Travel (☎ 020-7935 4775), 69 Wigmore St, London. There are occasionally some direct London-Samarkand charter flights; ask your travel agent.

Kyrgyzstan Airlines (☎ 0121-523 5277) flies from Birmingham to Bishkek via Istanbul once a week for a bargain UK£195/395 one way/return. For details call the airline. Complaints about in-flight service are common.

The cheapest flights to Ashgabat are with Turkish Airlines, from London via Istanbul (overnight) to Ashgabat, four times a week for UK£550 return. Turkmenistan Airways flies twice a week from London (6½ hours) and three times a week from Birmingham to Ashgabat.

British Airways flies to Almaty, Bishkek (via Tiblisi, importing Kyrgyz gold) and soon Tashkent, under the name British Mediterranean. Its fares are not the cheapest but sometimes it offers good deals.

The Saturday and Sunday papers have good travel sections, including ads for scores of bucket shops. Also check out the Travel Classifieds in London's weekly *Time Out* magazine. Trailfinders in west London produces a brochure, with airfares – start by looking outside the main train stations.

Most British travel agents are registered with the Association of British Travel Agents (ABTA). If you have paid for your flight to an ABTA-registered agent that then goes out of business, ABTA will guarantee a refund or an alternative. Unregistered bucket shops are riskier but also sometimes cheaper.

Some ABTA registered bargain-ticket agencies are:

Bridge the World
(☎ 020-7911 0900)
47 Chalk Farm Rd, Camden Town, London NW1 8AH
Council Travel
(☎ 020-7478 2000, fax 734 7322,
✉ infouk@councilexchanges.org.uk)
52 Poland St, London W1V 4JQ – Web site www.ciee.org/EUROPE
STA Travel
(☎ 020-361 6262)
Priory House, 6 Wrights Lane, London W8 6TA – Web site www.statravel.co.uk
Trailfinders
(☎ 020-7938 3366, fax 937 9294)
42-50 Earl's Court Rd, Kensington, London W8 6FJ
(☎ 020-7938 3939) 194 Kensington High St, W8 7RG – Web site www.trailfinders.com

Usit Campus Travel
(☎ 020-7730 8111) 52 Grosvenor Gardens, London SW1W 0AG – Campus is also found in many YHA shops.
Web site www.campustravel.co.uk

Continental Europe

The best fares from Europe to Almaty are probably with Turkish Airlines, via Istanbul, and with Air Kazakstan. There are occasional charter flights from Astana to Frankfurt, Hannover and Vienna. Connections include:

Air Kazakstan: Almaty to Vienna, Zurich, Frankfurt and Hannover
Austrian Airlines: Vienna to Almaty (twice weekly)
KLM: Amsterdam to Almaty (twice weekly) and on to Tashkent
Lufthansa: Frankfurt to Almaty (five weekly), Tashkent (three weekly) and Ashgabat (three weekly, via Baku)
Transasian: Almaty to Hannover and Frankfurt (weekly)
Turkmenistan Airways: Ashgabat to Frankfurt (weekly)
Uzbekistan Airways: Tashkent to Amsterdam, Athens, Frankfurt and Paris

A reliable source of bargain tickets is NBBS Travels (☎ 20-620 70 51), Leidsestraat 53, 1017 NV Amsterdam; it has another office (☎ 20-624 0989) at Rokin 38 in Amsterdam. STA Travel has offices in Paris; the main one (☎ 1-43 59 23 69) is at 49 rue Pierre Charron. Council Travel's headquarters in Europe (☎ 1-44 41 74 74, fax 43 26 97 45, @ infofrance@ciee.org) is at 1 Place de l'Odéon, F-75006 Paris. Its Web site is at www.ciee.org/EUROPE/france.htm.

Council also has some offices in Germany (☎ 030-28848 590, fax 2809 6180, @ info@councilexchanges.de) at Oranienburgerstr 13-14, 10178 Berlin, and Italy (☎ 39-06 8440561, fax 85355407, @ info@councilexchanges.it) at Corso Trieste 133, 00198 Rome. STA Travel has dozens of offices in Germany, including Bergerstrasse 118 Frankfurt-am-Main, 60316 (☎ 49-69 4301910). In Switzerland try SSR Travel (☎ 41-31 302 03 12) Falkenplatz 9 BERN, 3012, affiliated with STA Travel.

Russia

Air Kazakstan has daily Moscow-Almaty flights (US$190, five hours). Transaero does the same run daily for US$260. There are flights between Moscow and several other Kazak cities, such as Astana and Atyrau.`

Uzbekistan Airways flies from Moscow to Samarkand (US$66/180 for payment in *sum* at black market rate/US dollars), Urgench (US$75/214) and Bukhara (US$75 /214), once a week. Uzbekistan Airways also flies daily from Tashkent to Moscow (US$66/180) and to about twenty other Russian cities. Transaero flies daily from Tashkent to Moscow.

Flights between Bishkek and Russia include Moscow (three per week, US$160 with Kyrgyzstan Airlines; twice weekly, $200 with Aeroflot) and Novosibirsk (weekly).

Aeroflot has four Moscow-Dushanbe flights weekly for US$280 (one way).

Turkmenistan Airways flies daily between Ashgabat and Moscow (Moscow-Ashgabat is US$140, Ashgabat-Moscow US$220).

Other airline connections include:

Aeroflot: Moscow to Samarkand and Tashkent
Domodedovo Airlines: Moscow to Tashkent (daily)
Air Enterprise Pulkovo: St Petersburg to Almaty (twice weekly), Tashkent (weekly) and Bishkek (fortnightly)
Transaero: Moscow to Almaty and Tashkent (daily)
Xinjiang Airlines: Ürümqi to Novosibirsk and on to Moscow (weekly)

Note that Moscow has three airports; the international Sheremetevo (terminal two), and 'domestic' (ex-Soviet destinations) Domodedovo and Vnukovo. Flights to Central Asian states used to go from Domodedovo, but Aeroflot, Transaero, Uzbekistan Airways and Air Kazakstan now operate to/from Sheremetevo (terminal one).

This means that transit passengers don't have to get a pricey transit visa and haul themselves across Moscow to catch a connecting plane. (Note that when you change between terminals you will probably have to go through customs twice; if you are carrying over US$500 cash you will have to declare it going into Russia, in order to be able to take it out of Russia half an hour later). Turkmenistan Airways and Kyrgyzstan Airways (and minor airlines such as Domodedovo Airlines and Sayakhat Air Company) still use Domodedovo airport, though this may change in the future.

Many travel agencies, good and bad, advertise in the *Moscow Times* and *Moscow Tribune*. Among reliable agencies in Moscow that could help with air bookings are Intourist, which has many service bureaux in Moscow; IRO Travel (☎ 095-234 6555, fax 234 6556, Web site www.iro.ru), Komsomolsky prospekt 13, affiliated with the Travellers Guest House; and Andrew's Consulting (☎ 258 5198, fax 258 5199), Novaya Ploshchad 10, 5th floor.

Turkey

Turkish Airlines flies from Istanbul to Almaty (four weekly), Bishkek (twice), Tashkent (three) and Ashgabat (four). The various republics' national airlines also fly once or twice a week. Alternatively you could fly from Istanbul or Trabzon to Baku, take the ferry to Turkmenbashi and a 12 hour train ride across the desert to Ashgabat.

A good agency in Trabzon for Baku and other flights (plus visas) is Sarptur (☎ 462-123 995, fax 122 119), at K Maras Caddesi 35. There are numerous other agencies.

China & Hong Kong

Hong Kong is the discount plane ticket capital of the region, though its bucket shops are at least as unreliable as those of other cities. STA Travel, which is reliable, has a branch in Hong Kong.

The convenience of quick China visas makes Hong Kong a useful stop, but it's generally cheaper to fly directly into China. The cheapest routes from Europe and North America are via Beijing or Shanghai, and those from Australasia are via Guangzhou. The lowest fares are normally with Air China. If you do stop in Hong Kong, an alternative to flying from there is to take an overnight boat, morning hoverferry or fast train to Guangzhou and then take a cheaper flight on from there.

China Travel Service (CTS) can help with flights to Almaty via Ürümqi, or to Tashkent

from	to	one way (US$)
Almaty	Bangkok	400
	Beijing	435
	Delhi	320
	Frankfurt	295
	Istanbul	275
	Moscow	190/260[1]
	Tel Aviv	470
	Ürümqi	145
Ashgabat	Istanbul	250
	Karachi	160
Bishkek	Amsterdam	595
	Birmingham	320
	Delhi	230
	Istanbul	290
	London	405
	Moscow	160
	New York	860
	San Francisco	1185
	St Petersburg	220
	Ürümqi	190
Tashkent	Amsterdam	615
	Bangkok	535
	Delhi	350
	Istanbul	635
	London	650
Ürümqi	Beijing	235
	Islamabad	210
	Moscow	250

Airfares from Central Asia

The following gives a rough idea of one-way airfares to points outside the region.

[1] Air Kazakstan/Transaero

via Beijing. For details of offices in Hong Kong see Travel Agencies & Organised Tours later. In Beijing try China International Travel Service (CITS; ☎ 1-6515 8562, fax 6515 8603) at 28 Jianguomenwai Dajie.

From Beijing there are twice weekly flights to Tashkent on Uzbekistan Airways, and weekly flights to Almaty on Air Kazakstan and to Bishkek on Kyrgyzstan Airlines.

To Ürümqi, Xinjiang Airlines has daily flights from most Chinese cities, including

Beijing (US$240), Guangzhou (US$275), Lanzhou (US$125), Shanghai (US$275), Xi'an (US$160) and Hong Kong. From Ürümqi there are twice weekly flights to Almaty (US$200) and Bishkek (US$190). See Ürümqi in the Xinjiang chapter for details.

The only way to fly to Kashgar is from Ürümqi with Xinjiang Airlines. Flights depart daily in summer and four times a week in winter, for about US$180 (one way). You may have to stay the night in Ürümqi.

Pakistan

PIA flies from Islamabad and Lahore, each once a week, to Tashkent via Almaty. Fares are around US$230 to Almaty, or US$210 to Tashkent. From Karachi Uzbekistan Airways flies to Tashkent for around US$250, Kyrgyzstan Airlines flies to Bishkek and Turkmenistan Airlines flies to Ashgabat (all weekly). Xinjiang Airlines flies between Islamabad and Ürümqi twice a week for around US$210 one way.

If you want to travel the Karakoram Highway and will begin or end your trip in Islamabad you may find it cheaper to fly via Karachi than direct to Islamabad.

If you are thinking of travelling between Islamabad and Central Asia via the Karakoram Highway it's worth looking into an open-jaw ticket, either with PIA or KLM. This enables you to fly into Pakistan and out of, say, Almaty (or vice versa) on one ticket. This can be considerably cheaper than buying two one-way fares.

Elsewhere in Asia

Useful flight connections and airlines are listed below:

Air Kazakstan: Almaty to Baku, Delhi, Iran, Seoul, Sharjah, and Tel Aviv
Asiana: Seoul to Tashkent (weekly)
El Al: Tel Aviv to Tashkent (twice weekly)
Imair: Baku to Almaty and Tashkent (weekly)
Iran Air: Tehran to Tashkent and Almaty (weekly)
Turkmenistan Airways: Ashgabat to Abu Dhabi, Baku, Bangkok, Delhi, Karachi, Mashad and Yerevan
Uzbekistan Airways: Tashkent to Baku, Bangkok, Delhi, Jeddah, Karachi, Kuala Lumpur, Riyadh, Seoul, Sharjah and Tel Aviv

There are also irregular charter connections from the major Central Asian capitals to Karachi, Delhi, Aleppo, Beijing and Abu Dhabi, mainly for small-time importers. They fly out half empty but return overloaded with cargo; generally there is space only on flights *out* of Central Asia.

LAND
Border Crossings

Cross-border roads that are open to foreigners, (by bus, taxi or hired car) are listed here.

China to Kazakstan A year-round road crosses from Ürümqi in China to Almaty via the border post at Khorgos (Korgas on the Xinjiang side) and Zharkent (formerly Panfilov). See Getting There & Away under Almaty and the Zharkent, Dostyk and Khorgos sections of the Kazakstan chapter for details.

There are two other China-Kazakstan crossings farther north, at Bakhty (Tacheng on the China side) and Maykapchigay (Jeminay in China). The Jeminay crossing is the more reliable of the two, though neither is all that reliable. See the Jeminay and Tacheng entries in the Xinjiang chapter.

Foreigners can only cross the border at Dostyk by rail. See Dostyk under South-East Kazakstan and Getting There & Away under Almaty in the Kazakstan chapter for details.

China to Kyrgyzstan From at least June to September it's possible to cross the dramatic 3752m Torugart pass on a rough road from Kashgar into Kyrgyzstan. Chinese and Kyrgyz buses run over the pass but foreigners are forbidden from taking the bus and have to arrange their own pricey transport, at least on the Chinese side.

Even the most painstaking arrangements can be thwarted by logistical gridlock on the China side or by unpredictable border closures (eg for holidays or snow).

For more detail on this fine but frustrating trip – including transport and visa tips – see the boxed text 'Crossing the Torugart' and the Bishkek to Kashgar via the Torugart Pass section in the Kyrgyzstan chapter. Additional tips for crossing from China are covered in the 'Over the Torugart Pass' aside in the Kashgar section of the Xinjiang chapter.

Another warm-weather crossing is now open for commerce, from Kashgar via Irkeshtam to Osh, but so far not for individual tourists.

China to Tajikistan There are grand plans to build a road from near Murgab in eastern Tajikistan to near Bulunkul in China, to link up with the Karakoram Highway to Pakistan. It will take years (or decades) for this to happen and even then, for the first few years at least, it will be for local traffic only.

Pakistan to China The exciting trip on the Karakoram Highway over the 4730m Khunjerab pass, said to be the world's highest public international highway, is an excellent way to get to or from Chinese Central Asia. There are regular bus and 4WD services when the pass is open – normally May to early November. See Kashgar to the Khunjerab Pass in the Xinjiang chapter for details. For more detailed coverage of both the Chinese and Pakistan sections see Lonely Planet's *Karakoram Highway*.

Iran to Turkmenistan The Iran-Turkmenistan border is now open to foreigners at Sarakhs/Saraghs. If you have a Turkmen visa, with Saraghs specified as the entry point, it's possible to cross into Turkmenistan here, though you'll have to take a taxi or minibus to get to/from the border posts. On the Iranian side there is public transport between Sarakhs and Mashad (the last bus to Mashad leaves around 5 pm). On the Turkmenistan side there is one bus and train a day from Saraghs to Ashgabat and there are four or five a day to Tejen.

Direct buses currently run five times a week between Mashad and Mary, though they may not wait for you if you are delayed at the border controls.

There is another border crossing at Gaurdan/Bajgiran, through a pass in the Kopet Dag just south of Ashgabat. This is a more direct crossing between Mashad and Ashgabat. A daily bus leaves from both Mashad and Ashgabat at 6 am. Special permits are no longer required to cross at Gaurdan, though it does have to be listed as the entry or exit point on your visa. Tickets cost US$4/11 at the black market/official exchange rate.

Train
There are three main rail routes into Central Asia from Russia. One comes from Moscow via Samara or Saratov, straight across Kazakstan via Kyzylorda to Tashkent (3369km), with branch lines to Bishkek and Almaty (4057km). The second, the Turkestan-Siberia railway or 'Turksib', links the Trans-Siberian railway at Novosibirsk with Almaty. A third main route goes around the other side of the Aral Sea via Urgench, Bukhara and Samarkand to Tashkent, with a branch line to Dushanbe, but services on this line are now unreliable.

Another line crosses Kazakstan via Karaghandy. From the Caspian Sea yet another line crosses Turkmenistan. This is the so-called Trans-Caspian route, although only cargo trains run this route at present.

Completed in 1992, after being delayed almost half a century by Russian-Chinese geopolitics, is a line from China via Ürümqi into Kazakstan, joining the Turksib for connections to Almaty or to Siberia.

The 2½ day trip from Moscow to Tashkent and the 1½ day trip from Ürümqi to Almaty don't have quite the romance or the laid-back feel of the Trans-Siberian railway, but they are usually cheaper and more frequent than flying, and allow Central Asia to unfold gradually. A guidebook devoted entirely to the Moscow-Beijing rail route via Central Asia is Douglas Streatfield-James' *Silk Route by Rail*.

Types of Trains Trains into Central Asia are either Russian or, from the China side, Chinese. With minor exceptions carriages are the same in corresponding classes of each, with washrooms at either end with cold (and sometimes hot) water and a toilet, and a big samovar dispensing boiling water. Smoking is forbidden in the compartments, but permitted at the ends of the cars. Trains trundle slowly across the countryside, but don't expect much of a view: windows are usually filthy, and covered with steel screens to protect against stone-throwers. Windows are double-glazed and sealed, so carriages get stale, smoky and smelly after half a day or so. Carriages are often heated (hardly appropriate for crossing summer steppes and desert) and tend to be pretty decrepit, with the odd cockroach.

Chinese railway tracks are about 10cm narrower than the old Soviet ones, and at the Chinese-Kazakstan border the carriages are hoisted up and their 'bogeys' (wheel assemblies) changed.

Services A normal long-distance train is called a 'fast train': СКОРЫЙ, *skoryy* in Russian. In Uzbekistan, where Russian has disappeared from timetables, the Uzbek word is ЙУЛОВЧИ *(yulovchi)*. A *passazhirskiy* (passenger) train stops more often and may have a smaller proportion of more comfortable accommodation. Foreign tourists are usually put on one of these two types. The best of these often have names, eg the *Uzbekistan* between Moscow and Tashkent. These named trains (Russian: *firmennye poezdy*) tend to have cleaner cars, more polite staff, more convenient arrival/departure hours, sometimes fewer stops, more top-class accommodation and functioning restaurants.

Note that all trains numbered 900 and up are mail trains and therefore *extremely* slow.

Classes A deluxe sleeping carriage is called *spets-vagon* (SV, Russian for special carriage, abbreviated CB in Cyrillic; some say this means *spalnyy vagon*, sleeping carriage), *myagkiy* (soft) or 1st class. Closed compartments have carpets and upholstered seats, and convert to comfortable sleeping compartments for two.

An ordinary sleeping carriage is called *kupeynyy* or *kupe* (Russian for compartmentalised), *zhyostkiy* (hard) or 2nd class. Closed compartments are usually four-person couchettes. Seats are leather or plastic and also form the lower pair of bunks.

Chinese trains have something in between 1st and 2nd, called soft-sleeper *(ruǎnwò)*, with carpets, clean loos etc, but four to a compartment. All closed compartments

mercifully have a switch that allows you to turn off the piped Muzak.

A *platskartnyy* (reserved-place) or 3rd class carriage – also called hard-sleeper – has open-bunk accommodation. Bunks (not actually hard, just less soft) are partitioned, but not closed off, and more are squeezed into a carriage. The Chinese equivalent is hard sleeper *(yìngwò)*. *Obshchiy* (general) or 4th class is unreserved bench-type seating. In China this is called hard-seat *(yìngzuò)*.

With a reservation, your ticket normally shows the numbers of your carriage *(vagon)* and seat *(mesto)*. Class may be shown by what looks like a fraction: eg 1/2 is 1st class two berth, 2/4 is 2nd class four berth.

On Board Carriage attendants (Russian: *provodnik* (M) or *provodnitsa* (F), and Chinese: *fúwùrén*) are responsible for keeping things clean, filling and stoking the samovars, giving you a change of linen every few days and keeping track of you at halts. Especially on the ex-Soviet side they're a force all their own, ranging from bossy, lecherous young men to sturdy, tank-commander women with hearts of gold. It is worth being on good terms with yours if possible.

Experienced passengers bring comfortable 'lounging' clothes for long trips, eg track suits and slippers. Sleeping compartments are mixed-sex; when women show that they want to change or get out of bed, men go out and loiter in the corridor.

Take enough food for the whole journey. The food in restaurant cars is awful (less so in Chinese trains), and only gets worse and less plentiful as the trip wears on. On long trips locals bring great bundles of food that they spread out and offer to one another (you should do the same). This they may supplement with food bought at station halts.

At many stations, hawkers sell (or come aboard selling) fruit, bread, pasties, dried fish, hot potatoes, preserved food, beer, soft drinks etc. Be suspicious of all the preserved stuff because of the risk of food poisoning. You're expected to pay in local currency. Most carriages have a samovar with boiling water that's safe. If you don't always fancy tea, bring bottled water.

Local travellers generally love speaking with foreigners, and on long train rides, many love drinking with them as well. See Alcohol & Assault-by-Hospitality under Dangers & Annoyances in the Regional Facts for the Visitor chapter on the pressures to drink and the ways around it. If you're uneasy about your compartment-mates for any reason, you might persuade the attendant to make some rearrangements if you ask at the start. Foreigners are more carefully segregated on Chinese trains.

Stops are welcome as much for real air as for exercise. Toilets are locked during stops, and that can be a long time at the border. The 'pok, pok' you hear is a maintenance worker testing the bogeys with a little hammer.

Stops are from one to 20 minutes long except at borders; durations are in the timetable posted in each carriage, though these may be out of date. Departure comes without a whistle and the trains slip out almost soundlessly – and the engineer doesn't care whether a foreigner's been left behind. Be careful too about crossing tracks, which could be carrying a slow, 3km-long freight train just at departure time.

Theft Trains are the safest as far as accidents go, but some long-distance trains routinely experience midnight thefts, occasionally robberies and sometimes assaults. See Crime on the Rails under Dangers & Annoyances in the Regional Facts for the Visitor chapter, for suggestions on how to make your compartment hassle-proof. Never wander off and leave your bags unattended at station halts.

'Official' robbery seems to be a bigger problem. Police and customs officials at border crossings routinely try to shake down passengers for a few dollars. Potential hotspots include the Almaty-Ürümqi train and Tashkent-Urgench train that dips into Turkmenistan (officers may try to fine you for not having a Turkmen visa). Keep your wits about you, and stand your ground politely but firmly.

Buying Tickets Book at least a week ahead for international connections, though

as little as two days is probably safe for intra-CIS connections, even in summer. There's not much advantage in buying tickets abroad, and it's more expensive.

Foreigners are supposed to pay more than locals, typically 50% to 100% more, though in the ex-Soviet republics this is not always enforced at station ticket windows. A named train is usually more expensive than others on the same route. Fares frequently lurch upward to compensate for inflation, so we don't quote many in this book.

Keep to the place shown on your ticket. 'Helpful' train attendants may offer to upgrade you (eg from kupeynyy to SV) for a few unofficial dollars, but police or ticket masters may later want a few dollars more, a 'fine' for being in the wrong place.

In Kazakstan and Kyrgyzstan, trains still run on Moscow time. Check this when buying tickets.

To/From Russia Most trains bound for Central Asia depart from Moscow's Kazan(sky) station. Europe dissolves into Asia as you sleep, and morning may bring a vast panorama of the Kazak steppe.

Train connections between Russia and Central Asia have thinned out in recent years. Services no longer run from Russia to Samarkand or Dushanbe and connections to other cities have become less frequent. At the time of research, fast trains left three times a week to/from Tashkent (Nos 5/6 and 85/86, from 55 to 65 hours), twice a week to/from Almaty (No 7/8, 78 hours) and once or twice a week to/from Bishkek (No 17/18, 75 hours). There are other, slower connections but you could grow old and die on them. Trains out of Moscow have even numbers; those returning have odd numbers.

Typical fares for a 2nd class (kupeynyy) berth are US$100 Moscow-Bishkek, US$100 Moscow-Tashkent and US$110 Moscow-Almaty. The same ticket bought in Tashkent costs US$150 in *sum* changed at the government rate or US$50 in *sum* changed at the black market rate.

To/From China Apart from the long way around on the Turksib and Trans-Siberian trains, there's just one way to get in to or out of Central Asia by rail on the China side – the 1359km journey between Ürümqi and Almaty. Tickets are easily booked in either Ürümqi or Almaty (see those cities). One problem (which applies as well to the bus trip) is visas. It's not impossible to get a China visa in Central Asia, but awkward to get a Kazakstan (or Kyrgyzstan) visa from anywhere closer to the border than Beijing. You're better off bringing one from home. See Getting There & Away under Almaty in the Kazakstan chapter for details.

From Hong Kong to Ürümqi by rail is 4900km and takes a minimum of 4½ days, although few in their right minds would do this all at once, considering not only comfort but all there is to see en route. Other destinations east include Liuyuan (for Dunhuang, 15 hours), Lanzhou (35 hours), Xi'an (48 hours) and Beijing (60 hours).

To/From Iran A line now links Mashad in Iran with Tejen on the Trans-Caspian mainline, which completes the connection between Tehran and Ashgabat. This means that it only needs the reopening of the Van-Tabriz line to allow a rail trip from Hong Kong to London. The snag is that, at the time of research, only cargo trains are operating (though passenger trains do run on the Iranian side between Mashad and Sarakhs). When international services do eventually start expect a lengthy wait at the border while bogeys are changed.

Car & Motorcycle
Bringing your own car or motorbike to Central Asia is fraught with practical problems, the main one being fuel (unpredictable, often adulterated supplies and 'broken' pump counters) and wildly fluctuating prices. There are no motoring associations of any kind. Most seriously, in case of an accident in a remote place, you could be very much up the proverbial creek, and not just for spare parts. If you harm a person or property, you must settle on the spot, and you're at risk of robbery or violence.

The state insurance offices, splinters of the old Soviet agency Ingosstrakh, have no

overseas offices that we know of, and your own insurance is most unlikely to be valid in Central Asia. You would probably have to arrange insurance anew at each border.

Bringing a personal vehicle into China is even more difficult. We have met people who have driven their own vehicles over the Torugart pass to Kashgar and then beyond into Pakistan but you will have to arrange permission months in advance through a Kyrgyz or Chinese travel agency and it will not be cheap as you will need a guide/translator and a full pack of documents from Ürümqi. Edelweiss in Bishkek has had experience in arranging this. See the Bishkek section for contact details.

SEA
The only regular passenger service to Turkmenistan on the Caspian is from Baku, and it's not strictly a passenger service – nor, for that matter, is it very regular. For more information on the crossing, see the Turkmenbashi section in the Turkmenistan chapter.

Ships to/from Astrakhan, Iran, the Black Sea and even the Mediterranean occasionally call at Turkmenbashi, and individual captains may be willing to take on board a passenger.

TRAVEL AGENCIES & ORGANISED TOURS
In this section we list reliable agencies who can help you with the logistics of travel in the Central Asian republics and Xinjiang – whether it be visas, a few excursions or an entire trip. These include travel agencies, adventure tour operators and home-stay agencies – many combine these functions.

Agencies specialising in cheap flights are listed under Buying Tickets in the Air section of this chapter.

Tour Operators
Australia
Passport Travel
(☎ 03-9867 3888, ✉ passport@werple.net.au) Suite 11A, 401 St Kilda Rd, Melbourne VT 3004 – organises group and budget tours for Uzbekistan, Kyrgyzstan, Kazakstan and Xinjiang. Can arrange a visa with accommodation. Web site www.travelcentre.com.au.

Sundowners
(☎ 03-9600 1934, fax 9642 5838,
🖂 rail@sundowners.com.au)
Suite 15 Lonsdale Court, 600 Lonsdale St, Melbourne, 3000 – small-group tours and treks plus independent itineraries, particularly by rail from China or via the Trans-Siberian, with add-ons available. Web site www.sundowners.com.au.

France
Allibert Guides
(☎ 04-76 45 22 26, fax 76 45 50 75)
rue Longifan, 38 530 Chapareillan
(☎ 01-40 21 16 21, fax 40 21 16 20)
14 rue de l'Asile Popincourt, 75011 Paris

The UK
British Museum Traveller
(☎ 020-7323 8895/1234, fax 7580 8677)
46 Bloomsbury St, London WC1B 3QQ – cultural trips to Silk Road cities, esp Uzbekistan.
Exodus
(☎ 020-8675 5550, fax 8673 0779,
🖂 sales@exodustravels.co.uk)
9 Weir Rd, London SW12 OLT – treks to Pik Lenin and Muztagh Ata base camps, Heavenly Lake, 21 days Tashkent-Islamabad over the Torugart. Web site www.exodustravels.co.uk.
Explore Worldwide
(☎/fax 01252-760001) 1 Frederick St, Aldershot, Hants GU11 1LQ – offers a 23 day overland trip from Tashkent to Rawalpindi. Web site www.explore.co.uk.
Imaginative Traveller Ltd
(☎ 020-8742 3049, fax 8742 3045,
🖂 info@imaginative-traveller.com)
14 Barley Mow Passage, Chiswick, London W4 4PH – Silk Road by rail, trips and tours. Web site www.imaginative-traveller.com.
KE Adventure Travel
(☎ 017687-73966, fax 74693,
🖂 keadventure@ enterprise.net)
32 Lake Rd, Keswick, Cumbria CA12 5DQ – combination 16 day tour; trekking in the Tian Shan and sightseeing in Samarkand. Web site www.keadventure.com.
Naturetrek
(☎ 01962-733051, fax 736426,
🖂 info@naturetrek.co.uk)
The Cadam Centre, Brighton, Alresford, Hants SO24 9RE – botany tours to Kazakstan. Web site www.naturetrek.co.uk.
OTT Expeditions
(☎ 0114-258 8508, fax 255 1603,
🖂 andy@ottexpd.demon.co.uk)
Unit 5b, Southwest Centre, Troutbeck Rd, Sheffield S7 2QA – hard-core mountaineering including Khan Tengri and Pik Lenin. Web site www.ottexpeditions.co.uk.

Regent Holidays Ltd
(☎ 117-921 1711, fax 925 4866,
🖂 regent@regent-holidays.co.uk)
15 John St, Bristol BS1 2HR – nine-day and weekend tours. Web site www.regent-holidays.co.uk.
Russia Experience
(☎ 020-8566 8846, fax 8566 8843,
🖂 russ_exp@compuserve.com)
Research House, Frasier Rd, Perivale, Middx, UB6 7AQ – tours from Moscow into Uzbekistan and Kazakstan.
Steppes East
(☎ 01285-810267, fax 810693,
🖂 sales@steppeseast.co.uk)
Castle Eaton, Cricklade, Swindon, Wiltshire SN6 6JU – a variety of tours into Central Asia, including Shandur Polo tournament, Great Game Tours, horseback riding in the Karakoram, plus trekking. Web site www.steppeseast.co.uk.
Travelbag Adventures
(☎ 01420-541007, fax 541002,
🖂 info@travelbag-adventures.co.uk)
15 Turk St, Alton, Hampshire GU34 1AG – Silk Road China, Kyrgyzstan, Kazakstan. Web site www.travelbag-adventures.co.uk.

The USA
Adventure Center
(☎ 800-227 8748, 510-654 1879, fax 654 4200)
1311 63rd St, Suite 200, Emeryville, CA 94608 – can book passengers for several travel companies including Explore Worldwide (See UK listing). Web site www.adventurecenter.com.
Geographic Expeditions
(☎ 800-777 8183, 415-922 0448,
🖂 info@ geoex.com)
2627 Lombard St, San Francisco CA 94123 – rigorous touring and trekking, including the Torugart crossing. Web site www.geoex.com.
Journeys International, Inc
(☎ 800-255 8735, 734-665 4407, fax 665 2945,
🖂 info@journeys-intl.com)
107 Aprill Dr, Suite 3, Ann Arbor, MI 48103 – three-week Silk Road tour through Central Asia, specialised theme trips, family trips. Web site www.journeys-intl.com.
KE Adventure Travel
(☎ 800-497 9675, 970-925 8368, fax 925 6704,
🖂 ketravel@rof.net)
PO Box 10538, Aspen, Colorado 81612 – 16 day tour; trekking in the Tian Shan and sightseeing in Samarkand. Web site www.keadventure.com.
Mir Corporation
(☎ 800-424 7289, fax 206-624 7360,
🖂 mir@igc.apc.org)
85 South Washington St, Suite 210, Seattle, WA 98104 – specialists in travel to Central Asia, Russia and China; can arrange Central Asia home-stays. Web site www.mircorp.com.

Mountain Travel Sobek
(☎ 510-527 8100, fax 525 7710,
✉ info@mtsobek.com)
6420 Fairmount Ave, El Cerrito, California 944530 3606 – camel and horse trips, rafting, trekking in the Turkestan Mountains, Central Asian highlights. Web site www.mtsobek.com.

Red Star Travel
(☎ 800-215 4378, 206-522 5995,
✉ travel@travel2russia.com)
9705 Sand Point Way NE, Seattle, WA 98115 – Silk Road bazars and camel caravans. Web site www.travel2russia.com.

REI Adventures
(☎ 800-622 2236, 253-437 1100, fax 395 8160,
✉ travel@rei.com)
PO Box 1938, Sumner, WA 98390 – trekking in Central Asia, including Aksu, sightseeing in Samarkand. Web site merc.rei.com/travel/.

TCS Expeditions
(☎ 800-727 7477, 206-727 7300, fax 727 7309, ✉ travel@tcs-expeditions.com)
2025 First Ave, Suite 450, Seattle, Washington 98121 – to experience the Silk Road by private train. Web site www.tcs-expeditions.com.

Travel Agencies

The following agencies can arrange individual itineraries, accommodation, tickets and visa support.

Outside Central Asia Agencies outside Central Asia include:

Australia

Gateway Travel
(☎ 02-9745 3333, fax 9745 3237,
✉ agent@russian-gateway.com.au)
48 The Boulevarde, Strathfield NSW 2135 – airfares to Central Asia, hotel bookings, home-stays, visa invitations and airport transfers.

Passport Travel
(See under Tour Operators, earlier.) Individual and budget tours into Central Asia; offers visa support with accommodation and rail tickets.

Sundowners
(See under Tour Operators, earlier.) Small-group and independent tours into Central Asia, Silk Road; offers letters of invitation with accommodation booking.

Russia

HOFA
(☎/fax 812-275 1992,
✉ alexei@hofak.hop.stu.neva.ru)
Tavricheskaya 5-25, St Petersburg – home-stays in major cities; Web site www.spb.ru/homestays.

The UK

East-West Travel
(☎ 020-7938 3211, ✉ travel@east-west.co.uk)
Consular Service
(☎ 020-7376 1555, fax-back 7565 7770,
✉ consulareast-west.co.uk)
15 Kensington High St, W8 London – independent itineraries and flights to the entire ex-Soviet Union. The consular service can arrange visas to all ex-Soviet republics. Web site www.east-west.co.uk.

Regent Holidays Ltd
(See under Tour Operators, earlier.) They can cobble together an individual itinerary, minitreks, home-stays in Bishkek and Torugart crossings (UK£185 per person from Bishkek to Kashgar).

Steppes East
(See under Tour Operators, earlier.) Arranges individual itineraries, and assists with border crossings and visas in conjunction with ground transport.

The USA

American-International Homestays, Inc
(☎ 800-876 2048, 303-642 3088, fax 642 3365,
✉ ash@igc.apc.org)
PO Box 1754, Nederland, CO 80466 – specialises in (expensive) home-stays, also offers two and three-week itineraries.

Central Asia Adventures
(✉ CAADVTRS@aol.com)
5849 NE Simpson, Portland, OR 97218 – based in Almaty, arranges visa support, home-stays, individualised trips and treks. Web site members.aol.com/caadvtrs.

Mir Corporation
(See under Tour Operators, earlier.) Arranges independent tours, home-stays and visa support with accommodation.

Red Star Travel
(See under Tour Operators, earlier.) Organises individual itineraries, accommodation, train tickets; visa support with booking.

Within Central Asia Competent agencies within Central Asia are listed here. Look under Travel Agencies in their headquarters' cities in the country chapters for contact details.

Kazakstan (Almaty) – ACS Travel Agency, AMS CAT, Asia Tourism, Central Asia Tourism Corporation, Jibek Joly, Kan Tengri

Kyrgyzstan (Bishkek) – Celestial Mountains, Central Asia Tourism Corporation (CAT), Dostuk Trekking Ltd, Ecotour Ltd, Edelweiss, ITMC Tien-Shan, Kyrgyz Concept

Turkmenistan (Ashgabat) – Amado, Ayan, DN Tours, Latif

Uzbekistan (Tashkent) – Asia Travel, Sairam, Sambuh, Sportur

Uzbekistan (Bukhara) – Bukhara Visit, Farkhad & Maya's, Marvarid-95, Salom Travel

Chinese State Travel Agencies

CITS and CTS, the main Chinese state travel bureaux, will book flight and hotels, train tickets plus tours in China at high group rates and usually with a service charge. This can save you time and hassle getting to Xinjiang if you have a tight itinerary.

CITS The CITS (*zhōngguó guójì lǚxíngshè*; Web site www.cits.net) has offices throughout Xinjiang. The Ürümqi branch is quite good and the Kashgar office rents jeeps and offers package trips (see the Xinjiang chapter). Offices abroad include:

Australia
(☎ 03-9621 2198, fax 9621 2919)
99 King St, Melbourne 3000; Web site www
.travman.com.au.

Canada
(☎ 604-267 0033, fax 267 0032)
5635 Cambie St, Vancouver BC V5Z 3A3; Web site www.citscanada.com.

France
(☎ 01 42 86 88 66, fax 01 42 86 88 61,
✉ china.international@wanado.fr)
30 Rue de Gramont, 75002 Paris

Hong Kong
(☎ 852-2732 5888, fax 2721 7154)
New Mandarin Plaza, Tower A, 12th floor, 14 Science Museum Rd, Tsimshatsui East; Web site www.cits.com.hk.

Japan
(☎ 03-3499 1245, fax 3499 1243)
24-2 Shu Bldg, 6th Floor, Shibuya 1-Chome, Shibuya-Ku, Tokyo 150; Web site www.cits-japan.co.jp.

USA
(☎ 718-261 7329, fax 261 7569,
✉ citsusa@aol.com)
71-01 Austin St, Suite 204, Forest Hills, NY 11375
(☎ 626-568 8993, fax 568 9207,
✉ citslaz@aol.com)
975 East Green St, Suite 101, Pasadena, CA 91106; Web site www.citsusa.com.

CTS This is the clear choice for plans from Hong Kong. There is a competent CTS in

Ürümqi, at the Overseas Chinese Hotel (see the Xinjiang chapter). Offices abroad include:

Australia
(☎ 02-9211 2633, fax 9281 3595)
757-759 George St, Sydney, NSW

Canada
(☎ 1-800-663 1126, 604-872 8787, fax 873 2823)
556 West Broadway, Vancouver, BC V5Z 1E9
(☎ 1-800-387 6622, 416-979 8993, fax 979 8220)
Suite 306, 438 University Ave, Box 28, Toronto, Ontario M5G 2K8

France
(☎ 01-44 51 55 66, fax 44 51 55 60)
32 rue Vignon, 75009 Paris

Germany
(☎ 69-223 8522) Düsseldorfer Strasse 14, D-60329, Frankfurt-am-Main
(☎ 30-393 4068, fax 391 8085)
Beusselstrasse 5, D-10553, Berlin

Hong Kong
(☎ 2853 3888, fax 2854 1383)
4th Floor CITS House, 78-83 Connaught Rd, Central
(☎ 2315 7188, fax 2721 7757)
1st Floor, Alpha House, 27-33 Nathan Rd, Tsimshatsui

UK
(☎ 020-7836 9911, 7836 3121)
7 Upper St Martin's Lane, London

USA
(☎ 800-899 8618, 415-352 0399,
✉ info@chinatravelservice.com)
575 Sutter St, L/F, San Francisco, CA 94102
(☎ 800-890 8818, fax 626-457 8955,
✉ usctsla@aol.com)
119 S Atlantic Blvd, Suite 303, Monterey Park, CA 91754 – Web site www.chinatravelservice.com.

Others China Youth Travel Service (CYTS) offers most of the same services as CITS and CTS, at similar prices. They're no longer just for 'youth'. See that section in the Xinjiang chapter.

The Kashgar branch of China Mountaineering Association (CMA) can arrange trekking and other small group sports trips in the Kashgar region, as well as Torugart pass crossings and can also give on-the-spot help with guides, transport and equipment. They are the clear choice in Kashgar. See Information under the Kashgar entry in the Xinjiang chapter.

Getting Around the Region

Flying is the least interesting and arguably the least safe mode of transport in Central Asia, but to some destinations and in some seasons it's the only sensible alternative. Trains are slow and easy-going, but crowded, and the cheaper classes are sometimes crime-ridden and grotty. Buses are the most frequent and convenient way to get between towns cheaply, though long trips can be tedious and cramped, and vehicles are prone to breakdowns.

The best option in many areas is a car: taxis or private drivers are often willing to take you between cities for little more than a bus fare. In Kyrgyzstan, per person prices are cheap enough to buy all the seats in the car and stretch out.

The biggest headache for travellers crossing the region is that most inter-republic bus services have been cut. A few direct buses (ie Tashkent to Almaty) still run but in general travellers have to get a taxi to and from both sides of the border. See the boxed text 'Jigsaw Borders' for more on the logistical and visa hassles of inter-republic travel.

AIR

Flying saves time and takes the tedium out of Central Asia's long distances; from Tashkent, nothing is more than 1½ hours away by air. It's the only sensible way to reach some places, such as Dushanbe (very roundabout by train, but a gorgeous flight over the western Tian Shan) and, in winter, much of Kyrgyzstan and Tajikistan. But the Central Asian airlines (and a few smaller carriers) have some way to go before meeting international safety standards; for more on this see Airline Safety in the Getting There & Away chapter.

Domestic and inter-republic services are absolutely no-frills; for long flights consider packing lunch.

Helicopter flights were once popular in the Tian Shan and Pamir ranges but rising fuel costs have made most services prohibitively expensive (charter costs start at around US$1000 per hour in Kyrgyzstan). Moreover, maintenance standards have plummeted, as indeed do the helicopters themselves from time to time. Avoid them except in summer and go only if the weather is absolutely clear.

Connections

At time of research there was no Almaty-Bishkek service, and uncertain services between Dushanbe and other capitals; Almaty-Tashkent, Bishkek-Tashkent and Ashgabat-Almaty went just twice a week. Major internal connections still run daily.

Flights between the biggest cities generally stick to their schedules, but those serving smaller towns are often delayed without explanation and cancellations are common, usually a result of fuel shortages (big-city flights get priority). Printed schedules are unreliable; routes and individual flights are constantly being cancelled or reintroduced. The only sure way to find out what's flying is to ask at an air booking office. In any case, confirm any flight 24 hours beforehand.

Buying Tickets

A few western agencies can book intra-CIS flights, officially or otherwise. But as flights and information are more plentiful and prices usually lower from within Central Asia, this is not very useful. Also, flights are frequently cancelled, and foreigners tend to get priority when booking a ticket in any case.

Tickets for Central Asian airlines can be purchased from old Aeroflot municipal booking offices (most now renamed), from hotels' airline reservation desks (though they may attach fees of US$5 or more), at the airport right up to departure or increasingly at private travel agents, known as *aviakassa*. You'll often need your passport and visa. Many booking offices have a special window for foreigners and/or for international flights. It is rarely possible to book a return flight.

Check your ticket closely – mistakes are common. It might help to have a local friend look it over.

Jigsaw Borders

When Stalin drew the borders between different republics in 1924 no-one really expected them to become international boundaries. Areas were portioned off on the map according to the whims of Party leaders, without much regard to the reality on the ground. As these crazy jigsaw borders solidify throughout post Soviet Central Asia, many towns and enclaves are finding themselves isolated, as the once complex web of regional ties shrinks behind new borderlines.

There are now border checks at many hitherto disregarded borders, particularly in the Fergana valley. Kazakstan-Uzbekistan and Kazakstan-Kyrgyzstan border checks are still cursory.

The Fergana valley has been particularly affected. Travellers (and locals) may find it tricky to get to more remote areas or trekking bases by public transport. Problems arise when travelling on Kyrgyz buses that transit Uzbekistan, eg between Osh and Jalal-Abad. Borders are sometimes closed and travellers without an Uzbek visa often face hassles from Uzbek border guards, even though travellers are officially allowed 72-hours transit between republics. The transit agreement in Cyrillic and English appears in the Language chapter and may assist in these situations.

The political violence in Tajikistan has severely tightened up travel between Uzbekistan and Tajikistan. Cars with Tajik number plates can no longer cross into Uzbekistan and Uzbek border guards often give locals the third degree. If you are travelling from Uzbekistan to Tajikistan and back (ie from Samarkand to Penjikent or the Fan mountains) it's worth investing in a double or multiple-entry visa. Buses no longer run from central Uzbekistan into the Fergana valley along the natural route via Khojand but rather take the mountain road from Tashkent over the Kamchik pass. Only train connections exit the Fergana valley through its mouth.

Trains are not immune to these border shenanigans, as lines occasionally veer into other republics. Trains from Bukhara to Urgench and Urgench to Nukus dip into Turkmenistan territory and Turkmen guards regularly board the train to fine travellers without a Turkmen visa (Turkmenistan is not part of the 72 hour transit agreement).

These problems may be short lived, as new transport connections are springing up everywhere. Uzbekistan is building a railway line to bypass Turkmenistan and makeshift dirt roads have appeared in Kyrgyz parts of the Fergana valley to avoid Uzbek border guards. But these are just a few of the thousands of ties that bind the ex-Soviet republics to one another, and to Russia, and disentangling them will take decades.

Fares

Flights in Kyrgyzstan, Kazakstan and China are the same price for foreigners and locals, but Tajikistan, Turkmenistan and Uzbekistan operate two-tier pricing systems, with nonresident foreigners paying two to four times the local rate. In Uzbekistan, however, tickets can be paid for in *sum*, which if changed on the black market makes domestic flights very cheap.

Some Central Asian airlines fly to and from one another's republics, and fares can depend on the one you choose – eg Almaty-Tashkent is US$105 (one way) with Uzbekistan Airways but US$69 (one way) with Kazakstan Airlines.

At the time of research fares on Kyrgyzstan Airlines (Kyrgyz: Aba Joladru) were still heavily subsidised by the government (one reason why the airline is losing millions of US dollars every year) and so fares are very cheap (ie US$12 in som from Bishkek to Osh). In Kyrgyzstan a booking fee of 50 som is charged if booked less than three days in advance, 70 som if booked less than 24 hours.

The airfare diagram shows approximate one-way foreigners' fares in US dollar equivalents, for some major regional connections.

Departure Tax

Kyrgyzstan, Kazakstan and Uzbekistan have no domestic departure tax. Turkmenistan

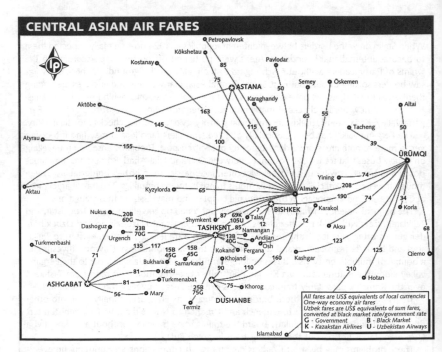

CENTRAL ASIAN AIR FARES

Petropavlovsk

Kökshetau

Kostanay

85

75

Pavlodar

ASTANA

50

Semey   Öskemen

Karaghandy

Aktöbe

163

Altai

145

115   105

65   55

Tacheng   50

120

100

39

Atyrau

155

ÜRÜMQI

158

Yining   74

208

Aktau   Kyzylorda   65   Almaty   190   74   34

Nukus   20B   BISHKEK   Karakol   Korla

60G   87 69K 7 Talas

Shymkent   105U   12   12

Dashoguz   23B   TASHKENT   85   Namangan   Aksu   68

70G   13B   Andijan Osh

Urgench   40G

135   117   15B   15B   Kokand Fergana   123   125

Bukhara   45G   45G   Khojand   160   Kashgar   Qiemo

81   71   Samarkand   90   110   210

Turkmenbashi   81   Kerki   Hotan

ASHGABAT   81   Turkmenabat

56   Mary   25B   75   Khorog

75G

Termiz   DUSHANBE

All fares are US$ equivalents of local currencies
One-way economy air fares
Uzbek fares are US$ equivalents of sum fares,
converted at black market rate/government rate
G - Government   **B** - Black Market
K - Kazakstan Airlines   **U** - Uzbekistan Airways

Islamabad

spasmodically enforces a US$5 tax. In China departure tax (or 'airport reconstruction fee') costs Y50, sometimes paid at check-in, sometimes (as at Kashgar) included in the price of the ticket. In Xinjiang you may be pressured to pay an optional Y20 insurance fee.

Check-In

Check-in is 40 to 90 minutes before departure and airlines are entitled to bump you if you come later than that. Some airports have special facilities for foreigners, allowing them to board early and miss out on the seating free-for-all (flights are generally single-class, with no assigned seats), especially if the flight is overbooked. To minimise the risk of loss or theft, consider carrying everything on board; many planes have special areas for large carry-ons.

BUS

This is generally the best bet for getting between towns cheaply. The major transport corridor (eg Almaty-Bishkek-Tashkent-Samarkand-Bukhara) is served by big long-distance coaches (often reconditioned German or Turkish vehicles), which run on fixed routes and schedules, with fixed stops. They're relatively problem-free and moderately comfortable, with windows that open and sometimes reclining seats. Luggage is locked safely away below. Journey times depend on road conditions but are somewhat longer than a fast train.

Regional buses are a lot less comfortable and a bit more ... interesting. Breakdowns are common. They are also used extensively by small-time traders to shift their goods around the region, and you could gradually become surrounded by boxes, bags, urns and live animals. Runs are occasionally cancelled, resulting in screaming matches as people storm the next available bus. Buses in the countryside are usually the ancient snub-nosed style.

Private minibuses, which often solicit passengers in front of bus stations, are a bit more expensive, sometimes faster, and usually more hair-raising. They may be called *marshrutnyy* (marsh-**root**-ni, Russian for fixed-route) or *arenda* (Russian for for-hire). They generally have fixed fares and routes but no fixed timetable (or no departure at all if there aren't enough passengers to satisfy the driver), but will stop anywhere along the route. They may be clapped-out heaps or spiffy new Toyota vans.

But you're at the mercy of the driver as he picks up cargo here and there, loading it all around the passengers, picks up a few friends, gets petrol, fixes a leaky petrol tank, runs some errands, repairs the engine, loads more crates right up to the ceiling – and then stops every half-hour to fill the radiator with water.

Good bladder control is needed as pit stops are irregular. Hawkers are periodically allowed on board the big buses to sell bread, fruit or snacks.

Buying Tickets

Most cities have a main intercity bus station (Russian: *avtovokzal*, Kyrgyz & Uzbek: *avtobekat*) where you can buy your own ticket. Almost no travel agencies will book buses.

Try to pick buses originating from where you are, enabling you to buy tickets as much as a day in advance. Tickets for through buses may not be sold until they arrive, amid anxious scrambles. In a pinch you could try paying the driver directly for a place; this is also a good way to avoid the police in Uzbekistan bus stations as long as you know how much the ticket should cost.

In Tashkent, and to a lesser extent in Samarkand, buying a long-distance ticket at the station can be a headache for a foreigner. You must first satisfy the station's Office of Visas and Registration (OVIR) that you have a visa for your destination, and at Tashkent they may insist on buying the ticket for you, with your dollars, never mentioning the true price. Long-distance bus stations are in general low-life magnets, rarely pleasant after dark. Disregard most bus station timetables.

Fares

Officially, the ex-Soviet republics and China have done away with two-tier bus prices.

Some routes have both 'hard' and 'soft' buses, with fares 15% to 35% higher for the latter. Hard/soft is *zhumsaq/qatty* in Kazak and Karakalpak, *yumshak/gaty* in Turkmen, and *yumshok/kattik* in Uzbek.

In Xinjiang sleeper buses (*wòpùchē* in Chinese; *qarvatlik mashina* in Uyghur) operate on long-distance routes, such as Kashgar-Ürümqi and Hotan-Ürümqi. These double-deckers have two levels of seats that fold flat (or almost flat) to become berths. Lower berths are a little more expensive than upper berths. Sleeper buses can be noisy and smoky but in general they are pretty good.

Inter-republic fares can depend on which side you start from (eg a ticket from Tashkent to Almaty costs US$8, while Almaty to Tashkent is US$11). Some sample fares (one way) on state-run long-distance coaches to and from Bishkek are: Tashkent US$4.50, Almaty US$3, and Karakol US$3. A private Bishkek-Osh bus costs about US$10. Bus fares in Uzbekistan are also cheap: Tashkent-Samarkand is US$1.50, Tashkent-Bukhara is US$3 and Bukhara-Urgench is US$2.20.

TRAIN

Lower-class train travel is the cheapest way to get around, but that also makes it attractive to everybody else, so it's the most crowded way. You can of course sleep or stretch on long journeys, and there is camaraderie if you want it, but you'll always attract lots of attention – everything you do, or pull from your bag, will be of interest to compartment-mates and their friends down the aisle. In general travelling in the summertime is best done at night.

SV (1st class) carriages are scarce for trips within Central Asia. See the Getting There & Away chapter about trains, classes and services.

Connections

Vast tracts of mountains or desert mean some journeys are a pain by train, eg between north and south in Turkmenistan (Ashgabat-Dashoguz goes via Turkmenabat) and Kyrgyzstan (Bishkek-Osh takes almost two days, via Tashkent). For these, buses or flights are more sensible.

Trains are most useful to cover the vast distances in Kazakstan. Certain corridors, eg the Turksib (Semey-Almaty), Tashkent-Andijan and Almaty-Tashkent, are well served by fast trains every other day. The daily overnight Tashkent-Bukhara run, which carries on to Urgench (for Khiva), is particularly useful. Train is the only real way to get into Khojand at the moment as buses and taxis no longer cross the Tajikistan border.

As an indication of journey times, Urgench-Tashkent and Tashkent-Almaty are each about 25 hours on a fast train.

Elsewhere connections are drying up as fast as the Aral Sea; few trains run to Dushanbe any more (those that do take a very roundabout route) and many services in Kyrgyzstan operate periodically. There are no direct lines, for example, between Ashgabat and any other Central Asian capitals; you must change at Turkmenabat (Charjou).

Many trains to and from Russia (see the Getting There & Away chapter) can be used for getting around Central Asia, and may be faster and in better condition. But any train originating far from where you are is likely to be filthy, crowded and late by the time you board it. Surprisingly, trains in Kazakstan and Kyrgyzstan still run on Moscow time, even for trips entirely within Central Asia. Some suburban trains run on local time, however.

Buying Tickets

Book at least two days ahead for CIS connections, if you can. You will probably need to show your passport and visa. A few stations have separate windows for advance bookings and for departures within 24 hours; the latter is generally the one with the heaving mob around it (beware of pickpockets).

Many tourist hotels have rail-booking desks (with their own mark-up). Few travel agencies are interested in booking trains.

If you can't get a ticket for a particular train, it's worth turning up anyway. No matter how full ticket clerks insist a train is, there always seem to be spare *kupeynyy* (2nd class or sleeping carriage) berths. Ask an attendant. You'll have to pay at least the equivalent price of the ticket, often more, and usually in dollars. Shop around the

attendants for the best offer (the money, of course, all goes into his/her pocket). You can also upgrade this way. But police or ticket masters may later make a fuss and demand a further 'fine' of a few dollars.

Fares

Foreigners pay roughly double local rate for train tickets in Russia and Uzbekistan, but fares are the same in Turkmenistan, China and Kazakstan. At major centres in Uzbekistan you may have to show your passport when you buy the ticket, but elsewhere the rule may not always be enforced. You might get a local person to buy you a ticket, but tickets are still pretty cheap and you're a sitting duck for any train official who wants to make a stink about it.

A few sample kupeynyy fares (one way) for trips from Tashkent are US$15 Bishkek, US$12 Almaty (24 hours), US$3 Andijan, US$6 Bukhara and US$4.50 Samarkand.

CAR & MOTORCYCLE

Car is an excellent way to get around Central Asia and it needn't be expensive. Main highways between capitals and big cities, eg Almaty-Bishkek-Tashkent-Samarkand-Bukhara, are fast and fairly well maintained. Mountain roads (ie most roads in Kyrgyzstan and Tajikistan) can be blocked with snow in winter and plagued by landslides in spring. See Self-Drive later for advice about riding a motorcycle through Central Asia.

Share Taxis

There are two main ways of travelling by car in Central Asia. The first is by share taxi, whereby a taxi or private car does a regular run between two cities and charges a set rate for each of the four seats in a car. These cars often wait for passengers outside bus or train stations and some have a sign in the window indicating where they are headed. Cars are quicker and just as comfortable as a bus or train, and can work out little more expensive than a bus. In Kyrgyzstan per person fares are so cheap that two or three of you can buy all four seats and stretch out. Otherwise smaller cars can be a little cramped. The most common car is the Russian Zhiguli.

These services are particularly useful in Kyrgyzstan along certain main routes such as Bishkek-Almaty, Bishkek-Osh, and Naryn-Bishkek. Other useful share taxi routes are Urgench-Khiva and Ashgabat-Mary. There are a few share taxis in Xinjiang (ie Yengisar-Kashgar) but they can be hard to find.

Ordinary Taxis

The other main kind of car travel is to hire a taxi for a special route. This is handy for reaching off-the-beaten-track places, where bus connections are hit-and-miss or nonexistent, such as Song-Köl in Kyrgyzstan. Taxis are often marked as such or have a checkerboard symbol on the dashboard. Hotel staff, travel agencies or local development agencies can sometimes help you find an English-speaking driver. Select your driver with care, look over his car (we took one in Kyrgyzstan whose exhaust fumes were funnelled through the back windows) and assess his sobriety before you set off. See Taxi in the Local Transport section later in this chapter for more on Central Asian taxis.

You'll have to negotiate a price before you set off. Along routes where there are shared taxis this is four times the per-person fare so if you can fill the car up, your share will be about the same as a bus fare. Make sure everyone is clear which route you will be taking, how long you want the driver to wait at a site and if there are any toll or entry fees to be paid. You will need to haggle hard. You can work out approximate costs by working out the return kilometre distance; assume the average consumption of cars is around 12 litres per 100km and times the number of litres needed by the per litre petrol cost (constantly in flux). Add to this a daily fee (anything from US$5 up to the cost of the petrol) and a waiting fee of around US$1 per hour and away you go.

Rental

A car and driver from Uzbektourism is about US$11 per hour. Almaty has a Hertz franchise. In general you are better off hiring a taxi for the day. Some Central Asian travel agencies have a fixed per-kilometre rate, eg US$0.25 per kilometre for a 4WD Niva.

Self-Drive

Driving your own car or motorcycle is fraught with problems (see the Getting There & Away chapter), and we don't recommend it. The biggest problem by far is fuel supplies, although new petrol stations are opening up; Uzbekistan does its own refining, while Kazakstan exports oil to China and then imports the petrol. Prices per litre swing wildly depending on supply. During research prices per litre in Uzbekistan were about US$0.10, in Kyrgyzstan US$0.20 and rising. Petrol comes in four grades – 76, 93, 95 and 98 octane. In the countryside you'll see petrol cowboys selling plastic bottles of fuel from their own trucks, often of very poor quality, adulterated with oil or water.

Distances are daunting; Almaty-Tashkent is about 800km (10 hours) and Tashkent-Khiva 1000km (14 hours). Tajikistan's roads have almost as many checkpoints as potholes. In Uzbekistan there are police at every province *(oblast)* border and at the limits of larger towns, most looking for excuses to hit drivers (local or otherwise) with a 'fine'.

It is possible to buy a car or motorbike in Central Asia, though you really have to know what to look for in a vehicle and how to repair it when it (inevitably) breaks down. Several cities have car markets (*glavnii avtorynok* in Russian) on the outskirts of town. Bishkek's is at Voyenny Antonovka, 10km west of the city. You'll definitely need a Russian-speaking intermediary to strike a deal and help with registration procedures.

HITCHING

Hitching is never entirely safe in any country, and we don't recommend it. Travellers who decide to hitch should understand that they are taking a small but potentially serious risk. If you do choose to hitch, you will be safer if you travel in pairs and let someone know where you are planning to go.

In Central Asia there is generally little distinction between hitching and taking a taxi. Anyone with a car will stop if you flag them down (with a low up-and-down wave not an upturned thumb) and almost any driver will expect you to pay for the ride. If you can negotiate a reasonable fare (it helps to know the equivalent bus or share taxi fare) this can be a much quicker mode of transport than the bus. There's also a good chance you'll be invited to someone's house for lunch or vodka, often a mixed blessing.

LOCAL TRANSPORT

Most sizable towns have public buses, and sometimes electric trolleybuses; bigger cities also have trams, and Tashkent has a metro system. Transport is still ridiculously cheap by western standards, but usually packed because there's never enough money to keep an adequate fleet on the road; at peak hours it can take several stops for those caught by surprise to even work their way to an exit.

Uzbekistan makes things extra hard by labelling all buses and trolleybuses in Uzbek only. See the Language chapter for translations. The supply of taxis is usually inadequate except around tourist hotels, but plenty of people will give you lifts.

Public transport in smaller towns tends to melt away soon after dark.

Bus, Trolleybus & Tram

Services are frequent in city centres, but more erratic as you move towards the edges.

Payment methods vary, but the most common method is to pay the driver cash on exit. In Tashkent and other big cities, you buy tickets *(talony)* in strips of five or 10 from drivers, or from street kiosks that display them in the window. You then punch them in little machines fixed inside the vehicles. Most passengers are perfectly honest, patiently passing one another's money and tickets up and down to the nearest conductor or punch.

Manoeuvre your way out by asking anyone in the way: '*Vykhodite?*' ('Getting off?').

Marshrutnoe Taxi

A marshrutnoe taxi (marsh-**root**-na-yuh tahk-**see**) is a minibus running along a fixed route. You can get on at fixed stops but can get off anywhere by saying *zdyes pazhalsta* (zd-**yes** pa-**zhal**-stuh, here please). Routes are hard to figure out and schedules erratic, and it's usually easier to stick to other transport. Fares depend on the distance travelled but are a little higher than the bus fare.

Taxi

There are two kinds of taxis: officially licensed ones and anything else. In bigger city entries we describe how to tell them apart from their licence plates. Official ones are more trustworthy, and sometimes cheaper – if you can find one. 'Taxi' painted on the door and a roof light are no guarantee of official licence. They may have meters but they're always 'broken' and you'll have to negotiate. Or let a local friend negotiate for you – they'll do better than you will.

Unofficial taxis are anything else you can stop. Some 'gypsy' taxis are also painted and have roof lights, while others are just private cars driven by people trying to cover their huge petrol costs. Stand at the side of the road, and extend your arm and wait, as scores of others around you will probably be doing. When someone stops, negotiate destination and fare through the passenger-side window or through a partially open door. The driver may say *sadytse* (sit down) or beckon you in, but sort the fare out first. It helps a lot if you can negotiate the price in Russian, even more so in the local language.

A typical fare across Tashkent at the time of research was around US$1; about half that for Ashgabat or Bishkek. Fares go up at night, and extra charges are incurred for radio calls (we note telephone numbers for these under individual town entries).

> ## Taxi Precautions
>
> Avoid taxis lurking outside tourist hotels – drivers charge far too much and get uppity when you try to talk them down. Know your route, be familiar with how to get there and how long it should take. Never get into a taxi with more than one person in it, especially after dark; check the back seat of the car for hidden friends too. Keep your fare money in a separate pocket to avoid flashing large wads of cash. If you're staying at a private residence have the taxi stop at the corner nearest your destination, not the specific address. Trust your instincts – if a driver looks creepy, look for another one.

Kazakstan

Kazakstan at a Glance

Official Name: Republic of Kazakstan
(Kazakstan Republikasy)
Area: 2,717,300 sq km
Population: 15.6 million (1999)
Ethnic Mix: 50% Kazak, 32% Russian, 5%
Ukrainian, 3% German, 2% Uzbek, 8%
Others
Capital: Astana
Currency: tenge (T)
Country ☎ Code: 7 (same as Russia)
Best Time to Go: May/June, September/
October; Trekking: July/August; Winter
Sports: January to April

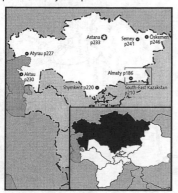

- **Almaty** – baths buildings and museums
  at the cultural centre of the country
- **Turkistan** – Kozha Akhmed Yasaui
  mausoleum, a blueprint for more
  famous ones in Samarkand
- **Altay Mountains** – the quintessential
  Central Asian landscape
- **Lake Burabay** – distinctive rock forma-
  tions and idyllic lakes
- **Aksu-Zhabaghly Nature Reserve** –
  birds and wildlife in this rugged region
- **Semey** – the former homes to the bard
  Abay and the writer Dostoevsky

Kazakstan, reaching from the Caspian Sea
to China and from Siberia to the Tian Shan
range, is more than twice as big as the four
other former Soviet Central Asian republics
put together. It's also the least densely
populated and potentially the area's richest
country, with huge mineral resources attracting serious investment from the west.
Though unquestionably Central Asian, and
aspiring to political and economic leadership of the region, it's set apart from the
other states in several important ways.

The ninth largest country in the world,
Kazakstan lies at the heart of the great Eurasian steppe, the band of grassland stretching
from Mongolia to Hungary, which has served
for millennia as the highway and grazing
ground of nomadic horseback peoples. Kazaks remained largely nomadic until well into
the 20th century and as a result have left no
ancient cities or ruins. The few historic remains are from non-Kazak cultures.

Because of the fertility of the steppe, and
because it's the only Central Asian territory
bordering directly on Russia, Kazakstan was
colonised by the tsarist and Soviet empires
far earlier, and to a far greater extent, than the
rest of Central Asia. Much of the steppe was
turned into farmland and grey industrial cities
were built to exploit the mineral resources.

The 'emptiness' and 'remoteness' of the
steppe also made Kazakstan a convenient
dumping ground for unwanted tsarist or Soviet subjects – from Dostoevsky, Trotsky
and Solzhenitsyn to whole peoples disliked
or feared by Stalin – as well as a place to
hide the USSR's chief nuclear testing zone
and its main space launching centre. Today,
Russians and other nationalities are leaving
and Kazaks have only recently begun to
number a majority once more.

For many, Kazakstan is a staging post for
more famous Central Asian destinations.
Almaty is one of Central Asia's main international gateways, and is linked to Ürümqi
in China by bus and train. All trains from
Russia to Central Asia also cross Kazakstan.

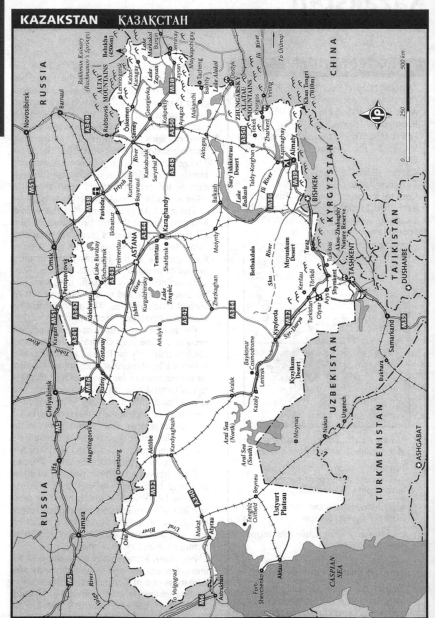

Despite appearing bleak – especially as you cross the treeless steppe and deserts, or find yourself in yet another drab and decaying industrial city – there are good reasons for making time for Kazakstan. Almaty, Central Asia's most cosmopolitan city, has a relaxed atmosphere and is particularly lovely in spring and summer when its streets are lined with shady trees and outdoor cafes. It's also an ideal base from which to explore the neighbouring mountains.

The new capital of Astana has little in it's own right to attract tourists, but it is en route to the beguiling Lake Burabay. The mausoleum of the Turkic Muslim mystic Kozha Akhmed Yasaui, in the southern town of Turkistan, is impressive despite being only part way through a long restoration program.

Above all, the mountains along Kazakstan's southern and eastern fringes (the Tian Shan, the Zhungar Alatau and the Altay) are Kazakstan's real attractions. With their icy peaks, forested valleys, swift rivers and clear lakes, the mountains are beautiful places to hike in summer and ski in winter. A five-day trek can take you across two Tian Shan ranges from Almaty to Kyrgyzstan's Lake Issyk-Kul. Ambitious trekkers can tackle the 7010m Khan Tengri in the south-east.

You'll meet as many Russians as Kazaks here, and probably a few other nationalities too; generally people are friendly and helpful. The Kazaks, descended from Jenghiz Khan's hordes, present great contrasts. Though mainly rural and still just two or three generations from nomadism (as is shown by their wild horseback sports, the lingering custom of bride-stealing and the collective farmers who disappear off to the hills with their herds and yurts for months on end), Kazaks in the cities can also be much more sophisticated and stylish than their Russian counterparts.

Facts about Kazakstan

HISTORY
The early history of Kazakstan is a shadowy procession of nomadic empires, most of whom swept into the region from the east and are shrouded with uncertainty, since they left few records. The Kazak people did not emerge as a distinct entity until the 15th century. Down the millennia, recurring historical threads include a great deal of large-scale slaughter and a contrast between the far south, which was within the ambit of the settled Silk Road civilisations of Transoxiana (modern Uzbekistan), and the rest of Kazakstan, which remained the domain of nomadic horseback animal herders until the 20th century. Since the 18th century the involvement of Russia has been paramount.

Early Peoples
Around 500 BCE (before common era) southern Kazakstan was inhabited by the Saka, a nomadic people considered part of the vast network of Scythian cultures which stretched across the steppes from the Altay mountains to Ukraine. One southern Saka clan, the Massagetes, succeeded in repelling Alexander the Great in the 4th century BCE. The Saka did leave at least one important relic to posterity – the Golden Man, a fabulously worked golden warrior's costume discovered in a tomb near Almaty, and now Kazakstan's greatest archaeological treasure. See the boxed text 'The Golden Man' in the Almaty section later in this chapter.

Around 200 BCE eastern Kazakstan was briefly under the control of the Hsiung-nu, a great nomad confederacy from China's northern borders, and probably ancestors of the Huns who later conquered large parts of Europe, Persia and India.

Turkic Peoples
Turkic peoples, again from the region of today's Mongolia and northern China, began moving into Kazakstan as the Huns were leaving. From about 550 to 750 CE (common era) the southern half of Kazakstan was the western extremity of the Kök (Blue) Turk empire, which reached across the steppe from Manchuria.

The far south of Kazakstan was within the sphere of the Bukhara-based Samanid dynasty from the mid-9th century and here the cities of Otyrar and Yasy (now Turkistan) developed on the back of agriculture and Silk Road trade. When the Karakhanid Turks from the southern Kazak steppe ousted the Samanids in the late 10th century, they took up the Samanids' settled ways (as well as Islam) and left probably Kazakstan's earliest surviving buildings (in and around Taraz).

Jenghiz Khan

Around 1130 the Karakhanids were displaced by the Khitans, or Liao, a Buddhist people driven out of Mongolia and northern China. The Central Asian state set up by the Khitans, known as the Karakitay empire, stretched at its height from Transoxiana to Xinjiang but in the early 13th century became prey to rising powers from both west and east. To the west was the Khorezmshah empire, based in Khorezm, south of the Aral Sea. In 1210 the Khorezmshah Mohammed II conquered Transoxiana and at the same time gained control over the southern tip of Kazakstan.

East of the Karakitay was Jenghiz Khan, and to make matters worse, a Mongolian named Kuchlug, enemy of Jenghiz Khan since the khan's early days, had set himself up as the ruler of Karakitay.

Jenghiz Khan sent an army to crush the Karakitay in 1218, then in 1219 turned to the Khorezmshah empire, which had misguidedly rebuffed his relatively peaceable overtures by murdering 450 of his merchants at Otyrar and killing one of his ambassadors at Samarkand. The biggest Mongol army yet (150,000 or more) sacked Samarkand, Bukhara and Otyrar, then carried on westwards to Europe and the Middle East. All of Kazakstan, like the rest of Central Asia, became part of the Mongol empire.

After Jenghiz Khan

On Jenghiz Khan's death in 1227, his empire was divided between his sons. The lands most distant from the Mongol heartland – west, north and north-east of the Aral Sea – went to sons of his eldest son Jochi, who had died before his father. This territory, which stretched as far as Ukraine and Moscow and included western and most of northern Kazakstan, came to be known as the Golden Horde. The bulk of Kazakstan went, along with Transoxiana and western Xinjiang, to Jenghiz Khan's second son Chaghatai, and became known as the Chaghatai khanate.

The Chaghatai khanate split in the mid-14th century between Transoxiana, whose rulers adopted that region's settled lifestyle and Islam, and the lands further north and east, where the Mongols maintained their nomadic ways. Timur, who invaded Transoxiana soon afterwards, wrecked Otyrar and constructed the grand Mausoleum of Kozha Akhmed Yasaui at Turkistan, but otherwise didn't bother much with Kazakstan.

The Kazaks

It was from the descendants of the Mongols, and of Turkic and other peoples who survived their coming in Kazakstan, that the Kazaks emerged. The story actually starts with the Uzbeks, a group of Islamised Mongols taking their name from an early 14th century leader Özbeg (or Uzbek), who were left in control of northern Kazakstan as the Golden Horde disintegrated in the 14th and 15th centuries. The Uzbeks spread southward, mingling with other peoples, adopting the Turkic language as they went, and eventually crossing the Syr-Darya river to attack the decaying empire of Timur's descendants.

Kazak, Kyrgyz or Cossack?

'Kazak' is a Turkic word meaning free rider, adventurer, outlaw – just what the Kazaks were to the settled Uzbeks south of the Syr-Darya river. Confusingly, the Russians used the same word to refer to the Cossacks, an entirely different group of free riders, and until the 20th century Russians called the Kazaks 'Kyrgyz', and the Kyrgyz – just to make things clear – 'Kara (Black) Kyrgyz'. When the Russians decided in the 1920s to call the Kazaks 'Kazakhs', they distinguished them from the Cossacks by using the Cyrillic letter x (kh) instead of the second k in Kazak. Thus in Soviet times Kazakstan was spelt Kasakhstan.

In 1468 an internal feud split the Uzbeks into two groups. Those who ended up south of the Syr-Darya ruled the old Timurid empire from Bukhara as the Shaybanid dynasty, settled down to agriculture and ultimately gave their name to modern Uzbekistan. Those who stayed north remained nomadic and became the Kazaks.

In the late 15th and 16th centuries the Kazaks established one of the world's last great nomadic empires, stretching across the steppe and desert north, east and west of the Syr-Darya. They menaced the remnants of the Chaghatai khanate in the Tian Shan and Xinjiang and raided Transoxiana. Haq Nazar's successor, Tevkel Khan, even briefly occupied Samarkand around 1590.

In the north, in 1563, a Kazak leader called Kuchum took over the Siberian khanate, a Golden Horde remnant with its capital deep inside present-day Russia at Sibir (modern Tobolsk). Sibir was captured by the eastward-advancing Russians in 1582, but Kuchum and his descendants harassed the Russian advance until the 1670s.

Those Russians who today claim that northern Kazakstan is 'traditionally part of Russia' seem unaware that, by similar logic, southern Siberia could be considered 'traditionally part of Kazakstan'.

The Hordes & the Great Disaster

After Haq Nazar the fissures between the three great hordes of Kazaks deepened, weakening their ability to resist external threats. The hordes – with which Kazaks today still identify – were the Great (or Elder) Horde in the south, the Middle Horde in the centre and north-east, and the Little (or Young or Lesser) Horde in the west. Each was ruled by a khan and was composed of a number of clans whose leaders held the title *aksakal, bi* or *batyr*.

The Kazaks' ruin came from the Oyrats, a warlike, expansionist Mongolian people who subjugated eastern Kazakstan, the Tian Shan and parts of Xinjiang to form the Zhungarian empire in the 1630s. The Kazaks were savagely and repeatedly pummelled, particularly between 1690 and 1720. They still remember this as the 'Great Disaster'.

The Russians Arrive

In 1640 Guriyev (now Atyrau), near the Caspian Sea, became part of the Russian empire. Russia's expansion into Siberia also ran up against the Oyrats, against whom the Russians built a line of forts along the Kazaks' northern border. The Kazaks, considering the Russians the lesser of two evils, sought tsarist protection from the Oyrats, and the khans of all three hordes swore loyalty to the Russian crown between 1731 and 1742. This brought little help to the Kazaks, but the Russians took it as an excuse to stretch their defensive line right across the north of the Kazaks' territory to the Ural river. In the 1750s this line began to move south and Russian, Cossack and Tatar settlers moved in behind it.

Russia chose to interpret the Kazak khans' oaths of allegiance as agreement to annexation, despite the annihilation of the Oyrats by the Manchurian Chinese in the 1750s. Spurred by Kazak attacks on Russian forts and by Kazak revolts against their own leaders which were provoked by the deterioration of the quality of life during the Great Disaster, Russia gradually extended its 'protection' of the khanates to their abolition by 1848. The khanates as political entities were abolished, but the hordes (as social/ethnic entities) remained.

Despite repeated Kazak uprisings, notably by Abylay Khan's grandson Kenisary Kasimov in the 1840s, Russia steadily tightened its grip. The last bits of Kazakstan to fall were northern outposts of Uzbekistan's Kokand khanate. In 1854 the Russians founded a fort in the south-east called Verny, which became Almaty.

Tsarist Rule

Revolts were brutally suppressed. By some estimates one million of the four million Kazaks died in revolts and famines before 1870. Movement of peasant settlers into Kazakstan was stimulated by the abolition of serfdom in Russia and Ukraine in 1861. One million came to the north in the 1890s. The tsarist regime also used Kazakstan as a place of exile for dissidents – among them Fyodor Dostoevsky and the Ukrainian nationalist writer and artist Taras Shevchenko.

Russia governed southern Kazakstan as part of its Turkestan region, which also included much of the other modern Central Asian republics. Northern Kazakstan was treated separately and known as the Steppe region.

In 1916, Russian mobilisation of Kazaks as support labour behind the WWI front caused a widespread uprising, led by Abdulghaffar and Amangeldy Imanov. It was brutally put down, with an estimated 150,000 Kazaks killed and perhaps 200,000 fleeing to China.

The Communist Takeover

In the chaos following the Russian Revolution of 1917, a Kazak nationalist party, Alash Orda (which had been formed as an underground movement by aristocratic Kazak intellectuals in 1905) tried to establish an independent government. Alash Orda's leader was Ali Khan Bukeykhanov, a prince and descendant of Jenghiz Khan, and ultimately a victim of Stalin's 1930s purges.

The Alash Orda government had two centres, Semey in the north-east and Zhambeyty in the west. As the Russian civil war raged across Kazakstan, Alash Orda vacillated between support for the Red and White factions, eventually siding with the Bolsheviks who emerged victorious in 1920 – only for Alash members to be purged from the Communist Party of Kazakstan (CPK) and executed or sent to labour camps from 1925. Meanwhile many thousands more Kazaks and Russian peasants had died in the civil war, which devastated the land and economy, and several hundred thousand fled to China and elsewhere.

Under Communist rule, southern Kazakstan was initially part of the Turkestan Autonomous Soviet Socialist Republic (ASSR), which included most of the rest of Soviet Central Asia. A separate ASSR covered northern Kazakstan, the old tsarist Steppe region, with its capital at Orenburg (now in Russia). From 1924 to 1925 the latter was enlarged by the addition of Kazak parts of the Turkestan ASSR, and its capital moved to Kyzylorda. The capital was shifted once more, to Almaty, in 1928. Kazakstan was made a full Soviet Socialist Republic (SSR) of the USSR in 1936.

Collectivisation & Colonisation

The next disaster to befall the Kazaks was denomadisation, which began in the late 1920s. The world's biggest group of semi-nomadic people was forced one step up the Marxist evolutionary ladder to become settled farmers in new collectives. They literally decimated their herds rather than hand them over to state control and, unused to agriculture, died in their hundreds of thousands from famine and disease. Those who opposed collectivisation were sent to labour camps or killed. Many more escaped to China. Kazakstan's population fell by more than two million between 1926 and 1933.

In the 1930s and 1940s more and more people from other parts of the USSR were settled in Kazakstan to work in its new industrial cities, or sent as prisoners to its many labour camps. The latter included whole peoples deported en masse from various parts of the USSR by Stalin around the time of WWII.

'Development' & Unrest

In the 1950s a new wave of around 800,000 migrants arrived when Russian president Nikita Khrushchev decided to plough up 250,000 sq km of north Kazakstan steppe to grow wheat in the Virgin Lands scheme, a bid to achieve Soviet grain self-sufficiency. One Leonid Brezhnev, as deputy head and later head of the CPK, improved his own political standing by making the Virgin Lands appear more of a success than it really was (storms and wind savaged nearly half the new land in the early 1960s). Kazakstan eventually accounted for over 20% of the agriculturally productive land of the Soviet Union and in terms of grain output ranked third after Russia and the Ukraine.

Though the labour camps were wound down in the mid-1950s, many survivors stayed on, adding to the country's highly varied ethnic mixture. Yet more Russians, Ukrainians and other Soviet nationalities arrived to mine and process Kazakstan's reserves of coal, iron and oil. By 1959, 43%

of Kazakstan's 9.3 million people was Russian, and only 29% was Kazak.

The CPK's first Kazak leader was Zhumabay Shayakhmetov, appointed during WWII but replaced in 1954 because of his lack of enthusiasm for the Virgin Lands campaign. A second Kazak, Dinmukhamed Konaev, was in charge from 1964 to 1986. Though he was corrupt, Konaev's replacement by a non-Kazak, Gennady Kolbin, in 1986 provoked big demonstrations and violent riots by Kazaks in many cities.

During the Cold War the USSR decided Kazakstan was 'empty' and 'remote' enough to use as its chief nuclear testing ground and the Soviet command's space launch centre (the Baykonur Cosmodrome). In 1989 Kazakstan produced the first great popular protest movement the USSR had seen: the Nevada-Semey (Semipalatinsk) Movement. This pressure forced the CPK to demand an end to tests in Kazakstan; there have been none since 1989. See the Ecology & Environment section later in this chapter for more on the nuclear tests.

The Rise of Nazarbaev

Nursultan Nazarbaev, a Kazak and former Konaev protege, took over from Kolbin in 1989 and has ruled Kazakstan since, with the title of president since 1990. In 1991 Nazarbaev did not welcome the break-up of the USSR and Kazakstan was the last Soviet republic to declare independence. Kazakstan's first multi-party elections, held in 1994, returned a parliament considered favourable to Nazarbaev, but were judged unfair by foreign observers. Complaints included arbitrary barring of some candidates, ballot rigging and media distortion.

The parliament, however, turned out to be a thorn in Nazarbaev's side, obstructing his economic reforms, which one deputy called 'shock surgery without anaesthetics'. Living standards across the country fell, in line with virtually all other post Soviet economies. In 1995, following a court ruling that the elections had been illegal, Nazarbaev dissolved parliament.

Soon afterwards, in the manner of Uzbekistan's Islam Karimov and Turkmenistan's

Nursultan Nazarbaev

For a man born to a peasant family in a rural village, who tended a blast furnace at Karaghandy Metallurgical Works in the 1960s, Nursultan Nazarbaev – President of Kazakstan since 1990 – has come a long way. In the process he has amassed himself not only political capital but also so much wealth that he's listed as one of the richest men in the world.

In the 1970s Nazarbaev began his rise up through the ranks of the Communist Party of Kazakstan to become the first secretary in 1989. This put him in the unenviable top position when the Soviet house of cards came tumbling down, but like fellow Central Asian Soviet leaders he has managed to hold on to the presidency in two elections by using a mixture of political pragmatism and force.

Together with his wife Sara, an economist and head of a children's charity fund, he has three daughters. The eldest Dariya, is in charge of Kazakstan's TV company, Khavar, and the youngest, Aliya, a student, was part of Central Asia's 'Royal Wedding' of 1998 when she married the son of the Kyrgyz president, Askar Akaev.

Saparmurat Niyazov, he held a referendum to extend his presidential term, without elections, until 2000, and won with an overwhelming majority. Elections for a new parliament, under a new constitution, were held in December 1995. The new constitution practically created a presidential dictatorship, with Nazarbaev head of state, commander-in-chief of the armed forces and able to veto any legislation passed by parliament.

Perhaps as a sop to the Russians but also as recognition of the overwhelming economic and military importance of Russia itself, Nazarbaev has said he favours much closer ties with Russia, even mentioning a single parliament and a single currency. In 1995 the two countries signed a common defence agreement, but the president's enthusiasm for Russia has since waned and a more placatory tone to the west has been adopted.

The country is still basically run by former communists, but there have been improvements. Local and national government was restructured throughout 1997, resulting in a significant reduction in governmental bodies and staff, including Cabinet changes that saw the sacking of the prime minister, Akezhan Kazhegeldin.

Kazakstan has introduced market-oriented economic policies, partly to secure aid from western governments. Privatisation is advanced and major western investments have been won, the biggest being multi-billion dollar deals with American and European companies to develop the Tenghiz oilfield and the Karachaganak gas field in western Kazakstan.

Strategy 2030

Many thought Nazarbaev crazy in wanting to move the capital from Almaty to the heartland steppe city of Akmola, but the change was made ahead of schedule in December 1997. On 6 May 1998, the president decreed the new capital should have a new name – Astana (imaginatively, 'capital city' in Kazak).

The move to Astana is part of the president's 2030 economic development strategy. Nazarbaev wants Kazakstan to be not so much an Asian tiger as 'a Central Asian snow leopard, creating a model to be followed by other developing countries.' Shrewdly enough, he has set the attainment date for economic prosperity well enough into the 21st century that he need not worry about what will happen if the dream doesn't quite come off.

Perhaps with the expectation that Kazakstan's economy would take a battering in the wake of the 1998 Russian economic crisis, the presidential election was called early in January 1999. Nazarbaev won again with a resounding 82% of the vote, securing the presidency until 2006. His nearest rival was a communist candidate Serikbolsyn Abdildin, who some said had been forced to stand to give the appearance of choice. The Organisation for Security and Co-operation in Europe said the election 'fell far short' of international standards. One of the two candidates banned from standing included, on a legal technicality, Nazarbaev's most serious rival, Kazhegeldin, the former prime minister and now chair of the new National Republican Party.

With parliamentary elections expected for December 1999, the government moved to further sideline Kazhegeldin by investigating him for tax evasion in May 1999. In the meantime, constitutional changes have given the parliament increased powers, including the ability to initiate laws and the right to choose the prime minister, currently an appointee of the president.

GEOGRAPHY

Covering 2.7 million sq km, Kazakstan is the ninth biggest country in the world, about the size of western Europe. Its border with Russia in the north and west is one of the world's longest, at 6846km. It borders Turkmenistan, Uzbekistan and Kyrgyzstan in the south, and China in the east. It has a lengthy shoreline (1894km) on the Caspian Sea, and a shrinking one of around a thousand km on the Aral Sea, which it shares with Uzbekistan.

The country is mainly flat except for its alpine south-east and eastern fringes. South-east Kazakstan lies along the northern edge of the Tian Shan, and Mt Khan Tengri (7010m), one of the great Tian Shan peaks, pegs the China-Kazakstan-Kyrgyzstan border. Lesser Tian Shan ranges straddling the border west of here, most topping 4000m, are the Küngey Alatau, Zailiysky Alatau, Kyrgyz Alatau and Talassky Alatau.

Kazakstan's eastern border, shared with China, is a series of alternating mountain ranges and gaps through which roads or railways pass. Further north are the Tarbagatay Hills (mostly 2000 to 3000m) and, north of the headwaters of the Irtysh river, the Altay mountains (4000m plus) which straddle Russia, Mongolia, Kazakstan and China.

The only serious elevations elsewhere in the country are the Karatau Hills, really a spur of the Tian Shan north-west of Taraz and Shymkent, and a band of upland that stretches west from the Tarbagatay Hills, occasionally topping 1000m as in the Shyngghystau Hills south of Semey.

The north of the country is flat, mostly treeless steppe, much of its original grassland now turned over to wheat or other agriculture. Further south the steppe is increasingly arid, turning into desert or semidesert (often with some scrub vegetation) across much of the southern third of the country.

The Ustyurt plateau, a stony desert, reaches west from the Aral Sea towards the Caspian; south-east of the Aral Sea, Kazakstan shares the Kyzylkum desert with Uzbekistan; the Betbakdala clay desert stretches between the Aral Sea and Lake Balkash; south of the Betbakdala is the Muyunkum desert, and south of Lake Balkash is the Sary Ishikotrau desert.

The most important rivers are the Syr-Darya (ancient Jaxartes), flowing north-west across the south of Kazakstan into the Aral Sea; the Ural, flowing south from Russia's Ural mountains into the Caspian Sea; the Ili flowing out of China into Lake Balkash; the Irtysh which flows across north-east Kazakstan into Siberia; and the Ishim and Tobol which flow north from northern Kazakstan to join the Irtysh.

Lake Balkash in the central east is the fourth largest lake in Asia (17,400 sq km) but very shallow – only 26m at its deepest point. Its eastern half is salty, and its western half is fresh water.

CLIMATE

Like the rest of the region, Kazakstan has hot summers and very cold winters. During the hottest months, July and August, the average daily maximums are 36°C in Almaty and 38°C in Semey, although such really hot days are never very numerous.

From November to March, frosty mornings are typical in Almaty and afternoon temperatures remain below freezing about a third of the time. The ground is snow-covered on average for 111 days a year, while the Altay mountains are snowcapped all year. Fogs and mists normally burn off by noon. In Semey only summer mornings are free of frost and from October through to April most mornings will be below freezing. Snow is usual in winter and the ground is usually thinly covered in snow 150 days a

year. Average daytime temperatures in January are -2°C in Almaty and -11°C in Semey, with average annual minimums as low as -26°C in Almaty and -37°C in Semey.

Annual precipitation ranges from less than 100mm a year in the deserts to 1500mm in the Altay mountains. Much of the summer rain on the steppes comes from violent thunderstorms, which often produce local flash floods. See also the Climate section in the Facts about Central Asia chapter.

ECOLOGY & ENVIRONMENT

Because of its vast size and relative emptiness Kazakstan, more than any other country in Central Asia, was forced to endure the worst excesses of the Soviet system – a fearful legacy it is only now feebly coming to grips with. The Aral Sea catastrophe (see the Ecology & Environment section in Facts about Central Asia) is the best known of these disasters, but the country also continues to suffer from the fallout, both literal and metaphorical, of past nuclear tests conducted mainly in the Semey area of East Kazakstan (although there were also tests in the region near Oral in the west and radioactive contamination from the Chinese Lobnor test site across the eastern border). The Caspian Sea is another environmental flashpoint, as oil and gas exploration in the region increasingly has an impact.

Nuclear Tests

When the USSR decided it had to test nuclear bombs, it chose – as nuclear powers always do – places a long way from where the decision makers lived and which looked, at that safe distance, 'empty' on the map. Several testing sites were used around the USSR during the Cold War, but the main ones were the Novaya Zemlya islands in the Arctic Ocean and, busiest of all, a tract of steppe between the big north-eastern Kazakstan cities of Semey and Pavlodar.

Between 1949 and 1989 about 470 nuclear bombs were exploded at the Polygon, as the Semey testing ground was known. The region around the Polygon certainly wasn't uninhabited: the very first bomb test drenched several villages with fallout after a 'late change of wind direction'. The nerve centre of the Polygon was the town of Kurchatov, on the Irtysh river about 150km north-west of Semey. Kurchatov is named after the scientist considered the father of the Soviet bomb, but locally it's better known as Konechnaya – Russian for 'the end'. Because of the secrecy surrounding the tests, no one was told what danger they might be in, even when some were given health tests. No one was ever evacuated from Semey or other cities.

The end for the Polygon came about as a result of the biggest environmental protest movement the USSR ever saw, the Nevada-Semey (formerly Nevada-Semipalatinsk) Movement. Nevada-Semey was founded in February 1989 on the initiative of Olzhas Suleymenov, a leading Kazak poet and politician (now ambassador to Italy), in the wake of two particular tests which created big shock waves and a radioactive cloud over northern Kazakhstan. Within a few days more than a million signatures had been collected on Kazakhstan's streets calling for an end to bomb tests by the two superpowers and the closure of the sites.

Support from antinuclear movements in the USA, Germany, Japan and other countries followed. Such pressure forced the Kazakhstan Communist Party to call for closure of the Polygon and no further tests took place there after October 1989.

In 1991, fears arose that the Soviet military were planning new tests at the Polygon, but in the wake of the abortive August coup in Moscow, Kazakhstan's president, Nursultan Nazarbaev, finally closed the Polygon, and announced compensation for the victims. The following year the area around the site was declared an ecological disaster zone, agriculture was banned, and foreign experts invited to help the clean-up.

Apart from the legacy of the Polygon, independent Kazakhstan also inherited 1400 nuclear warheads from the USSR. From early on it declared its intention to be a nonnuclear state, but Nazarbaev used the issue as a bargaining chip with Russia and the USA, and exactly when and how the warheads are to be dismantled is still not clear.

The Nevada-Semey Movement, meanwhile, now concentrates on reviving the earth, nature and humanity in the affected areas of Kazakhstan and on stopping nuclear testing worldwide.

The 'Virgin Lands' Campaign

In 1954 under Khrushchev, the Soviet government undertook to expand arable land on a massive scale by irrigating the steppes and deserts of Kazakhstan and Uzbekistan. The water was to come via canals from the Amu-Darya and Syr-Darya, and certain Siberian rivers would be tapped or even reversed.

The Siberian part was dropped but the rest went ahead with great fanfare. Only under *glasnost* (openness) has the downside become clear. In some areas of the Kazak steppe, for example, soil has become degraded or is so over-fertilised that local rivers and lands are seriously polluted. By some measures, the problems of erosion, aridity and salinity are on a larger scale than those associated with the Aral Sea. (See the boxed text 'Hope for the Little Aral Sea' in the Aralsk section later.)

The United Nations Development Programme reckons that the country is now losing around 25 billion tenge every year, mainly because no work is being done to recover exhausted land. Another 10 billion tenge is lost annually due to depletion of water resources.

The Caspian Sea

As the search for new oil and gas fields hots up around the Caspian Sea, the environmental future of the world's largest lake hangs in the balance. Ironically, the collapse of the Soviet Union and the reduced pace of oil exploration that followed gave the Caspian a crucial breathing space. At the northern shallow end, around Atyrau and Aktau the water is practically freshwater and a clear blue. How long this will last as Kazak and western oil companies gear up to exploit the Tenghiz oilfield – ranked as one of the world's 10 largest deposits – is anyone's guess.

For the time being, low world oil prices and debate on whether and where to build a new pipeline to transport the crude oil is keeping a lid on the problem. But the signs of trouble are already noticeable from the impact on the sea's 415 species of fish, including the famous beluga (white) sturgeon, source of the best caviar. A beluga can grow to 6m in length and the 100kg of caviar that it might yield can sell for a quarter of a million dollars. The Caspian is the source of 90% of the world's caviar, yet documented catches of all types of sturgeon have dropped dramatically during the 1990s, as over-harvesting, water pollution and poaching all take their toll.

But the most pressing problem for the people who live close by the shallower end of the Caspian around Atyrau is the sea's rising level. Protective coastal constructions cost Kazakstan at least 30 billion tenge a year, yet still small communities find themselves flooded out and forced to move.

GOVERNMENT & POLITICS

Since 1995, when Nazarbaev dissolved the elected parliament and took a more authoritarian line, government has slowly become more democratic in Kazakstan. The parliament now sits in Astana and has a lower house (the Majlis) and an upper house (the Senate). Forty members of the Senate are elected by members of the regional assemblies with a remaining seven senators appointed by the president (although this might change).

Party politics is developing, but generally personal and family ties play a more important role in who people vote for. In February 1999 the Party of People's Unity and the Democratic Party, two of the main pro-presidential parties, merged into one under the name Otan (fatherland). There are around 10 other smaller parties represented in the parliament, including the pro-presidential People's Cooperative Party, the Socialist and Communist parties, and Lad, which represents the interests of Slavs.

Radical nationalists – whether Kazak or Russian – have never been welcome in Nazarbaev's Kazakstan. The most radical Kazak group, Alash, founded in 1989 with Pan-Turkic, Islamic revivalist and Kazak supremacist policies, was harassed and pre-vented from registering as a political party. In any event, Nazarbaev was the sole candidate in the first direct presidential elections in 1991, and he received 99% of the vote.

A popular opposition force has been the citizens' movement Azamat, formed in December 1996, drawing support from across Kazakstan's ethnic spectrum.

In 1997, the administrative regions of Kazakstan were consolidated from 19 to 14. Each region has a provincial governor (akim) appointed by the president and a directly elected council. There are also city and village governments.

ECONOMY
Resources

In terms of natural resources Kazakstan is probably the richest country per capita on earth. The trick is to achieve sustainable development and spread the wealth around the population – not easy in a land of entrenched corruption and regionalism. The country has some 60% of the former USSR's mineral resources, extracting large quantities of iron from the Kostanay basin in the north-west and huge amounts of coal from around Karaghandy and Ekibastuz, plus oil, gas, land various metals used in electronics, nuclear engineering and rocketry.

Kazakstan accounted for 20% of the cultivated land in the former USSR. Much of the north was turned into one big wheat field in the 1950s Virgin Lands campaign (see the History section, earlier). Despite little success, Kazakstan continues to grow an awful lot of wheat, up to a third of the former USSR total. In arable areas in the south, fruit, vegetables, tobacco, rice, hemp and cotton are grown. Drier areas are used for seasonal grazing of sheep, cattle, horses and camels.

Problems & Policy

After the break-up of the USSR, Kazakstan suffered the universal former Soviet problems of collapsed trade and distribution systems, runaway inflation, lack of funds to modernise ageing equipment, drying up of state subsidies and a slump in production. In 1993 up to a third of a bumper wheat harvest was lost because of poor harvesting methods, lack of storage facilities and shortage of transport. Another problem has been that many of the key industrial and agricultural areas are in the heavily Slav-populated north. The loss of qualified and skilled Slavs and Germans (see Population & People later in this chapter) through emigration has not been good for the Kazakstan economy.

The government's consistent policy to bring the economy around has been privatisation and price liberalisation, with a big effort to lure foreign investment. In 1993 Kazakstan introduced its own currency, the tenge, which was floated in 1999. Though there's still a long way to go, the economy is picking up.

Privatisation

Much of Kazakstan's economy, almost exclusively run by the state before 1991, has now been privatised, including the broadcast television, electricity and oil companies. Some 17,000 entities have been sold off. The private sector is dominated by a handful of big companies with diverse interests, from banking and investments to shops and restaurants, and all with close, often family, connections to the government.

Privatisation of land and agriculture has been slower, with Kazaks worried that it would consolidate Russian colonial dominion and upset historical horde and clan land rights. Many Kazaks still live on the former collective farms, few of which are profitable.

POPULATION & PEOPLE

Kazakstan's population is around 16 million – down by nearly two million over the past decade, due to emigration and lower birth rates. It is one of the planet's least densely populated places (5.9 people per sq km), but most people are concentrated in the south and north – which are both the most fertile and most industrially developed areas.

Ethnic Composition

The total conceals an extraordinary, changing and potentially troublesome ethnic mixture. Kazaks now account for just over 50% of the population, Russians 32%, Ukrainians around 5%, Germans about 3% or less,

and Uzbeks and Tatars around 2%. Of about 100 other groups, the main ones are Belarussians, Koreans, Chechens, Poles, Uyghurs and Jews.

Although you're most likely to encounter them in the cities, looking no different from their fellow Kazakstanis, the Kazaks were nomadic horseback pastoralists until the 1920s and a majority still live in rural areas. Some maintain a seminomadic existence, moving out with herds, flocks and yurts from their farms to summer pastures every year. See the Peoples of the Silk Road special section in the Facts about Central Asia chapter for more details on Kazaks and other ethnic groups.

The Slavs and other non-Central Asian groups reached Kazakstan in several waves, chiefly as: peasant settlers from the 19th century on; industrial workers from the 1930s on; political prisoners from the 1930s to 1950s (many of these stayed on if they survived); and entire peoples deported before or during WWII because Stalin feared they would collaborate with the enemy. The latter included Germans from the Volga region, Ukraine and elsewhere; Ingush, Karachay, Balkar, Chechens, Meskheti Turks and Kalmyks from the Caucasus region; Crimean Tatars; and Koreans from areas of Russia bordering Korea. Many died on the way to Kazakstan or soon after arriving. Of the survivors, many Germans and Koreans subsequently moved into technical, professional and managerial jobs. The Caucasus peoples were permitted to return to their homelands in 1957, though many stayed on. There was also an influx of Virgin Land agricultural workers in the 1950s.

While migrants were flooding into Kazakstan, the Kazaks themselves suffered repeated devastating blows from famine, wars, repression and emigration (see the History section, earlier). Thanks to their relatively high birth rate, and the return of Kazak people to Kazakstan from China and elsewhere, the Kazak population has made a big comeback. Since independence, large-scale emigration by Russians Slavs and Germans has also tilted the ethnic balance further in the Kazaks' favour.

Large communities of Kazaks, many of them descendants of those who fled Russian and Soviet invasions, famines and repression, remain in nearby countries – an estimated 650,000 in China, 30,000 in northern Afghanistan and 70,000 in Mongolia. There are also some 900,000 Kazaks in Uzbekistan and 700,000 in other former Soviet states. Kazaks outside Kazakstan were invited to settle in Kazakstan after independence in 1991; an estimated 100,000 came.

Ethnic Politics

So far, serious ethnic conflict has been avoided but there are tensions, chiefly between Kazaks and Slavs, over issues like language, education and jobs.

Though President Nazarbaev is far from a rabid Kazak nationalist, there has been a clear swing towards Kazaks in awarding senior jobs, and Slavs also complain of discrimination in education – trends which have their origins in the 1986 riots. Many Slavs and Germans have already gone. Radical Kazak nationalists are happy about this but the losses of the generally more educated Slavs and Germans have damaged the economy. The Slav population is particularly concentrated in the economically important north, and there have been rumblings of a movement to unify some parts of the north with Russia, although this now seems unlikely.

ARTS
Music

The Kazak national instrument seen most often is the *dombra*, a small two stringed lute with an oval, guitar or rectangular box shape. It's used to play traditional songs known as *kyui*. Other stringed instruments include the *kobyz*, a two-stringed primitive fiddle (the playing of which is said to have brought Jenghiz Khan to tears), and the *zhetigen*, with seven strings and a rectangular body.

The main wind instrument is the *sybyzgy*, two flutes made of reed or wood strapped together like abbreviated pan pipes. Percussion instruments include the small, hand-held *dabyl* and *dauylpaz* drums.

The music is largely folk tunes, handed down like the area's oral literature through the generations, with the country's best known composer being Kurmanghazy, a 19th century musician. The most skilled singers or bards are called *akyns* (see the following Literature entry in this section).

Your best chance of seeing live performances of Kazak music will be in Almaty where several orchestras, incorporating traditional instruments are based, including the folk group Sazgen, the Kurmanghazy Orchestra and the Otrar Sazy Orchestra.

Literature

Before the 19th century, Kazak literature consisted chiefly of long oral poems, a reflection of the race's nomadic life. Recitals by bards *(akyns)*, and contests between them known as *aitys*, are still important and popular. The most famous akyn is Zhambyl Zhabayev, whose statue stands in Almaty on Dostyk.

The biggest name in Kazak literary history is Abay Kunabaev, a 19th century poet and man of letters who launched Kazak as a literary language (see the boxed text 'Abay – Literary Hero' and the Semey section in this chapter). He also translated Russian works into Kazak and had his mythical status endorsed by the epic Kazak novel *Abay Zholy* (The Path of Abay) by Mukhtar Auczov (1897-1968), another local literary hero.

Facts for the Visitor

SUGGESTED ITINERARIES

If you only plan a short stay, the best base is Almaty, which has sufficient attractions nearby to occupy most visitors for at least a couple of days. With a week in hand, you'll be able to strike out on some of the longer treks in the nearby mountains, go skiing in winter, or explore alpine countryside closer to the Chinese border.

Another week at least is needed to visit southern Kazakhstan, taking in the Aksu-Zhabaghly Nature Reserve, Shymkent and Turkistan. The same goes for a trip around East Kazakhstan setting off from Öskemen. With three weeks, both these areas could be visited along with Semey and possibly the lovely Lake Burabay near Astana.

Abay – Literary Hero

Writer, translator and educator Abay (Ibrahim) Kunanbaev (1845-1904) was born in the village of Kaskabulak on the northern fringe of the Shyngghystau hills in East Kazakstan. His translations of Russian and other foreign literature into Kazak, and his public readings of them, as well as his own work, were the beginning of Kazak as a literary language and helped broaden Kazaks' horizons. Other Kazak bards took up and passed on the stories he read so that, for example, Dumas' *Three Musketeers* became widely known.

Despite this, Abay was decidedly pro-Russian. He wrote: 'Study Russian culture and art – it is the key to life. If you obtain it, your life will become easier ...' Ironically, Abay suffered a brief period of disfavour years after he died, early in the Soviet period. The charge: Abay's politics were undeveloped and feudal.

But soon the Soviets needed to raise up native fathers for the decimated Kazak nation they were trying to reconstruct. Abay's reputation was at last 'officially licensed' by Moscow, and his Russophile writings were enshrined. Now he is Kazakstan's greatest literary figure, with museums both in Semey where he spent much of his life and the village of Zhidebai, where he died.

With a month you can get around the whole country, taking in the more acquired travel pleasures of the vast steppes and West Kazakstan, including the Aral Sea and Atyrau and Aktau, both on the Caspian Sea.

VISAS & DOCUMENTS

Don't risk coming into Kazakstan without a visa, since there may still be a visa check even if you travel overland by bus or train. There are always checks for flights arriving from outside the former Soviet Union, and at road and rail crossings on the Kazakstan-Uzbekistan border from Tashkent to Shymkent, and the Kazakstan-China frontier at Khorgos/Korgas or Dostyk/Alashankou. Fines of up to US$370 can be levied for not having a proper visa. Your visa will only list the city where you are initially registered, but in practice, apart from a few places, you're free to go almost anywhere. Kurchatov, the command town of the former nuclear testing zone near Semey, and the Baykonur Cosmodrome and its support town Leninsk, are off-limits to casual visitors. There are some areas of the country where you'll need special permits if you wish to travel there – see Travel Permits later in this section.

Visas

Visas can be obtained from Kazakstan embassies and consulates. If there is no Kazak embassy or consulate in your country, visas may be available from the Russian embassy. It is *not* possible to get a visa on arrival at the airport.

To obtain either a tourist or business visa you will need a properly registered invitation letter, generally obtained from tourism companies in Kazakstan. For a list of tour agents who can arrange such a letter see the Travel Agencies entry in the Almaty section of this chapter. You don't need to pre-book services, hotel rooms, etc, with an agent to get this invitation letter, but you almost certainly will have to pay a fee, from around US$20 to US$45. The fee may be waived if tourist services are booked.

You will need to provide your full name as it appears on your passport, date of birth, sex, nationality, passport number, validity of passport, Kazakstan cities to be visited, period of stay and the embassy where you intend to obtain the visa. Apply for the letter *at least* two weeks in advance of your intended departure, since the letter will take a week to be issued and then arranging a visa usually takes a week. Some agents, such as Central Asian Tourism Corporation (CATC), can issue the letter of invitation at shorter notice, but for twice the cost.

Take the letter of invitation (which can be faxed) along with your passport and two passport sized photos to a Kazak embassy or consulate (see the following Embassies & Consulates section in this chapter). The visa will be issued only after they have gained permission from the consular department of the Ministry of Foreign Affairs; this typically takes a week, but may take longer depending on the type of visa you're applying for.

At the time of research the fees at Kazak embassies or consulates for a single-entry visa for most nationalities were about US$60 for one to three weeks, US$170 for one to three months single entry, US$180 for a double entry visa, US$190 for a triple entry visa, US$200 for a multiple entry visa and US$260 for a year. For processing in less than one week, fees are doubled. Fees vary for visas issued through Russian embassies. Also note that some embassies and consulates will only issue visas of up to one month; any extension will have to be sorted out in Kazakstan.

Note that if you think you will be in Kazakstan for over a month it is probably cheaper to get a business visa, as tourist visas are only issued for one month and can be pricey to extend.

If you plan to stay in Kazakstan over three months you will need to present an AIDS examination certificate when registering your visa with OVIR (Office of Visas & Registration; see the following Registration entry in this section).

If you plan to cross overland from China to Kazakstan, the only reliable place in China to get a Kazak visa is Beijing, though there is a Kazak consulate in Ürümqi (see Embassies & Consulates in the Xinjiang chapter).

Transit Visas

Kazak embassies will issue extendible three-day transit visas for around US$90 without sponsorship, but they will want to see an onward ticket from Kazakstan and/or onward visa. But since visas for any CIS (Commonwealth of Independent States) country are good for 72 hours in Kazakstan, there's little reason to get one of these, save perhaps for peace of mind.

Registration

Once in Kazakstan, if you're staying more than three days you must register your visa

with OVIR. This should be done by the company/individual who issued your invitation letter. Some firms will charge an additional fee of between US$10 and US$25 for doing this, although many don't; it's best to check such details when initially contacting tourist firms for the invitation letter.

Registering your visa yourself will be difficult and time-consuming since it involves two visits to OVIR, much hanging around and the payment of a small processing fee at a specified bank.

In Almaty, OVIR (☎ 63 86 81, 62 54 62) is at Karasay Batyr, 86, just west of Masanchi. Hours for accepting visas to be registered are Monday, Wednesday, Thursday and Friday 11 am to 12.15 pm, and for the return of passports 5 to 7 pm the same days. In Astana, OVIR (☎ 32 77 51) is at Seyfullin 63. It's open Monday to Friday 8.30 am to 12.30 pm and 2.30 to 7 pm.

If you're moving around the country, keep in mind that you're supposed to re-register with OVIR at any place you stay more than 72 hours. So you can legally stay up to three days anywhere *without* re-registering. Your passport is likely to be checked on trains and at airports so it's a good idea to keep all ticket stubs and hotel receipts to prove when you arrived in a place and how long you've spent there. The smallest infringement of the rules lays you open to the imposition of a fine. If you don't register a visa within 72 hours the penalty is US$60. If you are caught at the airport this rises to US$150. Carry bus or hotel receipts as proof if you are leaving a city within three days.

Visa Extensions

For a fee it's possible to obtain a visa extension or a new visa in Almaty or Astana through OVIR. Again the company/individual who issued your letter of invitation should organise this. Visa extensions cost US$30 for up to seven days, US$50 up to two weeks and US$70 up to a month.

Travel Permits

Special permits (sometimes called a *propusk*) are needed for sensitive border areas in eastern Kazakstan and for the Aksu-Zhabagly

Nature Reserve in the south. Tour agents in Öskemen and Shymkent should be able to arrange such permits, as long as their services are used to visit the restricted areas.

Visas for Neighbouring Countries

If you haven't already obtained the visas you need for your Central Asian trip, Almaty is one of the best Central Asian cities for doing so, though the information given here is subject to change and many embassies may move to Astana (although the western ones are digging their heels in Almaty). Some travel agencies (see the Travel Agencies entry in the following Almaty section) may be able to speed up visa processes, or obtain otherwise difficult visas, for a fee.

Note – it's only possible to apply for a Chinese visa in Almaty if Kazakstan is your main residence. Tourists *must* apply for Chinese visas in their home country.

China Visas (usually for 30 days) are officially issued only to foreigners living in Kazakstan. Fees in this case depend on nationality – eg US$20 for Australians, US$60 for Americans and US$30 for Britons; an invitation is not required.

The consular section is open Mondays, Wednesdays and Fridays only, from 9 am to noon, and is usually a real scrum. For information only, go to reception in the main entrance at the front of the building.

CATC say they can get foreigners (not living in Kazakstan) a visa for a service fee of $30. Also required is a letter of invitation costing $60 and requiring 10 days, after which they submit your passport to the embassy for a visa. The best person to contact is Ms Li Kong, CATC's Chinese tour coordinator in Almaty.

Kyrgyzstan visas cost US$40 for up to a month and take up to a few days to issue. A letter of invitation from a Kyrgyz company/individual should not be necessary, see the Visas section in the Kyrgyzstan chapter.

Pakistan Visas are issued on the third working day from application. The embassy is open for submission of documents Monday to Friday from 10 am to noon, and for collection of documents from 4 to 5 pm. Costs vary from US$16 (Australians) to US$45 (Americans).

Tajikistan Visas are issued on the spot if you have an invitation from a Tajik travel agency (available from most agencies in Almaty and Bishkek).

Uzbekistan You must first book a hotel or service in Uzbekistan through a travel agency, for at least the value of US$60. The embassy will then issue a visa in about 10 days. You don't have to leave your passport with the embassy while your application is being processed. Hours are Monday to Friday from 3 pm to 5 pm. Note – US citizens may not need an invitation or prebooked accommodation for Uzbekistan; see the visa section in the Uzbekistan chapter.

Copies

It's important to carry a photocopy of your passport and visa stamp with you at all times, rather than the real thing, since it's not unknown for policemen and soldiers, bona fide or otherwise, to harass foreigners for their documents. The British and several other embassies will provide, free of charge, a photocopy with an attached letter in Russian for verification. It's worth taking the time to get this, especially if you're going to be travelling around the country, since this document works wonders with officious officials.

EMBASSIES & CONSULATES
Kazak Embassies & Consulates

Citizens of New Zealand should apply for a visa via Sydney, Irish citizens should apply via London and Dutch citizens should apply via Belgium. For embassies in Central Asia see the relevant country chapter.

Australia
   Consulate:
   (☎ 02-9365 3011, fax 9365 3044,
   @ consul@bb.com.au)
   144 Clyde St, North Bondi, Sydney 2026
Azerbaijan
   (☎ 8922-90 65 21, fax 90 62 49)
   Apt 82, Inglab 889, Baku
Canada
   Consulate:
   (☎ 1416-593 4043, fax 593 4037)
   Box 52, Suite 1014, 20 Queen St West, Toronto

China
(☎ 010-6532 6182, fax 6532 6183)
9 Dong 6, San Li Tun, Beijing
France
(☎ 01-45 61 52 00/02, fax 45 61 52 01)
59 rue Pierre Charron, F-75008 Paris
Germany
(☎ 030-302 9375, fax 301 9518) Berlin
Consulate: Bonn
Hungary
(☎ 01-275 13 00, 275 13 01, fax 275 20 92)
1025, Kapy 59, Budapest
India
(☎ 011-688 1461, fax 688 8464)
Er-16/17 Chandragupta Marg, Chanakyapuri,
New Delhi
Iran
(☎ 021-256 5933, fax 254 6400)
Darrus Hedayat, Masjed 1, N4, Tehran
Israel
(☎ 023-752 2147, fax 752 2142)
Tel Aviv
Japan
(☎ 03-3791 5273, fax 3791 5279)
9-8 Himonya 5-chome, Meguro-ku, Tokyo
Mongolia
(☎ 9761-31 22 40, fax 31 22 04)
House 95, Microregion 6, Ulan Bator
Pakistan
(☎ 051-26 28 07, fax 26 28 06)
House 2, Street 4 F-83, Islamabad
Russia
(☎ 095-208 98 52, fax 208 26 50)
Chistoprudny bulvar 3A, Moscow 101000
South Korea
(☎ 02-548 1415, fax 548 1416)
32-15 Nonhyun-dong, Kangnam-ku, Seoul
Turkey
(☎ 312-441 23 01/2, fax 441 23 03)
Ebùzziya Tevfik Sokak 6, TR-06680 Ankara
UK
(☎ 020-7581 4646, fax 7584 8481)
33 Thurloe Square, London SW7 23D
Ukraine
(☎ 044-290 2306, fax 290 7722)
Kiev 252000
USA
(☎ 1202-232 5488, fax 232 5845,
✉ kazak@intr.net)
1401 16th St NW, Washington, DC 20036

Embassies & Consulates in Kazakstan

A handful of embassies and consulates had moved to Astana at the time of research, but more may choose to do so as the city's infrastructure grows. It is a good idea to register with your embassy if you are staying for an extended period.

The following are embassies unless otherwise stated:

Afghanistan
(☎/fax 3727-32 37 29)
Zheltoksan 12, corner of Tashkentskaya, Almaty
Australia
(☎ 3727-63 94 18, 63 95 14, fax 58 26 01)
Kazybek Bi 20A, Almaty
Canada
(☎ 3727-50 11 51/52, fax 58 14 93)
Karasay Batyr 34, Almaty
China
(☎ 3727-63 92 91, fax 63 82 09)
Furmanov 137, Almaty
France
(☎ 3727-50 71 10, 50 62 36, fax 50 61 59)
Furmanov 173, Almaty
Georgia
(☎ 3172-37 11 17, 37 40 04)
Karaotkel, Astana
Germany
(☎ 3727-50 61 55, 50 61 56, fax 50 62 76)
Furmanov 173, Almaty
India
(☎ 3727-69 47 46, 67 14 11, fax 67 20 70)
Maulenov 71, corner of Kazybek Bi, Almaty
Iran
(☎ 3727-67 78 46, 67 50 55, fax 59 27 54)
Kabanbay Batyr 119, Almaty
Israel
(☎ 3727-50 72 15, 62 48 17, fax 50 62 83)
Zheltoksan 87, Almaty
Italy
(☎ 3727-63 98 14/04, fax 63 96 36)
Kazybek Bi 20A, Almaty
Japan
(☎ 3727-60 86 00, fax 60 86 01)
41A Kazybek Bi, Almaty
Kyrgyzstan
(☎ 3172-37 11 13) Kara Otkel settlement
(open Monday, Wednesday and Friday from 3
to 5 pm)
Consulate: Almaty
Mongolia
Consulate:
(☎ 3727-29 37 90, fax 60 17 23)
Sain, Aubakirov 1, Almaty
Pakistan
(☎ 3727-33 26 78, 33 35 48, fax 33 13 00)
Tölebaev 25, Almaty
Russia
(☎ 3727-44 66 44 (visas), 44 64 91, fax 44
83 23)
Zhandosova 4, Almaty

KAZAKSTAN

Tajikistan
(☎ 3727-45 56 56, fax 44 20 89)
Zhandosova 58, Almaty

Turkey
(☎ 3727-61 39 32, 61 81 53, fax 50 62 08)
Töle Bi 29, Almaty

Turkmenistan
(☎ 3172-28 62 06), prospekt Respublica 11,
Astana

UK
(☎ 3727-50 61 91, 50 61 92, fax 50 62 60)
Furmanov 173, Almaty

Ukraine
(☎ 3727-62 70 73, fax 69 40 62)
Chaikovkogo 208, corner of Kurmanghazy,
Almaty
Consulate: Astana

USA
(☎ 3727-50 76 21/23, 63 28 80, 63 24 26; fax
63 38 83)
Furmanov 99, Almaty
Consulate: Astana

Uzbekistan
(☎ 3727-61 83 16, fax 61 10 55)
Baribaev 36, Almaty

MONEY

The tenge (T) is divided into 100 *tiyn*, although in practice tiyn and even 1 T notes are virtually nonexistent; small change is often provided in the form of a box of matches or a stick of gum. Tenge notes are 5000, 2000, 1000, 500, 200, 100, 50, 20, 10, five and three.

At the time of research, exchange rates were:

country	unit		tenge
Australia	A$1	=	84 T
Canada	C$1	=	90 T
China	Y1	=	16 T
euro	€1	=	136 T
France	10FF	=	20 T
Germany	DM1	=	70 T
Japan	¥10	=	13 T
Kyrgyzstan	1 som	=	4 T
New Zealand	NZ$1	=	67 T
Pakistan	Pak Rs 10	=	26 T
Russia	R10	=	50 T
UK	UK£1	=	215 T
USA	US$1	=	132 T
Uzbekistan	10 *sum*	=	3 T

Make sure you change all local money before leaving Kazakstan since it's illegal to leave the country with any tenge.

Apart from Almaty and Astana, where there are several banks that will change travellers cheques (for a small commission), this form of money is useless in Kazakstan.

Only top hotels, restaurants and shops accept credit cards, so don't rely on them. This said, it's usually possible to get cash advances (for a percentage fee). Try the national banks, such as Narodny, Kazkommertzbank and Turan Alem. Centre Credit Bank in Almaty, next to the Hyatt Regency Hotel, is an agent for Western Union.

Alternatively, cash machines are increasingly found in the main hotels and shopping districts of the major cities. They accept overseas Visa and other credit cards and are a very handy and safe alternative to lugging around wads of cash. Often the machines have English instructions.

POST & COMMUNICATIONS
Post

The cost of an airmail letter under 10g to anywhere outside the CIS is 85 T. Postcards stamps cost 54 T. A 2kg parcel of books by surface mail costs around US$5, by airmail around US$15 or more (depending on the destination).

If you have anything of value or importance to post it's much safer to use one of the international courier firms, such as DHL, Federal Express or UPS, all of which have offices in Almaty (see the following Almaty section of this chapter).

Telephone & Fax

Kazaktelekom is the state telecommunications company with branches in all towns and cities. In the larger cities, such as Almaty and Astana, you can make long distance and international calls at their offices or via the many card-operated pay phones.

If you're staying in an apartment or a smaller hotel, local calls are usually free of charge, covered by the general rental fee for the line. Not all phones allow long distance or international calls. If a direct dial service is available (it will be on all card-operated phones) you will first have to dial 8 and wait for a long tone signal before continuing to dial the rest of the number.

To dial into Kazakstan:

☎ caller's country international access code + 7 + area code (eg 3272) + local number

If the phone you're using does not allow direct dial calls, it might be possible to book a long distance call by dialling ☎ 8 614, and ☎ 8 694 for an international call. Don't rely on an English-speaking operator being available.

At peak times, expect a one minute call to Europe or the US to cost around US$2, and to Australia US$3.50. Calls are cheaper from 8 pm to 8 am.

Fax services are available from Kazaktelekom offices and many hotels. To send a one-page fax to countries outside of the CIS costs around US$4, within the CIS US$2 and within Kazakstan under US$1.

Email & Internet Access

Although Kazaktelekom is pushing the Internet, it's yet to make much headway across the country, mainly because of poor telecommunications infrastructure. Outside of Almaty, which has at least two Internet cafes, your best bet for finding a computer terminal with email and Internet access is to head for the nearest major library or university. The cheapest connection rates are around US$3 an hour.

TIME

Kazakstan is so big that its territory spans three time zones. In the eastern half of the country, including Almaty and Astana, the time is six hours ahead of Greenwich Mean Time (GMT) and three hours ahead of Moscow – times for all long distance train services are still listed according to Moscow time. In the far western regions, including Atyrau and Aktau, the time is four hours ahead of GMT.

From the last Sunday in March until the last Sunday in September Kazakstan is on Daylight Savings Time, so all the clocks go forward by one hour. If you're doing any travelling by train around the change-over dates, take extra special care to make sure you know what *local* time the train actually departs.

FOOD & DRINKS

The food culture of Kazakstan is one of the strongest indications of the people's nomadic roots. Nomads eat the food most readily available, and in most cases this meant horses and sheep. Across the country you'll also find ubiquitous Central Asian dishes such *shashlyk* (kebab), *laghman* (noodles), *manty* (stuffed dumplings) and *plov* (fried rice). In the main cities and northern Kazakstan, Russian cuisine is prevalent, reflecting the tastes of the immigrant culture.

The national dish is *besbarmak*, chunks of long boiled beef, mutton and perhaps horsemeat and onions, served in a huge platter atop flat squares of pasta. The bouillon broth from the meat is drunk separately. Besbarmak is always served on special occasions, in particular if you're invited to a Kazak family's home.

In the bazars and a few restaurants, you'll come across *kazy*, a smoked horsemeat sausage (though beef is sometimes substituted). Served on special occasions sliced with cold noodles it's called *naryn*. *Karta* (literally 'horse intestines', used as the casing) and *chuchuk* (or *chuzhuk*) are two other kinds of horsemeat sausage. *Kuurdak* is a fatty meat, offal (including lungs and heart) and potato stew.

Kazaks make a sweet plov with dried apricots, raisins and prunes, while *plov askabak* is made with pumpkin. *Zhuta* is pasta shaped like a Swiss roll with a carrot and pumpkin filling.

A local snack is *baursaki*, fried dough balls, not unlike heavy doughnuts. Kazak apples are also famous in Central Asia (Almaty and its old form, Alma-Ata, literally mean 'father of apples').

As in Kyrgyzstan, *kumys*, fermented mares' milk, is popular, but on the steppes and in the desert regions, you'll also come across *shubat*, fermented camel milk, which has a somewhat less salty taste.

KAZAKSTAN

ORIENTATION

Most Kazak cities now have Kazak names instead of their Soviet-era Russian names. In many cases they are close to the Russian (eg Almaty instead of Alma-Ata, Karaghandy for Karaganda). Less obvious changes include Astana for Tselinograd, Aktau for Shevchenko, Aktöbe for Aktyubinsk, Atyrau for Guriyev, Dostyk for Druzhba, Oral for Uralsk, Öskemen for Ust-Kamenogorsk, and Semey for Semipalatinsk. You'll find Russian names still in use, particularly in the northern cities where there are still large Russian populations, such as Petropavlovsk.

Similarly, most cities have changed their street names from Russian to Kazak. Often the Kazak is similar to the Russian, with a different ending to the name and the substitution of *köshesi* for *ulitsa* (street); *prospektisi*, *prospekti* or *dangghyly* for *prospekt* (avenue); or *alangy* for *ploshchad* (square). It helps to be aware of both names, since not all signs have been changed, and in any case many people are still more familiar with the old names.

Almaty

☎ 3272 • pop 1.5 million

Founded in 1854 as a Russian frontier fort when the Kazaks were still nomads, Almaty has always been a very Russian place. Its long, straight avenues and uniform architecture bear the unmistakable thumbprint of the USSR. To the ear, the sound of Russian, spoken even by most Kazaks here, reveals the continuing hold of the colonising culture over much of Kazakstan's way of life.

But though neither old nor exotic nor even very Kazak, Almaty is a city on an upswing. It may no longer be the capital, but as the commercial heart of Central Asia's richest country, it's a honeypot not just to Kazaks but to a horde of foreigners ranging from Chinese, Uzbek, Russian and Turkish traders to big-time business folk, diplomats and financiers from the west and from east Asia. This exposure to the outside world has, in just a few years, turned a provincial outpost of the USSR into Central Asia's most cosmopolitan city. The goods in shops and markets, the range of good places to eat, the direct flights from several world capitals, the boom in banks, advertising and other trappings of capitalism, the new hotels, the casinos – all these would make Almaty unrecognisable to anyone who had been away since 1990.

Although, for many travellers, Almaty is little more than a way-station between Bishkek or Tashkent and Ürümqi or Siberia, lingering in the city has its rewards. It's a clean place (except sometimes for its air), easy on the eye, especially when the trees that line the streets are in full leaf, creating a city that feels as if it was built in the midst of a forest. The Zailiysky Alatau mountains rise like a wall along its southern fringes and form a superb backdrop when weather and smog permit. There are lots of parks and many of the monumental Soviet-era buildings are individually striking.

Apart from skiing and skating at nearby Medeu and Shymbulak in winter and plenty of hiking routes through the summer, there are several other fine trips into the surrounding region that can be undertaken year round. Almaty also has some of Central Asia's most experienced travel firms, which can also arrange trips further afield.

Most of the city's architecture is fairly low-rise, due to Almaty's earthquake-prone location. All this makes it a pleasant city to walk around, though the central area is very spread out. Public transport is frequent and cheap – virtually every car on the road is a potential taxi.

Almaty's people are a typical mix of dozens of nationalities but, untypically for southern Kazakstan, Russians and Ukrainians form the majority. To these have been added in the past few years several thousand Americans, Europeans, Turks and south and east Asians, all after a foothold in the developing Kazakstan economy. The expat scene is lively and if you can tap into it your time here will be more entertaining and informative.

The best times of year are mid-April to late May, and early September to mid-October, when it's neither too cold nor too hot.

History

The Russians built a frontier post called Verny here in 1854 on the site of the Silk Road oasis Almatu, which was laid waste by the Mongols. Cossacks and Siberian peasants settled around it, but the town was twice almost flattened by earthquakes, in 1887 and 1911. In the late 19th and early 20th centuries it was a place of exile, its best-known outcast being Leon Trotsky.

Renamed Alma-Ata (meaning Father of Apples, after the apple orchards that are still found on the city's outskirts), it became the capital of Soviet Kazakstan in 1927, and was connected to Siberia by the Turkestan-Siberia (Turksib) railway in 1930, by which time its population was about 50,000. The railway brought big growth and so did WWII, as factories were relocated here from Nazi-threatened western USSR and many Slavs came to work them. Large numbers of ethnic Koreans, forcibly resettled from the Russian Far East, came at the same time.

Almaty was the scene of the first unrest unleashed in Central Asia by the Gorbachev era of *glasnost* and *perestroika*. In December 1986, after Dinmukhamed Konaev, a Kazak, was replaced as head of the CPK by the Russian Gennady Kolbin, thousands took to the streets in protest. An apparently communist-organised counter-demo of workers armed with metal bars and cables turned the protest into riots, police opened fire and several people were killed, with hundreds injured. The riots spread to several other cities before being quelled by martial law.

Almaty made more headlines in 1989 as the focus of the successful campaign to stop nuclear testing near Semey, and in 1991 as the venue for a meeting at which the USSR was finally pronounced dead, when all five Central Asian republics (along with Azerbaijan, Armenia and Moldova) joined the CIS, founded by Russia, Ukraine and Belarus. The name Almaty, close to that of the original Silk Road settlement, replaced Alma-Ata soon after.

In Soviet times Almaty's off-centre location – just 25km from Kyrgyzstan, yet nearly 900km from the nearest point on Kazakstan's border with Russia – perhaps reduced the political heat on the USSR's rulers as they manoeuvred to maintain their grip on Kazakstan; the fact that north-west Kazakstan was nearer to Moscow than to Almaty, and northern Kazakstan closer to Siberia, would always strengthen Moscow's hand against Almaty's and balance any tendencies to independent-mindedness among the republican leadership.

But after independence, President Nazarbaev began to view this quirky political geography somewhat differently. In 1994 he announced, to universal amazement, a plan to transfer the capital to the northern city of Akmola, now renamed Astana. This has since happened – see the Astana section later in this chapter, for more details. Whether the move turns out to be a stroke of visionary genius or a divisive disaster remains to be seen. In the meantime, Almaty remains Kazakstan's business centre and a strong contender for Central Asia's most important city.

Orientation

Almaty can be a slightly disorienting place owing to the uniform appearance of its long, straight streets. Keep in mind that the mountains are to the south, and the city slopes upward from north (650m) to south (950m).

Almaty has done away with many Soviet street names and moved to Kazak rather than Russian on many signs. We use the Kazak street names wherever possible, although many local people are still more familiar with the old names than the new. See the Almaty map for the old name of each street (in brackets). If the name you give doesn't seem to work, try the old one instead.

The central area of Almaty is large, stretching 4km from Almaty-II train station in the north to the Respublika alangy ceremonial square in the south, and over 2km from Kaldayakov in the east to Seyfullin in the west. Blocks are long. The airport is a 20-minute bus ride north of the centre; Almaty-I train station is 15 minutes north; the Sayran long-distance bus station is half an hour west.

In the centre, the main north-south streets are Dostyk (Lenina), Konaev (Karl Marx), Furmanov and Abylay Khan (Kommunistichesky). The main east west streets are the

KAZAKSTAN

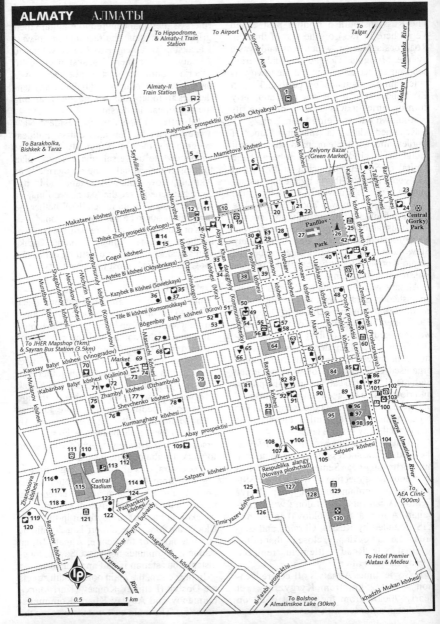

ALMATY АЛМАТЫ

PLACES TO STAY
11 Hotel Zhetisu; Jibek July
    Travel Agency
14 Kaezhol
15 Uyut
22 Hotel Otrar
52 Hotel Issik
53 Hotel Ambassador
56 Hotel Almaty
62 Hotel Daulet
76 Hotel Zerde
86 Hotel Kazakstan
90 Hotel Dostyk
97 KIMEP Gostinitsa No 1
114 Astana Hotel
118 Hyatt Regency Almaty;
    CATC Travel Agency;
    Rahat Travel International
124 CAA Guesthouse
125 Regent Almaty (Ankara)

PLACES TO EAT
5   Kafe Marmara
17 Rock Bar
18 Rodem
20 Korkim Ama
21 Seyhanlar
32 International
    Business Club
34 Stradivari
39 Solyanka
40 U Stary Varoty
44 Inara
46 Mad Murphy's
50 Old England
51 Shenyan
61 Jazz Rock Café
63 Stetson
66 Schwäbisches Häuschen
71 Ristorante Adriatico
77 Dastarkhan Kulinaria
80 Dastarkhan
82 Kolsay
83 L'Hermitage
87 Korean Restaurant;
    Osaka Japanese Restaurant
89 Barrakuda
92 U Alina
99 Pizzeria Venezia
106 Cadillac

109 Capos
117 Havana Club

OTHER
1   Sayakhat Bus Station
2   Buses to Taraz & Shymkent
3   Train Ticket Office
4   Mosque
6   Pakistan Embassy
7   AIDS Centre
8   Dom Takani Drapers Shop
9   Universam Supermarket
10 Zanghar (TsUM)
    Department Store
12 City Air Terminal (Aerovokzal)
13 Bus Stop from Airport
16 Bus Stop to Airport
19 Kazaktelekom (Main Office)
23 Main Entrance to Central
    (Gorky) Park
24 Uzbekistan Embassy
25 Museum of Kazak
    Musical Instruments
26 War Memorial
27 Zenkov Cathedral
28 Arasan Baths
29 Cash Machine
30 Akademkniga
31 US Embassy
33 Kazkontsert Hall
35 Indian Embassy
36 CATC Travel Agency
37 SMAT Supermarket
38 Old House of Parliament
41 Australian & Italian Embassies
42 Japanese Embassy
43 Dom Kino
45 Central Concert Hall
47 Stalker Internet
48 ACS Travel Agency
49 Main Post Office
54 Conservatory
55 Kazaktelekom
57 Chinese Embassy
58 Akademkniga
59 Rossia Supermarket
60 Archaeology Museum
64 Opera & Ballet Theatre
65 SMAT Supermarket
67 Nevada-Semey Movement

68 Kyrgyzstan Consulate
69 OVIR
70 Rainbow Bar
72 Kan Tengri Travel Agency
73 St Nicholas Cathedral
74 Ibragimov Cinema
75 ISAR
78 Peace Corps Office
79 Dinamo Stadium
81 Asia Tourism
84 Academy of Sciences
85 Guinness Pub
88 Kazak Business Centre;
    Geology Museum
91 British, French & German
    Embassies
93 Tengri Umai Modern
    Art Gallery; Lermontov
    Russian Drama Theatre
94 Belgium Pub
95 Agricultural Academy
96 KIMEP Main Entrance
98 KIMEP 24hr entrance
100 Cinema
101 Palace of the Republic
102 Internet Cafe
103 Cable Car to Köktyube
104 Republican Palace of
    Schoolchildren
105 Central Army Sports Club
107 Monument to Independence
108 British Council
110 Wedding Palace
111 Auezov Kazak
    Drama Theatre
112 Cash Machine
113 Swimming Pool
115 Fantasy World
116 Circus
119 Goethe Institute
120 Russian Embassy
121 Kusteyev Museum of Fine Arts
122 Daulet Gym
123 Bowling Alley
126 TV Centre
127 City Government Building
128 Presidential Residence
129 Central State Museum
130 Ramstor Shopping Mall;
    NOMAD Cinema

partly pedestrianised Zhibek Zholy (Gork-ogo) and Gogol north of the centre and Abay and Satpaev in the south. One slightly confusing aspect of Almaty's grid layout is that some streets end at one block and begin again on the other side, for example

Ualikhanov ends at the Academy of Sciences and restarts again south of Abay.

Maps & Guides JHER (☎/fax 68 40 19; also known as GEO), at Tole Bi 155, is Almaty's best map store, with topographic and trekking maps from 1:25,000 to 1:100,000, as well as more general maps.

A variety of Almaty city maps are sold in hotel kiosks and bookshops, some up-to-date, some not. The best is the *Almaty Guide* (around US$3, May 1996), an English map with a good close-up of the city centre.

Stranded on the Silk Road: the What Next?! Guide to Almaty by expat residents Amy Forster and Micheal Rothburt is the most current guide to the city and surrounding areas, and includes lots of good tips on what to do in town as well as trekking information if you want to explore further afield than the mountains immediately south of Almaty.

Another useful information source is the *Almaty Official Visitors Guide* (Baur, 1998), a slim booklet, with a handy map and background on Kazak culture.

The Hiker's Guide to Almaty by Arkady Pozdeyev (Real Virtuality Press, PO Box 338, Littleton, CO 80120, USA) is a useful book outlining some 40-odd day hikes and longer around Almaty. It also includes some walking routes around the city and an overview of the country's flora and fauna and some important tips on mountain safety. The book is available from most hotel bookshops in Almaty. A second edition is planned for 2000.

Information

Money There are exchange kiosks all over the place, including at the main transport terminals and the hotels, although you'll get better rates away from such places. Avoid kiosks on the street or in other very public places, such as the Zelyony Bazar, to minimise the risk of theft during or after the transaction.

The main banks are Narodny Bank, Kazkommertzbank and Turan Alem. Opening hours are 9 am to 6 pm. You'll be able to get cash advance on credit cards and change travellers cheques at some of their branches for a fee of about 1%. Centre Credit Bank, beside the Hyatt Regency Almaty accepts American Express travellers cheques in US dollars only and has a minimum charge of US$3. It's also an agent for Western Union money transfers.

Visa cash machines are outside the Kazakstan Institute of Management, Economics & Strategic Research (KIMEP), beside the Navigator discotheque on Abay, on the corner of Gogol and Furmanov and at several branches of Narodny Bank including those on the corners of Töle Bi and Dostyk, and Seyfullin and Zhambyl, where you can also change travellers cheques. There are also Visa cash machines in the Hotel Otrar, Hyatt Regency Almaty, Hotel Kazakstan and Regent Almaty.

Post The main post office is on Baysetova just off Bögenbay Batyr. It's open Monday to Friday, 8 am to 7 pm, and Saturdays and Sundays, 9 am to 5 pm. There's also a post office at the airport. The following international courier services are in Almaty:

DHL
   (☎ 50 94 16/17, fax 63 61 66) Abay 157
Federal Express
   (☎ 30 17 23, 69 55 36) Makataev 28
UPS
   (☎ 50 31 94/95, ☎/fax 41 49 80) Abay 153

Telephone & Fax Card payphones are located all over the city; cards can be bought for around US$3 from telephone offices and street vendors in kiosks.

The central Kazaktelekom office is at Zhibek Zholy 100, a block east of the Zanghar (TsUM) department store. It's open daily 8 am to 10 pm and you can send faxes from here. Another useful Kazaktelekom office is on Panfilov 129, behind the Hotel Almaty, open daily 8 am to 8 pm.

The upmarket hotels all have business centres offering long distance and international calls and fax facilities; the cheapest rates are at the press centre in the Hotel Otrar (room 101, ground floor).

Email & Internet Access The fastest and most reliable computers are at the Internet Café on the 2nd floor, at the back of the Palace of the Republic on Dostyk. It's open daily 10 am to around 1 am. Internet access is about US$3 per hour, computer games US$2. There's also a roomy cafe/bar area.

More a bar than a cafe, Stalker Internet, Töle Bi 20, is just off Dostyk near Mad

Murphy's. Open daily from noon to midnight, Internet access is also around US$3 per hour. Internet access is also available in the business centres of both the Regent Almaty and Hyatt Regency Almaty hotels, at vastly inflated rates.

Travel Agencies General travel agencies useful for air and rail tickets, hotel bookings, visa invitation letters, and the like include:

ACS
(☎ 62 22 44, 62 23 73, 62 26 15, fax 62 26 68,
🖂 gen@acs-almaty.kz)
Dostyk 27 – English speaking staff. Branch in Shymkent. They charge US$25/45 for visa registration/letter of invitation. Also excursions in Uzbekistan. Web site www.acs-almaty.kz
AMS CAT
(☎ 62 39 53, ☎/fax 69 23 63,
🖂 amsmax@online.ru)
Panfilov 92 – mainly for arranging business visas and travel; US$15/20 for visa registration/letter of invitation. Web site www.online.ru/people/amsmax/
Central Asia Tourism Corporation (CATC)
(☎ 50 10 70, fax 50 17 07,
🖂 catfvk@online.ru)
Seyfullin 537
(☎ 50 99 39, 50 17 00)
Hyatt Regency – staff speak several European languages; also have a section specialising in trips to China. Also rental cars and accommodation. US$10/30 for visa registration/letter of invitation.
Galaktika
(☎ 47 37 36, fax 50 62 68)
1 Kotkem-3, Apt 61 – small agency specialising in trips around Almaty. They can also arrange letters of invitation and visa registration.
Jibek Joly
(☎ 32 58 89, 32 56 40, 53 06 44, fax 50 92 66,
🖂 jjoly@kazmail.asdc.kz)
Hotel Zhetisu, Abylay Khan 55 – can arrange full board at six cottages in the Almaty region. Office has small library of English and Japanese guidebooks for around Asia. Can also arrange ISIC cards for US$8. US$20 for visa letter of invitation and registration.
Otrar Travel
(☎ 33 13 75, fax 33 12 34,
🖂 otrartravel@kaznet.kz)
Hotel Otrar, Gogol 73 – English-speaking staff
Rahat Travel International
(☎ 33 58 52, fax 33 56 74) Panfilov 109A
(☎ 47 30 11) Hyatt Regency

The following agencies specialise in mountaineering, trekking and tours, but some also do visa support and accommodation:

Asia Tourism
(☎ 63 12 27, 63 08 55, fax 63 12 56,
🖂 office@asiatour.org)
Zheltoksan 160 – a reputable operator offering trekking and mountaineering trips. Visas can be arranged for Kazakstan and neighbouring Central Asian countries. Web site www.asiatour.org
Central Asia Adventures
(☎ 43 27 92,
🖂 caadvtrs@aol.com, scott@pactec.org)
Kurmanghazy 179 – can tailor adventure trip itineraries around Kazakstan and neighbouring countries. They can also arrange home-stays, city tours, transportation and visas.
Kan Tengri
(☎ 67 78 66, 67 70 24, fax 50 93 23,
🖂 kazbek@kantengri.almaty.kz)
Michurin 89 – one of Central Asia's leading mountain tourism firms, focusing on climbs, trekking, heli-skiing and ski-mountaineering in the Central Tian Shan and the ranges between Almaty and Lake Issyk-Kul. For treks and climbs they charge around US$50 to US$70 per person per day, from Almaty. They also offer visa support for US$20. Web site www.kantengri.almaty.kz
Tour Asia
(☎ 48 25 73, ☎/fax 49 79 36,
🖂 tourasia@online.ru)
Morisa Tereza 359 – long established company offers possibilities including trekking or mountaineering in the Central Tian Shan, Alatau, Altay and Fan mountains (in Tajikistan). They can also arrange home-stays in Almaty for US$20 without meals, US$30 with meals, and provide visa support (US$25 if you don't book a tour, included in tour fee if you do). Web site www.tourasia.hypermart.net

Karlygash Makatova (☎/fax 32 27 67), a Kazak sportswoman, has long organised trips for the expat community and offers day trips to the Charyn canyon or Lake Issyk-Kul, car trips to Charyn canyon, day hikes to Bolshoe Almatinskoe lake or waterfalls near Medeu, skiing at Shymbulak, boating on the Ili river, climbing in the Zailiysky Alatau, riding and trekking. This is the one chance you might have to tag along on an otherwise extremely expensive helicopter trip.

Anatoli Nekhororshev (office ☎ 54 66 36, home ☎ 54 51 24, fax 54 52 24, @ nam@satsun.sci.kz) is a local guide who specialises in trekking trips in the Zailiysky Alatau.

Victor Sedelnikov (office ☎/fax 46 65 77, home ☎ 45 74 12) has been recommended for day tours to the Köl-Say lakes, Charyn canyon as well as other tours. He also arranges frequent helicopter tours to these places.

Bookshops & Other Media It's worth getting a copy of *Rizvi's Yellow Pages of Kazakstan*, an annual directory of useful addresses and telephones. It is published in English and Russian.

The lobby shop of KIMEP on Abay has a good selection of English books, magazines and newspapers. The Hyatt Regency Almaty and Regent Almaty both have reasonably well-stocked, expensive bookstalls. The cheapest selection of English books on local topics is at the Hotel Otrar.

Akademkniga at Furmanov 139, next to the Chinese embassy, and at Furmanov 91, next to the US embassy, has a range of maps of Kazakstan cities, districts and regions, including trekking and river maps. It also sells dictionaries and phrasebooks.

Western newspapers and magazines are sold at the major hotels, KIMEP and the Dastarkhan Kulinaria on Shevchenko.

You can pick up the BBC World Service on 15.070 MHz (short wave), and Voice of America on 1341 KHz (medium wave).

Cultural Centres & Useful Organisations
If you plan to stay for an extended period, it may be good to know about the following organisations:

British Council
(☎ 63 33 39, 63 77 43, fax 63 34 43,
@ bc@britcoun.almaty.kz)
Has recently moved to the south end of Baysetova, just off Respublika alangy. There's a good English library and Internet facilities, as well as a cafe.
Goethe Institute
(☎ 44 97 07) Zhandosova 2 – open Monday to Friday 9 am to 5 pm; library open Tuesday to Thursday 1.30 to 5 pm.

ISAR
(☎/fax 67 71 88), Shagabutdinov 128 – the US-funded environmental watchdog is on the 2nd floor of a building set back from the street between Zhambyl and Shevchenko.
Kazakstan Institute of Management, Economics & Strategic Research (KIMEP)
Abay 4 – Almaty's premier English language further education institution; a good place to meet young Kazaks and find out about the country.
Nevada-Semey Anti-Nuclear Movement
(☎/fax 62 54 70), Karasay Batyr 85, room 203 – Kazakstan's first nonprofit organisation campaigned successfully for the closure of the Polygon nuclear testing site near Semey, and is now working for regeneration of that region and for a worldwide end to nuclear testing. If you want to find out more the best contact is the volunteer Rima Dzimisova (☎ 28 60 57 or 67 63 23), who speaks English.
United Nations Development Programme (UNDP)
(☎ 58 26 46, 69 67 24, 69 60 34, fax 58 26 45) Tole Bi 67 – on corner with Zheltoksan, and in the same building as the Ministry of Foreign Affairs consular section.
US Peace Corps (Main Office)
(☎ 69 29 85, fax 62 40 30)
Corner of Seyfullin and Shevchenko

Medical Services The main international clinic with English-speaking staff is AEA (Asia Emergency Assistance), Luganskogo 11 (☎ 64 26 56, fax 50 73 35), at the southern end of the city. Interteach, the Kazak National Corporation of Health and Medical Insurance, also has a small clinic with English speakers at Furmanov 175, next to the British, French and German embassies. Both these clinics are expensive, but are preferable to the poorly run and supplied local health service.

A reliable US doctor is Dr Marty Basset, at Grace Clinic (☎ 46 94 48) and the Diagnostic Centre, Auezov 57 (☎ 42 29 79), Monday, Wednesday, Friday 9 am to 2 pm.

There are pharmacies (Kazak: *dorikhana*, Russian: *apteka*) all over Almaty where you can buy most western medicines.

If you need an AIDS test for visa purposes, the Aids Centre (☎ 30 69 15)) is at Talghar 7, on the corner of Makataev.

Emergency Police: ☎ 02; fire: ☎ 01; ambulance: ☎ 03.

Dangers & Annoyances Take care if walking on the streets after dark; try to go with at least one other person, and don't stop if you're approached by strangers. Be especially on your guard near obvious foreigners' haunts such as the expat bars and major hotels, where drunken foreigners have been targeted by muggers. Inside hotels, don't open your room door to a stranger.

Prostitution is common at many Almaty hotels: one traveller reported being phoned in the middle of the night by a prostitute who addressed him by name.

Walking Tour

Respublika alangy is the best place to start a walking tour; not only is it all downhill from here, on a clear morning the square provides a panoramic view of the snowcapped mountains. Head east along Satpaev past the Army's Central Sports Club on the right and the Agricultural Institute campus on the left. When you hit Dostyk, you'll notice an observatory building uphill; this is the **Republican Palace of Schoolchildren**. Downhill, behind the large statue of the writer Abay Kunabaev and the Palace of the Republic, you could make a detour to take the **cable car** to Köktyube for a view across the city.

A block north of the Hotel Kazakstan, turn west along Shevchenko to find the magnificent **Academy of Sciences** building, one of the true gems of Soviet monumental architecture. Fountains and parks around the building make this a cool spot to linger in summer. Check out the 'Eastern Calendar' fountain with Chinese zodiac creatures on the east side of the academy.

It's pleasant to continue heading north along tree-lined Tölebaev until you reach Kabanbay Batyr and turn west to reach the neo-classical **Opera and Ballet Theatre**. Two blocks north of here is a small park in front of what used to be Kazakstan's House of Parliament (before it shifted to Astana) and which now houses local government offices. In the park you'll find a statue to local war heroes Manshuk Mametova and Alie Moldagulova, which replaced the one of Lenin, removed after independence.

Heading east along Töle Bi, you can turn north to reach Panfilov Park (see the following section) on Dostyk, where you'll find Zenkov Cathedral, the imposing war memorial and the **Museum of Kazak Musical Instruments**, in a charming wooden building. Just to the east of the park along Gogol, you'll see another rare example of fine Russian nineteenth century wooden architecture. **Dom Takani**, an elegant drapers shop on Zhibek Zholy is also worth a look. To the east of here is the **Zelyony Bazar**, Almaty's most colourful market, with a true flavour of Central Asia.

Just north of the market you'll notice the turquoise dome of a large **mosque** on the corner of Pushkin and Mametova; after many years of slow work, this building is still to be completed.

Panfilov Park

This large rectangle of greenery, first laid out in the 1870s, makes a pleasant focus for the northern part of the central area. In the middle is the candy coloured **Zenkov Cathedral**, designed by AP Zenkov in 1904. This is one of Almaty's few surviving tsarist-era buildings (most of the others were wrecked in the 1911 earthquake). Though at first glance it doesn't look like it, the cathedral is built entirely of wood – and apparently without nails. Used as a museum and concert hall in the Soviet era, then boarded up, it was returned to the Russian Orthodox Church in 1995 and is now a functioning place of worship. The interior is festooned with icons and murals; it's well worth attending when a service is on, to get the full effect.

The park's rather fearsome full title – the Park Named After the 28 Panfilov Heroes – is explained by an equally fearsome **war memorial** east of the cathedral. This represents the 28 soldiers of an Almaty infantry unit who died fighting off Nazi tanks in a village on the outskirts of Moscow in 1941. An eternal flame commemorating the fallen of 1917-20 (the Civil War) and 1941-45 (WWII), flickers in front of the giant black monument of soldiers from all 15 Soviet republics bursting out of a map of the former USSR.

The park is on the routes of trolleybus No 1, 2, 8, 12 or 16 along Gogol from anywhere in the central area.

Arasan Baths

Facing the west end of Panfilov Park are these elaborate baths, a favourite Almaty relaxation spot. Arasan means 'warm spring' but the complex is also known as Kunaev Banya after the former Soviet leader of Kazakstan who had the baths built. The main entrance is on Atyteke Bi, and you can choose from two options; Russian *(Russkaya banya)* and Finnish *(Finskaya banya)* baths, which are straight ahead up the stairs, comprising of regular sauna, a giant steam room and a large circular plunge pool, or the Turkish *(Vostochnaya banya)* which is downstairs, with three different temperatures of heated stone platforms plus a plunge pool. There are separate sections in each for women and men and good massages are available for around US$15 (one hour).

The baths are open Tuesday to Sunday. Sessions begin every two hours from 8 am to 8 pm. Until 2 pm entry to either set of baths is around US$2, after 4 pm around US$4. There are also more expensive, private deluxe sections for four people. You should take along soap, a towel and some thongs (flip-flops) for walking around in (essential if you want to negotiate the scorching floor of the Russian baths!). If you don't have any bathing gear at hand, there's a shop in the lobby. There are sellers with bunches of myrtle leaves outside, if you fancy giving yourself a good thrashing.

Central (Gorky) Park

Almaty's largest recreational area, at the east end of Gogol, 1km from the Hotel Otrar, is still known as Gorky Park. It harbours boating lakes, funfair rides, a zoo, several cafes, shashlyk and beer stands. It's busiest on Sunday and holidays. Entry is 20 T. Trolleybus No 1, 8, 12 and 16 run along Gogol to the entrance from anywhere in the central area.

Museums

In a striking 1908 wooden building at the east end of Panfilov Park is the **Museum of Kazak Musical Instruments,** the city's most original museum. It has a fine collection of traditional Kazak instruments – wooden harps and horns, bagpipes, the lute-like two stringed *dombra* and the viola-like three stringed *kobiz*. Wait for a guided tour by an attendant who will press buttons on the displays to play tapes of the instruments, strum the dombra himself and offer to sell you a tape of the music at the end for 300 T, as good a souvenir of Almaty as you could wish for. The museum is open daily, 10 am to 6 pm except Monday and the last day of the month. Admission is 40 T.

The **Archaeology Museum** has four main display areas showing the history of civilisations in Kazakstan from ancient times to the Middle Ages. Here you'll find a full-size replica of the country's chief archaeological treasure, the Golden Man (see the boxed text 'The Golden Man'), a Scythian warrior dressed in a glittering funeral suit of armour. The museum is on the 2nd floor of the block with three 12-storey towers at Dostyk 44, behind the statue of the famous Kazak singer Zhambyl. It's open Monday to Friday, 10 am to 6 pm and entry is 60 T.

The intriguing **Geological Museum,** in the bowels of the Kazak Business Centre, is reached by a mineshaft-like elevator. On display are startling examples of much of the country's mineral wealth, including giant precious gems and crystals, plus touch screen computers to provide quick geology lessons in English. Entry is 60 T and it's open Tuesday to Friday, 9 am to 6 pm.

One of the city's best museums stands at Furmanov 44, 300m uphill from Respublika alangy. The **Central State Museum** gives a worthwhile if patchy picture of Kazakstan's history. The downstairs rooms cover geology, archaeology and early history, including another miniature replica of the Golden Man. There's also a missable section with precious metals that costs 30 T extra to view.

Upstairs covers the Soviet and modern eras, including exhibits on space flight from the Baykonur Cosmodrome, nuclear testing at Semey, and the Aral Sea; and the era of the Kazak khanates, the coming of the Russians and the changes in the country since

The Golden Man

The Golden Man (Russian: Zolotoy Chelovek) is a warrior's costume that was found in a Saka tomb near Esik, about 40km east of Almaty. It is made up of over 4000 separate gold pieces – many of them finely worked with animal motifs. It also has a 70cm-high headdress bearing sky-ward-pointing arrows, a pair of snarling snow leopards and a two-headed winged mythical beast. There's some confusion about its age – the Central State Museum says it's from about the 12th century CE but most other sources put its origin at about the 5th century BCE. Its Scythian-style artwork would certainly favour the latter. The original of this treasure, considered too fragile to be pieced together for display, resides in the vaults of Kazakstan's National Bank.

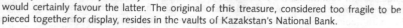

MICK WELDON

independence. One chief exhibit is a colour-fully kitted-out yurt.

The crafts stall in the foyer is worth a look. Also in the foyer are Kazak carpets and tapestries for sale, with prices starting at around US$50 for small pieces and rising sharply.

The museum is open daily except Tuesday from 10 am to 5 pm; entry is 60 T. Get there by bus No 2, 11 or 100 going up Furmanov from Gogol.

The **Kasteyev Museum of Fine Arts**, at Satpaev 30A, has the best collection of art in the country, including works of artists banned during the Soviet period. The two extensive floors crammed with paintings, sculpture and applied arts give a comprehensive view of Kazak art. There are also collections of Russian and West European art. Particularly interesting is a one-room section of Kazak fine carpets, wall carpets, saddle covers, wood carving and jewellery, and the Soviet-era paintings glorifying the workers in fields, mines and kitchens. It's worth taking a guided tour in English for around US$8.

The museum is open Tuesday to Sunday, 10 am to 5 pm; entry is 60 T. There are a couple of good craft shops on the ground floor. Get there by trolleybus No 16 heading west on Gogol then south on Zheltoksan; or

take any transport to the circus on Abay, then walk one block south.

Cable Car to Köktyube

This rickety thrill-ride runs from beside the Palace of the Republic on Dostyk up to Köktyube (green peak), a foothill of the Zalaisky Alatau, crowned by the landmark TV transmitter complex. There's a viewing platform, shashlyk and beer stands at the top cable car station and it's a good place to visit on a warm summer evening to take in the city panorama beneath. If you visit during the day, the hike down the hill back to Dostyk is a pleasant one. The cable car runs daily 11 am to 7 pm and costs 100 T each way.

Respublika Alangy

This broad ceremonial square at the high southern end of Almaty, created in Soviet times, is a block uphill from Abay. The focal point on the Satpaev side is the attractive **Monument to Independence**, erected in 1996. The column is surmounted with a replica of the Golden Man and flanked at its base by fountains and two bas-relief walls, depicting scenes from Kazakhstan's history. At the centre of the square is the neo-classical city government building and at the south-east corner, opposite the Central State Museum, the official **Presidential Residence**, an ugly modern building also known as the 'White House'.

You can reach the square on bus No 2, 11 or 100 going up Furmanov from Gogol, or bus No 32 or 70 up Zheltoksan from Gogol.

St Nicholas Cathedral

The pale turquoise St Nicholas (Nikolsky Sobor), with its gold onion domes stands out west of the centre, on Baytursynuly at the corner of Kabanbay Batyr. Built in 1909, it was later used as a stable for Bolshevik cavalry before reopening about 1980. Renovations of the extensive murals inside are still continuing. It's a terrifically atmospheric place, like a corner of old Russia, with icons and candles inside and black-clad old supplicants outside. For the best impression visit at festival times such as Orthodox Christmas Day (7 January) or Easter, for the midnight services.

Activities

The city's best public outdoor **swimming pool** is next to the Central Stadium on Abay, behind a building that looks like an aircraft hangar. In the winter the water is heated and there's a short underwater tunnel so you needn't even step out into the freezing cold. Tickets are bought from the women's entrance on the west side of the hangar; men enter on the east side in the door next to the cafe. You have to remove your shoes before entering the changing rooms and at busy times visits are supposed to last an hour. It's open daily 8 am to 9 pm, entrance is 300 T or 3000 T for 12 visits.

There are also indoor and outdoor public **swimming pools** at the Dinamo Stadium at Nauryzbay Batyr 89, on the corner of Shevchenko. In winter you can **ice-skate** here, too.

Daulet (☎ 67 20 69) at Shagabutdinov 183, just off Satpaev near the Central Stadium, is one of Almaty's best **gyms**; entry is around US$10. There are also a gym and good clay **tennis courts** for US$3 per hour at the Army's Central Sports Club on Satpaev near the crossing with Furmanov.

TPF Bowling at Satpaev 30, is a popular, large all-American **bowling** alley. Ultimate

Frisbee matches are held between April and November on Thursday at 7 pm and Saturday at 3 pm on the soccer pitch at the Agricultural Institute on Abay at the end of Tölebaev.

Fun runners can catch the **Hash House Harriers**, on the corner of Dostyk and Kurmanghazy, opposite the Hotel Kazakstan, November to April on Sunday at 3 pm and the rest of the year on Monday at 6.45 pm. Lone joggers (avoid jogging after dark) will find the safest tracks in Central Park at the east end of Gogol.

Places to Stay – Budget

There's a small *gostinitsa* (hotel; ☎ 60 42 13) upstairs from the international hall of Almaty-II train station, on the left as you enter the building. Dorms are small, with two hard beds, for US$2, but may be acceptable if you arrive late. Toilets are separate (there's no shower) and there's a restaurant.

KIMEP Gostinitsa (Hotel) No 1 (☎ 64 58 31, fax 65 10 88, Abay 4), in the campus of the Kazakstan Institute of Management, Economics & Strategic Research (KIMEP), has dorms and excellent cheap hotel rooms. During the day enter through the front entrance on Abay and cut through to the courtyard at the back by a door to the side of the elevators. At night, the only entrance is through the gate on Ualikhanov, on the west side, half a block uphill from Abay. The hotel reception is on the left inside this gate. Dorms, in a separate building from the hotel, are US$5; the comfortable, clean singles/doubles, with phone and shared bathroom cost US$18/26. Suites of rooms, with kitchen and TV from US$35 to US$56. All room prices include breakfast. There are also kitchen facilities and a good cafe. Trolleybus No 4 from Almaty-II station or any bus running up Dostyk or Furmanov will bring you close to KIMEP.

Hotel Zerde (☎ 67 14 24, Shevchenko 126), a kind of Soviet-style youth hostel, is where the Peace Corps station their volunteers on arrival in Almaty, so the army of stout, kindly women in charge are well used to dealing with foreigners. Spartan, but clean rooms with shared bathroom are US$4, deluxe doubles with ensuite and TV, US$10. There's also a canteen serving cheap meals and a sauna (150 T). There's no sign on the hotel; look for the building set back from the street, opposite Michurin.

Closer to Almaty-II station and the City Air Terminal are two small private hotels set back in a block at Gogol 117, between Nauryzbay Batyr and Seyfullin. The better one is the **Kaezhol** (☎ 32 33 00, 32 28 22, fax 32 42 00), with singles/doubles with fridge, TV and phone for US$20/30. The receptionist speaks a little English and they accept credit cards. The staff at the **Uyut** (☎ 32 32 88) are not as friendly, but singles start from US$5, rising to US$40 for deluxe doubles. There's a cafe, too.

Hotel Daulet (☎ 62 04 09, fax 50 71 01, Konaev 153) is a no-frills place, but the old-style rooms are fine for US$15/20 with en-suite, TV and phone.

The travel agency Tour Asia (☎ 48 25 73, ☎/fax 49 79 36, @ tourasia@online.ru) can arrange lodging in **private homes**, generally a few kilometres south-west of the centre, for US$30 with full board, US$25 without.

Places to Stay – Mid-Range
Hotels Almaty's oldest hotel, the **Hotel Zhetisu** (☎ 32 68 34, fax 39 24 85, Abylay Khan 55), conveniently located near the City Air Terminal and also about the nearest hotel to Almaty-II train station (1km by trolleybus No 4, 5 or 6), is showing its age. Rooms are clean and the receptionists seem to have improved their manners since our last visit. Rooms cost US$37/40 for ones with shared bathrooms, US$46/60 with en-suite and breakfast included. The helpful travel agency Jibek Joly is also in the hotel.

Hotel Almaty (☎ 63 09 43, fax 63 02 02, Kabanbay Batyr 85) is cheap but somewhat rundown. It has comfortable rooms at US$45/55 with breakfast, plus a restaurant and a lobby cafe. You can reach it by trolleybus No 4, 5, or 6 which run along Abylay Khan from Almaty-II station.

The small **Hotel Issik** (☎ 60 02 11, Bögenbay Batyr 140), just west of Zheltoksan, has singles/doubles for US$30 and up with TV and phones. A Soviet-era atmosphere prevails and while some rooms are nice, others are tatty. It's close to the routes of bus No

92 or 97 on Zheltoksan and trolleybus No 4, 5 or 6 along Abylay Khan.

Better is the 26 floor **Hotel Kazakstan** (☎ 61 91 65, 61 95 41 fax 61 98 98, Dostyk 52), built in 1977 and still Almaty's tallest building. Rooms are standard Soviet tourist-hotel issue, although the more expensive ones have been renovated and all include satellite TV. Prices start at US$43 rising to US$132 and all include a good buffet breakfast in the top floor Cosmos Café, which is also open to nonguests.

If you have transport or fancy a break from the city, the **Interlux Country Club** (☎ 54 97 65, 54 93 94, fax 54 97 67) is some 15km south of the centre in the village of Kamenka (best accessible via taxi). It's also known as the Alatau Sanatorium (this was once the resort for top party officials) and offers, in addition to comfortable rooms with satellite TV and phone, indoor swimming pool, gym, sauna, tennis courts and an 18-hole golf course, all for bargain rates beginning at US$40 per night.

Apartments Kupava Service Agency (☎ 68 63 25, fax 68 63 07, Schevchenko 129, Apt 35) and Charlotte Gaillard at **Check Point** (☎ 30 26 45, 30 80 40, Kurmanghazy 32, Apt 1) can help arrange apartments from around US$30 per night. If you can read/speak Russian, the weekly classified ads newspaper Karavan lists people renting out apartments and rooms. The staff at **Hotel Otrar** (see Places to Stay – Top End) are also helpful and might be able to find you an inexpensive apartment for around US$20 per night.

Places to Stay – Top End
The cheapest of the upmarket options is the **Hotel Otrar** (☎ 33 00 76, 33 00 46, fax 33 20 13, Gogol 73), the Intourist flagship in Soviet days. It's still a decent hotel with a good location facing Panfilov Park and comfortable rooms with cable TV for US$90, with a good help-yourself breakfast. It also has the cheapest hotel bookshop in Almaty. Take trolleybus No 1, 2, 8, 12 or 16 along Gogol from anywhere in the central area.

Also good value, with a central location, is the *Hotel Ambassador* (☎ 69 68 49, 69 17 50, fax 69 64 41, ✉ ambassador@nursat.kz, Zheltoksan 121), which is smart and modern. Single/doubles start at US$130/165 with breakfast, and have cable TV, minibar, and IDD phone. There's also a restaurant and bar.

A similar standard, although not as conveniently located, is the *Hotel Premier Alatau* (☎ 58 11 11, fax 58 15 55, Dostyk 105). It's recently been renovated and has huge rooms with cable TV, phone, minibar and small balcony for US$120/150 including tax and breakfast. It's about 2km south of the Hotel Kazakstan and can be reached by buses heading towards Medeu.

Astana Hotel (☎ 50 70 50, fax 50 10 60, Baytursynuly 113, ✉ aih@kaznet.kz) is a popular business choice. The rooms, inoffensively modern with thin walls, small balconies and cable TV, are US$150 for both singles and doubles. As well as a restaurant, business centre and sauna, the Astana also has a small bowling alley.

The former Communist Party choice, *Hotel Dostyk* (☎ 63 62 01, 63 63 01, fax 63 66 12, Kurmanghazy 36) on the corner of Konaev, was the best in Almaty till the Hyatt and the Regent Almaty came along. It's still quite grand, if somewhat subdued, with comfortable rooms with cable TV from US$110/257, the cheaper ones with showers only.

Almaty's first international luxury hotel, the *Hyatt Regency Almaty* (☎ 581 12 34, 47 36 30, fax 581 16 35, Akadamik Satpaev 29/6) is also known as the Rachat Palace. It's about 2km west of Respublika alangy, next to the Circus and Fantasy World. Although rather ugly outside, the rooms, around a central atrium, are all excellent with IDD phones, cable TV and minibar for US$290 single or double. There's also a business centre, an indoor swimming pool and gym, Turkish bath, sauna and tennis court and several good restaurants. A shuttle bus runs to/from the airport for international flights.

Rivalling the Hyatt is the glitzy *Regent Almaty* (☎ 50 37 10-19 (nine lines), Zheltoksan 181), just west of Respublika alangy. It used to be called the Ankara. Plush rooms

with all the usual five-star amenities start at US$295/320. The hotel has a health club, night club, casino, business centre and three restaurants. It too has complimentary pick-ups at the airport for international flights.

Places to Eat

Enjoy the good range of restaurants and cafes in Almaty – they're the best you'll find in the country. With a couple of exceptions, traditional Kazak cuisine is rare, but favourites such as shashlyk, laghman and manty abound, and in the spring and summer, shashlyk stands sprout all over the city. During the warmer months several of Almaty's cafes and restaurants have tables outside, too.

North of Töle Bi Of three good Turkish cafes and restaurants in this area, *Seyhanlar* (☎ 33 56 50, Konaev 64), on the first floor in a courtyard behind the Hotel Otrar, is the best. There's a photo menu and dishes on display so you can see exactly what you're getting. A shish kebab with salad is US$4; a meal should cost around US$6. No alcohol is served and it's open daily 8 am to midnight.

Less fancy is *Kafe Marmara* (☎ 39 85 62), on the corner of Mametova and Abylay Khan, a neat little place with friendly service, open daily from 11 am to 10 pm. Soup, bread and doner kebab with potatoes costs about US$4.50. The salads are good, too.

More a fast food option is *Korkim Ama*, on Zhibek Zholy near the corner of Konaev. Kebab and hamburger set meals with chips and drinks are around US$3. There's also a selection of sticky Turkish sweets and a play area for kids.

Zelyony Bazar has plenty of stalls selling plov, manty and shashlyk outside the main hall, while inside there are cafes overlooking the market action where a bowl of laghman, tea and bread will cost less than US$2.

Reasonably priced Korean food as well as a wide selection of Kazak and Russian dishes are available at *Rodem* on Abylay Khan, just south of TsUM and open daily 9.30 am to 11 pm. The 'sushi' is made with plain rice and mince meat, but still tasty and less than US$2.

Across the road, the *Rock Bar*, an imitation Hard Rock Café is a smarter hangout that's also a surprisingly quiet bar. There's a pleasant outdoor area beside a fountain, an English menu and passable Russian/European food for less than US$5.

Heading two blocks west, the *International Business Club* (☎ 32 27 01, Gogol 86), is also known as the 'yellow pub' and has a good restaurant and a happy hour on Friday 6 to 10 pm. The food is international, including Mexican, European and American dishes (around US$5). Open noon to 1 am daily.

The classy *Stradivari* next to the Kazkontsert Hall on Abylay Khan is worth searching out. Their *jarkoye*, a meat and potato stew in a clay pot, is excellent.

Heading back towards Panfilov Park, the restaurants at the Hotel Otrar are best for lunch, especially the Pakistani restaurant *Mughalia*, which does a buffet lunch for US$7 (the exact same meal is US$11 for dinner). The main restaurant is worth a look for its striking Kazak theme murals, fountain and domed ceiling.

Almaty's most popular shashlyk restaurant, *Inara,* on Kaldayakov opposite the Central Concert Hall, doesn't look much, but has friendly service, a buzzy atmosphere and big, cheap plates of barbecued meat with onion and cucumber trimmings. It's certainly a more authentic Kazak experience than *Mad Murphy's*, around the corner on Töle Bi, a quintessential Irish bar, with sandwiches from US$4, Irish Stew for US$10, and a full English breakfast for US$9.40.

Another pleasantly rustic place for shashlyk, especially in the summer (when you can sit outside on the veranda and look across to Panfilov Park) is *U Stary Varoty* (The Old Gatehouse), on the corner of Dostyk.

An old standby, *Solyanka (Panfilov 100)* is clean with good Russian and Kazak food and helpful staff. It's open from 10 am to 3 pm and 4 to 9 pm.

South of Töle Bi A popular expat hangout also favoured by nouveau-riche/Mafia types is *Stetson*, opposite the Opera & Ballet Theatre. It has an English menu and serves decent burgers for around US$6.

Heading up Furmanov, you'll find *Kolsay*, an inexpensive Azeri restaurant on the corner of Kurmanghazy and Panfilov. The decor is a bit tacky but the food, including spicy salads and manty, is fine; it's open from 11 am to midnight daily.

Also worth a look across the road, in a basement is *U Alina*. It has an English menu. The small pots of creamy mushrooms are tasty and the chicken and fish main dishes are also good.

Further west along Shevchenko is the excellent *Dastarkhan*, open 24-hours. The breakfast menu includes pancakes and omelettes; there's a discount lunch served until 4 pm and even dinner needn't break the bank with many dishes around US$5 (there are plenty more expensive foods on offer including a range of game meats). There's a no-smoking section and live music of the synthesiser and crooner variety.

The music is much better at the sophisticated *Jazz Rock Café* (☎ 62 94 93) on Shevchenko and Konaev. The menu is reasonable and includes a platter of kazy for US$4 and more conventional dishes for under US$5.

The Hotel Kazakstan, has the economical *Kafe Kosmos* on the top floor, open 7.30 am to 4 pm and 6 to 9 pm, with main dishes around US$3. A blow out buffet breakfast here is US$6.

Opposite the hotel there's a quiet, sophisticated cafe in the *Kazak Business Centre*; you can get lunch here and browse art displays and information on Kazakstan's mineral and oil wealth.

Inside *KIMEP* on Abay, you'll find a very cheap student *stolovaya* (canteen), and a more upmarket restaurant in the 'mirror hall', only open for lunch, but very good value for a three course meal at around US$2; head to the south end of the campus from the main building. There's also a decent cafe in the KIMEP Gostinitsa No 1, a fine option for breakfast or lunch.

Opposite KIMEP is *Barrakuda*, a deli with outdoor tables and a simple menu including blinis and laghman.

Tucked behind the *Hotel Dostyk* is an unmarked stolovaya, in which you can get a hearty lunch of Russian favourites, Monday to Friday noon to 2 pm. It's a bit school dinner-ish, but a bargain at US$2. Look for the wooden door in the building opposite the Hotel's casino.

Just off Respublika alangy there's a cafe inside the *British Council*. Across the road, *Cadillac* has a lovely view from its balcony, but only passable food. The *Ramstor* mall on Furmanov has a western-style food court with pizza, kebab, burger and cake stalls.

Top End Restaurants The Chinese *Shen-yan Restaurant* (☎ 69 19 71, Bögenbay Batyr 136), also known as China Town, is atmospheric and has a photo menu with main dishes starting at US$8. Servings are generous, but count on US$20 per person for a full meal. It's open daily 12.30 pm to midnight.

The German *Schwäbisches Häuschen* (Abylay Khan 121), next to the SMAT supermarket, is one of Almaty's quirkiest places, serving gut-busting platters of food under stuffed and mounted boars' heads. Entertainment is provided by a fraulein decked out in country costume who kicks her heels as an accordion player pumps out a jaunty ditty. Prices are all in Deutschmarks; expect to pay around US$20.

More elegant, but not so much fun, is the French *L'Hermitage*, on Furmanov. Best value is their business lunch Monday to Friday, noon to 3 pm, of salad, soup, a main course, dessert, tea or coffee for US$13.20. Opening hours are Monday to Friday noon to midnight, weekends 6 pm to midnight.

Back downhill, is *Old England* (☎ 69 51 04, Bögenbay Batyr 134), a stylish, but not particularly British looking place, with main dishes in the US$10-15 range. Roast beef and Yorkshire pudding and bread and butter pudding are on the menu along with caviar and blinis (US$14.50).

The Hotel Dostyk has the ground floor *Café Bastau* (☎ 63 92 42) with French cuisine, and the more formal 2nd floor *Dostyk Restaurant* (☎ 63 67 11) with international fare. A typical full meal in either will come to US$20, but there are cheaper offerings such as burgers and pizza for around US$10 in the restaurant.

Next to the Hotel Kazakstan is a *Korean restaurant* of variable quality – usually with a floor show, which may include Korean ethnic dance, in the evenings. The restaurant has an amazing ceiling. In the same room, at the back, is the *Osaka Japanese restaurant*. The fish for the sushi at US$30 is supposedly flown in from Korea. The beef stew dish shabu-shabu is better value at US$19 noon to 3pm; US$38 for dinner.

Further uphill, *Pizzeria Venezia* (☎ 64 09 95, Dostyk 87A), open daily noon to midnight, is a convivial place, famed for its thin crust, freshly baked pizzas for US$5-10. They also have pasta dishes, but they make very bad cappuccino.

The swanky Regent Almaty hotel's top restaurant is the *Belvedere Grill Room*, with a spectacular view from its top floor perch. The French food is around US$20. A little more affordable, but still very plush is their Turkish restaurant *Bosphorus*. There's a tempting *patisserie* on the ground floor, next to the buffet restaurant *The Asian Café*, where a slap-up breakfast is US$20 and Sunday brunch US$30. Saturday is their Kazak specialities night.

Set back from the street, *Capos* (Abay 32), just west of Seyfullin, is more of a bar, with western music and satellite TV, but serves OK US and Mexican-style food, too. There's a lunch all-you-can-eat deal for US$9 and a big breakfast for US$7 when it opens at 10 am on weekends only (Monday to Friday noon to 2 am). Dinner with drinks should come to US$15-20.

Ristorante Adriatico (☎ 67 29 44, Mechnikov 90) offers a long menu of reasonable Italian food in smart surroundings with good service, though portions can be small. Starters and pasta are US$8 to US$15, and main courses US$6 to US$20. Opening hours are noon to 3 pm and 7 pm to midnight.

The Hyatt Regency Almaty has the good *Café Vienna* on the ground floor with soups, salads, light main meals, sandwiches and coffees, open 24 hours with newspapers and magazines to browse. You can watch birds fly around its airy atrium. Also on the ground floor the *Zhambyl Restaurant* serves nightly buffets on different European and Asian themes; Sunday night is Kazak traditional food. There's also the dark, club-like *Grill Restaurant* for fine European cooking. In the warmer months a yurt restaurant/bar is open outside.

The *Havana Club* next door, run by the Hyatt, also does a good range of snacks, such as spring rolls and potato skins, salads, burgers, pizza, pasta and sandwiches, mostly for under US$10. It's open from 6 pm and, until the party crowd begins to arrive after 10 pm, you'll pretty much have the place to yourself.

Self-Catering Lots of vegetables, fresh and dried fruit, nuts and dairy products, including *kumyz* and shubat, are sold at the large central market, best known as the *Zelyony Bazar (Green Market)* *(Zhibek Zholy prospekti 53)*; open Tuesday to Sunday. You need to watch out for pickpockets here. There's also a smaller farmer's market by St Nicholas Cathedral, west of the centre on Baytursynuly.

Among the many small supermarkets across the city now, the best is the chain *SMAT*, selling reasonably priced local and imported goods; branches are on the corner of Seyfullin and Töle Bi, and Kabanbay Batyr and Abylay Khan. One of the older-style, more reasonably priced supermarkets is *Universam* on the corner of Zhibek Zholy and Furmanov.

Dastarkhan on Shevchenko between Baytursynuly and Masanchi is Almaty's best *kulinariya* (deli), with a tempting array of cakes, packaged delicacies and food specialities. There's also a cafe out front in summer. Another upmarket supermarket is *Rossia* on Dostyk and Kabanbay Batyr, with a good selection of picnic goodies.

At the huge supermarket in the *Ramstor* shopping mall at the south end of Furmanov, there's an impressive selection, but most items you'll find elsewhere in the city (albeit not under one roof) at vastly cheaper prices.

Entertainment

Nightclubs Come Friday night you'll find a fair percentage of Almaty's expat community at *Mad Murphy's*, the slick Irish bar on Töle Bi. It's loud, convivial and the beer, including Murphy's stout on draft, is expensive. The *Guinness Pub*, up Dostyk towards the Hotel Kazakstan, has the famous Irish stout in bottles only, but does have billiard tables, darts and backgammon.

Quieter bars include *Stalker Internet*, on Töle Bi near Mad Murphy's, where you can knock back cheap draft beer in a cavernous room after surfing the Internet, and the *Belgium Pub* at the top of Furmanov, which serves a pricey range of European bottled beers.

As for clubbing, the scene revolves around three main venues: *Havana*, *Capos* and *Tequilla Sunrise* at the Hotel Otrar, each jostling for top position depending on the fickle tastes of the expat and yuppie local community. Our winner is Havana, by far the most stylish of the three. You're supposed to purchase 1000 'Havanas' (costing 1000 T) on entry, which you can use to pay for drinks and food, but in practice this isn't always enforced and isn't necessary if you're staying at the Hyatt. Capos' disco is small and behind the main bar/dining room; it's more pleasant to hang in the courtyard outside on a warm evening. Tequilla Sunrise is the sleaziest of the three, with all the charm of a wild west saloon pumping out techno.

More of a teen-scene is the *KIMEP Fun Club* (☎ 64 07 34) in a grand two-level hall in a corner of the KIMEP campus on Abay. It's open on Tuesday, Friday and Saturday nights 10 pm to 3 am, with a cover charge of 350/500 T for women/men. Enter by the side gate on Ualikhanov and walk diagonally across the grounds to the left.

Casinos are attached to all of Almaty's top hotels but are best avoided unless you're up to rubbing shoulders with Mafia-types and their molls.

Gay & Lesbian Venues There's a small underground scene in Almaty of which the two main bars are *Spartacus* on Dosmukhamedov between Abay and Kurmanghazy, and *Rainbow* on Shagabutdinov and Kabanbay Batyr. Spartacus is a club with a strict door policy to keep out troublemakers, but has a very relaxed atmosphere inside where all sexual persuasions mingle freely. There's a professional strip show on Fridays, a transvestite show on Saturdays, good dance music and reasonably priced drinks. Entrance is 400/600 T for men/women.

Live Music Good jazz bands groove at *Jazz Rock Café* on Shevchenko and Konaev, on Wednesday, Thursday and Friday from around 8 pm. More cocktail lounge style jazz is played at the Regent Almaty's *Members Bar* daily from 4 pm to midnight (happy hour 7 to 8 pm). The *Aiia Disco* in the Fantasy World amusement park has live bands, usually on the weekend. Visiting CIS bands and singers and the odd washed up western act usually perform at the *Palace of the Republic* on Dostyk at the east end of Abay.

Concerts, Ballet, Opera & Theatre The two main concert halls are the *Central Concert Hall* (☎ 61 80 48, Kaldayakov 35), on the corner of Töle Bi, and the *Kazkontsert Hall* (☎ 62 01 26, Abylay Khan 83), south of Ayteke Bi. Inexpensive classical concerts are given at the *conservatory (Abylay Khan)* next to the main post office. Also keep your eye open for posters advertising the good Otyrar Sazy Kazak Folk Orchestra.

The main theatre is *Auezov Kazak State Academic Drama Theatre (Abay 105)*, a rather more elegant example of Soviet architecture. Further east is the *Lermontov State Academic Russian Drama Theatre (Abay 43)* which also stages plays by Kazak writers.

Cinema Many Almaty cinemas shut down in the immediate post Soviet period, when subsidies dried up and pirate video cassettes proliferated, but there's now a small revival going on. The *Ibragimov* on Masanichi, behind the St Nicholas Cathedral, is one place showing major recent US and European films, and so is the *Dom Kino* on the corner of Kazybek Bi and Kaldayakov, next to the Australian and Italian embassies, which hosts international film festivals occasionally.

The newest is *NOMAD Kinoteatr*, on the 3rd floor of the Ramstor shopping mall on Furmanov. It screens recent US films, first showing of the day 150 T, rising to 500 T.

The *Iskra* (☎ 50 50 10) on Dostyk, next to the supermarket Rossia, has been recently renovated with marble floors in the foyer, Dolby Digital surround sound, comfy seats and aircon. Tickets are US$4; half price on Monday.

KIMEP also has a *movie club*, screening British and German films usually on Monday; check notice boards around the campus for details.

Spectator Sports

Horse races and occasionally *kökpar* (traditional polo game; see the boxed text 'Buzkashi' in the Spectator Sports section of the Regional Facts for the Visitor chapter) are held at the Hippodrome *(Ippodrom)*, several kilometres north of the centre at Zhansugurov and Akhan Sere. Take a taxi or bus No 30 or 34 north on Seyfullin to Dulatov then walk three blocks west. Get someone to call ahead and see what's on (☎ 36 56 21).

Almaty's soccer team Kayrat plays its home games at the central stadium, Abay 48, which has a fantastic view of the mountains. Kazak baseball teams play regularly at a field behind the stadium on Saturday evenings in June and July, with equipment provided by the San Francisco Little League and the US oil company Chevron, which helped construct the field.

Shopping

Markets The Zelyony Bazar (see Places to Eat) is a sprawling place with a big indoor hall and vendors spread outside too. It's interesting to explore, but watch out for pickpockets. Much of it is devoted to food but there are stalls with clothing and other goods, as well as sad lines of people selling odd shoes, shirts and socks along nearby streets.

There's a big, busy flea-market known as the Barakholka, or Veshchevoy rynok out in the western suburbs. Uzbeks, Chinese, Uyghurs and others converge here selling everything from animals and cars to fur hats and (if you're lucky) carpets. Much of the stuff is cheap imported ware from China and elsewhere, but even if there's nothing you want to buy, it's a revealing Almaty experience. The pet section is among the most interesting. Weekends, especially early Sunday morning, are the busiest times (it's not always open other days). Watch out for pickpockets here, too. Buses going there include No 71, 140 and 530 westbound on Raiymbek (you can pick it up at Abylay Khan).

A curious flea market in stamps, coins and lapel pins is held in the Central Park, just north of the funfair area, on Sunday.

Shops Partly pedestrianised Zhibek Zholy is the street with the biggest cluster of shops, of which Zanghar, the central department store (commonly known by its Russian name TsUM) on the corner of Abylay Khan, is most worth a look. Downstairs all manner of electronic goods are sold; on the 2nd floor you'll mainly find clothes while on the top floor there are stalls selling a fairly similar selection of largely kitsch Kazak crafts and other souvenirs. Another good one-stop shopping destination is Rossia in the shiny fronted blue and gold building on Dostyk and Kabanbay Batyr.

The craft and carpet stalls in the Central State Museum are worth a look, as are the ones in the Kasteyev Museum of Fine Arts. The best selection of modern art is at the Tengri Umai Modern Art Gallery, Abay 43 on the ground floor of the Lermontov Russian Drama Theatre, where you'll find many original artworks and jewellery.

For fur hats (as well as other fur and leather items), try Mekha at Kurmanghazy 157, at the corner with Panfilov.

Ramstor, Kazakstan's first mall, opened in May 1999. Part of a Turkish chain, it's on Furmanov, just south of the Central State Museum and has a range of generally expensive import shops as well as a food court, small skating rink and a movie theatre. A few items that you'll find in the supermarket here that you won't find elsewhere include board games like Scrabble, a wide selection of tampons, many shampoos and plasticware.

Getting There & Away

Almaty is one of Central Asia's major transport hubs. It's served by a growing range of flights from European and Asian cities; flights from Moscow (twice daily) and other Russian cities; trains from Moscow, Siberia, and Ürümqi; and buses from Ürümqi. It has good bus services to Bishkek and south-east Kazakstan cities, and daily trains and several daily buses to Tashkent. Apart from daily flights to Tashkent, flights to other Central Asian cities are sparse.

Almaty is also the hub of internal Kazakstan flights and is linked to most major Kazakstan cities by daily trains. A good way of getting to Tashkent is to go by train to Shymkent, then by bus between Shymkent and Tashkent to avoid the long rail loop.

Air The airport, about 12km north-east of the city centre, undertook a drastic re-design by fire on 10 July 1999. The cause of the blaze is still officially unknown, although it is rumoured there may be a link to the jockeying between the city and oblast governors over the site of a new US$400 million international airport to be built by a Turkish concern.

The arrival and departure terminals for international flights were not damaged and thus *all* flights, international and domestic, are now being channelled through these buildings. To aid travellers, ticket holders for any domestic or CIS flight can check in at the City Air Terminal (Aerovokzal) in the centre of Almaty on Zheltoksan, and will then be bussed directly to their flight.

The main building has a left-luggage office in the basement, open 9 am to 7 pm and 8 pm to 8 am. There's a buffet on the ground floor, and a restaurant upstairs. There are also foreign exchange facilities.

To/From Non-CIS Countries Air Kazakstan is generally cheaper than foreign airlines. The list of carriers and destinations is in flux but at the time of research included the following:

Air China (Xinjiang Airlines)
    (☎ 30 04 86, fax 50 94 85)
    Arikova 36 – Ürümqi twice a week
Air Kazakstan
    (☎ 50 35 03, 50 36 19)
    Airport
    (☎ 32 73 00) Beibitshilik 24 – Bangkok, Beijing, Budapest, Delhi, Frankfurt, Hannover and Tel Aviv weekly; Istanbul and Sharjah twice a week

Asiana Airlines
(☎ 57 12 22, 57 11 66)
Airport Hotel Aksunkar – Seoul weekly, with connections to Asia, Australia and the US west coast
Austrian Airlines (Central Asia Tourism Corp)
(☎ 50 10 70, fax 50 17 07)
Seyfullin 537 – Vienna three times a week
British Airways
(☎ 63 62 67, 63 59 77, fax 63 83 64)
Travel Vision, Kurmanghazy 33 – London twice a week
Iran Air
(☎ 57 28 27, fax 57 28 47)
Airport Hotel Aksunkar, Rm 111 – Tehran weekly
KLM
(☎ 50 77 47, fax 50 91 83)
Hotel Otrar, Gogol 73 – Amsterdam three times a week
Lufthansa
(☎ 45 78 92, 45 55 12, fax 44 37 11)
Morisa Tereza 152 – Frankfurt five times a week
PIA
(☎/fax 57 29 48/02)
Airport Hotel Aksunkar, Rm 117 – Islamabad and Lahore weekly
Turkish Airlines
(☎ 50 62 20, 50 10 67, fax 50 62 19)
Kazybek Bi 81 – Istanbul four times a week

To/From Other CIS Countries The following flights are by Air Kazakstan and a few other Russian and CIS airlines. Fares are one way and subject to change.

To/from Russia there are daily Moscow flights (five hours) by both Air Kazakstan (US$190) and Transaero (☎ 63 95 06, 32 38 88, fax 69 55 72, Ayteke Bi 88; US$260); weekly to St Petersburg (US$210), Mineralnye Vody (US$240), Novosibirsk (US$130) and Samara (US$130).

To/from other Central Asian and CIS locations are daily Tashkent flights (US$69 Air Kazakstan, US$105 Uzbek Airlines); Dushanbe three times a week (US$160); Ashgabat twice a week ($135 Turkmenistan Airlines), weekly to Baku (US$140) and Kiev (US$235 Aerosweet).

To/From Other Kazak Cities Almaty has flights on Air Kazakstan to/from about 15 other cities in Kazakstan. Prices given are for one way flights from Almaty; they're often cheaper from regional cities back to Almaty.

Schedules are subject to change (including last-minute cancellations) but at the time of research, flights went once or more daily to the following destinations: Astana (US$115), Atyrau (US$155), Karaghandy (US$105), Öskemen (US$55), Pavlodar (US$50) and Shymkent (US$87); six times a week to Kyzylorda (US$65) and Kostanay (US $163); five times a week to Aktau (US$158), Aktöbe (US$145) and Kökshetau (US$75); four times a week to Petropavlovsk (US$85) and Semey (US$65); and three times a week to Oral (US$158).

Ticket Offices See Travel Agencies under Almaty earlier for agents to book air tickets and To/From Non-CIS Countries earlier for airline offices. You can buy tickets on Air Kazakstan and other CIS airlines, including Transaero, at the City Air Terminal at Zheltoksan 59. Windows 10 and 11, to the right as you enter, are where foreigners must go for *all* tickets, and are open daily from 9 am to 1 pm and 2 to 7 pm (to 6 pm on weekends). You'll need to show your passport. There are also ticket windows at the airport – worth trying for last-minute tickets.

Bus Long-distance buses use the Sayran bus station (☎ 26 28 55) on the corner of Töle Bi and Mate Zalki, 3.5km west of the centre. Sayran is also called the *novy avtovokzal* (new bus station) or *tsentralny mezhdugorodny avtovokzal* (central inter-city bus station). It has a left-luggage office, open daily from 5 to 3 am. Services include Balkash, Öskemen and Karaghandy (one bus each daily), Taraz and Shymkent (a few buses daily; Tashkent buses will normally take you to these cities too), Taldy-Korghan (daily) and Zharkent (a few buses daily).

Nearer destinations are served by the Sayakhat bus station (☎ 30 08 32) on Raiymbek prospektisi at the north end of Pushkin. Sayakhat is also called the *stary avtovokzal* (old bus station). Buses go at least hourly (8 am to 8 pm) to Yessik, Kapshaghay and Talgar, and between once and four times daily to Chilik, Kegen and Narynkol.

Buses to Taraz and Shymkent also depart from outside Almaty-II train station. They depart daily at 6.30 pm and cost around US$5 to Taraz and US$7 to Shymkent. On the return journey, they depart at 7.30 pm from Shymkent and 11 pm from Taraz.

Buses to Zharkent (430 T) leave daily at 9.30 am, 6.05 pm and 7.05 pm from Almaty-II station, and then Sayakhat bus station.

To/From China A year-round road crosses between Almaty and Ürümqi (in Xinjiang) via the border post at Khorgos (Korgas on the Xinjiang side; see Khorgos under South-East Kazakstan, later in this chapter).

A direct Almaty-Ürümqi bus runs Monday to Saturday in each direction, taking about 24 hours, with no stops except for food and toilets. Bring some food; if the bus is running late, you may get pretty hungry.

It costs US$50 in local currency. Buses for Ürümqi (Kazak: Urimshi) leave Sayran Monday to Saturday at 8 am. Schedules may change so check in advance – it's advisable to buy your ticket a day or two ahead. You might be asked for your China visa when you buy the ticket (about US$50) since you must already have a valid Chinese (or Kazak) visa to travel. No visas are issued at the border. See the Visas entry in the Facts for the Visitor section of the Xinjiang chapter.

Ürümqi buses bypass Yining (Xinjiang), about 100km from the border and the largest town en route, so if you want to stop off here or at Sayram lake (Xinjiang) take a daily Almaty-Yining bus for US$30. See the Xinjiang chapter for more details on Yining (also called Ely or Guldzha) and Sayram lake.

There are minibuses shuttling between the Kazak and Chinese border posts, and Chinese buses run between the border and Ürümqi (about US$10, 15 hours).

To/From Kyrgyzstan & Uzbekistan From Sayran, buses run the 240km to Bishkek roughly every half hour from 1 am to 11.30 pm. The journey takes five hours and costs around US$2. Marshrutnoe buses and taxis also wait at Sayran; they're faster and cost US$4. Buses also go to Tashkent (US$11, 860km, 18 hours) five times daily.

There are also daily buses to Cholpon-Ata (US$12) and Karakol (US$17) near Lake

Issyk-Kul in Kyrgyzstan, via Georgievka near Bishkek. No buses take the rougher and far more scenic easterly road to Issyk-Kul via Kegen, but see the Karkara Valley section later in this chapter for other options.

Train Almaty has two main stations. All main long-distance trains stop at Almaty-I, on the Turksib main line several kilometres north of the centre, but many trains (including those to/from Ürümqi) terminate at Almaty-II, at the end of a spur line much nearer the centre. Almaty-I is at the north end of Seyfullin prospektisi; Almaty-II is at the north end of Abylay Khan dangghyly. Tashkent trains use Almaty-I only. See the Getting Around section for city transport to/from the stations.

At Almaty-II the advance ticket office is outside the main building on Tuzova; open daily 8 am to 8 pm. You can buy tickets for trains leaving from Almaty-I, too. Tickets on the day of departure are bought inside the station. Apart from fares to Moscow, foreigners now pay the same as locals for tickets. You'll be asked to show your passport when buying tickets.

Remember when booking tickets that train timetables are in *Moscow time*, three hours behind Almaty time.

All prices quoted below are for *kupe* (sleeper) tickets, and vary depending on the grade of train (2nd/1st). From Almaty-II there are trains at least once a day to Astana (US$19/28, 20½ hours), Aktöbe (US$29/41), Kostanay (US$29/38), Turkistan (US$15/22); Kyzylorda (US$18/27); Novosibirsk (US$46, 35 hours), Pavlodar (US$35), Petropavlovsk (US$23/35); Semey (US$16/23, 20 hours) Shymkent (US$30, 16 hours), Taraz (US$17, 14 hours), and Zashita (for Öskemen) (US$19); every two days to Atyrau (US$30), Moscow (US$220, 77 hours), Omsk (US$60) and Oral (US$35/49); and twice a week to Sverdlovsk (US$57).

From Almaty-I there are trains occasionally to Tashkent (US$40, 24 hours) and every two days to Kostanay.

Note that all trains for Shymkent and Tashkent also stop at Taraz; for Semey you can also take a Novokuznetsk, Novosibirsk, Krasnoyarsk or Irkutsk train.

To/From China The 2nd or soft-class *Genghis Khan Express* (No 13/14) covers 1359km between Almaty and Ürümqi. It takes about 40 hours (depending on your misadventures at the border crossing at Dostyk – see the Dostyk entry of the South-East Kazakstan section, later), with two nights aboard in either direction. There's no guarantee of a restaurant car so bring your own food and drink and share, as everyone else does.

Trains to Ürümqi leave Almaty-II about 8.10 pm (local time and 9.10 pm between 28 March and 30 August), stopping at Almaty-I about 8.45/9.45 pm, on Monday and Saturday only, but check this yourself. A kupe berth to Ürümqi is US$50 (46 hours). You have to show your passport and Chinese visa when buying the ticket as no visas are issued at the border. It is possible (but tricky) to get a Chinese visa in Almaty, but unreliable to get a Kazak visa in Ürümqi. Generally, you're better off arranging visas at home. See the Visas & Documents entry in the Facts for the Visitor section of this chapter.

Car Hiring a car and driver for inter-city travel is common practice in Kazakstan. It's quicker than buses and can be economical. The best place to find drivers (taxis or personal vehicles) looking for inter-city passengers is outside Sayran and Sayakhat bus stations. Choose your driver and car with care. The normal fare is four or five times the bus fare, *for the car*, so if the car is full each passenger pays only a little more than the bus fare. Some drivers may ask for more from foreigners but you should be able to bargain them down. Joining a car that already has some passengers should ensure that you pay the local price.

Some sample fares per car are Kapshaghay (US$6), Talgar (US$3), Charyn canyon (US$45), Medeu (US$5), Shymbulak (US$12), Taraz (US$150), Shymkent (US$200), Balkash (US$100) and Taldy-Korghan (US$30).

Another option, if your Russian is good, is looking in the weekly classified ads newspaper *Karavan* under *transportenay uslugi* for a driver and vehicle for hire.

Rental Hertz (☎ 30 80 40, fax 30 26 45) has an operation near the airport on Suyubai dangghyly. Avis (☎/fax 50 35 55, 63 43 03, ✉ avis@kaznet.kz) is based at the Regent Almaty. Avis has only two vehicles for rent: a Ford Explorer 4WD for US$210 per day with unlimited mileage, insurance and tax, and a Fiat Tempra sedan for US$114 per day.

Getting Around

Almaty has a vast network of bus, trolleybus and tram routes. They can get very crowded, so if you have baggage or are short of time, it's much simpler to take a taxi. On city-owned buses, trolleybuses and trams, the fare is 15 T, for privately-owned services (those beginning with a 5), 20 or 25 T – there's generally a sign at the front of the bus. If an attendant isn't collecting money from passengers, pay the driver as you get off.

To/From the Airport Buses No 92, 97, 439, 492 and 597 go frequently from outside the arrivals terminal to the City Air Terminal on Zheltoksan, then on down Zheltoksan to Abay, then west on Abay. Minibus 526 goes along Furmanov to al-Farabi. It's a 30 minute ride from the airport to the city terminal. Going out to the airport, these buses stop on Zheltoksan and Furmanov.

Lots of taxis wait outside the airport and drivers will approach you inside the building. If you don't want a taxi you'll have to be firm. If you do want a taxi, you'll need to bargain – US$4 to the city centre is standard.

To/From the Train Stations Trolleybus Nos 4, 5 and 6 run the full length of Abylay Khan, north-south through the city centre between Almaty-II train station and Abay, passing close to several hotels and other useful places. No 4 continues east along Abay and north up Dostyk, passing near KIMEP and the Dostyk and Kazakstan hotels on the way. From Almaty-I train station bus No 30 or 34 and trolleybus No 7 go all the way down Seyfullin to Kurmanghazy or beyond.

To/From Sayran Bus Station A taxi costs US$1.50 to or from the Sayran bus station. By public transport, often crowded, it's about half an hour to/from the city centre. Bus No 43, heading west on Töle Bi from the corner of Zheltoksan, goes to Sayran. So do trams No 4 or 7 heading west on Shevchenko anywhere between Konaev and Seyfullin. Heading into the city from the bus station, catch any of these outside the station on Töle Bi, going east. An equally slow alternative is trolleybus No 19, from Pushkin opposite Sayakhat bus station. Going into the city from the bus station, wait for this on Mate Zalki, across the street from the west side of the station.

To/From Sayakhat Bus Station Bus No 92 and 97 (see To/From the Airport) stop on Raiymbek in front of Sayakhat. Bus No 32, between Sayakhat and Zhandosova in the south-west of the city, runs the length of Zheltoksan between Raiymbek and Respublika alangy. Trolleybus No 19 also connects both bus stations.

Bus, Trolleybus & Tram Routes The following is a summary of useful routes, or sections of routes. All run in the opposite directions too. Those numbers with a '5' in front indicate the slightly more expensive privately run services.

Bus Nos 2, 100
    south on Furmanov from Gogol to Ramstor and beyond
Bus No 29
    south on Kaldayakov at Gogol, Bögenbay Batyr, south on Dostyk
Bus No 30
    Almaty-I station, Seyfullin prospektisi, Kurmanghazy, south on Baytursynuly
Bus No 32
    Sayakhat station, Raiymbek, Zheltoksan, Timiryazev and south on Zhandosova
Bus Nos 34, 434
    Almaty-I station, Seyfullin, west on Abay
Bus No 43
    Töle Bi from Zheltoksan to Sayran station
Bus No 61
    Furmanov from Vinogradov to Respublika alangy and beyond
Bus Nos 66
    Dostyk and Töle Bi, Abay, Zhandosova
Bus Nos 92, 492
    airport, Sayakhat bus station, City Air Terminal, Zheltoksan, west on Abay

Bus Nos 97
    airport, Sayakhat bus station, City Air Terminal, Abay prospektisi, south on Baytursynuly
Trolleybus No 1
    Central Park, Gogol, south on Auezov
Trolleybus No 2
    Gogol at Kaldayakov, Nauryzbay Batyr, west on Abay
Trolleybus No 4
    Almaty-II station, Abylay Khan, Abay, north on Dostyk
Trolleybus No 5, 6
    Almaty-II station, Abylay Khan, west on Abay and beyond
Trolleybus No 7
    Almaty-I station, Seyfullin to Kurmanghazy
Trolleybus No 9
    Pushkin opposite Sayakhat bus station, Gogol, Kaldayakov, Bögenbay Batyr, Dostyk, Kabanbay Batyr, Masanchi, south on Baytursynuly
Trolleybus No 11
    Dostyk at Bögenbay Batyr, Abay, south on Baytursynuly
Trolleybus No 12
    along Gogol from Central Park to Mukanov and beyond
Trolleybus No 16
    Central Park, Gogol, Zheltoksan, Abay, Baytursynuly, Satpaev, Zhandosova
Trolleybus No 19
    Pushkin opposite Sayakhat bus station, Gogol, Kaldayakov, Bögenbay Batyr, Dostyk, Abay, Sayran bus station
Tram No 1
    Makataev at the Zelyony Bazaar, Baytursynuly, Töle Bi
Tram Nos 4, 7
    Shevchenko from Konaev to Seyfullin, Sayran bus station

Taxi There are a lot of official taxis – marked with chequerboard logos or other obvious signs – but many private cars will also act as taxis. A ride in the centre of Almaty should cost around 100 T during the day, double at night. For longer distances you'll need to agree a price before getting in.

If you book a taxi (dial ☎ 58 and speak Russian or Kazak), there's usually an extra charge of about US$1. See the Local Transport section in the Getting Around the Region chapter, including tips on personal safety.

AROUND ALMATY

There are many good excursions to be made from Almaty, notably into the Zailiysky Alatau range along the Kyrgyzstan border, a northern spur of the Tian Shan with plenty of spectacular scenery and good walking and skiing. Easy day trips include Medeu, Shymbulak, Bolshoe Almatinskoe lake and Talgar. Given the deteriorating state of the roads as you travel east from Almaty it's better to consider destinations such as the Charyn canyon and the Karkara valley as overnight trips. These are listed in the South-East Kazakstan section. See also the map in that section.

Medeu & Shymbulak

These are Almaty's playgrounds in the foothills of the Zailiysky Alatau, both easily visited on a day trip from the city. If you want to get away from crowds come on a weekday.

Medeu is a somewhat scruffy scattering of buildings around the huge Medeu ice rink, 1700m high, about 15km south-east of central Almaty up the Malaya (Lesser) Almatinka canyon. Shymbulak at 2300m, is one of Central Asia's top skiing centres. Both are starting points for treks in the Zailiysky Alatau, and for good day hikes (see Travel Agencies in the previous Almaty section in this chapter for information on guided trips and the boxed text 'Hiking in the Malaya Almatinka Gorge').

Medeu is always several degrees cooler than Almaty, and Shymbulak is cooler still. If it's raining in the city, Medeu will probably have snow and zero visibility. Your Almaty hotel might call about conditions and what's open.

The 10,500 sq m **Medeu rink**, built in 1972, is made for speed skating and many champion Soviet skaters have trained here. It normally functions from about November to March and is open to the public on weekends (US$4). You can hire skates for about US$2 on the first floor outside the rink. Even when the rink is closed people come to relax at the shashlyk and drink stands, and to take a walk in the surrounding valleys and hills.

Hiking in the Malaya Almatinka Gorge

The farther away from Medeu you hike, the prettier the landscape becomes. *The Hiker's Guide to Almaty* (see Maps & Guides in the Almaty section) details 19 hikes starting in the Malaya Almatinka gorge. If you're heading high into the mountains make sure you have a good map and/or a guide. In winter and spring you'll need to watch out for avalanches. See the boxed text 'Trekking Warning' in the Zailiysky Alatau & Küngey Alatau section.

Medeu to Butakovka Trek

This trek through the wooded Komissarov (also called Kim-Asar) valley and over the 2200m Komissarov pass can be completed in half a day, or extended to a full day if you continue on the 2870m Butakovsky pass. From the Premier Medeu Hotel take the paved road heading up the left side of the gorge from the ice rink, towards the Kazak Aul restaurant. From here keep going along the road until you reach the track that heads past some buildings belonging to the forest service. The trail rises steeply to the first pass. From here you can either hike along the north ridge of the Komissarov spur back to Medeu, or head east through a forest leading to a narrow ravine. The trail forks in several places but all routes will eventually bring you the Butakovka gorge. From here you can continue up to the pass or down to the village, from where bus No 29 returns to Almaty.

Stage 1	Medeu to Komissarov pass	(2 hours)
Stage 2	Komissarov pass to Butakovka gorge	(2-3 hours)
Stage 3	Butakovka gorge to Butakovka pass	(4 hours)
Stage 4	Butakovka pass to Butakovka	(2-3 hours)

The **Voice of Asia pop festival** is held at Medeu usually in early August and attracts big-name groups from China, Central Asia, Russia and elsewhere – though few from Kazakstan. It lasts about four days.

What looks like a dam in the main valley above the ice rink (about 1km by road or 800-odd steps on foot) is actually there to stop avalanches and mud-slides. The road climbs a further 4.5km from this barrier to the surprisingly swish **Shymbulak ski resort**, with a vertical drop of 900m and a variety of runs for all levels of skier. New lifts were installed here in 1998 and the ski rental equipment, including snowboards, is also in good condition and costs around US$15 a day. A day lift-pass starts at around US$40 at the beginning and end of the season, with individual lift tickets at US$2. Since it takes three lifts to reach the Talgar Pass at around 3200m, a day pass makes sense if you're going to ski the whole mountain. The resort has a Web site at www.chimbulak.kz.

The skiing season here runs from December to April but it's usually best in January, February and early March. Like the ice rink at Medeu, the slopes get crowded at weekends. The chair lifts run daily in winter from about 10 am to 6 pm, but the highest one may close in March because of avalanche danger. In summer and autumn they run at weekends, though they sometimes close early and may not work during the week.

You can take walks from Shymbulak itself. A track continues 8km up the Malaya Almatinka valley and, in summer, it's a 3km hike up to the Talgar Pass (warning: there is year-round avalanche danger wherever you see snow). Pik Komsomola (4375m) rises 3km south, the nearest of a ring of glacier-flanked peaks around the top of the Malaya Almatinka valley, which are favourites with Almaty climbers.

Places to Stay All places to stay are open in summer; discounts may be possible during this season.

The best deal is the *Hotel Chimbulak* (☎ 3272-33 33 16, 33 86 24, fax 33 80 82, ✉ chimbulak@nursat.kz) at the foot of the Shymbulak chair lifts. Doubles with ensuite

are US$12, rising to US$40 for deluxe rooms, with a sitting room, TV and scary pink bedspreads. The resort also has several *cottages* away from the main complex, which can sleep up to eight people; all reachable by car. All come with cable TV, phone, bathroom and kitchen and cost US$60 per person.

Just below the ice rink is the big *Premier Medeu* (☎/fax 3272-50 20 07). It's been smartly, if unimaginatively renovated and the comfortable rooms with cable TV and phone are good value for singles/doubles at US$50/60. Check out the bearskins on the wall in the bar.

Places to Eat A real treat is the *Kazak Aul (Kazak Village)* (☎ 3272-50 75 24), a restaurant in several traditionally decorated yurts, a short walk or drive above the ice rink. Squatting around low tables, you can enjoy local specialities such as kazy and manty, dumplings stuffed with meat and pumpkin. If you book in advance, the noodle and meat national dish, besbarmak is available. For a full banquet expect to pay US$20 per head; a simple meal will be US$10.

Around the ice rink and up at Shymbulak the main food option is shashlyk. The outdoor terrace by the old lift base at Shymbulak serves better food than the main cafe at the ski resort. If you're planning a hike or intend camping, bring food with you.

Getting There & Away From Almaty, bus No 6 goes to Medeu every 40 minutes from opposite the Hotel Kazakstan on Dostyk. They return until 10 pm. A taxi should be US$6 or less, including the US$2 payable at a vehicle checkpoint a couple of kilometres before Medeu. At weekends during the ski season, some buses will continue up the gorge to from Medeu to Shymbulak – this road is sometimes closed after bad weather. At other times, take a taxi or walk (three to four hours).

Bolshoe Almatinskoe Lake Area

West of the Malaya Almatinka gorge lies its 'big sister' the Bolshaya Almatinka gorge, the entrance to which, Kokshoky, is about

15km from central Almaty. Here you'll find the artisan's village of Sheber Aul, Bolshoe Almatinskoe lake, the Tian Shan Astronomical Observatory and many good hikes. The same warnings about the weather apply as at Medeu and Shymbulak; for information on the weather and road conditions at the lake, call ☎ 3272-61 27 55 or 29 04 66.

The artisan's village of **Sheber Aul** is five minutes' walk from the Kokshoky bus stop, just behind the GES-2 hydroelectric station. It was founded in 1987 as part of a government program to develop traditional Kazak arts and crafts. Master artists from around the country were relocated here, but then left as the country became independent. Today, 50 families live in the village, making traditional crafts including leather, wood and metalwork, jewellery, textiles (felt rugs, weaving) and musical instruments.

In May 1999, thanks to sponsorship by Texaco and the US government, two workshops and a *chaykhana* (teahouse) with a crafts store were opened. Previously, the artists had worked out of trailers and their apartments. You can watch the craftsmen at work and buy their work, from a US$1000 suit of armour to cheaper traditional felt slippers and hats. The chaykhana serves Kazak dishes.

A four to five hour hike up the valley is the picturesque 1.6km long **Bolshoe Almatinskoe lake**, resting in a rocky bowl in the foothills of the Zailiysky Alatau at 2500m. This is the starting point for treks into the mountains and across to Lake Issyk-Kul in Kyrgyzstan (see the boxed text 'Trekking to Lake Issyk-Kul').

The route up to the lake is scenic, though part of the gorge is slightly disfigured by minor hydroelectric installations.

The lake is frozen from November to June and only takes on its famous turquoise tinge once the silt of summer meltwater has drained away. It's well known as a good bird-watching spot.

Just visible from the lake, at 2800m, is the outlandish **Tian Shan Astronomical Observatory**, sometimes still referred to by its Soviet-era acronym, GAISH. Several of the observatory's telescopes remain in use,

but others, looking like giant Death Rays from a Flash Gordon movie, are running to rust. It's possible to stay here and take tours of the working observatories for US$10.

At the head of the Zhusalykezen Pass (3336m), the **Kosmostantsia** is a group of wrecked buildings belonging to various Russian scientific research institutes. It's all but abandoned now, though some meteorological research is still carried out here.

Places to Stay *Tian Shan Astronomical Observatory* is the best place to stay. The rooms are cosy with heaters and although the water in the accommodation block is cold, an authentic wooden *banya* will be fired up in the evenings. Without food it's US$15 per person, but it's well worth paying the extra US$10 for meals, which are excellent. There are also dorms for US$7.50 without food, and a kitchen. To make bookings and to arrange transport, contact the head of the observatory Kenes Kuratov (work ☎ 3272-25 20 92, home ☎ 21 11 44). He speaks some English. Also see Travel Agencies in the Almaty section.

There is basic *cottage* accommodation (US$15) in the hamlet of Ozyorny beside Bolshoe Almatinskoe lake; look for the white roofed buildings. It's also possible to camp beside the lake.

Getting There & Away From Almaty, get any bus heading to Orbita I, II, III or IV (listed as the last stop on the bus sign); these buses can be caught heading south on Zheltoksan or on Zhandosova at Abay. Get off at the big roundabout at the intersection of Navoi and al-Farabi at the city's edge. Then take bus No 28, 93 or 136 to Kokshoky, about half an hour. The last bus back is at about 9.45 pm.

The Kokshoky bus stop, just past the GES-2 hydroelectric station, is at a fork where a sign points to Alma-Arasan (4km) in one direction, and Kosmostantsia (23km) in the other. Bus 93 continues to Alma-Arasan if you want to hike from there. Bolshoe Almatinskoe lake is about 16km up the Kosmostantsia road, a climb of about 1100m.

Treks around Bolshaya Almatinka

Below is one of the easiest one-day treks starting from the Bolshaya Almatinka river valley. This can be extended to a two or three day 35km circuit if you also take in the 3660m Almaty-Alagir pass.

More challenging routes link the 'Two Sisters' – the Bolyshaya Almatinka and Malaya Almatinka gorges. To go from Kokshoky to Shymbulak via the Lokomotiv glacier and Lokomotiv pass (grade 1B, 4050m), the Tuyuksu glacier and the Malaya Almatinka river, takes two or three days. See the boxed text 'Trekking Warning' in the Zailiysky Alatau & Küngey Alatau section.

Kokshoky to Alma-Arasan Trek

You can start from where the bus stops at GES-2 hydroelectric station, but time and effort will be saved by taking a taxi farther to GES-1, where the broad water pipe rises sharply up the gorge. Climb the metal steps beside this pipe and then walk along the top of it for the most direct route to Bolshoe Almatinskoe lake. The road is a more serpentine, 10km route to the same place. From the lake, follow the road uphill to the right, past the observatory and up to the Kosmostantsia at the head of the Zhusalykezen Pass (3336m). From here a trail runs to the 3681m summit of Pik Bolshoy Almatinsky, or you can skirt the mountain and follow the Prokhodnaya river gorge, which eventually leads to the Alma-Arasan Resort. From here, bus no 93 runs back to the city or you can continue walking to Kokshoky.

Stage 1	Kokshoky (GES-2) to GES-1	(1-2 hours)
Stage 2	GES-1 to Bolshoe Almatinskoe Lake	(2-3 hours)
Stage 3	Bolshoe Almatinskoe Lake to Kosmostantsia	(3 hours)
Stage 4	Kosmostantsia to Alma-Arasan	(4-5 hours)

Alternatively, taxis run from the corner of al-Farabi and Navoi; expect to pay US$5 for a whole car to the GES-1. It's possible to drive to the lake and even as far up as the Kosmostantsia, but the road may well be impassable after bad weather. A 4WD helps in any case, though locals do it without. The observatory can also arrange transport – see Places to Stay.

Talgar & Almatinsky Nature Reserve

The village of Talgar, 45km east of Almaty, is the gateway to the **Almatinsky Nature Reserve**, a rugged area of about 750 sq km, and an important habitat of the rare snow leopard. Other inhabitants include the *arkhar* (a big-horned wild sheep) and the goitred gazelle, known locally as the *zheyran*. The reserve contains Mt Talgar, the highest peak in the Zailiysky Alatau at 4979m, which takes experienced climbers three days to climb.

Although you're supposed to have special permits to enter the reserve, in practice,

arranging a trip here is simple. Buses run from Sayakhat bus station in Almaty (40 T) to Talgar, from where it's US$1 for a taxi to the reserve entrance and 100 T to get in. Trails are well marked. For organised tours try Gallactica Tours (☎ 61 38 33 and ask for Olga or Vika) or other operators – see Travel Agencies in the previous Almaty section.

South-East Kazakstan

This section contains overnight trips from Almaty and trekking information, including details of routes to Lake Issyk-Kul in Kyrgyzstan, which can be reached in as little as four days. You'll also find details of the road and rail crossings to China.

The region from Almaty to Lake Balkash is traditionally called Zhetisu meaning 'land of seven rivers'. There are actually over 800, many fed by glaciers in the Zailiysky and

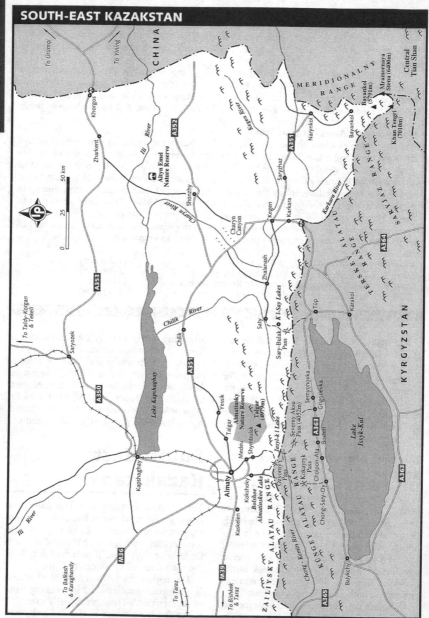

SOUTH-EAST KAZAKSTAN

C H I N A

To Ürümqi

To Yining

Khorgos

Zharkent

Ili River

A352

Altyn Emel
Nature Reserve

Shonzhy

Charyn River

50 km

25

0

A353

MERIDIONALNY RANGE

Mramornaya
Stena (6400m)

Central
Tian Shan

Narynkol

Bayankol

Bayankol

Khan Tengri
(7010m)

Sarybhaz

A351

SARYJAZ RANGE

Kegen

Karkara

Karkara River

A364

Charyn
Canyon

Zhalanash

TERSKEY ALATAU RANGE

To Taldy-Korgan
& Tekeli

Saryozek

Chilik   River

Chilik

A351

Saty

Sary-Bulak
Pass

K-I-Soy Lakes

Tüp

Karakol

K Y R G Y Z S T A N

Lake Kapshaghay

Yessik

Almatinsky
Nature Reserve

Talgar

Talgar
(4979m)

Semyonovka

Severny Aksu
Pass (4052m)

Grigorievka

A363

Bosteri

Talgar

Medeu

Shymbulak

Jasyk-I Lake

Ozyorny
Pass

A363

Kökaryyk
Pass

Cholpon-Ata

Lake
Issyk-Kul

A363

Kapshaghay

Kolchoky

Bolshoe
Almatinskoe Lake

Chong-Saty-Oy

Almaty

Kaskelen

Chong - Kemin River

KÜNGEY ALATAU RANGE

Balykchy

Ili   River

M36

M39

A365

To Balkash
& Karaghandy

To Bishkek
& Taraz

To Taraz

ZAILIYSKY ALATAU RANGE

Zhungar Alatau ranges, making it a rich area for agriculture. The largest river, the Ili, flows west out of China, forms Lake Kapshaghay reservoir near Almaty, then flows north into Lake Balkash. There are danger signs that Balkash may be suffering a similar fate to the Aral Sea (see the Aralsk section later in this chapter). Increased use of the Ili river for irrigation has led to a 1.5m drop in the water level, causing the coastline to recede and leave behind a salty strip of land as wide as 10km in some places.

ZAILIYSKY ALATAU & KÜNGEY ALATAU

The Zailiysky Alatau, and the Küngey Alatau further south of Almaty, are spurs of the Tian Shan running east-west between Almaty and Lake Issyk-Kul. Together with the Kyrgyz Alatau, which stretches from Taraz to Bishkek, they form the northern Tian Shan. South-west of Almaty the Kazakstan-Kyrgyzstan border runs along the Zailiysky Alatau ridgeline; eastward, it follows the Küngey Alatau ridgeline.

The mountains are high and beautiful, with many peaks over 4000m, lots of glaciers and wild rivers, and Tian Shan firs covering the steep valley sides. In summer the valleys are used as summer pasture and herders set up yurt camps. The summer snowline is around 3800 to 4100m. These mountains make for excellent trekking and there are dozens of trails of varying length and toughness, many starting from Medeu, Shymbulak, Kokshoky or Bolshoe Almatinskoe lake (see Around Almaty earlier), which are easily reached from Almaty. Some of the best-used trails go right across to Lake Issyk-Kul. Several travel agents (see the previous Almaty section) offer guided treks, with camping gear available.

Passes marked Unclassified (H/К) or 1A are simple, with slopes no steeper than 30° and glaciers, where they exist, are flat and without open crevasses. Grade 1B (1B) passes may have ice patches or glaciers with hidden crevasses and may require ropes. Passes of grade 2A and above may require special equipment and technical climbing skills. For a description of popular routes see the boxed text 'Trekking to Lake Issyk-Kul'.

Maps & Guides

The Hiker's Guide to Almaty (see Books & Maps in the previous Almaty section) has reasonable descriptions of many routes through the mountains.

The best Russian-language trekking maps are available in Almaty from JHER, in a seven storey building on the corner of Töle Bi and Baizakova, at US$8 per map. There may also be maps at the Akademkniga bookshops.

Most maps are 1:50,000 and called *Marshrutnaya Turistskaya Karta* (Tourist Route Map). The *Vysokogornye Perevaly Severnogo Tyan-Shanya* (High Mountain Passes of the Northern Tian Shan) map covers virtually the whole area between Almaty and Lake Issyk-Kul at 1:200,000 and grades all the passes in the region.

KÖL-SAY LAKES

These three pretty lakes lie amid the steep, forested foothills of the Küngey Alatau, 110km east of Almaty. With camping gear you can visit the lakes and trek or ride over to Lake Issyk-Kul, but be warned that if you plan on visiting independently by car a fee of at least US$20 is being charged. June to August are the best months, but as always be careful with the weather in the mountains.

Trekking Warning

It's feasible to trek unguided if you have suitable experience and equipment, but watch out for two things. One is the possibility of 'bandits' in the hills, who rob hikers especially when they are camped at night. The bigger hazard is the weather – be equipped for conditions to turn bad suddenly. The trekking season lasts from about mid-May to mid to late September; in July and August the weather should be OK, but outside those months it can often rain or even snow in the mountains when it's warm in Almaty. If you're caught unprepared by a sudden storm, it could be fatal.

Check what lies in store before embarking on any trek – some routes cross glaciers and tricky passes over 4000m high. When in doubt, use a guide.

KAZAKSTAN

Trekking to Lake Issyk-Kul

Before setting off on these treks make sure you have good maps and, better still, go with a guide. You will need to bring all food and camping equipment. The two most used routes run from Bolshoe Almatinskoe lake to Grigorievka on Lake Issyk-Kul, 35km east of Cholpon-Ata (or Semyonovka, 42km east of Cholpon-Ata); and from Kokshoky to Chong-Sary-Oy, on Lake Issyk-Kul 15km west of Cholpon-Ata. Routes also go via the Kol-Say lakes, east of Almaty.

The Bolshoe Almatinskoe lake-Grigorievka route and variations described here all pass through the Chong-Kemin valley, between the main ridges of the Zailiysky Alatau and Küngey Alatau, which is a summer pasture for yurt-dwellers. The glacial moraine lake Jasy-Köl towards the upper (eastern) end of the valley, at 3200m is one of the loveliest spots in these mountains. Times given here are for a fairly unstrenuous pace: one or two days can be cut off several routes if you wish.

Bolshoe Almatinskoe lake to Grigorievka

This route takes four to six days. From Bolshoe Almatinskoe lake (2500m), up the Ozyornaya river to the Ozyorny pass (3507m), on the Zailiysky Alatau main ridge. Down the Kol-Almaty river to the Chong-Kemin river (2800m). East up the Chong-Kemin valley to Jasy-Köl lake. Back west down the Chong-Kemin valley to the Aksu river. South up the Aksu river and the Vostochny (Eastern) Aksu glacier to the Severny (Northern) Aksu pass (4052m, on the Küngey Alatau main ridge). Eastward down to the Chong Aksu river, to the foot of Mt Autor Bashi. Finally follow the river eastward, then southward to Grigorievka.

Stage 1	Bolshoe Almatinskoe Lake to Ozyorny pass	(8-9 hours)
Stage 2	Ozyorny pass to Chong-Kemin river	(6 hours)
Stage 3	Chong-Kemin river to Aksu pass	(5-6 hours)
Stage 4	Aksu pass to foot of Autor Bashi	(6 hours)
Stage 5	Foot of Autor Bashi to Grigorievka	(8 hours)

Variation from Shymbulak

Three days can be added to the preceding route by going from Shymbulak, across Bolshoy Talgarsky pass (3160m) and down to the Levy Talgar river (2300m). South up the Levy Talgar river then west up the Turistov river to Turistov pass (3930m). South-west down the Kyzylsay river to the Ozyornaya river. Up the Ozyornaya river to Ozyorny pass then continue as on the preceding route.

Kokshoky to Chong-Sary-Oy

This is a more westerly route of about six days. From Kokshoky, head south through Alma-Arasan and up the Prokhodnaya river valley to the Almaty (Prokhodnoy) pass (3600m) on the Zailiysky Alatau main ridge. South past Primul lake below the pass and down the Almaty river to the Chong-Kemin river (2700m). West down the Chong-Kemin river then south up the Severnaya (Northern) Orto-Koy-Su river to the Kok-Ayryk pass (3889m), on the Küngey Alatau main ridge. South down the Yuzhnaya (Southern) Orto-Koy-Su river to Chong-Sary-Oy.

Stage 1	Kokshoky-Almaty pass	(8 hours)
Stage 2	Almaty pass to Chong-Kemin river	(8 hours)
Stage 3	Chong-Kemin river to Orto-Koy-Su river	(6 hours)
Stage 4	Orto-Koy-Su river to Kok-Ayryk pass	(6-7 hours)
Stage 5	Kok-Ayryk pass to Chong-Sary-Oy	(8 hours)

The lakes are strung along the Köl-Say (or Kolsai) river, about 1800 to 2200m high, south-west of the village of Saty on the bigger Chilik river. Saty is a five or six-hour bus ride from Almaty's Sayakhat bus station, across barren steppe via Chilik and Zhalanash. The road takes a very roundabout route (at least 250km, or 350km via Kegen). If there's no bus to Saty, get one to Zhalanash and hitch or catch a truck for the last 33km to Saty. Jibek Joly (see travel agencies in Almaty section) has wooden *guesthouses* both in Zhalanash and overlooking the Nizhny (Lower) Köl-Say lake, which is accessible by vehicle. Full board at either cottage is US$35 a day and the agency can also arrange horse riding and guides. Independently, you should be able to hire a horse and/or a guide in Saty for around US$20 per day.

From Saty it's about 15km to the 1km-long Nizhny Köl-Say lake at 1750m. The Sredny (Middle) Köl-Say lake, also called Minzhilka (Thousand Horses), is 9km away, a four hour steep hike rising to 2250m. The surrounding meadows are used as pasture and are a good camping spot. From the middle lake to the smaller Verkhny (Upper) Köl-Say lake at 2850m is about 4km and takes at least two hours.

The route over to Lake Issyk-Kul continues from here to the 3274m Saray-Bulak pass on the Küngey Alatau ridge (also the Kazakstan-Kyrgyzstan border), and descends to the village of Balbay (also called Saray-Bulak) on Issyk-Kul. By horse, this can be done in one day, on foot in two days. From the pass there are fine views north towards the Kazak steppe and south into the Issyk-Kul basin.

CHARYN CANYON

The Charyn river, flowing rapidly down from the Tian Shan, has carved a 150m to 300m deep canyon into the otherwise flat and barren steppe some 200km east of Almaty, and time has weathered this into all sorts of weird, wonderful and colourful rock formations. Although the canyon can be visited in a long day trip from Almaty, an overnight camping expedition is better, since the road there is in a shocking condi-

tion. It's too hot in summer; April to June or September to November are best.

The main *camp site* (around US$8 per tent) has toilets, but you must take all supplies and water with you, including fuel for cooking stoves, since there is little wood around.

To get here take a bus from Sayakhat bus station to Kegen or Narynkol. The buses cross the Charyn river just upstream from the canyon, which is as close as you can get by road. Travel agencies in Almaty arrange trips here, from at least US$25 per person. You can also hire a car from in front of Sayakhat bus station for around US$50.

KARKARA VALLEY

The valley of the Karkara river sweeping down northwards from the Central Tian Shan is an age-old summer pasture for herds from both sides of what's now the Kazakstan-Kyrgyzstan border. The river forms the border for some 40km before heading north to join the Kegen river, beyond which it becomes the Charyn. In its lower reaches the Karkara valley is up to 40km wide, a broad green expanse filled with wildflowers and grazing herds in summer.

From Kegen, 250km of bleak steppe by road from Almaty, a rough but scenic road heads south up the valley to the settlement of Karkara, then across the border into Kyrgyzstan about 28km from Kegen. There are said to be Scythian (Saka) burial mounds between Kegen and the border. The road then veers west towards Tüp and Lake Issyk-Kul.

Border formalities take place at Kegen. Travellers have reported being fined heading into Kazakstan without a valid Kazak visa, though there doesn't seem to be a problem heading into Kyrgyzstan without a Kyrgyz visa. Still, you are better off getting a visa in Almaty.

Depending on the strength of the local economy, the *chabana* (cowboy) festival, a bazar and 'rodeo' of local sports such as *kökpar* (traditional polo played with a goat carcass) and *kyz kuu* (where a man chases a woman on horseback) is held around 15 to 20 June. It brings together Kazaks and Kyrgyz in a reminder of the valley's historic role as a meeting place of nomads and Silk

Road traders. The location of the festival apparently changes from year to year, and the exact dates depend on weather, work requirements, etc. See Lake Issyk-Kul & the Central Tian Shan in the Kyrgyzstan chapter for more on the Issyk-Kul region, the Karkara valley and the festival.

The Almaty mountaineering and trekking companies Kan Tengri and Asia Tourism both maintain base camps on the Kazak side of the Karkara river. Kan Tengri's is about 35km south of Kegen, at 2200m. Accommodation is in yurts and tents and there is a bar and a sauna too. From here climbers go by helicopter to mountain base camps in the Central Tian Shan. See the Central Tian Shan section of the Kyrgyzstan chapter for details.

Though there are no buses taking this cross-border route, in summer you could take a Kegen, Saryzhaz or Narynkol bus from Almaty's Sayakhat bus station to Kegen, then hitch south from there – though traffic is thin. On the Kyrgyzstan side, the valley is an easy hitch from Tüp or Karakol. A taxi from Karakol to the border would be about US$40.

LAKE KAPSHAGHAY & THE ILI RIVER

Lake Kapshaghay is a 100km long reservoir formed by a dam on the Ili river near the town of Kapshaghay, 60km north of Almaty. Many Almaty residents have dachas (holiday bungalows) here and the lake has cold, fresh water. Its best beaches are on the north shore just past the dam.

The **Ili river** flows west out of China into the lake, then north-west to Lake Balkash. As it approaches the southern end of Lake Balkash, the Ili enters a delta wetland region of many lakes, marshes and thick, jungle-like vegetation. The river is navigable by kayak all the way from lake to lake (around 460km), and by raft at least some of the way. See the Travel Agencies entry in the previous Almaty section for companies running trips to the river. These trips usually include a visit to the **Tamgaly-Tas petroglyphs**, about 20km downstream from Lake Kapshaghay. Some of these thousand or more rock drawings are very old. Many depict deer and hunters, but there's also a large image of the Buddha or Shiva (depending who you believe), which probably dates from at least the 8th century CE when Chinese influence in Central Asia ended.

Kapshaghay is on the route of trains and buses between Almaty and Zharkent, Taldy-Korghan, Aktogay or Semey. There are also hourly buses to Kapshaghay from Almaty's Sayakhat bus station. A taxi from Almaty to the beaches will cost around US$9. The few small settlements along the Ili river are linked by road to Kapshaghay and/or to the Almaty-Karaghandy road.

ALTYN-EMEL NATIONAL PARK

Visited mainly for its prime attraction, the Singing Sands, the Altyn-Emel National Park is 35km east of Lake Kapshaghay. The sand dunes, as tall as 80m, make a low hum like an aeroplane engine whenever the wind picks up. The park is a habitat for wild donkeys, antelope, camels and a number of predatory birds, including golden eagles. Local legend attributes the name Altyn-Emel (Golden Horseshoe) to Jenghiz Khan: when he passed through here, his horse lost a gold horseshoe in the sand. He suspected his soldiers of theft, and reputedly killed every tenth man.

Entrance fees to the park vary widely; whoever is at the gate decides how much to charge that day, which could be as much as US$21 for the first day and $10 for additional days.

Because the park is remote and not easily accessible, the easiest way to get there is through an Almaty travel agent or, more cheaply, by hiring a taxi and a local guide.

TALDY-KORGHAN
☎ 32822 • pop 118,000
From this sleepy, mixed Russian-Kazak town (Russian: Taldy-Kurgan), 265km north-east of Almaty, you can reach the rarely visited Zhungar Alatau mountains along the Chinese border to the east, as well as scenic Lake Alakol and the southern shore of Lake Balkash.

Orientation & Information
The main street, Lenin (renamed Tauelsizdik, but rarely used by locals), runs east-

west from the Karatal river at the east end of the centre to a roundabout at the west end. Tölebaev (International) runs one block south of Lenin, Kabanbay (Octyabr) one block north. The main north-south streets, starting from the river, are Abylay Khan, Abay, Akinsara and Shevchenko. OVIR is on Abylay Khan and the corner of Tauelsizdik.

You'll find moneychangers in the bazar at the corner of Kabanbay and Birzhansau, open 9 am to 5 pm, closed Mondays. The post and telephone offices, open 8 am to 6 pm, are on Akinsara, west of the square on Lenin.

The Taldy-Korghan Business Center (☎/fax 712 34, ✉ laz@nursat.kz) at Birzhansau 102, promotes tourism in the region, among many other activities. For US$10 they will write an invitation and arrange the proper papers necessary for trekking in the Zhungar Alatau. They can also arrange for a jeep or horses and guide. Email is available at the business centre or the Internet cafe at the Astana restaurant on Tölebaev east of Ablai Khan.

Things to See & Do

The **City Museum of Regional Studies** at Abay 245, features Kazak traditions and a display of the region's flora and fauna, including Red Book species.

Around the corner at Lenin 1 is a **museum** in the house of the Soviet-era Kazak writer Ilyas Zhansugurov.

Club Shagan, a 10 minute ride from the city centre, is popular with young locals. From Lenin, take bus 5, 8, 17 or 23 west 4km to the Third Mikrorayon (microregion). Entrance is around US$1 and you can play billiards and eat here, too.

Places to Stay & Eat

Hotel Taldy-Korghan on Akinsara (☎ 423 96, Tölebaev 134) is the only hotel in town, with singles for US$5.50, doubles US$7.50 and deluxe rooms for US$16 (but avoid the dire restaurant). The business centre has information on guesthouses and can also arrange an *apartment* for US$10-50 per person per night, with meals.

The small *delicatessen* on Shevchenko and Kabanbay has excellent salads, cakes

and pies; you can eat for US$2.50. Across the street is *Choson (Shevchenko 121)*, where tasty Korean meals are US$4. *B&W* is a grill bar on the corner of Birzhansau and Kabanbai known for its chicken dishes. *Zhetisu* on Lenin near Birzhansau has decent local dishes for about US$6 a meal. *Astana* on Tölebaev east of Ablay Khan has similar fare but is more upscale.

Getting There & Away

Taldy-Korghan is on the main road from Almaty to north-east Kazakstan, but off the Turksib railway. Buses run about every two hours to Almaty (US$3, 265km, six hours). A taxi takes about four hours and costs around US$5 per passenger.

There is an occasional train service on the spur line linking Taldy-Korghan to Ushtobe, the nearest station on the Turksib, however buses are more frequent. Buses also serve Tekeli, Sarkand on the northern edge of the Zhungar Alatau and Ucharal, near Lake Alakol. It's 45km to Ushtobe and 35km to Tekeli. A taxi to either place costs less than US$1 and takes 40 minutes.

Taldy-Korghan's bus and train stations are at the end of Shevchenko, six blocks south of Lenin. Long distance taxis wait along the last two blocks of Shevchenko.

AROUND TALDY-KORGHAN

You'll need to pass through the border control post 2km north-east of the small town of **Tekeli**, 45km east of Taldy-Korghan, to trek in the Zhungar Alatau mountains. This mountain range, which forms the Kazak-Chinese border from Zharkent to Druzhba, has peaks over 4000m, heavily forested in birch and fir and covered with wildflowers in summer. Cold, steep rivers flow through the valleys and, unlike near Almaty, the range's isolation means you can hike for days without seeing crowds, vehicles or broken beer bottles.

From Tekeli you can hike on a dirt road 47km up the torrential Kara river to an impressive 60m **waterfall**. The head of the valley, 14km further on, is at 3000m and surrounded by glacier-covered peaks. There are numerous good **camping** spots, and the water in the creeks is safe to drink.

Horses can be rented at the Ninth Homestead (Devyati Passik) farm, about 20km up the valley from Tekeli, for US$5 per day. Beyond this farm (15km), a footbridge across the river is the trailhead for a trek up to the Bessonov glacier, a steep day hike. The trekking map *Po Dzhungarskomu Alatau Marshrut No 1*, available in Almaty, is useful.

Most of the **Zhungar Alatau** lie in a restricted border zone and you'll need written permission to visit here, although, as one local put it, 'the restrictions have changed before, and could change again tomorrow'. You must first register with OVIR in Taldy-Korghan, then visit the border control post in Tekeli with an invitation listing your full name, passport number, date of birth and reason for going (tourism). The permit costs under US$1, but getting it is a bureaucratic and laborious process. The Taldy-Korghan Business Center can pull strings to get it sorted out quickly for US$10.

Lake Alakol, a 90km-long saltwater lake named for its shores of black stone, is at the north-east end of the Zhungar Alatau. Fierce winds blow almost constantly from China, through a low pass between mountain ranges called the Zhungar Gates. The Almaty-Ürümqi train line runs through this pass.

From the town of **Koktuma**, which is on the southern shore of the lake, you can hire a motorboat and driver to go to 8km long Bird Island (Ptichiye Ostrov), where you might be able to see flocks of flamingos as well as 40 other species of bird. The uninhabited island takes 2½ to four hours to reach by boat, depending on winds. Lake Alakol's north end is connected to the smaller freshwater **Sasykkol Lake**. July and August is the best time to visit Alakol, when the winds are at their minimum. You can reach Koktuma by bus from Taldy-Korghan, or by train on the Almaty-Ürümqi line.

Lake Balkash is Asia's fourth largest lake at 17,400 sq km, but very shallow – only 26m at its deepest point. Its eastern half is salty, its western half fresh water. Pollution from copper smelters set up on its shores in the 1930s has diminished lake life, though it still supports a fishing industry.

The largest lakeside town of **Balkash** on the northern side is a dying industrial city. If you want to visit the lake, nicer places are found on its southern shore, accessible from Taldy-Korghan. The Karatal river has excellent fishing, especially in the remote region where it flows into Lake Balkash. You can get there from Ushtobe by taxi. At the eastern end of the lake, north of the small town of **Lepsy**, are wide empty beaches and a lake bottom so gradual that you can walk a kilometre out into the water. Lepsy can be reached via train or by northbound bus from Taldy-Korghan in three hours.

ZHARKENT

See the Getting There & Away entry in the previous Almaty section for the bus journey to China through Zharkent and Khorgos.

Zharkent (formerly called Panfilov), 340km north-east of Almaty on the northern fringe of the Ili river valley, is the last real town in Kazakstan on the bus route to China. It has a substantial Uyghur population. Its limited attractions include the **Yuldashev mosque**, named for the Uyghur migrant who initiated it. Like Almaty's Zenkov Cathedral, the mosque is built without nails, but the curious design incorporates a minaret in the form of a Chinese pagoda beside a more conventional Central Asian dome, with gates in the style of the Timurid epoch; adding to the cross-cultural symbolism, the mosque's ground floor windows look Russian.

Be ready for a local scam known as the 'Zharkent Free Trade Zone'. At a checkpoint a few kilometres before the town, all non-Kazak passengers, traders or not, must pay a 'fee'. Non-CIS travellers have been asked for US$10 or more, though you might persuade them to accept the CIS rate (around US$1) on the grounds that you're only passing through. There doesn't seem to be any way to avoid this municipally sanctioned highway robbery.

KHORGOS

See the Getting There & Away entry in the previous Almaty section for the bus journey to China through Zharkent and Khorgos.

The Kazak customs and immigration post, a foreign-exchange bank and the tiny, cheap *Khorgos Hotel* are at Khorgos, 40km east of Zharkent and about 4km west of the border. Taxis can go no further than Khorgos.

Be ready for tedious border formalities; the crossing is usually crammed with Kazak and Uyghur families and traders who can cross more easily than foreigners, but seem to have about 10 times as much baggage. You may also encounter Russian or Kazak officials looking for bribes or goodies, though travellers report few hassles in comparison with the train crossing (see the Getting There & Away entry in the previous Almaty section).

DOSTYK

See the Getting There & Away entry in the previous Almaty section for the train journey to China through Dostyk.

Like its widely used Russian name, Druzhba, Dostyk means 'friendship'. There is almost nothing here except border facilities and a local train station.

Border procedures take roughly eight hours (bogey changing and general waiting around). There are apparently no toilet facilities during the custom checks but at other times you can pop out and use the station toilet. Toilets are unlocked for the 10-minute dash between the Kazakstan and China posts, so get in line early!

Kazak customs officials at Dostyk have long been infamous for their rampant corruption and pilfering of travellers' goods, but recent reports suggest that things have improved. Still, you should be prepared. Have your papers in order, be deadly accurate on your customs form, and hang in there. Lying about your cash probably won't work because they want to see everything. One trick, however, is to carry mostly travellers cheques and next to nothing in cash (you can exchange cheques in both Ürümqi and Almaty), since officials haven't the first idea what to do with travellers cheques.

Officials at Alashankou on the Chinese side can be maddeningly thorough, but they are honest. Travellers report no such serious hassles on either side on the bus journey.

South Kazakstan

South Kazakstan, the region from Kyrgyzstan's western border to the Aral Sea, is the most Kazak part of Kazakstan. Kazaks form a higher percentage of the population here than almost anywhere else. The two main cities, Shymkent and Taraz, saw some of the worst of the December 1986 riots (after the Kazak Dinmukhamed Konaev was replaced by a Russian as head of the CPK), and both were under martial law for a year afterwards. Some anti-Russian sentiment remains today.

This is an arid region of deserts and barren steppe, dissected by the Syr-Darya but with only pockets of cultivation. You'll cross it if you travel by land between Tashkent and Almaty, or by rail between Moscow and Tashkent, Almaty or Bishkek. The chief reasons to stop lie in the mountainous Aksu-Zhabaghly Nature Reserve on the region's southern fringe, best reached from Shymkent, or the great 14th century mausoleum of the Sufi poet and teacher Kozha Akhmed Yasaui at Turkistan. Travellers in search of utter desolation may also want to aim for Aralsk to witness the effects of the region's biggest environmental disaster, the draining of the Aral Sea.

TARAZ
☎ 32622 • pop 310,000

Taraz (formerly Zhambyl) is renowned as the place where Kazakstan's favourite brand of vodka is produced, but it's mostly of interest to travellers as a possible jumping off point for side trips (see Around Taraz).

Evidence of the town's past as a 6th century Silk Road settlement was discovered in 1938. In the 11th century it was a capital of the Turkic (and Islamic) Karakhan state which also ruled Bukhara for a while. Levelled by Jenghiz Khan, it only rose again 600 years later, under the name Aulie-Ata (Holy Father), as a northern frontier fort of the Kokand khanate. It fell to the Russians in 1864. The whole town seems to have been demolished and rebuilt in Soviet times, when the town was renamed after the Kazak bard Zhambyl Zhabayev, who was born here.

Taraz is ringed by ugly, defunct phosphate factories. Now they're closed it's a much less polluted place than it once was.

Orientation & Information

The meeting of east-west Töle Bi with north-south Abay is the centre of town. West from here a government and ceremonial square, still called ploshchad Lenina, stretches along Töle Bi. East of Abay is Lenina park, which has a stadium in one corner and some shabby buildings and disused funfair rides.

There are exchange kiosks all around town, with one in the Kazaktelekom office on the corner of Töle Bi and Abay. Here you'll also find Internet access, Monday to Friday 9 am to 6 pm, at 300 T per hour. The main post office is on Töle Bi just west of Zhambyl.

Things to See

The **History Museum**, facing ploshchad Lenina and open Monday to Saturday 9 am to 1 pm and 2 to 6 pm, has some worthwhile exhibits. The tableaux of models recreating scenes from the past are excellent. There's the usual colourfully decorated yurt and, more intriguingly, a collection of ancient stone statues *(balbals)* in a courtyard between the main building and a hall containing artefacts from an 11th century bathhouse and aqueduct unearthed near the present bazar. The museum runs an **art gallery** with changing exhibitions just off Abay beside the Akim, the local government office.

Two small mausolea in a wooded park near the town centre, both 20th century reconstructions, are worth a look. The **Karakhan mausoleum** marks the grave of an 11th century Karakhan potentate. It does recycle a few old bricks. Nearby, the **Dauitbek mausoleum** was for a 13th century Mongol viceroy, and is said to have been built lopsided in revenge for the man's infamous cruelty. It's a place of worship now, with a shrouded tomb and carpets inside.

Park Ryskulbekova, a block west along Töle Bi from Abay is prettier than Park Lenina. There's a small, almost disguised mosque near the central bazar, and a new Russian Orthodox church on Töle Bi just west of Zhambyl.

Places to Stay & Eat

Hotel Zhambyl (☎ 425 52, Töle Bi 42), has adequate single/doubles with bathroom, phone, TV and fridge for US$16/28. Its clean, economical restaurant is also a good bet, serving a mixture of Kazak and Russian food (US$5).

Less conveniently located for the centre, the *Hotel Taraz* (☎ 334 91, Zhambyl 75) is near the corner of Sukhe-Bator. Basic rooms start at US$10 but ones with TV, fridge and phone are US$20. The staff are friendly and there's a restaurant. Buses No 10, 26 or 29 pass by.

Opposite the Hotel Zhambyl is *Oral*, a cheap cafe which also serves shashlyk. For a fancier meal, at around US$10, head towards the train station south along Abay to *Jasmine* (☎ 46 96 6), an upmarket Chinese restaurant on Baizakova, where dishes can be ordered in small, medium or large portions.

There are shashlyk stalls and lots of fruit and vegetables at the sprawling central *bazar* on Töle Bi and east of Park Lenina. Bus No 2 or 16 and trolleybus No 3, 4 or 5 run along Töle Bi from the park.

Getting There & Around

Taraz's airport, several kilometres west of town off the Shymkent road, is now only occasionally used for charter flights.

To get around this part of Kazakstan, buses are far cheaper, more frequent and faster than the train. From the bus station on Zhambyl, about 4km north-east of the centre, buses go three or four times daily to Almaty (US$6, 10 hours) and Bishkek (US$5, seven hours), at least seven times daily to Shymkent (US$2.50, four hours) and Tashkent (US$5, six hours). All Tashkent buses stop at Shymkent too. Marshrutnoe minibuses and taxis to Almaty, Shymkent and Bishkek also wait outside the bus and train station, on Baluan Shcholak about 4km south of the centre. Trains stop here daily to/from Almaty, Shymkent, Bishkek, Tashkent, Aktöbe and Moscow; and Semey, Karaghandy and Akmola on most days.

Since you'll have to take two buses (one along Zhambyl to the stop just before Töle Bi, then bus No 2 or 16 or any trolleybus running east) from the bus station to reach the town centre, you'd be better off hopping in a taxi (US$1).

Trolleybus No 4 or 6 from the train station run into the centre along Abay. Heading to the station, catch them on Abay south of Kazybek Bi.

AROUND TARAZ

Taraz can be used as a jumping off point from which to explore the Talassky Alatau range spanning the Kazak-Kyrgyz border and the Aksu-Zhabaghly Nature Reserve.

Aysha-Bibi & Babazhi Katun Mausolea

Near Aysha-Bibi village (formerly Golovachovka), 20km west of Taraz, are the tombs of two Karakhan women, though little else is known about them. The 12th century mausoleum of Aysha-Bibi (one wall) is probably the only authentically old building around Taraz. Made of splendid, delicate terracotta bricks in over 50 different motifs, it looks almost weightless. A Muslim shrine for centuries, it was damaged by the removal of bricks in Soviet times but later restored. It now stands in a glass box to ward off the corrosive air. Beside it is a recent reconstruction of the 11th century **tomb** of one Babazhi Katun, with a pointed, fluted roof.

Aysha-Bibi village is on the Shymkent road from Taraz. A sign points to the mausolea, about 1km south from the main road in the village. Shymkent or Tashkent buses will take you to Aysha-Bibi or you can hire a taxi in Taraz.

SHYMKENT

☎ 3252 • pop 400,000

South Kazakstan's most vibrant town, with a booming bazar, Shymkent is mostly of interest only as a jumping-off point for other places (Turkistan, Otyrar, and the Aksu-Zhabaghly Nature Reserve). The city's past reads like Taraz's – the Mongols razed a minor Silk Road stop here; the Kokand khanate built a frontier fort in the 19th century, Russia took it in 1864, and the whole place was rebuilt in Soviet times. These days the lead mining that used to keep the

economy ticking over has been replaced by a factory producing biscuits and chocolates.

Orientation & Information

The main central streets are north-south Kazybek Bi (formerly Sovietskaya) and east-west Turkistan and Tauke Khan (formerly prospekt Lenina). The bus and train stations are both a short ride by bus south of the MiG fighter plane, a monument to WWII pilots who trained at Shymkent.

There are exchange kiosks along Tauke Khan and Kazybek Bi and in the TsUM department store at the corner of Kunaev and Tauke Khan. There's also a cash machine for visa cards outside the museum on Kazybek Bi. Western Union transfers can be arranged through Centre Credit Bank (☎ 53 24 52) at Konaev 13.

The main post office is at Kazybek Bi 24, on the corner of Turkistan. There's a long-distance phone office opposite the post office and on Tauke Khan, opposite Karl Marx. Internet access at US$4 per hour is available in room 4 at the library on Baytursynov and open daily 9 am to 7 pm.

To arrange trips around the area, including to the Aksu-Zhabaghly Nature Reserve, Turkistan and Otyrar, contact the tour company Altex (☎ 52 54 36, fax 62 19 72) run by Shamil Rafikov, who speaks some English. ACS Travel Agency, based in Almaty, also have a branch at Turkestanskaya 2/2 (☎ 53 48 51, 53 49 52, fax 53 51 26).

Things to See & Do

The **Regional Studies & History Museum** on Kazybek Bi has dusty exhibits that may be of interest, including material on old Otyrar, a yurt, some fine old carpets, jewellery and costumes, and a nature section with a grinning stuffed wolf and some information on Aksu-Zhabaghly Nature Reserve. It's open Tuesday to Sunday, 10 am to 6 pm.

More entertaining is the big, bustling **bazar** sprawling around Titov and open daily from 8 am to 8 pm. Among the fresh produce, tins of imported food and household goods, cheap clothes, mechanical spare parts and spices, you can find some gaudy traditional skullcaps and coats, or a rather

KAZAKSTAN

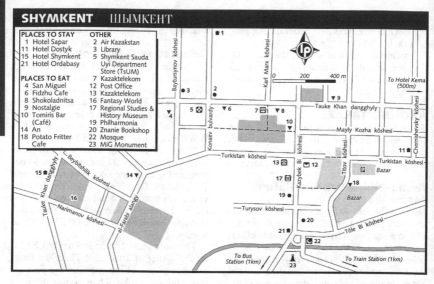

SHYMKENT ШЫМКЕНТ

PLACES TO STAY
1   Hotel Sapar
11 Hotel Dostyk
15 Hotel Shymkent
21 Hotel Ordabasy

PLACES TO EAT
4   San Miguel
6   Fidzhu Cafe
8   Shokoladnitsa
9   Nostalgie
10 Tomiris Bar
    (Café)
14 An
18 Potato Fritter
    Cafe

OTHER
2   Air Kazakstan
3   Library
5   Shymkent Sauda
    Uyi Department
    Store (TsUM)
7   Kazaktelekom
12 Post Office
13 Kazaktelekom
16 Fantasy World
17 Regional Studies &
    History Museum
19 Philharmonia
20 Znanie Bookshop
22 Mosque
23 MiG Monument

less portable wooden chest with colourful stamped tin decoration.

Shymkent also has a small **Fantasy World**, one in the chain of humble amusement parks that have sprung up around Kazakstan. It's on Tauke Khan opposite the Hotel Shymkent and open Monday to Friday 1 pm to 10 pm and Saturday and Sunday 3 pm to 11 pm.

Places to Stay

There are some nicely renovated rooms at the airy *Hotel Ordabasy* (☎ 53 64 21, *Kazybek Bi 1*), from US$10 to US$20 for a single, US$28 a double, with breakfast. The main problem is the noise from the traffic and the mosque across the road.

Hotel Dostyk (☎ 44 68 49), on the corner of Chernishevsky and Turkistan, is on a more peaceful, leafy back street and has friendly staff, but its rooms are shabbier, the hot water is likely to be limited to a couple of hours at night and it's a haunt of prostitutes. Singles/doubles are US$8/17.

Hotel Shymkent (☎ 21 55 41), on Tauke Khan, languishes from neglect west of the centre. Tatty rooms with bathroom, but no hot water, are US$12/16. Take bus No 16 from the bus station.

The best upmarket place is the modern *Hotel Kema* (☎ 23 79 23, *Tauke Khan 93A*), east of the centre. Newly furnished rooms with TV, phone and ensuite are US$64.

If you need lots of space, the *Hotel Sapar* (☎/fax 53 51 31, *Konaev 17*, @ sapar-shm@ nursat.kz) has suites of rooms only starting at US$135. The receptionists speak English.

Places to Eat

Among the several private restaurants that have sprung up along Tauke Khan, *Nostalgie* is one of the best, a convivial place, serving salads, chicken and beef dishes at around US$5 a meal. Further west is *Shokoladnitsa* a tiny Viennese-style cake and coffee shop, selling very tempting confections.

There are cheap cafes in the old TsUM building, and continuing west along Tauke Khan, you'll find *Fidzhu*, with a mixture of European and Chinese dishes at around US$3 a meal. More expensive is *San Miguel*, on Baytursynov – a convincing Mexican-style cantina, offering chilli, *buritos*, *quesedillas* and *fajitas* as well as Mexican beer and tequila.

Shashlyk stands abound in the spring and summer. At the entrance to the park on

Kazybek Bi, is the **Tomiris Bar** serving a 'gamburger' – tasty roll filled with charcoal grilled beef. There're outdoor karaoke performances here, too.

On the corner of al-Farabi and Momyshuly, **An** also has outdoor tables and serves excellent shashlyk, plov and laghman for less than US$2.

There's a *cafe* selling good potato fritters *(pirozhki s kartoshkami)* on Titov beside the steps leading to the upper half of the bazar. Here you'll also find plenty of fruit, vegetables and bread for picnics.

Getting There & Away
Between Shymkent and Tashkent bus is much quicker than train, as the latter goes round by Arys, the junction of the Tashkent-Moscow and Almaty-Moscow lines, 70km west of Shymkent.

There have been highway hold-ups on the Shymkent-Tashkent road, and north of the airport turn-off on the Turkistan road. Locals say it's safer to go by bus than by car, and safer in a local car than an expensive foreign one.

Taxis to Tashkent, Taraz and other places can be found at both the train and bus stations.

Border controls on the crossing to/from Tashkent have tightened, especially since terrorist bombings in Tashkent in 1999.

Air Tickets are sold at the Air Kazakstan office on the corner of Tauke Khan and Konaev, open daily 9 am to 7 pm. Scheduled flights include Almaty daily (US$80); Astana twice a week (US$100); and Moscow three times a week (US$159). There may also be flights to St Petersburg in the summer, and charter flights to Pavlodar and Kostanay.

Bus The bus station is about 1km south of the Hotel Ordabasy. Many buses from here are in transit, with tickets not usually sold till the bus has arrived; to reduce anxiety try to pick a bus that starts here. Buses for Tashkent may also wait outside the train station when trains arrive from Almaty or Bishkek.

Scheduled departures from the bus station include Almaty (US$8, 13 hours) and Bishkek (US$5, 11 hours), each with around 10 departures daily, most in transit; Tashkent (US$1.50, three hours) with 30 daily buses starting here; Turkistan (US$2.50, 3½ hours, nine daily); and Taraz (US$2.50, four hours, 11 daily).

A fleet of overnight buses also depart Monday to Saturday at 4 pm for the outskirts of Almaty from the car park beneath the MiG monument at the end of Kazybek Bi. The fare is US$6.50 and you'll be riding alongside the market traders who shuttle between Shymkent's bazar and the one held at Barakholka in Almaty.

Train The train station is at the end of Kabanbay Batyr in the south-east of town. Trains go several times a day to/from Turkistan, Aktöbe, Taraz (about five hours), Almaty (18 hours), Bishkek, Tashkent (six hours) and Moscow (60 hours); Semey, Karaghandy and Astana most days.

Getting Around
From the airport, about 12km north of Shymkent, bus No 12 goes occasionally to/from the Air Kazakstan ticket office. Going to the airport, catch it as it heads north on Konaev outside the office. A taxi is about US$5.

Bus No 2 from in front of the Hotel Ordabasy goes to the train station, then the bus station, then back to the Ordabasy. From the same stop, trolleybus No 6 goes to the train station and back, and bus No 9 or 16 and marshrutnoe taxi No 14 go to the bus station and back (bus No 16 also serves the Shymkent hotel). Bus No 2 or 6 runs from the train station to the bus station.

AROUND SHYMKENT
Sayram
About 10km east of Shymkent, Sayram is one of the oldest settlements in Kazakstan, reckoned to date back 2000 years. There's little to show for this, but it's a pleasant country town, mainly of interest as the birthplace of Kozha Akhmed Yasaui (see the following Turkistan section in this chapter) and can be visited en route to the Aksu-Zhabagly Nature Reserve. You can see three small 14th century **mausoleums** for Kozha's sons and

his mother, the later being a miniature copy of the holy man's own resting place in Turkistan. Regular buses run to Sayram from Shymkent – get off when you see the blue dome of a modern mosque at the cross roads with a small bazar. Kozha's mother's mausoleum is around 1km in the opposite direction from the mosque.

Aksu-Zhabaghly Nature Reserve

This beautiful 750 sq km patch of foothills and mountains in the Talassky Alatau range of the western Tian Shan is the longest established and one of the easiest visited of Kazakstan's nature reserves. It's promoted as the home of the tulip, and in May its alpine meadows are dotted with the wild crimson and yellow Grieg's Tulip. This is also one of only two places in Kazakstan where you can see the native Archa pine trees.

Getting into the reserve independently is tricky, making it essential that you go through a tour agent. Guided hikes or horseback trips and nights at huts in the reserve can be arranged either through agents in Almaty (see the Travel Agents entry of the previous Almaty section in this chapter), Altex in Shymkent (see the Information entry in the Shymkent section) or Zhenia and Lyuda in the village of Zhabagly (see the following Places to Stay entry in this section). May to October is the best time to visit.

The reserve stretches towards the border with Kyrgyzstan, and rises from about 1000m to over 4000m. The most dramatic scenery is on the west side; to visit this area you'll need to contact Altex, who run the camp there. From here it's possible to take a long day hike to two small lakes at 2000m, go in search of ancient petroglyphs, or tackle the more demanding 4236m Mt Sayramsky, a two day climb requiring equipment. There's a slim chance of spotting a bear, ibex and rare birds of prey. You're less likely to see a snow leopard, though this is an important habitat for it.

Access to the east side of the reserve is via the village of **Zhabaghly**, 100km west of Taraz and 75km east of Shymkent, where you'll also find the reserve office with a small museum on Abay, the main street. The eastern region is renowned for its bird and plant life.

There's a direct bus to/from Shymkent daily for about US$1.

Places to Stay Altex (☎ 3252-52 54 36, fax 62 19 72) maintains a permanent camp of metal box *cabins* in a pretty location in a canyon beside the Sayram river, 70km from Shymkent. The cabins are surprisingly comfortable, and there's a traditional log banya in the woods. The daily cost for accommodation, food and guide is US$50 per person, with transfers from Shymkent.

In Zhabaghly village *Zhenia & Lyuda's* (☎ 32538-568 96, Abay 36) is the place to stay. This friendly English-speaking couple have transformed their home into a cosy hotel with rooms sharing bathrooms at US$50 a night, with all meals, transfers and excursions within the reserve. There are plans to build a section with ensuite bathrooms, too.

Otyrar

About 150km north-west of Shymkent lie the scanty ruins of Otyrar (also called al-Farabi, Otrar or Utrar), the town that brought Jenghiz Khan to Central Asia. Much of the rest of Asia and Europe might have been spared the Mongols if Otyrar's 13th century governor had not murdered the Great Khan's merchant-envoys for it. There's little left of the town that once covered 20 hectares, save for hillocks which were once town walls, and a few bits uncovered by archaeologists.

Close to the ruins is the intact 11th century Arslan-Bab mausoleum, tomb of an early mentor of Kozha Akhmed Yasaui (see the following Turkistan section). The al-Farabi museum is 5km away at the village of Shauildir and includes some finds from Otyrar.

The road to Shauildir and Otyrar is from Törtköl, 95km north of Shymkent on the Turkistan road. Shauildir is 50km west of Törtköl. Altex (see Information in the previous Shymkent section) can take you there.

TURKISTAN
☎ 32533 • pop 70,000

At Turkistan, 165km north-west of Shymkent, past cotton fields and salt marshes at the edge of the Kyzylkum desert, stands

Kazakstan's greatest building and its most important site of Muslim pilgrimage. The mausoleum of the first great Turkic Muslim holy man, Kozha Akhmed Yasaui, was built on a grand scale by Timur in the late 14th century. Restoration work, largely funded by the Turkish government, is ongoing and although cranes dwarf the mausoleum's mighty proportions, it's certainly worth visiting.

Founded perhaps as early as the 5th century CE, and known as Yasy or Shavgar until the 16th century, the town was an important trade and religious centre by the 12th century, on a boundary between nomadic and agricultural societies. It once had 14 mosques. Later it became a northerly outpost of the Kokand khanate, falling to the Russian push of 1864.

Turkistan is an almost entirely Kazak town (some of whose people understand little or no Russian) with a thriving bazar. To visit the mausoleum takes no more than half a day and can easily be done as a day trip from Shymkent.

Orientation & Information

If you come by road from Shymkent, the mausoleum will loom into view on your left as you enter the town along Tauke Khan (formerly Lenina). Tauke Khan continues 1km or so past the mausoleum, to a fork where the Kyzylorda road goes straight on and the street to the left leads to the bus station (after about half a kilometre) and the bazar.

At the ticket office for the mausoleum and in the bazars in Turkistan and Shymkent you can buy a little photographic book on Turkistan with text in English, Russian and Kazak for around US$1.50

Kozha Akhmed Yasaui Mausoleum

The revered Sufi teacher and Turkic mystical poet was born at Sayram east of Shymkent in 1103. He underwent ascetic Sufi training in Bukhara, but lived much of the rest of his life in Turkistan, dying here, some say, about 1166. At the age of 63 he is said to have retired to an underground cell for the rest of his life, in mourning for the Prophet Mohammed who had died at the same age. He founded the Yasauia Sufi order.

Yasaui's original small tomb was already a long-time place of pilgrimage before Timur ordered a far grander mausoleum built here in the 1390s. The building has the biggest intact dome in Central Asia and is all that's left of the old town.

Timur died before it was complete and the front face was left unfinished, flanked by two round towers but still studded with wooden scaffolding, like whiskers. The loveliest parts are the exquisite tiling (mainly blue and turquoise) on the outer rear walls and on the small fluted rear dome rising over the burial chamber.

Approaching the mausoleum from the front, you'll walk along an avenue with rose bushes planted either side and a few trees for shade. To the right is a gift shop, cafe and a reconstructed wall, to the left a good replica of the small 15th century **mausoleum of Rabigha-Sultan Begum** (the original was torn down for tsarist building material in 1898), the wife of Abul-Khayir Kahn, a 15th century leader of the then-nomadic Uzbeks. Abul-Khayir was killed in the 1468 feud which split the Uzbeks and effectively gave birth to the Kazak people; his tomb is within the main building.

Restoration of Yasaui's mausoleum's **central chamber**, with a dome 39m above the floor and 18.2m wide, is finished, but work continues on the 35 smaller rooms on two floors that surround it. In the centre of the chamber is a vast goblet *(kazan)* cast from seven precious metals and donated by Timur. It weighs over 2000kg, and while it once held holy water it now contains donations from visitors. Yasaui's tomb lies beyond the ornately carved 14th century wooden door as the end of the chamber.

West of the mausoleum on a small hill is the entrance to the **Hal-wat mosque** and small museum, built underground with a wood-decorated interior. Next to the small prayer hall is the cell in which Yasaui is said to have withdrawn to. It's possible to crawl into the pitch black cave-like cavity.

Back towards the entrance is a traditional 15th century **bathhouse**. The interior has been well restored but the building is now just for show. It's open daily 9 am to 8 pm (40 T).

Places to Stay & Eat

The cheap option is *Hotel Saule* (☎ 318 96), a simple guesthouse behind the Nauryz restaurant, a 10 minute walk east of the mausoleum. Clean little single/doubles with shared bathroom cost US$5.50. There's no hot water, but the people are friendly and there's a pretty garden.

More upmarket, but cheaply decorated *Hotel Nurtas* (☎ 515 74) is closer to the bazar on Sultanbek Kozhanov. The beds in the US$10 rooms are hard and there's only hot water in the deluxe rooms, overpriced at US$20.

There are several cafes along the main road from Shymkent on the approach to the mausoleum, among which *Khan Taniri* does decent laghman and shashlyk.

The *Nauryz* restaurant, a block away from Tauke Khan, is built in a mock old Turkistan style and serves the standard menu of manty, laghman noodles and beefsteak. Another atmospheric place is *Karavansaray*, a teashop set around a colonnaded courtyard, opposite the bazar, where you'll find shashlyk stands.

The chock-a-block *bazar*, close by the bus station, heaves with produce and does justice to Turkistan's historic role as a market centre.

Getting There & Around

Buses come from Shymkent (US$2, 3½ hours, six daily), and from Kyzylorda (US$3, six hours, once a day). Marshrutnoe buses wait outside the bus station and are cheaper (US$1.50). A taxi to Shymkent costs around US$10.

The train station, out on the western edge of town, has at least four daily trains to/from Kyzylorda, Töretam (Leninsk), Aralsk, Aktöbe and Moscow. There are at least three daily trains to Shymkent, Taraz and Almaty, one to Bishkek, and two or three to Tashkent.

Public transport is infrequent. Flagging down a car or taxi will be easier for getting to/from the bus station, bazar or train station. Bus No 2 or 5 and marshrutnoe taxi No 5 run between the Hotel Turkistan, the bus station and the train station.

KYZYLORDA

☎ 32422 • pop 155,000

On the Syr-Darya river, 280km north-west of Turkistan, Kyzylorda (meaning Red Capital) was the capital of Soviet Kazakstan from 1925 to 1927 but was dumped in favour of cooler Almaty when the Turksib railway reached there. The only evidence you'll see of this former glory is the ornate train station, the rest of the city being depressingly bleak. Like Taraz, Shymkent and Turkistan, it was part of the Kokand khanate's 19th century frontier defences, and the first of these to fall to Russia in 1853. Today it's the capital of Kyzylorda oblys, which has the highest Kazak population in the country.

If you do need to stop here, the *Hotel Kyzylorda* (☎ 611 21) is closest to the train station and charges US$25 for basic rooms. At the luxury end of the scale, catering to the oil and gas prospectors is the *Hotel Samal* (☎ 616 17, fax 616 23), a foreign-run operation with singles at US$117 and doubles US$200. *Café Rosali* opposite the city's central square is a good spot for lunch, serving excellent laghman noodles.

The airport is 17km south of the city and there are six flights a week to/from Almaty (US$85, 2½ hours). Train services are the same as for Turkistan.

BAYKONUR COSMODROME

The Baykonur Cosmodrome, amid semi-desert about 250km north-west of Kyzylorda, has been the launch site for all Soviet and Russian-crewed space flights since Yuri Gagarin, the first human in space, was lobbed up in 1961. In fact the launch site isn't really in Baykonur, which is actually a town 300km to the north-east, but the USSR told the International Aeronautical Federation that Gagarin's launch-point was Baykonur, and that name has stuck.

The nearest town is the Russian military town of **Leninsk** on the Syr-Darya, south of the cosmodrome, which it was built to guard and service. The train station just north of Leninsk is called Töretam. A space tracking station is visible 2 to 3km north of the station; the launch site is about 30km farther north.

After the collapse of the USSR, the Cosmodrome became a useful card in Kazakstan's dealings with Russia, which inherited the Soviet space program. While Russia insisted that the cosmodrome and its associated military forces were its own, Kazakstan wanted them under joint control. A shortage of funds led to a number of space projects being suspended, falling living standards in the support towns, and riots by Kazak soldiers here in 1992 and 1993. Many Russians and Ukrainians left. In 1994 Kazakstan agreed to lease Baykonur and Leninsk to Russia for 20 years for about US$120 million a year. A few months later the Kazak cosmonaut Talgat Musabaev and the Russian Yuri Malenchenko took off on a symbolic joint visit to the Mir space station. Just to underline who is in charge, Russian rubles are the official currency in Baykonur.

This area is not open to travellers. Just fronting up and trying to talk or bribe your way into Baykonur from Töretam might work, but it certainly won't get you anywhere near the cosmodrome and will get you into a lot of trouble if you're caught. It's always possible the situation could loosen up. The best place to check is the Russian embassy in Almaty.

ARALSK
☎ 32422 • pop 40,000
Aralsk, about 220km north-west of Leninsk on the same road and railway, used to be on the Aral Sea, and was an important fishing port. In its train station waiting room, a mosaic covering an entire wall depicts how in 1918 Aralsk's comrades provided fish for people starving in Russia.

The fishing industry has long since died. At one point the sea had withdrawn at least 30km from Aralsk and it remains a dramatic shock to drive to the edge of the town and see the dip in the land where the water once

---

Hope for the Little Aral Sea

Svetlana Kamal-ad-Din points at the salt-encrusted desert before us and says:

As a child I remember learning to swim here. My father said, you live by the sea, so you must learn. When I told my children this, they didn't believe me. 'Where is the sea?' they asked.

The sea in question is the Aral, once smaller in size only than the Caspian Sea, Lake Superior and Lake Victoria. After decades of seeing its source waters from the Syr-Darya and Amu Darya rivers diverted to irrigate cotton fields, mostly in Uzbekistan and Turkmenistan, the Aral is a puddle of its former self, or more precisely two puddles, since its northern end is now a separate lake, dubbed the Little Aral Sea.

It is this lake that, together with Svetlana of Aralsk's UNDP office, I drive to see. Once we would have had to bump over the dried out sea bed for 30km or more to reach the water. Today, the trip is just 9km, with the water inching closer to Aralsk by the month. The reason for this is a 16km long dam built by the community across the mouth of the Syr-Darya. Nine million cubic metres of water has since flowed back into the Little Aral.

The dike is controversial in that it condemns the larger southern lake to accelerated evaporation. For the citizens of Aralsk, though, better the survival of Little Aral than the disappearance of the whole sea.

Svetlana gives the reasons why she believes there is hope. Ten years ago there were terrible noxious dust storms every day in Aralsk. These now happen once a week. The birds and fish are returning to the water. 'Most importantly,' she adds 'the people now believe the sea will return.'

Since my visit the dam has broken several times during storms. The World Bank has sent delegations to assess the project, but have yet to commit the US$80 million needed to secure the dam for good. The battle to save the Little Aral Sea is not over yet.

Simon Richmond

lapped. There's been an improvement (see the boxed text 'Hope for the Little Aral Sea') but Aralsk remains a bleak place, battered by dust storms and suffering polluted water supplies.

If you want to witness first hand this environmental disaster zone, Aralsk is much easier to visit than similarly defunct ports on the Uzbek side of the Aral. A lone rusting fishing boat, high and dry some 5km from the town stands like a sentinel warning of the folly of man, while at Dzhambul, 50km west of Aralsk, and another former fishing village, you can see a **ship cemetery**, where several abandoned hulks rust in the desert. On the way there, you'll pass a former Soviet missile-launch base that looks like the set from a post-apocalypse movie.

The UNDP have a project office in Aralsk (☎ 6 11 25, ask for Svetlana Kamalad-Din, who speaks English well), on the central square, where people with a serious interest in the region can drop by for information and assistance in touring the area. For more on the Aral Sea, see the Ecology & Environment section in the Facts about Central Asia chapter.

The old Hotel Aral, beside what used to be the town's beach, is now called *Yaksart Konak Uyi* (☎ 214 79). Rooms on the 3rd floor have been renovated with air conditioning and cost US$13. Rooms without bathrooms are US$7. Local police take an interest in any outsiders curious enough to call here.

West Kazakstan

North and west of the Aral Sea stretches more desert and steppe, significantly populated only towards the Russian border, but of crucial to Kazakstan because here lie great reserves of oil and natural gas, now being extracted by local and foreign companies under deals bringing millions of vital dollars into the country. The most important sites are the Tenghiz oilfield, near the eastern shore of the Caspian Sea, and the Karachaganak gas field, south of Oral (formerly Uralsk). See the Economy section in the introduction to this chapter for more on these projects.

The rail routes from Central Asia to Moscow and the Volga region cross this wilderness – ideal if you like taking slow trains across empty deserts relieved only by roaming camels, salt lakes and pink rock outcrops. In the summer, the Caspian Sea is warm enough for swimming in at Aktau, although parts of the 'beach' look like the D-day landings, making this one of the most bizarre seaside resorts you could come across. Atyrau has some old architecture that's worth a look, but otherwise, if you're not in the oil or gas business, there's little reason to drag yourself here and even less to go further north to Oral.

AKTÖBE
☎ 3132 • pop 260,000

Aktöbe, on the main rail line to Moscow, about a hundred kilometres from the Russian border in north-west Kazakstan, is a drab industrial city where you might need to change trains. The older part of town near the station is marginally more interesting than the modern centre several kilometres north.

If you have time to waste or food to get, there's a lively market, backed by some very satanic-looking factories, about a kilometre east of the train station: take Kökkhar köshesi, the main road heading right uphill from the station. Nearby is the local **museum**, open 9 am to 5 pm, Wednesday to Monday, where Rosa, an English speaking curator, may be available to give you a tour of the otherwise unremarkable natural and general history collection. To reach here from the station, take Ayteke Bi, the second street on the left off Kökkhar köshesi from the station, then turn right at the Hotel Ilek on Altynsarin; the museum is in a white building.

For places to stay, the economical answer is the *komnaty otdykha* at the train station, which has quite comfortable dorm beds costing US$2.50 for up to 24 hours. The shared toilets and showers are tolerable. Look for the bed sign in the station's main hall, and go up to the 3rd floor.

The best place to stay is *Hotel Aktyubinsk* (☎ 57 28 29, fax 57 77 72, Abylay Khan 44), which has clean Soviet-style rooms with TV and fridge from $29. To get here from the station take bus No 1 or a taxi (about $1).

The locals recommend eating at an Armenian restaurant *Uratu (Truda 139a)*, a short taxi ride from the Hotel Aktyubinsk. Otherwise there are several small *cafes* near the station serving the usual menu of dumplings and noodles.

Flights from Aktöbe are scheduled to Almaty and Moscow daily, Aktau and Astana twice a week. A taxi to/from the airport, south-east of the centre, is US$2. Bus No 8 also links the two.

Trains run to Aktau (US$10), Orenburg (US$10), Samara (US$20), Oral (US$8), Saratov, Moscow (US$43, 32 to 37 hours), Shymkent (US$20), Taraz (US$23), Turkistan (US$24), Tashkent (US$33, 31 hours) and Almaty (US$27, 42 hours) several times a day, and to Bishkek (US$35, 40 hours) once a day. There's also a daily train to Atyrau (14 hours) and Astrakhan (Russia), pulling carriages to Mangghyshlak near Aktau.

ATYRAU

☎ 31222 • pop 200,000

Atyrau, on the Ural river, 30km upstream from its mouth on the northern shore of the Caspian Sea, is 'Oil City Kazakstan', acting as command station for the main Tenghiz oilfield 350km further south. The giant USA oil company, Chevron, is one of the major players through its multibillion dollar joint venture, called Tengizchevroil, with the Kazakstan government. There are many other oil and gas fields in the Atyrau region, and offshore reserves in the Caspian may hold the greatest potential yet.

Not surprisingly, Atyrau sees a steady stream of western oil people, which keeps hotel prices higher than they should be, somewhat compensated for by a better than average range of restaurants. Because it was founded in 1640 by a Russian trader named Guriyev, whose name the town bore until 1993, there are also fascinating architectural remnants of bygone ages to be discovered.

Caviar used to be traded here until the oil business took off early in the 20th century. Some 80% of the town's population is Kazak, one of the highest levels in the country.

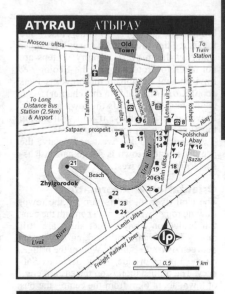

ATYRAU

PLACES TO STAY
2 Hotel Chagala
7 Hotel Ak Zhayyk
10 Hotel Kaspii
19 Atyrau Sanatoriyasi
23 Riverside Inn

PLACES TO EAT
12 Eurasia
13 Sernas
15 Maestro
16 McMagic
17 Svetlana

OTHER
1 Russian Orthodox Church
3 History Museum
4 Kazaktelekom
5 Bowling Alley
6 Akimat (Regional Government Office)
8 Central Telephone Office
9 Air Kazakstan
11 City Government Building
14 CATC Travel Agency
18 New Star Club
20 Kazkommetz Bank
21 Palace of Culture
22 Sports Stadium
24 Mustang (Pool Club)
25 OVIR

KAZAKSTAN

Spring floods in recent years have brought the Caspian shoreline closer, and it's feared that much of Atyrau will be under water by the mid-21st century if steps are not taken to protect it (see the Ecology & Environment section in the previous facts about Kazakstan entry in this chapter). As it is, the mud that engulfs the town after rain in winter is legendary; if you visit during this time, take appropriate footwear.

Atyrau is 2700km west of Almaty; the nearest sizeable town is Astrakhan in Russia, 350km to the west.

Orientation & Information

The Ural river meanders through the town, flowing roughly north-south beneath the central bridge on Abay (street signs are still mostly in Russian) and marking the border between Asia and Europe. West of the bridge, on the European side, Abay becomes Satpaev. The train station is on the eastern edge of town, about 6km from the centre, the bus station is about 2.5km west of the river on Avangard (turn right off Satpaev), and the airport is further out to the west.

Inside the *akimat* (regional government office), the unmissable white building on the west bank of the Ural just across the central bridge, is an information office (☎ 234 85, 277 86, fax 545 73, @ atyrau@asdc.kz) set up to assist foreign businesses and organisations operating in the area. The English-speaking assistants are also happy to help out travellers.

You'll get the best rates of exchange at the bazar on Makhambet, although you'll have to haggle. There are also currency exchange points at the airport, in the main hotels and in several banks. There are cash machines in the akimat, Hotel Ak Zhayyk, Hotel Chagala, Kazkommertsbank and Narodny Bank. The Hotel Chagala has a business centre with phone and fax. You can also phone worldwide from the Central Telephone Office next to the Hotel Ak Zhayyk, open Monday to Saturday, 8 am to midnight.

Almaty-based travel agency Central Asia Tourism Corp has a branch office at Lenin 25 (☎ 540 75/76 fax 540 77). British Airways has an office in the Hotel Chagala.

Things to See

The **Atyrau History Museum**, open daily 9 am to 4 pm, has recently moved to Lenin, about 100m behind the Hotel Ak Zhayyk. It has several interesting artefacts from the region, including a display on Saraichuk, a once grand city some 45km west of Atyrau, destroyed in the 13th century and since uncovered by archaeologists. Entrance is 100 T for foreigners.

At the heart of the visibly crumbling 'old town' on the west side of the river about 1km north-west of the bridge, a well-maintained **Russian Orthodox church**, emerges like a jewelled finger from the surrounding shacks. It dates from 1888 and its interior is plastered with icons.

A pleasant half day stroll starts at the central bridge following the east bank of the Ural south. Here you'll see some handsome, if run-down, turn-of-the-century villas. On reaching the riverside beach, complete with metal parasols, turn inland to find **Zhylgorodok**. This charming area of Mediterranean-looking whitewashed houses with blue-painted woodwork was built at the end of WWII by German, Italian and Japanese POWs. At its heart is a square with colonnaded arcades on two sides and a handsome **Palace of Culture** on another. Peep inside the upstairs hall, which has dazzling ceiling decoration.

Places to Stay

Hotel Kaspii (☎ 333 07, fax 379 36, Satpaev 15), down a side street by the Air Kazakstan office and through a gate to the right, is a good quality place with single rooms at US$40 with breakfast, doubles at US$70, a few expensive suites, a restaurant and a sauna. The only problem is that since it's a publicly owned hotel, bookings have been known to be suddenly cancelled in favour of visiting civil servants.

A reasonable alternative is the *Atyrau Sanatoriyasi (☎ 225 31, 233 60)*, just off Lenin. The entrance is around the back of the building facing on to the river. No-frills rooms are $15, while fancier suites are $30. The rates include all meals, although the food is pretty dire.

The big *Hotel Ak Zhayyk* (☎ 278 63, fax 278 82, Abay 4), just east of the central bridge, has seen better days. Very basic singles start from under $10, other rooms are overpriced at US$45. As with other tall buildings in Atyrau, above the 3rd floor there is only hot water.

The British-managed *Riverside Inn* (☎/fax 5 89 86, Smagulov 102A) is on the banks of Ural, behind Zhylgorodok. It's supposed to be for visiting oil company employees only, but you might be able to get a room; all have satellite TV and IDD phones for US$75 and up to US$95, with meals and laundry service.

Atyrau's most upmarket accommodation, though nothing extraordinary, is the *Hotel Chagala* (☎ 540 33, fax 540 34, Ismagulov 1, @ shagala@kaznet.kz), beside the river. Singles/doubles are US$138/216, with satellite TV, IDD phones, a swimming pool and gym, a restaurant and bar, business centre, shop and laundry service.

Places to Eat

Several good restaurants can be found along Lenin. One of the best is *Sernas*, next to the flower stalls, a small place serving spicy Korean dishes as well as local favourites such as laghman. Nearby, facing onto ploshchad Abay, is the more upmarket *Eurasia*, which, like *Maestro* and *Svetlana*, next to each other further down Lenin, offers a mix of local and European dishes, such as breadcrumbed chicken legs and beef stroganoff.

For something simpler, try *McMagic*, a reasonable western-style burger and pizza bar next to the bazar on Makhambet. There are also a couple of small *cafes* in Zhylgorodok.

At the opposite end of the price scale is the restaurant at the *Hotel Chagala*, where blowout breakfasts are US$12, buffet-style lunch $22 and dinner $26. The bar, which also serves food, is better value. The food at the *Riverside Inn* is also rated highly.

Entertainment

Apart from the *bar* at the Hotel Chagala, a good place to relax is *Mustang (Sharipova 6)*, where you can play Russian and US pool and drink beer.

A new *bowling alley* is behind the akimat, and a new municipal *gym* has opened south of the Hotel Chagala.

A reasonable club is *New Star* on Makhambet, serving 500ml beers for under US$1. Also hunt out the *Pivnoe Bar* in a circular building on Gagarina near the Chevron garage on the west side of town. Here you can try 500ml of good home-brewed beer for 60 T.

Getting There & Away

Air Kazakstan's ticket office (☎ 249 49) on Satpaev is open Monday to Saturday 8 am to noon and 1 to 7 pm. Flights are daily to Almaty, three times a week to Moscow, and weekly to Budapest.

There's a daily bus service to Oral, 500km to the north, taking around 12 hours. Take a taxi to the bus station.

There are daily trains to/from Aktöbe (US$6, 14 hours), Mangghyshlak (for Aktau, US$8, 22 hours) and Astrakhan (US$10). Services to/from Moscow (US$40), Volgograd (through Astrakhan), Tashkent (US$38) and Almaty (US$20) are scheduled every two days. When buying tickets, note that Atyrau is one hour ahead of Moscow and two hours behind Almaty.

AKTAU

☎ 3292 • pop 140,000

Stuck between the desert and the Caspian, hundreds of kilometres from anywhere, with all its water derived from a desalination plant powered by a nuclear reactor, Aktau is one of the strangest places scattered across the former USSR.

The reason anyone is here at all is local uranium deposits. In 1963, Soviet architects began to lay out a model town of wide, straight streets, dividing residential quarters into numbered *mikrorayony* (microregions) of apartment blocks, uncomplicated by street names. It was called Shevchenko, after the 19th century Ukrainian poet and artist Taras Shevchenko, who was exiled to Kazakstan for his nationalist views. Thanks to the nearby sandy beaches on the blue Caspian, the place was also developed as a holiday resort for the Soviet elite.

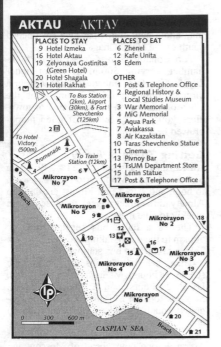

AKTAU АКТАУ

PLACES TO STAY
9 Hotel Izmeka
16 Hotel Aktau
19 Zelyonaya Gostinitsa
     (Green Hotel)
20 Hotel Shagala
21 Hotel Rakhat

PLACES TO EAT
6 Zhenel
12 Kafe Unita
18 Edem

OTHER
1 Post & Telephone Office
2 Regional History &
    Local Studies Museum
3 War Memorial
4 MiG Memorial
5 Aqua Park
7 Aviakassa
8 Air Kazakstan
10 Taras Shevchenko Statue
11 Cinema
13 Pivnoy Bar
14 TsUM Department Store
15 Lenin Statue
17 Post & Telephone Office

To Bus Station
(2km), Airport
(30km), & Fort
Shevchenko
(125km)

To Hotel
Victory
(500m)

To Train
Station (12km)

Promenade

Abay

Mikrorayon No 7

Mikrorayon No 6

Mikrorayon No 5

Mikrorayon No 2

Mikrorayon No 4

Mikrorayon No 3

Mikrorayon No 1

Beach

0   300   600 m

CASPIAN SEA

Beach

Now the uranium and tourism industries are in decline and Aktau has the feel of a place whose bubble has burst. The development of the Tenghiz oilfield, 200km north-east, and the prospect of offshore oil in the Caspian, offer the best hope of economic recovery. Already there's a steady trickle of westerners in town, mingling with the local population of Russians, Kazaks and Caucuses peoples.

Orientation & Information
The only street with a name is Abay (formerly prospekt Lenina), a broad avenue sloping down from north to south and running parallel to the coast. Other Aktau locations are identified by their mikrorayon and *dom* (building) numbers.

A huge statue of Lenin still stands at the southern end of Abay, opposite the Hotel Aktau. Another landmark, uphill on Abay, is an impressive war memorial with an eternal flame. A pedestrian promenade runs

from here to the coast road, where a MiG fighter plane is mounted on a pedestal.

There are several banks along Abay and a currency exchange booth on the 2nd floor of the TsUM department store opposite the Hotel Aktau. One post and telephone office is beside the Hotel Aktau; a bigger one is 2km north on Abay.

Things to See & Do
To best savour Aktau's bizarre atmosphere, head for the breezy **seafront**. There are cliffs and a promenade running to a rocky beach to the north, just beyond the MiG, and an **aqua park** of water slides and pools. Heading south you'll pass the brooding statue of the exiled poet Taras Shevchenko. Further south the beach is so rubble-strewn that it looks as if the D-day landings have just taken place. There are better beaches to be found if you drive out of town to where the locals have their dachas.

Interesting displays about the Caspian and surrounding area make the **Regional History & Local Studies Museum** well worth a visit. It's on Abay, with the entrance in a courtyard through a blue gate. Hours are Tuesday to Friday 9 am to 6 pm and Saturday 10 am to 5 pm, closed 1 to 2 pm.

If you're in search of desolation, head to **Fort Shevchenko**, 125km north up the coast, which originated in the 19th century as a Russian bridgehead, called Fort Alexandrovsk. Despite a new base here for the joint British and Kazak oil exploration firm OKIOK, the place is a ghost town, with Soviet-era fishing boats rusting in the harbour beside a row of attractive old Russian houses.

Get up early if you want to catch a bus (US$1) here from the bus station on the north edge of Aktau. Otherwise, haggle for a taxi (no more than US$20 round trip). Worth stopping at along the way is **Koshkarata**, a picturesque Muslim cemetery whose crenellated skyline of miniature domes and towers looks from a distance like some town out of an Arabian fairy tale.

Places to Stay
There's no bargain accommodation in Aktau although most hotel rooms come

with hot water, TVs and phones. At the time of research the *Hotel Aktau* at the fork in Abay was undergoing renovation.

The small *Zelyonaya Gostinitsa* (☎ 51 73 04) is set back slightly from Abay in mikrorayon 3. It's run by a friendly group of women and has roomy, good value single/double suites for US$20/40.

The next cheapest place, but nowhere near as nice, is *Hotel Izmeka* (☎ 51 18 75), on the second floor of an apartment building in mikrorayon 5. Very basic rooms here are US$28.

Best of the upmarket options is art-deco looking *Hotel Victory* (☎ 43 95 16, fax 43 95 01) on the seafront in mikrorayon 15. Rooms start at US$60/100. English is spoken and there's a decent bar and restaurant.

Heading south down Abay from the centre and towards the beach, the *Hotel Rakhat* (☎ 51 17 55) was also being renovated, but had small, modern-decorated rooms available on its 3rd floor from US$40.

More of a Soviet dinosaur is the nearby *Hotel Shagala* (☎ 51 22 59), which has huge, suite-style rooms from US$50.

Places to Eat

Kafe Unita, in the round-roofed building next to the TsUM department store, is a small, dark basement space serving standard meat and fish dishes for around US$3. There's an English menu and it's open from noon to 3 pm and 7 pm to 2 am. Next door is a *pivnoy bar* serving large mugs of beer.

Edem (☎ 51 77 66), in mikrorayon 3, is more convivial and serves better food for similar prices as Kafe Unita. There's also a bar, where you can get bottled American beer.

Zhenel is a swanky operation which, despite the good food, can work out expensively because of additional cover charges. Also bunging a cover charge on top of the bill is the restaurant in the *Hotel Victory*, an elegant place with an English menu, illustrated with photographs that bear a good resemblance to the food served.

Near the bus station is a large bazar where you can pick up picnic snacks. There's a grocery section in TsUM and during the summer, cafes open along the seafront.

Getting There & Around

Tickets for most places are sold at Air Kazakstan (☎ 51 23 68), on Abay, open daily from 8 am to 1 pm and 2 to 7 pm, or the *aviakassa* (private travel agent) for Caspian Transport, in the next building north along Abay, open daily 8 am to 8 pm. Flights are scheduled to Almaty six times a week; and Aktöbe, Astana, Baku (Azerbaijan), Mineralnye Vody (Russia) and Moscow twice a week. There may also be charter flights to Aleppo (Syria), Dubai and Istanbul.

The station for Aktau is Mangghyshlak (also called Mangghystau), about 12km east of the town. Daily trains run to/from Atyrau, 400km north as the crow flies, but 800km and about 24 hours by rail. A *kupe* (second class) ticket costs around $10. These trains also pull carriages to/from Aktöbe which is about 1400km and two days away, including 14 hours in a siding at Atyrau. Note – Aktau is one hour ahead of Moscow time and two hours behind Almaty time.

Bus No 101 runs between Mangghyshlak train station and Aktau bus station (avtovokzal or avtostantsia), around 3km north of the Hotel Aktau via Abay. The journey into town takes about half an hour across a wilderness strewn with pipelines and cables. The fare is 30 T. A taxi should cost around US$5, the same as the fare to the airport.

Bus No 3 runs along Abay to the bazar and bus station. Buses No 1 and 2 run along the seafront.

North Kazakstan

Until the 19th century, the flat steppe of northern Kazakstan was largely untouched except by Kazak nomads and their herds. Russia's bridgehead in the area was Petropavlovsk, still one of the most Russian of Kazakstan's cities. As the mighty neighbour's grip stretched southwards, immigrants from western USSR came in increasing numbers to farm the steppe. A million or more had settled in the north by 1900, displacing the Kazaks from their pastures. The Kazaks' resistance was largely futile and many thousands died in rebellions or famines

An even bigger transformation came in Soviet times. The nomadic Kazaks were forced into collective farms, with hundreds of thousands starving in the ensuing famine. New industrial cities like Karaghandy, Ekibastuz and Kostanay sprouted to process coal, iron ore and other minerals, and in the 1950s vast areas of steppe were turned over to wheat in Khrushchev's Virgin Lands scheme (see 'Development' & Unrest in the History section of this chapter), engendering yet more cities such as Akmola, recently elevated to become Kazakstan's new capital, Astana. A huge influx of Russians, Ukrainians and others came to work on the new projects. Despite wind erosion which turned a lot of the Virgin Lands wheat fields back into steppe, the area remains the country's breadbasket, accounting for over half of Kazakstan's grain and livestock.

The region was useful to Moscow for more sinister reasons, too. A network of Gulag labour camps was set up here, to which were sent deportees from other parts of the USSR around the time of WWII. In the 1950s most of the camps were closed, but many of the survivors stayed, including a large number of ethnic Germans. Since independence many have chosen to return to Germany.

The legacy of the Soviet era is a high Russian and Ukrainian population (Kazaks number less than 20% in several regions) and a lot of decaying, dirty industry. Many Slavs, disgruntled by economic decline and seeing little future in a Kazakstan dominated by Kazaks, are leaving like the Germans. Most of the cities are bleak, impoverished places.

Apart from Astana, which is principally of interest to those engaged in business, the highlight of the area is Lake Burabay, the most scenic and charming of several lakes that dot a wooded, hilly area south of Kökshetau. The major rail junction of Petropavlovsk near the Russian border also makes for a pleasant stop en route to joining up with Trans-Siberian trains.

The best months to visit are May to June and September to October. Winters are severe, with howling blizzards and temperatures to -40°C in January. In July and August you can expect the opposite extreme.

ASTANA
☎ 3172 • pop 400,000

During its lifetime, Astana, the new capital of Kazakstan, 1300km north-west of Almaty, has gone through several name changes. It was founded in 1830 as a Russian Cossack fortress, named Akmola (a Kazak name meaning 'white plenty' because the area was renowned for its dairy products and bread). When Nikita Khrushchev announced his Virgin Lands scheme (see 'Development' and Unrest in the History section of this chapter), Akmola became the project's capital and was renamed Tselinograd (Virgin Lands City) in 1961. Many immigrants from Russia and western USSR came to work here, bequeathing the city a sizeable Russian and Slav population.

After the break-up of the USSR, Akmola got back its old name, and would have kept it if President Nazarbaev's plan to shift the capital here from Almaty hadn't attracted such unfavourable comments. Although Nazarbaev cited the possibility of earthquakes in Almaty and its worrying closeness to conflicts in neighbouring countries as good reasons for making the change, critics said opting for a provincial town, plagued by extremes of weather, as the new capital would prove to be Nazarbaev's political grave – a pun on another translation of Akmola, as 'white tomb'. The president promptly renamed the city Astana (Kazak for Capital) and hastened along the program of change so that by December 1997 all government ministries and the parliament had moved here.

Astana's international debut was 10 June 1998, when visitors were greeted by what appeared to be a shiny new city centre. The reality, beyond a handful of new constructions, is that the old Soviet buildings have been given a lick of paint and plastic siding facelifts; look behind the facades and the same old crumbling concrete remains. There are grand plans to redesign the city completely, but these have been scaled back due to lack of funds.

Still, Astana is a friendly and fairly low-rise town with some attractive tree-lined streets, but prone to strong steppe winds and very harsh winters.

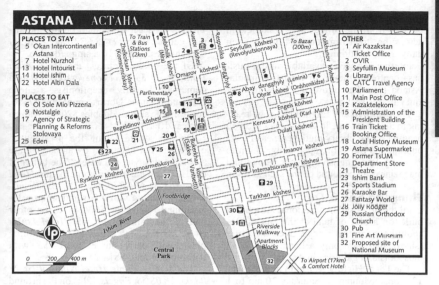

ASTANA АСТАНА

PLACES TO STAY
5 Okan Intercontinental Astana
7 Hotel Nurzhol
13 Hotel Intourist
14 Hotel Ishim
22 Hotel Altin Dala

PLACES TO EAT
6 Ol Sole Mio Pizzeria
9 Nostalgie
17 Agency of Strategic Planning & Reforms Stolovaya
25 Eden

OTHER
1 Air Kazakstan Ticket Office
2 OVIR
3 Seyfullin Museum
4 Library
8 CATC Travel Agency
10 Parliament
11 Main Post Office
12 Kazaktelekom
15 Administration of the President Building
16 Train Ticket Booking Office
18 Local History Museum
19 Astana Supermarket
20 Former TsUM Department Store
21 Theatre
23 Ishim Bank
24 Sports Stadium
26 Karaoke Bar
27 Fantasy World
28 Jolly Rodger
29 Russian Orthodox Church
30 Pub
31 Fine Art Museum
32 Proposed site of National Museum

Orientation

The city is centred around the square at the end of Beibitshilik (formerly Mira). Here you'll find major new government buildings, including the parliament at the north end, and the former TsUM department store, currently being redeveloped, to the south. Two blocks east is the main avenue Respublika (formerly Tselinnikov), which starts by the river Ishim in the south and changes its name to Pushkin as it nears the train station, 3km to the north.

The sprawling open-air bazar is five blocks east of Pushkin between Batyr Bogembai and Seyfullin prospekts. The airport is 17km south of the centre. The road from the airport into the city passes by a striking monument erected in memory of those who perished during Stalin's rule. Nearby is the city's central park, bordering the river Ishim. Around a kilometre east of here is a newly built district of *mikrorayony* (microregions), including a covered bazar, bowling alley and several restaurants.

Maps The best map you can buy of the city is the English-language *Astana* 1:20,000 scale map published by Comzemresursy in

1998. Copies can be bought at the major hotels in Astana and Almaty for around 300 T.

Information

OVIR (☎ 32 77 51) has an office at Seyfullin 63. They are open Monday to Friday 9 am to 5 pm. Almaty-based travel agency CATC has a branch at Respublika 66 (☎ 32 78 44, fax 32 45 38). It's open Monday to Friday 9 am to 7 pm and Saturday 9 am to 1 pm. As well as issuing international and internal air tickets, CATC offers visa support and registration and can arrange trips to local attractions such as Lake Burabay.

Foreign exchange booths are dotted around the city. The best exchange rates from banks are from branches of the Valut Transit Bank and Ishim Bank. There's also a Visa cash machine outside the Hotel Turist.

The main post office is behind the Hotel Intourist at the corner of Abay and Auezov. It's open Monday to Friday 8 am to 7 pm, Saturday 9 am to 5 pm and Sunday 9 am to 3 pm and you can change money here, too. Courier post is available through Pony Express (☎ 32 26 39) and Express Mail (☎ 26 19 24) at Auezov 71.

Long-distance phone calls and faxes can be sent from the offices of Kazaktelekom across the street from the post office, open daily 6 am to midnight.

Internet service is available in the business centre of the Okan Inter-Continental Astana (see the following Places to Stay entry in this section).

The dearth of any English language reading material for sale in Astana may see you heading to the library on the corner of Respublika and Seyfullin, open daily 10 am to 7 pm. A few English-language books and magazines can be found on the second floor.

Things to See & Do

Until the proposed new national museum is built (on a plot of land at the end of Respublika near the bridge over the river Ishim), there are only a handful of small museums and galleries in Astana.

The **Local History Museum** at Kenesary 107, open Monday to Saturday 10 am to 1 pm and 2 to 6 pm, is about the best. Highlights include a mildly diverting collection of costumes of different ethnic groups, a yurt, a collection of jewellery and yet another copy of the Golden Man armour (see the boxed text 'The Golden Man' in the Almaty section earlier in this chapter).

The entrance to the **Fine Art Museum**, Respublika 3, open Tuesday to Sunday 10 am to 6 pm, is on the side of the block. The small permanent collection includes some striking works and there are regularly changing exhibitions.

Close by the main library on Seyfullin is an attractive old Russian-style cottage, the former home of the Kazak writer Saken Seyfullin and now a **museum** dedicated to his memory. It's open daily 10 am to 7 pm.

A good place for a stroll is down the new promenade on the east bank of the Ishim between the road and the footbridges leading across to the central park. In winter the Ishim freezes over and people go ice fishing. Also on the east bank near the footbridge is the amusement park called **Fantasy World**, open Tuesday to Friday 4 pm to 11 pm and Saturday and Sunday 1 to 11 pm.

Places to Stay

There's an acceptable hotel beside the airport called *Airport* (☎ 33 37 18, 17 43 54) that charges US$10/16 a single/double.

Of the cheaper places, the *Hotel Altin Dala* (☎ 32 33 11, Peoneveskaya 19) is a gem, with friendly receptionists, a cheap cafe and a sauna. Dorms are around US$6, comfortable singles/doubles $20/40, with en suite and TV.

On the square facing the presidential office, but not identified by any signs, are a couple of Soviet-era hotels. The better of the two on the northern corner is the *Hotel Intourist* (☎ 32 01 30, fax 32 02 39, Beibitshilik 8), with a buffet bar and smart, old-fashioned rooms for $60/74. At the other end of the same block, the *Hotel Ishim* (☎ 32 82 03, Beibitshilik 8) is a rambling place, with basic singles for US$5, with bathroom from US$14/25.

The small, private *Hotel Nurzhol* (☎ 28 08 05, 28 08 58, Engels 69) is on the ground floor of an apartment block off Imanbaeva. Well-furnished rooms here cost around $25 with breakfast.

If you're really stuck you could try the dorms at the *komnaty otdyka* above the bus station. There's no hot water, but a bed is only US$5 for 24 hours.

A favourite among the expat business community is the Turkish-owned *Comfort Hotel* (☎ 37 10 21, fax 37 10 30, Kosmonavtov 60), a 10 minute drive from the centre towards the airport. Singles/doubles are US$144/216, but discounts may be available.

Astana's most prestigious hotel is the *Okan Inter-Continental Astana* (☎ 39 10 00, fax 39 10 10, Abay 144, ✉ astana@ interconti.com), a five-star establishment with plush rooms and facilities with satellite TV, health club, swimming pool, business centre and several restaurants. Even with all these comforts, the regular rate of US$354 per room is on the steep side.

Places to Eat

For a budget meal, try the *stolovaya* on the ground floor of the Agency of Strategic Planning and Reforms on the square at the end of Beibitshilik. It's open Monday to

Saturday, 9 am to 8 pm, with a break from 2.30 to 3 pm. It's also worth checking out the *cafe* in the Hotel Altin Dala. A good Russian-style meal here of salads, dumplings, or a meat dish should costs under US$4.

One of the city's most stylish restaurants, a favourite with the business sets, is *Eden* (☎ 39 14 10). The European-style food is pricey (around US$12) but excellent. Their cappuccinos are the best in town.

La Steppe (☎ 39 03 43), a short cab ride to the east of the city on Krasnyi Krest, is another classy operation serving a mixture of Russian and European dishes. Violin and piano players accompany dinner.

Decent pizza and pasta are available at *Ol Sole Mio Pizzeria (Abay 102)*, a couple of blocks east from the Okan Inter-Continental. Pizzas range from US$3.50 to US$8 and there's a good selection of bottled beer from US$2.50.

The mirrored ceiling and pink walls make *Nostalgie (Auezov 66)* a trial even before the food – standard European dishes – arrives. Expect to pay around US$8.

For a splurge try the restaurants in the Okan Inter-Continental. The *Alatau Grill*, daily 7 to 11.30 pm, serves local and Turkish dishes in a yurt-inspired setting. A mezze plate is US$7, shashlyk US$10.50 and bes-barmak US$8. Nightly entertainment is provided by a belly dancer. *Puccini's* is a very sophisticated Italian restaurant, while *Café Marco Polo* is an all-day operation with buffet meals at US$20 for lunch, US$22 for dinner.

If you're self-catering, or fancy a shashlyk snack, check out the giant *bazar*, four blocks east of Respublika. The Astana supermarket, opposite the local history museum on Kenesary, is a pricier alternative.

Entertainment

Astana's favourite pub is the *Jolly Rodger* on Respublika, where the staff wear stripey sailors' jerseys and draft beer is US$3.50 for a large mug. Watch the bill; they've been known to overcharge.

Cheaper, smaller and smokier is *Pub* across the street and a couple of blocks south along Respublika. A more sophisti-

cated option is the *Windsor Lounge* in the Okan Inter-Continental, but check the bill carefully here, too.

If you fancy a bit of a sing-a-long there's the Korean *Karaoke*, just off Kenesary. The snack bar is best here, serving food and draft beer.

Out east in mikrorayon 1, *Strike* is a bowling alley and restaurant complex serving fast food. *Discos* can also be found at the Okan Inter-Continental and Fantasy World.

Getting There & Away

There's an Air Kazakstan office at Beibitshilik 24. Flights go to/from Almaty daily, Moscow at least five times a week, Aktau twice a week and Kiev weekly. There are also occasional charter flights to Frankfurt, Hannover, Vienna and possibly other locations.

Trains go to/from Karaghandy, Almaty (kupe US$28, 24 hours) and Kökshetau (US$5, five hours) at least twice daily; and to/from Petropavlovsk (US$12, 11 hours), Kostanay (US$10, 16 hours) and Pavlodar (US$16, 10 hours). For daily services to Moscow and St Petersburg (every two days), foreigner prices still apply. There's service to/from Taraz, Shymkent and Kyzylorda every two days. You don't need to go to the station to buy tickets – there's a booking office at Zheltoksan 25 (☎ 32 82 82), behind the Presidential building. Note that Astana is three hours ahead of Moscow.

The bus station is next to the train station. Buses run to/from Karaghandy, Kökshetau, Omsk, Pavlodar, Shchuchinsk, Semey and Öskemen.

Getting Around

Bus No 10 (15 T) runs every half hour between the airport and Respublika. A taxi is about US$10. From the train and bus stations, bus No 9 or 25 and trolleybus No 2, 3, 4 or 5 go along Beibitshilik to the town centre. Taxis are numerous and cost 50-100 T per trip within the city centre.

AROUND ASTANA

Apart from Lake Burabay (see the following section), there are a couple more possible outings from Astana.

About 150km south-west of the capital, **Kurgalzhino Nature Reserve** includes both virgin feather-grass steppe and numerous lakes, making it a waterbird habitat of major importance. Between April and September, the salty Lake Tenghiz supports a large breeding colony of pink flamingos. This is the world's most northerly habitat of these graceful birds, which migrate to the Caspian Sea during winter. The reserve is undeveloped for visitors, but travel agencies in Astana can help arrange a car to take you there.

Around **Ereimentau**, 135km north-east of Astana, there are granite cliffs popular with climbers, and some fine scenery. It's two hours by daily train from Astana.

LAKE BURABAY
☎ 3142

For a preview of one of the most beautiful places in Kazakstan, look at the scenic drawing on the 10 tenge note. This is the classic view across **Lake Burabay**, 200km north of Astana and 95km south-east of **Kökshetau**, the nearest large town, which holds no interest to travellers. The area is known as 'Little Switzerland', though the mountains qualify only as steep hills. The dense forests, strange rock formations and scattered lakes, however, are in stark contrast to the surrounding flat, treeless steppe. Although it's possible to visit Lake Burabay in a day, the better option is to stay overnight. Apart from being an idyllic place to relax, Burabay is ideal for hiking, rock climbing or cross-country skiing in winter.

The gateway to the lake district is the run-down town of Shchuchinsk, itself on the edge of a lake. Lake Burabay and the village of **Burabay** are some 25km north. Here you'll find a rustic Museum of Natural History, open Tuesday to Sunday, 10 am to 6.30 pm, with good displays on local flora and fauna.

Although it's only 16km in circumference, in practice it's difficult to walk around Lake Burabay because part of the shoreline is blocked off for an army sanatorium. A pleasant walk (one hour) is from the village to **Okzhetpes** – the striking 380m-tall rock pile between the lake and the tallest peak, the 947m Kokshe (Russian: Sinyukha).

The formation of Okzhetpes is explained by a legend that also covers **Zhumbaktas**, the Sphynx-like rock that pokes out of the water in front of it. The story goes that while Abylay Khan's army was fighting the Oyrats, a beautiful princess was captured and brought to Burabay. It was decreed that she should marry a Kazak. The princess agreed, saying whoever could shoot an arrow to the top of the rock hill could have her hand. All her potential suitors failed first time, hence the name Okzhetpes which means 'the arrow cannot reach this place'. But on a second attempt her true love hit the target. His rivals were so angry that they killed him, and the princess, like a distraught Tosca, flung herself into the lake, thus creating the rock Zhumbaktas.

A short footpath heading north from Okzhetpes leads to a point from where both Lake Burabay and the neighbouring Lake Bolshoe Chebachye can be seen.

Places to Stay & Eat

The only accommodation is in the 'korpus 3' building of the Burabay *sanatorium* (☎ 715 45), about 1km west of the village along the lakeside road. The simply furnished rooms are clean and cost US$8 per person. There's no hot water, and though the rate includes meals in the attached refectory, you'll probably want to eat elsewhere or bring your own food after sampling the cooking. The sanatorium office is at the west end of the village, in a wooden cottage opposite the telephone and post office.

In the village you'll also find a *stolovaya* and a surprisingly fancy *restaurant*, serving good salads, meat dishes and even imported bottled beer. A meal here costs around US$6.

Camping is possible in a couple of spots on the east side of Lake Burabay, near the museum, and there's also a *campsite* on the rocky isthmus on the north side of Lake Bolshoe Chebachye.

The decrepit *Hotel Burabay* (☎ 443 25), in Shchuchinsk, has rooms for US$4. It's found opposite the town's grand former theatre, but the *Hotel Novy Kökshetau* on the central square in Kökshetau is probably a better option.

Getting There & Away

Burabay can be visited in a day trip, by train, from Astana, leaving on the local 8.10 am train to Shchuchinsk, the nearest station to the lake district, taking four hours, and returning on the 7.40 pm train. A one-way kupe ticket is US$3. Most trains to and from Kökshetau also stop in Shchuchinsk. From Shchuchinsk train station you may be able to catch a bus 25km to Burabay; a more reliable option is a taxi (US$2).

There are also buses from both Astana and, more frequently, Kökshetau to Shchuchinsk, although the train is easier.

Flights are scheduled to Kökshetau from Almaty five times a week (US$75).

PETROPAVLOVSK

☎ 3152 • pop 200,000

Older and architecturally more diverse than many places in Kazakstan, Petropavlovsk is the country's most northerly city, 475km north of Astana, and just 60km from the Russian border. It's an important rail junction, at the meeting of the north-south line through central Kazakstan with a branch of the Trans-Siberian railway, and Kazakstan's busiest freight terminal. It's also on the highway linking the Russian cities of Kurgan (270km west) and Omsk (260km east).

With a large Russian population, Petropavlovsk is as much a part of Siberia as of Kazakstan. Several 19th century brick buildings in the city centre, testaments to early attempts by the tsars to subjugate the Kazaks, remain, as does a handsome Russian Orthodox church near the Ishim river. Climatically it's certainly Siberian, with harsh winters and mild summers.

During Soviet times, four major defence plants were the backbone of the economy, making this a closed city. Now, it's a Turkish-funded pasta factory that keeps most people in work. You'll find that locals are curious about foreigners and that the relatively laid-back atmosphere is enticing.

Orientation & Information

Internatsionalnaya is the central axis of the city, running east-west from the train station. Lenina, tree-lined and pedestrian for much

of its length, runs parallel two blocks to the north. The main north-south street is Kirova.

There are many currency exchange kiosks. The best rates are offered by moneychangers in the central aisle of the bazar on Krasnoarmeskaya. The main post office, open daily, is opposite the drama theatre on Pushkin. The best place for long-distance phone calls is another post office on the corner of Kirova and Krasnoarmeyskaya (closed Sunday). Internet access is possible on the 3rd floor of the library on Lenina and Kirova.

If you're looking for an English guide to the city, approach the English department of North Kazakstan University, on the corner of Pushkin and Internatsionalnaya.

Things to See

One of the city's most attractive buildings (a pale green wooden villa that once belonged to a rich timber merchant) is behind the cinema on the corner of Internatsionalnaya and Kuybysheva. It houses an **art museum** (open daily 10 am to 5 pm) on two floors including modern and traditional paintings, and collections of *netsuke* (small wooden carvings), household objects and icons.

The **History & Local Studies Museum**, in a sturdy red brick building on the corner of Lenina and Kirova, traces the growth of Petropavlovsk from its origins as a Cossack fort built to protect Russia's Siberian frontier against the Kazaks. There's also a nature section with the usual stuffed animals. It's open Tuesday to Sunday 10 am to 5 pm.

Central Park, occupying several blocks in the city centre, has some rickety fairground rides, a cafe, karaoke and a large statue of Lenin, moved here from its original place on Lenina. It's a fun place to take the tempo of the city and perhaps hear some live music.

For a pleasant stroll, the Ishim river flows 2km east of the centre. Take trolleybus No 1 or 2 along Internatsionalnaya. On the way you'll pass the handsome blue onion-domed **cathedral**, surrounded by pretty gingerbread-style Russian cottages.

Places to Stay & Eat

The best place to stay is the *Hotel Kyzyl Zhar* (☎ 46 11 84), an unmissable 11 storey block opposite the park on Lenina. Comfortable, clean rooms with private bathroom are about US$30. It has a restaurant and a bar, but avoid both.

A much humbler option, *Hotel Express*, is a block east of the train station, where there are dorms for US$3.

Behind the university's first building *(pervay zadanay)* is a red brick building called the House of Mercy (Doma Molacaydee) with an excellent *stolovaya*, cheap and popular with students.

Between Mira and Kirova, on Internatsionalnaya, is *Day and Night Café*, with an English sign and good food at about US$8 for a meal with a couple of beers. The music is a bit loud, but they will turn it down if asked. Almost all of the booths have curtains that can be drawn around the table.

There's fine shashlyk, plus fruit and vegetables, available from stalls in the *bazar* on Krasnoarmeyskaya. Look for the old guy who serves the shashlyk with all the trimmings. Shashlyk is also available from outside the central park.

A better option is the *Ahotny Reodd* (Hunter's Row) in the courtyard behind the history museum, open evenings only. You can eat well here for less than US$10, but you might have to put up with the bartender launching into song.

Getting There & Around

Air tickets are sold at the Air Kazakstan office on the corner of Kirova and Lenina; look for the Aeroflot sign on the top of the building. Flights go to/from Almaty four times a week for US$85. The airport is a 20-minute ride from Kirova. A taxi is US$4.

Daily trains go to/from Almaty via Kökshetau, Astana and Karaghandy. There are also several daily trains heading across Siberia; west to Yekaterinburg and Moscow or St Petersburg, east to Omsk and beyond.

There are daily buses to Kökshetau (3½ hours) and Kostanay (11 hours) from the bus station next to the train station and plenty of taxi drivers willing to do a deal on rides to Kökshetau.

The train and bus stations are west of the city centre on Ruzaeva, at the end of Internatsionalnaya, about a 20 minute walk or a ride on bus No 1 or 2, or trolleybus No 2, 19 or 22.

KOSTANAY
☎ 3142 • pop 250,000
Kostanay, another Virgin Lands wheat centre, is also an industrial town processing the vast iron-ore deposits of the Kostanay basin. On the Tobol river in a remote corner of Kazakstan, 700km north-west of Astana, the town holds little interest for travellers.

The main drag is Lenina, with the train station at its west end. The heart of the town is about 2km from here, where Lenina is pedestrianised. The bus station, on Karbusheva, is around 10km south-east of the centre.

Hotel Tselinka (☎ 54 43 66) is at the corner of Sovietskaya and Pushkina, and the *Hotel Medeo (☎ 54 58 27)*, around the corner on Tarana. Both are a short walk up Lenina from the train station and cost around US$2 for a room.

Tobol, near Gogol, and *Medeo*, opposite the theatre on Baigamavetova, are recommended restaurants. Opposite the train station, *Surprise* is a cafe serving passable food.

The air ticket office is on Abay near the corner of Lenina. There are daily flights to/from Almaty, and most days to/from Moscow. Kostanay is on a rail route between Moscow (52 hours), Samara and Astana (kupe US$9, 16 hours), with services every day. Trains go to/from Almaty (kupe US$29, 40 hours) every two days.

Bus No 20 links the airport to the town centre. A taxi is about US$10. From the train station, any bus or trolleybus will take you to the centre; bus No 38 links the train and long distance bus station.

KARAGHANDY
☎ 3212 • pop 500,000
Kazakstan's second biggest city, Karaghandy, some 200km south-east of Astana and 1000km north-west of Almaty, is famous for two things: coal and Gulag labour camps. The two are intimately connected, as the big network of camps around Karaghandy was set up to provide slave labour for the mines.

Founded in 1926, much of Karaghandy was built by Gulag labour. The nearby Samarka and Kengir camps were the centre of a famous revolt in 1954 – 700 prisoners were killed when tanks moved in to put it down.

Mining continues today, although on a much smaller scale, with a large portion of the coal feeding the Indian-financed steelworks at Temirtau, 25km to the north. Sadly, Temirtau is now more famous for reportedly having over 80% of all HIV-infection cases in Kazakstan.

Despite being beset by such problems, Karaghandy is not an unpleasant place to visit. The city centre is much cleaner than it once was when heavy industry was more prevalent, and there are avenues of trees and a large central park to provide greenery.

Orientation

The train and bus stations are beside each other on Bukhar Zhirou (formerly Sovietsky prospekt), the main street off to the right. Follow it along and you'll pass the TsUM department store and the Central Park. A little further, at the end of Mira, is a pretty Neo-classical-style theatre, built of wood by Japanese prisoners of war. Yurabaev runs parallel to Bukhar Zhirou, one block south.

Things to See & Do

At the main entrance to the **Central Park** on Bukhar Zhirou, facing the Miners' Culture Palace (now a bank), stands a giant statue of two miners, an icon of Karaghandy. The park is a little shabby these days, but is large and has kids' playgrounds and places to eat.

On Bukhar Zhirou, near the train station, is a small **art museum**, open daily 10 am to 6 pm, with a diverting collection of works.

Places to Stay & Eat

The cheapest place to stay is the **komnaty otdykha** on the 2nd floor of the train station. Dorm beds are less than US$2, but the crude bathroom has no hot water.

The best value central hotel is the Soviet-style **Hotel Kazakstan** (☎ *41 03 00, Bukhar Zhirou 42*). Single/doubles with hot water and TV are US$7/15 and the staff are helpful.

More upmarket is the **Hotel Chayka** (*Krivoguza 36*), a short bus or taxi ride from the centre on the opposite side of Central Park. Once the Communist Party's hotel, it's still reasonably plush, with rooms around US$40. At the same price, **Kasmonaft**, on Mikhailovka, is further away from the centre, but the preferred choice of many expat business people.

One of the classiest restaurants is **Stary Gorad** (Old Town), serving good European dishes, on Lenina and Teatrana. On the opposite corner the **Country Club** is more of a bar, and serves draft beer. On Yerabaev, near the intersection with Mira, is a cheap **stolovaya** where you can get freshly-baked sugar-coated buns. Next to TsUM is the large and uninspiring restaurant **Orbita**; the nearby **Café Paradise**, serves acceptable shashlyk and salads for around US$3. **Blues Café**, opposite the Miners' Cultural Palace, is better for beer and live music than food.

Getting There & Around

Karaghandy has daily flights to/from Almaty (US$105) and three times a week to Moscow. Bus No 152 goes from the airport to the train and bus stations (one hour).

Trains run about three times daily to/from Almaty, at least daily to/from Astana, Petropavlovsk and Kostanay, and most days to/from Taraz and Shymkent.

There are buses to/from Almaty (about 20 hours), Astana (four hours), Pavlodar, Omsk, Novosibirsk and Bayanauyl, the gateway to the Bayanauyl National Park (see Around Pavlodar).

East Kazakstan

East of Astana, the train lines and roads reach out towards Russia, passing through the ravaged industrial town of Ekibastuz, one of the direst spots in Kazakstan, to Pavlodar, once an 18th century Russian fort.

The Soviet authorities chose this remote part of the country as their chief nuclear testing ground, causing untold health and environmental damage in an area inhabited by four million people.

Though obviously suffering economic depression, Semey remains eastern Kazakstan's most interesting and historical city, sporting notable architecture and literary connections with the great Kazak writer Abay Kunabaev and Russian novelist Fyodor Dostoevsky.

Öskemen is a centre for the ferrous metal industry, the region's capital and most prosperous city. It is also a pleasant place, best visited en route to the splendid Altay mountains and lakes in the far east of the region.

PAVLODAR
☎ 3182 • pop 335,000
On the Irtysh river, Pavlodar, 400km east of Astana and 110km from the Russian border, was developed as an industrial town in Soviet times. It's dominated by drab architecture and a largely redundant industrial plant, plus a tractor factory, that used to make tanks. (Pavlodar was closed to foreigners until 1992.) The extension of the railway south to Semey provides hope of a partial revival for the city.

Places to Stay & Eat
The *Hotel Sariarka* (☎ 76 18 27, *Toraygirova 1*), in a tower block overlooking the Irtysh, has good rooms with TV and hot water for US$15. There's also a nice buffet bar with a view on the 6th floor. More expensive and more western in ambience is the *Hotel Business Centre* on the corner of Lenin and Lermintov. Rooms start at US$30; prices decrease the longer you stay.

At the Turkish restaurant *Bosfor* on Lermintov, a good meal costs US$5 and you can bring your own alcohol. The *Osterbrau* opposite the Hotel Sariarka has German-style beer on tap and decent food for US$7. There's also a *stolovaya* in the TsUM on Dzerzhinskogo and shashlyk at the main bazar.

Getting There & Around
There are daily flights to/from Almaty (US$50) and occasional charter flights to Frankfurt and Hannover. Bus No 22 links the airport to the centre, 15km away, and the train station. A taxi to the airport is around US$7.

The train and bus stations are both at the north end of Toraygirova. The fastest way to Semey is by one of the two daily small minibuses *(kommerchesky)* which take around four hours and cost US$5. There are also at least a couple of slower buses daily to Semey, plus services to Astana, Karaghandy, Novosibirsk, Omsk, and Öskemen.

Trains run daily to Astana (12 hours), Barnaul, Omsk and Novosibirsk in Russia, and every other day to Almaty (36 hours) and Moscow (69 hours) via Astana. Note, Pavlodar is three hours ahead of Moscow time.

SEMEY
☎ 3222 • pop 340,000
North of Almaty by 850km and 700km east of Astana, Semey is better known to the world by its Russian name Semipalatinsk. For 40 years between 1949 and 1989, the Soviet military exploded 470 nuclear bombs in the Polygon, a vast area of the steppe southwest of the city. Locals say they knew when tests were going on because the ground would shake – often on Sunday mornings. An unprecedented wave of popular protest in Kazakstan, the Nevada-Semipalatinsk Movement (now the Nevada-Semey Movement), was largely instrumental in halting the tests in 1989. See the boxed text 'Living beside the Polygon' and the Ecology & Environment section later, in the Facts about Kazakstan section of this chapter for more information.

Despite the terrible health and environmental legacy of the tests, Semey is one of Kazakstan's more interesting cities. Set in the territory of the Middle Horde, who were noted for their eloquence and intellect, the city and its surrounding region have produced several major Kazak writers and teachers, among them the national poet Abay Kunabaev (1845-1904) and Mukhtar Auezov (1897-1968).

In 1917 Semey was the capital of the short-lived Alash Orda independent Kazakstan government. Its Russian past is interesting, too. The original fort was founded in 1718, a few kilometres away along the Irtysh river, as Russia's expansion across Siberia ran up against the war-like Mongolia-based

Top: National Heroes, Astana. Kazybek Bi, Töle Bi and Ayteke Bi were leaders of the three Kazak hordes.
Middle Right: Statue of the bard, Zhambyl Zhabaev. Like other heroes, an Almaty street bears his name.
Bottom Left: Ghosts of the Soviet era abound; a Kazak boy stands outside an old Soviet cinema.
Bottom Right: Zenkov Cathedral, Almaty, is built entirely of wood and apparently without nails!

The beautiful azure-blue dome of the Pahlavon Mohammed mausoleum, Khiva, is typical of Timurid architecture.

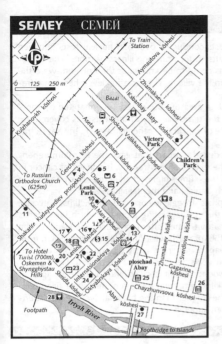

SEMEY СЕМЕЙ

To Train Station

Aymautova köshesi

Zhamakaeva köshesi

Kabanbay Batyr köshesi

Bazar

Aseta Naymanbaev köshesi

Shokan Valikhanov köshesi

Kulzhanovykh köshesi

125   250 m

Gerchena köshesi prospektisi

Dulatova köshesi

Shakarim Kudayberdiev

Lenin Park

Karl Marks köshesi

Victory Park

Children's Park

To Russian Orthodox Church (625m)

Simida köshesi

Internatsionalnaya köshesi

Lenina

Oktyabrskaya köshesi

Abay köshesi

Zhumabaev köshesi

Sverdlova köshesi

To Hotel Turist (700m), Öskemen & Shyngghystau Hills

ploschad Abay

Gagarina köshesi

Chayzhunrsova köshesi

Footpath

Irtysh River

Footbridge to Islands

SEMEY

PLACES TO STAY
3   Hotel Semey
24 Hotel Irtysh

PLACES TO EAT
4   Eldorado Supermarket & Cafe
12 Edem
16 Kafe Dostyk
17 Istanbul

OTHER
1   Bus Station
2   Don Quixote Bar
5   Air Kazakstan Ticket Office
6   Main Post Office
7   Kazaktelekom
8   Shanghai Bar
9   Abay Museum
10 OVIR
11 Old Fort Gate
13 Fire Station
14 Theatre
15 Narodny Bank
18 History & Local Studies Museum
19 University of Medicine
20 Communist Statue Graveyard
21 UNDP Office
22 Library
23 Old Cinema
25 Dostoevsky Museum
26 Fine Arts Museum
27 Children's Culture Palace
28 Boat Bar

Oyrat (Zhungarian) empire. Semey shifted to its present site in the 1770s and remnants of this fort still stand. In the 19th century the great Russian writer Fyodor Dostoevsky spent five years in exile here.

Semey is the most northerly major stop in Kazakstan on the Turksib railway which joins Almaty with Novosibirsk in Russia. Like most other Kazakstan cities, it's Russian-looking and increasingly down at heel since the collapse of industry in the area and its loss of oblast capital status in 1997. A major bridge building project across the Irtysh is the mainstay of the local economy.

The nuclear testing program helped maintain the intellectual traditions of the place by bringing in top scientists and teachers. Semey's university remains highly respected and you'll encounter students from all over Asia.

If you wish to go to Kurchatov itself without visiting some military or other important organisations, you do not need a permit. If you want to go somewhere in the Polygon or visit the nuclear centre or talk to some people relevant to nuclear or any 'closed' activity, you must get permission from the Ministry of Foreign Affairs in Almaty, or through an organisation in Semey; the first way is preferable.

Orientation
Semey is dissected from north-east to south-west by its main street, Shakarim Kudayberdiev (formerly called Komsomola), and from south-east to north-west by the Irtysh river. The older part of the city and nearly everything of use or interest is on the north-east side of the Irtysh. The train station is just off the north-east end of Shakarim Kudayberdiev, about 3km from the centre. Street names are now mostly in Kazak.

Living beside the Polygon

In Sarjal, just 30km from where Soviet scientists conducted over 550 nuclear tests between 1949 and 1991, almost all the 2600 inhabitants suffer from one illness or more. The explosions in the 18,000 sq km test area, which has come to be known as the Polygon, were the equivalent of one Hiroshima for every person in the village. The radiation levels here were frequently 100 times higher than normal.

Winds carried the fallout and contaminated an area of 300,000 sq km, inhabited by some two million people, yet during the Soviet era, the terrible legacy of the tests was covered up. Amazingly, some blamed the growing incidence of cancer and other illnesses on the Kazak tradition of drinking scalding tea.

In December 1998, the United Nations produced a report that gave the first comprehensive assessment of the situation, confirming the extent of the tragedy. Incidence of cancer in communities like Sarjal, close to the test site, is three times higher than in the rest of Kazakstan and there has been a dramatic increase in birth defects and mental illness.

Hardly having any money, Semey's local hospitals struggle to cope with the victims. Ironically, the situation has worsened due to the end of the nuclear testing program, which for decades was the mainstay of the area's economy. Kurchatov (named after Igor Kurchatov, leader of the team that developed the Soviet atom bomb), 150km north-west of Semey and just 20km from Sarjal, was the headquarters of the nuclear weapons program. Forty thousand troops and scientists were stationed here during the Cold War years; less than 8000 are there today.

Apart from sick people, the most overt evidence of the test program is Lake Balapan, a 400m wide, 800m deep crater left by a 130 kiloton nuclear explosion, and since filled with water. The base radiation in the lake is 200 times higher than the national average and scientists warn that no one should go near it without supervision.

Information

You can change money in the hotels, at the bazar and at exchange booths around town. There's a cash machine at Norodny Bank on Lenina.

The main post office, is behind the long-distance telephone office on the corner of Dulatova and Bauyrzhan Momyshuly. It's open Monday to Friday 8 am to 6 pm, Saturday 9 am to 4 pm, and until 3 pm on Sunday.

UNDP has an office at Lenina 4 (☎ 62 33 66), which may be able to put you in touch with an English-speaking guide.

OVIR (☎ 66 48 09), open Monday to Wednesday and Friday 9 am to 12.30 pm and 2 to 6 pm, is in the centre of the city at Ibraev 7 (on the corner of Baurzhan Momyshuly, opposite Park Lenina) in the five storey building of the City Department of Internal Affairs. The registration fee for visas is 71.50 T, which is to be paid at the post office. After paying the fee, one should submit a form to OVIR that should contain the following information: date of arrival in the city, place of stay and duration.

Abay Museum

This big complex at the corner of Dulatova and Internatsionalnaya was unveiled in 1995 for the 150th anniversary of Abay Kunabaev's birth and covers all aspects of his life, with sections on wider Kazak culture and other writers too. Abay was born in the Shyngghystau hills south of Semey (see the following Around Semey section) and spent much of his life there and in the city. He is the No 1 Kazak cultural guru – a 19th century humanist poet and teacher who valued Kazak traditions as well as aspects of the progress that came with the Russians. See the boxed text 'Abay – Literary Hero' in the Arts entry of the Facts about Kazakstan section of this chapter.

As well as many personal possessions of Abay (including his books and writing desk) there's a gallery, a fully decorated yurt,

The 150th birthday anniversary of Abay, a national hero, was celebrated in 1995.

sections on his literary successors (including his nephew, the bard Shakarim Kuday-berdiev), and Mukhtar Auezov, playwright and author of the epic Kazak novel *Abay Zholy* (The Path of Abay). This book, a tale of 19th century steppe life based on Abay and other historical figures, has been translated into many languages and has helped to perpetuate the memory of Abay among Kazaks.

The museum is open daily 10 am to 6 pm, with a lunch break from 1 am to 2 pm. Entrance is 125 T. The entrance is on Lenina and the wooden building in front is a recreation of the medressa where Abay studied as a child.

Museums

The well laid-out **Dostoevsky Museum** is just off Lenina, built alongside the wooden house where the writer lived from 1857 to 1859. There are exhibits covering both his life and work. It has a lot of pictures and photos and is worth a visit even if you can't understand its mainly Russian texts.

The two main parts of the museum are a display on Dostoevsky's life and works (with sections devoted to his childhood in Moscow, residence in St Petersburg, periods in Omsk and Semey, and creative life from 1860 to 1881), and the rooms where he lived, maintained in the style of his day. Don't bother getting an extra ticket for the *vystavka* (an exhibition from the museum's archives) unless you have a special interest.

The museum is open Tuesday to Sunday 9 am to 5 pm. Guided tours are available in Russian and Kazak only.

The **History and Local Studies Museum** at Lenina 5 has material on the growth of Semey, a small display on nuclear testing and the Nevada-Semey Movement, and a few old Kazak artefacts. It's only moderately interesting if you can't understand

Dostoevsky in Exile

In 1849, at the age of 28, Fyodor Dostoevsky was sentenced to death with several others for attending meetings of the Petrashevsky Circle, a group of utopian socialist intelligentsia who gathered in a St Petersburg house. The group was lined up before a firing squad – only to be told at the last moment that their sentences had been commuted to exile in Siberia.

Dostoevsky spent the next five years in a convict prison at Omsk – an experience which produced his first major novel, *The House of the Dead*. This was followed by five years of enforced military service in the garrison at Semey, which was then starting to prosper mildly as a trading town but was still as remote and inhospitable a place as the tsarist authorities could think of for dissidents. This didn't stop Dostoevsky from his writing, and it was in Semey that he began one of his most famous novels, *The Brothers Karamazov*.

It was also in Semey that Dostoevsky met and made friends with the extraordinary Shoqan Ualikhanov, a prince of the Middle Horde, explorer, artist, intellectual, and officer and spy in the Russian army. A statue of both men stands outside the museum. See the boxed text 'Renaissance Boy of the Steppes', in the History section of the Facts about Central Asia chapter, for more on Shoqan.

Russian or Kazak. It's open Tuesday to Sunday 10 am to 2 pm and 3 to 6 pm.

Located in a white colonnaded building, a couple of blocks east of the Hotel Irtysh, the **Fine Arts Museum** has some good work by Kazak, Russian and west European painters.

Old Semey

Looking somewhat forlorn on a concrete island on Abay, just before the railway bridge, is one of the **fort gates** built in the 1770s, flanked by a couple of cannons. Also still standing (and working), down the third street on the left after the bridge, is a pretty **Russian Orthodox church** with a blue tower and dome, which once stood at the centre of the fort. In the streets north-east of here, towards the bus station and bazar, are many old one-storey wooden houses.

On Internatsionalnaya, opposite Park Lenina, is a handsome red-brick **fire station** dating from the turn of the century. Further east, on Pavlov, is a 19th century **mosque** (a Russian-style building with a minaret sticking out of the top), used as an exhibition hall in Soviet times but back in religious use now.

Irtysh River

The walk along the north-east bank of the Irtysh is pleasant. There's a curious collection of Communist statues – a kind of graveyard of Lenin and Marx busts, presided over by the giant Lenin that used to stand on the nearby square, immediately north of the Hotel Irtysh and behind the old cinema. A footbridge about 700m south-east of here leads to a long island which, in summer, is the favourite local spot for sunbathing, sitting round campfires and watching members of the opposite sex. It's not a good idea to stroll here after dark.

Places to Stay

Hotel Irtysh (☎ 66 64 77, Abay 97) may be a chilly and off-putting Soviet-era establishment, but the staff are pleasant and rooms with bathroom, TV, fridge and hot water are good value at US$15/30.

There's been some renovation at the *Hotel Semey (☎ 62 25 08, Kabanbay Batyr 26)*, opposite Victory Park. It still has basic rooms, with just a sink and shared bathroom from US$4.50, but there are also more luxurious ones with TV, fridge and ensuites for US$20/40.

The most dilapidated of Semey's hotels is the *Hotel Turist (☎ 42 21 25, Zhambyl 9)*, just off Shakarim Kudayberdiev on the south-west bank of the river. Go up to room 211 to check in. Shabby rooms with bath are US$8/10.

Places to Eat

It's a sign of the times that the Dom Knigi bookshop in Semey is now *Eldorado*, a glitzy supermarket serving the city's best array of food. The attached *cafe* has a good range of cheap snacks including hamburgers, hot dogs and beer. It's open 24 hours.

Restoran Semey in the Hotel Semey is reasonable – three courses and a drink will cost you around US$3. It's open noon till midnight.

Near the University of Medicine on Bauyrzhan Momyshuly is a Turkish cafe, *Istanbul*, serving kebabs, chips and burgers – mainly to teenage tear-aways.

Kafe Dostyk, on Lenina, has music in the evenings and may be booked up with banquets. A more reliable bet is *Edem*, further down Lenina towards the park. The food portions are on the small side, but this is more a bar than a restaurant.

The *bazar*, off Kabanbay Batyr, sells a wide range of fresh and prepared food and is worth a visit.

Entertainment

Kazak, Russian, Ukrainian or German dance performances are staged occasionally in the orange *Culture Centre* building facing the park in front of the Hotel Semey. The *theatre* on ploshchad Abay has concerts by the Semey philharmonic orchestra and others. You may also find good concerts in the *Children's Culture Place*, the dome-topped building on Abay near the Hotel Irtysh.

Bars to check out include *Shanghai* on Internatsionalnaya and Naymanbaev, and *Don Quixote* on Kabanbay Batyr a couple of blocks north-west of the Hotel Semey. A boat docked on the Irtysh, docked near the

Hotel Irtysh, also acts as an outdoor bar in the summer.

Yelimay Semey is one of Kazakstan's top *soccer* teams and its home games are advertised on posters around town. The season runs from about April to September. To find the stadium, follow Lenina north-west from Shakarim Kudayberdiev, take the first street on the right after you go under the railway, and head for the floodlight pylons.

Getting There & Away

Air tickets are sold at the Air Kazakstan office (☎ 62 92 32) at Shakarim Kudayberdiev 38, open daily 8 am to 1 pm and 2 to 5 pm. Flights go to/from Almaty daily (US$65) and there are occasional charter flights to Germany on Vogelman.

From the bus station off Naymanbaev, next to the bazar, several daily fast and slow buses run to Pavlodar (four or seven hours) and Öskemen (three or six hours), and one to Barnaul in Russia (11 hours).

Trains from Semey run directly to Barnaul (US$23, nine hours) and Novosibirsk (US$32, 16 hours) three times a day. South bound trains head twice a day to Almaty (US$13), twice a week to Tashkent (US$39), and twice a week to Bishkek (US$29). If you're heading for China, you can connect with the Almaty-Ürümqi trains at Aktogay, 12 hours south of Semey. At the time of research these trains leave Aktogay for Ürümqi at 7.15 am (4.15 am Moscow time) on Sunday and Tuesday.

Since most trains from Semey are in transit, getting tickets at short notice can be a pain. Note that Semey is three hours ahead of Moscow time.

Getting Around

Bus No 11, 22, 33 or 44 run from the train station to the centre along Shakarim Kudayberdiev. Bus No 22 turns right along Kabanbay Batyr to the bazar; the others continue across the Irtysh, with bus No 33 going all the way to the airport. For the Hotel Irtysh get off when you see the river bridge ahead, and walk back to Abay; for the Hotel Turist get off after the bridge. A taxi from the train station to the centre is about US$1.

From the theatre on ploshchad Abay, bus No 2 and 35 run to the bazar and bus No 50 runs to the bus station. Buses run from about 6 am to 10 pm.

AROUND SEMEY
Shyngghystau Hills

The Shyngghystau is a range of rocky hills (1200m at their highest) 100 to 200km south of Semey. Apart from its natural beauty, this sparsely peopled area is full of Kazak legends and is famed as the homeland and inspiration of the writers Abay Kunabaev, Mukhtar Auezov and Shakarim Kudayberdiev. Abay was born in Kaskabulak on the northern fringe of the hills, but his last home, in the village of Zhidebai, is now a museum, and this is where you'll also find his mausoleum, together with that of Kudayberdiev – easily the area's most impressive building. Auezov's home, also a museum, is in Borli.

To get to these remote places you'll need to hire a guide and car in Semey. A good place to make inquires is the Abay Museum. Organised trips may be run by travel agencies in Semey over the summer.

ÖSKEMEN
☎ 3232 • pop 315,000

Still commonly known by its Russian name of Ust-Kamenogorsk, Öskemen is the starting point for trips to the remote Altay mountains and lakes in the far eastern corner of Kazakstan. Like Semey, Öskemen was founded as a Russian fort in 1720. It has grown from a small town since the 1940s when Russians and Ukrainians began to arrive to mine and process local minerals.

Mining of nonferrous metals, in particular copper, lead, silver and zinc, still continues, all of which makes Öskemen a relatively prosperous and lively place. Its location straddling the Ulba and Irtysh rivers, and at the foot of some small mountains, is appealing, as is the centre's generally low-key Soviet architecture, supplemented by a handful of pre-Communist era buildings.

Orientation

The centre of Öskemen is on a spit of land between the Irtysh and Ulba rivers. The

KAZAKSTAN

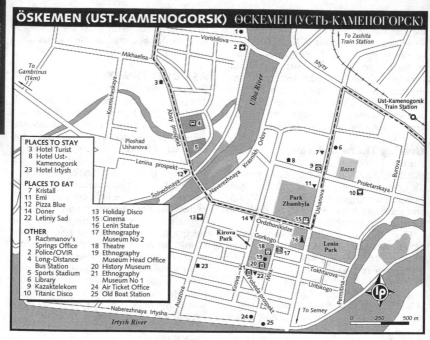

ÖSKEMEN (UST-KAMENOGORSK) ӨСКЕМЕН (УСТЬ-КАМЕНОГОРСК)

PLACES TO STAY
3 Hotel Turist
8 Hotel Ust-
   Kamenogorsk
23 Hotel Irtysh

PLACES TO EAT
7 Kristall
11 Emi
12 Pizza Blue
14 Doner
22 Letiniy Sad

OTHER
1 Rachmanov's
   Springs Office
2 Police/OVIR
4 Long-Distance
   Bus Station
5 Sports Stadium
6 Library
9 Kazaktelekom
10 Titanic Disco

13 Holiday Disco
15 Cinema
16 Lenin Statue
17 Ethnography
   Museum No 2
18 Theatre
19 Ethnography
   Museum Head Office
20 History Museum
21 Ethnography
   Museum No 1
24 Air Ticket Office
25 Old Boat Station

main axis is Ushanova, running north from the bridge over the Irtysh, past Lenin's statue, still facing the park that bears his name, and further north to the bustling bazar. Crossing Ushanova and leading to the main bridge across the Ulba is Ordzhonikidze, which splits into prospekt Abay and prospekt Lenina on the west bank of the river. The bus station is at the foot of prospekt Abay, while the main train station, Zashita, is around 5km further west.

Information

Kazaktelekom has its main office on the corner of Ushanova and Proletarskaya. At the central **library** on Ushanova, you'll find English speakers and books; Internet access is US$6 per hour. It's open daily 9 am to 6 pm.

Travel Agencies Former Soviet-team mountaineer Andrei Tselichev (☎ 47 93 43, fax 47 93 44) runs an adventure tourism outfit called Altay Trial and is also the owner of the Rachmanov's Springs resort in the Altay mountains (see the following Altay Mountains and Lake Markakol section). As well as organising hiking and sightseeing trips to the Altay (including special visas), Lake Markakol and the Black Irtysh river basin, he can arrange ascents of the 4506m Mt Belukha, cross-country skiing in winter and rafting along the Ulba and Bukhtarma rivers in early summer. The company also has a small skiing operation at Bubrovka, 35km north of Öskemen.

Another good contact is Boris Vasilevich Shcherbakov (☎ 25 76 29 home, 26 49 00 work) at the Unnatski Ekologik Sentir (Ecology Centre), Gorkogo 66. He's an ornithologist – with a collection of parrots – who with a bit of notice can organise trips to Altay's Lake Markakol and maybe Mt Belukha.

Things to See

Clustered around the pretty Kirova Park, are some of Öskemen's oldest buildings, plus several interesting museums. The **Ethnography Museum** is split into three sites: permanent exhibits are at the branch on the corner of Kirova and Uritskogo, including a recreation of a 19th century pioneer's log cabin, a room celebrating Öskemen's Korean residents, and some fine Russian Orthodox icons. The rest of the collection is rather kitsch.

The museum's second site is across the park on the corner of Mira and Gorkogo, and includes a Kazak section with a yurt, an area for visiting exhibitions and a gallery displaying local art.

The third site, primarily the museum's offices, is in the handsome red brick building on Mira beside Kirova park, dating from 1886. Next door, with its entrance facing the park, is the **History Museum**, with a natural history section on the ground floor, including a giant stuffed Maral deer (the antlers of which are considered an aphrodisiac in Korea), and interesting archaeological and contemporary history exhibits upstairs.

Places to Stay

The best hotel is the *Hotel Irtysh* (☎ 25 29 23, fax 25 09 85, Auzzova 22). The receptionists speak English, the restaurant is fine, there's a well stocked gift shop and an airline ticket booking office. Rates for good singles/doubles, with satellite TV, phone and hot water, are US$10/20 and include breakfast.

Hotel Ust-Kamenogorsk (☎ 26 18 01, Proletarskaya 158) is more along traditional Soviet lines, but has pleasantly furnished rooms with TV and ensuites for US$20/40.

As a fall-back, the *Hotel Turist* (☎ 22 26 42, Abay 9) is gloomy and cold compared with the other hotels and less centrally located. Rooms are US$10/14 or US$17 with TV and phone.

Places to Eat

While the restaurants at both the Hotel Irtysh and Hotel Ust-Kamenogorsk are OK, there are better options around town, including two modern Turkish cafes, both with outdoor tables and an excellent selection of sweet cakes and desserts to supplement the kebabs, burgers and salads. *Kristall*

is on Ushanova, just north of the bazar, while *Doner* is on the corner of Kirova and Ordzhonikidze; both have table service.

On the western side of the city, on Metallyurgov, is *Gambrinus*, a European-style restaurant with wooden booths and fine food for around US$8.

Facing the Ulba at the end of Lenina is *Pizza Blue*, serving some 10 different types of pizza and fine *solyanka*, a thick soup.

Letiniy Sad, on the corner of Kirova, is a pleasant beer garden dotted with funky wooden sculptures. Shashlyk and the like is served here; it's open May to September.

Another convivial cafe/bar with an outdoor area is *Emi* on Ushanova, which also serves ice cream.

Entertainment

Titanic and *Holiday* are Öskemen's top discos (US$5), both in former cinemas, and pounding out Russian techno from 9 pm onwards. There's a *cinema* on the corner of Ushanova and Ordzhonikidze. The *theatre* on Mira next to Kirova park dates from 1902 and still holds performances.

Getting There & Around

There are flights daily to/from Almaty (US$55) and weekly to/from Moscow. Tickets can be bought at the office on the second floor of the building facing the old boat station on the Irtysh on Nabereshnaya Irtysha, or at the Hotel Irtysh.

From Semey, the most direct way to Öskemen is by road. The fastest minibus takes 3½ hours and costs US$4.50.

The train to/from Semey follows a circuitous route, looping into Russia, and takes at least 10 hours. The main station for Öskemen is Zashita; the Ust-Kamenogorsk station at the end of Ushanova is on a branch line. For train times, note that Öskemen is three hours ahead of Moscow.

Buses No 12 or 39 run to the airport, around 10km west of the city. A taxi costs around US$2. Tram 3 connects Ust-Kamenogorsk and Zashita train stations, running along Ushanova, Ordzhonikidze and up Abay. Also you can take bus No 1 or 19 to Zashita from Lenina.

THE ALTAY MOUNTAINS & LAKE MARKAKOL

In the far north-eastern corner of Kazakstan the magnificent Altay mountains spread across the borders to Russia, China, and Mongolia, only 50km away. This is still considered a sensitive border zone and everyone, even Kazaks, needs special visas if they want to go beyond the village of Berel in the Bukhtarma valley, or visit the Markakol Nature Reserve in the southern Altay range. See the following Visas entry.

The hassle is well worth it. Endless rolling meadows, forested valleys, rocky, snow-covered peaks, pristine lakes and rivers, and rustic villages with Kazak horsemen riding by make for scenery of epic proportions. In fact, little has changed since US journalist George Kennan toured here in 1885 and proclaimed 'I had never seen such a picturesque alpine panorama that could compare with this in splendour, grandeur and beauty.' Small wonder that Asian legends call this area Shambhala, a paradisal realm that will be revealed after humanity destroys itself.

Huge collective farms dominated the lowland steppes during Soviet times, but they're all finished now. The area's largest town is Katon-Karagay, but the place to aim for is Rachmanov's Springs, an idyllic hot springs resort at the very end of the mountain road, 110km to the east. Alternatively, Lake Markakol to the south is a wildlife haven set amid a forest of birch, larch and fir trees.

Visas

The Altay mountains and Markakol Nature Reserve are classed as sensitive border areas and require a visa. Applications should be made at least 10 days in advance to the local police office on Voroshilova in Öskemen, but are best arranged via an agent (see the Travel Agencies entry in the previous Öskemen section).

Rachmanov's Springs

This charming health resort, 30km further up the mountain track from the village of Berel, was built in the 1960s by one of the local mining companies, but is now a private concern. Here you'll find pastel-painted wooden cottages linked by wooden boardwalks through pine forests, nestling in a mountain valley, one end of which is plugged by a mirror-like lake. Activities include trekking, horse riding, cross-country skiing in winter.

Accommodation starts at US$8 per day for a basic *cottage*, rising to US$14 for luxury ones with their own kitchens and TV. For three meals a day, plus afternoon tea at the resort canteen, add on US$4.20. Bookings should be made through the resort office in Öskemen (☎ 3232-47 93 43, fax 47 93 44).

This is an ideal base from which to tackle 4506m Belukha, the Altay's highest mountain, on the Kazakstan-Russia border. Its double-headed peak, linked by a glacier, is a two-day climb from the resort. Make sure you're thoroughly prepared, suitably experienced and preferably accompanied, as there are glaciers and 3000m-plus passes, which may require crampons, ropes and ice screws.

Markakol Nature Reserve

The Markakol Nature Reserve is centred on Lake Markakol, at 40km the largest lake in the Altay and 1500m above sea level, south of Katon-Karagay. The lake is noted for its pure waters and beautiful countryside. Accommodation is likely to be in *tents* or in *home-stays* at Urunkhayka village at the east end of the lake. In summer, in a 4WD, the lake can be reached by a mountain pass road built by POWs during WWII. At other times the only access is by a much longer southern route passing through the town of Kurchum on the north coast of Lake Zaysan.

Getting There & Away

Tour agencies in both Almaty and Öskemen are the best way to arrange trips to this remote area. See the relevant sections of this chapter for details.

Contact the Rachmanov's Springs office for details of the bus transport they arrange over summer, during which time it's also possible to hire cars to make the eight hour journey from Öskemen; expect to pay US $50 one way. If you're determined to go by public transport it's an all-day bus trip to Katon-Karagay, which has a small *hotel* and *stolovaya*. From here, you're on your own.

Uzbekistan

Uzbekistan at a Glance

Official Name: Uzbekiston Jumhuriyati
Area: 447,400 sq km
Population: 24 million (1999 estimate)
Ethnic Mix: 80% Uzbek, 5% Russian, 5% Tajik, 3% Kazak, 2% Tatar, 2% Karakalpak, 1% each Kyrgyz and Korean, and 1% others
Capital: Tashkent
Currency: *sum*
Country ☎ Code: 998
Best Time to Go: May to end June, September to November

- **Tashkent** – culture at the Alisher Navoi Opera & Ballet Theatre
- **Fergana Valley** – the quiet charm of orchards, canals and villages
- **Margilan** – the mystery of silk-worm farming
- **Shakhimardan** – unrestricted vistas of the Alay mountains
- **Samarkand** – a city resonant of the Silk Road, with fine monuments
- **Bukhara** – the bazars and ancient monuments of Central Asia's holiest city
- **Khiva** – dramatic history, plus mosques, tombs, palaces and *medressas*

Uzbekistan, the ancient cradle between the Amu-Darya and Syr-Darya rivers, is the most historically rich of the Central Asian republics. Within it are some of the world's oldest towns, some of the Silk Road's main centres and most of Central Asia's architectural attractions. Samarkand – capital of the cultured empire of Timur (Tamerlane) – plus Bukhara and Khiva are virtual outdoor museums.

Uzbekistan sees itself as the most important of the former Soviet Central Asian republics. In addition to being the 'spiritual home' of sizable Uzbek minorities in the other republics (and in Afghanistan), it is the only republic sharing borders with all the others and Afghanistan. Uzbeks are the most self-confident of the region's peoples, historically settled, pious and community-minded.

The president, Islam Karimov, the former Communist Party boss, keeps a tight grip on the country. Statues of Amir Timur (Tamerlane) and other Uzbek figures now stand on plinths once occupied by Marx and Lenin, the KGB has changed its name to the National Security Service, and politics remain as monolithic and shadowy as ever. The revival of Islam is causing great alarm to the government, and moderate opinions have been brutally suppressed along with the more extreme ones. Nevertheless Karimov does have some popular support, though it is unlikely ever to be tested in an election.

It has never been easier to travel on the golden road to Samarkand. Much of the economy is still stagnant but the basics are there for Central Asia's most diversified economy. Reforms have been only gradually, almost grudgingly, introduced but already the markets are thriving, new tourist-oriented businesses have emerged, and crafts and skills once thought lost are being revived. A vigorous black market hungry for hard currency has made travel much cheaper.

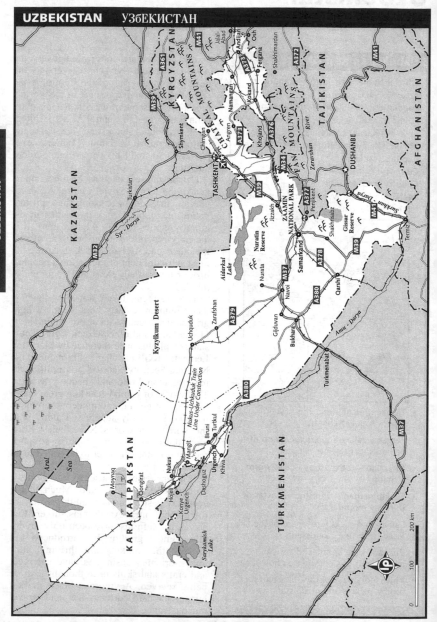

UZBEKISTAN

UZBEKISTAN УЗБЕКИСТАН

KAZAKSTAN

KYRGYZSTAN

TAJIKISTAN

AFGHANISTAN

TURKMENISTAN

KARAKALPAKSTAN

Aral Sea

Kyzylkum Desert

CHATKAL MOUNTAINS

FAN MOUNTAINS

Sarykamish Lake

Aidarkul Lake

ZAAMIN NATIONAL PARK

Nuratau Reserve

Gissar Reserve

Nukus-Uchkuduk Train Line Under Construction

Syr-Darya

Amu-Darya

Zeravshan River

Surkhan-Darya

TASHKENT
DUSHANBE

Jalal-Abad
Andijan
Osh
Shakhimardan
Fergana
Namangan
Kokand
Khojand
Angren
Chimgan
Shymkent
Turkistan
Penjikent
Jizzakh
Samarkand
Shakhrisabz
Termiz
Nurata
Navoi
Qarshi
Gijduvan
Bukhara
Zaratshan
Uchkuduk
Turkmenabat
Biruni
Turkul
Urgench
Khiva
Dashoguz
Mangit
Nukus
Hojeli
Konye Urgench
Qongrat
Moynaq

M41
A361
M39
M32
M41
A373
A372
A375
A376
A384
M39
A377
A378
A380
M37
A379
A380
M37
M41

200 km
100
0

Facts about Uzbekistan

HISTORY
The land along the upper Amu-Darya, Syr-Darya and their tributaries has always been different from the rest of Central Asia – more settled than nomadic, with patterns of land use and communality that changed little from the time of the Achaemenids (6th century BCE; before common era) right into the 19th century. An attitude of permanence and proprietorship still sets the people of the region apart.

Ancient Empires
The region was part of some very old Persian states, including Bactria, Khorezm and Sogdiana. Into Cyrus the Great's Achaemenid empire came Alexander the Great in the 4th century BCE. He stopped near Samarkand and married Roxana, the daughter of a local chieftain. Under the Kushan dynasty, Buddhism took hold and the Silk Road brought peaceful contact with the wider world and facilitated the growth of wealthy, culturally diverse towns. With its decline came a brief return to Persia under the Sassanians.

Then out of the northern steppes in the 6th century CE (common era) came the Western Turks – the western branch of the empire of the so-called Kök (Blue) Turks. They soon grew attached to life here and abandoned their wandering ways. The Arabs brought Islam and a written alphabet in the 8th century but found Central Asia too big and restless to govern.

A return to the Persian fold came with the Samanid dynasty in the 9th and 10th centuries. Its capital, Bukhara, was the centre of an intellectual, religious and commercial renaissance. In the 11th century the Ghaznavids moved into the southern regions. For some time the Turkic Khorezmshahs dominated Central Asia from present-day Konye-Urgench in Turkmenistan, but their fun was cut short and the region's elegant oases ravaged by Jenghiz Khan in the early 13th century.

Central Asia again became truly 'central' with the rise of Timur, the ruthless warrior and patron of the arts who fashioned a glittering Islamic capital at Samarkand.

The Uzbeks
Little is known of early Uzbek history. At the time the Golden Horde (see The Hordes & the Great Disaster in the History section in the Kazakstan chapter) was founded, Shibaqan or Shayban, a grandson of Jenghiz Khan, inherited what is today northern Kazakstan and adjacent parts of Russia. The greatest khan of these Mongol Shaybani tribes (and probably the one under whom they swapped paganism for Islam) was Özbeg or Uzbek (ruled 1313 to 40). By the end of the 14th century these tribes had begun to name themselves after him.

The Uzbeks began moving south-east, mixing with sedentary Turkic tribes and adopting the Turkic language, reaching the Syr-Darya in the mid-15th century. Following an internal schism (which gave birth to the proto-Kazaks), the Uzbeks pulled themselves together under Mohammed Shaybani and thundered down upon the remnants of Timur's empire. By 1510 all of Transoxiana ('the land beyond the Oxus') from the Amu-Darya (Oxus) to the Syr-Darya (Jaxartes) belonged to the Uzbeks, as it has since. They ruled at this time from Bukhara, with a separate line in Khorezm, at Khiva.

The greatest (and last) of the Shaybanid khans, responsible for some of Bukhara's finest architecture, was Abdullah II, who ruled from 1538 until his death in 1598. After this, as the Silk Road fell into disuse, the empire unravelled under the Shaybanids' distant cousins, the Astrakhanids. For a time Khorezm and the Astrakhanid lands again became part of Persia, after the warlord Nadir Shah defeated Bukhara and Khiva in 1740.

The Astrakhanid throne was usurped by the first of the Bukhara emirs, Masum Shah Murad, in 1785. By the start of the 19th century the entire region was dominated by three weak, feuding Uzbek city-states – Khiva, Bukhara and a Bukhara breakaway, Kokand.

UZBEKISTAN

The Russians Arrive

In the early 18th century the khan of Khiva made an offer to Peter the Great of Russia (to become his vassal in return for help against marauding Turkmen and Kazak tribes) stirring the first Russian interest in Central Asia. Peter's appetite had been whetted by Khiva's potential as a staging post for trade with India, by reports of gold along the Amu-Darya, and by a mistaken idea that the Amu-Darya could be made navigable right into the heart of Central Asia (by destroying the 'dams' that he believed forced it to run into the Aral Sea instead of the Caspian Sea). But by the time the Russians got around to marching on Khiva in 1717, the khan no longer wanted Russian protection, and after a show of hospitality he had almost the entire 4000-strong force slaughtered.

Their fingers burnt, the Russians only gradually renewed interest, starting with trade, mainly with Bukhara – buying raw cotton in exchange for textiles and tools. The slave market in Bukhara and Khiva was the excuse for further Russian visits, to free a few Russian settlers and travellers. In 1801 the insane Tsar Paul sent 22,000 Cossacks on a madcap mission to drive the British out of India, with orders to free the slaves en route. Fortunately for all but the slaves, Paul was assassinated and the army recalled while struggling across the Kazak steppes.

The next try, by Tsar Nicholas I in 1839 to 1840, was really a bid to pre-empt expansion into Central Asia by Britain, which had just taken Afghanistan, although Khiva's Russian slaves were the pretext on which General Perovsky's 5200 men and 10,000 camels set out from Orenburg. In January 1840, a British officer, Captain James Abbott, arrived in Khiva (having travelled from Herat in Afghan disguise) offering to negotiate the slaves' release on the khan's behalf, thus nullifying the Russians' excuse for coming.

Unknown to the khan the Russian force had already turned back, in the face of the worst winter for ages on the steppes. He agreed to send Abbott to the tsar with an offer to release the slaves in return for an end to Russian military expeditions against Khiva. Incredibly, Abbot made it to St Petersburg.

In search of news of Abbott, Lieutenant Richmond Shakespear reached Khiva the following June and convinced the khan to unilaterally release all Russian slaves in Khiva and even give them an armed escort to the nearest Russian outpost, on the eastern Caspian Sea. Russian gratitude was doubtlessly mingled with fury over one of the Great Game's boldest propaganda coups. (For more information see The Great Game in the Khiva section later in this chapter.)

But when the Russians finally got themselves together 25 years later, the khanates' towns fell like dominoes – Tashkent in 1865 to General Mikhail Chernyaev, Samarkand and Bukhara in 1868, Khiva in 1873, and Kokand in 1875 to General Konstantin Kaufman.

Soviet Daze

Even into the 20th century, most Central Asians identified themselves ethnically as Turks or Persians. The connection between 'Uzbek' and 'Uzbekistan' is very much a Soviet matter. Following the outbreak of the Russian Revolution in 1917 and the infamous sacking of Kokand in 1918, the Bolsheviks proclaimed the Autonomous Soviet Socialist Republic (SSR) of Turkestan. Temporarily forced out by counter-revolutionary troops and *basmachi* (Muslim guerilla fighters), they returned two years later and the Khiva and Bukhara khanates were forcibly replaced with 'People's Republics'.

Then in October 1924 the whole map was redrawn on ethnic grounds, and the Uzbeks suddenly had a 'homeland', an official identity and a literary language. The Uzbek SSR changed shape and composition over the years as it suited Moscow, hiving off Tajikistan in 1929, acquiring Karakalpakstan from Russia in 1936, getting bits of the Hungry Steppe (the Russian nickname for the dry landscape between Tashkent and Jizzakh) from Kazakstan in 1956 and 1963 and losing some in 1971.

For rural Uzbeks, the main impacts of Soviet rule were the forced and often bloody collectivisation of the republic's mainstay (agriculture) and the massive shift to cotton cultivation. Life hardly changed in

The Great Cotton Flim-Flam

The communist party chief comes up to a cotton farmer in Uzbekistan and says 'How much cotton do we have, comrade?'
The farmer replies 'Enough to pile up to Allah's feet, sir!'
The party chief says 'Fool, this is a communist state, there is no god here!'
The farmer replies 'Well, that's OK, because there's no cotton either.'

The feudal boss of the Communist Party of Uzbekistan, Sharaf Rashidov, was at the head of a mammoth, lengthy swindle over cotton harvests in the late 1970s and early 80s, during the years of Brezhnev (who himself rose to power from a Central Asia base). After spy satellites revealed that many 'cotton fields' were in fact empty, it was discovered that cotton production figures for Uzbekistan had been massively falsified for years, that cotton was being sold on the black market, and that some 5000 million roubles had been embezzled.

Rashidov was never prosecuted, but some 50,000 lesser officials were dismissed between 1984 and 1988. It's a fairly clear indication of how little has changed, that Rashidov (who was born in Karimov's own neighbourhood of Jizak) is now being posthumously 'rehabilitated' in Uzbekistan, and presented as a defender of Uzbek interests against Moscow.

Another figure in the scandal was the chairman of the Pap Agroindustrial complex, Akhmajon Adylov, who took a page straight out of the Emir of Bukhara's book – running a virtual slave labour plantation with the help of a private army, keeping a bevy of concubines and torturing those who crossed him. After the August 1991 coup in Moscow, the Russian Supreme Court dropped the charges against Adylov.

other ways. The Uzbek intelligentsia and much of the republic's political leadership was decimated by Stalin's purges. This and the traditional Central Asian respect for authority meant that by the 1980s *glasnost* (openness) and *perestroika* (restructuring) would hardly trickle down here; few significant reforms took place.

Towards Independence

Uzbekistan's first serious non-Communist popular movement, Birlik (Unity), was formed by Tashkent intellectuals in 1989 over issues that included Uzbek as an official language and the effects of the cotton monoculture. It immediately began gathering support, eventually claiming 1.5 million members, but was barred from contesting the election in February 1990 for the Uzbek Supreme Soviet (legislature) by the Communist Party. The resulting Communist-dominated body elected Islam Karimov, the First Secretary of the Communist Party of Uzbekistan (CPUz), to the new post of executive president.

During the abortive coup in Moscow in August 1991, Karimov was conspicuously quiet, but within days of its failure, he declared Uzbekistan independent on 31 August. Soon afterward the CPUz reinvented itself as the Popular Democratic Party of Uzbekistan (PDPU), inheriting all of its predecessor's property and control apparatus, most of its ideology, and of course its leader, Karimov.

In December 1991 Uzbekistan held its first direct presidential elections, which Karimov won with 86% of the vote. His only rival was a poet named Mohammed Solih, running for the small, figurehead opposition party Erk (Will or Freedom) party, who got 12% and was soon driven into exile. The real opposition groups, Birlik and the Islamic Renaissance Party (IRP), and all other parties with a religious platform, had been forbidden to take part.

Uzbekistan Today

The following years have seen Karimov consolidate his grip on power, and dissent shrivel – thanks to control of the media, police harassment and imprisonment on trumped up charges. Hundreds of activists have been arrested, and some jailed.

On 8 December 1992, the day the Uzbek Supreme Soviet adopted a new constitution committed to multiparty democracy and human rights, Abdumannov, founder of the Uzbek Human Rights Organisation, was abducted from a conference in the Kyrgyz capital, Bishkek, and charged with sedition. A few weeks later, Birlik was banned, and has now been essentially crushed.

Erk is officially still legal, though members have been hounded from the legislature, bumped out of jobs, detained and interrogated, and their newspaper banned. The IRP, with support in the Fergana valley, has gone underground. Most opposition leaders live in exile in Russia, Turkey or Afghanistan.

'Multiparty' elections were held in December 1994 for a new, streamlined parliament. The two participating parties were the PDPU and another set up with Karimov's blessing, Vatan Tarikiati or the National Progress Party. In March 1995, voters agreed to extend Karimov's term until 2000. He ran unopposed.

In 1998 a series of devastating bomb attacks in Tashkent led to a crackdown on a broad spectrum of opponents and on the Islamic resurgence. Mosques are no longer permitted to broadcast the *azan* (call to prayer), and mullahs have been pressured to praise the government in their sermons. Independent Muslims are invariably tagged 'Wahhabis' by the government and indeed even by ordinary people, though they may have nothing to do with this fundamentalist Arabian sect. Muslim reformers who want to change customs such as cripplingly expensive funerals and create a society that follows *sharia* (Islamic law) are often cast in with the real fundamentalists who fight in Tajikistan and Afghanistan. Attendance at mosques has fallen for fear of practising Muslims being observed and harassed by government agents.

Suppression of dissent is officially called a temporary necessity in a country new to democratic traditions, but it's hard to see how a democratic framework could grow here. It's no accident that Uzbekistan's newly adopted cultural role model is Timur (whose image has replaced Karl Marx's head in Tashkent's central square).

GEOGRAPHY

Uzbekistan sprawls over 447,400 sq km (about the size of Sweden), third in size after Kazakstan and Turkmenistan but the most populous (and densely populated) of the five former Soviet republics. Well over two-thirds (most of the central and western part) is flat, monotonous desert or steppe: the Ustyurt plateau in the far west with its salt marshes and streams that go nowhere, and the vast, barren Kyzylkum (Red Sands) desert in the middle. The only faint relief here is the delta where what remains of the Amu-Darya empties into what remains of the Aral Sea.

By contrast, eastern Uzbekistan tilts upward towards the mountains of Kyrgyzstan – Tashkent's Chatkal mountains running into the western Tian Shan range, and Samarkand's Fan mountains and a mass of ranges in the south-east flowing into the Pamir Alay. The mountains of Tajikistan and Kyrgyzstan encircle the Fergana valley.

The life-giving rivers all rise in these mountains. Central Asia's greatest waterway, the broad Amu-Darya, forms Uzbekistan's short border with Afghanistan and its long one with Turkmenistan, before a trickle enters the Aral Sea. The region's other defining artery, the Syr-Darya, originating in the Fergana valley from two rivers rising in Kyrgyzstan, arcs into Kazakstan on its way to the Aral Sea.

Arguably the most valuable river is the Zeravshan, nourisher of ancient Bukhara and Samarkand; theoretically the Amu-Darya's biggest tributary, it actually dies in the desert. Most other rivers are either emptied by irrigation or swallowed by the desert. The misnamed Soviet Ministry of Water Economy created two wide shallow lakes where there used to be desert, salt pans and marshes, Sarykamish in the west and Aidarkul north of the Nuratin range, as well as a host of smaller unplanned ones.

UZBEKISTAN

The bulk of Uzbekistan's population, and its richest farmland, are in gaps in the mountains (especially the Fergana valley), on the alluvial plains at their feet, and in the Amu-Darya, Syr-Darya and Zeravshan valleys.

Fully 37% of the country – the worst of it, probably – is occupied by the autonomous Republic of Karakalpakstan (see the boxed text 'Karakalpakstan' in the Nukus section later in this chapter).

CLIMATE

Large areas of Uzbekistan are desert. Summer is long, hot and extremely dry; spring is mild and rainy; autumn has light frosts and rains; and winter, although short, is unstable with snow and temperatures below freezing.

From June to August average afternoon temperatures hit 32°C or higher. The average annual maximum temperature is 40°C in June. Most rain falls in March and April.

GOVERNMENT

Formally speaking, under the terms of its December 1992 constitution Uzbekistan is a secular, democratic presidential republic. The president, who is both supreme executive and head of state, is directly elected for a five year term and may serve at most two consecutive terms. The president appoints the government (Cabinet of Ministers), subject to approval by the legislature; its chairperson becomes prime minister. The highest legislative body is the Oliy Majlis (Supreme Assembly), whose 150 members are also elected for five-year terms. The Oliy Majlis can be dissolved by the president with the approval of the Constitutional Court. The country is administratively divided into 12 *viloyati* (provinces), Tashkent *shahri* (city), plus the semi-autonomous Republic of Karakalpakstan.

In reality, while Uzbekistan is most certainly secular, with a determined separation between religion and state, it's decidedly not 'democratic'. The man ultimately in charge of everything from municipal gardeners' salaries to gold production quotas is President Islam Karimov – as he was, under a different title, even before independence. Trends towards pluralism evident in other Central Asian republics are absent here.

Social control is ensured by the government's grip on the traditional network of urban districts *(mahallas)*, a concept unique to Uzbeks in Central Asia. The neighbourhood in which an Uzbek is raised is comprised of a web of intimate social ties; neighbours attend one another's weddings, celebrations and funerals. Advice on all matters is sought from a revered elder (*aksakal*, literally 'white beard'), whose authority is conferred by the community. The government has usurped these structures by employing aksakals as district custodians and informants – to the extent that you cannot even sell your flat without their permission. Mahalla committees are required to take note of residents who attend mosques, wear Islamic garb, cultivate beards (facial hair indicating Islamic tendencies) or generally show any sign of stepping outside the line.

ECONOMY

Uzbekistan's economy is dominated by two realities. The first is the massive artificial irrigation and fertilisation of arid and semi-arid areas needed to sustain production of its major crop, raw cotton, and the resulting severe ecological and economic strains. The second (true of the other Central Asian republics too) is the crumbling of the old Soviet trade system, leaving the country a producer of far more raw materials than finished goods, despite industrialisation around Tashkent, Samarkand, Bukhara and the Fergana valley. Landlocked Uzbekistan faces great difficulties in getting its products to hard currency markets.

Uzbekistan is taking on the daunting job of curing its addiction to the cotton market and returning its rich soil to food production.

Other major agricultural sectors are fruit and rice, especially in the Fergana valley, which is also the main centre for silkworm cultivation. Animal husbandry dominates the dry west – most famously Karakul sheep, with their velvety wool of many colours, in Bukhara province.

Uzbekistan is the world's eighth largest producer of gold. The Murantau mine in the Kyzylkum desert is said to be the world's biggest open-cast gold mine. Other natural resources are coal, natural gas, petroleum, uranium and other nonferrous and rare-earth metals. Roughly 3% of the country is forest, and timber and lumber are imported. Most electricity comes from thermal plants, the remaining 15% from hydroelectric stations.

The government has invested in new infrastructure and attracted some large-scale foreign investment, particularly in textile and automobile manufacturing, and is busily making the country self-sufficient in electricity, food, oil and gas. Its main exports are of course raw cotton (over 40% of the value of all agricultural output) and cotton thread, cloth and clothing, plus some nonferrous metals. Over four-fifths of Uzbekistan's trade is still with Commonwealth of Independent States (CIS) countries.

The crisis in the Asian and Russian economies in 1998 prompted the government to raise the barriers on what was already a mostly closed economy, and the black market for hard currency reappeared. There has been no attempt to decollectivise agriculture or industry, and only the most hesitant stabs have been made at deregulation. Land is most definitely still in government hands, though it is possible to rent fields. The government's policy to gradually replace Russian workers with Central Asians has created a brain drain.

The economy is heavily protected behind steep tariff walls. The *sum* is not convertible except for government-approved projects, which in practice often means that only businesses connected to the elite can change *sum* into hard currency. These restrictions against exporting hard currency (ie profits) discourage foreign investors, and most of those who have invested are deeply in debt.

UN figures portray Uzbekistan as one of the world's most poorly developed countries, with a mean monthly income of around US$50 in the cities; much of the countryside employs a barter economy.

POPULATION & PEOPLE
In 1999 an estimated 24 million people lived in Uzbekistan. According to unofficial figures there were about 200,000 Arabs living in Kashkadarya province (around Qarshi) in 1990. Huge numbers of Slavs have emigrated, and the exodus is still running at a net rate of 60,000 people per year.

Some 38% of Uzbekistan's people are urban and 62% rural; 90% are Muslim (almost all Hanafi Sunni) and 8% Christian. A third of them live in the Fergana valley, Central Asia's mostly densely populated region.

The population growth rate has fallen since independence with the sudden disappearance of subsidies for large families, but is still high at 2.5% per year. Over half the population is under 15 years of age.

In the 1920s Stalin dismembered Turkistan and the Bukhara and Khorezm People's Republics and redrew the borders, ostensibly along ethnic lines but very often across them. The most blatant gerrymandering was in the Fergana valley (see the Fergana Valley map) where, for example, majority-Uzbek Khojand ended up in Tajikistan, and majority-Uzbek Osh in Kyrgyzstan.

On the other hand, Samarkand, Bukhara, Qarshi and Termiz went to Uzbekistan, although they are Tajik-speaking towns. But most people there call themselves Uzbeks, for the same reasons their parents or grandparents did in the 1920s, for their own protection or convenience. Says a young Tajik in Samarkand (quoted in the *International Herald Tribune*), 'In 1924 they started writing in our passports that we were all Uzbek. And if an old man insisted that, no, he was Tajik ... he ended up very far away from here.' Many Tajik speakers feel these cities should never have been part of Uzbekistan, and there is still wild-eyed talk of taking them back. The issue is complicated by ethnic Uzbek city dwellers who speak Tajik.

See History in this section and the Peoples of the Silk Road special section in the Facts about Central Asia chapter for more on the origins of the Uzbek people.

Facts for the Visitor

WHEN TO GO
The summer furnace of 35°C days lasts 40 days from mid-July to the end of August, while the worst of winter lasts 40 days from

Christmas to the first week of February. The best time to visit is in spring from May until the end of June, and in autumn from September until November. The mountains are pleasantly cool in summer, freezing in winter.

TOURIST OFFICES

Uzbektourism, the national tourist agency, is a direct descendant of Intourist and wants only tightly organised groups paying high tourist rates. There are a few helpful exceptions, including the Uzbektourism office in Fergana, and the occasional open-minded hotel excursion bureau. Seeking information at other offices can be either a waste of time or an encounter with the professionally rude. One of the worst has to be at the Hotel Tashkent.

For professional, switched-on help and some comprehension of budget travel, you should try one of the growing number of private firms (listed under individual cities).

VISAS & DOCUMENTS

First see the general Visas section in the Regional Facts for the Visitor chapter.

Getting a visa for Uzbekistan requires a visa support letter, and if you are flying into Tashkent you must have accommodation vouchers for the first three days of your stay. These aren't necessary if you arrive overland. Reliable travel agencies can supply these letters for US$15 to US$25 within a fortnight to three weeks. For a list of these see the Travel Agencies & Organised Tours section in the Getting There & Away chapter.

In 1999 Uzbekistan announced that US citizens no longer need an invitation to get a visa. Certainly at the time of research the Uzbekistan embassy in the US was issuing four year multiple entry visas to US citizens, valid for 30 days each visit, for a flat US$45, though it might take some time for this policy decision to filter down to other embassies.

Getting a Visa

Armed with the visa support letter from a travel agency, Uzbek embassies can issue visas on the spot; one-week visas cost US$40, 15-day visas US$50, one-month visas US$60 and two-month visas US$80.

Multiple-entry visas cost US$150 for a minimum validity of six months. Transit visas cost US$20 for one day, US$25 for two days and US$30 for three days. Visas for US citizens cost a flat US$45.

Visa Extensions

Visa extensions cost US$50 for 30 days and require another visa support letter. If you try to get a visa support letter from Uzbektourism they will most likely insist that you book expensive accommodation or a tour through them. Apply at the Ministry of Foreign Affairs in Tashkent (see the Tashkent map); the process can take several days.

Transit

A traveller with a valid Russian, Kyrgyz or Kazak visa can officially spend 72 hours in Uzbekistan, though some travellers report problems when they travel off the main routes. Tajik visas are not valid for transit.

Registration

The rules are a little complicated, but seem to be loosening up. Registration with the Office of Visas & Registration (OVIR) is not required for visits of less than 15 days, or for people under 18 years. For longer visits, it is necessary to register within three days of arriving; the easiest way is by staying at a hotel or official home-stay/B&B (bed & breakfast), who should register you with OVIR and give you a docket when you leave (they may need reminding). Though officials will rarely demand to see registration dockets, hang on to them anyway, especially if you are flying out from Tashkent. If you are staying in a private house (almost invariably the best value budget accommodation) you are required to register at the local OVIR office, but as this can create more problems than it solves for you and your hosts, it's probably best not to. There are fines if you get caught. Registration is important for long-term residents.

EMBASSIES & CONSULATES
Uzbek Embassies & Consulates

For embassies in other Central Asian countries see the relevant country chapter.

UZBEKISTAN

Azerbaijan
(☎ 12-982 2383, fax 97 25 48)
Hotel Azerbaijan, Baku
China
(☎ 10-6532 6304/6854, fax 6532 6203)
5-2-22 Taiyuan Diplomatic Office Bldg,
Chaoyang district, Beijing
France
(☎ 1-53 83 80 70, fax 53 83 80 77)
Ave Franklin Roosevelt 3, Paris 75008
Germany
(☎ 228-953 5711, fax 953 5799)
Deutschherrenstrasse 7, Bonn 53177
Consulate: Frankfurt
India
(☎ 11-614 9034, fax 587 3246)
D-2/5 Vasant Vihar-57, New Delhi 110057
Iran
(☎ 21-229 9158, ☎/fax 229 1269)
6 Nastaran St, Tehran
Pakistan
(☎ 51-26 4746, fax 26 1737)
House 2, 2nd St, F8/3, Kohistan Rd, Islamabad
Consulate: Karachi
Russia
(95-230 0076, fax 238 8918)
Pogorelski 12, Moscow
Turkey
(312-447 1571, fax 447 4398)
Ugur Mumju Sokak, Ankara
Consulate: Istanbul
UK
(☎ 020-7229 7679, fax 7229 7029)
41 Holland Park W11 9DL, London
USA
(☎ 202-887 5300, fax 293 6804,
✆ emb@uzbekistan.org)
1746 Massachusetts Ave NW, Washington
DC 0036; Web site www.Uzbekistan.org
Consulate-General: New York

Embassies & Consulates in Uzbekistan

All are in Tashkent (☎ code 371 or 71):

Afghanistan
(☎ 34 26 34) Murtazaev 6
Azerbaijan
(☎ 78 93 04, ☎/fax 77 72 13) Halqlar Dustligi 25
China
(☎ 133 80 38, fax 133 47 35) Gogol 79
France
(☎ 133 53 82, fax 133 62 10) Akhunbabayev 25
India
(☎ 133 82 67) Tolstoy 5
Iran
(☎ 68 82 47, fax 68 78 18) General Petrov 20

Kazakstan
(☎/fax 133 60 22)
Samatova 20 – many difficulties reported;
irregular working hours, consul often 'busy',
can take several days.
Kyrgyzstan
(☎ 133 89 41, fax 133 08 93)
Samatova 30 – visas issued on the spot, no
invitation needed.
Pakistan
(☎ 77 66 87, fax 77 14 42) Chilonzor 25
Russia
(☎ 55 92 18, fax 55 87 74)
Nukus 83 – very busy, long queues.
Tajikistan
(☎ 54 99 66, fax 54 89 69)
Tarobi 16 – same building as Turkmenistan
embassy.
Turkmenistan
(☎ 152 52 78, fax 152 52 81)
Tarobi 16 – open for visa collection 9 am to
12.30 pm, collect visa 4.30 pm; three day transit visa US$31 plus one photo.
UK
(☎ 120 62 88/64 51, fax 120 65 49) Gogol 67
USA
(☎ 77 14 07, consular section ☎ 77 22 31, fax
120 63 36) Chilonzor 82

MONEY

The Uzbek *sum* has notes in denominations
of 200, 100, 50, 20, 10, 5, 3 and 1, and the
currency is devaluing at a rate of 30% per
year. The black market (see Money in the
Regional Facts for the Visitor chapter) or
bazar rate for US dollars was about three
times the official rate at the time of research. Recent US dollar bills in good condition are the most acceptable. At the time
of research, the exchange rates were:

country	unit		sum
China	Y1	=	52.6 *sum*
Germany	Dm1	=	226 *sum*
euro	€1	=	442 *sum*
Kazakstan	1 T	=	3.3 *sum*
Kyrgyzstan	1 som	=	14 *sum*
Russia	Rb1	=	16 *sum*
Turkmenistan	100 M	=	8.3 *sum*
UK	UK£1	=	700 *sum*
USA	US$1	=	436 *sum*
			(1300 *sum**)

* black market (approx)

Visa and American Express credit cards can be used to get US dollars cash at branches of the National Bank of Uzbekistan with a 5% commission. Otherwise credit cards are only of use in top-end hotels.

POST & COMMUNICATIONS

An airmail postcard costs 50 *sum* and a 20g airmail letter costs 120 *sum*. The postal service is not renowned for speed or reliability in delivering parcels. International couriers are listed under Post & Communications in the Tashkent section.

Making phone calls is an uncertain and time-consuming business, especially from public offices, where you have to book calls and wait. International rates at these offices are US$1 per minute in *sum* to Europe or US$1.50 to North America in *sum*. Calls from upmarket hotels are generally easier to make, but cost differs widely depending on whether payment is in *sum* or US dollars – from US$2 per minute in *sum* to Europe up to US$9 per minute on a Visa card to Australia. Faxes everywhere are slow and ex-

pensive, US$5 to US$15 per page. At the time of research Uzbekistan had one set of area codes for incoming calls, and another for calls within the country. The latter will eventually be phased out.

To make a local call dial ☎ 0 + city code.
To dial into Uzbekistan from abroad dial ☎ 00 998 + incoming area code (see table).
To dial out of Uzbekistan dial ☎ 8, wait for a tone, then dial ☎ 10.

DANGERS & ANNOYANCES

The *militsiya* (police) have become much less of a nuisance to travellers in recent years. Dire threats from President Karimov have curbed the police habit of shaking down travellers for bribes, although one author had US$15 in *sum* taken by a policeman in Tashkent who wouldn't return his wallet.

Tashkent's international airport officials have a dodgy reputation but seem to be improving; either you'll sail through or be hit with the full force of venal bureaucracy. Have registration dockets and exchange certificates handy when leaving.

A police checkpoint on the Bukhara-Urgench road has occasionally demanded money from people travelling by car – taking a bus is one solution.

The road over the Kamchik pass into the Fergana valley sometimes has roadblocks where every car is searched, presumably to catch potential militants. Cities in the Fergana valley see the most police action against suspected opponents, but this doesn't impact on foreigners (Taliban members excepted).

The cities are quite safe: take the usual precautions if you are walking at night, but drunks are a far more likely hazard than muggers. The Uzbek mafia prefers to get the tourist dollar through black market moneychanging and restaurants rather than outright robbing and unless you fail to pay for a drug shipment or a hooker they won't bother you. Tashkent has a noticeably higher police presence than other cities, and it is important to always have your passport with you here. It's also riskier to change money on the black market in Tashkent, compared with other cities where deals are

Incoming Area Codes

When calling from outside Uzbekistan dial ☎ 998 plus the following area codes, depending on the length of the telephone number (six or seven digits).

area	area code (6 digits)	area code (7 digits)
Andijan	☎ 712	☎ 71
Bukhara	☎ 652	☎ 65
Fergana	☎ 732	☎ 73
Khiva	☎ 732	☎ 62
Kokand	☎ 732	☎ 73
Margilan	☎ 732	☎ 73
Namangan	☎ 792	☎ 79
Navoi	☎ 792	☎ 79
Qarshi	☎ 752	☎ 75
Samarkand	☎ 662	☎ 66
Shakhrisabz	☎ 752	☎ 75
Tashkent	☎ 712	☎ 71
Termiz	☎ 762	☎ 76
Urgench	☎ 662	☎ 62

UZBEKISTAN

done more or less openly. With the highest denomination note worth only a few US cents, one US$100 bill turns into bundles of at least 225 notes, usually hundreds more.

Finally, there seems to be an unspoken rule *against* seatbelts – we were once warned the police would be very suspicious if we were seen wearing one.

FOOD & DRINKS

Plov and *shashlyk* are the national staples, both noticeably free of the western obsession with low cholesterol. Plov (pilau) comes in a hundred variations based around steamed buttery rice mixed with carrot and mutton, piled on a dish for all to share. Shashlyk (skewered pieces of barbecued meat and fat) is ordered in batches of four or five and consumed with mouthfuls of onion followed by bread. Another common snack is the *samsa*, the ancestor of the Indian *samosa*, little fried parcels stuffed with meat and vegetables.

Round unleavened bread called *nan* and tea makes up the traditional diet of the poor. Every region has its own variation of nan; the raised rim of Kokand's speciality makes it a particularly fine shashlyk plate. The other vegetarian staple is fruit, which appears in extraordinary abundance in summer and autumn. Bazars are packed with luscious apples, grapes, apricots, plums, cherries, pomegranates and above all watermelons and melons.

Steamed pumpkin is a light treat. *Mosh-kichiri* and *moshhurda* are meat and mung bean gruels. *Dimlama* (also called *bosma)* is meat, potatoes, onions and vegetables braised slowly in a little fat and their own juices; the meatless version is *sabzavotli dimlama*. *Hunon* or *honum* is a noodle roll, usually with a meat and potato filling. Uzbeks are fond of stuffed cabbage and grape leaves *(dulma),* tomatoes, peppers and quinces.

After a century of Russian influence vodka is available everywhere, including in mouthful-sized plastic cups with foil tops. While some Muslims have rejected alcohol, it is still common to toast festivals (even Ramadan!) with shots of raw clear spirit. The most reliable (unadulterated) brands of vodka are sold in state-run stores, distinguishable because

they often sell little else. Local wines range from sweet to sickly sweet. The dry champagne is sweet but drinkable, the extra sweet variety of champagne is carbonated syrup. Besides green tea, nonalcoholic drinks include the usual soft drinks and the peculiar *gaz suzli* (fizzy water) sold from booths. Bottled waters include Coca-Cola's strongly mineral-flavoured Bonaqua brand, so heavily carbonated it practically erupts on opening.

SHOPPING

Bukhara carpets (see the special colour section in the Turkmenistan chapter) are actually Turkmen but are sold in abundance in tourist centres. Cheaply made touristy souvenirs and better quality goods can be found in Samarkand, Bukhara and Khiva.

There is a huge range of handicrafts available. Many on the verge of extinction by the end of the Soviet Union have been revived, though artisans are struggling to get their wares to hard currency markets. Some regional specialities include *khanatlas* silks from Margilan, ceramics from Rishdon, Gijduvan and Samarkand, and Bukhara silverware.

Clothing includes striped cloaks, skullcaps (black and white for Uzbeks, multicoloured for Tajiks), enormous woolly Turkmen hats, silk dresses, gold-embroidered slippers and colourful socks.

ORIENTATION

Uzbekistan has tried to erase Soviet names completely (in perfect imitation of the Soviets themselves). Streets everywhere have been renamed, sometimes several times, since 1991, often with unpronounceable new names. Some names have merely been shifted to other streets. Russian Cyrillic script has been aggressively eliminated too; even the signs on buses and in stations have mostly gone over to Uzbek Cyrillic and increasingly to a Roman script (see the Language chapter for some useful words in Uzbek Cyrillic).

But many people – Russians and Uzbeks alike, including taxi drivers – still use old names, complete with Russian endings and Russian words for 'street' etc, and these are still on available maps. In towns where these still seem to be the most common, we use them too. In Uzbek, a street is *kuchasi* (Russian: *ulitsa*), an avenue is *prospekti* (Russian: *prospekt)*, a boulevard *hiyaboni* (Russian: *bulvar)*, a square *maydoni* (Russian: *ploshchad* or *skver)*. In Karakalpakstan the words are different again.

Tashkent

☎ (3) 71 • pop 2.3 million

Tashkent, the Uzbek capital, is Central Asia's hub – its biggest and worldliest city (the fourth-biggest in the CIS after Moscow, St Petersburg and Kiev), bang in the middle of the Eurasian landmass, and better connected by international flights than any other city in the region.

Rebuilt after the 1966 earthquake as the very model of a modern Soviet city, Tashkent comprises concrete apartment blocks decorated with Uzbek motifs and illuminated slogans, yawning parade grounds around solemn monuments, hectares of parkland and a remarkably comprehensive public transport system. There's also the other, older city, a sprawling Uzbek country town with fruit trees and vines in every courtyard hidden behind secure walls.

Some of the region's Slavs have moved to the relative cultural security of Tashkent, which is still at least half Russian-speaking (if not Russian). It's also a haven for Uzbekistan's Koreans, Caucasians and Tatars, lending it a diverse and cosmopolitan edge.

It's hard to visit Uzbekistan without passing through Tashkent, and there are consular, communications, medical and other facilities you can't find elsewhere in the republic, along with a busy (and very affordable) cultural life and some interesting museums.

History

Tashkent's earliest incarnation may have been as the settlement of Ming-Uruk (Thousand Apricot Trees) in the 2nd or 1st century BCE. Known variously since then as Chach, Shash, Shashkent and Binkent, by the time the Arabs took it in 751 CE it was a major caravan crossroads. It got the name Toshkent or Tashkent ('City of Stone' in Turkic) in about the 11th century.

The Khorezmshahs and Jenghiz Khan stubbed out Tashkent in the early 13th century, though it slowly recovered under the Mongols and under Timur (who in 1404 bequeathed the town to his grandson Ulughbek). Despite the general decline of the cities of the Silk Road, the town once again grew prosperous under the Shaybanids in the late 15th and 16th centuries, and most of its surviving architectural monuments date from this period.

The khan of Kokand annexed Tashkent in 1809. In 1865, as the Emir of Bukhara was preparing to snatch it away, the Russians under General Mikhail Grigorevich Chernyayev beat him to it, against the orders of the tsar and despite being outnumbered 15 to one. They found a proud town, enclosed by a 25km-long wall with 11 gates (of which not a trace remains today). Installing General Konstantin Kaufman as governor general, the tsar made Tashkent the capital of his new Turkistan satrapy (territory), building a cantonment and town across the Ankhor (or Bozsu) canal from the Uzbek town and filling it with Russian settlers and merchants.

From Tashkent, General Kaufman was to gradually widen the imperial net around the other Central Asian khanates. Tashkent also became the tsarists' (and later the Soviets') main centre for espionage in Asia, during the protracted imperial rivalry with Britain known as the 'Great Game' (see History in the Facts about Central Asia chapter).

The city's bondage became literally iron-clad with the arrival of the Trans-Caspian Railway in 1889, and Russian workers on the railway were at the front of the revolution of 1917. With Osipov's treachery and Bolshevik reprisals this was a bloody place during the Russian Civil War. Peter Hopkirk's *Setting the East Ablaze* and FM Bailey's *Mission to Tashkent* document the cruelty, duplicity and mayhem at this time, as the Bolsheviks fought to get a grip on the region in the face of local and White Russian resistance.

Tashkent became the capital of the Turkestan Autonomous SSR, declared in

UZBEKISTAN

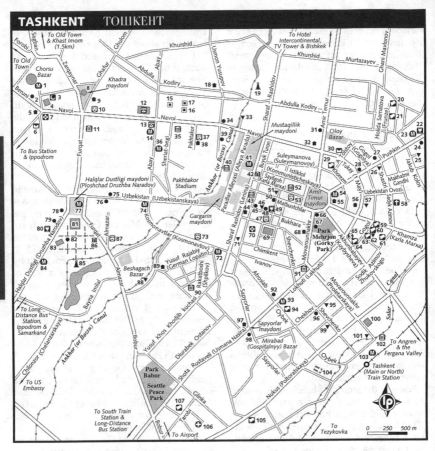

TASHKENT ТОШКЕНТ

1918. When this was further split, the capital of the new Uzbek Autonomous SSR was Samarkand until 1930, when this status was restored to Tashkent. The city acquired industrial muscle with construction of the agricultural machinery combine, Tashselmash, in the 1920s, and the wholesale relocation of factories from western Russia to Central Asia during WWII.

Physically, Tashkent was changed forever on 25 April 1966, when a massive earthquake levelled vast areas of the town and left 300,000 people homeless. Soviet historians made much of the battalions of 'fraternal peoples' and eager urban planners who came from around the Soviet Union to help with reconstruction and give the city its present-day face of shady streets, immense plazas, fountains and hectares of bland architecture.

But when Moscow later announced it would give 20% of the newly built apartments to these (mainly Russian) volunteers and invite them to stay, local resentment boiled over in the so-called 'Pakhtakor Incident' of May 1969.

At Pakhtakor stadium (by the present-day Shodlik Palace hotel), brawls erupted between Uzbeks and Russians, and Soviet

TASHKENT

PLACES TO STAY
5 Hotel Chorsu
9 Hotel Hadra
18 Hotel Turon
32 Hotel Dustlik
38 Hotel Shodlik Palace
44 Hotel Tashkent
55 Hotel Uzbekistan
56 Le Meridien; DHL
68 'House Market'
89 Hotel Turkiston
97 Hotel Rossiya

PLACES TO EAT
25 Tortoise & Violin
26 Gruziya Restaurant
33 Ankhor Chaykhana
46 New World Pizza & Bakery
51 Zeravshan Bars
    & Restaurants
57 Cassandra Restaurant
62 Dutika Canteen
    (Indonesian Embassy)
71 Blue Domes Café &
    Chaykhana
88 Shahshara Chaykhana
95 Taj Restaurant
99 The Café
101 Mama's Fun Pub

OTHER
2 Mustaqillik
   International Library
3 Juma (Friday) Mosque
4 Kukeldash Medressa
6 Post Office
7 GUM Department Store
8 Circus
10 Khamza Drama Theatre
11 Geology Museum
12 Central Telephone &
    Telegraph Office
13 Private Telephone Office
15 Yunus Khan Mausoleum
16 Sheikh Hobandi Tahur
    Mausoleum
17 Kaldergach Bi Mausoleum

19 Earthquake Memorial
20 Kyrgyz Embassy
21 Kazak Embassy
22 Lucky Strike Bar
24 Anglesey Supermarket
27 Mukhtar Ashrafi Conservatory
28 Dunyo Supermarket
29 Indian Embassy
30 Main Post Office
31 Ardus Supermarket
34 'Drugstore' Pharmacy
35 Navoi Literary Museum
37 Ilkhom Theatre
39 OVIR (Registration & Visa)
    Office
40 Bakhor Concert Hall &
    Mukarram Tuzunbayeva
    Museum
42 Romanov Palace
43 History Museum of the
    People of Uzbekistan
45 Asian Business Agency
47 Alisher Navoi Opera &
    Ballet Theatre; New World
    Restaurant
48 Turkish Airlines Booking
    Office
49 New World Bar
50 Ardus Supermarket;
    Ardus FM Burger
52 Open-Air Art Gallery
53 Gorky Drama Theatre
58 German Protestant Church
59 British Embassy
60 Afghan Embassy
61 Japanese Embassy
63 Chinese Embassy
64 French Embassy
65 National Bank of Uzbekistan
66 Clock Tower
67 Shahar Hokimiyat
    (City Hall)
69 Ministry of Foreign Affairs
70 TsUM Department Store
73 Republic Puppet Theatre
75 Systeme Educatif Français
76 Bookshop

78 Pakistan International Airlines
    Booking Office
79 Transaero Airlines Office
80 Blues Bar
81 Palace of the Friendship of
    Peoples
82 Abdul Khasim Medressa
83 Oliy Majlis
85 Navoi Monument
86 Wedding Palace
87 Muqimi Musical Theatre
90 Museum of Applied Arts
91 Fine Arts Museum of
    Uzbekistan
92 Ozbegim Supermarket;
    Zumrad Cultural Centre
94 Israeli Embassy
96 Asia Travel
98 Uzbekistan Airways
    Booking Office
100 Railway Booking Office
102 Railway Museum
104 Assumption Cathedral
    (Uspensky Sobor)
105 Russian Embassy
106 UN; Tashkent International
    Medical Clinic
107 Turkmen Embassy;
    Tajik Embassy

METRO STATIONS
1 Chorsu
14 Alisher Navoi
23 Khamid Olimjon
36 Pakhtakor (Pakhtakorskaya)
41 Mustaqillik maydoni
54 Amir Timur Hiyoboni
    (Oktyabrskoy Revolyutsii,
    Markaziy Hiyoboni)
72 Kosmonavtlar (Prospekt
    Kosmonavtov)
74 Uzbekistan
77 Halqlar Dustligi
    (Druzhba Narodov)
84 Yoshlik (Komsomol)
93 Oybek (Aybek)
103 Tashkent

UZBEKISTAN

troops had to be deployed on the streets. A series of bomb blasts in February 1998 killed an undisclosed number of people, and the security presence has remained high ever since. The blasts were attributed by the government to Islamic extremists, but it will probably never be known who was responsible.

Orientation

Tashkent sits at an elevation of 480m at the foot of the Chatkal mountains.

Before the 1966 earthquake the Ankhor canal separated old (Uzbek) and new (Russian) Tashkent, the former a tangle of alleys around the Chorsu bazar, the latter with shady avenues radiating from what is now

Amir Timur maydoni. Uzbeks perhaps still consider Chorsu their 'centre', though it now lies exposed at the edge of the old town, with the Hotel Chorsu planted beside it like a sword. Civil servants and diehard communists might home in on Mustaqillik maydoni (Independence Square, formerly Lenin Square), the vast parade grounds just east of the canal. The statue of Timur on horseback in the gardens of Amir Timur maydoni is a useful reference point, with the Hotel Uzbekistan on the eastern side of the park and the Broadway (Sayilgoh) strip of stalls, cafes and restaurants leading off to the west.

Tashkent airport is 6km south of Amir Timur maydoni. Tashkent train station (also called Main or North station) is 2.5km south of Amir Timur maydoni at the end of Movarounnakhr (formerly Proletarskaya), by Tashkent Metro station. South (Uzbek: *janubiy*, Russian: *yuzhniy*) train station is 7km south-west of Amir Timur maydoni at the end of Shota Rustaveli. The Tashkent long-distance bus station is 3km beyond this, at Sobir Rakhimov Metro station.

Information

The useful monthly expatriate's newsletter *Odd & Ads* has listings and reviews of restaurants and cultural events. It costs US$2.50 in *sum* at the Anglesey supermarket on Pushkin. The monthly *Tashkent Leisure Guide* in Russian and idiosyncratic English also has listings of cultural events and a side-splitting 'Army Humour' section. It's free and can be found at the Uzbekistan and Tashkent hotels (see Places to Stay).

City maps can be hard to find; try in the lobby of the Hotel Uzbekistan, the underground arcade of Amir Timur Hiyaboni Metro, or the bookshop on Uzbekistan near Halqlar Dustligi Metro.

Tourist Offices There is no tourist office as such, and no-one to help you with visa problems. The 'service bureau' on the ground floor of the Hotel Uzbekistan mainly seems to hire cars. If you're a guest there, you can arrange excursions (and visas) at the Tours & Options office (☎ 33 27 73) on the 3rd floor. There's an Uzbektourism office in the

Hotel Tashkent that we can't say much about since they told us to get lost.

For information on visas and the like it's best to go to one of the travel agencies listed later in this section.

Visas & Registration Theoretically the OVIR office (☎ 56 97 13) at Navoi 5 is the place for visa matters. Go in the morning. Bring a representative from a Tashkent agency with whom you have booked services, as well as passport photos and every relevant piece of paperwork you have. Vouchers from Uzbektourism might also help. There are passport photo studios on the Broadway near Buyuk Turon kuchasi.

If you're staying at a hotel, police registration is automatic. For long-term residents the OVIR office is at Navoi 5. The OVIR officer at the long-distance bus station might accost you on arrival to register.

Useful Organisations A place to meet young 'Tashkentliks' who speak some English is the little Mustaqillik International Library (satellite TV, email, and a modest collection of donated books, periodicals and English-language teaching materials) run by the Central Asian Free Exchange, at Navoi 48 at the edge of Chorsu bazar, opposite the Hotel Chorsu.

Another place to meet young people is the Language Faculty (Russian: *Fakultet zarubezhnoy filologiy*) at Tashkent State University. Follow *'na ulitsu Beruni'* signs out of Beruni Metro station and ask for Vuzgorodok or University Town.

Money The Hotel Uzbekistan's 24 hour desk changes US travellers cheques as well as cash in several major currencies at the official rates.

At the National Bank of Uzbekistan (☎ 133 60 70) at Akhunbabayev 23 you can get US dollars from Visa cards and travellers cheques (rooms 8 and 42). The bank is open Monday to Friday 8.30 am to 12.30 pm.

Black-market moneychangers work in all the bazars, but it's more dangerous to change money here than other places in Uzbekistan. Only change money in private with the help of someone you trust. The best rates are with nontourist oriented businesses.

Only upmarket places accept credit cards. Visa and American Express are accepted at the Uzbekistan, Le Meridien, Intercontinental and Shodlik Palace hotels and their restaurants, and for accommodation at the Sambuh Hotel.

Post The main post office (Uzbek: *pochta bulimi*, Russian: *glavpochtamt*; ☎ 133 47 49) is on May at the corner with Alexey Tolstoy. Poste-restante is dubious. DHL (☎ 133 56 53) has an office at the Le Meridien hotel and TNT (☎ 120 69 35) is at the Hotel Intercontinental.

Telephone & Fax For Central Asia's pre-eminent capital, Tashkent's telephone system is awful. Mobile phones are the only option for long-term residents. The cheapest and slowest place to make intercity and international calls is the central telephone and telegraph office, the big yellow building at Navoi 28, open 8 am to 11 pm daily. You can also call from the main post office. Making calls from the Le Meridien and Intercontinental hotels is more reliable and still reasonably priced as you can pay in *sum*; US$2 per minute to Europe, US2.30 to North America, US$2.70 to Australia. The Hotel Uzbekistan's business centre has quick, clear satellite-linked services but only takes payment in US dollars – for US$6 per minute to North America, US$8 to Australia. There's also a private calling office open until 11 pm daily on the corner of Navoi and Abay across from the central telephone building; calls cost US$4 per minute to Europe and North America.

Email & Internet Access Nuron Relcom (☎ 67 86 76, @ root@nuron.tashkent.su), Buyuk Ipak Yuli 42, has email access as well as fax and telex services. For an initial fee, plus monthly and kilobyte rates, anyone can get an email box and other services. From Pushkin Metro station go under the railway bridge; it's across the road beyond a nine storey blue and white building.

The Mustaqillik International Library has email facilities (not Internet) for US$1 per hour. The American Business Center (☎ 40 67 05, fax 40 66 76, @ office@csabc .silk.org), Buyuk Turon 41 (the highrise with the clock) can only be used by US citizens; email costs US$1.50 per hour.

Travel Agencies Several travel agencies in Tashkent have helpful English-speaking staff who can arrange home-stay accommodation and help with visas, tickets and activities like trekking and skiing.

Asia Travel
   (☎ 152 67 28, 56 37 62, fax 56 29 27,
   @ adventure@asia-travel.uz)
   Sharaf Rashidov 40 – visa support, tours, guides, activities like rafting, trekking, caving, specialists in mountain sports.
Sairam
   (☎ 133 35 59, fax 40 69 37,
   @ silkroad@sairamtour.com.uz)
   Movarounnakhr 16A – visa support, tours, guides, cars.
Sambuh
   (☎ 254 95 38, fax 24 91 74,
   @ sales@sambuh.com)
   Tsehovaya 1 – popular firm run by the Rasulev brothers; visa support, tours, home-stays, guides, air tickets, visas for neighbouring countries, treks, Hotel Tashkent. Web site www.sambuh.com
Sportur
   (☎ 186 86 48, fax 137 17 64,
   @ sport@airam.ilk.org)
   Flat 19, Bldg 65 Pushkin, Tashkent 700000 – arranges cars, guides, visas for neighbouring countries, home-stays and self-catering apartments in Tashkent, and a villa on the city outskirts.

Bookshops & Cultural Centres Other than slim paperbacks of Karimov's political philosophies, bookshops have little more than school textbooks in Russian or Uzbek; even the English titles of Soviet days have disappeared.

Systeme Educatif Français (☎ 45 19 41) is a language school on the 3rd floor of Dom Uchiteley (House of Teachers), Uzbekistan 80 near Halqlar Dustligi Metro station.

Medical Services The Tashkent International Medical Clinic (☎ 55 36 25, 120 60 92, emergencies ☎ 120 60 91, 185 60 93, 185

20 88, 185 84 81, fax 120 60 93), in the UN complex at Taroabi 14, is a joint project of the UN, the US embassy and the Peace Corps, meant for long-termers but available to visitors in emergencies. Visitors are asked for US$50 per visit. If that sounds expensive, remember that this is one of the few sources of western-quality medical care in Central Asia. They're open Monday to Friday 8 am to 5 pm, with western-trained personnel on call 24 hours a day. They can also advise you on dental emergencies.

Embassies maintain lists of other medical contacts.

Mountain Rescue Uzbekistan's mountain rescue service (☎ 68 67 95, fax 68 67 83) is in the offices of Uzbekmakhsustour (Uzbekspetstour), around the corner from the Hotel Sayokhat complex, Buyuk Ipak Yuli 115, near Maxim Gorky Metro station.

Emergency Police: ☎ 01 or 001; fire ☎ 02; ambulance ☎ 03, ☎ 133 26 24/25 or ☎ 133 19 03. See also Medical Services, earlier.

Old Town

The old town (Uzbek: *eski shakhar*, Russian: *staryy gorod)* starts beside Chorsu bazar and the Hotel Chorsu. A maze of narrow dirt streets is lined with low mud-brick houses and dotted with mosques and old medressas. These few handsome religious buildings date from the 15th and 16th centuries.

If you're lucky enough to be invited into someone's home, you'll discover that the blank outer walls of traditional homes conceal cool, peaceful garden-courtyards.

Kukeldash Medressa This grand 16th century medressa on a hill opposite the Hotel Chorsu has a domed courtyard at the rear which has been under restoration for years. On warm Friday mornings the plaza in front overflows with worshippers.

Behind Kukeldash is the tiny ruined 15th century Juma (Friday) Mosque, used in Soviet times as a sheet metal workshop.

Chorsu Bazar It's open every day, but on Saturday and Sunday morning this huge open market beside Kukeldash is a great place to find crowds of people from the surrounding countryside (many in traditional dress) along with fresh produce, prepared food, tea, traditional Uzbek clothes, carpets, tea sets and household items. You'll also find destitute people selling bits of glass, rusty nails, miscellaneous washing machine parts and other things you can't imagine anyone buying. Tashkent has at least 16 such farmers' markets. See the Shopping section later for information on these and other big bazars.

Khast Imom This is one name for the plain square 2km north of the Circus, on Zarqaynar kuchasi, which is the official religious centre of the republic. On the south-west corner the 16th century Barak Khan Medressa (Madrasa Barok Hon) houses the Central Asian Muslim Religious Board, whose Grand Mufti is roughly the Islamic equivalent of an archbishop for Uzbekistan, Kyrgyzstan, Tajikistan and Turkmenistan. Tourists can ask to see the rose garden courtyard inside.

East from here across Zarqaynar kuchasi is the **Telyashayakh Mosque**, also called Khast Imom Mosque. The Osman Quran, said to be the world's oldest, is kept in the mosque's library. A small financial inducement usually earns you a look at this enormous tome, brought to Samarkand by Timur, then taken to St Petersburg by the Russians and returned here in 1989.

The big block on the north side is the **Imam Ismail al-Bukhari Islamic Institute**, a two year post-medressa academy with more than one thousand students, the only one in Central Asia in Soviet times (when it had 25 students) and still the most important medressa in the region. Just west of this is the little 16th century **mausoleum of Abu Bakr Kaffal Shoshi**, an Islamic scholar of the Shaybanid period.

All these buildings are normally closed to tourists. Visitors who have made prior arrangements to go inside should be modestly dressed, and women should wear a scarf over their hair.

Yunus Khan Mausoleum Across Navoi from the Navoi Literary Museum are three

15th century mausolea, restored in the 19th century and now stranded in a forest of office and university buildings. The biggest bears the name of Yunus Khan, grandfather of the Mughal emperor Babur. The Uzbek Restoration Institute is at the rear of the building, where tiles are made for projects across the country. Two small mausolea are eastward inside a fence – **Sheikh Hobandi Tahur** (Shiekhhantaur) and the pointy roofed **Kaldergach Bi**, the latter now used as a neighbourhood mosque.

Getting There & Around The easiest way to the old town is by metro to Chorsu station. Alternatively, from near the Hotel Uzbekistan, tram No 16, trolleybuses Nos 4 and 8 and express bus No 28-3 go west down Navoi to Chorsu bazar. Russian taxi drivers, if they go into the old town at all, may get immediately lost. On foot, you could easily get lost too. Three major streets that head into Chorsu bazar are Forobi (Farabi), Sagban and Zarqaynar.

Museums & Galleries

A small admission fee in *sum* is charged at all the museums, and some charge extra for cameras and videos.

On the 1st floor of the **Fine Arts Museum of Uzbekistan** is a fine collection of the art of pre-Russian Turkestan – Zoroastrian artefacts, serene 1000-year-old Buddhist statues, Sogdian murals, royal furnishings too splendid to use. Down the hall is 19th and 20th century Uzbek applied art, notably the brilliant silk-on-cotton embroidered hangings called *suzani*. Less impressive is the Russian and Asian art upstairs. The ground floor often has exhibitions by local artists. The museum is in the giant cube-shaped building at Movarounnakhr (Prole-tarskaya) 16. The museum (☎ 136 74 36) is open daily except Tuesday 10 am to 5 pm.

At the **Museum of Applied Arts**, Alexander Polovtsev, a wealthy tsarist diplomat, originally commissioned this house to be built for him in traditional style by artisans from Tashkent, Samarkand, Bukhara and Fergana, but he was transferred before it was finished. After a post-Revolutionary

stint as an orphanage, the house was surrounded by modern museum buildings and opened in 1937 as a showcase for turn-of-the-20th century applied arts.

Full of bright carved plaster decorations *(ghanch)* and carved wood, the house itself is the main attraction, though there are also exhibits of rare ceramics, textiles, jewellery, musical instruments and toys, and a pricey gift shop. The museum (☎ 56 39 43), on Rakatboshi (ex-Shpilkov), is open daily except Tuesday 10 am to 5 pm. Look for the mosaics on the white walls.

The **History Museum of the People of Uzbekistan**, Tashkent's biggest museum (☎ 133 57 13), has 8000 exhibits in the former Lenin Museum at Sharaf Rashidov 30, presented with a nationalistic edge. One highlight in the museum is a small, peaceful Buddha figure from a Kushan temple excavated at Fayoz-Tepe near Termiz, but conspicuously absent is a famous big Buddha from Kuva in the Fergana valley. The museum is open daily, except Sunday, 10 am to 6 pm.

The **Amir Timur Museum**, Tashkent's newest museum (☎ 132 02 12), stands just north of the rehabilitated national icon's statue. It's quite an impressive structure with a brilliant blue ribbed dome and a richly

Festival Tunic, Fine Arts Museum: almost all Central Asian clans used embroidery to decorate clothing.

decorated interior. President Karimov and Amir Timur battle for attention in the murals; most of the displays are models of Timur's greatest building projects. The museum is open daily except Monday, 10 am to 5 pm.

The **Mukarram Tuzunbayeva Museum** in a courtyard behind the Bakhor concert hall on Mustaqillik maydoni, is a tiny museum dedicated to the first Uzbek woman to dance professionally in public. There are displays with photos, costumes, information about the Bakhor troupe, and a gift shop. It's open daily, except Sunday, 10 am to 5 pm.

Besides memorabilia of 15th century poet Alisher Navoi and other Central Asian literati, **Navoi Literary Museum** has replica manuscripts, Persian calligraphy, and 15th and 16th century miniatures. Open daily except Monday 10 am to 5 pm, it's at Navoi 69, a block east of Alisher Navoi Metro station.

This surprisingly grand **Geology Museum**, full of beautiful minerals, a dinosaur skeleton, natural history dioramas and a giant 3-D map of Central Asia, is open Monday to Friday 9 am to 5 pm.

The impressive collection of Soviet behemoths in the **Railway Museum** is at a railway siding near the main train station and Tashkent Metro station, at Movarounnakhr 1. The curator is friendly and happy to help you clamber all over the trains. Even if trains aren't really your thing it's a fun place to visit. Open Wednesday to Sunday (☎ 99 70 40), 10 am to 5 pm.

The **Central Exhibition Hall** of the Uzbekistan Union of Artists features an art gallery, occasional sponsored art exhibitions, and an 'antiques' shop. It's on Sharaf Rashidov, diagonally opposite the Hotel Tashkent; enter on the north side. It's open daily, except Sunday, 10 am to 6 pm.

Alisher Navoi Opera & Ballet Theatre

The interior of this theatre harbours various regional artistic styles – a different one in each room – executed by the best artisans of the day, under the direction of the architect who did Lenin's tomb in Moscow. There is a separate ticket office, inside the main door, just for guided tours of the place. The program changes daily, from Uzbek symphony to Russian opera.

The theatre (☎ 133 33 44, 133 59 09) faces Buyuk Turon kuchasi across from the Hotel Tashkent. See the Entertainment section later for programs at this and other theatres in the city.

Squares, Parks & Memorials

At the **Amir Timur maydoni**, a glowering bust of Marx has been replaced by a suitably patriotic statue of Timur on horseback. The gardens and fountains around it are some of the nicest in the city.

Mustaqillik maydoni or Independence Square (still Lenin Square to most Russians) is the place for parades. A brass globe emblazoned with an oversized neon map of Uzbekistan sits in the spot where the USSR's biggest Lenin statue used to be. The salmon-and-green building on the west side was Tashkent's first Soviet administration building (1930); it now has the city library, some embassies and government offices, and the Bakhor concert hall. The president's office and most ministries are just to the south, around Gagarin maydoni.

The New Soviet Men & Women who rebuilt Tashkent are remembered in stone at the **Earthquake Memorial**. Russian newlyweds still come here to have their photos taken. It's three long blocks north on Sharaf Rashidov from Mustaqillik Maydoni Metro station, barely worth the effort.

Palace of the Friendship of Peoples

This testament to Soviet gigantism contains (naturally) an enormous concert hall. It is stunningly, fascinatingly ugly, and the interior is even worse. Out the front is a bit of Soviet mythologising, a memorial to a blacksmith named Sham Akhmudov and his wife who adopted 15 war orphans (thousands were sent to Tashkent during WWII), all of whom are said to still live in the province.

Up behind the palace, meanwhile, is a vast promenade and a post-Soviet (but decidedly Soviet-scale) monument to Alisher Navoi, Uzbekistan's newly chosen cultural hero, with the eerie feeling of a Lenin shrine.

Other Things to See

The shiny new blue-domed **Oliy Majlis** (parliament) stands somewhat isolated near the Abdul Khasim Medressa. Currently it functions as a giant rubber stamp in its infrequent sessions; you can watch proceedings with a ticket organised through your embassy.

The **TV Tower**, a 375m three-legged monster, the epitome of Soviet design, stands north of the city centre and the Hotel Intercontinental on Amir Timur. There's a viewing platform and two revolving restaurants. You'll need your passport to buy a ticket. It's open daily except Monday 10 am to 9 pm.

Near Mirabad (Gospitalnyy) bazar is one of Tashkent's four Orthodox churches, the **Assumption Cathedral** (Uspensky Sobor), which is bright blue with copper domes. Around it you can find elderly Russians whose pensions collapsed along with the Soviet Union, reducing them to beggars.

Looking quite out of place is the **German Protestant Church**, once used as a recital hall and now holding Lutheran services again, on Sodik Azimov (Zhukovskogo) near Sovietskaya.

Places to Stay

Home-Stays Unofficial home-stays are a little hard to find in Tashkent. Try asking hotel staff or taxi drivers.

Sportur (see Travel Agencies earlier) has several self-catering apartments for US$25 per person in convenient city locations like Halqlar Dustligi and Khamid Olimjon. The knowledgeable manager Airat Yuldashev can also arrange a comfortable home-stay with a Russian woman named Flora in an apartment near Khamza Metro (US$25 per night).

Rental Accommodation Around a bus shelter about halfway along Movarounnakhr (Proletarskaya) people gather informally to swap information on flats for sale. The authorities tell them to move along periodically, but there are handbills stuck to poles with prices and phone numbers. Some may be willing to rent one to visitors for a few days or weeks. A sparsely furnished place goes for about US$30 per week; US$60 a week might get you TV, a telephone or other luxuries. Deal with the Russian grandmothers, not the Uzbek black marketeers. See Visas & Documents earlier in this chapter about registration.

Places to Stay – Budget

The decrepit but habitable *Hotel Hadra* (☎ 44 28 08, 56A Ghafur Ghulom) next to the Circus is a rock-bottom option with rooms from US1.50 to US$7 in *sum*. Only Russian is spoken. They can also register you with OVIR for a small fee if you are staying at an unofficial home-stay. There's a cheap and cheerful Pakistani restaurant here as well.

Travel back to the Soviet Union at the *Hotel Rossiya* (☎ 56 29 63, Sapyorlar maydoni 2), at the east end of Shota Rustaveli. Singles/doubles with TV (black & white sets, but they do show BBC and ESPN), toilet, hot water and the odd cockroach start at US$7/10 in *sum*. Some say it's quite good, others write of fascinatingly rude staff. It's an awkward location for transport (take west-bound tram No 28 from TsUM on Uzbekistan).

Rather better is the *Hotel Bakht* (☎ 78 95 25, Katartal 21), Chilanzor kvartal (quarter) 8, 15 minutes west of Khamza Metro. Reasonably clean rooms with functioning bathrooms cost from US$5/7 in *sum*.

Places to Stay – Mid-Range

The best option in this range is the *Sambuh Hotel* (☎ 54 95 38, fax 54 91 74, Tsehovaya 1), run by the recommended private travel agency of the same name. It costs US$60 per person in modern doubles with satellite TV, fridges and bathrooms. As it's quite hard to find you should arrange to be picked up – the hotel is set off the street in a neighbourhood south of the Hotel Rossiya.

Hotel Turkiston (☎ 56 45 35, fax 56 17 59) is a secluded former lodge for Soviet bigwigs with pleasant gardens. It's at the far end of Yusuf Rajabiy kuchasi (ex-German Lopatin), a five minute walk from Kosmonavtlar Metro station. The rooms are clean and comfortable but a bit spartan; renovations are pending. Singles/doubles cost US$35/50, suites US$110. There's a small, inexpensive restaurant with European and Asian dishes, and polite service.

The city-owned *Hotel Turon* (☎ 41 57 69), formerly the Leningrad, at the corner of Abdulla Kodiry and Usmon Yusupov, has plain rooms with toilet and shower (but dicey hot water) at US$20/30 and up. Take bus No 18 north from Pakhtakor Metro station, or tram No 23 or 27 west on Navoi from Amir Temur maydoni. The Georgian Table restaurant is in the basement.

Hotel Tashkent (☎ 152 43 75, fax 120 61 30, Sharaf Rashidov 50), very central, opposite the Navoi Opera Theatre, has plain but large rooms with shower, toilet, fridge, TV and balcony from US$25/50. Visa credit cards are accepted. There is a good snack and coffee shop at the north end and a restaurant underneath.

As a last resort there's the *Hotel Chorsu* (☎ 42 76 00, fax 42 87 00), the three-sided tower at Akhunbabayev maydoni 1 by Chorsu bazar. This used to be Tashkent's flagship hotel and the funky interior has great potential, but it's barely surviving on no maintenance and few guests. Singles/doubles cost US$35/44 in *sum*. The rooms have no air-con and a variable array of electrical appliances that actually work (like lights, for example).

Places to Stay – Top End

Uzbektourism's giant *Hotel Uzbekistan* (☎ 136 00 77, fax 40 61 15, Khamza 45) faces Amir Timur maydoni. Air-con rooms in the renovated wing cost US$130/160 with fridge, TV and telephone. The restaurants serve ordinary Uzbek/Russian fare, and service is slow if there's a tour group.

Behind the Hotel Uzbekistan looms the *Le Meridien* (☎ 120 66 00, fax 120 63 18, Uzbekistan Ovozi 2), an Indian-built concrete pile with several restaurants, swimming pool, gym and a business centre. The rooms are decent but overpriced at US$190/210 and US$320 for a suite; all have satellite TV. Credit cards are accepted.

Hotel Shodlik Palace (☎ 41 42 22, fax 41 44 06, Pakhtakor 5) has German management, tasteful renovations, a business centre and gym. Rooms with all mod cons costs from US$180/200, payment by credit card or dollars. There are also several expensive restaurants, including the gourmet La Strada with menus in English and German.

Hotel Intercontinental (☎ 120 70 00, fax 120 64 59, Amir Timur 107A, ✉ tashkent@interconti.com) is the city's best, with a full range of business and leisure facilities: indoor swimming pool, business centre, boutiques and several excellent restaurants including the Dome on the top floor. For those on expense accounts, rooms cost from US$255 up to US$1550 for the presidential suite. All credit cards accepted.

Places to Eat

Restaurants The ground floor restaurant at the Hotel Uzbekistan serves passable if unspectacular international dishes. It is better to eat elsewhere.

The *Allegro* at the Hotel Intercontinental (☎ 120 70 00) offers Italian cuisine and live music; pastas start at around US$12. There's also the cheerful *Los Amigos* Mexican bistro, and on the top of the building the Lebanese *Dome* with great views over the city. They're all pricey but regarded as some of the best in town.

The Shodlik Palace has the European *La Strada* (☎ 41 42 44) and the *Hemingway* bar/bistro, while the Le Meridien has the excellent Indian *Ragu* restaurant, with many veg dishes, the French *La Baguette* cafe and the *Scheherezade* restaurant with a jazz brunch on Sunday.

Georgian Table, in the basement of the Hotel Turon, has good cheap Georgian steaks and delicious *khajipuri* (bread with cheese filling) with loud music, good Georgian wine and a range of veg dishes. It's around US$5 in *sum* per person, not including alcohol.

The Hotel Hadra next to the Circus isn't anything special but the Pakistani *Hadra* (☎ 44 28 44) restaurant inside serves delicious food; trace the culinary connections between Central Asia and the subcontinent with nan breads and plov for a few dollars in *sum*.

One of the city's best *chaykhanas* (teahouses) is the *Shahshara*, beside the Ankhor (Bozsu) canal on Rakatboshi kuchasi. The canal gushes down a chute into a small lake, with tables set on terraces on one side, an open-air dance hall on the other, and smoke billowing from the shashlyk kitchen. There are several similar places on the east bank of the Ankhor just north of Navoi; the *Ankhor* is built right on the edge of the wide canal surrounded by trees.

The *Taj Restaurant* (☎ 133 53 92, Chekhov 5) does a large variety of great Indian food, including a lot of veg options, and the service is good too. Perhaps it's poor taste to recommend a restaurant for its toilets, but they were exceptionally clean.

Across from the Le Meridien on Tukay is the *Cassandra* (☎ 133 75 61), with an intriguing mix of Uzbek and European food, including quail and pizza, and a menu in English. It's fairly cheap at US$5 or so in *sum* for dinner.

The *Tortoise & Violin* (☎ 136 45 22, Jakub Kolos 11) is a gallery where Uzbek meals are served to the accompaniment of traditional music. It's open Wednesday, Thursday and Friday nights.

The Georgian *Gruziya* (☎ 136 35 37) is in a dark, cool basement on Pushkin across from the music conservatory, with a large menu of meat and veg dishes, a pianist for mood and karaoke for the seriously vodka-ed. Check the bill for extra charges.

The *New World Restaurant* (☎ 133 33 22) has a set price buffet of Korean, Japanese and western dishes for US$35. It's pricey by local standards but the Korean-style seafood is superb and the service is top-notch. It's upstairs in the Navoi Opera Theatre; enter through the foyer.

On the corner of Ataturk and the Broadway, the huge *Zeravshan* complex (☎ 33 43 76) has several restaurants and bars, dealing more in alcohol and atmosphere than decent food. The Georgian *Tbilisi* and the Chinese *Peking* are two of the better restaurants here.

Tashkent's Korean restaurants are renowned for their excellent service, and make a wonderful change from shashlyk. Two of the best are the *Seoul Restaurant* (☎ 53 14 14, Shota Rustaveli 65), two tram stops beyond Babur Park, and *Sam Yang* (☎ 74 45 71, Chilonzor 11) – take the westbound trolleybus No 11 from Mirzo Ulughbek Metro station. For a full meal figure at least US$30 per person at either place.

There are cheaper Korean restaurants in the southern suburb of Qoyloq. Several are on the Ring Rd about 500m west of Qoyloq bazar; look for the shed-like buildings (they turn into discos after dinner) and the strings of coloured lights. Expect to pay about US$5 in *sum* for excellent cold noodles, salads and dishes spiced with lots of chili.

Cafes & Streetstalls Chaykhanas abound in parks, bazars and transport stations, dishing up shashlyk, plov, *laghman* (noodles) and tea. Hygiene is variable; look for high turnover and service right off the fire. There's a string of open-air cafes along the pedestrian Sayilgoh kuchasi, known as the Broadway, some of which offer western fare like burgers and pastries.

The *New World Pizza & Bakery* on Bukhara across from the Navoi Opera Theatre has croissants, cakes, white bread and pizzas, and you can sit outside.

Ardus FM Burger on Ataturk near the Broadway, next door to the Ardus supermarket, is where well-heeled teenagers gather to preen in the city's best approximation of a western fast-food chain. Burgers and fries are US$2, and there's powerful air-con.

The Café (☎ 56 43 73, Shevchenko 52A) is open daily, has a cosy atmosphere and good pastas and salads as well as Turkish food. There's a menu in English and live music some nights; dinner is about US$5.

In the park between Sharaf Rashidov and Buyuk Turon, the *Blue Domes Café* (Kafe Golubye kupola) has good shashlyk, *samsa* (like a samosa) and plov in clean surroundings. It's self-serve at lunch and has waiters in the evening. Next door is a chaykhana.

The *Dutika Canteen* (Gogol 73), at the Indonesian embassy, serves terrific cheap Indonesian food and has veg options. It's only open on Monday and Thursday 12.30 to 2 pm, for a fixed price of US$1.25 in *sum*.

Home Restaurants One place to taste true Uzbek cooking is in one of the restaurants that people open in their homes in parts of the old town – just tables in a courtyard, where you're served one or two simple

UZBEKISTAN

dishes from the same pots that feed their families, plus tea or beer.

One such neighbourhood in Tashkent is a few minutes from Tinchlik Metro station. From the station, walk to the closest traffic signal on the main street, Beruni prospekti, and turn right into Akademik Sadikov kuchasi. Most of the home-restaurants are between five and 10 minutes walk along (or just off) this street.

There are no signs or shopfronts. Boys practically drag you off the street for the midday and evening (after 7 pm) meals. Try for a home, not one of the little cafes that seem to be run by post-adolescent kids. Most places are fairly clean, but it's OK to peek into the kitchen. Anything more than about US$1 per dish (in *sum*) is probably too much. Gentle bargaining is OK.

Self-Catering There are farmers' markets all over town; see the Shopping section for some near the centre. In season, an informal *melon bazar* springs up near the Navoi Literary Museum.

Entertainment

Folk Music & Dance Uzbeks delight in singing, although the style – a reedy sound from the front of the mouth, not the chest – is strange to western ears. And for a foreigner who doesn't know the words or traditions, the attraction can soon wear thin.

Less authentic but more accessible than traditional performances are the rousing instrumentals and lush choreography of the state-supported company, *Bakhor* (Spring). They have their own concert hall at Paradlar Alleyasi 5, at the north end of the long salmon-and-green building on Mustaqillik maydoni. The box office is open 9.30 am to 5 pm (or you can book a pricier ticket through Uzbektourism), but they're away on tour June to September.

Theatre & Concert Halls Tashkent has a full cultural life, some of it, like drama, of interest mainly to Uzbek and Russian speakers. But one of Asia's best cultural bargains is surely the *Alisher Navoi Opera & Ballet Theatre* (Ataturk 28) opposite the Hotel

Tashkent, where you can enjoy quality classical western opera almost any night (except June to August) for US$0.10 to US$1 in *sum*. The box office (☎ 133 33 44), in one of the columns out front, is open daily 10 am to 3 pm and 4 to 6 pm. Performances start at 6 pm Monday to Friday, and at noon and 5 pm on Saturday and Sunday, with a different show every day. In just a week you can see *Swan Lake, Carmen, Rigoletto* and the Uzbek opera *Timur the Great*. The quality of performances is high, though groups of schoolkids on a compulsory culture experience can add a circus-like atmosphere. Even if you don't like opera, the theatre interior makes a visit worthwhile, and the box office will arrange a tour for a small fee for any group of three or four who ask. Other theatres include:

Ilkhom Theatre
(☎ 41 22 52) Pakhtakor 5, Pakhtakor Metro – modern theatre with an experimental edge, often comprehensible to non-Russian speakers, occasional jazz concerts, with performances at 6 pm.
Khamza Drama Theatre
(☎ 144 35 42) Navoi 34 – Uzbek and classical western drama in Uzbek, performances at 5.30 pm Monday to Friday
Muqimi Musical Theatre
(☎ 45 36 55) Almazar 187, Halqlar Dustligi Metro – Uzbek operettas such as *Brothers, Matchmakers, Super Mother-in-Law* and *Bridegroom's Contest*, 6 pm Monday to Friday, 5 pm Saturday and Sunday
Palace of the Friendship of Peoples
Halqlar Dustligi maydoni – big events including pop concerts
Republic Puppet Theatre
(☎ 56 73 95) Kosmonavtlar 1 (Kosmonavtlar Metro) – performances at 11 am and 1 pm
Russian Drama Theatre of Uzbekistan
(☎ 133 81 65) Ataturk 24, Mustaqillik Maydoni Metro – classical western drama, with performances Monday to Friday at 6 pm, Saturday and Sunday at 5 pm
Tashkent State Conservatory
(☎ 133 52 74) Pushkin 31 – chamber concerts, Uzbek and western vocal and instrumental recitals, with announcements posted outside
Tashkent State Musical Comedy Theatre
(☎ 77 84 92) Volgogradskaya, Mirzo Ulughbek Metro – operettas (eg Strauss and Mozart) at 6 pm Monday to Friday, 4 pm Saturday and Sunday

Central Asia summons up images of desert and open steppe **(below)**, but the region has its own share of lakes, such as Toktogul **(top)** and Lake Issyk-Kul **(middle)**, both in Kyrgyzstan.

MARTIN MOOS

BRADLEY MAYHEW

BRADLEY MAYHEW

MARTIN MOOS

Top: Guards march with their flag in a ceremony at Bishkek, the capital of Kyrgyzstan.
Middle & Bottom Right: The Kyrgyz flag – the 40 flames represent the 40 Kyrgyz clans. The centre depicts the cross beams at the top of a yurt as shown **(bottom right)** in a partly built yurt.
Bottom Left: Art with a communist message, a mosaic typical of the Soviet era.

Bars & Discos The standard night out is a long, boozy dinner. The **Broadway** is the local version of Moscow's Arbat, with artists, buskers, cheap outdoor eateries and bars, and cheerful young Uzbeks after your dollars. The **Zeravshan** complex here has bars and nightclubs filled with all sorts of interesting denizens, such as freelance Russian prostitutes, local Mafia types and waitresses who gamely tack massive service charges onto bills.

The **Lucky Strike Bar** is popular with expats; it has draught beer, MTV and a less seedy atmosphere than most. It's in the basement of a massive apartment building lined with shops on the ground floor north-east of Khamid Olimjon Metro; the entrance is along a street next to a large corner store.

Mama's Fun Pub (Movarounnakhr 32) is a theme pub across from the Railway Museum, near the train station, with live jazz 7 to 9 pm and live rock 9 pm until closing time. It also serves good South-East Asian food.

The **New World Bar** on the corner of Bukhara and Ataturk across from the Opera Theatre has imported beer on tap and live jazz every night. The **Blues Bar** on Halqlar Dustligi across from the Oliy Majlis is similar. There are also hotel bars where you can mingle with maudlin businesspeople losing their shirts in the Uzbek economy; the best are the **Hemingway** in the Shodlik Palace, the **Salty Dog** in the Le Meridien and Uzbekistan's only **Irish Pub** at the Intercontinental. The bar in the lobby of the **Hotel Uzbekistan** has a chunky Soviet style all its own and massive leather couches to sink into.

Shopping

Handicrafts The Zumrad Culture Centre is run by the Businesswomen's Association of Uzbekistan and has a first-rate selection of handicrafts including ceramics, jewellery, embroidery, fabrics, paintings and traditional clothing. The knowledgeable staff speak English. Zumrad is at Afrosiab 41, next door to the Ozbegim supermarket close to Oybek Metro. It's open daily except Sunday 10 am to 7 pm.

The Abdul Khasim Medressa, close to the Oliy Majlis near Halqlar Dustligi Metro

station, is now the Meros Centre for Traditional Arts, with some attractive souvenirs by local artisans. It's open daily 9 am to 6 pm.

The Museum of Applied Arts, on Rakatboshi south of Kosmonavtlar Metro station, has a good but expensive shop with some genuinely old items and overpriced carpets. The museum is open daily 10 am to 5 pm. The shop in the Museum of Fine Arts also has a big selection, and sells good Turkmen rugs. You could also try the 'antiques' shop in the Union of Artists hall, diagonally across Sharaf Rashidov from the Hotel Tashkent.

Silk They don't have the atmosphere of the bazars, but for the best prices and a surprisingly good selection of silk by the metre, try the big department stores (univermag) – one across Uzbekistan from the Hotel Tashkent, the other south across the road from the Hotel Chorsu.

Art Galleries In the Exhibition Hall of the Uzbek Union of Artists, opposite the Hotel Tashkent, is the Union's own Hamar Gallery; enter on the north side. For kitsch street-level art and amusingly sarcastic Soviet era cartoons, try the little open-air galleries on the Broadway (Sayilgoh).

Open-Air Markets In warm weather, a big goods bazar sprawls by the Ippodrom every morning except Monday, but it's biggest by far on Sunday, with small-time biznesmen selling cheap goods of every kind. The Ippodrom is 2km south-west from Sobir Rakhimov Metro station, along Halqlar Dustligi prospekti on bus No 108 or tram No 17.

Tezykovka is the local name for a vast Sunday 'flea market' near the airport. Once a place for hobbyists, bookworms and talkers, it's now a sombre sea of junk – 'anything from nails to nukes' as one resident put it – some of it probably stolen. Take bus No 2 from Tashkent Metro station to the 'GAI' stop and walk south on Starodubtsev, or bus No 25 south on Movarounnakhr near the Hotel Uzbekistan to the 'Pervomaysky Rynok' stop and cross under the train tracks.

Watch your purse or wallet; gangs of pickpockets are said to work these bazars.

UZBEKISTAN

Farmers' Markets Tashkent has at least 16 open-air farmers' markets or bazars (Uzbek: *dekhqon bozori*, Russian: *rynok)*. The best for produce in season, say locals, are:

Chorsu – the central bazar for the old town, at Chorsu Metro station.
Farkhad (Russian: Farkhadsky) – six stops west from Khamza Metro station on tram No 9.
Mirabad (Russian: Gospitalnyy) – four blocks west of Tashkent Metro station on tram No 8, 9 or 24.
Oloy (Russian: Alaysky) – four blocks north of the Hotel Uzbekistan on Amir Temur Hiyaboni; being closest to the tourist zone, this one also has moneychangers, pickpockets and other lowlife.

Also worth a look is the modest 'Beshagach' bazar (Uzbeks write it Besh-Yoghoch, 'Five Karagach Trees'), in an isolated section of the old town near the Palace of the Friendship of Peoples (Halqlar Dustligi Metro station).

Supermarkets Western toiletries – including shampoo, scratch-free toilet paper and tampons – are available at the Ardus supermarkets on Amir Timur and on Ataturk near the Broadway; at the Anglesey supermarket on Pushkin near Khamid Olimjon Metro; and at Ozbegim on Afrosiab near Oybek Metro. Dunyo, on the corner of Pushkin and Navoi, has a good photo-developing centre as well as film supplies. All have imported western foods, though the selection tends to vary from week to week.

Getting There & Away

Air Tashkent airport is Central Asia's main international airport. The international arrivals area and domestic terminals are modern and reasonably efficient, while international departures are still in a grimy Soviet-era building. The domestic terminal is about 150m from the international terminal.

From Tashkent, Uzbekistan Airways flies three times a day to Bukhara (1½ hours), twice daily to Samarkand (one hour) and Urgench (2¼ hours), and once a day to Fergana (one hour). Other destinations with two or more flights a day include Namangan, Andijan, and Kokand in the Fergana valley; Qarshi and Termiz in the south; and Nukus. The inflight service on domestic flights is good if a touch quirky (care for a shot of vodka before takeoff?) and there is a modern plane maintenance facility in Tashkent.

There are two flights weekly to Ashgabat and Bishkek and daily flights to Moscow and Almaty. Direct international connections are in the Getting There & Away chapter.

Buying Tickets Outbound Uzbekistan Airways tickets are best bought a few days in advance, at the city booking office (☎ 066 or ☎ 56 38 37), Shota Rustaveli 9, opposite the Hotel Rossiya, open daily 9 am to 5 pm. Take tram No 28 west from the TsUM or tram No 7, 8 or 10 south on Sharaf Rashidov by the Hotel Tashkent. Some credit cards are accepted, though it is possible, and preferable, to pay for domestic flights in *sum*. International flights must be paid for in US dollars. Foreigners will be directed to the modern glass-walled offices on the right-hand side as you enter, where staff speak English and the service is good. Uzbektourism hotels will book flights for US$5.

You can also buy last-minute international tickets at a window on the departures level of the new terminal. Airport staff say the international dispatcher's office (just to the right of passport control on the departures level) might help if you have an open ticket and want to leave the same day. City offices of other airlines serving Tashkent are:

Aeroflot
(☎ 41 56 28) Qodiri 5A
Lufthansa
(☎ 137 60 65) Hotel Intercontinental, Amir Timur 107A
PIA (Pakistan International Airlines)
(☎ 45 35 68) Halqlar Dustligi 4
Transaero
(☎ 139 99 35) Halqlar Dustligi 6A
Turkish Airlines
(☎ 152 52 52) Ataturk 24

These also have offices at the airport, along with airlines such as Asiana (☎ 50 83 63), Iran Air (☎ 50 44 40), Ukraine Airlines (☎ 50 91 16) and Georgian Airlines (☎ 85 81 57).

Bus The Tashkent long-distance bus station is 200m north-west from Sobir Rakhimov

Metro station, through a complex of stalls and hawkers (don't confuse it with the regional bus stand beside the Metro station).

Ticket sellers or OVIR officers sometimes insist you register with the 24 hour passport (OVIR) office (upstairs to the left); formalities should only take a minute. Sometimes they'll also help you buy a ticket. The ticket 'queue' can be a struggle; beware pickpockets. If the bus you want is about to leave, try buying the ticket from the driver.

Major destinations and departure frequencies include Samarkand (hourly until 5 pm), Bukhara (five a day), Urgench/Khiva and Termiz (once a day), Shymkent (every 25 minutes until 6.30 pm), Bishkek (once a day) and Almaty (three times a day). There were no buses to the Fergana valley at the time of research. The new road over the Kamchik pass may be finished by the time this book goes to press, at which time bus journeys will be reinstated.

For buses to Chimgan go to the bus station at Mashinasozlar Metro.

Train Tashkent station, right by Tashkent Metro station, is mainly for destinations north and east of the city (eg the Fergana valley, Bishkek and Almaty) and for Moscow. South station is for those to the south and west (eg Samarkand, Bukhara, Urgench, Termiz and Dushanbe); take tram No 7 or 28 from near the Hotel Tashkent, or tram No 24 from Tashkent Metro station. Prices quoted in this section are for 2nd class *(kupeynyy)*.

Trains leave every day for Samarkand (US$3), Bukhara (US$6), Urgench (US$8) and Nukus; three times a week to Andijan via Kokand and Margilan in the Fergana valley; and three times a week to Bishkek (16 hours) and Almaty (24 hours). Trains to Moscow make the 55 to 65 hour odyssey on Tuesday, Wednesday and Thursday (US$50).

Buying Tickets Ticket counters for all destinations are on the ground floor of the Hotel Locomotif. However, foreigners may first be directed to the OVIR office and then to the special foreigners' booking office. The 24 hour passport (OVIR) office at Tashkent station is out onto the platform and down to the

left. They give you a chit for the railway booking office, or they might call ahead for you. It's a five minute walk from there (turn right from the station, left at the corner and across the canal) to the booking office (ТЕМУР ЙУЛ КАССАЛАРИ) at Movarounnakhr 51, opposite the old Railway Workers' Palace of Culture. The foreigners' hall at the right end is open daily 8 am to 5 pm.

Share Taxi These leave from several places around the city, including outside the main train station and around the fringes of the long-distance bus station. Seats cost US$5 to US$7 in *sum* to the Fergana valley, depending on the vehicle and your bargaining skills, slightly less for Samarkand.

Getting Around

To/From the Airport Buses are the cheapest way to/from the airport. Coming *from* the airport, they're also an alternative to the greedy, sometimes crooked, taxi drivers. Unfortunately they don't run late at night.

Bus No 25 and the infrequent express bus No 67-3 take 25 minutes to/from the clock tower on Movarounnakhr (Proletarskaya) near the Hotel Uzbekistan. The No 14 trolleybus takes 30 to 40 minutes to/from Alisher Navoi Metro station, near the Hotel Shodlik Palace. Express bus No 11-3 runs between the airport and the Hotel Chorsu.

The 6km, 20 minute taxi ride to/from the Hotel Uzbekistan should cost US$2, but drivers at the airport seem to have formed a cartel and won't accept less than about US$10 from foreigners.

Metro This is the easiest way to get around. During the day you'll never wait more than five minutes for a train, and the stations are clean and safe, if in need of new light bulbs. The Metro was designed as a nuclear shelter and taking photos inside is strictly forbidden.

There are two lines (the red-mapped Chilanzor and blue-mapped Uzbekistan lines), with a crowded pedestrian interchange between them at Pakhtakor and Alisher Navoi stations. A new line (the green-mapped Yunusabad line) seems to be permanently under construction. Plastic tokens, known

TASHKENT METRO

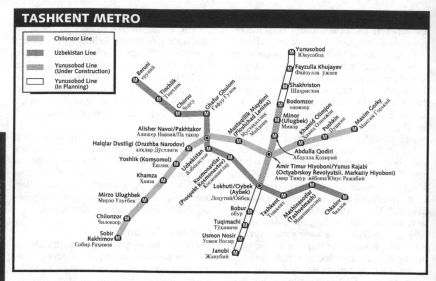

as *jetons*, good for a one-way journey between any two stations, cost 15 *sum*. The system runs daily 5 am until midnight.

Despite the use of Uzbek for signs and announcements, the system is easy to use, and well enough signposted that you hardly need a map. The most important signs are КИРИШ (entrance), ЧИКИШ (exit), and ЎТИШ (interchange).

If you listen as the train doors are about to close, you'll hear the name of the next station at the end of the announcement: *Ekhtiyot buling, eshiklar yopiladi; keyingi bekat ...* ('Be careful, the doors are closing; the next station is...').

Local Transport Buses, trolleybuses and trams cost 15 *sum* (30 *sum* for express buses), paid to the conductor or driver, who can sometimes give small change. Vehicles are marked in Uzbek, often *only* in Uzbek, so only the number is much use. Buses and trolleybuses are much faster but more crowded.

Taxi You can wave down practically any car and negotiate a price to where you want to go. There are licensed taxis also, with 'broken' meters. Except for a few rats at the airport, most are honest. You should be able to cross the whole city for under US$2 in *sum*.

You can book a taxi by dialling ☎ 062 or ☎ 34 51 60.

Car You can hire a car and driver from the service bureau at the Hotel Uzbekistan for US$10 per hour and up. A cheaper alternative is to hire a taxi for about half that.

AROUND TASHKENT

What opportunities there are for outdoor recreation near Tashkent are in the Chatkal mountains, an outrider of the Tian Shan, east of the city. Several rivers in this region offer the chance for rafting and kayaking. The Angren and Syr-Darya are for beginners. More experienced boaters will appreciate the Ugam and the Chatkal rivers, while the most challenging is said to be the upper Pskem. The white water season is September to October.

Chirchik Valley

A huge, partly moribund chemical factory dominates the industrial city of **Chirchik**. The next big town up the valley, **Gazalkent**, used to be predominantly German. All but a

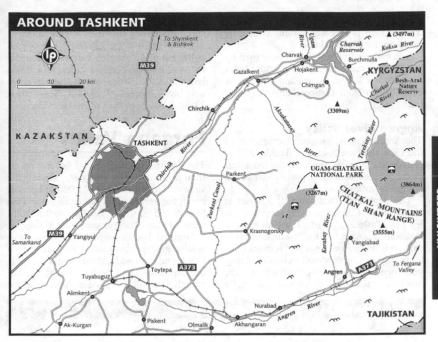

AROUND TASHKENT

UZBEKISTAN

handful of families have emigrated, and the mostly Uzbek inhabitants of today live in distinctly German houses with pitched roofs. Near the foot of the **Charvak reservoir** is a small park protecting 40,000-year-old petroglyphs of humans and antlered animals. The park lies on the right-hand side of the road as you face the dam wall, near a road sign for the village of Hojakent. Look for the rockface and some fruit trees.

Chimgan

This recreation zone on the south shore of the Charvak reservoir, 80km (2½ hours by bus) up the Chirchik river valley, is popular for winter sports (though it runs a poor second to those near Bishkek and Almaty). But it's open year-round, and there is some good walking here. Roadside stalls run by Kazak and Kyrgyz women sell *kumys* (fermented horse milk) in spring and summer.

Three rivers feed the reservoir – the Pskem from the north-east, the Koksu from the east and the Chatkal from the south-east – and a fourth, the Ugam, joins the outflow just below the dam at Charvak village. In the upper Chatkal watershed is a nature reserve, the **Ugam-Chatkal National Park**. Along the Tereksay (or Tereklisay) river, a tributary of the Chatkal, there are ancient petroglyphs. On the Kyrgyzstan side is the **Besh-Aral Nature Reserve**, taking in 3000 to 4000m peaks in the narrow ridge between the Koksu and Chatkal valleys. Visas are apparently not necessary for short treks into Kyrgyzstan and Kazakstan from here. It is possible to trek from here to Kyrgyzstan's Lake Sary-Chelek.

Accommodation at Chimgan includes Uzbektourism's massive and slightly decrepit *Hotel Chimgan* (☎ 274222- 444), where a standard double with breakfast is about US$50. There is also a spartan year-round *turbaza* (holiday camp) here. Uzbektourism, through the tour office or service bureau of any of its hotels, will sell you expensive guided walks (or winter skiing trips). There is a seasonal mountaineering camp on the upper Pskem.

You can get to Chimgan on your own by bus from the station at Mashinasozlar Metro, or as far as Charvak village and the dam by electric train from Tashkent's North (main) train station.

Angren River Valley

The Angren (or Akhangaran) drops out of the Tian Shan south-east of Tashkent. The canyon of the upper Angren is the most dramatic and least accessible part of Tashkent's natural surroundings.

The depressed coal town of **Angren** is about 100km (3½ hours by bus) up the valley from Tashkent. Nearby is a 12th century mausoleum. About 13km north up a side canyon is the grotty Yangiabad turbaza (better to stay at Angren's modest hotel or bring your own tent, say locals), from where there are fine walks past cliffs and waterfalls

towards the Ugam-Chatkal National Park, and a week-long trek over to Chimgan.

Crawling over the 2267m Kamchik pass at the top of the Angren valley is the winding road into the Fergana valley, which was being upgraded at the time of research to enable buses to avoid Tajikistan. See Getting There & Away in the following section.

Fergana Valley

The first thought many visitors have on arrival in the Fergana valley is, 'where's the valley?' From this broad (22,000 sq km) flat bowl, the surrounding mountains (the Tian Shan to the north and the Alay to the south) seem to stand back at enormous distances.

Drained by the upper Syr-Darya, funnelling gently westward to an outlet just a few kilometres wide, the Fergana valley is one big oasis, with perhaps the finest soil and climate in Central Asia. Already in the

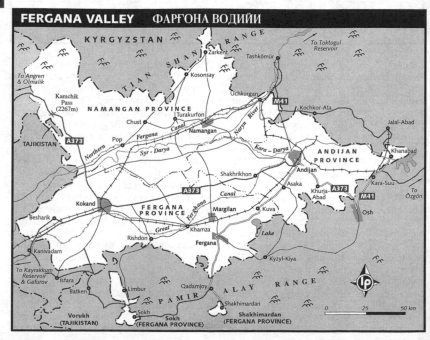

2nd century BCE the Greeks and Persians found a prosperous kingdom based on farming, with some seventy towns and villages. A major branch of the Silk Road wound through the valley.

The Russians were quick to notice the valley's fecundity, and Soviet rulers enslaved it to an obsessive raw-cotton monoculture that will only slowly be dismantled to allow Uzbekistan an economic equilibrium of its own. But there is also abundant seasonal fruit and this is the centre of Central Asian silk production (see the boxed text 'Silk Production in Uzbekistan' in the Rishdon section).

With eight million people (a third of Uzbekistan's population) the valley is the most densely settled area in Central Asia, and thoroughly Uzbek – 90% overall and higher in the smaller towns. But the Fergana valley has few architectural monuments and no tradition of religious or secular scholarship; on the whole its towns are architecturally uninspiring. The hotels are mostly bad and Uzbektourism keeps a stranglehold on home-stays. But it has always wielded a large share of Uzbekistan's political and religious influence. For the visitor its main assets are hospitable people, exceptional crafts, several kaleidoscopic bazars and the proximity of the mountains. The valley's landscape of cotton fields fringed by mulberry trees, interspersed with orchards, canals and villages, has its own quiet charm.

Although this is a kind of Uzbek heartland in terms of language, population and tradition (the people of Andijan are said to speak the purest form of Uzbek), it's not all part of Uzbekistan. The mutual boundaries of Uzbekistan, Tajikistan and Kyrgyzstan are crazily knotted together here – a giant Stalinist demographic fiddle to dilute the independent tendencies for which the valley has long been known. There are tiny pockets of territory scattered throughout the region, so small they don't make it onto maps. The valley's western 'gate' is plugged by a thumb of Tajikistan, and the surrounding mountains belong mostly to Kyrgyzstan (Khojand in Tajikistan, and Osh, Jalal-Abad and other towns in Kyrgyzstan, are described in those respective chapters). The Russian-era town of Fergana makes a convenient base for trips around the valley.

History

The first Chinese visitors to Central Asia, imperial envoys in search of allies in the 2nd century BCE, were also on the lookout for the swift 'dragon-horses' of the Fergana valley, celebrated in legends across Asia and India for their size, speed and endurance. The valley was already under cultivation and must have been a welcome oasis for travellers coming from the deserts in the east.

Temple remains at Kuva, about 35km north-east of Fergana, and elsewhere suggest the valley was Buddhist-ruled before the arrival of the Arabs in the 8th century. The valley's best-known son is probably Zahiruddin Babur (Bobur in modern Uzbek), founder of India's Mughal dynasty in the 16th century.

About 1709, valley tribes elected one Shahrukh Bey as their leader and the Kokand khanate split from its Bukhara parent. The bickering of the Khiva, Bukhara and Kokand city-states would thereafter dominate Central Asia until the mid-19th century. At its height the Kokand khanate's claims extended west to Tashkent, north to Shymkent (Chimkent) and cast as far as Kashgar. The last Kokand ruler was a Russian puppet named Khudoyar Khan.

Kokand, Andijan and Osh were taken by the tsar's troops in 1876 with little effort and the khanate was dissolved. Uncomfortable in the valley's medieval towns, the first military governor, General Mikhail Skobelev (soon to achieve infamy for the massacre of the Turkmen at Geok-Tepe) founded the New Margilan cantonment, later renamed as Fergana.

In trying to keep a grip on the tsar's domains, the Bolsheviks made one of their worst moves here. After a rival, moderate Islamic government was proclaimed in Kokand, Tashkent revolutionaries in 1918 sacked the town and slaughtered thousands of civilians. Central Asia's previously somnolent Muslims were electrified, the *basmachi* (Muslim guerilla fighters') rebellion was ignited in town after town; any trust

Muslims might have had in the revolution or in the Russians was permanently destroyed.

The valley's legendary fertility brought it to its knees in Soviet times. Less than 300km long, it was harnessed to provide nearly a quarter of the USSR's raw cotton. While the crops have diversified somewhat since independence, the region is still made up primarily of huge agro-industrial collectives.

The frustrations of this lopsided, seasonal economy, coupled with Stalin's invention of 'us-and-them' republican boundaries, stirred up intense ethnic tensions, and glasnost let these loose in the form of bloody violence that gave the valley a bad name in the final Soviet years and left hundreds dead. The ugliest incidents included riots against Meskhetian Turks in Fergana and other towns in 1989, an anti-Jewish pogrom in Andijan in the same year and mutual butchery between Uzbeks and Kyrgyz at Osh and Özgön (Uzgen) in 1990. There is a continuing exodus of non-Uzbeks.

The government cracked down on Islamic opponents in the late 1990s, raising tensions in the valley. An Uzbek Islamic militia took hostages and skirmished with Uzbek and Kyrgyz forces in 1999, sheltering in the mountainous valley fringes just as basmachi rebels did in the 1920s.

Religion

Muslims in this rural, conservative corner take their faith as seriously as any in Central Asia, and the end of Soviet rule has naturally led to a religious revival (or to an 'Islamic hotbed', as the media like to put it). The outlawed IRP enjoys strong support here. To the government's great unease, the eastern end of the valley – around Namangan, Andijan and over the border in Osh and Jalal-Abad – has proved a fertile ground for Islamic resistance to Karimov's regime. The Wahhabi branch of Islam offered by the Saudi-backed Ahle Sunnah movement flourished here for a time in the early 1990s and was then pushed underground by repression. Uzbekistan accuses Tajikistan of offering sanctuary to rebels.

In the 18th and 19th centuries, Kokand was Central Asia's second Islamic centre after Bukhara, its khans the bitter rivals of Bukhara's. Worship, forbidden in the 1920s, was later grudgingly allowed at a single mosque each in Kokand, Margilan and Fergana. The number of mosques mushroomed after independence, but the government closely vets Friday sermons and banned the broadcasting of the *azan* (call to prayer), from mosque loudspeakers in 1998.

Dangers & Annoyances

Although the valley is as hospitable as anywhere in Uzbekistan, perhaps more so, standards of dress are a source of misunderstanding. Except perhaps in the centre of Fergana town, too much tourist flesh will be considered an insult and a provocation. Dress modestly (no shorts or tight-fitting clothes for either sex, and preferably no short sleeves). Women travellers report being harassed when walking alone in cities like Andijan, especially at night.

Periodically the government cracks down on suspected Islamic opponents in the valley – Namangan seems to get the bulk of the attention. The police set up roadblocks and check vehicles and identity papers closely. The police are friendly enough but it does cause delays. The kidnapping of Japanese geologists by an Uzbek Islamic militia in 1999 in the Batken area of Kyrgyzstan may be an isolated incident, but keep an eye on developments and heed warnings.

Food

The valley is known for its cuisine but you won't find it in restaurants. The way to taste Fergana plov is to be invited to someone's home. Uzbek men here are proud of their cooking skills. The best chaykhanas include special rooms where guests can cook their own meals with ingredients from the nearest bazar. Hotel restaurants mainly limit themselves to dreary Russian fare and imitation laghman.

Vegetarians and self-caterers will do fairly well at the valley's well-stocked bazars. The most colourful bazar is Margilan's, on Thursday and Sunday. The biggest and perhaps most thoroughly Uzbek market is in Andijan.

Getting There & Away

Tashkent is linked to Andijan by three daily flights, to Kokand by two daily flights and to Fergana/Margilan by one daily flight.

Daily fast trains connect Tashkent with Gafurov (for Khojand), Kokand, Margilan and Andijan (there is no station at Fergana).

Overland to/from Tashkent The main route is the serpentine road via Angren over the 2267m Kamchik pass. A new tunnel and a wider road should allow buses to take this route by 2000. It takes five hours from Tashkent to Kokand this way. Buses and share taxis no longer travel via Khojand in Tajikistan.

Overland to/from Kyrgyzstan Osh is 115km east of Fergana town, but there are no direct bus connections. It is necessary to travel to Andijan and get a taxi from there to the border. Kyrgyz visas are not available at the border; you will need a valid visa from the Kyrgyz embassy in Tashkent (see Embassies & Consulates in the Facts for the Visitor section of this chapter), or any other Kyrgyz embassy. From Osh, via Jalal-Abad, a dramatic, two-lane mountain road snakes for 650km to Bishkek (with a change of bus at Toktogul). See the Bishkek to Osh & the Kyrgyz Fergana Valley section in the Kyrgyzstan chapter for more information. If you are headed north it's also possible to cross into Kyrgyzstan at Uchkurgan, northeast of Namangan.

A less travelled, less comfortable road climbs from Jalal-Abad, east via the goldmining town of Kazarman to Naryn, from where you can get to the Torugart pass into China. Jalal-Abad to Naryn takes at least two days. See the Naryn to Jalal-Abad section in the Kyrgyzstan chapter.

The Kyrgyz part of the Fergana valley has fewer services and poorer food, but lower prices and cooler air, than the Uzbek part.

KOKAND
☎ 73 • pop 176,000
This was the capital of the Kokand khanate in the 18th and 19th centuries and the valley's true 'hotbed' in those days – second only to Bukhara as a religious centre in Central Asia, with at least 35 medressas and hundreds of mosques. But if you walk the streets today, you'll find only a polite, subdued Uzbek town, its old centre hedged by colonial avenues, bearing little resemblance to Bukhara. The Roman Uzbek alphabet spells it Qoqon.

Nationalists fed up with empty revolutionary promises met here in January 1918 and declared a rival administration, the 'Muslim Provincial Government of Autonomous Turkestan' led by Mustafa Chokayev. Jenghiz Khan would have admired the response by the Tashkent Soviet, who immediately had the town sacked, most of its holy buildings desecrated or destroyed and 14,000 Kokandis slaughtered. What little physical evidence of Kokand's former stature remained was either left to decay, or mummified as 'architectural monuments'.

Many of the mosques and medressas that did survive are coming back to life now, but non-Muslim visitors are not welcome in some.

There's a hotel here, but you can do the town justice on a day trip from Fergana (1½ hours away by bus)

Orientation & Information
The khan's palace stands in the central Muqimi Park (called 'Russian Park' by locals). The remnants of pre-Russian Kokand are roughly between the park, the train station 2km to the south-west and the main bazar (and adjacent main bus station) to the south-east. Off Khamza and Akbar Islamov kuchasi are old-town lanes good for a wander, plus most of the town's surviving religious buildings. The centre of 'tourist' Kokand is Abdulla Nabiev maydoni, a 15 minute walk west of the park. The airport is about 10km south of town.

On Abdulla Nabiev maydoni are the main post and telegraph office and the National Bank (open Monday to Friday 8.30 to 11 am). On the east side of the park on Turkiston are OVIR and a police office. A small Uzbektourism office (☎ 417 82) on Khamza, south of the park, offers city tours for US$10 per hour.

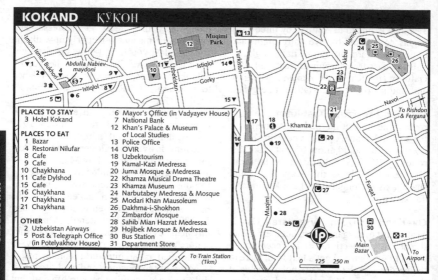

KOKAND КЎКОН

PLACES TO STAY
3 Hotel Kokand

PLACES TO EAT
1 Bazar
4 Restoran Nilufar
8 Cafe
9 Cafe
10 Chaykhana
11 Cafe Dylshod
15 Cafe
16 Chaykhana
17 Chaykhana
21 Chaykhana

OTHER
2 Uzbekistan Airways
5 Post & Telegraph Office
(in Potelyakhov House)

6 Mayor's Office (in Vadyayev House)
7 National Bank
12 Khan's Palace & Museum
of Local Studies
13 Police Office
14 OVIR
18 Uzbektourism
19 Kamal-Kazi Medressa
20 Juma Mosque & Medressa
22 Khamza Musical Drama Theatre
23 Khamza Museum
24 Narbutabey Medressa & Mosque
25 Modari Khan Mausoleum
26 Dakhma-i-Shokhon
27 Zimbardor Mosque
28 Sahib Mian Hazrat Medressa
29 Hojibek Mosque & Medressa
30 Bus Station
31 Department Store

To Train Station (1km)

0   125   250 m

UZBEKISTAN

Khan's Palace

The palace of the last khan, Khudoyar, now shares space in a former Soviet pleasure park with a mothballed Yak-40 plane. The park is being extensively remodelled.

The palace, with seven courtyards and 113 rooms, was completed in 1873 – just three years before the tsar's troops arrived, blew up its fortifications and abolished the khan's job. He fled, not from the Russians but from his own subjects (who were probably encouraged to ransack the palace); indeed he fled *to* the Russians at Orenburg and a comfortable exile (he was later killed by bandits as he returned through Afghanistan from a pilgrimage to Mecca).

The palace entrance is reached by a ramp, with strikingly gaudy tilework in a multitude of colours blaring out from the long facade. The palace's surviving two courtyards and 19 rooms house a staid **Museum of Local Studies**, with jewellery and musical instruments in the throne room, Uzbek furniture in the waiting room and Oriental porcelain in the khan's well-used bedroom. To the right of the entrance the former offices of the chief minister are now devoted to nature displays (ie mouldy stuffed animals). The main

courtyard to the left has an unusual slender Chinese cannon. At the rear left-hand corner of the complex is a small art gallery where dozy Uzbek matrons watch over landscapes of Russian forests – one curious item is a statue of a sleeping hermaphrodite.

The now-demolished harem used to stand at the rear of the palace, where Khudoyar's 43 concubines would wait to be chosen as wife for the night – Islam allows only four wives so the khan kept a mullah at hand for a quick marriage ceremony. The concubines lived in a complex of pavilions with the sultan's mother, whose Kyrgyz origins led her to shun her official chambers and sleep in a yurt set up in a courtyard. It's open Tuesday to Sunday, 9 am to 5 pm.

Narbutabey Medressa

The Bolsheviks closed the 1799 Narbutabey Medressa but it's now open again with about eighty students, one of two in town (the other is the 1818 Juma Medressa on Khamza kuchasi); visitors are not welcome at either medressa. To win wartime support from Muslim subjects, Stalin had the adjacent **mosque** reopened, the only one for all of Kokand at the time.

The first right turn beyond the medressa takes you into a **graveyard** with several prominent mausolea associated with another khan, Umar. To the right inside the graveyard is the bright sky-blue cupola of the unrestored **Modari Khan mausoleum**, built in 1825 for the khan's mother. To the left is the 1830s **Dakhma-i-Shokhon** (Grave of Kings), the tomb of the khan and other family members, with an elegant wooden portal carved with Quranic verses and/or Umar's poetry.

Nasrullah Khan, the Emir of Bukhara, is said to have kidnapped Umar's independent-minded wife, a poetess named Nodira, and demanded that she marry him. When she refused, Nasrullah had her beheaded, along with her children and her brothers-in-law. Originally buried behind Modari Khan, she was adopted by the Soviets as a model Uzbek woman and moved to a prominent place beneath a white **stone tablet**, beyond Dakhma-i-Shokhon.

Russian Buildings
Around Abdulla Nabiev maydoni (named for a prominent Kokand Bolshevik) is a knot of sturdy brick buildings, built by the Russians in turn-of-the-20th-century 'mixed style', with sculptured façades and copper cupolas. They include the former headquarters of the German-Turkestan Bank (still a bank), Potelyakhov House (1907; now the main post and telegraph office) and Vadyayev House (1911; now the mayor's office).

Sahib Mian Hazrat Medressa
From the uninteresting Kamal-Kazi Medressa on Khamza, walk five minutes down Muqimi to the truncated remnants of a big medressa called Sahib Mian Hazrat (1861). Most of it was appropriated in Soviet times for a factory, but in a couple of surviving cells the Uzbek poet and 'democrat' Mohammedamin Muqimi (1850-1903) is said to have spent his last days. For about US$0.25 in *sum* the caretaker will give you a tour.

Juma Mosque
The city's Friday mosque reopened in 1989 after decades of neglect under Soviet rule and today can accommodate up to 10,000 worshippers. Non-Muslims are usually not permitted to enter, though by asking politely and dressing modestly, men may be allowed to take a peek beyond the gateway at the enormous courtyard and a 100m-long ornately carved and painted *eivan* (study hall).

Khamza Museum
This could just as well be dedicated to Lenin – a fatuous shrine to a Soviet-imposed 'national hero', the poet Khamza Khakimzade Niyazi (who was born in Kokand) – full of manuscripts and Socialist-realism (and the odd photo of old Kokand) and staffed by guides who shadow you like the KGB. Kokand's main bazar was blasted away to make room for this Soviet-gigantic building and the twin Khamza Musical Drama Theatre – both now crumbling. The museum, on Akbar Islamov, is open Tuesday to Sunday, 9 am to 5 pm.

Places to Stay & Eat
The privatised *Hotel Kokand* (☎ 364 03) on Abdulla Nabiev maydoni is pretty grim but it usually has electricity and water; it's not overpriced with rooms for US$2/4 in *sum* and *lux* (deluxe) doubles for US$9 in *sum*. Get there from the bus station on southbound marshrutnoe taxi No 1 or 8, or bus No 3, 8 or 14. From the train station take almost anything north-bound on Istanbul.

The biggest place in town, with decent Russian and Uzbek dishes inside and shashlyk and plov outside, is *Cafe Dylshod* west of Muqimi Park. Opposite the Hotel Kokand, the *Restoran Nilufar* has good Uzbek food and cheap Russian grub. Fill up at either for about US$1. The *cafe* by the Hotel Kokand on Istiqlol kuchasi opens early.

There are chaykhanas dotted all over the place, some of them serving food, though hygiene is dubious. A pleasant *chaykhana* is in the little park near the Khamza Museum. Vegetarians and self-caterers can go to the big *bazar* by the bus station, or a small one near the hotel.

Getting There & Around
The only regular air connection is to/from Tashkent, twice a day for the equivalent of

UZBEKISTAN

US$13 in *sum*. The Uzbekistan Airways booking office is beside the Hotel Kokand.

The bus station, by the main bazar on Furqat, is to be phased out in favour of a new one out on the Tashkent road. Fergana and Margilan are 90km (two hours) away by bus, with departures about every half hour. Buses go hourly to Andijan and Namangan.

There are three trains a week to Tashkent from here for about US$3 in *sum* (2nd class) leaving at 8.30pm.

Share taxis leave when full for Tashkent from the main bazaar and from the bus station for a negotiable US$3 to US$5 per seat, or US$12 to US$20 for charter, depending on the vehicle.

Bus No 14 links the airport, train station and bus station, but apparently only to meet incoming and departing flights. Bus No 8 runs back and forth past the Hotel Kokand, Khan's Palace, Juma Medressa and the bus station and bazar. Bus Nos 16 and 23 go north from the bus station to the area around Narbutabey Medressa.

FERGANA
☎ 73 • pop 220,000
This is the valley's least ancient and least Uzbek city. It began in 1877 as Novy Margelan (New Margilan), a colonial annexe to nearby Margilan. The name Fergana (say **fair**-ga-na) dates from the 1920s.

With the central streets shaded by huge plane and poplar trees and dotted with pastel-plastered tsarist buildings, Fergana is a nice enough place to hang out, a mini-Tashkent with a relatively high proportion of ethnic Russian and Korean citizens but without the belittling Soviet architecture. It's the most convenient and comfortable town from which to look around the valley.

Orientation & Information
The streets radiate from what's left of the old tsarist fort, 10m of mud-brick wall within an army compound (off limits to visitors) behind the city and provincial administration buildings.

Uzbektourism (☎ 25 04 13, 25 06 35), on the 2nd floor of the Hotel Ziyorat, can arrange transport, home-stays and valley excursions for cash. They may try to sell you expensive tours, but are quite open to negotiation; around US$50 per day for an English-speaking guide/driver. English-speaking staff include Alex and Rustam, who make an effort to go beyond the tourist sites (eg informal home visits, local craft centres including Rishdon ceramics studios, silkworm nurseries and trips to the mountains).

At the National Bank (☎ 24 40 36) on al-Farghoni you can extract US dollars on Visa cards or change Amex and Visa travellers cheques, presuming they have US dollars in the first place.

The main post office is on Qosimov opposite the Hotel Fergana. Another post office and the telephone and telegraph office are near the east end of al-Farghoni.

Things to See
Fergana's most appealing attraction is the **bazar**, its good-natured Uzbek traders leavened with Korean and Russian vendors selling home-made specialities.

Despite labels exclusively in Uzbek, and staff who dog your steps, the **Museum of Local Studies** on Usmankhojayev is worth a look for its 3-D map of the valley, infrared satellite photos showing where all that cotton grows and some items on the valley's ancient Buddhist and shamanist sites. Other displays include natural history (animals taxidermed into permanent states of alarm), a fine collection of Rishdon ceramics and photos of pre-Soviet life. It's open daily except Tuesday 10 am to 5 pm (to 2 pm on Monday).

Places to Stay & Eat
Uzbektourism's flagship hotel, the Chinese-built *Hotel Ziyorat* (☎ 24 77 42, fax 26 86 02, Dodkhokh 2A) is close to the bazar and transport. Comfortable and clean singles/doubles with toilet and shower are expensive at US$50/70 (cash dollars only) with breakfast. There's no hot water in summer when the city's central heating is turned off. The clean, charmless restaurant here offers a small, unvarying selection of Russian and pseudo-international food.

Uzbektourism at the Hotel Ziyorat arranges *home-stays* for US$25 per day, including meals – a better deal and a more interesting experience than the Hotel Ziyorat offers.

Olga & Valentine Guesthouse (☎ 23 04 13, 25 06 35) is a long way from the city centre. Call in advance (Olga speaks English) and they'll pick you up. Staying in their comfortable apartment with hot showers and TV costs US$25 per night, including meals.

Hotel Dustlik (☎ 26 86 18, Skobelev 30) near Pushkin is a little decrepit, but not too bad, and stuck in the usual Soviet timewarp. Rooms with toilet and shower are advertised at an absurd US$7/12.

The gloomy *Hotel Fergana (☎ 26 95 01, Qosimov 29)* has rooms with toilet and shower for US$4 in *sum* and suites of sheer Soviet comfort for US$10. The restaurant in the east building has Uzbek dishes.

Restoran Saran is a well-regarded Korean restaurant close to the bazar. Dinner costs US$4 in *sum* for fresh noodles and salads; the service is excellent.

Self-caterers will enjoy the *bazar*, which is also a good place to go for lunch. There are several basic Uzbek canteens nearby. There are chaykhanas in Al-Farghoni Park but they tend to close early, usually by 8 pm.

Getting There & Away
Air The only regular flights are to/from Tashkent (1½ hours away) once a day for US$13 in *sum*. You can buy tickets through Uzbektourism at the Hotel Ziyorat or at the airport counter, which is open daily 8 am to noon and 1 to 7 pm.

Bus & Share Taxi Buses start from Fergana station (behind the bazar) for Shakhimardan, Kuva and a few local destinations, including the Margilan bus station. Long-distance coaches and regional buses use Yermazar station, out on the road to Margilan; some of the regional buses also stop at Fergana station. Departures from Yermazar include Namangan and Osh (every two hours, daily), and Kokand and Andijan (frequent departures each day). The main bazar has a few share taxis to Tashkent for around US$20 to US$25 to charter a Daewoo, US$15 for a Lada.

Train The station is at Margilan but it's possible to buy a ticket in Fergana. The booking office on al-Farghoni is open Monday to Friday 9 am to noon and 1 to 5 pm, and Saturday 8 am to noon. Trains depart three times a week for Tashkent.

Getting Around
The airport is a 25 minute trip on bus No 22; bus No 3 takes longer. Yermazar bus station is 10 minutes away on bus No 21, marked EPMO3OP-MAPKA3 (Yermazar-Centre). All these, and other local buses, depart from Mabrifat kuchasi near the bazar, returning to adjacent Kuvasoy kuchasi. There are also marshrutnoe taxis to Yermazar from Fergana station.

The easiest option for getting to the train station in Margilan is by taxi (locals estimate about US$1.50 in *sum*). If you arrive by train, take a taxi to Fergana, or one to Yermazar station and bus No 21 on to Fergana bazar.

In general, to home in on Fergana bazar, ask for *markaz* (centre).

MARGILAN
☎ 73 • pop 145,000
Often treated as if it were an appendage of Fergana, Margilan in fact came first by a couple of millennia, having been around (originally as Marginan) since at least the 1st century BCE.

Margilan's merchant clans, key players in Central Asia's commerce, are said to be a law unto themselves. In the closing decades of Soviet rule, this was the heart of Uzbekistan's black market economy. Margilan has long been known in Central Asia for its silks; Uzbekistan's most famous silk factory, the Yodgorlik, is here.

Hotel Margilan (☎ 646 42) opposite the bazar is very basic. A room is about US$1 in *sum*. It's simpler and more pleasant to come here on a day trip from Fergana.

Bazar
On Thursday and Sunday especially, Margilan's central bazar is a time capsule, full of weather-beaten Uzbek men in traditional clothing exchanging solemn greetings and gossiping over endless pots of tea, with

UZBEKISTAN

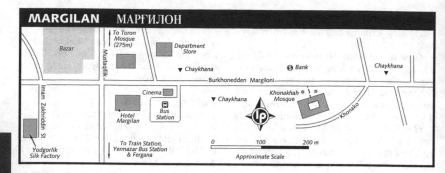

MARGILAN МАРГИЛОН

hardly a Russian or a tourist in sight. Uzbek matrons here dress almost exclusively in the locally produced khanatlas silk. In summer and autumn the stalls groan under fruit of all kinds and the air smells of spices. Some travellers say it's the most interesting bazar in the Fergana valley. There's another bazar about 2km out of town, best on a Sunday.

Yodgorlik Silk Factory
The Yodgorlik (Souvenir) factory employs traditional methods of silk production, unlike the vast and increasingly moribund Margilan and Khanatlas mass-production factories that are also in the city. It is possible to see the whole production process here, from steaming and unravelling the cocoons to the weaving of the dazzling khanatlas ('king of satins') patterned fabric. The factory has recently diversified into carpet making and embroidery.

A shop here sells silk for US$4 per square metre, plus khanatlas dresses, carpets and embroidered items for reasonable prices. The Yodgorlik factory is at 138 Imam Zakhriddin kuchasi, south-west of the bazar. It's open Monday to Friday 8 am to 5 pm.

Mosques
The modest **Toron Mosque** just to the north of the bazar is a fine example of the Fergana style with a gaily painted eivan; female visitors are prohibited from entering and male visitors may only enter with permission.

Half a kilometre east of the bazar is the reconstructed **Khonakah Mosque**, with two new 25m-high minarets out the front. Mod-

estly dressed male visitors may be welcomed into the courtyard and proudly shown the oldest part, an unrestored prayer room dating back, they say, to 1452. It seems to have been too small to catch the Bolsheviks' attention. The restored main building is a masterpiece of Fergana woodcraft, delicately painted in pale shades of blue, pink, yellow and green.

Getting There & Away
The trip from Fergana is simplest in a taxi, for the equivalent of about US$1.50 (ask for the bazar). A cheaper alternative is the slow, claustrophobic bus from Fergana station, half an hour via Yermazar bus station and the Margilan train station. It's marked simply ФАРГОНА-МАРГИЛОН.

Share taxis to Tashkent lurk around the train station car park; chartering a sturdy Volga sedan costs about US$20 in *sum*, or US$5 for a seat.

The bazar is right across the intersection from Margilan's bus station. From the train station it's a half hour trek north on Mustaqillik (formerly ulitsa Karla Marxa), or five minutes by almost any marshrutnoe taxi.

See the Fergana section for information on long-distance train and bus connections.

RISHDON
This mainly Tajik town near the border with Kyrgyzstan, 50km west of Fergana, is home to a group of master potters utilising the fine local clay. But unless you speak Tajik, or come here with Uzbektourism, it's difficult to find them on your own. Master of ceramics Rustam Usmanov (☎ 73-215 85) has

Silk Production in Uzbekistan

Although silk thread production and cloth-making have been largely automated, the raising of silkworms is still almost entirely a 'cottage industry', with most worms raised in individual farmers' homes, as they have been since perhaps the 4th century CE.

Out of its stock from previous years' husbandry, the Uzbekistan government distributes an average of 20g of young silkworm grubs to any farmer willing to 'raise' them in late April and early May. Each farmer prepares special rooms with large bedding boxes. The worms' entire diet consists of chopped up mulberry leaves culled from trees along lowland roads and canals. The farmers use the leftover branches as fuel, and the stripped mulberry trees regrow their branches the following year.

The initial 20g of grubs takes up about a square metre of space and consumes about 3kg of leaves a day. But each week, after a sleep cycle of a few days, the worms wake up and eat more than previously. At the end of just a month, each of those originally microscopic creatures has grown to the size of a little finger, and together they occupy two or three rooms and devour some 300kg of leaves each day! Then abruptly they stop eating altogether and spend a week or so rolling themselves up into a cocoon of silk fibres. The farmers (exhausted from trying to gather 300kg of leaves each day) sell the cocoons back to government silk factories – typically 80 to 120kg of cocoons at about US$1 to US$2 per kilogram.

Some worms, called 'seed-worms', are set aside and allowed to hatch as moths, which will lay eggs and produce the next generation of grubs. The rest are killed inside their cocoons by steaming (otherwise they would break out and ruin the silk filaments), and each cocoon is boiled and carefully unwound. A typical 3 or 4cm cocoon yields about 1km of filament! Several filaments are twisted together to make industrial thread, which is used to make clothing.

Uzbekistan as a whole produces about 30,000 metric tonnes of cocoons a year. The biggest silk factory in the former Soviet Union is in Margilan. Uzbektourism in Fergana can arrange tours of the factory.

his home and a studio featuring his own works and examples from his fellow artisans on the main road through town at Ar-Roshidony kochasi 230. He doesn't speak English but one of his sons speaks a little. He's a member of an association of master potters who have broken away from the collectivised workshops and are rediscovering techniques abandoned in Soviet times. Their ceramics use mostly traditional designs on a white background in shades of green and cobalt. They deserve more support than they're getting.

Local buses go to Rishdon from Fergana, Margilan and Kokand. The road to Kokand passes through a tiny enclave of Kyrgyzstan, unsignposted and almost invisible except for Kyrgyz vehicle number plates and the sight of farmers wearing white Kyrgyz hats instead of Uzbek skullcaps.

SHAKHIMARDAN

One of the odder results of Stalin's diabolical gerrymandering around the Fergana valley is the existence of an archipelago of tiny 'islands' of one republic entirely surrounded by another. One of these is the Uzbek enclave of Shakhimardan, 55km south of Fergana (another, equally scenic but less accessible, is Sokh, 60km west of Shakhimardan).

Shakhimardan's main appeal for visitors is that it's nestled in a 1500m-high alpine valley, a fine place to clear your lungs and take an easy look at the Alay mountains. Even at the height of summer the air is clean and cool, and above the village there are cheap turbazas within easy reach of trails that hardly anyone seems to use on weekdays. On Saturday and Sunday the town comes alive with cheery groups of families and friends quaffing vodka and plov in picnic spots with the favourite Uzbek setting of shady trees and a clear mountain stream.

Its main attraction for Muslims is that it's said to be the resting place of Ali, son-in-law of the Prophet Mohammed and fourth caliph, whose descendants Shia Muslims regard as the true heirs of the caliphate (at least seven places in the Middle and Far East make the same claim). *Shakh-i-mardan* is Persian for 'King of Men', a reference to Ali. For centuries pilgrims came to pray at the simple Hazrat Ali Mosque and mausoleum on a ledge above the village (*hazrat* is an honorific title meaning majestic or holy).

In an effort to suppress this traffic, successive Soviet administrations have tried to reinvent Shakhimardan. The mosque and mausoleum were burned down in the early 1920s by basmachi rebels trying to flush out 48 Red Army soldiers who had taken refuge there (according to Soviet historians); or by the Bolsheviks (according to local Uzbeks). In any case, the pilgrims stopped coming.

The village was later renamed Khamzaabad, in honour of one of the Bolsheviks' adopted martyrs, the secular Kokandi poet and playwright Khamza Khakimzade Niyazi. Khamza encouraged women to join his first-ever Uzbek theatre company and come out from behind their veils – for which, intoned the Soviets, he was stoned to death by Muslim fundamentalists here in 1929 and his body hidden in a rock crevice. The real story is undoubtedly more complex.

Following Uzbekistan's independence, local donations were used to build a simple replacement for an Ali shrine and pilgrims once again mingle with holidaymakers during the high season, April to September.

When a chunk of the Khrebet Katran Too glacier broke away in July 1998 it triggered a catastrophic flood that swept away the flimsy holiday homes close to the river; estimates of the number of people killed range from 100 to 3000. The small mosque south of the bazar by the river was spared; locals say the floodwaters parted around it.

Orientation

From the long-distance bus stand it's a 1.5km walk up to the village centre, where the valley splits. Up the right-hand canyon, 2.5km by road or a steep 1.5km on foot, is Turbaza Shakhimardan. Up the left-hand canyon, past dozens of workers' holiday camps, is Kuli Kulon (Sky-Blue lake).

Things to See & Do

At the end of the road, 4.5km from the village up the left-hand canyon, is an ageing diesel-powered cable car (or a farther steep 2 or 3km walk) to the icy **Kuli Kulon**, created centuries ago by a landslide. The 1998 flood wrecked the scenery somewhat. Crumbling statues of bears, wolves and mountain sheep set on boulders on the way up add a surreal touch. The shore of this alpine lake, at 1740m, is crowded in the high season and apparently deserted (but very cold) after that. A boat trip to the head of the lake is a small fee in *sum*. From its outlet flows a clear river called Kok-Sub (Green Water).

The dreary **Khamza Museum** behind Hazrat Ali is mostly full of Soviet-style propaganda (happy Uzbeks organising collective farms etc) but there are some photos of pre-Bolshevik Shakhimardan and the original Hazrat Ali mausoleum. The museum's opening hours are rather informal: usually Wednesday to Monday 9 am to 1 pm and 2 to 5 pm.

Treks

Turbaza Shakhimardan crawls with Uzbek holidaymakers during high season, enjoying volleyball, videos, excessive food and drink, clean air and the views.

Beyond the turbaza, about 15km from the village and above 2000m, is an ex-military training camp, now an international mountaineering camp (*alpinistskiy lager* or *alplager*) and trekking base called Dugoba. Most treks from here cross into Kyrgyzstan; you will need a valid Kyrgyzstan visa and possibly a special Alay Valley permit (see Permits in the Alay Valley section of the Kyrgyzstan chapter). A reputable travel agency with whom you book your trek may be able to help with this.

Established trekking routes lead from Shakhimardan over the Pamir-Alay to Daraut-Korgon in Kyrgyzstan. Routes head up the Ak Suu valley and then the Archa Bashi and Kara Kazyk valleys to the tricky 4440m Kara Kazyk pass and then over into the Kara Kazyk and Kök Suu valleys to Daraut-Korgon. An alternative route leads up the Eki Daban valley and over the 4296m Alaydin Daban pass into the Kök Suu valley. Other routes lead from nearby Khaidakan in Kyrgyzstan. All routes take a minimum of a about a week.

The best map coverage is the 1:100,000 *Pamiro-Alay Bisokiy Alay* (1992), often available at the office of Asia Travel (see the Travel Agencies section under Tashkent).

In the wake of (isolated) armed conflict in nearby Batken and Sokh trekkers are better off trekking with agency help. Fergana Uzbektourism can take you on treks from a day to a week or more. Guide, equipment (except sleeping bags) and three meals a day will cost about US$40 per person per day for a group of three or four, plus US$45 each way for transport from Fergana. Agencies in Tashkent and Samarkand also do trips up here. The trekking season is roughly May to October.

Places to Stay & Eat
The village has lots of chaykhanas, food stalls and a *bazar* and many holiday lodges. The main place to stay is *Turbaza Shakhimardon*, with 360 beds in very basic two-bed 'cottages' with common bathroom, for US$2 per person per day, including three plain meals. It's jammed in the high season but they can always squeeze in one or two extras. The *Sugurtachi Damolish Oye* is about 2km from the bazar in the outlying village of Vuardil, with clean rooms in a large Soviet building for US$1 per person in *sum*.

The *Dugaba alplager* has cabins with showers and a Russian sauna for US$5 per day and there are cooking facilities. To book call Rimma in Tashkent on ☎ (3)712-78 19 44; English is spoken.

Getting There & Away
Buses depart on the scenic 90 minute trip to Shakhimardon from Fergana station at least 10 times a day in the high season, or two or three times a day until 2 pm in the low sea-

son for US$0.30 in *sum*. There's no regular transport beyond Shakhimardan village.

ANDIJAN
☎ (3)74 • pop 350,000
Andijan dates to at least the 9th century CE, but its claim to historical fame is as the birthplace of Zahiruddin Babur (see the boxed text 'Zahiruddin Babur', below) in the 15th century, when it was the capital of the Fergana state and its main Silk Road trading centre.

It fell to the tsar in 1876, but was the scene of an abortive anti-Russian uprising in 1898. In 1902 an earthquake did what the Bolsheviks might have felt compelled to do two decades later – destroying the town and killing over 4000 people.

Andijan province, the most densely settled part of the valley, is today Uzbekistan's main oil-producing region and the town is its dour capital and industrial centre. Andijan has one of the most traditional bazars in the valley and the people of the region are said to speak the purest form of Uzbek.

UZBEKISTAN

Zahiruddin Babur

Born in 1483 to Fergana's ruler, Umar Sheikh Mirzo, Zahiruddin Babur (Bobur in Uzbek) inherited his father's kingdom before he was even a teenager, but his early career was less than brilliant. At 17 the young king (a descendant of Timur on his father's side and Jenghiz Khan on his mother's) took Samarkand, but was then abruptly driven right out of Fergana and into the political wilderness by the Uzbek Shaybanids. He found new turf in Afghanistan, where he ruled Kabul for two decades. Then in 1526 he marched into Delhi to found the line of Persian-speaking emperors of northern India known as the Mughals (a corruption of 'Mongol', local parlance for anybody from Central Asia). Though he died four years later in Delhi, his descendants ruled in Delhi until 1857.

Orientation & Information
Museums, medressa, bank, bookshop, department store, post and telegraph office and

a municipal hotel are clustered around the main bazar, about 3km north of the bus and train stations (which are a two or three minute walk from one another). Uzbektourism has a small office (☎ 610 22) in its own Hotel Zolotaya Dolina (Golden valley), almost 2km south of the bus and train stations, which means neither is much use unless you're in a group or have your own transport.

Things to See

The **bazar** is not the biggest in the valley but it's certainly colourful in the early morning. It's at its active peak on Thursday and Sunday. Across Oltinkul is the handsome 19th century **Juma Mosque and Medressa**, said to be the only building to survive the 1902 earthquake. A factory appears to have been dropped squarely upon most of it. What's left is now a working medressa again. Mosque attendances have fallen since a respected mullah was arrested and the police started taking note of worshippers here. It's normally closed to non-Muslims but a quick peek may be possible outside prayer times. Beside it is a **regional museum** with the usual historical exhibits and stuffed animals, open daily, except Sunday, 9 am to 5 pm (to 3 pm on Saturday).

The marginally more interesting **Babur Literary Museum**, surrounded by rose gardens in the lane behind the bazar, occupies the site of the royal apartments where Babur lived and studied as a boy within Ark-Ichy, the town's long-gone citadel. The museum, though visually pleasant, is more like a slicked-up shrine, with books, paintings and hyperbolic text about Babur and his literary friends. It's open daily, except Monday, from 9 am to 4 pm.

Places to Stay & Eat

Best bet to stay the night and see the bazar at its liveliest early in the morning, is the basic **Hotel Andijan** (☎ 587 07, Ralabi 241). Spartan rooms are about US$5 in *sum*; watch out for bedbugs. The hotel restaurant serves basic Uzbek food.

Uzbektourism's renovated **Hotel Zolotaya Dolina** (☎ 687 08, Mashrab 19) has fairly clean singles/doubles with toilet and shower for US$20/30.

Chaykhanas on Fitrat have shashlyk and laghman and of course the **bazar** has abundant fruit, vegetables, nuts and honey.

Getting There & Around

The easiest way to get between Andijan and other points in the valley is by bus. There are buses to Andijan about every 45 minutes for about US$1 from Fergana's Yermazar station (a 2½ hour trip), as well as frequent connections all day to/from Kokand, and Namangan every two to three hours. If you are headed to Osh or Jalal-Abad in Kyrgyzstan you will probably have to take a taxi to the border and change there. Share taxis and minivans leave from outside the bazar on Oltinkul and from the bus station.

From Andijan-I train station (not Andijan II) trains leave three times a week at 5.30 pm on a 12 hour journey to Tashkent (US$3.50 in *sum* for a 2nd class seat).

You can fly here from Tashkent (one hour) three times a day for US$13 in *sum*. Tickets are sold at the airport. The airport is 5km from the bazar by bus No 1A or 8; from the Zolotaya Dolina take bus No 6 or marshrutnoe taxi No 4. Bus No 2 connects the Zolotaya Dolina, the bus station and the bazar. Bus No 8 and trolleybus No 2 run between the Zolotaya Dolina and the bazar.

Central Uzbekistan

SAMARKAND

☎ (3) 66 • pop 404,000

No name is so evocative of the Silk Road as Samarkand. For most people it has the mythical resonance of Atlantis, fixed in the western popular imagination by poets and playwrights, sealed there by James Elroy Flecker with his 1913 poem *The Golden Journey to Samarkand*, and recycled in his play *Hassan*, which concludes with the lines:

We travel not for trafficking alone,
By hotter winds our fiery hearts are fanned.
For lust of knowing what should not be known
We take the Golden Road to Samarkand.

The reality is harsher, but not much. From the air your eye locks onto the domes and minarets, and on the ground the sublime, larger-than-life monuments of Timur, the technicolour bazar and the city's long, rich history do work some kind of magic. East of the centre, though, this is a sprawling Soviet-style city with few redeeming features. Ahead of spring and autumn the city can be engulfed by choking sandstorms.

Most of Samarkand's high-profile attractions are the work of Timur, his grandson Ulughbek and the Uzbek Shaybanids. You can visit them all, plus some ancient excavations, in two or three days. If you're short on time, at least see the Registan, Guri Amir, Bibi-Khanym Mosque, Shahr-i-Zindah and the bazar.

Note that the people of Samarkand, Bukhara and south-eastern Uzbekistan don't speak Uzbek but an Uzbek-laced Tajik (Farsi). Some members of the ethnic Tajik minority wish Stalin had made the area part of Tajikistan, but the issue is complicated by ethnic Uzbek cityfolk who speak Tajik.

History

Samarkand (Marakanda to the Greeks), one of Central Asia's oldest settlements, was probably founded in the 5th century BCE. It was already the cosmopolitan, walled capital of the Sogdian empire when it was taken in 329 BCE by Alexander the Great, who said, 'Everything I have heard about Marakanda is true, except that it's more beautiful than I ever imagined.'

From the 6th to the 13th centuries it grew into a city more populous than today, changing hands every couple of centuries: Western Turks, Arabs, Persian Samanids, Karakhan and Seljuq Turks, Mongolian Karakitay and Khorezmshah have all ruled here – before being literally obliterated by Jenghiz Khan in 1220.

This might have been the end of the story, but in 1370 Timur decided to make Samarkand his capital, and over the next 35 years forged a new, almost-mythical city, Central Asia's economic and cultural epicentre. His grandson Ulughbek ruled until 1449 and made it an intellectual centre as well.

When the Uzbek Shaybanids came in the 16th century and moved their capital to Bukhara, Samarkand went into decline. For several decades in the 18th century, after a series of earthquakes, it was essentially uninhabited. The Emir of Bukhara forcibly repopulated the town towards the end of the century, but it was only truly resuscitated by the Russians, who forced its surrender in May 1868 and linked it to the Russian empire by the Trans-Caspian Railway 20 years later.

Samarkand was declared capital of the new Uzbek SSR in 1924, but lost the honour to Tashkent six years later.

Orientation

Samarkand sits at 710m above sea level in the valley of the Zeravshan, Uzbekistan's third-biggest river, flowing down from the Alay mountains of Tajikistan.

A map of the centre reveals the city's Russian-Asian schizophrenia. Eastward are the tangled alleys of the old town, whose axis (and main shopping street) is the pedestrian section of Tashkent kuchasi between the Registan and the bazar. Shady 19th century Russian avenues radiate westward from Mustaqillik maydoni, the administrative centre of the modern city and province. The focus of this part of the city is the yawning open space in front of the Hokimiyat Tower, a multistorey Soviet monster with a golden lattice over its facade.

The main Russian-style shopping area is along Mustaqillik north of Gorky Park (sometimes called Tsentralnyy or Central Park). The decrepit multistorey Hotel Turist is a useful landmark on Gagarin, but you wouldn't want to stay there.

Almost everything of tourist interest is in the sun-dried old town, basically unchanged in its layout since the Middle Ages. Once you're off the main streets a good sense of direction helps in the web of mainly unsignposted alleys lined with high mud walls. A useful tourist landmark in the 'new' city is the Hotel Samarkand on the park-like boulevard called Universiteti.

Beyond Gorky Park, the Registan and the bazar, Samarkand is a sprawling, oversize city with a tedious transport system that

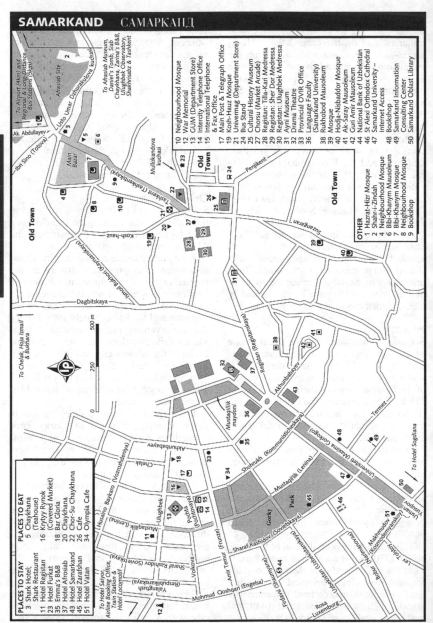

SAMARKAND   САМАРКАНД

PLACES TO STAY
3   Shark Hotel;
    Shark Restaurant
11 Hotel Registan
37 Hotel Furkat
35 Emma's B&B
37 Hotel Afrosiab
43 Hotel Samarkand
45 Hotel Zarafshan
51 Hotel Vatan

PLACES TO EAT
5   Chaykhana
    (Teahouse)
16 Krytoy Rynok
    (Covered Market)
18 Bar Gloria
20 Chaykhana
22 Chor-Su Chaykhana
26 Cafe
34 Olympia Cafe

10 Neighbourhood Mosque
12 War Memorial
13 GUM (Department Store)
14 Intercity Telephone Office
15 International Telephone
    & Fax Office
17 Main Post & Telegraph Office
19 Kosh-Hauz Mosque
21 Univermag (Department Store)
24 Cultural History Museum
25 Chorsu (Market Arcade)
27 Registan: Tilla-Kari Medressa
28 Registan: Sher Dor Medressa
29 Registan: Ulugbek Medressa
30 Registan: Ulugbek Medressa
31 Ayni Museum
32 Drama Theatre
33 Provincial OVIR Office
36 Language Faculty
    (Samarkand University)
38 Rukhobod Mausoleum
39 Mosque
40 Hodja-Nisbaddor Mosque
41 Ak-Saray Mausoleum
42 Guri Amir Mausoleum
44 National Bank of Uzbekistan
46 St Alexi Orthodox Cathedral
47 Samarkand University –
    Internet Access
48 Bookshop
49 Samarkand Information
    Consulting Center
50 Samarkand Oblast Library

OTHER
1   Hazrat-Hizr Mosque
2   Shahri-Zindah
4   Neighbourhood Mosque
6   Bibi-Khanym Mausoleum
7   Bibi-Khanym Mosque
8   Neighbourhood Mosque
9   Bookshop

means it takes a long time to get anywhere. The artery for municipal transport between the Russian town and the bazar is Dagbitskaya and Ismoil Bukhori.

The airport is 4km north of the bazar, along Akademik Abdullayev kuchasi. The long-distance and main regional bus stations are a farther 1km east from the airport. The train station is about 6km north-west of the centre.

Information

Tourist Offices The most capable of Uzbektourism's service bureaus is at the Hotel Samarkand (☎ 35 88 12, 35 71 51, fax 35 88 26), though they're not very enthusiastic if you're not a guest there. A three hour city tour costs US$30 each for a minimum of three people, not including entry fees.

Maps A detailed, fairly accurate 1991 map (scale 1:13,000) includes transport but has mostly Soviet street names. It's available from the hotels Samarkand and Afrosiab and from the Registan ticket booths. Many souvenir shops still fob off completely useless 1980 maps full of wrong and missing streets.

Useful Organisations The Samarkand Information Consulting Center (АХБОРОТ МАСЛАХАТ МАРКФЗИ) is a networking centre for local people and overseas non-governmental agencies, but visitors willing to stop and chat are welcome. For US$2 per hour you can use their email connection. It's in the Physics Faculty building just east off Universiteti, and open daily except Sunday 9 am to 1 pm and 2 to 5 pm.

A place you might find young Samarkandis keen to try out their English, French or German, and perhaps act as unofficial guides, is the Language Preparation Centre (Tsentr Yazykovoy Podgotovki) in room 52, two flights up at the university's Language Faculty, across the roundabout from the Hotel Samarkand. An informal English-language club operates from an office at the Samarkand Oblast Library, at the other end of Universiteti at No 21.

Money Hotel Samarkand has an exchange desk at the official rates, open 8 am to 8 pm.

At the National Bank of Uzbekistan, Firdavsi 7, travellers cheques and Visa cards can be used to extract US dollars, but they're only open from about 9 am to noon.

Post & Communications The unhelpful main post and telegraph office is on Pochta behind the small farmers' market, Krytyy Rynok. Hotel Samarkand's tiny stamp desk and drop-box seems to open mainly when tour groups are around.

The Hotel Samarkand has a 24 hour, direct-dial satellite telephone link with connections as clear as if they were next door, US$5 per minute (to Europe) to US$7 per minute (to Australia). With no three minute minimum this may actually be the cheapest place to make a *short* overseas call. The small international telephone and fax office on Shohrukh at the corner with Pochta (not the intercity office next door) has cheaper rates but dicier connections, and you pay even if the connection is lost.

The big Samarkand University building on the corner of Universiteti and Sharaf Rashidov has Internet and email access for US$2 per hour in room 306.

Travel Agencies Two agencies have offices on the second floor of the Hotel Samarkand – Asia Travel International (☎ 35 86 76, fax 33 06 86) and Afrosiab Travel Agency (☎/fax 35 82 50, ✉ busy@hotsam.samuni.silk.org). Both can set up conventional tourism or adventure travel in Uzbekistan, Kyrgyzstan and Kazakstan, plus local car rental, Uzbek home-stays and international flights. Although they are both group-oriented and not cheap, they are willing to do individual bookings. They prefer a few weeks' warning.

Cultural Centres Alliance Française, which mainly offers French tuition, is in the Samarkand Oblast Library at Universiteti 21 (☎ 233 66 27, speak to Nijina). They can arrange home-stays and act as informal guides.

The Registan

This ensemble of majestic, tilting medressas – a near-overload of majolica, azure mosaics and vast, well-proportioned spaces – is the centrepiece of the city, and one of the most awesome single sights in Central Asia. It was medieval Samarkand's commercial centre and the plaza was probably a wall-to-wall bazar. Heavy Soviet-era restoration included digging down 3m to its original level, exposing the buildings' full height.

Ulughbek Medressa on the west side is the oldest, finished in 1420 under Ulughbek (who is said to have taught mathematics there; other subjects included theology, astronomy and philosophy). Beneath the little corner domes were lecture halls, and at the rear a large mosque. About one hundred students lived in three storeys of dormitory cells, some of which are still visible.

The other buildings are imitations by the Shaybanid Emir Yalangtush. The entrance portal of the **Sher Dor (Lion) Medressa**, opposite Ulughbek's and finished in 1636, is decorated with roaring felines that look like tigers but are meant to be lions, flouting Islamic prohibitions against the depiction of live animals. In between is the **Tilla-Kari (Gold-Covered) Medressa**, completed in 1660, with a pleasant, garden-like mosque courtyard.

The hexagonal building in the square's north-east corner is a 19th century *chorsu* (market arcade).

The complex is a 10 minute walk from the Hotel Samarkand, and entry is US$0.50 in *sum*. Many inner rooms now serve as art and souvenir shops, and the Sher Dor's courtyard is favoured for lavish official banquets. On some summer evenings, there's a tacky sound-and-light show in the square.

Bibi-Khanym Mosque

The gigantic congregational mosque northeast of the Registan, powerful and shapely even in ruins, was finished shortly before Timur's death, and must have been the jewel of his empire. It's a victim of its own grandeur; once one of the Islamic world's biggest mosques (the main gate alone was 35m high), it pushed construction techniques to the limit. Slowly crumbling over the years, it finally collapsed in an earthquake in 1897.

Legend says that Bibi-Khanym, Timur's Chinese wife, ordered the mosque built as a surprise while he was away. The architect fell madly in love with her and refused to finish the job unless he could give her a kiss. The smooch left a mark and Timur, on seeing it, executed the architect and decreed that women should henceforth wear veils so as not to tempt other men.

Restoration of the main gate is underway (apparently with UNESCO patronage) and parts of the courtyard are closed off. Are they really going to try to *rebuild* this magnificent ruin?

It's worth going inside for a look at the enormous marble Quran stand in the open courtyard, and to get a feel for the scale of this place. Local lore has it that any woman who crawls under the stand will have lots of children. Entry costs US$0.50 in *sum*.

Across Tashkent kuchasi is Bibi-Khanym's own compact, 14th century mausoleum.

Shahr-i-Zindah

The most moving of Samarkand's sights is this street of tombs east of Bibi-Khanym. The name, which means Tomb of the Living King, refers to its original, innermost and holiest shrine – a complex of cool, quiet rooms around what is probably the grave of Qusam ibn-Abbas, a cousin of the Prophet Mohammed who is said to have brought Islam to this area. This is among the oldest standing buildings in the city. It's also an important place of pilgrimage, so enter with respect and dress conservatively.

Except for this and a few other early tombs at the end, the rest belong to Timur's and Ulughbek's family and favourites. Vaguely disfigured by donation boxes, they nevertheless feature some of the city's finest majolica tilework, largely unrenovated. The most beautiful is probably that of Timur's niece, second on the left after the entry stairs (which climb over the ancient city wall from the outside).

The site is open daily 8 am to 6 or 7 pm except national holidays and entry is US$0.50 in *sum*. You'll only have it more or less to yourself if you go very early or at lunchtime.

Guri Amir Mausoleum & Around

Guri Amir is Tajik for tomb of the emir. Timur, two sons and two grandsons, including Ulughbek, lie beneath this surprisingly modest mausoleum topped by a fluted azure dome, at the edge of the old town behind the Hotel Samarkand. One reason it looks small is that a medressa that used to be in front is now gone, except for the gate.

Timur had built a simple crypt for himself at Shakhrisabz, and apparently had this one built in 1404 for some of his sons or grandsons. But the story goes that when he died unexpectedly of pneumonia in Kazakstan (in the course of planning an expedition against the Chinese) in the winter of 1405, the passes back to Shakhrisabz were snowed in and he was interred here instead.

The simple inner room was originally decorated in gold (a 1970 restoration used some 2.5kg of the stuff). As with other Muslim mausolea, the stones are just markers; the actual crypts are in a chamber beneath, but to view these, the caretaker will expect a small consideration. In the centre is Timur's stone, once a single block of dark-green jade. In 1740 the warlord Nadir Shah carried it off to Persia, where it was accidentally broken in two – from which time Nadir Shah is said to have had a run of very bad luck, including the near-death of his son. At the urging of his religious advisers he returned the stone to Samarkand, and of course his son recovered.

The plain marble marker to the left of Timur's is that of Ulughbek, and to the right is that of Mersaid Baraka, one of Timur's teachers. In front lies Mohammed Sultan, Timur's grandson by his son Jehangir. The stones behind Timur's mark the graves of his sons Shah Rukh (Shohrukh in Uzbek/Tajik; the father of Ulughbek) and Miran Shah. Behind these lies Sheikh Umar, the most revered of Timur's teachers; the pole with the horse-hair tassel further identifies him as a Muslim 'saint'. Two other sons, Jehangir and Umar Sheikh, are buried at Shakhrisabz.

The Soviet anthropologist Mikhail Gerasimov opened the crypts in 1941 and, among other things, confirmed that Timur was tall (1.7m) and lame in the right leg and right arm (from injuries suffered when he was 25) –

and that Ulughbek died from being beheaded. According to every tour guide's favourite anecdote, he found on Timur's grave an inscription to the effect that 'whoever opens this will be defeated by an enemy more fearsome than I'. The next day, 22 June, Hitler attacked the Soviet Union.

In front of the gate are the remains of an earlier medressa, and to the right are the foundations of an even older *khanaka* (Uzbek: *hanako*, a Sufi contemplation hall and hostel for wandering mendicants). The complex is open daily 8 am to 8 pm, entry US $0.50 in *sum*.

Just behind Guri Amir is the derelict little **Ak-Saray mausoleum** (1470), said to have beautiful frescoes inside. From Guri Amir you can walk north through a patch of the old town, emerging near the weedy, crumbling **Rukhobod mausoleum**, dated 1380 and possibly the city's oldest surviving monument.

Main Bazar

Around and behind Bibi-Khanym is the best live show in town, the frenetic, colourful main farmers' market, called Siab Market on maps. It's a Tower of Babel, full of dresses and shawls, hats and turbans of every nationality, and great for photographers, souvenir hunters and vegetarians, especially in the early morning and on Saturday and Sunday. There's an extension on the other side of Tashkent kuchasi too.

The bazar is a 25 minute walk from the Hotel Samarkand, or take bus No 10 or marshrutnoe taxi Nos 17, 18, 19 or 23.

Ancient Samarkand

At a 2.2 sq km site called Afrasiab, north-east of the bazar, are excavations of Marakanda (early Samarkand) more or less abandoned to the elements. The **Afrasiab Museum** beside them has a site plan, chronological maps and models but nothing in English, and renovations have temporarily truncated everything in mid-history – overall a disappointment unless you have a guide. The only real attraction, in a ground floor room, is fragments of some striking 7th century frescoes depicting hunting, an ambassadorial procession and visits by local rulers.

UZBEKISTAN

The restored **tomb** of the Old Testament prophet Daniel lies on the eastern side of the Afrasiab site, on the banks of the Siab river, accessible by a new road with an ornate portal that turns left off Tashkent kuchasi just before the bridge. The building is a long, low structure topped with five domes, containing an 18m sarcophagus – legend has it that Daniel's body grows by half an inch a year and thus the sarcophagus has to be enlarged. His remains were brought here by Timur. The caretaker may show you a small cave nearby – the lion's den, or so he says. There are some chaykhana tables under trees by the river, making it a pleasant picnic site.

The Afrasiab Museum, 1.5km beyond the bazar on the Tashkent road, is open daily, except Thursday and the last day of the month, 9 am to 5 pm. Bus No 26 from the bazar, and marshrutnoe taxi Nos 17 and 45 from the Hotel Samarkand and the bazar, stop there.

Ulughbek Observatory

Ulughbek was probably more famous as an astronomer than as a ruler. About 1km beyond the Afrasiab Museum are the remains of an immense (30m) astrolab for observing star positions, part of a three storey observatory he built in the 1420s. All that remains is the instrument's curved track, unearthed in 1908. Next door is a little **museum**, open 9 am to 6 pm daily, about Uzbek astronomers. Entry is 30 *sum*. Transport is the same as for Afrasiab.

Other Mosques

The fine **Hodja-Nisbaddor Mosque**, a small 19th century summer mosque with open porch, tall carved columns and brightly restored ceiling, is on Suzangaran kuchasi. Don't confuse it with the smaller, less interesting mosque a block nearer the Registan.

Beside a scummy pool on Kosh-hauz behind the Registan is the peaceful, run-down **Kosh-hauz Mosque**. Across the intersection from the bazar is the neglected 19th century **Hazrat-Hizr Mosque**.

State Museum of the Cultural History of Uzbekistan

In the crumbling edifice east of the Registan are earnest exhibits on regional archaeology,

Ulughbek

Ulughbek, Timur's favourite grandson (son of Shah Rukh), became viceroy in Samarkand and ultimately ruler of Timur's Central Asian territories. But he broke the family pattern of savage grandeur with his intelligence, his breadth of knowledge and his love of science, especially astronomy.

In 1420 he opened the doors of Samarkand's greatest Islamic 'university', the Ulughbek medressa, on what is now Registan Square. Using a huge, specially constructed marble astrolab he charted star positions, discovered some 200 previously unknown stars, and did his own amazingly accurate calculations of the length of the year. Nowadays his reputation as an astronomer dominates his achievements as a Timurid sultan, although the west didn't learn of him until after his death.

This cultured man was to prove the exception to the rule, however, as small-mindedness and puritanism closed in. The Islamic clergy resented his preference for science over scripture as a source of truth, and their resulting loss of influence. His own son, Abdul Latif, arranged his murder by decapitation in 1449, and the observatory was razed to the ground, although his work was saved and published to posthumous acclaim in the west.

It was only in 1908 that a Russian teacher and amateur archaeologist, Vladimir Vyatkin excavated what he calculated to be the site of the observatory, and found the astrolabe's massive semicircular track, untouched. Vyatkin remained in Samarkand through the revolution, became the city's Director of Antiquities and after his death was buried beside the observatory.

Samarkand history, folk art (including a mock-up yurt) and some modern art. A semi-permanent exhibit of paintings of old Samarkand and Bukhara has a lingering aroma of Socialist propaganda but is still a good aid for the imagination. Admission is only a few *sum*. It's open daily except Wednesday, 9 to 5 pm (to 3 pm on Tuesday).

Special Events

During **Navrus** (at the vernal equinox, around 21 March) there is a parade and a giant fair, with food, music, dancing and lots of colour, around the old Cholpan-Ata Restaurant, east of town on the road to Shakhrisabz. Samarkand hosts the **Children's Peace & Disarmament Festival** every 23 October.

Places to Stay

Home-Stays The agencies listed under Information can put you in touch with people ready to give travellers bed and breakfast, typically for about US$20, or US$25 with an evening meal. Locals may offer cheaper places at around US$10 per person.

Hotel Furkat (*☎/fax 35 32 61, Mullokandova 105)* has an unbeatable location just a few hundred metres from the Registan in a quiet street. The rooms are clean, with aircon, cheerfully lurid furnishings and a pleasant courtyard. The family are very hospitable. It costs US$25 per person, or US$20 for the one room without air-con. Furkat has more accommodation at No 32 farther along the street, and an apartment on Registan kuchasi. He can arrange young English-speaking guides around Samarkand for about US$25 for four hours, not including transport.

Zarina's B&B (*☎ 35 41 53, fax 31 06 41, Obi-Rakhmat 2)* is off the Tashkent road, east of the Afrasiab site on the far side of the Siab river. It's quite hard to find, so call in advance and they'll pick you up. The rooms are pleasantly decorated but some guests report that they felt pressured to spend. They also have apartments closer to the Registan, and are opening another B&B.

Zoja Bulicheva (*☎ 33 64 73, Gagarina 230)* is a retired doctor who according to one happy guest does 'the most delicious cooking'; US$20 per night.

Emma's B&B (*☎ 33 54 77, Akhunbabayev 78)*, run by Emma Popova, is in an apartment block not far from the Hotel Samarkand. She has two flats in the building, and the food is reportedly very good.

Places to Stay – Budget

Travellers report being able to stay at the *Hotel Locomotif*, 500m to the left of the train station as you exit the building. 'Suites' with TV, bathroom and fridge cost US$5 in *sum*.

Shark Hotel (*☎ 35 64 42)* near the main bazar on Tashkent kuchasi has basic lodgings for farmers and is usually off limits to forcigners, but at US$1 to US$3 in *sum* it's worth a try.

Failing this, there's the truly awful *Hotel Registan* (*☎ 33 52 25, Ulughbek 36)*, once the Leningrad but none the better for privatisation. Noisy rooms with nasty common toilet and shower cost US$4; a few suites with toilet are US$6.

Places to Stay – Mid-Range

The renovated *Hotel Zarafshan* (*☎ 33 33 72, Sharaf Rashodiv 65)* is a Russian-era building on the edge of Gorky Park. Doubles with toilet and shower (hot water in the morning and evening) are about US$12 in *sum*; big corner suites with balcony are US$17. Trolleybus No 1 runs along Universiteti to/from the Registan.

The little *Hotel Vatan* (*☎ 33 18 14, Universiteti 17)* opposite the Navoi statue is one of two former mayoral guesthouses, with spotless singles/doubles with bath and toilet for US$25/50.

West of the centre is the three storey *Hotel Saiyor* (*☎ 21 49 16, Ulughbek 148a)*. Old, plain, clean rooms with toilet (and plenty of hot water) are US$20/40, and every room has a little balcony. Though far away, it's well connected to the centre (express bus No 21, bus No 2, trolleybus No 1 and marshrutnoe taxis). Across the road is a big department store.

Places to Stay – Top End

Uzbektourism's *Hotel Samarkand* (*☎ 35 88 12, Universiteti 1)* has a choice location, an eager service bureau and fairly clean, comfortable rooms, all with air-con. Facilities include a post office, coffee shop and souvenir shop. It costs US$42/56 for standard rooms and US$77/114 for suites.

Hotel Sogdiana (*☎ 35 14 76, 35 24 26, Usman Yusupov 33)* is the other former mayoral guesthouse. It's a peaceful, rather stately place with three hectares of trees and

UZBEKISTAN

gardens. Standard doubles cost US$70, suites US$100.

The Indian-built *Hotel Afrosiab* (☎ *231 20 80, fax 231 10 44,* ✆ *afrosiab@samuni.silk .org)* is Samarkand's priciest and best, and is popular with tour groups. Singles/doubles with satellite TV and ensuites cost from US$90/110; suites US$230. Payment is in US dollars, or with Visa and Amex cards plus a whopping 5.25% commission. Facilities include swimming pool, travel agency, plane tickets, two restaurants and a bar.

Places to Eat

Restaurants The restaurant in the *Hotel Afrosiab* generally gets good reports, at least if you're not competing for attention with a tour group, with European dishes such as veal cutlets, osso bucco and pizza as well as Uzbek standards like laghman and plov.

The restaurant at the *Hotel Samarkand* has adequate if unspectacular Uzbek and western food; the rooftop cafe has shashlyk, ice cream and fine views. There's a show nightly in the main restaurant featuring traditional Uzbek dancing with a Sovietised touch of Las Vegas.

The restaurant at the *Saiyor* is adequate (and apparently dishes up a good breakfast) but it's a thuggish, very overpriced scene in the evening. The friendly *cafe* in the office block next door serves good Russian standards.

The dining rooms at the *Hotel Vatan* and *Hotel Sogdiana* will apparently prepare whatever you want using local ingredients, if you order ahead.

One of the very best places for Uzbek food is the *Siab Chaykhana*, shaded by willow trees on the Siab river. It's down the first road on the right after the Afrasiab Museum on Tashkent kuchasi, at the fork in the road. Expect to pay US$1.50 in *sum* for a feast of shashlyk and plov.

The quiet *Shark Restaurant*, in front of the hotel of the same name, across Tashkent kuchasi from the bazar has good service and decent Uzbek dishes, but is apt to overcharge. Check prices first; dinner shouldn't cost more than US$3 in *sum*. They don't serve fish here: the *shark* in the name is Uzbek for 'east'.

Another best-bet is the popular outdoor *Yulduz Chaykhana*, beside Ulughbek Observatory on the Tashkent road (take the No 26 bus from the bazar, or marshrutnoe taxi No 17 or 45 from the Hotel Samarkand or the bazar). Fill up on well-prepared shashlyk, laghman, *shorpa* (meat and vegetable soup) or other standards, along with tea and excellent bread, for about US$2. It's packed out at lunchtime.

A busy place in the centre is the big chaykhana called *Chor-Su* at the south end of Tashkent kuchasi. A smaller *chaykhana* is nearby, just west of the univermag. Less interesting is the *cafe* at the rear of the Museum of the Cultural History of Uzbekistan.

In the Russian part of town restaurants tend to come and go; one of the better ones was the tidy little *Bar Gloria* on Ulughbek near the corner with Akhunbabayev, with aircon, western staples such as 'chizburger', tasty salads and cold meats for US$1 to US$2 in *sum*.

Cafes & Snack Shops The *Olympia Cafe* (also called Enterprice Olympia) is a cheap, fairly clean burger-and-sometimes-pizza joint with adequate offerings, on Shohrukh opposite Gorky Park. It is open daily except Sunday 8 am to 4 or 5 pm. Gorky Park is rimmed with shashlyk stands and other snack shops with bottom-end prices and dodgy hygiene.

Home Restaurants In summer in the old town between the bazar and Ismoil Bukhori, you can track down a simple home-cooked meal in one of the restaurants in the courtyards of private homes. There are said to be over fifty of them. Family members solicit customers; go with the women or kids, not the brash young men. If you're uneasy about hygiene, ask to have a look first. In Russian, 'can we have a look in the kitchen?' is *'mozhna posmotret v kukhne?'*. Agree on the price in advance. We enjoyed a steaming common plate of mutton stew, salad, bread and tea for US$1 each, in *sum*. Bargaining might be appropriate if you're asked for more than about US$2 or US$3.

Self-Catering The bazar has bread, boiled eggs, tomatoes, fruit and more, and there's a smaller bazar – the *krytyy rynok* (covered market) on Ulughbek near the main post office.

Shopping

A major shopping district is the pedestrianised Tashkent kuchasi near the bazar, heavy on Uzbek cloth (including silk), clothing and housewares, and some souvenirs. The main Russian-style shopping area is pedestrian Mustaqillik north of Gorky Park, with the GUM department store plus food, toiletries and electrical goods shops. Smaller department stores are at the south end of Tashkent kuchasi and opposite the Hotel Saiyor on Mirsharopov.

Down the middle of Gorky Park a kiosk minibazar takes shape every day, offering imported clothing, tapes, snacks, cheap beer and useful items like soap and toilet paper. The craftier vendors probably graduate to the tinselly *savdo dukoni* (commercial shops) scattered around town, good for anything from imported coffee to kitchen appliances, at wildly variable prices.

Afghan-Uzbek Joint Venture has its own carpet factory, and a small showroom in the Registan (☎ 35 07 36, 35 88 16; contact Ewat Badghissi Abdulwahet).

Silk prices in hotel kiosks are not too much higher than in the bazar, but the selection is poorer.

Getting There & Away

Air Uzbekistan Airways flies to Tashkent daily. Aeroflot goes to Ashgabat twice a week and Moscow three times a week in summer, once or twice a day in winter.

Tickets are best bought a few days in advance. Hotel service bureaus charge an extra US$5 or so to send someone over to the city booking office, on Gagarin south of the Hotel Turist. You can do it yourself on bus No 10 outbound on Universiteti near the Hotel Samarkand, or north-bound on Sharaf Rashidov near the Hotel Zarafshan; ask for *aerovokzal*. They'll also reconfirm flights at no charge. Check your tickets – mistakes are common.

Train One fast train departs for Tashkent on Tuesday, Thursday and Saturday at 10.40 am, and many others pass through to Tashkent. A fast Tashkent-Bukhara train passes here daily at 2.45 pm, and others depart three times a week to Dushanbe and once a week to Almaty. Two daily trains stop en route between Tashkent and Termiz. Trains no longer go to Moscow.

Buy tickets at the depressing train station in the north-west outskirts. Go to the end of the line on bus No 1, trolleybus No 1 or marshrutnoe taxi No 17 near the Hotel Saiyor; bus Nos 3 or 10 or marshrutnoe taxi No 22 near the Turist; or any of these plus express bus 103 near the Samarkand and Zarafshan.

Bus Tashkent is five hours away by bus across a flat, dry landscape that tsarist Russians nicknamed the Hungry Steppe, now a monotonous stretch of factories and cotton fields. There are hourly departures, and tickets (about US$1.50) are available as little as a few hours in advance. Other major destinations are Bukhara (six hours, six daily) and Urgench (twice each evening).

Buy tickets at one of the little booths outside the long-distance station (take bus No 10 past the Turist Hotel, Hotel Zarafshan and Hotel Samarkand); it's not clear who uses the huge, empty station building. You may encounter a police officer or two, but if your visa is in order you'll have none of the hassle typical of Tashkent. Travellers report gangs of pickpockets here, who board a bus or minivan, distract you with some kind of fuss, and dip into your pockets or slash your bag.

Just beyond the long-distance bus station entrance is a smaller regional bus station, mainly for points north (eg Hoja Ismoil). There is also a bus stand on Penjikent kuchasi east of the Registan, mainly for points south and east (eg Jumabazar and Penjikent).

Taxi & Share Taxi To charter a modern sedan to Tashkent will cost US$40 in *sum*, or US$10 for a seat; it's around US$5 for a share minibus or in an old Russian car.

UZBEKISTAN

Getting Around

To/From the Airport The No 10 bus goes from the long-distance bus station and the airport to the bazar and the Samarkand, Zarafshan and Turist hotels and the train station, and back, about every 20 minutes (express bus No 10-3 doesn't stop near Turist). Any marshrutnoe taxi at the airport goes to the Hotel Samarkand. A taxi from the airport to Samarkand will be the *sum* equivalent of about US$4, half that for the return journey.

Local Transport Buses and trolleybuses run from about 6 am until dusk. Pay cash to the conductor, or to the driver when you get off – 10 *sum* when we were there (20 *sum* for express buses). Marshrutnoe taxis (about 30 *sum*) disappear by 8 or 9 pm.

Taxi There are unlicensed and licensed taxis. You should be able to go from the Hotel Samarkand to the Ulughbek Observatory for US$0.50, or across town for under US$1. Rates jump after 8 pm when buses and marshrutnoe taxis start thinning out, and taxis themselves are scarce by 10.30 or 11 pm.

Don't expect Russian taxi drivers to know their way around the old town, nor to know all the post-Soviet street names. If you're alone, remember to be suspicious of any taxi that already contains more than just the driver.

AROUND SAMARKAND
Hoja Ismail

In Hoja Ismail, a village 30km north of Samarkand, is one of Islam's holier spots, the modest mausoleum of Ismail al-Bukhari (Uzbek/Tajik: Ismoil Bukhori, 810-87 CE). He was one of the greatest Muslim scholars of the *hadith*, the collected acts and sayings of the Prophet Mohammed. His main work is regarded by Sunni Muslims as second only to the Quran as a source of religious law. Following his refusal to give special tutoring to Bukhara's governor and his children, he was forced into exile here.

This is definitely more a place of pilgrimage than a tourist spot – just a courtyard, a mosque and a smaller courtyard around the tomb. On weekdays the loudest sound is that of boys chanting prayers in the mosque; on Friday and Sunday the pilgrims and the curious crowd in.

It's essential to dress conservatively, respect the calm and reverent atmosphere, and

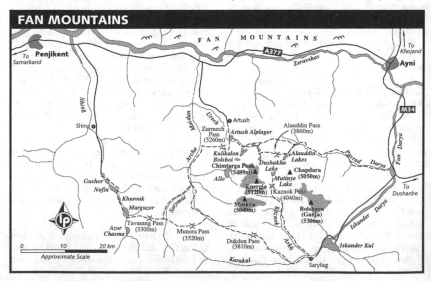

Trekking in the Fan Mountains

The Fannsky Gory – in Tajikistan but most easily accessed from Samarkand – are one of Central Asia's premier trekking destinations. The range is studded with dozens of turquoise lakes and alpine valleys inhabited by Tajik shepherds.

Many Uzbek travel agencies, such as Asia Travel, offer trekking programs here, as do many overseas trekking companies, though it is a possible destination for experienced and fit do-it-yourselfers, taking a shorter route.

To get to the Fans from Uzbekistan you will need a Tajik visa, though a single-entry Uzbek visa should suffice. The region has been unaffected by the Tajik civil war, though the border crossing into Uzbekistan has become much stricter in recent years.

Buses run from Penjikent in Uzbekistan to Artush or Shing, the main trailheads. You can get supplies in Penjikent, though it's better to bring your foodstuffs from Samarkand. The region can be hot and dry at the end of summer. It's possible to hire donkeys at the trailheads to carry rucksacks.

The best map is the 1:100,000 *Pamir Alay – Severo-Zapadnaya Chast* (1992 Tashkent) available from Asia Travel in Tashkent.

Routes from Artush

From Artush walk up to the *alplager* (mountaineers' camp) where rooms and possibly food are available. From here it's a hard uphill hike into the Kulikalon bowl, home to a dozen deep blue lakes. Excellent camping can be found near Dushakha lake, at the foot of Chimtarga (5469m, the highest in the region).

From here it's a hard slog up and over the Alauddin pass (3860m) to the Alauddin lakes, where you can find good camping and sometimes a food tent in summer. From here you can make a hard day hike up to Mutinye lake and back.

From Alauddin lakes you can head downstream to the Chapdara valley and then west up to Laudon pass (3630m) and back down into the Kulikalon bowl.

An alternative from Mutinye lake takes you over the difficult Kaznok pass (4040m; grade 1B), where you may need an ice axe. From here head down the long Kaznok valley to Sarytag village, the main road and Iskander Kul lake.

Routes from Shing

The other main trailhead is at Shing, from where you can walk up to the Marguzor lakes. From here trails lead over the Tavasang pass (3300m) to the Archa Maidan valley. Trails continue down the valley to the foot of the Zurmech pass and then over to Artush.

Alternatively, when you hit the Archa Maidan valley, you can climb up to the Munora pass and down into the valley, and then up over the Dukdon pass (3810m) into the Karakul valley and, eventually, Iskander Kul.

---

ask before you take photos. Take your shoes off before you step onto any carpet.

Getting There & Away Hoja Ismail village is 30km north of Samarkand, off the road to Chelek. Buses from the regional bus station (beside the long-distance bus station) to Oqqurghon (or Ak Kurgan) stop at Hoja Ismail, and there are said to be buses to Chelek from the bus stand on Penjikent kuchasi. A taxi should be under US$20 for the return trip plus a short wait.

With a day's notice the Hotel Samarkand service bureau can arrange a three hour excursion for up to four people in a car for US$40. They may tell you non-Muslims are not especially welcome, perhaps to encourage you to go with one of their guides.

Penjikent

On a high valley terrace on the banks of the Zeravshan river, 1.5km from the modern town of Penjikent, are the ruins of ancient Penjikent or Bunjikath, a major Sogdian town founded in the 5th century and abandoned in the 8th century when the Arabs came. The ancient city has not been built upon since. The foundations of houses, a citadel with a couple of Zoroastrian temples, and the city bazar are visible in the excavated ruins, but the best of the frescoes (some of them 15m long), sculptures, pottery and manuscripts have been taken off to Tashkent's history museum and St Petersburg's Hermitage. An annotated map at the site describes what all the furrows and mounds once were.

Some lesser finds are on display at the **Rudaki Museum** in modern Penjikent. The museum's name arises from the claim that Penjikent was the birthplace of Abu Abdullah Rudaki, the Samanid court poet considered by many to be the father of Persian poetry.

Getting There & Away Penjikent is 70km east of Samarkand, just across the border into Tajikistan. It's listed here because the only sensible way to get there is from Samarkand.

Currently it is possible, though difficult, to do this as a day trip from Samarkand, without a Tajik visa, through a travel agency that can arrange the permits. The Hotel Samarkand service bureau will arrange a half-day car trip to the excavations and museum for US$150 for up to four people (or three people and a guide). The Hotel Furkat can arrange a day trip for US$70 each for two people. Alternatively you could take a taxi from Penjikent kuchasi or Suzangaran kuchasi in Samarkand. Ask for *'drevniy gorod'* (ancient city), and don't pay until you get back. Crossing the border can take several hours, and the Tajik border guards sometimes demand bribes.

If you're coming from Khojand in Tajikistan, there's a fantastically scenic route between Khojand and Penjikent through the Turkistan range, climbing in places to 3500m. You might find a bus plying the route but you will probably have to hire a taxi. Check the security situation in the region before you go.

In summer, when the passes are clear of snow, there are also buses between Penjikent and Dushanbe, 255km to the south.

There are daily buses from Penjikent to Artush or Shing, the main trailheads for trekking in Tajikistan's Fan Mountains (see the boxed text).

SHAKHRISABZ

☎ (3) 75 • pop 60,000

Shakhrisabz is a small, un-Russified town south of Samarkand, across the hills in Kashka-Darya province. The town is a pleasant Uzbek backwater and seems to be nothing special – until you start bumping into the ruins dotted around its backstreets, and the megalomaniac ghosts of a wholly different place materialise. This is Timur's home town, and once upon a time it probably put Samarkand itself in the shade. It's worth a visit just to check out the great man's roots.

Timur was born on 9 April 1336 into the Barlas clan of local aristocrats, at the village of Hoja Ilghar, 13km to the south. Ancient even then, Shakhrisabz (called Kesh at the time) was a kind of family seat. As he rose to power Timur gave it its present name (Tajik for 'Green Town') and turned it into an extended family monument. Most of its current attractions were put here by Timur (including a tomb intended for himself) or his grandson Ulughbek.

The town was trashed in the 16th century by the Emir of Bukhara, Abdullah Khan II, in a quest for the Shaybanid throne. He is said to have been subsequently overcome with remorse for his stupidity. Nowadays its easy-going older generation is being displaced on the streets by post-Soviet, post-adolescent males sporting identical baggy trousers and twirling keychains.

The road from Samarkand to Shakhrisabz and on to the border at Termiz was once the main route for Soviet soldiers and hardware going into Afghanistan.

[Continued on page 307]

CENTRAL ASIAN ARCHITECTURE

The most impressive surviving artistic heritage of Central Asia is its architecture, and some of the world's most audacious and beautiful examples of Islamic religious buildings are to be found at Bukhara, Khiva and, especially, Samarkand, all in Uzbekistan.

Thanks in the main to the destructive urges of Jenghiz Khan, virtually nothing has survived from the pre-Islamic era or the first centuries of Arab rule. The Bolsheviks further destroyed many of Central Asia's religious buildings, except those of architectural or historical value.

Early Influences

Several technological advances have had a large effect on the development of fired brick in the 10th century, coloured tilework in the 12th century and polychrome tile work in the 14th century.

The squinch (the corner bracketing that enabled the transition from a square to an eight, then 16-sided platform), was essential to the development of the dome. This technology gave rise to the double dome, which made possible the huge domes of the Timurid era.

Other influences have been more climatic; the lack of wood or stone made Central Asian architects turn to brickwork as the cornerstone of their designs. Tall portals, built to face and catch the prevailing winds and running streams of water were designed to have a cooling effect in the heat of summer. Nomadic influence is particularly relevant in Khiva, where platforms were designed to hold winter-time yurts.

Timurid Architecture

Most of the monumental architecture standing today dates from the time of the Timurids (14th to 15th century), rulers who could be almost as savage as the Mongol warlords but who also had a bent for artistic patronage.

Like butterfly collectors, Timur and his grandson Ulughbek accumulated artists and craftsmen from Timur's conquered territories – Persia, the Caucasus and India – and brought them to his capital, Samarkand.

The Timurid architectural trademark is the beautiful, often ribbed, azure-blue dome. Other typical design elements include monumental, arched entrance portals *(pishtak)*, flanked by tapering minarets, a tendency towards ensemble design and exuberant, multicoloured tile work.

Other than in Central Asia, the best examples of Timurid architecture are to be found in Mashad or Tabriz, both in Iran, and Herat in Afghanistan.

Inset: The Sher Dor, or Lion, Medressa in the Registan.
Photo: Bradley Mayhew

Architectural Design

Khiva and Bukhara have the most homogenous architectural layout, highlighting the importance of the *shahristan* (inner city). An outer city wall surrounded most cities, protecting against desert storms and brigands.

In the town, monuments are often found facing each other in reflective pairs. Apart from Islamic monuments (see following), secular architecture includes palaces (such as the Tash Hauli in Khiva), forts (*arks*, as in Bukhara), multidomed bathhouses *(hammam)*, caravanserais *(rabat)*, shopping arcades *(tim)*, covered crossroad bazars *(tok)* and reservoirs *(hauz)* that supplied the city with its drinking water.

Mosques Islam dominates Central Asian architecture. Mosques *(masjid)* trace their design back to the house of the Prophet Mohammed, though later designs vary considerably. Most common is the use of the portal, which leads into a colonnaded space, sometimes open, and a covered area

MARTIN MOOS

for prayer. The entrance of many Central Asian mosques, such as the Bolo-hauz in Bukhara and many mosques in Kashgar and Yarkand, have, instead, a flat, brightly painted roof, supported by carved wooden columns. Other mosques such as the Juma Mosque in Khiva are hypostyle, that is, made up of an enclosed space, divided by many pillars.

Whether the place of worship is a *guzar* (local) mosque, serving the local community, a *jami* (Friday) mosque, built to hold the entire city congregation once a week, or a *namazgokh* (festival) mosque, the focal point is always the *mihrab*, a niche that indicates the direction of Mecca.

Medressas These are Islamic colleges, normally two storeys high and set around a cloistered central courtyard, punctuated with arched portals (or *iwans*) on four sides. Rows of little doors in the interior facades lead into *hujras*, cell-like living quarters for students and teachers – or *khanakas*, prayer cells for the ascetic wandering dervishes who stayed there. Most medressas are fronted by monumental portals. On either side of the entrance you will normally find a lecture room *(darskhana)* to the left, and mosque to the right. The niches in the medressas' front wall were once used as shopkeepers' stalls.

Left: Kalon Minaret and Mosque, Bukhara. The Mangit emirs in Bukhara used to throw criminals off the massive Kalon minaret.

Decorative and practical, minarets serve as a lookout for brigands and the tower from which the muezzins make their call to prayer.

The awesome architectural heritage of Uzbekistan: the Registan, Samarkand **(top)**; Guri Amir mausoleum, Samarkand **(middle left & bottom right)** and Mir-i-Arab medressa at sunset, Bukhara **(bottom left)**.

BRADLEY MAYHEW

BRADLEY MAYHEW

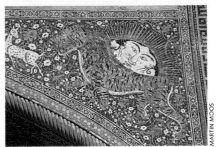

MARTIN MOOS

MARTIN MOOS

Glittering at a distance and stunning up close, the tilework of Central Asian architecture most commonly takes the shape of abstract geometric, floral or calligraphic designs.

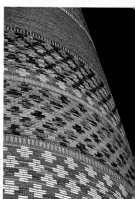

Awesome Khiva, mystical Samarkand and beautiful Bukhara – Uzbekistan's cities hold some of the most striking architecture in all of Central Asia.

Mausolea The *mazar* (mausoleum) has been a popular style of architecture for millennia, either built by rulers to ensure their own immortality or to commemorate holy men. Most consist of a prayer room (*ziaratkhana*), set under a domed cupola. The actual tomb may be housed in a central hall, or underground in a separate room (*gurkhana*). A complex of lodging, washrooms, and kitchens is often attached. Tombs vary in design from the cupola style, mentioned above, to the pyramid-shaped, tent-like designs of Konye-Urgench, or whole streets of tombs as found at the Shahr-i-Zindah in Samarkand.

Minarets These tall, tapering towers were designed to summon the faithful during prayer time, so most have internal stairs for the muezzin to climb. Other uses include supplying a lookout for brigands, and, in the case of the Kalon minaret in Bukhara, a means of execution. Some minarets (eg at Samarkand's Registan) exist purely for decoration.

Decoration

Tilework is the most dramatic form of decoration in Central Asia, giving huge Timurid buildings a much lighter feel. Colours were made especially bright to stand out in the bright sunlight of the desert. The deep cobalt and turquoise ('colour of the Turks') of Samarkand's domes have moved travellers for centuries. Greens are most common in Khorezm, khakis in Bukhara and blues in Samarkand.

Decoration almost always takes the shape of abstract geometric, floral or calligraphic designs, in keeping with the Islamic taboo on the representation of living creatures. Geo-

metric designs were closely linked to the development of Central Asian science – star designs were a favourite with the astronomer king Ulughbek. Calligraphy is common, either in the square, stylised Kufic script favoured by the Timurids or the more scrolling, often foliated *thulth* script.

Tiles come in a variety of styles, either stamped, faience (carved onto wet clay and then fired), polychromatic (painted on, then fired) or jigsaw-style mosaic. Carved *ghanch* (alabaster), patterned brickwork and carved and painted wood are also important methods of decorating architecture.

Right: Glorious Timurid tilework shines in the bright sunlight of the desert.

Architectural Highlights

Khiva's Ichon-Qala and Bukhara's historic centre are both UNESCO World Heritage Sites. Shakhrisabz is currently under consideration. Herat's old town is included in the list of the 100 most endangered sites in the world. The following sites are all in Uzbekistan, other than the Sultan Sanjar Mausoleum, which is in Merv, Turkmenistan.

monument	location	comments
Ismail Samani Mausoleum (900-1000)	Bukhara	mesmerising brickwork
Kalon Minaret (1127)	Bukhara	Central Asia's most impressive minaret, 48m high
Sultan Sanjar Mausoleum (1157)	Merv	huge double-domed Seljuq monument
Guri Amir (1404)	Samarkand	exquisite ribbed dome
Bibi-Khanym Mosque (1399-1404)	Samarkand	Timur's intended masterpiece, designed to be the architectural embodiment of heaven; unfortunately, it was erected so hastily that it was in ruins almost as soon as it was finished, only the entrance gate and three domed buildings remain to suggest the colossal dimensions of this folly
Ak-Saray (1400-1450)	Samarkand	tantalising remains of Timur's once opulent palace
Shahr-i-Zindah (1300-1400)	Samarkand	features Central Asia's most stunning and varied tilework
Registan (1400-1600)	Samarkand	epic ensemble of medressas; the Sher Dor (1636) flaunts Islamic tradition by depicting two lions chasing deer, looked down on by a Mongol-faced sun
Labi-Hauz Ensemble (1600)	Bukhara	featuring pool, khanaka and medressa
Char Minar (1807)	Bukhara	quirky ex-gateway, like a chair thrust upside down in the ground
Islom-Huja (Islam Khoja) Minaret (1910)	Khiva	reckoned by Central Asian archaeological specialist Edgar Knobloch to be the last notable architectural achievement of the Islamic era in Central Asia; we'd expand that to say the last notable architectural achievement in Central Asia, period

[Continued from page 302]

Orientation & Information

The town's main road is Ipak Yuli, Uzbek for 'Silk Road'. The long-distance bus station is at the south end of town, about 400m beyond the Kok-Gumbaz Mosque. The train station is several kilometres south of the centre, and a small airport is beyond that. There is a post office in the centre of town. There is no charge to enter any of the town's monuments.

Ak-Saray Palace

Just north of the centre, Timur's summer palace (White Palace) has as much grandeur per sq cm as anything in Samarkand. There's actually nothing left of it except bits of the gigantic, 40m-high entrance, covered with gorgeous, filigree-like blue, white and gold mosaics. It was probably Timur's most ambitious project, 24 years in the making, following a successful campaign in Khorezm and the 'import' of many of its finest artisans. It's staggering to try to imagine what the rest of it was like, in size and glory.

Kok-Gumbaz Mosque & Dorut Tilyovat

This big Friday mosque was completed by Ulughbek in 1437 in honour of his father Shah Rukh (who was Timur's son). The name means Blue Dome, though the luminous outer tiles are long gone and it's full of pigeons now. It appears to be under snail's-pace restoration.

Behind it was the original burial complex of Timur's forebears; the sign says Dorut Tilyovat (House of Meditation). On the left as you enter the complex is the **mausoleum of Sheikh Shamseddin Kulyal**, spiritual tutor to Timur and his father, Amir Taragay (who may also be buried here), completed by Timur in 1374. Inside are some fine carved columns, but the walls, coarsely restored in Soviet times, are already rotting.

On the right is the **Gumbazi Seyidan** (Dome of the Seyyids), which Ulughbek finished in 1438 as a mausoleum for his own descendants (though it's not clear whether any are buried in it).

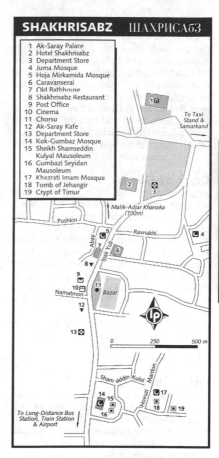

SHAKHRISABZ ШАХРИСАБЗ

1 Ak-Saray Palace
2 Hotel Shakhrisabz
3 Department Store
4 Juma Mosque
5 Hoja Mirkamida Mosque
6 Caravanserai
7 Old Bathhouse
8 Shakhrisabz Restaurant
9 Post Office
10 Cinema
11 Chorsu
12 Ak-Saray Kafe
13 Department Store
14 Kok-Gumbaz Mosque
15 Sheikh Shamseddin Kulyal Mausoleum
16 Gumbazi Seyidan Mausoleum
17 Khazrati Imam Mosque
18 Tomb of Jehangir
19 Crypt of Timur

UZBEKISTAN

Khazrati-Imam Ensemble

A few streets east of Kok-Gumbaz are a few melancholy remnants of a 70m by 50m mausoleum complex called Dorussiadat or Dorussaodat (Seat of Power & Might), which Timur finished in 1392 and which may have overshadowed even the Ak-Saray Palace.

The main survivor is the tall, crumbling **tomb of Jehangir**, Timur's eldest and favourite son, who died at 22. It's also the resting place for another son, Umar Sheikh (Timur's other sons are with him at Guri Amir in Samarkand). It's a mess inside, though restoration looks imminent.

You may find someone to unlock the tomb at the adjacent **Khazrati Imam Mosque**. The mosque itself dates only from the late 19th century, although the plane trees in its peaceful courtyard are probably much older. The name refers to a revered 8th century imam, or religious leader from Iraq, and the story goes that Abdullah Khan II spared the mausoleum because he was told the imam was buried there. The legend (and the name) have stuck, though there is no evidence that the Khazrati Imam ever came here.

Crypt of Timur
In an alley behind the mausoleum (and within the perimeter of the long-gone Dorussiadat) is a bunker with a green door leading to an underground room. The room, plain except for Quranic quotations on the arches, is nearly filled by a single stone casket. On the casket are biographical inscriptions about Timur, from which it was inferred (when the room was discovered in 1963) that this crypt was intended for him. Inside are two unidentified corpses.

Unfortunately the only way to see the crypt is to take an Uzbektourism guided city tour from the Hotel Shakhrisabz, at about US$35 per person.

Other Things to See
A small complex west of the Hotel Shakhrisabz called the **Malik-Adjar Khanaka** was once a khanaka, a Sufi meditation hall and hostel for wandering mendicants. Its mosque, built in 1904 and for a time a local museum and archives, has lately become a mosque.

In the centre of town is a 17th century bathhouse, in use right up until 1983, now under interminable restoration. Next door is a 1914 mosque which maps call **Hoja Mirk-amida**, converted into a chaykhana in the 1980s and recently reinstated as a mosque. Locals call it Abdushukur Okhoylik and say a mosque was first built here in 1705. About 500m west of here is the **Juma Mosque**, which was a museum in Soviet times.

Across the street is a 16th century **caravanserai**, now restored as a shopping complex. Originally it was a medressa. The round, five domed building in front of the bazar is a **chorsu** (arcade), possibly a copy of one here as early as the 15th century.

Places to Stay & Eat
Quiet, fairly clean singles/doubles with toilet and shower at Uzbektourism's **Hotel Shakhrisabz** (☎ *338 61, fax 357 09, Ipak Yuli 26*) cost from US$10 to US$40 with breakfast. The restaurant is the best in town.

For US$1 you can fill up with decent local food and gallons of tea in the chaykhanas on the main road. Flyblown but best of the lot, and friendliest towards women visitors, is the *Ak-Saray Kafe*. In the *bazar* you may find women dishing out a wonderful hot soup of noodles, vegetables and yoghurt.

Shopping
The local Khujum Arts Factory produces Uzbek dresses, carpets and embroidery. Uzbektourism will take you there or to a cap, silk, pottery or wine factory. All but the carpets and wine are easy to find in the bazar or the department stores.

Getting There & Around
Shakhrisabz is about 90km from Samarkand across the arid foothills of the Zeravshan range, over the 1788m Takhtakaracha (or Aman-kutan) pass. By car this takes 1½ to two hours. The pass is intermittently closed by snow from January to March, forcing a three hour detour around the mountains.

Taxis go from Suzangaran kuchasi in Samarkand for about US$30 per carload for the round trip and a wait. Drivers from Shakhrisabz will know more and may be keener to bargain, as they're trying to get home.

You can find taxis by the bus station, the bazar or the post office, or at a stand about 10 minutes walk north of the centre.

Buses depart Samarkand's main bus station two or three times each morning for about US$0.80, but may take the long way around the hills. Samarkand's Hotel Furkat B&B in Samarkand offers unguided day trips by car for US$35; Uzbektourism at the Hotel Samarkand charges twice as much.

Bus No 10 and marshrutnoe taxi No 10 run between the hotel and the bus station.

BUKHARA

☎ (3) 65 • pop 255,000

Central Asia's holiest city has buildings spanning a thousand years of history, and a thoroughly lived-in old centre that probably hasn't changed much in two centuries. Bukhara is one of the best places in Central Asia for a glimpse of pre-Russian Turkestan.

Most of the centre is an architectural preserve, full of former medressas, a massive, decaying royal fortress and the remnants of a once-vast market complex. The government is pumping a lot of money into restoration, even redigging several stone pools *(hauz)* filled in by the Soviets. Although the centre has become a bit too clean and quiet ('Ye Olde Bukhara' as one traveller put it), the 21st century has still been kept more or less at bay, and the city has some of the best accommodation options in the country.

Until a century ago Bukhara was watered by a network of canals and some 200 stone pools called hauz where people gathered and gossiped, drank and washed. As the water wasn't changed often, Bukhara was famous for plagues; the average 19th century Bukharan is said to have died by the age of 32. The Bolsheviks modernised the system and drained the pools.

Storks, considered good omens, roosted here for a thousand years, and some buildings and trees are still crowned with their huge nests. But with the loss of the hauz that bred bugs and frogs, the storks have disappeared and the nests are empty.

As in Samarkand, most people speak Tajik but tend to call themselves Uzbeks. There are a few self-declared Tajiks, and a dwindling minority of Russians, Tatars and Bukharan Jews.

You'll need at least two days to look around. Try to allow time to lose yourself in the old town; it's easy to overdose on the 140-odd protected buildings and miss the whole for its many parts. If you're short on time, at least see Labi-Hauz, the covered markets, the Kalon minaret and mosque, the mausoleum of Ismail Samani and the marvellously tacky summer palace of the last emirs.

History

When the Arabs arrived in 709 CE they found an already prosperous trading centre. Although they succeeded in Islamicising much of what they controlled, they faced almost continuous revolts and soon lost their enthusiasm for the place.

It was as capital of the Samanid state in the 9th and 10th centuries that Bukhara – *Bukhoro-i-sharif* (Noble Bukhara), the 'Pillar of Islam' – blossomed as Central Asia's religious and cultural heart, and simultaneously brightened with the Persian love of the arts. Among those nurtured here were the philosopher-scientist ibn Sina and the poets Firdausi and Rudaki – figures with the stature in the Persian Islamic world that, for example, Newton or Shakespeare enjoy in the west. It was said that 'while elsewhere light radiates from heaven onto the land, in holy Bukhara it radiates upward to illuminate heaven'.

After two centuries under the smaller Karakhan and Karakitay dynasties, Bukhara succumbed in 1220 to Jenghiz Khan – and in 1370 fell under the shadow of Timur's Samarkand.

A second lease of life came in the 16th century when the Uzbek Shaybanids made it the capital of what came to be known as the Bukhara khanate, which (along with its smaller Shaybanid cousin, the Khiva khanate) eventually embraced most of present-day Central Asia and parts of Iran and Afghanistan. The old town's present appearance owes most to that period, especially to the greatest of the Shaybanid khans, Abdullah II (ruled 1583-98).

The centre of Shaybanid Bukhara was a vast marketplace with dozens of specialist bazars and caravanserais, over one hundred medressas (with 10,000 students) and more than three hundred mosques.

Under the Astrakhanid dynasty, the Silk Road's decline slowly pushed Bukhara out of the mainstream. Then in 1753 Mohammed Rahim, the local deputy of a Persian ruler, proclaimed himself emir, founding the Mangit dynasty that was to rule until the Bolsheviks came. In a parody of its ancient glory, Bukhara had a final fling as a decadent, feudal city-state, one of three (with Khiva and

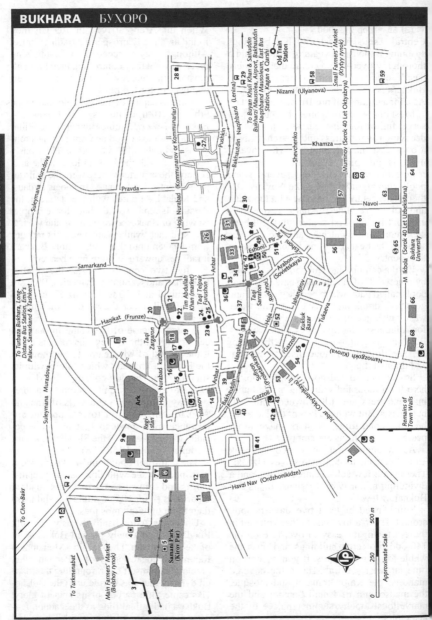

BUKHARA

PLACES TO STAY		
28 Sasha & Lena's B&B	11 Abdullah Khan Medressa	39 Medressa
30 Sasha & Son B&B	12 Modari Khan Medressa	40 Mausoleum of Imam
41 Nutfullo's B&B	13 Hoja Zaynuddin Mosque	Muhammad Gazzoli
42 Farkhad & Maya's B&B	14 Medressa	43 Ruined Mosque
48 Labi Hauz B&B	15 Women's Baths	44 Gaukushan Medressa
51 Muhinjon's Bukhara House	16 Kalon Mosque	45 Baths (Under Reconstruction)
61 Hotel Bukhara (Old)	17 Kalon Minaret	46 Bookshop
62 Hotel Bukhara (New)	18 Mir-i-Arab Medressa	47 Bukhara Information &
63 Hotel Varaksha	19 Amir Alim Khan Medressa	Culture Centre (BICC)
64 Hotel Zarafshan	20 Ulughbek Medressa	49 Salom Travel
68 Hotel Gulistan	21 Abdul Aziz Khan Medressa	50 Jewish Community Centre
	22 Site of Hindu Caravanserai	& Synagogue
PLACES TO EAT	23 Site of Former Raja Begi	52 Turki Jangi Mausoleum
7 Chaykhana	Caravanserai	53 Baths
	24 Spice Shop	54 Hoja Gazian Medressa
OTHER	25 Men's Baths (Under	55 Fayzulla Khujayev House
1 Marshrutnoe Taxi to Chor-Bakr	Reconstruction)	(National House)
2 'Bolshoy Rynok' Bus Stand	26 Kukeldash Medressa	56 Bukhara PDPU Central
3 Remains of Town Walls &	27 Char Minar	Committee Offices
Talli-Pach Gate	29 'Vokzal' Bus Stops	57 Provincial PDPU Central
4 Chashma-Ayub 'Mausoleum'	31 Nadir Divanbegi Medressa	Committee Offices
5 Ismail Samani Mausoleum	32 Hoja Nasruddin Statue	58 'Krytyy Rynok' Bus Stop
6 Ayni Uzbek Theatre of Drama	33 Labi-hauz	59 'Gorgaz' Bus Stop
& Musical Comedy	34 Nadir Divanbegi Khanaka	60 Telephone & Telegraph Office
8 Bolo-Hauz Mosque	35 Post Office	65 National Bank
& Minaret	36 Maghoki-Attar Mosque	66 OVIR
9 Water Tower	37 Site of Former Caucasus	67 Namozgokh Mosque
10 Zindon	Caravanserai	69 Mosque
	38 Museum of Art	70 Medressa

Kokand) that by this time dominated Central Asia and spent their time picking fights with one another.

The worst of the depraved Bukhara emirs was probably Nasrullah Khan (also called 'the Butcher' behind his back) who ascended the throne in 1826 by killing off his brothers and 28 other relatives. He made himself a household word in Victorian England after he executed two British officers (see the boxed text 'Stoddart & Conolly').

In 1868, Russian troops under General Kaufman occupied Samarkand (which at the time was within Emir Muzaffar Khan's domains). Soon afterward Bukhara surrendered, and was made a protectorate of the tsar, with the emirs still nominally in charge. The Russians did insist that the Bukharans discontinue their thriving slave-trade. The Trans-Caspian Railway arrived in 1888, but at Emir Abdallahad Khan's request the train station was built a respectful 15km away at Kagan, then called New Bukhara.

In 1918, as the Russian Revolution took hold in Central Asia, a party of emissaries and a military escort arrived from Tashkent (by then under Bolshevik control) to persuade Emir Alim Khan to surrender peacefully. The wily despot stalled long enough to allow his agents to stir up an anti-Russian mob that slaughtered nearly the whole delegation, and the emir's own army sent a larger Russian detachment packing, back towards Tashkent.

But the humiliated Bolsheviks had their revenge. Following an orchestrated 'uprising' in Charjou (now Turkmenabat) by local revolutionaries calling themselves the Young Bukharans and an equally premeditated request for help, Red Army troops from Khiva and Tashkent under General Mikhail Frunze converged on Bukhara on 2 September 1920, stormed the Ark (citadel) and captured Bukhara. Alim Khan fled with his entourage into the mountains and, in the following year, via Dushanbe into Afghanistan (where he died in Kabul in the 1940s). Local people are

MICK WELDON

Muzaffar Khan was the Emir of Bukhara while Russian troups occupied the city in 1868.

said to have swarmed into the Ark to free children kept as the emir's playthings.

Around this time a group of Bukhara women, members of a movement known as Khujum, achieved Soviet martyrdom when they gathered in front of the Ark and burned their veils – symbol of purity for Muslims and of religious tyranny for the Bolsheviks. Whether this was a spontaneous demonstration or a Bolshevik put-up, afterwards most of the women are said to have been killed by their humiliated husbands or brothers.

Bukhara won a short 'independence' as the Bukhara People's Republic, but after showing rather too much interest in Pan-Turkism it was absorbed in 1924 into the newly created Uzbek SSR.

Much of the town's old aristocracy – judges, merchants etc – had fled in the early post-Revolution years to Dushanbe, Afghanistan and Iran.

Orientation
An oasis in the enveloping Kyzylkum desert, Bukhara sits 250km downstream of Samarkand on the Zeravshan river. The bulk

of the modern town lies south of the historical centre. In between old and new, violating the otherwise low skyline, is a knot of tourist hotels and Party buildings.

The heart of the *shakhristan* (old town), is the pool and square called Labi-hauz, a 10 minute walk north-west of the Hotel Bukhara; the landmark Kalon minaret is five minutes farther, the Ark five more. Farther west are Samani Park and the main farmers' market (Russian: *bolshoy rynok*).

The long-distance bus station is 5km north of the centre by bus or taxi, and the airport is 4km east of the centre. The nearest functioning train station is 15km south-east at Kagan.

Information
Tourist Offices Bukhara has the best tourist office in the country, and not coincidentally it isn't government-run. The Bukhara Information & Culture Centre (BICC; ☎ 224 22 46, 🖂 bicc@bukhara.silk.org), on the south side of Labi-hauz on the corner with Eshoni Pir (former Tsentralnaya), is open daily 9 am to 6 pm. The friendly staff including Yuliya Shishova can help with finding B&Bs, arranging transport and guides, even somewhere to eat. There's also a useful folder with travel info as well. You can send email from here for US$0.50 per day, and make international phone calls and send faxes.

Registration If you're not staying in a tourist hotel, OVIR is in the four storey building east of the Hotel Gulistan on M Ikbola.

Money The National Bank of Uzbekistan on Sorok Let Uzbekistana 10 changes US dollar travellers cheques into US dollars, and it's possible to get cash advances on Visa cards. The exchange desk at the Hotel Bukhara will change US dollars.

Post & Communications The best place to mail anything is probably back in Tashkent, although the Hotel Bukhara has a desk with stamps and a postal drop-box, and there is a small post office near Labi-hauz.

The BICC has the best and cheapest international phone connections, and email facilities as well.

Stoddart & Conolly

On 24 June 1842 Colonel Charles Stoddart and Captain Arthur Conolly were marched out from a dungeon cell before a huge crowd in front of the Ark, the emir's fortified citadel, made to dig their own graves and, to the sound of drums and reed pipes from atop the fortress walls, beheaded.

Colonel Stoddart had arrived three years earlier on a mission to reassure Emir Nasrullah Khan about Britain's invasion of Afghanistan. But his superiors, underestimating the emir's vanity and megalomania, had sent him with no gifts, and with a letter not from Queen Victoria (whom Nasrullah regarded as an equal sovereign) but from the governor-general of India. To compound matters Stoddart violated local protocol by riding, rather than walking, up to the Ark. The piqued Nasrullah had him thrown into jail, where he was to spend much of his time at the bottom of the so-called 'bug pit', in the company of assorted rodents and scaly creatures.

Captain Conolly arrived in 1841 to try to secure Stoddart's release. But the emir, believing him to be part of a British plot with the khans of Khiva and Kokand, tossed Conolly in jail too. After the disastrous British retreat from Kabul the emir, convinced that Britain was a second-rate power and having received no reply to an earlier letter to Queen Victoria, had both men executed.

Despite general revulsion back in England, the British government chose to let the matter drop. Outraged friends and relatives raised enough money to send their own emissary, an oddball clergyman named Joseph Wolff, to Bukhara to verify the news. According to Peter Hopkirk in *The Great Game*, Wolff himself only escaped death because the emir considered him so hilarious, dressed up in full clerical regalia.

Travel Agencies Agencies worth contacting include:

Bukhara Visit
 (☎/fax 226 46 00, 224 49 65,
 ✉ visit@b1.silk.glas.apc.org)
 Jami 7, Bukhara 705030 – visa support.
Farkhad & Maya's
 (☎/fax 224 59 09, 223 03 26,
 ✉ mfarkhad@bcc.com.uz)
 Sufiyon 16, Bukhara 705000 – visa support, Bukhara B&B, English, French and German-speaking guides, drivers; gets uniformly good reports.
Marvarid-95
 (☎/fax 223 15 56, ✉ era@silk.org)
 Deputatskaya 103, Bukhara 705018 – Bukhara home-stays, visa support, tours, drivers; gets good reports.
Salom Travel
 (☎/fax 224 42 59, 223 72 77,
 ✉ raisa@salom.silk.org)
 Eshoni Pir 5, Bukhara 705000 – Raisa Gareyeva was one of the first private travel agents and is one of the best; Salom can arrange just about anything from visa support to B&Bs to camel treks.

Guides Guides recommended by travellers include Zinnat Ashurova (☎ 522 20 37), Dima Kulikov (☎ 223 41 22), Angelina Todorova (☎ 223 78 34) and Noila Kazidzanova (☎ 228 20 12), all charging around US$5 per hour. The BICC keeps up-to-date lists of guides.

Business Hours & Tourist Season Museums are open Thursday to Monday 9 am to 5 pm, to 3 pm Tuesday, closed Wednesday and closed for lunch. Some hotels drop their rates outside the tourist season, which is April to October.

Baths There are at least four public baths near the centre. Two old ones now under reconstruction (which may turn them into tourist traps) are a men's bath *(erkaklar hammomi)* just north of Taqi-Telpak Furushon and a bath just south of Taqi-Sarrafon. An operating women's bath *(ayollar hammomi)*, with common room *(hammomi kunjak)* only, is behind Kalon minaret. A bath on Jubar, south-west of Taqi-Sarrafon, has private rooms *(hammomi numur)* and both men's and women's common rooms.

A common room is less than US$0.20 (in *sum*) for as long as you want to stay. A private room, with tub, shower and endless hot water, is about US$0.50 for an hour – pure heaven. Bring your own towel, soap, flip-flops etc. They're all closed on Sunday.

Labi-Hauz

Labi-hauz, a plaza built around a pool in 1620 (the name is Tajik for 'around the pool') is the most peaceful and interesting spot in town – shaded by mulberry trees as old as the pool and peopled with street-sellers, crazies, old men hunched over chessboards or gossiping over tea, and anyone else with nowhere else to go. Pray that municipal officials don't decide to pretty it up.

On the east side is a statue of **Hoja Nasruddin**, a semi-mythical 'wise fool' who appears in Sufi teaching-tales around the world (see the boxed text).

To the east, the **Nadir Divanbegi Medressa** was built as a caravanserai, but the khan thought it was a medressa and it became one in 1630. On the west side of the square, and built at the same time, is the **Nadir Divanbegi khanaka**. Both are named for Abdul Aziz Khan's treasury minister, who financed them in the 17th century.

North across the street, the **Kukeldash Medressa**, built by Abdullah II, was at the time the biggest Islamic school in Central Asia.

South of Labi-hauz is what's left of the old town's unique **Jewish quarter.** There have been Jews in Bukhara since perhaps the 12th or 13th century, evolving into a unique, non-Hebrew-speaking branch of the Diaspora. They managed to become major players in Bukharan commerce in spite of deep-rooted, institutionalised discrimination. Since the collapse of the Soviet Union, Jews have dwindled from roughly 7% of the town's population to less than 2% at the last count, and even that is probably a big overestimate. This is probably a result of both Jews' new freedom to emigrate and others' freedom to act out prejudices.

Hoja Nasruddin

Hoja Nasruddin was a mullah and a Sufi (a *hoja* is someone who has made the pilgrimage *(hajj)* to Mecca). He was renowned for his sense of humour that he put to use in his teaching, if only to loosen his students up. Hundreds of tales about him are the theological equivalent of a running joke. Following is a good example:

One day the Hoja borrowed a pot from his neighbour. When he returned it the neighbour noticed a little pot nestled inside and called his attention to it. The Hoja exclaimed that the pot must have fallen pregnant and that this was its baby. Since the pot was the neighbour's, so was the baby! The neighbour went home, pleased.

Some time later, the Hoja came to borrow the neighbour's *kazan* (a large steel pan for making plov and other dishes). The neighbour was happy to lend it, thinking that this larger mother would surely produce an even bigger baby.

Time passed, and the kazan wasn't returned. Finally the neighbour inquired with the Hoja as to its whereabouts.

'Oh my!' the Hoja exclaimed, 'I was going to tell you, it's so very sad!'

'What?' asked the neighbour.

'I'm sorry to say your kazan has died, so I cannot return it to you!'

'What? Kazans are made of metal, they don't die.'

'Ah,' said the Hoja, 'but you were quite happy to learn that a pot could become pregnant and give birth, so it's only fitting that you also accept the consequences of a kazan's mortality!'

Down the lane opposite the west end of the pool is a relatively recent Jewish community centre, and around the corner a much older synagogue. A century ago there were at least seven synagogues here, reduced after 1920 to this one.

Covered Bazars

From Shaybanid times, the area west and north from Labi-hauz was a vast warren of market lanes, arcades, and crossroad minibazars whose multidomed roofs were designed to draw in cool air. Three remaining domed bazars, heavily renovated in Soviet times – Taqi-Sarrafon (No 1; Moneychangers), Taqi-Telpak Furushon (No 2; Cap-Makers) and Taqi-Zargaron (No 3; Jewellers) – were among dozens of specialised bazars in the town. They have been reborn with touristy souvenir shops, selling identical merchandise of dubious quality at highly negotiable prices. It's easy to change US dollars here, though they won't give the best rates.

Taqi-Sarrafon Area Just to the north, in what was the old herb and spice bazar, is Central Asia's oldest surviving mosque, the **Maghoki-Attar** (meaning 'pit of the herbalists'), a lovely mishmash of 12th century façade and 16th century reconstruction. This is probably also the town's holiest spot: under it in the 1930s archaeologists found bits of a 5th century Zoroastrian temple wrecked by the Arabs, and an earlier Buddhist temple. Until the 16th century Bukhara's Jews are said to have used the mosque in the evenings as a synagogue.

Only the top of the mosque was visible when the digging began; the present plaza surrounding it is the 12th century level of the town. A section of the excavations has been left deliberately exposed inside. Also here is an exhibition of beautiful Bukhara carpets and prayer mats (see the special colour section 'Bukhara Carpets' in the Turkmenistan chapter).

West of this bazar is the site of a caravanserai for traders from the Caucasus, destroyed by the Bolsheviks and replaced with a small park.

Taqi-Telpak Furushon Area On the north side is a men's **bathhouse**, still working a few years ago and now being rebuilt. The late 16th century covered arcade beyond it is called **Tim Abdullah Khan** (a *tim* was a general market, a kind of proto-department store, which it is again).

Two more caravanserai wrecked by the Bolsheviks were on the site of a fountain west of the path, and one for Hindu traders was north of Tim Abdullah Khan. A construction site beyond the fountain was to become a new, Saudi-financed medressa; however, the government, nervous about Islamic fundamentalism, has clamped down on such projects.

Taqi-Zargaron Area A few steps east of the bazar, on the north side of Hoja Nurabad, is Central Asia's oldest medressa, and a model for many others – the elegant, blue-tiled **Ulughbek Medressa** (1417), one of three built by Ulughbek (the others are at Gijduvan, 45km away on the road to Samarkand, and in Samarkand's Registan complex). For a time after Uzbekistan's independence this was again a working medressa, closed to visitors, but the government has since shut it down.

The **Abdul Aziz Khan Medressa** opposite was begun in 1652 by the Astrakhanid ruler of the same name, but left unfinished when he was booted out by the first of the Mangit emirs. This and the **Nadir Divanbegi Medressa** (built by his treasury minister) are the only ones in town to flout the Sunni Muslim prohibition against the depiction of living beings (Adul Aziz Khan was a Shia).

Inside, the former lecture hall on the left (now a shop) still has original frescoes, including one in Chinese style. Inside on the right is a little winter mosque. A single two storey students' cell is open in the courtyard.

Kalon Minaret & Around

When it was built by the Karakhan ruler Arslan Khan in 1127, the Kalon minaret was probably the tallest building in Central Asia (*kalon* means 'great' in Tajik). It's an incredible piece of work, 47m tall with 10m-deep foundations (including reeds stacked

UZBEKISTAN

underneath in an early form of earthquake-proofing), which in 850 years has never needed any but cosmetic repairs. Jenghiz Khan was so dumbfounded by it that he ordered it spared. It was also used as a beacon and watchtower, and the Mangit emirs threw criminals off it until forbidden to do so by the Russians.

Its 14 ornamental bands, all different, include the first use of the glazed blue tiles that were to saturate Central Asia under Timur. Up and down the south and east sides are faintly lighter patches, marking the restoration of damage by Frunze's artillery in 1920. Its 105 inner stairs are accessible from the Kalon Mosque for a small donation.

A legend says that Arslan Khan killed an imam after a quarrel. That night in a dream the imam told him, 'You have killed me; now oblige me by laying my head on a spot where nobody can tread', and the tower was built over his grave.

At the foot of the minaret, on the site of an earlier mosque destroyed by Jenghiz Khan, is the 16th century congregational **Kalon Mosque**, big enough for 10,000 people. Used in Soviet times as a warehouse, it was reopened as a place of worship in 1991. The roof, which looks flat, actually consists of 288 small domes. Tourists are only allowed into the central courtyard, where early in this century Emir Alim Khan added his own little prayer pavilion.

Opposite, its luminous blue domes in sharp contrast to the surrounding brown, is the **Mir-i-Arab Medressa** – a working seminary from the 16th century until 1920, but reopened by Stalin in 1944 in an effort to curry Muslim support for the war effort. It was Central Asia's only functioning medressa in Soviet times. Presently 250 young men, mostly from Uzbekistan, enrol for five years, normally from the age of 17 or 18, to study Arabic, the Quran and Islamic law. In fact most classes are now held in the Kalon Mosque, with Mir-i-Arab serving mainly as dormitories.

The medressa is named for a 16th century Naqshbandi sheikh from Yemen who had a strong influence on the Shaybanid ruler Ubaidullah Khan and financed the original complex. Both khan and teacher are buried beneath the northern dome. The tall pole with a horse-hair tassel at the north end of the tomb is a traditional marker for the graves of very revered figures in Islam. The hand symbolises the 'five pillars of Islam' (see the Religion section of the Facts about Central Asia chapter). The medressa is officially off limits to tourists (especially female visitors).

Behind Mir-i-Arab is the small **Amir Alim Khan Medressa**, built in the 20th century, and now used as a children's library.

The Ark & Around

This royal town-within-a-town is Bukhara's oldest structure, occupied from the 5th century right up until 1920, when it was bombed by the Red Army. Bits of it may go back two millennia, though the present crumbling walls are probably less than three hundred years old. It's about 75% ruins inside now, except for some remaining royal quarters, now housing several **museums**.

At the top of the entrance ramp is the 17th century **Juma (Friday) Mosque**, its porch supported by tall columns of sycamore. Inside is a little museum of 19th and 20th century manuscripts and writing tools.

Turn right into a corridor with courtyards off both sides. First on the left is the former living quarters of the emir's *kushbegi* (prime minister) now housing a seldom-shown exhibit on WWII and the Soviet period (including a little mechanical diorama depicting the celebrated post-Revolutionary burning of the veils).

Second on the left is the oldest surviving part of the Ark, the vast **Reception & Coronation Court**, whose roof fell in during the 1920 bombardment. The last coronation to take place here was Alim Khan's in 1910. The submerged chamber on the right wall was the treasury, and behind the room was the harem.

To the right of the corridor were the open-air royal stables and the *noghorahona*, a room for drums and musical instruments used during public spectacles. Now there are shops and a tedious natural history exhibit.

Around the *salamhona* (Protocol Court) at the end of the corridor are what remain of the royal apartments. These apparently fell into such disrepair that the last two emirs preferred full-time residence at the summer palace (see Around Bukhara). Now there are several museums, including ho-hum pre-Shaybanid history on the ground floor, and coins and bits of applied art on the top floor.

Most interesting is in between – Bukhara's history from the Shaybanids to the tsars. Among items to look for are the huge snakeskin 'Whip of Rustam' that once hung above the Ark's entrance; a 9kg royal robe, padded to make the emir look big; and a surprisingly negative, Soviet-style exhibit on Islam. One on Bukhara's slave trade has conspicuously shrunk since we first visited in Soviet times, with the more 'feudal' items (eg people selling their children, often to the royal court as sexual toys) now covered or missing. Also gone are grisly displays on public executions.

Entry to the Ark is about US$1 in *sum* and an English-language guided tour can be US$1 to US$5 – not a bad idea since there are no English labels on anything.

Out in front of the fortress is medieval Bukhara's main square, the **Registan** (meaning 'sandy place'), a favourite venue for executions, including those of the British officers Stoddart and Conolly (see the boxed text 'Stoddart & Conolly' in the Bukhara History section earlier).

Behind the Ark is **Zindon**, the jail, now a museum. Cheerful attractions include a torture chamber and several dungeons, including the gruesome 'bug pit' where Stoddart and Conolly languished in a dark chamber filled with lice, scorpions and other vermin.

Beside a pool opposite the Ark's gate is the **Bolo-hauz Mosque**, the emirs' official place of worship, built in 1718 and probably very beautiful at the time. The brightly painted porch, supported by 20 columns of walnut, elm and poplar, was added in 1917, as was the stubby minaret nearby. It's now a mosque again. Beside it is a now-disused water tower, built by the Russians in 1927 as part of their new water system.

Ismail Samani Mausoleum & Around

In Samani Park is one of the town's oldest monuments (completed about 905 CE) and one of the most elegant structures in Central Asia, the **mausoleum of Ismail Samani** (the Samanid dynasty's founder), his father and grandson. Its delicate baked terracotta brickwork – which gradually changes 'personality' through the day as the shadows shift – disguises walls almost 2m thick, helping it survive without restoration (except of the dome) for eleven centuries. The bricks predate the art of majolica tiles. Though dating from early Islamic times, the building bears Zoroastrian symbols such as the circle in nested squares – symbolising eternity – above the door. Jenghiz Khan overlooked it because it was partly buried in the dust of ages.

Behind the park is one of the few remaining, eroded sections (a total of 2km out of an original 12km) of the Shaybanid **town walls**, and a reconstructed gate called Talli-Pach. Another big section is about 500m west of the Hotel Gulistan.

At the edge of the main farmers' market is the peculiar **Chashma-Ayub 'mausoleum'**, built in the 12th century over a spring. Its middle domes were added in the 14th century, the front one in the 16th, but no-one was buried in it until even later. The name means 'Spring of Job'; legend says Job struck his staff on the ground here and a spring appeared. Inside you can drink from the spring and check out a little exhibit on the town's ancient waterworks.

Buyan Khuli Khan & Saifuddin Bukharzi Mausolea

One of Bukhara's oldest, prettiest and saddest 'monuments' is far off the tourist track, in the middle of factories and railway sidings east of the centre. It can only have survived the Soviet era through low-key patronage by some sympathetic non-Russian official.

The tiny, 14th century Buyan Khuli Khan mausoleum (now also used as a mosque) may be the tomb of a Karakitay ruler. On a trip to London, a sharp-eyed Uzbektourism guide discovered that the mausoleum's original gravestone, and large sections of its exterior tiles, had somehow found their way into the Victoria and Albert Museum. Some unrestored tilework, beautiful and delicate, remains over the portal.

Nearby is the Saifuddin Bukharzi mausoleum, resting place of a revered early 16th century teacher. The grave has been moved out in front (the horsehair tassel and sign-of-the-hand indicate a 'saint' on a level with Mir-i-Arab) and the mausoleum converted to another mosque.

Turki Jangi Mausoleum

Deep in the old town is a tiny mausoleum favoured as a place for getting one's prayers answered. It's the resting place of a holy man known as Turki Jangi, his two sons, several grandsons and numerous other relations. Its importance is signalled by the hundreds of other graves around it – allegedly in stacks 30m deep! The central chamber is under slow, devoted restoration. It's on Namozgokh about 500m south of Taqi-Telpak Furushon.

Char Minar

This photogenic little building, the gatehouse of a long-gone medressa built in 1807, bears more relation to Indian styles than to anything Bukharan. The name means 'Four Minarets' in Tajik, though they aren't strictly minarets but simply decorative towers. UNESCO restored one collapsed tower and fixed another in 1998. It's in a maze of alleys between Pushkin and Hoja Nurabad; everybody in the neighbourhood knows it by name. If it's locked, the friendly shopkeeper in the shop on the south side of the building has the key and is willing to lead you up to the roof for a small consideration.

Other Medressas & Mosques

West of Taqi-Sarrafon is the **Gaukushan Medressa**, now full of handicraft shops and workshops, and a summer chaykhana. Across the canal is a little brother of the Kalon minaret.

South-east of Samani park are two massive facing medressas, one named for the great Shaybanid ruler **Abdullah Khan** and one for his mother (**Modari Khan**, 'mother of the khan'). Another giant is the handsome 16th century **Namozgokh Mosque**, behind the Hotel Gulistan.

Fayzulla Khujayev House

Uzbektourism calls it 'National House' and the sign says 'The Daily Life of a Bukhara Merchant', but neighbours know it by its most infamous occupant, Fayzulla Khujayev, who plotted with the Bolsheviks to dump Emir Alim Khan. He was rewarded with the presidency of the Bukhara People's Republic, chairmanship of the Council of People's Commissars of the Uzbek SSR, and finally liquidation by Stalin.

The house was built in 1891 by his father, Ubaidullah, a wealthy merchant. There are said to be about twenty such merchants' houses left in Bukhara, out of hundreds at the turn of the 20th century. How these survived the anti-bourgeois fury of 1920 is a matter of wonder. Some may have been camouflaged with layers of adobe mud, but most were probably under the wing of Uzbek communist officials who hadn't completely lost touch with their traditions, or were willing to be bribed. After the revolution this house served as a Marxist school and then a museum in praise of Khujayev.

Since 1994 the state has let a few former museum employees live here and gradually restore the elegant frescoes, ghanch, latticework and ceiling beams (of carved, unpainted elm, Bukhara style), paying for the work with guided tours, special functions and a handicrafts shop. It's a bit contrived, but a very pleasant experience and a long step ahead of the usual sterile tours, for less than US$1 in *sum*. They say 'come anytime', but an advance booking is appreciated. They speak only Russian so bring a translator.

Museum of Art

The Museum of Art is in the former headquarters of the Russian Central Asian Bank (1912), just west of Taqi-Sarrafon. It has mostly 20th century paintings by Bukharan artists, and works of artists from other parts of the Soviet Union who now live in Bukhara.

Places to Stay

Home-Stays Travel agencies can arrange B&B accommodation in private homes, typically for about US$25 per person. You may also be approached by locals at the tourist spots. The BICC can help with cheaper, less official home-stays from US$5 per night. More official B&Bs are opening all the time, and the competition is lowering prices.

Mubinjon's Bukhara House (☎ 224 20 05, *Eshoni Pir 4)* is right in the middle of the old town and dates back to 1765. Traditional mattresses on the floor are a negotiable US$12 to US$15 each. The bathrooms are basic but Mubinjon can direct you to traditional baths. Crafty Mubinjon doesn't speak much English but makes himself understood. The house is in a cul-de-sac about 200m south of Labi-hauz down the lane from the BICC; look for the Olympic symbols painted on the garage door and turn down the alley to the gate.

In contrast to Mubinjon's very Asian B&B, *Sasha & Lena's B&B* (☎ 223 38 90, *fax 223 55 93, Molodyozhnaya 13)* is a spanking-clean, Europeanised place with sauna, spa, air-con and satellite TV. Five double rooms (and 'continental' breakfast) are US$20 per person in season; dinners by arrangement are about US$5. It's about a 10 minute walk east of Labi-hauz. Sasha Boltaev, a former Intourist guide, can arrange transport, tickets, onward bookings and other help. This is popular with Central Asia's expats and gets booked out early.

Sasha Boltaev has opened another B&B in the heart of the city, *Sasha & Son* (☎ 224 49 66, *Eshoni Pir 3)*, a traditional Bukhara-style house set around a courtyard with fabulously restored decorations and tasteful furnishings. It's quite easy to find, just south of the traffic circle on Bakhautdin Naqshband. The four doubles and one single room cost US$20 per person, with air-con, satellite TV and modern bathrooms.

Nutfullo's B&B (☎ 244 51 51, *fax 224 22 46, Vavilova 15,* @ *bakiev@bukhara.silk .org)* is in a quiet neighbourhood south of the Abdullah Khan and Modari Khan medressas. There are four rooms with modern bathrooms and air-con for US$25 per person and a traditionally decorated dining room. The Bakiev children speak English (Nutfullo only speaks a little English) and they're all very friendly; this place gets good reports.

Another friendly place with good food is *Farkhad & Maya's B&B* (☎/*fax 224 59 09, 223 03 26, Sufiyon 16,* @ *mfarkhad@ hotmail.com)*, near the Gaukushan Medressa and city bath No 1. There is space for eight guests in air-con rooms in an old courtyard house, this place also gets good reports for its atmosphere and its cooking. Farkhad has a computer with Internet access.

Labi Hauz B&B (☎ 224 84 24, 224 21 77, *Husainov 7)*, is close to Labi-hauz, of course, and has rather plain but comfortable rooms for US$25 per person, all with satellite TV and air-con. The highlight is the venerable eivan with carved wooden columns where breakfast is served.

Hotels The bug-ridden *Hotel Zarafshan* (☎ 223 41 73, *M Ikbola 7)* has huge threadbare singles/doubles with grotty baths and broken TVs from US$2/3. Surprisingly there's a decent Korean restaurant here.

The decaying *Hotel Gulistan* (☎ 223 38 10, *M Ikbola 19)* is 1km west. Transport there is poor. Typical Soviet rooms and service cost US$5 to US$15. Food may be hard to find except in summer or when a group is staying.

Hotel Varaksha (☎ 223 45 82, *fax 223 63 96, Navoi 5)* is a passable option with rooms for US$20/30 with toilet and shower. The restaurant is said to be reasonably good.

Hotel Bukhara (Old) (☎ 223 01 24, *fax 223 13 59)* is actually one of two places called the Hotel Bukhara. This one is a typical Soviet-built multistorey tower, recently renovated and in reasonable shape. Singles/doubles with bath cost US$60/100, and there's a bar, restaurant and shop to entertain the tour groups that mostly use the place.

Behind is the deluxe *Hotel Bukhara* (☎ 223 00 24, 223 50 04)*, similar to Samarkand's Afrosiab in its chunky Indian-built bulk. Prices quoted are around US$60/90 for a standard room and US$160 for a suite. There's a swimming pool, souvenir shops, two restaurants and Bukhara's most exclusive nightclub (which isn't saying much).

Places to Eat

Bukhara offers little in the way of 'dining' other than home-cooking at the B&Bs and hotel restaurants. The ***Europa Restaurant***, on the intersection of Naqshband and the former Gazliiskoe, across the road from the East bus station, has decent Russian food and pizza for US$3 to US$4 for dinner, plus Russian beer for US$1 per bottle.

During the day, dine al fresco at ***Labi-hauz*** with grey-beards, local families and other tourists. Tea and pastries appear by 7.30 am and shashlyk, samsas and laghman are dished up until sunset (pay separately for each). Hygiene is not always the best but prices are low and the setting is unmatched.

For vegetarians and other self-caterers there are farmers' markets. The main one by Samani park is known as the ***bolshoy rynok***; others include the smaller ***krytyy rynok*** near the Hotel Bukhara, and the Sunday-only ***Kukluk bazar*** in the old town, south of Labi-hauz.

Shopping

Nearly all of the tourist sights sell souvenirs on the side. Some shops to check out are in the Abdul Aziz Khan Medressa, the Maghoki-Attar Mosque and Taqi-Telpak Furushon. Although certain carpet designs originate here, the best 'Bukhara' rugs are made in Turkmenistan (as they have been ever since those regions were part of the Bukhara khanate).

Traditional Uzbek men's padded coats are US$25 in the Hotel Bukhora's gift shop, and the *sum* equivalent of about US$4 in the bazars!

Getting There & Away

Air There are regular flights from Bukhara to Tashkent (1½ hours away) at least three times a day in summer for US$15 in *sum*, and Moscow once a week for US$200. Bookings and tickets can be arranged through the Hotel Bukhara's service bureau or at the airport's 'international sector' office, to the right (south) of the main building.

Bus There are buses every hour to Tashkent (US$3 in *sum*, 12 hours) until 4 pm, and it's fairly easy to buy a ticket at the last moment. Six buses a day go to Samarkand (US$1.50 in *sum*, 6½ hours). On both, watch for the

unrestored gateway of a 12th century cara-vanserai called Rabati-Malik on the north side of the road about 80km before Samarkand. A single bus leaves each day for Urgench at about 2.30 pm, arriving around midnight. Frequent minibuses go to Gijduvan for about US$0.30 in *sum*. These buses leave from the long-distance station, 5km north of the centre.

For Qarshi as well as Shakhrisabz, go to the *sharq avtovokzal* (east bus station), on the road to Kagan. There are five daily departures to Qarshi (4½ hours) until 4pm, two of which go on to Shakhrisabz.

There are no longer any buses to Turkmenistan. See To/From Turkmenistan, later in this section.

Train Every evening a train goes from Kagan to Samarkand (US$4 in *sum* in 2nd class, 5½ hours) and Tashkent (US$6 in 2nd class, 12 hours), and another for Nukus (US$8, about 20 hours); one also passes each way between Nukus and Tashkent.

Share Taxi These leave from the long-distance bus station and from outside Kagan train station for Samarkand, Tashkent, and less regularly for Urgench. A seat in a minivan to Samarkand costs US$2 in *sum*, to Tashkent around US$4, and to Samarkand, around US$10 in a Daewoo sedan.

To/From Turkmenistan It is theoretically possible to take a car direct from Bukhara to Turkmenabat, but it's not advisable. Tourists have to wait for the car to be inspected at the border crossing, and pay additional fees for the car. It is much easier to take a car to the border (around US$40), walk across and hire another car from there to Turkmenabat (around US$60). From Bukhara's bolshoy rynok (farmers' market), you could also take a share minibus to Karakul in Xinjiang for US$0.65 in *sum*. From there, you can purchase a seat in a taxi to the border for no more than US$1.50 in *sum*. The trip to Turkmenabat by similar means should cost US$2.50 in Turkmen *manat*.

There is a train to Turkmenabat (75km or three to four hours away), and currently

Nukus trains pass through Turkmenabat. To transit in Turkmenistan you will need a transit visa from the Turkmen embassy in Tashkent.

Getting Around

The 10 minute taxi trip between the airport and the centre *should* cost about US$0.50 in *sum*; how much you'll end up paying depends on your bargaining abilities. Bus No 10 to/from the Vokzal, Krytyy Rynok or Gorgaz stops takes 15 to 20 minutes. Marshrutnoe taxi No 56 passes the Bukhara and Varaksha hotels.

Take the Kagan-Bukhara bus, or a marshrutnoe taxi, from the train station to the Vokzal stop (near Bukhara's disused train station), or a Bukhara-Kagan bus the other way.

Bus No 7 goes from Navoi, near the Hotel Bukhara to the long-distance bus station.

AROUND BUKHARA
Emir's Palace

For a look at the kitsch lifestyle of the last emir, Alim Khan, go out to Makhosa – Sitorai Mokhi Hosa, meaning 'Palace of Moon-like Stars' (or Moon & Stars) – his summer palace (now a museum) 3km north of the centre.

The present buildings were a joint effort for Alim Khan by Russian architects (outside) and local artisans (inside). A 50 watt Russian generator provided the first electricity the emirate had ever seen. The palace is a fascinating mix of taste and tastelessness – there's a fine collection of Asian porcelain displayed in a room with heart-shaped windows. Next door is the former harem, and beside a pool where the women frolicked is a wooden pavilion from which – says every tour guide – the emir tossed an apple to his chosen bedmate. The harem has a small **museum** devoted to the traditional silk-on-cotton dowry needlework called suzani.

The original complex was built by Alim Khan's father, Abdallahad Khan, who wanted a cool place to go in the summer. The story goes that he had a sheep slaughtered and the raw meat left in various suburban spots, and it was here that it rotted most slowly. The palace is open daily except Wednesday, 9 am to 5 pm; entry is US$0.50 in *sum*.

Bus Nos 9 and 13 go from the Krytyy rynok or Vokzal stop near the Hotel Bukhara, and bus No 12 goes from the Bolshoy rynok infrequently. The palace is at the end of the line. Taxis can be hard to find coming back.

Bakhautdin Naqshband Mausoleum

Just east of Bukhara in the village of Kasri Orifon is one of Sufism's more important shrines, the birthplace and the tomb of Bakhautdin (or Bakha ud-Din) Naqshband, the 14th century founder of the most influential of many ancient Sufi orders in Central Asia (see boxed text 'The Naqshbandis'), and Bukhara's unofficial 'patron saint'.

The huge main dome of the complex covers a 16th century khanaka. Beside it is a precariously leaning minaret and a courtyard with two old mosques, lovingly restored since independence. The tomb itself is a simple 2m-high block in the courtyard. Tradition says that it is auspicious to complete three anticlockwise circumambulations of the tomb. Beside it, beneath a mulberry tree, you may find a *mullah* (Islamic cleric) saying prayers for pilgrims with special requests.

The atmosphere here is amazingly serene compared to the other side of the walls. This is not a tourist attraction but a very sacred place for Muslims. Please dress conservatively, keep a respectful silence and be discreet with cameras.

Outside the courtyard is a small kitchen where wealthier visitors can have a sheep slaughtered and cooked, and the meat distributed among the poor. Nearby is the so-called 'Wishing Tree', the dead trunk of an ancient mulberry tree linked by legends to Bakhautdin himself, and one of those places where Islamic and pre-Islamic traditions mingle. Good luck (in particular for barren women) is said to come from crawling under it three times.

Also here are a small museum and restaurant, and outside the complex are chaykhanas and hostels for pilgrims. The entire village is a place of pilgrimage; in fact the usual first pilgrim stop is the tomb of Bakhautdin's mother, just north of the complex.

The Naqshbandis

Bakhautdin Naqshband was (meaning no disrespect) a kind of Islamic Gandhi, who emphasised the importance of work in a full spiritual life (a *naqshband* was a carver of wooden stamps for printing fabrics). The Naqshbandi are a clandestine, decentralised but non-fanatical, non-ascetic Sufi brotherhood (quite literally, since at least in Central Asia they apparently have little interest in women adepts) who share certain practices such as the *zikr* (recitation or contemplation of the names of God), sacred verses etc, sometimes combined with techniques of posture and breath control.

Naqshbandi groups exist all over the world, including almost all Muslim areas of the former Soviet Union. Naqshbandi fighters were at the centre of the 19th century struggle against the Russians in the Caucasus; several of the most famous basmachi guerillas were Naqshbandis.

Re-emerging Central Asian Islam has a strong Sufi flavour because it was mainly within such societies that it survived Soviet persecution. The KGB seems never to have managed to plant spies among them.

From Bukhara to Kasri Orifon is about 12km, past mulberry trees, vineyards and cotton fields. On your own, take an eastbound No 60 bus from the Vokzal stand or the bolshoy rynok. A taxi would be perhaps US$5 in *sum* for the round trip plus a wait. Tourist hotel service bureaus can arrange guided excursions.

Chor-Bakr

This haunting 16th century necropolis or 'town' of mausolea 10km west of Bukhara was built in Shaybanid times, but nobody seems quite sure for whom. The locally preferred story is that it was for Abu-Bakr, devoted friend of the Prophet Mohammed and later first caliph, and his family. Second choice is that it was built by and for a local dynasty called the Jubari Sheikhs.

Two massive structures, a Friday mosque on the left and a former khanaka on the right, dominate the complex. All around are small broken-down mausolea and simple graves built later to capitalise on the site's good vibes. There's little sign of recent restoration (save one small building apparently used by local people for 40-day intensive retreats), but this and the near-absence of visitors are part of its appeal.

For a donation of US$0.50 or so in *sum*, the caretaker may let you climb the (restored) circular staircase to the (restored) roof of the khanaka, for a bird's-eye view.

The complex is in a tiny village once called Sumitan, now Chor-Bakr. From the bolshoy rynok, take a bus labelled СВЕРДЛОВ Ш А БЕКАТИ (Sverdlov region) and ask for Chor-Bakr (about 10 minutes away), from where the complex is easily visible. There is also said to be a marshrutnoe taxi from the bazar directly to Chor-Bakr.

Kagan

This was the original Russian cantonment and train station of New Bukhara, placed far from old Bukhara to humour Emir Abdallahad Khan, who regarded trains as an evil influence. He apparently had a change of heart, and built a spur line (now disused) into the middle of Bukhara.

It's decidedly not worth a special trip, but if you're waiting for a train, have a look at its assortment of sturdy turn-of-the-20th century buildings, including an Orthodox church and an office of the Russian Central Asian Bank.

See the Bukhara Getting Around section for how to get to Kagan.

TERMIZ & AROUND

Modern-day Termiz bears few traces of its colourful cosmopolitan history. However, set in attractive landscapes on the fringes of town are some ancient monuments and sites attesting to more glorious times. These include the 2nd century BCE Zurmala Tower, the Mausoleum of al-Hakim at-Termizi, a revered Islamic philosopher-mathematician, the 2nd century Buddhist monastery of Fayoz-Tepe and the 12th century Djarkurgan Minaret. Termiz is currently off limits to foreigners, except for the rare tour group.

Khorezm & Karakalpakstan

URGENCH
☎ (3) 62 • pop 130,000

Urgench (Uzbek: Urganch) is a standard-issue Soviet grid of broad streets and empty squares, 450km north-west of Bukhara across the Kyzylkum desert, in the delta of the Amu-Darya river. Cotton motifs feature prominently in the seamless mix of Soviet and Uzbek monuments. It's the capital of Khorezm province, wedged between the Amu-Darya and the Turkmen border. Urgench is mainly of use to travellers as the transport hub for Khiva, 35km south-west, and somewhere to stay if you can't move right on to Khiva.

When the Amu-Darya changed course in the 16th century, the people of Konye-Urgench (Old Urgench), 150km downriver in present-day Turkmenistan, were left without water and started a new town here. There's virtually nothing to see in Urgench besides provincial propaganda, but if there's time to spare after Khiva you might fancy some ruined cities and fortresses in the vicinity or the Badai-Tugai Nature Reserve north of town (see the Around Urgench section).

There's a **statue of Mohammed Al-Khorezmi**, a local 9th century mathematician who invented algebra, in the park in front of the Hotel Urganch.

Orientation & Information

The town's axis is Al-Khorezmi (formerly Kommunisticheskaya), with the clock tower at its intersection with al-Beruni marking the centre of things. The train and bus stations are 1.5km south of the centre down Al-Khorezmi, the airport 3km north, and most hotels around the centre. Street numbering along Al-Khorezmi is haywire.

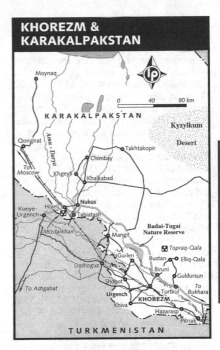

KHOREZM & KARAKALPAKSTAN

UZBEKISTAN

Uzbektourism (☎ 634 05, 664 55, fax 676 30) is at Al-Khorezmi 26, just south of the canal, but just as useful are the excursion bureaus at the Khorezm and Jayhun hotels. Hiring a car costs US$8 to US$20 per hour depending on the vehicle, and guides US$5 per hour. Both can arrange day trips to Konye-Urgench in Turkmenistan for a minimum US$130 between four people, but you will need a valid Turkmen visa.

The National Bank of Uzbekistan (☎ 626 44) at Pahlavon Mohammed 150 takes an hour or two to produce US dollars from Visa cards and travellers cheques. You can change money at the Khorezm or Jayhun hotels at the official rate, or with staff at the black market rate (negotiations reportedly difficult), or at the bazar if you're game.

The post, telephone and telegraph office is the building with the clock tower near the central roundabout.

The travel agency Gulnara (☎ 646 58, 405 26) at former ulitsa Nekrasova 191 offers airport and station pick-ups, accommodation in Urgench or at the Hotel Arqonchi in Khiva, and trips to Khiva or outlying sites as far away as the Aral Sea. Ask for Gulya or Svetlana, who speak some English.

Bahadir Rakhamov (☎ 352 41 06, 223 02 41) is an English-speaking driver offering excursions to Konye-Urgench for US$80, Moynaq US$100 and Badai-Tugai and the *kalas* (fortresses) for US$50 per carload.

Places to Stay & Eat
Hotel Bakht (☎ 224 05 15, fax 224 03 39, Samarkandskaya 3) has striking red decor and comfortable air-con rooms with satellite TV and clean bathrooms. It's good value at US$7/13 in *sum*. It's about 1.5km north of the post office on a street off the airport road.

Step into the Intourist past at Uzbektourism's large *Hotel Khorezm (☎ 226 56 66, 654 08, fax 661 80, al-Beruni 2)*. Simple, clean singles/doubles with satellite TV cost from US$38/44, plus US$5 for breakfast and US$7 for dinner (three meals US$20). Visa cards are accepted. The hotel has a restaurant, bar, coffee shop and bookshop.

Uzbektourism's swanky Hotel Jayhun (% 226 62 49, 226 62 23, fax 226 08 09, Al-Khorezmi 28) is 300m south of the clock tower. Rooms with private bath and satellite TV are US$25/35, 'apartments' are US$90. Like the Khorezm it's geared towards tour groups. Breakfast is US$4, dinner US$5, all meals US$15. The restaurant only seems to open when groups are in: at other times try the ground floor bar.

Gulnara travel agency can provide *B&B* in a clean house with hot water for about US$20. Taxi drivers can sometimes recommend home-stays for US$10 or less.

Chaykhana Mehribon, between the Hotel Urganch and Al-Khorezmi, has a small garden. The *Chaykhana Amizga*, 150m from the Khorezm on al-Beruni serves decent salads and shashlyk for US$2. The *bazar* is about 600m west of Al-Khorezmi. Follow the small street that starts almost opposite the Chaykhana Mehribon: the bazar actually begins as street stalls along this street. It has fresh fruit and vegetables, and shashlyk stalls.

Getting There & Away
Air Flights leave from the new airport twice daily to Tashkent (US$23 in *sum*) and once weekly to Moscow (US$214). The Uzbekistan Airways office is on Al-Khorezmi, a bit north of the clock tower.

Gulnara travel agency offers plane or helicopter trips to ancient sites around Urgench or to Moynaq, the former Aral Sea fishing port. The cost for a typical single-destination trip is around US$200 per plane (holding eight passengers) or helicopter (holding three).

Bus The bus station is on Al-Khorezmi just north of the train station. Scheduled departures include Tashkent (16 hours, daily) via Bukhara and Samarkand; Samarkand (12 hours, twice daily) via Bukhara; Bukhara (seven hours, daily); and Nukus (twice daily). There are no buses to Dashoguz or any other destination in Turkmenistan.

The Bukhara route sticks to Uzbekistan and passes no towns between Bukhara and Druzhba, 80km from Urgench. Take food and drink for the ride, which is across the scrub-covered edge of the Kyzylkum desert. There are occasional glimpses of the Amu-Darya, which forms a stretch of the border with Turkmenistan and broadens into a wide reservoir east of Druzhba.

If you find no direct bus to Nukus, you could get one to Hojeli (Uzbek Hujayli), a dreary 4½ hours away crisscrossing the Turkmen border (though without passport checks when we did it) – and then a local bus or taxi for the last 15km.

Train Trains leave daily for Tashkent (25 hours), Samarkand (18 hours), Bukhara (Kagan, 11 hours), passing through Turkmenabat in Turkmenistan; you'll need a transit visa. Daily Tashkent-Qonghyrat (Uzbek: Qunghirat, Russian: Kungrad) and Tashkent-Nukus trains stop here (though they may not have better than 3rd-class carriages). All go via Dashoguz for US$1 in *sum*, which is the cheapest way to cross into Turkmenistan. There are also daily Urgench-Qongirat and Ashgabat-Dashoguz services.

Taxi & Share Taxi Minivans and cars leave for Nukus and Bukhara from the bazar and from in front of the train station. There's a lot of waiting around for enough passengers to commit themselves to a vehicle. A seat in a car to Bukhara should cost US$12 to US$15, chartering a car costs around US$40 to US$60 (the upper limit should include air-con).

Share taxis to Khiva leave from Al-Khorezmi, south of the canal, at the cross-roads marked by a large billboard of Central Asian flags, and cost US$0.25 per person in *sum*. To charter a taxi will cost US$5.

Getting Around
Bus No 3 runs between the train station and the airport, stopping on Al-Khorezmi near the hotels en route. Bus Nos 2 and 19 also go between the station and the central roundabout. All supposedly run from 7 am to 11 pm.

Taxis should cost about US$0.25 per kilometre, though local drivers often ask for much more.

AROUND URGENCH
The Amu-Darya delta, stretching from south-east of Urgench to the Aral Sea, has been inhabited for millennia and was an important oasis long before Urgench or even Khiva were important. The historical name of the delta area, which includes parts of modern-day northern Turkmenistan, was Khorezm (see the Konye-Urgench section in the Turkmenistan chapter for more on old Khorezm).

The ruins of many Khorezmian towns and forts, some well over two thousand years old, still stand east and north of Urgench. None are major sights, nor have remains at all comparable with Khiva, but they may give you some fun. Place names in this section are given in Karakalpak, the official language of the region in which they lie.

Biruni (Uzbek: Beruni), formerly Shab-haz, 25km north-east of Urgench, is named for the 10th century mathematician and encyclopedist al-Beruni, who spent time here (and some say was born here).

Another possible trip is to the Badai-Tugai Nature Reserve, an area of jungle-like riverine *tugai* forest with some unusual wildlife. Uzbektourism in Urgench offers trips both here and into the Karakum desert.

Ruins around Bustan
The ruins of Topraq-Qala, Qavat-Qala and Ayaz-Qala lie on the fringes of the Kyzyl-kum desert, 10 to 20km north of Bustan, which is 50km north-east of Urgench.

Topraq-Qala is the westernmost and most impressive site, a fort and temple complex of the rulers of the Khorezm borders in the 3rd and 4th centuries, with high walls, three 25m round towers and rooms carved out of the rock on a hilltop. It was abandoned in the 6th century after the irrigation system was destroyed. Fragments of sculptures and colourful frescoes found here are kept in the Nukus museum and in St Petersburg

Qavat-Qala, east of Topraq-Qala, was an important oasis until Jenghiz Khan's arrival. There are substantial remains of fortress walls and towers.

Ayaz-Qala, east of Qavat-Qala, has an impressive mud-walled hilltop fortress from the 6th and 7th centuries.

There are more ruins in the town of **Elliq-Qala** (Fifty Cities), 3km north-east of Bustan. The base of the mud-brick fortresses is being dissolved by the waterlogged earth.

Ruins around Turtkul
At **Guldursun**, 20km south of Bustan on the road to Turtkul, are the high mud walls of a fortress dating from about the 4th century BCE to the 4th century CE. Nearby are two ruins both called **Qyrqqyz-Qala**. You'd have to be very dedicated to reach **Qoy Qyryl-ghan Qala**, a circular fort, temple and, it's thought, observatory complex dating from the same period. It had two rings of circular walls, and Uzbekistan's oldest known inscriptions were found here. Maps show it about 80km east of Turtkul, in the desert.

Badai-Tugai Nature Reserve
This is a strip of tugai forest about 30km long and a few kilometres wide between the east bank of the Amu-Darya and the barren Sultan Vai hills, beginning 30km north of Urgench. In the 1960s and 70s the Soviet

UZBEKISTAN

cotton-growing schemes unleashed a frenzy of forest clearing in the region, and this is one of the few areas preserved. Tugai is a very dense, jungle-like forest of trees, shrubs and prickly salt-resistant plants and creepers, unique to Central Asia's desert river valleys. Only about a fifth of the Amu-Darya's and Syr-Darya's tugai has survived the drying-up of the deltas and cotton farming.

Fauna includes the Karakal desert cat, jackals, wild boar, foxes and badgers. Bukhara deer have been introduced and there is an underfunded breeding station with 18 deer. The last Turan or Caspian tiger, which also used to inhabit the tugai, was killed in 1972 in the Kegeyli area north of Nukus.

The reserve was off limits in Soviet times but today park officials welcome visitors, as the US$5 per car entrance fee helps pay for food for the deer breeding program, government funding having almost dried up.

By the Amu-Darya on one edge of the reserve is **Janpyq-Qala**, an impressive fortress inhabited from as early as the 1st century CE (and until the 14th century). At the centre are remains of a colonnaded citadel.

Getting There & Away

All these places lie in Karakalpakstan, outside Khorezm province, so Nukus Uzbektourism is better informed and keener to show them than Urgench Uzbektourism. You could arrange a guide from Nukus, or settle for Gulnara travel agency or Uzbektourism in Urgench for some sites. Urgench Uzbektourism charges US$8 to US$20 an hour for a car and driver, and US$5 an hour for a guide.

If you go without a guide, the best bet is a taxi, as bus services to these places are rare or nonexistent. A taxi should cost about US$50 for a day's tour of Badai-Tugai and two or three of the ruined qalas. Make sure your driver knows where these sites are!

KHIVA
☎ (3) 62 • pop 40,000

Khiva's name, redolent of slave caravans, barbaric cruelty and terrible journeys across deserts and steppes infested with wild tribesmen, struck fear into all but the boldest 19th century hearts. Nowadays it's a mere 35km

south-west of Urgench, past cotton bushes and fruit trees.

Khiva (Uzbek: Hiva) is an odd place. Its historic heart, unlike those of other Central Asian cities, is preserved in its entirety – but so well preserved that the life has almost been squeezed out of it. As a result of a Soviet conservation program in the 1970s and 80s, it's now a squeaky-clean official 'city-museum'. Even among its densely packed mosques, tombs, palaces, alleys and at least 16 medressas, you need imagination to get a sense of its mystique, bustle and squalor. Remind yourself that in its heyday everything tended to be weedy, crowded and filthy. However, streets just a block or two away but still within the walled inner city, the Ichon-Qala, remain lived in and fairly dishevelled.

You can see Khiva in a day trip from Urgench, but you'll take it in better by staying longer. Morning and evening are the best times, and there are three decent places to stay. If your time is limited, don't miss the Kalta Minor minaret, Kukhna Ark, Juma Mosque and minaret, Tosh-Khovli Palace, Islom-Huja Medressa and minaret, and Pahlavon Mohammed mausoleum. A few historic buildings are functioning mosques or shrines, but most are museums. Some of the lesser museums are very missable. North-east of the old town the Isfandiyar Palace is worth a quick look.

Entry to the Ichon-Qala, where virtually everything of interest is clustered, is US$4 for tourists at its main West Gate. There are inconsistently applied additional charges of about US$0.25 to US$0.50 (bargainable, in some cases) for a few buildings inside. Attendants may offer to open locked rooms for a small tip, while others may show you around for free.

A visual surprise here, after Samarkand's blue and Bukhara's brown, is the use of turquoise tiles. Khivan art also displays an unusual fondness for plant motifs, which came into favour following a Persian invasion in the 18th century.

History

Agriculture and human settlement go back four, perhaps six, millennia in Khorezm, the

KHIVA (ICHON-QALA) ХИВА

To Bus Station & Urgench
To Hotel Khorezm (500m)
ulitsa Gagarine
Mustaqillik kuchasi (Lenina)
Allabergenov kuchasi (Budennogo)
North Gate

PLACES TO STAY
19 Hotel Khiva (Mohammad Amin Khan Medressa)
23 Mirzoboshi B&B
33 Hotel Arqonchi

PLACES TO EAT
16 Chaykhana
17 Cafe
18 Koop Chaykhana
21 Restoran Khiva (Matniyaz Divanbeg Medressa)

OTHER
1 Isfandiyar Palace
2 Navoi Cinema
3 Trolleybus Stop for Urgench
4 Kheivak Well
5 Toilets
6 Zindon
7 Mohammed Rakhim Khan Medressa
8 Arabhana Medressa
9 Dost Alimjob Medressa
10 Dost Alyam Medressa
11 Tosh-Khovli Palace
12 Alloquli Khan Caravanserai
13 Alloquli Khan Medressa
14 Kutlimurodinok Medressa
15 Matpana Bay Medressa
20 Kalta Minor Minaret
22 Sayid Alauddin Mausoleum
24 Qozi-Kalon Medressa
25 Juma Mosque
26 Juma Minaret
27 Abdulla Khan Medressa
28 Aq Mosque
29 Anusha Khan Baths
30 Islom-Huja Medressa
31 Islom-Huja Minaret
32 Pahlavon Mohammed Mausoleum
34 Sherghozi Khan Medressa

Kukhana Ark
Alloqulihon Bazar
Square
West Gate
East Gate
To Koy-darvoza
South Gate
0   100   200 m

UZBEKISTAN

large, fertile Amu-Darya river delta isolated in the midst of broad deserts. So Khiva, on the southern fringe of the delta, *may* be very old. Legend has that it was founded when Shem, son of Noah, discovered a well here; his people called it Kheivak, from which the name Khiva is said to be derived. The original well is in the courtyard of ulitsa Abdullah a-Baltal 50, in the north-west of the old town.

Khiva certainly existed by the 8th century, as a minor fort and trading post on a Silk Road branch to the Caspian Sea and the Volga. But while Khorezm prospered on and off from the 10th to the 14th centuries, its capital was at old Urgench (present-day Konye-Urgench in Turkmenistan), and Khiva remained a bit player. See the Konye-Urgench section in the Turkmenistan chapter for more on old Khorezm.

The Khanate It wasn't until well after Konye-Urgench had been finished off by Timur that Khiva's time came. When the

Uzbek Shaybanids moved into the decaying Timurid empire in the early 16th century, one branch founded a state in Khorezm, independent of the more powerful branch in Bukhara. They made Khiva their capital in 1592.

The town ran a busy slave market that was to shape the destiny of the khanate, as the Khiva state was known, for more than three centuries. Most slaves were brought by Turkmen tribesmen from the Karakum desert or Kazak tribes of the steppes, who raided those unlucky enough to live or travel nearby. To keep both of these away from its own door, Khiva eventually resorted to an alliance with the Turkmen against the Kazaks, granting them land and money in return.

Russian Interest Awakens Khiva had earlier offered to submit to Peter the Great of Russia in return for help against marauding tribes. In a belated response, a force of about four thousand led by Prince Alexandr Bekovich, arrived in Khiva in 1717.

UZBEKISTAN

Life & Death under the Khans

Richmond Shakespear, who rescued Khiva's Russian slaves in 1840, left behind far more slaves than he freed, mainly Persians and Kurds. The Russian envoy Captain Nikolai Muraviev, who had travelled here in 1819, estimated there were 30,000 of these, against 3000 Russians. Most of Khiva's slaves were men. Shakespear noted that nearly all the Russians were in good health, an able Russian male slave being worth four good camels.

The khans ruled Khiva by terror, with torture and summary execution among their weapons. The Hungarian traveller Arminius Vambéry in 1863 saw eight old men lying on the ground having their eyes gouged out, their tormentor wiping his knife clean on their beards as he proceeded. Muraviev reported that impalement was a favourite method of execution, with victims taking up to two days to die (you can see pictures of other methods in the Zindon prison at the city's Kukhna Ark). He also noted that people caught smoking or drinking alcohol, which the khan of the day had forsworn, had their mouths slit open to their ears, leaving them with a permanent silly grin.

The khans extorted huge taxes from their people thanks to their ownership of the state's entire irrigation system. Nevertheless Muraviev observed that the villages outside the city were prosperous, and that Khiva's richer citizens had gardens and palaces outside the city walls. His visit came at a time when trade through Khiva was on an upswing, engendering a boom in fine buildings and decorative arts like carving, painting and tilework – especially in the 1830s and 40s under Khan Alloquli who was responsible for the lovely Tosh-Khovli Palace and the nearby caravanserai and Alloqli Khan Medressa.

The number of medressas in Khiva is testament to its past importance as a centre of Muslim theology. But this didn't stop it being an isolated place ignorant of its own weakness, with horizons that didn't stretch far beyond the rival Uzbek khanate of Bukhara. James Abbott in 1840 recorded Alloquli's boast that he had all of 20 guns, and the belief of many Khivans that the British were a sub-group of the Russians. The khans resolutely opposed modernisation and secular education, and even after the Russian annexation, Khan Mohammed Rakhim II refused to allow electricity, schools or telephones. The clergy were a conservative lot who later engineered the murder of the modernising grand vizier, Islom Huja.

Khiva's renown and infamy, far out of proportion to its real significance, were a product of its remoteness, the extreme cruelty and backwardness of its regime, and the very real dangers to outsiders who ventured there: if they survived the surrounding deserts and their marauding clansmen, their lives were subject to the khans' caprice when they finally arrived.

Unfortunately, the khan had by that time lost interest in being a vassal of the tsar. He came out to meet them, suggesting they disperse to outlying villages where they could be more comfortably accommodated. This done, the Khivans annihilated the invaders, leaving just a handful to make their way back with the news. He sent Bekovich's head to his Central Asian rival, the Emir of Bukhara, and kept the rest of him on display.

In 1740 Khiva was wrecked by a less gullible invader, Nadir Shah of Persia, and Khorezm became for a while a northern outpost of the Persian empire. By the end of the 18th century it was rebuilt and began taking a small share in the growing trade between Russia and the Bukhara and Kokand khanates. Its slave market, the biggest in Central Asia, continued unabated, augmented now by Russians captured as they pushed their borders southwards and eastwards.

The Great Game In the early 19th century Russia sent two more armies, ostensibly to free Russian slaves, though neither got anywhere near Khiva. In 1801, 22,000 Cossacks got as far as the Kazak steppes, turning back when Tsar Paul was assassinated.

The second effort, in 1839 to 1840 by order of Tsar Nicholas I, came in response to British activity in Afghanistan. Learning of this, the British sent a single man, Captain James Abbott, to Khiva with an offer to negotiate the slaves' release with the approaching Russians on Khan Alloquli's behalf, which would eliminate the Russian excuse for being there.

Again the Russians were turned back, this time by the worst winter for ages, though no-one in Khiva yet knew this. Abbott, though initially treated with suspicion, persuaded Alloquli to send him to St Petersburg with a proposal to release the slaves in return for an end to military expeditions against Khiva and the freeing of Khivan hostages held at Orenburg. Surviving attack and capture, Abbott made it all the way to St Petersburg, only to have his thunder stolen by a fellow officer sent from Herat to find out what had happened to him.

Lieutenant Richmond Shakespear reached Khiva in June 1840. He got along better with Khan Alloquli than Abbott had, and even the news of the Russians' retreat did him no harm since the khan feared they might try again. Shakespear persuaded him to release all the Russian slaves in Khiva and even to give them an armed escort to Fort Alexandrovsk (present-day Fort Shevchenko in Kazakstan), a Russian outpost on the eastern Caspian. He delivered the 416 freed slaves to Russia, amid astonishment and rejoicing, obtained the release of 600 Khivans, and was personally thanked by a no doubt inwardly seething Tsar Nicholas in St Petersburg (see The Russians Arrive in the History section at the beginning of this chapter).

Russian Conquest When the Russians finally got around to sending a properly organised expedition against Khiva, it was no contest. In 1873 General Konstantin Kaufman's 13,000-strong forces advanced on Khiva from the north, west and east. After some initial guerilla resistance, mainly by Yomud Turkmen tribesmen, Khan Mohammed Rakhim II surrendered unconditionally.

To give his men a bit of action, Kaufman then indulged in a massacre of the Yomud. The khan became a vassal of the tsar and his silver throne was packed off to Russia. Khiva was not permitted an army of its own, while the Russians set up a big garrison at nearby Petro-Alexandrovsk (modern Turtkul).

The enfeebled khanate struggled on until 1920 when the Bolshevik general Mikhail Frunze installed the 'Khorezm People's Republic' in its place. This, like a similar republic in Bukhara, was theoretically independent of the USSR. But its leaders swung away from socialism towards Pan-Turkism, and in 1924 their republic was absorbed into the new Uzbek SSR.

Orientation & Information

The old city, the Ichon-Qala, still surrounded by its centuries-old walls, is in the southern part of a much bigger Soviet town. Transport from Urgench will probably take you straight to the Ichon-Qala's main entrance, the West Gate. Most sights are around its main axis, the former ulitsa Karla Marxa, running between the West and East gates.

Khiva's dusty bus station is on the Urgench road on the northern edge of town. From an intersection just to its south, ulitsa Gagarina runs 1.5km south to the Navoi cinema at the corner with Mustaqillik kuchasi (formerly ulitsa Lenina). About 150m east on Mustaqillik is the north-west corner of Ichon-Qala. The West Gate is 400m south and the North Gate 200m east.

The Khiva map with a colour picture of the Islom-Huja minaret, commonly sold at the West Gate, has the street plan printed upside down, leaving all the key numbers and street names in the wrong places.

Ichon-Qala Gates & Walls

The main entrance to the Ichon-Qala is the twin-turreted brick West Gate (Ota-darvoza, literally 'Father Gate'), a 1970s reconstruction – the original was wrecked in 1920. The picturesque 2.5km-long mud walls date from the 18th century, rebuilt after being wrecked by the Persians. The north-west sector, which greets approaching tourists, has been fully restored in recent decades;

other stretches are in a more tumble-down state. The walls also have North, East and South gates, respectively Buhoro-darvoza (Bukhara Gate), Polvon-darvoza (Strongman's Gate) and Tosh-darvoza (Stone Gate), as well as about forty bastions.

The first building on your right inside the West Gate is the **Mohammed Amin Khan Medressa**, built in the 1850s and serving since Soviet times as the Hotel Khiva (see Places to Stay). It's a nice enough building, with two storeys of cells around a broad courtyard, and certainly an exotic setting to lay your head, but it's not one of Khiva's major architectural highlights.

Outside stands the fat, turquoise-tiled **Kalta Minor minaret**, built at the same time and looking like it was originally meant to be far taller, which would have made it much higher than Bukhara's Kalon minaret.

Kukhna Ark

Opposite Mohammed Amin Khan stands the Kukhna Ark – the Khiva rulers' own fortress and residence, first built in the 12th century by one Oq Shihbobo, then expanded by the khans in the 17th century. The khans' harem, mint, stables, arsenal, barracks, mosque and jail were all here. Only parts have been restored.

The squat protuberance by the entrance, on the east side of the building, is the **Zindon** (Khans' Jail), with a display of chains, manacles and weapons, and pictures of people being chucked off minarets, stuffed into sacks full of wild cats, etc.

Inside the Ark, the first passage to the right takes you into the 19th century **Summer Mosque**, open-air and beautiful with superb blue and white plant-motif tiling and a red, orange and gold roof. Beside it is the old **mint**, now a museum that includes money printed on silk.

Ahead from the Ark entrance is another restored building that some say was the harem, but which its present guardians maintain was the **throne room**, where khans dispensed judgement (if not justice). The circular area on the ground was for the royal yurt, which the no-longer-nomadic khans still liked to use. It's said that if a victim

was ordered through the right-hand door behind this, it meant death; the left door meant freedom and the middle door, jail.

To the right of the throne room, a door in the wall gives onto a flight of steps up to the **Oq Shihbobo bastion**, the original part of the Kukhna Ark, set right against the Ichon-Qala's massive west wall. At the top is an open-air pavilion with good views over the Ark and Ichon-Qala.

Mohammed Rakhim Khan Medressa

Facing the Kukhna Ark, across an open space that was once a busy palace square (and place of execution), this 19th century medressa (Mukhammad Rakhimhon madrasasi) is named after Khan Mohammed Rakhim II. A hotch-potch of a museum within is partly dedicated to this khan, who surrendered to Russia in 1873 but had, after all, kept Khiva independent a few years longer than Bukhara. The khan was also a poet under the pen name Feruz.

Khiva's token camel stands burping and farting outside the medressa's south wall, waiting for tourists to ride it or pose with it.

Sayid Alauddin Mausoleum & Music Museum

Back on the south side of the main east-west axis (formerly Karla Marxa), beside the medressa housing Restoran Khiva, is the small, plain Sayid Alauddin mausoleum dating to 1310, when Khiva was under the Golden Horde of the Mongol empire. You may find people praying in front of the 19th century tiled sarcophagus.

To the east is a Music Museum in the 1905 Qozi-Kalon Medressa.

Juma Mosque & Around

East of the Music Museum, the large Juma Mosque is interesting for the 218 wooden columns supporting its roof – a concept thought to be derived from ancient Arabian mosques. The few finely decorated columns are from the original 10th century mosque, though the present building dates from the 18th century. From inside, you can climb the 81 very dark steps of the Juma minaret.

Opposite the Juma Mosque is the 1905 **Matpana Bay Medressa** (Abdullahon madrasasi), containing a museum devoted to nature, history, religion and the medressa itself. Behind this are the 17th century **Arabhana Medressa** and the 19th century **Dost Alyam Medressa**.

East of the Juma mosque, the 1855 **Abdulla Khan Medressa** holds a missable nature museum. The little **Aq Mosque** dates from 1657, the same year as the **Anusha Khan baths** (Anushahon hammomi) by the entrance to the long tunnel of the East Gate.

Alloquli Khan Medressa, Bazar & Caravanserai

The street leading north opposite the Aq Mosque contains some of Khiva's most interesting buildings, most of them created by Khan Alloquli in the 1830s and 40s – a testament to the wealth that Russian trade brought Khiva during his reign. First come the tall **Alloquli Khan Medressa** (1835) and the earlier **Kutlimurodinok Medressa** (1809), facing each other across the street, with matching tiled facades. Down a few steps under a small dome in the Kutlimurodinok's courtyard is an old drinking-water tank (don't try the water!).

North of the Alloquli Khan Medressa and built in the same year are the **Alloqulihon bazar and caravanserai** (Alloquli Khan Saroy-bozori va Karvon-saroyi). The entrance to both is through tall wooden gates, beside the medressa, which are closed from early to late afternoon. The bazar is a domed market arcade, still catering to traders, which opens on to Khiva's modern bazar, outside the Ichon-Qala walls, at its east end. The caravanserai, entered from the bazar arcade, was a travellers' inn with a large courtyard where traders could also sell their wares. Today the caravanserai houses Khiva's department store. Both the arcade and store have some quite attractive cheap pottery.

Tosh-Khovli Palace

Tosh-Khovli (Stone House), facing the caravanserai, contains Khiva's most sumptuous interior decoration, including ceramic tiles, carved stone and wood, and ghanch. Built by Alloquli Khan between 1832 and 1841 as a more splendid alternative to the Kukhna Ark, it's said to have over 150 rooms off nine courtyards, with high ceilings designed to catch any breeze. Alloquli was a man in a hurry – the Tosh-Khovli's first architect was executed for failing to complete the job in two years.

Only parts of the building are open. The biggest courtyard, immediately inside the entrance in the five recesses on the south side, is the **harem**, bedecked with gorgeous geometrical-motif tiles. The five recesses on its south side have beautiful bright patterned ceilings, held up by carved wooden pillars. The rooms off the harem's south-west corner hold craft exhibits. To see the other two main courtyards you'll probably have to ask the door attendants and pay a small fee. The **Ishrot-Khovli** was a ceremonial and banqueting hall with, like the Kukhna Ark, circles for yurts. The **Arz-Khovli** was a court of judgement, with one exit door kept exclusively for people condemned to death.

East Gate & Modern Bazar

The East Gate is a long, vaulted 19th century passage with several sets of immense carved doors. The slave market was held around here, and niches in the passage walls once held slaves for sale. Outside are a small working mosque and the long modern bazar (mostly food) on the left.

Islom-Huja Medressa

From the East Gate, go back to the Abdulla Khan Medressa and take the lane to the south beside it, to the Islom-Huja Medressa and minaret – Khiva's newest Islamic monuments, both built in 1910. The **minaret**, with bands of turquoise and red tiling, looks rather like an uncommonly lovely lighthouse. At 45m tall, it's Khiva's highest. You can climb its 118 steps for fine views across the Karakum desert.

The medressa holds Khiva's best museum, of Khorezm handicrafts through the ages – fine woodcarving, metalwork, jewellery, books, Uzbek and Turkmen carpets, pottery, stone carved with Arabic script (which was in use in Khorezm from the 8th to the 20th centuries), and large pots called *hum* for storing food underground.

Islom Huja himself was an early 20th century grand vizier and, by Khivan standards, a liberal: he founded a European-style school, brought long-distance telegraph to the city, and built a hospital. For his popularity, the khan and clergy had him assassinated.

Pahlavon Mohammed Mausoleum & Sherghozi Khan Medressa

Along the street west from the Islom-Huja minaret, this is Khiva's most revered mausoleum and, with its lovely courtyard and stately tilework, one of the town's most beautiful spots. Pahlavon Mohammed was a poet, philosopher and legendary wrestler who became Khiva's patron saint. His 1326 tomb was rebuilt in the 19th century and then requisitioned in 1913 by the khan of the day as the family mausoleum.

The beautiful Persian-style chamber under the turquoise dome at the north end of the courtyard holds the tomb of Khan Mohammed Rakhim II who ruled from 1865 to 1910. Leave your shoes at the entrance. Pahlavon Mohammed's tomb, to the left off the first chamber, has some of Khiva's loveliest tiling on the sarcophagus and the walls. Pilgrims press coins and notes through the grille that shields the tomb. Tombs of other khans stand unmarked east and west of the main building, outside the courtyard.

The 18th century Sherghozi Khan Medressa across the street holds a museum of ancient medicine. The khan it's named after was killed by the slaves he forced to build it.

Dishon-Qala

The Dishon-Qala was old Khiva's outer town, outside the Ichon-Qala walls. Most of it is buried beneath the modern town now, but part of the Dishon-Qala's own wall remains, 300m south of the South Gate. One or two Dishon-Qala gates survive too. The **Isfandiyar Palace** on Gagarina was built between 1906 and 1912, and like the Summer Palace in Bukhara displays some fascinatingly overdone decorations in a messy collision of east and west. The rooms are largely bare but the florid painted ceilings and garish tiled fireplaces hint at what it must have been like.

Places to Stay

There are three official places to stay in the Ichon-Qala, and one hotel not far outside. It is possible to arrange a stay in a home in the Ichon-Qala for US$5 to US$10 with the matrons at the Islom-Huja Medressa, but be warned that if the owner of the Arqonchi finds out there could be trouble for your hosts.

Mirzoboshi B&B (☎ 37 27 53) is the venerable rambling house next to the Qozi-Kalon Medressa on the main path through the old town; the entrance is at the back. It costs US$20 with all meals, US$10 for B&B, and the friendly owner seems happy to accommodate budget travellers. It is possible to roll out a mattress and sleeping bag on the floor of the eivan over the courtyard, which has a magical view of the Juma minaret.

The family-run ***Hotel Arqonchi*** (☎ 522 30, Pahlavon Mohammed 10), behind the Hotel Khiva, has pleasant double rooms set around a courtyard garden for US$25 a person including meals and free entry to all Khivan sites. The showers don't work particularly well but the bathrooms are clean and the food is excellent. Most travellers praise the place, but the owner can be rude to shoestring travellers.

Hotel Khiva is in fact the 19th century Mohammed Amin Khan Medressa, inside the West Gate. It's been used as a hotel since Soviet times and was being remodelled at the time of research, probably to be reborn as upmarket lodgings.

About 500m north of the north gate the Uzbektourism-run ***Hotel Khorezm*** (☎ 554 51) has singles/doubles for US$27/40, plus US$15 for all meals (dinner US$6). It has reliable hot water, ensuite bathrooms and large comfortable rooms, but manages to be slightly chilly and impersonal in a way that only Uzbektourism can do.

Places to Eat

The choices are limited, frankly. The best food is at the *Hotel Arqonchi*, but you probably need to be a guest. Likewise the *Mirzo-boshi* can probably arrange meals if you give them warning. A semblance of a meal can be had in the underground chaykhana in the *Hotel Khiva*. A better option is the cluster of eateries outside the Ichon-Qala's West Gate, including the *Koop Chaykhana* across from the gate with reasonable, moderately priced food and poolside tables, a stand-up *cafe* nearby and a *chaykhana* just outside the gate. These close by late afternoon. The *Restoran Khiva* in the Matniyaz Divanbeg Medressa, just east of the Hotel Khiva, mostly seems to operate for tour groups but they might let you in. The *bazar* has fresh fruit and vegetables and a couple of *shashlyk stands*.

Getting There & Away
The easiest way between Urgench and Khiva is the 45 minute trip by marshrutnoe taxi or taxi. Marshrutnoe taxis shuttle between the street outside Urgench's bus station and the West Gate 8 am to 8 pm, leaving when they're full, for US$0.25 (or more, depending on the driver). Trolleybuses to Urgench leave from Mustaqillik (the former ulitsa Lenina) but tend to stop inconveniently short of Urgench, delivering you into the hands of waiting taxis.

A taxi is US$5. In Khiva you'll find them outside the West Gate or at the east end of the bazar outside the East Gate.

Uzbektourism's standard Khiva tour for individuals takes just three hours from Urgench, at a cost of US$50 for car and guide, plus US$5 per person in entrance fees and US$2.50 per person to take pictures (US$10 for video).

Bus and marshrutnoe taxi Nos 1 and 2 go the length of Gagarina in Khiva between Mustaqillik and the intersection near the bus station. Bus and marshrutnoe taxi No 1 will take you to the North Gate (No 2 heads away from the Ichon-Qala at Mustaqillik).

A taxi between the Ichon-Qala and the bus station is about US$0.50.

NUKUS
☎ (3) 61 • pop 180,000
If desolation attracts you, welcome to the capital of Uzbekistan's Karakalpakstan

Republic, Nukus (Karakalpak: Nökis). Developed from a small settlement since 1932, Nukus might have been a bright and hopeful place two or three decades ago. Today it tries to present itself as the proud capital of newly 'sovereign' Karakalpakstan (see the boxed text 'Karakalpakstan'), but it's actually drab, impoverished, unhealthy and forlorn, its broad avenues and big public buildings now looking like jokes in poor taste. The city outskirts melt into barren, salt-scarred wastes where camels wander aimlessly. The economy of the town, a long way from anywhere at the back end of Uzbekistan, has suffered badly since the collapse of the USSR. In Soviet times the city was also home to the Chemical Research Institute, a major research and testing site for 300 scientists working on illegal chemical weapons. The institute was abandoned in 1992, and the government has been cleaning up the site with US help.

The city's isolation also made it a safe refuge for thousands of artworks preserved here at the Karakalpakstan Art Museum.

Nukus has felt – like the rest of poor Karakalpakstan – the full force of the health and environmental disaster from irrigated

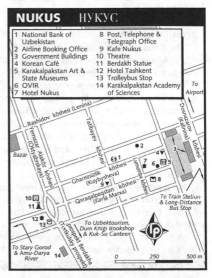

1	National Bank of Uzbekistan	8	Post, Telephone & Telegraph Office
2	Airline Booking Office	9	Kafe Nukus
3	Government Buildings	10	Theatre
4	Korean Café	11	Berdakh Statue
5	Karakalpakstan Art & State Museums	12	Hotel Tashkent
6	OVIR	13	Trolleybus Stop
7	Hotel Nukus	14	Karakalpakstan Academy of Sciences

agriculture in the Amu-Darya basin, in particular the depletion of the Aral Sea (see the Ecology & Environment section in the Facts about Central Asia chapter). In this dust-storm-prone wasteland of chemical-doused food and water, there are high rates of birth deformities, infant mortality, and diseases like cancer, typhoid, hepatitis and immune depression. Furtive drinking seems to be one of the few pleasures left to the inhabitants.

Orientation & Information

'Street' in Karakalpak is *köshesi*. The main central streets are Qaraqalpaqstan and Ghar-ezsizlik, both ending on the east at a square surrounded by government buildings. The city centre is bounded on the west by Yernazar Alaköz (which becomes prospekt Berdakha south of Qaraqalpaqstan) and on the east by Dosnazarov. The airport is north of the centre on Dosnazarov, and the train station and most useful long-distance bus stop about 3km from the centre at Dosnazarov's south end.

Russian street names have been replaced by Karakalpak ones on most signs, but Russian ones are still more familiar to most. Uzbektourism (☎ 709 14, 443 81, fax 714 07,

Karakalpakstan

The Republic of Karakalpakstan is Uzbekistan's biggest 'province', its 165,000 sq km occupying the whole western end of the country. Much of the fertile but environmentally blighted Amu-Darya delta lies in Karakalpakstan, and is home to most of the republic's population.

Karakalpakstan gets its name from the Karakalpak people whose homeland it is – though they number only about 400,000 of its 1.2 million population. It's also home to about 400,000 Uzbeks and 300,000 Kazaks. The Karakalpaks are a formerly nomadic and fishing people, first recorded in the 16th century and now struggling to recapture a national identity after being collectivised or urbanised in Soviet times. (In her book, *Turkestan Solo*, Ella Maillart gives a glimpse of Karakalpakstan in the early years of Soviet rule, when she travelled through by river boat and camel – see Books in the Regional Facts for the Visitor chapter).

The name Karakalpak means 'Black Hat People' but such has been their cultural decline that the Karakalpaks have had to set up a research project to find out just what this black hat was. Since the break-up of the USSR, there have been rumblings of nationalist discontent against Uzbek rule.

The Karakalpak language – now the official language of the republic – is Turkic, close to Kazak and less so to Uzbek. Its alphabet, written in modified Cyrillic since Soviet times, was due to switch over in 1996 to a modified Roman alphabet.

Life can never have been very easy here, though the Amu-Darya delta has supported irrigation-based agriculture for probably four thousand years, and Khorezm (the historical name for the delta area) has at times attained considerable importance and prosperity. Cotton, rice and melons are Karakalpakstan's main products. Tahiatash, 20km south-east of Nukus on the Amu-Darya, has a big hydroelectric station supplying the whole of Karakalpakstan plus Horazm province of Uzbekistan and the Dashoguz region of Turkmenistan.

One thing you'll see a lot of is camels, used less as a means of transport than for their milk, meat and hides.

Karakalpakstan was probably at its most prosperous in the 1960s and 70s when the fruits of expanded irrigation from the Amu-Darya were coming on stream, and before the disastrous effects of that same expansion were felt. But the republic has borne the brunt of the environmental, economic and health problems that have taken hold since then, and today the age-old oasis of rivers, lakes, reed beds, marshes, forests and farmland that constitute the Amu-Darya delta is being steadily dried up and poisoned. It's really one of the saddest places on the planet.

777 69 Attn Uzbektourism) is at prospekt Berdakha 48, 1km south of the Hotel Tashkent. The staff are keen to interest foreigners in Karakalpakstan and will set up excursions to almost anywhere. OVIR is at the east end of Qaraqalpaqstan by the museum.

You can change money at the National Bank on Gharezsizlik, which can provide US dollars on Visa credit cards and travellers cheques as long as they have dollars in cash. Street moneychangers will approach you outside the bazar.

The post, telephone and telegraph office is on Qaraqalpaqstan opposite the Hotel Nukus.

Museums

The Karakalpakstan Art Museum and State Museum are in the same building at the east end of Qaraqalpaqstan.

The **Art Museum** upstairs is an Aladdin's Cave of stunning Russian and Uzbek art on the lost period between 1918 and the late 1930s. Stalin tried to erase all of the non-Socialist art from this period, but the sheer isolation of Nukus helped the remarkable archaeologist, ethnographer and artist Igor Savitksy preserve this world-class collection. Many of the artists were sent to the gulags.

Paintings from landscapes to Cubist and Surrealist works cover nearly every available wall, and are still only a fraction of the over eighty thousand items that Savitsky rescued from oblivion. The collection was barely known until the Soviet Union collapsed, and the museum has had to struggle through with little official support since. There are replicas of paintings on sale, plus works by local artists and some handicrafts.

The curator Marinika Bobonazarova speaks English and can give a guided tour, as can some of the junior art historians on staff. They can also help arrange home-stays.

In the **State Museum** there are interesting displays on the fauna and flora of the Karakalpakstan region, including the Karakai desert cat, goitred gazelle *(geran)*, saiga antelope, wild boar *(kaban)*, cheetah *(gepard)* and Bukhara deer. The very last Turan (or Caspian) tiger, killed in 1972, stands stuffed and mounted in a corner. There are also displays on the Aral Sea and local health problems, on archaeology and early history, and of traditional jewellery, costumes, musical instruments and yurt decorations.

The third branch of the museum is the **Museum of Applied Arts**, with Karakalpak handicrafts, traditional dress and jewellery. It's a few hundred metres away. All the museums are open daily except Sunday 9 am to 1 pm and 2 to 5 pm, and they're well worth a look. Entry is US$1 in *sum*.

Other Things to See

A **statue of Berdakh**, the Karakalpaks' 19th century cultural guru, poet and thinker, stands outside the theatre opposite the Hotel Tashkent. The building with the big boiled egg on top and a statue of Ulughbek out the front, on prospekt Berdakha just south of the Hotel Tashkent, is the **Karakalpakstan Academy of Sciences**.

The **Amu-Darya river** curves around the west side of town, 3km from the centre. To see it, head west on Qaraqalpaqstan. The area on the right after you cross a wide canal (not the river) is pre-1932 Nukus – **Stary Gorod** (Old Town) in Russian. A pontoon bridge crosses the Amu-Darya, providing a short cut for drivers to Hojeli. You can judge the river's former breadth from the trees and buildings now set far back from its banks.

Special Events

Karakalpaks apparently still play the wild Central Asian polo-like game – with a goat carcass instead of a ball, and teams of dozens of riders – which they call *ylaq oyyny*. This and other traditional sports like wrestling, ram-fighting and cock-fighting are included in Nukus' **Pakhta-Bairam** (cotton) harvest festival in December.

Places to Stay & Eat

There are two hotels, one of which is actually pretty good.

The newly renovated *Hotel Nukus (☎ 217 88 00)* on Lumumba between Qaraqalpaqstan and Gharezsizlik has clean, comfortable singles/doubles for US$6 and triples for US$10. There is also a mini-apartment for four people with a kitchen for US$30. A restaurant is planned as well. Even before it opens, they should be able to rustle up some food if you give them notice.

The towering and largely empty *Hotel Tashkent* (☎ 213 13 67) at the corner of prospekt Berdakha and Qaraqalpaqstan has spartan but clean singles/doubles for US$8 /18 in *sum*, and no water supply. For once it actually looks better on the inside than the outside. The manager laments how far the hotel has fallen since the days when it was the lodgings of choice for party officials who used the 'secret' bar in the basement. The restaurant block is barely functioning. The ground floor bar has decent coffee and the odd snack.

Nukus is definitely not a culinary capital. Close to the museum is a *Korean cafe* with simple but palatable noodle dishes for US$1 in *sum*. The Korean *Kuk-Su* canteen is on prospekt Berdakha, about 2.5km south of the Hotel Tashkent. A decent bowl of noodles, vegetables and meat, with bread and tea, costs US$0.35. From the Hotel Tashkent, take a ЖД Вокзал or Т ЖВокзал trolleybus south on prospekt Berdakha for about seven stops, getting off before Berdakha climbs onto a bridge. The Kuk-Su has a blue door on the west side of the street; enter at the side. It's open till 6 pm.

Kafe Nukus on Qaraqalpaqstan at the corner with Tatibayev is another possibility. There's a sizable *bazar* 500m north of the Hotel Tashkent along Yernazar Alaköz.

Getting There & Away

The only flights are to/from Tashkent (US$20, four daily). The airline booking office is set back from Gharezsizlik köshesi, opposite the Hotel Nukus.

Buses to Tashkent, Urgench and Moynaq go from the yard in front of the train station *(avtovokzal)* at the south end of Dosnazarov – not from the bus station, 7km away at the north end of town (but bus No 15 runs between the two if you get confused). Buses leave for Urgench and Moynaq (both US$1, three to four hours, twice daily) and Tashkent (US$8, 20 hours, daily) via Bukhara and Samarkand. If Urgench buses are not running, try changing at Hojeli, 15km west of Nukus.

For trians, Nukus is currently on a branch line with daily trains to/from Tashkent, via Hojeli, Dashoguz and Urgench. Nukus is about four hours from Urgench. A new line is being built to connect the city with Uchquduq and thus bypass Turkmenistan. In the meantime the train to Tashkent is the easiest and cheapest way to cross into Turkmenistan, stopping at Dashoguz and Turkmenabat, although you will need a Turken transit visa.

Given the vagaries of public transport, taxis may have advantages for some long trips. To Moynaq and back, figure on US$50. If you can't find a willing taxi, try outside the train station or the Hotel Tashkent.

Getting Around

Bus No 3 runs between the airport and the bazar. A taxi between the airport and the centre is under US$1.

To reach the centre from the train station, take any trolleybus from the west end of the station yard (to the left as you exit the station). From the centre to the station, take a Ж Д Вокзал or Т Ж Вокзал trolleybus south on prospekt Berdakha by the Hotel Tashkent.

HOJELI
☎ (3) 61 • pop 55,000

Hojeli (Uzbek: Hujayli, Russian: Khodzheyli), 15km west of Nukus, is Karakalpakstan's second city. It's a local transport hub and otherwise a mundane place, apart from the atmospheric holy site of ancient Mizdakhan, on a hill 4km south-west of town beside the road to Konye-Urgench. Mizdakhan was a big Khorezm trading centre, inhabited from the 4th century BCE until Timur's coming. Even then it remained a sacred place, and tombs and mosques continued to be built there right up to the 20th century. Karakalpak cultural festivals are sometimes held here.

The hill is littered with ruined and intact mausolea, mosques and medressas from the 11th to 20th centuries, of which the most impressive is the restored **mausoleum of Mazlum Khan Slu**, dating from the 12th to 14th centuries. On the neighbouring hill towards Konye-Urgench are the remains of a 4th to 3rd century BCE fortress called Gyaur-Qala.

Nukus and Urgench buses use a new station on the edge of town, going to Nukus every 20 minutes until 5.50 pm, and to Konye-Urgench every 45 minutes until 2.15 pm. They can be very crowded, and taxis at the station nonexistent. More taxis are at the old bus station (Russian: *staryy avtovokzal*), reached by bus No 4 from the new station, or at the train station, a five minute walk off bus No 4 route. A taxi to/from Nukus is US$2.

MOYNAQ
☎ (3) 61• pop 2000
Moynaq (Uzbek: Muynoq, Russian: Muynak), 210km north of Nukus, encapsulates more visibly than anywhere the absurd tragedy of the Aral Sea. Once one of the sea's two major fishing ports, it now stands at least 40km from the water. What remains of Moynaq's fishing fleet lies rusting on the sand, beside depressions marking the town's last futile efforts in the early 1980s to keep channels open to the shore.

Moynaq used to be on an isthmus connecting the Ush Say (Tiger's Tail) peninsula to the shore. You can appreciate this on the approach to the town, where the road is raised above the surrounding land. The former shore is about 3km north.

Moynaq's shrinking populace suffers the full force of the Aral Sea disaster, with hotter summers, colder winters, debilitating sand-salt-dust storms, and a gamut of health problems (see the Ecology & Environment section in the Facts about Central Asia chapter). Not surprisingly the mostly Kazak residents are deserting the town.

Things to See
Poignant reminders of Moynaq's tragedy are everywhere: the sign at the entrance to the town has a fish on it; a fishing boat stands as a kind of monument on a makeshift pedestal at the bus station.

The **beached ships** are near the Niftibaza (a gas storage facility). Locals, seemingly embarrassed about them, might tell you they have been taken away for scrap, but plenty are still there. Head up the ramshackle main street for about 3km from the bus station and turn right just before the Kinoteatr Berdakh cinema, then fork left just after an electricity substation. About 2km along this track you'll see the ships poking up from the sands to your left. It's all rather unearthly.

Back beside the Kinoteatr Berdakh, the main road leads 2km out of town to a **war memorial** at the top of a small hill with cliffs along the former seashore. Looking back over the town there is a lake in the distance, created in an attempt to restore the formerly mild local climate.

Past the memorial the track continues 3km or so to a group of desolate buildings that were once **beach installations**. The wind through the bushes sounds eerily like waves on a shore.

Places to Stay
If you're stuck in Moynaq, there's the *Hotel Oybek*, a two storey building set back to the right of the main street a short distance past the Kinoteatr Berdakh. The very spartan rooms (with toilets outside) are US$1.50/3 in *sum*. Food can be provided for US$3 per day.

Getting There & Away
The bus station is at the south end of the long main street. Decrepit buses run twice daily between Moynaq and Nukus (US$1, three to four hours), departing both towns at 9 am and 3 pm. It isn't really feasible to take the morning bus from Nukus, walk out to the stranded boats and still catch the 3 pm bus back. A taxi is easier; a day trip from Nukus costs about US$50, US$100 from Urgench. The drive is across salt-scarred cotton fields at first, then a bizarre mix of marshes, waterlogged fields and desert – the unnatural result of the irrigation schemes. At Qonghyrat, about halfway, there is a basic roadside cafe, and a bazar.

Kyrgyzstan

Kyrgyzstan at a Glance

Official Name: Kyrgyz Republic
(*Kyrgyz Respublikasi*)
Area: 198,500 sq km
Population: 4.92 million (2000 estimate)
Ethnic Mix: 61% Kyrgyz, 15% Russian,
14% Uzbek, 1.5% Ukrainian, 1% Tatar, 1%
Dungan, 1% Uyghur, 1% Tajik, 1% Kazak,
3.5% Others
Capital: Bishkek
Currency: som
Country ☎ Code: 996
Best Time to Go: May to September

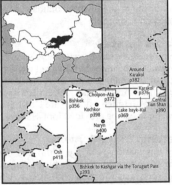

- **Lake Issyk-Kul** – the second-highest
  lake in the world

- **Altyn Arashan** – a beautiful alpine
  valley, perfect base for the Tian Shan

- **Osh Bazar** – one of the most eclectic
  bazars in Central Asia

- **Song-Köl** – a lakeside dotted with
  yurts and herders

- **Torugart Pass** – the most exciting
  (and frustrating) way into or out of
  Central Asia

- **Inylchek Glacier** – a stunning helicopter ride to the base of Khan Tengri

What Kyrgyzstan lacks in settled history it
makes up for in a wealth of nomadic traditions, including laid-back hospitality and a
healthy distrust of authority. What it lacks in
development it makes up for in determination. What it lacks in historical architecture
it more than makes up for in Central Asia's
finest mountain 'architecture' – the highest
and most dramatic parts of the central Tian
Shan and Pamir Alay ranges. When you tire
of Uzbekistan's *shashlyk* and *chaykhana*
(teahouses), trade them in for a night in a
yurt and a horse trek into the mountains of
Kyrgyzstan.

In Soviet times, because it also appealed
as a site for military development, most of
the country was closed to foreigners. The
Tian Shan abounds in uranium and other
valuable metals, although investment is low,
and secret mining towns grew at the heads
of remote valleys: Mayluu-Suu above the
Fergana valley, Ming-Kush in the interior,
Kaji-Say at Lake Issyk-Kul. Their imported
Russian workers were well provisioned and
well paid. Issyk-Kul itself was the perfect
place for naval weapons development, from
a top-secret research complex at its eastern
end. But independent Kyrgyzstan has closed
most of the mines and institutes (and begun
to grapple with the environmental health
problems they created), and Kyrgyz are
gradually replacing the departing Russians.

The collapse of the USSR has left this
tiny, underequipped republic out on a limb,
seemingly without the resources to survive
on its own. So far it is getting by on pluck,
a liberal agenda surprisingly free of self-
interest, and goodwill from western donor
countries. It is doing more than any other
Central Asian republic to encourage and
simplify tourism, at least partly because this
is one of the few things it has to sell to the
outside world.

It has some way to go; away from Bishkek, Issyk-Kul and a few parts of the high
Tian Shan, Kyrgyzstan is not yet very
switched on to the needs of tourists. Many

smaller cities lack the resources to deal with decaying soviet-era hotels, limited transport and growing crime, driven by alcohol and desperate poverty. And still, at every turn you will find a family offering to put you up for the night, or a group of herdsmen who will eagerly invite you into their yurt for a cup of tea and a bowl of fresh yoghurt. Most travellers vote this the most appealing, accessible and welcoming of the former Soviet Central Asian republics.

The capital, Bishkek, is a pleasant, leafy, cosmopolitan base from which to start, with 'alps' right in its backyard. Osh is one of Central Asia's oldest and most significant towns, with one of its most exciting markets. Arguably the biggest attraction is Lake Issyk-Kul and the adjacent Terskey Alatau range at the edge of the Tian Shan. And the Torugart pass is certainly the most challenging and spectacular way to cross to/from China.

Facts about Kyrgyzstan

HISTORY
The earliest notable residents of what is now Kyrgyzstan were warrior clans of Saka (also known as Scythians), from about the 6th century BCE (before common era) to the 5th century CE (common era). Alexander the Great met perhaps the stiffest resistance in his 4th century BCE advance through Central Asia from Scythian (Saka) clans. Rich bronze and gold relics have been recovered from Scythian burial mounds at Lake Issyk-Kul and in southern Kazakstan.

The region was under the control of various Turkic alliances from the 6th to 10th centuries. A sizeable population lived on the shores of Lake Issyk-Kul. The Talas valley in southern Kazakstan and north-west Kyrgyzstan was the scene of a pivotal battle in 751, when the Turks and their Arab and Tibetan allies drove a large Tang Chinese army out of Central Asia.

The cultured Turkic Karakhanids (who finally brought Islam to Central Asia for good) ruled here in the 10th to 12th centuries. One of their multiple capitals was at Balasagun (now Burana, east of Bishkek). Another major Karakhanid centre was at Özgön (Uzgen) at the edge of the Fergana valley.

Ancestors of today's Kyrgyz people probably lived in Siberia's upper Yenisey basin until at least the 10th century, when under the influence of Mongol incursions they began migrating south into the Tian Shan – more urgently with the rise of Jenghiz Khan in the 13th century. Present-day Kyrgyzstan was part of the inheritance of Jenghiz's second son, Chaghatai.

Peace was shattered in 1685 by the arrival of the ruthless Mongol Oyrats of the Zhungarian empire, who drove vast numbers of Kyrgyz south into the Fergana and Pamir Alay regions and on into present-day Tajikistan. The Manchu (Qing) defeat of the Oyrats in 1758 left the Kyrgyz as de facto subjects of the Chinese, who mainly left them to their nomadic ways.

In the 18th century the feudal tentacles of the Kokand khanate, centred in Uzbekistan's Fergana valley, began to encircle them, though the feisty Kyrgyz constantly made trouble from their Tian Shan redoubts. As the Russians moved closer in the 19th century, various Kyrgyz clan leaders made their own peace with either Russia or Kokand. Bishkek – then the Pishpek fort – fell in 1862 to a combined Russian-Kyrgyz force. Russian forces slowly rolled over the towns of Kokand, their advance culminating in the defeat of Tashkent in 1865. The Kyrgyz were gradually eased into the tsar's provinces of Fergana and Semireche.

The new masters then began to hand land over to Russian settlers, and the Kyrgyz put up with it until a revolt in 1916, centred on Tokmak and heavily put down by the Russian army. Out of a total of 768,000 Kyrgyz, 120,000 were killed in the ensuing massacres and another 120,000 fled to China. Kyrgyz lands became part of the Turkestan Autonomous Soviet Socialist Republic (ASSR) within the Russian Federation in 1918, then a separate Kara-Kyrgyz Autonomous Oblast (an *oblast* is a province or region) in 1924.

KYRGYZSTAN

KYRGYZSTAN

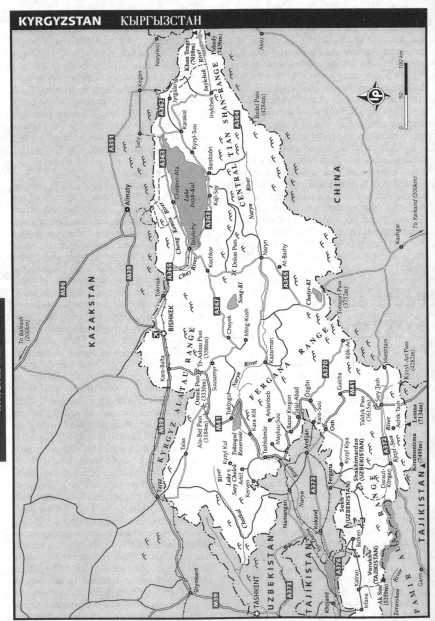

Finally, after the Russians had decided Kyrgyz and Kazaks were separate nationalities (they had until then called the Kyrgyz 'Kara-Kyrgyz' or Black Kyrgyz, to distinguish them from the Kazaks, whom they called 'Kyrgyz' to avoid confusion with the Cossacks) a Kyrgyz ASSR was formed in February 1926. It became a full Soviet Socialist Republic (SSR) in December 1936, when the region was known as Soviet Kirghizia.

Many nomads were settled in the course of land reforms in the 1920s, and more were forcibly settled during the cruel collectivisation campaign in the 1930s, giving rise to a reinvigorated rebellion by the *basmachi*, Muslim guerilla fighters, for a time. Vast swathes of the new Kyrgyz elite died in the course of Stalin's purges.

In the days of *perestroika* under Mikhail Gorbachev, and despite conservative Kyrgyz leadership, several groups were founded to fight the issues of unemployment and homelessness. Some activists went so far as to seize vacant land and build houses on it. One group, Ashar (Mutual Help), soon widened its scope as an opposition movement.

Land and housing were in fact at the root of Central Asia's most infamous 'ethnic' violence, between Kyrgyz and Uzbeks in 1990 around Osh and Özgön (Uzgen), a majority-Uzbek area stuck onto Kyrgyzstan in the 1930s (see the History entry in the following Osh section), during which at least three hundred people were killed.

Elections were held in traditional Soviet rubber-stamp style to the Kyrgyz Supreme Soviet (legislature) in February 1990, with the Kyrgyz Communist Party (KCP) walking away with nearly all the seats. KCP First Secretary Absamat Masaliev was made chairman but, discredited by the Osh violence, failed to get the nod the following October for the new post of president. After multiple ballots a compromise candidate, Askar Akaev, a physicist and president of the Kyrgyz Academy of Sciences, was elected.

Akaev has since gone on to establish himself as a persistent reformer, restructuring the executive apparatus to suit his liberal political and economic attitudes, and instituting reforms considered the most radical in the Central Asian republics, making the other republics nervous in the process. He faced down an attempt to depose him at the time of the *putsch* in Moscow in August 1991, came out strongly against the coup and resigned from the KCP, which was soon afterward dissolved.

On 31 August 1991, the Kyrgyz Supreme Soviet reluctantly voted to declare Kyrgyzstan's independence, the first Central Asian republic to do so. Six weeks later Akaev was re-elected president, running unopposed. Though he was at first reluctant to take part in Commonwealth of Independent States (CIS) peacekeeping efforts in Tajikistan, he joined up after armed Islamic groups were alleged to have crossed from there into Kyrgyzstan in January 1993. While that conflict may set nerves jangling in Bishkek, Islamic fundamentalism is not officially seen as a serious threat here, as it is in Uzbekistan.

On 5 May 1993 a brand-new Kyrgyzstan constitution and revamped government structure became law, dispensing with the last structural vestiges of the Soviet era. Akaev and his economic program got a solid popular vote of confidence in a referendum (called by him) in January 1994.

Kyrgyzstan was woken from relative complacency in August 1999 when four Japanese geologists were taken hostage in Kyrgyzstan's southern Batken district, between the Tajik enclave of Vorukh and the Uzbek enclave of Sokh. The geologists were prospecting for gold when they were abducted by a group of several hundred Islamic militants, who were hiding out in the hills after being flushed out of Tajikistan. The militants asked for US$2 million ransom. Kyrgyzstan's Minister for Interior Security flew down to oversee the rescue operation and was himself promptly kidnapped. The hostages were finally released in October 1999, but Islamic groups remain at large on the remote Kyrgyz-Tajik border.

GEOGRAPHY

Kyrgyzstan occupies an area of 198,500 sq km, a bit larger than Austria plus Hungary, about 94% of which is mountainous. The country's average elevation is 2750m. About 40% of it is over 3000m high, with three-quarters of that under permanent snow and glaciers.

The dominant feature is the Tian Shan range in the south-east. Its crest, the dramatic Kokshal-Tau, forms a stunning natural border with China, culminating at Pik Pobedy (7439m), Kyrgyzstan's highest point and the second-highest peak in the former USSR. The Fergana range across the middle of the country and the Pamir Alay in the south hold the Fergana valley in a scissor-grip.

In a vast indentation on the fringes of the Tian Shan, Lake Issyk-Kul, almost 700m deep, never freezes. One of the country's lacustrine jewels is tiny Song-Köl lake, in a smaller pocket to the south-west. Kyrgyzstan's only significant lowland features are the Chuy and Talas valleys, adjacent to Kazakstan. Its main rivers are the Naryn, flowing almost the full length of the country into the Syr-Darya in the Fergana valley, and the Chuy along the Kazakstan border. The Ak Shyrak, Inylchek and Sary Jaz rivers in the mountainous south-east flow into China's Tarim basin. The Kyzyl-Suu river in the far south of the republic is the only river to flow into the Amu-Darya (Oxus).

The mountains effectively isolate the country's northern and southern population centres from one another, especially in winter. A major road links them over two 3000m-plus passes, but a train journey between them means going around via Tashkent. There has been talk of building a trans-Kyrgyzstan railway, though it's hard to see this happening for decades.

CLIMATE

The climate of this mountainous region is influenced by its distance from the sea and the sharp change of elevation from neighbouring plains. Conditions vary from permanent snow in high-altitude cold deserts to hot deserts in the lowlands. From the end of June through mid-August most afternoons will reach 32°C or higher, with a maximum of 40°C, though mountain valleys are considerably cooler. Average annual precipitation is 380mm, but there's rain on less than

half the days of the year. Like most of the region, Bishkek gets most of its rainfall in spring and early summer.

During the winter months (November to February) about 40 days will be below freezing, with an average minimum of -24°C, which is most likely to occur in January when the cold winds blow in from Siberia. Snowfalls are common in Bishkek with snow remaining on the ground for days. During the cooler months (October to March) Bishkek is often covered by fog when the higher slopes behind the city are clear and sunny.

GOVERNMENT & POLITICS

Under the terms of the May 1993 constitution, legislative power belongs to the parliament, the Jogorku Kenesh or Supreme Council. In September 1994 the parliament failed to obtain a quorum when only about one-quarter of the deputies came to work; this eventually led to the creation of a smaller, two-chamber legislature. All new members were elected to the legislature in February 1995.

In its revamped form the Supreme Council consists of two chambers, a 35-seat standing Legislative Assembly elected nationally and a 70-seat People's Assembly based on regional representation. All members are elected to five-year terms. (Three MPs were arrested for corruption in 1999.) The south is represented by 48 deputies compared to the north's 57, guaranteeing the north control of central decision-making. A 1996 referendum expanded the powers of the president at the expense of the legislature.

The president, who is head of state, is also directly elected for a five year term. He appoints the prime minister, who forms the Cabinet of Ministers. The next elections are due to take place in 2000.

For administrative purposes the country is divided into seven oblasts or *duban*s (provinces). Local self-government is executed through local councils called *keneshes*.

ECONOMY

Agriculture – mainly farming and livestock raising – has traditionally accounted for about one-third of the country's production and employs about one-third of the workforce. (Kyrgyz are outnumbered almost three to one by their livestock). Only about 7% of the land is arable (and most of it needs irrigation); the major crops are grains, vegetables, fruit, cotton and tobacco (and some 600,000 hectares of walnut groves).

The government has gone a long way towards privatisation of agriculture but has seen a simultaneous drop in productivity. It's hoped that the introduction of inheritable leaseholds and the further break-up of collective farms and grazing lands may provide a sense of proprietorship and give the agricultural sector a boost.

Industry (mainly mining, hydroelectric power generation, agricultural machinery, food processing, electronics and textiles) accounts for about one-quarter of production, employing 27% of workers.

Kyrgyzstan has some important mineral resources, including coal, gold, uranium and other strategic metals. The Kyrgyz-Canadian gold mining company Kumtor single-handedly produces 18% of the republic's GDP. There has been a catastrophic fall in coal output in recent years, testaments to which can be witnessed in the deserted slag heaps and depressed economies around towns like Tashkömür and Mayluu-Suu. Kyrgyzstan has few gas or oil reserves of its own, depending heavily on imports and suffering for it after the Soviet collapse. Its mountain rivers offer vast hydro-power potential, though so far this only fulfils about 25% of its requirements, and expanded development will inevitably collide with environmental considerations. Uranium mining in Soviet times has left a fearsome legacy of untended tailings, contaminated water supplies and health problems that are only just becoming understood. Still, the country's reserves of fresh water, locked up in the form of glaciers, remain its greatest natural resource.

Despite the fastest privatisation program and the most liberal attitudes in Central Asia, Kyrgyzstan still has the region's shakiest economy. Between 1990 and 1996 industrial production fell by 64%, dragging the economy back to the levels of the 1970s when it was one of the lowest in the USSR.

Kyrgyzstan currently owes Moscow over US$130 million. Only in 1996 did the economy stop shrinking.

Unemployment is rife (estimated at 20% in 1998), and the average monthly wage is currently about US$55 in Bishkek, less than half this in the countryside. The banking system remains fairly primitive, offering only short-term loans suitable to a 'kiosk economy'.

Tightly integrated into the old Soviet system, Kyrgyzstan hung onto the rouble a little too long, and the Russian economic collapse dragged the republic down with it. Recent economic crises in Asia and Russia (again) have further stunted economic growth. The sudden introduction of the Kyrgyz som in May 1993 plunged Kyrgyzstan into conflict with Uzbekistan and Kazakstan, still then in the 'rouble zone'. In July 1994, however, all three cemented a closer economic union and in 1996 Kyrgyzstan joined a customs union with Kazakstan, Belarus and Russia, the first step to some kind of Central Asian common market.

POPULATION & PEOPLE

There is a total of 80 ethnic groups in Kyrgyzstan, plus up to 16,000 Tajik refugees.

Since 1989 there has been a major exodus of Slavs and Germans (see the Peoples of the Silk Road section in the Facts about Central Asia chapter) – more than 200,000 Russians and at least 75% of all Germans between 1989 and 1998 – amid dire forecasts of its economic effects. At its peak in 1993, 130,000 people left Kyrgyzstan, of whom 90,000 were Russians. Among the leavers was one of Akaev's closest allies, the Russian First Deputy Prime Minister, German Kuznetsov.

The country's largest cities are Bishkek (800,000), Osh (300,000), Jalal-Abad (74,000), Tokmak (71,000), Toktogul (70,000) and Karakol (64,000). About two-thirds of the population lives in rural areas.

The geographically isolated southern provinces of Osh and Jalal-Abad have more in common with the conservative, Islamised Fergana valley than of the industrialised, Russified north. Over 55% of the republic's population live in these two provinces, on

Manas – the Kyrgyz National Epic

The *Manas* epics have been called the 'Iliad of the steppes'. They are a collection of tales, 20 times as long as the *Odyssey*, which tell of the formation of the Kyrgyz people. They did not merely transplant their tradition from the classical world; *Manas*, acclaimed as one of the finest of all epic traditions, is the product and highpoint of a widespread Central Asian oral culture.

The super-hero of the poems is the khan, or *batyr*, Manas. The narrative revolves around his exploits in carving out a homeland for his people in the face of hostile hordes. (Subsequent stories deal with the exploits of his son Semety and grandson Seitek). Manas is of course big, strong, brave, and a born leader; he is also, to an important extent, the embodiment of the Kyrgyz' self-image.

This is how a 20th century *manaschi* (*akyn* or bard who improvises from the Manas cycle of legends) sends Manas' swarming armies off on a warring campaign, and how the bantamweight Kyrgyz propagate their endearing, larger-than-life national élan through the archaic medium of epic:

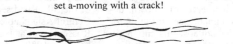

> Not a space there was between flag and standard;
> the earth's surface could not be seen!
> Not a space there was between banner and standard;
> the range of the Altay could not be seen!
> Points of lances gleamed; men's heads bobbed;
> the earth swayed on the point of collapse.
> Flags on golden standards fluttered,
> and a ground-splitting din was heard...
> The army, marching with a terrible noise,
> was greater than the eyes could take in –
> eyes were bowed with all the looking!
> Black plains, grey hills,
> the face of the earth was beaten down!
> Coats of mail all a-glitter,
> racers and chargers bursting forth neighing...
> the enormous warrior host
> set a-moving with a crack!

Unfortunately, visitors to Kyrgyzstan are lucky indeed to hear a manaschi in performance. There are few left. Latter-day bards wear sequined costumes and recite short, memorised snippets of the great songs in auditoriums. Traditionally the illiterate bards would belt out their epics in yurts, to enthralled audiences for whom the shifting, artful improvisations on timeworn themes were radio, television, rap music, performance poetry and myth rolled into one,

less than 15% of the land. Many feel underrepresented by the government in Bishkek. Ancient but still-important clan affiliations reinforce these regional differences. In a recent survey, 63.5% of Kyrgyz people thought that north-south contradictions were the main destabilising factor within society.

Kyrgyz (with Kazaks) in general, while probably the most Russified of Central Asian people, were never as deeply 'Leninised', judging by the casual ease with which they have turned away from the Soviet era. There has been none of the wholesale, hypocritical race to cleanse all Soviet terminology that afflicts Uzbekistan.

Islam has always sat lightly on the Kyrgyz people too. One consequence is a high profile for women here.

Manas – the Kyrgyz National Epic

but that tradition is dead.

The end of the oral tradition was inevitable with the advent of literacy (though the Soviets tried to pack it off early in the 1950s when there was a movement to criticise the epic as 'feudal'). Yet interest in *Manas* is on the rise. Books, operas, movies, comic books, and television serials based on *Manas* have appeared.

Manas mania received an exponential boost when the Kyrgyz government and UNESCO declared 1995 the 'International Year of *Manas*' and the '1000th Anniversary of the *Manas* Epos'. A grand festival was held. Visiting heads of state were feted, and President Askar Akaev held forth from the world's first (and probably last) three-storey yurt.

When a small, poor country spends US$8 million (by some estimates) on celebrating an oral epic, one can be pretty sure it's not just because the government really digs rhyming verse. Manas has become, once again, a figure for the Kyrgyz to hang their dreams on. Legend has even assigned Manas a tomb, located near Talas and supposedly built by his wife Kanykey, where Muslim pilgrims come to pray.

Churned out from the death throes of the Soviet empire, Kyrgyzstan is now charting its course into the 21st century with the aid of an epic poem.

ILLUSTRATIONS BY THEODOR HERZEN

KYRGYZSTAN

For more on the Kyrgyz people refer to the Peoples of the Silk Road section in the Facts about Central Asia chapter.

ARTS
Manas
Central Asian literature has traditionally been popularised in the form of songs, poems and stories by itinerant minstrels, called *akyn* in Kyrgyz (for more on this oral tradition, see the Arts section in the Facts about Central Asia chapter). Among better known 20th century Kyrgyz akyns are Togolok Moldo (real name Bayymbet Abdyrakhmanov), Sayakbay Karalayev and Sagymbay Orozbakov.

But the Kyrgyz have also come to be associated with something rather more complex – an entire cycle of oral legends, 20 times longer than the *Odyssey* and 2½ times the length of the *Mahabharata*, about a hero-of-heroes called Manas (see the boxed text). Akyns who can recite or improvise from these are in a class by themselves, called *manaschi*.

There were originally lots of epics, about various khans or leaders of the so-called Nogay people, who may be related to a clan by that name that apparently lives near the Aral Sea. The epics have gradually coalesced as bards improvised, attributing everybody's exploits to one person.

Manas in fact predates the Kyrgyz, in the same sense that Achilles or Agamemnon predate the Greeks. The stories are part of a wider, older tradition, but have come to be associated with the Kyrgyz people and culture partly because Soviet scholars 'gave' Manas to them in efforts to create separate cultures for the various Central Asian peoples.

Modern Literature

Kyrgyzstan has two well-known living authors – Chinghiz Aitmatov (born 1928) and Kazat Akmatov (born 1942).

Aitmatov is better known, having not only been published in Kyrgyz and Russian but translated into English, German and French. Among his works, which are also revealing looks at Kyrgyz life and culture, are *Djamila* (1967), *The White Steamship* (1970), *Early Cranes* (1975), *Piebald Dog Running Along the Shore* (1978), *A Day Lasts Longer Than a Century* (1980) and *The Place of the Skull* (1986).

Among Akmatov's works (according to Tiziano Terzani in *Goodnight, Mister Lenin*) are a play called *The Night of the Divorce*, about a corrupt Party official, and a novel called *Time*, about the repression of ethical values in the Stalin era. Both were instantly banned. Oddly, he eventually became chief of ideology for the Kyrgyz SSR. He was instrumental in the founding of the national-rebirth Movement for Democracy in 1989.

Shyrdaks

Kyrgyz specialise in felt rugs with appliqued coloured panels *(shyrdak)* or pressed wool designs *(ala-kiyiz)*. Shyrdaks are pieced together in the summer months after weeks of washing and drying and dyeing sheep's wool. Brightly coloured designs were introduced after synthetic dye became readily available in the 1960s, though neutral-coloured shyrdaks are still easy to find and resist fading. Patterns are usually of a *kochkor mujuz* (plant motif), *teke mujuz* (ibex horn motif), or *kyal* (fancy scrollwork), bordered in a style particular to the region. Working together, Kyrgyz women can knock out a beautiful carpet that will last for over three decades with two to three months diligent work – each stitch sewn by hand, using camel thread.

Facts for the Visitor

PLANNING
When to Go

Throughout the country springtime buds appear in April-May, though nights can still be below freezing. Mid-May to mid-June is pleasant though many mountain passes will still be snowed in. August is the hottest month. Overall, the republic is best for scenery and weather in September, with some rain and occasional freezing nights in October. Snow appears from mid-November through March.

Of course in the mountains the 'warm' season is shorter. The best time is July-September, although camping and trekking are pleasant from early June through mid-October. Avalanche danger is greatest in March through April and from September to mid-October. Winter brings ferocious cold in the mountains. See the previous Climate section for more information.

Maps

The Kyrgyz Cartographic Agency in Bishkek (see that section) has, in addition to maps of Bishkek in Cyrillic, a Kyrgyzstan country map using the roman alphabet and an interesting 'Silk Road of Kyrgyzstan' map. There are also trekking route maps and 1:200,000 Soviet topographic maps of various parts of Kyrgyzstan. Almost all maps are in Russian, though an English-language map of Ala-Archa was printed in 1999.

Trekking maps available at the agency include:

Ala-Archa (1:50,000) routes up to Ak-Say glacier and the ski base.

Cherez Talasskii Khrebet k Ozeru Sary-Chelek (1:200,000) from Leninopol to Sary Chelek over the Talas mountains.

Vorukh (1:100,000) Turkestan mountains.

Sokh (1:100,000) Alay mountains.

K Verkhvyam Sary-Dzhaza (1:200,000) routes to Chong-Tash and the Inylchek glacier.

Po Tsentralnomu Tyan-Shan and *Lednikam Terskey Ala-Too* (1:150,000) Terskey Alatau around Karakol, from Chong-Kyzyl-Suu valley to Jeti-Öghüz, Karakol and Arashan valleys.

Tsentralniy Tyan-Shan (1:150,000) schematic map of Inylchek glacier and around.

Ozero Issyk-Kul (1:200,000) topo map, covering trekking routes to Kazakstan via the Chong-Kemin valley.

Kirgizskii Khrebet (1:200,000) topo map, covering the Kyrgyzsky mountains south of Bishkek. There's also a separate 1:150,000 schematic map showing peaks in the same region.

VISAS & DOCUMENTS

First check the general Visas section in the Facts about the Central Asia chapter.

Kyrgyzstan is generally the easiest of the Central Asian republics for which to get a visa. In fact, in August 1999 President Akaev stated that by 1 January 2000 visas will be gradually annulled for visitors from World Trade Organisation member countries. The US and Japan are to be the first countries to benefit from the visa-free program.

Visa checks are rare on any ground or air approach to Kyrgyzstan from other CIS states; if you enter overland (eg by bus from Almaty or Tashkent) you'll just get a cursory passport check. Checks are possible on flights *from* Kyrgyzstan to other former USSR states, especially Russia. They're 100% certain on flights arriving from outside the former USSR.

Kyrgyz visas generally do not list specific towns, and you can go almost anywhere. If you're crossing the Torugart pass in either direction, you'll definitely need a Kyrgyz visa. If you're leaving Kyrgyzstan from the Torugart pass you must have a Bishkek registration stamp too; you can't just speed through from Almaty or Tashkent and count on the 72-hour rule in this case. See Registration, later in this section.

There are fines for visa violations, but most officials are fairly casual. If the police find you have no visa or no entry stamp, they'll probably just stamp the date in your passport and bundle you off to Bishkek to get one.

Visas

Many Kyrgyz embassies now issue visas without letters of support. At the time of research the embassy in Washington would give you a one month visa in a week for US$50, in three days for US$75 or immediately for US$100. In the UK 30-day visas cost UK£40 (longer-stay visas cost UK£66). Kyrgyz embassies in Almaty and Tashkent were issuing visas without support for around US$40. The embassy in Brussels is another easy place to get a hassle-free Kyrgyz visa.

It is possible to obtain a visa from the consular office at Bishkek's Manas international airport but finding the relevant official can take hours. Use this option only as a last-ditch plan.

If you arrive with only a Russian or Kazak visa, you can stay 72 hours, during which time you should be able to get a Kyrgyz visa on your own at the Consular Department of the Ministry of Foreign Affairs in Bishkek (see the Bishkek section later in this chapter). In practice it's easier to pay a local travel agency for help. Your sponsor or a local agency can also help with extending a visa or registering, both for a fee.

Transit

A traveller with a valid Russian, Uzbek or Kazak visa or an international ticket leaving Bishkek can automatically spend 72 hours in Kyrgyzstan.

Registration

Almost all foreigners staying in the country more than three days are expected to register once with OVIR (Office of Visas and Registrations; UPVR in Kyrgyzstan), preferably in Bishkek, though it is possible in Osh and, in theory at least, in Naryn. Swiss citizen do not need to register; the Swiss embassy can give you a letter to this effect to show police. A stamp from Bishkek is normally valid for a month for the entire country.

If OVIR can prove that you've been in the country longer than three working days without registering, you could be fined the equivalent of US$25. Some travellers report being fined even though OVIR had no proof, so keep hold of bus tickets, hotel receipts or any kind of evidence that shows when you entered the country. With weekends and irregular working hours it can sometimes take up to a week for the relevant OVIR office to open and so you'll have little choice but to hang around for the duration.

Registration takes a few minutes but the whole process takes most of the morning; get there as soon as the office opens. Registration costs 50 som if you've already got a visa. OVIR staff don't take the money themselves; you must first stop at a branch of the AKB Bank, say *'OVIR registratsiya'*, pay and get a receipt for OVIR. There's no real need for travel agency help with this but some agencies offer this service and it can gain you an extra morning's sightseeing.

Not everyone bothers to register, though OVIR officers will normally check your stamp at least once during your stay. If you are leaving over the Torugart pass, officials there will want to see a Bishkek registration stamp along with your visa.

If you are staying more than a month check that the date on your registration covers the duration of your visa or intended stay; if not you may have to register again.

Trekking Permits

To trek in any of the areas listed below you need an easily obtained permit from the Ministry of Tourism and Sport. See the Tourist Offices entry in the following Bishkek section. The permit can be issued on the spot and costs US$8 for three days or less, and US$30 for more than three days. The permit must list the dates of the trek and names of trekkers, but can include any number of treks and regions, so make sure you list all the regions you might possibly want to trek in. Permits are required for:

Ak Suu, Karakol, Jeti-Öghüz, Chong-Kyzyl-Suu, Juku valley, Jyrgalang region, Kaindi region (Chong-Kemin valley), Inylchek, Shakhimardan, Sokh, Khaidakan, Isfana, Achik Tash, Kamansu, Kyzyl Ünkür, Chatkal.

There are also peak fees of US$100 to climb Pobedy, Khan Tengri or Lenin (though you get a discount if you buy more than one). Ask your trekking agency for more details of these. In addition, certain sensitive border areas require a military border permit (cost US$10), for which you need trekking agency support.

EMBASSIES & CONSULATES

If you intend to cross into Kyrgyzstan from China over the Torugart pass, note that Beijing is the only place in China where you can get a Kyrgyz visa.

Kyrgyz Embassies & Consulates

If there is no Kyrgyz embassy in your country, inquire at the Kazak or Russian embassy. For embassies in Central Asia see the relevant country chapter.

Austria
   (☎ 01-535 0378, fax 535 0379)
   Naglergasse 25/5, 1010 Vienna
Belarus
   (☎ 0172-34 91 03, fax 34 91 17)
   ulitsa Starovilenskaya 57, Minsk
Belgium
   (☎ 02-534 6399, fax 534 2326,
   ✉ aitmatov@infonie.be)
   133 rue de Tenbosch, 1050 Brussels – Ambassador Chingiz Aitmatov issues visas on the spot for US$50.
China
   (☎ 010-6532 6458, fax 6532 6459,
   ✉ kyrgyz@public3.bta.net.cn)
   2-4-1 Ta Yuan Diplomatic Office Bldg, Chaoyang District, Beijing – there is no Kyrgyz consulate in Kashgar.
Germany
   (☎ 0228-36 52 30, fax 36 51 91)
   Koblenzei Strasse 62, 53173 Bonn
   Consulate: Frankfurt-am-Main
India
   (☎ 011-614 0917, fax 614 0372)
   BV 8125 Vasant Vihar, New Delhi 110057
Iran
   (☎ 021-229 8323/7729, fax 229 4607)
   Bldg 12-4th Naran, Jastan All Pasaran, Tehran

Russia
   (☎ 095-237 4601/4481/4571, fax 237 4452)
   ulitsa Bolshaya Ordynka 64, Moscow 109017
Turkey
   (☎ 312-446 84 08, fax 446 84 13)
   Boyabat Sokak 11, Gaziosmanpasa, 06700 Ankara
   Consulate-General: Istanbul
Ukraine
   (☎ 044-229 0308, ☎/fax 229 0307)
   Hotel Moscow, Institutskaya 4, Kiev
UK
   (☎ 020-7935 1462, fax 7935 7449
   ✉ kyrembuk@aol.com)
   Ascot House, 119 Crawford St, London W1H
   1AF – a one month tourist visa costs UK£40;
   Web site members.aol.com/kyrembuk.
USA
   (☎ 202-338 5141, fax 338 5139,
   ✉ embassy@kyrgyzstan.org)
   1732 Wisconsin Ave, NW, Washington, DC
   20007 – a single entry, one month visa costs
   US$50, ready in five days; Web site www
   .kyrgyzstan.org.

Embassies & Consulates in Kyrgyzstan

Note that some of the smaller embassies listed below are little more than a rented room in an obscure apartment block and can therefore be hard to find. All the following are in Bishkek (dialling code 312):

Belarus
   (☎ 24 29 52, fax 24 28 84) Moskva 210
Canada
   (☎ 65 02 02, fax 65 02 04, ✉ aki@infotel.kg)
   Moskva 189, crossing with Turusbekov
China
   (☎ 22 24 23, fax 21 25 47)
   Toktogul 196 – visas: Monday, Wednesday and
   Friday 9.15 to noon; you won't get a visa if
   you mention Torugart but should if you say
   you are flying to Ürümqi. Thirty-day visas cost
   US$30 for Americans, US$60 for Brits.
Germany
   (☎ 22 48 11, fax 22 85 23) Razzakov 28
India
   (☎ 21 08 62, fax 62 07 08)
   3rd Floor, Chuy 164-A – weekdays 9 am to
   5.30 pm, closed 1 to 2 pm; accepts visa application Monday to Friday, 2 to 4 pm. Standard
   six month tourist visas cost 1835 som for US
   citizens, 1105 som for most other nationalities.
   Two photos are necessary. Visas take around
   five days to issue and can be picked up from 4
   to 5 pm. Look out for the flag when looking for
   the embassy.

Iran
   (☎ 22 69 64, fax 62 00 09)
   Razzakov 36 – Monday to Friday 9 am to 5
   pm. Transit visas of 10 days duration are issued in one week. You need a letter of invitation for a tourist visa.
Kazakstan
   (☎ 66 01 64, fax 22 54 63)
   Togolok Moldo 10 – Monday to Thursday 10 am
   to noon.
Netherlands
   Honorary Consulate:
   (☎ 66 02 22, fax 66 02 88)
   Suite 1, Tynistanov 199
Pakistan
   (☎ 22 72 09, fax 62 15 50
   ✉ pakemb@asiainfo.kg)
   Panfilov 308 – open Monday to Friday 9 am to
   noon but may well refer you to a visa agency
   such as Ak Jolty (☎ 21 33 63), Panfilov 178.
Russia
   (☎ 22 17 75, fax 22 18 23)
   Razzakov 17 – Monday, Tuesday, Wednesday
   2.30 to 3.30 pm, and Friday 10 to 11 am.
Turkey
   (☎ 22 78 82, fax 66 14 58)
   Moskva 89 – open weekdays 9 to 12 am.
UK
   The nearest UK embassy is in Almaty,
   Kazakstan.
USA
   (☎ 55 12 41, ✉ pao@usis.gov.kg)
   Mira prospektisi 171
Uzbekistan
   (☎ 22 61 71) Tynistanov 104

MONEY

The Kyrgyz *som* is divided into 100 *tiyin*. Notes come in 100, 50, 20, 10, five and one som denominations. At the time of research the som was devaluing at a rate of 10% per month. However, prices in this chapter are still listed in som as the som rate was more stable than the dollar equivalent. Exchange rates at the time of research were:

country	unit		som
China	Y1	=	5 som
euro	€1	=	32 som
Germany	Dm1	=	21 som
Kazakstan	10 T	=	3 som
Russia	Rbl1	=	1.5 som
USA	US$1	=	42 som
Uzbekistan	100 *sum*	=	7 som

KYRGYZSTAN

POST & COMMUNICATIONS

An airmail postcard costs 6.2 som and a 20g airmail letter costs 12.2 som.

International telephone rates are 97 som per minute to Europe or 137 som to America or Australia. Calls to the CIS are 7 som per minute. To send a fax, telecom offices charge a minimum three minute telephone charge, plus a service charge, bringing the rate for a one-page fax to a whopping 549 som to the US or 366 som to the UK or Australia.

International calls from Kyrgyzstan are normally booked through the operator (☎ 105) otherwise dial ☎ 00 + the international code of the country you wish to call.

To call within the CIS dial ☎ 00.

To make a local call dial ☎ 0 + the city code.

To dial into Kyrgyzstan from abroad dial ☎ 00 996 + the local code.

FOOD & DRINK

Spicy *laghman* (noodle) dishes reign supreme, partly the result of Dungan (Muslim Chinese) influence. Apart from standard Central Asia dishes (see Food in the Regional Facts for the Visitor chapter), *besbarmak* (literally 'five fingers', since it is traditionally eaten by hand) is a special holiday dish consisting of large flat noodles topped with lamb and/or horsemeat cooked in vegetable broth. *Kesme* is a thick noodle soup with small bits of potato, vegetable and meat. *Jarkop* is a braised meat and vegetable dish with noodles.

Hoshan are fried and steamed dumplings, similar to *manty* (stuffed dumplings), best right off the fire from markets. Vendors also carry bags of them to sell in bus stations, or to bars, outdoor cafes etc. Horsemeat sausages known as *kazy*, *karta* or *chuchuk* are a popular vodka chaser, as in Kazakstan.

In Dungan areas (eg Karakol or certain suburbs of Bishkek), ask for *ashlyanfu*, made with cold noodles, jelly, vinegar and eggs. Also try their steamed buns made with *jusai*, a mountain grass of the onion family, and *fyntyozi*, spicy cold rice noodles. *Gyanfan* is rice with a meat and vegetable sauce. Dungans maintain a spirited rivalry with Uyghurs for noodle supremacy.

Kumys (fermented mare's milk), available in spring and early summer, is the national drink. *Bozo* is a thick fizzy drink made from boiled fermented millet or other grains. *Jarma* is a fermented barley drink. Shoro is the brand name of a similar drink, available at most street corners in Bishkek.

Issyk-Kul honey is said to be the best in Central Asia, and locally made blackcurrant jam is a treat. Kids and elderly people in Balykchy and Cholpon-Ata sell strings of dried fish and you can buy larger smoked fish in the bazars, though you should check that these have been cooked properly.

Tea is traditionally made very strong in a pot and mixed with boiling water and milk in a bowl before serving.

SHOPPING

Look out for shyrdaks, heavy rugs made from multiple layers of home-pounded felt in varying colours, with patterns created by cutting away the upper layers to reveal different coloured patterns beneath. Check that the Shyrdak is hand-made by irregular stitching on the back and tight, even stitching around the panels. Also check the colour will not run (lick your finger and run lightly over the colours to see that they do not bleed). The best Shyrdaks are said to be made around Naryn and there are several women's cooperatives in the surrounding towns.

Small pottery figurines shaped as bread sellers, musicians, and 'white beards' are for sale everywhere but most are made at the Arts Faculty in Osh. Hats are also for sale everywhere but most are factory-made in Toktogul, sold cheaply at the bazar in Osh.

Other souvenirs include miniature yurts and embroidered bags, chess sets featuring Manas and company, horse whips, kumys shakers, leather boxes, and musical instruments, such as the mouth harp *komuz*.

ORIENTATION

The Kyrgyz language has not been so bluntly imposed on nonspeakers in Kyrgyzstan as has Uzbek in Uzbekistan. In larger towns in the north at least, streets and squares are labelled in both Kyrgyz and Russian. In some smaller towns, the old Russian signs are still in place and Russian forms persist (in Osh and other towns in the south you'll hear Uzbek terms as well). Many Soviet-era names have been retained.

We try to use the most current names, but in each town we use the grammatical forms (Kyrgyz, Russian or Uzbek) that seem to be in common use.

A Kyrgyz street is *köchösü* (Russian: *ulitsa*), an avenue *prospektisi* (Russian: *prospekt*), a boulevard *bulvary* (Russian: *bulvar*), a square *ayanty* (Russian: *ploshchad*).

Bishkek

☎ 312 • pop 800,000

Bishkek, now the capital and industrial centre of independent Kyrgyzstan, is a relaxed and handsome place with wide streets, Ukrainian-style backstreet houses and mainly good-natured people of many races (47% are Russian and only about a third are Kyrgyz).

Bishkek wears its recent history without embarrassment. Lenin is still here in his concrete overcoat, gesturing at the mountains from the vast central square. A larger-than-life Frunze still sits on a bronze horse facing the train station, though his name has been removed. You can still visit the museum built over Frunze's birthplace, if you can keep a straight face.

There's nothing else old here, and little even predating WWII. Even old people now seem sadly marginalised, with some to be seen selling their belongings on street corners to make ends meet, and a few begging.

And yet amid the economic malaise the city is attracting a small flow of foreign businesspeople, embassy staff and aid workers, as well as a small but growing Kyrgyz middle class, and a network of bars, restaurants and well-stocked shops is sprouting rapidly to support them. In many ways, Bishkek feels like Almaty's naive younger brother.

For travellers, Bishkek is mainly a jumping-off point for the Tian Shan mountains and Lake Issyk-Kul, and for the overland crossing to China via the Torugart pass. The city can catch heavy weather, with snow here when it's raining elsewhere, even in October.

History

In 1825, by a Silk Road settlement on a tributary of the Chuy river, the Uzbek khan of Kokand built a little clay fort, one of several along caravan routes through the Tian Shan mountains. In 1862 the Russians captured and wrecked it, and set up a garrison of their own. The town of Pishpek was founded 16 years later, swelled by Russian peasants lured by land grants and the Chuy valley's fertile black earth.

In 1926 the town, re-baptised Frunze, became capital of the new Kyrgyz ASSR. The name never sat well; Mikhail Frunze (who was born here) was the Russian Civil War commander who helped keep tsarist Central Asia in Bolshevik hands and hounded the basmachi rebellion into the mountains.

In 1991 the city became Bishkek, the Kyrgyz form of its old Kazak name. A *pishpek* or *bishkek* is a churn for kumys. Numerous legends (some quaint, some rude) explain how it came to be named for a wooden plunger. Dan Prior, in his *Bishkek Handbook* (see the Information, following), concludes disappointingly that this was simply the closest familiar sound to its old Sogdian name, Peshagakh, meaning 'place below the mountains'. With the 4800m, permanently snow-capped rampart of the Kyrgyz Alatau range looming over it, the Sogdian name fits.

Orientation

Bishkek sits 800m above sea level on the northern hem of the Kyrgyz Alatau mountains, an arm of the Tian Shan. Nineteenth century military planners laid out an orderly, compass-oriented town and getting around is quite easy.

Jibek Jolu prospektisi (Silk Road Ave), just north of the centre, was old Pishpek's main street. Now the municipal axes are Chuy prospektisi and park-like Erkindik prospektisi. The busiest commercial streets are Kiev and Soviet. At the centre yawns Ala-Too Square, flanked by Panfilov and Dubovy (Oak) parks. Street numbers increase as you head north or west.

Bishkek's Manas international airport is 30km north-west of the centre, and the west or long-distance bus station is 4km out in the same direction. The east or regional bus station is east along Jibek Jolu. The train station is at the south end of Erkindik prospektisi by the Hotel Ala-Too.

The best view of the city and the mountains is probably from either the square in front of the Hotel Dostuk, or the top of the Ferris wheel in Panfilov Park!

Maps Kyrgyz Cartographic Agency (☎ 21 22 96, fax 21 07 72, ✆ geodes@imfiko .bishkek.su) at Kiev 107 sells recent Bishkek city and bus maps in Cyrillic, as well as trekking and other maps. For more information, see Maps in the Facts for the Visitor section, earlier in this chapter. The office is open 8 am to 4.30 pm, closed noon to 1 pm. The building is set back off the main road and the sales room is on the ground floor to the left.

The relatively useful 3D *Bishkek i Biznes Putyevodityel* map of Bishkek is available at many kiosks.

Information

Check hotels and shops for the *Bishkek Handbook*, a thorough look at Bishkek's history, sights and nearby excursions by ex-Bishkek resident and Kyrgyzophile Dan Prior. Written in 1994, the practical details are, however, well out of date.

Tourist Offices For general tourist information try the Tourist Information Office (☎ 21 48 54, fax 22 05 49), at the Ministry of Tourism and Sport on Togolok Moldo 17, near the stadium. From the street entrance go just inside the arch and turn left. For information on visas, border crossings and the like you are better off asking at one of the travel agencies listed later in this section.

Visas The place to get a Kyrgyz visa or visa extension is the Consular Department of the Ministry of Foreign Affairs (☎ 22 14 63), on the 3rd floor of a building on the east side of Ala-Too Square. It's open Monday, Tuesday, Thursday and Friday, 2 to 5.30 pm. The office can give visa extensions (for a stay of up to 40 days), can extend a transit visa (for a stay of up to 10 days) and can issue a month-long tourist visa, all for US$30. The

bureaucracy can be slow, however, and you may get farther faster with the help of one of the travel agencies listed in this section.

Registration Foreigners must register at OVIR within 72 hours of arriving in Kyrgyzstan (see the Registration section earlier in this chapter). To compound an already confusing set of rules, in Bishkek foreigners must register in one of four different OVIR offices, dependent upon which *rayon* (district) your hotel falls under. If in doubt, your hotel should be able to tell you which office to head for.

If you are staying at the Business School or Hotel Sary Chelek the place to head for is the OVIR office at Jibek Jolu 285, on the corner with Tynystanov (go in, turn to the left and take the last office on the left). Opening hours are inconvenient to say the least: officially open Tuesday, Thursday and Friday 9 am to 5.30 pm, closed noon to 1 pm, and Saturday 9 am to noon (though you'll be lucky to get much business done in the afternoons). If you are staying at the Hotel Dostuk, head to the office at Suyumbaev 73 (former Karpinsky). Other offices are at the corner with Moskva and Umetaliev and 86 Skryabina, about 4.5km south of the city.

After filling in the requisite registration forms, you have to pay the 50 som fee at the AKB Bank (room 113) on Togolok Moldo. You'll need help filling out the indecipherable forms, which cost 2.5 som. Get a receipt (*kvitansiya*) and sprint to the OVIR office before it closes. OVIR will give you a registration stamp next to your visa.

If in doubt, the central OVIR office (☎ 269 06 27/05 98) is at Kiev 58 near Shopokov (left-hand door, room 3 on the ground floor), open Monday to Friday 9.30 am to 12.30 pm, and 2 to 5 pm. They can advise you which office to register at, though they currently only register Chinese visitors.

Visas for Other Central Asian Republics Both the Kazak and Uzbek embassies in Bishkek require visa support before they will issue a visa. CAT (see Travel Agencies, later in this section) can provide a letter of invitation for Uzbekistan or Kazakstan for US$35.

The procedure takes a week and usually results in a 30 day visa.

The nearest Tajik or Turkmen embassies are in Almaty (Kazakstan). For a letter of visa support try ITMC, Kyrgyz Concept or the other agencies listed later in this section.

Customs If you've bought anything that looks remotely antique and didn't get a certificate from the shop saying it's not, you can get one from the 1st floor (room 210 or 214) of the Foreign Department of the Ministry of Education, Science and Culture, at the corner of Tynystanov and Frunze.

Useful Organisations Peace Corps volunteers are scattered to every tiny village in Kyrgyzstan and they can be a good source for local information. The head office (☎ 65 09 89) is at Chokmorov 304 (formerly Engels) to the extreme west of town.

A Kyrgyz-run information and contact point, Interbilim Centre (☎ 66 04 25, fax 66 44 34, @ ccpub@infotel.kg), at Razzakov 16, links local interest groups and foreign organisations. They may also be able to help visitors interested in teaching English or doing volunteer work in Kyrgyzstan.

There is a British Council representative on the 2nd floor of the Business School (☎ 63 33 39).

Money There are exchange desks in most hotels. Licensed private moneychangers in numerous tiny shopfronts give slightly better rates and will change most currencies, though new, high value US dollar bills are the preferred currency. There's a particularly high concentration of moneychangers along Soviet. Exchange receipts don't seem to be an issue any more, but it doesn't hurt to collect a few if you can, particularly if you plan to sell back your som.

Bank Eridan (☎ 65 06 10) on Kalyk Akiev charges 3% commission for cash advances off Visa, MasterCard and Eurocard and will give cash US dollars. They are open Monday to Friday 8 am to noon, and 1 to 3.30 pm.

AKB Bank, on Togolok Moldo, changes major travellers cheques for an eye-watering 5% commission (room 109). US dollar cash advances are relatively quick off Visa or MasterCard, for 3% commission (room 210).

Bishkek Bank at Toktogul 87 (the funky pink and yellow building) changes US dollar travellers cheques only into US dollars or som for a 5% commission, open Monday to Friday 9 am to 4 pm, closed noon to 1 pm. Foreigners can also open an account here.

You can arrange a money wire (minimum US$500) at Amanbank (☎ 66 41 49, fax 66 24 39), Tynystanov 249, for a fee of US$25 or 0.2% of the total amount wired, whichever is greater. You must first establish an account at their bank with a minimum of US$35.

Post, Telephone & Fax The main post and telephone offices face Soviet, south of Chuy. The post office is open Monday to Friday 7 to 11 am and 1 to 7 pm, Saturday and Sunday 9 am to 5 pm. There is a separate mailroom for poste restante, EMS and parcels – enter the first door on the left (north) side of the post office, turn left and go through another door, cross to the far right corner and go through a third door. It's possible to pick up poste restante letters here. Mail to your name, Glavpochtamt, Bishkek 720000.

Western priority mail services in Bishkek include DHL (☎ 61 11 11), at 107 Kiev, FedEx (☎ 65 00 12, fax 65 01 28) at Moskva 217, and Overseas Courier Service (☎ 28 43 46) in the Hotel Dostuk.

American Resources International (☎ 66 03 77, fax 66 00 77, @ casia@imfiko.bishkek.su, Web site www.its-ship.com/bishkek), Soviet 170, Room 15, ships larger items if you are moving to/from Bishkek.

The main telephone office also provides international fax service. There are smaller telephone offices on the corners of Chuy and Erkindik and Chuy and Isanov.

Email & Internet Access ElCat (☎ 22 75 85), at Razzakov 56, charges US$7 per month for an email account, plus a US$0.15 per kilobyte charge, or a straight US$8 per hour for Internet access (this figure will probably drop). Hotmail access is slow and you will have to queue for a computer, or bring your own. It is open Monday to Friday 9 am to 6 pm, closed 1 to 2 pm.

The Business Center Hotel (☎/fax 22 28 43, @ hotel@infotel.kg), 4th floor, Panfilov 237, offers a whole range of business services, including Internet access. To send or receive a 1 kilobyte message costs 12 som. To receive a fax costs only 2 som per page.

Dostuk Travels, in room 221 of the Hotel Dostuk, offers Internet access for US$8 per hour and will send messages for US$2 each (there's no charge to receive).

Since researching this edition, a 24 hour Internet cafe has apparently opened at Soviet 176, a five minute walk south of the post office. Internet access costs from US$2 to US$3 per hour, depending on the time of day.

Travel Agencies The following agencies are starting to figure out what budget-minded individual travellers want and how much they can get for it. For details on help and transport to the Torugart pass, see the Torugart Pass section later in this chapter.

Ak-Kuu
(☎ 47 22 62, fax 22 54 21)
Soviet 3U – Boris 'No Problem' Borkeyev speaks little English but can set up budget walking, horseback and ski excursions and, he says, local and long-distance transport, train and air tickets; he also has a little guesthouse with the same name.

Celestial Mountains
(☎ 21 32 78, fax 62 04 02,
@ celest@infotel.kg)
Kiev 131-4, Bishkek – western-run agency, specialises in the Torugart pass, but can also offer visa support and tours and runs a hotel in Naryn. Contact Ian Claytor. Web site www.celestial.com.kg.

Central Asia Tourism Corporation (CAT)
(☎ 66 02 77, 21 97 85, fax 66 56 92, 21 95 38,
@ cat@imfiko.bishkek.su, cat@asiainfo.kg)
Chuy prospektisi 124, Bishkek 720021 – visa support, rental cars, air tickets, accommodation and inclusive tours; contact Eduard Hrustalev. Web site http://cat.com.kg.

Dostuk Trekking Ltd
(☎ 42 74 71, ☎/fax 54 54 55,
@ dostuk@imfiko.bishkek.su)
Vosemnadsataya Liniya St 42-1, Bishkek 720005 – ascents to peaks including Khan Tengri, Pobedy and Lenin, treks, Torugart crossing. Web site http://alpha.bishkek.su/dostuk.

Ecotour
(☎/fax 21 34 70, @ ecotour@infotel.kg)
Moskva 145, Bishkek 720017 – green tourism: stay in a traditional yurt with horses, solar-heated water, and small hydroelectric turbines; local guides at Temir Kanat and Song-Köl. Contact English-speaking Elmira or German-speaking Zamira. Web site www.kg/ecotour.

Edelweiss
(☎ 28 07 28/42 54, fax 68 00 38,
@ edelweiss@imfiko.bishkek.su)
Usenbayev St 68/9, Bishkek 720021 – trekking, mountaineering, heli-skiing, horse tours, ski trips, visa support. Contact Slava Alexandrov.

International Mountaineering Camp Pamir (IMC Pamir)
(☎ 66 04 69, fax 66 04 65,
@ imcpamir@imfiko.bishkek.su)
Kiev 133, Apt 30, Bishkek 720001 – trekking and mountaineering programs and operate the Achik Tash base camp at the foot of Peak Lenin. Contact Bekbolot Koshoev. Web site www.bishkek.su/imcpamir.

ITMC Tien-Shan
(☎ 65 12 21/14 04, fax 65 07 47,
@ itmc@imfiko.bishkek.su)
Molodaya Gvardia 1A, Bishkek 720035 – competent adventure-travel operator offering package and piece-wise help, including visa support, mountaineering, trekking, heli-skiing, mountain biking and crossing the Torugart. They also run a string of yurt camps at Tash Rabat, Song-Köl, Naryn, Salkyn Tör (near Naryn) and Kurumdu (near Cholpon-Ata), for between US$7 and US$20 per person per day with food. Not to be confused with their former partners at Tien-Shan Travel. Contact Alex Timofiev.

Kyrgyz Concept
(☎ 21 05 56, 26 58 22, fax 21 05 54,
@ akc@mail.elcat.kg)
Razzakov 100, Bishkek 720001 – emphasis on cultural programs at the pricier end of the travel spectrum. Can arrange visa support, Bishkek home-stays for US$20 per person, horse trekking, cultural shows and can even put you in touch with a Kyrgyz costume designer. They are also a reliable international ticket agency. Credit cards accepted. Contact Ainura Sydykova or Emil Umetaliev. Web site www.akc.com.kg.

Tien Shan Raft
(☎/fax 28 41 42)
Musa Jalil 104, Bishkek 720051 – river raft and kayak trips on the Chuy and Chong-Kemin rivers; contact Alexander Kandaurov.

Tien-Shan Travel
(☎/fax 27 05 76,
✉ tienshan@travel.bishkek.su, tienshan@
imfiko.bishkek.su)
Tcherbakov 127 – out-of-work cartographers
with expedition gear and a menu of set group
tours into the mountains, but unaccustomed to
walk-in clients. Contact Vladimir Birukov.
Top Asia
(☎/fax 21 16 44,
✉ topasia@imfiko.bishkek.su)
Toktogul 175 – trekking and mountaineering.
Web site www.bishkek.su/topasia.

Two competent non-Bishkek agencies accustomed to serving tourists in Bishkek are Yak Tours in Karakol (see the following Lake Issyk-Kul & the Central Tian Shan section), and Alptreksport in Osh (see the following Bishkek to Osh & the Kyrgyz Fergana Valley section).

Bookshops Bishkek's bookshops have little of interest in English. Aeropag Books on the corner of Erkindik and Kiev has a few postcards and a few tourist brochures.

Akademkniga, on Moskva 141, has the odd English book, plus souvenirs, Soviet medals, pre-Soviet coins and stationery. There are a few English-language books for sale in the lobby of the Business College.

Newspapers & Magazines The *Times of Central Asia* is the local English-language newspaper. The Pub (see the Pubs & Bars entry of the following Entertainment section) has a decent collection of western newspapers and magazines, such as *Time* and the *International Herald Tribune*.

Bathhouses You can get unlimited hot water at the Zhirgal Banyo on the corner of Sultan Ibraimov and Toktogul. A private room with bath and shower costs 20 som for one person, 30 som for two. A Finnish sauna (women only) costs 40 som per person, and a Russian sauna (men only) costs 35 som. The baths are open 8 am to 9 pm; buy tickets from the *kassa* (ticket office) around the side. Old ladies sell birch twigs outside the baths for those who are into a bit of self-flogging.

Toilets There is a public toilet at the south end of Dubovy Park and a new one on Soviet south of Kiev.

Emergency & Medical Services ARMS clinic (☎ 22 63 49, emergency ☎ 517-77 09 11, fax 22 65 12), Kiev 74, is run by the mining company Kumtor and is the best contact for medical attention, though you must have medical insurance to receive treatment. Initial consultations cost US$40; English is spoken. You can also get vaccinations, imported medicines or even an HIV test here, if you need this for onward travel. Contact Dr Munara Davletova.

Other options include the Kyrgyz Republic Hospital (outpatients ☎ 22 89 60, 24 hour duty officer for emergencies and hospital ambulance ☎ 26 69 16) at 110 Kiev.

In an emergency, call police: ☎ 02; fire: ☎ 01; ambulance: ☎ 03.

Dangers & Annoyances Bishkek smiles during the day but is neither safe nor well lit after dark. Both locals and foreigners have been roughed up, sometimes by young cops on the take. An American woman was raped in a Bishkek park in November 1997. If you're out after dark, stick to main streets, avoid the parks and steer clear of the area around the train station. All the normal Central Asian security rules apply (see the Dangers & Annoyances section of the Regional Facts for the Visitor chapter).

Osh bazar is home to the odd pickpocket and bag-slashing thief, so keep your valuables out of sight. Don't wave your money pouch around, try not to fish in it for money, and stay sharp in close crowds.

A common and unpleasant scam here involves what looks like accidentally dropped money. If you pick it up, someone rushes up saying it's his; if you hand it back you may be accused of substituting a smaller note. A crowd (his cronies) can gather and unpleasantries can escalate. Let it lie and move on.

If you encounter problems, the US embassy publishes a list of lawyers and doctors based in Kyrgyzstan. It also suggests that US citizens register with them and leave a photocopy of their passport.

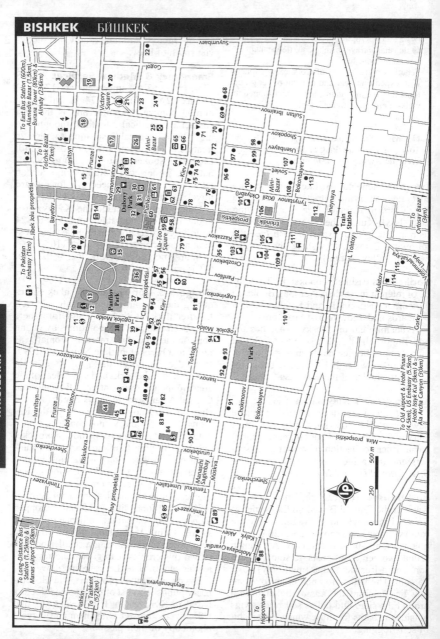

BISHKEK

KYRGYZSTAN

Ala-Too Square

This sea of concrete ceased to be called Lenin Square in 1991. Lenin remains on his plinth, but his days up there are probably numbered.

The brutal block behind him, once the Lenin Museum, has become the **State Historical Museum**, with two yurts, a small archaeology exhibit and a beguiling display of Kyrgyz carpets, embroidery and other applied crafts on the ground floor. The original, stupendously posh shrine to Lenin and the Revolution in Kyrgyzstan was still in place upstairs when we visited, and is worth seeing. The museum is open daily except Monday, 10 am to 3 pm; admission is 10 som, and no photography is allowed.

The grand facades across Chuy prospektisi from Lenin are just that – facades – about 10m deep, erected in Soviet times in front of the venerable but unsuitably drab Ilbirs knitwear factory.

The unmarked marble palace full of chandeliered offices just west of the square, the **'White House'**, is the seat of the Kyrgyzstan government, including the President's office and the republic's parliament. Behind this is **Panfilov Park**, whose rusting rides and arcades make it the centre of Bishkek for kids, and a great place to head for on a national holiday.

The conspicuously older structure east of Ala-Too Square at 68 Pushkin was the headquarters of the Central Committee of the Kyrgyz ASSR, declared in 1926. It's now home to the **Dom Druzhby** community centre, a centre for advocacy and self-help groups, as well as a drab zoology museum.

Beyond this is **Dubovy (Oak) Park**, full of strollers on warm Sundays, a few open-air cafes and some neglected modern sculpture. The century-old oaks here and along **Erkindik prospektisi** (Freedom Avenue) make Bishkek a candidate for the greenest city in Central Asia. Where Erkindik enters the park, a smouldering bust of Felix Dzerzhinsky, founder of the Soviet secret police, dares you to pass. His name has been removed; despite Kyrgyzstan's laid-back attitude to recent history, this name, like Lenin's, disappeared quickly in 1991.

State Museum of Fine Arts

This decaying museum, also called the Museum of Applied Art, at Soviet 196 near Abdymomunov (Kirov), features Kyrgyz embroidery, jewellery, utensils, eye-popping felt rugs, works by local artists, and a startling collection of reproduction Egyptian and classical statuary. It's open daily, except Monday, 9 am to 4 pm (from 10 am Friday) and admission is 10 som.

Frunze House-Museum

Is this thatched cottage really where the little Frunze played with his toy soldiers, or just the Soviet way with history? In any case the meticulous two storey museum engulfing it – showcasing Frunze as military and family man, plus the requisite posters, weapons, flags and statues – has itself become a piece of history. It's at the corner of Frunze and Razzakov, and is open Wednesday through Sunday 9 am to 4 pm, admission 5 som. The back of the museum also houses a video playstation for 12 som per hour!

Victory Square

This weedy plaza with an immense yurt-shaped memorial, erected on the 40th anniversary of the end of WWII, sprawls across an entire city block near the Hotel Dostuk. On cold evenings you may see a knot of young men passing the bottle and warming themselves at its eternal flame. On weekends it's the destination for an endless stream of wedding parties posing for photographs.

Russian Remnants

Among poignant reminders that there is still a Russian community here are the pretty, blue-steepled Orthodox church on Jibek Jolu near Togolok Moldo, and an incongruous, well-preserved Russian-style log house on Moskva, west of Togolok Moldo, which is now the Ecotour office.

Gosudarstvenny (Government) Bank at the corner of Erkindik and Frunze was the

Mikhail Vasilievich Frunze

Frunze was born in what was then Pishpek in 1885. After an early adulthood full of revolutionary excitement in Moscow, and numerous arrests, he eventually commanded the Red Guards who occupied the Moscow Kremlin in October 1917. He was a major player in the Russian Civil War, directing the defeat of the White forces of Admiral Kolchak in Siberia and the route of General Wrangel in the Caucasus. It was Frunze who led the Bolshevik forces that seized Khiva and Bukhara in 1920, and pushed the *basmachi* rebels out of the Fergana valley.

Replacing Trotsky as War Commissar, Frunze introduced compulsory peacetime military service, and moulded the Red Army into a potent tool of the Revolution. After Lenin's death, he survived several mysterious auto accidents, but died a victim of Stalin's paranoia in 1925, during an officially ordered stomach operation.

Bolsheviks' first capital construction project here (built in 1926). It was designed by one AP Zenkov, best known for the far lovelier wooden cathedral (1904) in Almaty.

Places to Stay – Budget

Bishkek International School of Management & Business (☎ 22 25 85, 22 28 43, fax 66 06 38, Panfilov 237), behind Panfilov Park, is far and away the best value accommodation in Bishkek. Clean doubles, with two rooms sharing toilet and shower (hot water most of the time) and a private balcony are 280 som. A larger *lux* (deluxe) room costs 726 som, and there are cheaper *pol lux* (semi deluxe) rooms somewhere between the two. (The thumping disco music coming from Panfilov Park stops abruptly at 10.30 pm.) The hotel is sometimes known as the 'Salima'.

Hotel Sary Chelek (☎ 22 14 67, Orozbekov 87) is not bad if the nearby Business School is full. Singles/doubles/triples with bath and cold showers run to 111/223/341 som. Also available are larger singles with hot shower and TV for 235 som or a lux suite that sleeps four for 450 som. Check that the door locks, and ignore the cockroaches.

Hotel Semetey (☎ 21 83 24, Toktogul 125) (formerly Polyot) has a good location and gloomy but clean and spacious singles/doubles with shared bath for 230/320 som. The lux suite is good value with private bath, refrigerator, TV and telephone for 520 som, and a bargain if you are a volunteer worker and get it for half-price.

There are three rock-bottom hotels in a scruffy district north-east of town. Best of the lot (not saying much) is probably **Hotel Ak-Say** (☎ 26 14 65, Ivanitsyn 117) behind the circus. Though it has decent enough rooms with squat toilets and cold-water basins (upstairs for the men; downstairs for the ladies), it's not great value at 120/240 som for singles/doubles. Locals pay 40 som.

The truly desperate might try **Gostinitsa Tsirki**, just west of the Ak Say, at 80 som per person, no bath, and usually full of long-term guests.

Gostinichny Komplex Ilbirs (☎ 23 13 04) on Ivanitsyn just north of the Dostuk has a

back (east) entrance on the high-rise side. Mouldy, basic rooms with common toilet and cold shower are 40 som per person. Its saving grace is large windows and cheerful staff.

Rahat Hotel (Kulatov 64), not far from the train station, is in the same league as the Ak Say. Though difficult to find the dubious neighbourhood, three surprisingly clean rooms are available for 100 som each.

Hotel Kyrgyz Altyn (☎ 21 97 78), on Manas, has basic singles/doubles for 131/198 som, with a common toilet but no place to wash. It's often full.

Home-Stays Dostuk, Kyrgyz Concept and probably other travel agencies listed in the Bishkek Information section earlier can arrange bed and breakfast in private homes, typically for around US$20 per person per night.

Places to Stay – Mid-Range

A group of old, smoky Soviet-style hotels offer run-down rooms with standard refrigerator and TV (one of which may work), and disappointing leaky bathrooms.

Hotel Bishkek (☎ 22 02 20, fax 62 03 65, Erkindik 21) is essentially clean and better value than the over-priced Dostuk (see Places to Stay – Top End). Singles/doubles with water heater cost US$65/75. You can receive faxes at the business centre for 10 som per page.

Hotel Issyk Kul (☎ 55 07 46, fax 55 04 85, Mira prospektisi 301), 9km south of the centre near the old airport, has small but comfortable rooms with balcony, hot water, refrigerator and local TV. Singles/doubles start at US$40/50, with a larger 'pol lux' at US$70 or huge, apartment-style lux for US$90.

Hotel Ala-Too (Erkindik 1), near the train station, is currently undergoing renovation by a German company and is expected to open soon at the higher end of the price scale.

Places to Stay – Top End

Business Center Hotel (☎ 22 25 85, 22 28 43, fax 66 06 38, @ hotel@infotel.kg, Panfilov 237), on the 4th floor of the Bishkek

KYRGYZSTAN

International School of Management & Business, offers comfortable top-end suites complete with kitchens, private baths and satellite TV. Conveniently located on the same floor is the well-run business centre. Prices for singles/doubles start at US$110/160, with discounts for longer stays; major credit cards accepted.

Hotel Dostuk (☎ 28 42 78, fax 68 16 90, *Frunze 429*), once Bishkek's flagship hotel, is looking pretty mediocre. Small but clean singles/doubles with satellite TV are overpriced at US$80/106. The near-empty hotel also has a friendly business centre, travel agency, exchange desk, two restaurants, souvenir stand and bookshop. Major credit cards accepted.

Hotel Pinara (☎ 54 01 44, fax 54 24 08, ✆ pinara@elcat.kg), formerly the Hotel Ak Keme, is a giant, Turkish-built attempt at a four star hotel near the airport, with barely functioning business centre, sauna, swimming pool, casino, two restaurants, but poorly trained staff. Singles/doubles go for US$130/170, suites for US$240 and the presidential suite is US$320. Major credit cards are accepted. They have a Web site www.pinara.com.kg.

Hyatt Regency (☎ 68 01 44, *Soviet 191*) is scheduled to open in 2000 on the site of the former Hotel Kirghizstan. Expect five star service and prices to match.

Places to Eat

We never dreamed the day would come when Bishkek had too many restaurants to list on a map! Pseudo-western restaurants with ruthlessly efficient staff have popped up everywhere, but beware: the menu rarely has what it claims, service charges are strapped on at random and portions can be small. Furthermore, due to lack of patrons, many will have closed by the time we type this sentence. The more established favourites are listed here.

Restaurants The Hotel Dostuk has two restaurants: the upstairs Russian menu offers dishes for around 20 som, while the downstairs *Arizona* western menu charges US$2 to US$3 for the same food. Arizona's menu is in English and also has a few western dishes for US$3 to US$5.

The *Consul Restaurant*, opposite the Hotel Sary Chelek, is quite popular with expats but its promising menu doesn't match the stock in the kitchen and they will double your portions and then charge you for it.

The recommended *Balasagun Restaurant*, just off Kiev, beside the Rossiya Cinema, serves Chinese dishes and bottomless cups of tea. A filling dinner costs about 120 som, or have a tasty lunch of fried noodles for 20 som.

Also recommended is the *Orient International*, on Kiev opposite Ala-Too Square, a Turkish restaurant with an English menu, outdoor seating and a good choice of main courses for around 100 som and desserts for 50 som. Huge *lavash* bread and *cacik* (cucumber and yoghurt dip) make a cool lunch on a hot day for 60 som.

Another good Turkish restaurant is the *Yusa* (*Logvinenko 14*), west of the embassy district, with good Turkish kebabs, cheese *pides* (Turkish-style pizzas) for 50 som, baklava, salads, vegetarian dishes and cold beer. The Iskender kebab is particularly good.

Travellers report that *Nooruz Restaurant* (☎ 22 17 44, *Moskva 73*) (the Cyrillic looks like 'Hoopys') has good food. The European and Turkish menu is served in grand ambience at fair prices.

Café Classic on Manas south of Kiev is bright and airy and a good place for drinks. The mushroom pizza is recommended (though it also contains beef) for 33 som.

Two decent Chinese restaurants have opened side by side in the plaza on the south side of Victory Square: the friendly *Khodeli*, serving main dishes for around 120 som and the *Kontinental*, with the same menu for about 20 som less per dish.

Khanguk Koan is a Korean restaurant and karaoke bar at the east side of the same plaza, featuring a fantastic picture menu. Dishes (150 som) come with side salads and appetiser. Try the excellent *namche*, a salad made of raw vegetables, meats and seafood sauce.

Just east of Victory Square, near the Hotel Dostuk is the *Indus Valley Restaurant* (☎ 29 36 62, *Ibraimova 105*), a Pakistani restaurant with a good selection for vegetarians. Chicken *karahi* (braised or stir-fried with tomato sauce) for three costs 200 som. Next door is the unique *Restaurant Polonia*, cooking up Polish and German food, including rabbit and sausages, for around 150 som a dish. They also serve a set breakfast for 100 som and carry an impressive selection of French wine.

The pretentious *Santa Maria* on Chuy boasts European and Korean cuisine. Main dishes start at 60 to 100 som, but you'll need plenty of add-ons to make a full meal and so it is poor value.

Adriatico Paradise, a couple of doors down on Chuy underneath the ice cream sign, is also pricey, but better value than the Santa Maria, and it offers excellent Italian food prepared by a genuine Italian chef. They even play Puccini on the stereo. A 12-inch pizza costs 150 som and pasta dishes run at around 120 som. If nothing else, order the bread basket, a delicious bargain at 15 som. There's a 10% service charge.

If you have a larger budget, the swanky *Café Catrin* (☎ 66 25 44), on Kiev, can spoil you with shrimp, salmon or caviar for around US$20 per person for dinner; you can pay with any major credit card.

Bombay Restaurant (☎ 22 87 17, Chuy 110) has upscale Indian food for around 160 som for a main dish.

Cafes & Chaykhanas

Dozens of *chaykhanas* (teahouses) dot the city but many have become vodka fests, so check the clientele first. The *Kafe Ersay (Kiev 49)* is a good place to get an English description of Kyrgyz dishes. Lunch will run to about 40 to 80 som, plus a 5% service charge.

Astana Café, across the street, has a great atmosphere and cheap Uyghur food, including chicken shashlyk for 20 som and good, cheap salads. At night the place is jumping and there's a small cover charge for the (for once) decent live music. The next-door *Nayuz Café* is similar.

Chaykana Jalal-Abad at the corner of Kiev and Togolok Moldo has pleasant gazebos for afternoon tea, but the menu is limited to cheap laghman and shashlyk.

The canteen in the basement of the *Slavic University* on the corner of Kiev and Shopokov slops out cheap Russian goulash, borshch, salads and chips for under 20 som a dish.

MacBurger (Soviet 137) near Toktogul (almost a Macdonald's) does a decent hamburger with chips and a drink for 45 som. Other attractions are an English menu and the cleanest toilets in Kyrgyzstan! Next door is a pastry and ice cream shop.

Kafe Altyn-Kush, below MacBurger serves up good chicken, salads and soups. Expect to pay around 100 som for lunch.

Several fast-food stands around town sell dangerous-looking doner kebabs (sometimes called 'gamburgers') for around 10 som.

Self-Catering The mini-bazar on Moskva near Soviet is a great place for do-it-yourselfers to pick up dinner from around 5 to 6 pm (bring your own bags and containers) – hot bread, manty and *piroshki* (Russian-style pies) – plus vegies, fruit, beer and sweets. Bishkek also has three farmers' markets (see the following Shopping section), with abundant fresh vegetables, fruit and snacks.

The *Eridan Supermarket* on Chuy is the place to buy all your imported western goodies, as well as tampons and decent toilet paper, at western prices. On the other side of town the *Europa Supermarket (Sultan Ibraimov 70)* is another well-stocked western market with a small department store and souvenir shop attached.

Entertainment

Pubs & Bars *The Pub* (☎ 21 76 64, Chuy 168A) is a new American venture serving up Tex-mex, burgers and baked potatoes (120 to 200 som) with cold beer (70 som for 500ml). Happy hour is Monday to Friday 6 to 8 pm and a popular disco is set up in the back. Weekends in particular are a good time to meet expats.

Eridan Bar next to the supermarket on Chuy is a trendy, smoky bar popular with the locals. A small beer costs 30 som.

Bar Navigator is a classy little spot on the corner of Moskva and Razzakov, where embassy workers shell out 100 som for a gin and tonic or 30 som for a cappuccino. They also serve salads (30 to 60 som), ice cream (15 to 50 som) and main dishes like Chicken Kiev (65 som).

Planet Holsten in Dobovy Park is a nice place to sit outside on balmy nights and order a cold beer and a hot pizza.

Theatres & Concert Halls The *Philharmonia* (☎ *21 92 92, 21 96 34)*, at the corner of Chuy and Belinsky, features western and Kyrgyz orchestral works and the occasional Kyrgyz song-and-dance troupe, but you may need a local person to identify these from the playbills. A 1½ hour performance by the excellent Kyrgyz troupe Kambarkan costs about 20 som and is well worth making the effort to see (see the boxed text). Check out the interesting old black-and-white photos on the 1st floor.

In front of the Philharmonia is a statue of the legendary hero Manas slaying a dragon, flanked by his wife, Kanykey, and his old adviser, Bakay, and a statue gallery of modern Kyrgyz akyn. The kassa (ticket office) is on the west side.

At the *State Opera & Ballet Theatre* (☎ *26 13 89, Soviet 167)* opposite the State Museum of Fine Arts, classical western as well as local productions play to half-empty halls. There are also occasional concerts in the *Palace of Sport* on the west side of Panfilov Park.

The *State Academic Drama Theatre*, on the east side of Panfilov Park, presents popular Kyrgyz-language works, more often than not written by Chinghiz Aitmatov, Kyrgyzstan's premier man of words.

The *Russian Drama Theatre* is on Tynystanov in Dubovy Park.

Other Entertainment The *Ala Too Cinema*, in Dubovy Park, has western films (in Russian) and the occasional Kyrgyz film. You can play pool for 80 som an hour in the *billiards club* (☎ *22 83 42)* underneath the Consul Restaurant.

There's a thumping open-air *disco* nightly in Panfilov Park for 4 som, though expats recommend more sophisticated clubs such as *San Fedele*, near the Consul Restaurant, and *UFO*, underneath the Philharmonia. Entry to these last two is 200 som.

The *Circus*, on Frunze east of Soviet, played to packed houses in Soviet times but is now in a state of extreme disrepair.

Spectator Sports

Once upon a time, on summer Sundays, you might have seen traditional Kyrgyz horseback games at the Ippodrom (Hippodrome), south-west of the centre. Lately the best you can expect around Bishkek are exhibition games in Ala-Too Square during the Navrus festival and on Kyrgyz Independence Day, 31 August. See the Spectator Sports section in the Regional Facts for the Visitor chapter for more information.

Shopping

Bishkek has the country's best collection of souvenirs and handicrafts, though you can often find individual items cheaper at their source (eg shyrdaks in Naryn, hats in Osh). The main general shopping district is on Soviet between Kiev and Bokonbayev.

TsUM This state-run department store is surprisingly well stocked with a photo shop, photocopying, a large selection of made-

---

Kambarkan

While in Bishkek try to catch a performance of Kambarkan, a 10-piece Kyrgyz musical troupe that plays regularly at the Philharmonia. The band plays music by Kyrgyz and Kazak composers, in a variety of styles ranging from bard-like storytelling to orchestral pieces, all highly evocative of high pastures and the nomadic Kyrgyz character. The music is played on a mixture of *komuz* guitars, a vertical violin known as a *kyl kyayk,* double bass, Andean-style pipes, flutes, drums, mouth harps (*temir komuz,* or *jygach ooz* with a string) and long horns. There are also four dancers, and an excellent finale featuring circus-style wrestling midgets. Performances cost about 20 som.

for-tourists souvenirs and essential hardware such as miniature water heaters (perfect for making your own hot drinks).

Markets On warm days the streets are lined with people selling everything from radio parts to Brazilian oranges, but mostly imported booze and cigarettes. An informal mini-bazar has sprung up along Chuy by TsUM. The best place for self-caterers is another mini-bazar on Moskva at the corner with Soviet.

The city has three daily farmers' markets, all fairly distant from the centre. Osh bazar, 3km to the west, though not very colourful, offers a glimpse of Kyrgyz and Uzbeks from the more conservative south of the republic. Produce is sold inside the main bazar and all around the outside of the complex. There is a separate clothes market south of the main produce bazar. To get there take trolleybus No 14 on Chuy, bus No 20 or 24 on Kiev or 42 from Soviet.

Smaller markets include the Alamedin bazar to the north-east (trolleybus No 7 or 9 from TsUM, return by bus No 20 or 38) and Ortosay bazar, 6km to the south (trolleybus No 12 on Soviet). All are open daily but are biggest on weekends.

A huge 'flea market' of imported consumer goods and junk, nicknamed Tolchok, 'jostling crowd', comes to life at 8 am on Saturday and Sunday, about 7km north of the centre. Special 'Tolchok' buses run along Soviet all day Saturday and Sunday, from the corner by TsUM for 4 som. Watch your wallet or bag.

Carpets Carpets and the brightly coloured Kyrgyz felt-applique floor coverings called shyrdaks are sometimes sold for reasonable prices in the lobby of the Museum of Fine Arts at Soviet 196. Overpriced, inferior ones can also be found at Alamedin bazar, and a few at Osh bazar.

The Talent Support Fund is a nonprofit NGO that sells high quality shyrdaks, *ala kiyiz* (felt rugs featuring coloured panels), hats, bags and slippers to support social development in Kyrgyzstan. The showroom at Moskva 53 goes under the name of Kyrgyz Style *(kyrgyz korku)* (☎ 28 27 02).

The Antiquarian Shop Bishfar (☎ 66 49 16, Kiev 76), carries a private collection of old and new carpets from throughout Central Asia. The Afghan owner Mr Akram can give you a stamped receipt for customs.

Handicrafts Zhambulat Souvenirs, at Moskva 162, has a good general selection of Kyrgyz handicrafts and Soviet memorabilia. Go into the room on the right from the sparsely filled anteroom and search for treasures among the bric-a-brac.

Iman Souvenirs (☎ 21 24 05) at Chuy 128 has a small collection of jewellery, wooden soldiers (Manas and company) and Kyrgyz handicrafts. Tumar Art Salon (☎ 21 26 53), at Togolok Moldo 36, sells high-quality, high-priced embroidery.

You may find Kyrgyz men's hats – the familiar white felt *ak-kalpak* or the fur-trimmed *tebbetey* – for sale in TsUM or in the bazars. Also check the dusty souvenir shops in the Museum of Fine Arts and Dostuk and Bishkek hotels for fair-priced local handicrafts.

Artwork To buy a print of one of the fabulous woodcuts shown in this book (or many other designs) visit the artist Theodor Herzen (☎ 22 54 68), on the 3rd floor of the Asia Gallery, Chuy 108. Other artists work in the yard out the back and sell their pieces in the gallery upstairs. The gallery is open Monday to Friday 10 am to 5 pm.

Saimaluu Tash Art Gallery, at Pushkin 78 (north side of Dom Druzhby), sells interesting but pricey pottery, open Monday through Saturday, 10 am to 5 pm.

Stroll along the covered gallery in Dubovy Park to see local artists selling woodcarvings, oil paintings and charcoal portraits most afternoons.

Getting There & Away

Air The Kyrgyzstan Airlines main office is at Soviet 105 (☎ 28 08 86), though there are now also many *aviakassas* (air booking offices) that can both book and issue domestic flight tickets.

Kyrgyzstan Airlines flies several times a day to Osh (500 som), every few days to

Jalal-Abad (500 som), Talas (300 som) and Kazarman (500 som), and irregularly to Karavan (Kerven), Batken and Kyzyl-Kiya – cheap and spectacular trips by Yak-40, between the mountain tops and the clouds.

Regional and CIS connections include Tashkent twice a week, Moscow four times a week, various Siberian destinations once or twice a week, and St Petersburg seasonally. Some one-way Kyrgyzstan Airlines fares at the time of research were US$85 to Tashkent, US$110 to Dushanbe, US$160 to Moscow and US$190 to Ürümqi. Other airlines, such as Uzbekistan Airways, are more expensive.

For details of international flights into and out of Bishkek see the Getting There & Away chapter. Bishkek's Manas airport has a US$10 international departure tax, but no domestic tax.

It's only three hours by road to/from Almaty, which has many international flights. A Kazak visa is not necessary if you're going straight to/from the Almaty airport, but from Bishkek it's a good idea to have something like a hotel receipt or bus ticket showing you have not been in Kazakstan for more than 72 hours. KLM is set to start a free Almaty-Bishkek ground shuttle service for their customers; Austrian Airlines currently offers one for an exorbitant US$60 per person.

The following travel agencies are reliable for booking domestic and international air tickets:

Central Asia Tourism Corporation (CAT)
 (☎ 66 02 77, fax 66 56 92)
 Chuy prospektisi 124 – IATA member
Glavtour
 (☎ 22 12 53/02 55, fax 62 08 96)
 Toktogul 93 – visa cards accepted
L-Tour
 (☎ 22 44 48) Toktogul 84
Realtur
 (☎ 66 33 77)
 Bokonbayev 95 – can book Aeroflot, Uzbekistan Airlines and Air Kazakstan

The following international airline offices are useful for reconfirming or changing the dates of an existing flight but are not the cheapest places to book an international ticket:

British Airways
 (☎ 66 00 92/09 00, fax 66 08 68)
 Ground floor, Toktogul 93
KLM – Royal Dutch Airlines
 (☎ 22 54 03, fax 62 15 47)
 1st floor, Toktogul 93
Turkish Airlines
 (☎ 66 00 08, fax 66 15 80)
 Soviet 136 (corner of Bokonbayev)

Bus The west (or new) bus station is the place for long-distance buses; get there via bus No 7 on Kiev, bus 35 or 48 or minibus 113 or 114 from Jibek Jolu, or trolleybus No 5 on Manas. There's an information office next to counter 21 and a 24 hour exchange booth on the upper floor. Don't trust the schedule board at the station, and first ask the price for a seat in a private car going in your direction – always a more comfortable option. See the Car entry later in this section.

Comfortable luxury buses depart hourly in the morning to Karakol (127 som, 8½ hours) stopping at Balykchy, Cholpon-Ata and most places in between. The private minivans out on the road only depart when full. A daily bus to Naryn (99 som, seven hours) and At-Bashy (80 som, eight hours) departs at 6.40 am.

For Osh and the Fergana valley you must change at Toktogul (118 som, nine hours); a single bus goes there daily at 7.15 am. Alternatively, ramshackle minibuses and private cars to Osh wait at the Osh bazar bus stand, departing in the late afternoon when full, for between 300 and 400 som for a seat in a minibus, or 500 som for a seat in a car. The overnight trip takes around 15 hours depending on the road and vehicle – we saw some old wheezers disabled on the Tör-Ashuu pass.

Comfortable Mercedes buses go from the west station to Tashkent (via Kazakstan, though no Kazak visa is needed if you don't get off) three times a day between 6 and 9 pm for about 185 som, taking as little as 10 hours. Buses go directly to Almaty (115 som, 4½ hours) every hour or two all day, plus hourly all night with a change at Zhambyl. There is a passport check at the border by the Chuy river but you don't necessarily need a Kazak visa if you are in transit.

The east bus station is for regional points east such as Kant, Tokmak, Kemin, Kegeti and Issyk-Ata.

The Osh bazar bus stand has daily overnight buses to Tashkent (150 som, 10 hours) departing at around 5 pm. There are also local buses to destinations west such as Tash-Bulak, Sokuluk, Kashka-Suu and Chong-Tash. Bus Nos 160, 169 and 177 go several times a day to Kashka-Suu, for Ala-Archa Park; inquire at the ticket office at the entrance to the bus stand.

Kashgar Bus A Chinese-run outfit departs for Kashgar via the Torugart pass every Thursday (US$50). At the time of writing, however, foreigners were being turfed off the bus by Kyrgyz officials at the Torugart pass; you must have proof of onward Chinese transport before being allowed over the pass. (See the Bishkek to Kashgar via the Torugart Pass section later in this chapter for more details.)

The office (☎ 22 36 70) is in a house at Razzakov 7, not far from the train station, and is open 9 am to 5 pm. It's also the office of Kashgar CITS.

There is also said to be a Kyrgyz bus that runs on Sunday from a *turbaza* (holiday camp) at ulitsa Fere 8 in north Bishkek. There are also one or two buses a week to Artush, near Kashgar, but the same restrictions apply.

Train Very few people use the trains to get from Bishkek to anywhere, except Moscow. Trains start here three times a week for Tashkent (16 hours) and the Fergana valley (16 hours farther). Three trains a week also go to Almaty (16 hours) and Krasnoyarsk in Siberia, and there's a daily express to Moscow (72 hours). There are trains to Balykchy on Lake Issyk-Kul but the timings are awkward. Incredibly, we found schedules still using Moscow time, two hours earlier than Bishkek time.

You can try for your own ticket at the station (open daily 7 am to noon and 1 to 5 pm), or pay a travel agent a few US dollars to buy it for you. Avoid the touts infesting the station.

Car Private cars and taxis to places outside Bishkek scout for passengers at the west bus station and Osh bazar bus stand. Cars from the former run to Kochkor (80 som), Naryn (150 som), Karakol and Almaty. The starting price for a Mercedes car to Almaty is US$50.

Cars and taxis to Osh run from the Osh bazar bus stand and cost around 500 som per person for the overnight trip.

For longer trips choose your car and driver with care! Check for small things like an exhaust pipe and at least one handle that can be passed around to roll down windows. Taxis are often cheap enough to buy the extra seats and ride in comfort.

Getting Around

To/From the Airport Express bus No 153 runs every 30 minutes all day between Manas airport and the old airport, but the closest it gets to the centre is a stop in front of the Philharmonia. The 35km trip takes one hour and costs 15 som. You may see the odd minibus marked MAHAC running from Manas airport to the long-distance bus station.

A taxi between the airport and the centre should be around US$2 to US$3 in som with baggage, more at night or on Saturday or Sunday. See Getting There & Away about getting to Almaty airport.

Public Transport Municipal buses cost 2.5 som, payable as you disembark at the *front*. At rush hour these are so crammed that you must plan your escape several stops ahead. Old school-bus shaped marshrutnoe (fixed-route; also called *jitney*) buses ply some routes for a slightly higher fare. Minibuses (3.5 som) are generally a better bet as they are faster and less crowded.

Some useful minibus routes include:

Nos 113, 114
    From the west (long-distance) bus station, down Jibek Jolu to Alamedin Bazar.
Nos 125, 126
    From Soviet (opposite the Orient International restaurant) south down Mira prospectisi to the old airport, US embassy and Hotel Issyk-Kul.
No 110
    From Osh bazar, along Moskva to Soviet and then south.

Car Most agencies listed in the Travel Agencies section earlier can arrange a car and driver but you are better off just hiring a taxi for the day at a fraction of the price (see following). Dostuk Travels in the Dostuk Hotel charges US$5 per hour or US$25 per day for a car and driver.

Taxi Essentially anyone with a car is a taxi. Official taxis, with ФИА or БИА number plates, are cheapest and most reliable. It should cost no more than 20 som for a ride within the city. Flag a car and if you don't like the look of the driver or his price, flag the next one. You can book a taxi 24 hours a day at ☎ 182, for a small surcharge.

AROUND BISHKEK

Rolling out of the Kyrgyz Alatau, the Ala-Archa, Alamedin and dozens of parallel streams have created a phalanx of high canyons, good for everything from picnics to mountaineering. Some highlights are noted here. Dan Prior's *Bishkek Handbook* (see the Information entry in the previous Bishkek section), with exceptional detail on these canyons as well as historical sites in the Chuy valley, is essential reading for those who want to linger.

There are plenty of possible do-it-yourself summer treks, but bring your own food and gear and be prepared for cold weather and storms even in summer. There is limited public transport and you are best off hiring a taxi to drop you at the trailheads, though travel agencies listed in the Bishkek Information section can provide transport and arrange guided trips. Winter excursions are best arranged through an agency, who should know about avalanche and other risks. A recommended reference for treks here is Frith Maier's *Trekking in Russia & Central Asia*.

To check the location of places mentioned in this section, see the Bishkek to Kashgar via the Torugart Pass map in the section of the same name, later in this chapter.

Ala-Archa Canyon

In this very grand, rugged but accessible gorge south of Bishkek, you can sit by a waterfall all day, hike to a glacier (and ski on it, even in summer) or trek into the region's highest peaks. Most of the canyon is part of a state nature park, and foreigners must pay an entrance fee of 50 som per car plus 15 som per person. For some hiking routes see the boxed text 'Trekking in Ala-Archa'.

The park gate is 30km from central Bishkek. Some 12km beyond the gate, at 2150m, the sealed road ends at a shabby base camp or *alplager* with a weather station and a simple hotel (a bigger complex burned down a few years ago). In summer it has recreational facilities, baths and a sauna. Beyond this point the only transport is by foot or 4WD.

Places to Stay & Eat The best way to enjoy Ala-Archa is by bringing your own tent and sleeping bag. The only year-round accommodation is a wooden *hotel* in the alplager, with a dozen spartan doubles with common toilet and no shower for about 120 som per person. There may be some food available in summer, but it would be wise to bring your own and cook it in the kitchen. Try to avoid visiting on Saturday or Sunday, when 'biznezmen' turn up by the BMW-load to drink vodka and eat salami.

Getting There & Away Bishkek travel agencies can arrange pricey day and longer trips including guides and gear. The best budget alternative would be to hire a taxi or hitch (though you'll still end up paying for the ride).

Bus From Osh bazar bus stand in Bishkek, catch the occasional clapped-out *arenda* bus No 160, 169 or 177 as far as Kashka-Suu village, 7km from the park gate (itself 12km from the alplager), and hitch or hike from there. The No 177 occasionally goes right to the gate, at least in summer. Ask *'vorota zapovednika?'* ('nature park gate?') when you board. Bus No 177 is scheduled to depart at 5.20 and 8.20 am, and 1.50 and 4.45 pm but don't count on these times. No public buses go beyond the gate, and you may not always find one there to take you back to Bishkek.

Also from Bishkek, on Moskva, westbound No 11 buses, and on Soviet, west-

Trekking in Ala-Archa

There are dozens of trekking and climbing possibilities, but three main options. The gentlest walk runs 300m back down-valley from the *alplager* (base camp), then across a footbridge and southwest up the **Adygene valley**. Along this way is a climbers' cemetery in a larch grove, a pretty and poignant scene. The track continues for about 7km to 3300m, below Adygene glacier.

The most popular trek goes straight up the main canyon on a poor jeep track, about 18km to the **Upper Ala-Archa Mountain Ski Base**. From there in July and August a 2km-long ski lift climbs between glaciers to a 3900m ridge (other lifts also run during the winter ski season, December through April). There's a ski chalet here, where trekkers can stay if it's not full.

Most demanding and dramatic is **Ak-Say canyon**, with access via Ak-Say glacier to the area's highest peaks. A trail climbs steeply to the east immediately above the alplager, continuing high above the stream. A strenuous three hours brings you to the Raztek Stop camping area at the base of the icefall at 3350m (with a backpackers' tent city in summer). Another hour or two's graft brings you to the beautiful glacial valley. Beyond here, climbers use a steel hut beside the glacier at 4150m (accessible only with some glacier walking). Serious climbing routes continue up to the peaks of Korona (4860m) and Uchityel (4572m). Semenov Tianshanskii (4895m), the highest peak in the Kyrgyz Alatau, is nearby.

You should be particularly careful about altitude sickness on this route. Try to do at least one day hike before tackling this route and don't sleep any higher than the Raztek Stop on the first night. See Altitude Sickness under Health in the Regional Facts for the Visitor chapter.

The trekking season around Ala-Archa is May through September or October, though the trail to the Ak-Say glacier can be covered in snow even in August.

The Kyrgyz Cartographic Agency (see the Bishkek Information section) sells a good 1:50,000 topographic map of the entire park, called *Prirodnyy Park Ala-Archa*. An English version was printed in 1999.

---

bound No 26 buses, go about 12km south to the end of the line near the city limits, from where you can hire a taxi or hitch (ask for 'alplager', not just 'Ala-Archa').

Car A taxi from Osh bazar costs around 150 som one way to the gate, or 200 som to the alplager. If you are planning to return the same day negotiate a rate for the day, otherwise you face a long 7km hike back to the gate or leave yourself to the mercy of the taxi sharks at the alplager.

Other Canyons

Several valleys east of Ala-Archa have good walks and fewer visitors. In next-door **Alamedin canyon**, 40km from Bishkek, the main destination for local people is an old sanatorium called **Tyoplye Klyuchi** (Hot Springs) run by the Ministry of Power, with cheap accommodation and food. Though unprotected

by a national park, the scenery above and beyond this is as grand and walkable as Ala-Archa's, but there are no facilities.

On your own, take arenda bus No 145 from Alamedin bazar in Bishkek, get off at Koy-Tash village and hitch the 14km to the gate. Buses are said to depart frequently throughout the day in summer.

Another thermal-spring complex *(kurort)* and guesthouse is about 45km east of Bishkek in **Issyk-Ata canyon**. A *guesthouse* here has foreigners' rooms for US$40, or a spartan hostel for around 100 som. A single late afternoon bus goes there from Bishkek's east bus station, returning the next morning.

Some travel agents take hiking or horseriding groups to a lake and waterfalls in **Kegeti canyon**, which is 75km east of Bishkek. Buses to Kegeti depart from Bishkek's east bus station on Saturday at 9.30 am and 3.30 pm.

South-west of Ala-Archa lies the village of Tash-Bulak, from where you can make nice overnight trips up the **Sokuluk canyon** and even (with a guide) make a three day trek over the Sokuluk pass (3775m) into the Suusamyr valley. Accommodation is available for around 100 som per person at the *Yuri Gagarin Pioneers' Camp*, 4km south of Tash-Bulak. Buses to Tash-Bulak leave every hour or so from the Osh bazar bus stand. Alternatively take a bus 20km west to the village of Sokuluk and then hitch the remaining 24km south to Tash-Bulak. For locations, see the Bishkek to Kashgar via the Torugart Pass map.

Burana Tower
Beyond Kegeti at the mouth of the Shamshin valley, 80km from Bishkek, is a sterile but thorough Soviet restoration of the so-called Burana Tower, an 11th century monument that looks like the stump of a huge minaret. A mound nearby is all that's left of the ancient citadel that Dan Prior records as Balasaghun, founded by the Sogdians and later, in the 11th century, a capital of the Karakhanids, which was excavated in the 1970s by Russian archaeologists. The Shamshin valley itself has yielded a rich hoard of Scythian treasure, including a heavy gold burial mask, all either spirited away to St Petersburg or in storage in Bishkek's State Historical Museum.

There is a small **museum** inside the minaret, open 9 am to 5 pm daily; entry costs 10 som. Climb the mound behind the minaret to get an overview of the old city walls. On the other side of the mound is an interesting collection of *balbals*, stone grave markers.

To get to Burana on your own, take an hourly bus from Bishkek's east bus station to Tokmak (10 som, one hour), from where it's about 15km (about 100 som round trip) by taxi. The minaret can be easily visited en route to or from Issyk-Kul.

Chong-Tash
Along a 16km dirt road linking Kashka-Suu village in Ala-Archa valley with Koy-Tash village in Alamedin valley is a historical spot of interest if you're in a car. About 9km

from Kashka-Suu turn south to a small local sanatorium, situated at what was, until at least the 1950s, a KGB 'facility'.

On one night in 1937, the entire Soviet Kyrgyz government – nearly 140 people in all – were rounded up, brought here and shot dead, and their bodies dumped in a disused brick kiln on the site. Apparently almost no one alive by the 1980s knew of this, by which time the site had been converted to a ski resort. But a watchman at the time of the murders, sworn to secrecy, told his daughter on his deathbed, and she waited until *perestroika* to tell police.

In 1991 the bodies were moved to a mass grave across the road, with a simple memorial apparently paid for by the Kyrgyz author Chinghiz Aitmatov (whose father may have been one of the victims). The remains of the kiln are inside a fence nearby.

There are three buses a day to Chong-Tash (10 am, 1.15 and 3.40 pm) from the Osh bazar bus stand.

Chong-Kemin Valley
The 80km-long Chong-Kemin valley and national park lies about 140km east of Bishkek, along the Kazak border. The valley is famous locally as the birthplace of current President Akaev but, more importantly for travellers, it provides another great opportunity to roll up your sleeping bag and trek into the hills.

Trekking routes lead up the valley to Jasy-Köl lake and either the Ozyorny pass (3609m) to Kazakstan's Bolshoe Almatinskoe region or the Aksu pass (4062m) to Grigorievka on the northern shores of Issyk-Kul. See the boxed text 'Trekking to Lake Issyk-Kul' in the South-East Kazakstan section of the Kazakstan chapter for more details.

There's no formal accommodation in the valley but the travel company Ecotour (see the Bishkek Travel Agencies section) sets up yurts here in summer. A bus to Chong-Kemin (2½ hours) leaves Bishkek's east bus station daily at 12.30 pm. Otherwise take a more frequent bus to Kemin and then take a taxi the remaining 50km to Chong-Kemin.

Lake Issyk-Kul & the Central Tian Shan

Lake Issyk-Kul is basically a huge dent, filled with water, in the Alatau ranges that form the northern arm of the Tian Shan. The name (we use the more familiar spelling of what is properly Ysyk-Köl from the Kyrgyz) means 'warm lake'. A combination of extreme depth, thermal activity and mild salinity means the lake never freezes; its moderating effect on the climate, plus abundant rainfall, have made it something of an oasis down through the centuries.

After Tsarist military officers and explorers put the lake on Russian maps, immigrants flooded in to found low-rise, laid-back, rough-and-ready towns. Health spas lined its shores in Soviet days, with guests from all over the USSR, but spa tourism crashed along with the Soviet Union. Today Slavs and Kyrgyz live in roughly equal numbers in the lake's major towns.

The part of the central Tian Shan range accessible from the lake comprises perhaps the finest trekking territory in Central Asia.

The most popular treks lead from Almaty to the lake, or hop between valleys south of Karakol. If you need a rest you can lie on a beach in Cholpon-Ata. If heading back to Almaty, another option is to go via the Karkara valley (see the Karkara Valley entry later in this section). Give yourself at least four or five days to take in this region. A week is better, more if you'll be hiking.

Issyk-Kul's main town is no longer the spa centre of Cholpon-Ata but the provincial headquarters town of Karakol at the east end of the lake, at the foot of the mountains.

History

The Kyrgyz people migrated in the 10th to 15th centuries from the Yenisey river basin in Siberia, and in all probability arrived by way of Issyk-Kul. This high basin would be a natural stopover for any caravan or conquering army as well. It appears to have been a centre of Scythian civilisation and legend has it that Timur used it for a summer headquarters (see the following Karkara Valley section).

The first Russian, Ukrainian and Belarussian settlers came to the east end of the lake in 1868. Karakol town was founded in the next year, followed in the 1870s by Tüp,

KYRGYZSTAN

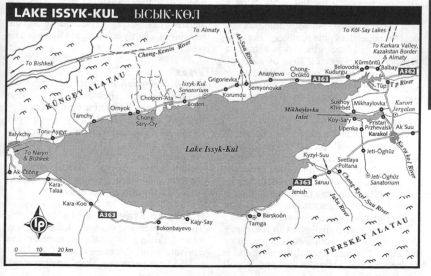

LAKE ISSYK-KUL   ЫСЫК-КӨЛ

To Almaty

To Köl-Say Lakes

Chong-Kemin River

Ak-Suu River

To Bishkek

To Karkara Valley, Kazakstan Border & Almaty

Kürmöntü   Balbay   A362

KÜNGEY ALATAU

Issyk-Kul Sanatorium   Grigorievka   Ananyevo   Chong-Orüktü   Belovodsk   Kudurgu

A363   Tüp   Tüp River

Cholpon-Ata   Korumdu   Semyonovka

Bosteri   Mikhaylovka Inlet   Sukhoy Khrebet   Mikhaylovka   Kurort Jergalan

Tamchy   Ornyok   Chong-Sary-Oy

Koy-Sary   Pristan Przhevalsk   Ak Suu

Balykchy   Toru-Aygyr   Lipenka   Karakol

To Naryn & Bishkek   Lake Issyk-Kul   Kyzyl-Suu   Jeti-Öghüz   Karakol River

Ak-Ölöng   Svetlaya Poltana   Jeti-Öghüz Sanatorium

Kara-Talaa   A363   Saruu   Jata River   Chong-Kyzyl-Suu River

Kara-Koo   Jenish

Barskoön   Tamga   TERSKEY ALATAU

Bokonbayevo   Kajy-Say

0   10   20 km

Teploklyuchenka, Ananyevo, Pokrovka (now Kyzyl-Suu) and a string of others, many of whose Cossack names have stuck. Large numbers of Dungans and Uyghurs arrived at Issyk-Kul in the 1870s and 1880s following the suppression of Muslim uprisings in China's Shaanxi, Gansu and Xinjiang provinces. Local Kyrgyz and Kazaks were still at that time mostly nomadic.

The Issyk-Kul region (and in fact most of Kyrgyzstan beyond Bishkek) was off limits to foreigners in Soviet times. Locals mention vast, officially sanctioned plantations of opium poppies and cannabis around the lake, though most of these had disappeared under international pressure by the early 1970s (Kyrgyzstan narcotics squads still swoop on isolated plots in the mountains).

More importantly, Issyk-Kul was used by the Soviet navy to test high-precision torpedoes, far from prying western eyes. An entire polygon or military research complex grew around Koy-Sary, on the Mikhaylovka inlet near Karakol. In 1991 Russian President Boris Yeltsin asked that it be continued but Kyrgyzstan's President Askar Akaev shut down the whole thing, ordering it converted to peaceful pursuits. Little conversion has taken place, though the old facilities have been closed down. Akaev did agree to try to limit western access, but with little success; local tour operators now routinely take visitors camping in the area. Jokes about the 'Kyrgyz navy' refer to a fleet of some 40 ageing naval cutters, now mothballed at Koy-Sary or decommissioned and hauling goods and tourists up and down the lake.

Geography

Issyk-Kul, 170km long and 70km across, is said to be the world's second-largest (in area) alpine lake, after Lake Titicaca in South America. It sits 1600m above sea level and reaches a depth of 695m, folded between the Küngey (Sunny) Alatau to the north and the Terskey (Dark) Alatau to the south. Both ranges rise straightaway to over 4000m.

The north side is shallow, with flat, sandy shores, while the south side is steep, stony and deep. The land around the west end is dry and barren, while the east end is well watered by air masses that collect moisture from the lake and then rise into the mountains. Most of the population and agriculture, and all the decent roads, are along the north shore.

Scores of streams enter the lake along its 600km shoreline, but there is no outflow – at least there has been none due to evaporation for some centuries – and consequently the lake is slightly salty. This, plus the physics of deep water and some underground thermal activity, mean that it never freezes, though in January it drops to 4° or 5°C. In June it's still only about 15° to 16°C. The warmest it gets – 18° to 20°C (even warmer in the shallows on the north side, where most lake shore spas are) – is from July through October.

Some people say the lake level has periodically risen and fallen over the centuries, inundating ancient shoreline settlements. There has been some fluctuation but the geological evidence points to a long-term drop – some 2m in the last 500 years. Nobody is sure why, although the interruption of inflowing streams for irrigation may play a part. Artefacts have been recovered from what is called the submerged city of Chigu, dating from the 2nd century BCE, at the east end. Mikhaylovka inlet near Karakol was apparently created by an earthquake, and the remains of a partly submerged village can be seen there.

Visas

Issyk-Kul remains a special military zone, and the higher reaches of the central Tian Shan are in a still-sensitive border zone. Police and other officials may check your Kyrgyzstan visa and registration stamp (see the Visas section earlier in this chapter). The old military zone at Mikhaylovka inlet, including the villages of Mikhaylovka, Lipenka and certain parts of Pristan Przhevalsk, is off limits to foreigners.

Places to Stay

The most pleasant, cheapest and safest way to bunk down at Issyk-Kul in summer is in a private home. Prices are cheap, from US$1 to US$5 per person per day, usually includ-

Issy-Kul Biosphere Reserve

The Issyk-Kul region has an astonishing array of ecosystems, from desert and semidesert in the south-west to steppe, meadow, forest, sub-alpine and glacial to the north and south-east. Local fauna includes Marco Polo sheep, ibex, wild boar, snow leopards, ibisbill, manul, Himalayan snowcocks, wild geese, egrets and other waders, pheasant partridges and wild turkeys. Water is a particularly important natural resource; some 4300 sq km of glaciers provide run-off water for Uzbekistan, Kazakstan, the Aral Sea and even parts of Xinjiang. The lake is an important ecological indicator of the entire region.

Plans are therefore afoot to create a reserve the size of Switzerland around the lake. This would consist of a mountainous core area, a buffer zone that would allow seasonal land use, and a transition and rehabilitation zone. The proposals will link up several existing reserves. Tourism is part of the program and a series of ecofriendly tourist yurts are planned.

The importance of environmental protection was highlighted in 1998, when almost two tonnes of sodium cyanide was spilled into the Barskoön river and thence Issyk-Kul, causing 700 locals to be hospitalised. As tourism and industry develops around Issyk-Kul, conflicts of interest are bound to increase in frequency, one reason why the reserve is being proposed now.

ing a meal or two, or if not then with cooking facilities provided. The best way to find a place is to ask the elderly ladies at the local bazar; before you know it, several people will offer a room.

Issyk-Kul's health resorts now seem a dying breed, although they still fill up with Bishkekers and local tourists in the hot months. Of at least 115 shoreline sanatoria before 1991, only a handful remain open. See the Cholpon-Ata Places to Stay section for details.

Some sanatoria may let you pitch your tent on their grounds or beach, and use their facilities for a small fee. Camping in the open is pretty safe, but regulations prohibit cars and camping within 200m of the shore.

Getting There & Away

Comfortable modern buses run every hour between Bishkek and Karakol, stopping in the towns of Balykchy, Cholpon-Ata and anywhere else en route.

The western road access to Issyk-Kul is a 40km-long, landslide-prone, slightly sinister canyon called Shoestring Gorge (Boömskoe ushchelie), which climbs into the Alatau east of Tokmak, with a howling wind funnelling up it most of the time. The Chuy river thundering down through it appears to drain the lake but doesn't (perhaps it once did, when the lake was higher). At the west end of the canyon is the Konorchek canyon, which travel agencies' hype likens to the red stone canyons of the American south-west.

There's a police checkpoint just west of Balykchy, where cars are searched for drugs and an 'eco-tax' is collected from each inbound vehicle from outside Issyk-Kul and Naryn provinces.

Balykchy is the place to change buses if you're going directly between Karakol and Naryn.

You can fly to/from Issyk-Kul too, though these flights only operate in summer and are among the first to be cancelled when fuel supplies get tight. They include Karakol-Almaty, Karakol-Bishkek, Karakol-Osh and Cholpon-Ata-Osh.

BALYKCHY
☎ 3944

There is no good reason to stop in this lifeless industrial town, except to change buses between Karakol and Naryn, or to change from train to bus en route between Bishkek and Karakol.

The old Soviet name was Rybache, derived from *ryba* (fish) and the post-independence name was merely translated into Kyrgyz (*balyk* is Kyrgyz for fish). You may find either name on old maps.

Ulitsa Frunze is the through road. The bus station is about 1km north-east of the train station. To get there from the train station, walk east on Ozyornaya ulitsa, take the first left, then left again (north-west) on Frunze.

Places to Stay & Eat

The only obvious choice is the run-down *Hotel Ak-Kuu* (☎ 255 59), also called the 'Chinese hotel', among apartment blocks north of the centre, two or 3km from the bus station. Small and stuffy singles/doubles with toilet (no hot water) are 42 som or 52 som for a lux. The *Kafe Bar Berek* is nearby, on the corner.

From the train station, go east on ulitsa Ozyornaya, take the first left, then go right on ulitsa Frunze for about 1.5km to ulitsa Gagarin (a boulevard). Go left there for three blocks to ulitsa 40-let Kirgizii, turn right and take the first left for 1½ blocks to the hotel. A taxi from the bus station costs around 15 som.

Getting There & Away

The most comfortable option to either Bishkek (56 som) or Karakol (69 som) is to take one of the modern Bishkek-Karakol coaches that pass through Balykchy bus station every hour or so. Scheduled local buses are slower and much less comfortable. There are local buses to Tamga and Bokonbayevo on the southern shore of the lake, and to Naryn.

In theory two trains a day run the 4½ hour trip between Balykchy and Bishkek but in reality the service is patchy and few people bother with the train.

You can get a seat in a shared taxi to Naryn (80 som, three hours), Kochkor (30 som, one hour) or Bishkek (60 som, three hours). Multiply the fare by four for the entire taxi fare. Taxis lurk on the north side of the bus station.

CHOLPON-ATA
☎ 3943

Cholpon-Ata is no longer worth a stop for its sanatoria, but if you want to see some ancient rock inscriptions or spend a day on a beach about as far away from the ocean as you can possibly get, then this is the place.

Orientation & Information

The town has two reference points: the bus station and adjacent summer-only bazar, and

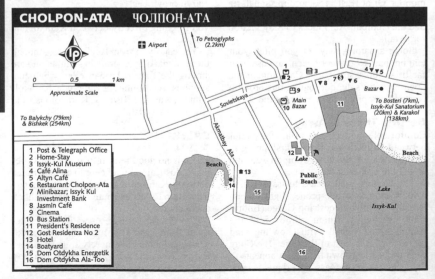

CHOLPON-ATA ЧОЛПОН-АТА

To Petroglyphs (2.2km)
Airport
To Bosteri (7km), Issyk-Kul Sanatorium (20km) & Karakol (138km)
To Balykchy (79km) & Bishkek (254km)
Sovietskaya
Almaty Ata
Main Bazar
Bazar
Lake
Beach
Public Beach
Lake
Beach
Lake
Issyk-Kul

0   0.5   1 km
Approximate Scale

1 Post & Telegraph Office
2 Home-Stay
3 Issyk-Kul Museum
4 Café Alina
5 Altyn Café
6 Restaurant Cholpon-Ata
7 Minibazar; Issyk Kul Investment Bank
8 Jasmin Café
9 Cinema
10 Bus Station
11 President's Residence
12 Gost Residenza No 2
13 Hotel
14 Boatyard
15 Dom Otdykha Energetik
16 Dom Otdykha Ala-Too

KYRGYZSTAN

the mini-bazar about 2km east on the main road. There is an exchange booth at the bank in the mini-bazar. The small airstrip is 1.5km west of the bus station, then about 1km up the hill away from the lake. Kyrgyz President Akaev owns a house in Cholpon-Ata, on the beach, so surrounding access can be tricky and you may have to show your passport.

Boatyard & Boat Trips
About 600m west of the bus station is a turn-off south to a bulge of shoreline. One kilometre down this road (officially Akmatbay Ata köchösü) is a tiny boatyard, now known as the Kruiz Yacht club (☎ 443 73), with a handful of sailboats and launches under repair or restoration. The once sleepy yacht club might be worth a poke around if you like boats, but the place now has tour group US dollars firmly in its gaze. Prices now run at an over-the-top US$10 to US$20 per hour for a four to six person yacht – more for an ex-Kyrgyz navy motorboat. You'll need to negotiate hard to get a decent price or else try arranging it through Valentin of Yak Tours in Karakol. It's even possible to arrange scuba gear here but this is really only an economical option for groups.

Beaches
South of the boatyard is a small, clean beach with shallow, warm water. Another much larger public beach lies 2km south of the bus station. Walk south from the bus station to the chalets of the Gost Residenza No 2 and then head east, across a bridge over a lagoon to the beach (plaj in Russian). You may have to show your passport to get to the beach.

There is another beach called Alytn Kul, 4km east of Cholpon-Ata.

Petroglyphs
Above the town is a huge field of stones, many with pictures scratched or picked into their south-facing surfaces. They apparently date from about 500 BCE to the 1st century CE, and were probably made by Scythian (Saka) people, predating the arrival of the Kyrgyz in the area. Most are of long-horned ibex, along with some wolves, deer and hunters, and some rocks appear to be ar-ranged in patterns. The stones with petro-glyphs are those with green inventory num-bers painted on them (which unfortunately takes away a bit of the mystique).

Take the road opposite the boatyard turn-off north for 2.2km, keeping to the asphalt, to a section of black iron fence. The stones are behind this.

Issyk-Kul Museum
This small regional museum is worth a quick visit. The emphasis is on archaeology, with displays of local Scythian (Saka) gold jewellery, balbal gravestones and local pet-roglyphs. Other rooms are devoted to ethnography, Kyrgyz bards, music and cos-tume. The museum is open daily 8 am to 5 pm; entry costs 10 som.

Places to Stay & Eat
Plenty of families rent out rooms or flats in Cholpon-Ata. The best people to ask are the elderly ladies in the mini-bazar, though some-one may approach you directly if you have a backpack on and look lost. There is supposed to be a kvartirnoe byuro (apartment bureau) at the main bazar where you can rent a flat but it wasn't operating when we visited in May.

The best place we found is the *home-stay* of Natalia Verenikova at Sovietskaya 81-4, about 300m east of the bus station, next to the post office. A bed in a comfortable four-bed room is a bargain at 50 som per person, in-cluding dinner and a hot shower. This is one of those rare occasions in Central Asia when you should actually consider paying more than is asked. Natalia can also book rooms at local sanatoria; she speaks only Russian.

For a few som you can pitch your tent in the sandy grounds of the *boatyard*, or sleep in the claustrophobic cabin of a rusty old boat for an overpriced 300 som. A small house next to the boatyard also has cheap rooms; look for the 'welcome' sign.

The town has a few cafes, including the *Jasmin Café, Café Alina* and *Altyn Café* and the Soviet-style *Restaurant Cholpon-Ata*, all of which serve up standard fare. Between October and May (inclusive) most of these are shut and you're better off eat-ing at your home-stay or self-catering.

KYRGYZSTAN

Sanatoria Along the shore on both sides of Cholpon-Ata is Issyk-Kul's largest concentration of old sanatoria. Prices tend to be excessive but they are very seasonal, and bargaining is in order.

By far the most famous is the year-round *Issyk-Kul Sanatorium* (*☎/fax 43 10 35)*, a Soviet monstrosity so big that from the road it obscures half the lake. It is nicknamed 'Avrora' (Aurora) after the cruiser that was involved in the starting of the October Revolution in St Petersburg. Rates for a single/double range from US$25/50 out of season (December to April) to US$65/110 and up per person at high season (July through August). For this you also get three modest meals and the chance to wander idly around 47 hectares of woods, sculpted gardens and a private beach. It's 20km east of Cholpon-Ata between the hamlets of Bosteri and Korumdu.

The year-round *Kyrgyz Seaside Resort* (*☎ 356 48)* is even bigger, with spa facilities, tennis courts, sailing boats, gym, swimming pool and over one thousand rooms. Rooms with full board range from US$15 in March/April to US$40 in summer, or from US$30 to US$80 for a lux. The resort is 3km south of Bosteri. A taxi from Cholpon-Ata costs 25 som.

Other, cheaper giants include the *Pansiyonat Stroitel* and *Goluboy Issyk-Kul*, just east of the centre of Cholpon-Ata, both probably US$20 to US$30 per person in summer. In Cholpon-Ata itself are two *dom otdykha* (like a sanatorium but without the in-house medical staff), the *Ala-Too* and *Energetik* and the turbaza-style *Gost Residenza No 2*. All charge about US$10 per person but aren't up to much and are closed outside of May to September.

Getting There & Away

Most bus connections are on through-buses between Karakol and Balykchy or Bishkek. A new road to Almaty is being constructed via the Chong-Kemin valley and the Kokayryk pass, but this will take years to complete. In summer there may be flights on Wednesday and Saturday to/from Osh (500 som), and maybe even Almaty, depending on passengers and fuel.

ANANYEVO

At Ananyevo, 52km farther east, is the Issyk-Kul state nature reserve, founded in 1948 and home to pheasants and shore birds. It's 3km south of the main road. Ananyevo's other attraction is some cheap, peaceful accommodation.

There's a small family-style *turbaza* in the middle of the reserve, but a better deal is in the adjacent townlet, called Turgorodok, where the reserve's staff live. Two *private*

Trekking North of Issyk Kul – the Küngey Alatau

Semyonovka, 42km east of Cholpon-Ata, is basically a bus stand and a few shops, but above here is the best local access to treks across the Alatau to/from Almaty. A road runs for about 15km into the mountains up the Chong Ak-Suu valley, becoming a jeep track after that. Up this road there was once a good trekking base, the Turbaza Kyrchyn, where you could get help and hire a guide, but for now at least, it's closed. The trail can also be reached from nearby Grigorievka. See the Zailiysky Alatau & Küngey Alatau section in the Kazakstan chapter for trek details.

From **Balbay** village (also called Sary-Bulak), at the north-east corner of the lake, it's a two day walk north over the 3274m Sary-Bulak pass and across the Kazakstan border, down to the pretty Köl-Say lakes, east of Almaty. From the upper lake it's another two or three days to Saty, the nearest trailhead in Kazakstan. A variant on the same route can take you over the nearby 3350m Kurmenty pass. See the Köl-Say Lakes section in the Kazakstan chapter.

A few trekkers across the Alatau to/from Almaty have been robbed, and there is some risk on any low-traffic, long-distance trekking route here.

Hidden Treasures

Large mounds on both sides of the road just west of the village of **Belovodsk** (50km east of Ananyevo or 15km west of Tüp) are said to be unexcavated Scythian (Saka) burial chambers. Other mounds excavated near Barskoön, across the lake, yielded bronze vessels and jewellery (now in museums in St Petersburg). There are more in the Karkara valley just across the Kazak border. One near the town of Yessik in Kazakstan yielded a fabulous golden warrior's costume, now Kazakstan's greatest archaeological treasure (see the boxed text 'The Golden Man' in the Almaty section of the Kazakstan chapter).

At Belovodsk is a turn-off south to the hamlet of Svetyy Mys, which at least one Soviet archaeologist insisted was the site of a 4th or 5th century Armenian Christian monastery. The story goes that its inhabitants were driven out by surrounding tribes, but not before hiding a huge cache of gold (and, some say, the bones of St Matthew) that has never been found. From the hills above, the village roads can be seen to trace something approximating an Orthodox cross.

---

houses (☎ 3942-627 66) have been converted to secure accommodation for independent travellers. A bed (one of 10 in plain doubles with common toilet and hot shower) and three square meals is around 200 som; there's also a sauna for an extra charge. Lyudmila Mirozhnichenko, the friendly *khozyayka* (landlady), can also arrange excursions, transport and horse trips into the hills, though she speaks little English. Take the road south towards the nature reserve, turn right 1km along, then left after 200m, and call at the third house on the right.

There is a small *bazar* on the corner of the main road and the road to the reserve, a *cafe* in the bazar and a *restaurant* just outside.

Bishkek-Karakol buses call at the bazar. There is also one direct Ananyevo-Bishkek bus each morning, plus arenda buses.

KARAKOL
☎ 3922 • pop 64,000

Karakol is a peaceful, low-rise town with backstreets full of Russian gingerbread cottages, shaded by rows of huge white poplars. Around the town are apple orchards for which the area is famous. This is the administrative centre of Issyk-Kul province, and the best base for exploring the lake shore, the Terskey Alatau and the central Tian Shan. It also has a very good Sunday market.

It's not quite paradise for those who live here – the economic stresses of independence and the decline in spa tourism have led to considerable hardship, thinned out available goods and services, and returned a kind of frontier atmosphere to this old boundary post – but hardly anybody talks about leaving. For better or worse, Karakol looks like headquarters for a new wave of tourism, from overseas.

The name means something like 'black hand/wrist', possibly a reference to the hands of immigrant Russian peasants, black from the valley's rich soil. Karakol is not to be confused with dismal Kara-Köl on the Bishkek-Osh road.

History

After a military garrison was established at nearby Teploklyuchenka in 1864, and it dawned on everybody what a fine spot it was – mild climate, rich soil, a lake full of fish and mountains full of hot springs – the garrison commander was told to scout out a place for a full-size town. Karakol was founded on 1 July 1869, with streets laid out in a European-style checkerboard, and the garrison was relocated here. The town's early population had a high proportion of military officers, merchants, professionals and explorers.

It was called Przhevalsk in Soviet times, after the explorer Nikolai Przhevalsky, whose last expedition ended here, and who is buried on the lake shore nearby (see the boxed text 'Przhevalsky' in the Around Karakol section). It didn't escape a trashing by the Bolsheviks. Its elegant Orthodox church lost its domes and became a club; only one small church on the outskirts was

KYRGYZSTAN

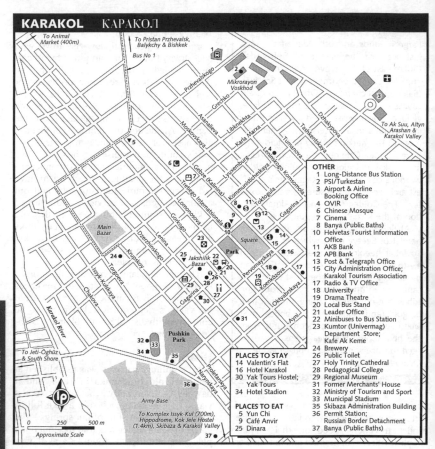

KARAKOL КАРАКОЛ

OTHER
1 Long-Distance Bus Station
2 PSI/Turkestan
3 Airport & Airline
  Booking Office
4 OVIR
5 Chinese Mosque
6 Cinema
7 Cinema
8 Banya (Public Baths)
10 Helvetas Tourist Information
   Office
11 AKB Bank
12 APB Bank
13 Post & Telegraph Office
15 City Administration Office;
   Karakol Tourism Association
17 Radio & TV Office
18 University
19 Drama Theatre
20 Local Bus Stand
21 Leader Office
22 Minibuses to Bus Station
23 Kumtor (Univermag)
   Department Store;
   Kafe Ak Keme
24 Brewery
26 Public Toilet
27 Holy Trinity Cathedral
28 Pedagogical College
29 Regional Museum
31 Former Merchants' House
32 Ministry of Tourism and Sport
33 Municipal Stadium
35 Skibaza Administration Building
36 Permit Station;
   Russian Border Detachment
37 Banya (Public Baths)

PLACES TO STAY
14 Valentin's Flat
16 Hotel Karakol
30 Yak Tours Hostel;
   Yak Tours
34 Hotel Stadion

PLACES TO EAT
5 Yun Chi
9 Café Anvir
25 Dinara

allowed to remain open. Of nine mosques (founded by Tatars, Dungans and various Kyrgyz clans), all but the Dungan one were wrecked.

Orientation
Karakol has a central square, but the real centre is the Jakshilik bazar, nicknamed *gostinny dvor* (the Russian equivalent of a caravanserai or merchants' inn, after its namesake in St Petersburg), built in the 1870s. The long-distance bus station is about 2km to the north, and the small airport is right at the north-eastern edge of town.

Russian street names are still in common use in spite of many official changes to Kyrgyz names, and we use the Russian ones here.

Information
Tourist Offices The Karakol Tourism Association, on the 4th floor of the City Administration Office, has largely disbanded and now acts much like a private agency, putting tourists in contact with chosen guides.

The Swiss development agency Helvetas (under the name Novinomad) (☎ 560 00), at 61 Pervomayskaya, is in the process of setting up a tourist information office (☎ 511 15) at 263 Toktogula, between Gebze (formerly Kalinina) and Tretiego Internatsionala, which will offer information and connect tourists with local guides and agencies, possibly for a commission.

Registration & Visa Extension To register (see the Facts for the Visitor section earlier in this chapter) or try for a visa extension, go to OVIR on Leninskogo Komsomola, at the corner with Kommunisticheskaya. The office in room 106 is open Tuesday, Thursday and Friday, 8 am to noon and 1 to 5 pm, and Saturday 8 am to noon. You need to pay the 50 som registration fee at the APB Bank.

Permits If you plan to head up to Altyn Arashan to spend the night or intend to go trekking anywhere in the Terskey Alatau mountains behind Karakol you need a permit from the Ministry of Tourism and Sport. See the Trekking Permits section under Visas at the beginning of this chapter for more details. Permits are issued on the spot and cost US$8 for three days or more, and US$30 for more than 30 days. Contact English-speaking Ermek (☎ 298 42) for information and help with filling out the form. There is theoretically a 1000 som fine for trekking without a permit.

To go up into the Tian Shan past Inylchek town, eg towards Inylchek glacier or Khan Tengri (see the following Central Tian Shan section in this chapter), you also need a military border permit *(propusk)* from the permit station of the Russian border detachment stationed at the army base here (at the site of Karakol's original garrison). Trekking agencies normally need two weeks to arrange this, so contact your agency well in advance. The permit costs US$10, though agencies charge up to US$35.

Money Moneychangers everywhere will change cash US dollars and deutschmarks. Try the small shops around the Jakshilik bazar or the exchange office next to the Investment Bank Issyk-Kul.

AKB Bank on Toktogula at the north-east corner of the square changes US dollar travellers cheques into US dollars for a 2%

commission, or into som for a 3% commission. Bank hours are 8 am to 3.30 pm, closed noon to 1 pm.

Post & Communications The post and telegraph office, on the east side of the square, is the place to mail postcards or make an international call or fax.

The travel agency PSI, operating under the name Turkestan (☎/fax 598 96, ✉ psi@ glob-x.karakol.su), offers email services (see also the following Travel Agencies entry in this section). Email is free for clients; US$1 per page for everyone else, or you can get Internet access for US$6 per hour. You can also make cheap international calls here through the Internet for US$2 to the USA and US$1.50 to Europe.

Valentin of Yak Tours (see the following Travel Agencies entry in this section) is hoping to add email to his facilities, at a few som per page.

Travel Agencies There are two main outfits in town. The veteran of the two is Valentin Derevyanko of Yak Tours (office ☎ 569 01, home ☎/fax 223 68, ✉ Yak Tours@ infotel.kg), with offices at their hostel at 10 Gagarina. In addition to running the town's only backpackers' hostel, they'll do on-the-spot arrangements for individuals, including trekking and horse trips (US$25 to US$35 per day), jeep transport and equipment rental. They can provide information on visits to a yak farm in the remote Sary Jaz valley and can even arrange a display of eagle hunting. They're environmentally switched-on, and sympathetic to budget needs if you ask. Valentin is a walking encyclopedia of the region, and speaks good English, though it's important that you make it clear exactly what kind of arrangements you want at the outset.

Across town is PSI/Turkestan (☎/fax 598 96, ✉ psi@glob-x.karakol.su, Web site www .oasis.fortunecity.com/myrtle/168; contact Sergey Pyshnenko) at flat 50, 3rd floor, building 10, mikrorayon Voskhod (the forest of high-rise apartment blocks opposite the bus station). PSI specialises in trekking and is pricier, but more professional, than Yak Tours. They can arrange horse treks into the

KYRGYZSTAN

Küngey Alatau mountains, north of Issyk-Kul, as well as providing no-strings-attached Kyrgyz (and other republics) visa support for US$10. They also have a nearby apartment for rent at US$8 per person and a camp site in town with places for US$2 with hot shower. Combined tent and sleeping bag rental costs about US$5 per day. They have a great selection of topo maps on the walls if you are planning a trek in the region.

A new company is Kok Jele (☎ 257 30, 422 78, ✉ kokjele@pari.el.cat.kg), Dzerzhinskogo 116. They hold the lease on the former mountain rescue hostel to the south of town and can arrange treks in the Terskey Alatau.

Equipment Hire The NGO Leader (☎/fax 541 84) rents out trekking equipment to fund its youth development programs. Equipment includes backpacks (US$2 per day), tents (US$3 to US$5), sleeping bags (US$2), sleeping mats (US$1), stoves (US$1) and mountaineering equipment. You can find them at Gagarina 15, on the corner of Gorkogo. No deposit is required but you do need to supply a copy of your passport.

Bathhouses There is a *banya* (public bath), ingeniously called 'Baths No 1', on Gebze near Toktogula, where a good soak is 20 som, or you can just use the hot showers at the back for 17 som. Bath toiletries are on sale at the ticket stand up front. Another banya, inside the Hotel Stadion, costs 40 som for a shower or 80 som per hour for a sauna and shower.

Chinese Mosque

What looks for all the world like a Mongolian Buddhist temple on the corner of Libknekhta and Tretiego Internatsionala is in fact a mosque, built without nails, completed in 1910 after three years' work by a Chinese architect and 20 Chinese artisans, for the local Dungan community. It was closed by the Bolsheviks from 1933 to 1943, but since then has again been a place of worship.

Sunday Market

This is no match for Kashgar's Sunday Market, but is still one of the best weekly bazars

we saw in Central Asia. The big **animal market** *(mal bazari)* in the northern outskirts of town, in particular, is a must-see: several blocks jammed with people from throughout the region – an array like you won't see down in Bishkek – here to buy and sell horses, cattle, sheep, pigs and other creatures. You can buy a good horse for US$150 to US$300, or at US$20 a sheep makes a nice gift. There is no evidence of the pickpockets or other low-life that inhabit urban markets. Go early: it starts at 5 am and is over by 10 am.

The regular **bazar** back in town is also particularly busy on Sunday, though unlike the animal market it's also open and less crowded on other days of the week. Across the road is a brewery, built before the Revolution with the latest technology of the day. Locals say, not surprisingly, that it once made the best beer in the region but has gone downhill since independence.

Holy Trinity Cathedral

A handsome cathedral is rising again from the rubble of Bolshevism, among birch and poplar trees at the corner of Lenina and Gagarina. Karakol's first church services were held in a yurt on this site after the town was founded. A later stone church fell down in an earthquake in 1890 (its granite foundations are still visible). A fine wooden cathedral was completed in 1895 (you can see a photo of it in the Regional Museum). But the Bolsheviks closed it in the 1930s, destroyed its five onion-domes and turned it into a club. Serious reconstruction only began in 1961, proceeding at a snail's pace as available money and materials permitted. Services are again being held, since its formal reconsecration in 1991 and again in 1997. Listen for its chimes on Sunday morning.

Other Colonial Buildings

The colonial-era part of town sprawls southwest from the cathedral and the Hotel Karakol – lots of single storey 'gingerbread' houses, mostly plain but some (eg those built by wealthier officers and scientists) quite pretty, and a few (those of Russian merchants and industrialists) with two storeys. Among decaying former merchants' houses are the Pedagogical College on Gagarina opposite the cathedral, the radio and TV office on Gebze (Kalinina), a block south of the Hotel Karakol, and another old merchant's home at the corner of Koenközova and Lenina.

Regional Museum

Karakol's modest regional museum is in a sturdy colonial brick building, once the home of a wealthy landowner, on Dzerzhinskogo near Toktogula. It's of interest for exhibits on the petroglyphs around Issyk-Kul, a few Scythian bronze artefacts, a Soviet history of the Kyrgyz union with Russia, some Kyrgyz applied art, and photographs of old Karakol – all of it better with a guide, since nothing is in English. It's allegedly open daily 8 am to noon, and 1 to 5 pm. Entry is 10 som, plus another 10 som for an English-speaking guide.

One exhibit features Nikolai Andreevich Nestorov, a Bolshevik hero who later took up life here as a trapper and naturalist (and built the tiny museum at Altyn Arashan). Strangely enough, he died in Karakol on the day we were at the museum.

Other Things to See

The leafy **Pushkin Park** by the stadium, four blocks south of the centre, includes the collective grave of a squad of Red Army soldiers killed in the pursuit of basmachi rebels.

About 3km south of the centre (on bus No 1) is Central Asia's very first **hippodrome**, still in use, though fewer and fewer people have the resources to keep racehorses.

Places to Stay

Cheapest by far, and fairly good value, is *Hotel Stadion (☎ 246 27)*, a spartan hostel on the west side of the municipal stadium, a 10 minute walk south of the centre. Beds in a small clean single or double are 120 som. There's a clean, communal washroom and you can get a hot shower in the adjoining sauna for 40 som.

Yak Tours Hostel (☎ 569 01, ☎/fax 223 68, Gagarina 10 ✉ YakTours@infotel.kg,) is the first backpacker-style hostel in Central Asia (or will be when its grand scheme is

complete). Facilities include baggage hold, equipment rental, an info board, a kitchen and a small collection of videos on Central Asia (including the LP video on Kyrgyzstan and Uzbekistan). Cozy doubles with bunks cost the som equivalent of US$1 to US$3 per person, or there are doubles for US$5 per person. You can also throw down your sleeping bag or pitch a tent in the yard for a few som. Unfortunately there is currently only one bathroom. Valentin also has an *apartment* in the centre of town, which is sometimes available for rent.

The Soviet-style *Hotel Karakol (☎ 214 5, 22 Gebze)* has plain and fairly clean singles/doubles/triples with toilet and bathtub (but no hot water) for 130/208/240 som. There are also lux rooms with separate sitting rooms for 320 som. Floor ladies provide a bucket of hot water for a few som. It's a 15 minute walk from the bus station.

One of the best mid-range hotels we found is the so-called 'government hotel', a former Party compound called *Komplex Issyk-Kul (☎ 207 10)*, 2.5km south of the centre at Fuchika 38 (take bus No 1). Plain, carpeted singles/doubles are US$18/22, and the more deluxe building of the two has plush doubles for US$30, US$36 or US$40 (locals pay a fraction of this) All rooms have hot water. Also in the leafy grounds are a dining room and a sauna, which can be booked for 75 som per hour.

The travel company Kok Jele currently holds the lease on a small A-frame *hostel*, once run by the mountain rescue service, at Fuchika 119, 3km south of the centre opposite the hippodrome (take bus No 1). Rooms cost around US$6 and you can pitch a tent, though you are better of contacting Kok Jele direct before heading out here (see the Travel Agencies entry earlier in this section).

Places to Eat

It's nearly impossible to find food in the evening in Karakol. Choices seem to be grotty Russian canteens, shifty vodka-goulash joints or instant noodles in your room. Lunches are easier to come by, and food stalls often serve until late in the afternoon, if you can adjust accordingly.

Café Anvir, on the north side of the central square, does cheap, filling lunches in a bright and pleasant little cafe. Try the French salad (vegetarians should ask for *nye myasa* – without meat), or *azu*, sweet and sour beef over chips.

Dinara on Lenina has also been recommended by expats for its local dishes.

Kafe Ak Keme in the basement of the Kumtor Department store does a decent hamburger for the bargain rate of 7 som.

Chef Babalina at the **Yak Tours Hostel** makes the best food in town and she understands vegetarians' needs; meals are a bit pricey at US$5 for lunch or US$4 for dinner, but prices are negotiable.

Dungan Food This is more or less traditional Chinese cuisine, adapted to local ingredients. The most common dish is ashlyanfu – meatless, cold, gelatine noodles in a vinagery sauce. It can be quite spicy so watch the red stuff. Even Dungan laghman and *pelmeni* (ravioli-like dumplings) are tastier than the stodgy Kyrgyz variants.

You can find Dungan snacks in the *bazar* for only a few som. One Dungan restaurant that might be worth trying is the **Yun Chi** in the north of town, on Przhevalskogo, though it was closed when we visited.

The best Dungan food is of course in Dungan homes, where a slap-up meal may have eight to 10 courses (Dungan weddings can have up to 30 courses). Yak Tours can arrange a good Dungan feast for between US$6 and US$10 per person, if you can get a group together.

Self-Catering Along with vegetables and fruit, the well-stocked main bazar also features lots of Russian and Dungan home produce, including a yoghurt drink called *kefir* by Russians and *ayran* by Kyrgyz, sausage, honey (Karakol honey is renowned in the region) and bread.

The Jakshilik bazar is also a good place to stock up on all kinds of foodstuffs, and there are plenty of private shops nearby that carry western brands of cheese, biscuits, sweets and tinned foods. This is a good place to stock up if you are planning a trek.

The Yak Tours Hostel will let you use the kitchen if you are staying there.

Shopping

The Kumtor (previously Univermag) Department store has overpriced made-for-tourists items similar to those found in Bishkek's TsUM. Artistik Salon in the Jakshilik bazar (the sign says 'Folkart') has some nice, neutral-coloured shyrdaks as well as some machine-stitched items; they're mid-priced but worthy of haggling. A poorly stocked souvenir shop on the ground floor of the city administration building has a few nice pieces at fair prices.

A pitiful shoebox-sized shop on Toktogula, north-west of the department store, sells some great Lenin pins and miscellaneous Soviet memorabilia.

Getting There & Away

Kyrgyzstan Airlines has daily flights to/from Osh (500 som), and sometimes Almaty and Bishkek, though at the time of writing these last two weren't operating. Ticket sales and the booking office are at the airport.

Comfortable modern buses to Bishkek's long-distance station (124 som, seven to eight hours) go roughly hourly, 6.30 am to 2.30 pm, via Cholpon-Ata (43 som) and Balykchy (69 som, three hours). There is a luggage charge of 5 som per bag. Slower buses run via the southern shore and depart at 8, 9 and 10 am and 3 pm. There are also daily buses at 12.50 pm to Tamga, 3.50 pm to Barskoön, at 2.20 and 3 pm to Bokonbayevo and at 11.50 am to Kaji-Say.

Out in front of the station are faster arenda minibuses (eg six hours to Bishkek), and private cars looking for passengers. Buses go to Balykchy every hour from 6.45 am to 4.30 pm, and via the south road about hourly until 12.30 pm. For Naryn and Kochkor, change at Balykchy.

Most local buses (eg to Pristan Przhevalsk, Ak Suu, Jeti-Öghüz, Barskoön) go from the centre, east of the Jakshilik bazar. Buses to anywhere farther away (eg, Tüp or beyond) go from the bus station.

Almaty buses via the Karkara valley are for hire only, and only run in summer. There is said to be one daily Karakol-Almaty bus in summer around the west end of the mountains, not stopping at Bishkek.

Unofficial taxis are relatively easy to hire in the centre for trips around the region, but agree on a price and waiting time beforehand.

Getting Around

The only remaining scheduled local route is the north-south bus No 1 (see the Karakol map), whose old German school buses link the centre, bazar, army base, Komplex Issyk-Kul and old mountain rescue hostel (now the Kok Jele hostel) for two som. Marshrutnyy minibuses trundle back and forth between the bus station and the centre, whenever one can coax in more than about 10 passengers.

Taxis are fairly plentiful and cost around 10 som anywhere in town, or 15 som out to the Komplex Issyk-Kul. The sharks at the bus station may ask for more but hold your ground.

AROUND KARAKOL
Przhevalsky Memorial, Grave & Museum

Thanks perhaps to the efforts of Soviet historiographers, and to the fact that he died here, the Russian explorer Nikolai Przhevalsky (see the boxed text 'Przhevalsky', later) is something of a local icon, an increasingly poignant reminder of what the Russians accomplished in this part of the world. His grave, a memorial park and museum are 7km north of Karakol on the Mikhaylovka inlet. A visit with a Russian guide still has the flavour of a pilgrimage.

Przhevalsky died in 1888, and a huge monument and tiny chapel were erected by his grave six years later. The museum and garden are Soviet creations opened in 1957, displacing the rest of a village graveyard.

The museum, a branch of the one in Karakol, features a huge map of Przhevalsky's explorations in Central Asia and a gallery of exhibits on his life and travels, plus a roll call of other Russian explorers. Captions are in Russian. There is usually a Russian-speaking guide on duty, delightful in her earnest explanations. Look out for the murals that change perspective from different angles.

The grave and monument overlook the Mikhaylovka inlet, though it's a rather different scene than that beloved by Przhevalsky. The shore has receded hundreds of metres since 1888, and the area – called Pristan Przhevalsk or just Pristan – is a clutter of cranes, docks and warehouses, all once part of the old Soviet top-secret 'polygon' for torpedo research.

To get there on your own, take bus No 37, marked ДАЧИ (Dachi) from the centre of Karakol, departing every two hours or so, or a taxi (budget about 200 som for the return trip, including waiting time). There is a museum entry fee of 20 som.

Pristan Przhevalsk

'Pristan' (Russian for pier) is a strip of lake shore several kilometres long that includes a sea of dachas to the north-east, a beach to the west, and in between various factories, warehouses and workers' homes. The beach is a jumping local scene in summer, with swimming, boats for hire, carts for hire, food, and occasional live music. Some of the dachas are in the restricted military zone and you may have problems staying here.

From Karakol centre to the beach, take any of the buses marked ПЛЯЖ Plaj (Beach), which run every hour. A return taxi will cost around 100 som.

Altyn Arashan

Probably the most popular destination from Karakol is a spartan hot spring development called Altyn Arashan (Golden Spa), set in a postcard-perfect alpine valley at 3000m, with 4260m Pik Palatka looming at its southern end. From the turn-off to Ak Suu Sanatorium it's an often-steep, five to six hour (14km) climb south on a track beside the Arashan river, through a piney canyon full of hidden hot and cold springs.

Much of the area is a botanical research area called the Arashan state nature reserve. Somewhere up here President Akaev and some other government bigwigs are said to have holiday yurts.

Altyn Arashan has several small hot-spring developments. In the order that you come to them, they belong to the government

KYRGYZSTAN

AROUND KARAKOL

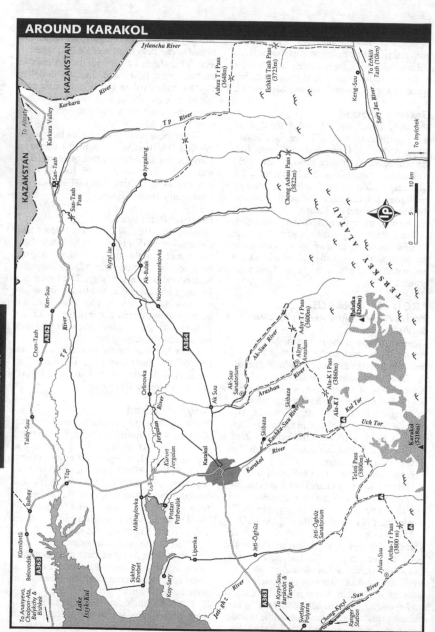

Przhevalsky

The Golden Age of Central Asian exploration was presided over by Nikolai Mikhailovich Przhevalsky. Born in Smolensk on 12 April 1839, his passion from an early age was travel. His father was an army officer and young Nikolai, under heavy pressure to be one too, apparently decided that an army career would give him the best chance to hit the road, though he never enjoyed the military life.

To prove to both the Russian Geographical Society and his senior officers that he would be a good explorer, he persuaded the Society to sponsor his first expedition, to the Ussuri river region in the Russian Far East in 1867-69. The results impressed everyone, the Society agreed to help finance future trips, and the army gave him the time he needed, insisting only that on his return from each trip he be debriefed first before saying anything to the Society.

Przhevalsky's Faustian bargain got him his freedom to travel in return for being, in effect, an army agent. He never married, going on instead to become a major general and the most honoured of all the tsarist explorers. He focused on Central Asia, launching four major expeditions in 15 years:

- Mongolia, China and Tibet   (1870-73)
- Tian Shan, Lop Nor, Taklamakan desert and northern Xinjiang   (1876-77)
- Mongolia, China and Tibet   (1879-80)
- Mongolia, China, Tibet, Taklamakan desert and Tian Shan   (1883-85)

Those starting in Mongolia were devoted to finding a route into Tibet. He finally made it to Lhasa once, and had an audience with the then Dalai Lama.

He was thwarted and threatened at many points in Mongolia, China and Tibet by local people who had no interest in letting foreigners come and look around. On the one non-Tibet trip, he discovered the tiny steppeland horse that now bears his name – Przhevalsky's Horse (now gone from its old habitats, surviving only in zoos around the world).

On the last of these trips he arrived via the Bedel pass at Karakol. In 1888 he was at Bishkek (then Pishpek) outfitting for his next, grandest, expedition. While hunting tiger by the Chuy river he unwisely drank the water, came down with typhus and was bundled off to Lake Issyk-Kul for rest and treatment. From here he wrote to the tsar asking to be buried beside the lake, dressed in his explorer's clothes. He died at the military hospital on 20 October 1888.

meteorological service, the Teploklyuchenka collective farm, and the forestry service. The collective farm has three concrete hot pools in wooden sheds, open to all for about 10 som a soak.

Across the stream is a little log house and museum with stuffed animals of the region. From the springs it's about five hours on foot to the snout of the Palatka glacier, wrapped around Pik Palatka.

Places to Stay & Eat Only the collective farm site is open to all (in summer). It has 30 beds (in two plain 10 bed dorms, a cramped triple and a porch) for about US$3 each, plus abundant free tent space, a kitchen, outside pit toilets and a full-time caretaker. Valentin of Yak Tours also runs a yurt here in summer for about US$3 a day and offers food. Your best option is to take a tent and camp somewhere undisturbed in the valley.

You can buy a few things here in summer but it's better to bring your own food (and purifying tablets for the water), plus a bit of tea, salt, sugar or coffee for the caretaker.

Getting There & Away A jeep road leads up to the springs from 5km south of Ak Suu (former Teploklyuchenka) village. You can walk five or six hours from the junction or hire a horse from one of the Karakol agencies. A taxi to the junction will cost 200 som from Karakol. Valentin of Yak Tours will bring you up to Altyn Arashan from Karakol in his jeep for about US$25 per person per day all in, including hotel accommodation at the start and finish. PSI charges considerably more. There's little traffic so hitching isn't really an option. You can hike in as the climax of several possible treks to/from the Karakol valley (see the boxed text 'Trekking around Karakol').

Ak Suu

Also known as Teploklyuchenka (Russian for hot springs), 12km east of Karakol, Ak Suu is typical of Issyk-Kul's original Cossack-settled villages. It was founded just before Karakol, on the banks of the Arashan river.

South of the village, past the derelict Orthodox church, the road forks where the river forks. To the right is the jeep track to Altyn Arashan and to the left, 6km from the centre of town, beside the murmuring Ak Suu (White Water) river, is the small

---

Trekking around Karakol

The Terskey Alatau range that rises behind Karakol offers a fine taste of the Tian Shan. Of numerous possible routes that climb to passes below 4000m, the best of them take in the alpine lake Ala-Köl above Karakol, and the Altyn Arashan hot springs above Ak Suu (Teploklyuchenka). Altyn Arashan is described in the Around Karakol section, and the trailheads at Jeti-Öghüz and Kyzyl-Suu are described under separate headings.

Routes
Established routes include:

Ak Suu to Altyn Arashan and back (minimum one or two nights) Five hours up the Arashan river valley, climbing from 1800 to 3000m. A day-hike extension could take you 4½ hours farther up the valley, branching east and then south for views of Palatka (4260m).

Karakol valley to Arashan valley, via Ala-Köl (minimum three nights) Hike up from the end of the No 1 bus route for about four hours to where the Ala Köl valley branches to the left. Two hours up takes you to the carved wooden Sirota camp; another five hours takes you past waterfalls to the high-altitude and barren Ala Köl lake. A 30 minute walk along the north shore offers camping at the base of the pass. The trail to the 3860m Ala-Köl pass is indistinct and the pass crossing can be tricky at the end of the season, so consider a guide from September onwards. Five hours downhill from the pass brings you to Altyn Arashan, from where you can hike down to Ak Suu the next day.

Jeti-Öghüz to Altyn Arashan via the Karakol valley (minimum four or five nights) The trail heads up the Jeti-Öghüz river valley, crossing east over the 3800m Teleti pass into the Karakol valley. From here head up to Ala-Köl, and then over to Altyn Arashan and Ak Suu (see previously).

Kyzyl-Suu (Pokrovka) to Altyn Arashan, via the Jeti-Öghüz and Karakol valleys (minimum six to eight nights) From Kyzyl-Suu head up the Chong-Kyzyl-Suu river valley to the Jyluu-Suu hot springs or on to a camp site below the 3800m Archa-Tör pass. Next day cross the pass, head down the Asan Tukum gorge into the Jeti-Öghüz valley. From here it's over the Teleti pass to the Karakol valley and to Ala-Köl, Altyn Arashan and Ak Suu, as described previously.

You can combine any number of these parallel valleys to make as long a trek as you like. You can also add on radial hikes up the valleys, for example from Altyn Arashan to Pik Palatka or up the Kul Tor valley at the head of the Karakol valley for views of Karakol peak (5218m).

Ak Suu Sanatorium. Here you can take a post-trek hot bath for 4 som or stay the night in a spartan dormitory for 65 som per person including meals. There is another bath complex just up the road.

Buses go every hour or so from Karakol's local bus stand and there are shared taxis from Karakol to Ak Suu village for 8 som per person, from where you can walk, hitch or hire a local taxi. A taxi to the spa from Karakol would be about 200 som, or 400 som to wait and return.

Karakol Valley

Due south of Karakol lies the Karakol valley. The beautiful valley offers some fine hikes, though you really need a tent, stove and a day's hiking before the valley reveals its charm. There is talk of upgrading the valley to national park status, largely it seems so that a US$20 park fee for foreign visitors can be introduced, *in addition* to the trekking permit already required (see the Permits entry in the previous Karakol section), potentially making this a relatively pricey valley to visit.

Trekking around Karakol

There are also longer, more technical variations on these that climb as high as 4200m and cross some small glaciers, but these should not be attempted without a knowledgeable guide and some experience with glacier walking.

Permits
Trekking permits are needed from the Ministry of Tourism and Sport in Karakol (see the Karakol section). There is apparently only one inspector working in the entire region and he spends most of his time at Altyn Arashan. Trekkers who are not in possession of a permit face a theoretical 1000 som fine but will probably just have to buy a permit on the spot.

When to Go
The season for the treks noted here is normally late June to early October. August is a popular time for picking mushrooms; blackcurrants are in season in September. For Altyn Arashan only, you could go as early as May or as late as the end of October, but nights drop below freezing then and the surrounding mountain passes are snowed over. Local people say that Altyn Arashan is loveliest in June and in September.

Maps
These routes are indicated on the Around Karakol map. The only good maps we have seen for these routes – part of an old Russian series called *Gornyy Turizm* (Mountain Tourism) – are the 1:150,000 *Lednikam Terskey Ala-Too* and the 1:150,000 *Po Tsentralnomu Tyan-Shan,* for sale at the Kyrgyz Cartographic Agency in Bishkek (see the Bishkek Information section).

Dangers & Annoyances
Weather is perhaps the biggest danger, with unexpected chilling storms, especially May through June and September through October. Streams are in flood in late May and early June; if you go then, plan your crossings for early morning when levels are lowest.

Getting to the Trailheads
For access to trailheads, refer to the Altyn Arashan, Karakol Valley, Jeti-Öghüz and Kyzyl-Suu sections of this chapter. Reliable Kyrgyz agencies who can arrange treks in this area include Dostuk Trekking and IIMC Tien-Shan in Bishkek; Yak Tours and PSI in Karakol; and Kan Tengri and Asia Tourism in Almaty (Kazakstan). See the Travel Agencies sections for those towns.

About 7km on a steep, snaky road south up the valley of the Kashka-Suu, a tributary of the Karakol river, is a **skibaza** (ski base). A small hotel there is open in winter (usually mid-October to mid-March), and you can rent ski gear, ride a 3km lift and shush down from 3000 to 2000m. Jeep-buses leave from beside the municipal stadium from the skibaza's administration building in Karakol town, at 7 am and 1 pm, returning at 11 am and 4 pm.

About 13km above the skibaza is a make-shift base (a fenced patch for tents, a radio shack, field hospital and caravan, and a generator to run a small lift), from which experts can ski on the Terim-Tör glacier in summer.

From May to mid-October you can make a strenuous three hour climb from the upper base to a crystal-clear lake called **Ala-Köl** at 3530m. It can be reached more easily in a day's hike from the Karakol river valley, or in 3½ to four hours over the ridge from Altyn Arashan; in fact this is on several alternative trek routes to/from Altyn Arashan (see the boxed text 'Trekking around Karakol').

A taxi from Karakol to the park gate is 80 som. The No 1 bus will drop you part of the way, from where you can start hiking.

Jeti-Öghüz

About 25km west of Karakol, at the mouth of the Jeti-Öghüz canyon, is an extraordinary formation of red sandstone cliffs that has become a kind of tourism trademark for Lake Issyk-Kul.

A village of the same name is just off the main round-the-lake road. Beyond it the earth erupts in red patches, and soon there appears a great splintered hill called **Razbitoye Serdtse** or Broken Heart. Legend says two suitors spilled their blood in a fight for a beautiful woman; both died, and this rock is her broken heart.

Beyond this on the west side of the road is the massive wall of Jeti-Öghüz. The name means Seven Bulls, and of course there is a story here too – of seven calves growing big and strong in the valley's rich pastures. Erosion has meant that the bulls have multiplied. They are best viewed from a ridge to the east above the road. From that same ridge you can look east into Ushchelie Drakonov, the Valley of Dragons.

Below the wall of Seven Bulls is one of Issyk-Kul's surviving spas, the ageing *Jeti-Öghüz Sanatorium*, built in 1932 with a complex of several plain hotels, a hot pool, a restaurant and some woodland walks. It's open to all, but in summer only. Russian President Boris Yeltsin and Kyrgyzstan's President Askar Akaev had their first meeting here, in 1991.

From here you can walk up the park-like lower canyon of the Jeti-Öghüz river to popular summer picnic spots. Some 5km up, the valley opens out almost flat at **Dolina Svetov**, the Valley of Flowers; it's a kaleidoscope of colours as summer passes and has poppies in May. There are also said to be pre-Islamic petroglyphs up here, similar to those at Cholpon-Ata. You really need a tent to make an enjoyable couple of days trip here. Bridges sometimes get washed out so check the best route with locals before setting off.

Jeti-Öghüz canyon is one of several alternatives for treks to/from Altyn Arashan and Ala-Köl (see the boxed text 'Trekking around Karakol', earlier).

Getting There & Away Buses run from Karakol local bus stand to Jeti-Öghüz village only at 10 am, and continue 6km to the spa at 1 and 4 pm. There are said to be shuttle buses and overpriced taxis between the village and the spa in summer. A taxi from Karakol centre to the spa would be about 300 som return, plus waiting time.

THE SOUTHERN SHORE
Kyzyl-Suu
☎ 3946

The town of Kyzyl-Suu (Pokrovka in Soviet times) is of no interest, but this is the turn-off for the Chong-Kyzyl-Suu river valley, including a primitive hot-spring development – both of which can form part of a trek to/from Altyn Arashan and Ala-Köl (see the boxed text 'Trekking around Karakol', earlier).

A few kilometres west of Kyzyl-Suu is the valley of the Juku river, the last leg of

Nikolai Przhevalsky's final expedition (see the boxed text 'Przhevalsky' in the Around Karakol section, earlier), and once such a popular smugglers' route – for Issyk-Kul opium, among other things – that there used to be a customs post at the top of the valley. Przhevalsky's route is now paralleled by a 4WD track from Saruu village up and then west to the Barskoön valley.

The hot spring is about 10km on a rough road above Kyzyl-Suu or 8km above the next-door village of Svetlaya Polyana. There are hourly buses to both places from Karakol's local bus stand, 40km away, and a local taxi might take you up to the spring if you're not a walker. From the Kyzyl-Suu bus stand it's 1.2km east to the Chong-Kyzyl-Suu river (or just ask the driver for *reka*, river); ulitsa Yumatovoy up the west side of the river becomes the valley road. There is a forest ranger station *(kardon)* at the lower end of the valley. The Jyluu-Suu hot spring site, a different site about 20km above the village, consists of a plain building with one hot pool, open to all at no charge, and a disused hostel.

Barskoön

Barskoön village was an army staging point in the days of Soviet-Chinese border skirmishes, and the small adjacent settlement of Tamga is built around a former military sanatorium, now open year-round to all. Barskoön is all Kyrgyz, with more horses than cars; Tamga is mainly Russian.

Locals pack a picnic and head 20km up the huge Barskoön valley to the Barskoön waterfall. The area's most illustrious resident was the 11th century scholar Mahmud al-Kashgari (see the boxed text).

Barskoön is about 90km from Karakol, with daily morning buses to/from Karakol and Balykchy, which stop at the sanatorium gate. From outside the gate a road runs to the left (east) for about 3km to the mouth of the valley. One to the right goes to the municipal baths (an alternative to the spa, with a shuttle bus in summer), or 1.5km to the lake shore. There's also a small airfield, mainly used by Canadian and Turkish mining engineers on the look out for gold.

Mahmud al-Kashgari

Mahmud al-Kashgari (also called al-Barskhani) was born in the 11th century at what was then the settlement of Barskhan. He is best known as the author of the first-ever comparative dictionary of Turkic languages, *Divan Lughat at-Turk* (A Glossary of Turkish Dialects), written in Baghdad during 1072-74 and including specimens of pre-Islamic Turkic poetry. He travelled widely to collect his information, his version of the known world, with Barskhan/Barskoön at the centre. His tomb is at Upal, south of Kashgar on the road to Pakistan.

THE KARKARA VALLEY

The eastern gateway to the Issyk-Kul basin is an immense, silent valley called Karkara, straddling the Kyrgyzstan-Kazakstan border. On the Kyrgyzstan side it begins about 60km north-east of Karakol and widens out to 40km or more, shoulder-deep in good pasture during summer. The name means Black Crane, after the graceful migratory birds that stop here (and at Chatyr-Köl near the Torugart pass) in June and again in August-September, en route between South Africa and Siberia. In contrast to the windy Shoe-string gorge (Boömskoe ushchelie) at the lake's west end, this is a lovely way in and out, but the road is poorer and far less used.

Every herder in the Karakol region (and in the Kegen region on the Kazakstan side) brings animals up here in summer to fatten, and the warm-weather population is an easy-going mix of Kyrgyz and Kazak *chaban* (cowboys) and their families. The valley is dotted with yurts at that time, and people are disarmingly friendly, as yet unaffected by tourism. The Karkara (or Karkyra) river – which forms the Kyrgyzstan-Kazakstan border through part of the valley – and its tributaries are said to yield abundant fish.

Every summer, around mid-June, all these good vibes come together in the form of the **Chabana festival**, a good-natured, non-touristic gathering of cowboys and herders, with horseback games and a big bazar. The

KYRGYZSTAN

Welcome to our Yurt

Warm in winter, cool in summer, relatively light and portable, the traditional nomadic yurts (*kiiz-uy* in Kazak, *bosuy* in Kyrgyz) once dominated the countryside like giant mushrooms. Today you are more likely to see an idealised version of a yurt in the local museum or mock-ups used as vodka bars and tourist attractions or reserved for special occasions such as weddings. Urbanised Kazaks have forsaken the yurt altogether, but many Kyrgyz still head out to the *jailoos* (summer pastures) and set up summer bosuy.

Yurts are made of multi-layered felt (*kiyiz* or *kiiz*) stretched around a collapsible wooden frame, often made of willow. The outer felt layer is coated in waterproof sheep fat, the innermost layer is lined with woven mats from the tall grass called *chiy* to block the wind. The lattice framework (*kerege*) make up the main walls, connected to long poles (*uyuk*) rising up to the apex (*shanrak*), the hole that controls the temperature of the yurt and allows air and light to get in and smoke from the fire to escape. Looking up the shanrak, you'll see the *tyndyk*, a wheel with two three-ply struts, which supports the roof and which also inspired the Kyrgyz flag. Long woven woollen strips of varying widths, called *tizgych* and *chalgych* in Kyrgyz, secure the walls and poles and embroidered bags are hung to be used as storage. Start to finish, a yurt requires three to four hours to set up or pull down.

The entrance to the yurt, usually facing east, has a door carved from pine or birch wood, or rolled chiy. Floors are lined with thick felt *koshma* and covered with bright *shyrdaks*, *ala-kiyiz*, and sometimes yak skin. The interior is richly decorated with handsome textiles, including colourful wall coverings, quilts, cushions, camel and horse bags, and ornately worked caskets. Large tassels hang from the tyndyk. The more elaborate the decoration, the higher the social standing of the yurt's owners.

The hearth is central to the yurt, above which hangs a metal cauldron, or *kazan* (or more often these days an iron stove). The place by the hearth farthest away from the door is always reserved for guests and the back right of the yurt is the 'master bedroom'. Harnesses and saddles are stored to the left of the entrance, bedding is stored along the wall opposite the entrance. Men's and women's sections are often divided by a chiy partition, the women's area (kitchen) to the right of the entrance. Lambs, kids and calves are kept near the door.

Traditionally, the collapsed yurt was transported via horse-cart, often an ox burdening the heavy roof wheel. Today it's more common to see one strapped down to a tractor and heading into the hills.

THEODOR HERZEN

KYRGYZSTAN

border seems especially nonexistent at this time. The location of the festival apparently shifts around the valley (and from one side of the border to the other) from year to year, and the exact time is only fixed at the last moment, depending on work requirements and weather. (This is not to be confused with an entirely different event called the Karkara Fair, a commercial and trade fair held in either Kegen or Almaty.)

The ancients liked Karkara too. In his *A Day Lasts Longer Than a Century* the Kyrgyz writer Chinghiz Aitmatov has the ancient Kyrgyz peoples arriving from the Yenisey via Karkara.

Some people suggest that Timur made Karkara his summer headquarters for several years, and point to a house-size pile of round stones in the south-west part of the valley. These, they say, were Timur's way of estimating his losses in eastern campaigns – each departing soldier put a rock on the pile, each returnee removed one, and the stones that remained represented the dead. The name of the site, San-Tash, means 'Counting Stones'. The whole idea was recently given a push by a slick television advertisement by a Russian bank, showing Timur kneeling distraught beside the remaining stones.

Sceptics and amateur historians point to an adjacent, stone-lined pit that appears to be the remnant of a burial chamber, and suggest that the football-size stones were just used to cover the chamber, and were removed by archaeologists or grave-robbers. Either way, the site has a dreamy, magical feel.

Places to Stay & Eat

Save for a few collective farm settlements, there are almost no buildings to be seen out here, certainly no such thing as a hotel or restaurant. Bring your own tent and food if you plan to stay the night, although you may well be invited into someone's yurt. Visitors are welcome especially those who have brought along a few supplies; tea and salt are especially well received, and cigarettes and vodka also make good gifts. These might also be traded for fresh milk, ayran (yoghurt), *kurut* (hard cheese) or *sary-may* (butter) – or even for the rental of a horse!

Getting There & Away

From Karakol the Karkara valley is about 90km via Tüp or 70 much prettier kilometres via Novovoznesenovka, but the road deteriorates about 40km outside Karakol in either case. The Kyrgyz border post is at the west end of the valley.

On the Tüp route a round trip by taxi from Karakol would probably be about US$40 for the day. Ask for *'pamyatnik San-Tash'*, just opposite a small collective farm settlement, 4.7km from the Kyrgyz border post or 19km from the Kazakstan border. There are regular daily buses to Tüp, and apparently some to settlements beyond the stones. It's also an easy hitch in summer, and the cheerful Kyrgyz border guards might even flag down a car for you.

The Novovoznesenovka route passes through the wettest and lushest part of the Issyk-Kul region, then past a former Soviet army training base and over the low San-Tash pass (closed by snow in winter) into a western arm of the Karkara valley.

There are daily buses from Karakol as far as Kyzyl Jar (former Sovietskoe) or the mining town of Jyrgalang (Russians call it Jergalan *shakhta* or mine), from where you might hitch. The border is about 90km from Karakol on this route. This would make a fine horseback trip from Karakol.

From Karkara you could also trek east or south into the Terskey Alatau; from Jyrgalang routes lead to the Inlychek glacier. See the boxed text 'Trekking to the Inylchek Glacier' for details.

From the Kazakstan side, you can get a Kegen, Saryzhaz or Narynkol bus from Almaty and get off at Kegen. The Kazak border post is there but it's a difficult 25 to 30km hitch south to the border itself. Travellers have been shaken down and fined for arriving in Kazakstan without a Kazak visa so don't just trust the 72 hour transit rule here. A taxi from Karakol to Almaty via Kegen takes about seven hours and costs around US$120, including car customs fees.

THE CENTRAL TIAN SHAN

This highest and mightiest part of the Tian Shan system – the name means Celestial

KYRGYZSTAN

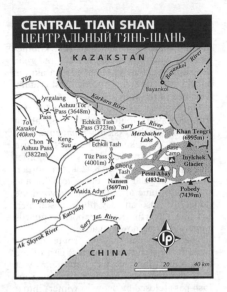

CENTRAL TIAN SHAN
ЦЕНТРАЛЬНЫЙ ТЯНЬ-ШАНЬ

Mountains in Chinese – is at the eastern end of Kyrgyzstan, along its borders with China and the very south-east tip of Kazakstan. It's an immense knot of ranges, with dozens of summits over 5000m, culminating in Pik Pobedy (Victory Peak, 7439m, second-highest in the former USSR) on the Kyrgyzstan-China border, and Khan Tengri ('Prince of Spirits' or 'Ruler of the Sky', 6995m), possibly the most beautiful and demanding peak in the Tian Shan, on the Kazakstan-Kyrgyzstan border. A 1990 Kazak geographical survey declared the height of Khan Tengri to be 7010m, though this figure has been greeted with scepticism. Locals call the peak 'Blood Mountain', as the pyramid-shaped peak glows crimson at sunset.

The first foreigner to bring back information about the central Tian Shan was the Chinese explorer Xuan Zang (Hsüan-tsang), who crossed the Bedel pass in the 7th century, early in his 16 year odyssey to India and back (see boxed text 'Great Chinese Explorers' in the History section of the Facts about Central Asia chapter). His journey nearly ended here; in the seven days it took to cross the pass, half his 14 person party froze to death.

The first European to penetrate this high region was the Russian explorer Pyotr Semyonov in 1856 (for his efforts the tsar awarded him the honorary name Tian-Shansky). In 1902-1903 the Austrian explorer Gottfried Merzbacher first approached the foot of the elegant, Matterhorn-like Khan Tengri, but it was only climbed in 1931, by a Ukrainian team.

Of the Tian Shan's thousands of glaciers, the grandest is 60km-long Inylchek (or Engilchek), rumbling westward from both sides of Khan Tengri, embracing an entire rampart of giant peaks and tributary glaciers. Across its entire northern arm where it joins the southern one a huge, iceberg-filled lake – Lake Merzbacher – forms at 3300m every summer, and some time in early August bursts its ice-banks and explodes into the Inylchek river below.

Along with the eastern Pamir, the central Tian Shan is Central Asia's premier territory for serious trekking and mountaineering. Several Central Asian adventure-travel firms will bring you by helicopter, 4WD and/or foot right up to these peaks. Even intrepid, fit do-it-yourselfers can get a look at Inylchek glacier (see the following Getting There & Away entry in this section).

Information
July through August is the only feasible season to visit at these elevations. This is a sensitive border zone, and to go anywhere in the upper Sary Jaz valley or beyond Inylchek town – even just to have a look at the glacier – you'll need a permit from the Russian border detachment at the army base in Karakol (see the Information entry in the earlier Karakol section). You must have a letter with the stamp of a recognised travel agency in Karakol, Bishkek or Almaty, a list of everyone in your party, and your itinerary.

Books & Maps You're best off bringing maps from home (see Maps in the Regional Facts for the Visitor chapter). The only good place in Kyrgyzstan for maps is the Kyrgyz Cartographic Agency in Bishkek (see the Information entry in the Bishkek section earlier), where you'll find selected topographic

Trekking to the Inylchek Glacier

The most common trekking route to the Inylchek glacier is the remote and wild five or six day trek from Jyrgalang, 70km east of Karakol. Most trekkers will need support for this trek, not least because you will need a military permit from Karakol to head up the Sary Jaz valley. To get to the trailhead at Jyrgalang you'll need to hitch or, more reliably, hire a jeep for about US$35.

Stage 1   From Jyrgalang the trail heads south up the valley, before cutting east over a 2800m pass into the Tüp valley (seven to eight hours).

Stage 2   Over the 3648m Ashuu Tör pass into the Janalach valley (six hours).

Stage 3   Head south over the 3723m Echkili-Tash pass into the Sary Jaz valley.

Stage 4   Seven hours hike up the Tüz valley to camp at the junction of the Achik Tash river.

Stage 5   Cross the river and head up four hours to the tricky Tüz pass (4001m), from where there are stunning views of the Inylchek glacier, Nansen Peak and Khan Tengri. From here it's a long descent to the Chong-Tash site at the snout of the Inylchek glacier.

It's possible to hire a jeep (US$80 from Yak Tours in Karakol) to the yak farm in Echkili-Tash and join the trek there, leaving only two or three days to reach Chong-Tash. From Chong-Tash you face a two day hike back west to Maida Adyr camp and Inylchek town.

To continue from Chong-Tash on to the Inylchek glacier you definitely need the support of a trekking agency to guide you over the glacier, keep you in supplies and let you stay in their base camps. With an experienced guide it's possible to continue from Chong-Tash over the glacier for one long day to Merzbacher lake and to continue the next day to the camps. A popular excursion for trekking groups based here is to make a trekking ascent of Mt Diky (4832m) or Pesni Abaji (4901m), or to hike up the Zvozdochka glacier to the foot of Pik Pobedy (7439m). Most groups take in a stunning helicopter route around the valley and out to Inylchek town and you might be able to buy a ride back for up to Inylchek for US$100.

The best time for trekking in this region is July and August. See the Central Tian Shan section in this chapter for information on permits, maps and agencies.

and trekking maps – all supposedly cleared of the deliberate distortions that infected Soviet-era maps. A map of trekking routes that approach Khan Tengri from the Sary Jaz valley in Kyrgyzstan and Bayankol valley in Kazakstan is the 1:200,000 *K Verkhvyam Sary-Dzhaza*, available in Bishkek.

The best book to take along is Frith Maier's comprehensive *Trekking in Russia & Central Asia*, with several maps and basic route descriptions in this region.

Dangers & Annoyances This is not a place to pop into for a few days with your summer sleeping bag – be properly equipped against the cold, which is severe at night, even in summer, and to give yourself plenty of time to acclimatise to the altitude.

Helicopters do fall out of the sky from time to time, or crash into mountainsides when bad weather unexpectedly descends; ride them only in absolutely clear summer weather.

Places to Stay & Eat
There are several *base camps* in the Inylchek valley: Maida Adyr below the snout of the glacier, with wagons and tents, mess hall and sauna; and tent-towns at several locations up on the glacier, owned and run by ITMC Tien-Shan and Dostuk Trekking in Bishkek and Kan Tengri in Almaty, among others. ITMC's camp costs around US$6 per night for accommodation, more for food.

Kan Tengri also maintains a *yurt camp* at 2200m at the edge of the Karkara valley. All

KYRGYZSTAN

these are intended for trekkers and climbers, but anybody with the urge to see this cathedral of peaks can make arrangements with those firms, and pay a visit.

Getting There & Away

Firms organising climbs and treks in the central Tian Shan include Dostuk Trekking, Edelweiss, ITMC Tien-Shan and Tien-Shan Travel in Bishkek; PSI in Karakol; and Kan Tengri and Asia Tourism in Almaty (see the Travel Agencies sections for those towns).

Access to the region surrounding Khan Tengri is by road, by air or on foot. It's a four hour (150km) trip on a roller-coastering, all-weather road from Karakol via Inylchek town, a mining centre at about 2500m and 50km west of the snout of the Inylchek glacier. Do-it-yourselfers could hire a 4WD or other reliable vehicle from Karakol, for around US$90 (for the vehicle, not per person) return. Local mountaineers on the cheap hang out at the intersection outside Karakol airport, the conventional place to catch a ride to Inylchek for around US$10 (in som).

If you've got the dosh, take a mind-boggling helicopter flight over the Tian Shan to Khan Tengri base camp – with Kan Tengri from their Karkara valley base camp, or with other agencies from Karakol or Maida Adyr. Once it was possible to hitch a lift on a helicopter taking climbers or mining engineers up from Karakol, for US$40. Fuel costs have curtailed these flights, but there's no harm in asking the various tour companies (these days you'll be asked more like US$150).

To Khan Tengri's north face you can trek from Narynkol (Kazakstan) or Jyrgalang (Kyrgyzstan). See the boxed text 'Trekking to the Inylchek Glacier' for more details.

Bishkek to Kashgar via the Torugart Pass

Kyrgyzstan's primo trip for non-trekkers – and the most exciting overland route into or out of Central Asia – is the 700km journey between Bishkek and Kashgar via the 3752m Torugart pass.

It's not for everyone, being long, sometimes cold, uncomfortable, plagued by uncertainties and not all that cheap, but it's the sort of absorbing and grandly beautiful trip you're glad you made once you've made it.

A major, and indeed probably the original, branch of the Silk Road crossed the Tian Shan between Kashgar and the Fergana valley, probably near Kök-Art, 85km southwest of Torugart. The Chinese emissary Zang Qian went that way in 138 BCE on an astonishing 13 year search for allies, and for the Heavenly Horses of Fergana, on behalf of the Han emperor (see the History section in the Facts about Central Asia chapter). You can't tread these paths today, but you can come pretty close on the Torugart.

This section is mainly about the Bishkek-Kashgar route and all there is to see on the way, but you don't have to be en route to China to visit most of the places mentioned here. Indeed, places like Kochkor, Song-Köl and Tash Rabat are worth visiting even if you don't make it to the pass.

From a purely physical standpoint the whole journey to Kashgar could be done in a sturdy, well-equipped 4WD in under 15 hours, but the country along the way reveals too much about the region's history, geography, people and wildlife to rush through it (and contains formidable official obstacles to slow you down even more). The actual trip, via Balykchy and Naryn, takes a minimum of two days.

The Torugart pass is open to all now, but ranks of officials on both sides still make it hard for individual budget travellers. The only way to take (most of) the uncertainty out of the trip is to spend money on it – crossing with the help of accredited and experienced local agencies on both sides. If you have time but no money, and are simply trying to get into or out of China, it's easier and surer to cross to/from Kazakstan.

When to Go

The Torugart pass is normally snow-free from late May through September, though in late May/early June 1999 the pass was

[Continued on page 397]

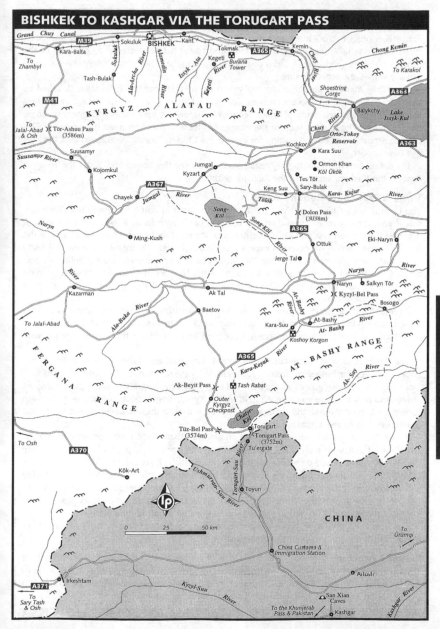

BISHKEK TO KASHGAR VIA THE TORUGART PASS

Crossing the Torugart

Torugart is one of Asia's most unpredictable border posts, with reliable information scarce, many decisions taken seemingly at random, and closures unexpectedly by one side or the other for holidays, road repair, snow or heaven knows what else, and nobody (even ambassadors) knows the score for sure.

Essentially many of the difficulties boil down to the fact that the Torugart is classified by the Chinese as a 'class 2' border crossing, for local traffic only, and so special regulations are in force for foreigners, many of which seem deliberately set up to milk foreigners for some hard currency. The bottom line, for the moment at least, is that you must have onward Chinese transport arranged and waiting for you on the Chinese side to be allowed past the Kyrgyz border post.

For details on crossing into Kyrgyzstan from China see the boxed text 'Over the Torugart Pass' in the Kashgar section of the Xinjiang chapter.

Visas & Transport Requirements

You cannot get a Chinese or Kyrgyz visa at the border, and you'll be turned back on either side if you don't have an onward visa (in fact you can't even *leave* Kyrgyzstan here without a proper Kyrgyzstan visa and OVIR registration). It's possible to get a Chinese visa in all the former Soviet Central Asia capitals except Dushanbe, though it's not all that easy in Almaty or Bishkek (and you mustn't mention the Torugart pass). In general, you are better off getting a Chinese visa before you come to Central Asia. No special endorsement is required on your Chinese visa, despite what Chinese embassies might tell you. In China, you can get a Kyrgyzstan visa only in Beijing.

At research time, Kyrgyz border officials were also insisting on written confirmation of onward transport into China, and detaining visitors until this transport arrived at the border arch from Kashgar. The best thing to have is a fax from an accredited Chinese tour agency, who will come and meet you.

The three-point border – two border controls 12km apart and a security station/arch in between – makes for further confusion, especially in trying to connect with onward transport. Normally the Chinese guards at the arch radio to Kyrgyz immigration when your transport arrives and only then are you allowed to leave the Kyrgyz border post. Sometimes groups are turned back even with all the right papers, because their transport never turned up or was not allowed up to the actual border.

Avoid arranging your Torugart crossing on any day that might even conceivably be construed as a holiday on *either side, or in Russia*, as the border will probably be closed. Note that the border is closed on weekends too. Tourist traffic is heaviest on Friday when groups cross into China to catch Kashgar's Sunday market; however, attempting to cross on a Friday is dangerous, as if the border is temporarily closed for snow or some other reason you won't be able to retry for another three days. Try to arrive at the border as early as possible (the Kyrgyz side opens at 9.30 am) as things tend to grind to a halt at lunchtime.

In summer (roughly April through September) China (ie Beijing) time is two hours later than Kyrgyzstan time, and in winter three hours later.

Travel Agencies

Given the difficulties, most people arrange the crossing with an agency in Bishkek. Arranging the whole trip from Bishkek to Kashgar currently costs from around US$120 to US$200 per person in a group of four, depending on the agent and the vehicle.

Crossing the Torugart

The standard trip takes two days, overnighting in Naryn or Tash Rabat (although you might want to add a third day to visit Song Köl and Tash Rabat). The second day involves a very early start and gets you into Kashgar that evening. Travel agencies are normally able to arrange accommodation in a yurt camp or home-stay in Naryn or Tash Rabat that costs around US$20 per person per night. Be aware that you should be able to do things cheaper yourself.

Most, but not all, agents can make arrangements with a cooperating Chinese agency for onward transport. The charge for this is set by the Chinese agency and normally paid in US dollars to the Chinese driver once in China. If this is the case, get a printed confirmation of the price from your Kyrgyz agent to avoid any dispute later. You could deal directly with a Chinese travel agency from abroad but it's generally easier to let a Bishkek agency make the arrangements. Try to make arrangements at least 10 days in advance, especially if you're setting up onward Chinese transport too.

Be suspicious of bargain-basement costs – this is not a trip to cut corners on. Ask for a breakdown, since some firms fail to mention all costs. Check that petrol, oil and food and accommodation for the driver are included, as well as the state transport duty (gosposhlina), a per-vehicle customs tax paid when you exit Kyrgyzstan.

Check also that you will be taken across to the Chinese checkpoint at the arch; only drivers with a Kyrgyz Foreign Ministry special permit can go that far. Your driver should have previous experience with Torugart – both getting there and getting across – eg minimising customs rip-offs, jumping truck queues, handling greedy officials, and of course repairing the vehicle. Those with a Foreign Ministry permit usually do.

You could also check that the driver has a current passport – we've heard of drivers being stopped at the outer checkpoint because they had the old-style (red) Soviet passport, not the new (blue) Kyrgyz one.

And ask to see what you'll get there in! This is a high-elevation road with steep grades, and even the sturdiest vehicles tend to have trouble. Little 2WD cars or minivans use less fuel but are dangerously lightweight and uncontrollable on rainy roads, snow or ice. A 4WD will get you out of all sorts of trouble. Check the tyres too. There is almost no reliable petrol, oil or parts along the way, so the vehicle must carry everything for the round trip, including several hundred litres of fuel in jerry cans.

At the time of research in Bishkek, Kyrgyz Concept were offering a jeep for US$350 or minivan for US$450 for the two day trip to Torugart. Dostuk and ITMC Tien-Shan were charging about US$330 for the same, while Edelweiss was asking a little less. Celestial Mountains was charging US$660 per car for a two-day trip, with a visit to Song Köl.

To book Chinese transport from Torugart to Kashgar Kyrgyz Concept was charging US$110 per person, Celestial Mountains was charging US$140 per person (minimum two people, plus a US$50 booking charge), and ITMC Tien-Shan was charging US$250 per car, or US$65 per person.

The Bishkek-Kashgar trip can also be arranged in advance from overseas, either by contacting a local Kyrgyz agency direct or by letting a foreign travel agency do it for you (for a price). See the Travel Agencies & Organised Tours section in the Getting There & Away chapter for some contact details.

Agencies may also have packages with excursions (eg to Issyk-Kul) and longer stays, as well as round trips to Kashgar and back.

Crossing the Torugart (continued)

By Bus

Weekly Bishkek-Kashgar, Bishkek-Artux, Naryn-Artux and Naryn-Kashgar buses make the nonstop 1½ day trip to China over the Torugart (US$50 from Bishkek, US$25 from Naryn) but foreigners aren't allowed to take these. You are allowed to buy a ticket but at the time of research foreigners were being regularly thrown off the bus at the Kyrgyz border post (and no, you won't get a refund).

Cutting Costs

To avoid the costs of hired transport within Kyrgyzstan you can take cheap scheduled buses from Bishkek to Naryn (three daily) or At-Bashy (one daily), but no farther. From there, taxis will take you to the border for around US$50 (for the car), though they may be turned back or shaken down at the outer checkpoint.

The problem with cutting costs this way is that you still must have your Chinese transport arranged and therefore you'll have to make sure that you get to the border in time to meet it. Moreover, you still need to find a way to cross the 7km of no man's land to meet your transport at the arch. There's always a risk that you won't be able to find a lift or that the Kyrgyz officials will not let you cross.

If the Torugart is Closed

If either the China or Kyrgyz side of the pass is closed (and unfortunately no one could ever possibly tell you this in advance), you face a serious dilemma. There are places to spend the night at the pass, so you could try again the next day (unless that's a Saturday), though you can't be sure that your Chinese arranged transport will bother to try again the next day. If you've cut your visa too fine, you might well have the extra headache of an expired visa to contend with.

At this point, you can either dial up the travel agency who has arranged your trip (the better companies carry their own long-distance radio set) and ask them to contact their Chinese partners urgently to confirm a next day re-try, or alternatively go back three hours to Naryn and start arranging the whole thing all over again.

It is possible to get a short visa extension in Naryn, though you'll need your travel agency's help with this. If all else fails you'll have to rush back to Bishkek, catch the thrice weekly flight to Ürümqi (US$180) and then the daily flight (US$125) or sleeper bus (US$30, 30 hours) on to Kashgar.

To reduce the possibility of this nightmare scenario:

- don't pay for Chinese transport until you see it
- try not to cross on a Friday
- always give yourself a few days leeway on your Kyrgyz visa
- book all your Torugart transport with one agency

A final piece of advice: if you decide to cross the Torugart, be stubborn, expect the unexpected, and don't count on getting across until you have.

[Continued from page 392]

blocked for over a week due to heavy snow. The crossing is apparently kept open all year, but is icy and dangerous in winter, and as soon as there is significant snow officials tend to turn back anything without snow-tyres or tracks. Nights at higher elevations are still bitterly cold in April, and again by September.

What to Bring
Besides your visas and papers, and winter clothes, gifts are useful to loosen up drivers and guards – cigarettes, western candy bars and dashboard stickers go over well, and may also do in lieu of money as petty bribes. Tea, salt and sugar come in handy to trade with herders at Song-Köl for milk, cheese or yoghurt. Vodka will make you lots of friends in the high pastures, but you're better off keeping that out of your driver's hands. Bring at least a couple of meals worth of food. Instant noodles make a good emergency stand-by.

Money
You can change US dollars into som and vice versa in Naryn. You'll find only private traders at the Kyrgyzstan customs station, though you can pay for food and accommodation in US dollars if you have small bills. There is a small Bank of China office at the Chinese customs post but most people wait until they get to their hotel in Kashgar. To change som into Chinese yuan in Kashgar you'll probably have to change with the shifty Uyghur black market moneychangers.

BISHKEK TO NARYN
The route begins as you would for Lake Issyk-Kul, winding up the **Shoestring Gorge** (Boömskoe ushchelie) towards Balykchy. A short cut past the azure **Orto-Tokoy reservoir** is full of twists and turns but saves an hour by cutting off the Balykchy corner and offers fine views. Only taxis (not buses) can take this route.

Three hours or 185km from Bishkek is the town of **Kochkor** (see the following entry). About 38km onward is tiny Sary-

Bulak, where you can buy laghman and snacks by the roadside. Five kilometres south of Sary-Bulak is the turn-off to **Lake Song-Köl** (see the following section). It's about 11km on to the 3038m summit of the **Dolon pass**, the highest point on the Bishkek-Naryn road, and a farther 19km to a dirt track that apparently climbs the Song-Köl river valley to the lake. About 16km on is **Ottuk**, a tidy Kyrgyz settlement with a representative of the Shepherd's Life organisation (see the boxed text), and 24km farther is a fork in the road, both branches of which take you about 10km into Naryn.

Altogether Bishkek-Naryn, without a stop at Song-Köl, is about 310km (six to 6½ hours).

Kochkor
☎ 3535
This sleepy little Kyrgyz village (Kochkorka in Russian) is a good stopping point en route to Naryn or the Suusamyr valley. It is the base for the 'Shepherd's Life' home-stay project (see the boxed text, later), and as such is a good base from which to make trips into the surrounding countryside or to Song-Köl, to experience traditional life in the Kyrgyz jailoos (summer pastures).

There's not much to actually do in the town itself except visit the small **Regional Museum**. A fine yurt is on display along with a collection of local Kyrgyz crafts, plus all the usual Soviet-era local heroes, such as the local scientist Bayaly Isakeev. More Soviet heroes are celebrated in the busts to the east of the museum.

There is said to be a good livestock market in town on Saturday morning. Locals also recommend walks down to Kara-Too village and along the riverbank.

Places to Stay & Eat The best value in town is *Mairam's B&B (Kuttuseyit uulu Shamen 111)*. Beds are traditional style (a comfortable pile of traditional duvets on a shyrdak) and cost 40 som, or 100 som including dinner and breakfast. Vegetarian meals (eg plain rice, tomato salad) can be prepared if you explain exactly what you want. Buckets of hot water can be arranged

KYRGYZSTAN

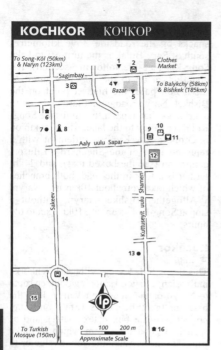

KOCHKOR КОЧКОР

1	Restoran Song-Köl
2	Shared Taxis to Balykchy & Bishkek
3	Telephone Office
4	Saikal Café
5	Chaykhana
6	Government Guest House No 2
7	Hakimyat (Mayor's Office)
8	Lenin Statue
9	Regional Museum
10	Cinema
11	Men Disco Bar
12	Dom Kultura
13	Alytyn Kol Shop
14	Bus Station; Shared Taxis to Naryn & Bishkek
15	Stadium
16	Mairam's B&B

for washing. Mairam Ömürsakova is also the co-ordinator for Shepherd's Life and can arrange jailoo stays and horseback riding to Song Köl and beyond. She speaks Russian and Kyrgyz only.

You can also stay at the *Government Guest House No 2*, just to the side of the hakim (mayor)'s office in the centre of town. Enter from the west via the aluminium gates (there's no sign). Basic triples with common toilet and cold-water bathroom cost 35 som per person. The 'pol lux' gets you essentially the same with a TV for 66 som, but the best bet is the huge lux suite, with a private cold-water bathroom and bathtub for 120 som.

Several cafes offer an uninspiring lunch, but dinner can be tricky. You're better off eating at Mairam's B&B if you are staying there.

Restoran Song-Köl offers the standard laghman and goulash but also some fish and chicken for tiny prices.

Saikal Café serves more Russian and Kyrgyz standards and acts as a contact point for the Shepherd's Life program.

The small bazar sells hot snacks out front and there's a dingy *chaykhana* inside that sells decent laghman.

Shopping A local women's collective known as Altyn Kol (Golden Hands) has a shyrdak showroom in the house of Jumagal Akhmadova, at Shamen 48. A 0.9 by 1.5m (three by five feet) shyrdak costs around US$15 and a 1.5 by 2.1m (five by seven feet) costs between US$40 and US$50. The money goes directly to the women who make the shyrdaks.

Getting There & Away Most people take a seat in a shared taxi to/from Bishkek (80 som), Balykchy (30 som, one hour) and Naryn (60 som). Taxis to Bishkek and Balykchy wait opposite the bazar while others to Bishkek and Naryn wait at the otherwise deserted bus stand.

Around Kochkor

Shepherd's Life can arrange home-stays at the jailoos of Ormon Khan, Tes Tör, Köl Ükök, Kök Bulak and Kara Kuchur and at Oktorkoi, Kölmö and Sandyk in the Jumgal valley and can help with getting there.

You can make an extended trip into the countryside by linking several home-stays on horseback or foot. Locals suggest the four day trip from Kara Suu to Köl Ükök (four hours), Mazar-i-Kök (four hours) and back to Kara Suu, or a three day trip from Kara Suu to Tes Tör and on to Köl Ükök. The Shepherd's Life co-ordinator in Kochkor can give information on the trip and help arrange it.

Lake Song-Köl

Alpine Lake Song-Köl (or Son-Kul, or Song-Kyol), at 3530m, is one of the loveliest spots in central Kyrgyzstan. All around it are lush pastures favoured by herders from the Kochkor valley and farther, who spend June, July and August here with their animals. Visitors are welcome, and this is a sublime place to camp and watch the sun come up. You can make any number of day hikes into the surrounding hills for excellent views. The lake is jumping with fish, and you might be able to trade tea, salt, sugar, cigarettes or vodka with the herders for milk, kurut (hard cheese) or full-bodied kumys. In any case bring plenty of food and water.

Shepherds Life can put you in touch with a yurt home-stay on the lake, where you can also ride horses (see the boxed text 'Shepherd's Life' below). Bishkek-based travel companies such as Ecotour and ITMC Tien-Shan operate yurt camps in the summer, where you can stay for about US$20 per person, including food, if there are no groups.

Shepherd's Life

Shepherd's Life is a new local initiative inspired by the Swiss development-based program Helvetas in 1997. A network of shepherds' families willing to take in guests in the villages and *jailoos* (summer meadows) surrounding Kochkor has been established. This not only provide tourists with a means to see the daily life of shepherds and farmers in central Kyrgyzstan, it also provides local families with a means to earn some extra income.

The network has now spread all over Naryn *oblast* (region) and includes bed and breakfast-style village houses along popular tourist routes as well as summer-time yurts. Accommodation on the jailoos operates from June to September only.

The five coordinators, in Kochkor, Chayek, At-Bashy, Ottuk and Kurtka (near Ak Tal), can put you in touch with families, local drivers and even shyrdak makers, for a flat fee of 50 som. Prices are very reasonable and currently fixed at 40 som a day for accommodation, plus another 60 som for breakfast and dinner. You can expect a traditional diet of home-made bread, *ayran* (yoghurt) *sary may* (butter), local jam, *kaimak* (cream), *kymys* (fermented mares' milk) and tastier than normal local dishes such as *pelmeni* and *laghman*. In most jailoos you can also hire a horse and guide for 30 som per half day. Drivers involved in the program charge a fixed per kilometre rate, plus a 50 som daily wage. Prices will of course change with inflation.

There is currently a network of over 18 homestays in the region and it's impossible to recommend one over the other, though it's worth making it out to one of the lesser-visited jailoos. Some jailoos are accessible by car as an overnight trip, while others require a day's hike to reach. It's possible to link a series of jailoos together to form a great trek or extended trip, safe in the knowledge that you have a meal and a place to sleep in the evening. Organisers recommend that you spend the night in the village from where you intend to hike or hire a horse in order to give people time to make arrangements (there are no phones in the region). It's a good idea to bring a sleeping bag, though there are normally plenty of guest duvets available.

How long the fledgling program survives remains to be seen but for the moment at least it's a great way for travellers to glimpse real life in Kyrgyzstan, while promoting low-impact tourism and providing some tourist income directly to local families.

To get in touch with the program, see Places to Stay & Eat in the Kochkor section earlier.

KYRGYZSTAN

The lake and shore are part of the Song-Köl zoological reserve. Among animals under its protection are a diminishing number of wolves. Weather is unpredictable and snow can fall at any time so dress and plan accordingly.

Getting There & Away It's 50km from the Bishkek-Naryn road to the lake: 6km to Keng-Suu (or Tölök) village, 21km to the end of the narrow valley of the Tölök river, and then a slow 23km (1½ hours) up, over and into the basin. This upper road is normally open only from late May to late October. The valley has little traffic and no regular buses.

A car hired from Kochkor through Shepherd's Life is the best value option. Prices depend upon the price of petrol but this will still be cheaper than a taxi from the bazar. Local Zhigulis (Soviet-made cars) can make it but you are far better off with a 4WD Niva or jeep as the tracks around the lake can get very boggy with rain.

There are at least three other unpaved 4WD tracks to the lake – from west of the lake at Chayek, from the Naryn-Kazarman road, and another from the Bishkek-Naryn road. It's therefore possible to drive in from Kochkor and out to Naryn or Chayek, making a nice loop route.

It's also possible to trek in to the lake on foot or horseback from Kyzart, near Jumgal, north of the lake, in one or two days. The Shepherd's Life representative in Kochkor or Chayek (Guljan Mykyeva) can arrange accommodation, horses and a guide for around 120 som per day, plus food.

NARYN
☎ 3522 • pop 45,000

Naryn is at about the right place for an overnight stop on the Bishkek-Torugart road, but it's a fairly dismal place. A Russian border detachment and a Kyrgyz army unit are based here, and the streets are full of officers and soldiers. Nearly everyone else (98% of the oblast) is Kyrgyz, most are desperately poor, and many are unemployed. The biggest problem for visitors is multiple drunks, some of them aggressive, and this is no place to be out on the streets after dark. Naryn is derived from the Mongolian for 'sunny' – a rare moment of Mongol irony.

The Naryn region's one real claim to fame is that the best quality shyrdaks are said to be made here.

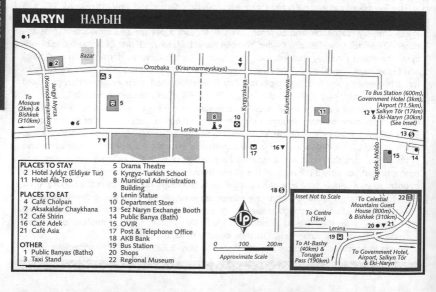

NARYN НАРЫН

PLACES TO STAY
2 Hotel Jyldyz (Eldiyar Tur)
11 Hotel Ala-Too

PLACES TO EAT
4 Café Cholpan
7 Aksakaldar Chaykhana
12 Café Shirin
16 Café Adek
21 Café Asia

OTHER
1 Public Banyas (Baths)
3 Taxi Stand
5 Drama Theatre
6 Kyrgyz-Turkish School
8 Municipal Administration Building
9 Lenin Statue
10 Department Store
13 Sez Naryn Exchange Booth
14 Public Banya (Bath)
15 OVIR
17 Post & Telephone Office
18 AKB Bank
19 Bus Station
20 Shops
22 Regional Museum

Bazar

Orozbaka (Krasnoarmeyskaya)

Jangyl Myrza (Kosmodemyanskoy)

Kyrgyzskaya

Kulumbayeva

Togolok Moldo

Lenina

To Mosque (2km) & Bishkek (310km)

To Bus Station (600m), Government Hotel (3km), Airport (11.5km), Salkyn Tör (17km) & Eki-Naryn (30km) (See Inset)

Inset Not to Scale

To Celestial Mountains Guest House (800m) & Bishkek (10km)

To Centre (1km)

Lenina

To At-Bashy (40km) & Torugart Pass (190km)

To Government Hotel, Airport, Salkyn Tör & Eki-Naryn

0 100 200m
Approximate Scale

Orientation & Information

Naryn is spread along the Naryn river for 15km, but is just one to 2km wide. The road from Bishkek forks north of town, each branch of the fork leading to one end of town. A trolleybus line runs along the main street, ulitsa Lenina, for its entire length.

If there's a centre it's probably the municipal *hakimyat* or administration building on Lenina. Travellers' landmarks are a small bazar 500m north-west of this on ulitsa Orozbaka (formerly Krasnoarmeyskaya), and the bus station, 1.2km east on Lenina. Naryn's small airport is about 11.5km east of the centre but there were no flights at the time of writing.

The post and telephone office is half a block east of the town centre on ulitsa Kyrgyzskaya. You can change only cash US dollars at the AKB Bank in the centre (1st floor, open Monday to Friday, 8.30 am to noon and 1 to 3 pm), the Sez Naryn exchange booth 500m east or in the bazar. This is the last place to change money before the border.

OVIR is east of the centre on ulitsa Togolok Moldo if you need to register. Head for the 1st floor of the building in the far left corner as you go through the entrance. There is apparently a consular office in the city administration building, which can extend your visa in emergencies (ie if you were turned back at the Torugart pass).

Things to See & Do

If you have some time to kill you could check out the new **Regional Museum**. Most interesting is the ethnological room featuring a dissected yurt and every accessory a nomad could ever need. Other halls include various stuffed animals, exhibits by local painters and on Soviet Kyrgyz heroes such as Jukeev Tabaldy Pudovkin, a local Bolshevik hero. The museum is open daily 9 am to noon, and 1 to 5 pm. Entry is 15 som, plus 25 som to take photos.

There's little else to see except the town's garish new **mosque**, 2.5km west of the centre – apparently built with Saudi money, and finished in 1993.

There are a couple of public *banyas* in town, one just up the road from the Hotel Jyldyz and another opposite the exchange office on Lenina. Book a time slot in advance and bring all your dirty clothes as the hot water is unlimited. An hour costs 30 som.

Places to Stay

Stay away from the dilapidated and overpriced *Hotel Ala-Too* on Lenina, unless you enjoy paying over the odds (180 som) for a filthy box with a stinking toilet attached.

The main budget choice is the very spartan but hospitable *Hotel Jyldyz (☎ 248 92)* on Orozbaka, half a block west of the bazar. The place is a converted playschool (ask for *detskiy sad* or kindergarten), with 25 beds in four barren rooms, some with washstands, with no hot water or shower, and a particularly nasty pit toilet in the garden. In summer it's about 60 som per person, plus 80 som for delicious supper and breakfast by arrangement with owners Manas and Roza Beksulmanov (they speak no English).

The *Government Hotel (☎ 226 21)*, 3km east of the centre, has small singles, pleasant doubles and large suites, all with common toilet and shower, for 65, 86 and 122 som per person respectively (though they may try to enforce a 100% foreigner surcharge). There's no hot water (sometimes no water at all) but the scowling ladies who run the place can heat up a tub of hot water for around 5 som. You might well be able to camp in the lovely orchard next to the hotel for about a dollar in som. You can get there on bus No 2, or it's a 45 minute walk from the centre.

In summer you can stay in the *Satar Yurt Inn*, a collection of seven or eight slightly fake-looking tourist yurts behind the government hotel, equipped with beds, western toilets and a small restaurant. A bed costs around US$15 per person with dinner and breakfast. A lot of Torugart-bound groups stay here.

The most luxurious place in town is the clean and modern *Celestial Mountains Guest House (☎/fax 504 12, Moscovskaya 42)*, also known as the English Guest House. The hotel, run by the Bishkek travel agency of the same name, offers comfortable rooms with spotless shared bathrooms, dinner and breakfast included, western videos and guidebooks on the region and the only hot shower between Bishkek and Kashgar. All this decadence doesn't come cheap at US$20 per person but if you need to escape the rigours of the road, this is the place. The hotel is 1km north of the eastern crossroads and is signposted from the road.

Places to Eat
There are numerous uninspiring canteens where you can get standard laghman, borshch or goulash, including the *Café Asia, Café Adek, Aksakaldar Chaykana, Café Shirin* and *Café Cholpan* (probably the best of the lot). There are some cheap snacks to be had in the bazar and this is also the place to come if you are self-catering. You can also get good-quality canned goods, biscuits, sausage and excellent cheese in several private shops at the eastern crossroads.

Getting There & Away
Scheduled buses depart at 9.30 am on the tedious trip to Bishkek (97 som, seven hours), stopping everywhere in between. Buses to At-Bashy (14 som, one hour) leave at 12, 1 and 3 pm. There are buses to Kazarman (100 som, seven hours) on Tuesday and Friday at 8.30 am.

Shared taxis are a good alternative but the shark-like taxi drivers outside the bus station go into a feeding frenzy at the sight of a foreigner. Beware of the friendly guy who grabs your bag and takes you to a car that conveniently happens to be going your way and then charges you a 'finder's fee'. A seat in a full taxi costs 30 som to At-Bashy, 60 som to Kochkor and 150 som to Bishkek. To hire your own taxi costs 600 som to Bishkek, 800 som to Tash Rabat, 400 som to Eki-Naryn or 2000 som to Torugart.

A Naryn-Kashgar bus leaves on Tuesday and a Naryn-Artush bus leaves on Monday, both at 6 am at a cost of US$25 but there isn't much chance that you'll be allowed to continue into China (see the 'Crossing the Torugart' boxed text at the beginning of this section).

The owners of the Hotel Jyldyz run a small company called Eldiyar Tur and can arrange return transport to Song-Köl, via Ak

Tal, for US$50 and to Tash Rabat for US$30. They can also arrange a four day horseback trip to Song-Köl, starting from Jerge Tal. The trip costs US$100, including car transport, the horses, a guide, and food – apparently regardless of the number of people in the group. The company can also arrange horseback trips east of Naryn to the Eki-Naryn valley and even an eight day trip to Issyk-Kul for around US$240 per person.

Around Naryn
Salkyn Tör At this former Pioneer youth camp, 17km east of the centre, a posh *guesthouse* is open May through October with 15 places for around US$20 per person, but you must bring your own food. Alternatively, trek past the camp into the pretty canyon and pitch a tent. In summer there is also a small *yurt camp* run by ITMC (see the Travel Agencies entry in the previous Bishkek section), a little higher up the valley, again for about US$20 a head, including dinner and breakfast.

Hitch east for 10.5km beyond the end of the No 2 trolleybus line to a turn-off with a big rainbow arch. The guesthouse is 1.5km up the turn-off. A ride from Naryn should cost around 50 som.

Eki-Naryn The scenic Kichi (Little) Naryn valley stretches to the north-east of Naryn and offers plenty of opportunities for exploration. The main settlement is at Eki-Naryn, 30km north-east of Salkyn Tör, close to where the Kichi Naryn meets the Naryn.

Buses leave Naryn for Eki-Naryn at 8 am on Monday, Wednesday and Friday, or you could take a taxi for around 400 som. There's no place to stay but there's plenty of good camping in the valley. With your own transport it's possible to continue north-east and then swing west to follow the Kara-Kujur valley back to Sary-Bulak and the main Naryn-Kochkor road.

NARYN TO JALAL-ABAD
If you're planning to go directly between the Fergana valley and the Bishkek-Torugart road, it's possible to cut right across central Kyrgyzstan between Jalal-Abad and

Naryn instead of going around via Bishkek. But the gruelling trip over the Fergana range has few rewards other than the rugged scenery en route.

The route goes via Kazarman, a gold-mining town in the middle of nowhere where you change buses. The old snub-nose buses on this trip don't look like they could climb a curb, let alone a mountain, stop everywhere, and don't even start unless they have enough passengers. In a sturdy 4WD you might do it in one long day; by hitching, figure on two or more, depending on weather and road conditions. Don't try it until the snow has melted off the passes in late May/early June. There are stops for food, but you'd be wise to bring your own.

Naryn to Kazarman

Buses depart Naryn bus station for Kazarman every Tuesday and Friday at 8.30 am (100 som), but only if there are enough passengers. The return trip departs Kazarman on Wednesday and Saturday. It's a seven to eight hour trip (about 350km) to Kazarman, over several minor passes and along the Naryn river valley.

At the village of Ak Tal there is apparently a 4WD track that leads up to the southern shore of Song-Köl. There is a Shepherd's Life co-ordinator (Sveta Jusupjanova, Yntymak 45) at the village of Kurtka, a couple of kilometres from Ak Tal.

Kazarman

This village of 15,000, at 1230m, serves the open-cast Makhmal gold mine about an hour to the east, and an ore-processing plant nearby. Gold seems to attract trouble, and Kazarman has an uncomfortable, untamed feel.

There are two hotels: a two storey white building (shy of foreigners) on the square where Naryn-Kazarman buses terminate, and a single storey white building, the *government hotel*, just east of the bazar, where Kazarman-Jalal-Abad buses terminate.

The bazar is a 20 minute walk south through backstreets from the square. There don't appear to be any restaurants, but there is a chaykhana.

Kazarman also has an airport, with flights to/from Bishkek (and possibly Jalal-Abad and Naryn) for 500 som that are frequently cancelled for lack of passengers.

Kazarman to Jalal-Abad There are no scheduled buses, only when-and-if-it-fills-up buses and cars for about 250 som per person, and taxis offering the trip for about US$30. They'll go only if the weather is good.

The slightly unnerving 6½ hour trip (about 150km) climbs a narrow dirt track over a 3100m pass in the Fergana range, and finishes at Jalal-Abad bazar. From the scenery on the Fergana side you can see why the Fergana valley is Central Asia's breadbasket.

For more information on Jalal-Abad, see the Bishkek to Osh & the Kyrgyz Fergana Valley section later in this chapter.

NARYN TO TORUGART

It's about 130km from Naryn to the outer checkpoint and a farther 60km to the main customs station at Torugart, a total of about 4½ hours driving if you make no stops. But there are two very worthwhile stops, at At-Bashy and Tash Rabat (see following).

From Naryn it's 24km to the low **Kyzyl-Bel pass**, with a stupendous view south and west, right down along the crest of the At-Bashy range (highest point 4786m). The road runs along the foot of this range and around the far (west) end of it to Torugart. About 13km and 20km from the pass are two turn-offs to the village of **At-Bashy** (see the following entry), the closest point to the border accessible by regular bus, and an hour's drive from Naryn.

West of At-Bashy is a yawning, red-walled notch on the north side of the valley; the road crosses a stream that drains everything through this notch and down to the Naryn river. Low bluffs west of the stream partly conceal a bizarre landscape of perfectly rounded, sandy hills. By the roadside is a splendid Kyrgyz graveyard.

About 14.5km west of the second At-Bashy access road is a turn-off to Kara-Suu village and the ruins of **Koshoy Korgon** (see later in this section).

Some 40km west of At-Bashy the road turns to gravel, but for a startling 3km before it does so, it becomes as wide and smooth as a four-lane superhighway: a military airstrip, apparently never used. About 19.5km off the end of the airstrip (about 99km from Naryn or 90km before the main Torugart customs station) is a completely unmarked turn-off south to **Tash Rabat** (see later in this section).

About 28km west of this turn-off is the low **Ak-Beyit pass** at the end of the At-Bashy range. Then it's 4km to the **outer checkpoint**, an hour's drive from At-Bashy, and another fine view – to the crestline, on the border itself.

At-Bashy

At-Bashy is off the Naryn-Torugart road, 6km by an easterly access road, 4km by a westerly one, and truly the far end of Kyrgyzstan. Sandwiched between the At-Bashy and Naryn Tau ranges, the town has a great location and can be used as a springboard for visits to Tash Rabat, Koshoy Korgon and the Torugart pass. Through the Shepherd's Life program you could also arrange visits to the surrounding villages of Tus Bogoshtu, Kök Köl, or farther afield to Bosogo and Tus Ashuu. It's tricky to arrange time to explore At-Bashy if you are en route to the Torugart but otherwise the valley is a great place to explore if you have the time.

Orientation From the bus station at the east end of town head 1.5km west past the new mosque to the cinema and city administration building. Turn right at the administration building and head north 300m to the Koshoy hotel on the right. Continue four blocks and turn left down a dirt road, Arpa köchösü, for 150m to get to Tursan's home-stay.

Places to Stay & Eat The small government-run *Koshoy Mehmonkanas (Aity Suleymanov 29)* tries hard with what are limited materials but rooms still aren't really up to much, though they are cheap at 50 som per person.

One of the best places we stayed in Kyrgyzstan was the *home-stay* of Tursan Akiev (☎ 3534-219 44, Arpa köchösü 25), the local co-ordinator of the Shepherd's Life program (see the boxed text in the Kochkor section). Tursan and her husband Beyshanbek are wonderful hosts and offer a warm, family atmosphere with beds in a comfortable room for 40 som, plus filling dinner and breakfast (vegetarian if you ask) for another 60 som. Tursan can also help out with transportation to Tash Rabat and Torugart and she houses the showroom of the local shyrdak cooperative.

There are a couple of grotty *cafes* at the bus station and beside the hotel, plus there's a small bazar about 600m west of the bus station.

Getting There & Away There are scheduled daily buses to Naryn (15 som, 1½ hours) at 9 am, Bishkek (80 som, eight hours), Kochkor (40 som, four hours) and Kara-Suu (7 som, 30 minutes), all at 8 am.

At the time of research taxis were asking 700 som return to Tash Rabat, though you could get it cheaper through Tursan at the Shepherd's Life program. A seat in a taxi to Bishkek costs 200 som, or 30 som to Naryn.

Koshoy Korgon

In a field behind the village of Kara-Suu are the surprising ruins of a small citadel, occupied during the 10th to 12th or early 13th century, and probably Karakhanid. The rapidly eroding walls are now only a couple of metres high, though a local farmer claimed (with mysterious authority) that they were originally 13m high and 4m thick. They form a big square, perhaps 300m long per side.

A more appealing local legend is that the Kyrgyz superhero Manas built the citadel and a mausoleum here for his fallen friend Koshoy.

Kara-Suu village was founded in 1919 by Kyrgyz refugees from Bolshevik oppression in the Chuy valley near Bishkek.

A taxi from At-Bashy to the site costs about 100 som for a return visit. About 14.5km west of the western access road to At-Bashy on the Naryn-Torugart road, turn south to Kara-Suu village. Take the first left turn in the village, go out past all the houses and look to the right for the ruins.

[Continued on page 410]

THE SILK ROAD

The Early Years

No-one knows for sure when the miraculously fine, light, soft, strong, shimmering, sensuous fabric spun from the cocoon of the *Bombyx* caterpillar first reached the west from China. In the 4th century BCE (before common era), Aristotle described a fibre that may have been Chinese silk. Some people give credit for history's first great industrial espionage coup to a Chinese princess who was departing to marry a Khotanese king: the legend goes that she hid live worms and cocoons in her elaborate hairstyle to fool customs agents so she would be able to wear silk in her 'barbarian' home. Others give the credit to Nestorian monks who allegedly hid silkworm eggs in their walking sticks as they travelled from Central Asia to Byzantium. The Romans probably first laid eyes on silk when the Parthians unfurled great banners of the stuff on the battlefield.

But even after the secret of sericulture arrived in the Mediterranean world, the Chinese consistently exercised the advantage of centuries-acquired know-how. Writing a short while after the time of Christ, Pliny the Elder was scandalised by the luxurious, transparent cloths, which allowed Roman women to be 'dressed and yet nude'. He fell wide of the mark in describing silk's origin and processing, though, believing silk to literally grow on trees in a land called Seres. The Chinese, had they known, would most likely have done little to disillusion him.

Parthia, on the Iranian plateau, was the most voracious foreign consumer of Chinese silk at the close of the 2nd century BCE, having supposedly traded an ostrich egg for its first bolt of silk. In about 105 BCE, Parthia and China exchanged embassies and inaugurated official bilateral trade along the caravan route that lay between them. With this the Silk Road was born – in fact, if not in name.

The Silk Routes

It was said to take 200 days to traverse the route, though geographically the Silk Road was a complex and shifting proposition. It was no single road, but rather a fragile network of intercontinental caravan tracks that threaded through some of the highest mountains and bleakest deserts on earth (see the accompanying map). Though the road map expanded over the centuries, the network had its main eastern terminus at the Chinese capital Ch'ang-an (modern Xi'an); west of there, the route passed through the Jade Gate and divided at Dunhuang, one branch skirting the dreaded Taklamakan desert to the north through Loulan, Turfan, Kucha and Aksu, while the other headed south via Miran, Khotan (Hotan) and Yarkand. The two forks met again in Kashgar, from where the trail headed up to any of a series of passes

Inset: The riches of the silk road were hauled on the backs of camels and horses.
Photo: Martin Moos

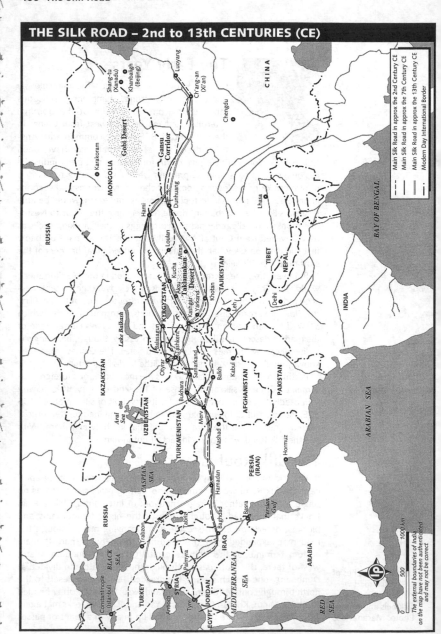

THE SILK ROAD – 2nd to 13th CENTURIES (CE)

confronting the traveller who attempted to cross the Pamir and Tian Shan (one pass again in use today is the Torugart on the border with Kyrgyzstan).

Beyond the mountains, the Fergana valley fed westward through Kokand, Samarkand and Bukhara, past Merv and on to Iran, the Levant and Constantinople. Goods reached transhipment points on the Black and Mediterranean seas, where caravans took on cargo for the march back eastward over the same tracks. In the middle of the network, major branches headed south over the Karakoram range to India and north via the Zhungarian Gap and across the Saka steppes to the Volga.

Caravans & Trade

Goods heading west and goods heading east did not fall into discrete bundles. In fact there was no 'through traffic'; caravanners were mostly short and medium-distance haulers who marketed and took on freight along a given beat according to their needs and inclinations. The earliest exchanges were based on mercantile interactions between the steppe nomads and settled towns, when barter was the only form of exchange. Only later did a monetary economy enable long-distance trade routes to develop.

Bottom: Tash Rabat caravanserai, once a popular stop on the old Silk Road, Central Kyrgyzstan.

BRADLEY MAYHEW

At any given time any portion of the network might be beset by war, robbers or natural disaster; the northern routes were plagued by nomadic horsemen and a lack of settlements to provide fresh supplies and mounts; the south by fearsome deserts and frozen mountain passes.

As with motion in an anthill, trends are visible when one steps back. In general, the eastern end was enriched by the importation of gold, silver, ivory, jade and other precious stones, wool, horses, Mediter-ranean coloured glass (an industrial mystery originally as inscrutable to the Chinese as silk was in the west), cucumbers, walnuts, pome-granates, grapes and wine, spices, ivory and – an early Parthian craze – acrobats and ostriches. Goods enriching the western end included silk, porcelain, paper, tea, lacquerware, spices, medicinal herbs, gems and perfumes.

And in the middle lay Central Asia, a great clearinghouse that pro-vided its native beasts – horses and two-humped Bactrian camels – to keep the goods flowing in both directions. The cities of Bukhara and Samarkand marked the halfway break, where caravans from Aleppo and Baghdad met traders from Kashgar and Yarkand. Caravanserais (*rabat*) grew up along the route, offering lodgings, stables and stores. Middlemen like the Sogdians amassed great fortunes, much of which went into beautifying cosmopolitan and luxuriant caravan towns such as Gurganj and Bukhara. The cities offered equally vital services such as brokers to set up contracts, banking houses to set up a line of credit and markets to sell the goods.

Bottom: Loading up the camels was a big task.

THEODOR HERZEN

Technology Transfer

The Silk Road gave rise to unprecedented trade, but its true glory and unique status in human history were the result of the interchange of ideas, technologies and religions that occurred among the very different cultures that used it. Religion alone presents an astounding picture of diversity and tolerance that would be the envy of any modern democratic state. Manichaeism, Zoroastrianism, Buddhism, Nestorian Christianity, Judaism, Confucianism, Taoism and the shamanism of grassland nomads coexisted and in some cases mingled, until the coming of Islam. In the course of his archaeological expeditions in Xinjiang, Albert von Le Coq brought back examples of 17 different languages written in 24 different scripts.

The Silk Road passed music and dance from west to east and enabled Indian, Chinese, Greek and Tibetan artistic styles to merge and fuse to form the Serindian art of Chinese Turkestan and Gandharan art of Pakistan and Afghanistan.

Buddhism spread along the trade routes to wend its way from India to China and back again. It's hard to imagine that Buddhist monasteries once dominated cultural life in Central Asia. Today only the faintest archaeological evidence remains in ex-Soviet Central Asia, at Adjina-Tepe in Tajikistan, Kuva in the Fergana valley, Termiz in Uzbekistan, and Ak Beshim in Kyrgyzstan.

The Death of the Silk Road

The Silk Road never regained its vitality after the cosmopolitan Tang dynasty. The destruction and turbulence wreaked by Jenghiz Khan and Timur (Tamerlane) dealt an economic blow to the region and the literal and figurative drying-up of the Silk Road lead to the abandonment of cities along the southern shore of the Taklamakan. The nail in the Silk Road's coffin was the opening of maritime trading routes between Europe and Asia.

Central Asia remained largely forgotten by east and west until the arrival of Russian and British explorers in the 19th century and the rediscovery of the glory of Xinjiang's Silk Road cities (see the boxed text 'Foreign Devils on the Silk Road' in the Xinjiang chapter). Ironically, it was only then, 20 centuries after the first Chinese missions to the west, that the term 'Silk Road' was even used, coined for the first time by the German geographer Ferdinand Van Richthofen, the uncle of the Red Baron.

[Continued from page 404]

Tash Rabat

At a completely unmarked turn-off, 55 to 60km from At-Bashy or 32km from the outer Kyrgyz checkpoint, a sometimes washed-out dirt track heads into a surprisingly level and very lovely valley in the At-Bashy range. It's the perfect shelter, with lush corduroy hillsides, small farmsteads and the occasional yurt encampment. Indeed it must have been attracting well-to-do travellers for centuries, for about 15km in is a solitary fortified caravanserai, looking rather like a little mausoleum.

Local sources say it dates from the 15th century, though a clumsy total restoration was completed in 1984. There is an entry fee of 10 som, payable at a gate 10km before the site. Keep the ticket to show the caretakers at the site, who will unlock the site compound. A few fragments of the original interior are visible in the main chamber; leading off this are many other chambers, including a well and a dungeon. An opening in the far right corner leads to what the caretakers say is a tunnel, explored generations ago as far as about 200m, and perhaps once leading to a lookout point to the south.

From Tash Rabat you can climb to a broad ridge overlooking Chatyr-Köl lake, but watch out: you're about 3500m high, and a short walk could set your head pounding. Chatyr-Köl is four or five hours away on horseback, longer on foot, but it's just a big, flat puddle surrounded by a boggy plain. Neither Tash Rabat nor Chatyr-Köl are in a restricted border zone, so no permits are needed. It's normally possible to hire horses from the caretakers for around 60 som per day.

A day trip by taxi from Naryn or At-Bashy to Tash Rabat is around 800 som.

Places to Stay You can stay at the *caretaker's house* across from the caravanserai and a few yurts are set up in summer in conjunction with ITMC in Bishkek for around US$7 per person.

It's cheaper at the *gatekeeper's house*, about 10km before the caravanserai. A quilt on the floor in the guestroom or nearby yurt

costs around 20 som and there's basic food available. Bring your own sleeping bag, as well as some munchies and supplies for your host family.

The valley is a fine place to camp and very peaceful if you happen to have it to yourself. If you do want to camp, bring all your own supplies – plus tea, cigarettes or vodka to trade with the lonely caretakers.

THE TORUGART PASS

South from the outer checkpoint the road rapidly degenerates as views of the Fergana range rise to the west. About 26km on, at the 3574m **Tüz-Bel pass**, it swings east and skirts Chatyr-Köl. The same black cranes that pause on their journey at the Karkara valley east of Issyk-Kul also stop here, and along with its broad, marshy shoreline the lake comprises the Chatyr-Köl zoological preserve. An old Soviet-era double electrified fence runs near the road, still patrolled by Russians but supposedly no longer charged up. As the road climbs, the surrounding mountains seem to shrink.

Fifty kilometres from the outer checkpoint and 7km from the Kyrgyzstan customs & immigration station, a big red and yellow sign says 'Narzan'; 50m off the road in a field of bubbling mud is a gushing cold spring, fizzy and tasty.

Kyrgyzstan Side

The customs & immigration facilities are open 10 am to 5 pm Monday to Friday, but in reality you must cross between 9 am and noon. Besides the various customs sheds, inspection pits and immigration offices, there is a spartan state 'hotel', though most people stay in *caravans*, 1km before the customs area.

Each of these caravans is a little private 'guesthouse' where you can take simple meals and sleep on cotton mattresses on the floor (family in one end, three or four guests in the other) for around 100 som per person with a basic dinner and tea. There's a couple of pit toilets around the back but no running water, and the grounds are pretty foul.

Most of the traffic through the pass is trucks carrying scrap metal and animal hides from Kyrgyzstan, or porcelain, thermoses, beer and clothing from China. The trucks accumulate in huge tailbacks at both sides, for 500m or more in the mornings.

From the Kyrgyzstan customs & immigration station it's 6.8km to the summit. There the Chinese have built a miniature redbrick Arc de Triomphe and a small house with Chinese guards. Below this, about 5km away, is a checkpoint, though the main Chinese customs & immigration post is another 70km away.

Crossing the Pass

Following is what we did on our way from Kyrgyzstan into China. Travellers coming the other way reported roughly the same in reverse.

Kyrgyzstan – Procedures If your vehicle made it to Torugurt, both sets of border guards showed up for work and your Chinese transportation arrived, you're in business. When both sides of the border finally open, you and your driver show confirmation of onward transportation on the Chinese side. Kyrgyzstan immigration will then delay you and your vehicle until the radio call comes from the Chinese side that your transportation has arrived. This can be a long, cold, frustrating wait. After confirmation of onward transport you march into customs, bags in tow, where officials collect the customs form you filled out when you entered the CIS and try (and probably succeed) to sell you a customs form for 30 som. You then proceed through immigration, where they'll want to see your Kyrgyzstan visa, OVIR registration, and a China visa. Meanwhile, your vehicle is being strip-searched in a garage next door.

After inspection you jump back into your vehicle and continue 7km to the arch. If you don't have transport for this section this is where your headache begins, as you'll have to negotiate with a driver to give you a lift and with the officials to let you pass.

Summit In the border zone, roughly between the two customs & immigration stations, permitted vehicles are allowed, but apparently no pedestrians other than guards

(although some travellers are said to have cycled it). At the arch at the summit, your new driver and some tiny little Chinese soldiers will be waiting for the transfer. Big handshakes all around. Don't forget to take a look at the beautiful pass, which you just fought so hard to cross.

China – Torugart to Kashgar Another 5km later you will arrive at the original Chinese border post, where the Bishkek-Kashgar bus passengers will be patiently unrolling every carpet and draining every thermos for the customs patrol. Just to keep up appearances, the guards will have you line up all your baggage and then choose one at random to dig through. You then file through the beeper machine to check for dangerous metals. Then you are off.

It's surprising how the climate and landscape change when you cross the pass. The China side is abruptly drier, more desolate and treeless, with little physical development other than adobe Kyrgyz settlements. The road runs through Kyzylsu Kyrgyz Autonomous County.

The 100km of road closest to the border, south through crumbling, red-walled canyons, is a miserable washboard surface, spine-shattering to travel along and choked with dust. At 45km is the hamlet of **Toyun** and about 10km farther, the Torugart-Suu canyon from the border post enters the equally immense Ushmurvan-Suu canyon from the north-west, flowing down to Kashgar. It's 41km from here to a river bridge, and a farther 7km to the spanking new **China customs & immigration station**, at the junction of the Torugart (Kyrgyzstan) and Irkeshtam (Tajikistan) roads.

Chinese immigration is open 1 to 5 pm Beijing time but they will wait for you if you are late. Here you fill out entry forms, get your passport stamped, and send your luggage through the x-rays, all relatively painless. The post has a Bank of China branch, a couple of simple noodle shops and a small guesthouse, though travellers in either direction are discouraged from staying.

From here to Kashgar it's 60km of paved road, passing several poplar-lined Uyghur villages and later the San Xi'an Caves (see the Around Kashgar section of the Xinjiang chapter).

The whole Torugart-Kashgar trip is 160km, a 3½ to four hour 4WD trip.

Bishkek to Osh & the Kyrgyz Fergana Valley

From the standpoint of landscape, the Bishkek-Osh road is a sequence of superlatives, taking the traveller over two 3000m-plus passes, through the yawning Suusamyr valley, around the immense Toktogul reservoir, down the deep Naryn river gorge and into the broad Fergana valley.

The road is rough but has improved dramatically over the last few years as the government tries to solder the two halves of the country together using better transport and communications links. The Bishkek-Toktogul stretch is still blocked occasionally by rockfalls, and in winter frequently by avalanches. Even in summer the passes are icy cold – no place to be stranded with a disabled bus. Snow fills the passes from October or November until February or March; the road is kept open but is dangerous then. Scheduled buses thin out by October and stop over winter, although cars continue to push through.

Regular buses do not go all the way; you must normally change at Toktogul. Smaller arenda minibuses and taxis do go direct, and you can find drivers waiting for passengers at the Osh bazar bus stand in Bishkek and at the old bus station in Osh.

BISHKEK TO TASHKÖMÜR
Bishkek to Toktogul

Even before you climb out of the Chuy valley from Kara-Balta, the craggy Kyrgyz Alatau range rises like a wall. The road climbs through a crumbling canyon towards the highest point of the journey, the 3586m **Tör-Ashuu pass** (Russian: Tyuz-Ashuu) at the suture between the Talas Alatau and Kyrgyz Alatau ranges. But instead of climbing over, it burrows through near the top, in a dripping tunnel (built by the same team

that constructed the metros in Leningrad and Moscow) that opens onto an eagle's-eye view of the Suusamyr basin. In summer there are plenty of yurt stands along the next section of road, offering fresh kumys and other dairy products.

About 4½ hours out of Bishkek a road shoots off straight as an arrow across the basin towards Suusamyr, Chayek and eventually the Bishkek-Naryn road. There are no buses along this route and you would have to hitch as far as Chayek, probably with one of the many coal trucks headed to a mine near Song-Köl. There's no accommodation along this route and local people don't seem to be all that friendly to outsiders.

After another 1¼ hours another road branches right, over the 3330m Otmek pass towards Talas, and Zhambyl in Kazakstan. There's no public transport along this route and not much to see in Talas except the 14th century tomb of Manas, east of town in the village of Tash Aryk.

In another 30 minutes the road climbs again, to the 3184m summit of **Ala-Bel pass** over the Suusamyr-Too mountains. Lower, broader and longer than the Tör-Ashuu pass, it is nevertheless colder, and said to be the bigger wintertime spoiler.

The beautiful valley down the south side of the pass, though partly in the Chychkan state zoological reserve, is defaced by three ranks of crackling high-voltage lines, running up from the dam at the head of the **Toktogul reservoir**, which now spreads out below. Most buses terminate at Toktogul on the lake's north side. Bishkek-Toktogul is an eight hour (about 300km) trip by minibus.

Toktogul
☎ 3747 • pop approx 70,000

This town is named for a well-known Kyrgyz akyn, Toktogul Satilganov, who was born here in 1884 (died 1933). It has nothing to recommend it, but is the usual bus changeover point between Bishkek and Osh, and you'll probably have to spend the night and push off again at sunrise.

From the bus station entrance, walk right (west) and immediately left (south) along a boulevard for about 400m. Just off to the right is the grotty town hotel **Ketmen-Töbö**, with beds for 40 som per person in doubles or triples, with shared bathroom – or a ridiculously huge apartment for 100 som per person. Hot water is unlikely.

Another option, back on the main road a few minutes walk from the bus station is the **Gostinitsa Kunduz**, a private chalet-style hotel with rooms for 30 som per person. It's not bad but the wooden walls make the rooms noisy, there's no place to wash and only a filthy pit toilet outside.

Getting There & Away Around 6 am a single bus departs for Bishkek (118 som), and another for Jalal-Abad (97 som, seven hours). Others go to Osh at 7.10 am (110 som), and to Kara-Köl at 10.30 am and noon (40 som 2½ hours). Private cars and jeeps wait for passengers at the station but most charge over the odds. It's possible to flag cars on the main highway running through town. A ride to Bishkek costs around 150 som per person.

Toktogul to Kara-Köl

The two to 2½ hour journey is mainly occupied with detouring around the vast, flat reservoir. If you have your own transportation, there's a trucker's hostel and restaurant, 1¼ hours south on the other side of the reservoir, though at the time of research it was occupied with Iranian roadworkers upgrading the highway. Some tour groups camp near here and it's not a bad choice; bring all your water with you. Several roadside stalls on the south side of the lake serve delicious fried *farel* (trout).

Kara-Köl

☎ 3746 • pop approx 22,000

Scribbled on a wall in the outskirts of town is a greeting: 'wellcome to fucking Kara-Kul'. Just about everybody here works for the hydroelectric station Toktogulsky Gidroelektrostantsia or GES. The sole reason to alight is to ask for a tour of the dam. Kara-Köl is not to be confused with the much pleasanter town of Karakol on Lake Issyk-Kul.

Orientation & Information Ask to be dropped, not at the bus station at the far east

of town, but about 2km west by a tiny 'Gostinitsa Turist' sign. This is also close to the dam administration offices. The town spreads lethargically below the main highway and is quite spread out.

The Kaskad The dam is part of the Nizhnenarynskiy kaskad, a series of five dams down the lower gorge of the Naryn river. This cascade, topmost in the series, was completed in 1976 after 14 years' work. More and bigger ones are under construction or in planning. Their power is distributed into the grid Kyrgyzstan shares with Uzbekistan and Kazakstan. Hydroelectric power is in fact one of the few things other than tourism that Kyrgyzstan has to sell to the outside world.

You can't see the Toktogul dam (behind a ridge to the west of the hotel) from town or from the road, and you can't just trek over to it – you won't get in without a pass. You might succeed in getting this and a guided tour by asking at kaskad headquarters, a two storey yellow brick building just off the highway near the hotel. Go upstairs to the director's office, where we found one English-speaking staff member.

The massive dam, wedged in the canyon, is a pretty awesome feat of Soviet engineering: 210m high, 150m wide at the top, and holding back a 19 billion cubic metre lake. Photographs are not allowed of the dam.

Places to Stay There's only one place to stay, the quiet **Hotel Turist**, where mouldy triples/doubles with bath and hot water are about 150/200 som per person. The dining room does a dreary set meal, but book ahead or you may find it shut. It's on the western edge of town, near the kaskad headquarters but over 2km from the eastern bus station.

Getting There & Away Buses to Jalal-Abad (60 som, 4½ hours) or Osh (70 som, seven hours) depart around 6.30 am (ask at the hotel for the exact times), and the bus station is a long, cold, dark walk from the hotel. You're better off flagging the bus down from near the kaskad headquarters, though you can't be sure of a seat. For Bishkek, change at Toktogul.

KYRGYZSTAN

A better bet is to take a seat in one of the shared taxis, which wait at the bus station. Fares are around 40 som to Tashkömür and 50 som to Toktogul.

Kara-Köl to Tashkömür

The gorge of the lower Naryn river is an impressive passage, with sheer walls and towering pillars of red sandstone, and a little road clinging to the side – but keep your gaze upwards. Looking down you will see that there is no longer any river at all, just a depressing series of narrow, utterly still lakes behind the dams of the Nizhnenarynskiy kaskad. At lower elevations the gorge bristles with pylons. Sit on the 'west' side of the bus for the best views of this ruination.

Tashkömür

☎ 3745

About 5½ hours from Toktogul is the coal-mining town of Tashkömür, strung for miles along the west side of the river below one of the dams. The town itself is one of the most surreal in all of Kyrgyzstan, but it is one of the main starting points to beautiful Lake Sary Chelek, 70km west.

Places to Stay & Eat Avoid the hotel near the bus station, unless you enjoy sharing your room with drunks and down-and-outers.

Instead head for the town *gostinitsa*, where beds in a decent four-bed room cost 33 som. There's a shared bathroom with an extremely dodgy water supply; both the water and electricity may temporarily be turned off if there aren't any other guests. There is a single pit toilet outside.

There are a few cheap *cafes* serving lukewarm laghman near the bus station along with what may well be Central Asia's most pitiful bazar. You are better off bringing your own supplies and self-catering.

Getting There & Away

Buses leave at 5.40 and 11.20 am and 3 pm for Osh and at 6.40 and 7.20 am and 12.20 pm for Jalal-Abad from the bus station in the centre of town.

To get a shared taxi head 3km from town to the Naryn river bridge, where there is a

collection of kiosks and food stalls. A taxi to Kara Köl costs 40 som per seat. This is also the place to pick up the infrequent and often packed through buses to Kara Köl or Toktogul.

If you are headed to Sary-Chelek take the 10 am bus to Kara Jigach.

LAKE SARY CHELEK

This beautiful 7km-long alpine lake, nature reserve and biosphere reserve lies hidden in the northern flanks of the Fergana valley amid groves of wild pistachios, walnuts and fruit trees. The lake is thought to have been created by an earthquake that caused a giant landslide about 800 years ago. Its remote location means that without your own transport the lake is hard to reach. In addition, the lake is not yet really tourist-friendly and visitors can only visit on a day trip, which essentially requires you to drive up to the lake. The only way to camp officially around the lake is to get permission beforehand from the Ministry of Environmental Protection in Bishkek.

There is a run down *turbaza* in Jilgen village, where it should be possible to stay for the night but it makes sense to bring a tent and all your food with you. From Jilgen it is another 10km to the lower park gate, another 2km to Arkit village and the bus terminus, and from here another half-day's hike to the lake. It's possible to drive right up to the lake shore in your own transport. If you arrive in Arkit on the evening bus you will probably not be allowed to proceed to the lake the same day and will have to return 12km to the turbaza.

It's possible to make a five day trek in to the lake from Leninopol (catch a daily bus from Talas). An easier trek starts from Kyzyl Kul in the next-door valley. From here it's a long day's walk up the valley to Kara Suu lake and then another day's hard slog over the 2446m Kemerty pass and down to either Sary Chelek or nearby Iyri Köl lake. Both routes are marked on the 1:120,000 *Cherez Talasskii Khrebet k Ozeru Sary-Chelek*, available in Bishkek at the Kyrgyz Cartographic Agency.

Sary Chelek is only open May to September. There is an entry fee of around 400 som (50 som for locals).

Getting There & Away

From Tashkömür take the morning bus to Kara Jigach (20 som, three hours) and then hitch or wait for the afternoon bus from Kerven (Karavan) to Arkit to pass through. There are also three buses a day between Kerven and neighbouring Kyzyl Kul, which also pass through Kara Jigach. Heading back, there are buses from Kara Jigach to Tashkömür at around 2 pm and to Kerven at around 12.30 pm. The decrepit local snub-nosed buses are packed, hot, uncomfortable and mind-numbingly slow; taxis are a sensible choice around here.

JALAL-ABAD

☎ 3722 • pop 74,000

Jalal-Abad is mainly a dried-up, washed-out resort town seemingly stuck in a Soviet time-warp. If you're not just changing buses here, the only thing to do is head up the hill for a soak at the sanatorium.

Rise above it all on a 3km walk (or five minute ride) up a tree-lined road to the peaceful, threadbare **Jalal-Abad Sanatorium**, with fine views of the almond-grove-blanketed countryside and the Babash-Ata mountains to the north. Head to the rear of the grounds, staying to the right; near a small cafe are the baths (open to the public) with mud and mineral water baths, massage, sauna and all the mineral water you can drink. Unless you go with someone who knows, you'll have to grab one of the white-cloaked health workers who shuffle between the dozens of unmarked blocks to help you find the correct building.

Surprisingly, it's possible to send and receive emails in Jalal-Abad at ElCat2 on Toktogul. Messages cost around 30 som each to send or receive.

A taxi from the centre is about 20 som (ask for 'kurort'), and there are usually a few hanging around the bus stand.

Places to Stay

The old Hotel Jalalabad has been renamed the *Hotel Mölmöl* (☎ 550 59). Spartan but essentially clean singles/doubles cost 151/221 som, with a private cold-water bathroom and huge lux suites with a sitting room, water heater and fridge, cost around 540 som. In

Border Shenanigans

If you are travelling between Tashkömür and Osh beware that most buses travel via Uzbekistan. In theory, you are allowed 72 hours transit to get through Uzbekistan but Uzbek police are increasingly ignoring this rule and you may face a shakedown when you leave Uzbekistan. Locals are occasionally refused entry to pass through Uzbekistan at times of political tension in the Fergana valley.

To avoid the border, you need to take a shared taxi from Tashkömür to Jalal-Abad and then another one from here to Özgön, before you can safely board a bus to Osh. See those cities' entries for transport details.

As the Uzbek border continues to solidify, new roads will spring up to help locals circumvent border shakedowns. The road from Tashkömür to Jalal-Abad already does a several kilometre detour up the Mailuu-Suu valley in order to avoid the Uzbek border crossing at Kochkor-Ata.

theory there is a small business centre and airline ticket office in the hotel.

The sanatorium allegedly has a pricey *government guesthouse* near the baths, though we couldn't find it. Sanatorium workers apparently rent out their flats here for around US$10 per night.

Places to Eat

Islam Sydyk Restaurant, near the square, has cheap, tasty Kyrgyz dishes on its 'first-course' menu, including soups *(manpar, kesme* or *shorpa)* and little dumplings called *chuchvara,* as well as pricier salads and European offerings. Go for lunch; after 6 pm the scene is set for a Russian-style blowout: shattering music, flashing lights, the works. It's on Lenin, a block west of the square; the building has '1917-1977' on the side.

The privately run canteen-style *Kafe Amir Temur* on the north-east side of the bazar has good, very cheap food and plenty of options for vegetarians. Just point to any of the dozen or so things on display to make a hearty meal for about 20 som.

The *Restaurant Ala-Too* opposite the Hotel Mölmöl has decent soups and Russian standards at lunch, but more blow-you-away music in the evening.

More of the same but in a fancier setting can be found at the *Café Abdykaar-Ata* on Lenin.

Getting There & Around

Air Marshrutnyy minibus No 1 from the centre and No 5 from the bus station go to the airport, north-west of the centre. A taxi is about 100 som. On paper there are flights to/from Bishkek twice a week; buy tickets at the airport or inside the Hotel Mölmöl.

Bus The bus station is two or 3km west of the centre; minibuses clearly marked *avto-vokzal* run frequently along Lenin near the bazar.

Scheduled buses depart for Kara-Köl at 8.20 am, and Toktogul at 6 and 10.20 am. Osh buses leave every half-hour or so until 6 pm, via Uzbekistan (see the boxed text 'Border Shenanigans' earlier in this chapter). For Uzbekistan, change at Khanabad (formerly Sovietabad) en route to Osh, though you might find a direct bus from Jalal-Abad to Andijan.

At a stand on the south-west corner of the bazar you can find arenda minibuses and private cars going all the way to Bishkek for 500 som a seat, especially in the late afternoon. You can also find shared taxis and jeeps for the tough mountain route to Kazarman (250 som per seat; see the previous Bishkek to Kashgar via the Torugart Pass section of this chapter).

Train The train station is a 10 minute walk south from Lenin on Toktogul. At the time of research all trains had been suspended, partly because of a blockade by Uzbekistan and partly because of a lack of passengers. If services resume there should be passenger trains to Bishkek (30 hours) and Tashkent (14 hours).

ARSLANBOB

Better than looking at the mountains from Jalal-Abad is to go up into them. An adventurous do-it-yourself trip goes up to Arslanbob, a totally Uzbek village of about 12,000 with a turbaza that swarms all summer with CIS holidaymakers.

Reasons to come here are the mountain air, grand setting, abundant fruit, the area's famous walnuts, and – for those who can tear themselves away from the turbaza bar and video salon – some fine walking and climbing in the Babash-Ata mountains. 'Instructors' lead reasonably priced day hikes or treks to waterfalls, caves or Ketmen-Köl lake, or into adjacent valleys. Alpinists can take on 4427m Babash-Ata (or Weber) Peak. Most day hikes start from the right-hand fork of the main road, just before the turbaza, and head up over successive ridges to meadows at the foot of the mountains.

Outside the season (June through September), shops are empty and it's *cold*. Arslanbob is over 3000m and even in summer it's considerably cooler than Jalal-Abad. May and October can still be good times to visit, though, as you'll likely have the place to yourself. You'll need at least two nights here if you want to do any walking.

The only English speaker is the village's schoolmaster, and even Russian is scarce. This is a fairly conservative village, so don't go up in shorts and singlets.

American *biznezmen* are said to have their eyes on the area's vast walnut groves, and not for the nuts.

The adjacent **Kyzyl-Ünkür** valley also has a small turbaza and a network of hiking and fishing routes equal to, if not grander than those at Arslanbob. It's sensible to bring a tent and supplies if you are headed here.

Places to Stay & Eat Prospects of a space at Arslanbob are good even without a booking. The run down but rustic *Turbaza Arslanbob* has over 500 beds, for a couple of hundred som each per night, in bungalows scattered around 29 hectares of grounds, with common showers and toilets; or you can pitch your own tent for free. A huge dining hall and a chaykhana serve Uzbek dishes in season.

If the turbaza is closed it's possible to stay in the guestroom of the caretaker Abdul

Rakhim, at ulitsa Turbaza 77, a five minute walk downhill from the turbaza. In fact, if you get the chance then stay here instead of the turbaza. There are no washing facilities but a traditional Uzbek bed of quilts on the floor only costs 30 som and the place has a very Central Asian feel to it (unlike the Sovietised turbaza).

Getting There & Away From Jalal-Abad, take a bus to Bazar Korgon (40 minutes, departs hourly). Change there for an Arslanbob bus and take it to the end of the line (20 som, three hours, hourly until 4.30 pm). It's a 1.5km uphill walk to the turbaza gate. A day trip would be possible by car but not by bus.

There are three buses daily from Bazar Korgon to Kyzyl-Ünkür, at 9.20 am, and 12.20 and 4.20 pm. A taxi from Bazar Korgon to Tashkömür costs around 150 som.

OSH
☎ 3222 • pop 300,000

Osh is Kyrgyzstan's second-biggest city and the administrative centre of the huge, populous province that engulfs the Fergana valley on the Kyrgyzstan side. It suffers a kind of demographic schizophrenia, being a major centre of Kyrgyzstan but with a dominantly Uzbek population more in tune with Uzbekistan and the rest of the Fergana valley, but isolated from it by one of the world's more absurd international borders. The resulting tension has had Osh on a communal knife-edge ever since Stalin drew the line, as Uzbek-Kyrgyz violence in 1990 emphatically showed.

There is almost nothing architecturally fascinating here, but it's still an interesting place to visit because of its long history. It's one of the region's genuinely ancient towns (with a history dating back at least to the 5th century BCE), it was an important crossroads for Silk Road trade, it maintained a broad mixture of peoples, and it continues to boast a huge market.

It's still a very Soviet place: while other cities scrubbed Lenin's name from their street maps after the collapse of the USSR, Osh merely shifted it politely one block away. There's a huge Lenin statue opposite the administration building and a huge metal-cut of Lenin still peers down from the rooftops west of the bazar.

Osh is the anchor-point of not only the Pamir Highway into Tajikistan but, branching off this, the main road access to the Pamir Alay on the Kyrgyzstan-Tajikistan border, and in the other direction the (currently closed) Irkeshtam border crossing to/from Kashgar in China.

The city is also a common travellers' base for trekking and mountaineering in the spectacular Pamir range.

History

The standard refrain from anyone you ask is that 'Osh is older than Rome'. Legends credit all sorts of people with its founding, from King Solomon (Suleyman) to Alexander the Great. Certainly it must have been a major hub on the Silk Road from its earliest days. The Mongols smashed it in the 13th century but in the following centuries it bounced back, more prosperous than ever.

Its late fame, however, is of a different kind. 'Osh' has become a byword for ethnic conflict in the festering, gerrymandered closeness of the Fergana valley. In fact the worst of 'Osh' took place 55km away in Özgön (Uzgen), during three nights of savage Uzbek-Kyrgyz violence in June-July 1990, during which at least three hundred people (some unofficial estimates run to over one thousand) died a variety of ugly deaths while Soviet military and police authorities stood oddly by.

When post-Soviet Kyrgyzstan adopted its own currency, Uzbekistan accused it of trying to sabotage Central Asian unity and imposed a blockade on exports of oil and gas to Kyrgyzstan; Osh, caught in the middle, felt the temperature rise again. While the majority Uzbeks dominate local business, Kyrgyzstan has forced upon them an almost totally Kyrgyz (and apparently widely corrupt) municipal administration, by which they feel constantly 'plundered'.

Rumours abound of weapons stockpiled for future conflicts. But considering the likelihood that most people around Osh and Özgön – Kyrgyz and Uzbek alike – have

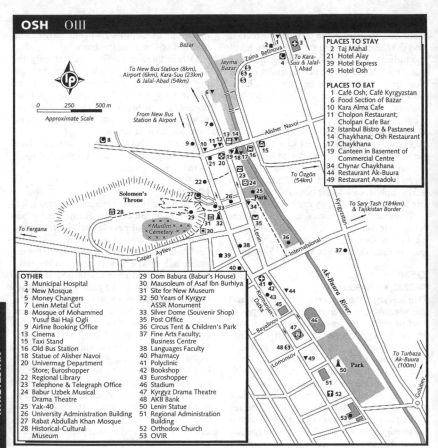

OSH OIII

Bazar

To New Bus Station (8km),
Airport (6km), Kara-Suu (23km)
& Jalal-Abad (54km)

Jayma
Bazar

Zaina Betinova

To Kara-
Suu & Jalal-
Abad

Alisher Navoi

From New Bus
Station & Airport

0   250   500 m

Approximate Scale

Solomon's
Throne

To Özgön
(54km)

Park

To Sary Tash (184km)
& Tajikistan Border

To Fergana

Muslim
Cemetery

Park

Gapar Aytiev

International

Ak-Buura River

Kurmanjan
Datka

Lenin

Bayalinov

To Turbaza
Ak-Buura
(100m)

Lomonsov

Goubev

Park

PLACES TO STAY
2   Taj Mahal
21 Hotel Alay
39 Hotel Express
45 Hotel Osh

PLACES TO EAT
1   Café Osh; Café Kyrgyzstan
6   Food Section of Bazar
10 Kara Alma Cafe
11 Cholpon Restaurant;
    Cholpan Cafe Bar
12 Istanbul Bistro & Pastanesi
14 Chaykhana; Osh Restaurant
17 Chaykhana
19 Canteen in Basement of
    Commercial Centre
34 Chynar Chaykhana
44 Restaurant Ak-Buura
49 Restaurant Anadolu

OTHER
3   Municipal Hospital
4   New Mosque
5   Money Changers
7   Lenin Metal Cut
8   Mosque of Mohammed
    Yusuf Bai Haji Ogli
9   Airline Booking Office
13 Cinema
15 Taxi Stand
16 Old Bus Station
18 Statue of Alisher Navoi
20 Univermag Department
    Store; Euroshopper
22 Regional Library
23 Telephone & Telegraph Office
24 Babur Uzbek Musical
    Drama Theatre
25 Yak-40
26 University Administration Building
27 Rabat Abdullah Khan Mosque
28 Historical-Cultural
    Museum
29 Dom Babura (Babur's House)
30 Mausoleum of Asaf Ibn Burhiya
31 Site for New Museum
32 50 Years of Kyrgyz
    ASSR Monument
33 Silver Dome (Souvenir Shop)
35 Post Office
36 Circus Tent & Children's Park
37 Fine Arts Faculty;
    Business Centre
38 Languages Faculty
40 Pharmacy
41 Polyclinic
42 Bookshop
43 Euroshopper
46 Stadium
47 Kyrgyz Drama Theatre
48 AKB Bank
50 Lenin Statue
51 Regional Administration
    Building
52 Orthodox Church
53 OVIR

friends or family members who were murdered in 1990, the wonder is how many Kyrgyz and Uzbeks remain close friends (or married couples) and how determined most of them are to get along.

Perhaps to stir up some post-independence patriotism and improve morale, the government has decided that 2000 should be marked as the 3000th year of Osh. A program of cultural events has been planned and a new museum is being built to celebrate the occasion. No dates have been set so far, largely because no one knows when there will be enough money to kick off the celebrations.

Orientation

Osh sprawls across the valley of the Ak-Buura river, flowing out of the Pamir Alay mountains. The city's most prominent landmark is 'Solomon's Throne', a craggy mountain that squeezes right up to the river from the west.

Along the west bank run two parallel main roads – one-way-south Kurmanjan Datka kuchasi and one-way-north Lenin kuchasi. To confuse matters, Lenin kuchasi used to be ulitsa Sverdlova, while Kurmanjan Datka kuchasi used to be ulitsa Lenina! Be careful with older maps, which may still immortalise

Lenin one block over. From the Hotel Osh to the bazar is a 20 to 25 minute walk.

Osh's old bus station *(starry avtovokzal)* is on Alisher Navoi kuchasi just east of the river, while the new one *(novyy avtovokzal)* is about 8km north of the town centre. The airport is about five minutes by bus beyond the new bus station. The nearest train station is at Kara-Suu, halfway to Jalal-Abad.

Information

Registration & Visas If you've just arrived from Uzbekistan you need to register with OVIR within three days of arrival in Kyrgyzstan. The office is at the back (south-west corner) of a building a block south-east of the City Administration Building on Lenin. Go to the Inspector's office (room four). You'll need to pay the 50 som fee at the AKB Bank.

No visa is needed to stay in Osh for less than three days if you have a Tajik visa endorsed for Khorog, or if you have an international flight ticket leaving Bishkek within three days of your arrival in Osh. Otherwise you may have problems visiting from Uzbekistan without a valid Kyrgyz visa.

Visa extensions can be given at the 4th floor of the City Administration Building but you will probably need a letter of visa support from a travel agency such as Alptreksport (see Travel Agencies).

Useful Organisations You might find keen students of English or other languages to act as unofficial guides to the city at Osh University's Languages Faculty (Infac), at Kurmanjan Datka 250, north of Internatsional.

Money A branch of the AKB bank, at Kurmanjan Datka 119, a block south of the Hotel Osh, will change US dollar travellers cheques for a commission of 5% and might be able to give an advance on a Visa card in an emergency. In general it's easier to change cash (US dollars, marks, Uzbek sum and Tajik roubles) at the various moneychangers' kiosks, a collection of which can be found east of the Jayma bazar.

Post & Telephone & Fax International calls can be made from the main telephone and telegraph office, on Lenin kuchasi south of Navoi. Faxes can be sent from the main post office, two blocks south of the telephone office.

Email & Internet Access The BIM Business Centre at the Faculty of Business, Kyrgyzstan 80, plans to have a public email and fax service running by the time this book comes out. There is an email service at the regional library (along with UNESCO and Soros Foundation offices), though strictly speaking this is for locals to use.

Travel Agencies Alptreksport (☎ 230 01, ☎/fax 779 06; contact Yury or Sasha Lavrushin), run by veterans of the Soviet sports agency Sovintersport's Pamir International Mountaineering Camp (IMC), does mainly mountaineering, trekking and caving trips for US$25 to US$40 per person per day. They prefer advance bookings but can accommodate drop-ins. Set programs include two-week treks around Sary Chelek, from Jalal-Abad to Chatyr-Köl, from Shakhimardan to Daraut-Korgon and around Achik Tash. Yury speaks English. Their address is Gogol kuchasi 3, Osh 714018.

The manager of Turbaza Ak-Buura, Jenishbek Ajimamatov, can arrange transport, excursions and other services. His office (☎ 220 36) is at Golubev kuchasi 82, Osh 714017.

Medical Services The municipal hospital is at the intersection of Zaina Betinova kuchasi and Kyrgyzstan kuchasi, north-east of the bazar. There's a polyclinic (health centre) on Internatsional between Kurmanjan Datka and Lenin.

Bazar

The thunderous daily Jayma bazar is one of Central Asia's best open markets, teeming with Uzbeks, Kyrgyz and Tajiks dealing in everything from traditional hats and knives to pirated cassettes, horseshoes (forged at smithies in the bazar), Chinese teasets, plus abundant seasonal fruit and vegetables. It stretches for about one kilometre along the west side of the river, and crosses it in several places. It's most kinetic on Sunday morning, and almost deserted on Monday.

Solomon's Throne & Around

Solomon's Throne, a jagged, barren rock that seems to loom above the city wherever you go, has been a Muslim place of pilgrimage of some importance for centuries, supposedly because the Prophet Mohammed once prayed here. From certain perspectives it looks like a reclining pregnant woman, and it's especially favoured by women who have been unable to bear children.

In 1497, 14-year-old Zahiruddin Babur, newly crowned king of Fergana (and later to found India's Moghul dynasty), built himself a little shelter and private mosque on the rock's high eastern promontory. In later years this came to be something of an attraction in its own right. It collapsed in an earthquake in 1853 and was rebuilt. Then in the 1960s it was destroyed by a mysterious explosion; most local people are convinced it was a Soviet attempt to halt the persistent pilgrim traffic and put a chill on 'superstition' (ie Islam) after failing to persuade Uzbek authorities to do so. After independence it was rebuilt.

Local people call it **Dom Babura**, Babur's House. If you speak Russian, the friendly Uzbek caretaker will tell you more, and he's always grateful for a few som for 'upkeep'. The steep 25 minute climb begins at a little gateway behind a futuristic silver dome (a souvenir shop) on Kurmanjan Datka. The promontory offers long views but little to see except for a vast **Muslim cemetery** at the foot of the hill.

Carry on around the south side for another 15 minutes to see Central Asia's most ridiculous museum – the **Historical-Cultural Museum**. With typical Soviet subtlety, a hole was blasted in the side of this sacred mountain into one of its many caves, and a grotesque sheet-metal front stuck on – a carbuncle now visible from great distances. Inside is a series of badly lit, unintelligible exhibits of potsherds, old masonry, rocks, bugs and mangy stuffed animals; upstairs is a huge, forlorn yurt. It's open daily except Monday and Tuesday, 9 am to noon and 1 to 5 pm. Admission is 10 som.

A new **museum** is currently being built behind the 50 Years of Kyrgyzstan monument to tie in with the Osh 3000 celebrations but the whole project is dependent upon funding and could take years to realise.

Back down at the bottom of the hill is the small **Rabat Abdullah Khan Mosque**, dating from the 17th or 18th century but rebuilt in the 1980s. It's a working mosque (ie male visitors only, and by permission only; shoes off at the entrance). The small **Mausoleum of Asaf Ibn Burhiya** is to the south along the base of the hill but is of little historical or architectural interest.

Other Sights

There isn't much, other than a long riverbank **park** stretching from Navoi to Internatsional. A central feature is an old Yak-40, now a video salon, looking poised to leap over the river. There's a *palvankhana* (wrestling hall) and sauna complex here, though there are only wrestling bouts every month or so.

Places to Stay

Taj Mahal (☎ 396 52), above the Demir Kyrgyz Bank, at the corner of Zaina Betinova and Kyrgyzstan, is currently the best bet. The new and bright Indian-built hotel has clean and pleasant doubles with hot water for 400 and 600 som. If you can afford it look no farther.

Hotel Osh (☎ 756 14, fax 563 26, Bayalinov 1), between Kurmanjan Datka and Lenin, is the time-capsuled former Intourist hotel. Faded but clean rooms with toilet and bath cost US$32/36 in som for a single/double; the lux suite costs US$84. All are overpriced and the place lies mostly deserted.

Hotel Alay (☎ 577 33), on Navoi, is the only budget choice if the Taj is full. It's centrally located but a bit depressing, with no hot water and dubious security. The rooms aren't that bad but the attached toilets are pretty grim. Singles cost 108 or 120 som. Doubles vary from 196 to 312 som; lux suites on the 4th floor are much better for 434 som. There are plenty of places to eat nearby.

The year round *Turbaza Ak-Buura* (☎ 220 36) in the south-eastern suburbs seems like a quiet option – set in 24 hectares of woods, peaceful and cool in summer, with rooms and bungalows with common toilet and shower. Unfortunately the place has acquired a reputation for sleaze, and travellers report drunks trying to enter lock-less doors at night. Rooms in the hotel just inside the main gate and to the right costs 50 som for locals but a negotiable US$10 for foreigners.

To get there take marshrutnyy minibus No 2 south on Kurmanjan Datka until it doubles back and crosses the river; from the traffic roundabout walk up the middle road, Golubev kuchasi (ulitsa Golubeva), for 2½ blocks, carrying on past the gate to reception at the top of the road.

Do not confuse this with the utterly wretched, broken-down *Turbaza Osh*, farther out of town (20 minutes from the centre) on the No 2 line.

Hotel Express (☎ 249 23), in an apartment block near the Languages Faculty, isn't actually a hotel but a private apartment that longer-stay visitors can rent for around US$20 a day. Get someone from the English Faculty to help you phone first (no English is spoken at the hotel) as there's no way anyone could find it without being taken.

Places to Eat

Restaurants Our favourite is the *Istanbul Bistro*, a Turkish restaurant on Navoi with good salads, eggplant dishes and kebabs for about 20 som a dish. The attached *Istanbul Pastanesi* next door sells great baklava and sesame sticks; take out or eat in at the bistro.

You can get more expensive Turkish food at the *Restaurant Anadolu*, which is on Kurmanjan Datka, just south of the Kyrgyz Drama Theatre.

Kitaiski Pelmeni (Chinese Dumpling) restaurant attached to the Hotel Alay serves excellent *jiaozi* (ravioli) and other Chinese dishes at around 40 som each. The Russian menu is largely unintelligible so you're probably best trying out the Chinese menu in the language section at the back of this book.

Cholpon Restaurant, opposite the Hotel Alay, serves standard Soviet canteen food. A better bet is the *Cholpan Cafe Bar* next door where you can get good roast chicken, salad and bread for 60 som,

Restaurant Ak-Buura across Lenin from the Hotel Osh offers the standard Russian evening – pretentious atmosphere, loud music and dreary (but cheap) food.

Cafes & Chaykhanas If you haven't already tired of laghman and shashlyk, there's good cheap grub at the city's chaykhanas, though hygiene is always dubious.

The best places are probably the *Kara Alma Cafe* opposite the Hotel Alay, and the *Chynar Chaykhana*, just north of the post office; the latter has huge *samsas* (envelopes of meat) baked on site. Pay in advance (and separately for tea).

If you just want tea there are several places in Navoi Park popular with the locals. There's also a good traditional *chaykhana* at the southern entrance to the bazar.

In the basement of the commercial centre with the clock tower and stepped roof at the corner of Lenin and Navoi, we found a little *canteen* run by three Uzbek brothers, with a small, changing menu of delicious, well-prepared Uzbek and Kyrgyz dishes for incredibly tiny prices. There's no sign; from Lenin, walk around to the basement stairs at the rear (south-east) corner, and it's halfway down the corridor on the right. It's open daily except Sunday but only from 11.30 am to 2 pm. Clear your own dishes.

Self-Catering The bazar is a good place to stock up, as are the *Euroshopper* supermarkets, one next to Univermag department store, another farther down on Kurmanjan Datka. Here you'll find European brand muesli, toilet paper, milk goods, canned fish, chocolate spread, pasta etc. It's a good place to stock up on trekking supplies.

Shopping

The entrance to the Jayma bazar is one of the best and cheapest places in Kyrgyzstan to buy an *ak kalpak* (felt hat worn by Kyrgyz men). The silver dome at the base of Solomon's Hill has a few lonely souvenirs, including komuz guitars, miniature yurts and the odd carpet. Pottery and clay Central Asian figurines can be bought cheaply in the Arts Faculty at ulitsa Kyrgyzstan 80.

KYRGYZSTAN

Getting There & Away

Especially in bus stations, don't be confused by the Kyrgyz names for Fergana valley towns on the Uzbekistan side – eg Anjiyan for Andijan and Margalan for Margilan.

Air The main airline booking office is at the airport but foreigners will be directed to a separate booking office to the right as you face the main terminal. This office was introduced to help collect a US$15 foreigners' departure tax but this tax has since been discontinued.

There's another booking office (☎ 222 11), at Kurmanjan Datka 287, just north-west of the Hotel Alay, open 8 am to noon and 1 to 6 pm daily.

A third office is inconveniently situated in the outer suburbs 2.5km north of the centre near the Kinoteatr Semetey.

The only regular flight to/from Osh is the daily flight to Bishkek (630 som leaving the same day; 560 som booked one to three days in advance; 510 som booked farther in advance). Flights to Cholpon-Ata (400 som) and Talas (300 som) operate when there are enough passengers (and petrol). Flights may soon recommence to Almaty and Moscow.

Bus & Car The old bus station, near the bazar, is mainly for buses to Özgön (13 som, every 40 minutes), Daraut-Korgon (depart 7 am, 100 som, 10 hours) and all points in Kyrgyzstan's southern arm (Sary Tash, Kyzyl Kiya, Aravan, Gulcha and others). There are slightly more expensive minibuses to Özgün and Kara-Suu. This is also the place to track down an arenda minibus (400 som) or shared taxi (500 som) to Bishkek.

Just about everything else goes to/from the new station, eg Jalal-Abad (15 som, every 20 minutes, via Uzbekistan), Toktogul (110 som, 7 am, nine hours), Tashkömür (37 som, three daily) and Kerven (Karavan).

There are no buses into Uzbekistan but taxis will take you as far as Andijan for 100 som. Taxis are also available to Jalal-Abad (150 som) and Kara-Suu (80 som).

If you want to hire transport to take you into Tajikistan and the Pamir Highway, you could ask around the old bus station. Travel agents charge around US$100 for a trip to Achik Tash in the Alay valley.

Getting Around

Marshrutnoe minibus No 2 runs southbound on Kurmanjan Datka from the old bus station to the Hotel Osh and Turbaza Ak-Buura; it returns northbound down Lenin.

Minibus Nos 2a and 7a shuttle between the airport and the centre of town. From the new bus stand to the airport take the 2a. To get to the long-distance bus stand from the old bus stand take minibus Nos 13 or 7 from opposite the old bus station.

A taxi costs 15 to 20 som from the centre to the new bus station and 50 som to the airport.

ÖZGÖN
☎ 3233

Özgön, 55km north-east of Osh, is today best known as the centre of three nights of ferocious Kyrgyz-Uzbek fighting in 1990 (see the introduction to the previous Osh section). Few outward scars are evident today. The town is nominally 85% Uzbek; locals say it was about two-thirds Uyghur in pre-Soviet days, and it seems likely that these account for many of the 'Uzbeks', as they may have called themselves for the sake of convenience in the early days of the Uzbek SSR.

This is claimed to be the site of a series of citadels dating back to the 1st century BCE; there is also a story that Özgön began as an encampment for some of Alexander the Great's troops. Some sources say it was one of the multiple Karakhanid capitals in the 10th and 11th centuries.

All that remains of this history is a quartet of Karakhanid buildings – three joined mausolea and a stubby minaret (whose top apparently fell down in an earthquake in the 17th century), faced with very fine ornamental brickwork, carved terracotta and inlays of stone. Each mausoleum is unlike the others, though all are in shades of red-brown clay (there were no glazed tiles at this point in Central Asian history). The complex was recently restored with German financial and technical assistance. At the rear of one of the flanking mausolea, a small section has been deliberately left off to reveal older layers of the middle one.

There are some pre-restoration photos of these buildings, as well as artists' renderings of more ancient structures, in Fergana's Regional Museum (see the Fergana Valley section of the Uzbekistan chapter).

Apart from the architectural attractions Özgön is an interesting place to wander around, particularly if you haven't seen much of Uzbekistan.

Places to Stay & Eat
There are several chaykhanas, a bazar, and plenty of interesting faces, but really no decent places to stay overnight. In an emergency *Hotel Özgön* on Manas köchösü has beds (but not much else) for 15 som.

Tourist Café down the road from the Hotel Özgön, near the defunct theatre serves cheap Russian food.

Kafe Shodlik on Manas (look for the clever tilework on the front of the building) serves Russian fare for under 10 som per dish.

The best atmosphere comes free with the shashlyk in the bazar Chaykanas.

Getting There & Away
Özgön is a pleasant half-day trip by bus from Osh's old station, and the closer you get the prettier the landscape becomes – open, rolling, fertile land, past mainly Kyrgyz villages and collective farms, finally to the edge of the broad Kara-Darya or Özgön valley, ringed with big peaks of the Fergana range.

To get to the mausolea turn right out of the bus station on Manas. The road curves to the right past 'minarets' at the entrance to the bazar. Minibuses usually drop off passengers right at the bazar. It's a 10 minute walk to the big administration building on the right (opposite the post office), from where you can see the minaret behind it.

Shared taxis to Jalal-Abad wait a block east of the bazar and cost 30 som a seat.

THE ALAY VALLEY
The far southern arm of Kyrgyzstan is the exclusive turf of trekkers and mountaineers, consisting as it does mostly of the Pamir Alay range, a jagged, 500km-long suture running from Samarkand to Xinjiang. The range is threaded right up the middle by the muddy Kyzyl-Suu river (known as the Surkhob farther downstream in Tajikistan – the two names mean Red Water in Kyrgyz and Tajik respectively) to form the 60km-long Alay valley, the heart of the Kyrgyz Pamir. Two of Central Asia's earliest and busiest Silk Road branches crossed the Pamir Alay from Kashgar, at Kök-Art and at Irkeshtam. The area was formerly the southern frontier of the Uzbek Khanate of Kokand.

With civil unrest in Tajikistan closing off other bases and access routes, Osh and the Alay valley are the main access points for mountaineering expeditions into Tajikistan's High Pamir – to 7495m Kuh-i-Samani (formerly Pik Kommunizma, the highest point in the former USSR), 7134m Kuh-i-Garmo (formerly Pik Lenina) or 7105m Pik Korzhenevskaya.

The only road into and through the Alay valley is the A372 from Osh, via Sary Tash and the 3615m Taldyk pass. This is also the main route into Tajikistan's Gorno-Badakhshan region.

A trip into the Alay region is not a lightweight jaunt. This is still a semi-restricted area (see Permits later in this section) and there are Russian border troops stationed at Sary-Tash. There is little traffic on the main roads and food supplies are limited, even in summer. From October through May the A372 is often closed by snow, and even in summer snow and rainstorms can appear without warning. The best trekking months are July and August. Whenever you head to the Alay, bring warm clothes, a raincoat, sunscreen and provisions.

Beware also that the A372 west of Daraut-Korgon runs through Tajikistan's Garm valley, the scene of heavy fighting in the past and still politically unstable and inadvisable. Check the current situation before setting out.

Refer to the Pamir Highway section of the Tajikistan chapter for information on taking the M41 Pamir Highway to Gorno-Badakhshan.

Information

Permits You still need an OVIR permit to go within 50km of the CIS/Chinese border. Strangely enough, this also applies to the whole of the Kyrgyz Alay valley, a remnant from the days of the Tajik civil war, when the valley was subject to incursions from Tajik rebels and off limits to travellers. The CIS border guards check passports and permits at Sary Tash. In our experience, however, if you are en route to/from Tajikistan and can show a Tajik visa, they'll let you pass even without an OVIR permit.

Trekking agencies operating in the area (see following) can arrange a permit with a minimum of two week's notice, for about US$15. Getting one of these will minimise the hassle and chances for a police shakedown. Make sure that the permit clearly mentions the Chong-Alay and Alay rayons of Osh oblast.

If you plan to trek around Pik Lenina, you'll also need a blue cardboard permit from the Ministry of Sports and Tourism (a 'Special Tour Zone Permit' – basically an official scam), which can be arranged by the same trekking agencies for about US$35.

Trekking Agencies The Pamir Alay is one of the most remote and rugged parts of Central Asia – this is one place where you can't just head off with a 1970s Soviet map and a handful of Snickers bars. ITMC Tien-Shan, IMC Pamir, Dostuk Trekking and Top Asia (see the Travel Agencies entry in the previous Bishkek section) all organise trekking and mountaineering trips in both the Kyrgyz and Tajik sides of the valley. Alptreksport in Osh (see the Travel Agencies entry in the previous Osh section) also has a lot of experience in the region. We found no useful agencies on the Tajikistan side, in either Dushanbe or Khorog.

Pik Lenin and Achik Tash

Trekking possibilities in the Alay valley are legion, but serious trekkers head for Pik Lenina (now officially called Kuh-i-Garmo, though everyone still calls it by its Soviet name). The peak is known as one of the most accessible 7000-ers in the world. It is the highest summit of the Pamir Alay and lays right on the Kyrgyz-Tajik border. The snow-covered ridges and slopes are not difficult to climb, though altitude sickness and avalanches are a serious problem; in 1990 a single avalanche killed over 40 climbers.

A lighter hike can take you to nearby Lukovaya Polyana, or Wild Onion Meadow, the last outpost of greenery before the glacial moraine takes over. For more details on trekking around Pik Lenina, see Frith Maier's *Trekking in Russia & Central Asia*.

At Achik Tash meadows (3600m), 30km south of Sary Moghol, IMC Pamir and most of the trekking agencies mentioned above operate Pik Lenina base camps and programs in summer. To get there you'll have to fix arrangements in advance with one of the trekking agencies (jeep transport to/from Kashka-Suu to the base camps costs a negotiable US$30 per ride). Otherwise, try your luck and arrange a ride in a 4WD in one of the villages along the road. A hired jeep from Osh bazar to the Achik Tash base camp can be negotiated down to US$100 for the ride. Trekking agency vehicles come at about US$160 one way.

Places to Stay & Eat

Bring your tent. There are cottages at the IMC Pamir base camp, while the others have spare tents. Sary Tash, Kashka-Suu and Daraut-Korgon all have derelict, Soviet-era guesthouses but you'll have more joy asking around for a home-stay. A reasonable amount for a night's accommodation and some basic food is around US$2 in som; to avoid embarrassment and disappointment on both sides, fix a sum in advance.

There are weekly farmer's markets in Daraut-Korgon (on Tuesday), Kashka-Suu (Wednesday) and Sary Moghol (Thursday) where you can buy basic foodstuffs. Several trailer shops offer the usual kiosk fare in Sary Tash, while you can buy bread in the villages and milk products at the yurt camps en route. Beyond this bring all your own food.

Getting There & Away

A daily bus leaves Osh's old bus station for Daraut-Korgon at 7 am (10 hours, 100 som).

Avoid taking the Monday morning bus; people head home from the Osh market and the bus is absurdly filled up with passengers and freight, making the ride a hideous ordeal. There is also a daily bus to Sary Moghol (70 som, 7½ hours).

From Daraut-Korgon, two buses a day leave for Osh, at 5 and 8 am, calling at Kashka-Suu and Sary Moghol en route. You might well find a seat or two in a private car; in Osh try the parking lot right next to the old bus station.

The Irkeshtam Pass

At the time of research, the Sino-Kyrgyz border post at Irkeshtam was open to official barter trade truck convoys only. Every year the Kyrgyz and Chinese authorities promise that this 'new Silk Road' crossing will open to tourists 'soon'. When exactly soon is, no one can tell – not even the Russian commander of the CIS border guards at Irkeshtam.

Mixed teams of Uzbek and Kyrgyz road workers are currently upgrading the gravel road east of Sary Tash. The Uzbeks, in particular, are keen to open a trading route between Kashgar and the Fergana valley. The Chinese, however, have less to gain – the route is perilously close to a major drug smuggling artery and also to ex-mujaheddin training camps (two of Afghanistan's major regional exports).

Kyrgyz travel agencies can arrange permits to visit the pass as a day trip, however, and the landscape en route is said to be sublime. The only transport option for the 180km return ride from Sary-Tash is to organise a 4WD, either in Osh or, less reliably, in Sary Tash. The going rate for the latter is

about 600 som for the return ride, 150 to 200 som more if you spend the night en route.

You will see no signs for Irkeshtam, only for the hamlet of Nura, 7km before the border. The border post itself consists of a gloomy, almost abandoned truck control post. An electric fence parallels the road. Two kilometres farther on, there is a small CIS border guard compound from where you have a view of the Chinese watchtowers and a huge Chinese flag painted on a hillside.

SOUTHERN KYRGYZSTAN

The southern wall of the Fergana valley forms a curious claw of Kyrgyz territory, though access to most of the mountain villages here comes from the Fergana valley territory of Tajikistan or Uzbekistan. The Turkestan ridge in particular offers superb trekking territory and was once a popular destination for climbers from the eastern bloc.

This is not a particularly easy place to make your first Central Asian trek. Access can prove tricky as inter-republic buses have ground to a halt, you'll need an Uzbek or Tajik visa to transit hassle-free through these republics, as well as a Kyrgyz trekking permit, and you'll need a range of different currencies (though Uzbek sum is the most widely accepted).

A more worrying development was the kidnapping of four Japanese geologists in the region in August 1999 by Islamic militants (see the History section earlier in this chapter). For the time being, it seems, you are better off planning any trek in the region with an established trekking operator in Bishkek or Tashkent.

KYRGYZSTAN

Tajikistan

Tajikistan at a Glance

Official Name: Jomharrii Tojikiston
Area: 143,100 sq km
Population: 6.76 million (2000 estimate)
Ethnic Mix: 65% Tajik, 25% Uzbek, 4% Russian, 6% Others
Capital: Dushanbe
Currency: Tajik rubl (R)
Country ☎ Code: 992
Best Time to Go: north and west – mid-March to May, September to November; Gorno-Badakhshan – June to September
Travel Warning: see the boxed text, p 428

- **The Pamir** – a flight through (not over) the Pamir, for a sheer adrenaline rush

- **Pamir Hwy** – the rollercoaster highway from Khorog to Murgab

- **Fan Mountains** – beautiful trekking, accessible from Samarkand

Tajikistan has its own flag, a national airline and a scattering of embassies abroad. Despite this, it's a curiously incomplete country, much less than the sum of its parts. The north is a part of Uzbekistan in all but name. Despite Soviet-era attempts to populate it, the mountainous Pamir region remains al-most a vacuum, and the capital, Dushanbe, a city not yet three-quarters of a century old, has yet to take on any character, like an apartment block awaiting its tenants.

That Tajikistan was easily the most artificial of the five Soviet-fashioned Central Asian republics was tragically illustrated by the bloody way it fell apart as soon as it was free of Moscow rule. In its brief post-Soviet history, the conflict in this remote pocket of the Commonwealth of Independent States (CIS) has seen far greater loss of life than in anywhere else in the old empire.

Peace has only been imposed by Russia's support of Tajikistan's current ruling clan. In doing so the country has been made a virtual protectorate. It's a fragile peace and one unlikely to last.

For the moment a trip to Tajikistan requires a good briefing on the political situation and as much help as you can get. This is not the place for the casual traveller. Nevertheless, Tajikistan's unparalleled scenery beckons seductively to those prepared to plan ahead. The Pamir range dwarfs anything found outside Nepal and even for non-mountaineers the Pamir Hwy provides plenty of high-altitude thrills. Anyone following this road has the added thrill of knowing that few 'foreign devils' have passed this way since Francis Younghusband, the consummate 'Great Game' player (see the 'Great Game & the Basmachi' in the following History section), was expelled from the region by the Russians in 1891, marking its closure (first by the Tsarists and then the Soviets) to the outside world for the next 100 years.

Facts about Tajikistan

HISTORY
Tajik Ancestry

In predominantly Turkic Central Asia, the Persian-descended Tajiks are firmly in the minority, yet they can legitimately claim to be the region's oldest residents.

Tajik ancestry is a murky area but the lineage seems to begin with the Bactrians and the Sogdians. In the 1st century BCE (before common era) the Bactrians had a large empire covering most of what is now northern Afghanistan, while their contemporaries, the Sogdians, inhabited the Zeravshan valley in present-day western Tajikistan (where a few traces of this civilisation remain, at a site near Penjikent) until they were displaced in the Arab conquest of Central Asia during the 7th century CE (common era).

The invaders succeeded in bringing Islam to the region but the Arab domination wasn't secure and out of the ensuing melee another Persian dynasty, the Samanids, took hold. The brief era of the Samanids (during 819-992 CE) was a period of frenzied creative activity.

Bukhara, the dynastic capital, became the Islamic world's centre of learning, nurturing great talents like the philosopher-scientist Abu Ali ibn Sina (also known commonly as Avicenna) and the poet Rudaki – both now claimed as sons of Iran, Afghanistan and Tajikistan.

A Blurring of Identity

Under the Samanids, the great towns of Central Asia were Persian (the basis of Tajikistan's modern-day claims on Samarkand and Bukhara), but at the end of the 10th century came a succession of Turkic invaders who followed up their battlefield successes with cultural conquest. Despite different ethnicities the two races cohabited peacefully, unified by religion – the Persian-speaking Tajiks absorbed Turk culture and the numerically superior Turks absorbed the Tajik people. Both were subject to the vicissitudes of Central Asia and weathered conquests first by the Mongols then later by Timur (Tamerlane; see Timur & the Timurids under History in the Facts about Central Asia chapter).

From the 15th century onwards, the Tajiks were subjects of the emirate of Bukhara,

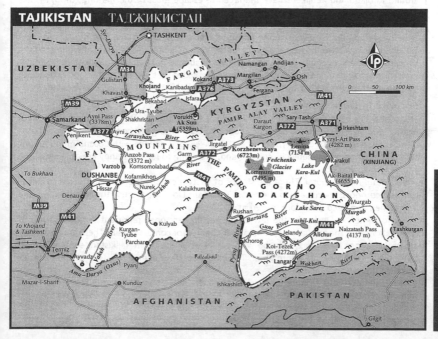

although in the mid-18th century the Afghans moved up to engulf all lands south of the Amu-Darya (Oxus) river along with their resident Tajik population (the Amu-Darya still delineates much of the Afghan-Tajik border today).

Safety in Tajikistan

Tajikistan's bloody civil war has formally ceased, but political violence in the republic continues to claim lives.

In November 1997 two French UN aid workers were abducted (one was later killed in a rescue attempt), and in 1998 another four UN staff were killed in eastern Tajikistan. Several kidnappings also occurred in 1998 along with political assassinations, car bombings, and five people were killed in a shootout in Dushanbe's city centre. As a reaction to this, the US embassy, UN and most aid workers pulled out of the country in 1998, the last two of these temporarily. The biggest potential dangers to travellers come from street crime in Dushanbe and being (literally) caught in political crossfire.

As a rule of thumb, anywhere near the Tajik-Afghan border is out of bounds and to this effect there's a 25km exclusion zone along its length. An exception is the Pamir town of Khorog, which is usually open to travellers wanting to take the road to the east through Murgab and into Kyrgyzstan. The stretch of the M41 Pamir Hwy between Dushanbe and Khorog remains unsafe, as does the nearby Garm region and the A372 highway to Kyrgyzstan.

Southern Tajikistan, including the towns of Kulyab and Kurgan-Tyube, is generally safe away from the immediate border areas, which are unpredictable. The more northerly regions around Khojand and Penjikent have managed to escape most of the fighting, though small gangs of Uzbek militia and Islamic rebels remain in the hills around here, so it is inadvisable to just head off into the hills with a tent.

Before setting out, you should also consult travel advisories at home (see the Government Travel Advice section in the Regional Facts for the Visitor chapter). At the time of writing the US, UK and Australian governments were advising their nationals not to travel to Tajikistan. It is, however, still possible to travel to and within Tajikistan provided that you're cautious and take advice on your itinerary. Anybody who goes off without first being briefed is asking for trouble.

Security in Dushanbe

The capital has been relatively peaceful for a while now, though street crime is a problem at night. If you do have to go out at night, order a taxi and arrange to be picked up at your hotel. Don't try to flag down a car on the road as it's unlikely that anyone with decent intentions will stop. The police are completely ineffective and, according to rumours, they are as likely to rob you as to help you.

Be careful in your hotel. There are stories of nasty incidents that have occurred in elevators and corridors, specifically in the Hotel Tajikistan. Do not advertise the fact that you are a foreigner, and keep your door locked at all times.

For foreigners in Dushanbe the few embassies that are open represent the best source of information – see the Dushanbe section of this chapter for contact details. There are also many aid organisations based in Dushanbe with operatives throughout Tajikistan, some of which can provide good localised information. The embassies have complete lists of all the agencies and their areas of operation.

The United Nations Military Observers Team (UNMOT) offers a security report on Tajikistan through the 24 hour dispatch number ☎ 201 47. For details of news services on the Web see the Internet Resources section in the Regional Facts for the Visitor chapter.

The 'Great Game' & the Basmachi

As part of the Russian empire's thrust southwards, St Petersburg made a vassal state of the emirate of Bukhara, which also meant effective control over what now passes for northern and western Tajikistan. But the Pamirs, which account for the whole of modern-day eastern Tajikistan, were literally a no-man's-land, falling outside the established borders of the Bukhara emirate and unclaimed by neighbouring Afghanistan and China. Russia was eager to exploit this anomaly in its push to open up possible routes into British India.

The Pamirs became the arena for the strategic duel that British poet and author Rudyard Kipling was to immortalise as 'the Great Game', a game in which Russia's players eventually prevailed, securing the region for the tsar.

Following the Russian revolution of 1917, new provisional governments were established in Central Asia and the Tajiks found themselves part of first the Turkestan (1918-24), then the Uzbekistan (1924-29) Soviet Socialist Republics (SSRs), though they wanted an autonomous Islamic-oriented republic. The following year Muslim *basmachi* guerillas began a campaign to free the region from Bolshevik rule. It took four years for the Bolsheviks to crush this resistance and in the process entire villages were razed, mosques destroyed and great tracts of land laid waste. The surviving guerillas slipped into Afghanistan from where they continued for years to make sporadic raids over the border.

Statehood

In 1924, when the Soviet Border Commission set about redefining Central Asia, the Tajiks got their own Autonomous SSR (ASSR). Although only a satellite of the Uzbek SSR, this was the first official Tajik state. In 1929 it was upgraded to a full union republic, although (in reprisal for the basmachi revolt?) Samarkand and Bukhara – where over 700,000 Tajiks still lived – remained in Uzbekistan. As recently as 1989 the government of Tajikistan was still trying to persuade the Soviet leadership to 'return'

these areas. Territorial tensions continue with the modern government of Uzbekistan.

The Bolsheviks never fully trusted this republic and during the 1930s almost all Tajiks in positions of influence within the government were replaced by stooges from Moscow. The industrialisation of Tajikistan was only undertaken following WWII, after the loss of much of European Russia's manufacturing capacity. But living standards remained low and in the late 1980s Tajikistan endured 25% unemployment, plus the lowest level of education and the highest infant-mortality rate in the Soviet Union.

Civil Unrest

In the mid-1970s, Tajikistan began to feel the impact of the rise of Islamic forces in neighbouring Afghanistan, particularly in the south around Kurgan-Tyube. This region had been neglected by Dushanbe's ruling Communist elite, who were mainly drawn from the prosperous northern province of Leninabad (now known as Khojand). In 1976 the underground Islamic Renaissance Party (IRP) was founded, gathering popular support as a rallying point for Tajik nationalism. Although in 1979 there had been demonstrations in opposition to the Soviet invasion of Afghanistan, the first serious disturbances were in early 1990 when it was rumoured that Armenian refugees were to be settled in Dushanbe, which was already short on housing. This piece of Soviet social engineering sparked riots, deaths and the imposition of a state of emergency. Further opposition parties emerged as a result of the crackdown.

On 9 September 1991, following the failed coup in Moscow and declarations of independence by other Central Asian states, Tajikistan proclaimed itself an independent republic. Elections were held 10 weeks later in which the Socialist Party (formerly the Communist Party of Tajikistan or CPT) candidate, Rakhmon Nabiev, was voted into power. Six years earlier he had been the First Secretary of the CPT but was removed on charges of corruption. There were charges of election rigging but what riled the opposition was Nabiev's apparent consolidation of an old guard Leninabad-oriented power base that refused to accommodate any other of the various clan-factions that make up the Tajik nation.

Sit-in demonstrations on Dushanbe's central square escalated to violent clashes that spread beyond the capital. In August 1992 anti-government demonstrators stormed the presidential palace and took hostages. Nabiev escaped, but he was captured a few days later at Dushanbe airport trying to flee to Khojand (the post-USSR renaming of Leninabad). He was replaced as head of state by Akbarshah Iskandarov, who headed a coalition government, that included the IRP and secular democratic parties.

But sharing power between regional clans, religious leaders and former Communists proved impossible. Tajikistan descended into civil war.

Civil War

During the Soviet era, Moscow and the party had been the lid on a pressure-cooker of clan-based tensions that had existed long before Russian intervention. Tajikistan's various factions – Leninabaders from the north, Kulyabis from the southern province of Kulyab and their hostile neighbours from Kurgan-Tyube, Garmis from the Garm valley in the east, and Pamiris from the mountainous province of Gorno-Badakhshan – had all been kept in line under Soviet rule. When independence came, the lid blew off. Civil war ensued and the struggle among clans has since claimed around sixty thousand lives and made refugees of over half a million.

Iskandarov's supporters were attacked by forces remaining loyal to the deposed Nabiev. As a way out of the internecine conflict Iskandarov stepped down and the government reconvened in Khojand to select a new front man. Imamali Rakhmanov was chosen from the Kulyab district. However, to the Islamic-democratic coalition (now fighting as the Popular Democratic Army or PDA) this was no improvement on Nabiev because in their eyes Leninabaders and Kulyabis had always been in each others' pockets. The Kulyabis then simply fought their way to power with a scorched earth policy against their Islamic-leaning rivals from the Garm valley and Kurgan-Tyube.

Rakhmanov was sworn in as president after a disputed election. The PDA refused to allow the new president into Dushanbe and it took an all-out assault from Kulyabi and Leninabad forces to get him into office. Kulyabi forces, led by Sanjak Safarov (who had previously spent 23 years in prison for murder) then embarked on an orgy of ethnic cleansing directed at anyone connected with Kurgan-Tyube and the Garm valley – mother and child were treated as equally as political activist and soldier.

The November 1992 elections did nothing to resolve the conflict (the opposition in exile refused to take part in the voting) and the PDA and its supporters continued the war from hideaways in the Pamirs and from Afghanistan, echoing the basmachi campaigns of 70 years earlier.

Rakhmanov was propped up by Russian-dominated CIS forces who had been drawn into the conflict as de facto protectors of the Kulyab regime. There are now 25,000 Russian troops inside the country operating some 50 border posts along the Afghan border. Boris Yeltsin has made no secret of why the Kremlin moved to intervene in what was a domestic struggle. 'Everyone must realise,' he said in a 1993 pronouncement 'that this is effectively Russia's border, not Tajikistan's'. The Russian (and Uzbek) fear is that if Tajikistan falls to Islamic rebels, then Uzbekistan could be next.

In late 1994 a second presidential election was held, in which Rakhmanov romped to victory, which was unsurprising, as he was the only candidate. All opposition parties had been outlawed.

Precarious Peace

Pressure on Rakhmanov from Russia, and several of his own commanders forced the government to negotiate with the opposition, then in exile in Iran. Finally in December 1996 a ceasefire was declared, followed up by a peace agreement on 27 June 1997. The agreement set up a power-sharing organisation, the National Reconciliation Commission, headed by the opposition leader Sayid

Abdullo Nuri, which guaranteed the United Tajik Opposition (UTO) 30% of the seats in a coalition government, in return for a laying down of arms.

Spirits were lifted in September 1998 when the Aga Khan, spiritual leader of the Islamic Ismaili sect, visited Gorno-Badakhshan for the first time. The Aga Khan Foundation has effectively fed the Pamir region since the start of the civil war and some 80,000 Pamiris came out to hear their spiritual leader tell them to lay down their arms, while another 10,000 Afghan Tajiks strained their ears across the river in Afghanistan.

And yet problems remain. The northern Khojand faction, headed by former premier Abdumalik Andullojonov and the large Uzbek minority in general, are angered that they have been largely excluded from the power-sharing process. In November 1998, fierce fighting broke out in Khojand as the northern Uzbek faction of Mohammed Khudoberdiev fought pitched battles in Khojand's central citadel with government troops. Two hundred people were killed before the rebels, who were demanding representation in the coalition government, fled into the hills around Ayni. Since then, relations between Tajikistan and Uzbekistan have become increasingly tense, with both sides accusing the other of sheltering opposition rebels.

Moreover, the pace of reform has been achingly slow, and the UTO has repeatedly threatened to pull out of the peace process unless the pace of reform quickens. The current political climate resembles a match of *buzkashi* (see the Spectator Sports section of the Regional Facts for the Visitor chapter), full of political manoeuvring, temporary allegiances and violent skirmishes, as local warlords with names like 'Ali the Boxer' and 'Hitler' continue to stir up trouble in an attempt to claim their share of the Peace Agreement pie.

The various militia groups are slowly being assimilated into the national army but the number of arms that have been handed in has so far been disappointingly low, hinting that weapons may be stockpiled in the hills in case the violence flares up again.

Like many Central Asian republics, Tajikistan treads a dangerous tightrope between authoritarianism and Islamisation as it faces the long-term challenge of meeting both the religious and the secular aims of its people.

GEOGRAPHY

At 143,100 sq km, landlocked Tajikistan is Central Asia's smallest republic. More than half of it lies 3000m or more above sea level. The central part encompasses the southern spurs of the Tian Shan mountain range while the south-east comprises the Pamir plateau. Within these ranges are some of Central Asia's highest peaks, including Pik Lenina (7134m) and Pik Kommunizma (7495m). The Fedchenko glacier, a 72km-long glacial highway frozen to the side of Pik Kommunizma, is one of the longest glaciers in the world outside of the polar region.

The western third of the country is lowland plain, bisected to the north by the Gissar, Zeravshan and Turkistan ranges – both western extensions of the Tian Shan that cross into Uzbekistan. The remote Zeravshan valley is cradled between them. The mountain peaks with their sun-melted icecaps are the source of a fibrous network of fast-flowing streams, many of which empty into Tajikistan's two major rivers – the Syr-Darya (Jaxartes), rising in the Fergana valley, and the Amu-Darya (Oxus), formed from the confluence of two Pamir rivers, the Vakhsh and the Pyanj.

Together, the Amu-Darya and the Pyanj mark most of the country's 1200km border with Afghanistan. Tajikistan's other borders are much less well defined: in the east, 430km of border meanders through Pamir valleys, while to the north and west are the seemingly random borders with Kyrgyzstan and Uzbekistan.

CLIMATE

Lowland Tajikistan weathers a climate that is 'extreme continental', with temperatures ranging from an average minimum of -12°C in January to an average maximum of 42°C in July. Spring (March-May) brings mild temperatures and frequent heavy showers. Summer (June-August) is hot, generally

35°C to 40°C with temperatures always a couple of degrees higher in the south of the country and cooler in the north. In winter, temperatures in Dushanbe hover around freezing.

In the Pamirs an average January temperature is -20°C, but up on the windswept plateaus it can drop to -45°C. In the eastern Pamir temperatures have reached 60°C below zero. From October through May fierce snowstorms rage in the mountains, making getting around almost impossible.

Strong dust storms can be expected from June through October.

GOVERNMENT & POLITICS

Since 1992 Tajikistan has been a parliamentary republic with legislative power vested in an elected 230 member parliament or *Oli majlis*. The parliament is fronted by a speaker or chairperson who is head of state, or president – Imamali Rakhmanov at the time of writing. The highest executive body is the Council of Ministers, whose chairperson becomes prime minister. The UTO's deputy leader, Akbar Turojonzoda, was made first deputy prime minister as part of the peace accords.

The National Reconciliation Commission (CNR), the parallel body that has to implement the 1997 peace agreement, is comprised of equal numbers of government and opposition members. There are about a dozen registered political parties, which tend to be mostly made up of government stooges. Opposition parties were banned until 1997.

The main political parties are Rachmanov's People's Democratic Party (PDP) of Tajikistan (formerly the Socialist Democratic Party and before that the Communist Party of Tajikistan) and the United Tajik Opposition (UTO). The National Revival Movement is the major political force in Khojand. Other groups include the Islamic Renaissance Party (IRP), the secular nationalist Democratic Party of Tajikistan (DPT), the Pamiri separatist party Lale Badakhshan (Ruby of Badakhshan), which wants to establish an Ismaili Pamir Republic, and Rastokhez (Rebirth), a nationalist-religious

party. The political landscape remains heavily clan-based. Presidential elections were scheduled for November 1999 and parliamentary elections for November 2000.

For administrative purposes the country is divided into three *viloyat* or provinces: Khojand, Khatlon and the 60,000 sq km autonomous mountain region of Gorno-Badakhshan.

ECONOMY

Independence proved catastrophic for Tajikistan, which had always been the poorest of the Soviet republics. The civil war completely destroyed any hope of economic self-sufficiency.

With the imposition of Soviet rule in the 1920s, most of Tajikistan's available arable land (only about 7% of the country, the rest being mountains) was turned over to intensive cotton farming. Tajikistan was heavily reliant on imports from the Soviet Union – not just food, but fuel and many other standard commodities.

With the disintegration of the Soviet trading system, Tajikistan was left badly equipped to fend for itself and dangerously unbalanced. Northern Tajikistan (the power base of the Soviet ruling elite and part of the cotton-growing Fergana valley) holds 75% of Tajikistan's arable land and generates over two-thirds of the national GDP. The country might have survived by augmenting the established cotton industry with its considerable deposits of gold, silver and other precious minerals, but the outbreak of fighting brought Tajikistan to a standstill.

The main agricultural areas of the southwest were badly hit by the fighting and two complete harvests were missed. Tajikistan's GDP per capita has fallen to US$330 (1998), putting it among the 30 poorest countries in the world. The annual national budget of Tajikistan remains less than the budget of a major Hollywood movie, and 40% of that is required for the upkeep of the military presence on the Afghan border.

In 1997 the government privatised 20% of the country's irrigated land, an act that has brought produce back into most town's markets. The Tajik government is still virtually the country's sole employer. Anybody still receiving a salary (teachers make about US$5 per month) is often supporting up to 30 relatives, neighbours and friends. Even the government is reduced to barter – Tajikistan currently pays for gas from Uzbekistan by allowing Uzbek rail shipments across its northern territory.

Presently, the country exists on a drip-feed of credits and loans from the World Bank and Moscow (Tajikistan's national debt is currently US$1.2 billion, US$141 million of which is owed to Russia). In return, Tajikistan has been forced to mortgage its future to the Kremlin, giving Russia half of the shares in the Nurek hydroelectric plant as well as controlling interests in other national industries. Russia realises that if the Tajiks ever stop shooting each other, one day they might have quite a prosperous country.

POPULATION & PEOPLE

Year 2000 estimates put the population of Tajikistan at 6.7 million. Population figures are only approximate because the demographics of Tajikistan have been fluctuating wildly since the start of the civil war in 1992. In addition to the 60,000 or so killed, more than half a million Tajiks were displaced from their homes during the war, while around two-thirds of the country's 600,000 Russians headed north. Another 60,000 Tajiks fled to Afghanistan, joining the 4.4 million fellow Tajiks that have lived there since being annexed by Kabul in the 18th century.

It's only in this century that 'Tajik' came to denote a distinct nationality. Previously 'Taj' was just a term for a Persian speaker (all the other Central Asian peoples speak Turkic languages). Despite their predominantly Persian ancestry, there has been so much intermarrying that it's often hard to distinguish Tajiks from their Mongol Turkic neighbours. Pure-blooded Tajiks tend to have thin faces, with wide eyes and a Roman nose.

There are some recognisable ethnic subdivisions among the Tajiks. As well as the Pamiri Tajiks (see the following section), there are dwindling numbers of Yaghnabis

(or Jagnobis), direct descendants of the ancient Sogdians, in the villages of the Zeravshan valley. In *The Lost Heart of Asia* (around 1992) Colin Thubron describes visiting a Yaghnabi settlement and discovering that Sogdian, the de facto language of the Silk Road, last widely spoken in the 8th century, is still spoken there.

Common to all Tajiks is a preference for rural life. Only around a third of their number live in towns and cities, the majority preferring to settle in *kishlaks*, small villages of wooden, one-family houses usually huddled on the sloping valley sides above a mountain stream or river. Average family sizes remain high, with seven or eight kids the norm.

Many older Tajik men continue to dress in the traditional manner of a *chapan* (long, quilted jackets), knee-length boots and a *tupi* (black, white-embroidered caps). Women of all ages favour the psychedelically coloured, gold-threaded long dresses *(kurta)* with head scarves *(rumol)* to match, and underneath the dress, striped trousers *(izor)* with brightly coloured slippers on their feet.

Pamiri Tajiks

Centuries of isolation in high-altitude valleys has meant that the Pamiris of Gorno-Badakhshan speak languages different not only from those of lowland Tajiks but from one another. Each mountain community has its own dialect of Pamiri, a language that, although sharing the same Persian roots as Tajik, is as different as English is from German. The different Pamiri tongues, named for the settlements where they're spoken (Ishkashimi, Rushani, Vanchi etc), are not necessarily mutually comprehensible.

The mountain peoples are, however, solidly bound by their shared faith: Ismailism (sometimes referred to locally as Suleymanism). Ismailis are a breakaway sect of Shia Islam with no mosques, no clerics and no weekly holy day. One of the few visible manifestations of the religion is the small roadside shrines at which passers-by stop to ask for a blessing. The shrines also act as charity stations; in return for the blessing the Ismaili customarily leaves some money or bread for anyone in need.

TAJIKISTAN

The spiritual leader of the Ismailis is the Aga Khan, a Swiss-born businessman and horse-breeder revered by Pamiris as a living god. But he's no remote, abstract deity – it's the Aga Khan's charity that currently provisions Gorno-Badakhshan, keeping certain starvation at bay (see The Pamirs section later in this chapter); Pamiris venerate him as 'Our God who sends us food'.

Not having two potatoes to fry together has done nothing to lessen the hospitality of the Pamiris, whose natural inclination is to share. Invitations to sit, eat and drink are free-flowing, though unlike some other peoples of Central Asia, the Pamiris allow you the choice of refusal.

If the chance arises it is worth accepting an offer to see inside a traditional Pamiri house. They're built as one large room with raised areas around four sides of a central pit. There are few if any windows; illumination comes through a skylight in the roof. Carpets and mattresses take the place of furniture and also serve as decoration along with panels of hand-coloured photographs – the most prominent of which is often a portrait of the Aga Khan. For more information on the people of Tajikistan, see the Peoples of the Silk Road special section in the Facts about Central Asia chapter.

ARTS
When Tajikistan was hived off from Uzbekistan in 1929, the new nation-state was forced to leave behind all its cultural baggage. A Moscow-drawn border delivered the glories of Bukhara and Samarkand, to which the Tajiks had a legitimate claim, into the cultural treasure chest of Uzbekistan.

The new Soviet order set about providing a replacement pantheon of arts, introducing modern drama, opera and ballet and sending stage-struck Tajik aspirants to study in Moscow and Leningrad. The policy paid early dividends and the 1940s are considered a golden era of Tajik theatre. A kind of Soviet fame came to some Tajik novelists and poets, such as Mirzo Tursunzade and Sadriddin Ayni, the latter now remembered more as a deconstructor of national culture because of his campaign to eliminate all

Arabic expressions and references to Islam from the Tajik tongue.

Since independence there has been something of a cultural revival in an attempt to foster a sense of national identity. Ancient figures of art and learning from the region's Persian past are being popularised.

The most famous of these figures is the 10th century philosopher-scientist Abu Ali ibn Sina (known in the west as Avicenna), author of two of the most important books in the history of medicine (the most famous being *The Medical Canon*). He was born in Bukhara when it was the seat of the Persian Samanids, to whom Rudaki (exact place of birth unknown), now celebrated as the father of Persian verse, served as court poet. Tajiks also venerate Firdausi, a poet and composer of the *Shah-nameh* (Book of Kings), the Persian national epic, and Omar Khayyam, of *Rubiayat* fame, both born in present-day Iran but at a time when it was part of an empire that also included the territory now known as Tajikistan.

Critics attribute the success of Tajikistan's most popular living writer of the moment, Taimur Zulfikarov, to his ability to mimic the ancient Persian style of writing and, in doing so, to appeal to nationalist sentiments.

Facts for the Visitor

PLANNING
When to Go
If you decide to go at all (see the boxed text 'Safety in Tajikistan' at the beginning of this chapter) bear in mind that northern, central and southern Tajikistan all sizzle in summer. March, April, September and October are probably the best times to visit. The Navrus festival in March is a particularly good time to visit. The best time of year for trekking is September. The Pamir region is best visited in July and August.

VISAS
Tajik visas are not issued at the airport or at any borders. In fact, more often than not there is no Tajik border control when you enter Tajikistan on the Termiz-Dushanbe train, the

Kokand-Khojand, Tashkent-Khojand or the Samarkand-Penjikent road.

By contrast there are many internal checkpoints, particularly in Gorno-Badakhshan, and if you intend moving outside Dushanbe you must have impeccable documents. As a result of border tensions and the increase in drugs and gun smuggling, the army and militia do not appreciate the presence of foreigners, and if anyone is not completely satisfied with your papers you will probably be deported. At any given time certain areas will be completely out of bounds because of military skirmishing (see the boxed text 'Safety in Tajikistan' at the beginning of this chapter).

Leaving Tajikistan for Uzbekistan has become increasingly difficult in recent years as the Uzbeks tighten the screw on the border. Note that you may need a double-entry Uzbek visa to return to Uzbekistan after a visit to Tajikistan.

Getting a Visa

At present the only accredited Tajik consular representation outside the former USSR is in Bonn (Germany gave them the building rent-free) and Austria, and even there they apparently only issue a letter for the Russian embassy.

The embassy in Almaty will issue a two week visa on the spot for US$50 if you have a visa invitation, available from many travel agencies in Almaty or Bishkek for a fee. Travel agencies in Tashkent can arrange Tajik visas for a fee, within a week or so. There have been reports of travellers getting a visa from the Tajik consulate in Moscow in return for a US$50 'fee'.

If you do arrive in Tajikistan without a visa, the immigration department of the Ministry of Foreign Affairs (see Information in the Dushanbe section, later in this chapter) may give you one. If your Tajik visa was issued through a Russian consulate you will probably have to go there anyway to get the Russian visa (which comes on a piece of paper) transferred into your passport.

Every Tajik town that you intend visiting or even passing through should be listed on your visa.

Visa Extensions

If you need an extension, see Tajik Intourist in Dushanbe. If you speak Russian well and want to try it yourself, go to the Ministry of Foreign Affairs in Dushanbe.

Registration

You should register at the Ministry of Foreign Affairs in Dushanbe (see Information in the Dushanbe section, later in this chapter) within 72 hours of arriving in Tajikistan.

EMBASSIES & CONSULATES
Tajik Embassies

For countries without a Tajikistan embassy, check with the Russian embassy (for a list of these see the Regional Facts for the Visitor chapter). For embassies in Central Asia see the relevant country chapter.

Austria
  (☎/fax 1-409 8266)
  Universitates strasse 8/1A, 1090 Wien
Germany
  (☎ 0228-972 950, fax 972 9555)
  Hans Böckler Strasse 3, D-53225 Bonn
Russia
  (☎ 095-290 61 02, fax 290 06 09)
  Skatertny pereulok 19, Moscow

Embassies in Tajikistan

No embassies in Dushanbe can issue visas, even for transit purposes. Exceptions may be made under persuasive circumstances but the embassy in question has to seek special permission from home and the process could take up to a month. The consulate of Afghanistan may be an exception, but at present there are no crossing points to Afghanistan from Tajikistan open to travellers. The nearest entry to Afghanistan is at Termiz in Uzbekistan, but this crossing has been tightly controlled since the Taliban seizure of northern Afghanistan. In any case frontier guards there will apparently only recognise documentation that was issued in Tashkent.

The US embassy is currently closed due to the perceived risk of terrorism from neighbouring Afghanistan. Americans in need of consular services should contact the US embassy in Almaty. Brits should contact the UK embassy in Tashkent.

There is no Kyrgyz or Uzbek embassy in Tajikistan.

Afghanistan
(☎ 27 60 58, 27 60 61) ulitsa Pushkina 25
China
(☎ 21 01 39, 21 01 94, fax 21 02 11)
ulitsa Parvina 8
Germany
(☎ 21 21 89, 21 21 98)
ulitsa Proyezd Azizbekova 21, off Mirzo
Tursunzade by the Badakhshan Kafe
Pakistan
(☎ 21 04 33) prospekt Rudaki 37a, opposite
Firdausi Library
Russia
(☎ 21 10 15) Hotel Oktyabrskaya, 3rd floor,
prospekt Rudaki 105a
USA
(☎ 21 03 56, fax 21 03 62)
Hotel Oktyabrskaya, 4th floor, prospekt
Rudaki 105a; currently closed

MONEY

In May 1995 Tajikistan began issuing its own money, the Tajik *rubl* (R). Notes come in one, three, five, 10, 100, 200, 500 and 1000 R denominations.

Tajikistan is a cash only economy. You'll find little use for travellers cheques or a credit card. Exchange rates, current at time of research, are listed below, though private moneychangers will give around 20% more:

country	unit		Tajik Rubl
euro	€1	=	R900
German	DM1	=	R460
Kyrgyzstan	1 som	=	R28.7
Russian	R1	=	R33.7
USA	US$1	=	R900
Uzbekistan	1 *sum*	=	R2.0

POST & COMMUNICATIONS

Couriers are the reliable way to send important documents, though they are pricey. DHL has offices in Khojand and Dushanbe (see Information in those sections). Tajikistan's country telephone code is ☎ 992.

FOOD

For a general rundown of common dishes see the Regional Facts for the Visitor chapter.

In these days of Tajik civil strife and economic chaos, meat often gives way to vegetables. Try chickpea samsas *(nahud sambusa)* or porridge *(nahud shavla)*. Tajiks also prepare many bean and milk soups, while *oshi siyo halav* is a unique herb soup. *Tuhum barak* is a tasty egg-filled ravioli coated with sesame seed oil. *Chakka* (*yakka* to Tajik speakers around Samarkand and Bukhara) is curd mixed with herbs, and delicious with flat-bread.

ORIENTATION

Few cartographical changes accompanied the transformation of the Tajikistan Soviet Socialist Republic to the independent Republic of Tajikistan. Dushanbe was once Stalinabad but shed that unfashionable name in the 1950s. Only with the demise of Russian communism did Tajikistan's second city, Leninabad, revert to its ancient name of Khojand, and the eponymous *oblast* of which it is the capital became Khojand province. Ordjonikidzeabad (25km east of Dushanbe), named for the Georgian who imposed Bolshevism in the Caucasus, reverted to Kofarnikhon.

Tajik was made the state language in 1989, though Russian was reintroduced as the second state language in 1995. Street signs in Dushanbe have begun to sport the Tajik forms *kuchai* (street) and *khiyeboni* (avenue), though the Russian *ulitsa* and *prospekt*, as well as *ploshchad* for square, are still the more common.

Dushanbe

☎ 372 • pop 700,000

With a cool backdrop of mountains, lazy tree-lined avenues and pale oriental-fringed buildings, Dushanbe is a good-looking city, but personality-wise it's a dead loss. It is a historically isolated backwater settlement that's just a little bit boring during the day. At night it's plain scary and more than a little dangerous. For the visitor who can't or won't pay upwards of US$40 a night for a bed there are discomforts in the form of some terrible accommodation.

Despite being the capital, the city is more like a cul-de-sac than a transport hub. Other than a couple of daily trains in and out via Termiz in southern Uzbekistan, the only other connections are badly oversubscribed flights to Khojand (from where it is easy to get to Tashkent) and to Khorog in the Pamirs, where onward transport requires a lot of forward planning or extraordinary luck.

Unless you have some specific agenda, a trip to Dushanbe in the current situation isn't particularly rewarding.

History

Although the remains of a 5th century BCE settlement have been found here, modern-day Dushanbe has little history beyond this century. As recently as 80 years ago, Dushanbe (then spelled Dushyambe) was a small, poor village known chiefly for its weekly bazar ('Dushanbe' means 'Monday' in Tajik).

In 1920 the last emir of Bukhara took refuge in Dushanbe, fleeing from the advancing Bolsheviks. He was forced to continue his flight early the next year as the Red Army swept remorselessly on to add the Tajik settlement to the expanding Bolshevik empire. The Russian hold was shaken off for a spell when in 1922 Enver Pasha and his basmachi fighters liberated Dushanbe as part of their crusade to carve out a pan-Islamic empire, but following his death in a gun battle in southern Tajikistan, Bolshevik authority was quickly reasserted.

With the arrival of the railroad in 1929, Dushanbe was made capital of the new Soviet Tajik republic and renamed Stalinabad – a name it bore until the historical reinvention of the Khrushchev era. The region was developed as a cotton and silk processing centre and tens of thousands of people were relocated here, turning the rural village into a large, urban administrative and industrial centre. The city's numbers were further swollen by Tajik emigres from Bukhara and Samarkand, which had been given over to Uzbek rule.

After almost 70 uneventful years of relative peace, if not prosperity, 1990 saw festering nationalistic sentiments explode into rioting, triggered by rumoured plans to house Armenian refugees in Dushanbe. Twenty-two people died in clashes with the militia.

There were further demonstrations in the autumn of 1991 organised by opposition factions dissatisfied with the absence of political change in Tajikistan. The statue of Lenin that stood opposite the parliament building disappeared overnight and guards had to be set to watch over all other communist-era monuments. Young bearded men and veiled women took to the streets of Dushanbe calling for an Islamic state. In May 1992 these demonstrations escalated into violence and then civil war. The fighting within the capital itself ended in December 1992 following a successful assault by the Kulyabi militia, supporters of the present government.

The city remained as a capital of chaos. It was kept under a dusk-to-dawn curfew with armed gangs controlling the roads both in and out and lawless brigands patrolling the streets. Most Russians fled.

Since then the situation has become considerably calmer and now the only soldiers and tanks on the streets belong to the Russian 201st Armoured Division, part of the resident peacekeeping force stationed on the Afghan border. Random acts of violence do occur, such as the storming of the Presidential Palace in 1997 and shootouts between rival clans, but these are impossible to predict.

Orientation

The focus of Dushanbe is the wide, tree-lined prospekt Rudaki, which runs from the train station on ploshchad Kuybysheva, 5.5km north to ploshchad Rudaki. Roughly central on Rudaki is ploshchad Azadi, surrounded by government buildings, now under the stern gaze of a sorcerer-like Firdausi (see the Arts section earlier in this chapter) in place of Lenin.

Almost everything useful or interesting is within a 15 minute walk of here. The exception is the central bus station, which is some 3km distant on ulitsa Profsoyuzov in the western part of town. The airport is on the opposite side of the city, roughly 5km southeast from ploshchad Ayni, along ulitsa Ayni.

Information

Tourist Offices It's been so long since Tajik-Intourist (☎ 21 68 92, fax 21 52 36), room 11, 1st floor, Hotel Tajikistan, had any foreigners to march around that the staff are at a total loss when any turn up. At present their major business is arranging shopping trips to Abu Dhabi, Aleppo and Karachi. With a couple of days warning they can arrange escorted trips to Hissar, Varzob and other local destinations, but probably nothing more ambitious. They quote US$30 for a half-day trip to Hissar with a guide, but prices are probably negotiable.

Some travellers have had help from the Ministry of Tourism/Tajiktourism (☎ 23 14 01) at ulitsa Pushkina 14.

Visas All Tajik visa problems are dealt with at the Ministry of Foreign Affairs, which is the big pink building at prospekt Rudaki 42, on ploshchad Azadi. As you face the building, you need to take the small door on the far right of the facade where you'll be given a pass to enter the building proper and told where to go. Nobody there speaks English.

In theory permits for Khorog are available from this office for US$40, but you may have trouble persuading them to give you one.

Money There are licensed moneychangers throughout the city and this is where most people change (US dollars cash only). There's a bank on prospekt Rudaki opposite the Hotel Vakhsh and at the big hotels, but they don't always have money and rates are low. If you find somewhere with a stash of rubls, change what you might need for your whole stay because sources tend to dry up (though of course you won't be able to reconvert any of it to foreign currency; also remember that foreigners must pay for flights in US dollars). Travellers cheques are of little use.

Post & Communications The Post and Telegraph office at prospekt Rudaki 57, on ploshchad Azadi, is open 8 am to 6 pm. The telephone office is one door south at prospekt Rudaki 55. At the time of writing it was

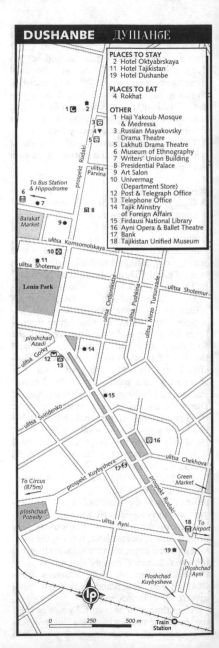

DUSHANBE ДУШАНБЕ

PLACES TO STAY
2 Hotel Oktyabrskaya
11 Hotel Tajikistan
19 Hotel Dushanbe

PLACES TO EAT
4 Rokhat

OTHER
1 Haji Yakoub Mosque & Medressa
3 Russian Mayakovsky Drama Theatre
5 Lakhuti Drama Theatre
6 Museum of Ethnography
7 Writers' Union Building
8 Presidential Palace
9 Art Salon
10 Univermag (Department Store)
12 Post & Telegraph Office
13 Telephone Office
14 Tajik Ministry of Foreign Affairs
15 Firdausi National Library
16 Ayni Opera & Ballet Theatre
17 Bank
18 Tajikistan Unified Museum

possible to make international and long-distance calls there, but not local ones. DHL (☎ 24 62 79, 21 76 53) is at 18 prospekt Rudaki, but even it takes three weeks to get mail to/from the USA or Western Europe.

Travel Agencies Alp-Navruz (☎/fax 24 53 73) specialises in mountaineering and trekking tours. Another one to try is Tajik Travel Co (☎ 21 72 46, fax 21 14 22, ✪ dmelnichkov@hotmail.com), 8th floor, 35/1 Bokhtar St.

Medical Services Dial ☎ 02 for the police and ☎ 03 for an ambulance. Your best bet in case of illness is to call the nearest embassy (see the previous Embassies & Consulates section in this chapter), which should have contact details for recommended doctors, medical services and hospitals.

Museums

The two room **Museum of Ethnography** at ulitsa Ismaili Somony 14, opposite Barakat market, is a very professional showcase of 20th century Tajik art. The collection includes pottery, carpets, cloaks, embroidery, jewellery, musical instruments, woodwork and more. It's open Monday to Saturday 10 am to 6 pm.

The **Tajikistan Unified Museum**, on a commanding site on ploshchad Ayni, includes exhibits on history, natural history and art. Among the more interesting items are exhibits on Islamic Samarkand and Bukhara, including a beautiful 10th century carved-wood mihrab (prayer niche) and a great 12 panel painting of the Russians entering Bukhara. The top floor is given over to a quirky collection, from Italian film festival programs to Olympic wrestling medals. Opening hours seem variable, but in theory they are Monday to Saturday 10 am to 5 pm. Admission costs US$0.20.

Mosque, Monuments & Markets

With its burnished golden dome and crescent-topped minaret, the **Haji Yakoub mosque & medressa** just west of the Hotel Oktyabrskaya is one of the few visible manifestations of Islam in Dushanbe. It was begun in 1990 and financed by contributions from Iran, Pakistan and Saudi Arabia; construction continues with private funds only. The mosque is named after Haji Yakoub, a Tajik religious leader who fled to Afghanistan.

Tajikistan's Persian past is invoked in the facade of the **Writers' Union Building** on ulitsa Ismaili Somony. It's adorned like a medieval cathedral with saintly, sculpted-stone figures of Sadriddin Ayni, Omar Khayyam and other poets and writers from the Tajik pantheon. Beside it is a striking **monument to Gorky & Ayni**, in the form of giant statues of the two writers seated on a lawn. West beyond the river, ulitsa Ismaili Somony is flanked by expansive **parks** with uplifting views of the mountains.

While not particularly exotic or eastern in flavour, the stalls around the large, covered **Barakat market** are the centre of activity in Dushanbe. It's north of the Hotel Tajikistan, on ulitsa Ismaili Somony. A second central bazar, the **Green market**, devoted to fruit and vegetables, lies a block north of ploshchad Ayni. Many more makeshift bazars are scattered around the outskirts. They are harrowing affairs composed of lines of people trying to sell whatever they can find at home – a pair of old shoes, some coverless books, a dismantled washing machine motor – anything that somebody might conceivably trade for a little cash.

Places to Stay & Eat

For travellers with a budget that stretches, the *Hotel Tajikistan* (☎ 27 43 93, 21 82 28, 21 33 56, ulitsa Shotemur 22) is a concrete oasis of luxury amid the deprivations of Dushanbe. The rooms are extremely comfortable and the miraculously clean bathrooms have the only hot water on tap in the city (just possibly related to the fact that two floors are permanently occupied by officers of the 201st division). South-facing rooms also benefit from mountain-edged views over the park. Singles/doubles are US$35/40.

Judging by rates of US$72/90, the *Hotel Oktyabrskaya* (☎ 21 12 80, 21 12 07, prospekt Rudaki 105a) aspires to be the classiest

TAJIKISTAN

hotel in town, but the cold marbled walls and guest-free corridors give it the feel of a morgue and there's no hot water. Moreover, it can be difficult to get a room here as much of it is occupied by aid agencies and embassies.

Hotel Dushanbe (☎ *23 36 60)*, on ploshchad Ayni, just 500m from the train station has been renovated and looks pretty sharp. Rooms are around US$75.

Restaurants and bars have opened again after the 'troubles'. The main options are the restaurants at the hotels *Tajikistan* and *Oktyabrskaya*, where the menu seems limited to a dish of the day – or maybe even a dish of the week. Whatever's available costs roughly US$2.

Bar Vistochny (prospekt Rudaki 56) has Tajik and Russian food and outdoor seating. *Café Romashka*, nearby at No 33, is similar.

An interesting place to snack during the day is the *Rokhat (prospekt Rudaki 84)*. It's an unusual, Soviet-era attempt at a grand Persian-style *chaykhana* (teahouse).

Fruit is available at the bazars, while imported cheese, frankfurters, cake and other edibles can be found in kiosks around town.

The best place in town is the *Restaurant Elite* (☎ *21 25 12),* ulitsa Chapaev, but the western ambience doesn't come cheap at around US$20 per person.

Entertainment

There's still life left at the *Ayni Opera & Ballet Theatre (prospekt Rudaki 28)*, a building that has possibly the finest interior in Dushanbe. The *Tajik Lakhuti Drama Theatre (prospekt Rudaki 86)* and the nearby *Russian Mayakovsky Drama Theatre (prospekt Rudaki 76)* also have regular performances.

Nightlife is limited to the ground floor bar of the *Hotel Tajikistan* where expats sink imported beers at a dollar a go, and keep their heads down when Russian soldiers, on leave from the Afghan border, let off steam loudly and sometimes violently. When the lights go on, we were told, you can still see the bullet holes in the ceiling. Anyone looking to wind down over a cold beer should take it to their room.

Shopping

For thick, colourful Pamiri socks, silver jewellery with lapis inlay, assorted handicrafts and even busts of Lenin, try the art salon at prospekt Rudaki 89. There is a gallery above with a permanent exhibition of paintings that are for sale. Barakat market is the place to pick up tupi for US$1.50 to US$3, and chapan for around US$8. You'll also find plenty of sequined, gold-stitched trousers and colourful dresses.

The bazar-like Univermag (department store) at prospekt Rudaki 83 is the place for everything from toilet paper to cassettes and Mars bars.

Getting There & Away

Air In theory Tajikistan Airlines flies from Dushanbe to Garm, Kulyab, Murgab and quite a few other towns in Tajikistan. In practice the only reliable regular services are several times daily to Khojand (US$90) and daily to Khorog (US$75), weekly to Bishkek, Ashgabat, Munich and Sharjah (United Arab Emirates), and three or four times a week to Almaty (US$150) and Moscow (US$310). Even these are frequently cancelled and rescheduled, either due to bad weather or fuel shortages. Often you can't buy a ticket until three days before the flight.

The separate foreigners' booking office is at the airport, through a door at the left end of the terminal entrance hall; it's open from about 8 am to 4 pm. Apparently you can only *buy* the ticket here; to make a reservation you first have to go to the Centralnaya Agenciya in the former Aeroflot office, near the Green market on ulitsa Chekhova.

Bus During the summer there is a daily service from Dushanbe to Samarkand via Penjikent, and a daily bus to Termiz. Domestic routes are mainly to southern Tajikistan, eg Kurgan-Tyube and Kulyab, and as far down as Pyanj and Ayvadz – but see the boxed text 'Safety in Tajikistan' earlier in this chapter. Services to the east reach only around 100km, as far as Komsomolabad.

Train At the time of writing there were few train services travelling in to or out of

Dushanbe. The main service, the No 23/24 Dushanbe-Moscow (via Termiz, Qarshi, Samarkand and Tashkent) train was suspended in May 1999 after Moscow declared the Tajik trains a risk to public health. When it resumes, the train takes 85 hours to reach Moscow. A 26 hour Dushanbe-Tashkent service departs early each evening.

Getting Around

Dushanbe is served by bus and trolleybus, but a lack of petrol and spare parts keeps half the fleet off the road and masses of people tapping their feet at bus stops. Fares rarely seem to be collected, and the buses are massively overcrowded. The state bus service is supplemented by an entrepreneurial fleet of less crowded private *marshrutnoe avtobusi*.

The airport is a quick ride on marshrutnoe avtobus No 8, or bus No 3 or 12, all caught from prospekt Rudaki or ulitsa Ayni. From the train station, trolleybus No 1 heads north up prospekt Rudaki passing close by all the city's hotels. To get to the bus station take bus No 18 or trolleybus no 12 west from in front of the Museum of Ethnography, a 10 minute ride.

Because of the scarcity of petrol, taxis are rare. You may be able to flag one down during the day on prospekt Rudaki, but the only place you are sure to find them is outside the Hotel Tajikistan. The government-fixed rate at the time of writing was about US$0.30 per kilometre but it's rare that a driver will agree to that – settle on a price before your journey. Private cars are too wary to stop for strangers.

There are no self-drive car-hire services but Tajik-Intourist can probably organise a car and driver for about US$30 per day. NGOs often know of reliable drivers who are used to dealing with foreigners.

AROUND DUSHANBE

The main M34 Ura-Tyube road winds north through the valley of the Varzob river and, though there's no one particular place to head for, there are plenty of picturesque locations, including the **Varzob gorge** 56km out of Dushanbe. There may be buses up to

the village of Varzob during the summer, otherwise Tajik-Intourist can arrange a half-day's drive for about US$20.

Dramatic but no longer picturesque, the **Vakhsh gorge** used to be a big favourite with Intourist because of its 300m-high hydroelectric dam, the world's highest. The dam is 80km east of Dushanbe near the new town of Nurek (from which it takes its name). If you are travelling on your own, take a Dangara bus.

The remains of a Buddhist temple were found at **Adjina-Tepe** near Kurgan-Tyube, 95km south of Dushanbe, but everything that could be moved – including a large reclining Buddha figure – was shipped off to the Hermitage in St Petersburg, leaving nothing left to see at the site.

Hissar

On a wide mountain-fringed plain, 30km west of Dushanbe, are the remains of an 18th century fortress, occupied until 1924 by Ibrahim Beg, the local henchman of the emir of Bukhara. Once a basmachi stronghold, the fortress was destroyed by the Red Army and all that remains is a reconstructed stone gateway in the cleavage of two massive grassy hillocks. A scramble to the top is rewarded with some excellent views.

Beside the fortress are two plain medressas, one dating from the 18th century and the other from the 19th century. Beyond them is the mausoleum of a 16th century Islamic teacher named Makhtumi Azam. The older medressa (facing the fortress gate) contains a small museum with displays of clothing, ceramics and jewellery.

At the foot of the grassy slopes around the fortress is a pleasant *chaykhana*.

Getting There & Away Take bus No 70 which departs frequently from ulitsa Komsomolskaya just south of Barakat market in Dushanbe. In the town of Hissar, walk down the main street past the market and take the right fork at the bus park. About 50m along is a stop for the marshrutnoe avtobus that terminates at the small settlement beside the fortress, some 7km farther. Ask for '**krey**-past' (fortress).

TAJIKISTAN

Northern Tajikistan

Tajikistan in the north squeezes between Uzbekistan and Kyrgyzstan before exploding in a splurge across the mouth of the Fergana valley, the Uzbek heartland. This jigsaw of boundaries is in fact the result of sober thought. Before 1929 Tajikistan was an autonomous republic within the Uzbek ASSR, but because of its sensitive location on the edge of the Islamic world, Stalin wanted it upgraded to a full republic. But, there weren't enough Tajiks; full-republic status required one million inhabitants. They simply topped up numbers by adding the (mainly Uzbek) population of the Khojand region (then Leninabad) to Tajikistan's. There may also be some truth in the theory that this was in partial recompense for the loss of Bukhara and Samarkand; a bum deal if ever there was one.

The only other settlement of any size in northern Tajikistan is Ura-Tyube, which has an interesting bazar. Shakhristan, 40km to the south, boasts some old Islamic monuments.

Farther south, the twin Turkestan and Zeravshan ranges, western outriders of the Pamirs, sever northern Tajikistan from the bulk of the country's landmass. Collectively known as the Fannsky Gory (Fan mountains), these are impassable from October through May. The highest passes, like the Anzob (3372m) and Ayni (3378m), are securely plugged with snow.

Since the collapse of the Soviet Union this region has become one of the world's most productive opium-growing centres. Police estimate that up to 25% of the rural workforce is involved in poppy growing.

The western Fan mountains are a favoured place for trekking and climbing, being only a couple of hours from both Samarkand and Dushanbe. See the boxed text 'Trekking in the Fan Mountains' in Around Samarkand of the Uzbekistan chapter for route details.

KHOJAND
☎ 3422 • pop 164,500

Khojand (**ho**-jan) is the capital of northern Tajikistan (known administratively as the Khojand province) and the second-largest city in the country. It's also one of Tajikistan's oldest towns, founded by Alexander the Great as his easternmost outpost, Alexandreia-Eskhate, more than 2300 years ago. Commanding the entrance to the Fergana valley, Khojand enjoyed prosperity and its riches spawned palaces, grand mosques and a citadel before the Mongols steamrolled the city into oblivion in the early 13th century.

A much-reduced Khojand subsequently arose on the site and unobtrusively weathered the course of Central Asian history on the Fergana plain: Uzbek khanates, tsarist Russia and eventually the Bolsheviks. But whereas the rest of Fergana was incorporated into the Uzbek SSR, in 1929 Khojand was scooped out for the newly formed Tajik SSR, where it has remained, albeit not always contentedly.

Majority-Uzbek Khojand has remained aloof from Dushanbe, although its 'good communist' credentials meant that it always provided Tajikistan's ruling elite. When Nabiev, a Khojand man, was unseated in 1992 and Tajikistan appeared to be becoming an Islamic republic, Khojand province threatened to secede. Secure behind the Fan mountains, it managed to escape the ravages of the civil war and remains the wealthiest part of the country, producing two-thirds of all Tajikistan's industrial output with only one-third of the population.

Fighting broke out for the first time in November 1998 between the rebel Uzbek warlord Mohammed Khudoberdiev and government troops. Two hundred people were killed in shootouts in the city streets. The city has since returned to normal, but rail and road communications between Khojand and the rest of the Fergana valley have been tightened considerably and you can expect delays and headaches if you are crossing to Tashkent or Kokand. Even if you are just transiting through Tajikistan between Samarkand and Kokand you should get a Tajik visa. Until travel connections become more convenient most travellers will probably find it more worthwhile to bypass the city if they are headed to the Fergana valley.

See the Uzbekistan chapter for more on the Fergana valley.

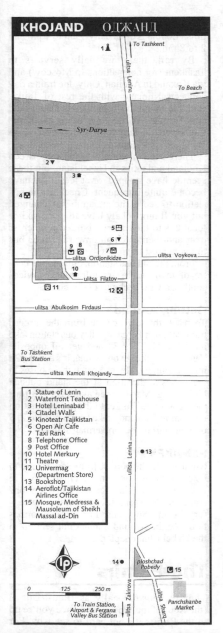

KHOJAND ОДЖАНД

To Tashkent

ulitsa Lenina

To Beach

Syr-Darya

ulitsa Voykova

ulitsa Ordjonikidze

ulitsa Filatov-

ulitsa Abulkosim Firdausi

To Tashkent
Bus Station

ulitsa Kamoli Khojandy

1 Statue of Lenin
2 Waterfront Teahouse
3 Hotel Leninabad
4 Citadel Walls
5 Kinoteatr Tajikistan
6 Open Air Cafe
7 Taxi Rank
8 Telephone Office
9 Post Office
10 Hotel Merkury
11 Theatre
12 Univermag
   (Department Store)
13 Bookshop
14 Aeroflot/Tajikistan
   Airlines Office
15 Mosque, Medressa &
   Mausoleum of Sheikh
   Massal ad-Din

ulitsa Lenina

13

0   125   250 m

To Train Station,
Airport & Fergana
Valley Bus Station

ulitsa Zakirova

ploshchad
Pobedy

ulitsa Sharq

Panchshanbe
Market

14

15

Orientation & Information

Khojand sprawls either side of the great Syr-Darya river, which is a little less than half a kilometre wide at that point. The centre of town is on the south bank, along the main artery of ulitsa Lenina, which runs from north of the river, over the bridge and 1.5km south to ploshchad Pobedy and the market. South of Pobedy, the street becomes ulitsa Zakirova and continues south a farther 5km to the train station, the new bus station (for buses east along the Fergana valley) and the airport. A second, older bus station, for services to Tashkent and south, is on ulitsa Kamoli Khojandy, west of ulitsa Lenina, 600m south of the river.

The post office and adjacent telephone office are on ulitsa Ordjonikidze, west off Lenina, 300m south of the river. Most people change money in the bazar.

Things to See & Do

The city's oldest remains are the formless baked-earth walls of the 10th century **citadel**, which could just as well be the residue of last summer's ditch-digging. The fort was the site of pitched battles during the political disturbances in November 1998. A building beside the walls that once housed the local archaeological museum is long-deserted, but the surrounding **park** is well kept and pleasant.

At the south end of ulitsa Lenina, east of ploshchad Pobedy, is the **Panchshanbe market**, a typical Central Asian bazar that bombards you with sights, smells and sounds, and also presents great temptations to the taste buds. The core of the bazar is an elegant, purpose-built hall (1954) with arched entrance portals that are patterned with brilliant designs.

Opposite the bazar, shielded from the hubbub by a calm white wall, are the **mosque**, **medressa** and **mausoleum of Sheikh Massal ad-Din**, a modest, relatively modern complex that is quietly busy with chattering young boys clutching Qurans and sage-like old men reclining in the shade. Take a look at the wooden canopy in the courtyard. It's sumptuously decorated like the market arches, but here, unusually, instead of abstract designs, the motifs are recognisable fruits and flowers.

TAJIKISTAN

Since the removal of its giant rival in Tashkent, Khojand's **statue of Lenin** is now probably the largest in Central Asia. Considering the town has already ditched its Soviet-era name, surely their monster communist can't have long to go either. He's on the north bank of the river, 300m beyond the bridge.

Places to Stay & Eat

Khojand has two accommodation options, both good. The unfashionably named *Hotel Leninabad* (☎ 669 27) is superbly placed on the corniche beside the Syr-Darya with great views, but only from its north-facing rooms. The clean, well-tended rooms have hot water in the attached bathrooms. Singles/doubles cost US$8/15.

Hotel Merkury (☎ 649 90, ulitsa Filatov 2), on a side street that runs off ulitsa Lenina beside the Univermag, couldn't be more different – a two storey villa with painted ceilings, polished banisters, creaky carpeted stairs and possibly the only full-size snooker table in Central Asia. The dozen enormous, very comfortable rooms are excellent value at US$10/20 for a single/double. The best thing about the place is the sauna around the back which guests can rent for a small fee if it has not been booked by a partying local bigwig.

The restaurant at the *Hotel Leninabad* is reasonable, if unexciting, with typical meat-and-rice fare for about US$2. The *Hotel Merkury* has no restaurant but you can often use the kitchen for a small fee. There are many chaykhanas, *shashlyk* grills and vats of *plov* around the bazar. Nearer the hotels is a small open-air *cafe* on ulitsa Lenina next to the Kinoteatr Tajikistan, serving shashlyk, soup and *gulyash*, while on the corniche by the Hotel Leninabad is a waterfront *chaykhana*, great for green tea and boiled eggs first thing in the morning. The bread is particularly good in Khojand, glazed and sprinkled with sesame seeds.

Getting There & Away

There are daily flights from Khojand to Dushanbe (US$90) and Moscow, and occasional services to Orenburg, Novosibirsk and Yekaterinburg in Russia. The Aeroflot/Tajikistan Airlines sales office (☎ 602 49) on ploshchad Pobedy at the southern end of ulitsa Lenina is open daily 9 am to 1 pm and 2 to 8 pm.

By rail, there are daily services to Tashkent (for connections to Moscow) and via Kokand to Andijan. Only one train a day connects Khojand with the rest of Tajikistan, the No 68 to Dushanbe via Samarkand and Termiz. At the time of research the trains were the only form of transport crossing the Uzbek-Tajik border.

There used to be frequent buses between Khojand and cities in Uzbekistan, but these seem to have stopped, or at least they have become quite infrequent. Check at the bus station to see if the situation has changed but you'll most likely have to get a taxi or local bus to the relevant border post, cross over and then catch an onward taxi or bus to the nearest town.

From the old bus station, close to the centre of town, there are infrequent services south via Ura-Tyube to Penjikent.

Getting Around

To reach the town centre from the airport, train station or Fergana valley bus station take local bus No 2 or 34 and get off opposite Kinoteatr Tajikistan on Lenina. It's about a 20 minute journey. You can catch these buses in the opposite direction at the stand outside Univermag. Marshrutnoe avtobus No 3 runs the same route. To get to the old bus station on Kamoli Khojandy take trolleybus No 2, 5 or 7, also from the Univermag stand.

PENJIKENT

Right across the border, from Samarkand in Uzbekistan, are the ruins of a major town in one of Central Asia's forgotten civilisations – ancient Penjikent, founded in the 5th century by the Sogdians. For more information, see the Around Samarkand section in the Uzbekistan chapter.

The Pamirs

They're known locally as Bam-i-Dunya (the Roof of the World), and once you're up in the Pamirs it's not hard to see why. For

Trekking to Ak Suu Peak

The beautiful valleys of the Turkestan range remain one of Central Asia's best kept secrets. Popular with climbers for years, the range has been compared to the spires of Patagonia. Ak Suu peak (5359m) is a beautiful pyramid-shaped peak with a sheer 2km-high wall, which makes it one of the world's best extreme rock-climbing destinations. The hike up to the Ak Suu wall is a worthwhile trip for independent hikers with a tent, stove and enough food for a few days, and there are also several longer treks that require agency support.

Ak Suu peak is actually in Kyrgyzstan, though most approach routes lead from Uzbekistan via Tajikistan. You will therefore need Uzbek, Tajik and Kyrgyz visas (though you might get away without a Tajik visa by saying you are in transit). You will need a Kyrgyz trekking permit (US$10 for three days, US$35 for more), which can be purchased at the base camp.

To get to Ak Suu by public transport will take most of the day. Hiring a vehicle will save you a lot of time and discomfort. Buses run from Khojand to Proletarsk and then to Isfana, where you change again for Katran and Ozgeryosh. Isfana has a small market, where militsia will check your visa.

The trek to base camp takes you up the Lyailyak valley and then the Ak Suu (or Jeti Kupryok) valley. The Ak Suu (white water) and Kara Suu (black water) rivers form parallel valleys. The climbers' camp is a long day's hike from Ozgeryosh and offers lovely views of the valley. From here you can take short day hikes up to the rock wall and surrounding glaciers. The afternoon offers the best light.

Longer trekking extensions include heading east over Ak Tyubek pass (4390m) down into Orto Chashma valley, then Rtachashma river and Karavshin valley to Vorukh, a Tajikistan enclave. The Karavshin valley makes an excellent trekking destination in itself.

Alternative routes include the three day trek west over the Uryam pass to Uryam river (with an optional day hike up to the glacier), then 8km down to the junction of Lyailyak river. A longer trek goes over the next pass into the Ashat valley and up to the glaciers at the foot of Sabakh peak (5282m).

---

centuries a knot of tiny valley emirates, the Pamirs feel like a land a little bit closer to the heavens. They are the node from which several of the world's highest ranges radiate, including the Karakoram and Himalaya to the south, the Hindu Kush to the west and the Tian Shan straddling the Kyrgyz-Chinese border to the north-east.

Though they don't quite compare with the pinnacles of the Himalaya, the Pamirs do contain three of the four highest mountains in the former Soviet Union, the apex of which is Pik Kommunizma at 7495m. Less than an Empire State Building behind is Pik Lenina at 7134m and Pik Korzhenskaya at 7105m. Where the Pamirs cannot be topped, however, is in the sheer prosaic quality of their names: as well as Lenina and Kommunizma (formerly Pik Stalina) there are the

Victory and Revolution peaks and, the most romantically impaired of all, an Academy of Sciences range. In mid-1997, Pik Kommunizma was renamed Kuh-i-Samani, and Pik Lenina, Kuh-i-Garmo, but everyone sticks with the Soviet names.

For the most part, the Pamirs are too high for human settlement. The autonomous region of Gorno, which means mountainous, to Badakhshan accounts for 45% of the country's territory but only 3% of its population. The 220,000 souls that do live here are divided equally between Tajiks, Kyrgyz and Pamiri (Mountain) Tajiks.

The slopes and high valleys are inhabited by hardier creatures, near-mythical animals like the giant Marco Polo sheep, which sports curled horns that would measure almost 2m were they somehow unfurled, and the rarely

Tajikistan's Sword of Damocles

As if Tajikistan didn't have enough to worry about, geologists warn that the country faces a potential natural disaster of biblical proportions. The watery sword of Damocles lies high in the Pamir in the shape of Lake Sarez, a body of water half the size of Lake Geneva, which was formed in 1911 when an earthquake dislodged an entire mountainside into the path of the Murgab river. The 500m-deep lake formed behind a 60m-high natural dam of rocks and mud. If this plug were to break, as some experts think it could, a huge wall of water would sweep down the mountain valleys, wiping away villages, even into Uzbekistan, Turkmenistan and Afghanistan, with flood waters reaching as far as the Aral Sea. Experts warn that it would be the largest flood ever witnessed by human eyes.

seen but very popular snow leopard. And that's not to mention the similarly elusive 'giant snowman'.

Chance encounters with Yetis aside, most of the Pamir region is reasonably safe excepting the stretch of the M41 Hwy between Komsomolabad and Rushan (see the boxed text 'Safety in Tajikistan' at the start of this chapter and the following Dangers & Annoyances section). The entire area is under the de facto administration of Russian CIS border guards, whose task it is to control smuggling and prevent fundamentalist infiltration from Afghanistan. There are, however, plenty of other problems and pitfalls, the biggest of which is the absolute dearth of transport and food.

Regional Crisis

With no arable land to speak of and no industry, the region of Gorno-Badakhshan has always relied heavily on Dushanbe for its upkeep, with 80% of the region's food and all its fuel coming from outside the region. The collapse of the USSR was a particularly vicious blow for the region.

Frustrated by its marginal position and seeing no future in a collapsing Tajikistan,

Gorno-Badakhshan nominally declared its independence in 1992 and chose the rebel side in the civil war. Since then, the government hasn't been sending much in the way of aid. Some even claim the M41 to Khorog is deliberately kept unstable by pro-government militias to keep supplies from the Pamir and 'punish' the Pamiri for choosing the rebel side.

At present, the people of the Pamirs are reliant on subsistence agriculture and humanitarian aid for their continued survival. Funded primarily by the Aga Khan Foundation, convoys of trucks shuttle between Khorog and supply depots at Osh (Kyrgyzstan), ferrying in wheat, rice, salt and other staples. As well as providing short-term food aid, the Aga Khan Foundation is setting up programs to create some degree of self-sufficiency, such as dams for electricity and irrigation. It is hoped that a new road, co-funded by the Islamic Development Bank, the Aga Khan Foundation and Pakistan, which is being constructed between Murgab and Tashkurgan in China will provide another supply link and lift the region out of its isolation.

Dangers & Annoyances

The Pamirs have seen relatively little of the political violence that devastated the republic throughout the 1990s. Today it is one of the most politically stable areas of the country. However, this already poor and remote region has suffered dramatically from Tajikistan's economic collapse and theft can be too tempting for some. So hide your greenbacks deep, dress modestly, and conceal flashy and obviously expensive equipment.

The Pamir is also a pivotal point in the trans-Asian drug-smuggling route. There is little chance of westerners seeing any of it, apart from the long and tedious checks by the CIS border guards along the Pamir Hwy.

At the time of research, the aid agencies operating in the region advised against using the M41 between Khorog and Dushanbe, via Komsomolabad, Rushan and Kalaikhum, as it is still plagued by political violence and banditry. Most Pamir travellers fly to Khorog to pick up the Pamir Hwy, which still has 728km of quite literally breathtaking high-altitude passes and plateaus to negotiate before finishing up in Osh.

There is now an alternative route to Dushanbe through Kuljab (hugging the Afghan border), but check the situation there thoroughly before setting out.

A second Pamir road, the A372, forks off from the M41 some 150km north-east of Dushanbe to make a 200km-long beeline for the Kyrgyz border (see Alay Valley in the Kyrgyzstan chapter). At the time of writing the Garm valley was still considered unsafe – check the current situation before setting out.

If you're going to be driving on the Pamir Hwy, where many of the passes are well over 4000m, read the Health section in the Regional Facts for the Visitor chapter – especially about the serious risks associated with altitude sickness.

Visas & Registration

It is essential to have a Tajik visa mentioning Khorog and/or Gorno-Badakhshan (Murgab) as your destination. Checks are strict at both Khorog and Sary Tash at either end of the Pamir Hwy. To get a visa you'll need an invitation/visa support letter mentioning the same destinations. Visas can be obtained in two weeks through the ITMC Tien Shan trekking agency in Bishkek. A visa support letter costs US$15 per person.

In our experience, the best place in Central Asia to get a visa for the Pamirs is either Dushanbe or Almaty. Make sure your visa clearly mentions Khorog as your destination. In the past Tajik officials in Dushanbe have been reluctant to help travellers visit Gorno-Badakhshan.

There seems to be no obligation to register with the Office of Visas & Registration (OVIR) during the trip, but nevertheless, when you plan to stay overnight in Murgab, it's prudent to inform the Office of the Ministry of Internal Affairs (the ex-KGB). They'll refer you to the OVIR office, where your name and passport details are put in a register.

If you plan to trek or stay several days in Karakul or Murgab, it's wise to inform the commander of the local CIS border guards as well.

When to Go

Travel is possible from mid-May to early November. Outside these months, it's unbearably cold, snow storms often close passes for days, food is very hard to get and the landscape is not as rewarding.

What to Bring

You can now buy basic foodstuffs like bread, potatoes and *kumys* (fermented mare's milk) along the way and there are a few grotty truckers' canteens, but availability of food is absolutely not reliable, so bring all your own high-protein provisions. You should bring 25% more than you'll actually need, since bad weather, cancelled flights and vehicle breakdowns will probably keep you in the region longer than you expect.

It's also essential to have warm clothing and thermal underwear even in mid-summer, as night-time temperatures on the Murgab plateau can drop as low as -25°C (-40°C in winter). To avoid looking like a cooked lobster and having to adopt a permanent Clint Eastwood squint, bring along sunscreen and sunglasses too.

Maps The best maps for the region are to be found in Bishkek and Almaty. For the northern stretch (ie Osh to Sary Tash) the best choices are the *Osh and Surroundings* and the *Pik Lenina* 1:200,000 map sheets of the Kyrgyz Cartographic Agency in Bishkek (see Bishkek in the Kyrgyzstan chapter).

For the southern part, the 1:1,000,000 scale J-42 *Dushanbe* and J-43 *Kashgar* maps (from a series called *Generalnii Shtab*) are available at the Zher Cartographic Agency in Almaty (see the Almaty section in the Kazakstan chapter). All maps are in Russian.

Money

With the increase in truck traffic on the Pamir Hwy, there is now a rudimentary cash economy in the Pamirs. Stock up on Kyrgyz som, Tajik rubl and small US dollar bills. Between Khorog and Murgab, everyone asks for Tajik rubls. From Murgab to the Kyrgyz-Tajik border, the Kyrgyz som is the de facto currency. There are no formal moneychangers along the route, though in an emergency you might find someone willing to change dollars in Murgab.

Trekking

Several great treks can be organised from Murgab (eg the Sarez Lake circuit, then on to Yashilkul lake), but you will need professionals with you on these demanding treks. Several routes are described in Frith Maier's *Trekking in Russia and Central Asia*.

Accommodation

Outside of the regional capital of Khorog there is no hotel or hostel accommodation. However, there are plenty of isolated farmsteads along the mountain routes that operate as very rough-and-ready guesthouses. What you can expect is some floor space, a pungent sheepskin blanket and probably a hot bowl of *sher chay*, tea with goats' milk, salt and butter. All drivers in the Pamirs know the whereabouts of such places.

Getting There & Away

The major transport options for the 728km Pamir Hwy are hitching on trucks or renting a 4WD with driver. It's worth allowing four to six days to complete the trip. As a general rule, it makes far more sense to organise everything from Osh than from Khorog, as fuel costs half the Khorog price, provisions are plenty and cheap in the markets and you will find far more drivers interested in taking you to the Pamirs.

Hitching Dozens of lorries make the journey between Osh and Khorog every day, so finding a ride shouldn't be too much of a problem. Figure on around US$50 for a ride from Osh to Khorog. However, you can end up waiting a long time for another ride if you break the journey, as trucks mid-route are often full. Moreover, drug smuggling controls at checkpoints tend to be tedious, with waiting lines that can last half a day or more.

In Osh, lorries heading for Gorno-Badakhshan can basically be found at two places. The first is the Kontor Aga Khana close to the train station, where trucks transporting humanitarian aid wait for their loads. The second (for all non-Aga Khan transport)

is the Avtostantsya Patu at Gagarin köchösü, also east uphill of the centre. You'll have far more choice there. Look for trucks with GB (Gorno-Badakhshan) in the licence plate.

In Khorog, the trucks going to Osh hang out at ulitsa Lenina, which runs right around the university.

Renting a Vehicle Renting a private vehicle (normally a Russian UAZ jeep) and a driver is expensive, but gives you flexibility. Travel agencies in Bishkek (see the Bishkek section of the Kyrgyzstan chapter) may be able to help with this, but if you want to organise it by yourself, you can speak with 4WD drivers who gather at the taxi stand next to the old bus station. A bottom-dollar rate is currently around US$250 for the 1500km ride to Khorog and back. This includes petrol, vehicle maintenance and the driver's pay, food and accommodation for four days on the road.

For every extra day, add about US$10. For side trips, add the extra petrol cost. You should try to organise this at least a week in advance. Give the vehicle the once-over, check that the 4WD is operational and check that the driver has the necessary documents to drive in Tajikistan. If you do not speak Russian, try to get help from an English, French or German-speaking student from the Language Faculty of Osh to ensure clear and proper negotiation.

Bus There are rumours about a weekly Osh-Khorog-Osh bus in summer, but there has been no official confirmation of this. There are occasional private vans between Osh and Murgab. Public buses run from Osh as far as Sary Tash (see the Osh and the Pamir Alay sections in the Kyrgyzstan chapter). From Khorog, buses go as far as Jelandy.

KHOROG

☎ 35220 • pop 22,000

A small mountain-valley town, Khorog is the capital of the autonomous Gorno-Badakhshan region. It lies 2000m above sea level, strung out irregularly along the slopes either side of the dashing Gunt river. A few kilometres downstream, the Gunt merges

One of Central Asia's premier trekking destinations, the Fan mountains are studded with turquoise lakes and alpine valleys. Swirls of snow and ice make trekking within the region both magical and challenging.

Top Left: Bright and colourful, Ashgabat's Tolkuchka bazar sprawls across acres of desert.
Top & Middle Right: The tombs of Najm-ed-Din Kubra in Konye-Urgench are said to have healing properties.
Bottom: Children take a break from studying outside a yurt at Darvaza, Turkmenistan.

with the Pyanj, the river that marks the border with Afghanistan.

Until the late 19th century, present-day Khorog was a tiny Sart (Tajik) settlement that loosely belonged to the domain of local chieftains, the Afghan shah or the emir of Bukhara. Russia installed a small garrison here following the Anglo-Russian-Afghan Border Treaty of 1896 that delineated the current northern border of Afghanistan on the Pyanj river. Khorog was made the administrative centre of Gorno-Badakhshan in 1925.

Settlers were encouraged to populate the town with the promise of a medal and a free Volga sedan to any mother spawning 16 or more children. Quite what these offspring were supposed to do on maturing is unclear, as Khorog has no industry and no cultivable land. Exacerbated by the civil war and Gorno-Badakhshan's ostracism by Dushanbe, unemployment here presently stands at almost 100%. Almost the only people with work are drivers employed by the Aga Khan Foundation, and at the depths of the economic crisis money disappeared altogether, replaced by barter.

Khorog time is one hour ahead of Dushanbe but all official business and office hours run on Dushanbe time, including those of international agencies.

Information

If you need an interpreter you can find students at the Language Faculty of the university who will be glad to practise their English. It's on ulitsa Lenina in the same premises as the police and the OVIR, across the main university building.

The university also has an email centre on the 1st floor. It's open 8 am to 4 pm (closed noon to 1 pm).

The post office, at ulitsa Lenina 40, is the place to make calls to Dushanbe.

A person to contact to arrange private transport, village home-stays and excursions to pre-Islamic fortresses and to the Afghan border is Mosalam Anvarov (☎ 3206 home, ☎ 4057 office). He previously ran Khorog's tourism department in Soviet times and is still able to set up travel arrangements at negotiable prices, given a few days notice. He lives close to the bazar at ulitsa Lenina 133/3, apartment 34.

Travellers have also recommended Molo Abdul Shagarf (☎ 3796 office, ☎ 5926 home) as a useful source of information and travel arrangements.

Things to See

Khorog has a surprisingly good **Regional Museum**, on ulitsa Lenina, with decent historical and ethnographic displays. Admission is US$0.50. History students speaking some English can act as guides.

There is allegedly a **botanical garden** on the slopes high above the town. To get there, begin at Khorog's only traffic light and take the road north that crosses the river and stick with it for about 5km.

Places to Stay & Eat

The spartan, almost derelict, **Dostay Maimankhana** (Russian: Gostinitsa Druzhba) has rooms (some with a toilet and basin) for about US$1.50 per person. The Dostay is by the river, just off ulitsa Lenina. If you're coming from the airstrip it's the first side street on the right after the little silver bust of Lenin.

Several international agencies now have their own guesthouses that are open to travellers if none of their own people are staying there.

The comfortable and well-located guesthouse of the **Mountain Society Development Support Programme (MSDSP)**, a branch of the Aga Khan Foundation, comes at a negotiable US$30 for a double, including breakfast. It's at ulitsa Lenina 54 (right next to the museum).

The **World Food Programme guesthouse** (ulitsa Aini 9/1; top floor), costs US$10 per person, and they can provide food as well. Check at the World Food Programme (WFP) office (☎ 4913) at ulitsa Lenina 10 (next to the post office) to see if there is room.

For **home-stays** (which should not cost more than US$2 per night), one possibility is to ask Mosalam Anvarov (see earlier).

The **bazar** on the outskirts of town has recently come to life again, offering produce from the nearby villages (especially in August and September).

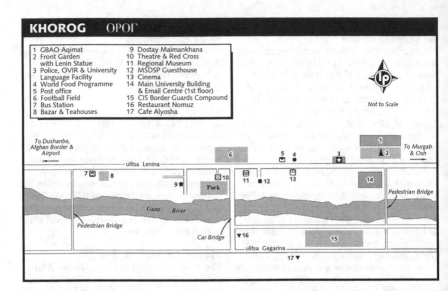

KHOROG ОРОГ

1 GBAO Aqimat
2 Front Garden
   with Lenin Statue
3 Police, OVIR & University
   Language Facility
4 World Food Programme
5 Post office
6 Football Field
7 Bus Station
8 Bazar & Teahouses
9 Dostay Maimankhana
10 Theatre & Red Cross
11 Regional Museum
12 MSDSP Guesthouse
13 Cinema
14 Main University Building
   & Email Centre (1st floor)
15 CIS Border Guards Compound
16 Restaurant Nomuz
17 Cafe Alyosha

Not to Scale

To Dushanbe,
Afghan Border &
Airport

To Murgab
& Osh

ulitsa Lenina

Park

Gunt   River

Pedestrian Bridge

Pedestrian Bridge

Car Bridge

ulitsa Gagarina

There are basic *chaykhanas* in the bazar. A little uphill, right at the crossing of the car bridge and ulitsa Gagarina, is the *Restaurant Nomuz*, which serves plov and fish for about US$0.50. Farther along Gagarina, the *Cafe Alyosha* has similar fare.

Getting There & Away

For details on transport along the Pamir Hwy see the Getting There & Away section of The Pamirs, earlier in this chapter.

Air One of the main attractions of Khorog is the flight in from Dushanbe which, depending on your confidence in the pilots of Tajikistan Airlines, will be one of the most exhilarating or terrifying experiences of your life.

In Soviet days this was the only route on which Aeroflot paid its pilots danger money. For most of the 45 minute flight the aircraft scoots along mountain valleys, flying in the shadow of the rockface with its wingtips so close you could swear they kick up swirls of snow. It may be reassuring to know that only one flight has failed to make it safely in recent years and that that incident was apparently not as a result of pilot error or mechanical failure but because the plane was brought down by rocket fire from Afghanistan.

There are two flights a day each way, though at the first sign of bad weather (which is frequent outside of the summer months) they're grounded. Passengers must then take their chances the next day, tussling for seats with those already booked on that flight. It can happen that, after a run of bad weather, hundreds turn up to fight for the first flight's 40 available seats. As a foreigner paying the hard currency rate (US$75 one way) you will be given preference.

The mountain-flanked airstrip at Khorog is 3km outside town at the western end of ulitsa Lenina. There is no bus service to or from the airstrip.

Bus There are daily buses to Dushanbe from the bus station, but check the security situation of the route. Four to five times a week, sturdy 4WD vans leave the bazar early in the morning for Osh. Services are regularly cancelled if there aren't enough passengers. There are also several buses a day to Jelandy, Rushan and Ishkashim on the Afghani border.

TAJIKISTAN

AROUND KHOROG

South of Khorog a side road loop traces the Tajik-Afghan border, swinging north-east to Langar before meeting the Pamir (M41) Hwy. The trip takes in hot springs, mountain lakes and the ruins of pre-Islamic fortresses. Another 4WD road heads up the Shakhdara valley south-east from Khorog and over to Turuntai-kul (see below), offering fine views of Pik Karla Marxa (6723m). Mosalam Anvarov (see the Khorog entry earlier) can arrange itineraries here. Apparently you need a special permit from OVIR to make this trip – it's not enough just to have Khorog or Murgab on your visa.

THE PAMIR HIGHWAY

The route from Khorog to Osh on the Pamir Hwy (a section of the M41) is a suspension-wrenching 728km of badly surfaced road. The route, the vast majority of which is higher than 3000m, takes you to Tibetan-style high plateaux grazed by yaks and studded with deep-blue lakes.

The Pamirskoe Shosse – as the Russians call it – was built by a batch of the best Soviet engineers in 1931, in order to facilitate troops, transport, and provisioning to this very remote outpost of the Soviet empire. Along the road, you will still see rusty Soviet propaganda signs, hailing the 'brave Pamir drivers who are the lifeblood of the region'. Until very recently, the road was virtually off limits to travellers.

Muscular, high-clearance 4WDs have been known to cover the distance in 20 hours, but a more realistic estimate is two full days. Blue kilometre posts line the way with the distance from Khorog marked on one side and from Osh on the other.

Being a major drug-smuggling artery, the road has numerous CIS border guard checkpoints, which can cause considerable delays. As with the Karakoram Highway, foreigners are supposed to register at every one of them, but there's little hassle.

Khorog to Jelandy

The initial 120km stretch out of Khorog belongs to the attractive and friendly Gunt valley. Lush poplars amid arid mountains shelter traditional Pamiri villages, and the people are very friendly and curious.

As the road relentlessly hauls itself up a succession of switchbacks, climbing 2000m in less than 100km, there are countless spectacular views back along the Gunt valley.

About 1km before Jelandy, at the 120km post, there is a spartan but clean and friendly *guesthouse* with hot springs and a rudimentary sauna. This is a favourite stop for truck drivers out of Khorog, a town with no hot water. A dorm bed here costs barely US$1 in Tajik rubls. It's a bit off the road, so when you're looking around, ask for the sanatorium. Behind the guesthouse, a track leads to Turuntai-kul lake, which makes a fine 15km return day hike. Jelandy is already close to 4000m above sea level so take things easy.

Jelandy to Murgab

Soon after leaving Jelandy the road climbs to 4272m as it crests the Koi-Tezek pass, after which the mountains pull back from the road to create a barren kilometre-wide plain. This is the Pamir plateau; 'the Roof of the World'. The road is raised on a 1m-high embankment barely wide enough for oncoming vehicles to pass and quite hazardous for over-tired drivers (drifting trucks have been known to slide off the crumbling embankment edge and roll onto the plain).

Murgab

☎ 82130 • pop 4300

The plateau town of Murgab, some 310km from Khorog, is where many drivers on the highway aim to finish up at the end of the first day. A Soviet-era settlement like Khorog, Murgab is a drab huddle of single storey white buildings in a forest of telegraph poles. The town is roughly half Kyrgyz, half Tajik.

Coming from Khorog, the first Pamir militsia checkpoint is on the outskirts of Murgab; anyone who doesn't have the town listed on their visa might have difficulties proceeding any farther.

The town's run-down truck-stop *hotel* (*ulitsa Sovietskaja 24*) has basic accommodation at around US$1.50.

Failing that, the Mountain Society Development Support Programme (MSDSP) has its own *guesthouse* on ulitsa Lenina where travellers can stay at a negotiable price when there is space. It is in a small compound whose light blue gate is marked 961. Contact Abubakir Ubaderdiev (who speaks some English) at ☎ 383 or ☎ 261 (office), or ☎ 706 (home). The guesthouse might be able to help arrange local *home-stays*, at around US$2 per person, including basic meals.

There is a *bazar* where you can buy basic foodstuffs or get a standard chaykhana meal.

Murgab is a good place to drum up a truck ride. Otherwise, daily 4WD vans leave for Osh from the bazar when full (usually around lunchtime) for US$7, returning the next day.

Murgab to Sary Tash

Beyond Murgab, the highway hugs the Chinese border and in places the twin barbed-wire-topped fences run less than 20m from the road. Despite this, there is no crossing between China and Tajikistan; the closest official breach in the Chinese border is at the Torugart pass in Kyrgyzstan.

Soon after Murgab (around the 371km-post) the mountains close in as the road climbs towards the Ak-Baital (White Horse) pass, at 4655m, the highest point of the journey. From there it's a long descent of some 70km to Kara-Kul, the highest lake in Central Asia.

Created by a meteor approximately ten million years ago, **Kara-Kul lake** has an eerie, Twilight-Zone air about it. Local Kyrgyz call the deep blue, lifeless lake Ulyy Kara-Kul (Big Black Lake), compared to Kishi Kara-Kul (Lesser Black Lake) along the Karakoram Highway in China. Although salty, the lake is frozen and covered in snow until the end of May.

Treks around Kara-Kul lake are described in Frith Maier's *Trekking in Russia and Central Asia*, but come prepared. This is already 4000m (water boils at 86°C here), and a local guide with a gun is more than an expendable luxury, as wolves roam the area. The only settlement of any significance here is the lakeside village of Karakul. The people are friendly, although after living in a high-security zone for decades, somewhat suspicious about why you are there.

Karakul lies right next to the CIS-Chinese border security zone (the electric fence is right at the outskirts of the village). In the past foreigners have been detained here for up to four hours while officers probe passports and visas for possible defects. If you've taken any photographs while in the Pamirs do not admit to it or you risk having your film confiscated. If you plan to camp and walk for more than just overnight, you'd better inform the *aqimat* (administration) and the commander of the CIS border guards.

No sooner do you get through the Russian checkpoint than the Tajiks bring all traffic to a halt with their own checkpoint.

The actual border between Tajikistan and Kyrgyzstan is some distance farther away at the crest of the Kyzyl-Art pass (4282m). There follows a rapid rollercoaster descent down a mountainside strewn with the skeletons of overly hasty trucks before the road levels out for the approach to the Kyrgyz border town of Sary Tash. At Sary Tash, after a succession of thorough Kyrgyz border formalities, the A372 branches off southwest to the Pamir Alay valley in Kyrgyzstan and the A371 heads north-east to the Kyrgyz-Chinese border post of Irkeshtam (see the Alay Valley entry in the Bishkek to Osh & the Kyrgyz Fergana Valley section of the Kyrgyzstan chapter).

Turkmenistan

Turkmenistan at a Glance

Official Name: Turkmenistan
Area: 488,100 sq km
Population: 4.7 million
Ethnic Mix: 82% Turkmen, 9% Uzbek, 3% Russian, 2% Kazak, 4% Others
Capital: Ashgabat
Currency: manat (M)
Country ☎ Code: 993
Best Time to Go: March, April, September, October

Turkmenbashi p477

Ashgabat p465

Merv p483

Mary p481

- **Konye-Urgench** – ancient buildings strung across a plain of graves – testaments to a city vaporised by Timur

- **Tolkuchka Bazar** – an amazing spectacle, with its colourful cast of thousands

- **Ancient Merv** – barren ruins and a series of dead cities sprawling over an ancient oasis

- **Turkmen Dress** – women in brightly embroidered robes and flowery headscarves, old *aksakals* (white beards) with knee-high boots and massive shaggy hats

- **Monuments, Public Portraits and Nonstop Propaganda** – the jaw-dropping personality cult of President Saparmurat 'Turkmenbashi' Niyazov

Arid and sparsely populated Turkmenistan's past mostly lies in ruins, shattered by earthquakes and murderous invasions. It's future depends on unexploited wealth in oil and gas. Enjoying the present requires a little imagination and good timing – while the country enjoys 300 days of sunshine a year, summer temperatures can hit 50°C.

While the capital, Ashgabat, has been livened with monuments, Turkmenistan's other centres are almost memorably dull. Cities that represented 2500 years of civilisation, built by Alexander the Great, the Persians, the Arabs – whose ancient city of Merv is said to be the setting for Scheherazade's tales – and the Russians are almost gone.

Much of the landscape recalls a spaghetti western, with snaking dunes, stark mountain ranges, scrappy villages and ramshackle railway towns. For relief the eye tends to settle on odd details like wandering camels, abandoned Soviet jet fighters and massive billboards of President Saparmurat Niyazov, also known as Turkmenbashi (Head of all Turkmen), and his ubiquitous motto 'Halk, Watan, Turkmenbashi' (people, nation, me).

The real attraction is the Turkmen people, only a generation or two removed from roaming the shifting desert sands on horseback. Speaking a language likened to 800-year-old Turkish, the Turkmen look back to a rural life revolving around their famous, traditionally patterned carpets and Akhal-Teke horses, supposedly the ancestor of Arabian horses. Turkmen women brighten up the dusty landscape in iridescent embroidered velvet gowns and flowery headscarves, while some dignified old *aksakals* (white beards) still stride about in cloaks and massive shaggy wool hats. Although Turkmen tend to be reserved with strangers, should you be invited into a home, you will share in mountains of steaming *plov* (rice dish), gallons of tea and perhaps the national obsession, chess. Very few people speak English; basic knowledge of Russian is vital, and basic Turkmen is a great bargaining aid (see the Language chapter).

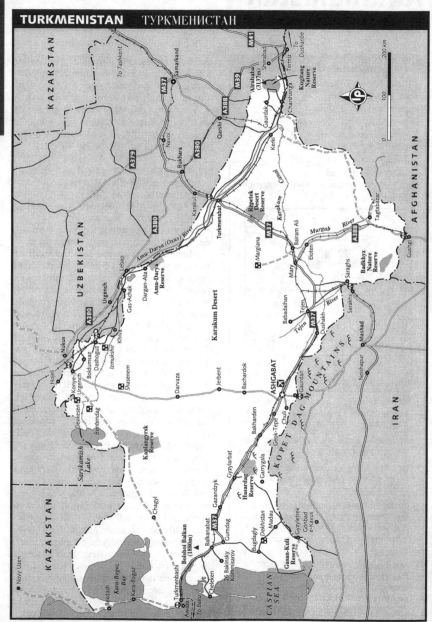

TURKMENISTAN ТУРКМЕНИСТАН

Facts about Turkmenistan

HISTORY
Ancient Armies

Though not a goal in itself, the sun-scorched, barren land between the Caspian Sea and the Oxus river (now the Amu-Darya) passed in ancient times from one empire to another as campaigning armies decamped on the way to richer territories. Alexander the Great established a city here on his way to India. Around the time of Christ, the Parthians, Rome's main rivals for power in the east, set up a capital at Nisa, near present-day Ashgabat. In the 11th century the Seljuq Turks appropriated Alexander's old city and Silk Road staging post, Merv, as a base from which to expand their empire into Afghanistan.

Two centuries later, the heart of the Seljuq empire was torn out as Jenghiz Khan stormed down from the steppes and through Trans-Caspia (the region east of the Caspian Sea) on his way to terrorise Europe.

Desert Raiders

It's not known precisely when the first Turkmen appeared, but most historians think they drifted here in the wake of the Seljuqs, some time in the 11th century. A collection of displaced nomadic horse-breeding tribes, possibly from the foothills of the Altay mountains, they found alternative pastures in the oases fringing the Karakum desert and in Persia, Syria and Anatolia (in present-day Turkey). They rode shy of any regional powers and remained largely unaffected by all the dynastic musical chairs.

With the decline in the 16th century of the Timurids, the last of Central Asia's empire-builders, Trans-Caspia became a backwater, punctuated with feudal islands like the khanates of Khiva and Bukhara. From their oasis strongholds the Turkmen preyed on straggling caravans and raided the peaceable settlements of northern Persia to steal hostages for sale in Turkic markets. According to Arminius Vambéry, a 19th century traveller in the region, the Turkmen 'would not hesitate to sell into slavery the Prophet himself, did he fall into their hands'. When not harassing and pillaging their neighbours, the Turkmen tribes would fall on one another with equal zest.

Geok-Tepe

The Turkmen bit off more than they could chew when they began kidnapping parties of Russians in Trans-Caspia, who were the vanguard of a rapidly expanding tsarist empire. At one time there were perhaps as many as 3000 Russians enslaved in Bukhara, most of them former captives of the Turkmen. In 1877 the empire struck back. A series of military actions was launched from the newly founded Caspian port of Krasnovodsk (now Turkmenbashi). The first, against the Turkmen encampment of Kyzyl-Arvat (Gyzylarbat), succeeded in routing the tribesmen but the second, against the earthen fortress of Geok-Tepe, resulted in an ignominious retreat for the Russians.

Desperate to save face and put down the now wildly uncontrollable Turkmen, the tsar gave command of his Trans-Caspian forces to General Mikhail Dmitrievich Skobelev, a soldier with a bloody career. In 1881, under Skobelev, Russian forces again marched on Geok-Tepe. This time its mud walls were blasted apart with gunpowder and the Russians streamed in to massacre an estimated 7000 Turkmen. In adherence to Skobelev's maxim of 'the harder you hit them, the longer they remain quiet', a further 8000 were cut down as they fled across the desert. With the diplomatically stated aim of 'putting an end to the depredations of the Turcoman tribes,' the Russians went on to seize Ashgabat and Merv. Not surprisingly, they met little further resistance and by 1894 had secured all Trans-Caspia for the tsar.

Tsarist Trans-Caspia

During the Trans-Caspian campaign, the Russians' biggest problem had been keeping the army provisioned on its trek through the inhospitable sands of the Karakum. The solution was to build a railway. Work on the Trans-Caspian line began at what was to be the western terminus, Krasnovodsk, in 1881 and, via Ashgabat and Merv, it had reached Charjou (now called Turkmenabat) and the Amu-Darya by 1886. Two years later trains were steaming into Samarkand and, not long after, Tashkent.

Although the swift annexation of Trans-Caspia had alarmed the British, who suspected Russian designs on Afghanistan and ultimately Imperial India, the outbreak of WWI unexpectedly threw the two Great Game rivals (see The Great Game in the History section of the Facts about Central Asia chapter) together as allies against two of the central powers, Germany and Turkey. The situation took another twist in 1917 with the Bolshevik coup and the signing of a peace treaty between Russia and Germany. Amid the chaos a loose grouping of counter-revolutionaries seized power in Ashgabat, only to come under attack from the Bolsheviks, who had a strong Central Asian power base in Tashkent. A small British force, dispatched from northern Persia to back up the provisional Ashgabat government, skirmished with the Bolsheviks at a place called Dushakh.

With the end of WWI the British withdrew and the Bolsheviks took Ashgabat in 1919. For a while the region existed as the Turkmen *oblast* (province) of the Turkestan Autonomous Soviet Socialist Republic (ASSR), before becoming the Turkmen Soviet Socialist Republic (SSR) in 1924.

The Turkmen SSR

Inflamed by Soviet attempts to settle the tribes and collectivise farming, Turkmen resistance continued and a guerrilla war raged until 1936. More than a million Turkmen fled into the Karakum desert or into northern Iran and Afghanistan rather than give up their nomadic ways. The Turkmen also fell foul of a Moscow-directed campaign against religion. Of the 441 mosques in Turkmenistan in 1911, only five remained standing by 1941.

A steady stream of Russian immigrants began arriving in the 1920s to undertake the modernisation of the SSR, and a big part of the plan involved cotton. Turkmenistan's arid climate was hardly conducive to bumper harvests, and to supply the vast quantities of water required the authorities began work in the 1950s on a massive irrigation ditch – the Karakum canal. The 1100km-long gully they built runs the length of the republic, bleeding the Amu-Darya to create a fertile band across the south. Cotton production quadrupled, though the consequences for the Aral Sea have been disastrous (see Ecology & Environment in the Facts about Central Asia chapter). Around Dashoguz the drive for cotton spurred the annihilation of nearly all the riverine *toghay* forest, plus more canals from the Amu-Darya, dumping the agricultural run-off into the enormous evaporation pan of Sarykamish lake. Up to 70% of the diverted water is lost to evaporation and seepage; unplanned lakes and swamps have appeared deep in the desert, miles from the canals.

Supremely Soviet

Turkmenistan was slow to pick up on the political changes in the other Soviet republics during the 1980s. The first challenge to the Communist Party of Turkmenistan (CPT) came in 1989 when a group of intellectuals formed Agzybirlik (Unity), a socially and environmentally progressive party whose name revived the fallen banner of the anti-Soviet rebels of the 1920s and 30s. The party was officially, if reluctantly, registered but in 1990, but when it showed signs of garnering too much support, it was promptly banned.

As a concession to dispossessed Agzybirlik supporters, the CPT adopted Turkmen as the official state language and on 22 August 1990 made a declaration of sovereignty which meant that Turkmenistan's laws were put above those of the USSR. On 27 October 1990 the Communist Party boss Saparmurat Niyazov, unopposed and supposedly with the blessing of more than 98% of voters, was elected to the newly created post of president.

Reluctant Independence

Despite all these preliminaries, the collapse of the Soviet Union came as a great shock to the Niyazov government. The underdeveloped economy and the republic's dependence on Moscow for subsidies meant that

Turkmenistan wasn't ready to go it alone. But just as the Turkmen hadn't been consulted about joining the Soviet Union, they had no say when it came time to leave. Despite voting overwhelmingly to remain a part of the USSR in a 1991 referendum, Turkmenistan accepted the inevitable following the unsuccessful coup attempt in Moscow several months later, and on 27 October 1991 the country became independent.

One Man, One Nation

The years since independence have belonged to President Niyazov, authoritarian head of the Democratic Party of Turkmenistan (DPT), the new name judiciously adopted by the old (and in no way altered) CPT.

Niyazov presents himself as the embodiment of Turkmen nationalism – if you don't love Turkmenbashi then how can you love your country? It's a policy not without effect and Niyazov does have some popular appeal, which is unlikely to ever be measured in a fair election. His opinion of the political opposition is simple – he simply denies it exists. All opposition parties are banned, as are opposition newspapers and any newspapers published in Moscow.

Of course there is dissent, especially among the educated, who are frustrated at Turkmenbashi's extravagance, the clannish dealing-out of favours, the glacial pace of economic and political reform, and the airy promises of future prosperity from oil and gas. Niyazov's talk of a 'new Kuwait' rings a little hollow when 70% or more of the population struggle beneath the poverty line, and government employees are paid only sporadically, if at all.

Relations with the Kremlin cooled distinctly after Niyazov declared the country neutral in 1995 and ordered the withdrawal of Russian troops guarding the Iranian and Afghan frontiers. There are mutterings that Russia's powerful oil and gas barons are plotting against plans to export Turkmenistan's energy wealth.

Meanwhile Niyazov has cultivated close cultural and economic links with Turkey (and styles himself as a nation-builder on a par with Kemal Atatürk, the founder of the Turkish republic) to counter the potentially domineering influences of Russia, Uzbekistan and Iran.

GEOGRAPHY

Bounded by the Caspian Sea in the west and the Amu-Darya river to the east, Turkmenistan covers 488,100 sq km and is the second largest of the former Soviet Central Asian republics after Kazakstan. It's also very sparsely populated, one major reason being that four-fifths of the country is waterless desert. The Karakum (Black Sands), one of the largest sand deserts in the world, fills the entire central region of the country with great crescent-shaped sand dunes, scrubby *saxaul* bushes and cracked, baked-clay surfaces, known as *takyr*.

To the south the Karakum is fringed by the Kopet Dag (literally: 'lots of mountains'), a jagged earthquake-prone escarpment forming a formidable 1500km natural border with Iran. Smaller ranges on the north-west edge of the desert mark Turkmenistan's border with Kazakstan. Apart from the Amu-Darya there are precious few watercourses to bring life to this arid region. In prehistoric times the Amu-Darya flowed across the Karakum and into the Caspian near Turkmenbashi, its ancient course still marked by a string of salt pans. The small Tejen and Murgab rivers run off the eastern end of the Kopet Dag but barely make it down from the mountains before they're swallowed up by desert. The Soviet answer was the ambitious Karakum canal, but even so, less than 3% of Turkmenistan's land is irrigated.

The most densely populated areas are the valleys of the Amu-Darya and Murgab rivers, the partitioned chunk of the ancient former state of Khorezm around Dashoguz, and the necklace of canal-fed oases that form the Akhal chain, strung between Gyzylarbat and Mary.

CLIMATE

Turkmenistan is unsurprisingly characterised by a lack of rainfall, lots of searing sunshine and high temperatures. During summer, daytime temperatures are rarely lower than 35°C, with highs in the south-east Karakum

Turkmenbashi

With his statue on every available pedestal, his face on every banknote, a growing clutch of streets, towns, squares and airports renamed after him and enough public portraits to fill the world's galleries, Saparmurat Niyazov is the focus of a personality cult that makes Lenin look shy and retiring. From the 12m-high golden revolving statue atop a 75m tower in central Ashgabat, to his specially built gold-domed presidential palace, billions of dollars have been spent on nurturing the Niyazov cult and projecting his image as a much-needed strong desert clan leader.

After being re-elected president in October 1992 (99.5% of the votes cast in favour) parliament awarded him the Order of the Hero of the Turkmen People, making him officially Turkmenistan's first hero. The following year he adopted the modest title of Turkmenbashi (Head of all Turkmen) and parliament extended his term in office until 2002 (this time with a less-than-credible claim of 99.9% of all votes in favour), sparing him the bother of constitutionally required five-yearly elections. There are calls for him to become president for life.

When an 820kg meteor landed near Konye-Urgench in 1998 it was named, perhaps predictably, the Turkmenbashi Meteor, and widely believed to be an auspicious sign for the legitimacy of Turkmenbashi's rule. In an attempt to lift the country's international image Niyazov recently commissioned an English-language soap opera about a western businesswoman who visits and falls in love with the country. The title is *Turkmenbashi, My Leader*. In 1999 he sparked a minor crisis when he dyed his hair black and thousands of old silver-haired portraits had to be hurriedly replaced.

desert of up to 50°. In winter daily temperatures average around 0°C to 10°C, falling as low as -15°C. It can snow in Konye-Urgench and Dashoguz.

In the capital, Ashgabat, there are rarely more than a couple of days when it drops below freezing and by April the heat is already uncomfortable.

Humidity is very low and rainfall meagre. Any rain that falls, does so around March, although summer rains occur up in the mountains.

GOVERNMENT

To outside appearances the government of Turkmenistan *is* Saparmurat Niyazov. Since 1990 he has been head of state (president), and since 1992 he has also been head of government (prime minister). In addition to this he is the Chairman of the Democratic Party of Turkmenistan (DPT) – the former Communist Party and the country's only legal political organisation. Despite the egalitarian title of his party, Niyazov is on record as saying he is against 'formal democracy', which he considers would be a burden to the people.

Niyazov's leadership style is shown on televised cabinet meetings. Ministers behave like students in a classroom, and stand up before answering his questions. He once sacked an education minister live on TV, and threw him out with the parting words 'And you'll never get another job either!'

The government has been largely successful in keeping the country's human rights record out of negotiations over oil and gas projects. Government opponents have variously been imprisoned in psychiatric hospitals, sent to forced labour camps, assaulted and kept under surveillance. Their families have found it difficult to find work, as the government is practically the only employer. Members of the 'Ashgabat Eight' who led a 1995 demonstration to protest unpaid wages and the lack of democracy, were released in 1998 after sustained international pressure.

Behind Niyazov is the Turkmen parliament, or Majilis. Elected in December 1994, this is a 50 member version of the 175 member Supreme Soviet of Soviet days. All successful candidates stood unopposed and were DPT members.

For administrative purposes the country is divided into five provinces (Turkmen: *velayaty*) – Akhal, Mary, Lebap, Dashoguz and Balkan. Their five symbols are set vertically on the maroon strip that decorates Turkmenistan's beautiful national flag.

ECONOMY

Turkmenistan was ill-prepared to go it alone after the collapse of the Soviet Union. Decades of dependence on the centralised Soviet market system left it with virtually no manufacturing capability. Since the 1930s it had been developed as a virtual monoculture, with cotton cultivation the backbone of the economy. This was supplemented by natural gas, one of the country's abundant resources. Both cotton and gas were sold raw to Moscow at rouble prices well below world rates. As a virtual colony, Turkmenistan never had any processing facilities.

The centrally controlled economy remains largely unreformed, although agriculture has shifted from growing cotton to producing food to the extent that the cotton harvest has sunk by 75% to 250,000 tonnes per year. Agricultural collectives are now deemed to be self-managing, but farmers still don't own their land.

The country has been mildly successful in attracting foreign investment, mostly in the oil and gas sector, but also in textiles and transport. Visa regulations have helped keep tourism to a minimum. While there is corruption, the government has a reputation for being less obstructionist to foreign businesses than several neighbouring countries.

Although there has recently been a mild economic upturn, this hasn't translated into higher living standards; the rising number of destitute people suggests the opposite. Pensions for some elderly are only sufficient to buy bread, if they are paid at all. Drug abuse is growing among the masses of unemployed young people.

With the withering of the state economy the black market has grown so large that it is really a parallel market. Underground businesses run largely by Turkmen women have mastered the skills of unofficial capitalism, dealing in food, cars, clothing, hard currency, camels, carpets and lots more. Ashgabat's Tolkuchka market gives just a hint of its true scale.

While food prices are now officially determined by the market, the government subsidises the price of petrol and has declared domestic gas, electricity and water free. This has given rise to some peculiar customs; people leave taps running so they don't miss the irregular daily water supply. Some people keep the gas stove burning all day, regarding matches as an unnecessary expense.

The country's long-term economic prospects are promising. Turkmenistan has considerable oil reserves (an estimated 700 million tonnes). Gas reserves are estimated at 13 trillion cubic metres, and only the USA, Canada and Russia are bigger exporters of natural gas.

The major obstacle is getting the gas to paying markets. A small pipeline carrying 2 million cubic metres of gas per year across Iran was finished in 1998, but the only other pipelines run north into the post-Soviet economic black hole. In today's hard currency market Turkmenistan is owed several billion dollars by equally impoverished former Soviet states, debts that are sometimes repaid by barter.

Plans for big new pipelines have come and gone as neighbouring countries and multinational companies bicker over routes and costs. Estimates run from US$2 billion to US$7 billion for the most commonly touted route running under the Caspian Sea, through the Caucasus republics and into Turkey (see the boxed text 'Pipe Dreams' in the Facts about Central Asia chapter), the cost of which is far beyond Turkmenistan's strained financial reserves. If and when a major pipeline is built and hard currency starts rolling in, it then remains to be seen if the elite builds Turkmenistan into a new Kuwait or a new Nigeria.

POPULATION & PEOPLE

The population of Turkmenistan stands at around 4.7 million; since independence the percentage of Turkmen has risen to 82%. The remainder are mainly Uzbeks and Kazaks; the Russian minority has shrunk from 13% to 3% since independence, with most of the remainder living in Ashgabat. Flights to Moscow are often full; return flights are almost empty. The recent introduction of compulsory exit visas for its citizens may be a attempt to stem the emigration tide, or simply another totalitarian policy. The once-alarming population growth rate has collapsed to 1.6% per year since the end of Soviet subsidies for large families.

Turkmen are more likely to live in rural areas, though with the exodus of Russians and other non-Turkmen nationalities a rising number have moved into the cities. Significant numbers of Turkmen have also drifted across the country's borders; some 650,000 live in Afghanistan, where they fled to escape collectivisation in the 1920s, and over one million live in northern Iran.

For more information on the Turkmen, see the special section 'Peoples of the Silk Road' in the Facts about Central Asia chapter.

ARTS

In the pantheon of national icons, second only to the self-proclaimed hero of the Turkmen, Saparmurat Niyazov, is the poet and thinker Feragi Magtumguly (Makhtumkuli) (see the boxed text 'Magtumguly – Bestower of Happiness').

The father of Turkmen literature and poetry, Magtumguly (1770-1840) is regarded by his people almost as a saint, and his words are held in greater reverence than even that of the Quran. The influence of Magtumguly was such that later Turkmen literature became a compendium of copyists. Of those who managed to struggle out

---

Magtumguly – Bestower of Happiness

Turkmenistan's national poet Magtumguly (also spelt Makhtumkhuli) Feraghy is regarded almost as a saint in his homeland. He is believed to have been born in 1733 near Garrygala, and to have died around 1800.

Magtumguly's poetry blends Islamic imagery with Turkmen proverbs. He was the first Turkmen writer to use colloquial expressions instead of the stilted literary language of Chaghatai Turkic, which originated in the 14th century. His poetry is also suited to Turkmen folk music, and today singers and *dutar* (two-stringed guitar) players still put his words to music.

Magtumguly studied at a *medressa* (Islamic college) in the great learning centre of Bukhara, where he mastered classical Arabic, Persian and several Turkic languages. Unfortunately, while he was away studying, his beloved Mengli married another man. His own marriage appears not to have been a happy one, and his two sons died as children.

One of his most famous lyrics, said to have been inspired by losing Mengli, is from his poem 'Nightingale'– 'I'm a nightingale. Here's my sad song/From my garden of roses. Now I've begun/See the tears in my eyes. There they belong/What pleasure in life when loving is done?'

During the increasing inter-clan warfare of the Turkmen during the 18th century, neighbouring rulers launched invasions and on at least one occasion Magtumguly was taken captive. This drove him to write for Turkmen unity; this was the first time a nationalist theme emerged in Turkmen literature.

He tried to negotiate between disputing Turkmen clans, and many folk tales survive about his tragic personal life, his struggle for Turkmen unity, his spiritual journey, even his advice to spurned lovers. The Turkmen revere him up as 'Magtumguly, bagtung guly' – Magtumguly, the bestower of happiness.

So far there are no translations of Magtumguly available in Turkmenistan. The book *Songs from the Steppes of Central Asia*, containing 40 translations of Magtumguly's poems, is available from the Society of Friends of Makhtumkhuli, 152 Lowfield Avenue, Caversham, Reading RG4 6PQ, United Kingdom.

of the shadow of the great scribe, the most noted are the 19th century writers Kemine, whose satirical rhymes castigated the ruling circles, and Mollanepes, the author of popular lyrical poems.

Surprisingly, the Soviet era actually led to a flourishing of the arts in Turkmenistan, though the penalties for not producing work that satisfied, if not flattered the authorities could be considerably worse than just a rejected manuscript. For daring to criticise local officials in her poetry, in 1971 Annasultan Kekilova was locked away in a mental asylum, where she remained until her death a short time later.

Today, much of the arts in Turkmenistan suffer, in common with most post-Soviet republics, from a lack of funding, particularly those areas which formerly enjoyed the support of the Russian community. By contrast, institutions that serve to buoy Turkmen national pride are thriving – the Mollanepes Drama Theatre in Ashgabat draws a full house for most performances, while the new National Museum and Carpet Museum are some of the swishest state-owned buildings in town.

Magtumguly's *qoshuk* lyrics, four-line poems with a distinctive rhyming scheme, are revered classics in Turkmen folk music, and a favourite of *baghsys* folk singers, accompanying themselves on the two-stringed *dutar*. Many Turkmen songs feature the name of the writer in the last stanza, a tradition in oral literature to prevent other poets or lyricists stealing their work.

Facts for the Visitor

WHEN TO GO
Spring and autumn are the best seasons. The Karakum flowers after the spring rains in April or May, and June is pleasantly sunny. Summer (July and August) is hot, damn hot – rarely less than 35°C and as high as 50°C in the south-eastern Karakum around Mary. Turkmenistan is no fun in the summer.

Autumn is the harvest season, when the bazars are overloaded with fresh fruit, and national events such as Melon Day take place.

VISAS & DOCUMENTS
For information about visas, see the Visas section in the Regional Facts for the Visitor chapter. Turkmenistan has bucked the regional trend and made it harder to get visas. They are no longer available at the borders or at Ashgabat airport, unless you are armed with a visa support letter and someone from the sponsoring agency is there to help. Visa checks are very common when travelling. Turkmen visas must list every town where you'll spend a night, plus the entry and exit points from the country, which are:

border town	country
Ashgabat	(airport)
Dashoguz	Uzbekistan
Gaurdan-Badzgiran	Iran
Gushgi	Afghanistan
Konye-Urgench	Uzbekistan
Saraghs	Iran
Turkmenabat	Uzbekistan
Turkmenbashi	Azerbaijan/Russia

Getting a Visa
The travel agencies listed in the Ashgabat section of this chapter can supply visa support letters for around US$35, plus expensive tours aimed more at groups than individual travellers. To issue the visa support letter the travel agency requires the dates of your visit, the name of every town or city which you intend to stay the night, and the entry and exit points to and from the country. Visa support letters take about a fortnight to be organised, at which point you either head to the nearest convenient Turkmenistan embassy (see the following Embassies & Consultants section) to collect the visa, or fly to Ashgabat where you can pick up the visa at the airport.

Niyazov refused to sign the agreement which allows a 72-hour transit if you have a visa for a neighbouring country. *Everyone* must have a visa. With a visa for a neighbouring country (Uzbekistan, Iran, Azerbaijan and Afghanistan), three to five-day transit visas can be obtained from Turkmenistan embassies for US$20-30, depending on which embassy you visit and how they're feeling on the day.

Visa Extensions

Visa extensions require another letter of support from the agency or company that sponsored your visa, who will deal with the formalities. It may also be possible to get a support letter from Turkmensiyahat in Ashgabat if you ask nicely enough. It takes up to five working days for the extension, perhaps less if your visa is about to expire; costs are US$30 for one month, US$20 for 20 days, and US$10 for 10 days.

Permits

Areas requiring permits from the Ministry of Foreign Affairs in Ashgabat include Dekhistan, Kerki, Gushgi and Saraghs, Badkhyz Nature Reserve and Kugitang Nature Reserve. You have a better chance of getting one if you visit the tourist office in the Hotel Ashgabat or Turkmensiyahat first (see the following Ashgabat section in this chapter) and get a letter supporting your application. The area along the Iranian border was fenced off in Soviet times and thus part of the Kopet Dag to Ashgabat route is inaccessible.

EMBASSIES & CONSULATES
Turkmen Embassies & Consulates

The following are embassies unless otherwise stated. For embassies in Central Asia see the relevant country chapters.

Azerbaijan
  (☎ 12-40 99 00, 61 62 03, fax 61 39 69),
  Tariverdiyev 4, Baku – will issue a four to
  seven day transit visa on the spot for US$31
Belarus
  (☎ 172-22 34 27, fax 27 23 39)
  Kirova 17, Minsk 220000
China
  (☎ 10-532 6975)
  Diplomatic Office Bldg 1-15-2, Sanlitun,
  Beijing
France
  (☎ 1-67 55 05 38, fax 47 55 05 68)
  13 rue Picot, Paris F-75116
Germany
  (☎ 228-361150, fax 361190)
  Konstantinstrasse 29A, Bonn D-53179
India
  (☎ 11-611 8054, fax 611 8332)
  1/13 Shanti Niketan, New Delhi 110021

Iran
  (☎ 21-254 2178, fax 258 0432)
  Dr Shariati Ave, 8 Maleka St, Tehran
  Consulate: Mashad
Pakistan
  (☎ 51-278 699, fax 278 799)
  22A F-7/1, Nizam-ud-din Rd, Islamabad
Russia
  (☎ 95-2 91 66 36, fax 2 91 09 35)
  Filippovsky 22, Moscow
Turkey
  (☎ 312-441 7122, 441 7123, fax 441 7125)
  28 Koza Sokak, Cankaya, Ankara
  Consulate: Istanbul
UK
  (☎ 020-7255 1071, fax 7323 9184)
  St Georges House, 14-17 Wells St, London
  W1P 3FP
Ukraine
  (☎ 44-229 3449, fax 229 3034)
  Pushkinskaya 6, Kiev
USA
  (☎ 202-588 1500, fax 588 0697/2207)
  Massachusetts Avenue NW, Washington DC
  20008

Embassies in Turkmenistan

At the time of research, some embassies were not yet in permanent accommodation, so be aware that their addresses are liable to change.

Many foreign representations in Ashgabat are not full-fledged consular offices and are not set up to issue visas. Even when an embassy does issue visas it can be much more complicated and expensive than elsewhere. The British embassy can help citizens of Ireland, the Netherlands and unrepresented Commonwealth countries.

China
  (☎ 51 87 03, fax 51 14 50) Razina
France
  (☎ 51 06 23, fax 51 06 99)
  Hotel Ak-Altyn Plaza
Germany
  (☎ 51 21 44, fax 51 09 23)
  Hotel Ak-Altyn Plaza
India
  (☎ 41 89 23, fax 35 09 44) Nogina
Iran
  (☎ 34 14 52, fax 35 05 65)
  Tehranskaya 3 – will issue transit visas but
  only if proof of onward travel is given, and
  each case is considered individually with no
  guarantees

Kazakstan
(☎ 39 55 48, fax 39 59 32) Gyorogly 14
Kyrgyzstan
(☎ 39 20 64, fax 35 55 06) Gyorogly 14
Pakistan
(☎ 35 00 97, fax 35 09 44) Kemine 92
Russia
(☎ 39 15 05, fax 39 84 66) Turkmenbashi 11
Tajikistan
(☎ 35 56 96, fax 39 31 74) Gyorogly 14
UK
(☎ 58 08 61, fax 58 73 61)
Hotel Ak-Altyn Plaza
USA
(☎ 35 00 45, 51 13 06, fax 51 13 05)
Pushkin 1
Uzbekistan
(☎ 36 23 65, 36 00 06 (visas), fax 36 23 85)
Gyorogly 50A – does not issue visas without
visa support letters

CUSTOMS

Customs officials at Ashgabat airport are notorious, both at arrival and departure. The
noble option is to refuse to pay until they
give up, although they are very persistent
and experts at threatening newcomers with
deportation, bigger fines, etc. For tips on
how to deal with such situations, see the Tipping & Bargaining entry and the Crooked
Officials entry of the Dangers & Annoyances
section, both in the Regional Facts for the
Visitor chapter.

No carpet made prior to 1970 can be exported. Carpets bigger than 6 sq m need to
get a registration certificate from the Ministry of Culture official based at the Carpet
Museum in Ashgabat. Carpets bought at the
Carpet Museum shop are an exception – airport officials only need the receipt. For
carpets bought from private sources the
government takes its pound of flesh. On
balance though, good carpets are still cheap
enough here to be worth the hassle.

Paintings, antiques (pre-1970) and sil-
verwork bought from private sources must
also be assessed for their cultural value.
Take the item to the Ministry of Culture in
Ashgabat (☎/fax 35 35 60) ulitsa Pushkina
14, opposite the US embassy. Here you can
check if you need written permission to take
it out of the country, and if duty has to be
paid at the Customs Office Operations Sec-

tion office. Ministry staff take several days
to pass judgement, but are nowhere near as
ruthless as customs officials.

Once at the airport the customs officials
check luggage carefully. They may well
claim the paperwork is incorrect and try to
'fine' you. Again, patient but steadfast negotiation is the key.

MONEY

The *manat* (M) has been rapidly devaluing
since it was introduced in 1993. At the time
of writing the highest denomination note
was 10,000 M, with notes of 500 M, 1000
M, 2000 M and 5000 M also commonly
used. While the official exchange rate was
5370 M to one US dollar at the time of research, the black market rate of 14,500 M is
the rate quoted by taxi drivers, guides and
restaurants, and so it is the rate used in this
chapter.

country	unit		manat
Azerbaijan	1 M	=	1.35 M
euro	€ 1	=	5550 M
Germany	Dm1	=	2880 M
Iran	1R	=	3 M
Russia	Rbl	=	208 M
USA	US$1	=	5370 M
			(14,500 M)[1]
Uzbekistan	1 *sum*	=	34 M

[1]black market rate

POST & COMMUNICATIONS

A postcard costs 2000 M and a 20g airmail
letter costs 5000 M. The service is slow and
reasonably reliable (parcels excepted).

International telephone rates are US$2 per
minute to Europe, US$2.50 to North Amer-
ica from Ashgabat's post office if you can get
through, and US$8 per minute from luxury
hotels if you can't. The internal telecommunications system is in a poor state.

To make a local call dial ☎ 0 + the city code.
To dial into Turkmenistan from abroad dial ☎ 00
993 + the local code
To dial out of Turkmenistan dial ☎ 8, wait for a
tone, then dial ☎ 10

DANGERS & ANNOYANCES

The complex visa rules serve as a warning that Turkmenistan excels in paperwork and officials. Ashgabat is a happy exception; police in the capital rarely if ever bother foreigners unless they pounce on an illegal currency exchange deal.

Travelling outside the capital leads to frequent encounters with officials checking passports, both on trains and at road checkpoints. Tour groups are largely immune from impromptu passport checks.

Border guards also have a well-earned reputation for angling for bribes, especially if you try driving across a border. You must fill out two copies of the customs declaration, and keep one copy for when you depart.

FOOD

Surprisingly for a country that is mostly desert, some of the more interesting Turkmen dishes are vegetarian. Herb-filled pastries are common in the markets. Cornmeal pancakes and breads are a change of pace from Turkmen *chorek* or flat-bread. Porridges made with either mung beans *(mash-ishulye)*; cornmeal and pumpkin; or rice, milk and katyk, can make a decent meal. Spinach or pumpkin pie, called *kutab*, is a decent snack. The Turkmen make a tasty meatless plov with dried fruit.

Meat dishes tend to be big on fat. *Gouk* is a round flat bread with mutton fat, *kuurma* is lamb cooked in its own fat, and the local *shashlyk* and *lyulya kebab* (seasoned minced lamb) literally drip with the stuff. Peace Corps volunteers tell horror stories of dinners of fat soup followed by fatty camel intestine.

A delightful alternative is fresh fish from the Caspian Sea – the smoked sturgeon is delicious.

ORIENTATION

Since independence, Krasnovodsk has become Turkmenbashi, Charjou has changed to Turkmenabat, Nebit Dag has been renamed Balkanabat and Tashauz has gone through a couple of names to become Dashoguz (travellers from Uzbekistan may see Uzbek variants including Toshhovuz, Toshauz and Tashavuz as well). As part of the same promotion of national identity, Turkmen versions of place names (in a new Turkmen Roman alphabet with Turkish modifications are being popularised at the expense of Russian. During the 20th century Turkmen has changed from Arabic to Roman script, then to Cyrillic, and finally back to modified Roman script. In most cases the differences are minor – Turkmen 'Tejen' instead of Russian 'Tedzhen', Turkmen 'Saraghs' instead of Russian 'Sarakhs', Turkmen 'Garrygala' instead of 'Kara-Kala'.

The authorities have made a start on replacing Russian Cyrillic street signs with new ones in Turkmen Roman, or in some cases Turkmen Cyrillic too. Most streets are still known by their old names.

Ashgabat

☎ 12 • pop 550,000

Ashgabat is a small, tree-lined, quietly poor city, home to the country's biggest Russian community. Turkmenistan's out-of-sight-out-of-mind distance from Moscow, and its proximity to less-than-progressive Iran and Afghanistan, has led to a languorous sort of existence.

It might not live up to the seductive imagery of its name (the city of love, from the Arabic *ashk* – to love), but Ashgabat's unexpected emergence as a capital city has brought a few cosmopolitan graces. The backdrop of the rugged Kopet Dag escarpment changes with the seasons: dusted with snow in winter, raw and parched in summer.

Niyazov's flamboyant buildings are a mix of western and eastern styles on a grandiose Soviet scale. The Arch of Neutrality, the Palace of Turkmenbashi and the National Museum next to the bizarre hotel strip in Berzengi have sprung up in just a few years; upcoming extravagances include the world's biggest fountain. Many government buildings have been given facelifts, some more than once.

From Ashgabat there are easy excursions to hidden mountain valleys, archaeological sites, the national horse stud and, most

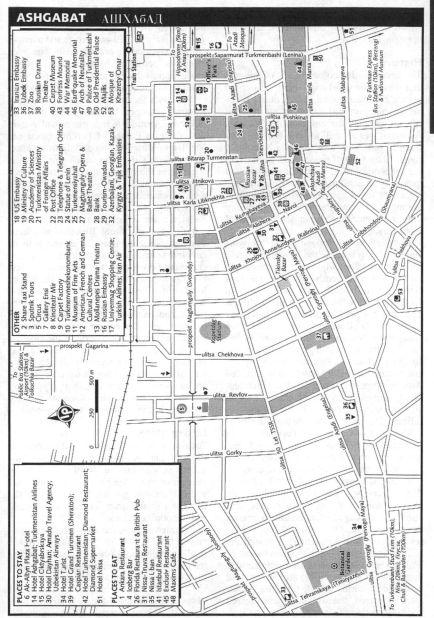

ASHGABAT АШХАБАД

PLACES TO STAY
6 Ak-Altyn Plaza I-otel
14 Hotel Ashgabat; Turkmenistan Airlines
15 Hotel Oktyabrskaya
30 Hotel Dayhan; Amado Travel Agency; Uzbekistan Airways
34 Hotel T urist
39 Hotel Grand Turcmen (Sheraton);
Caspian Restaurant
42 Hotel Turkmenistan; Diamond Restaurant;
Diamond Supermarket
51 Hotel Nissa

PLACES TO EAT
1 Ankara Restaurant
4 Iceberg Bar
26 Florida Restaurant & British Pub
31 Nissa-Truva Restaurant
35 Nissa L'Dan
41 Istanbul Restaurant
45 Exclusiv Restaurant
48 Maxims Café

OTHER
2 Share Taxi Stand
3 Sputnik Tours
5 Circus
7 Gallery Ensi
8 Kinoteatr Mir
9 Carpet Factory
10 Museum of Fine Arts
11 Turkmenvneshekonombank
12 American, French and German
Cultural Centres
13 Mollanepes Drama Theatre
16 Russian Embassy
17 Univermag Shopping Centre;
Turkish Airlines; Iran Air

18 US Embassy
19 Ministry of Culture
20 Academy of Sciences
21 Turkmenistan Ministry
of Foreign Affairs
22 Post Office
23 Telephone & Telegraph Office
24 Statue of Lenin
25 Turkmensiyahat
27 Magtumguly Opera &
Ballet Theatre
28 Bank
29 Tourism-Owadan
32 Azerbaijani, Georgian, Kazak,
Kyrgyz & Tajik Embassies

33 Iranian Embassy
36 Uzbek Embassy
37 Zoo
38 Russian Drama
Theatre
40 Carpet Museum
43 Fortress Mound
44 War Memorial
46 Earthquake Memorial
47 Arch of Neutrality
50 Palace of Turkmenbashi
50 Old Presidential Palace
52 Majlis
53 Mosque of
Khezrety Omar

TURKMENISTAN

famously, the colourful Tolkuchka bazar, which is at its best on Sundays, but also open on Thursdays.

History

The first recorded comment on Ashgabat is that they made good wine there, written on a Parthian-era (around 2nd century BCE; before common era) tablet noting a gift of several casks to the emperor. At that time Ashgabat was a small town within the Parthian empire, whose capital was Nisa (now ruins, 10km west of the modern capital). In the 1st century BCE Ashgabat was reduced to dust by an earthquake, but thanks to trade with Silk Road merchants travelling over the mountains into Persia it was gradually rebuilt, prospering again under the name of Konjikala.

Konjikala was destroyed by the Mongols and the region became the prowling ground for Turkmen tribes who never had much use for towns. Consequently, when the Russians arrived in 1881, fresh from their victory at Geok-Tepe, they found only a small village. The major Trans-Caspian town had been Merv, but the Russians chose to develop Ashgabat as a regional centre, possibly because of its more strategic location on the fringes of British-dominated Persia. By the end of the 19th century Ashgabat was graced with European shops and hotels, an architecturally impressive train station and a bicycle club that held glittering balls for the Russian officers. The city was even on the itinerary of a Thomas Cook tour. The population was overwhelmingly Russian, with some Armenians, Persians and Jews, even today Ashgabat has a large non-Turkmen population.

At around 1 am on 6 October 1948, the city that had become so popular with 19th century tourists vanished in less than a minute, levelled by an earthquake that measured nine on the Richter scale. Over 110,000 people died (two-thirds of the population), although the official figure was 14,000; this was the era of Stalin, when Socialist countries didn't suffer disasters. For five years the area was closed to outsiders during which time the bodies were recovered, the wreckage was cleared and construction of a new city was begun.

Orientation

Replanned after the quake, Ashgabat is a grid of precisely laid-out streets and avenues with barely a curve among them. The main artery is prospekt Magtumguly. Second most important is prospekt Saparmurat Turkmenbashi, running roughly north-south.

The city's focus is the 75m-high Arch of Neutrality topped by the gilded statue of Niyazov. Around it lies ploshchad Azadi, with the new Palace of Turkmenbashi and Majilis buildings facing an adjoining plaza on its south side. One block north of the square lies the busiest street, ulitsa Gyorogly/Shevchenko, with the Grand Turkmen and Turkmenistan hotels, several restaurants and the Carpet Museum on it. The Russian bazar is just north of this street.

Prospekt Saparmurat Turkmenbashi leads from the train station past the university to the new Independence Park. Near the site of the enormous new fountain in the park, the New Powrize highway leads west past the wacky hotel strip of Berzengi. The highway is Niyazov's own route between his city and country palaces, and is closed for an hour each day in the morning and evenings while he's in transit. The airport is 10km north of the city.

A fairly detailed colour map of the city is on sale in souvenir shops in the Ak-Altyn and Grand Turkmen hotels for US$4. Maps are hard to find elsewhere, though you may see some on sale in kiosks around the city centre or in the vicinity of the university.

Information

Tourist Offices The information desk at the airport is usually closed. The Hotel Ashgabat's service bureau (☎ 39 00 26) on the third floor has some English-speaking staff and can arrange guides, trips around Ashgabat and air and train tickets for reasonable and negotiable prices.

Turkmensiyahat, the state tourism corporation (☎ 35 57 77, 39 86 91, fax 39 67 40) at ulitsa Pushkina 17 has English-speaking staff who can help with permits to places such as Garrygala and Dekhistan.

Visas The Turkmenistan Ministry of Foreign Affairs is at prospekt Magtumguly 83, with the immigration and visa department through a separate door just to the left of the main entrance. It's open for visa extensions and inquiries Monday, Thursday and Friday between 9 am and 1 pm.

Money The most convenient place to change money at the official rate is the bureau in the Hotel Ashgabat, theoretically open seven days a week until 8 pm.

Black marketeers urgently whisper 'Dollar? Dollar?' in the Univermag shopping centre and outside the Florida restaurant, but if you are going to do it, don't change money openly on the street. It is illegal after all. It's best to inquire in private; nontourist oriented businesses offer the best rates. Restaurants such as the Nissa-Truva, Diamond and the British Pub at the Florida accept payment in US dollars and give change in manat at slightly less than the bazar rate.

Visa cards and Visa travellers cheques can be converted into US dollars for a 5% commission at the catchily named Turkmenvneshekonombank (☎ 229 78 69), ulitsa Jitnikov 22, the modern green and white building next to Mollanepes Park.

The Western Union money transfer agent is the Rossiysky Kredit Bank, prospekt Magtumguly 73.

Post & Communications The main post office is at ulitsa 50 Let TSSR 16. It's open weekdays, 8 am to noon and 1 to 7 pm, closing on Saturday at 5 pm and Sunday at noon.

The central telephone and telegraph office (Russian: *peregovorny punkt*, Turkmen: *gepleshik punkty*), 100m south of the post office at ulitsa Karla Libknekhta 33, is open daily from 8 am to 7 pm. Fax (US$3 per page) and telegram services are available in the same building, through the door marked 'exchange'.

International calls can also be placed from the reception of the Hotel Ashgabat but they cost more. Phone calls from luxury hotels cost US$8 per minute to Europe, and faxes US$12 per page! With luck and patience you might be able to get through at the main post office, where calls cost US$2 a minute to Europe and US$2.50 to North America.

Travel Agencies Agencies worth contacting include:

Amado
   (☎ 39 73 68, fax 51 04 12, 51 11 76,
   @ amado@online.com)
   Hotel Dayhan, ulitsa Azadi 60 – guides, excursions around Ashgabat, camel tours, air tickets, Uzbekistan visa support contacts, agents for Uzbekistan Airways
Ayan
   (☎ 35 29 14, 35 07 97, fax 39 33 55,
   @ ayan@cat.glasnet.ru)
   prospekt Magtumguly 14 – visa support, package tours, camel and horse treks
DN Tours
   (☎ 47 92 17, fax 47 01 21, 51 16 60,
   @ dntour@cat.glasnet.ru)
   prospekt Magtumguly 18/1, 74400 – guides, package tours, horse and camel tours, Uzbekistan visa support contacts; Web site www .wildox.com/dntour
Latif
   (☎ 41 40 87, fax 41 90 39, 41 50 77,
   @ latif@cat.glasnet.ru)
   Khoudaiberdiev 36A, Ashgabat 74400 – package tours, guides, air tickets, Uzbekistan visa support contacts; they have a Web site www .turkmenistan-travel.com
Tourism-Owadan
   (☎ 39 18 25, fax 35 48 60,
   @ trowadan@cat.glasnet.ru)
   ulitsa Azadi 65, Ashgabat 744000 – air tickets, guides
Sputnik Travel
   (☎ 25 12 79, fax 29 89 65)
   ulitsa Kemine 162 – specialises in hiking trips, mostly on or around the lower slopes of the Kopet Dag, also hang-gliding and camel treks

Cultural Centres The American Cultural Centre (☎ 39 90 66) is on the 2nd floor of the old Pioneer building diagonally opposite the US embassy on prospekt Magtumguly. There are email facilities here, and it's a good place to meet local students learning English. The German (☎ 39 80 89) and French (☎ 39 90 87) cultural centres are in the same building.

Emergency & Medical Services Medical facilities are seriously underfunded. Doctors can be contacted through embassies or luxury hotels. Hotels and embassies can also arrange to transport you to a hospital. A new

Turkish clinic was said to be opening. For an ambulance call ☎ 03, police ☎ 02.

Things to See

In the middle of ploshchad Azadi stands the 75m-high **Arch of Neutrality** (or, more jokingly, 'the Tower of Power'). The 12m golden statue of Niyazov positioned at its zenith revolves daily, his arm raised to summon the sun in the east and farewell it in the west. The three-legged base was chosen by Niyazov himself to represent the stability of the Turkmen cooking pot tripod. Glass booths creep up two of the legs to a reasonably priced cafe-bar, from where there is an elevator to the viewing platforms. Tickets cost a small amount in manat.

At the foot of the monument is the **Earthquake Memorial**, with a display of once-forbidden photographs of the 1948 catastrophe that levelled the city.

South of the Neutrality Monument on an adjoining square is **the Palace of Turkmenbashi**, made of white marble and gold mirrored glass, mixing classical columns with a dome adorned by Islamic motifs. The nearby **Majilis**, or parliament building, is in a similar style on a similarly monumental scale.

The plaza to the east of the Neutrality Monument is the scene of national festivities such as Independence Day, Sorrow Day, Carpet Day and everybody's favourite, Melon Day. At the eastern end is the **War Memorial**, with the **old presidential palace** (still adorned with Soviet emblems) next to it.

The statue of Lenin in the park south of ulitsa Azadi is one of the few structures to have survived the 1948 earthquake and the only one of a supposed 56 Lenin monuments in the city to have survived the collapse of Communism. A wonderful mix of Soviet iconoclasm and mock Turkmen nationalism, the statue stands on a large tiered plinth decoratively tiled with traditional carpet patterns.

South through the park and across ulitsa Shevchenko is a large earthen mound, considered by archaeologists to be the site of the original **fortress** of Ashgabat. Excavations here have unearthed artefacts dating from the Parthian era (around the 2nd century BCE).

The most pleasant of the city's green spaces is the **Officer's Park** on the corner of Magtumguly and Turkmenbashi.

More a statement of foreign-policy leanings than a sign of religious awakening, the **Azadi mosque** stands just south of prospekt Magtumguly, 600m east of the junction with Turkmenbashi. Similar in appearance to the Blue Mosque in Istanbul, the mosque sees few worshippers because of several accidental deaths during its construction.

The modern **mosque of Khezrety Omar**, off ulitsa Chekhova, is also worth visiting for its wonderfully garish painted ceilings. The angular, futuristic **Iranian mosque**, illuminated with green neon, is on ulitsa Gyorogly on the western outskirts of the city, on the way to Nisa.

North of the city centre, near Tolkuchka bazar (see the following Shopping entry in this section), the Karakum canal feeds a reservoir called **Kurtly lake.** Locals like to bathe here and lie on the sandy shores, but it's not particularly clean.

Museums

The **National Museum of Turkmenistan** stands alone on a grassy hillside on the New Powrize highway in Berzengi. The lavish Ancient History Hall includes neolithic tools from western Turkmenistan and relics from the Bronze Age Margiana civilisation (see the Margiana entry of the Eastern Turkmenistan section later in this chapter), including beautiful amulets, seals, cups and cult paraphernalia. There is also a model of the walled settlement uncovered at Gonurdepe. The Antiquity Hall has the amazing *rhytons*, horn-shaped vessels of intricately carved ivory used for Zoroastrian rituals and official occasions.

The Middle Ages hall has several Buddha images from Merv, but mostly displays objects from the early Islamic era. Other sections of the museum are the Nature Hall (stuffed animals) and the Ethnography Hall, which holds a huge collection of Turkmen weapons, wedding outfits, jewellery, old Qurans and carpets. The museum is open daily except Tuesday from 10 am to 6 pm. Admission is a steep US$10.

The **Museum of Fine Arts** at prospekt Magtumguly 84, has some great Soviet-Turkmen painting: happy peasant scenes where at least one stereotyped-Turkmen has a chest adorned with Order of Lenin medals, and lurking beyond the yurts and tethered horses is a productively smoking chimney. There is also a collection of Russian and western European paintings, including one by Caravaggio, and a fine selection of Turkmen jewellery and traditional costumes. The museum is open from 10 am to 6 pm Wednesday to Monday.

The **Carpet Museum** *(muzey kovra)*, at the junction of ulitsa Shevchenko and ulitsa Karla Libknekhta, has a pristine marbled foyer and a fleet of young, traditionally dressed women to lead tours (in Russian and Turkmen only) along its air-conditioned corridors. While there's a limit to the number of rugs the average visitor can stand, the central exhibit, the world's second-largest hand-woven rug, really is something to see. The biggest hand-woven rug in the world is in one of Niyazov's palaces. The museum, is open weekdays only, from 10 am to 1 pm and 2 to 6 pm. Admission is US$3. A museum store, open only on request, sells carpet bags, *telpek* hats, bright scarves and other small handicrafts.

More carpets and traditional handicrafts, plus some items not to be seen elsewhere, like patterned carpet saddles for motorbikes, are at **Gallery Ensi** (☎ 24 19 25), a private collection maintained by husband and wife Bairam Kovus and Leyli Haidova. There's no charge, but you can leave a dollar in the box by the door. The gallery is at ulitsa Reutov 8, two minutes walk from the Ak-Altyn Plaza Hotel.

Places to Stay – Budget

There are no official home-stays in the city (or the country, for that matter); you could try asking students at the American Center on ulitsa Magtumguly about unofficial ones.

One unusual budget option is actually the *dormitory* of a psychiatric institute (☎ 39 36 72) – ask for Mikhail. The institute has several surplus rooms and rents out beds for US$5 a night. The rooms (with air-con) are clean and guests have the use of a well-maintained bathroom, toilet and kitchen. The patients are not dangerous. Other guests include Iranian and Afghan merchants. The institute is at ulitsa Gobshoodova 106, about 1.5km south of Tikinsky bazar.

A little out of the centre is the *Hotel Turist* (☎ 24 41 19, 24 40 17, ulitsa Gyorogly 60). It's a six-storey Soviet-era block where some guests indulge in drinking sessions at all hours, but the staff are friendly. The rooms are quite clean but the bathrooms are in varying states of disrepair. Those facing south have good views of the Kopet Dag mountains. Singles/doubles cost from US$3 /6 in manat. The Turist is a 45-minute walk from the train station, or take trolleybus No 6 south from the junction of Turkmenbashi and Magtumguly.

Hotel Dayhan (☎ 25 30 78, 25 56 72, ulitsa Azadi 60) has a much better location close to the city centre. Clean air-con doubles with balconies cost US$12 in manat. Peace Corps volunteers often stay here.

Hotel Ashgabat (☎ 39 04 47, fax 51 23 80, ulitsa Magtumguly 74) also gets good reports from Peace Corps volunteers, which might indicate what they normally have to deal with. It's a typical Soviet place on a slightly grander scale, with a range of rooms costing from US$10/13 in manat.

Hotel Oktyabrskaya (☎ 25 65 28), the colonial-looking white building on the corner of prospekt Saparmurat Turkmenbashi and prospekt Magtumguly, gets very mixed reports. Some of the rooms are OK, others are filthy, and a few of the staff have reputations for unprecedented rudeness. The less crappy rooms cost US$5/8 in manat.

Places to Stay – Mid Range

Hotel Turkmenistan (☎ 35 06 30, fax 35 09 55), a large classically styled building on ulitsa Shevchenko, has a great location in the city centre and is good value. Air-con rooms with satellite TV, comfy beds and decent bathrooms cost US$40/50.

Lovers of the bizarre will appreciate Berzengi, Turkmenistan's Las Vegas. 10km south of the city, rising up out if the desert like a mirage, is a strip of more than twenty postmodernist hotels (one looks like a spaceship, the facade of another is decorated with a carpet design, a third resembles a sheikh's palace) all oozing money and almost all empty. Stranger still, despite their great size none has more than 20 rooms. They're actually government guesthouses built in anticipation of the rush of official visitors to be attracted by gushing oil pipelines. Two mid-range options are the *Hotel Rahat* (☎ *52 02 05)*, with rooms for US$50/60, and the *Hotel Akhal* (☎ *52 00 45)*, with rooms for US$50/70 and an Italian restaurant. Prices are negotiable for longer stays.

Places to Stay – Top End

Hotel Grand Turkmen (☎ *51 20 50, fax 51 20 49)* has recently been bought by the Sheraton chain, and so may have a new name. It's the modernist orange pile on ulitsa Gyorogly. Its facilities make it the best in town, with tennis courts, a swimming pool, souvenir shops, several restaurants, sauna, casino and gym. The walk-in rates are US$175/250.

The *Ak-Altyn Plaza Hotel* (☎ *51 21 81, fax 51 21 77, 51 21 79)* is just south of prospekt Magtumguly, near the circus. A five-storey slab of orange panels and copper-tinted glass, the Ak-Altyn has 137 air-conditioned rooms with a health centre, pool, tennis courts, a casino and other amenities. Singles/doubles are US$125/200; credit cards are accepted.

The *Hotel Nissa* (☎ *41 69 82, fax 41 95 51)* has similar facilities, yet is conspicuously cheaper; it could have something to do with being owned by one of Niyazov's sons. The hotel is on ulitsa Atabaeva, near the junction with prospekt Saparmurat Turkmenbashi, and has a swimming pool, the best Italian restaurant in town, a fitness centre and a nightclub. Doubles cost US$100.

In Berzengi *Hotel Independent* (☎ *52 00 02, fax 52 00 01)* has rooms for US$100/140 and suites for US$200, and the *Gara Altin* (☎ *51 01 72, fax 51 01 75)* charges US$100/125 for a standard room. Both offer full business facilities and accept Visa, Euro-Card and MasterCard.

Places to Eat

Cafes & Snacks The cheapest places to buy food are the *Tikinsky* and *Russian* bazars, both on ulitsa Azadi. They also have a couple of cheap plov eateries. Shashlyk stalls also appear in the evening in the park between the earthquake and war memorials (the atmosphere is surprisingly jolly).

McDonald's has yet to arrive but the nearest equivalent is the *Florida*, with reasonable hamburgers for US$1.50 in manat, as well as various types of Turkish kebab for similar prices. It's open from 11 am to 11 pm.

Anyone staying in the Hotel Turist will benefit from the outdoor cafes and kebab stalls that line ulitsa Gyorogly between the hotel and ulitsa Chekhova. There is also a basic restaurant inside the hotel.

A slightly pricier option is *Maxims Café*, an airy glass-walled structure in the park behind the Grand Turkmen hotel. You can sit outside under an umbrella and relax over coffee and pastries.

Restaurants The *Nissa-Truva* (☎ *39 16 28)* on the corner of ulitsa Gyorogly and ulitsa Alishera Navoi does Turkish and western dishes (including the best pizza in town), attracting an interesting crowd of regulars. Dinner costs between US$3 and US$5 per person in manat, not including imported beers and spirits. A trio of musicians led by an excellent violinist plays every night. It has air-con and is open daily from 8.30 am to midnight.

The *Exclusiv* (☎ *48 23 45)* is that rare beast, an Iranian restaurant/nightclub with alcohol and dancing girls. It is in the oddtriangular-roofed concrete bunker near the Earthquake Memorial. Dinner comes to about US$4 per person for excellent Iranian fare.

Also recommended is the *Ankara* (☎ *24 97 98)*, a Turkish-run restaurant on the north edge of town at prospekt Gagarina 11. The menu is confined to kebabs (spicy, lamb, kofta etc) served with salad and rice for US$2, but the side orders include some excellent spicy dips. A decent meal for two comes to around US$6. The Ankara is open 11 am to midnight. To get there it's about US$0.20 in manat in a taxi from the city centre, or two stops north on Chekhova from the prospekt Magtumguly bus stop.

The *Diamond* restaurant in the Hotel Turkmenistan building has a more Russian-oriented menu, including smoked sturgeon from the Caspian. The decor is impressively ornate. Without drinks the bill is about US$8 per person.

Between the Kino nightclub and the Carpet Museum on Gyorogly, is the *Istanbul Restaurant*. The service can be a bit indifferent and it's a little overpriced at between US$10 and US$20 for dinner.

The courtyard of the *Florida* complex on ulitsa Shevchenko is a popular meeting place for expats. The food is basically pub grub – steaks, fish & chips and pasta. Main courses cost around US$10. Upstairs is the startlingly grand Florida restaurant. The dishes on the extensive international menu are all around US$20 with soups and salads at US$3 to US$4. Visa, EuroCard and MasterCard are accepted for bills over US$50. Both the courtyard and the restaurant have a half-price 'happy hour' between noon and 2 pm and 6 and 7 pm.

Hotels such as the Grand Turkmen, Ak-Altyn and Nissa have international standard upmarket restaurants. The Italian *restaurant* at the Nissa is good value at US$15 per head; the Grand Turkmen's *Caspian Restaurant* with European cuisine is probably the best in town; dinner costs US$40 per person. The Grand Turkmen also hosts popular weekend afternoon barbecues around the swimming pool US$8. In addition, all these hotels also have buffet lunches for around US$8.

Entertainment

The Turkmen, or *Mollanepes Drama Theatre* at prospekt Magtumguly 76 and the *Magtumguly Opera & Ballet Theatre* on Azadi just west of the Russian bazar are the representatives of high culture in Ashgabat. Many plays at the Mollanepes are of Turkmen origin, some of them extremely colourful affairs featuring traditional music. With tickets at just US$0.30 in manat it's worth a gamble. The Magtumguly theatre season runs from October to the end of June, with performances at 6pm from Thursday to Sunday.

Ashgabat's nightlife isn't exactly Ibiza, but it can be fun. Freelance prostitution is very common, though. The *disco* underneath the circus on prospekt Magtumguly, across the road from the Ak-Altyn Plaza Hotel, is popular with local couples and relatively tame.

The courtyard of the Florida complex, on ulitsa Shevchenko, has a floorshow every night, and a theme night on Saturday. It is popular with expats and wealthier locals. Also at the Florida is the *British Pub*, with antique fittings and pictures of John Bull. A pint of Efes beer costs US$4.

The *Iceberg* bar, on ulitsa Kemine, is the country's only microbrewery, though supplies tend to run out early in the evening. In such cases the nearby kiosks do a roaring trade in cans of beer. There are trestle tables outside under the trees, and there's shashlyk if you feel the need for fatty snacks. It's on ulitsa Kemine close to the Circus.

Hippodrome The hippodrome itself, built in the 1980s, is nothing to see, but Turkmen are celebrated riders so the horse races here ought to be a spectacle. Races are held every Sunday from 21 March until May, and from late August until mid-November. Anyone more interested in riding than spectating can get a spell in the saddle by turning up in the morning and making a deal with one of the stable boys. The hippodrome is 5km east of the city centre; take bus No 4 along prospekt Magtumguly; a taxi journey should cost the equivalent of about US$0.50.

Shopping

See the Customs section earlier for details on taking goods out of the country.

Souvenirs include carpets, embroidered silk, slippers embroidered with silk, ceramics, Turkmen tea sets, headscarves and bright woolly socks. Tolkuchka bazar has all of these, but there are also handicrafts on sale at the Russian bazar on ulitsa Azadi.

The shop attached to the Carpet Museum sells carpets, telpek hats, felt rugs and other textiles.

Carpets are still produced in the villages of Turkmenistan, woven by family groups of women who carry the complex patterns in their heads. More commonly now, since the advent of the Soviet era, carpet-making has entered the machine age. The foreign dealers who prowl Ashgabat's Tolkuchka market (*the* premiere carpet showplace) dismissively pass over the factory pieces that tend to be uninspired and coloured with synthetic dyes that are prone to fading. The carpets with an angular Lenin image are absolute masterpieces of kitsch. See also the 'Bukhara' Rugs colour section in this chapter.

There are a couple of souvenir shops in the small arcade beneath the Arch of Neutrality that sell telpeks, T-shirts and little hand-painted wooden camels and handmade dolls dressed in traditional Turkmen garb.

The Magtumguly theatre on ulitsa Azadi, near the Russian bazar, has a gallery for local artists, and also sells jewellery, sculpture, clothes and carpets in the theatre shop.

The Diamond Supermarket in the Hotel Turkmenistan building is an oversized convenience store with erratic supplies of mostly imported food, toiletries and household goods. When word gets around the expat community of a sudden abundance of snow peas or pasta sauces for example, a stampede invariably follows.

Tolkuchka Bazar Tolkuchka (from the Russian *tolkat*, to push), with its teeming cast of colourful thousands, is a Central Asian bazar as staged by Cecil B De Mille. It sprawls across acres of desert on the outskirts of town, with corrals of camels and goats, avenues of red-clothed women squatting before silver jewellery, and villages of trucks from which garrulous Uzbeks hawk everything from pistachios to car parts. Whatever you want, it's sold at Tolkuchka. Expect to haggle. The wily old men selling telpeks always pitch an inflated price; if they ask for US$15 they'll probably settle for US$10, although the best telpeks do go for US$15 or more. The women give way less (or offer more honest opening prices). At the time of research, a fair price for a khalat (the attractive red and yellow-striped robe) was roughly US$15, while sequined skull caps and embroidered scarves cost between US$2 and US$3.

Above all, Tolkuchka is the place for carpets. Hundreds are laid out in a large sandy compound or draped over racks and walls. Predominantly deep red, most are the size of a double bed or a bit smaller, and the average price is US$200 to US$300. Haggling might shave off US$50.

Tolkuchka is in full swing every Sunday from around 7 am to 1 pm and, on a slightly smaller scale, on Thursday morning. Watch out for pickpockets. The site is about 8km north of prospekt Magtumguly, past the airport and just beyond the Karakum canal. Tolkuchka buses depart irregularly from Ashgabat bus station on prospekt Gagarina. A taxi should cost US$2 to US$3.

Getting There & Away

Air Turkmenistan Airlines links Ashgabat with Istanbul daily, Abu Dhabi three times a week, Karachi and Mashad in north-eastern Iran twice a week and Delhi and Damascus once a week. Commonwealth of Independent States (CIS) connections include two or three times a day to Moscow, four times a week to Tashkent, three times a week to Almaty and Baku, twice a week to Yerevan and once a week to Orenburg and Samarkand.

Domestic connections include numerous daily flights to Turkmenabat (US$81), Mary (US$56), Dashoguz (US$71) and Turkmenbashi (US$81), with daily flights to Kerki in the far east (US$81), and Balkanabat. The Turkmenistan Airlines booking office (☎ 29 05 73, 29 34 69) is in a bunker under the Hotel Ashgabat on prospekt Magtumguly.

International airlines serving Ashgabat include THY Turkish Airlines, which flies four times a week to/from Istanbul, and Iran Air, which flies every Tuesday to Tehran. Lufthansa flies to Frankfurt. Iran Air (☎ 51 06 41) and Turkish Airlines (☎ 51 06 66, 51 16 66) are both on the ground floor of the Univermag shopping complex on prospekt Magtumguly, opposite the Hotel Ashgabat. Lufthansa's office is located at the airport (☎ 51 06 84).

Bus The Turkish-owned Turkmen Express bus company has comfortable modern buses with fans and attendants serving drinks. One bus a day goes to Dashoguz (US$3 in manat, 11 hours) at 10 am, to Turkmenbashi at 11 am (US$3, 8 hours), and there are three buses a day to Turkmenabat (US$2.30, eight hours) via Mary (US$1.50) from 6.30 am to 10 am.

The ticket office (☎ 44 53 12) is on ulitsa Moscowski on the southern outskirts of the city, in the basement of an apartment building just to the right of the modern blue and yellow Corek Zawody building. The buses leave from the depot 100m away across the road. It's best to buy tickets a day in advance.

Public buses are cheaper, slower and more crowded. They leave from the old airport terminal off prospekt Gagarina. A Saraghs bus leaves around midday, which takes five hours. There are also four buses a day to Mary (six hours).

Share Taxis Share taxis and minivans leave when full from the train station forecourt, mostly heading east to Mary (US$3 in manat). Choose your vehicle according to how many passengers are already on board and how old the car is.

Train The following trains depart daily from the train station at the northern end of prospekt Sapurmarat Turkmenbashi. Westward, there's one overnight train to Turkmenbashi (12 hours), plus a slower early morning departure that takes all day. Eastward, two overnight trains depart in the early evening to Turkmenabat (11 to 14 hours), one continuing to Dashoguz. Another Dashoguz-bound train stops here at around 9 am. There's also a daily overnight Ashgabat-Gushgi service via Mary, although Gushgi is off-limits without permits because of its Afghan border location. See the Permits entry in the Facts for the Visitor section at the beginning of this chapter; if you don't speak Russian or Turkmen you'll have to have someone from a travel agency or the info desk at the Hotel Ashgabat with you.

You need to change at Turkmenabat for trains to Bukhara, Samarkand and Tashkent.

At the Ashgabat train station, windows Nos 6 and 7 are for advance booking. Don't forget that you will need your passport to purchase train tickets.

Getting Around
To/From the Airport The modern Saparmurat Turkmenbashi airport is 10km north of prospekt Magtumguly. Taxis should cost no more than US$3, but drivers will probably try for much more.

Public Transport Public buses and trolleybuses are cheap and often crowded. Bus No 13 and trolleybus No 2 run the length of Magtumguly to the Hotel Jubileynaya. Trolleybus No 6 goes down ulitsa Azadi to the Hotel Turist. You pay for your ride by punching a ticket in one of the punches fixed inside the vehicle. Tickets (pilet) are sold at street kiosks beside major stops and cost a minimal amount in manat for 10 tickets.

Just about any private vehicle without passengers can be flagged down as a taxi. Some have checkerboard pieces of cardboard attached to the windscreen. You should agree on the fare before you set off.

Cars and minivans can be hired at the Russian Bazar; about US$4-6 per hour, or US$25 for a day. It helps greatly if you can bargain in Turkmen.

AROUND ASHGABAT
Nisa & Around
Standing a little short of the swelling foothills of the Kopet Dag, 10km west of Ashgabat, is a lone green hillock. On a high grassy plateau at the top is a warren of earthen trenches and pits, like an extensive sand castle, blurred and partly demolished by the incoming tide, as Geoffrey Moorhouse put it in *Apples in the Snow*. It takes some imagination to see it, but these are the sun-baked bones of the royal fortress-city, Nisa, that existed 2300 years ago.

Nisa was founded as the capital of the Parthians, nomads who pushed back Alexander's Greek armies and gained an empire stretching to the Euphrates and to the Indus. In its prime Nisa was reinforced with 43 towers that sheltered the royal palace and a couple of temples. It was surrounded by a thriving commercial city. One ruling dynasty replaced another until the 13th century when the Mongols arrived, laid siege to the city and after 15 days razed it to the ground.

The ridges surrounding the plateau were the fortress walls; the steep modern approach road follows the route of the original entrance. In the northern part of the city are the remains of a large house built around a courtyard, with wine cellars in nearby buildings.

The main complex on the western side includes a large circular chamber thought to have been a Zoroastrian temple. Adjoining it is the partly rebuilt 'tower' building. On the far side of the western wall are the ruins of a medieval town, today the village of Bagyr.

All the finds from Nisa – pottery, tiles, coins, statuettes – have been carried off, some to Ashgabat's National Museum and some to the Hermitage in St Petersburg.

Entry costs US$2 per person. Coming by car from Ashgabat it is possible to take the road past Berzengi along the presidential

hwy. On the way you'll pass the **Palace of Orphans**, another bizarre Niyazov project with massive futuristic marble buildings, sporting facilities and its own mosque. The children in this village are educated to be government officials. Niyazov himself was raised in an orphanage after his mother died.

Although you may not drive to the **Firyusa Palace** in your own vehicle, it is still possible to visit this green valley by taking a public minibus from the Ashgabat bus station for a small amount in manat. Once a popular mountain escape, Firyusa is now the site of Niyazov's vast pink palace. Expect trouble if you're caught taking photos.

Turkmenbashi Stud Farm
The national horse stud is near the village of Bekrewe, about 10km from Ashgabat. By car

THEODOR HERZEN

Turkmen are celebrated riders who once roamed the shifting desert sands on horseback.

you can combine a stop here with a visit to Nisa. Strictly speaking you should arrange a visit through a travel agency, but no-one seems to mind if you just call in. These pure-bred Akhal-Teke horses are lithe, regal creatures, many with a beautiful golden colouring. Some horses are given to foreign leaders by the president.

Anau

Anau is the site of another of Turkmenistan's vanished cities. Inhabited since Neolithic times, it was known as Bagabad to Silk Road travellers. By the 15th century it was a fortified town famous for its mosque, the size and beauty of which rivalled many in Bukhara and Samarkand with its double domes, double minarets and, most strikingly, the tiled mosaic above the main entrance, depicting two sinuous 8m-long dragons facing each other. Bagabad dwindled but the mosque, albeit in a badly reduced state, survived and attracted attention right up until the earthquake of 1948, when it was completely demolished (the 50 manat note has a picture of the mosque before the quake).

Today the mosque is mainly an object of study for archaeologists. The site is still considered holy by locals and a new, smaller mosque has been built with bricks from the old one. Amid the ruins a kiosk-sized **shrine** is also the venue for some very un-Islamic rituals in which, along with their prayers, women offer up torn strips of cloth and items of babies' clothing, dummies and cheap plastic dolls in the hope of conceiving a child.

The modern settlement of Anau – after which the mosque is now named – is 20km east of Ashgabat city centre on the Mary road. A few kilometres after leaving the city limits, bear right at a big green 'Turkmen' hoarding at the centre of a fork in the road. After about 1km there's a dusty track to the left beside some buildings; beyond the buildings turn right then immediately left and the ruins of the mosque are a farther 500m along the road. There's no public transport, so you'll have to take a taxi. The whole round trip should take no more than two hours.

Chuli

This mountain resort offers a cool retreat from Ashgabat. The Turkish-built hotel complex, burdened with the title of *Annaniyazaga International Centre of Mountain Tourism* (☎ 12-31 31 58, fax 31 31 61) has comfortable singles and doubles with bathrooms for US$30/40, and suites from US$55. There's a good restaurant here, and the chance to eat outdoors in the hotel grounds. The 2462m-high Erekdag mountain looms over the establishment to the west, and as this peak is wholly within Turkmenistan it is possible to do some climbing.

There is no public transport so a taxi is the only option; it's a pleasant drive up a winding gorge, passing a portrait of Lenin carved into the rock and several tumbledown *turbaza (holiday) camps*. The shaded Chulinka rivulet is a popular picnic spot with locals. The drive up to the hotel takes about an hour.

Bakharden

Buried 60m underground in the lower slopes of the Kopet Dag mountains is a hot-water mineral lake (known in Turkmen as Kov-Ata or 'Father of Lakes') where you can take a swim in the 36°C waters if you don't mind the rotten egg smell. The lake is at the foot of a steep 250m stairway, descending through a damp and pungent chamber that spotlights struggle to penetrate.

There are changing rooms for swimmers at the water's concreted edge. While the water is supposedly good for your health, it's recommended that you don't stay in for more than 20 minutes.

Plodding back up towards the pinprick of daylight that is the cave mouth, reflect on the locals who, not too long ago, used to lower themselves into the bat-filled blackness on ropes and swim by the light of burning torches. Admission fee costs US$5 for foreigners.

Midway on the main road between Ashgabat and Bakharden is the village of **Geok-Tepe** (Green Hill), site of the Turkmen's last stand against the Russians (see the History section in Facts about Turkmenistan for details). During the Soviet era the uncommemorated site of the breached earthen fortress where 15,000 Turkmen died was part of a collective farm. Today a large futuristic mosque with sky blue domes stands beside the telltale ridges and burrows.

Getting There & Away For the underground lake *(podzemnoe ozero)* take a bus to Bakharden, 100km west of Ashgabat. From the capital the buses run four times a day, taking 2½ hours. Westbound trains out of Ashgabat also stop at Bakharden, but services are infrequent.

From the bus station at Bakharden the lake is 16km back towards Ashgabat along the main M37 Hwy, then 7km south along a dusty minor road. There's usually a taxi lurking at the bus station which will run visitors to the lake for US$2 to US$3.

The last Ashgabat bus from Bakharden leaves at 3 pm. A later bus can be flagged down in Akdepe, nearby, at about 4.30 pm.

Western Turkmenistan & the Caspian

Although the Caspian Sea sparkles turquoise-blue, the flat, pocked, desert shoreline seems to be composed not of sand, but of grey dust frosted with salt. It looks more like NASA footage of the moon than anything else.

Apart from the port of Turkmenbashi, all the Caspian coastal towns are centred around industrial plants and are very missable. **Bekdash**, the farthest settlement north before Kazakstan, is little more than a large salt-refining plant while **Cheleken**, across the bay from Turkmenbashi, is an extremely unhealthy chemical town.

Inland, the provincial capital Balkanabat is a modern oil town of negligible interest. **Gyzylarbat**, some 100km east of that, has a richer history as a 19th century Turkmen fortress but there's now nothing to see there either. The ruins of Dekhistan south of Balkanabat are interesting more for the sense of utter desolation than the surviving monuments. One rare highlight is the mountain village of **Garrygala** (or Kara-Kala), 80km south of Gyzylarbat in the Kopet Dag

range. The scenery is very attractive, with forests and waterfalls. The place used to be favoured by Party bosses as a secluded hideaway. However, sitting only 30km north of the border with Iran, it is only possible to visit with special permission from Turkmensiyahat in Ashgabat.

Some maps show a road running from Turkmenbashi north-east across the Karakum desert to Konye-Urgench and Dashoguz. In reality, this is an unsurfaced track, negotiable only with a truck or 4WD and there is no regular transportation travelling this route.

TURKMENBASHI
☎ 222 • pop 60,000

Though the climate is hot and humid, and very little goes on, Turkmenbashi is attractive in a sleepy Mediterranean sort of way. It sits in a bone-dry hollow enclosed by a crescent of mountains and faces the Caspian Sea. The waters of the Caspian are clean and blue, and a refreshing place for a dip after struggling through the humid coastal microclimate. The mostly ethnic Russian and Azeri population are poor but friendly, and relaxed about dress codes. It's a pleasant place to stay for a day or two. About 10km farther west is the barren resort of Awaza.

The first settlement here was established when a detachment of Russian troops under Prince Alexandr Bekovich set ashore in 1717 with the intention of marching on Khiva. They chose this spot because it was close to the place where the Oxus (now the Amu-Darya) had once drained into the Caspian, and the long-dry river bed provided the best road across the desert. But the mission failed, Bekovich lost his head (see the Khiva entry in the History section of the Uzbekistan chapter) and the Russians didn't come back for over 150 years.

It was 1869 when the next expedition put ashore and built a fortress at Krasnovodsk (Red Water). The fortress became Russia's base of operations in its campaign to break the troublesome khanate of Khiva and subdue the Turkmen tribes, and later became the western railhead of the new Trans-Caspian line, built to consolidate Tsarist gains.

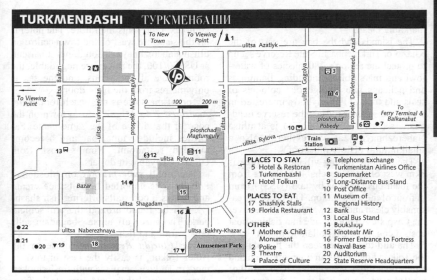

TURKMENBASHI **ТУРКМЕНБАШИ**

PLACES TO STAY		6	Telephone Exchange
5	Hotel & Restoran	7	Turkmenistan Airlines Office
	Turkmenbashi	8	Supermarket
21	Hotel Tolkun	9	Long-Distance Bus Stand
		10	Post Office
PLACES TO EAT		11	Museum of
17	Shashlyk Stalls		Regional History
19	Florida Restaurant	12	Bank
		13	Local Bus Stand
OTHER		14	Bookshop
1	Mother & Child	15	Kinoteatr Mir
	Monument	16	Former Entrance to Fortress
2	Police	18	Naval Base
3	Theatre	20	Auditorium
4	Palace of Culture	22	State Reserve Headquarters

Since then new rail routes have eroded the importance of the Trans-Caspian but Turkmenbashi remains Central Asia's sole port and sea link to European Russia and, via the Volga and Sea of Azov, to the Black Sea and the Mediterranean. These days the main trade is in oil; western Turkmenistan is the site of major reserves and the country's largest refinery is at Turkmenbashi.

Orientation & Information

The hub of the town is ploshchad Pobedy, with the playfully Moorish-style train station on its southern side. Facing the station is the Palace of Culture; on the west side of the square is the post office, and on the east side are the Hotel Turkmenbashi and a small supermarket. Below the hotel is the telephone exchange and next door is the sales office of Turkmenistan Airlines. Long-distance buses depart from outside the train station.

The sparse commercial district is about 500m west of ploshchad Pobedy centred on parallel streets, prospekt Magtumguly and ulitsa Turkmenistan. The bank on prospekt Magtumguly will change money. Ulitsa Naberezhnaya, south-west of the train station, features the Hotel Tolkun, the Florida

restaurant and the Turkmen navy base, whose sailors seem to mostly hang around cadging cigarettes.

The town's water supply is irregular and often limited to an hour in the morning and an hour in the evening.

Things to See & Do

The **Museum of Regional History** is on ulitsa Rylova, a 10 minute walk west of the station, in what used to be the old Russian fort. It is open Monday to Saturday from 9 am to 1 pm and 2 to 6 pm. A block south of the museum, the two things that look like Thunderbird Ones (from the old sixties TV show) topped by red stars mark the former entrance to the **fortress-town**. About 100m on is the gate to the one-time main pier and terminal.

One of the most pleasant things to do is to walk up into the mountains for the beautiful **views** over the town; there's a path behind the mother-and-child monument at the top of ulitsa Garayeva, and a steep but manageable scree-slope route off ulitsa Balkan. The best **beaches** are 50km north of town (there are no buses), but there are places to swim within walking distance if you head west along ulitsa Naberezhnaya. The Caspian around this part of Turkmenbashi seems remarkably clean.

The islands and the bay are part of the Khazar or Turkmenbashi State Reserve set up to protect the region's 280 species of waterfowl and marsh birds, including flamingos and pelicans, plus indigenous colonies of seals and turtles. For anybody interested in seeing the seals or turtles, the reserve headquarters (☎ 7 50 58, 7 42 76) is at ulitsa Naberezhnaya 42a, where there's also a small **natural history museum**.

The scrappy fishing village of **Awaza** is 8km west of town, reachable by buses from the local bus stand or by taxi (US$1) from in front of the train station. The beach is reasonably clean and you watch the sunset over the Caspian. An hour's ride in a fishing boat costs a couple of US dollars in manat.

The **auditorium** between the Florida and the Tolkun hotel hosts an open-air disco and bands on holiday weekends. The handful of local **discos**, such as at the Kinoteatr Mir, on ulitsa Shagadam, are drunken and sleazy.

Places to Stay & Eat

The front wall of the train station, either side of the entrance, serves as a notice board for apartments for rent. A decent place big enough for three or four people with a fridge, TV and functioning bathroom should cost about US$25 for five days. It pays to look around a few flats and bargain vigorously. Awaza has quite a few cheap *turbaza* holiday camps in varying states of disrepair.

The town's cheapest hotel is the all-too-familiar Soviet concrete monster, the *Hotel Turkmenbashi* (☎ 7 46 33) on Pobedy. The large, airy rooms have balconies (nice if you have one facing the square), but antiquated, smelly bathrooms. The fridges, TVs, air-conditioners and light switches mostly either don't work or give a small electric shock when touched. For this you pay US$3/7 for a single/double. The restaurant in the same building is cheap and not great. Try to have the fish instead of the meat dish, then wash it down with vodka, and pretty soon you won't mind the taste.

If the Turkmenbashi represents the past then the small *Hotel Tolkun* (☎ 7 30 59,

fax 7 30 31), also known as the Turkish complex, represents the future. The hotel is on the seashore west of the town centre on ulitsa Naberezhnaya. Though not a bargain at US$70/100, the prices are negotiable, the rooms have all mod-cons, and the sea is only metres from the back door.

Top of the scale is the beachfront *Hotel Awaza* (☎ 7 45 44), 8km from town on the edge of the village of the same name. Facilities include sauna, bar and a recommended restaurant. Rooms cost from US$100, payable in dollars.

The small *supermarket* on ploshchad Pobedy sells imported biscuits, ice cream and drinks. Food stalls offering fish shashlyk can be found around the amusement park. The *bazar* off ulitsa Shagadam sells bread, fruit and fish.

The *Florida Restaurant,* close to the Hotel Tolkun, is easily the best in town, a modern Turkish-run place with fresh smoked sturgeon, tasty kebabs and even steaks for a modest price – around US$4 per person, though this can soon rise if the cold beer tempts. If you pay in dollars they'll give you change in manat at the black market rate.

Getting There & Away

Turkmenistan airlines have flights that go twice daily to Ashgabat (US$81) and three times a week to Dashoguz. The booking office (☎ 7 54 74, 7 58 04) is just off ploshchad Pobedy, below the Hotel Turkmenbashi, open from 8 am to 6 pm. The airport is tucked away in the mountains that encircle the town. To get there, take a taxi for US$1 in manat.

From the stand in front of the train station, a morning public bus goes to Balkanabat (two hours). The Turkmen Express bus to Ashgabat (eight hours) also leaves from here at 11 am, but it's best to buy tickets (US$2 in manat) from the driver an hour or so earlier.

There are two trains a day at 4.30 pm and 7.05 pm, one terminating at Ashgabat (12 hours) and one continuing to Dashoguz via Turkmenabat. A *kupeynyy* (2nd class) berth to Ashgabat is US$4.50; the SV (1st class) closed cabins are comfortable at night, but hell on a hot day and cost US$6.

It's possible to cross the Caspian from Turkmenbashi to Baku, the Azerbaijani capital, by rusty ferry. Schedules are erratic but there's usually one boat every evening making the 14-hour (240km) voyage. Tickets cost US$50 for a chair and US$75 for a cabin; pay for a seat and a crewman will often offer a cabin with shower for US$10. Those arriving in Turkmenbashi this way must have a Turkmen visa already, as immigration is tightly controlled.

The sea terminal and sales office are on the eastern outskirts, just off the Ashgabat highway; you'll need to take a taxi out which will cost about US$2 in manat.

BALKANABAT
☎ 243 • pop 87,000

Less than 60 years old, Balkanabat (formerly Nebit Dag) is a desolate town in an even more desolate desert. Oil was discovered in the vicinity in 1874 and a small refinery was built, only to be abandoned for 50 years after being bankrupted by competition from the Baku oil industry.

Oil aside, there's little to bring anyone here. The main axis is prospekt Magtumguly, running east-west parallel with the railway. At its mid-point is ploshchad Niyazov, watched over by a lonely statue of the president. The train station is 1km west and 400m south of ploshchad Niyazov. Its forecourt also serves as the long-distance bus terminus.

If you speak Russian or Turkmen you might contact the local branch of the Department of Tourism, Balkansiyahat (☎ 2 25 67, 4 91 86) at Kvartel 145, building 2, some 100m south-east of ploshchad Niyazov. They can arrange trips to Garrygala and Dekhistan, and may be able to arrange hiking on the 1880m-high Bolshoi Balkan range north of the town.

Rooms at the *Neftyannik* (☎ 3 09 19), at Kvartel 225, are gloomy but comfortable and have attached showers and toilets. A plus is the hotel's leafy garden. The hotel is 1km north of prospekt Magtumguly, beside the children's hospital best reached by car or taxi. A standard double room is US$6.

The nearby *Hotel Nebitchi* (☎ 4 96 50, fax 4 96 57) couldn't be more different. This luxury hotel features the town's best restaurant and a bar. Rooms cost US$160/220.

The *bazar*, one block south of Niyazov, is the best place to get cheap food.

There are two trains a day to Turkmenbashi (3½ hours), and two to Ashgabat, one of which continues to Turkmenabat and Dashoguz. From the forecourt of the train station there are morning buses to Turkmenbashi and Cheleken, both taking 2½ hours. Balkanabat also has an airfield with daily flights to/from Ashgabat. The Turkmenistan Airlines booking office is in the train station.

DEKHISTAN

The ruined city of Dekhistan (also known as Misrian) lies deep in the barren wastelands south of Balkanabat, midway between the tumbledown villages of Bugdagly and Madau. The surrounding desolation begs the question of how a city came to be here in the first place. Yet in the 11th century it was a silk road oasis city with a sophisticated irrigation system rivalling Merv and Konye-Urgench, and it even managed to revive itself after destruction by the Mongols. It seems that some time in the 15th century the region suffered an ecological catastrophe. The forests of the Kopet Dag to the east had been exploited for centuries until the water supply failed and the well-watered slopes finally became a barren, deeply eroded lunar landscape.

Not much remains on the 200 hectare site apart from a truncated 20m-high **minaret** and two jagged and richly decorated mosque pylons. Tellingly, the buildings are made of baked rather than sun-dried brick, a sign of what use timber was put to.

The **cemetery** 7km north of Dekhistan features five semi-ruined mausoleums, including the Shir-Kabir mosque-mausoleum, the earliest mosque in the country.

Unless you have your own vehicle, Dekhistan is difficult to get to. Public transport is pretty much nonexistent. Balkansiyahat in Balkanabat are quite keen to promote the site in conjunction with a visit to Garrygala, and may be able to arrange transport. Ashgabat travel agencies are another possibility (see Information in the Ashgabat section, earlier).

Eastern Turkmenistan

With savannah-like plains, cave cities and dinosaur footprints, the eastern region is by far the most interesting part of Turkmenistan. Unfortunately, because of its proximity to Afghanistan and Iran, many of the more worthwhile destinations are out of bounds to the casual traveller. Once off the M37 Ashgabat-Turkmenabat highway, checkpoints are frequent and wayward foreigners are held until they can be put on a bus heading out of the 'sensitive' zone.

If you have your heart set on seeing something here, the surest route is through a semi-official channel like one of the Ashgabat tourism firms. Agencies listed in Travel Agencies under Ashgabat can organise visits to the Kugitang and Repetek reserves, or you can entrust yourself to a packaged expedition taking in Badkhyz, Gushgi and the cave city of Ekedeshik, near the village of Tagtabazar.

SARAGHS
☎ 134 • pop approx 6000
As a happening town, Saraghs peaked in the 12th century and it's been downhill ever since. It had its beginnings as an oasis on the upper reaches of the Tejen river, inhabited since perhaps the 4th century BCE. The town benefited from trade brought by the Arab conquest, and grew into a crowded walled city, dominated by a large citadel.

The fortifications proved useless against the Mongols, from whose assaults Saraghs never quite recovered.

The Saraghs of today is a small farming village. The only evidence of former glories is the unimposing 11th century **mausoleum of Abu Fazl**, erected over the grave of a Sufi teacher who died in 1023. It's about 2.5km south of the centre of the village, through a gateway in a long wall, and barely worth the half-hour walk.

The *Saraghs District Hotel* is a small, single storey whitewashed building 100m north of the bus stand. A bed in a twin room is US$3 per person.

There is one bus daily to Ashgabat (six hours), departing at midday, and one to Mary (four hours), departing at 8 am, both via Tejen. There are no buses south to the Badkhyz Nature Reserve or Gushgi, or across into Iran (though with an Iranian visa you can cross into Iran here – the border is 5km away). At the time of research it wasn't possible to cross the border by train.

MARY
☎ 522 • pop 95,000
The second biggest industrial centre in Turkmenistan, Mary (ma-**rih**) has nothing going for it except for the excellent Mary Regional Museum.

Because it is located on one of Turkmenistan's few watercourses, the Murgab river, Mary (as the town was renamed in 1937) developed as a cotton-growing centre. Its continued prominence was assured in 1968 when prospectors discovered huge reserves of gas 20km west of town, at a site since named Shatlik (Joy). Gas or not, the name seems something of a black joke for a place that roasts on a summer day at 45°C and higher.

Right from the start, Mary was destined never to become a tourist hot spot. In 1886, when Mr Boulangier, a visiting Frenchman, complained of his insect-ridden room he was told to consider himself lucky as the week before the town had suffered a plague of scorpions. By comparison, the modern-day visitor – suffering nothing more than over-priced rooms, a lack of anywhere decent to eat, and possibly, overwhelming boredom – has little to complain about.

But Mary is the closest transport hub to the ruins of ancient Merv, and may be an unavoidable part of your itinerary, in which case aim to arrive early and leave on the same day.

Orientation & Information
The modern glass domed bazar on ulitsa Mollanepes, the town's main thoroughfare, running roughly east-west, parallel to the railway line, is about as good as the city gets for landmarks. The seven-storey Hotel Sanjar is also on ulitsa Mollanepes. The adjacent train and bus stations are about 200m north of the Sanjar.

'BUKHARA' CARPETS

Purchased from traders in Samarkand and Bukhara (hence the name), handwoven carpets are valued for their quality, the richness of the natural plant and beetle dyes used (predominantly a deep wine red) and the beautiful simplicity of their geometric designs.

Originally the work of the Turkmen people, it's possible to identify exactly where a carpet was made from the motif (*gul*), as each design is unique to a particular Turkmen clan. For instance, a stylised anchor means that the carpet was woven by members of the Ersari clan from eastern Turkmenistan beside the Caspian Sea.

For the nomadic Turkmen the only piece of furniture worth having was a carpet or three. Easily transportable, the carpets served not just as floor coverings, they lined the walls of the yurt providing a highly decorative form of insulation.

Right & Inset: Brilliant colours and simple designs – Central Asia's carpets are magnificent even as wall hangings.

MARTIN MOOS

ANDREW HUMPHREYS

Top: A large part of Turkmenistan's economy, carpets are highly valuable, being the result of intense work. Often they are the main component of a bride's dowry.
Bottom: A woman proudly displays her rugs for sale, Turkmenistan.

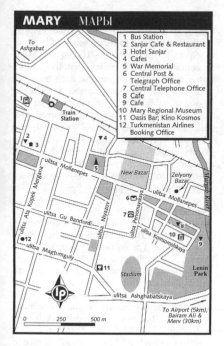

MARY МАРЫ

1 Bus Station
2 Sanjar Cafe & Restaurant
3 Hotel Sanjar
4 Cafes
5 War Memorial
6 Central Post & Telegraph Office
7 Central Telephone Office
8 Cafe
9 Cafe
10 Mary Regional Museum
11 Oasis Bar; Kino Kosmos
12 Turkmenistan Airlines Booking Office

series of deaths and misfortunes among museum staff persuaded them to have the original returned to where it was found. The fine quality and design of household items from Margiana artefacts is striking.

Other displays include an exhibition of Turkmen carpets from the museum's huge collection, an excellent collection of Turkmen household items, wedding and ceremonial clothing, and a fully decorated yurt. Some of the museum staff speak English and give guided tours for a few dollars. If you plan to visit Merv, a recommended guidebook, *Ancient Merv* by Georgina Herrmann and Andrew Petersen, is on sale here for US$4. The museum is in a former merchant's house at ulitsa Komsomolskaya 1, in the park beside the Murgab river. It's closed Monday.

There is also a Sunday morning market, **Tikinsky bazar**, held 4km out of town. Tikinsky is reportedly similar to Ashgabat's Tolkuchka bazar but, so locals claim, with more and cheaper carpets. The simplest way to get there is by taxi, which should cost US$2 at most.

Places to Stay & Eat

Staff at the Regional Museum are happy to arrange *home-stays* for US$10-20 per night including decent home-cooked meals.

The *Hotel Sanjar* (☎ 5 77 03, fax 5 71 44, ulitsa Mollanepes 58) is well located just south of the train and bus stations. The rooms are nondescript but fairly comfortable. Rooms cost US$10/13 in a manat.

Next door to the Sanjar is a cheap *cafe* with basic grub. It's greatest asset is proximity to the hotel; open from 9 am to 7 pm. That's about it for fine dining in Mary, though there is plenty of fresh food at the bazar.

There are a couple of shashlyk stalls in the park by the museum, one of which serves great chunks of rapidly congealing fat thinly marbled with tough meat. Better food can be found at stalls and cafes in the new bazar. There are also some cafes serving plov behind the war memorial.

For nightlife, Peace Corps volunteers recommend the *Oasis Bar* under the Kino Kosmos on ulitsa Magtumguly.

The central post and telegraph office is 1km east of the Sanjar on Mollanepes, while the central telephone office is 50m south of the post office on ulitsa Pervomayskaya. There is a currency-exchange service in the Sanjar, whose foyer seems to have the only working private telephone in town.

Golubeva Yevgeniya (☎ 3 42 14, 9 20 29), the assistant director at the museum, is a hugely knowledgeable English-speaking guide to the ruins of Merv. She charges individuals US$20 and groups of four US$10 each for a three-hour tour, not including travel time to and from Mary. The director of the Hotel Sanjar can also arrange tours; ask at reception for details.

Things to See & Do

The **Mary Regional Museum** shouldn't be missed. The display of artefacts from Merv and Margiana is attractively laid-out and features a large model of Merv. The skeleton of a Margiana priestess is a replica – after a

TURKMENISTAN

Getting There & Away

There are several flights a day to Ashgabat (US$56). The Turkmenistan Airlines booking office (☎ 3 27 77) is at ulitsa Magtumguly 11. The airport is 5km east of town on the Bairam Ali road. Take a Bairam Ali bus and ask for 'aeroport'; or take a taxi, which shouldn't cost more than US$2.

Three trains a day go to Ashgabat, one at 11.30 am goes on to Turkmenbashi, one at 10.30 pm and another at midnight. The trip is six to seven hours, and a kupe berth is less than US$1. There's a Turkmenabat service at 4.30 pm plus one train that halts at Turkmenabat en route to Dashoguz. There's also an overnight train to Gushgi.

Mary is well served by buses, with five a day to Ashgabat (five hours away) and three to Turkmenabat (4½ hours). Two daily buses go to Gushgi (10 hours), two to Saraghs (four hours) and one to Kerki (four hours). Turkmen Express buses leave from the same bus station (US$2 to Ashgabat).

Share taxis leave from the train station forecourt, taking about four hours to Ashgabat (not including delays at police checkpoints) and three hours to Turkmenabat.

BAIRAM ALI

This small, drab settlement, 30km east of Mary, is notable only for the extremely low humidity, which is supposedly good for the kidneys. Tsar Nicholas II had a palace built here but his R&R plans were interrupted by the Bolshevik Revolution of 1917 and his subsequent execution. The palace is now a **sanatorium**, with extensive gardens.

Bairam Ali is also the closest settlement to the ruins of ancient Merv. The ruins of the last and smallest city, the Timurid-era **Abdullah-Khan Kala**, merges with the northern outskirts. The area's biggest market and camel fair is held at the foot of the walls of Abdullah-Khan Kala every Sunday.

Buses shuttle between Mary and Bairam Ali stations every half hour or so.

MERV

Merv, the site of one of Central Asia's once-greatest cities, may be a treasure trove for archaeologists and may have moved travel writers to muse for pages on the life and death of civilisations, but casual visitors will need a guide to make sense of it all.

Spread over more than 100 sq km, Merv is actually the site of no less than five walled cities from different periods, each built beside the last. But don't expect an alfresco museum of ancient architecture. What you will see is a lumpen landscape scarred with ditches and channels, grazed by camels and the odd earthwork mound or a battered sandy-brick structure. Still, Merv does have a certain melancholy attraction, and Sultan Sanjar's mausoleum certainly impresses with its size and solidity.

History

Merv's origins are shrouded in conjecture and romance. It was definitely a Silk Road staging post. The earliest settlements in the Murgab oasis date back to 6,000 BCE, and in the desert on the northern fringes Bronze Age cities are still being excavated. Merv was known as Margiana in Alexander the Great's time. Under the Persian Sassanians it was a melting pot of religious creeds with Christians, Buddhists and Zoroastrians cohabiting peacefully. However, as a centre of power, culture and civilisation, Merv reached its greatest heights in the 11th and 12th centuries when the Seljuq Turks made it their capital and (after Baghdad) the greatest city in the Islamic world. Marv-i-shahjahan, or 'Merv, Queen of the World' as it was then known, may even have been the inspiration for the tales of Scheherazade's *Thousand and One Nights*.

Under Sultan Alp Arslan, Seljuq Merv became the centre of a dominion that stretched from Afghanistan to Egypt, a city rich with palaces and treasuries, libraries and observatories. The Seljuqs dammed the Murgab and dug irrigation ditches to the city's fields, parks and lush gardens.

All of this was completely eradicated in 1221 under the onslaught of the Mongols. In 1218 Jenghiz Khan demanded a substantial tithe of grain from Merv, along with the pick of the city's most beautiful young women. The unwise Seljuq response was to slay the tax collectors. In retribution Tuluy, the most brutal of Jenghiz Khan's sons, arrived three years later at the head of an army, accepted the peaceful surrender of the terrified citizens, and then proceeded to butcher every last one of the city's inhabitants. Each Mongol fighter had orders to decapitate 300 to 400 civilians. That done, the city was literally torn to pieces and put to the torch. With just swords, knives and axes the Mongols slaughtered perhaps a million people. Days later, after they had left, the few survivors crept back into the ruins, only for Tuluy's soldiers to reappear and viciously finish the job.

After this, Merv lay empty for more than a century. Eventually settlement did return, but the domain remained a political no-man's-land, tussled over by Bukhara, Khiva and the Persians. It wasn't until the 18th century that an echo of former glories was heard when a Persian noble, Bairam Ali Khan, rebuilt the old dam and returned a measure of prosperity to the city. That lasted

until 1795 when the Emir of Bukhara, covetous of Merv's strategic location as the gateway to Persia, undid the dam and led an army against the city, once again reducing it to dust.

After 1795 Merv existed only as an oasis camp for Turkmen tribes who were in the habit of conducting slave-raids on the villages of northern Persia. Such was the ire the Turkmen roused that a common saying of the time was: 'If you meet a viper and a Mervi, kill the Mervi first.'

An end to the Persian torment came in 1884 when the Russian army annexed Merv. Choosing not to garrison themselves on the doorstep of the Turkmen, they established their own town some distance away, closer to the shifting Murgab river. They took the name 'Merv' for their new town, leaving the Turkmen settlement to be known as Bairam Ali. In 1937 the Russian town changed its name to Mary, and Merv as a city ceased to exist.

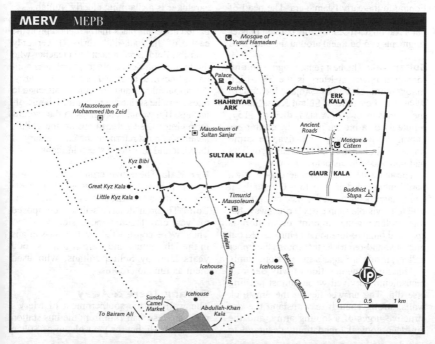

Things to See

Earliest Remains The oldest of the five Merv cities is **Erk Kala**, an Achaemenid city thought to date from the 6th century BCE. Today it's a big earthen doughnut about 600m across. There are deep trenches dug into the ramparts by Soviet archaeologists. The ramparts are 50m high, offering a good view of the surrounding savannah-like landscape.

From this vantage point it can be seen that Erk Kala forms part of the northern section of another, larger fortress – **Giaur Kala**, constructed during the 3rd century BCE by the Sassanians. The fortress walls are still solid, with three gaps where the gates once were. The city was built on a Hellenistic grid pattern; near the crossroads in the middle of the site are the ruins of a 7th century mosque. At the eastern end of the mosque there is an 8m-deep **water cistern** dug into the ground.

In the south-eastern corner of Giaur Kala a distinct mound marks the site of a **Buddhist stupa** and monastery, which was still functioning in the early Islamic era. The head of a Buddha statue found here is now in Ashgabat's National Museum. Little painted plaster fragments can be found around the site.

Sultan Kala The best remaining testimony to Seljuq power at Merv is the 38m-high **mausoleum of Sultan Sanjar**, located in what was the centre of Sultan Kala. Sanjar, the grandson of Alp Arslan, died in 1157, reputedly of a broken heart when, after escaping from captivity in Khiva, he came home to find that Jenghiz Khan's soldiers had laid waste to his beloved Merv.

The mausoleum is a simple cube with a barrel-mounted dome on top. Originally it had a magnificent turquoise-tiled outer dome, said to be visible from a day's ride away, but that is long gone. Interior decoration is sparse, though restoration is being carried out on a blue-and-red frieze that adorns the upper gallery; inside is Sanjar's simple stone tomb.

This raises the question of why Sanjar's mausoleum survived when almost nothing else did. The answer lies in the 3m-thick walls, strong enough to withstand the destructive urges of a looting army, and the 6m-deep conical foundations, designed to allow the structure to ride out any of the earthquakes to which this region is prone.

The **Shahriyar Ark** or citadel of Sultan Kala is one of the more interesting parts of Merv, with walls, a well-preserved *koshk* (fort) with corrugated walls, and the odd grazing camel.

North of the Shahriyar Ark outside the city walls lies the **Mosque of Yusuf Hamadani**, built around the tomb of a 12th century dervish. The complex has been largely rebuilt in the last 10 years and turned into an important pilgrimage site; it is not open to non-Muslims.

Mausoleum of Mohammed Ibn Zeid

About 1km west of Sanjar's tomb, just north of the dusty main road, is another Seljuq monument, the 12th century mausoleum of Mohammed ibn Zeid. The small, unostentatious earthen-brick building, heavily restored earlier this century, benefits greatly from an attractive setting in a hollow that is ringed by spindly saxaul trees, all combining to lend the scene a very Quranic air. The caretaker is a charming elderly mullah.

There's confusion as to who is actually buried under the black marble cenotaph in the centre of the cool, dark shrine. It certainly isn't ibn Zeid, a prominent Shia teacher who died four centuries before this tomb was built and is known to be buried elsewhere. Nearby, the colourful rags and tiny cradles attached to trees near the shrine are rather un-Islamic offerings. If a woman conceives in the months following a visit here, to ensure the child's health she must return on the anniversary of the visit and sacrifice a sheep in thanks.

Kyz Kala These two crumbling, 7th century *koshks* or fortress-palaces are interesting for their 'petrified stockade' walls, as Colin Thubron describes them, composed of 'vast clay logs up-ended side by side'. They were constructed by the Sassanians in the 7th century and were still in use 600 years later by Seljuq sultans, who used them as function rooms.

Getting There & Away

The walls of the southernmost of Merv's ruins are less than 1km from the bus station at Bairam Ali, but the mausoleum of Sultan

Sanjar and much else of interest is a good 6-8km away. While it's possible to spend a day hiking round the site, with summer temperatures in the region of 40°C it's not recommended. Watch out for snakes and scorpions, and bring food and water. It's more convenient to hire a taxi for a couple of hours – from the Bairam Ali bus station or from Mary – to chauffeur you around the sites and take you back again. From Mary expect to pay US$7.50 for a car and driver for four hours. Buses shuttle between Mary and Bairam Ali every half hour or so and the journey takes approximately 45 minutes.

If you intend heading east from Merv by bus, it's better to backtrack to Mary to be sure of getting a seat.

MARGIANA

Roughly 80km north of Merv beyond the edge of the Murgab oasis, where the river channels once ran, a Bronze Age civilisation flourished in the second millennium BCE. Today the area is barren flat desert, empty but for archaeologists uncovering an early urban culture with a place among ancient Egypt, China, Sumer and India as one of the oldest centres of civilisation. More than 150 settlements of Margiana (also called Margush) have been located.

The site at Gonurdepe (Gonur hill), once an undistinguished mound of earth, has been excavated to reveal a settlement surrounded by an almost perfect square of thick adobe walls, with a sturdy fortress at its centre. Bronze seals, ceremonial items, and surprisingly elegant pottery and jewellery from Gonurdepe can be seen in the Mary Regional Museum and Ashgabat's National Museum.

Chief archaeologist Victor Sarianidi believes that Zoroaster, founder of the first monotheistic religion, Zoroastrianism (often mistakenly called 'fire-worshipping'), may have lived in Margiana. The sites have revealed fire temples as well as evidence of a cult based around a drug potion prepared from poppy, hemp and ephedra plants. This potent brew is almost certainly the *haoma* elixir used by the fire priests or Magi whom Zoroaster began preaching against in Zoroastrian texts.

Golubeva Yevgeniya at the Mary Regional Museum can arrange transport to Gonurdepe; it would be hopeless trying to find it on your own. Even the locals have trouble giving directions. From Mary to Gonurdepe takes about two hours on rough tracks; a car for four people will cost about US$50.

TAGTABAZAR

About 230km south of Mary off the road to Gushgi is the small village of Tagtabazar, notable for its 7th century cave city, Ekedeshik. Dug into the banks of the Murgab river, the 'city' is a five-storey complex of interconnected chambers and passages wide enough to accommodate a camel-drawn cart.

The floors are tiled with bricks said to have been scavenged from a bridge built by the armies of Alexander the Great. The cave city was created by Christians as a refuge from the Arab conquest and forcible Islamisation, although the last storeys were hollowed out almost a thousand years later in the 16th century. Today only the upper two storeys are open to visitors, because the lower ones are subject to occasional collapse.

There is one bus a day to/from Mary, but special permission is probably needed to visit Tagtabazar (see the introduction to this Eastern Turkmenistan section).

GUSHGI

Also called Kushka, this small outpost on the Afghan border was the southernmost town in the former Soviet Union. It was founded as a military garrison in 1887 following an incident in which the Russians provoked the Afghans of Pandjeh into firing on them so that they might seize this little-known oasis, bringing the Tsar's influence that much closer to Herat. The annexation brought Russia within a hair's breadth of war with Britain, who felt its interests in Afghanistan to be under threat. The matter was resolved by the 1887 Joint Afghan Boundary Commission which allowed the Russians their gains in exchange for concessions elsewhere.

With a visa for Afghanistan and Gushgi listed as the exit point on your visa, it is possible to cross the border. It's 3km south of the town to the Turkmen border, from where you have to walk across no-man's-land unless the guards drive you. From the Afghan border point there's a 2km walk to the first Afghan village of Towraghondi (Torghuni). Buses to Herat have to negotiate a terrible road.

Visitors to Gushgi will need some convincing documentation to avoid being detained and put on the next bus out (see the introduction to this Eastern Turkmenistan section).

BADKHYZ NATURE RESERVE

Nestled at the south-eastern tip of Turkmenistan, close to the borders of both Afghanistan and Iran, the Badkhyz Nature Reserve is a region of rolling savannah landscape scored by ravines. Thanks to an impervious rock water table, Badkhyz is carpeted by tulips every spring and has great groves of pistachio trees. The wildlife is no less impressive, with roaming herds of goitred gazelles (known locally as *jieran*) and the rare Asiatic wild asses (Kulan), the preservation of which was a major factor in setting up the reserve in 1941.

Anyone interested in Badkhyz should get hold of *The Realms of the Russian Bear* by John Sparks (see the Books section of the Regional Facts for the Visitor chapter), which has a good, detailed section on the reserve's indigenous flora and fauna. There are no major settlements within the reserve, and no roads through it; you can only get there by special arrangement. Try the Ministry of Nature and Environmental Conservation (☎ 12-26 33 54, 29 04 33, fax 26 96 09) at ulitsa Kemine 192 in Ashgabat, or one of the tourist organisations listed in the Information entry of the Ashgabat section of this chapter.

TURKMENABAT

☎ 422 • pop 161,000

Now an unsightly industrial sprawl, Turkmenabat (formerly Charjou) has actually existed for more than 2000 years.

Travellers between Uzbekistan and Turkmenistan will probably land in Turkmenabat at some point because the only major land route passes through here. As a place to kill an hour or two between transport connections, Turkmenabat just about suffices, but there's no reason to stay longer.

The centre is ploshchad Niyazov, at one of the corner of prospekt Niyazov and ulitsa Shaidakova. Most amenities are within a 10 minute walk of this square: the post office is 400m north-west, the train station is 400m farther north, and the telephone and telegraph office are 300m south. You can change money at the official exchange rate at the Turkmen Bank, 100m south of the square (Monday to Saturday, 9 am and 1 pm).

The bus station is about 4km south of the city centre, beside a large roundabout on prospekt Niyazov.

Travellers report staying in a *train carriage* permanently shunted next to the main platform for less than a dollar in manat, but there are no showers.

The moderately shabby *Hotel Amu-Darya* (☎ 2 24 34, 2 58 22, prospekt Saparmurat Niyazov 14) is as good as it gets. Opposite the train station, it has basic but reasonably clean rooms and dilapidated bathrooms for US$10/13 in manat. It's also possible to leave luggage here for a small fee. The restaurant is popular with vodka swilling locals and serves up almost passable grub (salad and reconstituted meat) plus cold drinks.

There are a couple of *cafes* selling plov, shashlyk and greasy pastries around the entrance to the train station.

The best (least worst?) food in Turkmenabat is in the *bazar*, which boasts countless stalls selling plov, chicken legs, shashlyk with heaps of onions and herbs, decent bread, fresh honey and, of course, lots of fruit.

Getting There & Away

Turkmenabat is connected by five flights a day to Ashgabat (US$81). The airline booking office is 300m south of ploshchad Niyazov, in the second street on the left; it's open daily 9 am to 2 pm and 3 to 8 pm. The airport is about 5km out on the eastern edge of town.

Two trains a day go to Tashkent (17 hours away) via Bukhara (3½ hours) and Samarkand, leaving at 1 pm and 8 pm though delays are common. This is still the easiest and cheapest way to cross into Uzbekistan, though train services may drop off or disappear altogether when the Uzbeks finish a train line bypassing Turkmenistan. Tickets to Bukhara cost US$3 in manat, and the scrum at the ticket office is hard work unless someone buys a ticket for you (for a fee).

Daily trains go to Nukus via Urgench and Dashoguz, and there are two other Dashoguz services. Two trains go to Ashgabat (US$3.50, 14 hours) and one continues to Turkmenbashi.

The train station has a 24-hour left-luggage room located off the main concourse.

There are no buses to/from Uzbekistan. A taxi to the border should cost US$2 in manat, from where you must walk to the Uzbek checkpoint and hope there's another vehicle to take you onwards. The cheapest option is a taxi to Karakul (US$2 in Uzbek *sum*), from where share taxis/minivans go to Bukhara for less than US$1. Turkmen Express buses leave from in front of the train station to Ashgabat via Mary at 9 am and 2 pm daily (US$3 in manat). From the main bus station four public buses a day go to Kerki.

REPETEK DESERT RESERVE

With recorded air temperatures over 50°C and the surface of the sand sizzling at 70°C, nobody expects the Karakum desert to be inhabited by cuddly creatures, but the animals that do call the rolling ridges of sand home are a particularly repulsive lot. Among the thousand-plus indigenous species of insects, spiders, reptiles and rodents are prehistoric-looking monitor lizards that grow to over 1.5m but still put on an alarmingly good show at the 100m dash (see the boxed text). There are also bronze-coloured cobras, large black scorpions and tarantulas. All are studied at the Repetek Desert Research Centre. The research centre was set up in 1928 and has a visitors' centre with a museum and herbarium.

Visits can be arranged through Repetek Tours (☎ 422-4 44 70) in Turkmenabat.

The reserve is 70km south of Turkmenabat on the Mary road – Mary buses will stop there on request, and one train a day halts at the neighbouring shanty village of Repetek.

Entry costs US$30 with a tour, or U$1.25 per hour just to look around. There is a basic *lodge accommodation* here (not advisable in summer) for US$15 per person.

Desert Crocodiles

The giant grey striped lizards of the Karakum are sometimes known as desert or land crocodiles, an apt epithet for a beast that can grow up to 1.8m long. Despite their size and sharp teeth, in Turkmen tradition people were happy to have a *zemzen* dig a burrow near their home, as the giant lizards devoured or scared away snakes such as cobras, and eradicated colonies of sandflies.

Zemzens usually live for eight years or so, though in captivity they have lived for twice as long; they feed primarily on rodents, as well as a diverse mix of insects, snakes, frogs, other lizards and even scorpions. In winter they block their burrow's entrance hole (they often adopt the burrows of their rodent prey) and hibernate. They lay up to 24 eggs, which are almost the size of poultry eggs.

In the desert zemzens leave a distinctive track; a line left by the dragging tail swishing between the footprints. Should you be lucky enough to see one in the wild, rest assured that they don't normally attack unprovoked. A zemzen's bite is said to be extremely painful, as they have powerful jaws and sharp backward-angled teeth, and once attached they aren't inclined to let go.

While they are a protected species nowadays, and Turkmen tradition forbids killing them due to their pest-clearing qualities, in the past zemzens were killed to make shoes and luxury goods, and they have disappeared from several areas. Aside from a visit to Repetek Desert Reserve or Ashgabat's forlorn zoo, you are unlikely to see a zemzen unless it lies squashed on a road.

GAURDAK

GAURDAK is in the extreme eastern corner of Turkmenistan, squeezed between the Amu-Darya and Uzbekistan. The mountainous landscape is starkly beautiful with gorges, waterfalls and cave complexes forested with stalactites and stalagmites. Right on the Uzbek border is the **Kugitang Nature Reserve**, a geological research centre, the pride of which is a rock plateau imprinted with hundreds of dinosaur footprints. It's believed that 150 million years ago, in the Jurassic period, the plateau was the bed of a lagoon that dried up, leaving the wet foot-printed sand to bake in the sun. The reserve also includes the country's highest peak, Airababa (3137m).

The research centre has a lakeside *tourist lodge* and they are willing to host visitors and ferry them to the dinosaur plateau, an hour away by 4WD, and to a 9km cave system near Karlouk.

Contact them well in advance at 746680 Turkmenistan, Gaurdak, Kugitang Geological Reserve (746680 Туркмениста, Лебабский Велоят Ша□ер Говурдак Кугитанг Заповедник, Овуинников Александр), attention Alexandr Ovuinnikov (☎ Gaurdak 2 19 19). Staying at Kugitang costs US$50 per person per day.

Turkmenabat is the only place from which you can fly to Gaurdak (US$47); the flights leave once a week, but schedules change frequently. Visitors can be collected from Gaurdak airport, or from Charshanga, a stop on the Turkmenabat-Kelif railway line.

Travel agencies in Ashgabat can also arrange visits to Kugitang (see Information in the Ashgabat section of this chapter).

Northern Turkmenistan

Dashoguz is the only sizeable city in northern Turkmenistan, the focus of the country's portion of the environmentally blighted Amu-Darya delta. Salinity is steadily ruining miles of flat farmland, and fields encrusted with salt and brackish puddles can be seen everywhere. Dashoguz and northern Turkmenistan share, with the rest of the delta in Uzbekistan, the full force of the Aral Sea disaster (see the Ecology & Environment section in the Facts about Central Asia chapter). The region has a mixed Turkmen and Uzbek population.

The highlight of the region is the ruins of Konye-Urgench, home of Central Asia's tallest minaret and distinctive medieval Khorezm architecture.

DASHOGUZ
☎ 322 • pop 140,000

Founded as a fort in the early 19th century, Dashoguz is an entirely Soviet creation of straight streets lined by enormous blocks of flats, interspersed with desolate empty spaces. Nukus-Urgench-Turkmenabat-Bukhara trains come through here, at least until Uzbekistan finishes building a train line bypassing Turkmenistan. The town is a useful staging post for Konye-Urgench as well as smaller forts and ruined cities in the region.

In Uzbekistan you may find Dashoguz spelt 'Toshhovuz', 'Tashavuz', 'Tashauz' or 'Toshauz'. After independence it was first renamed 'Dashkhowuz', then Dashoguz.

The main axis of Dashoguz is Karla Marxa, running roughly north-south, with the bazar and bus station near its north end about 2km from the town centre. Dashoguz street signs, such as they are, are beginning to go over to new Turkmen names, though the old ones are still more familiar to most people.

Places to Stay & Eat

The *Hotel Dashoguz (Dashkhowuz)* (☎ 257 85, Andaliba 4), about 600m east of (former) ulitsa Karla Marxa, asks for US$7/10 in manat for basic but clean air-con singles/doubles. As Soviet-era state-owned hotels go, it is not bad, with the rare bonus of a smiling welcome from the receptionist.

The Turkish-owned *Hotel Diyabekir* (☎ 232 35, fax 232 36) is 500m west of the Hotel Dashoguz on Andaliba. The rooms are functional and comfortable, with satellite TV and probably the best bathrooms in town. Rooms are US$60/80 in US dollars only.

Midway between the two hotels on the opposite side of the road is the *Nuh Restaurant*, with air-con and pavement tables. The mostly Turkish menu of kebabs and salads is good value at US$1 in manat for a kebab. Expect to pay about US$3 in manat for dinner.

Getting There & Around

There are several daily flights to/from Ashgabat (US$71). The air ticket office (with belligerent staff) is in an annexe of the Hotel Dashoguz. The taxi ride to the airport takes 30 minutes and costs US$2 in manat.

The bus station *(avtostantsia)* is in the north of town on ulitsa Karla Marxa, just north of the bazar. There are buses to Konye-Urgench every hour until 6 pm and to Khiva twice a day.

One or two Turkmen Express buses leave from the front of the train station every morning, charging US$2 in manat and taking about 11 hours to Ashgabat. They go via Konye-Urgench.

The new train station is on ulitsa Wokzal, about 600m east of the northern end of the former ulitsa Karla Marxa. There are daily Tashkent-Nukus service and Dashoguz-Ashgabat services, both of which pass through Urgench in Uzbekistan. Tickets for open cabins cost US$6 in manat to Ashgabat, US$1 or so to Urgench.

Buses and share taxis run up and down Karla Marxa, some continuing to the train station. Share taxis to towns in the region wait to fill up in front of the train station.

IZMUKSHIR

The ruins of the Khorezm city once known as Zamakshar stand 25km south-west of Dashoguz on lands of a collective farm near the small town of Tagta. Thought to have been founded as early as the 3rd century BCE, the city reached its peak in the 9th and 10th centuries CE (common era). The scientist, poet and linguist Az-Zamakshari (1074-1144 CE) was born here. Best known for a commentary he wrote on the Quran, legend has that he once boasted 'Arabs, come to me to study your language.'

The city gates are the most impressive remnants. You enter between great drum-shaped brick towers into a second row of walls. The city fortress, or kala, is surrounded by a deep moat.

Taxis from Dashoguz takes 30 minutes. Expect US$10 for a three-hour round-trip.

KONYE-URGENCH

The ancient state of Khorezm, which encompassed the whole Amu-Darya delta area in northern Turkmenistan and western Uzbekistan, rose to its greatest heights at Konye-Urgench (Old Urgench), 480km north across the Karakum desert from Ash-gabat, and 100km north-west through cotton fields from Dashoguz.

Modern Konye-Urgench is a humdrum place, but its handful of beautiful old buildings (from before, between and after those invasions) make it well worth a day trip if you're in the area. What isn't here is almost as impressive as what is, because it serves as evidence of the annihilatory capacity of the armies of Timur and Jenghiz Khan.

In town there's the *Restoran Gurgench* on Gurgench shayoli. Near the southern monuments there's a meagre *cafe* at the ticket office, close to the Turabeg Khanym mausoleum.

History

Khorezm, located on a northerly Silk Road branch that leads to the Caspian Sea and Russia, has been an important oasis of civilisation in the Central Asian deserts for thousands of years. The Persians took it into their empire as long ago as the 6th century BCE, and the Arabs brought Islam to it in the 8th century CE. Old Urgench began its upward path when its ruler Mamun succeeded in uniting Khorezm in 995 AD. At this time the Amu-Darya flowed through the city.

Khorezm fell to the all-conquering Seljuq Turks, but rose in the 12th century, under a Seljuq dynasty known as the Khorezmshahs, to shape its own far-reaching empire. With its mosques, medressas, libraries and flourishing bazars, old Urgench became the centre of the Muslim world, until Khorezmshah Mohammed II moved his capital to Samarkand after capturing that city in 1210.

In 1216 Mohammed II, a man who thought of himself as a second Alexander the Great, received from that other empire-builder of the day, Jenghiz Khan, a collection of lavish gifts, along with an offer of trade and a message that Jenghiz Khan regarded Mohammed as his 'most cherished son'. Two years later, 450 merchants travelling from Jenghiz Khan's territory were murdered at Otyrar, a Khorezmshah frontier town east of the Aral Sea. Jenghiz Khan sent three envoys to Samarkand to demand reparation, but Mohammed had one killed and the beards of the other two burnt off.

Within two years Mongol armies had sacked Samarkand, Bukhara, old Urgench and Otyrar and massacred their people. Old Urgench withstood several months siege, but eventually the Mongols smashed the nearby dam on the Amu-Darya, let the river flood through the city, and massacred the survivors. Other great Khorezmshah cities (Merv, Balkh, Herat) went the same way, and then the Mongols carried on to the Caucasus and Russia. Mohammed II died in rags on an island in the Caspian Sea in 1221. The tombs of his father Tekesh and grandfather Il-Arslan survive, two of old Urgench's monuments.

In the following period of peace, Khorezm was ruled as part of the Golden Horde, the huge, wealthy, westernmost of the khanates into which Jenghiz Khan's empire was divided after his death. Old Urgench, rebuilt, was again Khorezm's capital, and grew into what was probably Central Asia's major trading city – big, beautiful, crowded and with a new generation of monumental buildings.

Then came Timur, five times. Considering Khorezm to be a rival to Samarkand, he comprehensively finished off old Urgench in 1388. The city was partly rebuilt in the 16th century, but it was abandoned when the Amu-Darya changed its course (modern Konye-Urgench dates from the construction of a new canal in the 19th century). When a new line of independent Khorezm rulers arose (Uzbek Turks who moved in from the steppes in the early 16th century) they started off at Devkesen, out in the desert west of Konye-Urgench, and made Khiva their capital in 1592.

Other fortresses in the region include Bentendag (Ak Kala), 100km west of Konye-Urgench on the way to Sarykamish lake. The fortress of Shasenem measures 250m long by 250m wide, set on a high artificial platform. It lies 100km south of Konye-Urgench, close to the Ashgabat road.

Orientation

The road from Dashoguz passes the bus station as it enters Konye-Urgench along Gurgench shayoli (ulitsa Kalinina). About 500m west of the bus station is a set of traffic lights where the road from Hojeli and Nukus, ulitsa Karla Marxa, comes in from the north.

To reach the monuments, go west along Gurgench shayoli from the traffic lights. After about 1km, just past the Restoran Gurgench on the right, turn right (north), then take the first left into G Atabayev, for the Najm-ed-din Kubra mausoleum and nearby sights. For the southern monuments, head to the west end of Gurgench (about 1km from the Restoran Gurgench intersection), then travel 1km south along the Ashgabat road.

Najm-ed-din Kubra Mausoleum & Surrounds

The sacred Najm-ed-din Kubra mausoleum is the most important of a small cluster of sights near the middle of the town. An intermittently open **museum** is housed in the early 20th century Dash mosque, facing G Atabayev kochasi where it turns a right angle into ulitsa Lenina. It includes some finds from old Urgench, and some ancient Arabic texts. To one side is the **Matkerim-Ishan mausoleum** also early 20th century.

The path past here leads to the **Najm-ed-din Kubra mausoleum** on the left, and the **Sultan Ali mausoleum** facing it across a shady little courtyard. The Najm-ed-din Kubra mausoleum is Konye-Urgench's holiest spot. Najm-ed-din Kubra was a famous 12th and 13th century Khorezm Muslim teacher and poet who founded the Sufic Kubra order, with followers in Turkmenistan and Karakalpakstan (in Uzbekistan). His tomb is believed to have healing properties and you may find pilgrims praying here. The building has three domes and a fine, unrestored, tiled portal. The tombs inside – one for his body and one for his head, which were separated by the Mongols – are colourful with floral-pattern tiles.

The Sultan Ali mausoleum was built in 1580. Sultan Ali was a 16th century Uzbek Khorezmshah.

Southern Monuments

These are Konye-Urgench's most striking monuments, dotted like a constellation across an empty expanse straddling the Ashgabat road 1km south of the end of Gurgench shayoli. What makes them all the more evocative is that across the empty expanse are scattered brick-studded mounds – indicating that this was once a city. Entry costs US$2 in Manat, which is payable at the kiosk near the Turabeg Khanym mausoleum.

Turabeg Khanym mausoleum, on the west side of the road, is proof of the comeback that old Urgench made the great Mongol destruction. It was built in the mid-14th century as the family tomb of a Sufi dynasty then ruling Khorezm under the Golden Horde. Turabeg Khanym was wife to Kutlug Temir, one of this dynasty, and a daughter of Khan Uzbek, the leader of the Golden Horde who converted the horde to Islam (and from whom the modern Uzbeks trace their origins).

The mausoleum is one of Central Asia's most perfect buildings (though it has recently been obscured by reconstruction work). Its geometric patterns are in effect a giant calendar signifying humanity's insignificance in the march of time. There are 365 sections on the sparkling mosaic on the underside of the dome representing the days of the year, 24 pointed arches immediately beneath the dome representing the hours of the day, 12 bigger arches below representing the months the year, and four big windows representing the weeks of the month.

Across the road, along the path through a modern cemetery and the 19th century **Sayid Ahmed mausoleum**, stands the **Kutlug Timur minaret**, built in the 1320s. It's the only surviving part of old Urgench's main mosque. Decorated with bands of brick and a few turquoise tiles, at 67m it's the highest minaret in Central Asia – though not as tall as it once was, and leaning noticeably.

Farther along the track is the **Sultan Tekesh mausoleum**. Tekesh was the 12th century Khorezmshah who made Khorezm great with conquests as far south as Khorasan (present-day northern Iran and northern Afghanistan). He built this mausoleum for himself, along with a big medressa and library (which did not survive) on the same spot. After his death in 1200 he was buried here. The conical dome with a curious zigzag brick pattern is typical of old Khorezm. Nearby is the mound of graves called the **Kirkmolla** (Forty Mullah's

Hill), a sacred place where Konye-Urgench's inhabitants held their last stand against the Mongols.

Continue along the track to the **Il-Arslan mausoleum**, Konye-Urgench's oldest standing monument. Il-Arslan, who died in 1172, was Tekesh's father. The building is small but well worth a close look. The conical dome with 12 faces is unique, and the floral terracotta moulding on the facade is also unusual. Farther south lies the base of the **Mamun II minaret**, which was built in 1011, reduced to a stump by the Mongols, rebuilt in the 14th century and finally toppled by an earthquake in 1895.

It's a longer walk to the last monument along this track, the main gate of a 14th century building, usually called the **Dash Kala Caravanserai portal**, though some archaeologists believe it to have been the gate of a palace or medressa. It lies in the middle of the pre-Mongol Dash Kala walled city, about 1.5km from the **Turabeg Khanym Mausoleum**. East of here is the **Ak Kala fortress**, which was smashed by the Mongols. To the west on the other side of the Ashgabat road are the walls of **Khorezm Dag**, rebuilt by Khan Mohammed Amin of Khiva in the mid-19th century. It was intended to be his new capital, but he was decapitated by a Turkmen horseman before the move could go ahead.

Getting There & Away

Konye-Urgench is about 100km north-west of Dashoguz, 160km north-west of Urgench and Khiva, and 45km south-west of Nukus. You can reach it from any of these places, but make careful inquiries about the situation on the border if you're coming from Uzbekistan. Even if you're just doing a day trip from Uzbekistan, you will need a Turkmenistan visa; make sure that your Uzbek visa isn't cancelled as you leave Uzbekistan.

Buses run from Dashoguz to Konye-Urgench every hour until 6 pm.

A taxi from Nukus and back, with a few hours to look around Konye-Urgench, should cost between US$10 and US$20. For a taxi day trip from Khiva or Urgench you're looking at US$50 to US$80.

Xinjiang

Xinjiang at a Glance

Official Name: Xinjiang Uyghur Autonomous Region
Area: 1,600,000 sq km
Population: 16.9 million
Ethnic Mix: 42% Uyghur, 40-50% Han Chinese, 6.5% Kazak, 1% Kyrgyz
Capital: Ürümqi
Currency: yuan (Y)
Country ☎ Code: 86
Best Time to Go: April, May, June, September, October

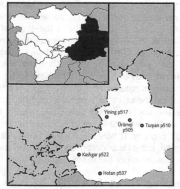

Yining p517
Ürümqi p505
Turpan p510
Kashgar p522
Hotan p537

- **Kashgar Market** – technicolour sea of people, animals and pony carts

- **Kashgar Old Town** – the exotic eastern feel of the fabled Silk Road oasis

- **Turpan** – a desert oasis, the lowest and hottest spot in China

- **Sayram Lake** – beautiful lake set on the grasslands between Yining and Ürümqi

- **Heavenly Lake** – alpine scenery that looks like a Swiss postcard

- **Hotan** – traditional Uyghur old town

- **Karakul** – stunning turquoise lake

- **Hanas Lake** – gorgeous in the autumn and inhabited by seminomadic Kazaks

Central Asia properly includes 'Chinese Turkestan' too – those parts of what is now China's Xinjiang Uyghur Autonomous Region, sharing the former Soviet Central Asian republics' culture, language and history. Only gradually has the old, hypersensitive USSR-China border opened enough for individuals to travel easily over ancient routes between the two regions, and to appreciate how much these corners of empire still have in common after decades of almost total political separation.

Xinjiang is the largest Chinese province, comprising 16% of the country's land surface. The province was made an autonomous region in 1955 and named after the majority Turkic-speaking Muslim Uyghurs *(wéiwúěr)* at a time when more than 90% of the population was non-Chinese. The north has traditionally consisted of nomadic pastoralists, such as the Kazaks, while the Uyghurs in the south settled in fertile oases scattered along the ancient Silk Road. Today the character *jiāng* of Xinjiang consists of the root symbols for bow, land, field and border, encapsulating the mix of settler and nomad in this wild land. With the building of the railway from Lanzhou to Ürümqi and the development of industry, the Han Chinese now form a majority in the northern area, while the Uyghurs continue to predominate in the south.

Xinjiang is a huge, geopolitically strategic area, four times the size of Japan, which shares an international border with eight other nations. Vast deserts and arid plains stretch for thousands of kilometres here before ending abruptly at the foot of towering mountain ranges. The ruins of Buddhist Silk Road cities pepper the deserts as reminders of the past, while newer Islamic monuments point the way to the future. For travellers, the region is one of the most interesting in China, packed with history, archaeological remains, ethnic variety, superb landscapes and a vibrant Central Asian culture. Memories of a cold Xinjiang beer under the grape trellises of Turpan, of wandering the bustling

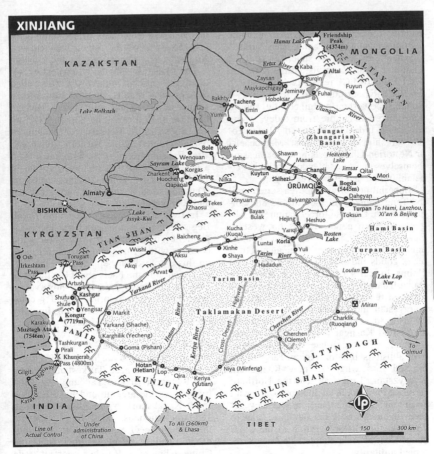

bazars of Hotan or Kashgar, and of the poplar-lined Uyghur villages will remain long after the end of most peoples' trips.

This chapter introduces Xinjiang within Central Asia. For more on travel from the Chinese side see Lonely Planet's *China*.

Facts about Xinjiang

HISTORY

Han Dynasty China had already pioneered its new trade routes (later named the Silk Road) through this region by the 2nd century BCE (before common era). In 138 BCE the Chinese envoy Zang Qian passed through the region in his search for potential allies against the Xiongnu tribes who were pummelling the Chinese heartland. In 102 BCE the Chinese even conquered as far as Kokand in the Fergana valley.

The first Chinese conquest of Xinjiang was between 73 and 97 CE (common era), led by the brilliant Chinese general Pan Zhao (Ban Chao) (32-102 CE). Zhao stayed in the region for 31 years, establishing contact with Syria and Babylonia. But despite the expenditure of vast resources in policing the 'Western Region', Han dynasty control eventually succumbed to northern nomadic warrior tribes, Mongols and, later, Turks.

When the Buddhist super-pilgrims Fa Xian and Xuan Zang visited the region in 400 CE and 644 CE respectively in a search for Buddhist scriptures, the region was a Buddhist powerhouse. Ruined cities show a quite different culture from today, where red-haired Indo-European and Altaic peoples worshipped at Buddhist, Manichaeist or Nestorian Christian temples, expressing themselves in art that blended Kashmiri, Tibetan, Indian and even Greek styles.

Imperial power was not reasserted until the Tang Dynasty in the 7th and 8th centuries, when Chinese forces captured Kashgar, and even penetrated as far west as Bukhara (659 CE). Even then, control amounted to little more than an annual tribute of goods and envoys. Chinese territorial claims to parts of the Pamir and Lake Balkash date from this period and were only resolved recently in talks with Kazakstan, Kyrgyzstan and Tajikistan.

In the 8th century, Arab armies from Persia visited Kashgar (713 CE) and Gilgit, though it wasn't until later that Islam began to establish itself in this region. Tang armies crossed into what are now Kazakstan, Kyrgyzstan, Tajikistan and the Northern Areas of Pakistan in an attempt to deal with Arab and Tibetan expansion. But they got their fingers burnt at the Battle of Talas in 751 (see the History section in the Facts about Central Asia chapter) and never returned militarily.

Tang control of Kashgaria came to an end about this time with the arrival of the Uyghur Turks from the borders of Mongolia and Siberia, and the area was ruled by a succession of small kingdoms — Uyghur, Karakhanid and Karakitay — for more than four centuries. It was during Karakhanid rule in the 11th and 12th centuries that Islam took hold here. Karakhanid tombs are still standing in Kashgar and nearby Artush.

Ili, Hotan and Kashgar fell to the Mongols in 1219, and Timur sacked Kashgar in the late 14th century. The area remained under the control of Timur's descendants or various Mongol tribes until a Manchurian army marched wrested control of the Tarim basin in 1755. In 1768 the region was renamed Xinjiang (New Dominions) by the Chinese.

The Manchus remained for a century, although resentment of their rule often boiled over in local revolts. In 1847 Hunza, then an independent Karakoram state, helped the Chinese quell a revolt in Yarkand. During the 1860s and 1870s a series of Muslim uprisings erupted across western China, and after Russian troops were withdrawn from a ten-year occupation of the Ili region in 1871, waves of Uyghurs, Chinese Muslims (Dungans) and Kazaks fled into Kazakstan and Kyrgyzstan.

In 1865 a Kokandi officer named Yakub Beg seized Kashgaria, proclaimed an independent Turkestan and made diplomatic contacts with Britain and Russia (for more on this extraordinary episode, see the History section in the Facts about Central Asia chapter). A few years later, however, a Manchurian army returned and Beg committed suicide. In 1884 Xinjiang formally became a province of China.

Playing the Game

As early as 1851 Russia had extended its influence into Chinese Turkestan, opening consulates in Ili and Tacheng. An 1864 treaty gave the area around Lake Balkash (now Kazakstan) to the Russians and in 1871 the Russians added the Ili valley to their province of Semireche. In 1881 another 'unequal treaty' returned Ili to the Chinese but gave Russia important trade concessions and let them open a consulate in Kashgar in return.

Already nervous of Russian expansion into the region, the British urgently reopened the British agency at Gilgit after the Mir of Hunza entertained a party of Russians at Baltit in 1888. In 1890 Britain set up its own Kashgar office.

On his way back from a mission to Kashgar through the Pamir in that year, Francis Younghusband (later to head a British invasion of Tibet) found the range full of Russian troops and was told to get out. A year later the British invaded Hunza. After a burst of diplomatic manoeuvring, Anglo-Russian boundary agreements in 1897 and 1907 gave Russia most of the Pamir and established a no-man's-land in the form of the Wakhan Corridor, the awkward tongue of Afghan territory that stretches across to meet Xinjiang.

The Pamir settlement shifted the focus of the Great Game towards Kashgar, where the two powers went on conniving. But in the chaos following the Chinese Revolution of 1911 the British were no match for Russian economic and political influence in western Xinjiang, despite Russian absence from Kashgar for almost a decade after the 1917 Bolshevik Revolution.

Warlord Anarchy

With the fall of the Qing dynasty in 1911, Xinjiang came under the rule of a succession of warlords, over whom the Chinese governments had very little control. The first of these warlord-rulers was Yang Zhengxin, who ruled from 1911 until his assassination in 1928 at a banquet in Ürümqi.

Yang was followed by Jin Shuren, another tyrannical overlord who, after being forced to flee in 1933, was replaced by a more oppressive leader, Sheng Shicai. The latter remained in power almost until the end of WWII, when he too was forced out. Sheng initially followed a pro-communist policy, then suddenly embarked on an anti-communist purge.

XINJIANG

Foreign Devils on the Silk Road

Adventurers on the road to Xinjiang might well like to reflect on an earlier group of European adventurers who descended on Chinese Turkestan, as Xinjiang was then known, and carted off early Buddhist art treasures by the tonne at the turn of the century. Their exploits are vividly described by Peter Hopkirk in his book *Foreign Devils on the Silk Road – the Search for the Lost Cities & Treasures of Chinese Central Asia* (Oxford Paperbacks, 1984).

The British first began to take an interest in the Central Asian region from their imperial base in India. Initially, the so-called 'pundits', local Indian traders trained in basic cartography and surveying, were sent to investigate the region. They heard from oasis dwellers in the Taklamakan desert of legendary ancient cities buried beneath the sands of the desert. In 1864 William Johnson was the first British official to sneak into the region, visiting one of these fabled lost cities in its tomb of sand close to Hotan. He was soon followed by Sir Douglas Forsyth, who made a report on his exploits entitled *On the Buried Cities in the Shifting Sands of the Great Desert of Gobi*. Not long afterwards, the race to unearth the treasures beneath the desert's 'shifting sands' was on.

The first European archaeologist/adventurer to descend on the region was the Swede Sven Hedin. A brilliant cartographer and fluent in seven languages, Hedin made three trailblazing expeditions into the Taklamakan desert, unearthing a wealth of treasures and writing a two-volume account of his journeys: *Through Asia*. The second explorer, in pursuit of Buddhist art treasures, was Sir Aurel Stein, a Hungarian who took up British citizenship. Stein's expeditions into the Taklamakan, accompanied by his terrier Dash, were to culminate in his removing a gold mine of Buddhist texts in Chinese, Tibetan and Central Asian languages from Dunhuang and taking them to the British Museum.

Between 1902 and 1914 Xinjiang saw four German and four French expeditions, as well as expeditions by the Russians and Japanese, all jockeying for their share of the region's archaeological treasures. While these explorers were feted and lionised by adoring publics at home, the Chinese today commonly see them as robbers who stripped the region of its past. Defenders point to the wide-scale destruction that took place during the Cultural Revolution and to the defacing of Buddhist artworks by Muslims who stumbled across them. Whatever the case, today most of central Asia's finest archaeological finds are scattered across the museums of Europe.

New Muslim uprisings exploded across Xinjiang in the early 1930s. In 1933 Kashgar was occupied by rebels and declared the capital of the Republic of Eastern Turkestan – which lasted only two months. By the mid-1930s an odd coalition of Chinese soldiers, immigrant White Russians and Soviet troops had stamped out these revolts.

The only real attempt to establish an independent state was in the 1940s, when a Kazak named Osman led a rebellion of Uyghurs, Kazaks and Mongols. He took control of south-western Xinjiang and established an independent eastern Turkestan Republic in January 1945.

Big Horse

Ma Zhongyin, or Big Horse as he was known, was one of Xinjiang's most enigmatic warlords. A Dungan (Hui Chinese Muslim) from Gansu, Ma led the great Muslim rebellions of 1933 and 1934, seizing towns throughout Xinjiang and reaching the gates of Ürümqi three times.

Ma was only turned back when the Soviets, sensing a Japanese-backed pan-Turkic rebellion that had the potential to spread into Soviet Turkestan, sent in troops, tanks and even bombers, all in unmarked convoys, to help put down the rebellion. After 2000 rebels were slaughtered, Ma quickly retreated to nearby Korla, stole four of Swedish explorer Sven Hedin's expedition trucks and drove off in a cloud of Taklamakan dust to the relative safety of Kashgar, where he was later seen playing tennis at the Swedish Mission.

Suddenly and without warning, the next day he relinquished control of all of his troops and was last seen bundled into the back of a Russian truck headed for the Soviet Union. Quite why he accepted a life of exile in the USSR (or even how much he was paid) will never be known, but with him died the Muslim rebellion. He was never to be seen again, though it is said that he lived a comfortable life in Moscow, until he was finally liquidated in Stalin's purges.

The Kuomintang convinced the Muslims to abolish their new republic in return for a pledge of real autonomy. This promise wasn't kept, but Chiang Kaishek's preoccupation with the civil war left him with little time to re-establish control over the region. The Kuomintang eventually appointed a Muslim named Burhan as governor of the region in 1948, unaware that he was actually a communist supporter.

A Muslim league opposed to Chinese rule was formed in Xinjiang, but in 1949 a number of its most prominent leaders died in a mysterious plane crash on their way to Beijing to hold talks with the new communist leaders. Muslim opposition to Chinese rule collapsed, although the Kazak Osman continued to fight until he was captured and executed by the Chinese communists in 1951.

Communist China

The People's Republic of China was declared in 1949, and the Kashgar consulates were shut down. In 1955 the communists declared Xinjiang an autonomous region, though it would never really know anything like true autonomy. It is fascinating to compare the Russian and Chinese versions of communist treatment of minority ethnic groups and religious affiliation at vitally strategic corners of the empire.

In the 1960s a rail link to Ürümqi was completed and massive resettlement tilted northern Xinjiang's population in favour of Chinese, although Uyghurs are still a majority in the Tarim basin. The railway has been extended to join the old Soviet rail system at the Kazakstan border and now stretches all the way to Kashgar.

Friction with the Chinese has continued, including riots in Kashgar in the 1970s, an armed uprising by Muslim nationalists in October 1981, and another in 1990 in which scores of protesters were said to have been killed by government troops.

GEOGRAPHY

Xinjiang is characterised by three mountain ranges (the Altay, Tian Shan and Kunlun), separated from each other by two depressions (the Tarim and Jhungarian).

The Beginning or the End?

Relations between Uyghurs and Han Chinese have never been good but ties have become increasingly strained since the early 1950s, when communist China began its policy of bolstering Xinjiang's population with Han settlers. In 1949 there were 200,000 Han Chinese in Xinjiang – the figure in 1993 stood at well over six million, with 300,000 immigrants a year swelling the ranks.

Perhaps to ward off these tensions China has invested considerable amounts of money in developing Xinjiang's economy and infrastructure (though Uyghurs frequently argue that all the good jobs and business opportunities are dominated by Han Chinese). Han migration, birth control policies, nuclear testing in the east of the province and the exploitation of oil reserves from outside of the province remain flashpoints of Uyghur contention. Just as importantly, the two cultures are split by deep religious, linguistic, cultural and even culinary differences. A survey of Xinjiang's towns and cities shows little integration between the two nationalities, although there seems to be more Han-Uyghur interaction in the capital, Ürümqi. Even there, however, it's possible to detect the underlying tension.

Long-simmering Uyghur resentment has boiled over on several occasions, notably in the form of bus bombings in Kashgar in 1990 and Ürümqi in 1992, pitched battles between Uyghurs and Chinese police in Baren township (outside Kashgar) in 1990, and rioting in Hotan in 1995, when the Chinese authorities removed a popular local imam. The most serious incident of recent years took place in February 1997 when Muslim separatists in the northern city of Yining started riots that led to a swift crackdown by Chinese security forces. At least 25 people died and nearly two hundred were injured, making the protest the most violent to date.

A wave of arrests, executions and patriotic re-education followed the riots; many Uyghurs were executed on the day of their trial. These arrests sparked several deadly responses. In late February (during Chinese New Year) separatists blew up three buses in Ürümqi, killing at least nine passengers and wounding many others. The bombing campaign reached as far as Beijing in March 1997.

Many Uyghurs eye the neighbouring newly independent nation states of Central Asia with envy and Uyghurs in exile have vowed to continue the campaign of violent protest until Xinjiang ('Uyghuristan', or Eastern Turkestan, as they would have it) gains its freedom from Beijing.

Communist officials take the Uyghur threat seriously and apparently now regard Uyghur insurrection as a more serious threat to national unity than the more widely reported independence demonstrations in neighbouring Tibet. Uyghurs, after all, enjoy the support and solidarity of the Islamic world. Beijing is keeping a particularly close eye on mujaheddin training camps in Afghanistan and Tajikistan and has put considerable political and economic pressure on Kazakstan and Kyrgyzstan to expel Uyghur rebel leaders based there. Local state propaganda is uncompromising, stating that China will deal with Uyghur 'minority splittists' 'like with a rat, of whom, when it crosses the street, everyone shouts 'kill it!''.

The question now is: were the February riots the start of a long march towards secession or the last gasp of a hopeless cause? Ironically, the answer to this may ultimately depend more on political developments in Beijing than in Xinjiang.

The Tarim basin, a 1500km-long depression covering most of southern Xinjiang, consists almost entirely of the hostile and shifting Taklamakan (Go-in-and-you-won't-come-out) desert, with a string of oases around its rim. To the east is the Turpan basin, the second-lowest basin in the world at 154m below sea level, and the remote salt lake of Lop Nur where the Chinese tested nuclear bombs from 1964 to 1997.

Another basin, the Jungar (or Zhungarian), marks the ancient gateway to the steppes of Central Asia. Farther north are the grasslands and alpine scenery of the Altay, shared between China, Kazakstan, Russia and Mongolia. The border is marked by Friendship Peak (4374m); standing on the glacier-covered summit allows you to be in three nations at once.

South of the Taklamakan the dramatic crests of the Karakoram and Kunlun ranges rise like a mirage from the desert sands. The second-highest mountain in the world, K2, marks the Chinese border with Pakistan. The Chinese recently discovered the world's 15th highest mountain, 8011m Central Peak, not far from here. The Kunlun marks the gradual transition from the Central Asian deserts to the Tibetan plateau and remains one of the least explored mountain ranges in the world.

In the south-west corner of the province a dramatic mountain cul-de-sac is formed by the merger of the Tian Shan, the Pamir and the Kunlun ranges. The Pamir range might be better described as a plateau, with broad, flat valleys nearly as high as the lower peaks. The western border is defined by the impressive Tian Shan, which peaks at 7439m Tomur peak (known as Pobedy in Kyrgyzstan). The Sino-Kyrgyz-Kazak border is marked by 6995m Khan Tengri.

Xinjiang's rivers, such as the Tarim and Yarkand, rise in the snowy peaks of the Tian Shan and Kunlun and drain through fertile oases before being swallowed up by the sands of the Taklamakan. The Ertix river, farther north in the Altay region (including the Altay mountains), is the only river in China to flow into the Arctic Ocean.

CLIMATE

In Kashgar the average annual maximum is 37°C, and most likely to occur in July or August. The average minimum will be around -18°C, usually in January. Xinjiang has no measurable rainfall on 93% of the year's days. When it does rain, flash floods can sweep through the otherwise dry stream beds.

ECONOMY

Xinjiang is one of the poorest provinces in China. Though it's trying to catch up through a lot of investment and the setting up of special economic zones in Tacheng, Bole and Yining, it still remains about 20 years behind the east coast of China.

Oil has become an increasingly important part of Xinjiang's economy. It is estimated that the Taklamakan holds 74 billion barrels of oil, more than three times the US's proven reserves. Oil roads are being forged through the desert sands, joining iron railroads to echo ancient silk roads. Gas and uranium are other important resources.

Silk Road trade has been on the rise for several years now. The 1300km Karakoram Highway has boosted trade with Pakistan since 1982, and the opening up of border crossings with Kyrgyzstan and Kazakstan has provided huge markets for Chinese made goods.

Yet unemployment remains high among rural Uyghur communities and even government-inspired success stories turn sour. Rebiya Kadir, a Uyghur millionaire businesswoman, once hailed as an ethnic success story, was stripped of her seat in the Chinese parliament after refusing to criticise her husband, who is accused of supporting Uyghur independence.

POPULATION & PEOPLE

Xinjiang's population currently stands at about 17 million. The majority of the inhabitants, until recently, have been Uyghur but immigration by Han Chinese settlers from the east of the country has pushed the Han population towards (some say over) the politically sensitive 50% mark. The 1990 census puts the Uyghur population at 7.2 million. For information on the Uyghurs see the Peoples of the Silk Road section in the Facts about Central Asia chapter.

Xinjiang is home to a total of 13 ethnic groups, including Han, Uyghur, Kazak, Hui (Chinese Muslims), Mongolian, Kyrgyz, Xibe, Tajik, Uzbek, Manchu, Daur (descendants of Manchu guards), Tatar and Russian.

Uyghurs live mostly in the southern Tarim basin. The summer villages in the Karakul region and settlements along the Torugart-Kashgar road are mostly Kyrgyz. In evidence near the Pakistan border are Tajiks, most of whom live in Tashkurgan Tajik Autonomous County, south of Kashgar. It's a surprise to encounter occasional Russians, descendants of White Russians who fled after the Bolshevik Revolution of 1917. The Ili valley in particular holds small pockets of Xibe, descendants of Manchu soldiers sent from north-east China by the Qing dynasty.

The official language of Xinjiang is Mandarin Chinese but Xinjiang's lingua franca is Uyghur. Uyghur is written in both Arabic and Roman scripts, the latter introduced for a time in an unpopular Chinese attempt to reduce illiteracy. Uyghur was once written in its own script and was the court language of the Mongols.

Facts for the Visitor

PLANNING
When to Go
High season for tourists (and peak demand for rooms and transport) is from late June through September. Most of Xinjiang is sizzling hot at this time but the crossings into Pakistan and Kyrgyzstan are at their most reliable. Xinjiang's famous melons and grapes ripen in August. Outside the summer you can find good deals on accommodation and transport in Kashgar in particular. Winter can be bitterly cold in northern Xinjiang and hovers around freezing in Kashgar. Many tourist hotels and restaurants close for the winter.

The Khunjerab pass to Pakistan is formally open to travellers from 1 May to 30 November – weather permitting. At other times the pass is snowed over. The Torugart pass to Kyrgyzstan is theoretically open year round though snow can be a real problem from November to May (see the Torugart Pass section of the Kyrgyzstan chapter for more details). The road and rail crossings into Kazakstan are open year-round.

Maps
China's National Tourist Administration produces an excellent Tourist Map of North-West China, which covers Xinjiang as well as neighbouring provinces of China. Xinhua bookshops sell provincial maps in Chinese. The best selection is in Ürümqi, though you can find Chinese-language versions in Kashgar.

TOURIST OFFICES
China National Tourist Offices offer brochures, maps and information. Their offices abroad include the following:

Australia
(☎ 02-9299 4057, fax 9290 1958)
CNTO, 19th floor, 44 Market St, Sydney NSW 2000
France
(☎ 01-44 21 82 82, fax 44 21 81 00)
Office du Tourisme de Chine, 116 Avenue des Champs-Elysées, 75008, Paris
Germany
(☎ 069-520135, fax 528490)
CNTO, Ilkenhansstr 6, D-60433 Frankfurt-am-Main
UK
(☎ 020-7935 9787, fax 7487 5842)
CNTO, 4 Glenworth St, London NW1
USA
(☎ 818-545 7507, fax 545 7506)
CNTO, Los Angeles Branch, 333 West Broadway, Suite 201, Glendale CA 91204
(☎ 212-760 9700, fax 760 8809)
CNTO, New York Branch, 350 5th Ave, Suite 6413 Empire State Bldg, New York, NY 10118

VISAS & DOCUMENTS
Everyone needs a visa to enter the People's Republic of China (PRC). Most tourists are issued a single-entry visa, valid for entry within three months of the date of issue, and good for a 30 day stay (see the following Getting a Chinese Visa in Central Asia entry in this section). With it you can visit any open city or region, and while in China you can extend it, and get travel permits for some restricted areas. You cannot get a visa at the border.

Visas are readily available from PRC embassies in most western and many other countries. The easiest place is probably Hong Kong, most cheaply from the Visa Office (☎ 2585 1794/1700) at the Ministry of Foreign Affairs of the PRC, 5th floor,

Low Block, China Resources Building, 26 Harbour Rd, Wanchai. Fees are HK$100 (single entry), HK$150 (double entry) or HK$200 (multiple entry) – US passport holders face an additional surcharge. Visas are issued in two or three working days; 24 hour and same-day service cost more than double. The office is open Monday to Friday 9 am to 12.30 pm and 2 to 5 pm, and on Saturday 9 am to 12.30 pm.

Elsewhere, processing times and fees depend on where you're applying. Express services cost twice the normal fee. Fees must be paid in cash at the time of application and you'll need two passport photos.

On the visa application you must identify an itinerary and entry/exit dates and points, though nobody will hold you to them once you're in the country. To avoid snags, don't mention Tibet or bicycles and don't give your occupation as journalist or writer. Just to be safe you may also want to leave off Ürümqi or Kashgar, since at the time of writing some embassies were making life difficult for travellers who mentioned these destinations. The visa you end up with is the same regardless.

Chinese embassies abroad have been known to stop issuing visas to independent travellers during the height of summer or in the run up to sensitive political events or conferences, in an attempt to control the numbers of tourists entering China at peak times.

Visas valid for more than 30 days are often difficult to obtain anywhere other than in Hong Kong, though some embassies abroad (for example the UK) may give you 60 days out of high tourist season if you ask nicely. If you have trouble getting more than 30 days or a multiple-entry visa, head to a visa or travel agency in Hong Kong (see the Travel Agencies & Organised Tours section in the Getting There & Away chapter).

Note that a 30 day visa is activated on the date you enter China, and must be used within three months of the date of issue. Longer-stay visas often start from the day they are issued, not the day you enter the country, so you should double-check this.

Getting a Chinese Visa in Central Asia

This is possible but difficult and unpredictable so you are better off getting a Chinese visa before leaving home. At the PRC embassy in Tashkent (see the Uzbekistan chapter) you must have a letter (or arrange a telex) of invitation or confirmation of pre-booked services from a Chinese state travel organisation; a 30 day visa will probably take a week and cost about US$20.

They said the same at the embassy in Bishkek, but two travellers there picked up a 10 day China transit visa simply by showing Chinese consular staff their valid onward visas for Pakistan (which were examined closely); they needed no letter of support. You stand a much better chance if you don't mention Torugart, though it's theoretically possible that your visa may be stamped 'by air only'.

Officially, only foreign residents in Kazakstan can get a Chinese visa in Almaty. The PRC embassy in Ashgabat will issue a visa in three days but you need an invitation. The embassy in Dushanbe doesn't issue visas.

Try to get your visa specifically endorsed for the place where you will cross – Alashankou on the train to/from Kazakstan (Dostyk in Kazak or Druzhba in Russian, on the Kazak side) and Korgas on the road to/from Kazakstan. Though the vast majority of travellers cross without problems, a few have been asked by Chinese border guards at Korgas for such endorsements (though fast talking got them one on the spot). It's also worth mentioning to immigration officials that you will be leaving China through another border crossing. In the past, some travellers have been given a border stamp that requires them to exit China by the same border post and, when reaching the border with Hong Kong, have been told that they have to return to Korgas to leave China!

Visa Extensions

You can normally get at least one 30 day extension at the Foreign Affairs office of any Public Security Bureau (PSB), though this does depend on the type of visa you have. A second extension is much harder to get.

The cost depends upon your nationality (eg Y160 for Brits, Y100 Australians, Americans, French).

Travel Permits

Besides the open areas you can visit with just a visa, there are others you can go to by applying at the PSB for an Alien's Travel Permit (*wàibīn lüxíngzhèng*, or *tōngxíngzhèng*). Examples include Karakul in the Kashgar area and Hanas lake in northern Xinjiang. Permits cost Y50 a pop.

EMBASSIES & CONSULATES
Chinese Embassies & Consulates

For embassies in Central Asia see the relevant country chapter. Chinese consular addresses in major cities abroad include:

Australia
    (☎ 02-6273 4780/4781)
    15 Coronation Drive, Yarralumla, ACT 2600
    Consulates: Melbourne, Perth, Sydney
Canada
    (☎ 613-789 3509)
    St Patrick St, Ottawa, Ontario K1N 5H3
    Consulates: Toronto, Vancouver
France
    (☎ 01-47 36 02 58, fax 47 36 34 46)
    9 Ave Victor Cresson, 92130 Issy-Les Moulineaux, Paris; Web site www.amb-chine.fr
Germany
    (☎ 0228-361 095)
    Kurfislrstenallee 125-300 Bonn 2
India
    (☎ 011-600328)
    50-D Shantipath, Chanakyapuri, New Delhi 110021
Netherlands
    (☎ 070-355 1515)
    Adriaan Goekooplaan 7, 2517 JX, The Hague
New Zealand
    (☎ 04-587 0407)
    104A Korokoro Rd, Petone, Wellington
Pakistan
    (visa office ☎ 051-821114)
    Diplomatic Enclave, Islamabad
Russia
    (☎ 095-143 1540, visa inquiries ☎ 143 1543, fax 938 2132)
    ulitsa Druzhby 6, 101000 Moscow
    Consulate: Griboedova
Turkey
    (☎ 312-436 0628, 436 1453)
    Gölgeli Sokak 34, Gaziosmanpasa, Ankara
    Consulate: Istanbul

UK
    (☎ 020-7636 8845, 7631 1430, 24 hour premium-rate visa information 0891-880808, fax 436 9178)
    31 Portland Place, W1N 5AG, London – visas cost UK£25 and are issued in three days; Web site www.chinese-embassy.org.uk
    Consulate: Rusholme
USA
    Embassy Consular Department:
    (☎ 202-338 6688, fax 588 9760, faxback 265 9809, ✉ visa@china-embassy.org)
    Room 110, 2201 Wisconsin Ave, NW Washington DC, 20007 – single-entry visas cost US$30, double-entry cost US$40; Web site www.china-embassy.org has downloadable visa forms
    Consulates: Chicago, Houston, Los Angeles, New York, San Francisco

Embassies & Consulates in Xinjiang

There is a Kazakstan consulate in Ürümqi. See Information in the Ürümqi section for details.

MONEY

The Chinese currency is known as *renminbi* (RMB) or 'People's money'. The basic unit is the *yuan* (Y) divided into 10 *jiao* or 100 *fen*. But in spoken Chinese, the yuan is called *kuai* (*koi* in Uyghur) and jiao is called *mao* (*mo* in Uyghur). Notes come in denominations of 100, 50, 10, five, two and one *yuan*, five and two *jiao*, and five, two and one *fen*, and there are still a few five, two and one *fen* coins about.

To change money in China you must go to the Bank of China, of which there are branches in most tourist hotels. Outside of Ürümqi, Turpan, Kashgar and Hotan changing money can be tricky. Exchange rates are standard and there is a 0.75% commission. Travellers cheques actually get around a 3% higher rate of exchange in the banks than cash.

You can't officially trade *yuan* in Pakistan nor *rupees* in China, though money-changers in Kashgar and Tashkurgan will oblige.

You can get a cash advance off most credit cards at the Bank of China. There is a minimum transaction of Y1200 and a 4% commission.

XINJIANG

country	unit		yuan
Australia	A$1	=	Y5.2
Canada	C$1	=	Y5.6
euro	€1	=	Y8.4
France	1FF	=	Y1.3
Germany	DM1	=	Y4.4
Hong Kong	HK$1	=	Y1.1
Japan	Y100	=	Y6.8
Kazakstan	100 T	=	Y6.2
Kyrgyzstan	10 som	=	Y2.6
Netherlands	DM1	=	Y3.8
New Zealand	NZ$1	=	Y4.3
UK	UK£1	=	Y13.3
USA	US$1	=	Y8.2

POST & COMMUNICATIONS

From China, airmail letters and postcards will probably take under 10 days, even from Kashgar. Airmail letters are Y5.4, postcards Y4.2. Parcels can be sent air, sea or train mail; a 5kg parcel to the US by sea/airmail costs Y194/602. Rates to the UK and Australia are a little cheaper.

Calls are easily made from China Telecom offices, or from top-end hotels (for a cost). Calls from the former are Y15 per minute to Europe and North America and Y30 to Australasia, with no three minute minimum.

Which Time Is It?

Xinjiang is several time zones removed from Beijing, which prefers to ignore the fact. While all of China officially runs on Beijing time *(běijīng shíjián)*, most of Xinjiang runs on an unofficial Xinjiang time *(xīnjiāng shíjián)*, two hours behind Beijing time. Thus 9 am Beijing time is 7 am Xinjiang time. Almost all government-run services such as the bank, post office, bus station and Xinjiang Airlines run on Beijing time. To cater for the time difference, government offices (including the post office and CITS) generally operate 10 am to 1.30 pm and 4 to 8 pm. Unless otherwise stated, we use Beijing time in this book. To be sure, though, if you arrange a time with someone make sure you know which, as well as what, time.

Another option is to dial the home country direct dial number (☎ 108) and then your country code, which puts you through to a local operator there. You can then make a reverse charge (collect) call or a credit card call. The major snag is that most telecom offices in Xinjiang are unaware that this system exists. Also the direct dial number seems to change subtly from place to place (eg 001 or 010 for the USA). Country direct codes include:

country	code
Australia	☎ 108-61
France	☎ 108-33
New Zealand	☎ 108-64
UK	☎ 108-440
USA	☎ 108-001

For faxes most places charge the basic three minute telephone rate, plus a per page fee, bringing the total to Y54 per page in Kashgar.

INTERNET RESOURCES

East Turkestan Information Center
www.uygur.org/English.htm
(German Web site affiliated with the Eastern Turkestan National Center for the Freedom of Uyghurs; lists links to history, literature, newsletters, and human rights groups)

Eastern Turkestan
www.ccs.uky.edu/~rakhim/et.html
(news, photographs, maps, music and some travel)

Nathan Light's Web Page
www.utoledo.edu/~nlight/mainpage.htm
(links related to Uyghur culture and history, with less emphasis on political rhetoric)

BOOKS

Aurel Stein – Pioneer of the Silk Road by Annabel Walker. Definitive biography of the Hungarian-born archaeologist.

China's Last Nomads: The History and Culture of China's Kazaks by Linda Benson & Ingvar Svanberg. This scholarly tome examines the effect of government policies on the Kazak's traditional lifestyle.

In Xanadu: A Quest by William Dalrymple. Dalrymple tries to follow in the footsteps of Marco Polo from Jerusalem to Xanadu, Kublai Khan's fabled city on the Mongolian steppe. His trip turns out rather grittier – and far more entertainingly narrated – than Polo's.

Islamic Frontiers of China – Silk Road Images
by How Man Wong. Coffee-table look at traditional life of the Kazaks, Kyrgyz and Tajiks in Xinjiang.
Lost Camels of Tartary by John Hare. Expeditions into remotest Xinjiang and Mongolia to track the wild Bactrian camel and visit the remote site of Loulan. Written in 1998.
News From Tartary by Peter Fleming. Classic travelogue. Recommended.
Xinjiang, the Silk Road; Islam's Overland Route to China by Peter Yung. Another wonderfully photographed coffee table book and a great souvenir of the region. A similar volume is entitled *Bazaars of Chinese Turkestan; Life and Trade along the Old Silk Road.*

DANGERS & ANNOYANCES

Xinjiang is generally a safe region to travel through, though pickpockets are a problem in Ürümqi and at many bus stations.

There are occasional bombings in public buses and municipal areas (see the boxed text 'The Beginning or the End?', earlier), though these are few and far between and never specifically aimed at tourists. February seems to be a particularly unstable time, with a combination of uprising anniversaries, Chinese New Year and, recently, Muslim Ramadan. The Kazakstan-China border is often closed at times of political instability, though air connections are usually kept open. The Kashgar area and the Pakistan border were closed from 1990 to 1992 in response to rioting.

One common annoyance is that many Chinese still consider it their patriotic duty to charge double prices for foreigners, despite the recent changes in state policy. There's not much you can do except keep a close eye on what locals are paying.

FOOD & DRINK

For a rundown of Uyghur specialities see the boxed text on the following page. Chinese food is also available anywhere wherever there is a sizeable Chinese community (just about everywhere) and is generally excellent. For a basic list of dishes see the menu guide in the Language chapter at the back of this book. Chinese snacks are a cheap lifesaver when confronted with a Chinese-only menu. Some popular snacks are:

bāozi – steamed buns stuffed with meat; delicious dipped in soy sauce.
huǒguō – hotpot; another trusty standard, especially in winter. You pay individually for ingredients such as noodles, mushrooms and beef, which you dip into a boiling cauldron of broth – a great group meal.
húntun – smaller ravioli, known in the west as wanton and normally served in a soup.
niúròumìan – beef noodles, available everywhere.
shāguō – an earthenware pot full of broth and vermicelli noodles, vegetables, mushroom, tofu and meat.
shuǐjiǎo – Chinese ravioli, served dry by the *jin* (500g) and then dipped into vinegar and soy sauce, or in a soup by the plate.

Hui Muslim food is also popular in the northern part of Xinjiang and is recognisable by its lack of pork and the green flag and Arabic script on the outside of the restaurant.

Xinjiang is also famous for its fantastic fruit, particularly its honeydew melons from Hami, grapes and raisins from Turpan, pears from Korla, apples from Ili, pomegranates from Karghilik and apricots from Kucha.

Alcohol is available everywhere. Xinjiang, Kashgar, Yellow River and Beijing beer are available in non-Uyghur restaurants. A regional favourite is wine from Turfan – red or white, both of them sickly-sweet like sherry.

SHOPPING

Inlaid knives, atlas silks, carpets, musical instruments, jade carvings, pottery, metal ware, wooden carvings, paintings, hats, Silk Road T-shirts ... the shopping list for Xinjiang is endless. Though most things come together in Kashgar's giant market, better value – and often better pieces – can be found in the smaller towns. For knives see Yengisar; for carpets and silk see Hotan; for hats try Kashgar; for books see the main tourist hotels.

ORIENTATION

Most Uyghur towns are divided into the old town *(kadimi shahr)* and Han-Chinese dominated new town *(yangi shahr)*.

Street names are mostly in Chinese and are named after communist ideals such as Renmin (People's), Jiefang (Liberation) and

XINJIANG

Uyghur Food

Uyghur cuisine includes all the trusty Central Asian stand-bys such as kebabs, *pulau* (plov – rice with meat and vegetables) and dumplings *(chuchura)*, but has benefited from Chinese influence to make it the most enjoyable region of Central Asia in which to eat.

Uyghurs boast endless varieties of *laghman* (Chinese: *lāmián*), though the usual topping is some combination of mutton, peppers, tomatoes, eggplants, green beans and garlic. *Suoman* are noodle squares fried with tomatoes, peppers, garlic and meat, sometimes quite spicy. *Suoman goshsiz* are the vegetarian variety. Noodles can be very spicy so ask for *lazasiz* (without peppers) if you prefer a milder version.

Kebabs are another staple and are generally of a much better standard than the ropey shashlyk of the Central Asian republics. *Jiger* (liver) kebabs are the low-fat variety. *Tonur kebabs* are larger and baked in a *tonor* oven – tandoori style.

Breads are a particular speciality, especially when straight out of the oven and sprinkled with poppy seeds, sesame seeds or fennel. They make a great plate for a round of kebabs. Uyghur bakers also make wonderful bagels called *girde nan*.

Other snacks include *serik ash* (yellow meatless noodles), *nokot* (chickpeas with carrot), *pintang* (meat and vegetable soup) and *gangpen* (rice with fried vegetable and meat). Most travellers understandably steer clear of *opke*, a nauseating broth of bobbling goat's heads and coiled, stuffed intestines.

Samsas (baked envelopes of meat) are available everywhere, but the meat-to-fat ratio varies wildly. Hotan and Kashgar offer huge meat pies called *daman* or *gosh girde*. You can even get *balyk* (fried fish) here, where it is as far away from the sea as it is humanly possible to be.

For dessert you can try *maroji* (vanilla ice cream churned in iced wooden barrels), *matang* (walnut fruit loaf), *kharsen meghriz* (fried dough balls filled with sugar, raisins and walnuts) or *dogh* (sometimes known as *durap*), a delicious, though potentially deadly, mix of shaved ice, syrup, yoghurt and iced water. *Tangzaza* are triangles of glutinous rice wrapped in bamboo leaves covered in syrup.

Xinjiang is justly famous for its fruit, whether it be apricots *(uruk)*, grapes *(uzum)*, watermelon *(tawuz)*, sweet melon *(khoghun)* or raisins *(yimish)*. The best grapes come from Turpan, the sweetest melons from Hami.

Meals are washed down with beer or green tea *kok chai*, often laced with nutmeg. Uyghur restaurants usually provide a miniature rubbish bin on the table in which to dispose of the waste tea after rinsing out the bowl.

Dongfeng (The East Wind). Streets are divided into sections called *běi* (north), *nán* (south), *dōng* (east) and *xī* (west).

Central Xinjiang

ÜRÜMQI
☎ 0991 • pop 1.5 million

The capital of Xinjiang, Ürümqi has little to distinguish itself other than the claim to being the farthest city in the world from the ocean (2250km). About 80% of the residents are Han Chinese, and much of the city looks like it was transplanted from eastern China. Ürümqi means 'beautiful pastureland' in Mongolian. There are few 'sights' as such, but it's an important transport crossroads and the gateway to the province, through which most travellers pass at some point.

Orientation
Most of the sights, tourist facilities and hotels are scattered across the city, although they're all easily reached on local buses.

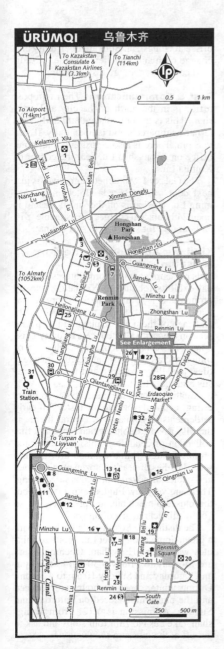

ÜRÜMQI 乌鲁木齐

ÜRÜMQI

PLACES TO STAY
3   Huadu Hotel
8   Hongshan Hotel; CYTS; CITS
9   Holiday Inn
12   Western Hotel
13   Bogeda Hotel;
18   Xinjiang Electric Power Hotel
21   Hoi Tak Hotel
27   Hualian Hotel
31   Ya'ou Hotel
32   Overseas Chinese Hotel; CTS; Siberia Airlines

PLACES TO EAT
16   John's Information Service & Café
17   Dong Nan Wei
23   Yuqing Restaurant
26   Meisheng Banquet Hall

OTHER
1   Youhao Department Store
2   Xinjiang Autonomous Region Museum
4   Main Post Office
5   Hongshan Department Store
6   Bank of China
7   Buses to Tianchi & Baiyanggou
10   CITS; Lüyou Hotel
11   Kyrgyzstan & Uzbekistan Airways Office;
     Yingjisha Hotel
14   Galaxy 169 Internet Bar
15   Xinjiang Airlines Booking Office
19   PSB
20   Tianshan Department Store
22   Post & Telephone Office
24   Bank of China
25   Long-Distance Bus Station
28   Buses to Turpan (Hengyuan Hotel)
29   Altai Regional Bus Station
30   Kashgar Bus Station

XINJIANG

The train and long-distance bus stations are in the south-western corner of the city. The 'city centre' revolves around Minzhu Lu, Zhongshan Lu and Jianshe Lu. Here you'll find most of the government offices, fancier hotels and upmarket department stores. In the north of town are two major intersections, called Youhao and Hongshan, which are very popular shopping areas and the latter an important local transport hub.

Information

Tourist Offices & Travel Agencies The Lüyou Hotel (just behind the Holiday Inn) is home to several tourist and travel agencies. On the ground floor is the China

International Travel Service (CITS; ☎ 282 6719, fax 281 0689).

A more useful place is CYTS (China Youth Travel Service; ☎ 282 4761, ext 130) in the Hongshan Hotel that seems relatively efficient and cheap for organising tickets and tours. CITS also has an office here that is a bit more helpful than the one in the Lüyou Hotel.

China Travel Service (CTS; ☎ 652 1440) is in the grounds of the Overseas Chinese Hotel. Most of Ürümqi's hotels have travel agents offering similar deals for trips around Xinjiang. Agents from both the Hongshan and Ya'ou hotels have been recommended by readers.

Consulates Kazakstan has a consulate (*hāsàkèsītǎn lǐngshìguǎn*; ☎ 383 2324) in the northern section of the city, just off Beijing Lu. Three-day transit visas are issued to those who have an onward visa for Kyrgyzstan, Russia or Uzbekistan. The visa takes a week to be issued and costs US$15, plus a Y65 processing fee. Some travellers report having to pay US$35 for a three day transit visa if they don't have another Central Asian visa. Longer stay tourist or business visas are generally best processed at the embassy in Beijing, though you could theoretically have your visa invitation sent directly in advance to the consulate.

It is theoretically possible to enter the country with a Kyrgyz visa using the 72 hour rule but Chinese customs may not let you on a plane without a Kazakstan visa. Visa regulations change regularly so give them a ring before you head out to the consulate.

The visa section is only open Monday to Thursday 10.30 am to 1.30 pm. A taxi to the consulate will cost about Y15.

Visa Extensions The foreign affairs office of the PSB, on Jiankang Lu, just north of Minzhu Lu, is the place to come for a visa extension. Look out for the sign 'Aliens Reception Room'. It is open Monday to Friday 9.30 am to 2 pm and 4 to 8 pm.

Money The main Bank of China is at 343 Jiefang Lu, next to South Gate. There is another Bank of China opposite the main post office at Hongshan. Both are open daily and change cash and travellers cheques. Credit card cash advances are also available.

Post & Communications The main post office is in the north of the city at Hongshan. This is the only place that handles international parcels and is open daily 10 am to 8 pm. There is also a post and telephone office on Zhongshan Lu, near the corner of Xinhua Lu.

The Galaxy 169 Internet Bar (*yīnyu*) is just next door to the Bogeda Hotel on Guangming Lu. The bar is on the 2nd floor and is open 24 hours and charges a reasonable Y10 an hour (Y5 for students) to surf the net.

Xinjiang Autonomous Region Museum

This museum contains some interesting visual exhibits relating to Xinjiang minority groups and is worth a look. There are at least 13 different ethnic groups in Xinjiang, and each of them are displayed in a special section covering all the facets of daily existence. There is a fascinating collection of minority clothing, musical instruments, textiles, jewellery, cooking and farming utensils and tools for hunting.

Another wing of the museum has an interesting section devoted to the history of early settlements in Xinjiang. A central theme is the Silk Road exhibits, which include a fine collection of ceramics, tools, tapestries and bronze figures. Prime exhibits are the preserved bodies of nearly a dozen men, women and babies discovered in tombs in Xinjiang. There are very few English explanations but the museum's exhibits are pretty visual, so you'll still get the gist of things.

The distinctive Soviet-style building with a green dome is on Xibei Lu, about 20 minutes walk from Hongshan. Opening hours are Monday to Friday 9.30 am to 6.30 pm and Saturday and Sunday 10 am to 4.30 pm. During winter, opening hours are reduced and the museum is closed on Saturday and Sunday. Admission is Y12. From Hongshan, take bus No 7 for four stops and ask to get off at the museum (*bówùguǎn*).

Parks

The scenic, tree-shaded **Renmin Park** is about 1km in length and can be entered from either the northern or southern gates. The best time to visit is early in the morning when the Chinese are out here doing their exercises. There are plenty of birds in the park, a few pavilions and a lake where you can hire rowboats. The park is open 7.30 am to 10 pm and admission is Y5.

Hongshan Park is Xinjiang's premier amusement park, complete with a Ferris wheel, bumper cars and swinging gondolas designed to bring up your lunch. Other attractions include an eight storey pagoda and sweeping views of the city. Entry is Y3; open daily.

Places to Stay

During the peak summer months (June to October) most hotel rooms double in price.

Places to Stay – Budget

Hongshan Hotel (hóng-shān bīnguǎn; ☎ 282 4761) is a good base in the centre of town and is popular with budget travellers. Dorm beds cost Y40 in a three bed dorm with private bath. However, it also has the most unhelpful desk staff in Ürümqi and charges foreigners more than Chinese.

Instead, try the nearby two star *Bogeda Hotel (bógédá bīnguǎn;* ☎ 282 3910), which has five-bed dorms for Y45 per person and beds in a triple with bath for Y60. Nice twins cost a reasonable Y144 or Y288 during the peak summer period.

Just next door to the train station is the *Ya'ou Hotel (yǎ'ōu bīnguǎn;* ☎ 585 6699), where basic dorm beds start at Y12 in an eight person room and beds in quads/triples with bath are Y40/50. Their singles/twins are a little overpriced at Y130/158, but you should be able to bargain them down. The other plus with this place is they can purchase train tickets for guests, free of charge.

For relatively cheap twins, there's the *Overseas Chinese Hotel (huáqiáo bīnguǎn;* ☎ 286 0793, fax 286 2279, 51 Xinhua Lu), which charges Y100 for compact rooms in the older, Russian-style building and Y180 in the newer wing.

Hualian Hotel (huálián bīnguǎn) is also on Xinhua Lu, but a little closer to the city centre. It has unexciting twins for Y80, even worse ones for Y100 and surprisingly good value twins for Y150. The last of these can be bargained down to Y120. The staff are friendly and inquisitive.

Places to Stay – Mid-Range

In the city centre, the *Xinjiang Electric Power Hotel (xīnjiāng diànlì bīnguǎn;* ☎ 282 2911, fax 282 6031) is actually a pretty good place, despite the silly name. Comfortable twins range from Y250 to Y366. Breakfast is included and they offer free airport and train station transfers for guests.

Western Hotel (xīnjiāng xīyù dàjiǔàn; ☎ 282 6788, fax 283 3613, 84 Xinhua Beilu) has twins/singles for Y200/280 and includes breakfast and dinner. The hotel is quite new, but is already showing signs of poor maintenance.

Huadu Hotel (huádū dàfàndiàn; ☎ 452 9922, fax 452 2708) at the Hongshan intersection has nice twins for Y180.

Places to Stay – Top End

Hoi Tak Hotel (hǎidé jiǔàn; ☎ 232 2828, fax 232 1818, ✉ hthxjbc@mail.wl.xj.cn) has five-star services and facilities, but is still waiting for the official stars. Standard rooms are Y665 and superior rooms Y735, plus 15% service charge and 3% tax. Even if you can't afford to stay here, they have great coffee and an excellent buffet.

Holiday Inn (jiàrì dàjiǔàn; ☎ 281 8788, fax 281 7422, ✉ holiday@mail.wl.xj.cn) is a popular choice with western tour groups. Standard rooms range from Y680 to Y935, while singles are Y580, plus a 15% service charge. There is a cake shop on the 1st floor that sells a good range of pastries and after 8 pm everything is discounted by 25%. During the summer months they also offer a number of deals on their buffets and barbecues.

Places to Eat

Ürümqi is not a bad spot to try Uyghur foods (see the boxed text 'Uyghur Food' earlier in this chapter). There is a row of restaurants on Jianshe Lu.

XINJIANG

Meisheng Banquet Hall (měishēng yàn-huìtīng) is a large Uyghur restaurant that is popular with locals. Both Uyghur and Chinese food is on offer and there are traditional dancing and singing performances most nights, usually starting after 10 pm. Most of the dishes are very generous, so you may prefer asking for an entree serving *(bàn pán)*. The restaurant is on the 2nd floor of the large building adjacent to the Hualian Hotel on Xinhua Lu. The entrance is just to the left of the Bank of China.

For cheap and tasty Chinese fare, the *Yuqing Restaurant (yuīng fànguǎn)* on Wenhua Lu hits the spot. Their spicy chicken *(làzi jīdīng)* and Japanese-style caramel tofu *(rìběn hóngshāo dòufu)* are worth trying. There is no English menu or sign, just look out for the white writing on a green sign.

Hongqi Lu, in the city centre, is another good street to go restaurant hunting, with lots of noodle and dumpling shops and other small eateries. One place that locals speak highly of is *Dong Nan Wei (dōng nán wèi)*. It's little more than a hole in the wall, but has a good reputation for its fish *(huángyú)* and spare rib *(páigu)* dishes. There's no English to be found anywhere, though you can always resort to pointing at meals on other people's tables.

John's Information Café has Chinese food as well as some reasonably priced western fare, and is a good place to meet up with other travellers and down a few beers.

If you've been in rural Kazakstan for too long and are craving real western food, then head for either the *Hoi Tak Hotel* or *Holiday Inn*. Their all-you-can-eat breakfast and lunch buffets will do the trick, though they're pricey at more than Y100 per person.

At night the footpath areas along Minzhu Lu and around the Youhao and Hongshan intersections become bustling *night markets* with fresh handmade noodle dishes, shish kebab skewers and a whole range of point-and-choose fried dishes.

During July and August, the markets are packed with delicious fresh and dried fruit. The best is the *Erdaoqiao Market (èrdào-qiáo shìchǎng)* in the southern end of the city, not too far from the Turpan bus station.

Getting There & Away

Air Ürümqi is well served by domestic services and has several international connections to neighbouring Central Asian countries. International departures include flights to Almaty (Y1660 with Xinjiang Airlines; one month return fare Y2370), Bishkek (US$190), Hong Kong, Islamabad, Novosibirsk (Russia), and Moscow (US$250). It's not uncommon for these flights to be suspended, especially during the winter months.

Domestic flights connect Ürümqi with Beijing (Y1930), Chengdu (Y1350), Chongqing (Y1460), Lanzhou (Y1040), Guangzhou (Y2270), Shanghai (Y2240), Xi'an (Y1330), and most other major cities in China.

There are regular flights from Ürümqi to these towns in Xinjiang: Aksu (Akesu), Hotan (Hetian), Karamai (Kelamayi), Kashgar (Kashi), Korla (Kuerle), Tacheng and Yining. See those town entries for details. Airline offices in town include:

Kazakstan Airlines
 (☎ 382 5564) next to the Kazakstan consulate, off Beijing Lu
Kyrgyzstan Airlines
 (☎ 231 6638/6333) 1st floor, Yingjisha Hotel
Siberia Airlines
 (☎ 286 2326) Overseas Chinese Hotel
Uzbekistan Airways
 (☎ 231 6333) shares an office with Kyrgyzstan Airlines
Xinjiang Airlines
 (☎ 264 1826) 2 Xinmin Lu, 1st floor, China Construction Bank Bldg

Bus The long-distance bus station is on Heilongjiang Lu. While there are buses here for most cities in Xinjiang (the notable exception being Turpan), many destinations have their own bus station elsewhere in town.

Large public buses and more comfortable minibuses to Turpan (Y23, three hours) run from near the Hengyuan Hotel on Quanyin Dadao, in the southern part of the city. The best way to get there is to hop in a taxi: just tell the driver you want to go to the *tuān qìchē zhàn*. The ride shouldn't cost more than Y10 to Y15 from anywhere within the city.

If you're heading to Kashgar (Y210 to Y240, 30 hours), you can get a sleeper bus from either the main station or the Kashgar bus station, which is just east of the train station. Sleeper buses depart between 4 and 8 pm daily.

Buses north to Burqin (Y50/108 normal/sleeper bus, 15 hours) leave in the evening. Tickets can be bought at either the main bus station or the alternative bus station for the Altay region, which is on Hetian Dongyijie, just after the overpass and north of Qiantangjiang Lu.

Buses to Yining (Y65) depart between 9 am and 6 pm from both the main bus station and the Yining bus stand. Buses to Jeminay (Y52 to Y100, 14 hours) leave around 4 pm from the main bus station.

To Kazakstan At the time of research buses to Almaty (*ālāmùtú*) were leaving the long-distance bus station once daily at 6 pm; check at window No 8 for the latest on this service. The 1052km trip takes 24 hours straight through with three stops for meals, and costs Y450.

Crossing the border shouldn't really be a problem as long as you have a valid Kazakstan visa. See Getting There & Away under Almaty in the Kazakstan chapter for more details.

Train The new 31 hour service between Ürümqi and Kashgar costs Y185 to Y199 for a hard sleeper berth and from Y301 for a soft sleeper. The train leaves Kashgar at midnight and takes in some interesting scenery.

For details of train services to provinces outside Xinjiang see the Getting There & Away entry in the Almaty section of the Kazakstan chapter.

To Kazakstan Trains run Monday and Saturday from Ürümqi to Almaty. The trip takes a very slow 35 hours, eight of which is spent at the Chinese and Kazak customs, and the hard sleeper fare is around Y400. At the Ürümqi station there's a special ticket window for these trains, inside the large waiting room in the main building. It's only open Monday, and Thursday to Saturday, 10 am to 1 pm and 3 to 7 pm. You will, of course, need a visa for Kazakstan. See Getting There

& Away under Almaty in the Kazakstan chapter for more details on the route.

Getting Around

To/From the Airport Minibuses (Y8) head out to the airport half-hourly from 6 am. They depart from the Xinjiang Airlines office and pass through the Hongshan intersection. The same minibuses also greet all incoming flights.

The airport is 16km from the Hongshan intersection. A taxi should cost between Y40 and Y50. If you're in no hurry, bus No 51 runs between Hongshan and the airport gate, but takes about an hour.

Bus Ürümqi's public buses are packed to the roof and beyond. It's better to spend an extra few mao for a minibus.

Some of the more useful bus routes include No 7, which runs up Xinhua Lu to the Youhao intersection, linking the city centre with the main post office; and No 2, which runs from the train station, past the main post office and way up along Beijing Lu, past the Kazakstan consulate.

AROUND ÜRÜMQI
Heavenly Lake

Halfway up a mountain, at 1900m, in the middle of a desert, this small, deep-blue lake looks like a chunk of Switzerland or Canada that's been exiled to Central Asia. The surrounding hills are covered with fir trees and grazing lands peppered with the yurts of Kazak herders who inhabit the mountains. In the distance are the snow-covered peaks of the Tian Shan range. It's a heavily touristed spot, especially in the peak summer season, but is beautiful nonetheless and you can climb the hills past the tourist groups right up to the snow line.

The lake is 115km east of Ürümqi at 1980m above sea level. Nearby is Bogda Feng (5445m), the Peak of God, which can be climbed by well-equipped mountaineers with permits (ask CITS). It's possible to hike to Bogda base camp and back in four days (including the trip from Ürümqi). The lake freezes over in Xinjiang's bitter winter and roads up here are open only in summer.

The best way to spend your time is to hike around the lake and even up into the hills. Follow the track skirting the lake for about 4km to the far end where there is a small nursery and PSB office. From here you can just choose your valley. From personal experience, avoid trying a circuit of the lake as a day trip.

During the summer, Kazaks set up yurts in this area for tourist accommodation at Y40 per person, with three meals. This is not a bad option; during the day the area can get quite cramped with day-trippers, but you'll pretty much have the place to yourself after 4 pm and in the morning. Readers recommend *Rashits Yurt*, which is about halfway around the lake; the owner can speak English. Some people have also brought their own tents and camped up here.

Admission to the lake area costs Y24. It is possible to hire horses for treks around the lake; a trip to the snow line costs about Y80. The return trek takes between eight and 10 hours, depending on where the snow line is.

Buses to Tianchi leave Ürümqi between 9 and 9.30 am from the north gate of Renmin Park and return between 5 and 6 pm. Tickets are sold from the desks to the left of the park entrance. The return fare is between Y25 and Y50, depending on the size and quality of the bus. The trip takes about 2½ hours and the road is improving all the time. There are also usually private buses leaving from in front of the Hongshan Hotel, and return fares from here are about Y30. Buses back to Ürümqi leave between 4 and 5 pm.

TURPAN
☎ 0995

East of Ürümqi the Tian Shan mountains split into a southern and a northern range; between the two lie the Hami and Turpan basins. The Turpan basin is the hottest, lowest and driest in China; the region was traditionally known to Chinese as Huozhou, the Land of Fire.

Turpan holds a special place in Uyghur history, since nearby Gaochang was once the capital of the Uyghurs. It was an important staging post on the Silk Road and was a centre of Buddhism before being converted to Islam in the 8th century. During the Chinese occupation it served as a garrison town.

Turpan is also the hottest spot in China – the highest recorded temperature here was 49.6°C (121.3°F). Fortunately, the humidity is low – so low that your laundry is practically dry by the time you hang it out. Turpan is famous for its grapes and is an important producer of sultanas and wine.

Turpan County is inhabited by about 240,000 people – just over half are Uyghurs and the rest mostly Han. The centre of the county is the Turpan oasis, a small city set in a vast tract of grain fields and grape vines. Despite the concrete-block architecture of the city centre, it's a pleasant, relaxing place. Some of the smaller streets have pavements covered with grapevine trellises, which are a godsend in the fierce heat of summer.

Orientation & Information

The centre of the Turpan oasis is called 'Old City' *(lǎochéng)* and the western part is called 'New City' *(xīnchéng)*. The Old City is where you'll find the tourist hotels, shops, market, long-distance bus station and restaurants – all within easy walking distance of each other. Most of the sights are scattered

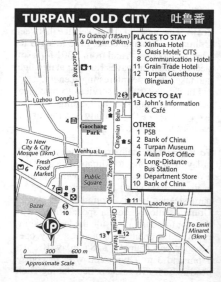

TURPAN – OLD CITY 吐鲁番

PLACES TO STAY
3 Xinhua Hotel
5 Oasis Hotel; CITS
8 Communication Hotel
11 Grain Trade Hotel
12 Turpan Guesthouse (Binguan)

PLACES TO EAT
13 John's Information & Café

OTHER
1 PSB
2 Bank of China
4 Turpan Museum
6 Main Post Office
7 Long-Distance Bus Station
9 Department Store
10 Bank of China

on the outskirts of the oasis or in the surrounding desert.

CITS (☎ 852 1352) has a branch in the grounds of the Oasis Hotel, and can help book train and plane tickets, as well as arrange tours of local sights.

The Bank of China has two branches that can change cash and travellers cheques. Both are open daily. The PSB is on Gaochang Lu in the north of town.

The main post office is west of the bus station or there is also a small post office inside the Oasis Hotel that handles parcels.

Things to See & Do

While the **bazar** is fun to poke around, it's nothing like its more exotic counterpart in Kashgar. At the front you'll find a few stalls selling brightly decorated knives, Muslim clothing and some other interesting items, but as you move towards the back it's mainly household goods and synthetic fabrics.

There are several mosques in town. The **City Mosque**, the most active of them, is on the western outskirts about 3km from the town centre. Take care not to disturb the worshippers. You can get here by bicycle.

Also known as Sugongta, the **Emin Minaret** and adjoining mosque are just 3km from Turpan on the eastern edge of town. It's designed in a simple Afghani style and was built in 1777 in memory of the local ruler, Emin Hoja. The minaret is circular, 44m high and tapers towards the top. The temple is bare inside, but services are held every Friday and on holidays. The surrounding scenery is nice, and from the roof of the mosque you can get a good view of the Turpan oasis. You can't climb the minaret: it was closed off to tourists in 1989 to help preserve the structure. You can walk or bicycle here, although many people stop here on a minibus tour. The mosque is open during daylight hours and entry is Y12.

Places to Stay

All hotels in Turpan increase their already inflated prices during the hot summer months. During this period the first thing you will probably be looking for, other than a pool, is an air-conditioner.

Right next to the bus station, ***Communication Hotel*** *(jiāotōng bīnguǎn;* ☎ *853 1320)* is pretty noisy, but is definitely the cheapest spot in town. It has very basic dorms with fans from Y8 to Y18 per person. Twins with bath and air-con cost from Y40 to Y80.

The most popular abode of backpackers is the ***Oasis Hotel*** *(lǜzhōu bīnguǎn;* ☎ *852 2491)*. Beds in a quad with air-con and common showers cost Y27. Twins, including a Uyghur-style room, are a ridiculous Y350. The hotel enjoys a quiet location and has a fairly nice courtyard with grapevine trellises and tree-lined walkways. Web site www.the-silk-road.com

Xinhua Hotel *(xīnhua bīnguǎn;* ☎ *852 0169)* is just north of the Oasis and has clean dorms in quads/triples for Y30/35. Good value singles are Y80 and a bed in a twin costs Y60. The only drawback is the common toilets, which are often filthy.

Turpan Guesthouse *(tuān bīnguǎn;* ☎ *852 1416, fax 852 3262)* has a nice vine-trellised courtyard, beer garden, quiet rooms and even a swimming pool. It has air-con dorms for Y30, triples for Y220 and overpriced twins for Y350, that CITS will book you into for Y200.

Grain Trade Hotel *(liángmào bīnguǎn;* ☎ *852 4301)* is an uninteresting but friendly place that has dorm beds from Y20 and twins for Y160, although it should be easy to bargain them down.

Places to Eat

There is a string of small restaurants along Laocheng Lu, between Gaochang Lu and Qingnian Lu. Quite a few have English menus, and the food is generally good and reasonably priced. Most of the places serve Sichuan and other Han-style dishes, but you can also get Uyghur food on request.

Opposite the Turpan Guesthouse is ***John's Information & Café*** *(*☎ *852 4237)*. This is the only place in town that does good western food, but there are Chinese meals available too. The menu is in English, prices are reasonable and you can even get cold drinks with ice (much appreciated in Turpan's heat!).

Entertainment

A traditional Uyghur music, song and dance show is staged in the courtyard of the *Turpan Guesthouse* (Binguan) under the trellises almost nightly in summer. In the off season performances take place on the 2nd floor of the hotel restaurant building. It's possible to order a decent meal here prior to the performance. During the summer, the shows are held almost every night from around 10 pm. They're fun nights that usually end up with the front row of the audience being dragged out to dance with the performers. Tickets are Y20.

Getting There & Around

The bus station is near the bazar. There are 10 to 12 buses a day to Ürümqi between 8 am and 6 pm. The 185km journey costs Y23 and takes 2½ to three hours on the new freeway.

Minibuses to the railhead at Daheyan (Y6, 1½ hours) run approximately once every 30 minutes between 8 am and 6 pm. For information on travelling from Daheyan to Turpan, see the Daheyan section, later in this chapter.

Public transport around Turpan is by minibus, pedicab, bicycle or donkey cart. John's Information Café and the Turpan Guesthouse have bicycle rental. Pedicab drivers usually hang around the hotel gates – negotiate the fare in advance. Donkey carts can be found around the market, but this mode of transport is gradually fading.

AROUND TURPAN

There are many sights in the countryside around Turpan, and it requires at least a day to see everything of importance.

The only way to see the sights is to join a tour or hire a minibus for a full day (about 10 hours). You won't have to look for them – the drivers will come looking for you, and will find other travellers to share the expense. Figure on paying between Y40 and Y60 per person, depending on your bargaining skills. Both the tours organised by the Oasis and Turpan hotels include an English guide and are cheap, reliable and recommended by readers.

Make sure it's clearly understood which places you want to see. A trip might include Astana graves, Gaochang ruins, Bezeklik caves, Grape valley, Emin Minaret, the Karez underground irrigation channels and Jiaohe ruins (usually in that order). Practically no drivers speak English, but many speak fluent Japanese, a testament to the popularity of Turpan with Japanese tourists.

Don't underestimate the weather. The desert sun is hot and it can bake your brain in less time than it takes to make fried rice. Essential survival gear includes a water bottle, sunglasses and a straw hat. Some sunscreen and chapstick for your lips will prove useful.

Astana Graves

These graves, where the dead of Gaochang are buried, lie north-west of the ancient city. Only three of the tombs are open to tourists, and each of these is approached by a short flight of steps that leads down to the burial chamber, about 6m below ground level.

One tomb contains portraits of the deceased painted on the walls, while another has paintings of birds. The third tomb holds two well-preserved corpses (one mummy from the original trio seems to have been removed to Turpan's museum).

Some of the artefacts date back as far as the Jin dynasty, from the 3rd to 5th centuries CE. The finds include silks, brocades, embroideries and many funerary objects, such as shoes, hats and sashes made of recycled paper. The last turned out to be quite special for archaeologists, since the paper included deeds, records of slave purchases, orders for silk and other everyday transactions. Admission is Y10; open daily.

Gaochang Ruins

About 46km east of Turpan are the ruins of Gaochang, the capital of the Uyghurs when they moved into the Xinjiang region from Mongolia in the 9th century.

The town was founded in the 7th century during the Tang dynasty and became a major staging post on the Silk Road. The walls of the city are clearly visible. They were as much as 12m thick, formed a rough square with a perimeter of 6km, and were

Karez

The *karez* is a peculiarly Central Asian means of irrigation that can be found in Xinjiang, Afghanistan and Iran. Like many dry, arid countries Xinjiang has great underground reservoirs of water, which can transform otherwise barren stretches of land – if you can get the water up. However, this subterranean water is often so far underground that drilling or digging for it with primitive equipment is virtually impossible.

Long ago the Uyghurs devised a better way. They dig a well (*karez*), known as the 'head well', on higher ground, where snowmelt from the mountains collects (in Turpan's case the Bogda mountains). A long underground tunnel is then dug to conduct this water down to the village farmland. A whole series of vertical wells, looking from above like giant anthills, are dug every 20m along the path of this tunnel to aid construction and provide access. The wells are fed entirely by gravity, thus eliminating the need for pumps. Furthermore, having the channels underground greatly reduces water loss from evaporation.

Digging a karez is skilled and dangerous work and the *karez-kans* are respected and highly paid workers. The cost of making a karez and later maintaining it was traditionally split between a whole village and the karez was communally owned.

The city of Turpan owes its existence to these vital wells and channels, some of which were constructed over 2000 years ago. There are over 1000 wells, and the total length of the channels runs to an incredible 5000km, all constructed by hand and without modern machinery or building materials.

surrounded by a moat. Gaochang was divided into an outer city, an inner city within the walls, and a palace and government compound.

A large monastery in the south-western part of the city is in reasonable condition, with some of its rooms, corridors and doorways still preserved. The entry fee is Y10; open daily.

Flaming Mountains

North of Gaochang lie the aptly named Flaming mountains (*huǒyànshān*) – they look like they're on fire in the midday sun. Purplish-brown in colour, they are 100km long and 10km wide. The minibus tours don't usually include a stop here, but they drive through on the way to Bezeklik caves. Uyghurs call the mountains Kyzyl Tag, or Red mountains.

The Flaming mountains were made famous in Chinese literature by the classic novel *Journey to the West*. The story is about the monk Xuan Zang (Tripitaka) and his followers who travelled west in search of the Buddhist sutra. See the boxed text 'Great

Chinese Explorers' in the Facts about Central Asia chapter for more information.

Bezeklik Thousand Buddha Caves

On the north-western side of the Flaming mountains, on a cliff face fronting a river valley, are the remains of these Buddhist cave temples. All the caves are in dreadful condition, most having been devastated by Muslims or robbed by all and sundry.

The large statues that stood at the back of each cave have been destroyed or stolen, and the faces of the buddhas ornamenting the walls have either been scrapped or completely gouged out. Particularly active in the export of murals was a German, Albert von Le Coq, who removed whole frescoes from the stone walls and transported them back to the Berlin Museum – where Allied bombing wiped most of them out during WWII.

Today the caves reveal little more than a hint of what these works of art were like in their heyday. Those that remain are usually tacky replicas. Fortunately, the scenery just outside the caves is fine. Admission is Y12; open daily.

XINJIANG

Grape Valley

In this small paradise – a thick maze of vines and grape trellises – stark desert surrounds you. Most of the minibus tours stop here for lunch; the food isn't bad, and there are plenty of grapes in season (late August to early September is best).

There is a winery near the valley and lots of well-ventilated brick buildings for drying grapes – wine and raisins are major exports of Turpan. CITS runs an annual 'grape festival' in August, featuring dancing, singing, wine-tasting and, of course, a lot of grape eating.

Tempting as it might be, don't pick the grapes here or anywhere else in Turpan. There is a Y15 fine if you do. Considerable effort goes into raising these grapes and the farmers don't appreciate tourists eating their profits. There's a Y10 entry fee for the Grape Valley; open daily.

Jiaohe Ruins

During the Han dynasty, Jiaohe was established by the Chinese as a garrison town. The city was decimated by Jenghiz Khan's 'travelling road show' and there's little left to see.

The buildings are rather more obvious than the ruins of Gaochang though, and you can walk through the old streets and along the roads. A main road cuts through the city, and at the end is a large monastery with figures of Buddha still visible.

The ruins are around 7km to 8km west of Turpan and stand on an island bound by two small rivers – thus the name Jiaohe, which means 'confluence of two rivers'. During the cooler months you can cycle out here without any problem. Entry costs Y12; open daily.

DAHEYAN

The railway jumping-off point for Turpan is signposted 'Turpan Zhan' (tuān zhàn). In fact, you are actually in Daheyan, and the Turpan oasis is a 58km drive south-east across the desert. Daheyan is not a place you'll want to hang around, so spare a thought for the locals who have to eke out a sane living here.

The bus station is a five minute walk from the train station. Walk up the road leading from the train station and turn right at the first main intersection; the bus station is a few minutes walk ahead on the left-hand side of the road.

Minibuses run from here to Turpan about once every 30 minutes during the day. The fare is Y5, and the trip takes 1½ hours.

Although Daheyan train station is rarely crowded, it can be difficult to get onward hard-sleeper tickets, as most of these will have already been sold from Ürümqi. The best option is to just board the train and try your luck with an upgrade. There are daily trains to Beijing, Chengdu, Lanzhou, Xi'an and Kashgar.

KUCHA (KUQA)
☎ 0997

This oasis town was another key stop on the ancient Silk Road. Scattered around the area are eight Thousand Buddha Caves (qiānfó dòng) which rival those of Dunhuang, Datong and Luoyang. There are also at least four ancient ruined cities in the area.

The Buddhist cave paintings and ruined cities in the area are remains of a pre-Islamic Buddhist civilisation. When the 7th century Chinese monk Xuan Zang passed through Kucha he recorded that the city's western gate was flanked by two enormous 30m-high Buddha statues, and that there was a number of monasteries in the area decorated with beautiful Buddhist frescoes; 1200 years later the German archaeologist-adventurers Grünwedel and Le Coq removed much of this art and took it to Berlin.

Sadly, modern-day Kucha retains little, if any, of its former glory. There is still some traditional architecture remaining, and traffic jams of donkey-cart taxis add some appeal. But for most people, it's the sights outside the town that would justify a stop here.

Orientation

There is no real town centre as such, but the main thoroughfare is Renmin Lu, which connects the new and old parts of town. The bus station is in the east of town and the train station is an isolated 5km south-east of here.

Qiuci Ancient City Ruins

These ruins are all that is left of the ancient capital of Qiuci. Qiuci was one of several ancient feudal states in what was once loosely called the Western Region of China.

Qiuci has had several name changes. During the Han dynasty it was named Yancheng, but in the Tang era (when Xuan Zang dropped in) it was called Yiluolu. The ruins are along the main road, about a 10 minute walk west of the Qiuci Hotel.

Bazar & Great Mosque

Every Friday a large bazar is held about 2.5km west of town next to a bridge on Renmin Lu. Traders come in from around the countryside to ply their crafts, wares and foodstuffs. While the local tourism offices are trying to make it a sightseeing draw, the bazar is thus far largely a local event, and is worth a visit.

About 150m farther west from the bazar is the Great Mosque, Kucha's main centre for Muslim worship. Though large in size, the mosque is a fairly modest affair, but some of the carvings around the main gateway are quite elaborate.

Places to Stay & Eat

The cheapest spot in town, without question, is the *Jiaotong Hotel (jiāotōng bīnguǎn;* ☎ *712 2682)*, which is next door to the bus station. Dorm beds in quads/twins are Y10/20, while twins with bath are Y60. There is usually hot water after 10 pm. If you are staying in the dorms, there are public showers next door for Y1 a wash.

Small Kuqa Hotel (kùchē xiǎo bīnguǎn; ☎ *712 2844)* offers nicer surroundings with a large courtyard. Simple, but clean twins go for Y40 a bed; however, they might try to add a foreigner's surcharge. Be polite but firm and they may back down. If not, go elsewhere. Hot showers are available in the evenings or on demand. The hotel is in the north-west of town, just off the end of Jianshe Lu – look for the small sign.

Kuqa Hotel (kùchē fàndiàn; ☎ *712 0285)* is a little out of town, but offers the best value accommodation. In addition to spacious twins/triples for Y80/100, they also have a

swimming pool, sauna, spa and beauty salon the size of a cinema. You will probably need a guided tour to avoid getting lost. The No 6 bus that travels to and from the train station can drop you off here, or otherwise it's a 10 minute walk east of the bus station.

The restaurant at the *Kuqa Hotel* serves tasty Chinese food, but the best place to get a bite to eat is at one of the stalls in the market. There are the usual kebabs, noodles and breads available for a few yuan.

If you would prefer to eat indoors, try the *Muslim Restaurant (mùsīlín cāntīng),* on Wenhua Lu, near the corner of Jiefang Lu. It has cheap and tasty kebabs, laghman *(lāmiàn)* noodles and cold beer.

Getting There & Away

With the completion of the train line to Kashgar in late 1999, the bus station will be of minor consequence for most travellers. If you prefer the rattle and bump of bus travel, then there is a daily sleeper to Kashgar (Y120) that takes around 16 hours, barring breakdowns and bad weather.

From Kucha there are four daily sleeper buses to Ürümqi (Y120, 22 hours). There is also one daily bus to Yining (Y56, 22 hours): a spectacular 24 hour trip which takes you up through the Tian Shan mountains and onto the grasslands around Bayan Bulak. There are plenty of beautiful places to camp en route if you have a tent.

The best way to visit Kucha is by train from either Kashgar or Turpan (Daheyan). If you want to purchase sleeper tickets, then it would be best to get to the train station at least 10 minutes before the office opens at 10.30 am on the day of departure. There is also a ticket office at the bus station that sells tickets for trains that depart from Korla and Ürümqi.

Getting Around

Kucha's sights are scattered around the surrounding countryside, and the only way to get to see them is to hire a vehicle. CITS (☎ 712 2005) is in the Quici Hotel, an inspiring hotel in the west of town on Tianshan Lu. They can arrange jeep or car hire for the day; however, taxi drivers offer better rates.

Within town, taxi rides are a standard Y10 per trip, while horse or donkey carts are generally Y2 to Y3, depending on the distance.

AROUND KUCHA
Kizil Thousand Buddha Caves
There are quite a lot of Thousand Buddha Caves around Kucha, but the most important site is this one, 72km to the west of Kucha in Baicheng County. The caves date back to the 3rd century CE and are believed to have taken over 500 years to complete.

Although there are more than 230 here, only 24 are generally open to the public. Sadly, most of the caves have suffered from religious attacks and the elements over the centuries. The caves are divided into eastern and western sections. The caves in the eastern section are more general in style and include many depictions of the Buddhist legends. The western caves contain paintings that depict the life of Sakyamuni (the 'historical Buddha').

Entry to each of the sections costs Y25. Access to additional caves can cost up to Y150 per cave. More caves are planned to be open to the public within the near future. If you visit during the hot summer months, you are compensated with delicious berries and grapes that can be freely picked from the orchard in front of the caves. The caves are open daily 9.30 am to 8 pm.

The easiest way to get to the Kizil caves is to hire a vehicle. CITS charges Y300 for the return trip, while private taxi drivers offer rates of around Y150 to Y200. It is also possible to catch the Baicheng bus from Kucha and get off at the turn-off. It is still another 11km along a dirt track, so you will need to hitch the rest of the way.

Other Buddhist cave sites around Kucha include **Kumtura** and **Kizilgaha**. Kumtura is theoretically closed, but CITS can arrange exclusive visits. The catch: Y450 for the privilege of viewing the caves here. Considering that it takes most of the day to get there and back, most travellers opt to forgo this particular trip. The one-way journey to Kizil or Kazilgaha takes 1½ hours, that to Kumtura, closer to four.

Ancient City Ruins
In addition to Qiuci (in Kucha itself), there are several other ruined cities in the region. Around 23km to the north-east of Kucha is the ancient city of **Subashi**. About 20km to the south of Kucha is the ancient city of **Wushkat**.

About 60km south-west of Kucha is **Tonggusibashi**, one of the largest and best preserved of the ruined cities. Again you'll need to hire a vehicle to get to these spots; rates are similar to those for the Kizil caves.

Northern Xinjiang

This part of Xinjiang is positively stunning, a land of thick evergreen forests, rushing rivers and lakes. The highlight of the area is beautiful Hanas lake and the surrounding mountainous valleys.

Until recently, the area was a quiet backwater of China's far north-west and closed to foreigners due to the proximity of the Russian, Mongolian and Kazakstan borders. The area is rich in ethnic groups and despite constant Han migration, continues to remain predominantly Kazak. Tourism is just starting to take off and the region remains relatively untouched by pollution.

YINING
☎ 0999
Also known as Gulja, Yining lies close to the Kazakstan border, about 390km west of Ürümqi. It is the centre of the Ili Kazak Autonomous Prefecture.

The Ili valley has in times past been an easy access point for invaders, as well as for the northern route of the Silk Road. The Russian influence has probably been the most predominant, not counting the obvious Han influence. Yining was occupied by Russian troops in 1872 during Yakub Beg's independent rule of Kashgaria. Five years later, the Chinese cracked down on Yakub Beg and Yining was handed back by the Russians. In 1962 there were major Sino-Soviet clashes along the Ili river.

Today, Yining has little to show for this influence, save for a few faded remnants of

YINING 伊宁

To Airport (500m)

To Bank of China (150m), Bus Station (200m), Sayram Lake (120km) & Ürümqi (581km)

Feijichang Lu

Jiefang Lu

Shengli Lu

Yingbin Lu

Sidalin Jie

To Yilite Grand Hotel (250m), CAAC (250m) & Kuqa (549km)

Night Market

Sidalin Jie

Qingnian Lu

Hongqi Square

Xinhua Donglu

To Ili River (3km)   *To Ili River (4km)*

0   250   500 m

1 Post, Telephone & Internet
2 Asia Hotel
3 Friendship Hotel
4 Ili Hotel; Restaurant
5 Jiahe Meishilin Restaurant
6 PSB
7 Hongqi Department Store
8 Main Post Office
9 Tianma Hotel

XINJIANG

Russian architecture and street names. Overall there's not much to the town itself, other than enjoying the surrounding scenery, the best of which can be seen along the roads from Ürümqi and Kucha, which pass through some spectacular desert, grassland and alpine landscapes.

The Ili valley is pretty – the roads are lined with tall birch trees and there are farms everywhere. This is home to some 20,000 Xibe people, who were dispatched to safeguard the region by the Manchus. They have proudly retained their own language and writing system and continue to live in a relatively closed community.

More recently, Yining was the scene of violent riots started by Uyghur separatists, resulting in a number of deaths (see the boxed text 'The Beginning or the End?' earlier in this chapter). Although the riots were swiftly put down, underlying tension and resentment continues under the surface.

Information
The PSB is opposite the Yilite Grand Hotel on Stalin Jie. The Bank of China is opposite the bus station on Jiefang Lu and the post and telephone office is right on the big traf-fic circle in the centre of town. There is also another post and telephone office east of the bus station on Jiefang Lu. Internet access is available on the 2nd floor of this office.

The Xinhua Bookstore is next to the bus station, on the 2nd floor of the department store. You can pick up a city map here.

Things to See
Just to the south of town is the Ili river, a popular recreational area with the locals. Down by the river are some pleasant restaurants, *chaykhana* (teahouses) and bars. It's a good place to relax and enjoy watching the river pass you by. To get here, hop on a No 2 bus and get off at the last stop, just before the bridge over the river.

Places to Stay & Eat
Budget travellers can try the *Friendship Hotel* (*yǒuyì bīnguǎn;* ☎ 802 3901), which has dorm beds in triples for Y32. Twins start at Y90. It's about 10 minutes walk southeast of the bus station, but isn't that easy to find – it's down an obscure side street and the only sign pointing the way is in Chinese.

Nearby is the *Asia Hotel* (*yà ʾyà bīnguǎn;* ☎ 803 6077), which has beds in triples/twins for Y32/40 and doubles for Y88.

Tianma Hotel (*tiānmǎ bīnguǎn;* ☎ 802 2662) is a nine storey white-tiled building on Qingnian Lu. A bed in a quad with common bath is Y18 and a twin room costs Y80. Other than the cigarette burns in the carpet, the rooms are clean and good value. Look out for the small English sign that reads 'Fixed Hotel for overseas visitors'.

Closer to all the action (such as it is) is the *Ili Hotel* (*yīlí bīnguǎn;* ☎ 802 3799, fax 802 4964), where a bed in a clean triple is Y40. Twins range from Y150 in the older wing to Y360 in the brand new three star wing. The hotel has very pleasant tree-shaded grounds.

There are plenty of street markets that set up stalls in the evenings around town. The *Jiāhé měishílín* is a popular local restaurant adjacent to the entrance of the Ili Hotel. It serves a pretty tasty *dàpánjī* (whole or half chicken chopped up, stir-fried with potatoes, herbs and other vegetables and served with noodles), as well as lots of snacks.

Getting There & Away

There are daily flights between Ürümqi and Yining for Y590. There is a Xinjiang Airlines office inside the Yilite Grand Hotel, opposite Hongqi Square. A taxi to the airport costs Y7.

Buses to Ürümqi (Y56 normal bus, Y87/ 97 upper/lower berth sleeper bus, 14 to 20 hours) run between 8 am and 6 pm.

The spectacular bus ride to Kucha in the south passes over the Tian Shan and through the small Mongolian village of Bayan Bulak, a good place to break the journey. A daily bus leaves at 10.30 am and seats cost Y56 for the 22 hour trip.

It is possible to travel by bus from Yining to Almaty in Kazakstan. Buses leave Yining on Monday, Wednesday, Thursday and Saturday between 3.30 and 4 am. The ticket office is in the main waiting hall, next to the customs office. Tickets cost US$30.

AROUND YINING
Sayram Lake

The large and beautiful Sayram lake is 120km to the north of Yining, and offers some nice hiking opportunities. The lake is especially colourful during June and July, when alpine flowers blanket the ground.

A very yurty village has sprung up on the main road to cater for the influx of tourists during July and August. There are horses and speedboats for hire here.

If you prefer peace and tranquility then pack a tent and just hop off the bus anywhere along the lake. There is food up here, but the selection is limited and prices expensive, so bring what you need. Otherwise there are plenty of Kazak yurts around the lake willing to take a boarder. The usual fee is Y30 per night including meals.

Buses from Yining to Sayram lake take about three hours (Y10). All buses between Ürümqi and Yining pass by the lake, so there is usually no problem finding onward transport. Just stand by the road and wave a passing bus down.

TACHENG
☎ 0901

Located in a lonely corner of north-west Xinjiang, Tacheng is a relatively obscure border crossing into neighbouring Kazakstan. Life here is usually pretty slow and relaxed, even more so since the closure of the Kazak side of the border. Locals report that the Kazak customs have been, shall we say, a little 'erratic' in charging duties and were therefore shut down. However, now and then the gates are opened and a rush of trade starts to flow through the main streets again. If you do make it here and discover the border is closed, don't despair; Tacheng is a pleasant enough place to relax before catching a bus south to Alashankou or north to Jeminay.

The Bank of China, on Guangming Lu, can change both cash and travellers cheques.

Places to Stay & Eat

Tacheng Guesthouse (tǎchéng bīnguǎn; ☎ 622 2093) is tucked away in the north-west of town on Youhao Jie. It has dorm beds in a Russian-style building for Y20 and Y30. The rooms come complete with cracked ornate plaster, broken windows, peeling paint and wet carpet. If the place smelled of vodka it would be the authentic Russian experience. More comfortable twins in the main hotel range from Y80 to Y160. All rooms have bathroom and 24 hour hot water.

Tacheng Travellers Hotel (tǎchéngshì kèyùn bīnguǎn; ☎ 622 2544) is the cheapest option in town with dorm beds from Y10 to Y18 with common shower. A bed in a simple twin is Y25 or Y50 in a triple with a large sofa. There is hot water from 10 pm to 2 am.

Yinxiang Hotel (yínxiáng bīnguǎn; ☎ 622 2222 ext 2666) is the most upmarket option with standard twins for Y124 or suites for Y188, complete with living room and a large double bed. They have 24 hour hot water and can usually offer a bit of a discount on all rooms. You can't miss this place, as it is the biggest white tile and blue reflective glass building in town.

There is a great *night market* in front of the cinema on Xinhua Lu, just opposite the Yinxiang Hotel. It has an amazing array of dishes for all budgets and tastes.

Yuèliangchéng Restaurant has a good range of cheap Chinese dishes. It's adjacent to the post office on Ta'er Bahetai Lu; look for the pink characters on the window.

Getting There & Away

There are flights on Tuesday and Saturday to/from Ürümqi (Y310). Tickets can be purchased from the CAAC office (☎ 622 3428) on Guangming Jie. The shuttle bus to the airport also departs from here.

There are three daily buses to Ürümqi (Y52, 15 hours), the first of which is a sleeper (Y84/97 upper/lower berth).

Taxis to the border cost Y20, or Y5 each if there are enough passengers.

JEMINAY

The only reason you would want to visit this forlorn little town is if you are heading to or from Kazakstan. The border checkpoint is 18km from town. The border crossing has become more popular in recent years due to the irregularity of the crossing at Tacheng but border guards are still not used to foreigners and you should come armed with a plan B in case you don't get through. The first major town in Kazakstan is Maykapchigay, from where you can catch a taxi to Zaysan and then a bus to Semey (12 hours).

A couple of buses depart for Ürümqi (Y52/100 normal/sleeper bus, 14 hours) from the bus station and main intersection between 4 and 5 pm daily. Four daily buses make the dusty trip to Burqin (two hours, Y11).

There is no reliable public transport to the border, but you can catch a taxi there for Y25. Coming the other way you can share a taxi to Jeminay for Y5.

BURQIN
☎ 0906

Burqin, meaning dark green water in Mongolian, is named after the nearby Burqin river, which is a tributary of the Ertix river. The Ertix is the only river in China to flow into the Arctic Ocean. Burqin, 620km north of Ürümqi, marks the end of the desert and the beginning of the grasslands and mountains to the north. The town's population of 60,000 is mainly Kazak (57%), but there are also Han, Uyghurs, Tuvan Mongolians and Russians.

There isn't much to see in Burqin, but it is a convenient transit stop if you're heading for Hanas lake or Kaba.

CITS (☎ 652 2652), 4 Huancheng Xilu, can arrange jeeps, guides and permits, but it would be cheaper and quicker dealing through one of their drivers who will greet you at the bus station.

The PSB is on the corner of Qinfu Lu and Wenming Lu. This is where you come to pick up a permit for Hanas lake.

There is nowhere to change travellers cheques in Burqin, but the local Industrial & Commercial Bank of China can change major currencies.

The most convenient place to stay is the *Jiaotong Hotel (jiāotōng bīnguǎn)*, at the bus station. Beds in quads/triples/singles cost Y9/17/40. The rooms are nothing special and there is often no hot water, but the staff are friendly.

A more comfortable option is the *Tourist Hotel (bùerīn lüvyóu bīnguǎn; ☎ 652 1325)*. It has comfortable twins for Y58 per person and 24 hour hot water. There are also dorms in quads/triples for Y20/30 and singles for Y88.

Another reasonable option is the *Jiakesi Hotel (jiākèsī jiuàn; ☎ 652 1716)* on Xiang Lu. It has dorm beds for Y20 and a bed in a twin with bath for Y55. The hot water is turned on from 10 pm to 1 am.

Just north of the bus station on Wenmin Lu is the *Yinchuan Huimin Restaurant (yínchuān húimín fàndiàn)*, which serves up a tasty bowl of spicy *niúròumiàn* noodles. A good plate of *bànmiàn* noodles can be found opposite the bus station at the *Nánqiáo dìèrhúimín shítáng Restaurant*.

Buses from Ürümqi take around 15 hours to get to Burqin – see the Ürümqi Getting There & Away section. Heading back to Ürümqi there are departures at 4, 5 and 6 pm.

There are two daily buses to Chonghu'er (Y10, two hours) at 4 and 5 pm. There are regular buses to Kaba (Y6.70, one hour) and to Jeminay (Y11, two hours).

HANAS LAKE NATURE RESERVE

The most splendid sight in the Altay region is Hanas lake *(kānàsīhú)*, an alpine lagoon surrounded by pines, boulders and mountains. In the autumn the aspen and maple trees provide a scenic backdrop of riotous colour.

XINJIANG

The area shelters a diverse range of flora and fauna, including eagles, brown bears, lynx, snow leopards, black storks and lots of squirrels. The forests are dominated by spruce, birch, elm, poplar, Korean pine and Siberian larch.

The trip up to Hanas lake is stunning, with beautiful vistas that range from desert, to grasslands, to alpine wilderness. Along the way you pass hundreds of seminomadic Kazaks, who are either on their way up or down the valley, depending on the season.

There are many possibilities for hiking in and around the lake. In fact, there is even more incredible scenery in the neighbouring valley of **Hemu Hanas** and **Bai Kaba** village. For those more content with day hikes, there are a couple of paths that lead out from the tourist village of Hanas.

A popular day walk is the trip up to **Guanyuting Pavilion** (2030m), the peak on the far side of the lake. It's a 1½ hour walk from the river up the steps to the pavilion. From the top you are rewarded with panoramic views of the lake, mountains and grasslands. It is possible to return to Hanas via a circuitous scenic route down the eastern slope by following the dirt road. The round walk takes a lazy five hours.

It's also possible to climb the mountains behind the tourist camp or even partly around the lake to some nearby rock paintings.

Boats leave from the pier to **Twin Lakes** (shuānghú) and the headwaters of the lake.

The area is really only easily accessible from June to early October, with ice and heavy snow closing the road between October and May. There isn't really any summer up here, more a gradual transition from spring to autumn, with the temperature remaining pleasant throughout.

During June and July a blanket of alpine flowers carpets the region; in August wild berries litter the ground. In September and October the first snow starts to fall and the forests begin to turn a brilliant red and yellow. Winter trips are also possible by trekking in on horseback, on skis, or for those with the money, snowmobiles.

Entrance to the Hanas Lake Reserve costs Y40, but foreigners are also expected to pay an extra Y6 per day to ensure the ongoing protection of the area. Presumably, larger noses and feet are a larger cause of pollution in the area. You will only pay this fee if you are unfortunate enough to bump into an environmental bureau officer. They usually hang around the pier area on the other side of the lake.

Permits

Before you head up to Hanas lake, drop into Burqin's PSB to arrange an Alien's Travel Permit. It costs Y52, plus an extra Y50 deposit, which they give back to you when you return from your trip. If you are interested in visiting other areas or villages, make sure you include them on the permit. There are a number of checkpoints throughout the whole region, where you will be asked to hand over your permit and sometimes your passport.

Places to Stay

An accommodation construction boom is currently underway and no doubt the area will undergo changes. Hopefully the impact on the environment can be minimised.

Officially, the only options for foreigners are the tourist bureau's *cabins* and *yurts*, most of which are located in the northern section of the tourist village. Rates range from Y25 per person in a yurt to Y200 for a twin room with bathroom. During the peak summer months, there are nightly barbecues around the yurts, accompanied by Kazak and Mongolian dancing and a large bonfire.

A better option is to either stay in a yurt with some Kazaks and Mongolians, or bring your own tent and camp out in the wilderness. Some of the best places for camping are actually along the route up to Hanas lake after the town of Chonghu'er. Chinese tourists do this quite a lot, but the officials are still a bit nervous about foreigners making their own plans. If you do head off, make sure you are equipped to deal with freezing temperatures and heavy rain, both of which are common throughout the year.

Getting There & Away

The lake is a stunning 145km journey from Burqin. During July and August there are tourist buses (Y50) that head up to the lake from Burqin's bus station. A more flexible option is to hire a 4WD and driver (Y400/500 one way/return), which allows you to stop and take photos along the way. The drive takes about five to six hours.

The road from Burqin passes through Chonghu'er, Heliutan and Jiadengyu before reaching the tourist town of Hanas. All of these towns have restaurants and small supply shops. The main road is sealed to just past Chonghu'er, but there are plans to widen and seal the road all the way to the lake. In fact, the tourist bureau also plans to construct a runway up here, but hopefully this will take years.

South-West Xinjiang (Kashgaria)

Kashgaria is the historical name for the western Tarim basin. Despite its present isolation, Kashgaria was a major hub of the Silk Road and has bristled with activity for over 2000 years. A ring of oases lined with poplar trees and centred on weekly bazars remain a testament to the mercantile tradition. The region remains the heartland of the Uyghurs.

KASHGAR
☎ 0998 • pop approx 180,000
Even at the dawn of a new millennium, the name Kashgar still sparks images of a remote desert oasis, the sole outpost of civilisation separating the vast deserts of Xinjiang from the icy peaks of the Karakoram. Desert brigands, exotic bazars and colourful silks spring to mind at the mention of China's westernmost city.

Kashgar is no longer that remote, and the modern age has certainly taken its toll, emphatically symbolised by the statue of Chairman Mao – one of the largest in China. Kashgar is now only 1½ hours by plane from Ürümqi, or less than two days by sleeper bus. The old town walls have been torn down, flashy red taxis with blaring horns congest the footpaths and Chinese super-freeways encircle the beleaguered old town. In October 1999 the railway link from Ürümqi was formally opened, sounding what many fear will be the death knell for traditional Kashgar.

Even so, Kashgar retains an intoxicating air of the exotic, due mainly to its fascinating ethnic mix of Uyghurs (who comprise the majority of the population), Tajiks, Kyrgyz, Uzbeks and a growing number of Han Chinese. Some things haven't changed since medieval times – blacksmiths, carpenters and cobblers hand tool in the old quarter and Id Kah Mosque draws the town's faithful as it has since 1442. Markets with rows of shimmering silks, knives and jewellery vie for your attention and narrow backstreets lined with earthen-walled homes beckon for exploration.

Kashgar has been a Silk Road trading centre for two millennia and traders from Kazakstan, Kyrgyzstan, Pakistan and even Russia (along with travellers from around the globe) continue to fuel the city, with impromptu street-corner negotiations, perpetual bazars, and hotel-room deals with Gilgit traders. Shifting geopolitics have reopened lines of communication and it's not hard to imagine a new high-tech Silk Road recrossing the Tarim basin one day. Kashgar's future, it seems, lies firmly rooted in its past.

With all the trading activity, one couldn't call Kashgar 'laid-back', but it has a great atmosphere and it is a fine place to settle back for a week or so. The town is also a good launching pad for trips along the southern Silk Road to Hotan, over the Torugart pass to Kyrgyzstan or south to beautiful Karakul lake and the stunning Karakoram Highway to Pakistan.

Kashgar experiences blistering hot summers, although at 1290m above sea level it's cooler than Turpan, Kucha and other stops along the Xinjiang section of the Silk Road.

Orientation
Official (Chinese) street names are given here. The town centre is a Tiananmen-style square north of Renmin Park, dominated by a statue of Mao Zedong. The Uyghur old town lies just north of here, bisected by

XINJIANG

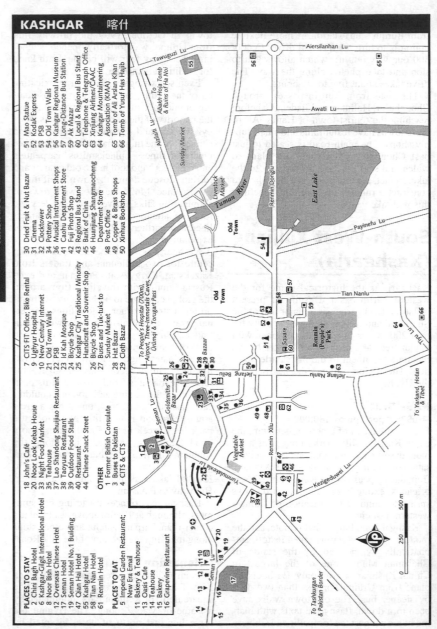

KASHGAR 喀什

PLACES TO STAY
2 Chini Bagh Hotel
6 Kashgar-Gilgit International Hotel
8 Noor Bish Hotel
12 Overseas Chinese Hotel
17 Seman Hotel
19 Seman Hotel No.1 Building
47 Qian Hai Hotel
55 Kashgar Hotel
58 Tian Nan Hotel
61 Renmin Hotel

PLACES TO EAT
5 Imperial Garden Restaurant;
   New Era Email
11 Bakery & Teahouse
13 Oasis Cafe
14 Teahouse
15 Bakery
16 Grapevine Restaurant
18 John's Café
20 Noor Look Kebab House
33 Night Food Market
35 Teahouse
37 Lao Shandong Shujiao Restaurant
38 Taoyuan Restaurant
39 Outdoor Food Stalls
40 Restaurant
44 Chinese Snack Street

OTHER
1 Former British Consulate
3 Buses to Pakistan
4 CITS & CTS
7 CITS FIT Office; Bike Rental
9 Ughyur Hospital
10 New Century Internet
21 Old Town Walls
22 PSB
23 Id Kah Mosque
24 Bicycle Shop
25 Kashgar City Traditional Minority
   Handicraft and Souvenir Shop
26 Bicycle Shop
27 Buses and Tuk-tuks to
   Sunday Market
28 Hat Bazar
29 Cloth Bazar
30 Dried Fruit & Nut Bazar
31 Cinema
32 Clocktower
34 Pottery Shop
36 Musical Instrument Shops
41 Caohu Department Store
42 Fuji Photo Shop
43 Regional Bus Stand
45 Bank of China
46 Huanjiang Shangmaocheng
   Department Store
48 Post Office
49 Copper & Brass Shops
50 Xinhua Bookshop
51 Mao Statue
52 Kodak Express
53 PSB
54 Old Town Walls
56 Kashgar Regional Museum
57 Long-Distance Bus Station
59 Ak Mazar
60 Local & Regional Bus Stand
62 Telephone & Telegraph Office
63 Xinjiang Airlines/CAAC
64 Kashgar Mountaineering
   Association (KMA)
65 Tomb of Ali Arslan Khan
66 Tomb of Yusuf Has Hajib

Jiefang Beilu (North Liberation Rd). The budget travellers' enclave is on the west side. The Sunday market is on the east side.

Buses from Pakistan normally arrive at the Chini Bagh Hotel. If you arrive by air a bus brings you to the China Xinjiang Airlines (CAAC) booking office on Jiefang Lu. The airport is 12km north-east of the centre. The new train station (not yet open at the time of research) is said to be out in the east of town near the Abakh Hoja tomb.

Information
Tourist Offices & Travel Agencies
There isn't really a 'tourist office' here. The state-run China International Travel Service (CITS) and China Travel Service (CTS) are basically travel agencies. Both can arrange air tickets or transport, but they're not reliable sources of information on off-route places. The FIT (Foreign Independent Traveller) branch of CITS, just inside the Chini Bagh gate, caters more to independent travellers. The main CITS office (☎ 282 8473, fax 282 3087) is up two flights of stairs in a building farther inside the gate. CTS (☎ 283 2875, fax 282 2552) is up two more flights in the same building. CTS also has an independent office for small groups and individuals in the plaza, outside the Chini Bagh gate. CTS is consistently cheaper than CITS.

The Kashgar Mountaineering Association (KMA; Uyghur: *takka chkesh*, Chinese: *dēngshān xiéhuì*) is a government liaison office for expeditions and group sports travel and will help individuals with guides or vehicles, though both are scarce in high season. The office (☎ 282 3680, fax 282 2957) is far away at 45 Tiyu Lu (Sports Rd), off Jiefang Lu beyond Air China.

Private Agents
From John's Café (☎/fax 282 4186, ✉ Johncafe@public.qd.sd.cn or Johncafe@hotmail.com), opposite the Seman Hotel, John Hu also organises bookings, transport and excursions and can link you up with other budget-minded tourists to share costs. He can arrange a bus ticket for a Y15 commission or a plane ticket for Y50. The cafe is probably the best place in town to meet travellers and swap information.

At some point in your stay you are bound to bump into Ablimit Ghopor (aka Elvis). Elvis' main business is buying and selling carpets but he also takes tourists on excellent tours of the old town to off-beat sites such as a local *pir* (holy man) and a traditional Uyghur house, where he acts as translator and cultural interpreter. He has recently started cheap trips into the Taklamakan desert and also sells his own Uyghur-English phrasebook for Y50. He can normally be found at the Oasis Cafe between 4 and 6 pm (Beijing time).

Travel Permits & Visa Extensions
The Division of Aliens and Exit-Entry Administration of the regional Public Security Bureau is in the right-hand door of PSB headquarters on 111 Yunmulakexia Lu. A friendlier office is at 67 Renmin Donglu, north-east of Renmin Park. Alien Travel Permits are theoretically available here, for places like Karakul lake, but you may well be told to arrange one (and a tour) with CITS. You can get a month-long visa extension here. Some staff speak English. The office is open Monday to Friday only, 9.30 am to 1.30 pm and 4 to 8 pm.

Money
Bank of China branches at most tourist hotels will change cash and, for a better rate, travellers cheques in major currencies. Exchange rates are uniform throughout China. The central Bank of China at 239 Renmin Xilu can also give quick cash advances on major credit cards with a minimum withdrawal of Y1200 at 4% commission. Bank summer hours are Monday to Friday 9.30 am to 1.30 pm and 4 to 8 pm, and Saturday and Sunday 11 am to 3 pm. You can also sell RMB back into dollars at the bank's foreign exchange desk if you have exchange receipts – a good idea if you are headed to Tashkurgan, where the bank hours are erratic.

Uyghur moneychangers loiter outside the Chini Bagh Hotel and in the bazar. There's little to be gained from dealing with them because their rates are so similar to the banks, and plenty to be lost because some are accomplished cheats. They will, however, exchange Pakistan rupees.

Post & Telephone The post office at 40 Renmin Xilu is open daily 10 am to 8 pm. Overseas stamps, international parcels and poste restante are all located together on the ground floor. There's a Y2.30 charge for each letter you pick up from poste restante. Take unsealed parcels in early, fill out a customs form, and be prepared to wait. Tourist hotels and smaller post office branches can also post letters and postcards.

Across the road is China Telecom, open daily 9.30 am to 8 pm. Kashgar now has international direct dialling (IDD), so calls go through fairly fast. You must leave a Y200 deposit before making an international call. Collect (reverse charge) calls can (in theory) be made here but you need to know the correct codes. See the Telephone section at the front of this chapter for details. IDD prices from tourist hotels and agencies are all grossly inflated.

Faxes cost a pricey Y54 a page to most countries. You can receive a fax here for Y9.

Email & Internet Access New Century, (📧 abdul-ks@mail.xj.cninfo.net), at 243 Seman Lu offers email and Hotmail for Y30 an hour, as well as copier services and some travel information. New Era in the plaza outside the Chini Bagh gate also charges Y30 an hour and has four computer stations. Both are theoretically open 24 hours. Try going online early in the morning or late at night to avoid slow downloads. John's Café has Internet access at Y40 an hour.

Bookshops The Xinhua Bookshop on Jiefang Beilu has a few Stalin posters and maps of Xinjiang in Chinese or Uyghur, but not much else. The best places for coffee table books on Xinjiang are the souvenir shops of the Kashgar-Gilgit International Hotel and Seman Hotel (No 1 Building).

Film & Photography You can get western print film and Chinese black & white, plus some western E6 slide film, in department stores and, increasingly, shops and kiosks. Decent colour print processing is available at Kodak Express, 61 Renmin Donglu, but duck around the corner to 59 Renmin Donglu for cheaper Kodak film. There is also a Fuji processor behind the clock tower on Jiefang Beilu and one just west of the bank on Renmin Xilu. Print film (100ASA) costs around Y21 for 36 exposures.

Laundry You can get your laundry done for Y5 to Y10 per piece at tourist hotels. The Oasis Cafe charges a flat rate of Y3 per piece.

Toilets While your hotel room is always your best bet, public toilets are available throughout the city. The most useful are at the main entrance to Renmin Park and in the centre of the Sunday market, behind the carpet pavilion.

Medical Services The main Chinese hospital is the People's Hospital *(rénmín yīyuàn)* on Jiefang Beilu north of the river. There's a Hospital of Traditional Uyghur Medicine on Seman Lu about 500m east of the Seman Hotel, though it is reportedly none too clean. A small clinic under the CITS building in the Chini Bagh compound can administer first aid and medicines; some staff speak English.

Dangers & Annoyances Travellers have lost money or passports to pickpockets at the Sunday market, in the ticket scrum at the bus station, and even on local buses, so keep yours tucked away.

Some foreign women walking the streets alone have been sexually harassed, by both locals and visiting Pakistanis. The Muslim Uyghur women here dress in long skirts and heavy stockings like the Uyghur women in Ürümqi and Turpan, but here one sees more female faces hidden behind veils of brown gauze. It's probably wise for women travellers to dress as would be appropriate in any Muslim country; long, loose skirts and blouses are the most comfortable. This should be second nature for travellers who have come from Pakistan but it may come as a surprise if you've come from Kyrgyzstan or Kazakstan.

Sunday Market

Once a week Kashgar's population swells by 50,000 as people stream in to the Sunday market – surely the most mind-boggling bazar in Asia, and not to be missed. By sunrise the roads east of town are a sea of pedestrians, horses, bikes, motorcycles, donkey carts, trucks and belching tuk-tuks, everyone shouting *'boish-boish!'* (coming through!).

In arenas off the livestock market, men test-ride horses or look into sheep's mouths. A wonderful assortment of people sit by their rugs and blankets, clothing and boots, hardware and junk, tapes and boomboxes – and, of course, hats. In fact the whole town turns into a bazar, with hawkers everywhere. It's wonderfully photogenic so bring twice as much film as you think you might need and get there early to avoid the tour groups.

The grounds are on Aizilaiti Lu, a 30 or 40 minute walk from the Chini Bagh or Seman hotels. You can take a bike and park it in the bike-lot in front of the entrance to the carpet pavilion. Taxis are plentiful outside tourist hotels on market day; cost should be about Y10 from the Seman, less from the Chini Bagh. You might catch a donkey cart outside the city centre, but negotiate a price beforehand. You can also get a minibus or passenger tuk-tuk from the east side of Id Kah Square. Ask for the *Yekshenba bazar* (Sunday market). John Hu offers a free one-way minibus shuttle from his cafe after breakfast in July and August.

If the tourist crush gets to you, try the Sunday market at Hotan (see the Southern Silk Road section later in this chapter).

Id Kah Mosque

The big yellow-tiled mosque is one of the largest in China, with a courtyard and gardens that can hold 20,000 people during the annual Kurban (Qurban) Bairam celebrations (see Muslim Holy Days in the Public Holidays & Special Events section of the Regional Facts for the Visitor chapter). It was built in 1442 as a smaller mosque on what was then the outskirts of town. During the Cultural Revolution, China's decade of political anarchy from 1966 to 1976, Id Kah suffered heavy damage, but has since been restored. There are also more than 90 tiny neighbourhood mosques throughout the city.

It's acceptable for non-Muslims to go into Id Kah; there's a Y3 fee. Local women are rarely seen inside but western women are usually ignored if they're modestly dressed (arms and legs covered and a scarf on the head). Take off your shoes if entering carpeted areas, and be discreet about photos. In front of the mosque is Id Kah Square, swarming on sunny days with old men in high boots and long black coats, women with brown veils, and quite a few down-and-outers waiting for Muslim charity.

At night the square comes alive with exotic food vendors and blaring televisions surrounded by dozens of onlookers.

Old Town

Sprawling all around Id Kah are roads full of Uyghur shops, and narrow passages lined with adobe houses that seem trapped in a time warp. Look for religious books to the north of the mosque, regional handicrafts and hats to the east and south, and dowry chests, brightly painted cradles and hardware of every kind on the road south to the post office. Several streets sport bright new buildings in traditional Uyghur style. Behind a wall of department stores opposite Id Kah is a dusty labyrinth of blacksmiths, farriers, carpenters, jewellers, chaykhana, bakeries and noodle shops.

At the east end of Seman Lu stands a 10m-high section of the old town walls, at least five hundred years old. Another rank of them are visible from Yunmulakexia Lu opposite the vegetable market. Construction around, on and in them makes access impossible, and there's clearly no interest in preserving them.

Abakh Hoja Tomb

Kashgar's best example of Muslim architecture is an elegant mausoleum built in the mid-17th century for the descendants of a Muslim missionary named Muhatum Ajam (or Mukhram Azan). With its tiled dome and four minarets, it resembles a brightly coloured, miniature Taj Mahal. Beneath the tiled stones in the main chamber are more than 70 graves, including some small ones of children. These include Muhatum

Ajam's grandson Abakh Hoja, a local Uyghur aristocrat and spiritual leader who ruled southern Xinjiang for 16 years in the 17th century and is sometimes called the 'patron saint of Kashgar'.

Also buried here is Abakh Hoja's granddaughter Ikparhan, known to the Chinese as Xiang Fei, the 'Fragrant Consort', who led the Uyghurs in an abortive revolt against the Qing emperor Qianlong in 1759. She subsequently became the emperor's concubine until she was forced to commit suicide by Qianlong's mother, the empress dowager, two years later. Behind the mausoleum is a vast run-down graveyard.

The main mausoleum costs Y6 and separate fees total Y15 for the surrounding mosques and exhibits, though on a slow day no-one seems to care where you go.

The tomb is a half hour bike ride or a two hour walk north-east of town to Nazirbagh village and then marked by a small sign on the left. A taxi is about Y30 and bus No 8 leaves from Renmin Park for Y2.

Tomb of Yusup Has Hajib

A grand, newly restored mausoleum with a purple dome on Tiyu Lu, off Jiefang Lu, marks the grave of an 11th century Sufi teacher and Uyghur scholar. Yusup Has Hajib was the author of a famous Uyghur epic poem, *The Wisdom of Royal Glory*, an encyclopedic look at Karakhanid life. The tomb is Xinjiang's most important Uyghur monument, though there's only a restored gravestone to see inside if you pay the Y5 to have them unlock the door.

Tomb of Ali Arslan Khan

Another historical site is this tomb and small mosque, which are quite modest considering they mark the grave of a Karakhanid ruler, Ali Arslan Khan (ruled 970-998). At the end of Renmin Donglu, at the roundabout, turn right and go about 750m south; the tomb is on the right, through an eerie sea of graves, mounded up like giant ant hills.

Ak Mazar

Just east of Renmin Park, about 200m down a back lane, is an old tomb, now in a sad state of disrepair and with most of its blue tiles stripped off but still carrying echoes of grandeur. The signpost names it the 'White Tomb of Eskander Wang' (King Alexander). The story goes that after many failed attempts to destroy the tomb the Chinese finally gave up – and built a toilet in front of it instead.

Other Things to See

At the time of research a new 'Silk Road Cultural Relic Show' was due to open at the **Kashgar Regional Museum** out on the eastern edge of Kashgar. The museum is open daily 9.30 am to 1.30 pm, and 4 to 8 pm and entry costs Y10.

Renmin (People's) Park (*rénmín gōngyuán*), south of the Mao statue, is a thirsty arboretum with tall poplars, a pitiful zoo and Uyghurs lounging about on 'beer beds', eating shashlyk and listening to local musicians play the long-necked *dutar*. Entrance is Y1.

East of the centre, along Renmin Donglu, is a willow-lined artificial lake, a popular spot for migratory birds and a good place for a picnic or a lazy afternoon. In the summer it may be possible to rent little boats here. There is an entrance fee of Y1 to walk across the bridge into the park, though they may try to charge foreigners Y2.

Places to Stay

Accommodation is tighter on the days preceding the Sunday market than afterward. In the low season, or for stays of more than a few days, you may be able to coax some discounts. Not listed are a growing number of hotels uninterested in foreign guests.

Places to Stay – Budget

Chini Bagh Hotel (*qíníwǎké bīnguǎn;* ☎ 282 2084, fax 282 3842, 93 Seman Lu) is a five storey tower where the British consulate's front gate used to be, located conveniently close to the old town. Spartan but clean quads/triples with hot shower are Y20/25 per bed. Clean doubles with hot shower in the main building are Y120; very nice carpeted singles/doubles with TV in the Jingyuan annexe are Y120/180; however, at the time of research the annexe was being renovated and

Listening Posts of the Great Game

The British and Russian rivalries of the Great Game (see the History section in the Facts about Central Asia chapter) across the Pamirs were matched by personal rivalries across town – for information, influence and even Silk Road antiquities – and the Russian and British consulates in Kashgar quickly became listening posts on the front line of the Great Game. While opening up mountain routes and expanding trade, the consul-generals kept an anxious ear open for news of political alliances and military manoeuvres.

In 1890, 24-year-old George Macartney arrived with Francis Younghusband to set up the British office in Kashgar. Younghusband left a year later; Macartney remained for the next 28 years. Eventually George was joined by his wife Catherine, who gradually turned the British consulate, known as the Chini Bagh (Chinese garden), into an island of European civility, with cuttings from English gardens, exotic flowers, and pear and apple trees. Table tennis tables were set up indoors and tennis courts were built nearby. Brahms records provided melodious lullabies and eventually a piano was shipped over the mountain passes. Explorers such as Aurel Stein and Albert Von Le Coq called at the Chini Bagh on their way to the sandy wastes of the Taklamakan, and Peter Fleming enjoyed his first bath and coffee there for over five months. Subsequent consuls included Percy Etherton, Clarmont Skrine (1922), George Gillan, Thompson Glover, and Eric Shipton (1940 to 1942 and 1946 to 1948).

Across town the Russian consuls made similar attempts at introducing luxuries, vying for the company of passing westerners and gaining the favour of information. The Russian consul Nikolai Petrovsky once gave Macartney a much-coveted pane of glass, only to demand it back (secured by his Cossack guard) after a sensitive issue involving a political cartoon. Following the incident the two didn't speak to each other for 2½ years. Subsequent Russian consuls included Mestchersky, who, after leaving his post, fled the Bolshevik Revolution in Russia and ended up working as a waiter while his wife became a chambermaid in Paris. Ironically, the Russian consulate in Kashgar became a safe haven for White Russians, including Paul Nazarov, who sought refuge here for four years, until the Bolsheviks took the consulate in 1925.

Both consulates were closed down in 1949, though the Chini Bagh functioned as a British representative office to India and Pakistan for a while. The consulates remain today as the Chini Bagh and Seman hotels.

The Chini Bagh Hotel is built right smack in front of the old consulate, whose main floor is now a Chinese banquet hall. The upper three room suite, finished in 1913, is awaiting renovation, but you may be able to talk your way upstairs to the living quarters and enjoy the view from the flat roof, where one consul's wife was shot through the shoulder during the Dungan rebellion of 1934.

The Russian consulate has fared better than the Chini Bagh and remains as atmospheric suites, in the courtyard behind the Seman Hotel. The well-appointed suites cost Y400 and Y600 and are a must for Great Game buffs and romantics.

To recreate a flavour of these lost times try reading Diana Shipton's *The Antique Land* (her husband Eric ran the consul from 1940 to 1942 and 1946 to 1948) or Catherine Macartney's *An English Lady in Chinese Turkistan*.

XINJIANG

prices may have gone up. All rooms are discounted by Y20 without breakfast. The complex has Chinese and Uyghur restaurants, souvenirs, travel agencies, and a coffee shop.

Seman Hotel (sèmǎn bīnguǎn; ☎ 282 2147, fax 282 2861, 170 Seman Lu) – 'si-**maan**' not 'semen' – dominates the courtyard of the old Russian consulate, and is probably the most popular place for back-packers, due more to the good amenities nearby than the quality of the rooms. The 500 bed complex has three buildings, a restaurant, laundry service, shady gardens and enough overpriced souvenir shops to occupy days.

Dorms of two to six beds with common bathroom are Y15 per person. Spartan doubles with common bath cost Y30 per person, while small, musty and overpriced doubles with private bathroom in No 2 block go for Y60 per person. Second floor rooms are dangerously close to the hotel's karaoke bar. Better doubles in No 1 block go for Y280.

Building No 3 is actually across the street above John's Café. Compact but carpeted doubles cost Y30 per person here and come with hot-water bathroom. Standards vary, so check more than one room. The place is particularly popular with Pakistani traders.

Overseas Chinese Hotel (huáqiáo bīng-uǎn; ☎ 283 3262), across the road (on the site of a building bombed by militants in 1993), has hot, decaying rooms for a negotiable Y30 per person and medieval plumbing.

Tian Nan Hotel (tiānnán fàndiàn), near the bus station, has dreary doubles for Y30, Y50 or Y90 per bed, depending on the building. Building No 1 also has grim quads/triples for Y16/20 per bed. Showers are communal except for the most expensive doubles; hot water is available in the evening only.

Noor Bish Hotel (nǎobĕixī lüvshè; ☎ 282 3092) is a small Uyghur guesthouse just off the road that connects the Chini Bagh to the Id Kah Square. Basic rooms set around a pleasant courtyard cost between Y10 and Y20, though you might well get unwelcome attention from the PSB for staying here.

Renmin Hotel was under renovation at the time of research.

Places to Stay – Mid-Range

Kashgar Hotel (kāshí gě'ěr bīnguǎn; ☎ 261 4954, fax 261 4679), also called Kashgar Guesthouse, has seen better days. The spacious, dusty 200 room compound has Chinese and Uyghur restaurants and a beer garden. Carpeted doubles with telephone and hot shower are Y200, or Y250 with TV and

bathtub. Quads with bath and TV are better value at Y200. The drawback is that it's 3km east of the centre, although taxis (about Y5 to the centre) linger at the gate, the No 10 bus goes to Id Kah and Renmin Park and back, or you can rent a bike from the hotel for Y3 an hour.

Qian Hai (qiánhǎi bīnguǎn; ☎ 282 2922, 48 Renmin Xilu), tucked back about 50m from the street, is aimed squarely at cell phone-toting Chinese *nouveaux riche*. Plush but smoky air-con doubles are a decent Y240, or larger suites are Y500. The hotel has two restaurants, a business centre, meeting hall, and some basic exercise facilities.

Kashgar-Gilgit International Hotel (yǒuyì bīnguǎn; ☎ 282 4173, fax 282 3842), the high-rise tower in the Chini Bagh's front yard, is a joint venture between CITS and Gilgit's Northern Areas Trading Cooperative. It's poor value for tourists; comfortable but damp doubles with bath are an undeserving Y280 with breakfast, but Y700 gets you an alarmingly large, plush suite. The friendly staff accept all major credit cards and there's a branch of the Bank of China here.

The former Russian consulate at the back of the *Seman Hotel* has been converted into five standard rooms (Y400) and two suites (Y600). Nicely decorated and oozing atmosphere, this is the must-stay choice of the well-heeled Great Game afficionado.

Places to Eat

Uyghur Food The best place to sample Uyghur food is at the food stalls outside Id Kah Mosque. Vendors sell noodles, chick-peas, poached eggs, kebabs, breads, boiled goat heads, chicken and fried fish; bring your own fork. For dessert you can try watermelon by the slice, vanilla ice cream, *tangzaza* (triangles of glutinous rice covered in syrup), *kharsen meghriz* (fried dough balls filled with sugar, raisins and walnuts), or just a glass of hot milk and a pastry.

Imperial Garden Restaurant in the plaza outside the Chini Bagh gate has good, cheap Uyghur food, quick service and clean surroundings. Recommended is the *suoman* (spicy noodles) or *suoman goshsiz* (spicy noodles without meat) for Y4.

Noor Look Kebab House (285 Seman Lu), inside a cool courtyard, specialises in kebabs, but they will cook up anything if you can explain it.

The *Chini Bagh*, *Seman* and *Kashgar* hotels have clean, but boring Muslim dining halls where you can eat fixed Uyghur meals during limited hours.

Chinese Food Chinese fast-food stalls serve up oily but cheap lunches in an alley behind the Bank of China off Renmin Xilu. There's a good choice for vegetarians; just point and pay. A tray of ready-cooked food costs about Y5. Go at noon when the food is hot.

At night tables are set up outside the Chinese restaurants on Yunmulakexia Lu north of Renmin Xilu for beer and cheap snacks. Among the snails and chicken's feet are more appealing offerings such as *shāguo* (vegetables, tofu and mushroom broth in an earthenware pot), *shuǐjiǎo* (ravioli) and *húntun* (wanton soup). The nearby *Lao Shandong Shuijiao Restaurant* is also recommended for shuǐjiǎo – order by the bowl or the jin (500g, enough for two).

Taoyuan Restaurant is one of several alongside the night market that offer good-value authentic Chinese food, but the menus are in Chinese. Check the Language chapter at the back of this book for more information.

The *Chinese Restaurant* at the Chini Bagh and the *Grapevine Restaurant* (*pútaojià cānfīng*) inside the courtyard of the Seman serve decent Chinese food off an English menu at mid-range prices. Better to go across from the Seman Hotel to *John's Café* or the even better *Oasis Cafe*. Both offer big quasi-Chinese menus, in English, from which you can satisfy a raging hunger for under Y15 (they also do chips and adequate western breakfasts in a street cafe atmosphere).

Self-Catering

A small *vegetable bazar* on Yunmulakexia Lu has fresh fruit and vegetables, hard-boiled eggs (dyed red), dried fruits and nuts. Early in the morning, small bakeries everywhere churn out delicious nan bread (the flat ones are *ak nan*, the bagels *girde nan*).

The best department stores are to be found just off Renmin Donglu – the *Huanjiang Shangmaocheng* is probably the best for foodstuffs. The best *dried fruit market* is on the south side of the cloth bazar on the east side of Id Kah Square.

Yoghurt is available in sweetened, mass-produced tubs but Uyghur women still sell the real thing – thick and tasty – in ceramic bowls for under Y1, around 8 to 9 am (Beijing time) in the bazar and the streets near the Seman and Chini Bagh hotels. Bring your own spoon and scrape away the top crust.

Shopping

Souvenirs For serious shopping go to the old town; Sunday market prices tend to be higher. The citizens of Kashgar have been selling things for 2000 years, so be ready to bargain. It helps to listen in on what local people pay (a good reason to learn Uyghur numbers).

Look for hats, teapot sets, copper/brassware and handicrafts along the south side of Id Kah Mosque. A better place for hats is behind the cloth bazar. A big favourite with tourists is Uyghur knives with colourfully inlaid handles, but don't try to fly out of Kashgar with them in your hand luggage.

There are a couple of high quality but pricey handicraft stores on the east side of the Id Kah Mosque. These and the bazar have a depressing line-up of snow leopard pelts. Aside from the moral issues of buying the skins of endangered species, bear in mind that you may not be able to import such items into your own country.

Hotel gift shops have convenient selections of overpriced Chinese souvenirs.

Musical Instruments Beautiful long-necked stringed instruments run the gamut from junk to collector's items. They include the bulbous two-string dutar, larger three-string *khomuz*, small *tambur* and elaborately shaped *rabup* with five strings and a snake or lizard-skin sounding board. The small reed horn is a *sunai* or *surnai*. A *dab* is a type of tambourine. The friendly Ababekry Seley shop on the street north of the post office sells these, plus miniature tourist versions.

XINJIANG

Try to negotiate a carrying case if you buy an instrument as this will greatly increase the chances of it getting home in one piece.

Gold An arcade of goldsmiths is just south-west of Id Kah Mosque. At the rear of some you can see young apprentices at work making jewellery. Typically heavy and ornate, the jewellery is designed for dowry pieces.

Carpets There are a few dealers in the bazar and some bargains in small shops, but most have moved out to the Sunday market pavilion. Do some carpet homework if you plan to buy one in Kashgar. A small carpet factory is located in the 'Kashgar City Traditional Minority Handicrafts and Souvenir Shop' at the far end of the goldsmiths' arcade (see the Gold entry earlier in this section). Regionally, the best carpets are said to be in Hotan.

Getting There & Away

Air The only place you can fly to/from is Ürümqi, in a Russian Tu-154 jet (Y980, daily flights in summer, four flights weekly in winter). These flights are sometimes cancelled because of wind or sandstorms. If so, just show up for the next flight and you get priority; there's no need to change the ticket (but you must change any ticket for a connecting flight out of Ürümqi).

You should try to book at least a week ahead in summer. CITS will book a ticket for a Y30 fee; John Hu will do the same for Y50. Alternatively go to the China Xinjiang Airlines/CAAC ticket office (☎ 282 2113) at 95 Jiefang Lu on the ground floor of a blue four storey building, open daily 10 am to 1 pm and 4.30 to 8 pm (this is also the terminus for the airport shuttle). You can buy tickets here for other domestic flights.

There is a Y50 domestic departure tax, unreassuringly called an 'airport reconstruction fee', which is normally paid at the airport.

Bus Bus services to and from Kashgar include the following.

To Kyrgyzstan There are public buses to Kyrgyzstan over the Torugart pass, but at the time of writing foreigners were not allowed

to use these services. For the record, a Chinese sleeper bus runs from the Chini Bagh Hotel to Bishkek on Monday and Friday and a normal Kyrgyz bus runs on Thursday at 9.30 am (US$50). Another Kyrgyz bus runs to Naryn on Friday (Y205). Services also go to Bishkek and Naryn from nearby Artush.

Both bus companies are more than happy to sell you a ticket for these buses, but without a permit you'll be thrown off the bus at the customs post (see the boxed text 'Over the Torugart Pass').

To Pakistan The terminus for buses to/from Sost (Y270, two days) in Pakistan is the customs shed beside the Chini Bagh Hotel. From June to September they lay on as many buses as needed, so you needn't book very far ahead. Earlier or later in the season there may not be buses on some days. Landslides can cancel departures even in summer.

The bus leaves about noon Beijing time. The 500km trip takes two days, with an overnight at Tashkurgan. Bring water, snacks and warm clothes as nights can be cold in any season. Sit on the left side for the best views.

Customs procedures are conducted at Tashkurgan. Drivers like luggage to go on the roof, though most people load up the back seats if there aren't too many passengers.

If buses have stopped for the season but you're desperate to cross the border, Pakistani traders may have space in a truck or chartered bus. You can also hire a 4WD; see 4WD later in this section.

To Ürümqi You can now make the 1480km trip to Ürümqi in a nonstop, soft-seat coach (Chinese: *hàohuàchē*, Uyghur: *ali mashina*) or sleeper coach (Chinese: *wòpùchē*, Uyghur: *qarvatlik mashina*) in around 30 hours, for Y210 (upper berth) or Y240 (lower). You can also go in an ordinary bus (Chinese: *pûtōngche*, Uyghur: *adetki mashina*) for about Y138.

All of these depart from the long-distance bus station three times daily – the regular and soft-seat buses at 1 and 6 pm, the sleepers at 9 am and 9 pm. Tickets are on sale up to four days ahead, at the station or more expensively through CITS; the sleepers sell out quickly.

Over the Torugart Pass

Officially the Torugart pass is a 'second grade' pass and therefore for local not international traffic. Except of course that it straddles an international border. What you require on the Chinese side is a *xuězhèng* permit from the PSB entry-exit section in Ürümqi. Most agents in Kashgar can get this (CTS claim in two working days), though at the time of research no-one would arrange a permit without transport.

You can hire a 4WD Land Cruiser holding four to six passengers (see the 4WD entry in the Getting There & Away section of Kashgar) and minibuses holding eight to 12 from the Kashgar Mountaineering Association, CTS, CITS or John Hu.

It's unclear whether you can get into Kyrgyzstan without booking Kyrgyz transport. Officially the Chinese won't let you leave the arch at the summit of the pass without onward transport into Kyrgyzstan, and Chinese travel agencies are reluctant to take you to the arch without booking onward transport – but it looks likely that the Chinese guards will let you cross if you can find a lift from the arch to the Kyrgyz border post. If you do manage to get to the Kyrgyz border post you will need to find onward transport to Naryn or Bishkek. Taxi sharks may open the bidding at US$200 or more to Bishkek (and may lead you to think that's for the vehicle, then later tell you it's per person), though US$50 for the car is a more realistic amount.

There are public buses to Kyrgyzstan over the Torugart pass, but at the time of writing foreigners were not allowed to take these services. Without a permit you'll most likely be thrown off the bus at the customs post. You must of course already have a Kyrgyzstan visa. There are local buses from Kashgar to the customs post but this doesn't help much.

For more on the Kashgar-Torugart road, as well as the onward journey into Kyrgyzstan, see Bishkek to Kashgar via the Torugart Pass, in the Kyrgyzstan chapter.

Other Destinations Other buses use the long-distance bus station *(aptoos biket)*. There have been instances of theft at the bus station, especially in the early-morning crush, so keep a close watch on your bags.

Local buses to Tashkurgan leave daily except Sunday at 9 am (Y37) and charge the full fare to drop you off in Karakul. There are also sleeper buses to Toksun (for Turpan) for Y188 or Y213 (30 hours).

Overnight buses leave for Hotan (Y51, 10 hours) daily at 8 pm. Buses and minibuses to Yengisar (Y7, 1½ hours), Yarkand (Y19, 3½ hours) and Karghilik (Y24, five hours) depart every half hour or so until 8 pm.

Train The new Kashgar-Ürümqi service leaves at midnight (Y185 to Y199 hard sleeper, from Y301 soft sleeper, 31 hours).

4WD You can hire 4WD Land Cruisers (holding four to six passengers) and minibuses (holding eight to 12) from the Kashgar Mountaineering Association, CTS, CITS or John Hu at John's Café. At the time of research a Land Cruiser to meet you or drop you off at Torugart was from about Y1200, plus Y250 to Y300 per person to arrange the requisite permits. CTS were offering the cheapest rates, while John Hu was charging Y2000 for a car (up to four people). Land Cruiser rates with CTS all the way to Bishkek were around US$430 for four people, plus US$30 per person for permits. A Land Cruiser to Sost was Y5000. Food and lodging are extra, and the driver pays for his own. Book ahead, a week or more in high season. Just because you are paying through the nose, don't expect high standards – our driver was so exhausted when he arrived that we had to drive ourselves all the way from the Torugart pass to the customs post.

Hitching You might hitch a lift to Tashkurgan, but from there to Pakistan you'll probably have to wait for an empty seat on the bus. There are plenty of cargo trucks crossing the Torugart pass to Kyrgyzstan, but you'll probably have problems getting past the customs post (see the Bishkek to Kashgar via the Torugart Pass section in the Kyrgyzstan chapter).

Getting Around

To/From the Airport A (Y4) CAAC bus leaves from the China Xinjiang Airlines/CAAC ticket office on Jiefang Lu 2½ hours before all flight departures, and one meets all incoming flights. A taxi is about Y30.

Local Transport A local bus stand at the west end of the square, opposite the Mao statue, is the terminus for bus No 2 (airport), bus No 10 (Kashgar Hotel), bus No 20 (Abakh Hoja tomb) and bus No 9 (Seman, Chini Bagh, People's Hospital and Artush).

A new fleet of noisy red taxis clogs every street and alley. About Y5 to Y10 should get you anywhere within the city.

The traditional Kashgar 'taxis' (donkey carts) are getting scarcer. They're not allowed in the centre in the daytime, so routes are circuitous. If you hire your own, set the price and destination before you go. Don't pay until you get there, and have exact change.

Bicycle A bike is the cheapest and most versatile way to get around Kashgar. One-gear clunkers can be hired by the hour (Y2) or the day at many hotels and John's Café. A deposit is required; don't leave your passport with them, even if asked. You can negotiate a daily rate with most hotels.

AROUND KASHGAR
San Xian Caves, Ha Noi & Mor Pagoda

Twenty kilometres north of Kashgar is one of the area's few traces of the flowering of Buddhism, the San Xian (Three Immortals) caves, three grottoes high on a sandstone cliff, one of which has some peeling frescoes. Unfortunately, the cliff is too sheer to climb, so it's disappointing. Watch for them if you enter Kashgar via the Torugart pass.

At the end of a jarring 35km drive northeast of town are the ruins of Ha Noi, a Tang dynasty town built in the 7th century and abandoned in the 12th century. Little remains except a great solid pyramid-like structure and the huge Mor Pagoda or stupa.

CITS will take you to Ha Noi for Y200 per Land Cruiser, or you can hire a car from CTS for Y63 per person. John Hu charges Y350 per car.

KASHGAR TO THE KHUNJERAB PASS

To the Chinese the road from Kashgar to the Pakistan border is the China-Pakistan Highway (zhōngbā gōnglù). It's a fantastic trip along a deep gorge, past giant sand dunes and up onto the eastern Pamir plateau – well worth taking even if you aren't headed all the way to Pakistan. Travelling times given here are for bus travel.

Kashgar to Karakul

As you leave Kashgar the main attraction, rising up from the plain to the west, is the luminous rampart of the Pamir. An hour down the road is **Upal** village (Chinese: wūpàěr), where the Kashgar-Sost bus normally stops for lunch. There's an interesting weekly market here every Monday. About 3km off the road here is the small tomb of Mahmud al-Kashgari, an 11th century Uyghur scholar (born at Barskoön in Kyrgyzstan) famous for writing the first comparative dictionary of Turkic languages. Most settlements as far as Karakul are Kyrgyz.

Two hours from Kashgar you enter the canyon of the Ghez river (Uyghur: Ghez Darya), with wine-red sandstone walls at its lower end. **Ghez** itself is just a checkpoint; photographing soldiers or buildings here can result in confiscated film. Upstream the road is cut into sheer walls or inches across huge boulder fields. At the top of the canyon, 3½ hours above the plain, is a huge wet plateau ringed with sand dunes, aptly called the Kumtagh, or Sand mountain, by locals.

The corridor from here to the Pakistan border is the **Sarikol valley**, and the mountains on either side are the Taghdumbash (or Sarikol, or Chinese Pamir). Half an hour south, at the foot of Mt Kongur, is the Kyrgyz settlement of **Bulun Kul**, 3700m above sea level. An hour south of Bulun Kul is **Karakul** – properly Lesser Karakul, as there's a bigger lake of the same name in Tajikistan.

Karakul Lake

Many travellers come to Kashgar hoping to rub shoulders with Kyrgyz nomads in the pastures around Karakul. On a clear day this is one of the most beautiful places in western China, the deep blue waters (*kara kul* is Uyghur for 'black lake') nestled between two Pamir giants, 7546m Muztagh Ata to the south and 7719m Mt Kongur to the north-east.

With a tent you could spend days at the lake or on the flanks of Muztagh Ata, and trekking possibilities are good. Karakul is theoretically a restricted area, for which you need a travel permit from the PSB in Kashgar or Tashkurgan, but many travellers just turn up without a permit and no-one seems to mind.

There are several Kyrgyz summer villages in the area (the nearest, just south of the lake, is Subash). You can walk around the lake in half a day; the downstream outflow can be forded at the village nearby, where you can also sit on a camel or arrange an excursion on mangy, bad-tempered horses up to high pastures (*jailoo*), about three hours away at the foot of Muztagh Ata.

Go between June and September; at other times the villages and the yurt site are usually closed down. The lake is at 3800m and nights are below freezing even in summer; one camper awoke to find snow in the middle of August!

Places to Stay & Eat Unless you make arrangements in advance, the only alternative to camping appears to be tacky mock-up yurts (around Y40 per person) in a tour group site by the lake. If you are camping, head at least 15 minutes around the lake to avoid hassles and take fresh water with you. There is also a restaurant at Muztagh Ata base camp.

Getting There & Away The public Kashgar-Tashkurgan bus will stop at Karakul, though you may have to fight to pay less than the full fare to Tashkurgan. Some travellers have had problems getting a seat on an onward bus, which probably won't even stop if it's full. Empty seats as far as Karakul are available on the Kashgar-Sost bus on a stand-by basis for Y44.

Another option is to hire a taxi or Land Cruiser from Kashgar, though this isn't cheap at between Y800 and Y1000 for a day trip or Y1200 to Y1500 for an overnight stop. You should be able to persuade a taxi to do the return trip from Kashgar for around Y400.

The Kashgar Mountaineering Association in Kashgar can arrange treks in the region and can also arrange stays in a Kyrgyz house or yurt, or a Tajik home in Tashkurgan.

Karakul to Tashkurgan

From the high ground west of Muztagh Ata, called the **Subash plateau**, the highway comes within about 10km of Tajikistan, and several jeep tracks run that way. At the turn of the century this area was still in dispute, never having been properly mapped. Two to three hours south of Karakul is a disused police checkpoint at **Kekyor**. From there, across the marshy **Tagh Arma basin**, it's about 1½ hours to Tashkurgan. Settlements from Tagh Arma to the border are mainly Tajik.

Tashkurgan

This is the administrative centre of the Tashkurgan Tajik Autonomous County, stretching from Muztagh Ata to the border, and home to most of China's 20,000 Tajiks. By bus in either direction between Kashgar and Sost, you'll probably have to spend the night here, so make the best of it.

In Uyghur *tash kurgan* means stone fortress. The ruins of a mud-brick fort still stand on the edge of town, and although this one is estimated to be approximately 600 years old, local lore says Tashkurgan has been a citadel for more than 2300 years. The Chinese Buddhist pilgrim Xuan Zang (Hsuan Tsang) wrote about the fortress in the 7th century, when it was the farthest frontier outpost of the Tang dynasty. There is also said to be another fortress high in the mountains south of Tashkurgan, though this remains off limits at present.

There's only one street, 1km long. A small bazar is on a side street 400m down from the main road. A department store and post office are at the other end of town.

Customs & Immigration Just south of Tashkurgan is the huge Chinese customs and immigration post. Buses arrive in Tashkurgan late and leave early the following morning, although customs may not open until 10 am. The Bank of China at the customs post is closed indefinitely. Most people swap RMB for rupees or dollars at the shops opposite the entrance to immigration.

Fort The massive, crumbling fort is at the north-east corner of town, on the only hill in the Tashkurgan river's flood plain. Most of its multilayered walls and battlements are still intact. A fancy entrance to the site is being built up some steps at the east end of the main road, though this is essentially just a scam to get an entry fee off you. You can also reach the fort from the far end of town, up the fort's east side.

Places to Stay & Eat The bus will probably dump you at the *Transport Hotel* (jiāotōng bīnguǎn), also called the Communications Hotel, with plain quads for Y15 per bed and OK doubles with a bathroom for Y50 per bed.

The nearby *Ice Mountain Hotel* (bīngshān bīnguǎn) is a better bet for budget travellers. Pleasant doubles with a common toilet cost Y25 per person and beds in a quad cost Y15.

Most groups go to the *Pamir Hotel* (pámǐ'ěr bīnguǎn; ☎ 342 1085), where a comfortable double with (sometimes) a hot-water bathroom goes for Y200. The older block also has triples with a cold water bathroom for Y30 per person and beds in an eight/four bed dorm for Y10/15. The Tajik staff are very friendly here.

Khunjerab Hotel (hóngqilafu ilāfu), right next to customs, has some cheap dorms but generally isn't up to much.

There are plenty of private Chinese restaurants lining the main street, though some travellers have complained of overcharging here. Current restaurants include the *Paradise Restaurant*, *Muslem Restaurant*, *Border City Restaurant* and the snappily named *UBLZC House*, but others are opening and closing all the time.

If you can grapple with a Chinese menu the best place we found is the *Hongxuelian Restaurant* (hóngxuělían jiuā), which has big portions of excellent food for reasonable prices.

There's also a decent restaurant at the *Pamir Hotel* but if there are no groups about they may have nothing at all.

Getting There & Away A public bus runs between Kashgar and Tashkurgan daily except Sunday (Y36). The Kashgar-Sost bus departs Tashkurgan at about 9 am and, if there are seats, tickets cost Y225. Under the terms of a Sino-Pakistani agreement the same bus must return from Sost empty but can take travellers from Tashkurgan back to Kashgar for Y77. Ask at the bus station or customs post.

Tashkurgan to the Khunjerab Pass

This level stretch along the Tashkurgan river is grand and picturesque in fine weather. About 1½ hours south of Tashkurgan is **Dabdar**, the largest permanent Tajik settlement along the road. Look out for small groups of wild Bactrian camels here. South of Dabdar, the road passes the mouth of an enormous opening westward into the Pamir – the **Mintaka valley**, once a major Silk Road branch and historically one of the main routes to Hunza and Afghanistan's Wakhan Corridor. Two hours from Tashkurgan is **Pirali**, the former Chinese customs post. South of here the Pamir gradually becomes the Karakoram and the road rises to the border at the 4730m Khunjerab pass.

The Southern Silk Road

The Silk Road east of Kashgar splits into two threads in the face of the huge Taklamakan desert. The northern thread follows the course of the modern road and railway to

Kucha and Turpan. The southern road charts a remoter course between the desert sands and the huge Pamir and Kunlun ranges. This ancient route is marked by a ring of abandoned cities, deserted by retreating rivers and encroaching sands. Some cities like Niya, Miran and Yotkan remain covered by sand, others like Yarkand and Hotan remain important Uyghur centres.

From Kashgar you can visit the southern towns as a multi-day trip from Kashgar, en route to Ürümqi or as part of a rugged backdoor route into China's Qinghai or Gansu provinces.

YENGISAR

The sleepy town of Yengisar, 58km south of Kashgar, is synonymous with knife production. There are dozens of knife shops here (though prices are not much better than in Kashgar) and it's possible to visit the **knife factory** (Chinese: *xiǎodāochǎng*, Uyghur: *pichok chilik karakhana*) in the centre of town to see the knives actually being made. Each worker makes the blade, handle and inlays himself with only the most basic of tools. Try not to time a visit between noon and 4 pm when most workers head off for lunch. From the main highway walk south past the Yengisar Hotel then turn left to the bazar. The factory is just north of the bazar.

Places to Stay

There's no real need to overnight at Yengisar but if you decide to then the **Yengisar Hotel** (*yīngjíshā bīnguǎn;* ☎ *0998-3622 390*) is a pretty good choice. Building No 1 has beds in a triple/double with hot shower for Y40/50. Building No 2 is more spartan, with beds in a quad/triple/double for Y20/25/30, with solar-heated hot water. There's no English sign so look out for the 'Handicraft of National Store' at the entrance gate.

Another **Yengisar Hotel** (*yīngjíshā dàjiuàn*) is on the main road from Kashgar. Beds in a quad/triple/double cost Y25/30/40.

Getting There & Away

Buses pass through the town regularly en route to Yarkand (Y13, 2½ hours) and Kashgar (Y7, 1½ hours). Share taxis wait at the main crossroads to speed passengers to the Kashgar bus station for Y10 per person, whenever there are three passengers or more.

YARKAND
☎ 0998

Yarkand is one of those Central Asian towns, like Samarkand and Kashgar, whose name still resonates deeply with Silk Road romance. At the end of a major trade route from British India, over the Karakoram pass from Leh, Yarkand was for centuries an important caravan town and centre of Hindu tradespeople and moneylenders. Robert Shaw, Francis Younghusband's uncle, visited the town in 1868 and dreamed of opening up China to the joys of British tea.

Today Yarkand is dominated by its large Chinese new town, which is little more than a single street of department stores and Sichuanese restaurants. The old town to the east is of far more interest, and is an excellent place to explore traditional Uyghur life.

Things to See

Yarkand's main 'sight' is the **Altyn Mosque** complex. In the central courtyard of the mosque, near to where worshippers carry out their pre-prayer ablutions, is the newly built **tomb of Aman Isa Khan** (1526 to 1560), musician, poetess and wife of the khan of Yarkand. From here you can access the **tombs of the Kings of Yarkand**. The complex has an entry fee of Y10. Across from the mosque is the solitary gateway, or *orda darvaza*, all that remains of the former citadel.

The huge sprawling **cemetery** behind the mosque is a fascinating place, especially at dawn when mourners are out in force. Amid the endless graves are the blue tilework and the Yeti Sultan Mosque and *mazar* (tomb) at the back of the cemetery. There should be no charge to visit the cemetery.

If you turn left out of the mosque and then left again after 30m, this road takes you down into the centre of the traditional old town and the back of **Wenhua Park**, where there is a small bazar and several traditional Uyghur chaykhana.

Other tombs for mausolea maniacs to track down 2km or 3km out of town include

XINJIANG

Hajiman Deng mazar, Sud Pasha mazar and Hayzi Terper mazar. There's plenty of scope here to take many interesting walks in the surrounding countryside.

Yarkand also has a large **Sunday market**, untouristed but smaller than Kashgar's or Hotan's. The market is held a block north of the Altyn Mosque.

Places to Stay & Eat

Finding a cheap place to stay can be a problem in Yarkand. The only hotel that officially accepts foreigners is the *Shache Hotel* (*shāchē bīnguǎn;* ☎ *851 2365*), where comfortable triples/doubles cost Y120/160. This is particularly bad value for single travellers who must pay for all the beds in the room. Rooms in the old block are laughably overpriced at Y100, without a bathroom.

Yarkand's other hotels include the *Traffic Hotel* (*jiāotōng bīnguǎn*) by the bus station, with beds in a quad/triple/double for Y15/20/35 and the *Gulbagh Guesthouse* (*guèbāgé bīnguǎn*), with beds in a double for Y50, but neither will take foreigners.

The only place we found willing to take in a cash-starved foreigner was the *Hedu Hotel* (*hèdū bīngu;* ☎ *851 4850*), one block left out of the bus station, which has beds in a clean and spacious double for Y45, with private hot-water bathroom. There are also cheaper triples and quads with shared facilities. The more Chinese you speak the more willing they will be to take you in.

There are Uyghur *food stalls* in front of the bus station and on most street corners. For Chinese snacks there are several places just west of the Shache Hotel. The *Ali Baba Restaurant* on the main road looks interesting.

Getting There & Around

Buses leave hourly for Kashgar (Y19, four hours) and Yengisar (Y12.50, 2½ hours). Buses leave at 11 am for Hotan (Y30, six hours) and at 9.30 am to Ürümqi (Y205, 36 hours).

From the bus station it's about 1.5km to the Shache Hotel and the same again to the start of the old town. Cycle rickshaws cost Y1 or Y2.

KARGHILIK
☎ 0998

Karghilik is a convenient place to break the long trip to Hotan. There are decent places to stay and you could enjoyably spend several hours exploring the interesting Uyghur old town. Karghilik is also of importance to travellers as the springboard for the long overland trip to Tibet.

The main thing to see in town is the 15th century *Jama Masjid*, or Friday Mosque. The mosque is surrounded by an interesting covered bazar, while the traditional mudwalled backstreets of the old town spread south behind the mosque.

The town of Charbagh, 10 minutes drive towards Yarkand, has an interesting Tuesday market.

Places to Stay & Eat

Jiaotong Hotel (*jiāotōng bīnguàn;* ☎ *728 5540*), right by the bus station, has comfortable carpeted doubles for Y80 per person, though they'll probably take Y50 if it's late. Hot water can be temperamental on the upper floors.

Next door to the main hotel is a cheaper *guesthouse* (*jiāotōng zhàodàisu*), where beds in a quad/triple/double with common bathroom cost Y20/26/30.

The other main choice is the *Mountaineering Hotel* (*dēngshān bīnguǎn*), one block south and 2½ blocks east from the bus station, where beds start at Y30.

Yecheng Hotel (*yèchéng bīnguǎn*) does not accept foreigners.

There are some busy 24 hour *food stalls* across the main road from the bus station and some good Uyghur places in front of the mosque.

Getting There & Around

Pedicabs charge a flat Y1 anywhere in town. There are buses every two hours to Hotan (Y23, five hours) and to Yarkand/Kashgar every half hour until 8 pm (Y6/23). There are also daily sleeper buses to Korla (Y154) and Ürümqi (Y216).

To Tibet The 1100km-long road to Ali in western Tibet branches off from the main

Kashgar-Hotan road 6km east of Karghilik. There are no buses along this road so you'll have to hitch a ride with a truck. This is a very tough road with several passes over 5400m and several foreigners have died, either from exposure or in traffic accidents. You should come equipped with warm clothes and enough food for a week (though the trip to Ali can take as little as three days). In addition, the route is officially off limits to foreigners and there are numerous checkpoints en route (though surprising numbers of travellers have been making it through in recent years). See Lonely Planet's *Tibet* for more details.

HOTAN
☎ 0903

About 1980km south-west of Ürümqi by road, dusty Hotan (or Khotan) is one of the most remote parts of Xinjiang, sitting at the southern boundary of the Taklamakan desert.

The main reason to haul yourself all the way out here is to catch the fantastic Sunday market (see following), but Hotan is also renowned for its silk, carpets and jade, which are considered the finest in China. You can even see deposits of white jade along the Jade Dragon Kashgar river, which passes to the east of town. You can check out the local selection at the rows of stores and stalls along the town's main street.

For those setting off on the infrequently explored southern Silk Road, via Keriya (*yútián*), Cherchen (*qiěmò*), Charklik (*rùoqiāng*) and on to Golmud, this is the last place to take care of important errands like changing money, stocking up on supplies or extending your visa.

Information

Hetian International Travel Service (*xīnjiāng hétián guójì lüvxíngshè;* ☎ 202 8994), in room 228 of the Hetian City Guest House, can arrange a car and guide to Yotkan and Melikawat for Y350 for three people or to the Silk Factory for Y150. They also offer an adventurous (and expensive) week-long trip into the Mushi mountains 150km south of Hotan, and trips into the Yengi Eriq desert to the north.

The Bank of China cashes travellers cheques and is open Monday to Friday, 9.30 am to 1.30 pm, and 4 to 8 pm. The branch on Nu'erbage (Noorbagh) Lu changes cash US dollars only.

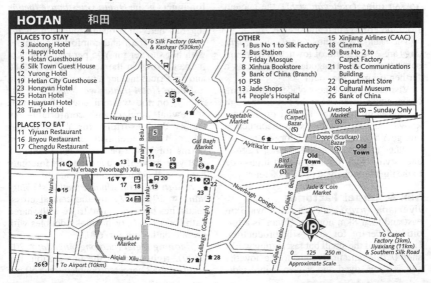

HOTAN 和田

PLACES TO STAY
3 Jiaotong Hotel
4 Happy Hotel
5 Hotan Guesthouse
6 Silk Town Guest House
12 Yurong Hotel
19 Hetian City Guesthouse
23 Hongyan Hotel
25 Hotan Hotel
27 Huayuan Hotel
28 Tian'e Hotel

PLACES TO EAT
11 Yiyuan Restaurant
16 Jinyou Restaurant
17 Chengdu Restaurant

OTHER
1 Bus No 1 to Silk Factory
2 Bus Station
7 Friday Mosque
8 Xinhua Bookstore
9 Bank of China (Branch)
10 PSB
13 Jade Shops
14 People's Hospital
15 Xinjiang Airlines (CAAC)
18 Cinema
20 Bus No 2 to Carpet Factory
21 Post & Communications Building
22 Department Store
24 Cultural Museum
26 Bank of China

(S) – Sunday Only

To Silk Factory (6km) & Kashgar (530km)
Aiyitika'er Lu
Nawage Lu
Tanayi Beilu
Gul Bagh Market
Nu'erbage (Noorbagh) Xilu
Pesitan Nanlu
Tanayi Nanlu
Gulbage (Gulbagh) Lu
Nuerbagh Donglu
Guijang Nanlu
Guijang Beilu
Vegetable Market
Aiqiali Xilu
To Airport (10km)
Vegetable Market
Gillam (Carpet) Bazar (S)
Aiyitika'er Lu
Bird Market (S)
Old Town
Doppi (Scullcap) Bazar (S)
Livestock Market (S)
Old Town
Jade & Coin Market
To Carpet Factory (3km), Jiyaxiang (11km) & Southern Silk Road
0   125   250 m
Approximate Scale

XINJIANG

Sunday Market

Hotan's biggest draw is its traditional weekly market, which rivals Kashgar's in both size and interest. The market swamps the old town and reaches a pitch between noon and 2 pm Xinjiang time. The most interesting parts to head for are the *gillam* (carpet) bazar, which also has a selection of *atlas* (tie-dyed) silks, the *dopy* (skullcap) bazar, and the livestock bazar.

Hotan Cultural Museum

Also known as the 'Historical Relics Ancient Corpses Exhibit' this small archaeological museum is worth a brief visit. The main attractions are two mummies, both over 1500 years old – ostensibly a 10-year-old girl and a 35-year-old man. There's also a useful map showing the location of the region's buried cities, essential viewing for all foreign devil explorers and Aurel Stein wannabes. It's open daily 9 am to 7 pm, closed Monday to Friday for lunch 2 to 4 pm. Entry costs Y7.

Ancient Cities

The deserts around Hotan are peppered with the faint ruins of abandoned cities. Ten kilometres to the west of town are the **Yotkan ruins** *(yuètègān yízhǐ)*, the ancient capital of a pre-Islamic kingdom dating from the 3rd to 8th centuries CE.

The **Melikawat ruins** *(málìkèwǎtè gùchéng)* are 25km south of town, and there are some temples and pagoda-like buildings a farther 10km to the south.

Visiting either of these places will require hiring a taxi, arranged at the hotels, through the museum, or with any taxi driver who knows the way. The two sites theoretically charge Y5 for entry and Y5 for photos.

Other ruins such as the **Rawaq Pagoda** and city of **Niya** (Endere) are off limits due to the high fees charged (US$5000 for Niya).

Silk & Carpet Factories

Jiyaxiang *(jíyàxiāng)*, a small town 3km east and then 8km north of Hotan, is a traditional centre for *atlas* silk production. Look around the small but fascinating workshop (*karakhana* in Uyghur) to see how the silk is spun, dyed and woven using traditional methods. A taxi from Hotan to the village costs Y10.

En route to the village, on the eastern bank of the Jade Dragon Kashgar river, is a small **carpet factory** (Uyghur: *gillam karakhana*), which is also worth a quick look around. Take the No 2 minibus from in front of the Hetian City Hotel and then change to the No 3 or walk 20 minutes over the bridge.

Hotan Silk Factory *(hétián sīchóu chǎng)* uses a less traditional form of silk production, employing over 2000 workers. Staff (*guǎngbàn*) will give you a tour of the plant to see the boiling of cocoons and spinning, weaving, dyeing and printing of silk. It's open Monday to Friday, 9 am to 1.30 pm, and 3.30 to 7.30 pm, though if you don't speak at least some Chinese you are better off arranging a visit through Hetian Travel Service. No photos are allowed. To get there, take minibus No 1 (8 mao) to the end of the line from outside the bus station and then walk back 150m.

None of the above factories charge for a look around, though all have shops that you are expected to at least look in.

Places to Stay

The cheapest reliable accommodation for foreigners is the *Hotan Guesthouse* (*hétián yínbīnguǎn;* ☎ 202 2203). The north building has beds in a quad/triple with shared bath for Y15/20, and comfortable doubles with hot shower for Y45 per bed. More upmarket rooms in the new block cost Y180 and up. Prices include a miserable breakfast.

Hotan Hotel (*hétián wài bīnguǎn;* ☎ 202 3564), on the western edge of town, is somewhat fancier, with comfortable but smoky doubles/triples for Y240/260 per room. There are also carpeted six-bed dorms for Y30 a bed – the bathrooms are pretty grim but if you are the only foreigner here you'll get the room to yourself.

Hetian City Guesthouse (*hétián shì bīnguǎn;* ☎ 204 6101), by the central crossroads, has beds in a quad/triple with shared bath for Y15/20, or in smoky doubles with private bathroom for Y40.

Jiaotong Hotel (*jiāotōng bīnguǎn;* ☎ 203 2700), right next to the bus station, has comfortable, carpeted doubles for Y60 per bed. The cheaper hostel (lüvshé) next door doesn't take foreigners.

A basic Uyghur-style alternative is the **Happy Hotel** (xìngfú lüvshé), a couple of minutes walk to the right from the bus station. Rooms are a little grimy, but there are hot showers. The owner asks around Y30 per bed but will take less. The 100% Uyghur **Silk Town Guest House** is ultra-basic but ultra-cheap (Y5 a bed).

There are several other Chinese hotels on Gulbagh Lu, such as the **Hongyan**, **Huayuan** and **Tian'e**, all with beds in a double for Y30 to Y50. The new **Yurong Hotel** (yùróng bīnguǎn; ☎ 202 5242) in the centre has clean doubles for Y138 and triples at Y30 a bed.

Places to Eat

There are plenty of standard Chinese (new town) and Uyghur (old town) restaurants in Hotan, though few places speak English. One to recommend is the hole-in-the-wall **Jinyou Restaurant** (jīnyǒu cāntīng). There's no English but everything on the menu costs a flat Y6. There's also a more expensive menu. The **Chengdu Restaurant** nearby is of a similar standard. **Yiyuan Restaurant** (yíyuàn kuàicān) is another good cheap Chinese menu place 60m south of the Hotan Guesthouse gate (not the fancy place to the left).

Getting There & Around

Donkey carts go to or from the Sunday market for five mao. Taxis cost a flat Y5 and there are also three-wheeler motorcycles.

Air There are four flights weekly between Hotan and Ürümqi (Y1000), departing at 2 pm. The CAAC/Xinjiang Airlines office (☎ 202 2178) is on Positan Nanlu. The airport is 10km south of town and the taxi ride from town costs Y20.

Bus Buses from Ürümqi to Hotan now travel along the recently opened Cross-Desert

Hwy, which spans 500km of almost completely deserted land between Luntai and Niya (mínfēng). The roadway is actually built on a raised roadbed and surrounded by squares of netting and grasses to help prevent sandstorms from building up dunes on the tarmac. Sleeper buses leave Hotan twice a day at 4 and 7 pm (Y290, 30 hours). Express sleeper buses (Y340 or Y360, 22 hours) leave at noon on Tuesday, Thursday and Saturday. There are also plenty of sleeper buses to Aksu (Y146, 15 hours).

There are two daily buses between Hotan and Kashgar – one in the morning (Y34) and a 'luxury' one in the evening (Y55). The 530km trip takes around 10 hours. At the time of research, the sleeper bus service had been discontinued due to insufficient demand. There are also several buses daily to Yarkand (Y21) via Yecheng (Y17 to Y28).

HOTAN TO GOLMUD

To continue along the southern Silk Road into China proper catch an early-morning bus from Hotan to Cherchen (qiěmò), 580km to the east. The trip takes two days and costs Y55 and goes via the Uyghur towns of Keriya (yútián) and Niya (mínfēng).

From Cherchan buses continue another 320km east to Charklik (ruòqiāng). The trip takes anywhere from 13 to 16 hours under good conditions, and tickets are around Y35. From Charklik you may be able to get a bus to Golmud, although some travellers have had to resort to private jeep services that take you the nine hours to the border with Qinghai. From there you can reportedly take a series of buses on to Dachaidan in Qinghai Province, and from there connect with buses to Golmud. This route requires a few overnight stops, and roads in this area are plagued by washouts and landslides, so don't try this route if you're in a hurry. See Lonely Planet's China guide if you are headed into China proper.

XINJIANG

Afghanistan

Afghanistan at a Glance

Official Name: Islamic Emirate of Afghanistan
Area: 650,000 sq km
Population: 23.74 million (1997)
Ethnic Mix: 38% Pashto, 25% Tajik, 19% Hazara, 6% Uzbek, 3% nomad, 2% Turkmen, 1.5% Baluch, 5.5% Others
Capital: Kabul
Currency: Afghani
Country ☎ Code: 93
Best Time to Go: don't go
Travel Warning: see the boxed text

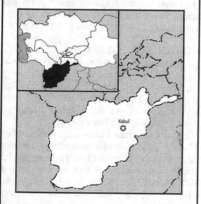

Kabul ✪

At the time of writing the sound of gunfire and shelling still reverberates over parts of Afghanistan as it has done with depressing regularity since the late 1970s. Hopes are high that the latest faction to win control over the war-torn capital, the Islamist Taliban fighters, may eventually succeed in bringing peace but for the time being Afghanistan is unsafe to visit. This is tragic for the country and unfortunate for travellers, as Afghanistan is vastly appealing, with endless empty deserts, soaring barren mountains, old historic towns and, best of all, the proud, independent and immensely hospitable Afghans.

HISTORY

Afghanistan's history as a country spans little more than two centuries, but in the past it has been part, or the centre, of many great empires. As with much of the region, the rise and fall of political power has been inextricably tied to the rise and fall of religions.

It was in Afghanistan that the ancient religion of Zoroastrianism began in the 6th century BCE (before common era). Later, Buddhism spread west from India to the Bamiyan valley where it remained strong until the 10th century CE (common era). The eastward sweep of Islam reached Afghanistan in the 7th century and the entire country to this day remains Muslim.

Empires & Invaders

Afghanistan has weathered invasions by such historical superstars as the Aryans, Darius of Persia, Alexander the Great, the Kushans, Hephalites, Sassanids, the Arab armies, Jenghiz Khan, Timur (Tamerlane), Babur (the founder of the Moguls) and even the Soviet Red Army. Between 1220 and 1223 Jenghiz Khan tore through the country destroying everything before him. Balkh, Herat, Ghazni and Bamiyan were all reduced to rubble. When the damage was finally repaired Timur swept through in the early 1380s and reduced the region to rubble again.

In contrast to Jenghiz, Timur's reign ushered in the golden Timurid era, when poetry, architecture and miniature painting reached their zenith. Timur's fourth son Shah Rukh in particular, devoted much wealth and energy to the arts; he built shrines, mosques and medressas throughout Khorasan, from Mashad, in modern-day Iran, to Balkh in modern-day Afghanistan. Herat continued to prosper under Sultan Hussain Baykara (died 1506), producing such great Central Asian poets as Jami and Alisher Navoi.

The rise of the Great Mogul empire again lifted Afghanistan to heights of power. Babur had his capital in Kabul in 1512, but as the Moguls extended their power into

Warning

! Lonely Planet strongly advises against travelling to Afghanistan, as do both the British Foreign Office and the US State Department. Although much of the country is no longer at war, the situation remains extremely volatile and there are recurrent outbreaks of fighting throughout the country. Visitors should be aware that there is no British or US mission in Afghanistan to provide consular help and there are almost certainly no other consular missions other than for Pakistan. The country is awash with arms and warlords steeped in a culture of guns, kidnappings and banditry and there are over 10 million unexploded land mines in Afghanistan. At the time of research Afghan embassies and consulates were only issuing visas to accredited journalists and aid workers. It was not possible to visit Afghanistan for the update of this edition. Occasional adventurers do make it, though many of them have come unstuck and have even been killed in the process.

India, Afghanistan's status declined as it went from being the centre of the empire to simply being a peripheral part of it. In 1774, with European strength threatening the declining Moguls on the Indian subcontinent, the kingdom of Afghanistan was founded.

The Afghan Wars

The 19th century was a period of often comic-book confrontation with the British, who were afraid of the effects of unruly neighbours on their great Indian colony. The rise of Great Game tensions (see the Facts about Central Asia chapter at the start of this book) and the internal weakness of the Afghan kingdom resulted in a series of remarkably unsuccessful and bloody, preventative wars being fought on extremely flimsy pretexts.

The first war took place between 1839 and 1842. Dost Mohammed, ruler of Kabul, had made approaches to the British and Russians in turn. In 1841 the British garrison in Kabul found itself under attack after Alexander 'Bokhara' Burnes was hacked to pieces by an Afghan mob. The British attempted to retreat to India and were almost totally wiped out in the Khyber pass – out of 16,000 persons only one man survived. The British managed to re-occupy Kabul and carried out little razing and burning to show who was boss, but Dost Mohammed ended up back in power, just as he had been before the war.

Following local wars, from 1878 to 1880, Afghanistan agreed to become more or less a protectorate of the British, happily accepted an annual payment to keep things in shape and agreed to a British resident in Kabul. No sooner had this diplomatic mission been installed in Kabul than all its members were murdered. This time the British decided to keep control over Afghanistan's external affairs, but to leave the internal matters strictly to the Afghans themselves.

Treaties between Britain and Russia in 1895 and 1907 took much of the heat out of the Great Game, when they agreed to establish a little strip of no-man's land between themselves, resulting in the strange little finger of Afghanistan, the Wakhan Corridor, poking out of the top north-eastern corner. In 1893 the British also drew Afghanistan's eastern boundaries with the so-called Durand Line and neatly partitioned a large number of the Pathan tribes into imperial India, in what today is Pakistan. This has been a cause of Afghan-Pakistani strife for many years and is the reason the Afghans refer to the western part of Pakistan as Pashtunistan.

From WWI onwards the US replaced Britain in worrying about Russian influence. Nevertheless, the US tacitly recognised that Afghanistan was firmly in the Soviet sphere of influence and the Soviet presence was strongly felt. Afghanistan's trade tilted heavily towards the USSR and Soviet foreign aid to Afghanistan far outweighed western assistance. Only in tourism did the western powers have a major influence on the country.

Despite its relatively untroubled external relations, internally Afghanistan remained precariously unstable. Attempts to encourage Turkish-style progress in the country failed dismally between WWI and WWII. The post-war kingdom ended in 1973 when the king, a Pathan like most of those in

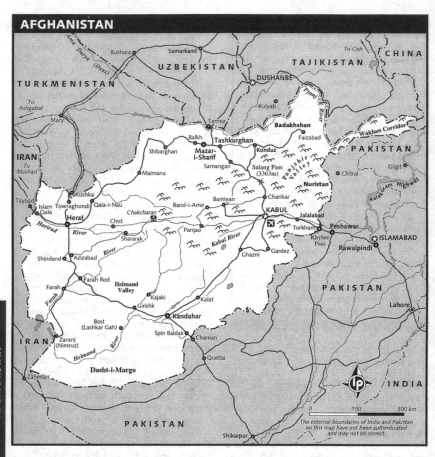

AFGHANISTAN

power, was neatly overthrown while away in Europe. His 'progressive' successors were hardly any more progressive than he had been, but the situation under them was far better than that which was to follow.

After the bloody pro-Moscow revolution that took place in 1978, Afghanistan rapidly deteriorated into turmoil and confusion. Its pro-communist, anti-religious government was far out of step with the strongly Islamic situations that prevailed in neighbouring Iran and Pakistan, and soon the ever-volatile Afghan tribes had the countryside up in arms. A second revolution brought in

a government leaning even more heavily on Soviet support and the country took another lurch towards anarchy.

The Soviet Invasion

Finally in late 1979, the Soviet regime decided that enough was enough. Another 'popular' revolution took place and a Soviet puppet government was installed in Kabul, with what looked like half the Soviet army lined up behind it. Despite an ineffectual storm of western protests it soon became clear that the Soviets were there to stay. An Islamic jihad (holy war) was called and seven mujaheddin factions emerged. The Soviets soon found themselves mired in what later became known as 'Russia's Vietnam'. They had the advantage of short supply lines, no organised protests from home and a divided enemy but, divided or not, the Afghan mujaheddin were every bit as determined as the Viet Cong.

The war ground on through the 1980s. The Afghan clan warriors remained disorganised and badly trained but to their determination and undoubted bravery they also began to add modern weaponry; the CIA pumped up to US$700 million a year into the conflict in one of the largest covert operations in history. Soon the Soviet regime held only the cities and soon even supplying the cities became increasingly difficult as road convoys were ambushed and aircraft brought down with surface-to-air missiles. In the late 1980s Gorbachev's new pragmatic mood of *perestroika* (restructuring) weakened the Russians' will to fight such an intractable opponent and suddenly the Russians wanted out.

The decade-long war had cost the Soviets over 15,000 men, produced a wave of nationalism in the Central Asian republics and contributed significantly to the collapse of the USSR. In Afghanistan over a million Afghans lay dead and 6.2 million people, over half the world's refugee population, had fled the country.

Civil War in the 1990s

The Soviet withdrawal in 1989 weakened the Russian-backed government of President Najibullah. In an attempt to end the civil war, Najibullah proposed a government of national unity but the mujaheddin refused to participate in any government which included him or his Watan (Homeland) Party. In April 1992 Najibullah was ousted and a week later fighting erupted between rival mujaheddin factions in Kabul. An interim president was installed and replaced two months later by Burhanuddin Rabbani, a founder of the country's Islamic political movement.

The accession of Rabbani did nothing to stop the fighting. Constant warfare between the presidential forces of Rabbani and the rival mujaheddin armies of Gulbuddin Hekmatyar and Rashid Dostum devastated the country, doing more damage than the Soviet occupation.

The Taliban

The two bitter rivals were, however, forced into an alliance in May 1996 by the spectacular military successes of a group of Islamic fighters called the Taliban. The Taliban are a group of ethic Pashtuns ('talib' is a Pashto word meaning 'religious student' or 'seeker of knowledge' – 'taliban' is the plural), backed by Pakistan and educated in Pakistani medressas. The Taliban took Kandahar in 1994, Ghazni, Helmand and Herat in 1995 and in September 1996 they entered Kabul unopposed – Rabbani and Hekmatyar's forces had already fled north. The former communist president Najibullah was not so foresighted, and one of the first acts of the new rulers of Kabul was to drag him from the UN compound where he had been sheltering for the last 4½ years, execute him and string up the body for all to see.

In 1997 the Taliban took Mazar-i-Sharif only to be pushed back in their first ever military setback, but by September 1998 they had taken Mazar in the north and Bamiyan in the central region of Hazarajat (with the alleged massacre of over 8000 Hazaras). At the time of writing, the Taliban controlled 90% of Afghanistan's territory and only the Tajik mujaheddin Ahmed Shah Masood provided an active opposition in the Panjshir valley.

On the international field the Taliban have enjoyed fewer successes. In 1998 the US pulverised parts of south-east Afghanistan with Tomahawk cruise missiles in an attempt to flush out Osama bin Laden, the multi-millionaire Saudi dissident suspected of the 1998 bombings of US embassies in Kenya and Tanzania. In retaliation a UN official was murdered in Kabul and all UN staff and aid agencies temporarily pulled out of the country. That same year Iran mobilised up to 100,000 troops on its eastern borders as tension between the two countries (one Sunni, the other Shia) reached a peak after the murder of eight Iranian diplomats in Mazar-i-Sharif. The Iranian Ayatollah Khamanei has described the Taliban as 'ignorant and immature'.

Talibanned

The Taliban are a group of ethic Pashtuns, backed by Pakistan and educated in the medressas of Peshawar, Lahore and Karachi. Their aim is simple – to create the world's purest Islamic state – but their unprecedentedly severe interpretation of Islamic sharia law (which includes forbidding women to work, closing girls' schools and making beards compulsory for men) has caused great unease in the traditionally relaxed cities of Kabul and Herat.

The list of unnecessary evils banned by the Taliban's 'Department to Propagate Virtue and Eliminate Vice' runs to music, television, magazines, photography, kite flying, pigeon flying, paper bags, long hair and drums. Cassette and video tape flutters like bunting from many Taliban checkpoints. With other forms of entertainment banned, Kabul's sports stadium packs a crowd every Friday afternoon, when thieves have limbs surgically amputated (under anaesthetic), female adulterers are stoned and murderers beheaded. Others open to arrest or beating include men whose beard is less than fist-length (the punishment is imprisonment until the facial hair grows to the requisite length), anyone absent from daily prayers and taxi drivers who take unaccompanied female fares.

In March 1999, for the first time, the Taliban and the leaders of the Anti-Taliban Northern Alliance brokered an agreement in Ashgabat in Turkmenistan to share power. The agreement quickly collapsed and further talks in Tashkent failed to achieve a concrete solution (the implementation of Islamic law for one proving a sticking point), but for a nation weary of war the agreement marks the most positive development for a decade.

Reports from within indicate that if the Taliban can enforce peace and unity throughout the land and rebuild at least some of the country's shattered infrastructure then imposed Islamic law may be an acceptable price to pay. However, for the traveller, one of the most interesting countries in Asia looks likely to remain off limits for some time to come.

GEOGRAPHY

Afghanistan is a totally landlocked country slightly larger than France, with an extremely rugged topography. It borders Iran, Turkmenistan, Uzbekistan, Tajikistan, China and Pakistan and is strategically important to all.

The mighty Hindu Kush (Killer of Hindus) range, the western extremity of the Himalaya, runs across the country from east to west. The average elevation of this mountainous interior is a lofty 2700m and the highest peaks reach 7500m in the north-east. From here rise

the major rivers of Afghanistan. The Kabul river flows east into the Indus while most others such as the Helmand, Farah and Harirud disappear into the desert sands.

To the north of the Hindu Kush lie the low-lying plains of Afghan Turkistan and the border marked by the Amu-Darya (Oxus). To the south stretches the dry, dusty Dasht-i-Margo, or Desert of Death.

Afghanistan is very seismically active. Two major quakes in 1998 and then again in February 1999 killed hundreds of people, the latter leaving over 30,000 homeless.

GOVERNMENT & POLITICS

According to Afghanistan's 1987 constitution the Loya Jirga, a traditional gathering of clan leaders, elects an executive president for a seven-year term. The president then appoints a Council of Ministers which must be approved by the bicameral National Assembly.

The country is presently without elected leaders. The UN and most western governments continue to recognise the government of ex-President Burhanuddin Rabbani and the Northern Anti-Taliban Alliance, despite the fact that they now control less than 10% of the country. Power is in the hands of the Taliban who are led by Maulana Mohammed Omar, a one-eyed former mujaheddin cleric. Only Pakistan, Saudi Arabia and the UAE recognise the Taliban diplomatically.

On taking the capital the Taliban announced that Afghanistan would be ruled by an interim six-member inner *shura* (council) led by Omar's deputy, Mullah Mohammed Rabbani (no relation to the fleeing president). The country has since been renamed the Islamic Emirate of Afghanistan.

ECONOMY

A country primarily of agricultural and nomadic shepherds, Afghanistan traded chiefly with the former republics of the Soviet Union and Eastern Europe. The only natural resource exploited was natural gas, most of which was piped into the former USSR.

Constant war for 20 years has destroyed all industry. Today's biggest earner is smuggling, either of goods (imported duty free from Dubai and then 'exported' to Pakistan) or drugs (Afghanistan is the world's largest producer of hashish and opium). Traditional exports include karakul pelts from Turkistan, dried fruit and nuts, handwoven carpets and gemstones from Badakhshan. Indeed in the 1980s lapis and heroin financed many of the mujaheddin groups. Drug money is often still laundered through the gemstone market.

Foreign aid remains vital to Afghanistan's economy. It is hoped that transit fees from Central Asian oil and gas pipelines could become a major earner, as – once again – could tourism. See the boxed text 'Pipe Dreams' in the Facts about Central Asia chapter.

POPULATION & PEOPLE

The population of Afghanistan is about 23 million although exact figures are hard to come by due to nomadic wanderings and large numbers of internally displaced peoples. Afghanistan is split sharply along ethnic lines and these ethnic and cultural differences continue to profoundly shape Afghan politics. Approximately 40% of the population is Pashto. There have been allegations of ethnic cleansing against the Taliban troops in northern Afghanistan.

SOCIETY & CONDUCT

Afghanistan's geographical position – for centuries crisscrossed by armies, empires and trade routes – combined with its varied geological terrain have given rise to the great diversity of languages and traditions that form Afghanistan's cultural heritage. The turmoil produced by the civil war and the enormous number of displaced peoples have put great pressure on Afghan cultural life.

The seclusion and veiling of women has not been enforced since 1959, but the Taliban's accession to power has brought great changes to women's lives. Afghan women can be flogged or otherwise punished for being on the street without the company of a male relative or for not wearing the shuttlecock-shaped *burqa*. Women can only attend single sex hospitals (of which there are few) and may not seek employment or education.

Aid workers tell of women dying after being refused treatment because the only available doctors were male, and of women having their thumbs cut off for wearing nail varnish. The Taliban have stated that girls' schools will be set up but only when the country can afford them – little consolation to Afghan women, whose literacy rates remain as low as 15%. The ban on seeking employment has had a particularly painful affect on Kabul's estimated 50,000 war widows. If the extreme orthodox Islamic regime persists great care will be needed to exercise respect for prevailing customs.

RELIGION

Afghanistan is an intensely Muslim country. Although the Blue Mosque in Mazar-i-Sharif is one of the most important Shia Muslim shrines, the country is 85% Sunni. The Hazaras of central Afghanistan form the bulk of the Shias and as such have strong links to Iran. The country has historically been a great centre of Sufism.

LANGUAGE

Afghanistan has two main languages. One is Dari, a Persian dialect very similar to the Fārsī spoken in Iran and Tajik spoken in Tajikistan. The second language is Pashto, which is also spoken in the Pathan (Pashtun) regions of Pakistan. Persian is the language of the Taliban and thus most officials, and is the one to generally use.

AFGHANISTAN

INTERNET RESOURCES

Afghanistan Online
www.afghan-web.com
(news searches, books, culture and cookery)
Afghanistan Today
http://frankenstein.worldweb.net/afghan/
(music, history, culture, restaurants, publications, news and aid organisations)
Taliban Online
www.ummah.net/dharb
(the Taliban and their Islamic aims)

BOOKS

Afghanistan – Essential Field Guides by Edward Girardet and Walter Jonathan (ed). Excellent introduction to Afghanistan, aimed at journalists and aid workers. The only practical source of information for travelling in the region.
An Historical Guide to Afghanistan by Nancy Hatch Dupree. This was written in 1977, so is well out of date but still offers interesting historical details for armchair travellers.
Road to Oxiana by Robert Byron. Still, more than 60 years after it was written, the best travel book on Persia and Afghanistan. Few characters in the travel literature genre are as memorable as the show-stealing Afghan consul to Iran.
A Short Walk in the Hindu Kush by Eric Newby. One of the modern classics of travel writing, the book describes the (mis)adventures of two Englishmen who trekked through the Hindu Kush to Nuristan, north of Kabul, in the 1950s. One of the best endings of any travel book.

USEFUL ORGANISATIONS

The following organisations can give advice on security as well as private flights and guesthouses for aid workers and journalists:

Agency Coordinating Body for Afghanistan (ACBAR)
(☎ 091-44392, fax 840471,
@ acbaar@radio.psh.brain.net.pk)
3 Rehman Baba Rd, University Town, Peshawar
United Nations Office for the Coordination of Humanitarian Assistance to Afghanistan (UN-OCHA)
(☎ 051-211451, fax 211450,
@ unocha@undpafg.org.pk)
House 292, St 55, F-10/4, Islamabad

KABUL

The capital of Afghanistan was never a terribly attractive or interesting city and that has certainly not been improved by the last twenty years of conflict. The Soviets left the city reasonably intact in 1989, but since then Kabul has been virtually destroyed by bombardments and street battles, with an estimated loss of some 30,000 lives.

The **Kabul Museum**, which used to have one of the finest collections of antiquities in Asia, has had nearly three-quarters of its finest collections looted. It was once possible to walk the five-hour length of the crumbling walls of the old citadel, **Bala Hissar**, but they are now off limits and extremely dangerous due to unexploded bombs and local landmines. The pleasant **Gardens of Babur** were once a cool retreat near the city walls.

AROUND KABUL

Nuristan (Land of Light), north-east of Kabul, is mountainous, remote, little visited and of great ethnological interest – and memorably described in Eric Newby's hilarious *A Short Walk in the Hindu Kush*.

The **Red City** (Shahr-i-Zohak), the remains of an ancient citadel which guarded Bamiyan, is about 17km before Bamiyan itself and 180km north-west of Kabul. This was once the centre of the Ghorid kings.

Within Bamiyan are the great **buddhas**. The smaller of the two buddhas stands a towering 35m high. This buddha is thought to have been carved out in the 2nd or 3rd century CE (common era), but it is badly disfigured. The better and larger buddha, which stands 53m high, is estimated to be two or three centuries younger and is in a later, more sophisticated style. The buddhas were carved roughly out of their niches, then built up with mud and straw, covering them in a type of

The Hidden Costs of War

There are over 10 million unexploded land mines in Afghanistan. Some 400,000 Afghans have already been killed and 4000 a year continue to die violently. Some 80% of the casualties are civilian. Worse still, mines will continue to take lives indiscriminately for decades to come. In September 1998, 45 people were killed when a public bus hit an anti-tank landmine.

The Golden Crescent

For years Afghanistan has been the world's largest exporter of hashish and it recently overtook Myanmar to become the world's leading supplier of opium. It is estimated that 200,000 farmers cultivate 2200 tons of opium a year. Although the Taliban has condemned drug production (it controls 95% of opium land) and promised to cut down on production in return for international recognition, it is uncertain whether it has enough support in the countryside to do this.

Opium poppies, which are harvested in June and July, are often shipped for production to mobile labs in Pakistan's tribal areas, where Pakistani law doesn't apply. They are then packed back over the mountain passes into Afghanistan and beyond. The so-called 'Golden Crescent' now supplies Europe with 80% of its heroin, 65% of which is smuggled through Central Asia.

Tajik officials say that 200,000 tons of drugs are stockpiled at the border, about a ton of which crosses over each day. Known locally as *khanka*, raw opium costs US$30 per kg in Afghanistan's Helmand valley. The same kg costs US$800 in Osh and then US$6000 in Moscow. In 1995, Kyrgyzstan alone exported more narcotics then either Myanmar (Burma) or Thailand.

Most of the business is controlled by narco-clans, although the army, police and border guards all have fingers in the opium bowl. Drugs have even turned up on Russian military aircraft. It is feared that Tajikistan in particular could degenerate into a major 'narcocracy' like Colombia. And it's big business. Central Asia's drugs industry is valued at an annual turnover of US$1 billion to US$14 billion. In 1999 alone the UN gave US$6 million to fight the drugs war and US$30 million worth of opium was seized in a single haul near the Pyanj river. Police estimate that they catch about 5% of all shipments.

Not all of the drugs are exported; addiction in Central Asia is mushrooming. The average age of addicts in Bishkek is 17 years. In Kazakstan, 85% of those HIV positive are drug addicts.

In post-Soviet Central Asia, camel caravans of exotic silks and spices have been replaced, it seems, by Ladas packed with opium. The Silk Road has become an opium highway.

Production centres and shipment routes in Afghanistan are well protected by armed warlords and trafficking carries the death sentence in many countries in the region.

---

cement. Cords draped down the body were covered to form the folds of the figures' robes.

Shar-i-Gholgola is the main ruined city in the valley – the name means 'city of sighs'; climbing to the top of the cliff on the other side of the valley to look across at the buddhas used to be a popular activity.

The incredible lakes of **Band-i-Amir** (Dam of the King), clear blue water dammed by sulphurous deposits and surrounded by towering pink cliffs, are 75km beyond Bamiyan.

SOUTH & WEST OF KABUL

The modern town of Ghazni is just a pale shadow of its former glory. The city is only 150km south-west of Kabul but poor roads mean the trip still takes most of the day. Ghazni today is known mainly for its fine bazar. The restored **tomb of Abdul Razzak**

and the museum within are of interest. There are also some very fine minarets, the excavations of the **Palace of Masud** and, most surprisingly, a recently discovered **Buddhist stupa** which has survived from long before the Arab invasion of the 7th century CE.

Kandahar is in the far south of Afghanistan, midway between Kabul and Herat. It is the second largest city in Afghanistan and lies at an important crossroads where the main road from Kabul branches north-west to Herat and south-east to Quetta in Pakistan. Kandahar lies in the Pashto heartland and has gained modern significance as the power base of the Taliban militia. Kandahar's great treasure, a **cloak** which once belonged to the Prophet, is safely locked away from infidel eyes in the mosque of the Sacred Cloak, known locally as Da Kherqa Sharif Ziarat.

AFGHANISTAN

A few kilometres from the centre of Kandahar towards Herat are the **'Forty Steps'** (Chihil Zina). They lead up to a niche carved in the rock by Babur, founder of the Mogul empire, guarded by two stone lions.

KANDAHAR TO HERAT

Ruins and drugs are the features of this route across western Afghanistan. The Helmand valley was once the centre of a sophisticated *karez* (underground irrigation system; see the boxed text 'Karez' in the Around Turpan section of the Xinjiang chapter). Today the region has gained infamy as Afghanistan's largest drug-producing area (see the boxed text). **Bost (Lashkar Gah)**, 150km west of Kandahar, today is a jumble of ruins and remains – shattered remnants of a once mighty city. The superb arch, **Qalai Bost**, was the high point of a visit to this old centre.

HERAT

Herat was a small, provincial, relatively green, laze-about place which everyone seemed to like. It was an easy-going oasis after a lot of hassle and dry desert. In the fifteenth century Herat was the Timurid centre of art, poetry, miniature painting and music, blending Persian, Central Asian and Afghan cultures to create one of Central Asia's cultural highlights. Today the city sits particularly uneasily under puritan Taliban rule.

The **Friday Mosque**, or Masjid-i-Jami, is Herat's number one attraction and one of the finest Islamic buildings in the world, certainly the finest in Afghanistan. It has some exquisite Timurid tilework to complement its graceful architecture. Herat's ancient citadel, or *qala*, built in 1305, is today used as a base by the Taliban so you can't get in for a look around, although you could once walk right round its outer wall. The **covered bazar** in Char souq is a complex of all sorts of shops and artisans' workshops.

A short walk from the centre of Herat on the road that runs north are a number of interesting sights. First there is a small **park** with a beehive-shaped tomb then, farther on, four immense, broken **minarets**. They are all that remains of an old medressa, which was built in 1417 by the Queen Gaur Shad (who also built the fabulous Masjid-i-Azim Gohar Shah mosque at Mashad in modern-day Iran). As the wife of Timurid ruler Shah Rukh, Gaur Shad was Timur's daughter-in-law and a remarkable woman in her own right, who kept the empire intact for many years. Her mausoleum still stands near the medressa, a carbon copy of the Gur Emir in Samarkand.

The shrine complex of **Gazar Gah**, dating from 1425, is about 5km east of Herat. The tomb of Abdullah Ansar, a famous Sufi mystic and poet who died in Herat in 1088, is the main attraction. The Afghan King Dost Mohammed and the famous Persian poet Jami are also buried here.

The 65m high **Minaret of Jam**, 313km from Herat and around 550km from Kabul is the second highest in the world and one of the oldest at over 800 years old.

AFGHAN TURKESTAN

North of the Hindu Kush is a quite different Afghanistan – if the south is related to the Iranian plateau, the north is akin to the Central Asian steppes and indeed, prior to the modern obsession about borders, the Afghan nomads were quite at home on both the Russian and Afghan sides of the border. Until the Salang pass tunnel was completed in the mid-1960s this was also a totally isolated part of the country. To get there before that time you either had to climb up and over the highest part of the Hindu Kush, north of Kabul, or cross the lower western extremity near Herat and make a long desert crossing.

Archaeologists have found remains of Greek cities from the days of Alexander the Great near Mazar-i-Sharif but there is nothing much for the visitor to view. In Mazar-i-Sharif itself is the **Blue Mosque**, supposedly the Tomb of Ali, the adopted son of the Prophet, and the holiest spot in Afghanistan.

Although **Balkh** was, until Jenghiz Khan, a flourishing city of beautiful buildings, today all that is left are a few time-worn buildings and the crumbling remains of the city walls.

The 15th century **Green Mosque** (Mosque of Abu Nasr Parsā), Masjid-i-Nau Gumbad and the rubble of the pre-Mongol city walls are pretty much all there is to see.

Language

Central Asia is a multilingual area, and so this chapter includes words and phrases from eight different languages which you may find useful. The official languages of the former Soviet Central Asian countries are Kazak, Kyrgyz, Tajik, Turkmen and Uzbek, but Russian is still the language of government and academia (rather like English in India). Therefore the one language most useful for a visitor is still Russian; you'll find that it's the second language for most adults, who were taught it in school. A few words of the local language will nonetheless give a disproportionate return in goodwill. At home, educated people normally speak a mishmash of Russian and their native tongue.

If you can read Russian Cyrillic characters, then most of the Cyrillic-based alphabets of Central Asia will be familiar also. Knowing how to count in local languages will allow you to listen in on discussions of prices in the markets. In public it's now often worthwhile letting non-Russians know in advance that you're not Russian, either by saying so or by starting out in English. For an excellent guide to the languages of Central Asia, get a copy of Lonely Planet's *Central Asia phrasebook*.

RUSSIAN

Two words you're sure to use during your travels are Здравствуйте *(zdrastvuyte)*, the universal 'hello' (but if you say it a second time in one day to the same person, they'll think you forgot you already saw them!), and Пожалуйста *(pazhalsta)*, the multipurpose word for 'please' (commonly included in all polite requests), 'you're welcome', 'pardon me', 'after you' and such.

The easiest way to turn a statement into a question is just to use a rising tone and a questioning look, or follow it with *da?*, eg 'Is this Moscow?', Уто Москва да? *(eta maskva?)*. A sentence is made negative by putting не *(ni)* before its main word, eg 'This is not Moscow', Уто не Москва *(eta ni maskva)*.

Two letters have no sound, but modify others. A consonant followed by the 'soft sign' ь is spoken with the tongue flat against the palate, as if followed by the faint beginnings of a 'y'. The rare 'hard sign' ъ after a consonant inserts a slight pause before the next vowel.

Greetings & Civilities

Hello.
    zdrastvuyte   Здравствуйте.
Goodbye.
    da svidaniya   До свидания.
How are you?
    kak dila?   Как дела?
I'm well.
    kharasho   Хорошо.
Yes/No.
    da/net   Да/Нет.
good/OK
    kharasho   хорошо
bad
    plokha   плохо

Thank you (very much).
    (bal'shoye)   (ольшое) спасибо.
    spasiba
What's your name?
    kak vas zavut?   Как вас зовут?
My name is ...
    minya zavut ...   Меня зовут ...
Where are you from?
    atkuda vy?   Откуда вы?
Australia
    afstraliya   Австралия
Canada
    kanada   Канада
France
    frantsiya   Франция
Germany
    germaniya   Германия
Ireland
    irlandiya   Ирландия
New Zealand
    novaya zelandiya Новая Зеландия
the UK (Great Britain)
    velikabritaniya   Великобритания

LANGUAGE

The Russian Cyrillic Alphabet

Cyrillic	Roman	Pronunciation
А, а	a	as the 'a' in 'father' (in stressed syllable)
		as the 'a' in 'about' (in unstressed syllable)
, б	b	as the 'b' in 'but'
В, в	v	as the 'v' in 'van'
Г, г	g	as the 'g' in 'god'
Д, д	d	as the 'd' in 'dog'
Е, е *	e	as the 'ye' in 'yet' (in stressed syllable)
		as the 'yi' in 'yin' (in unstressed syllable)
Ё, ё **	yo	as the 'yo' in 'yore'
Ж, ж	zh	as the 's' in 'measure'
З, з	z	as the 'z' in 'zoo'
И, и	i	as the 'ee' in 'meet'
Й, й	y	as the 'y' in 'boy'
К, к	k	as the 'k' in 'kind'
Л, л	l	as the 'l' in 'lamp'
М, м	m	as the 'm' in 'mad'
Н, н	n	as the 'n' in 'not'
О, о	o	as the 'o' in 'more' (in stessed syllable)
		as the 'a' in 'hard' (in unstressed syllable)
П, п	p	as the 'p' in 'pig'
Р, р	r	as the 'r' in 'rub' (rolled)
С, с	s	as the 's' in 'sing'
Т, т	t	as the 't' in 'ten'
У, у	u	as the 'oo' in 'fool'
Ф, ф	f	as the 'f' in 'fan'
Х, х	kh	as the 'ch' in 'Bach'
Ц, ц	ts	as the 'ts' in 'bits'
Ч, ч	ch	as the 'ch' in 'chin'
Ш, ш	sh	as the 'sh' in 'shop'
Щ, щ	shch	as 'sh-ch' in 'fresh chips'
ъ	(no symbol)	'hard sign' (see p.549)
Ы, ы	y	as the 'i' in 'ill'
ь	'	'soft sign'; (see p.549)
Э, э	e	as the 'e' in 'end'
Ю, ю	yu	as the 'u' in 'use'
Я, я	ya	as the 'ya' in 'yard' (in stressed syllable)
		as the 'ye' in 'yearn' (in unstressed syllable)

* Е, е is transliterated *Ye, ye* when at the beginning of a word

** Ё, ё is often printed without dots

USA, America
(se she a), (США),
shtaty/amerika Америка

Language Difficulties

I don't speak Russian.
ya ni gavaryu pa ruski
Я не говорю по-русски.
I don't understand.
ya ni panimayu
Я не понимаю.
Do you speak English?
vy gavarite pa angliyski?
Вы говорите по-английски?
Could you write it down, please?
zapishite pazhalsta
Запишите пожалуйста.

Transport & Travel

Where is ...?
gde ...? Где ...?
airport
aeraport аэропорт
bus
aftobus автобус
railway station
zhileznadarozhnyy vagzal
железно дорожный (ж. д.) вокзал
train
poyezt поезд

When does it leave?
kagda atpravlyaetsya?
Когда отправляется?
What town is this?
kakoy eta gorat?
Какой єтот город?

hotel
gastinitsa гостиница
square/plaza
ploshchat' площадь (пл.)
street
ulitsa улица (ул.)
toilet
tualet туалет

Money & Shopping

How much is it?
skol'ka stoit? Сколько стоит?
Do you have ...?
u vas est'...? У вас есть ...?

Non-Russian Cyrillic Letters

Cyrillic	Roman	Pronunciation
Kazak		
Ә, ә	a	as the 'a' in 'man'
Ғ, ғ	gh	as the 'gh' in 'ugh'
Қ, қ	q	a guttural 'k'
Ө, ө	ö	as the 'eu' in 'bleu'
Ү, ү	u	as the 'u' in 'full'
Ұ, ұ	ü	as the 'oo' in 'fool'
Ш, ш	i	as the 'i' in 'ill'
Ң, ң	n	as the 'ng' in 'sing'
h, h	h	as the 'h' in 'hat'
Tajik		
Ғ, ғ	gh	as the 'gh' in 'ugh'
Й, й	ee	as the 'ee' in 'fee'
Қ, қ	q	as the 'k' in 'keen'
Ӯ, ӯ	ö	as the 'eu' in 'bleu'
Х, х	kh	as the 'h' in 'hat'
Ч, ч	j	as 'j' in 'jig'
Uzbek		
Ғ, ғ	gh	as the 'gh' in 'ugh'
Ж, ж	j	as the 'j' in 'jail'
И, и	i	as the 'i' in 'bit'
Қ, қ	q	a guttural 'k'
Щ, щ	o	as the 'o' in 'wrong'
Ў, ў	u	as the 'oo' in 'book'
Х, х	kh	as the 'ch' in 'Bach'
Х, х	h	as the 'h' in 'hat'
Kyrgyz		
Ж, ж	j	as the 'j' in 'jail'
И, и	i	as the 'i' in 'bit'
Ң, ң	ng	as the 'ng' in 'sing'
Щ, щ	o	as the 'o' in 'wrong'
Ө, ө	ö	as the 'eu' in 'bleu'
Ү, ү	ü	as the 'ew' in 'few'
Turkmen		
Г, г	g	a rolled 'r'; 'g' as in 'get' at the beginning of a word
Х, х	h	as the 'h' in 'hat'
Ә, ә	a	as the 'a' in 'camera'
Ж, ж	j	as 'j' in 'jump'
Ң, ң	n	soft 'n' hardly sounded
Ө, ө	ö	as the 'eu' in 'bleu'
Ү, ү	ü	as the 'ew' in 'few'

money
  den'gi деньги
currency exchange
  abmen valyuty обмен валюты

shop
  magazin магазин
bookshop
  knizhnyy книжный
  magazin магазин
market
  rynak рынок
pharmacy
  apteka аптека

Time, Days & Dates

Dates are given as day-month-year, with the month usually in Roman numerals. Days of the week are often represented by numbers in timetables; Monday is 1.

When?
  kagda? когда?
today
  sivodnya сегодня
yesterday
  vchira вчера
tomorrow
  zaftra завтра

Monday
  panidel'nik понедельник
Tuesday
  ftornik вторник
Wednesday
  srida среда
Thursday
  chitverk четверг
Friday
  pyatnitsa пятница
Saturday
  subota суббота
Sunday
  vaskrisen'e воскресенье

Emergencies

I need a doctor.
  mne nuzhin vrach
  Мне нужен врач.
hospital
  bal'nitsu больница
police
  militsiya милиция
Fire!
  pazhar! Пожар!

Help!
*na **pomashch**'!* or *pamagiti!*
На помощь! or Помогите!
Thief!
vor!   Вор!

Numbers
How many?
skol'ka?   Сколько?

0	*nol'*	ноль
1	*adin*	один
2	*dva*	два
3	*tri*	три
4	*chityri*	четыре
5	*pyat'*	пять
6	*shest'*	шесть
7	*sem'*	семь
8	*vosim'*	восемь
9	*devit'*	девять
10	*desit'*	десять
20	*dvatsat'*	двадцать
30	*tritsat'*	тридцать
40	*sorak*	сорок
50	*pyat'disyat*	пятьдесят
60	*shest'disyat*	шестьдесят
70	*sem'disyat*	семьдесят
80	*vosimdisyat*	восемьдесят
90	*divyanosta*	девяносто
100	*sto*	сто
1000	*tysyacha*	тысяча

Food
restaurant
ristaran   ресторан
cafe
kafe   кафе
canteen
stalovaya   столовая
bill
schyot   счёт
bread
khlep   хлеб
water
vada   вода
boiling water
kipyatok   кипяток
tea
chay   чай
meat
myasa   мясо

I can't eat meat.
ya ni em maysnova
Я не ем мясного.

Russian Menus
A typical menu is divided into *zakuski* (cold appetisers), *pervye* ('first' courses, ie soups and hot appetisers), *vtorye* ('second' or main courses), and *sladkye* (desserts). Main dishes may be further divided into *firmennye* (house specials), *natsionalnye* ('national', ie local, dishes), *myasnye* (meat), *rybnye* (fish), *iz ptitsy* (poultry), or *ovoshchnye* (vegetable) dishes.

Salads & Vegetables
Frantsiskiy salat (Французкий салат) – beetroot, carrots and French fries
olivye salat (оливые салат) – potato, ham, peas and mayonnaise
chuiskiy salat (чуйский салат) – spicy carrot salad in vinaigrette
kapustiy salat (калусты салат) – cabbage salad
morkovi salat (моркови салат) – carrot salad
salat iz svezhei kapust (салат из свежей капусты) – raw cabbage salad
Stolichny (столичный) – beef, potatoes, egg, carrots, mayonnaise and apples
agurets (огурец) – cucumber
pomidor (помидор) – tomato
gribi (грибы) – mushroom
kartofel pure (картофель) – mashed potato
kartofel fri (картофель фри) – French fries, chips
kartoshka (картошка) – potato

Meat, Poultry & Fish
befstroganov (бефстроганов) – beef stroganoff
gavyadina (говядина) – beef
lyulya kebab (люля кебаб) – beef or mutton meatballs
bifshteks (бифштекс) – 'beefsteak', glorified hamburger
bitochki (биточки) – cutlet
frikadela (фрикадела) – fried meatballs
gulyash (гуляш) – a dismal miscellany of meat, vegetables and potatoes
ragu (рагу) – beef stew

antrecot (антрекот) – steak
kotleta po-Kievski (котлета по киевски) – chicken Kiev
tabak (табак) – chicken
kuritsa (курица) – chicken
tsyplyonok tabaka (цыплёнок табака) – grilled chicken with a spicy sauce
sudak zharen (судак жарен) – fried pike or perch
farel (форель) – trout
galuptsi (голубцы) – cabbage rolls stuffed with rice and meat
shashlyk iz pecheni (шашлык из печени) – liver kebabs
shashlk iz okorochkov (шашлык из окорочков) – chicken kebabs
shashlyk iz baraniny (шашлык из баранины) – mutton kebabs
sosiski (сосиски) – frankfurter sausage
kolbasa (колбаса) – sausage

Pasta, Noodles, Rice & Grains

laghman (лагман) – noodles, mutton and vegetables
chuchvara (чучвара) – dumplings
pelmeni (пельмени) – small dumplings in soup
makaron (макарон) – macaroni, pasta
ris (рис) – rice
grechka (гречка) – boiled barley

Dairy & Farm Produce

seer (сыр) – cheese
smetana (сметана) – sour cream
marozhnoe (мороженое) – ice cream
yitsa (яйцо) – eggs

Soups

okrochka (окрошка) – cold or hot soup made from sour cream, potatoes, egg and meat
borshch (борш) – beetroot and potato soup, often with sour cream
rassolnik s myasam (рассольник с мясо) – soup of marinated cucumber and kidney

KAZAK

Kazak is a Turkic language. Since 1940 it has been written in a 42-letter version of the Cyrillic alphabet. At least as many people in Kazakstan speak Russian as Kazak. Any

political tension over language issues has been rather neatly sidestepped by making Kazak the official state language, but permitting the majority language in local regions to be used in written government business there, and giving Russian national language status as 'language of inter-ethnic communication'.

Russian is the first language for some urban Kazaks as well as the large Russian minority who form about 35% of the population. Few people speak English or other western languages, but many of those who do tend to work in the tourist industry or with foreigners.

Street signs are sometimes in Kazak, sometimes in Russian, sometimes in both. In this book we use the language you're most likely to come across in each town.

Kazak Basics

Peace be with you.	*asalam aleykum*
Hello.	*salamatsyz ba?*
Goodbye.	*qosh-sau bolyngdar*
Thank you.	*rakhmet*
Yes/No.	*ia/zhoq*
How are you?	*khal zhagh dayyngyz qalay?*
I'm well.	*zhaqsy*
Do you speak English?	*aghylshynsa bilesiz be?*
I don't understand.	*tusinbeymin*

police	*militsia*
doctor	*dariger*
hospital	*aurukhana*
bus station	*avtobus vokzal*
train station	*temir zhol vokzal*
airport	*aeroport*
toilet	*azhetkhana*
friend	*dos*
good	*zhaqsy*
bad	*zhaman*

Where is...?	*... qayda?*
How much?	*qansha?*
hotel	*qonaq uy/ meymankhana*
restaurant	*restoran*
tea	*shay*
expensive	*qymbat*

bread	*nan*
boiled water	*qaynaghan su*
rice	*kurish*
meat	*yet*
Monday	*duysenbi*
Tuesday	*seysenbi*
Wednesday	*sarsenbi*
Thursday	*beysenbi*
Friday	*zhuma*
Saturday	*senbi*
Sunday	*zheksenbi*

1	*bir*
2	*yeki*
3	*ush*
4	*tört*
5	*bes*
6	*alty*
7	*etti*
8	*sakkiz*
9	*toghyz*
10	*on*
100	*zhus*
1000	*myng*

KYRGYZ

Kyrgyz is a Turkic language which has also been transliterated using a Cyrillic script since the early 1940s.

Along with neighbouring Uzbekistan and Turkmenistan, Kyrgyzstan is in the process of changing over to a modified Roman alphabet. While international Roman letters have already been adopted for vehicle number plates, Kyrgyzstan is the slowest of these three countries in implementing the change from a Cyrillic to a Roman alphabet.

Kyrgyz Basics

Peace be with you.	*salam aleykum*
Hello.	*salam*
Goodbye.	*jakshy kalyngydzar*
Thank you.	*rakhmat*
Yes/No.	*ova/jok*
How are you?	*jakshysüzbü?*
I'm well.	*jakshy*
Do you speak English?	*siz angliyscha süylöy süzbü?*
I don't understand.	*men tüshümböy jatamyn*
police	*militsia*

doctor	*doktur*
hospital	*oruukana*
bus station	*avtobiket*
train station	*temir jol vokzal*
airport	*aeroport*
toilet	*darakana*
friend	*dos*
good	*jakshy*
bad	*jaman*
Where is ...?	*... kayda?*
How much?	*kancha?*
hotel	*meymankana*
restaurant	*restoran*
tea	*chay*
expensive	*kymbat*
bread	*nan*
boiled water	*ysyk suu*
rice	*kürüch*
meat	*et*
Monday	*düshömbü*
Tuesday	*seyshembi*
Wednesday	*sharshembi*
Thursday	*beishembi*
Friday	*juma*
Saturday	*ishembi*
Sunday	*jekshembi*

1	*bir*
2	*eki*
3	*üch*
4	*tört*
5	*besh*
6	*alty*
7	*jety*
8	*segiz*
9	*toguz*
10	*on*
100	*jüz*
1000	*ming*

MANDARIN CHINESE

Mandarin (or *putonghua*, 'people's speech') is China's official language, the dialect of Beijing and the language of bureaucrats.

In this guide we use mainland China's official Romanised 'alphabet' of Chinese sounds, Pinyin. It's very streamlined, but the sounds aren't always self-evident.

The most difficult aspects of Chinese for westerners to master are the tones and pronunciation. A given sound has many meanings depending on its tone. There are four tones – the following examples show the accents used to represent them: high (*mā*, 'mother'), rising (*má*, 'hemp'), falling-rising (*mǎ*, 'horse'), and falling (*mà*, 'to sweat'). With common phrases you'll probably be understood even if you get the tones wrong.

Consonant and vowel sounds are mostly pronounced as per their English counterparts. Here are a few that may cause confusion:

Consonants
q (flat 'ch'); **x** (flat 'sh'); **zh** ('j'); **z** ('dz'); **c** ('ts'); **r** (tongue rolled back, almost 'z').

Vowels
a ('ah'); **er** ('ar', American pronunciation); **ui** ('oi' or 'wei'); **iu** ('yoh'); **ao** ('ow' as in 'now'); **ou** ('ow' as in 'low'); **e** ('uh' after consonants); **ian** ('yen'); **ong** ('oong'); **u** ('oo', or sometimes like 'ü': say 'ee' with your mouth rounded as if to say 'oo').

Mandarin Basics

Hello.
   nǐ hǎo 你好

Goodbye.
   zàijiàn 再见

Thank you.
   xièxie 谢谢

I'm sorry.
   duìbùqǐ 对不起

Yes, there is/No, there isn't.
   yǒu/méiyǒu 有/没有

No. (not so)
   búshì 不是

How much is it?
   dūoshǎo qián? 多少钱?

Is there a room vacant?
   yǒu méiyǒu kōng 有没有空房间?
   fángjiān?

hotel
   lǚguǎn 旅馆

I want to go to ...
   wǒ yào qù ... 我要去 ...

What time does it depart/arrive?
   jǐdiǎn kāi/dào? 几点开/到?

bicycle
   zìxíngchē 自行车

bus
   gōnggòng qìchē 公共汽车

taxi
   chūzū chē 出租车

train
   huǒchē 火车

long-distance bus station
   chángtú qìchē zhàn 长途汽车站

railway station
   hǔochē zhàn 火车站

one ticket
   yìzhāng piào 一张票

Where is the ...?
   ... zài nǎlǐ? ... 在哪里?

post office
   yóujú 邮局

telephone office
   diànxùn dàlóu 电讯大楼

toilet (restroom)
   cèsuǒ 厕所

today
   jīntiān 今天

tomorrow
   míngtiān 明天

yesterday
   zuótiān 昨天

Help!
   jiùmìng a! 救命啊

I'm sick.
   wǒ shēng bìng 我生病

emergency
   jǐnjí qíngkuàng 紧急情况

hospital
   yīyuàn 医院

police
   jǐngchá 警察

0	*líng*	零
1	*yī, yāo*	一, 么
2	*èr, liǎng*	二, 两
3	*sān*	三
4	*sì*	四
5	*wǔ*	五
6	*liù*	六

7	*qī*	七
8	*bā*	八
9	*jiǔ*	九
10	*shí*	十
11	*shíyī*	十一
12	*shí'èr*	十二
20	*èrshí*	二十
21	*èrshíyī*	二十一
100	*yìbǎi*	一百
200	*liǎngbǎi*	两百
1000	*yìqiān*	一千
10,000	*yíwàn*	一万

Food

spicy chicken with peanuts		
gōngbào jīdīng	宫爆鸡丁	
chinese ravioli		
shuǐjiǎo	水饺	
shredded pork & green beans		
biǎndòu ròusī	扁豆肉丝	
pork & sizzling rice crust		
guōbā ròupiàn	锅巴肉片	
double cooked sweet & sour pork fillets		
tángcù lǐjǐ/	糖醋里脊/	
gǔlǎo ròu	古老肉	
pork cooked with soy sauce		
jīngjiāng ròusī	精酱肉丝	
'wooden ear' mushrooms & pork		
mù'ěr ròu	木耳肉	
pork & green peppers		
qīngjiāo ròu piàn	青椒肉片	
dry cooked beef		
gānbiān niúròu sī	干煸牛肉丝	
sizzling beef platter		
tiěbǎn niúròu	铁板牛肉	
'fish-resembling' meat		
yúxiāng ròusī	鱼香肉丝	
egg & tomato		
fānqié chǎodàn	番茄炒蛋	
red cooked aubergine		
hóngshāo qiézi	红烧茄子	
'fish-resembling' aubergine		
yúxiāng qiézi	鱼香茄子	

fried vegetables		
sùchǎo sùcài	素炒素菜	
garlic beans		
sùchǎo biǎndòu	素炒扁豆	
spicy tofu		
málà dòufu	麻辣豆腐	
'homestyle' tofu		
jiācháng dòufu	家常豆腐	
I'm vegetarian.		
wǒ chī sù	我吃素	
Muslim noodles		
lāmiàn	拉面	
Muslim noodles & beef		
gànbàn miàn	干拌面	
noodles, tofu & vegetables in soup		
dàlǔmiàn	大鲁面	
fried noodle squares		
chǎopàozhàng	炒泡涨	
water (boiling)		
kāi shuǐ	开水	
mineral water		
kuàng quán shuǐ	矿泉水	
tea		
chá	茶	
Muslim tea (in Muslim restaurants)		
bābǎo wǎnzi	八宝碗子	
hot		
rède	热的	
ice cold		
bīngde	冰的	
beer		
píjiǔ	啤酒	

TAJIK

Tajik, the state language of Tajikistan since 1989, belongs to the south-west Iranian group of languages and is closely related to Farsi. This sets it apart from all the other Central Asian languages which are Turkic in origin. Tajik was formerly written in a modified Arabic script and then in Roman, but since 1940 a modified Cyrillic script has been used.

In Dushanbe most people speak Tajik and Russian. Uzbek is also spoken by a significant number of the population.

Tajik Basics

Peace be with you.	*assalom u aleykum*
Hello.	*salom*
Goodbye.	*khayr naboshad*
Thank you.	*rakhmat/teshukkur*
Yes/No.	*kha/ne*
How are you?	*naghzmi shumo?*
I'm well.	*mannaghz*
Do you speak English?	*anglisi meydonet?*
I don't understand.	*man manefakhmam*

police	*militsia*
doctor	*duhtur*
hospital	*bemorhona/ kasalhona*
bus station	*istgoh*
train station	*istgoh rohi ohan*
airport	*furudgoh*
toilet	*khojat'hona*
friend	*doost*
good	*khub/naghz*
bad	*ganda*

Where is ...?	*... khujo ast?*
How much?	*chand pul?*
hotel	*mekhmon'hona*
restaurant	*restoran*
tea	*choy*
expensive	*qimmat*
bread	*non*
boiled water	*obi jush*
rice	*birinj*
meat	*gusht*

Monday	*dushanbe*
Tuesday	*seshanbe*
Wednesday	*chorshanbe*
Thursday	*panjanbe*
Friday	*juma*
Saturday	*shanbe*
Sunday	*yakshanbe*

1	*yak*
2	*du*
3	*seh*
4	*chor*
5	*panj*
6	*shish*
7	*khaft*
8	*khasht*
9	*nukh*
10	*dakh*
100	*sad*
1000	*khazor*

TURKMEN

Turkmen, the state language of Turkmenistan since 1990, has been described as '800-year old Turkish'. It belongs to the south-western group of Turkic languages together with the Turkish spoken in Turkey and Azerbaijan. In Turkmenistan virtually everyone speaks Russian and Turkmen (except for Russians, who speak Russian only). English speakers are generally only found in the tourist industry and some universities.

There's been a significant infiltration of Russian words and phrases into Turkmen, especially in this century (words to do with science and technology particularly). Native-tongue Turkmen conversation is punctuated with Russian, to the extent that sentences will begin in Turkmen, then slip into Russian midway through.

Three different scripts have been used to transliterate Turkmen; Arabic, Roman and Cyrillic. Arabic was the first, though little Turkmen was ever written in it (there's a popular style of calligraphy, often used on monuments, in which Cyrillic script is rendered in such a way that it almost resembles Arabic script). A modified Turkish Roman alphabet was introduced in 1940. The Turkmen Cyrillic is identical to its Russian progenitor but with the addition of five supplementary characters and two sound modifications. On 1 January 1996, Turkmen Cyrillic was officially replaced by a newly created, modified Turkmen Roman alphabet. Signs are still being changed over, and the process is progressing slowly.

Turkmen Basics

Peace be with you.	*salam aleykum*
Hello.	*salam*
Goodbye.	*sagh bol*
Thank you.	*tangyr*
Yes/No.	*howa/yok*
How are you?	*siz nahili*
Fine, and you?	*onat, a siz?*
I don't understand.	*men dushenamok*

Do you speak English?	*siz inglische gepleyarsinizmi?*
police	*militsia*
doctor	*lukman*
hospital	*keselkhana*
bus station	*durolha*
train station	*vokzal*
airport	*aeroport*
toilet	*hajat'hana*
friend	*dost*
good	*yakhsheh*
bad	*ervet*
Where is ...?	*... niredeh?*
How much?	*nyacheh?*
hotel	*mikmankhana*
restaurant	*restoran*
tea	*chay*
expensive	*gummut*
bread	*churek*
boiled water	*gaina d'lan su*
rice	*tui*
meat	*et*
Monday	*dushanbe*
Tuesday	*seshenbe*
Wednesday	*charshanbe*
Thursday	*penshenbe*
Friday	*anna*
Saturday	*shenbe*
Sunday	*yekshanbe*

1	*bir*
2	*ikeh*
3	*uch*
4	*durt*
5	*besh*
6	*alty*
7	*yed*
8	*sekiz*
9	*dokuz*
10	*on*
100	*yuz*
1000	*mun*

UYGHUR

Uyghur is spoken all over Xinjiang and in parts of Kyrgyzstan and Uzbekistan. In China, written Uyghur uses an Arabic script, although for a time children were taught a Romanised alphabet.

Most sounds in Uyghur correspond to those found in English, with the following exceptions:

ö	as the 'e' in 'her', said with well-rounded lips
ü	as the 'i' in 'bit', said with lips rounded and pushed forward
kh	slightly gutteral sound as the 'ch' in Scottish 'loch'
gh	similar to the French 'r' – produced by moving the bulk of the tongue backward while the tip rests behind the lower front teeth
zh	as the 's' in 'pleasure'

Uyghur Basics

Hello.	*assahlahmu alaykum* (lit: peace be upon you)
How are you?	*kahndahk ahhwah-lingiz?*
Fine (and you?)	*yahkhshi (siz chu?)*
Goodbye.	*her khosh*
Thank you.	*rahmat sizga*
Yes.	*ha'a*
No.	*yahk*
Excuse me.	*kachürüng*
Sorry.	*kechiresiz*
Never mind.	*kerak yok* or *hichkisi yok*
I don't understand.	*chüshanmidim*
Do you speak English?	*siz englizchi sözliyahlahysiz?*
I don't speak Uyghur.	*man uyghurcha sözliyalmayman*
I don't speak Chinese.	*man khanzucha sözliyalmayman*
police	*sahkchilahr*
doctor	*doktor*
toilet	*oburni (hahli jahy)*
bus (terminal)	*ahptobus (ning ahkhirki bikiti)*
train station	*poyiz istahnzisi*
airport	*ahyrudurum*
taxi stand	*taksi bikiti*
Where is the ...?	*... kayarda?*
How much?	*kahncha pul?*
That's very expensive.	*u bak kimmat ikan*
restaurant	*resturahn*
flat bread	*nahn*

rice	gürüch
tea	chahy
water	su

Monday	düshanba
Tuesday	sahyshanba
Wednesday	chahrshanba
Thursday	payshanba
Friday	jüma
Saturday	shanba
Sunday	yakshanba

0	nöl
1	bir
2	ikki
3	üch
4	töt
5	bash
6	ahlta
7	yatta
8	sakkiz
9	tokkuz
10	on
11	on bir
20	yigirma
21	yigirma bir
100	bir yüz
1000	bir ming

UZBEK

Uzbekistan has three major languages Uzbek, Russian and Tajik. Uzbek is a Turkic language and is the official language of Uzbekistan, and with 15 million speakers it is the most widely spoken of the non-Slavic languages of the former Soviet Union. Uzbekistan has been the most publicly anti-Russian of the Central Asian countries, virtually eliminating the language from public view, in favour of written Uzbek.

Uzbek was written in Roman letters from 1918 to 1941. Since then it has used a modified Cyrillic script, which differs from the Russian script by only a few letters.

Uzbekistan (like Kyrgyzstan and Turkmenistan) is gradually changing over to a Roman script in order to align itself more closely with Turkey, and gain better access to western markets.

Uzbek Basics

Peace be with you.	asalom u alaykhum
Hello.	salom
Goodbye.	hayr
Thank you.	rakhmat
Yes/No.	kha/yuk
How are you?	qanday siz?
Do you speak English?	inglizcha bila sizmi?

police	militsia
doctor	tabib
hospital	kasalhona
bus station	avtobeket
train station	temir yul vokzali
airport	tayyorgokh
toilet	hojat 'hona
friend	urmoq/doost
good	yakhshi
bad	yomon

Where is ...?	... qayerda?
How much?	qancha/nichpul?
hotel	mehmon 'hona
restaurant	restoran
tea	choy
expensive	qimmat
bread	non
boiled water	qaynatilgan suv
rice	guruch
meat	gusht

Monday	dushanba
Tuesday	seyshanba
Wednesday	chorshanba
Thursday	payshanba
Friday	juma
Saturday	shanba
Sunday	yakshanba

1	bir
2	ikki
3	uch
4	turt
5	besh
6	olti
7	etti
8	sukkiz
9	tuqqiz
10	un
100	yuz
1000	ming

GAZETTEER

Kazakstan	Қазақстан
Akmola	Ақмола
Aksu-Zhabaghly Nature Reserve	Ақсу-Жабағлы Қорығы
Aktau	Ақтау
Aktöbe	Ақтөбе
Almaty	Алматьч
Altay mountains	Алтай
Aralsk	Аральск
Astana	Астана
Atyrau	Атырау
(Lake) Balkash	Балқаш Көл
Baykonur Cosmo-drome	Байконур Космо-дром
Bolshoe Almatin-skoe lake	Озеро Бопьшое Алматинское
(Lake) Burabay	Бурабай Көл
Charyn canyon	Чарынскии Каньон
Dostyk (Druzhba)	Достық (Дружба)
Ili river	Реука Или
(Lake) Kapshagay	Су Қоймасы Қалшағай
Karaghandy	Қарағанды
Karkara valley	Каркара Долина
Korgos	Хоргос
Kökshetau	Көкшетау
Köl-Say lakes	Озера Колсаи
Kostanay	Қостанай
Küngey Alatau	Күнгей Алатау
Kyzylorda	Қызылорда
Leninsk	Ленинск
(Lake) Markakol	Маркакол Көл
Medeu	Медеу
Öskemen/ Ust-Kamenogorsk	Өскемен/ Усть-Каменогорск
Otyrar	Отырар
Pavlodar	Павлодар
Petropavlovsk	Петропавловск
Rachmanov's springs	Рахмановские Ключи
Sayram	Сайрам
Semey	Семей
Sheber Aul	Шебер Аул
Shymbulak	Шымбудақ
Shymkent	Шымкент
Shyngghystau Hills	Шыңғыстау
Taldy-Korghan	Талды-Қорған
Taraz/Zhambyl	Тарас/Жамбыл
Tekeli	Текелы
Turkistan	Туркістан
Zailiysky Alatau	Заилийский Алатау
Zharkent	Жаркент
Zhungar Alatau	Жунгар Алатау

Kyrgyzstan	Кыргызстан
Ak-Suu	Ак- Суу
Ala-Köl	Ала-Көл
Alay valley	Алайская Допина
Altyn Arashan	Алтын Арашан
Ananyevo	Ананьево
Arslanbob	Арспанбоб
At-Bashy	Ат- аши
Balykchy	Балыкчы
Barskoön	Барскоон
Belovodsk	Беловодска
Bishkek	Бишкек
Central Tian Shan	Центральный Тянь-Шань
Cholpon-Ata	Чолпон-Ата
Jalal-Abad	Жалал-Авад
Jeti-Öghüz	Жети-Өгүз
Kara-Köl	Кара-Көл
Karakol	Каракол
Karkara valley	Өрөөн Каркара
Kashgar	Кашгар
Kochkor	Кочкор
Koshoy Korgon	Кошой Коргон
Kurort Jergalan	Курорт Джергалан
Kyzyl-Suu	Кызыл-Суу
Naryn	Нарын
Özgön	Өзгөн (Kyrgyz) Үзган (Uzbek)
Osh	Ош
Pristan Przhevalsk	Пристань Прже-валск
(Lake) Sary-Chelek	Сары-Чҿпҿк
Semyonovka	Семёновка
Skibaza	Скибазы
(Lake) Song-Köl	Соң-Көл
Sukhoy Khrebet	Суой Ребет
Tashkömür	Ташкөмүр
Tash-Rabat	Таш-Рабат
Teploklyuchenka	Теплоключенка
Toktogul	Токтогул
Torugart	Торугарт
Torugart Pass	Перевал Торугарт

Tajikistan	Таджикистан
Dushanbe	Душанбе
Hissar	Гиссар

Khojand	Оджандюучанд
Khorog	Орог
Pamir Highway	Памирское Шоссе
Penjikent	Пенджикент

Turkmenistan — **Туркменистан**

Anau	Анау
Ashgabat	Ашхабад
Badkhyz	Ьадхыз
Bairam Ali	Ваирам Апы
Bakharden	Ьахарден
Balkanabat	Ьалканабад
Charjou	Чарджев
Dashoguz	Дашховуз
Firuza	Фируза
Gaurdak	Говурдак
Könye-Ürgench	Көне-Ургенч
Gushgi	Гчшгы
Mary	Мары
Merv	Мерв
Nisa	Несса
Saraghs	Серахс
Tagtabazar	Тахта-Базар
Turkmenbashi	Туркменбаши

Uzbekistan — **Узбекистан**

Andijan	Андижон
Bukhara	Ьуоро
Chimgan	Уимган
Fergana	Фарғона
Hoja Ismoil	Жа Исмоил
Hojeli	Ожели
Jumabazar	Жумоңозор
Khiva	Иива
Kokand	Ққон
Margilan	Марғилон
Moynaq	Мойнақ
Nukus	Нукус (Нөкис)
Penjikent	Пенджикент
Qarshi	Қарши
Samarkand	Самарқанд
Shakhimardan	Шоҳимардон
Shakhrisabz	Шаҳрисабз

Tashkent	Тошкент
Termiz	Термиз
Urgench	Урганч

Xinjiang

Burqin		
	bùěrjīn	布尔津
Daheyan		
	dàhéyàn	太河沿
Hanas lake		
	kānàsī hú	喀纳斯湖
Heavenly lake		
	tiānchí	天池
Hotan		
	hétián	和田
Jeminay		
	jímùǎi	吉木乃
Karghilik		
	yèchéng	叶城
Kashgar		
	kāshí	喀什
Khunjerab pass		
	hóngqílāfǔ shānkǒu	红其拉甫山口
Kucha		
	kùchē	库车
Sayram lake		
	sàilǐmù hú	赛里木湖
Tacheng		
	tǎchéng	塔城
Tashkurgan		
	tǎshíkù'ěrgān	塔什库尔干
Torugart pass		
	tǔěrgātè shānkǒu	吐尔尕特山口
Turpan		
	tǔlǔfān	吐鲁番
Ürümqi		
	wūlǔmùqí	乌鲁木齐
Yarkand		
	shāchē	莎车
Yengisar		
	yīngjíshā	英吉沙
Yining		
	yīníng	伊宁

Glossary

Abbreviations
A – Arabic
R – Russian
T – all the Turkic languages
U – Uyghur

-abad – suffix meaning 'town of' (T)
adetki mashina – ordinary bus (U)
administrator – general word for chief or manager (R)
aeroport – airport (R)
aerovokzal – airport bus station (R)
ak kalpak – felt hat worn by Kyrgyz men
ak nan – flat nan bread
akimat – regional government office (T)
aksakal – revered elder (Uzbek)
akyn – minstrel, bard (Kyrgyz)
ala kiyiz – Kyrgyz felt rug with coloured panels pressed on
alangy – square (Kazak)
Ali Majlis – Uzbek Supreme Assembly
ali mashina – soft seat coach (U)
alpinistskiy lager – see *alplager*
alplager – mountaineer's camp (R)
apparatchik – bureaucrat (R)
apteka – pharmacy (R)
aptoos biket – long-distance bus station (U)
arashan – springs (T)
arenda – literally 'lease' or 'rent', referring usually to buses that make a trip only if there are enough passengers (R)
ASSR – Autonomous Soviet Socialist Republic (R)
atlas – tie-dyed silks, known as ikat or khanatlas in Uzbekistan (T)
aul – Kazak nomadic encampment
aviakassa – private travel agent (T)
avtobiket – bus station (T)
avtobus – bus (R)
avtostantsia – bus stop or bus stand (R)
ayanty – public square (Kyrgyz)
ayil – village (Kyrgyz)
ayollar hammomi – women's baths (Uzbek)
azan – the call to prayer; translates as 'God most great. There is no God but Allah. Mohammed is God's messenger. Come to prayer, come to security. God is most great.' (A)

balbal – Turkic totem-like gravestone (T)
banya – public bath (R)
basmachi – literally 'bandits'; Muslim guerilla fighters who resisted the Bolshevik takeover in Central Asia (R)
batyr – warrior hero in Kyrgyz and Kazak epics
bazar – open market (R)
B&B – bed and breakfast accommodation
BCE – before common era; equivalent to BC
beg or bay – landlord or gentleman (T)
besbarmak – flat noodles with lamb or horsemeat or vegetable broth
bishkek – see *pishpek*
biznes tsentr – business centre (R)
biznesmen – businessmen (R)
bolnitza – hospital (R)
bolshoy rynok – 'big-farmer's market' (R)
bosuy – Kyrgyz *yurt*
bufet – snack bar selling cheap cold meats, boiled eggs, salads, breads, pastries etc
bulvar – boulevard (R)
bulvary – boulevard (Kyrgyz)
burqa – all-over body veil (A)
buzkashi – traditional polo-like game played with a headless goat carcass rather than a ball (also kökpar, kozlodranie)
byuro puteshestviy i exkursiy – excursion bureau (R)

caravanserai – a travellers' inn
CATC – Central Asian Tourism Corporation
CE – commn era; equivalent to AD
chaban – cowboy (Kyrgyz, Kazak)
chay – tea (T)
chaykhana – teahouse (T); has various transliterations, eg chaykhana, choyhona, shaykhana
chorsu – market arcade (T)
choy – see *chay*
choyhona – see *chaykhana*
chuchuk – see *kazi*
chuchvara – dumplings
CIS – Commonwealth of Independent States; the loose political and economic alliance of most former member republics of the USSR

(except the Baltic states); sometimes called NIS, for newly independent states
CPK – Communist Party of Kazakstan

dacha – a holiday bungalow, usually in the countryside just outside a town (R)
dangghyly – avenue (Kazak)
darikhana – pharmacy (Kazak)
darya – river (T)
dastarkhan – literally 'table cloth'; also feast (T)
dervish – a Sufi ascetic
dezhurnaya – 'floor-lady', the woman attendant on duty on each floor of a Soviet-style state hotel; literally 'on duty' (R)
dom – building (R)
dom otdykha – rest home (R)
dopi – see *dopy*
doppe – see *dopy*
dopy – black, four-sided skullcap embroidered in white and worn by Uzbek men (Uzbek)
drevniy gorod – ancient city (R)
duban – province (Kyrgyz)
Dungan – Muslim Chinese

eivan – study hall in a *medressa*
erkakli hammomi – men's baths (Uzbek)

GAI – traffic police (R)
gastronom – speciality food shop (R)
ghanch – carved and painted plaster (T)
gillam – carpet (T)
glasnost – literally 'openness'; the free expression that was one aspect of the Gorbachev reforms (R)
glavpochtamt – main post office (R)
gorod – town (R)
gosposhlina – state transport duty (R)
gosudarstvenny pvirodny park – national park (R)
Great Game – the geopolitical 'Cold War' of territorial expansion between the Russian and British empires in the 19th and early 20th centuries in Central Asia
gril-bar – grill bar serving roast chicken and other meats (R)
guligans – hooligans (R)
gulyash – goulash (R)
GUM – 'gosudarstvennyy universalnyy magazine', or state department store (R)

Hadith – collected acts and sayings of the Prophet Mohammed (A)
hajj – the pilgrimage to Mecca, one of the 'five pillars of Islam'; to be made at least once during one's lifetime by devout Muslims (A)
hakimyat – town/city administration building (Kyrgyz)
hammomi – baths (hammomi kunjak means common baths, hammomi numur means private baths) (Uzbek)
hanako – (Uzbek) see *khanaka*
hauz – an artificial pool (T)
hazrat – honorific title meaning 'majesty' or 'holy' (A)
Heartland – the area comprising Central Asia and including Mongolia and Siberia
Hegira – flight of Mohammed and his followers to Medina in 622 CE (A)
hiyoboni – boulevard (Uzbek)
hokimyat – mayor's office (Uzbek)

IRP – Islamic Renaissance Party, a grouping of radical activists dedicated to the formation of Islamic rule in Central Asia
Ismaili – a branch of Shia Islam

jailoo – summer pastures (Kyrgyz)
Jami Masjid – a large mosque
jarma – fermented barley drink
jeiran – Persian gazelle
jiao – Chinese currency, 1/10 of a *yuan,* pronounced mao
Juma Mosque – see *Jami Masjid*

kadimi shahr – old part of Uyghur towns
kala – fortress (T)
kalon – great (Tajik)
karakhana – workshop, factory (Uyghur)
karez – well; ancient system of irrigation (A)
karta – see *kazi*
kassa – cashier or box office (R)
kazan – cauldron (T)
kazi – horsemeat sausage
-kent – suffix meaning 'town of' (T)
kesh-kumay – traditional game in which a man chases a woman on horseback and tries to kiss her (Kyrgyz)
khanaka – a Sufi contemplation hall and hostel for wandering ascetics; the room of an Eshon (Sufi leader) in which he and other Sufis perform their *zikr*

khanatlas – see *atlas*

kino, kinoteatr – cinema (R)

kiosk economy – small-time dealers buying goods and reselling them at a higher price

köchösü – street (Kyrgyz)

kökör – kumys-shaker

kökpar – see *buzkashi*

kolkhoz – collective farm (R)

kommerchesky – private enterprise (R)

komnaty otdykha – rest rooms (R)

kontrolno propusknoy punkt – permit station (R)

köshesi – street (Kazak, Karakalpak)

koshk – desert fortress (Uzbek)

koshma – multicoloured felt mats (Kazak)

kozlodranie – see *buzkashi*

krytyy rynok – covered market (R)

kuai – see *yuan*

kuchasi – street (Uzbek)

kulinariya – canteen (T)

kumys – fermented mares' milk, popular in Kazakstan, and Kyrgyzstan

kupeynyy – 2nd class or sleeping carriage on trains (R)

kyrort – thermal spring complex (R)

kyz kuu – (Kazak) see *kesh-kumay*

laghman – noodles

lux – deluxe (R), though often a euphemism

mahalla – an urban neighbourhood (Uzbek)

majolica – earthenware tiles with baked enamel finish

Manas – legendary hero revered by the Kyrgyz

manaschi – type of *akyn* who recites from the Kargyz cycle of oral legends

manat (M) – Turkmen currency

manty – small stuffed dumplings

mao – see *jiao*

markaz – centre (T)

maroji – vanilla ice cream

marshrutka – see *marshrutnoe*

marshrutnoe – a small bus or van that follows a fixed route but stops on demand to take on or let off passengers, with fares depending on distance travelled; a *marshrutnyy avtobus* is a larger bus that does the same; a short term for either one is *marshrutka* (R, T)

marshrutnyy avtobus – see *marshrutnoe*

maydoni – public square (Uzbek)

mazar – tomb or mausoleum (T)

medressa – an Islamic academy or seminary (A)

mikrorayon – micro region (R)

militsia – police (R, T)

muezzin – the man who calls the Muslim faithful to prayer (A)

mufti – Islamic spiritual leader (A)

mujaheddin – Muslim freedom fighter engaged in jihad, or Holy War (A)

mullah – an Islamic cleric (A)

nan – flat-breads

Naqshband – the most influential of many Sufi secret associations in Central Asia

Navrus – 'New Days', the main Islamic spring festival; has various regional transliterations: Nauroz, Nauryz, Norruz, Novruz

NIS – Newly Independent States

non – see *nan*

oblast – province or region (R)

oblys – province or region (Kazak)

otdel exkursii – excursion office (R)

OVIR – Otdel Vis I Registratsii, literally 'Office of Visas and Regulations' (R)

pakhta – cotton; pakhtakor: cotton worker (T)

panjara – trellis of wood, stone or *ghanch* (T)

perestroika – literally 'restructuring'; Gorbachev's efforts to revive the economy (R)

petrol hookers – roadside fuel dealers who buy fuel in Russia and undersell local distribution outlets

piala – bowl (T)

pilau – see *plov*

pishpek – churn for *kumys*

pishtak – entrance portals

platskartnyy – hard sleeper (R)

ploshchad – square (R)

plov – a rice dish with meat, carrots or other additions (traditionally prepared by men for special celebrations)

pochta – post office (R)

pochta bulima – main post office (Uzbek)

pol-lux – semi-deluxe (R), see *lux*

polyclinic – health centre (R)

propusk – military border permit (T)

prospekt – avenue (R, T) also *dangghyly*

provodnik – male attendant on a long-distance train (R)

provodnitsa – female attendant on long-distance train (R)

qala – fortress (Uzbek)
qarvatlik mashina – sleeper coach (Uyghur)
Quran – Islam's holiest book, the collected revelations of God to the Prophet Mohammed
qyz-quu – (Kazak) see *kesh-kumay*

rayon – district (R)
remont – repair service, or under repair (R)
renmimbi (RMB) – Chinese currency, literally 'Peoples' Currency'

salam aleykhum – traditional Muslim greeting, meaning 'peace be with you' (A)
samovar – urn used for heating water for tea, often found on trains (R)
samsas – baked envelopes of meat
savdo dukoni – commercial shops (U)
sharia – Islamic Law (A)
sharq – east (Tajik and Uzbek)
shashlyk – meat roasted on skewers over hot coals
shay – (Kazak) see *chay*
shaykhana – see *chaykhana*
Shia – one of the two main branches of Islam (A)
Shi'ite – another name for *Shia*
shishbesh – game like backgammon (Tajik)
shosse – highway (R)
shubat – camel's milk (Kazak and Tajik)
shyrdak – felt rug with coloured panels sewn on (Kyrgyz)
Sinkiang – old Wade-Giles transliteration of Xinjiang
skibaza – ski base (R)
skotovod – see *chaban*
som – Kyrgyz currency
SSR – Soviet Socialist Republic
stolovaya – canteen/cafeteria (R)
Sufi – the mystical tradition in Islam
sum – Uzbek currency
suzani, **suzana** or **suzane** – bright Uzbek silk embroidery on cotton cloth (Uzbek)

Taliban – plural of Talib, meaning student or seeker of knowledge, most powerful political group in Afghanistan

talon – coupon (R)
tebbetey – round fur-trimmed hat worn by Kyrgyz men
telpek – sheepskin hat worn by Turkmen males (T)
tenge (T) – Kazakstan currency; 1 T is 100 tiyn
tim – an arcade, eg in a market (T)
toi – celebration (T)
Transoxiana – 'the land beyond the Oxus'; a historical term for the region between the Amu-Darya and Syr-Darya rivers
TsUM – 'Tsentralnyy universalnyy magazin' or central department store (R)
turbaza (turistskaya baza) – holiday camp typically with spartan cabins, plain food, sports, video hall and bar; usually only open in summer (R)
Turkestan – literally 'the Land of the Turks', covers Central Asia and Xinjiang

ulak-tartysh – (Kyrgyz) see *buzkashi*
ulama – class of religious scholars or intellectuals (A)
ulitsa – street (R)
umuvalnik – portable washing basin (R)
univermag – universalnyy magazin or department store (R)
uulu – son of (Kyrgyz); equivalent in Arabic is 'ibn'

viloyat – province (Uzbek)
vodopad – waterfall (Russia)

yangi shahr – new part of Uyghur towns, usually Han-dominated
ylag oyyny – see *buzkashi*
yuan – Chinese currency, pronounced kuai
yurt – the traditional nomadic 'house', a collapsible cylindrical wood framework covered with felt

zakat – obligatory alms tax, one of the Five Pillars of Islam (A)
zapovednik – nature reserve (R)
zhyostkiy – hard carriage on trains
zikr – recitation or contemplation of the names of God, recitation of sacred writings, one part of traditional Sufi practice (A)

Acknowledgments

Many thanks to the travellers who used the last edition and wrote to us with helpful hints, useful advice and interesting anecdotes:

A. Griffin, Aarif Meghani, Al Karim Govindji, Albert Kratzer, Aldo Vietti, Alison Griffin, Alison Stern, Ana Burbano, Andreas Setzepfandt, Andrew Connel, Andrew Miller, Andrew Yim, Anne Miehe Zeegers, Annelize Muraczewski, Annemiche Zeegers, Annette den Ouden, Anthony Williams, Anton Jacobus, Anton Kos, Aravind Narasipur, Ari Katz, Arkady Divinsky, Aziz Atakuziev, Bakhodir Irhanov, Barbara Balkwill, Barbara Hay, Beate Gross, Ben Barlow, Ben Vroom, Bill Bearnson, Bill Iler, Bill Williamson, Billy Willy, Blasé Reardon, Boaz Rottem, Bonnie McCormick, Boris Habets, Brendan Whyte, Brett King, Brian Randall, Bruno De Cordier, Carol Finnegan, Casimir Paltinger, Cate Turk, Catherin Joley, Christian Koeppe, Christian White, Christopher Cerisier, Clare Bateson, Colin Taylor, Crystal Zibas, Dale Myers, Damian McCormack, Danny & Yael Golan, Darren McLean, Darren Schwab, Dave Quinn, David A Hicks, David Berner, David Mallette, David Raterman, David Tomlinson, David Zetland, Diane Mew, Dovlet Amanov, Dr Wolfgang Neumann, Dr. A.D. Miller, Dr. Scott Kirby, Dre Visscher, Ed Tockman, Eden Scott, Edward Schoolman, Elad Yom-Tov, Elaine Rati Kochar, Elizabeth King, Eric Poupon, Esther Stone, Fabrizio Beverina, Fernando Marques da Silva, Feruza Kulturaeva, Flouis Bylsma, Francois Gossiaux, Frank Becker, Gene Jannotta, George & Lisa Horsington, George Craig, Gerald Fimberger, Gerald Sorg, Gianni Gambillara, Gilda Davies, Glen Reynolds, Graham Bate, Gregor Preac, Guy de Bruyn, Guy Gagne, H J S Dorren, Harald Legge, Harm Dorren, Harold Garcke, Herman van Banning, Herman Wierenga, Hitesh Parmar, Hugo Van Hecke, Ian Millard, Ian Williams, Igor Vislyansky, Inge Haegeman, Inge Sollerud, Irene Rietmann, Iver Munk, J A Riches, J Edhouse, J J Matze, Jane M Materna, Jane M. Materna, Jane Tate, Jarek Rudnik, Jason Thomson, Jean Harrison, Jean-Luc Widlowski, Jeff Whitbeck, Jeffrey Paulsen, Jen Aldridge, Jerry Azevedo, Jessica Barry, Jill Going, Jim Findlay, Joe Higham, Johan Van Audekerke, John & Dianne McKinnon, John Ellis, John McKinnon, Jonathan Harris, Jonathan Kells Phillips, Jonathan Turner, Joost van der Ven, Jose de Ory, Jurjen Berends, Kai Kaninth, Karl Bach, Keith Leitich, Keith Potter, Krzysztof Obara, L H van Keijzerswaard, Leesa Peters, Liba Eichner, Liliane Metz-Krencker, Linda MacLachlan, Lisa Marie Leef, Lorainne Hatch, Lorraine Hatch, Lynn Grantz, Maarten van Baggum, Manfred Weis, Manucher & Khurshed, Marc De-Haut, Marcia Peerlinck, Marco Priebe, Maria Mack, Marianne Heredge, Marion Marquand, Mark Carrera, Mark Turpin, Mark Zhong, Martin Harris, Martyn Rasche, Mathias Metzdorf, Matt Murphy, Matteo Fumagalli, Max Altantsev, Megan Falvey, Melinda Niekum, Meredith Perish, Michael Banker, Michael Bell, Michael Fergus, Michael Wyzan, Michael Zeilinger, Michel Steger, Mick Lloyd, Mike Crostini, Mike Leon, Mirjam Gelinck, Mona Megalli, Monique Verschuren, Mrs. J. Edhouse, Nancy Kalajian, Nanna Koekoek, Neil Poulter, Nicolass Jourdier, Norbert Zimmermann, Norm R. Loeffler, Odd Staurset, P.J. & A.P. Hanson, Patrick Joseph Becker, Paul C Holtz, Paul Deborger, Paulus Geraedts, Pavel Hortlik, Pekka Saavalainen, Peter & Arnie Hanson, Peter Holdforth, Peter van Alen, Piotr Gaszynski, Pomme Clayton, Quintin Anderson, R A Baller, Rachel Dornhelm, Ralph West, Ray Bayliss, Richard Bardua, Richard Heeps, Richard Manning, Rick Porter, Robert Walker, Robyn Larbalestier, Rodney Lax, Roger Lewer, Ronald Gossiaux, Ronald V Plant, Rowene Z. Neodow, Rupert Fiennes, Sandra Basic, Sarah Rennie, Sarlas Vasilis, Sayat Ozcan, Scott Eden, Scott Kirby, Scott Mitic, Scott Smith, Seffy Efrati, Seibert Adams, Sergey Pyshnenko, Simon Farley, Soichi Arai, Stefan Smith, Stephane Muller, Stephen Jones, Stephen McFarlane, Stephen McPhillips, Stephen Winterstein, Stuart Horsman, Susan Richardson, T Last, Tanya Shabalkina, Ted Elder, Thorsten Swoboda, Tim Chevassut, Tim Edmunds, Timur Duisengaliev, Tobias Skog, Toke Rude, Tom & Anna Longworth, Tom Weller, Trygve Inda, Ulrike Schueler, Valeri Denisov, Valerie A Smith, Vanessa Baethe, Wee-Cheng Tan, William Boyd, Wim Oostindier, Wojciech Kwarcinski, Wolf Gotthilf, Zoltan Nagy.

LONELY PLANET

Phrasebooks

Lonely Planet phrasebooks are packed with essential words and phrases to help travellers communicate with the locals. With colour tabs for quick reference, an extensive vocabulary and use of script, these handy pocket-sized language guides cover day-to-day travel situations.

- handy pocket sized books
- easy to understand Pronunciation chapter
- clear & comprehensive Grammar chapter
- romanisation alongside script to allow ease of pronunciation
- script throughout so users can point to phrases for every situation
- full of cultural information and tips for the traveller

'... vital for a real DIY spirit and attitude in language learning'
– *Backpacker*

'the phrasebooks have good cultural backgrounders and offer solid advice for challenging situations in remote locations'
– *San Francisco Examiner*

Arabic (Egyptian) • Arabic (Moroccan) • Australian *(Australian English, Aboriginal and Torres Strait languages)* • Baltic States *(Estonian, Latvian, Lithuanian)* • Bengali • Brazilian • British • Burmese • Cantonese • Central Asia (Uyghur, Uzbek, Kyrghiz, Kazak, Pashto, Tadjik • Central Europe *(Czech, French, German, Hungarian, Italian, Slovak)* • Eastern Europe *(Bulgarian, Czech, Hungarian, Polish, Romanian, Slovak)* • Ethiopian (Amharic) • Fijian • French • German • Greek • Hebrew • Hill Tribes • Hindi & Urdu • Indonesian • Italian • Japanese • Korean • Lao • Latin American Spanish • Malay • Mandarin • Mediterranean Europe *(Albanian, Croatian, Greek, Italian, Macedonian, Maltese, Serbian, Slovene)* • Mongolian • Nepali • Pidgin • Pilipino (Tagalog) • Quechua • Russian • Scandinavian Europe *(Danish, Finnish, Icelandic, Norwegian, Swedish)* • South-East Asia *(Burmese, Indonesian, Khmer, Lao, Malay, Tagalog Pilipino, Thai, Vietnamese)* • South Pacific Languages • Spanish (Castilian) *(also includes Catalan, Galician and Basque)* • Sri Lanka • Swahili • Thai • Tibetan • Turkish • Ukrainian • USA *(US English, Vernacular, Native American languages, Hawaiian)* • Vietnamese • Western Europe *(Basque, Catalan, Dutch, French, German, Greek, Irish, Italian, Portuguese, Scottish Gaelic, Spanish (Castilian), Welsh)*

LONELY PLANET

Lonely Planet Online

Whether you've just begun planning your next trip, or you're chasing down specific info on currency regulations or visa requirements, check out Lonely Planet Online for up-to-the-minute travel information.

As well as miniguides to more than 250 destinations, you'll find maps, photos, travel news, health and visa updates, travel advisories and discussion of the ecological and political issues you need to be aware of as you travel. You'll also find timely upgrades to popular guidebooks that you can print out and stick in the back of your book.

There's an online travellers' forum (The Thorn Tree) where you can share your experience of life on the road, meet travel companions and ask other travellers for their recommendations and advice.

There's also a complete and up-to-date list of all Lonely Planet travel products including travel guides, diving and snorkeling guides, phrasebooks, atlases, travel literature and videos, and a simple online ordering facility if you can't find the book you want elsewhere.

Lonely Planet Diving & Snorkeling Guides

Beautifully illustrated with full-colour photos throughout, Lonely Planet's Pisces books explore the world's best diving and snorkeling areas and prepare divers for what to expect when they get there, both topside and underwater.

Dive sites are described in detail with specifics on depths, visibility, level of difficulty, special conditions, underwater photography tips and common and unusual marine life present. You'll also find practical logistical information and coverage on topside activities and attractions, sections on diving health and safety, plus listings for diving services, live-aboards, dive resorts and tourist offices.

Index

Abbreviations

A – Afghanistan
C – Xinjiang (China)
Kaz – Kazakstan

Kyr – Kyrgystan
Taj – Tajikistan
Tur – Turkmenistan

U – Uzbekistan

Text

A

Abay Museum (Kaz) 242-3
Abbott, Captain James 329
Abu Ali Ibn-Sin 61
accommodation 128-31
   home-stay 79, 129-30
   Shepherd's Life program 399
Achik Tash (Kyr) 424
Adjina-Tepe (Taj) 441
Afghan Turkestan (A) 548
Afghanistan 540-8, **542**
   books 546
   civil war 543
   cultural considerations 545
   Internet resources 545
   people 545
   safety 541, 546
Aga Khan 431, 434, 446
agriculture 34-5, 49
air travel 141-50, 158
   safety 122-3
   to/from Central Asia 141-50
   to/from Kazakstan 201-2
   to/from Tajikistan 440
   to/from Turkmenistan 472
   to/from Uzbekistan 274-337
   to/from Xinjiang 508
   within Central Asia 158
Aitmatov, Chinghiz 346
Ak Suu (Kyr) 384-5
Akaev, Askar 341
Akmatov, Kazat 346
Ak-Saray Palace 307
Ak-Say canyon (Kyr) 367
Aksu-Zhabaghly Nature Reserve (Kaz) 222
Aktau (Kaz) 229-32, **230**
Aktöbe (Kaz) 226-7
Ala-Archa canyon (Kyr) 366 71
Alamedin canyon (Kyr) 367
Alay mountains 287

Alay valley (Kyr) 423-5
Al-Beruni 61
al-Bukhari, Ismail 300
Alexander the Great 15-16, 251
Algorismi, see Al-Khorezmi
Ali 288
al-Kashgari, Mahmud 387
Al-Khorezmi 61
Almantiskoe Lake (Kaz) 207-9
Almatinsky Nature Reserve (Kaz) 209-11
Almaty (Kaz) 184-205, **186**
   baths 192
   entertainment 199-200
   getting around 204-5
   getting there & away 201-4
   Gorky Park 192
   information 188-91
   medical services 190
   museums 192-3
   places to eat 196-9
   places to stay 194-6
   postal services 188
   safety 191
   shopping 200-1
   travel agencies 189
   walking tour 191
Altay mountains (Kaz) 248
altitude sickness 109
Altyn Arashan (Kyr) 381-4
Altyn-Emel National Park (Kaz) 214
Amazons of Central Asia 18
Ananyevo (Kyr) 374-5
Anau (Tur) 474
Andijan (U) 289-90
Angren (U) 278
animal husbandry 43
animals, see fauna
Aral Sea 38, 39-42, 225, **40**
Aralsk (Kaz) 225-6
archaeology expeditions 495
architecture 303-8
Arslanbob (Kyr) 416-17

arts 61-4
   books 99
Ashgabat (Tur) 464-76, **465**
   getting there & away 472-3
   information 466-8
   medical services 468
   museums 468-9
   places to eat 470-1
   places to stay 469-70
   things to see 468
   travel agencies 467
Askar, Akaev 368
Astana (Kaz) 172, 232-5, **233**
Astana Graves (C) 512
Astrakhanids 24
astronomy 61
At-Bashy (Kyr) 404
Atyrau (Kaz) 227-9, **227**
Avicenna 434, see Abu Ali Ibn-Sin
Ayaz-Qala (U) 325
Ayni, Sadriddin 434
Aysha-Bibi (Kaz) 219

B

Babur, Zahiruddin 279, 289
Bactrian camels 45
Bactrians 427
Badai-Tugai Nature Reserve (U) 325-6
Badkhyz Nature Reserve (Tur) 486
Bai Kaba (C) 520
Bairam Ali (Tur) 482
Bakharden (Tur) 475-6
Balbay (Kyr) 374
Balkanabat (Tur) 479
Balkash (Kaz) 216
Balkchy (Kyr) 371-2
Balkh (A) 548
Bam-i-Dunya, see Pamirs (Taj)
Bamiyan (A) 546
Band-i-Amir (A) 547
bargaining 92-3

Bold indicates maps.

Bold indicates maps.

Boxed Text

MAP LEGEND

CITY ROUTES

Freeway	Freeway
Highway	Primary Road
Road	Secondary Road
Street	Street
Lane	Lane
	On/Off Ramp
	Unsealed Road
	One-Way Street
	Pedestrian Street
	Stepped Street
	Tunnel
	Footbridge

REGIONAL ROUTES

	Tollway, Freeway
	Primary Road
	Secondary Road
	Minor Road

BOUNDARIES

	International
	State
	Disputed
	Fortified Wall

HYDROGRAPHY

	River, Creek
	Canal
	Lake
	Dry Lake; Salt Lake
	Spring; Rapids
	Waterfalls

TRANSPORT ROUTES & STATIONS

	Train
	Underground Train
	Metro
	Tramway
	Cable Car, Chairlift
	Ferry
	Walking Trail
	Walking Tour
	Path
	Pier or Jetty

AREA FEATURES

	Building
	Park, Gardens
	Market
	Sports Ground
	Beach
	Cemetery
	Campus
	Plaza

POPULATION SYMBOLS

✪ CAPITAL	National Capital	● CITY	City
◉ CAPITAL	State Capital	● Town	Town
		● Village	Village
			Urban Area

MAP SYMBOLS

✿	Place to Stay	▼ Place to Eat	● Point of Interest

✈	International Airport	▣	Embassy	▥	Museum
⊖	Bank	❿	Golf Course	⌸	National Park
⊕	Border Crossing	✚	Hospital	)(	Pass
⊟	Bus Stop	◙	Internet Cafe	✪	Police Station
▣	Bus Terminal	❋	Lookout	▭	Post Office
✚	Church	⚲	Monument	▢	Pub or Bar
▤	Cinema	☾	Mosque	✪	Ruins
				✪	Shopping Centre
				✡	Synagogue
				☎	Telephone
				▲	Temple
				◿	Theatre
				➊	Tourist Information
				▢	Zoo

Note: not all symbols displayed above appear in this book

LONELY PLANET OFFICES

Australia
PO Box 617, Hawthorn, Victoria 3122
☎ 03 9819 1877   fax 03 9819 6459
email: talk2us@lonelyplanet.com.au

USA
150 Linden St, Oakland, CA 94607
☎ 510 893 8555   TOLL FREE: 800 275 8555
fax 510 893 8572
email: info@lonelyplanet.com

UK
10a Spring Place, London NW5 3BH
☎ 020 7428 4800   fax 020 7428 4828
email: go@lonelyplanet.co.uk

France
1 rue du Dahomey, 75011 Paris
☎ 01 55 25 33 00   fax 01 55 25 33 01
email: bip@lonelyplanet.fr
www.lonelyplanet.fr

World Wide Web: www.lonelyplanet.com *or* AOL keyword: lp
Lonely Planet Images: lpi@lonelyplanet.com.au